EUROPEAN FAMILY LAW IN ACTION

EUROPEAN FAMILY LAW SERIES

Published by the Organising Committee of the Commission on European Family Law

EUROPEAN FAMILY LAW IN ACTION

Volume III: Parental Responsibilities

Edited by

KATHARINA BOELE-WOELKI

BENTE BRAAT

IAN CURRY-SUMNER

intersentia

Antwerp – Oxford

Distribution for the UK:
Hart Publishing
Salter's Boat Yard
Folly Bridge
Abingdon Road
Oxford OX1 4LB
UK
Tel: + 44 1865 24 55 33
Fax: + 44 1865 79 48 82

Distribution for North America:
Gaunt Inc.
Gaunt Building
3011 Gulf Drive
Holmes Beach
Florida 34217-2199
USA
Tel: + 1 941 778 5211
Fax: + 1 941 778 5252

Distribution for Switzerland and Germany:
Stämpfli Verlag AG
Hallerstrasse 7
Postfach
CH-3001 Bern
Switzerland
Tel: + 41 31 300 66 77
Fax: + 41 31 300 66 88

Distribution for other countries:
Intersentia Publishers
Groenstraat 31
BE-2640 Mortsel
Belgium
Tel: + 32 3 680 15 50
Fax: + 32 3 658 71 21

European Family Law in Action. Volume III: Parental Responsibilities
Katharina Boele-Woelki, Bente Braat, Ian Curry-Sumner (eds.)

ISBN 90-5095-443-X
D/2005/7849/55
NUR 822 and 828

PREFACE

This third volume of the European Family Law in Action publications contains detailed information concerning the law on parental responsibilities in twenty-two European jurisdictions. The first two volumes, which were published in 2003 under the same editorship, include national reports on the grounds for divorce and maintenance between former spouses (Nos. 2 and 3 of this series). Upon the basis of this comparative material the Commission on European Family Law has formulated the *Principles of European Family Law regarding Divorce and Maintenance Between Former Spouses,* which were published in December 2004 as No. 7 in this series. In order to prepare the second set of Principles of European Family Law the expert members of the CEFL have once again drafted comprehensive national reports on the basis of a detailed questionnaire in the field of parental responsibilities (see p. xi-xviii). These national reports, together with the relevant legal provisions, are available on CEFL's web site (www.law.uu.nl/priv/cefl). This book integrates all the given answers in order to provide an overview and a straightforward simultaneous comparison of the different solutions chosen within the national systems. On the basis of this comparative material the CEFL will be able to draft *Principles of European Family Law regarding Parental Responsibilities.*

The question arises whether and how the CEFL can contribute to the further harmonisation of this field of family law in Europe. For many decades important international organisations have been engaged in the field of parental responsibilities in order to improve the legal position of the child. Under the auspices of the United Nations, the Hague Conference on Private International Law and the Council of Europe a number of international conventions have been drafted. Many European countries are bound by these conventions, most of which deal with cross-border relationships. In addition to the international unification of the law relating to the protection of children including all civil matters concerning the attribution, exercise, delegation, restriction or termination of parental responsibilities, the European Union has unified the rules concerning jurisdiction and the recognition and enforcement of judgments on parental responsibilities. From 1st March 2005 these matters are governed by Council Regulation (EC) No. 2201/2003 concerning jurisdiction and the recognition and enforcement of judgments in matrimonial matters and the matters of parental responsibility (Brussels II*bis*). This Regulation repealed and replaced Council Regulation (EC) No. 1347/2000 on jurisdiction and the recognition and enforcement of judgments in matrimonial matters and in matters of parental responsibility for children of both spouses (Brussels II), which was in force from 1st March 2001 until 28th February 2005. Not only the Brussels II Regulation but, in particular, the widening of its scope by the Brussels II*bis* Regulation supported the choice for parental responsibilities as the CEFL's second working field. Besides, there are significant and natural links between, on the one hand, the question of divorce and its consequences and, on the other, between the question of parental responsibilities and the financial consequences of divorce. In addition to legally binding instruments (conventions and regulations), the Council of Europe has drafted Principles Concerning the Establishment and Legal Consequences of Parentage in its White Paper of 15th January 2002. The drafters noted that 'with the legal and social changes which have occurred at the national and international level, in particular, as regards human rights and the protection of the rights of the child, as well as the newly available medical techniques, there is an increased need for the Member States of the Council of Europe to update their laws in order to clarify and reinforce the legal status of the child.' For the CEFL the White Paper contains interesting perspectives and choices that will be used as a frame of reference. Already at this stage it can be noted that, to a certain extent, the content of the CEFL's Principles regarding Parental Responsibilities will probably be quite similar to the Council of Europe Principles regarding the legal consequences of parentage (Principles 18-25). However, with respect to the presentation of the choices that have already been made by the Council of Europe and will be made by the CEFL, considerable differences will exist since the White Paper does not delve into the origins of its Principles. In contrast, comparative overviews and explanations as to why a certain rule has been chosen is one of the main characteristics of the CEFL's Principles. Explicit comparisons between the European jurisdictions will be undertaken and an exposition of the variations in the underlying rules themselves will systematically reveal and explain why a particular Principle was selected and drafted. Only reliable and comprehensive comparative material should be used in carrying out such an endeavour. The book at hand fulfils this fundamental requirement.

Katharina Boele-Woelki
Utrecht, May 2005

AUTHORS

AUSTRIA	*Prof. Marianne Roth* University of Salzburg
BELGIUM	*Prof. Walter Pintens* Catholic University Leuven
	Dominique Pignolet Catholic University Leuven
BULGARIA	*Dr. Velina Todorova* Plovdiv University
CZECH REPUBLIC	*Prof. Milana Hrusaková* Masarykovy University, Brno
DENMARK	*Ingrid Lund-Andersen* Department of Private Law, University of Århus
	Christina Jeppesen-de Boer Molengraaff Institute for Private Law, Utrecht University
ENGLAND AND WALES	*Prof. Nigel Lowe* Law Department, University of Cardiff, Wales
FINLAND	*Dr. Kirsti Kurki-Suonio* Office of the Parliamentary Ombudsman, Helsinki
FRANCE	*Prof. Frédérique Ferrand* University of Lyon

GERMANY	*Prof. Nina Dethloff* University of Bonn
	Prof. Dieter Martiny European University Viadrina
GREECE	*Prof. Achilles G. Koutsouradis* Faculty of Law, University of Thessaloniki
	Helen Zervogianni University of Athens
HUNGARY	*Prof. Emila Weiss* Civil Law Department, University of Eötvös Loránd
	Dr. Orsolya Szeibert Civil Law Department, University of Eötvös Loránd
REPUBLIC OF IRELAND	*Prof. Geoffrey Shannon* Law Society of Ireland, Dublin
ITALY	*Prof. Salvatore Patti* Department of Private Law, University La Sapienza of Rome
	Dott. ssa Elena Bellisario University Roma Tre
	Prof. ssa Liliana Rossi Carleo University Roma Tre
LITHUANIA	*Prof. Valentinas Mikelenas* Supreme Court of Lithuania

THE NETHERLANDS	*Prof. Katharina Boele-Woelki* Molengraaff Institute for Private Law, Utrecht University
	Dr. Wendy Schrama Molengraaff Institute for Private Law, Utrecht University
	Machteld Vonk Molengraaff Institute for Private Law, Utrecht University
NORWAY	*Prof. Tone Sverdrup* Department of Private Law, Faculty of Law, University of Oslo
	Prof. Peter Lødrup Department of Private Law, Faculty of Law, University of Oslo
POLAND	*Prof. Andrzej Mączyński* Jagiellonian University of Kraków
	Prof. Jadwiga Mączyńska Jagiellonian University of Kraków
PORTUGAL	*Prof. Guilherme de Oliveira* University of Coimbra
RUSSIA	*Prof. Masha Antokolskaia* Free University of Amsterdam
SPAIN	*Dr. Cristina González Beilfuss* University of Barcelona
SWEDEN	*Prof. Maarit Jänterä-Jareborg* University of Uppsala
SWITZERLAND	*Prof. Heinz Hausheer* University of Bern

SWITZERLAND (*cont.*)

Cornelia Achermann-Weber
University of Bern

Dr. Stephan Wolf
University of Bern

INTRODUCTION TO QUESTIONNAIRE

The following definitions of parental responsibilities are used in international instruments:

1. **Hague Convention of 19 October 1996 on jurisdiction, applicable law, recognition, enforcement and co-operation in respect of parental responsibility and measures for the protection of children**

   Article 1 sub 2: For the purposes of this Convention, the term ' parental responsibility' includes parental authority, or any analogues relationship of authority determining the rights, powers and responsibilities of parents, guardians or other legal representatives in relation of the person or the property of the child.

2. **Council Regulation (EC) No 2201/2003 of 27 November 2003 concerning jurisdiction and the recognition and enforcement of judgments in matrimonial matters and the matters of parental responsibility, repealing Regulation (EC) no 1347/2000**

   Article 2 sub 7: The term 'parental responsibility' shall mean all rights and duties relating to the person or the property of a child which are given to a natural of legal person by judgment by operation of law or by agreement having legal effect. The term shall include rights of custody and rights of access.

3. **Council of Europe: 'White Paper' of 15 January 2002 on principles concerning the establishment and legal consequences of parentage**

   Principle 18: Parental responsibilities are a collection of duties and powers, which aim at ensuring the moral and material welfare of children, in particular:
   - Care and protection
   - Maintenance of personal relationships
   - Provision of education
   - Legal representation
   - Determination of residence and
   - Administration of property.

This questionnaire uses the definition of the Council of Europe (White Paper) as a working definition.

QUESTIONNAIRE

A. GENERAL

1. Having regard to the concept of parental responsibilities as defined by the Council of Europe (see above), explain the concept or concepts used in your national legal system.

2. Explain whether your national concept or concepts encompass:
   (a) Care and protection;
   (b) Maintenance of personal relationships;
   (c) Provision of education;
   (d) Legal representation;
   (e) Determination of residence;
   (f) Administration of property.

3. In what circumstances (*e.g.* child reaching majority or marrying) do parental responsibilities automatically come to an end?

4. What is the current source of law for parental responsibilities?

5. Give a brief history of the main developments of the law concerning parental responsibilities.

6. Are there any recent proposals for reform in this area?

B. THE CONTENTS OF PARENTAL RESPONSIBILITIES

7. Describe what the contents of parental responsibilities are according to your national law including case law.

8. What is the position taken in your national law with respect to:
   (a) Care;
   (b) Education;
   (c) Religious upbringing;
   (d) Disciplinary measures and corporal punishment;
   (e) Medical treatment;
   (f) and legal representation.

9. What is the position taken in respect of the child's right to be heard with regard to the issues mentioned under Q 8a - 8f. What relevance is given to the age and maturity of the child?

10. Do(es) the holder(s) of parental responsibilities has(have) the right to administer the child's property?

11. If yes, explain the content of this right.

12. Are there restrictions with respect to:
    (a) Certain goods and/or values (inherited property, gift...);
    (b) Salary of the child; or
    (c) Certain transactions?

13. Are there special rules protecting children from indebtedness caused by the holder(s) of parental responsibilities?

14. Do the contents of parental responsibilities differ according to the holder(s) of parental responsibilities (*e.g.* married, unmarried, parents not living together, stepparents, foster parents or other persons). If so, describe in some detail how it differs.

C. ATTRIBUTION OF PARENTAL RESPONSIBILITIES

I. Married parents

15. Who has parental responsibilities when the parents are:
    (a) Married at the time of the child's birth;
    (b) Not married at that time but marry later?

16. How, if at all, is the attribution of parental responsibilities affected by:
    (a) Divorce;
    (b) Legal separation;
    (c) Annulment of the marriage;
    (d) Factual separation.

17. To what extent, if at all, are the parents free to agree upon the attribution of parental responsibilities after divorce, legal separation or annulment of the marriage? If they are, are these agreements subject to scrutiny by a competent authority.

18. May the competent authority attribute joint parental responsibilities to the parents of the child even against the wish of both parents/one of the parents? To what extent, if at all, should the competent authority take account of a parent's violent behaviour towards the other parent?

19. Provide statistical information on the attribution of parental responsibilities after divorce, legal separation or annulment of the marriage.

II. Unmarried parents

20. Who has parental responsibilities when the parents are not married?

21. Does it make a difference if the parents have formalised their mutual relationship in some way (registered partnership, civil union, *pacte civil de solidarité…*).

22. Under what condition, if at all, can
    (a) The unmarried mother;
    (b) The unmarried father,
    obtain parental responsibilities.

23. How, if at all, is the attribution of parental responsibilities affected by the ending of the unmarried parents' relationship?

24. May the competent authority attribute joint parental responsibilities to the parents also against the wish of both parents/one of the parents? To what extent, if at all, may the competent authority take into account a parent's violent behaviour towards the other parent?

25. To what extent, if at all, are unmarried parents free to agree upon the attribution of parental responsibilities after the ending of their relationship?

26. Provide statistical information available regarding the attribution of parental responsibilities for unmarried parents.

III. Other persons

27. Under what conditions, if at all, can the partner of a parent holding parental responsibilities obtain parental responsibilities, when, he/she is:
    (a) Married to that parent;
    (b) Living with that parent in a formalised relationship (registered partnership, civil union, *pacte civil de solidarité…*);
    (c) or living with that parent in a non formalised relationship?

28. Does it make any difference if the partner of the parent holding parental responsibilities is of the same sex?

29. How, if at all, is the attribution of parental responsibilities in the partner affected by the ending of his/her relationship with the parent? Distinguish according to the different relationships referred to in Q 27 and Q 28.

30. To what extent, if at all, is the parent holding parental responsibilities and his/her partner free to agree upon the attribution of parental responsibilities after the ending of his/her relationship with the parent? Distinguish according to the different relationships referred to in Q 27 and Q 28.

31. Under what conditions, if at all, can other persons not being a parent or a partner of a parent holding parental responsibilities, obtain parental responsibilities (*e.g.* members of the child's family, close friends, foster parent...)? Specify, where such other persons may obtain parental responsibilities, if it is in addition to or in substitution of existing holder(s) of parental responsibilities.

32. Under what conditions, if at all, can a public body obtain parental responsibilities? Specify, where it is so obtained, if it is in addition to or in substitution of existing holder(s) of parental responsibilities.

33. To whom are the parental responsibilities attributed in the case of:
    (a) The death of a parent holding parental responsibilities;
    (b) The death of both parents of whom at least one was holding parental responsibilities at the time of the death?

34. To what extent, if at all, may the holder(s) of parental responsibilities appoint a new holder(s) upon his/her/their death? If such an appointment is permitted, must it take place in a special form, *e.g.* will?

D. THE EXERCISE OF PARENTAL RESPONSIBILITIES

I. Interests of the child

35. In exercising parental responsibilities, how are the interests of the child defined in your national legal system?

II. Joint parental responsibilities

36. If parental responsibilities are held jointly by two or more persons, are they held equally?

37. If parental responsibilities holders cannot agree on an issue, how is the dispute resolved? For example does the holder of parental responsibilities have the authority to act alone? In this respect is a distinction made between important decisions and decisions of a daily nature? Does it make any difference if the child is only living with one of the holders of the parental responsibilities?

38. If holders of parental responsibilities cannot agree on an issue, can they apply to a competent authority to resolve their dispute? If applicable, specify whether this authority's competence is limited to certain issues *e.g.* residence or contact.

39. To what extent, if at all, may a holder of parental responsibilties act alone if there is more than one holder of parental responsibilities?

40. Under what circumstances, if at all, may the competent authority permit the residence of the child to be changed within the same country and/or abroad (so called relocation) without the consent of one of the holders of parental responsibilities?

41. Under what conditions, if at all, may the competent authority decree that the child should, on an alternating basis, reside with both holders of parental responsibilities (*e.g.* every other month with mother/father)?

III. Sole parental responsibilities

42. Does a parent with sole parental responsibilities have full authority to act alone, or does he/she have a duty to consult:
    (a) The other parent;
    (b) Other persons, bodies or competent authorities?

E. CONTACT

43. Having regard to the definition by the Council of Europe (see above), explain the concepts of contact used in your national legal system.

44. To what extent, if at all, does the child have a right of contact with:
    (a) A parent holding parental responsibilities but not living with the child;
    (b) A parent not holding parental responsibilities;
    (c) Persons other than parents (*e.g.* grandparents, stepparents, siblings etc)?

45. Is the right to have contact referred to in Q 43 also a right and/or a duty of the parent or the other persons concerned?

46. To what extent, if at all, are the parents free to make contact arrangements? If they can, are these arrangements subject to scrutiny by a competent authority?

47. Can a competent authority exclude, limit or subject to conditions, the exercise of contact? If so, which criteria are decisive?

48. What if any, are the consequences on parental responsibilities, if a holder of parental responsibilities with whom the child is living, disregards the child's right to contact with:
    (a) A parent;
    (b) Other persons?

F. DELEGATION OF PARENTAL RESPONSIBILITIES

49. To what extent, if at all, may the holder(s) of parental responsibilities delegate its exercise?

50. To what extent, if at all, may a person not holding parental responsibilities apply to a competent authority for a delegation of parental responsibilities?

G. DISCHARGE OF PARENTAL RESPONSIBILITIES

51. Under what circumstances, if at all, should the competent authorities in you legal system discharge the holder(s) of his/her/their parental responsibilities for reasons such as maltreatment, negligence or abuse of the child, mental illness of the holder of parental responsibilities, *etc.*? To what extent, if at all, should the competent authority take into account a parent's violent behaviour towards the other parent?

52. Who, in the circumstances referred to in Q 51, has the right or the duty to request the discharge of parental responsibilities?

53. To what extent, if at all, are rights of contact permitted between the child and the previous holder of parental responsibilities after the latter has been discharged of his/her parental responsibilities?

54. To what extent, if at all, can the previous holder(s) of parental responsibilities, who has been discharged of his/her parental responsibilities, regain them?

H. PROCEDURAL ISSUES

55. Who is the competent authority to decide disputes concerning parental responsibilities, questions of residence of the child or contact? Who is the competent authority to carry out an investigation relating to the circumstances of the child in a dispute on parental responsibility, residence or contact?

56. Under what conditions, if any, may a legally effective decision or agreement on parental responsibilities, the child's residence or contact, be reviewed by a competent authority? Is it, *e.g.*, required that the circumstances have changed after the decision or agreement was made and/or that a certain period of time has time has passed since the decision or agreement?

57. What alternative disputes solving mechanisms, if any, *e.g.* mediation or counselling, are offered in your legal system? Are such mechanisms also available at the stage of enforcement of a decision/agreement concerning parental responsibilities, the child's residence or contact?

58. To what extent, if at all, is an order or an agreement on parental responsibilities, the child's residence or contact enforceable and in practice enforced? Describe the system of enforcement followed in your national legal system. Under what conditions, if at all, may enforcement be refused?

59. To what extent, if at all, are children heard when a competent authority decides upon parental responsibilities, the child's residence or contact, *e.g.*, upon a dispute, when scrutinizing an agreement, when appointing or discharging holder(s) of parental responsibilities, upon enforcement of a decision or agreement?

60. How will the child be heard (*e.g.* directly by the competent authority, a specially appointed expert or social worker)?

61. How, if at all, is the child legally represented in disputes concerning:
    (a) Parental responsibilities;
    (b) The child's residence; or
    (c) Contact?

62. What relevance is given in your national legal system to the age and maturity of the child in respect of Q 59-61?

QUESTION 1

A. GENERAL

Having regard to the concept of parental responsibilities as defined by the Council of Europe, explain the concept or concepts used in your national legal system.

AUSTRIA

The Austrian term for parental responsibilities is *Obsorge, i.e.* caring for and supervising the child. This encompasses the entire care relationship of the parents or other person(s) entrusted with the custody of the child. It involves rights as well as duties of the holder(s) of parental responsibilities. Under Sec. 144 Austrian CC, parental responsibilities include care and education, administering the child's property, and legal representation of the child in all these matters.

BELGIUM

Parental responsibilities are a collection of rights necessary for the parents to properly fulfil their duties relating to person and property of their minor children.[1]

BULGARIA

Bulgarian family law originates from the Roman legal family. It was constructed at the end of the 19th century.[2] A national law making tradition did not exist at that time, since the State was still recovering from 5 centuries of Ottoman occupation. Therefore the lawmakers chose to adopt foreign solutions. The Law of family relations was taken from the French Code Civil via the Italian Civil Code. In 1907 the Bulgarian Act on Persons introduced the concept of 'parental power', however this was abolished by the Bulgarian Persons and Family Act of 1949.

During the years 1944-1989 Bulgarian family law developed under the influence of the relevant Soviet legislation. In the years 1945-1949, new concepts were introduced including 'parental rights and duties'. The Bulgarian Family Code of 1968 substituted this with the concept of 'parental power'. The current

---

1 H. DE PAGE, *Traité élémentaire de droit civil belge*, T. II (Les Personnes), Vol. 2 (by J.-P. MASSON), Brussels: Bruylant, 1990, p. 947; J. GERLO, *Handboek voor Familierecht, 1. Personen- en familierecht*, Bruges: Die Keure, 2003, p. 298.

2 Bulgarian civil law is not codified. Separate pieces of legislation regulate its various branches. Currently, the Bulgarian Contracts and Duties Act, the Bulgarian Civil Registration Act, the Bulgarian Inheritance Act and the Bulgarian Family Code are in effect. The Bulgarian Family Code regulates parent-child relationships, as well as marriage and its dissolution, financial and property issues between spouses, parentage and adoption. Courts apply the law, but do not make law. Supreme courts, in addition to law enforcement, also interpret the statutory provisions, binding courts of lower instances.

Bulgarian Family Code (1985) utilises the concept of 'parental rights and duties'.

The main provision in the Bulgarian Family Code speaks only of parental obligations: 'The parents are obliged to care for their children and to prepare them for socially useful activity' (Art. 68). The Code further stipulates that 'parental rights and obligations are exercised by both parents jointly and separately' (Art. 72). The Bulgarian Constitution of 1991 also speaks of parental rights and obligations: 'Raising and bringing up of children until they are the age of majority is both a right and an obligation of their parents' (Art. 47 § 1).

It has been stated that 'the parental rights and obligations are functions with social importance that are assigned to parents to be exercised exclusively in the interests of children'.[3] This legal theory underlines the unity of the rights and obligations: 'all parental conduct towards a child has the features of both a parental right and a parental duty. Child support and consent for adoption are the only exceptions; child support is solely a parental obligation, and consent for adoption is only a parental right.' The Bulgarian Family Code uses the term 'care' for children to express the unity between the rights and duties of the parent.

Family law literature defines the parental functions as 'all the rights and duties for the rearing and upbringing of a child, including care for its property'.[4] Both natural and adoptive parents hold parental rights and duties and both exercise them jointly and separately.[5] In case of conflict between parents, each parent may submit a claim to the court to decide how to perform parental rights and duties. Parents cannot decline or transfer their parental rights and duties to any third party. The restriction or termination of parental rights may be effected only by court intervention.[6] Even in such cases no one can become the recipient of such rights and duties (except through adoption). Under certain conditions stipulated by the Bulgarian Family Code, care for the upbringing of the child may be exercised by grandparents or other members of the extended family. However, these persons do not become holders of parental rights and duties.

The Bulgarian Child Protection Act (2000) introduced a new obligation of parents: 'The parents are obliged to bring into effect the measures undertaken under the Act and shall provide assistance towards the implementation of child protection measures' (Art. 8 § 4).

---

3 L. NENOVA, *The Bulgarian Family Code and the Family Law Reform*, Sofia, 1971, p. 199.

4 See: L. NENOVA, *Family Law of the Republic of Bulgaria*, Sofia, 1994, p. 407 *et seq.*; A. STANEVA, *Representative and Custodial Functions of Parents*, Sofia, 1992.

5 Art. 72 Bulgarian Family Code reads: 'Parental rights and obligations are exercised by both parents jointly and separately....'.

6 Art. 47, § 5 of the Constitution (1991) and Art. 74 -76 Bulgarian Family Code (1985).

CZECH REPUBLIC

Under Czech law, every parent is awarded parental responsibility provided the parent has full legal capacity, regardless of whether the parents are spouses or the child is born out of wedlock. Court determined fathers also hold parental responsibility.[7] If a parent is dead, unknown, or does not have full legal capacity, their right to exercise parental responsibility transfers to the second parent. This also applies if one of the parents is deprived of parental responsibility or if their exercise of parental responsibility has been suspended (Sec. 34 § 2 Czech Family Code).

The 1998 reform of family law strengthened the position of the minor parent who, due to lack of legal capacity, cannot be awarded parental responsibility by operation of law. The court may award parental responsibility to the minor parent taking care of his or her child if the parent has attained sixteen years of age and is duly qualified for the exercise of rights and duties of parental responsibility (Sec. 34 § 3 Czech Family Code).

The practical importance of this provision is that when a minor mother does not cohabit with a father who has obtained majority (and who would be the sole holder of parental responsibility), the court may award the minor mother parental responsibilities of care for the child, and at the same time, according to Sec. 50 Czech Family Code, the mother may be awarded the upbringing of the child (the exercise of personal care) and the father may be ordered to pay a certain amount of maintenance.[8] If the father of the child is also a minor, or unknown, a guardian determined by court will be appointed the legal representative of the child, compare with Sec. 78 Czech Family Code.

Parental responsibility is defined in the Czech Family Code (Sec. 31 § 1) as a sum of rights and duties:

- when caring for a minor child, which includes in particular caring for its health and physical, emotional, intellectual and moral development,
- when legally representing a minor child,
- when administering its property.

All the rights and duties mentioned above are also held by an adoptive parent because adoption establishes the same relationship between the adoptive parent and adopted child as between a biological parent and child (Sec. 63 Czech Family Code).

Parenthood is also protected by the Czech Charter of Basic Rights and Freedoms. Pursuant to Art. 32 of the Charter, care of children and their

---

7 M. HRUSAKOVA and Z. KRALICKOVA, *Ceske rodinne pravo, 2. vyd,* Brno: MU, 2001, p. 194.

8 M. HOLUB and H. NOVA, *Zakon o rodine. Komentar a predpisy souvisici. 6. vyd,* Prague: Linde, 2004, p. 72; M. HRUSAKOVA, *Zakon o rodine. Komentar. 2. vyde.* Prague: C.H.Beck, 2001, p. 104

upbringing is a parental right, and children have a right to parental upbringing and care. Rights of parents may be restricted and minor children may be separated against their will from their parents only by court under the law.

Beside parental responsibility the parental legal relation to children also includes other rights and duties of parents such as the right and duty to determine the name and surname of the child, and the maintenance duty of the parent in relation to the child.[9]

DENMARK

The Danish concept is *forældremyndighed* which is best translated as parental authority.[10] The holder(s) of parental authority have certain duties and powers and decisions must be made from the perspective of the child's interests and needs, Art. 2(1) Danish Act on Parental Authority and Contact.[11] The holder(s) of parental authority is/are also the child's guardian(s), which entails a right to act on behalf of the child in legal and financial matters.

It has been considered on a number of occasions whether the concept of parental authority should be changed into a concept which better reflects the responsibility of the holder(s).[12] When the Act was changed in 1985 the concept of parental authority was retained, the underlying reasoning being that a change in concept would not change the legal content of the concept. It was further stressed that the concept of parental authority entailed not just a right to decide for the child, but also a duty to protect and care for the child.[13]

In general it is the parents or one of the parents who is/are the holder(s) of parental authority. Parental authority can be transferred to a non-parent (for example, a step-parent) or to two non-parents (this must be a married couple), but there can never be more than two holder(s) of parental authority at the same time, Art. 11 Danish Act on Parental Authority and Contact. If child protection measures are taken, the holder(s) of parental authority retain

---

9 J. PETRULAKOVA, *Prava uprava vychovy deti v rodine*, Obzor, Bratislava, 1970.

10 There are no official translations of Danish legislation. At http://www.jur.ku.dk/biblioteker/infosoeg/ a number of unofficial translations of different acts can be found. The Danish Act on parental authority has not been translated. However, the unofficial translation of an older version of the Act on the formation and dissolution of marriage, Act No. 148 of 08.03.1991 with later amendments, uses the concept of custody. The concept of custody can also be found in a number of older articles and governmental reports. The concept of parental authority is chosen as a better direct translation of the Danish concept *forældremyndighed*.

11 *Lov om forældremyndighed og samvær*, Act No. 387 of 14.06.1995 with the following amendments No. 752 of 15.08.1996, No. 416 of 10.06.1997, No. 147 of 09.03.1999, No. 461 of 07.06. 2001 and No. 446 of 09.06.2004.

12 S. DANIELSEN, *Lov om forældremyndighed og samvær*, Copenhagen: Jurist- og Økonomforbundets Forlag, 1997, p. 54.

13 Commission report No. 985/1983, p. 24-25.

parental authority but their rights and duties are accordingly restricted. When a child is taken into care as a child protection measure, the local authorities and/or the foster parents with whom the child is placed are not endowed with parental authority. Their rights and duties stem from the care order.

ENGLAND & WALES

So far as English law is concerned the controlling statute, the English Children Act 1989, refers to 'parental responsibility' rather than 'parental responsibilities'. The English concept of parental responsibility very much accords with Principle 18 of the Council of Europe's White Paper on Parental Responsibility. As Lord MACKAY LC said[14] when introducing the Children Bill to Parliament, the concept of 'parental responsibility':

> 'emphasises that the days when a child should be regarded as a possession of his parent - indeed when in the past they had a right to his services and to sue on their loss are now buried forever. The overwhelming purpose of parenthood is the responsibility for caring for and raising the child to be a properly developed adult both physically and morally'.

The comment is echoed by the Department of Health's introductory guide to the Children Act[15] which states that parental responsibility:

> 'emphasises that the duty to care for the child and to raise him to moral, physical and emotional health is the fundamental task of parenthood and the only justification for the authority that it confers'.

Both these comments reflect in turn the earlier landmark decision of *Gillick v West Norfolk and Wisbech Area Health Authority*[16] in which, at any rate, Lords FRASER and SCARMAN emphasised that parental power to control a child exists not for the benefit of the parent but for the benefit of the child.

As well as embracing the idea that parents must behave dutifully towards their children, the English concept of responsibility also embodies the concept that responsibility for childcare belongs to parents and not to the state. By providing that responsibility should continue despite, for example, a court order that the child should live with one of them, parents 'are to understand that the state will not relieve them of their responsibilities'.[17] This is underscored by the fact that responsibility cannot be voluntarily surrendered to a public body[18] and that

---

14 502 HL Official Report (5th series), col 490.

15 'Introduction to the Children Act 1989', HMSO 1989, para 1.4.

16 [1986] AC 112, [1985] 3 All ER 402, HL.

17 CRETNEY, 'Defining the Limits of State Intervention: The Child and Courts' in: FREESTONE, (ed.), *Children and the Law*, 1990, p. 67.

18 *I.e.* where the child is 'accommodated' by a local authority under Sec. 20 of the 1989 Act parental responsibility is not acquired by the authority, see the discussion by

even where a care order is made compulsorily placing the child in local authority care parents still retain their responsibility. In short the English Children Act 1989 through the concept of parental responsibility emphasises the idea that 'once a parent, always a parent' and that prima facie responsibility for deciding what should happen to their children even upon their separation should rest with the parents themselves.

This enduring aspect of parental responsibility is in marked contrast to the concept of 'rights of custody' espoused by many continental European legal systems inasmuch as under English law it is not possible following divorce, for example, to divest a married parent of parental responsibility and thus to vest sole responsibility in the other. Any dispute between the parents over the upbringing of their child can be solved by the making of an appropriate court order.[19]

FINLAND

The central concept is child custody. According to the Finnish legal system the custodian of the child shall provide daily care and protection for the child and moreover provide for the child's well-being in general. The custody of the child includes the child's personal relationships to other persons close to the child, especially its parents. Child protection is a concept of public law whereas child custody belongs to private law. Child protection is a task of the local social authorities, which above all, shall provide support to the custodian of the child. But if the circumstances at home seriously endanger the child's well-being or if the child seriously endangers its own well-being, the child can be taken into care by the local social authorities, to whom a considerable part of the custodial rights will be transferred. According to the Finnish legal system a guardian oversees the administration of the property of incompetent persons. However, the custodians of a minor are also its guardians unless the court appoints another person.

Approximately one hundred unaccompanied minors arrive in Finland per year. Every unaccompanied minor must have a representative appointed who will represent the child in applying for asylum. According to the Sec. 26 Finnish Act on the Integration of Immigrants and Reception of Asylum Seekers (No. 493/1999):

> A representative may be assigned to a refugee child, or a child applying for a residence permit or seeking asylum, who is in Finland without a guardian or other legal representative. The representative

---

EEKELAAR 'Parental Responsibility. State of Nature of Nature of the State?' [1991] 37 *JSWFL* 4042.

19 The courts have powers under Sec. 8, English Children Act 1989 to make residence, contact, prohibited steps and specific issue orders. These powers are wide enough to cover virtually any kind of dispute over a child's upbringing. For a discussion of these powers see *e.g.* LOWE/DOUGLAS, *Bromley's Family Law*, 1998, 9th Ed, Ch. 12.

exercises a guardian's right to be heard in matters pertaining to the child's physical care and assets, decides living arrangements and manages its assets.

Because of its rather limited application, reference will no longer be made to the concept of the representative of an unaccompanied minor. The Finnish social security system provides services for custodians, such as the right to public day care or free education. Within the concepts of Finnish child law, this may be important to take into consideration from a comparative perspective.

FRANCE

French legal provisions use the terminology *autorité parental'* (parental authority). Until the Act of 4 April 1970, the French CC used the terms '*puissance paternelle*', which states the power of decision the father had over his children (this power belonged only to the father). In Art. 371-1 French CC the '*autorité parentale*' is now defined as "a collection of rights and duties aimed at the child's interests.' This concept of parental authority encompasses several aspects, including care and protection, the maintenance of personal relationships, determination of the child's residence, the child's education, legal representation, a maintenance obligation towards the child, administration of property, and civil liability of the parents for damages caused by their child. See also Q 2.

GERMANY

Until recently the term 'parental responsibility' (*elterliche Verantwortung*) was used only in some legal provisions (*e.g.* § 52 para. 1 German Act on Voluntary Jurisdiction[20]), but was not used as basic concept in German law. However, due to the use of this concept in the Brussels II and II A Regulations and other international and European instruments, this term is employed more and more in German legal literature.[21] The basic concept in German family law is still parental custody (*elterliche Sorge*), which includes the care of the child (*Personensorge*) and the care for the property of the child (*Vermögenssorge*), § 1626 para. 1 German CC. All other issues (legal representation, determination of residence, *etc.*) are either consequences of this parental custody or - as the right of contact - additional legal positions.

GREECE

The concept of parental responsibilities, as defined by the Council of Europe, encompasses the Greek concepts of parental care and guardianship. Parental care is the usual situation where parents have parental responsibilities for their child. If, for any reason, parental care does not exist, the court will place the

20 Act on Voluntary Jurisdiction (Gesetz über die Angelegenheiten der freiwilligen Gerichtsbarkeit; FGG) of 20.05.1898, *Imperial Gazette* (*Reichsgesetzblatt; RGBl.*) 1898 p. 771, as amended.

21 See D. SCHWAB, *Familienrecht*, 12th Edition, Munich, 2003, No. 436 *et seq*, which also includes child maintenance as an issue of parental responsibility.

child under guardianship, meaning that it attributes parental responsibilities to a third person, the guardian, who is assisted and controlled by a supervisory council and the court (Art. 1590 Greek CC). Both parental care and guardianship consist of a bundle of rights and duties, which have to be exercised in the best interests of the child (Art. 1511 and 1648 Greek CC). Those rights and duties pertain to the physical care of the child, the administration of its property, and the child's legal representation (Art. 1510 para. 1 and 1603 Greek CC). A supplementary institution to parental care and guardianship is foster care (Art. 1655-1665 Greek CC). The foster parents may be charged with the actual care of the child, but the child's legal relationship with its parents or guardian remain, in principle, unaltered.

HUNGARY

The Hungarian family law title, 'The Rights of Parental Supervision,' regulates the main principles of exercising parental responsibilities, the children's rights in issues of parental responsibilities, the elements of parental responsibilities and the control of the authority exercised over the parental responsibilities.

When parental responsibilities are exercised by a guardian instead of the parents, the rules of parental responsibilities, as regulated by the Council of Europe, are somewhat adjusted. If the parents are alive they may be able to observe or even take part in the child's continuing care.

It is when the duties of the guardian are carried out by the child's close relatives (by 'another person' according to the White Paper) that parental responsibilities most closely resemble those of the parents. The guardians can exercise parental responsibilities temporarily or for the child's entire minority, depending on the reasons for the guardianship. If the unmarried mother is a minor when the child is born, her parental responsibilities are suspended until she reaches majority. In this situation, a temporary guardian, usually one of the child's close relatives, will exercise temporary parental responsibilities. This may also happen when the parents are temporarily prevented from exercising their parental responsibilities and they agree that another person should take the child into his or her household. It is, of course, a different situation when both parents die and the child comes under the guardianship of a close relative.

In a 'traditional guardianship,' the child's guardian is a close relative of the child. The parental responsibilities exercised by this guardian are very close to the parental responsibilities of the child's parents. This guarantees that the child's familial identity and relationships can be maintained, as well as that the child should grow up in its family.

The 'Child Welfare Guardianship' differs from the traditional guardianship. The state takes the child into a child welfare guardianship if living with the parents puts the child in danger. The child taken into state care is not under the guardianship of the authorities. If the child lives with foster parents, the exercise of the parental responsibilities belongs to the foster parent. If the child lives in a children's home, the exercise of the parental responsibilities belongs to the supervisor of the children's home.

Strong efforts are taken to place children with foster parents rather than in children's homes. The parental responsibilities of foster parents are closer to those of the child's natural parents. As many as forty children can live in each children's home. Children may live in the 'SOS Children's Village,' a special form of children's home which work according to international principles and rules.

A child that is taken into state care is not necessarily completely separated from its parents. Strong efforts are taken to maintain the child's personal family relationships while the child is in state care. State care should be a temporary solution, preserving the possibility that the child may live with its family again.

The parental responsibilities arising from an adoption differ from those in a guardianship. The only difference between a parent-child relationship established by adoption and a parent-child relationship established by descent is the method of establishment. Once the adoption is completed, the adoptive parent has parental responsibilities identical to those of a biological parent.

IRELAND

The matters covered in the Council of Europe definition of parental responsibility broadly equate with the concept of parental responsibility as understood in the Irish legal system. The term 'parental responsibility' is taken to mean rights of custody, rights of access (contact) and guardianship. Parental responsibility also equates to the basis of the exercise of jurisdiction by the Irish courts of their wardship jurisdiction.

ITALY

In the Italian legal system, there is no agreed definition of the term 'parental responsibility'. The Italian legislature uses the expression 'parental authority' (Title IX, Book 1, Italian CC). The concept of 'parental responsibility,' joined with 'authority,' implies the totality of rights and duties exercised exclusively in the interests of the child by the parents. It must be remembered that the Italian concept of parental responsibility includes both authority (the totality of rights and duties) and responsibility (the attribution of those rights and duties); the terms 'authority' and 'responsibility' are used as synonyms.

Parental authority is conferred in order to ensure the moral and material well-being of the child; the exercise of authority is one of the duties used to comply with the rest of the parental duties.

The concept of parental authority has not been defined by the legislature, nor has its content has been wholly specified. Italian legal literature has developed parental authority's characteristics and determined its limits.

Generally, parental authority is a civil law institution that includes rights and duties that are exercised exclusively in the interests of the child. Legal literature distinguishes the internal aspects of authority (concerning the relationship of parents and child) from the external ones (concerning the relationship of parents and third parties), and personal aspects (concerning the care and the growth of the child) from those of property (concerning the management of minor's properties).[22]

If the parents are deceased or for any other reason cannot exercise the authority, the legal authority of the child's place of residence will appoint a guardian for the child. The institution of guardianship, aiming to protect the child, has a function similar to but not identical with parental authority; the content of guardianship is more limited than that of parental authority.[23]

Finally, the Italian system provides (though often in an incomplete and incoherent way) for a 'special curator' who is entitled to represent the minor in all legal proceedings affecting her or his interests and if there are conflicts of interest between the child and the child's parent(s) or guardian(s) charged with the exercise of the parental responsibilities (Art. 360 § 6 Italian CC).[24]

---

22 See P. PERLINGIERI and P. FEMIA, in: P. PERLINGIERI, *Manuale di diritto civile*, Naples, 2000, p. 119.

23 The guardian must provide for the education and moral guidance of the child, but not for the child's support. In addition, the guardian has the power to represent the child and manage the child's properties; however, the guardian's actions are limited to the more pertinent forms of legal supervision and control due to the lack of a parent-child relationship. Regarding the education of the minor and the management of his properties: the guardian must follow the instructions set by the guardianship judge following the guardian's suggestions (Art. 371 Italian CC), the guardian must inventory the minor's properties, (Art. 362 *et seq* Italian CC), the authorisation of the guardianship judge is needed for extraordinary acts of disposition of the minor's property (Art. 374 Italian CC) and the court's authorisation is needed for the more burdensome acts. Finally, if the child's interests should conflict with the guardian's, taking the opinion of the guardianship judge into consideration a substitute guardian will be appointed to represent the minor (Art. 360 Italian CC). If there is a conflict between the substitute guardian and the minor as well, the guardianship judge will appoint a special curator (Art. 360 Italian CC). The guardianship can be qualified as a civil law institution characterised by obligation and gratuity, except for adequate compensation for the guardian, taking into account the amount of the properties and the difficulties relating to its management (Art. 379 Italian CC). See P. PERLINGIERI and P. FEMIA, in: P. PERLINGIERI, *Manuale di diritto civile*, Naples 2000, p. 121.

24 The Italian legal system does not explicitly provide for a special curator acting as the minor's lawyer in all legal proceedings affecting his interests (for example, those concerning the termination or modification of the parental responsibilities pursuant to Art. 330 and 333 Italian CC), nor can provisions of that kind (for example, adoption proceedings) be de facto implemented where they exist due to the absence of a specific, free, court provided, procedural defence. In this respect, the Supreme Court has stated (Supreme Court, 30.01.2002, No. 1, *Giust. Civ.*, 2002, I, p. 1467, commented by A.G. CIANCI) that the incompleteness of the legislation is in principal compatible with the *New York Convention on the rights of child* of 20.11.1989 (ratified

The main function of 'parental responsibilities' in the Italian legal system falls within the definition provided by the Council of Europe.

LITHUANIA

The concept of parental responsibilities derives from Art. 3.155 - 3.158, among others, of Book Three, Lithuanian CC. According to Art. 3.155 Lithuanian CC, the substance of paternal authority is defined in the following way:

> Until they attain majority or emancipation, children shall be cared for by their parents, *i.e.*, a child is subject to the supervision of its parents until majority or emancipation;
> Parents have a right and a duty to properly educate and bring up their children, care for their health and, having regard to their physical and mental state, to create favourable conditions for their full and harmonious development so that the child will be able to live independently in society.

Thus, Art. 3.155 defines the notion of parental authority. This notion is not absolutely new; it was espoused in the legal acts of Lithuania pre-World War II. Parental authority, the whole complex of parental rights, powers, duties and responsibilities connected with their minor children, has existed in all the periods of development of Lithuanian society. The essence of parental responsibilities (or parental authority, using the terminology of the Lithuanian CC) is established by Part. 6 of Art. 38 1992 Lithuanian Constitution as the right and duty of parents to raise their children to be honest individuals and loyal citizens, as well as to support them until they reach the age of majority (18 years of age). In fact, parental authority includes considerably more familial relationships than are defined by the law. Besides the legal aspects of parental authority, there are moral aspects, also the aspects determined by customs, which, though not determined by laws, nevertheless exist and develop alongside legal relationships.

In defining legal aspects of parental authority, the law combines personal interests of parents and children with those of the State. Therefore, the proper exercise of parental authority is not only a responsibility of the parents themselves, but of the State as well. The principle of care and protection of the family, motherhood, fatherhood and childhood is a Constitutional principle, therefore the point of view of the State in this sphere is established in Part 2 of Art. 38 Lithuanian Constitution. The Lithuanian CC provides for such cases when the State interferes or must interfere in family relationships if parental authority is not exercised in a proper way.

---

and implemented in Italy by the Law of 27.03.1991, No. 176), according to which the child must be party to all proceedings which may have implication for his or her life and personal development.

Legally, parental authority commences from the moment the legal relationships between a child and its parents are established and continues until the child's majority *i.e.* its characteristic feature is temporal; a time period defined by the law. Part 1 of Art. 3.155 Lithuanian CC establishes the legal essence and duration of parental authority: until the age of majority, children are under the supervision of their parents. Parental supervision also comes to an end when a child enters into marriage before attaining the age of 18, or if the child is emancipated (Part 4 of Art. 3.194 Lithuanian CC).

All these provisions are closely connected and compose an integrated whole. They are established in the law as the personal and patrimonial rights and duties of the parents (Art. 3.165-3.172 Lithuanian CC). If any of the provisions on parental responsibilities are ignored, other provisions can not be exercised to their full extent, or at all. For instance, if the parents fail to provide maintenance for their child, it will be impossible to provide favourable conditions for the health, education and development of the child, and for the welfare of the child *etc.* The main provisions of parental responsibilities are closely related with the rights of the child. Rights of minor children are implemented by their parents (Part 1 of Art. 3.163 Lithuanian CC), so the parental responsibilities must be orientated to the implementation of the rights of the child. In essence, parental responsibilities and the child's rights and duties are in conformity with each other.[25]

THE NETHERLANDS

According to Dutch law parental responsibilities comprise the duty and the right of the parent to care for and raise his or her minor child. This includes the care and responsibility for the mental and physical well being of the child, and fostering the development of its personality (Art. 1:247 Dutch CC). In addition, parental responsibilities relate to the minor, the administration of his or her estate and his or her representation in civil acts, both judicially and extra-judicially (Art. 1:245 § 4 Dutch CC). Parents are vested with parental responsibilities in the interests of their child(ren), therefore the ensuing rights and duties cannot be disconnected from the parents' obligation to pursue these interests. The freedom of parents to raise their children in accordance with their own outlook on life, within the framework of the law, is central.[26]

NORWAY

The concept of parental responsibilities may be described as duties and rights relating to a child. According to Art. 30 Norwegian Children Act 1981, the concept includes both a duty to care for the child as well as a right to make decisions on behalf of the child. The concept as laid out in the Norwegian

---

25 V. MIKELENAS *et. al.*, *Commentary of Book Three of the Civil Code of Lithuania* (in Lithuanian), Vilnius: Justitia 2002, p. 297-298.

26 ASSER-DE BOER, Mr. C. *Asser's Handleiding tot de beoefening van het Nederlands Burgerlijk Recht. Personen- en Familie Recht*, 2002 No. 818; *Personen- en familierecht, Tekst en commentaar*, 2004, Art. 247 and Supreme Court 25.9.1998, *NJ* 1999, 379.

Children Act 1981 does not include duties and rights relating to the property of a child nor legal representation (guardianship). Since guardianship, however, is an automatic consequence of parental responsibilities, the person(s) having such responsibilities will also decide financial matters for the child, within the limits set in the Norwegian Act on Guardianship of 8 April 1927, No. 7.

POLAND

Polish law concerning parental responsibilities is defined by the Polish Constitution of 2 April 1997.[27] According to Art. 48 sec. 1 Polish Constitution, 'parents have the right to rear children in accordance with their own convictions [...]'. Article 48 sec. 2 Polish Constitution only permits the limitation or deprivation of parental rights as specified by statute or on the basis of a final court judgment. Furthermore, Art. 72 sec. 2 Polish Constitution ensures that a child deprived of parental care shall have the right to care and assistance provided by public authorities.

The constitutional regulation of parental responsibilities is further developed in the provisions of the statute of 25 February 1964 namely the Polish Family and Guardianship Code (*Kodeks rodzinny i opiekuńczy* further quoted as Polish Family and Guardianship Code).[28] The main principle is that a minor child remains under parental authority (Art. 92 Polish Family and Guardianship Code), which is held, as a rule, by both parents (Art. 93 § 1 Polish Family and Guardianship Code) and in exceptional cases by one of the parents. Parental authority, regulated as one of the elements of relationships between parents and children, is the key element to parental responsibilities in Polish law. This notion also finds direct application in field of adoption.

This idea is complimented in that respect by the concept of custody. If neither of the parents have parental authority over the child, a family court should appoint and supervise a curator to exercise guardianship over the child. The provisions on the exercise of parental authority are applicable to the exercise of guardianship (Art. 155 § 2 Polish Family and Guardianship Code), but the provisions on guardianship state that the rights and obligations of the guardian are different from those of parents who have parental authority over the child. The Polish Family and Guardianship Code permits the establishment of guardianship over a child, with the guardian being a child-care institution or some other institution or social organisation (Art. 150 Polish Family and Guardianship Code), but the Ministry has not yet issued a regulation on this issue.

In an adoption, all previous parental authority (or guardianship) over the child ceases to exist (Art. 123 § 1 Polish Family and Guardianship Code). The legal relationship, between those adopted and those who are adopting is equivalent to a child and a parent (Art. 121 § 1 Polish Family and Guardianship Code);

---

27 Published in *Dziennik Ustaw* of 1997 r., No. 78, pos. 483 with rectifications.

28 Published in *Dziennik Ustaw* of 1964 r., No. 9, pos. 59.

which also embraces the concept of parental authority. Should the child be placed with a foster family or in a child-care institution, some of the obligations and rights (namely those concerning the care of the child, the child's upbringing and representation in claiming means of subsistence) are vested in the foster family or in a child-care institution. The remaining obligations and rights vest with the child's parents (Art. 112[1] Polish Family and Guardianship Code).

The preliminary question with regard to parental responsibility is the existence of parenthood. In practice, parenthood is indicated by a relevant annotation on the child's birth certificate. The woman who gave birth to the child is indicated as the child's mother.

If the mother of the child is married at the time of the child's birth, the mother's husband is indicated as the child's father. It is, however, possible to deny the fatherhood in a court judgment. If the mother of the child is not married at the time of the child's birth, but her marriage ended (*e.g.* by the spouse's death or by divorce) less than 300 days before the child was born, the mother's former husband is indicated as the child's father.

In all remaining situations, the law acknowledges either the man who was either declared to be the child's father or who was declared in a court judgment to be the child's father.

PORTUGAL

Under Portuguese law, parental responsibility (literally, 'parental power') is seen both as a way to compensate for the incapacity of the non-emancipated minor to exercise his or her rights (Art. 122, 123, 124, and 129 Portuguese CC) and as a collection of rights and duties that the legal system confers to or imposes upon both parents. Thus, parents are expected, in the interests of their child, to look after all aspects of the child, particularly the child's maintenance, health, safety, education, legal representation and administration of property (Art. 1878 No. 1 Portuguese CC). Parental responsibility cannot be renounced (Art. 1882 Portuguese CC), is non-transferable *(inter vivos* and *mortis causa),* and the exercise of it can be objectively controlled.[29]

RUSSIA

Russian law and legal literature use the concept of parental rights, which includes the rights and duties of the natural and adoptive parents regarding the person and the property of their minor children. To understand the Russian notion of parental responsibilities the following points are essential:

- The concept of parental responsibility is only reserved for the rights and duties of the natural and adoptive parents only. The rights and duties of natural or legal persons other than parents, who acquire responsibility over minor children by court or administrative order

---

29 F. PEREIRA COELHO and G. DE OLIVEIRA, *Curso de Direito da Família,* Vol. I, 3rd Ed., Coimbra: Coimbra Editora, 2003, p. 173.

(full guardians,[30] guardians with limited capacity[31] and child institutions[32]) fall outside the concept of parental responsibility.

- Parental responsibility should be executed in the best interests of the child (Art. 65 (1) Russian Family Code).
- Parental responsibility is regarded to be both public and private in nature. The execution of parental rights is considered to be a duty of parents to their children and the society at large.[33] Not fulfilling these duties leads to the application of sanctions.
- Parental responsibility is a constitutional right. Art. 38 (2) of the Constitution of the Russian Federation states the equality of parental rights and duties of both parents. According to Russian law, parents always have joint parental responsibility. This means that parents enjoy a formal equality in their parental rights irrespective of whether they are or have been married, or whether parentage has been established by voluntary recognition of a child or by a court order against the will of the parent (generally the father).
- Parental rights are not at the parent's free disposal. The rights cannot be terminated, restricted or transferred to other persons by the parents alone.
- Parental rights are temporal in nature. They exist as long as the child is under age.[34] If parents are appointed guardians of their legally incapacitated children of full age, the parents' rights and duties fall outside the scope of parental responsibility.[35]

SPAIN

Since Spain's system of law regarding parental responsibility is not uniform, it is necessary to distinguish between the so-called common civil law that is the Civil Code regime and the law of Navarra, Aragon and Catalonia. However, there are no marked differences among the regulations of parental responsibility in the different Spanish subsystems of law.[36] This national report will therefore only refer to differences when relevant.

The Spanish CC uses the general concept of *patria potestad* (Art. 154 Spanish CC), which embraces all issues mentioned in Principle 18 of the Council of Europe's White paper. This concept is also used in the laws of Navarra and

---

30 A full guardian is appointed to a child under the age of fourteen if the child is left without parental care. Art. 145 (2) Russian CC.

31 A guardian with limited capacity is appointed to a child between the age of fourteen to eighteen if the child is left without parental care. Art. 145 (2) Russian CC.

32 Art. 147 (1) Russian CC.

33 M. ANTOKOLSKAIA, *Family Law* (*Semeinoe pravo*), Moscow: Jurist, 1999, p. 196; L. PCHELINTZEVA, *Family Law* (*Semeinoe pravo*), Moscow: Norma-Infra M, 1999, p. 298.

34 Art. 61 (2) FC.

35 M. ANTOKOLSKAIA, *Family Law* (*Semeinoe pravo*), Moscow: Jurist, 1999, p. 195.

36 As regards Catalan Law and the Spanish CC see J. FERRER RIBA, 'Comentari a l'article 132' in: EGEA FERNÁNDEZ-FERRER RIBA, *Comentaris al Codi de Família, a la Llei d'unions estables de parella i a la Llei de situacions convivencials d'ajuda mutua*, Madrid, 2000, 610.

Aragon, whereas Catalan law speaks of the *potestad del pare i la mare* in order to stress that this *potestas* or authority is usually jointly exercised by both father and mother.[37]

It is generally admitted that neither of these terms adequately reflects the contents of the concept. When the Spanish CC was reformed in 1981 to adapt the regulation of *patria potestad* to the 1978 Spanish Constitution (see Q 5), a change of terminology was discussed. It was, however, finally decided to keep the term because it is rooted in society, and was not contradictory with a profound change of the concept.[38]

Patria potestad is not defined by the law. The Spanish Supreme Court has defined *Patria potestad* as a function, established in the interests of children, whose contents consist more of duties than rights (*e.g.* STS 31.12.1996). The contents of the concept will be further developed under Q 7.

If parental responsibility is held by persons who are not parents, Spanish law uses the concept of guardianship, or *tutela,* as a surrogate. For differences between *patria potestad* and *tutela* see Q 31.

SWEDEN

The concept of parental responsibilities is not used in autonomous Swedish legislation.[39] Instead, Swedish law distinguishes between the concepts of custody (*vårdnad,* Chapter 6 Swedish Children and Parents Code) and guardianship (*förmynderskap,* Chapters 9-15 in part Swedish Children and Parents Code). Seen together, the content of these two concepts corresponds to the Council of Europe's definition of the concept of parental responsibilities.

In Swedish law, custody refers to the legal responsibilities a custodian has for the child, including the duty to provide for the child's needs for care and protection, good upbringing, education and maintenance. In personal affairs, the custodian represents the child and also determines the child's residence. Normally, custody also involves the actual care of the child, meaning that the custodian personally lives with and looks after the child. However, it is not necessary for the child to live with a custodian. The child's parents have a joint responsibility to ensure that the child's right of contact with the parent the child

---

37 See Preamble of the Catalan Codi de Família.

38 J. CASTAN VAZQUEZ, Comentario al Tìtulo VII' and M. ALBADALEJO (Dir.), *Comentarios al Código civil y Compilaciones forales,* Madrid, 1982, 66; J. CASTAN PEREZ GOMEZ, 'La patria potestad', in: J.F. DELGADO DE MIGUEL, *Instituciones de Derecho Privado,* T.IV. Familia Vol. 1, 2001, 641.

39 The introduction of the concept of parental responsibilities was considered, but rejected in Sweden in the 1970's and 1980's. The issue of terminology re-emerged in the mid 1990's. The present terminology, consisting of concepts such as custody, contact, the child's residence, and guardianship was each time found adequate and well-established. See Å. SALDÉN, *Barn och föräldrar,* Uppsala: iustus Förlag, 2001, p. 71-72.

is not living with is met. The custodian(s) shall ensure that the child's right of contact with any other person particularly close to the child is met.

Guardianship refers to administration of the child's property and legal representation of the child's financial matters. Normally a child's parents are both the child's custodians and guardians. If custody is transferred from a parent or parents to one or two specially appointed custodians, they normally also become the child's guardians. As long as either of the parents has custody, it is not possible to appoint any other person as the child's custodian.

SWITZERLAND

Parental responsibilities are an individual right of each parent,[40] consisting of both rights and duties that cannot be renounced in the interest of a third-party. They are bound to a certain purpose, the exercise of which changes as the child grows up (Art. 301 § 1 and 2 Swiss CC). Parental responsibilities are the legal basis for education, legal representation and the administration of property. This is reflected in the parents' authority to take all necessary decisions in regard to the child's welfare (Art. 301 § 1 Swiss CC); in particular (based on the right of custody), to determine the child's place of residence (Art. 301 § 3 Swiss CC), to give the child a christian name (Art. 301 § 4 Swiss CC) and to raise the child. Apart from being directly responsible for the child's care, parental authority also ensures the child will receive a general education and an adequate vocational education (Art. 302 *et seq* Swiss CC), representation in dealings with third parties (Art. 304 *et seq* Swiss CC) and administration of his or her property (Art. 318 *et seq* Swiss CC).[41]

---

40 Swiss Federal Court Decision (BGE) 67 II 11.

41 Further details in this connection to be found inter alia I. SCHWENZER passim on Art. 301 and 302 in: H. HONSELL, N.P. VOGT, TH. GEISER (ed.), *Basler Kommentar zum Schweizerischen Privatrecht, Zivilgesetzbuch I*, Art. 1-456 ZGB, Basel: Helbing & Lichtenhahn, 2002.

QUESTION 2

A. GENERAL

Explain whether your national concept or concepts encompass:
(a) Care and protection;
(b) Maintenance of personal relationships;
(c) Provision of education;
(d) Legal representation;
(e) Determination of residence; and
(f) Administration of property.

AUSTRIA

(a) Care and protection

Under Sec. 144 Austrian CC, the care of minor children is part of parental responsibility. This encompasses protection of the child's physical welfare and health as well as direct supervision and upbringing, particularly the development of the child's physical, mental, psychological, and moral strengths, the fostering of its aptitudes, abilities, inclinations, and developmental capabilities, and its education in school and in an occupation (Sec. 146 (1) Austrian CC).

(b) Maintenance of personal relationships

Sec. 148 Austrian CC ensures the maintenance of the child's personal contact with his or her parent and other persons who do not live in a common household with the child, but are nevertheless very close to him or her *(Besuchsrecht)*. A parent not holding parental responsibilities also has the right to be informed of important matters concerning the child and to express himself or herself about them (Sec. 178 Austrian CC).

(c) Provision of education

Under Sec. 144 Austrian CC, education of minor children is also a part of parental responsibility. It includes but is not limited to development of the child's physical, mental, psychological, and moral strengths, the fostering of its aptitudes, abilities, inclinations, and developmental capabilities, and its education in school and in an occupation (Sec. 146 (1) Austrian CC).

(d) Legal representation

Under Sec. 144 Austrian CC, legal representation of minor children is also a part of parental responsibility. This relates to matters of care, education, administration of property, and all other matters in which parents are required to act in the child's best interests with respect to third parties.

(e) Determination of residence

The parents have the right to determine the child's residence to the extent required for the care and education of the child. If contrary to this determination a child is staying elsewhere (*e.g.* if the child has run away or has been kidnapped), the authorities must, upon request from an authorized parent, cooperate in determining where the child is staying and bringing the child back, if necessary (Sec. 146b Austrian CC). Each parent entitled to the child's care and education is also independently entitled to this protection (*e.g.* if the child stays with the other parent who refuses to surrender the child at the end of his/her visit).[1] The parents' right to demand the return of a child presupposes it is still necessary and possible to care for and educate the child. This right may not be exercised in a way that is contrary to the child's interests.[2] Thus, from the age of 14, a youth can generally determine where he or she will vacation. On the other hand, the child's parents can forbid the youth from taking a trip to India to take drugs, for example, and can bring the child back from there.[3]

(f) Administration of property

Under Sec. 144 Austrian CC, administration of the child's property is part of parental responsibility. The parents must administer a child's property with the care of proper parents. They must maintain and, if possible, increase the property unless the child's interests require otherwise (Sec. 149 Austrian CC).

BELGIUM

(a) Care and protection

Parental responsibilities include the duty of contact with the child (Art. 374(4) Belgian CC) and the authority over the child (Art. 373-375 Belgian CC), which encompasses the right to the care of the child.[4] (See Q 8a).

(b) Maintenance of personal relationships

Parental responsibilities include the right of contact with the child (Art. 374(4) Belgian CC) and the authority over the child (Art. 373-375 Belgian CC), which encompasses the right to administer the contacts and personal relationships of the child with third parties. (See Q 8a).

(c) Provision of education

Parental responsibilities include the authority over the child (Art. 373-375 Belgian CC), which encompasses the right to decide on fundamental options such as the philosophical, religious and ideological upbringing of the child, its language, school, type of education. (See Q 8b).

---

1 *Oberster Gerichtshof*, 28.08.1997, *Sammlung der Entscheidungen des Obersten Gerichtshofs in Zivilrechtssachen (SZ)*, Vol. 70, No. 163 = *Juristische Blätter*, 1998, p. 243.

2 *Landesgericht für Zivilrechtssachen Vienna*, 07.04.1992, *EFSlg*. 68.622 (Rejection of the parents' right to bring the child home because the child's interests were endangered at home).

3 For further examples see M. SCHWIMANN in: M. SCHWIMANN, *Praxiskommentar zum ABGB*, Vol. I, 2nd Edition, Vienna: Orac, 1997, § 146b Marg. No. 2. Regarding the applicability of the Hague Convention on the Civil Aspects of International Child Abduction (25.10.1980) see *Oberster Gerichtshof*, 11.07.1990, *EFSlg*. 63.879.

4 H. DE PAGE, *Traité élémentaire de droit civil belge*, T. II (Les Personnes), Vol. 2 (by J.-P. MASSON), Brussels: Bruylant, 1990, p. 960.

(d) Legal representation

The parents may represent their child in all civil actions, including their representation in court as either plaintiff or defendant. This competence is linked to the right to administrate the property of the child.[5] (See Question 8f.)

(e) Determination of residence

A distinction must be made between 'domicile' and 'residence'. 'Domicile' is the place a person is principally established (Art. 102 Belgian CC),[6] while 'residence' refers to the place where a person has fixed his or her dwelling for a certain time.[7]

According to Art. 108 Belgian CC, the child's domicile is at the communal residence of its parents, when they live together or, if they are separated, at the residence of one of them. Following the principle of joint parental responsibilities, the parents decide together where the domicile of the child will be fixed, even in case of separation (See Q 15a). When no consent can be reached, the dispute is submitted to the Juvenile Court (See Q 37).[8] The determination of residence is encompassed in the exercise of the parental authority over the child (Art. 374 Belgian CC). (See Q 8a).

(f) Administration of property

The concept of parental responsibilities also includes the administration of the property of the child and his legal representation (Art. 376-379 Belgian CC) and the right of use and enjoyment of its property (Art. 384-387 Belgian CC) (See Q 10 and Q 11).

BULGARIA

The concept of 'parental rights and duties' encompasses all of the types of parental responsibility listed below. The family law legal literature has adopted one general typology of parental rights and duties – 'rights/duties on personal relationships' and 'rights/duties on property of the child'.[9]

---

5 E. DE WILDE D'ESTMAEL, 'Que recouvre l'authorité parentale?', *Div. Act.*, 1995, p. 24-26.

6 According to Art. 36 Belgian Judicial Code, 'domicile' is the place where a person is principally registered in the registers of the population. However, this definition is limited to the application of the Belgian Judicial Code and, therefore, does not modify the Belgian CC.

7 *R.P.D.B.*, See Domicile (N. GALLUS), compl. T. VIII, No. 36; *Rép. Not.*, 'Domicile', T. I, 2, VII, p. 55.

8 However, the Juvenile Court is the natural judge for matters concerning children, the Justice of the Peace is competent for interim measures between spouses and the President of the Court of First Instance for interim measures when a divorce-claim has been introduced.

9 See: L. NENOVA, *Family Law of the Republic of Bulgaria*, Sofia, 1994, p. 407.

(a) Care and protection

This is the main duty of the parents. According to Art. 47 § 1 Bulgarian Constitution: 'Raising and bringing up of children until their age of majority is both a right and an obligation of their parents and is supported by the State.' The Bulgarian Family Code states: 'The parents are obliged to care for their children and to prepare them for socially useful activity.' (Art. 68 § 1)

The raising of children comprises care for the physical development of the child: life and health, support for development, both in kind and financially. 'Care' includes mainly all the everyday regular activities of the parents to supervise and raise the child. The content of the supervision should be interpreted according to the age-specific needs of the child. Violation of these obligations where it jeopardises child's development leads to criminal liability of the parent (Art. 182 § 1 Bulgarian Penal Code).

(b) Maintenance of personal relationships

The Bulgarian Family Code does not explicitly provide for such a right or obligation of the parent, however it could be implied from the obligation of the child to reside with his or her parents (Art. 71 § 1). It may also be stated that the law views maintenance of personal relationships as a prerequisite for the exercise of parental rights and obligations.

In cases of divorce and separation however, a personal relationship between the child and the non-custodial parent should be arranged either via court order[10] or agreement between parents.[11]

(c) Provision of education

The Bulgarian Family Code does not explicitly impose a parental obligation to provide education. The legal literature however interprets the parental obligation to 'prepare them (children) for socially useful activity' (Art. 68 § 1) as a parental obligation to provide for the education of children.[12] In addition, the child has a constitutional right to education that is obligatory up to the age of 16.[13] It is a parental duty to guarantee the observance of that right by enrolling the child in school, ensuring his or her attendance at school *etc.*[14]

The regulation of parental support in the Bulgarian Family Code indirectly suggests a parental duty towards the child's education. If the child continues its education beyond the age of majority (18), parents are obliged to support the child.

---

10 In cases of divorce based on irretrievable breakdown of the marriage (Art. 106 linked to Art. 99 § 2 Bulgarian Family Code) or in case of parental dispute where parents do not live together (Art. 71 § 2 Bulgarian Family Code).

11 In cases of divorce based on mutual consent (Art. 100 Bulgarian Family Code).

12 See: L. NENOVA, *Family Law of the Republic of Bulgaria*, Sofia, 1994, p. 413.

13 Art. 53 Bulgarian Constitution.

14 Art. 47 Bulgarian Public Education Act.

As for Art. 82 (Amended, SG, No. 11/1992):

> (1) The parents are obliged to support their children who are not of full age regardless of whether they are fit for labour or can support themselves from their own properties.
>
> (2) The parents are obliged to support their children who have come of age, if the latter cannot support themselves from their income or use of their properties, when they study at secondary, undergraduate and higher education establishments, for the specified term of education, up to 20 years of age in the case of study at secondary school and up to 25 years of age in the case of study at undergraduate or higher education establishment.
>
> (3) The support under the preceding sub Art. is due provided it does not create undue inconvenience for the parents'.

(d) Legal representation

Children below the age of 14 are minors and have no legal capacity. Therefore their parents (adopters) represent them.[15] Children that have reached the age of 14 have limited capacity and may act on their own with the consent of their parents or guardians.[16] If the adolescent acts without that consent the contract is void.[17]

A conflict may occur between the interests of children and their parents while their parents are acting as their representatives/guardians.[18] The Bulgarian Family Code does not stipulate for the assignment of a special (*ad hoc*) representative to protect the interests of children in such situations.[19] This may be done only when the conflict occurs in the context of court proceedings.[20] The Bulgarian Child Protection Act envisages that in each court or administrative procedure, the court or the administrative body will either summon the Child Protection Department to prepare a social report concerning the interests of the child or will send a social worker to take part in the proceedings (Art. 15 § 6).

(e) Determination of residence

The child is obliged to reside with its parents until the age of majority. As the Bulgarian Family Code states in Art. 71: 'Children who are not yet of full age are obliged to live with their parents unless valid reasons necessitate that they live elsewhere. If the child is at least ten years of age and departs from this obligation, the court of jurisdiction in the parent's residence will order the child to return, if the parents so request, after hearing the child. The order is subject

---

15 Art. 3 Bulgarian Persons and Family Act.

16 Art. 4 § 3 Bulgarian Persons and Family Act.

17 Art. 27 Bulgarian Contracts and Obligations Act.

18 For instance in claims for affiliation, division or acquisition of property *etc.*

19 To the contrary the abolished Art. 90 Bulgarian Persons and Family Act had envisaged that special representative for children in cases of conflict of interests.

20 Art. 16 § 6 Bulgarian Civil Procedure Code.

to appeal to the President of the county court, but the appeal does not stop its execution. The order is executed through administrative channels.'

Legal literature justifies this rule in two ways, underlying the interests of children. Firstly, the common residence provides the opportunity for the parents to fulfil their duties of care and upbringing of children. Otherwise the everyday supervision and care would not be possible. Secondly, the existence of a common residence is also ground for the return of their children in cases of unlawful removal.[21] Case law rules that 'children from dissolved marriages should live with the parent assigned with the exercise of parental rights and obligations'.[22] The district court of the parent's residence determines whether to return a child that has been removed from the parent's home. The ground is 'unlawful removal of the child'. This could either be an action of the child or of a third person who removes the child unlawfully from its parent's home.[23] In such a situation, the court will issue an order for the return of the child which is enforceable by the police.

An exception is possible if there are well-founded reasons for the child to live elsewhere. The court has the discretion to determine the 'well-founded reasons' in each particular case. Such reasons might be the contracting of a marriage by the child (if the child is at least 16), the child studies in another location, or the child is placed in public care under the Bulgarian Child Protection Act. In these cases the court will not issue an order to return the child.

If the parents do not live together and are unable to reach an agreement as to with whom the children will live, the dispute is resolved by the district court of the children's residence. The court will hear the children if they are at least ten years of age. The decision of the court is subject to appeal according to the general rules (Art. 71 § 2). According to case law, this claim belongs to parents not living together and not married. In this situation the court decides not only on the child's residence but also on the exercise of parental rights and contact matters, applying the provision of Art. 106 § 1 Bulgarian Family Code:[24] parental rights after the divorce: 'With the pronouncement of the divorce the court decrees, *ex officio*, to which spouse the exercise of the parental rights shall be granted, orders measures in connection with the exercise of these rights and also as to the personal relations between the children and the parents, as well as the support of the children'.

(f) Administration of property

Parents, in their capacity as representatives or guardians, may perform two types of actions in relation to the property of the child. Firstly, ordinary

21 See: L. NENOVA, *Family Law of the Republic of Bulgaria*, Sofia, 1994, p. 414-415.
22 Decision of the Supreme Court, 822-1991 (Civil Division).
23 Keeping and not returning a child by a person other than the parent is a crime according to Art. 185 and 186 Bulgarian Penal Code.
24 Decision of the Supreme Court, 1218-1999 (Civil Division).

administration or management of property, either by one parent or jointly by both of them. This follows *per argumentum a contrario* from the provision of Art. 73 § 2 Bulgarian Family Code: 'The expropriation of real property and chattels, with the exception of fruits and perishables, the encumbering thereof with liabilities and in general the undertaking of acts of disposition, related to the property of minors, are allowed, with the permission of the district court, at the place of residence only in case of necessity or where this is in their obvious interests.'

The Bulgarian Family Code does not define the concept of 'ordinary administration or management'. The Supreme Court has defined it as actions that do not expropriate the property but maintain it and make use of it.[25] It is in the court's discretion to decide the meaning on a case-by-case basis.

Secondly, transactions with the child's property only after the court's permission. According to the abovementioned decision of the Supreme Court, 'transaction' comprises actions that change the right to property - it is transferred, limited, or ceased. The court would grant this permission only if it is 'of necessity or where this is in the obvious interests' of the child. A transaction undertaken without court's permission is void.[26]

The Bulgarian Family Code prohibits some type of actions with the child's property. According to Art. 73 § 3: 'The donation, waiver of rights, lending and guaranteeing the debts of third persons by pledge, mortgage or endorsement, effected by children not yet of full age are null and void. This does not apply to the transactions executed by married minors to whom only the limitation of Art. 12, § 3 is relevant'.[27] These actions are not allowed even with the permission of the court because they are considered not to be in the child's interests. Any such transaction is void. A dissent to the theory suggests that circumstances of the case might compel such transactions in order to protect the best interests of the child (for example the child's education or payment for health intervention).[28]

CZECH REPUBLIC

(a) Care and protection

The content of parental responsibility pursuant to the Czech Family Code means care and protection. Care means upbringing on the one hand but at the same time it also means deciding about the child's matters.[29] The parents are not obliged to take personal care of the child but may entrust the personal care to a third person (in practice, this frequently means the grandparents).

---

25 Decision of the Supreme Court, 91-1974.

26 Art. 27 Bulgarian Contracts and Obligations Act.

27 Real property is the only property which they are not allowed to transfer.

28 See A. STANEVA, *Representative and Custodial Functions of Parents.*

29 M. ARNOLDOVA, 'Pojem vychova v rodinnom prave', *Justicna revue,* 3/1991.

(b) Maintenance of personal relationships

A maintenance duty is not considered as part of parental responsibility because Czech law requires even a parent who lacks parental responsibility to fulfil a duty of maintenance towards the child (Sec. 44 § 4 Czech Family Code). the duty to maintain does not expire when the child attains the age of majority but only when the child is able to make its own living, which may be either before or after attaining the age of majority (a child studying at a university, a handicapped child *etc*).[30]

(c) Provision of education

The Czech Family Code does not include any special regulations concerning education of the child. The choice of education method, including a particular type of school, may be seen as an essential matter, therefore the parents should agree on the method of the child's education. If the parents disagree, the method of education may be determined by court. Pursuant to Sec. 31 § 3 Czech Family Code, the child has the right to free expression on all parental decisions concerning essential matters relating to its personality, including the choice of profession and education method. Courts have repeatedly emphasised the child has a right to an education that corresponds with its abilities *i.e.* that the maintenance duty of parents does not expire when the child leaves primary school. Czech Act No. 3/2000 Coll. regulates that the parents determine the religious education of the child under fifteen.

(d) Legal representation

The parents represent the child in legal acts for which the child does not have full legal capacity (Sec. 39 Czech Family Code). Pursuant to Sec. 9 Czech CC, minors possess the capacity to perform acts in law only if the nature of such acts corresponds to the mental and moral maturity of their age.

Neither parent may represent their child in legal acts concerning matters in which a conflict of interest may occur between the parents and the child, or between the child and other children of these parents (Sec. 37 § 1 Czech Family Code). In this situation the court shall appoint a custodian who will represent the child in the proceedings or in a certain act. The custodian is usually an authority of social and legal protection of children, but another natural person, most frequently some other relative of the child, may also be appointed as custodian. The conflict of interests need not arise in practice; it is sufficient that such a possibility exists. Typically, in these situations the parents and the child are parties to proceedings that determine various issues about the child (upbringing, establishing maintenance, regulating the other parent's contact with the child, deciding about placing the child in a substitute family and probate proceedings to which the child and the other parent are parties).

---

30 H. NOVA and O. TEZKA,Vyživovací povinnost v rodinnem pravu.

(e) Determination of residence

Determination of residence of the child is known in Czech law as the concept of awarding custody, or exercising care of the child. In view of the fact that by operation of law both parents are entitled the same rights and duties in relation to the child, the Family Code provides for entrusting the care of the child to one of the parents, or alternating care, or the so-called joint care in the situation when the parents of the child do not cohabit (regardless of whether they are spouses or they have never been spouses). Joint care (custody) in the Czech Family Code ultimately means that the child's terms are not legally regulated at all.[31]

(f) Administration of property

Both parents are entitled and obligated to administer the child's property. The Czech Family Code imposes on them the duty to administer the child's property with 'due care' (Sec. 37a Czech Family Code). The parents are not obliged to strive to increase the child's property but they are obliged to preserve the property's essence until the child attains majority. The law allows them to use interest from the child's property for maintenance of the child and only then may it be used for reasonable family needs. The principal may be affected only when a gross disproportion in respect to social and economic conditions arises between the minor child and the persons obligated to maintain it, through no fault of those who maintain the child. However, in most cases the parents would need the consent of custody court (court for custody of minors) for such a use of the child's property. The parents are obligated to give an account of their administration of the property, if the child so requires, within one year after termination of their administration. The child's rights from liability for damage and unjust enrichment remain unaffected (Sec. 37a § 3 Czech Family Code).

DENMARK

(a) Care and protection

Care and protection are the core elements in the Danish concept of parental authority. They are directly mentioned in Art. 2 Danish Act on Parental Authority and Contact.

(b) Maintenance of personal relationships

The maintenance of personal relationships (between the holder(s) of parental authority and the child) is not mentioned in the Danish Act on Parental Authority and Contact or in legal doctrine as an aspect of parental authority. Considering that the holder(s) of parental authority has/have the right to decide where the child should live and the right and duty to care for the child, one may argue that there is an inherent right to maintain personal relationships.

---

[31] M. HRUSAKOVA, *Zákon o rodine. Komentar. 2. vyd*, Prague: C.H.Beck, 2001, p. 178.

(c) Provision of education

The provision of education is not directly mentioned in the Danish Act on Parental Authority and Contact. It follows from the travaux préparatoires that the holder(s) of parental authority has/have a duty to provide education taking into account the child's abilities and interests.[32]

(d) Legal representation

The holder(s) of parental authority is/are also almost always the guardian(s) of the child. The holders(s) of parental authority and the guardian(s) are the child's legal representative, Art. 2 Danish Act on Parental Authority and Contact.[33]

(e) Determination of residence

The holder(s) of parental authority has/have the right to decide where the child should reside/live. This right is only restricted where the authorities have decided that the child should be taken into care.

(f) Administration of property

The holder(s) of parental authority is/are also almost always the guardian(s) of the child. The guardian(s) has/have the right to administer the child's property.[34]

ENGLAND & WALES

(a) Care and protection

There is no doubt that parental responsibility embraces care and protection of the child and it is undoubtedly an aspect of parental responsibility to afford physical protection to the child.[35] Whether the duty exists in any given case depends *inter alia* upon the necessity of protection. A crippled mother, for example, would not be under any duty to protect a healthy son aged 17.[36]

This common law of protection has largely been replaced by the English Children and Young Persons Act 1933, Pt I, which makes certain forms of behaviour criminal offences. The offences are dependent on the likelihood of

---

32 Commission report No. 985/1983, p. 60.

33 Danish Act on Guardianship, *Værgemålsloven,* Act No. 388 of 14.06.1995, Art. 1 and 2.

34 Danish Act on Guardianship, *Værgemålsloven,* Act No. 388 of 14.06.1995, Art. 1 and 2.

35 In fact the common law duty is owed by anyone who willingly undertakes to look after another who is incapable of looking after himself. It can therefore continue after the child's majority, see *R v Chattaway* (1922) 17 Cr App Rep 7, CCA (starvation of a helpless daughter aged 25), and can extend to a stepchild or foster child, see *R v Bubb* (1850) 4 Cox CC 455; *R v Gibbons and Proctor* (1918) 13 Cr App Rep 134, CCA.

36 *Cf R v Shepherd* (1862) Le & Ca 147 where a girl aged 18 (the age of majority was then 21), who normally lived away in service but who returned home from time to time, died in childbirth. It was held that her mother was under no duty to send for a midwife because the girl was beyond the age of childhood and was entirely emancipated.

the child being caused unnecessary suffering or injury. Sec. 1(1) of this Act provides:

> 'If any person who has attained the age of 16 and has responsibility for any child or young person under that age, wilfully assaults, ill-treats, neglects, abandons or exposes him, or causes or procures him to be assaulted, ill-treated, neglected, abandoned, or exposed in a manner likely to cause him unnecessary suffering or injury to health... that person should be guilty of [an offence]...'

This is subject to Sec. 1(7) under which parents' right[37] to administer corporal punishment is preserved. Among those expressly made liable for a Sec. 1 offence is by Sec. 17(a)(i) any person who "has parental responsibility for him (within the meaning of the English Children Act 1989)".

(b) Maintenance of personal relationships

Parental responsibility encompasses seeing or otherwise having contact with the child. While not an absolute right since in any litigation it will be contingent upon the child's welfare, nevertheless as Lord OLIVER said in *Re KD (A Minor)(Ward: Termination of Access)*:[38] 'As a general proposition a natural parent has a claim to [contact with] his or her child to which the court will pay regard and it would not I think, be inappropriate describe such a claim as a "right"'. This 'claim' is protected to the extent that there is a statutory presumption of reasonable contact between a child in local authority care or under emergency protection and, *inter alia*, those with parental responsibility.[39] These latter provisions were enacted following the European Court of Human Rights ruling[40] that the absence of any right to challenge a termination of contact by a local authority amounted to a breach of Art. 8 and 13 of the Convention.

Given that it is a normal assumption that a child will benefit from continued contact with both parents[41] it may be that parental responsibility properly encompasses the prima facie duty to allow the child to have contact with either

---

37 This right can be delegated but corporal punishment is now forbidden in schools, see the s 548 (as substituted by Sec. 548, English Education Act 1996, (as substituted by Sec. 131, English School Standards and Framework Act 1998), children's homes (Reg. 17(5)(a), English Children's Homes Regulations 2001, SI 2001/3967), and foster placements (Reg. 28(5)(b), English Fostering Services Regulations 2002, SI 2002/57). Note: As of 15 January 2005, this defence has been abolished by Sec. 58, Children Act 2004. See further Q 8d.

38 [1988] AC 806 at 827. *Cf Sanderson v McManus* 1997 SLT 629, sub nom *S v M (Access Order)* 1997 1 FLR 980, HL (Scotland) in which Lord HOPE held that the onus was on the unmarried father to establish that continued contact was for the child's welfare.

39 Sec. 34(1) and 44(13), English Children Act 1989.

40 See *R v UK* [1988] 2 FLR 445.

41 See *e.g.* Lord OLIVER in *Re KD* [1988] AC 806 at p. 827 and *M v M (child: access)* [1973] 2 All ER 81, *per* WRANGHAM J at p. 85 and *per* LATEY at p. 88.

or both parents. Whether such responsibility extends to a parent having an obligation him or herself to maintain contact with the child can be debated.[42]

(c) Provision of education

As WARD LJ has observed[43] 'arranging for education commensurate with the child's intellectual needs and abilities is [an] incident of the parental responsibility which arises from the duty of the parent to secure the child's education'. This responsibility derives from the common law right of a parent to determine what education the child should receive.[44] Parents' rights to determine their children's education are also protected by the European Convention on Human Rights to the extent of respecting their religious and philosophical convictions.[45]

At common law, because the duty was unenforceable,[46] parents could formerly choose not to have their children educated. However, since the Education Act 1944 (now consolidated by the English Education Act 1996) parents of every child between the ages of five and 16 have had to ensure that the child receives 'efficient full-time education suitable (a) to his age, ability, aptitude and (b) to any special education needs he may have, either by regular attendance at school or otherwise'.[47] 'Parent' for these purposes includes any person who is not a parent but who has parental responsibility for the child or who has care of the child.[48] Failure to perform this duty can result in a criminal prosecution[49] and the child may be subject to an education supervision order.[50]

(d) Legal representation

Based on common law and practice rather than statute[51] a parent (and presumably any person with parental responsibility) has the right to act as a legal representative of the child[52] though this might be challenged.[53] Children of

---

42 In Scotland, Sec. 1(1)(d), Children (Scotland) Act 1995, clearly states that a parent has a responsibility to maintain personal relations and direct contact with the child.

43 *Re Z (A Minor)(Identification: Restrictions on Publication)* [1997] Fam 1 at 26, CA.

44 For a striking example, see *Tremain's Case* (1719) 1 Stra 167. See also *Andrews v Salt* (1873) 8 Ch. App. 622 – father's wishes to be respected after his death.

45 Art. 2, Protocol No. 1.

46 *Hodges v Hodges* (1796) Peake Add Cas 79.

47 Sec. 7 and 8, English Education Act 1996.

48 Sec. 576(1), English Education Act 1996.

49 Sec. 443, English Education Act 1996. Formerly, parents could be fined but not imprisoned for a breach of a school attendance order for failure to secure regular attendance at school. However, under Sec. 444(8A), English Education Act 1996, parents can now be imprisoned for up to three months where they know that their child is failing to attend regularly at the school and fail without reasonable justification to cause him to do so.

50 Sec. 36, English Children Act 1989.

51 *Cf* in Scotland where Sec. 2(1)(d), Children (Scotland) Act 1995, expressly confers the right of a parent to act as the child's legal representative.

52 In general a child can only bring legal proceedings by an adult acting on his behalf. Such persons were generally known as "next friends" but now, ironically outside the

sufficient age and understanding, however, can effectively litigate for themselves when seeking a Sec. 8 order or an order under the High Court's inherent jurisdiction.[54]

(e) Determination of residence

Based upon the common law right of a person to possession of his child,[55] it now seems better to say that those with responsibility have a prima facie[56] responsibility to provide a home for the child and the power to determine where the child should live.[57] This responsibility is protected by the criminal law to the extent that persons without responsibility commit the crime of child abduction if they remove the child without lawful authority.[58] As between individuals with parental responsibility the right is qualified to the extent that removal of a child outside the United Kingdom without the consent of other individuals with parental responsibility can amount to a crime.[59] Associated with providing a home is the necessary accompanying power, *inter alia*, physically to control children at any rate until the years of discretion. As Lord LANE CJ once commented, restraint of a child's movement is usually well within the realms of reasonable parental discipline.[60] Responsibility also includes the power to control the child's movements whilst in someone else's care.[61] On the other hand a parent and, presumably therefore, any other person with parental responsibility, can commit the common law crime of kidnapping[62] or unlawful imprisonment[63] if a child (old enough to make up his own mind) is forcibly taken or detained against his will.

---

context of family proceedings, they are known as "litigation friends": Civil Procedure Rules 1998, Pt 21.

53 *Woolf v Pemberton* (1877) 6 Ch D 19. There is a power of removal if a proper case is made out, see *Re Taylor's Application* [1972] 2 QB 369.

54 Family Proceedings Rules 1991, Rule 9.2A, on which see *Re T (A Minor)(Child: Representation)* [1994] Fam 49 and SAWYER, 'The competence of children to participate in family proceedings' (1995) *CFLQ* 180.

55 See *e.g. Re Agar-Ellis* (1883) 24 Ch D 317.

56 *I.e.* unless a court order (*viz* a residence, care or emergency protection order) has been made giving someone else that prima facie right.

57 See *Re M (Minors)(Residence Order: Jurisdiction)* [1993] 1 FLR 495 at 499 per BALCOMBE LJ.

58 Sec. 2, Child Abduction Act 1984.

59 Sec. 1, Child Abduction Act 1984. Certain defences, however, are provided for by Sec. 1(5).

60 *R v Rahman* (1985) 81 Cr App Rep 349 at 353, CA. See also *Re K (A Child)(Secure Accommodation: Right to Liberty)* [2001] Fam 377. CA (but *cf* BUTLER-SLOSS P and THORPE LJ applying *Nielson v Denmark* (1989) 11 EHRR 175. E Ct HR), *Hewer v Bryant* [1970] 1 QB 357 at 373, CA, per SACHS LJ.

61 *Fleming v Pratt* (1823) 1 LJ OS KB 194.

62 *R v D* [1984] AC 778, HL.

63 *R v Rahman*, supra.

(f) Administration of property

Sec. 3(1), English Children Act 1989 provides that parental responsibility means "all the rights, duties, powers, responsibilities and authority which by law a parent of a child has in relation to the child *and his property*" (emphasis added). While, according to Sec. 3(2), English Children Act 1989 parental responsibility includes the rights, powers and duties which a guardian of the child's estate (appointed before the 1998 Act came into force)[64] would have had in relation to the child and his property. Such rights include, pursuant to Sec. 3(3), the right "to receive or recover in his own name, for the benefit of the child, property of whatever description and wherever situated which the child is entitled to receive or recover". Parental responsibility does *not* include rights of succession to the child's property.[65]

FINLAND

(a) Care and protection

The custodian shall provide daily care and protection for the child (Sec. 1 Finnish Child Custody and the Right of Access Act), but the factual care provider must not be the custodian him or herself. If the child has been taken into care, the local social authority has the right to decide about care for the child.

(b) Maintenance of personal relationships

The objects of the custody of the child are to ensure close and affectionate human relationships for the child, particularly between the child and its parents. The right of access shall ensure a child the right to meet the parent with whom it does not reside and to maintain contact with this parent. The custodian shall therefore allow the child to have access to its parent (Sec. 1 and 2 Finnish Child Custody and the Right of Access Act). The social authorities have the power to restrict the child's right to remain in contact with its parents or to other persons close to the child, if the child has been taken into care (Sec. 25 Finnish Child Protection Act).

(c) Provision of education

The custodians have the right to make decisions concerning the education of the child. However, the concept of child custody does not include providing the means for education; that is encompassed by the parental duty to support the child. The Finnish Constitution grants everyone a right to basic education free of charge (Sec. 16). Basic education in the public basic school system normally lasts nine years beginning the year the child reaches the age of seven.

(d) Legal representation

The custodian has the right to represent the child in matters relating to the child's physical care, unless otherwise provided by law (Sec. 4 Finnish Child Custody and the Right of Access Act). If a special guardian has been appointed

64 *Viz* 14 October 1991.
65 Sec. 3(4)(b), Children Act 1989.

to administer the child's property, the guardian has the right to represent the child in cases concerning this property. The right of a minor to represent itself in court or to take authority in other matters concerning parental responsibility as well as the contingency of ordering a guardian in case of a conflict of interest between the child and his or her custodian is described in Q 8f.

(e) Determination of residence

The concept of child custody encompasses the right to determine the child's place of residence. Joint custodians shall make decisions concerning the child's residence together, if not otherwise ordered by the court. A sole custodian has the power to decide the child's place of residence alone (Sec. 4 and 5 Finnish Child Custody and the Right of Access Act). A court order or an agreement approved by the local social authority, according to which the child shall reside with one of the custodians does not impact the custodians' duty to make joint the decisions concerning the child's place of residence.

A child's removal from Finland or retention abroad is considered to be wrongful if the removal or retention is not approved by the other custodian (Sec. 32 Finnish Child Custody and the Right of Access Act). Thus the return of the child according to the 1980 Hague Convention is possible if a custodian with whom the child resides according to a parental agreement or a court order abducts the child. If the child has been taken into care, the local social authority has the right to decide the child's place of residence (Sec. 19 Finnish Child Protection Act).

(f) Administration of property

A special guardian may be appointed for the administration of the child's property, although normally the custodians of a minor are also responsible for the administration of the child's property as guardians of the child (Sec. 4 Finnish Guardianship Services Act).

FRANCE

The French concept of '*autorité parentale*' (parental authority) encompasses several different parental rights and duties. The child, regardless of age, owes honour and respect to his or her parents (Art. 371 French CC). Art. 371-1 French CC gives a broad definition of parental authority: it is a collection of rights and duties aimed at the interests of the child. The parental authority belongs to the father and mother until the child reaches the age of majority or is *émancipé* (emancipated). This authority is used for the protection of the child's safety, health and morality. The rights and duties also ensure the child's education and allow for its personal development. The parents should make the child a party to the decisions relating to him, allowing for the child's age and degree of maturity.

(a) Care and protection

Yes. The fundamental function of parental authority is protection.[66] French legal provisions require the parents to protect the child's safety, health and morality (Art. 371-1 C.C.). Although the 4 March 2002 reform of the French CC no longer mentions the classical triptych that formed the contents of parental responsibilities (*garde, surveillance, éducation*),[67] French authors assert that these three fundamental parental tasks still exist and remain part of the parental responsibilities.[68] *Garde* meant that the parents should live with their child or, more generally, determine where their child should live. It is therefore part of the '*communauté de vie*' (living together, community of living) between parents and children. *Surveillance,* a term no longer used in the new legal provisions, still exists as a parental duty to take care of, to protect, and to pay attention to the child and its needs.[69] This is indirectly stated in Art. 371-1 French CC, which requires that the exercise of parental responsibilities should be used to protect the child's safety, health and morality. Education is still mentioned in the legal provisions of the French CC concerning the parental authority.

(b) Maintenance of personal relationships

Yes. The child cannot leave the family home without the parents' permission (Art. 371-3 French CC). The European Court of Human Rights decisions interpreting Art. 8 of the European Convention on Human Rights insist that the parent and child living together is an essential and fundamental part of the right to respect for family life.[70] The maintenance of personal relationships between parent and child is not expressly stated in the French CC except as it relates to the divorce or separation of the parents; even if the parents get divorced or separated and only one parent retains parental responsibilities, the other parent has the right and the duty to maintain personal relationships with the child. See Art. 373-2 para. 2 French CC: "The father and mother shall maintain personal relationships with the child and respect the bonds between the child and the other parent.' The use of the word 'maintain' shows that this duty also existed when the parents lived together.

(c) Provision of education

Yes. Each parent shall contribute to the education and support of the child in proportion to his or her means, to those of the other parent and in proportion to

---

66 See G. CORNU, *Droit civil, La famille*, 2001, Paris : Montchrestien, 7th Ed., No. 71: *l'autorité parentale est en soi un droit-fonction*; see also No. 73: *l'autorité parentale est fondée sur la vocation naturelle des parents à protéger leur enfant*).

67 See G. CORNU, *Droit civil, La famille*, 2001, Paris : Montchrestien, 7th Ed., No. 77.

68 See, for example, Th. FOSSIER, *L'autorité parentale*, 2002, ESF, 2nd Ed., p. 4. A reason for this solution is not only the contents of Art. 371-1 French CC, which defines parental responsibilities and their aims, but also Art. 213 French CC. that states that spouses are jointly responsible for the moral and material guidance of the family. They shall provide for the children's education and prepare their future.

69 *Cf.* G. CORNU, *Droit civil, La famille*, 2001, Paris : Montchrestien, 7th Ed., No. 77, p. 164.

70 See ECtHR, 13.07.2000, *Elsholtz v. Germany,* Appl. No. 25735/94, (2001) I *JCP* 291; 26.02.2002, *Kutzner v. Germany,* Appl. No. 46544/99.

the child's needs (Art. 371-2 French CC). Education has several aspects, including school education and studies, moral education, professional orientation and religious upbringing.

(d) Legal representation

Yes. Parents are the legal representatives of their minor child if they have parental responsibilities (see Art. 389 French CC). If the parents have joint parental responsibilities, they are both *administrateurs légaux* of the child; they both represent the child in all legal transactions (*actes civils*) except those where law allows the minor child to act on its own behalf (see Art. 389-3 French CC). If only one parent has parental responsibilities, that parent alone is *administrateur légal* (legal representative, Art. 389 para. 2 French CC).

(e) Determination of residence

Yes. See Art. 108 and 108-1 French CC. Spouses are allowed to have separate domiciles, but only if this does not undermine the legal provisions concerning the community of living (Art. 108 French CC). Regardless, the spouses shall jointly determine the family residence (Art. 215 para. 2 French CC) where the children will live. The domicile of a minor child who has not been emancipated is at the domicile of his parents (Art. 108-2 French CC). If the parents have different domiciles, the child's domicile is at the domicile of the parent with whom he lives (Art. 108-2 para. 2 French CC).

(f) Administration of property

Yes. See Art. 382 to 387 French CC. The parents have the right to administer their child's property and the right of usufruct (*droit de jouissance légale*).

GERMANY

(a) Care and protection

As stated in the answer to Q 1, the German concept of parental custody specifically encompasses the care of the child; §§ 1626 para. 1, 1631 para 1 German CC. The statute mentions the care (*Sorge*) of the person, including education and supervision, but does not give details. Care means to take responsibility for the child in a very broad sense.[71] Protection as such is not expressly mentioned as a part of parental care, but there is a general consensus that the person and the property of the child have to be protected.[72]

(b) Maintenance of personal relationships

Maintenance of personal relations - seeing, visiting, staying together or otherwise having contact - is called *Umgang* (personal contact) in German law. According to § 1626 para. 3 German CC, personal relations are in general in the

---

[71] See J. GERNHUBER and D. COESTER-WALTJEN, in: *Lehrbuch des Familienrechts*, 4th Edition, Munich: Beck, 1994, § 57 I, p. 856 *et seq.*

[72] See J. GERNHUBER and D. COESTER-WALTJEN, in: *Lehrbuch des Familienrechts*, 4th Edition, Munich: Beck, 1994, § 57 IX , p. 892 *et seq*; L. M. PESCHEL-GUTZEIT, in: STAUDINGER, *Kommentar zum Bürgerlichen Gesetzbuch*, 13th Edition, Berlin: Gruyter, 2002, § 1626 German CC No. 56 *et seq.*

best interests of a child with respect to both parents (sent. 1), and also with other persons (sent. 2). § 1684 German CC grants the child a right to contact. The corresponding parental right and duty to contact with the child is a separate legal position and is constitutionally protected by Art. 6 German Basic Law.[73]

(c) Provision of education

The provision of education is a part of personal care. A person having personal care over the child has the right and obligation to educate the child, § 1631 para. 1 German CC. Today, however, the public law of the respective state (*Land*) defines the extent to which regular attendance at school is compulsory.[74] Failure to perform this duty will mean an administrative offence and can lead to educational measures.

(d) Legal representation

Legal representation of the child means that the holder of parental custody can act as a legal representative of the child, see Q 8f. This is a consequence of parental custody. Custody over personal or property matters bestows representation in these matters, § 1629 German CC.

(e) Determination of residence

The determination of the residence of the child is generally not a separate issue under German law; see Q 40. The right and duty to determine the child's place of abode (*Aufenthaltsbestimmungsrecht*) form part of the responsibility for the child. Therefore the determination of residence is generally a part of the custodian's care (§ 1631 para. 1 German CC.). This also applies for the domicile in the sense of § 11 German CC. There can be restrictions by the family court, however, and a custodian may lose the right to determine the residence of the child, see Q 51. The abduction of a child outside the Federal Republic without the consent of the holder of parental responsibility amounts to a crime under § 235 German Penal Code.

(f) Administration of property

The German concept of parental custody also encompasses the 'care for the property' of the child, which includes administration of property, § 1626 para. 1 sent. 2 German CC, see Q 10, 11. One consequence is that the holder of parental responsibility has possession of the property (*Besitz*), in the sense of the law of property.[75]

---

73 Federal Constitutional Court (Bundesverfassungsgericht; BVerfG), 31.05.1983, *Entscheidungen des Bundesverfassungsgerichts* (*BVerfGE*) 64, 180, 188 = *Familienrechtszeitschrift* (*FamRZ*) 1983, 872.

74 *E.g.* ten years according to § 38 para. 1 School Law of Brandenburg of 02.08.2002.

75 D. SCHWAB, *Familienrecht*, 12th Edition, Munich, 2003, No. 606.

GREECE

(a) Care and protection

The Greek concepts of parental care and guardianship encompass the care and legal protection of the child. This obligation forms part of the physical care of the child and, more specifically, its upbringing.[76]

(b) Maintenance of personal relationships

When the child lives with the holder(s) of parental duties and responsibilities, the maintenance of personal relationships constitutes a daily practice. Communication with the child forms part of this duty.[77] Nevertheless, a parent who is not entrusted with the physical care of the child still has the right to contact that child (Art. 1520 para. 1 and 3 Greek CC). According to the prevailing opinion, this right does not form part of parental care, but is a distinct right stemming from the ties of kindred between the child and its parents.[78]

(c) Provision of education

According to Art. 1518 para. 1 Greek CC, the education and instruction of the child form part of the duty to provide parental care.

(d) Legal representation

Both parental care and guardianship encompass the legal representation of the child in any matter, transaction, or litigation regarding its person or its property (Art. 1510 para. 1 and 1603 Greek CC). This is a necessary complement to the care of the child and the administration of its property.

(e) Determination of residence

The determination of the child's residence forms part of the duty of care of the child's person (Art. 1518 para. 1 Greek CC).[79]

---

76 A. POULIADIS, in: A. GEORGIADIS and M. STATHOPOULOS (eds.), *Civil Code commentary, Vol. VIII, Family Law (Arts. 1505-1694)*, 2nd Edition, Athens: Law & Economy, P.N. Sakkoulas, 2003, Art. 1518 Greek CC, p. 259-260, No. 12 [in Greek]. According to Art. 1606 Greek CC, the provisions of Art. 1518 Greek CC apply also, by analogy, when the child is subject to guardianship.

77 S. KOUKOULI-SPILIOTOPOULOU, in: A. GEORGIADIS and M. STATHOPOULOS (eds.), *Civil Code commentary, Vol. VIII, Family Law (Arts. 1505-1694)*, 2nd Edition, Athens: Law & Economy, P. N. Sakkoulas, 2003, Introductory Remarks on Arts. 1505-1541 Greek CC, p. 74, No. 159 [in Greek]; A. POULIADIS, in: A. GEORGIADIS and M. STATHOPOULOS (eds.), *Civil Code commentary, Vol. VIII, Family Law (Arts. 1505-1694)*, 2nd Edition, Athens: Law & Economy, P.N. Sakkoulas, 2003, Art. 1520 Greek CC, p. 308-309, No. 16.

78 S. KOUKOULI-SPILIOTOPOULOU, in: A. GEORGIADIS and M. STATHOPOULOS (eds.), *Civil Code commentary, Vol. VIII, Family Law (Arts. 1505-1694)*, 2nd Edition, Athens: Law & Economy, P. N. Sakkoulas, 2003, p. 70, No. 154, with further references.

79 See also Art. 56(1) and (2) Greek CC.

(f) Administration of property

Parental care and guardianship include the administration of the child's property (Art. 1510 para. 1 and 1604 Greek CC). Special provisions of the Civil Code (Art. 1521-1528 and 1611-1630 Greek CC) regulate the formalities of and restrictions on the management of the child's assets.

HUNGARY

Answering this question cannot be separated from Q 7 and 8 and from Q 10-13. considering the administration of property. The Hungarian national concept of parental responsibilities encompasses:

(a) Care and protection

The care and protection of the child is the first, privileged element of the parental responsibilities. The duties of parental responsibilities cannot be enumerated fully. The rules regulating the parental responsibilities, the Family Act, the Child Welfare Act and the Orders of Guardianships, describe only some of these duties. The duties aside from the ones stated in Q 2b, 2c and 2e guarantee: the child's physical, mental and moral development, the determination of the child's name, the determination of the child's career, the child's health care and the child's permanent residence.

(b) Maintenance of personal relationships

The maintenance of the personal relationship is also part of the parental responsibilities. This right, as emphasised in the Convention on the Rights of the Child, belongs to the parents and to the child. The maintenance of the personal relationship is defined in a broad sense, including the child's personal relationship not only with its parents, but also with other relatives.

The maintenance of personal relationships is especially important when the child lives apart from one of the parents or both of them, or if the child has been taken into state care. The maintenance of the earlier personal relationships must be ensured.

In the first situation, the legal rules enlarge and ensure the right of contact with the child to the circle of relatives beyond the parents. In the other situation, if more than one of the parents' children is taken into state care, the legal rules guarantee siblings the right to have the same residence in order to maintain their personal relationship. In these situations, the belief that state care should not separate the child from its relatives influences both the legal rules and the practice of the public guardianship authority.

(c) Provision of education

Education is one of the rights of the parental responsibilities that belongs to the 'child's care'. A parent living apart from the child has the right to decide together with the holder of the parental responsibilities on the education of the child. If the child is capable of forming its own views, the child also has the right to express its views on its education. The views of the child should be given due weight, based on the child's age and maturity. The acts require, if possible, the participation of children 12 and older.

(d) Legal representation

The legal representation of the child is one of the duties and powers of the parental responsibilities. In exercising this power, the Civil Code distinguishes between the legal representation of the child under 14, who is incapable of representing self-representation, and of the child over 14, whose capacity to represent itself is restricted. (See Q 8f).

(e) Determination of residence

The determination of the child's residence is a right of the parental responsibilities which belongs to the 'child's care'. The parent living apart from the child has the right to decide the child's residence along with the holder of the parental responsibilities.

(f) Administration of property

The administration of the child's property is one of the duties and powers of the parental responsibilities. See Q 10-13.

Hungarian family law grants parents one more parental responsibilities' right: they can appoint, or exclude persons from being, a guardian for their child if they should die, even without giving the grounds for their disposition. Only the parents can exercise the right of appointing a guardian or excluding someone from the guardianship. This right cannot be exercised by any other guardian of the child who exercises the parental responsibilities.

IRELAND

(a) Care and protection

Yes, it does. The Irish Child Care Act 1991[80] provides a definitive legal structure for the protection of children at risk.

(b) Maintenance of personal relationships

Yes, it does. Where a parent who is a guardian does not obtain custody, he or she may nonetheless apply for access to the child. The general rule is that contact between a child and his or her parent is to be maintained wherever practicable. Where immediate direct contact cannot be ordered, supervised or indirect contact will generally be granted.

(c) Provision of education

Yes, it does. The concept of guardianship relates not to the specific matter of a child's daily life, but to its overall welfare and upbringing, such as the provision of education.

---

[80] No. 17 of 1991.

(d) Legal representation
Yes, it does.

(e) Determination of residence
Yes, it does.

(f) Administration of property
Yes, it does.

ITALY
(a) Care and protection
'Parental responsibilities' includes the power to make all decisions necessary for the care and the moral and material assistance of the child. In fact, Art. 30 § 1 Italian Constitution denotes the right and duty of the parents to support, educate and provide moral guidance to their children; Art. 147 Italian CC states that in doing this, the child's abilities, natural inclinations and ambitions should be taken into consideration. Therefore, parents must provide for the physical and mental growth of their child, protect and support him or her, and also supervise and form the child, develop his or her personality and promote the child's psychological and physical well-being.

A duty to support the child is one of the obligations of material assistance. This implies satisfying the child's ordinary needs, in line with the material conditions of the family. These obligations of support are not limited to just the basic needs of the minor, but also to any other expense necessary for the development of the child.

(b) Maintenance of personal relationships
Material assistance is joined to a moral one: parental responsibilities imply the obligation to maintain an intense and constant personal relationship with the minor, to spend time with him or her, and to provide care and attention, always with respect to the child's moral and material needs. The Italian legal system normally implies that living with the minor is an attribution of the parental responsibilities.[81] However, the parent not living with the child still has the right and duty to maintain a personal relationship with the child (so-called visiting right, see Q 43-48). The non-compliance of this right and duty can effect

[81] The link between living together and parental responsibilities is evidenced in Art. 317 *bis*, which confers authority over a child born to an unmarried mother onto the parent with whom the child lives. However, it is also possible for a child and the parent not to live together (such as with joint custody, when one parent, separated or divorced and not living with the child continues to hold parental responsibility. See, among others, Supreme Court, 17.09.1992, No. 10659, *Mass. Giust. Civ.*, 1992, p. 1378, which grants custody to the parents but decides that the child should live with his grandparents). In our legal system there is one-way relationship between living together and parental responsibilities in the sense that although living together is always linked with the exercise of the parental responsibilities, the exercise of the parental responsibilities is not linked with living together.

the limitation or termination of parental responsibilities, and may even constitute criminal behaviour as contemplated by Art. 570 Italian Criminal Code ('Violation of the duty of supporting the family').

Moreover, taking care of the moral and material interests of the child, the fundamental task conferred on the parents, can only be realised if there is close and daily contact with the child. The obligation to maintain a personal relationship with the minor 'naturally' implies 'loving the child' and showing him or her affection, even if the parents cannot be obligated to do so.

(c) Provision of education

The obligations of moral assistance include educating the child and providing moral guidance. The parent's educational obligation and responsibility is linked to that of the State (Art. 34 Italian Constitution), which has the duty to provide institutions that enable parents to fulfil their obligations and the duty to supervise the parent's compliance with their obligations. The legislature, without indicating an aim, has specified that parents must take the child's abilities, natural inclinations and ambitions into account.

Potential conflicts that arise between the child's freedoms (religious, ideological, sexual, freedom *etc*) and the parent's rights and duties must be resolved by balancing the opposing needs, respecting the capacity of the child's judgment.[82] Case law recognises the parent's duty to respect their child's choices. In particular, parents have been denied the right to choose their child's religion; a 17 year old teenager has been recognised as having the capacity to choose his own religious creed.[83] Moreover, it is has been stated that parental responsibilities cannot include the right to oppose the cultural-ideological choices of the child, but that the responsibilities must instead be exercised with full respect of the child's fundamental freedoms and inviolable rights.[84] Finally, the Supreme Court has established that using violence to educate children is unlawful.[85] Such decisions point out that a child is no longer only an object to protect, but also a holder of rights.

---

82 See M. SESTA, *Diritto di famiglia*, Padua 2003, p. 383.

83 The Family Proceedings Court of Genoa, 09.02.1959, *Giur. Cost.* 1959, p. 1278. With regard to religious education, a specific provision has been issued (Law 18.06.1986, No. 281 'capacity of choosing the type of the school to be attending and of enrolment for high schools') that expressly established that high school students (and in general students older than 14 years) have the right to choose whether to attend religious lessons and also to choose other optional classes and any other cultural or educational activity (Art. 1).

84 The Family Proceedings Court of Bologna 13.05.1972, *Giur. it.*, 1974, I, 2, c. 329, with comments by M.E. POGGI.

85 Supreme Court, 16.05.1996, *Dir. Fam. Pers.*, 1997, p. 509, with comments by D. BONAMORE.

(d) Legal representation

In order to attend to all the interests of the child, parents exercising parental responsibilities have the right and duty to represent their children and to manage their property (Art. 320 Italian CC).

Legal representation aims at allowing the child to participate in his or her own legal life; this includes acts regarding both personal and property issues. However, legal representation excludes 'very personal acts' (for example, the recognition of a natural child; the testament). Still, even if the child is incapable of acting, he or she can validly perform certain acts (*e.g.* a child can exercise the rights and duties deriving from an employment contract, pursuant to Art. 2 § 2 Italian CC). Representation also includes the power to act to protect the minor's personal rights, such as in a civil action for compensating damages resulting from a violation of the minor's rights, or for status actions not implicating conflicts of interest with the minor. Italy's legal system has developed a general principle that grants a child autonomy over his or her person if the child has the requisite power of judgment or is mature enough to make decisions with the necessary awareness.[86] If the child does not have the requisite maturity, the legislation for the minor's representation contemplates property management (see Q 8f.). These acts grant parents the right to represent an unborn as well as a born child (Art. 462 and art. 784 Italian CC).

(e) Determination of residence

Parental authority implies the power to determine the minor's residence. Because a child's residence coincides with the residence of the family in Italy's legal system, the parental responsibilities imply that the parents will live with the minor. Art. 318 Italian CC states the child has a duty not to leave the parent's home, thus affirming the parental power to exercise parental responsibilities in the return of the child through physical coercion and, if necessary, the intervention of the guardianship judge.

(f) Administration of property

Parental responsibilities include the right and duty to represent the child and to manage her or his property (Art. 320 Italian CC). If parental responsibilities are jointly exercised, each parent can individually make ordinary acts of disposition of the minor's property; however, extraordinary acts of disposition (alienation, the establishment of pledges or mortgages; acceptation or renouncement of inheritances, legacy and donation; dissolution of common ownerships, contract loans, initiation of court proceedings regarding those acts, reference to an arbitrator, settlements) can only be exercised out of necessity or if they are

---

86 Concerning the general freedom of a child that is capable of judgment in the exercise of the non-familial rights and, more generally, the conduct of personal affairs, see, among others, P. STANZIONE, *Capacità e minore età nella problematica della persona umana,* Camerino: Naples, 1975; ID., *Diritti fondamentali dei minori e potestà dei genitori,* in *Rass. Dir. Civ.*, 1980, p. 425; F. GIARDINA, headword *Minore,* in *Enc. Giur. Treccani,* XX, Rome 1990, p. 1.

obviously beneficial for the child and presuppose the authorisation of the guardianship judge (Art. 320 § 3 Italian CC). There must also be an authorisation to collect principal, and the judge will determine how it shall be invested (Art. 320 § 4 Italian CC). In addition, the continual running of a commercial enterprise presupposes the authorisation of the court, given after prior consultation with the guardianship judge (Art. 320 § 5 Italian CC).

If there is a conflict of interests among the children, or among the children and parent(s) exercising the parental responsibilities, involving property, the guardianship judge has the power to appoint a special curator for the children (Art. 320 § 6 Italian CC). In order to avoid possible conflicts of interest, parents are prohibited from acquiring, even through an intermediary, goods or rights of the child that are objects of their parental authority. Acts performed in violation of this rule can be annulled at the request of the parents exercising the authority, or on the request of the child, his heirs or successors in interest (Art. 322 Italian CC); the action is proscribed until five years after the child reaches the age of consent.

Parents have the legal usufruct of their child's property for the support of the family and the education and moral guidance of the child (Art. 324 Italian CC).

LITHUANIA

(a) Care and protection

Yes, the Lithuanian national concept of parental authority encompasses the notion of care and protection. According to Part 2 of Art. 3.155 Lithuanian CC, parents have the right and the duty to properly educate and bring up their children, care for their health and, having regard to their physical and mental state, to create favourable conditions for their full and harmonious development so that the child will be able to live independently in the society. According to Part 1 of Art. 3.165, parents have the right and duty to raise their children; they are responsible for their children's education and development, their health and spiritual and moral guidance.

In performing these duties, parents rights have priority over the rights of other persons. According to Part 2 of Art. 3.159 Lithuanian CC, parents are jointly and severally responsible for the care and education of their children. According to Art. 3.170 Lithuanian CC, a father or a mother who lives separately from the child has the right to have contact with the child and be involved in the child's education. The father or the mother with whom the child resides may not interfere with the other parent's contact with the child or involvement in the child's education. Where the parents cannot agree as to the involvement of the separated father or mother in the education of and association with the child, the procedure of the separated parent's association with the child and involvement in the child's education is determined by the court. The separated father or mother has a right to receive information about the child from all the institutions and authorities concerned with the child's education, training, health care, protection of the child's rights *etc.* Such information may be denied only if the child's life or health is imperilled by the mother or the father, and in situations provided for by the law. The authorities, organisations, institutions or natural persons who refuse to provide information to the parents about their children may be brought before the court. According to Art. 3.171 Lithuanian CC, parents can maintain contact and be involved in the education of the child who is placed in a special situation (detention, arrest, imprisonment, in-patient clinic *etc.*) in the procedure laid down by the law.

(b) Maintenance of personal relationships

Yes. According to Art. 3.156; 3.161 Lithuanian CC, a child has a right to live with its parents, be brought up and cared for in the parents' family, have contact with its parents no matter whether the parents live together or separately, and to have contact with its close relatives, unless that is prejudicial to the child's interests.

(c) Provision of education

Yes, according to Part 2 of Art. 3.165 Lithuanian CC, parents must create conditions for their children to learn during their compulsory school age (16 years). The parents' additional educational duties are established by Art. 21 Law on Education of 25 June 1991 (parents must create living and studying conditions for their children that guarantee sound and secure development of their mental and physical abilities as well as their moral growth, parents must send their children who are at least 6 or 7 years old to schools of general education if they are of sufficient physical and psychological maturity, parents must co-operate with educational institutions in questions concerning their child's education *etc.*).

(d) Legal representation

Yes. According to Art. 3.157 Lithuanian CC ('Representation of children'), legally incapable children are represented by their parents, except where the parents have been declared legally incapable by a court judgment. Parents represent their children on the presentation of the child's birth certificate (Art. 38 Lithuanian Code of Civil Procedure).

(e) Determination of residence

Yes. According to Art. 3.168 Lithuanian CC, an underage child's residence is determined in accordance with the provisions of Book Two of the Lithuanian CC (Art. 2.12-2.17). This means that the child's place of residence is the place of residence of its parents. A child may not be separated from its parents against the child's will, except in cases provided for in Book Three Lithuanian CC.`This norm corresponds to the provision of Art. 9 of the United Nations Convention on the Rights of the Child). Parents have a right to demand the return of their children from any person who keeps them against the law.

Art. 3.169 Lithuanian CC establishes a child's residence if the parents are separated. When the parents are separated, the child's residence is decided by mutual agreement of the parents. If there is a dispute about the child's residence, it will be determined by a court judgment in favour of one of the parents. If the circumstances change or if the parent with whom the child is to live allows the child live with and be brought up by the other parent, the other parent may file a suit for a re-determination of the child's residence.

(f) Administration of property

Yes. These relationships are regulated by Art. 3.185-3.191 Lithuanian CC establishing parental rights and duties related to the property owned by the children. According to Art. 3.185 Lithuanian CC, property owned by underage children is managed by the parents under the right of usufruct. The parents' right of usufruct may not be pledged, sold, transferred or encumbered in any way, and no execution may be charged against it; parents manage the property that belongs to their underage child by mutual agreement. In the event of a dispute over the management of the child's property, either parent may petition for a judicial order establishing the management procedure of the property; where the parents, or one of the parents, cause harm to the child's interests by mismanaging their underage child's property, the state institution for the protection of the child's rights or a public prosecutor may apply to the court for the removal of the parents from the management of the property that belongs to their underage child. Where warranted, the court shall remove the parents from the management of their underage child's property, revoke their right of usufruct to the child's property and appoint another person as the administrator of the minor's property. Where the grounds for the removal no longer exist, the court may allow the parents to resume the management of their underage children's property under the right of usufruct.

THE NETHERLANDS

(a) Care and protection

According to Art. 1:247 Dutch CC care and protection are important features of parental responsibility; it is both a right and a duty of a parent with parental responsibilities to care for and protect the child.

(b) Maintenance of personal relationships

There is no provision relating explicitly to the maintenance of personal relationships in the Dutch CC. However, it can be deduced from provisions in the title on parental responsibilities and the title on contact that there is a right to maintain personal relationships. For instance, Art. 1:277a and 1:277b Dutch CC state that a parent without parental responsibilities has the right to maintain a personal relationship with his or her child (contact and information). The same applies to a parent with parental responsibilities after divorce, even though this as such is not explicitly stated in the Dutch CC.

(c) Provision of education

Parental responsibilities include fostering and guiding the minor in the development of its personality, in particular with regard to its education (Art. 1:247 Dutch CC).[87]

---

[87] ASSER-DE BOER, *Mr. C. Asser's Handleiding tot de beoefening van het Nederlands Burgerlijk Recht. Personen- en Familie Recht*, 2002 No. 818.

(d) Legal representation

Parental responsibilities include the judicial and extra-judicial civil representation of the minor (Art. 1:245 § 4 Dutch CC). If there is a dispute between the child and the holder(s) of parental responsibilities, the sub-district court may appoint a special guardian to represent the minor, both judicially and extra-judicially at the request of an interested person or *ex officio*, if there is a conflict of interest that could harm the best interests of the minor (Art. 1:250 Dutch CC). There are a number of exceptions to this rule. A minor may represent himself in some summary proceedings, or may lodge an appeal against placement in a closed institution (Art. 1:261 § 3 Dutch CC) and file a request to be placed under a care and supervision order.[88] If the parents have joint parental responsibilities, they each have the capacity to represent the child in civil law acts alone, provided there are no objections from the other parent (Art. 1:253i § 1 Dutch CC).

(e) Determination of residence

Parents with parental responsibility are free to determine the residence of their child, unless a care and supervision order is in place and the child's court judge pursuant to Art. 1:261 Dutch CC decides that the child is to be placed outside the home. If the parents with parental responsibilities do not live together and cannot come to agreement about the child's residence, they may ask the court to decide the residence of the child (Art. 1: 253a Dutch CC).[89]

(f) Administration of property

According to Art. 1:254 § 4 Dutch CC, the holder(s) of parental responsibility are under the duty to administer the minor's estate. The holders of parental responsibilities must act as good administrators in administrating the capital of the minor. In case of bad administration they shall be liable for the loss attributable to them, except for the benefits the law confers to them for the enjoyment of the capital (Art. 1:253j Dutch CC).

NORWAY

(a) Care and protection

It follows from Art. 30 Norwegian Children Act 1981 that the child may claim that the person or persons attributed parental responsibilities should provide the child with care and consideration. It is expressly stated that parental responsibilities shall be exercised on the basis of the child's interests and needs. Those who are attributed parental responsibilities are under an obligation to raise and maintain the child in a proper manner.

---

88 S.F.M. WORTMANN, *Losbladige Personen- en familierecht*, Art. 245, No. 13.

89 Supreme Court 15.12.2000, *NJ*, 2001, 123. During divorce proceedings the court may determine the residence of the child.

(b) Maintenance of personal relationships

The concept of parental responsibilities includes the maintenance of personal relationships. The parents shall give the child love, security and care while it is young.

(c) Provision of education

As regards education, it follows from the Art. 30 sec. 2 Norwegian Children Act 1981 that parental responsibilities entail the duty to ensure that the child obtains an education according to its interests and abilities. It is expressly stated in Art. 32 Norwegian Children Act 1981 that a child of 15 or older may make all decisions concerning his or her education without the consent of the parents.

(d) Legal representation

The legal representative for a person under 18 is the guardian. But since guardianship follows from the attribution of parental responsibilities, it may be said that for all practical purposes guardianship is included in parental responsibilities.

(e) Determination of residence

The determination of a child's residence is decided by the person(s) to whom parental responsibilities are attributed. This is not expressly stated in the Norwegian Children Act but it is assumed that it lies within the concept of parental responsibilities.

(f) Administration of property

Administration of property is carried out by the guardian(s) who according to Art. 3 Norwegian Act on Guardianship 1927 is the person(s) attributed parental responsibilities. However, a child of 15 or older may dispose of income he or she has earned through work, or received as gifts or through inheritance if the donor or testator has expressly declared that the child shall have full control over the gift or inheritance, Art. 33 Norwegian Act on Guardianship 1927.

POLAND

The general scope of parental authority is determined by the provisions of Art. 95 and 96 Polish Family and Guardianship Code.

(a) Care and protection

Yes. The provisions refer to custody over the child and the child's upbringing (Art. 95 § 1 Polish Family and Guardianship Code), and the care of the child's physical and intellectual development (Art. 96, sentence 2 Polish Family and Guardianship Code).

(b) Maintenance of personal relationships

Yes. Polish legislation indicates that the right to personal contact with the child is included in the parental rights and obligations. It is not, however, included in the concept of parental authority and does not form a part of this authority (*dziecka*).[90]

Parents deprived of parental authority maintain the right to personal contact with the child. This can however be prohibited by the family court, when the child's interests so require (Art. 113 § 1 Polish Family and Guardianship Code). In exceptional cases the family court can limit the parents' personal contact with the child by limiting their parental authority by placing the child with a foster family or child-care institution (Art. 113 § 2 Polish Family and Guardianship Code).

(c) Provision of education

The Polish Family and Guardianship Code does not refer specifically to education, but more generally to the obligation to care for the child's intellectual development and to prepare the child for future work that will benefit society, in accordance with the child's abilities (Art. 96 Polish Family and Guardianship Code).

(d) Legal representation

Yes. Parents are the legal representatives of a child by virtue of their parental authority (Art. 98 § 1 Polish Family and Guardianship Code). The limitation of their representation is prescribed by Art. 98 § 2 Polish Family and Guardianship Code, which states that no parent should represent a child in legal actions involving other children remaining under their parental authority, or in legal actions between a child and the other parent or the parent's spouse (except for the cases when the legal act is gratuitous and for the child's benefit or concerns the means of child's subsistence and upbringing due from the other parent). If neither of the parents can represent the child, the child is represented by a curator appointed by the family court (Art. 99 Polish Family and Guardianship Code).

(e) Determination of residence

For a child remaining under parental authority, the Polish CC binds the child's place of residence with that of the child's parents, or with the parent who has sole parental authority or who the family court entrusted with the exercise of the parental authority (Art. 26 § 1 Polish CC).[91] If parents having joint parental authority over a child do not have a common place of residence, the child's residence is with the parent the child stays with on a regular basis. If the child does not stay with either parent on a regular basis, the child's place of residence is defined by the court (Art. 26 § 2 Polish CC).

---

90 Supreme Court judgment of 05.05.2000, II CKN/761/00.

91 *Kodeks cywilny*, statute of 23.04.1964, published in *Dziennik Ustaw* of 1964, No. 16, pos. 93.

(f) Administration of property

The parents shall administer the property of a child under their parental authority with due care (Art. 101 § 1 Polish Family and Guardianship Code). The administration exercised by the parents does not encompass the child's earnings or objects given to the child for the child's free use (Art. 101 § 2 Polish Family and Guardianship Code). Parents cannot, without the authorisation of the family court, perform acts exceeding the regular management standard, nor can they agree to such acts being performed by the child (Art. 101 § 3 Polish Family and Guardianship Code). Analogously, the property management is generally exercised by the guardian, under the supervision of the family court (Art. 155 Polish Family and Guardianship Code).

PORTUGAL

(a) Care and protection

As the concept of parental responsibility is understood to be a collection of powers and duties that the legal system confers upon parents so that they, in the interests of their children, will look after them, then the dimensions of care and protection can be understood as manifested in that concept.

(b) Maintenance of personal relationships

If 'looking after children' includes the parents' right and duty to keep their children close to them, then it must also include the maintenance of a close personal relationship with their child.

(c) Provision of education

The obligation of parents to ensure that their children receive an education is one of the mainstays of parental responsibility, expressly stipulated in the law (Art. 1878 No. 1 Portuguese CC).

(d) Legal representation

In accordance with the notion of parental responsibility given above, the legal representation of children is one of the main aspects of parental responsibility (Art. 1878 No. 1 Portuguese CC).

(e) Determination of residence

The right to establish the child's residence and the power to demand that she or he remains there (Art. 1887 No. 1 and 2 Portuguese CC) are included in the concept of parental responsibility.

(f) Administration of property

The administration of their children's property is another of the rights and duties that parents hold as part of parental responsibility, expressly stipulated in the law (Art. 1878 No. 1 Portuguese CC).

RUSSIA

(a) Care and protection

Parents have the right and are under the duty to care for the health, physical, psychological, spiritual and moral development of their children. (Art. 28 (2) of the Russian Constitution, Art. 63 (1) Russian Family Code).

Parents have the right and the duty to protect the rights and interests of their children. (Art. 64 (1) Russian Family Code). This duty of protection is seen not as the duty of physical protection of the children, which is regarded to reside under the duty of care, but as the duty of legal protection.[92]

(b) Maintenance of personal relationships

Maintenance of personal relationships is regarded as indispensable to the execution of the parental rights of personally caring for and educating the child. Maintenance of personal relationships is safeguarded by granting the parents the right and the duty[93] to live together with their children.[94] Art. 68 (1) Russian Family Code provides parents the right to reclaim their child from any person who holds the child other than by authorisation of a court order. If the parents are not living together, the right of the non-residential parent to maintain personal relationships with the child is safeguarded by granting that parent the right to maintain contact with the child (Art. 66 (1) Russian Family Code).

(c) Provisions of education

Right and duty to educate their children is regarded as a core element of parental responsibility. This right is laid down in Art. 28 (2) of the Russian Constitution, and developed in Art. 63 Russian Family Code.

(d) Legal representation

Parents are the legal representatives of their child by operation of law (Art. 64 (1) Russian Family Code).

(e) Determination of residence

Parents who do not live together are entitled to determine by agreement wth whom of them the children shall reside (Art. 65 (3) Russian Family Code). The parents have to make this decision 'according to the best interests the child and taking into consideration his or her wishes'(Art. 65 (2) Russian Family Code).

(f) Administration of property

Parents are entitled to administrate the property of their child in their capacity as the legal representatives of the child. While executing this right the parent has the same rights and responsibilities as the civil law (Art. 37 Russian CC)

92 A. NETCHAEVA, 'Commentary to art. 79 Russian Family Code', in: I. KUZNETZOVA (ed.),*Commentary on the Family Code of Russian Federation*, Moscow: Jurist, 2000, p. 121.

93 Parent(s) are obliged to live with their children if the children are younger than fourteen years of age.

94 Parents may, however, allow a child under the age of fourteen to live temporarily with the other persons (family, friends) or in an internat.

attributes to a guardian of an legally incapable adult (Art. 60 (3) Russian Family Code).

SPAIN

(a) Care and protection

Although Spanish law does not use the exact concepts of care and protection, care and protection are implicit in the duties enumerated in Art. 154 Spanish CC and Art. 143 Catalan Family Code. The Spanish Constitution refers to care and protection as well, Art. 39 establishes that parents must provide assistance of all kinds to their children. See for further explanations Q 8a.

(b) Maintenance of personal relationships

Spanish law refers to a duty of living with the child or having the child in one's company (Art. 154 Spanish CC and Art. 143 Catalan Family Code). This duty does not exclude the children living outside their parents' domicile for justified reasons, such as *e.g.*. education.[95] Legal literature therefore equates the duty with an emotional and intellectual communication equivalent to that required to maintain personal relationships.

It should be noted, however, that the maintenance of personal relationships is an effect of parenthood (160 Spanish CC and Art. 135 Catalan Family Code), that is, parents who do not hold parental responsibility also have a duty and a right to maintain personal relationships with the child. The child also has a right to maintain personal relationships with other relatives and persons the child is close to. See Q 44.

(c) Provision of education

The provision of education is expressly mentioned in Art. 154 Spanish CC and Art. 143 Catalan Family Code as one of the duties of parental responsibility. Education is moreover a fundamental right under Art. 27 of the Spanish Constitution. See further explanations under Q 8b.

(d) Legal representation

According to Art. 162 Spanish CC and 155 Catalan Family Code, legal representation is part of the content of parental responsibility: Spanish law establishes a general power of representation. See further explanations under Q 8 f.

(e) Determination of residence

The determination of residence is not statutorily mentioned as a specific issue among the duties comprised by *patria potestad*. As mentioned under Q 2b, the Spanish CC and the Catalan Family Code assume that children will live with their parents who jointly hold parental responsibility.

---

95 The Catalan Family code actually clarifies this in Art. 143. 2 Catalan Family Code.

Parental responsibility holders who live together with their child are free to choose where they establish their domicile. If they choose a residence which is damaging to the child however, public bodies will intervene and eventually decree that the child is in a situation of bereavement or abandonment (see Q 32).

The legal concept of living together is not identical to what, in ordinary language, would normally be understood as living together. As has been pointed out, it is more an intellectual and emotional communication, which is compatible with the situation in which a child that does not physically reside with the parents who hold responsibility. Provided that parents keep this communication (otherwise it would be understood that they abandoned the child, which is a criminal offence) and that there is a justification, parental responsibility holders are free to determine their child's residence outside their domicile *e.g.* send the child to a boarding school or summer camp, or leave the child with grandparents.

Another issue, dealt with under Q 40, is when parental responsibility is held jointly and there is disagreement as to the determination of the child's residence.

(f) Administration of property.

The administration of the child's property is specifically mentioned as part of parental responsibility in Art. 155 Spanish CC and Art. 145 Catalan Family Code. See Q 10-12.

SWEDEN

(a) Care and protection

According to Chapter 6 Sec. 1 Swedish Children and Parents Code, children are entitled to care, security and a good upbringing. They shall be treated with respect and may not be subjected to corporal punishment or any other humiliating treatment. A person who has custody of a child shall ensure that the above-mentioned needs of the child are met, Chapter 6 Sec. 2 Swedish Children and Parents Code. The custodian's obligation to protect the child encompasses the necessary supervision of the child and assuring that the child does not cause damage to any other person.

(b) Maintenance of personal relationships

In assessing the best interests of the child, particular attention shall be paid to the child's need of close and good contact with both parents, Chapter 6 Sec. 2a Swedish Swedish Children and Parents Code. The child's parents have a joint responsibility to ensure that, as far as possible, the child's right of contact with the parent the child is not living with is met (Chapter 6 Sec. 15 para. 2). Furthermore, a person with custody of the child has a responsibility to ensure, as far as possible, that the child's right of contact with any other person particularly close to the child is met (Chapter 6 Sec. 15 para. 3).

(c) Provision of education

The obligation to see to that the child receives an adequate education is included among the duties of the custodian, Chapter 6 Sec. 2 para. 2 Swedish Children and Parents Code.

(d) Legal representation

In matters relating to the personal affairs of the child, the custodian acts as the child's legal representative. The guardian acts as the child's legal representative in matters relating to the economic affairs of the child. Normally, in Swedish law both parents are the custodians and the guardians of their children. This means that they jointly represent their children in personal and economic affairs.

(e) Determination of residence

Parents sharing the custody of a child may enter into an agreement concerning the child's residence. In addition, a court may, on application of one or both parents sharing custody, decide with which of the parents the child is to live. Such a decision can include residing with both parents on an alternate basis. The relevant rules are found in Chapter 6 Sec. 14a Swedish Children and Parents Code.

(f) Administration of property

The guardian of a child is responsible for administrating the child's property and representing the child in legal proceedings concerning that property, Chapter 12 Sec. 1 Swedish Children and Parents Code.

SWITZERLAND

(a) Care and protection

Parental responsibilities comprise care and protection: 'The parents are in charge of the child's care and upbringing with a view to the child's welfare,' (Art. 301 § 1 Swiss CC) and must 'facilitate and protect the child's physical, mental and moral development' (Art. 302 § 1 Swiss CC).

(b) Maintenance of personal relationships

Parental responsibilities not only constitute the right but also the obligation to maintain a personal relationship with the child. However, parental responsibilities are not necessarily a prerequisite for a right to personal contact (Art. 273 Swiss CC). In those cases in which no parental responsibilities exist (*i.e.* because there was no marriage or they were withdrawn from one parent in connection with a divorce or were withdrawn for the protection of a child [Art. 311 Swiss CC]), the existence of a parent-child relationship is sufficient (Art. 252 *et seq* Swiss CC, Art. 273 § 1 Swiss CC).

(c) Provision of education

Parents provide for their child's education within the limits of the parents' individual economic situation and with a view to the child's welfare, in accordance with the child's abilities and predisposition. Necessary decisions concerning this are subject to the child's capacity to act, so they change or become superfluous as the child grows older (Art. 301 § 1 Swiss CC). The parents must facilitate and protect the child's physical, mental and moral development and must provide an appropriate education that corresponds as far as possible to the child's abilities and predisposition, especially if the child is physically or mentally impaired (Art. 302 § 1 and 2 Swiss CC).

(d) Legal representation

By virtue of law parents have the right to represent their child in dealings with third parties to the extent of the parental responsibilities appertaining to them (Art. 304 § 1 Swiss CC). If one parent has no parental responsibilities in a marital-type cohabitation, the father has the status of a foster father or step-father in regard to the right to represent the child within the meaning of Art. 299 and 300 Swiss CC.[96]

(e) Determination of residence

Parental responsibilities also include the right to determine the child's place of residence (custody right, Art. 301 § 3 Swiss CC). Parents only determine their child's place of residence indirectly insofar as the child's place of residence is derived from their own place of residence. 'The child's domicile is deemed to be the place of residence of his or her parents with parental responsibility. In the case where his or her parents do not have a common residence, the child's domicile will be deemed to be that of parent with custody over the child. In all other cases, the child's domicile is deemed to its place of residence (Art. 25 § 1, Swiss CC). The parent's domicile is determined in accordance with Art. 23 *et seq* Swiss CC. In principle the place of residence is the place where a person stays with the intention of permanently remaining.

(f) Administration of property

'As long as parents hold parental responsibilities they have the right and the obligation to administer the child's property' (Art. 318 § 1 Swiss CC).

---

96 For one example representing many, see: C. HEGNAUER, *Grundriss des Kindesrechts*, Bern: Stämpfli Verlag, 1999, No. 25.22.

QUESTION 3

A. GENERAL

In what circumstances (*e.g.* the child reaching the age of majority or marrying) do parental responsibilities automatically come to an end?

AUSTRIA

Since parental responsibilities are restricted to minor children, they end automatically when the child reaches majority (Sec. 172(1) Austrian CC), *i.e.* at 18 years of age (Sec. 21(2) Austrian CC). The holder(s) of parental responsibilities shall release any property administered by them and all documents relating to the child to any child who has come of age (Sec. 172(2) Austrian CC).

Marriage makes a minor child equal to an adult in his or her personal relationships for the duration of the marriage (Sec. 175 Austrian CC). These personal relationships include using a name and applying for personal documents, but not the legal capacity to commit and dispose of property, *e.g.* for purposes of support or to furnish a dowry.[1] A child may marry after completing his or her 16th year if the future spouse is an adult and the minor appears to be mature enough for this marriage (Sec. 1(2) Austrian Marriage Act [*Ehegesetz*]).

BELGIUM

Parental responsibilities automatically come to an end when a child reaches majority, which is at the age of 18 (Art. 388 Belgian CC). This is also the case when both parents or the only surviving parent die, when both parents (or the only surviving parent) are continuously unable to exercise their parental responsibilities or when the parent(s) are discharged of their parental responsibilities by a Juvenile Court (Art. 32-35 Belgian Law of 8 April 1965 concerning Juvenile Protection. See Q 51-54). The parental responsibilities of the parents also come to an end if the child is adopted.[2] The minor is judicially removed from guardianship by its marriage (Art. 476 Belgian CC).

BULGARIA

The parental rights and duties automatically come to an end in the following circumstances:

---

1 M. Schwimann, *Familienrecht*, 5th Edition, Vienna: LexisNexis ARD Orac, 2004, p. 9; H. PICHLER, 'Der Unterhalt der Ehefrau unter 18 Jahren', *Österreichischer Amtsvormund*, 1985, p. 68-69.

2 M. VERRYCKEN, 'Openvallen en organisatie van de voogdij', in: P. SENAEVE, J. GERLO and F. LIEVENS (eds.), *De hervorming van het voogdijrecht*, Antwerpen: Intersentia, 2002, p. 1-20.

- Children attain the age of majority at 18 years. According to the Bulgarian Persons and Family Act: 'At the age of 18 persons obtain full age and capacity to acquire rights and to take obligations' (Art. 2), and to the Bulgarian Child Protection Act 'a child is every person under 18 years of age' (Art. 2).
- In contracting of marriage by the child, which by exception is allowed at the age of 16.[3]
- In cases of death of the child or of the parent.

CZECH REPUBLIC

Parental responsibility automatically comes to an end when the child reaches majority. A minor older than sixteen acquires majority by contracting marriage (Sec. 8 § 2 Czech CC). Court consent is needed for contracting a valid marriage (Sec. 13 Czech Family Code). If the marriage is contracted without the court consent majority will still be acquired, even though the marriage will be void. Such a majority is not lost if the marriage is ended by other means.

Parental responsibility also comes to an end by adoption. At the moment the legal relationship between the parents and the child ceases to exist, the adoptive parents are placed into the legal position of parents (including family relationships).

DENMARK

Parental authority automatically comes to an end when the child becomes 18 or enters into a marriage or a registered partnership, Art. 1 Danish Act on Parental Authority and Contact.[4]

ENGLAND & WALES

The duration of parental responsibility depends in part on how it is initially acquired but in all cases it automatically ends upon the child attaining his majority. This is because responsibility can only exist in respect of a "child" which Sec. 105(1), English Children Act 1989 defines as "a person under the age of eighteen". It will clearly end upon the child's death.[5] There is pre-Children Act 1989 authority for saying that the right of custody ended upon the child's marriage[6] and that it was suspended whilst the child was serving in the armed

---

3 Art. 12 § 3 reads that 'With the contraction of marriage a minor becomes competent but can dispose of real estate only with the permission of the District court at the place of its residence.'

4 A child under the age of 18 needs the consent of the holder(s) of parental authority and permission from the administrative authorities in order to marry or enter into a registered partnership. If permission is granted the child is no longer subject to parental authority. Such permission may stipulate that the child is still subject to guardianship, Art. 1 Danish Act on Guardianship.

5 Though parents retain the right to dispose of the child's corpse, see *R v Gwynedd County Council ex p B* [1992] 3 All ER 317, CA.

6 *Hewer v Bryant* [1970] 1 QB 357 at 363, CA, per SACHS LJ; *R v Wilmington Inhabitants* (1825) 5 B Ald 525 at 526 and *Lough v Ward* [1945] 2 All ER 338 at 348.

forces[7] but it remains to be seen whether a similar position will be taken with regard to parental responsibility.

The making of a parental order[8] or an adoption order[9] operates to extinguish the parental responsibility of existing holders and to transfer it to the person or persons in whose favour the order is made. This in fact is the only means by which mothers and married fathers can be deprived of their responsibility during the child's minority since the court's have no general divesting powers. The position is different with respect to unmarried fathers for regardless of how responsibility is acquired it can be ended by a court order.[10] Non-parents who have responsibility by reason of a residence order and local authorities that have responsibility by reason of a care order only have responsibility for the duration of the order.[11] In other words in these cases responsibility automatically ends upon the cessation of the residence or care order.

FINLAND

The custody of the child ends at the age of majority, which is the age of 18 or before this, if the child marries (Sec. 3 para. 2 Finnish Child Custody and the Right of Access Act).[12]

FRANCE

In three circumstances parental responsibilities automatically come to an end:

- when the child reaches majority (Art. 371-1 para. 2 French CC);
- when the child is emancipated. This takes place when the child, who must be at least 16, obtains the capacity to enter in legal transactions (*faire les actes civils*, Art. 481 French CC). The parents can petition jointly or one parent can act alone. If the *juge des tutelles* (guardianship court) believes after the child is heard that there are *justes motifs* (serious reasons) for the emancipation, an emancipation order will be issued (Art. 477 French CC); or
- when the minor child gets married (Art. 476 French CC).

---

7 *R v Rotherfield Greys Inhabitants* (1823) 1 B & C 345 at 349-50.

8 *Viz* an order made under Sec. 30, British Human Fertilisation and Embryology Act 1990. The effects of such orders are governed by the Parental Orders (Human Fertilisation and Embryology) Regulations 1994, SI 1994/2767.

9 See Sec. 12(3), English Adoption Act 1976 (prospectively Sec. 46, English Adoption and Children Act 2002).

10 See Sec. 4(3), English Children Act 1989.

11 Sec. 12(2) and 33(3), English Children Act 1989. A similar position obtains in respect of parental responsibility acquired by reason of an emergency protection order, see Sec. 44(4)(c).

12 A person who is under 18 years of age can marry if the Ministry of Justice grants him/her permission to marry on special grounds (Chapter 2 Sec. 4 Finnish Marriage Act 411/1987).

In other cases, it is possible for the court to discharge parents of their parental responsibilities (*retrait de l'autorité parentale*, see Art. 378 *et seq* French CC and Q 51).

GERMANY

Under some circumstances parental custody automatically comes to an end. One reason is the child attains majority, § 1626 para. 1 sent. 1 German CC. Another is adoption of the child by other persons, which extinguishes the parental responsibility of the former holder (see § 1755 German CC).[13] Marriage of the child does not terminate parental custody.[14] However, care for an underage child who is or was married is restricted to representation in personal affairs, § 1633 German CC. A parent's care also expires with his or her death (see § 1680 para. 1 German CC).[15] It is also automatically terminated when there is a declaration of death of the parent (§ 1677 German CC). Personal care cannot exist after the child dies.[16] The parents, however, shall attend to those affairs which cannot be delayed without jeopardy until the heir is able to attend to them; see § 1698b German CC. In other cases of a legal or actual obstacle for the custodian there is only a suspension of care, §§ 1673 et seq German CC. However, when persons other than the parents have only limited personal responsibility, these rights automatically end upon the cessation of living together, see Q 14.

GREECE

Parental responsibilities automatically come to an end when the child reaches the age of majority, dies or is declared to be a missing person (Art. 1538 Greek CC). The child's marriage does not formally amount to the cessation of parental care, but it does restrict its scope:[17] Art. 137 Greek CC provides that a married minor can, of its own accord, enter into every legal transaction which is necessary in order to conserve or enhance its property, or to provide the needs for its personal maintenance and education, as well as to support its family. In addition, the child is entitled to manage its own assets to a certain extent, and to ensure its own legeal representation. Finally, the obligations of the spouses to

---

13 L. M. PESCHEL-GUTZEIT, in: STAUDINGER, *Kommentar zum Bürgerlichen Gesetzbuch*, 13th Edition, Berlin: Gruyter, 2002, § 1626 German CC No. 40.

14 L. M. PESCHEL-GUTZEIT, in: STAUDINGER, *Kommentar zum Bürgerlichen Gesetzbuch*, 13th Edition, Berlin: Gruyter, 2002, § 1626 German CC No. 41.

15 L. M. PESCHEL-GUTZEIT, in: STAUDINGER, *Kommentar zum Bürgerlichen Gesetzbuch*, 13th Edition, Berlin: Gruyter, 2002, § 1626 German CC No. 42.

16 L. M. PESCHEL-GUTZEIT, in: STAUDINGER, *Kommentar zum Bürgerlichen Gesetzbuch*, 13th Edition, Berlin: Gruyter, 2002, § 1626 German CC No. 38.

17 A. POULIADIS, in: A. GEORGIADIS and M. STATHOPOULOS (eds.), *Civil Code commentary, Vol. VIII, Family Law (Arts. 1505-1694)*, 2nd Edition, Athens: Law & Economy, P.N. SAKKOULAS, 2003, Art. 1518 Greek CC, p. 297 - 299, No. 142-143; S. KOUKOULI-SPILIOTOPOULOU, in: A. GEORGIADIS and M. STATHOPOULOS (eds.), *Civil Code commentary, Vol. VIII, Family Law (Arts. 1505-1694)*, 2nd Edition, Athens: Law & Economy, P. N. Sakkoulas, 2003, p. 57, No. 126.

cohabit (Art. 1386 Greek CC) and to engage in conjugal life (Art. 1387 Greek CC) further restrict the scope of parental responsibilities.

The duties of a specific holder of parental responsibilities come to an end when he dies, is declared to be a missing person, or is legally discharged from this task (Art. 1510 para. 2 and 3, 1538 and 1650-1651 Greek CC), as well as when the child is adopted (Art. 1561 Greek CC). In such cases another person (a guardian or adoptive parent) will take over these responsibilities.

HUNGARY

The parental responsibilities automatically end when the child reaches majority, even if the child continues to live with its parents and the parents continue to provide the child's board and education. The parental responsibilities also end, with the permission of the public guardianship authority, if the child marries before reaching the age of majority. Hungary's age of majority is 18; both men and women can marry from the age of 16 with the permission of the public guardianship authority. In this situation the marriage will result in the child's majority.

If the parental responsibilities of the parents end as before the child's majority or marriage, the child must come under the parental responsibilities of another person.

IRELAND

Parental responsibilities arise only in respect of 'a person who has not attained full age'.[18] By virtue of Sec. 2 Irish Age of Majority Act 1985[19] a person reaches full age on attaining the age of 18. In respect of maintenance obligations, a dependent child is defined to include a person who has attained the age of 18 years but is under the age of 23 and is receiving or undergoing a full-time course of education at a recognised educational establishment, or is suffering from a mental or physical disability to such an extent that it is not reasonably possible for him or her to maintain him or herself fully.

ITALY

Parental responsibilities expire when the child reaches the age of consent (18 years), or with emancipation (Art. 316 Italian CC). The only existing form of emancipation is the legal one: children older than 16 who marry with the authorisation of the Court (Art. 390 Italian CC). The emancipated minor has a partial capacity to act: with respect to his or her legal actions, he is no longer substituted by the parents (or by the guardian) but a curator assists him or her with extraordinary acts of disposition. This curator, differing from the guardian, has neither the power of representation nor the management of the minor.

---

18 Per Sec. 2(1) Irish Guardianship of Infants Act 1964 (No. 7 of 1964).
19 No. 2 of 1985.

Parental responsibilities expire through: death of the child or the parent, declaration of adoptability, legal termination of the parental responsibilities, or declaration of the lack of biological parentage (a disclaimer of paternity or impugnation of the acknowledgment of a natural child).

The termination of parental responsibilities when the child attains majority does not signal an end to all parental obligations. The duty to support the child persists until the child is economically independent, unless the child refuses to work without just cause. Italian case law[20] has consistently upheld this principle. Judges will equate the child's economic independency with negligent behaviour if the child fails or refuses to earn his or her own income. A parent's duty to support their child ends if the child marries; the obligation of the child's partner to support him or her prevails over the obligation of the parents.

Neither does the obligation to provide moral guidance to the child automatically expire once the child has reached the age of consent; the child has the right to finish her or his studies, allowing the child to acquire the necessary skills to find a job and become economically independent.

LITHUANIA

This issue is specified in Art. 3.160 Lithuanian CC, according to which parental rights and duties shall end when the child attains majority (18 years of age) or full active legal capacity (*e.g.* in the event of the emancipation of the child who has attained 16 years, or in the event of marriage before the age of 18 years). In certain cases considered in the light of the child's interests, parental authority may be limited on a temporary or permanent basis, or the child may be separated from the parents in the procedure laid down by Book Three Lithuanian CC.

THE NETHERLANDS

All minors are subject to parental responsibilities (Art. 1:245 § 1 Dutch CC). Minors are persons who have not reached the age of eighteen, are not married or involved in a registered partnership nor have been married or registered, or have been declared of age pursuant to Art. 1:253ha Dutch CC. Art. 1:253ha Dutch CC states that where a minor woman with parental responsibilities wishes to care for and raise her child, she may before or after the birth having reached the age of sixteen, apply to the children's court judge to declare her of age. Parental responsibilities automatically come to an end when the child reaches majority (Art. 1:246 Dutch CC). A parent's responsibilities end with death. If there is no other person with parental responsibilities and the parent

---

20 Among the most recent Case-Law, see Supreme Court, 03.04.2002, No. 4765, in *Famiglia*, 2003, p.195, with comments by A. QUADRUCCI; Supreme Court 16.02.2001, No. 2289, in *Fam. dir.*, 2001, p. 275, with comments by W. FINELLI. Among the more previous ones see Supreme Court 07.11.1981, No. 5874, *Giust. civ.*, 1981, I, p. 2837.

did not appoint a guardian by will, the court must appoint a guardian over the minor (Art. 1:245 § 1 and 1:295 Dutch CC).

NORWAY

The right to make decisions for the child comes to an end when the child reaches majority (18 years), according to Art. 33 Norwegian Children Act 1981. There are no general provisions in the Norwegian Children Act on when parental responsibilities cease, but it is generally assumed that after the child has reached the age of majority, he or she has full capacity in all respects. However, when the act was debated in parliament, it was agreed that the 18 year limit in itself should not be relevant to that part of parental responsibilities that refers to the feeling of responsibility and concern for the child.[21] The functions of the guardian(s) cease at the age of 18, Art. 1 Norwegian Act on Guardianship 1927. Parental responsibilities do not cease if a child under 18 marries.

POLAND

The parental authority ceases when the child attains the age of majority (Art. 92 Polish Family and Guardianship Code); *i.e.* when the child either reaches 18 years of age or marries before then (Polish law prescribes that a minor attains the age of majority by virtue of a marriage - Art. 10 § 2 Polish Civil Code). Previous parental authority or guardianship also ceases when a child is adopted (Art. 123 § 1 Polish Family and Guardianship Code). The adoption creates the equivalent of a parent-child relationship between the adopted and the adoptive persons (Art. 121 § 1 Polish Family and Guardianship Code) which also encompasses parental authority. Parental authority may also cease when a parent holding it loses the full capacity to perform acts in law (*e.g.* by the parent's legal incapacity) as the result of a judgment terminating the parental relationship (*e.g.* denial of the paternity) or in case of parent's or child's death.

PORTUGAL

Children are subject to parental responsibility until they reach majority or are emancipated (Art. 130, 132, 133 and 1877 Portuguese CC). These are the normal ways in which parental responsibility will automatically come to an end.

There are, however, other ways that parental responsibility may end: the death of the parents or of the child, and full adoption (Art. 1979 *et seq* especially Art. 1986 No. 1 Portuguese CC) or simple adoption (Art. 1992 *et seq* and especially Art. 1997 and 1998 Portuguese CC). Upon the death of one of the parents, parental responsibility falls to the surviving parent (Art. 1904 and 1911 No. 3 Portuguese CC). With full adoption, 'the adoptee acquires the status of son/daughter of the adopter and becomes part of his or her family alongside other descendents, while family ties between the adoptee and his or her natural ascendants and siblings are extinguished'; the biological parents' parental responsibility is therefore extinguished (Art. 1986 No. 1 Portuguese CC). With

---

21 Innst. O. (1980-81) nr. 30, p. 10.

simple adoption, parental responsibility falls exclusively to the adopter, although the natural bond of parentage is not extinguished (Art. 1997 Portuguese CC).

RUSSIA

Parental responsibility automatically ends in the following circumstances:

- The death of a parent or a child;
- a child reaches the age of eighteen - the age of majority under Russian law (Art. 61 (2) Russian Family Code);
- a child acquires full legal capacity by entering a marriage before the age of majority after being granted dispensation (Art. 61 (2) Russian Family Code, Art. 21 (2) Russian CC[22]).
- a child acquires full legal capacity by way of emancipation (Art. 61 (2) Russian Family Code and Art. 27 (1) Russian CC). A child who has reached the age of sixteen and has paid employment, or, with consent of his or her parents, is carrying out a business activity, can be emancipated by the Guardianship and Curatorship Department upon consent of his or her parents or guardians, or by a court order of the District Court if the parents or guardians do not give their consent (Art. 27 (1) Russian CC).

SPAIN

Art. 158 Catalan Family Code and 169 Spanish CC establish that parental responsibility automatically comes to an end in the following cases:

- upon the death or declaration of death of either the child or the parental responsibility holder. It should, however, be considered that if parental responsibility is held jointly by the father and mother of the child, the death of one of the holders does not mean an automatic end of parental responsibility but instead a change in the subject. Jointly held parental responsibility will be held, after the death of one of the holders, by the other holder alone.
- if the child or the parental responsibility holders are declared absent. The former reasoning applies if parental responsibility is held jointly.
- if the child is adopted, except in the case of step-parent adoption. If a child is adopted by the parent's spouse or cohabitee, parental responsibility is not terminated but changes subjectively because both the parent and the adopter will hold it jointly.
- if the child reaches majority (18 years).
- if the child is emancipated. This can occur in three situations:
  - Art. 314 Spanish CC[23] establishes that a child becomes emancipated by judicial decision. This can occur if the child is 16 and the child

---

22 Civil Code of the Russian Federation of 1994. *Sobranie Zakonodatel'stva Rossiiskoi Federatsii*, 1994, No. 32, item 3301. Further referred to as Russian CC. For an English translation see: *21 Review of Central and Eastern European Law*, 1995, No. 3/4, p. 245-430.

23 This regulation is applicable in Catalonia as well.

requests it himself or herself (Art. 320 Spanish CC). The parental responsibility holders must be heard and there must be a reason for the emancipation; either that the parental responsibility holder marries or cohabitates with a person who is not a parent, or that the parents live apart, or any other reason which gravely disturbs the exercise of parental responsibility.
- A child also becomes emancipated if he or she marries. This is possible with parental consent or judicial authorisation if the child is older than 16. Children older than 14 and younger than 16 need judicial permission in order to marry, notwithstanding the fact that parental responsibility holders' consented. Younger children cannot marry.
- Emancipation can also be a concession of those exercising paternal responsibility. This requires that the child is older than 16 and consents to the emancipation. This kind of emancipation must be formalised in a public document (notarial deed) or before the Civil Registrar. It has to be registered in the Civil Registry in order to be enforceable *vis a vis* third parties. Such an emancipation is irrevocable.

With emancipation, however, *patria potestad* is not extinguished completely because the child will need the authorisation of his or her parents in order to borrow money and sell or burden valuable properties (Art. 323 Spanish CC). This rule is also applicable in the case of married children unless the property is common and the child's spouse is older than 18, in which case his or her consent will suffice.

SWEDEN

The custodian's responsibilities end when the child reaches the age of eighteen, which in Sweden is the age of majority,[24] or when the child enters into marriage or registered partnership, if younger than eighteen, Chapter 6 Sec. 2 Swedish Children and Parents Code. The responsibilities of the guardians, however, do not come to end until the child reaches the age of majority, even if the child contracts a marriage or a registered partnership before eighteen, Chapter 9 Sec. 1 and Chapter 10 Sec. 4 Swedish Children and Parents Code.

SWITZERLAND

An individual basically reaches his or her majority upon reaching his or her 18th birthday, whereupon parental responsibilities automatically cease (Art. 14 Swiss CC, Art. 296 § 1 Swiss CC). Parental responsibilities also lapse upon the death of both parents; in this case a guardian must be appointed for any child who is still a minor (Art. 368 Swiss CC). Since the age for reaching majority and the age at which the child is permitted to marry (Art. 94 Swiss CC) now coincide, marriage no longer results in an early end to parental responsibilities.

---

[24] The age of majority was lowered to 18 years in 1974, compared with the previously applicable 20 years (1969-1974). Before 1969, a child reached majority at the age of 21.

QUESTION 4

A. GENERAL

What is the current source of law for parental responsibilities?

AUSTRIA

The most important source of law governing parent and child in Austria is the Austrian CC (*Allgemeines Bürgerliches Gesetzbuch*, abbreviated ABGB).[1] It contains substantive law provisions governing the exercise of parental responsibilities (Sec. 137 to 267 Austrian CC). The religious education of children is governed by the Federal Act on the Religious Education of Children (*Bundesgesetz über die religiöse Kindererziehung*).[2] In the area of public assistance, the 1989 Youth Welfare Act (*Jugendwohlfahrtsgesetz*)[3] and the individual regional assistance acts are relevant.[4] The procedural provisions relating to the exercise of parental responsibilities (*custody matters*) are contained in sections 104 *et seq* Non-Contentious Proceedings Act (*Außerstreitgesetz,* abbreviated *AußStrG*).[5]

BELGIUM

The Belgian CC contains the principles of parental responsibilities, which form the basic source of law. However, this basic source must be completed with other laws that regulate certain aspects of the parental responsibilities. The sources of law for parental responsibilities are:

- Belgian CC
    - Art. 108 concerning the domicile of the child;
    - Art. 148 concerning the parental agreement with marriage;
    - Art. 203 concerning the right to maintenance;
    - Art. 221-223 concerning the disputes about parental responsibilities, questions of residence of the child or contact in the context of interim measures between spouses;
    - Art. 319 concerning the mother's agreement about the acknowledgement of her extra-marital child by a man;
    - Art. 348, 368(4) and 349(4), (5) and (6) concerning the adoption agreement;
    - Art. 371-388 concerning parental authority;
    - Art. 389 - 420 concerning guardianship;
    - Art. 475 *bis* – 475 *septies* concerning custodianship;
    - Art. 476 - 487 concerning judicial removal from guardianship (emancipation);

---

1 01.06.1811, JGS 946, http://www.ris.bka.gv.at.

2 Federal Law Gazette *[Bundesgesetzblatt, BGBl.]* 1985/155.

3 *BGBl.* 1989/161.

4 For details see E. STREINESBERGER/TH. HACKER, 'Jugendwohlfahrtsrecht', in: O. LEHNER, *Kinder- und Jugendrecht*, 2nd Edition, Vienna: Orac, 1998, p. 159-183.

5 *BGBl.* I 2003/111, in force since 01.01.2005, http://www.ris.bka.gv.at.

  - Art. 487 *ter* concerning the demand of prolonged minority;
  - Art.1397 concerning the right to assist with a (change of) marriage contract;
- Belgian Judicial Code:
  - Art. 734 *bis* - 734 *sexies* concerning family mediation;
  - Art. 931 concerning the child's general right to be heard;
  - Art. 1232 - 1237 concerning procedural issues about guardianship;
  - Art. 1258 concerning procedural issues about disputes arisen in the context of interim measures between spouses;
  - Art. 1280 concerning interim measures when a claim for divorce has been introduced in court;
  - Art. 1288-1304 concerning divorce by mutual consent;
  - Art. 1322 *bis* - 1322 *octies* concerning protection of cross-border rights of contact;
- Belgian Law of 8 April 1965 concerning Juvenile Protection (LJP)
  - Art. 32-35 and 60 concerning discharge of parental responsibilities;
  - Art. 51 and 56 *bis* concerning the hearing of the minor in the Juvenile Court;
- Others:
  - Art. 391 *bis* Belgian Penal Code concerning the criminal action that can be taken against the parent who disregards his maintenance-obligation;
  - Art. 432 Belgian Penal Code concerning the criminal action that can be taken against the parent who disregards someone's right of contact;
  - Art. 63 Belgian Law on the Public Social Welfare Centre concerning the guardianship over particular categories of children;
  - Art. 44 Belgian Law on the Labour Contract;
  - Art. 2 Belgian Law of 15 May 1987 on Surnames and First Names concerning the demand of a change of name;
  - Art. 3 Belgian Law of 28 May 2002 concerning Euthanasia;

Art. 12 Belgian Law of 22 August 2002 concerning the rights of minor patients.

BULGARIA

The Bulgarian Family Code passed in 1985.

CZECH REPUBLIC

Parental responsibility is regulated by the Czech Family Code (Act No. 94/1963 Coll. as amended in 1998, Act No. 91/1998 Coll. with effect from 1 August 1998, especially in provisions of Sections 26-28, 31-37b and 44).

DENMARK

The main source is the Danish Act on Parental Authority and Contact, *Lov om forældremyndighed og samvær*, Act No. 387 of 14 June 1995 as amended by the following acts; No. 752 of 15 August 1996, No. 416 of 10 June 1997, No. 147 of 9 March 1999, No. 461 of 7 June 2001 and No. 446 of 9 June 2004. Under the authority of the Act, Art. 17, 4 and 31, the Minister of Justice can issue rules regarding the way in which the administrative authorities and the courts hear cases under the Act, and he/she can also issue rules regarding the conditions under which agreements on joint parental authority may be registered and rules regarding supervised contact. Such rules have been issued and can be found in Departmental order No. 874 of 24 October 2002. A number of guidance notes and instructions lay down the rules and practices followed by the administrative authorities in cases concerning parental authority and contact.[6]

A child under 18 is also subject to guardianship and these rules may be found in the Danish Act on Guardianship, *Værgemålsloven*, Act No. 388 of 14 June 1995.

ENGLAND & WALES

The main controlling statute is the English Children Act 1989 which came into force in October 1991, a key aim of which was to replace the concept of parental rights of and duties with the concept of parental responsibility. However, the Act itself does not contain a comprehensive definition. Sec. 3(1) merely states that:

> 'parental responsibility' means all the rights, duties, powers, responsibilities and authority which by law a parent of a child has in relation to the child and his property'.

This admittedly disappointing definition means that reference must also be made to the pre-Children Act position[7] including the common law (i.e. case-law going back to at least the eighteenth century) bearing in mind that that law concerned notions of parental rights and duties rather than responsibilities. Reference of course must also be made to post-Children Act 1989 case-law on parental responsibility.

FINLAND

The main source for the Finnish law concerning parental responsibility is the Finnish Child Custody and the Right of Access Act of 1983 with amendments, especially those from 1994.[8] Two other important Acts are the Finnish Act of the

---

6 Guidance notes, *Vejledninger*, No. 11049 of 1999 and No. 214 of 20.12.1995. Instructions, *Skrivelser*, No. 9555 of 08.11.2002, No. 9556 of 28.10.2002, No. 11491 of 12.11.1997, No. 11195 of 23.04.1997, No. 11271 of 28.06.1996, No. 10357 of 28.06.1996, No. 11092 of 08.12.1995 and No. 10360 of 02.10.1995.

7 For which see EEKELAAR, 'What are Parental Rights?' (1973) 89 *LQR* 210, HALL, 'The Waning of Parental Rights' [1972B] *CLJ* 248, MAIDMENT, 'The Fragmentation of Parental Rights' [1981] *CLJ* 135 and LAW COMMISION, *Working Paper No. 91: Guardianship*, para. 2.25 *et seq*.

8 Finnish Child Custody and the Right of Access Act, No. 361/1983 with amendments 186/1994, 620/1996, 818/2000.

Enforcement of a Decision on Child Custody and Right of Access, reformed in 1996, and the Finnish Child Protection Act of 1983 with amendments, especially those from 1990. The main source of law concerning the administration of property is the Finnish Guardianship Services Act of 1999.

FRANCE

The legal provisions concerning parental responsibilities are contained in Art. 371 to 387 French CC. These provisions have been amended several times. The latest reform is the Act No. 2002-305 of 4 March 2002, which was integrated into the parental responsibilities' provisions of the French CC.

GERMANY

There are several important legal sources for parental responsibility. They are found in German constitutional law, European human rights law, German substantive civil law, the law of civil and non-contentious procedure and in social security law.

According to Art. 3 para. 2 of the Constitution (*Grundgesetz* or German Basic Law) there is equality of the sexes.[9] This provision, which came into force in 1953, made the former provisions of the Civil Code giving 'parental authority' to the father unconstitutional. Later the Constitutional Court also struck down a provision which gave the father the right to decide, if there was a conflict between the parents.[10]

Another important provision is Art. 6 para. 1 of the German Constitution, which states that marriage and family shall enjoy the special protection of the State. This means that in addition to the subjective rights embodied in Art. 6 of the German Basic Law this provision also contains a constitutional 'institutional guarantee' and a 'basic norm decisive as to value.'[11] 'Family' includes the relationship between parents and their children, whether legitimate or illegitimate[12].

According to Art. 6 para. 2 of the Constitution, the care and raising of children is the parents' natural right and foremost obligation. Therefore parents enjoy the fundamental right to determine the upbringing of their offspring as they think fit. Art. 6 para. 2 first sentence, guarantees the exercise of parental responsibility in the interests of welfare of the child.[13] This is considered to be

9 Grundgesetz für die Bundesrepublik Deutschland of 23.05.1949, *Federal Gazette (Bundesgesetzblatt; BGBl)* 1949 I p. 1.

10 BVerfG, 29.07.1959, *BVerfGE* 10, 59 = *Neue Juristische Wochenschrift (NJW)* 1959, 1483 = *FamRZ* 1959, 416.

11 See BVerfG, 17.01.1957, *BVerfGE* 6, 55, 71 *et seq*; 29.07.1968, *BVerfGE* 24, 119, 135; 04.05.1971, *BVerfGE* 31, 58, 67 *et seq*; 18.07.1979, *BVerfGE* 51, 386, 396 *et seq*; 30.11.1982, *BVerfGE* 62, 323, 329.

12 See BVerfG, 29.07.1959, *BVerfGE* 10, 59, 66 = *FamRZ* 1959, 416.

13 See BVerfG, 18.07.1979, *BVerfGE* 51, 386, 398; 09.02.1982, *BVerfGE* 59, 360, 381 *et seq.*

not only the constitutional basis for the principle that the best interests of the child are paramount, but also a barrier to State intervention. The State nevertheless has to fulfil its role as guardian of the child's own basic rights.[14] Therefore the State is authorized to curtail parental rights in order to protect children where there is abuse or neglect. The State also has to guarantee that the child's position is represented in custody court proceedings.[15]

Art. 6 para. 5 of the German Constitution states that legislation shall provide illegitimate children with the same opportunities for their development and their place in society as are enjoyed by legitimate children. This constitutional mandate was the basis for the reform statutes of 1969 and 1997. A different treatment of illegitimate children is only acceptable if there are reasons that flow from the special situation of these children.[16] In the field of parental responsibility, this provision and Art. 3 of the Constitution were the legal basis for several judgments of the Federal Constitutional Court, giving unmarried fathers a better legal position.[17] However, the Court recently upheld § 1626a German CC, according to which it is the mother who has parental responsibility if there is not a common declaration of joint parental responsibility,[18] see Q 22b.

Another important legal source is the European Convention on Human Rights, especially Art. 8 on the respect of family life.[19] The convention, however, has only the same status as a German federal statute. For this reason, German courts must observe and apply the Convention in interpreting national law. But on the level of German constitutional law, the text of the Convention and the case-law of the European Court of Human Rights (ECtHR) serve as interpretive aids when determining the scope and contents of the fundamental rights and constitutional principles of the German Basic Law, to the extent that this does not restrict or reduce the protection of the individual's fundamental rights under the German Basic Law.[20]

However, in practice the implementation of the rules of the European Convention on Human Rights can be difficult, as the case of *Görgülü* shows. He is the Turkish father of a child born out of wedlock in 1999. The mother of the child gave the child up for adoption one day after the birth and declared her consent prior to adoption by the foster parents, with whom the child has been living since its birth. Since October 1999, the father has unsuccessfully endeavoured in a number of judicial proceedings to obtain custody and gain a

---

14 See BVerfG, 15.06.1971, *BVerfGE* 31, 194, 208 = *FamRZ* 1971, 421.

15 BVerfG, 20.08.2003, *FamRZ* 2004, 86 = *NJW* 2003, 3544.

16 BVerfG, 07.05.1991, *BVerfGE* 84, 168, 185 = *FamRZ* 1991, 913; BVerfG, 06.05.1997, *BVerfGE* 96, 56, 65 = *FamRZ* 1997, 869.

17 See BVerfG, 07.03.1995, *BVerfGE* 92, 158 = *FamRZ* 1995, 789 (adoption without consent of the father); 23.04.2003, *FamRZ* 2003, 1447 annotated by M. COESTER.

18 BVerfG, 29.01.2003, *BVerfGE* 107, 150 = *NJW* 2003, 955 = *FamRZ* 2004, 285.

19 See C. LENZ/J. BAUMANN, 'Umgangsrecht auf internationaler Ebene, insbesondere vor dem EGMR', *FPR* 2004, 303 *et seq.*

20 See BVerfG, 14.10.2004, *NJW* 2004, 3407 = *FamRZ* 2004, 1857.

right of contact. In a judgment of 26 February 2004, the ECtHR declared that the German decision on custody and the exclusion of the right of access violated Art. 8 of the European Convention.[21] The father was also successful in a constitutional complaint.[22] The Appellate Court of Naumburg nevertheless again denied contact to the child. Then, realising that the Appellate Court seemingly was not willing to follow the applicable legal norms, the German Constitutional Court itself issued a preliminary injunction in favour of the father.[23]

The primary source of German family law is the Fourth Book of the Civil Code (§§ 1297-1921 German CC; Bürgerliches Gesetzbuch) with its three sections, 'Civil Marriage' (bürgerliche Ehe, §§ 1297 - 1588), 'Family Relationships' (Verwandtschaft, §§ 1589 - 1772) and 'Guardianship' (*Vormundschaft*, §§ 1773 - 1921). The statutory provisions on custody and contact are set out in section 2. The current source of law for parental responsibilities is mainly §§ 1626 - 1698b German CC. The provisions in this area of law were reformed in 1979[24] and again substantially amended by a reform statute of 16 December 1997 (*Reform des Kindschaftsrechts*),[25] which came into force on 1 July 1998. However, judge-made law still dominates the details of the allocation of custodial rights.

There are also provisions on the parental responsibility of the registered partner of a parent in § 9 of the Registered Partnership Act (LPartG; *Lebenspartnerschaftsgesetz*).

'Non-contentious' procedural issues are dealt with in the Act on Voluntary Jurisdiction (FGG; *Gesetz über die freiwillige Gerichtsbarkeit*).[26] Matters of parental responsibility are family matters in the framework of the Act on Voluntary Jurisdiction, see §§ 35b *et seq* German Act on Voluntary Jurisdiction.

The details of divorce proceedings and parental responsibility proceedings in this framework are regulated by the Code of Civil Procedure (§§ 606 *et seq Zivilprozessordnung*; German Code of Civil Procedure).[27] Especially in the context of divorce the relevant provisions are found in the Code of Civil Procedure. The subject matter jurisdiction of the family court and other courts is dealt with in the Court Organisation Act (*Gerichtsverfassungsgesetz*).[28]

---

21 ECtHR (Third Section), *Görgülü* v. *Germany*, 26.02.2004, *NJW* 2004, 3397 = *FamRZ* 2004, 1456. A. ZEYCAN, Der Fall Görgülü/BRD im Lichte der Menschenrechtskonvention, *FuR* 2004, 443 *et seq.*

22 See BVerfG, 14.10.2004, *NJW* 2004, 3407 = *FamRZ* 2004, 1857.

23 BVerfG, 28.12.2004, *FamRZ* 2005, 173 annotated by G. RIXE.

24 Gesetz zur Neuregelung des Rechts der elterlichen Sorge of 18.07.1979, *BGBl.* 1979 I p. 1061.

25 *BGBl.* 1997, p. 2942.

26 Gesetz über die Angelegenheiten der freiwilligen Gerichtsbarkeit of 20.05.1898, *Reichsgesetzblatt (RGBl).* 1898 p. 771, as amended.

27 Zivilprozessordnung of 12.09.1950, *BGBl.* 1950 I p. 533, as amended.

28 Gerichtsverfassungsgesetz of 09.05.1975, *BGBl.* 1975 I p. 1077, as amended.

Of particular importance is the Children and Young Persons Assistance Act (KJHG; *Kinder- und Jugendhilfegesetz*) of 8 December 1998[29] (as amended), which forms Book Eight of the Social Security Code (*Sozialgesetzbuch*; SGB VIII). According to this statute, the State Youth Welfare Office (*Jugendamt*) plays a central role.[30] The Youth Welfare Service (*Jugendhilfe*) gives, among other things, advice on partnership, separation and divorce (§ 17), on the exercise of contact rights (§ 18 para. 3), on education, adoption and guardianship (§§ 28, 51, 52a *et seq* of the Act), supervises foster parents (§ 44), commits children and young persons into custody (§ 34), participates in court proceedings (§§ 50 *et seq*), and acts as legal adviser, legal curator and guardian (§§ 55 *et seq*). Another task is the authentication of statements such as an acknowledgement of paternity or a commitment to pay maintenance (§ 59). The State youth welfare office can give advice and support (*Beratung und Unterstützung*). It also can be a legal adviser (*Beistand*, §§ 1712 *et seq* German CC) and in some cases the legal curator (*Amtspfleger*) for the child. Its task is mainly to promote the rights and interests of the child in relation to determination of paternity and maintenance (§§ 52 a *et seq* Social Security Code VIII).

GREECE

The provisions of the Greek CC and particularly Art. 1505-1541 (Relations between Parents and their children), 1589-1654 (Guardianship) and 1655-1665 (Foster Care), constitute the main source of law for parental responsibilities. The Constitution,[31] European law,[32] as well as International Conventions[33] influence

29 German Social Security Code (Sozialgesetzbuch; SGB) Achtes Buch (VIII) Kinder- und Jugendhilfe of 08.12.1998, *BGBl.* 1998 I, p. 3546.

30 See U. Lohrentz, 'Aufgaben des Jugendamtes bei Elterntrennung nach der Kindschaftsrechtsreform', *Kind-Prax* 2001, 43 *et seq.*

31 The most relevant provision is that of Art. 21 para. 1 of the Greek Constitution, which pertains to the protection of the family, marriage, maternity, and childhood.

32 The most significant legislation by the European Union on this issue is the new Council Regulation (EC) No. 2201/2003 on the jurisdiction and the recognition and enforcement of judgments in matrimonial matters and the matters of parental responsibility, which repealed Regulation (EC) No. 1347/2000. Also relevant is Art. 24 of the EU's Charter of Fundamental Rights.

33 The most relevant International Conventions on the issues dealt with here, which Greece has signed and ratified are, *inter alia*: the (1989) United Nations Convention on the Rights of the Child (Law 2101/1992), the (1950) European Convention on Human Rights (Law 2329/1953, Legislative Decree 53/1974), the (1996) European Convention on the Exercise of Children's Rights (Law 2502/1997), the (1967) European Convention on the Adoption of Children (Law 1049/1980), the (1975) European Convention on the Legal Status of Children Born out of Wedlock (Law 1702/1987), the (1980) European Convention on Recognition and Enforcement of Decisions Concerning Custody of Children and on Restoration of Custody of Children (Law 2104/1992), and the (1980) Hague Convention on the Civil Aspects of Child Abduction (Law 2102/1992). Finally, Greece has signed the (1996) Hague Convention on Jurisdiction, Applicable Law, Recognition, Enforcement and Co-operation in Respect of Parental Responsibility and Measures for the Protection of Children, but has not yet ratified it.

the interpretation of these provisions, complement the relevant legal framework and, in the case of conflict of laws, they prevail as *leges superiores*.[34] Nowadays, custom hardly plays a role in this field. Finally, legal literature and court decisions constitute informal sources of law.

HUNGARY

The current sources of law for parental responsibilities are the following:

- The Hungarian Family Act, the Act No. IV. 1952. on marriage, family and guardianship, as amended. It was last amended through the Act No. IX. 2002. and Act No. IV. 2003. concerning the issues of parental responsibilities.
- The Hungarian Child Welfare Act, the Act No. XXXI. 1997. on the Child Welfare and guardianship administration, as amended by Act No. IX. 2002. and Act No. IV. 2003.
- The Hungarian Order of Guardianship, the Order of Government No. 149/1997. on public guardianship authority and proceeding in Child Welfare and guardianship cases, as amended by the Order of Government No. 262/2001., No. 14/2003. and No. 203/2003.
- The Hungarian Act No. XV. 2001. on amending several Acts in connection with legal capacity and curatorship. This Act concerns the legal representation and administration of property.

IRELAND

The central concepts governing parental responsibilities in Ireland are guardianship, custody and access. The law relating to guardianship, custody and access is contained in the Irish Guardianship of Infants Act 1964 as amended by the Irish Status of Children Act 1987, the Irish Judicial Separation and Family Law Reform Act 1989, the Irish Family Law (Divorce) Act 1996 and the Irish Children Act 1997.

ITALY

Current sources of law for parental responsibilities can be found in the Italian Constitution (Art. 30 § 1), the Italian Civil Code, (Art. 417, 155, 315 *et seq* and 2048), Italian Divorce Law (Art. 6 Law of 1 December 1970, No. 898, as modified by the Law of 6 March 1987, No. 74) and Italian Adoption Law (Law of 4 May 1983, No. 184, as modified by the Law of 28 March 2001, No. 149).

LITHUANIA

Art. 3.2 Lithuanian CC, which defines sources of family law, establishes the sources of law for parental responsibility as well. The current sources of law for parental responsibilities are: the Constitution of the Republic of Lithuania (Parts 5 and 6 of Art. 38 establish that 'in the family, spouses shall have equal rights', 'the right and duty of parents is to bring up their children to be honest individuals and loyal citizens, as well as to maintain them until they come of

---

[34] Art. 28(1) Greek Constitution.

age'. Art. 26 and 40 of the Lithuanian Constitution establish the right of parents to educate their children, including education of religion).

The main source is Chapter XI of Book Three Lithuanian CC. Also special laws such as the Law on the Protection of the Rights of the Child of 14 March 1996, the Lithuanian Law on Education of 25 June 1991 *etc.* International treaties such as the United Nations Convention on the Rights of the Child of 1989, the Council of Europe Convention on the legal status of children born out of wedlock of 1975 and others are also very important.

The Government and other state institutions may adopt legal acts on family law matters only as provided for by the Lithuanian CC and other laws (*e.g.* the Government may adopt regulations regarding the organization of provisional care of the child). Important sources also are court practice and the legal literature, *e.g.* Commentary of the Lithuanian CC, which interprets and explains the content of parental responsibilities.

THE NETHERLANDS

Book 1 of the Dutch CC and in particular Title 14: Custody over minor children, Title 15: Right to contact and information and Title 16: Appointment of a Curator are the main current sources of law for parental responsibilities. The Supreme Court has clarified the law on a number of important issues such as when sole parental responsibilities can be attributed to one parent after divorce, which factors need to be taken into account if there is a request for a transfer of parental responsibilities, etc. Dutch law makes a distinction between parental responsibilities and guardianship. Parental responsibilities can be exercised by one parent alone, by two parents jointly or by a parent and his or her partner jointly. Guardianship can be exercised by a person or persons other than the child's parent(s). The umbrella term for both concepts is custody (Art. 1:245 § 2 and 3 Dutch CC). Custody (*gezag*) regulations apply to parental responsibilities (*ouderlijk gezag*) as well as guardianship (*voogdij*). Regulations specific to parental responsibilities do not apply to guardianship, and vice versa.

NORWAY

The current source of law for parental responsibilities is the Norwegian Children Act 1981. The main rules on parental responsibilities are found in Chapter 5, which contains provisions on the nature of parental responsibilities and to whom such responsibilities are attributed. Case law plays an important part as a source of the current law. The rights and duties related to the property of a child (guardianship) are laid down in the Norwegian Act on Guardianship 1927.

POLAND

The principal source regulating parental responsibility in Polish law is the Polish Family and Guardianship Code.[35] In Title II: *Kinship,* Part I: *Parents and*

[35] Statute of 25.02.1964, published in *Dziennik Ustaw* of 1964, No. 9, pos. 59.

children (Art. 62 - 113 Polish Family and Guardianship Code) and Part II: *Adoption* (Art. 114 – 127 Polish Family and Guardianship Code). Within Part I, in particular Chapter II *Relations between parents and children* (Art. 87 – 113 Polish Family and Guardianship Code), and within this chapter, Section II *Parental authority* (Art. 92 – 113 Polish Family and Guardianship Code). In Title III *Guardianship and custody* Part I: *Guardianship of a minor* (Art. 145 – 174 Polish Family and Guardianship Code). Provisions on substitute families are regulated in Social Assistance Act of 12th March 2004 (Art. 72 - 79). Procedural provisions regulating the proceedings in parental responsibility cases are regulated by the Polish Civil Procedure Code.[36]

PORTUGAL

The Constitution of the Portuguese Republic, the Portuguese CC and Portuguese Child Protection Law regulate parental responsibility. Thus, the Fundamental Law establishes various constitutional principles that directly affect parent-child relationships. These are: the principle of equality between spouses as regards the maintenance and education of their children (Art. 36 No. 3 Portuguese Constitution); the principle of awarding parents the right and duty to educate and maintain their children (Art. 36 No. 5 Portuguese Constitution); and the principle of the inseparability of children from their parents (Art. 36 No. 6 Portuguese Constitution).

The Portuguese CC has a section on parental responsibility, divided into six subsections: general principles (Art. 1877 to 1884, Portuguese CC); parental responsibility regarding their child (Art. 1885 to 1887-A Portuguese CC); parental responsibility regarding their child's property (Art. 1888 to 1900 Portuguese CC); the exercise of parental responsibility (Art. 1901 to 1912 Portuguese CC); restrictions upon parental responsibility (Art. 1913 to 1920-A Portuguese CC); and the recording of decisions relating to parental responsibility (Art. 1920-B and 1920-C Portuguese CC).

The Portuguese Child Protection Law lays down the rules for the regulation of the exercise of parental responsibility and its incidents (Art. 174 to 183 Portuguese Child Protection Law), and allows either parent the possibility of applying for court intervention when there is disagreement between them as to some matter of particular importance (Art. 184 Portuguese Child Protection Law).

RUSSIA

The current source of divorce law in the Russian Federation is the Russian Family Code of Russian Federation[37] of 8 December 1995, enacted on 1 March

---

36 *Kodeks postępowania cywilnego*, statute of 17.11.1964, published in *Dziennik Ustaw* of 1964, No. 43, pos. 296 with amendments.

37 *Semeinyi Kodeks Rossiiskoi Federatsii, Sobranie Zakonodatel'stva Rossiiskoi Federatsii*, 1996, No. 1, item 15. For an English translation see: W. BUTLER and J. HENDERSON, *Russian*

1996. The most relevant provisions are: Chapter 11 entitled 'Rights of Minor Children', Chapter 12 entitled 'Rights and Duties of the Parents', and Art. 24.

SPAIN

There is no single law which contains all the relevant rules. Public and private law rules are embodied in different sources. There is also a jurisdictional division between the central legislative power and the autonomous communities, both in Public and Private law.

Private law rules on parental responsibility are basically contained in:

- In Aragon: Title II of Book I of the *Compilaciòn de Derecho civil de Aragón* (Art. 9-14). These Art. were reformed in 1985 (*Ley 3/1985 de 21 de mayo*).
- In Navarra: Title V of Book I of the *Compilación de Derecho civil foral o Fuero Nuevo de Navarra* (*Leyes 63-67 and 72*). These dispositions were modified in 1987 (*Ley foral 5/1987 de 1 de abril*).
- In Catalonia: Title VI of the Catalan Family Code (Art. 132-163) which was introduced in 1998 (*Ley 9/1998 de 15 de julio*).
- The Spanish CC regulates *patria potestad* in Title VII of Book I (Art. 154-171) which was last reformed in general terms in 1981 (*Ley 11/1981, de 13 de marzo*). The Spanish CC also contains rules on parental responsibility in Chapter IX of Title IV of Book one in connection to divorce, annulment and judicial separation. These rules were introduced in 1981 as well, but in a different law: *Ley 30/1981 de 7 de julio*.

According to relevant private international law rules, the applicability of these rules depends on a personal quality: the child's *vecindad civil* (Art. 9.4 Spanish CC). Every Spanish national and only Spanish nationals have a *vecindad civil* which is acquired at birth.

Public law rules: There are general laws on the protection of children and the exercise of children's rights, such as the *Ley Orgánica de Protección Jurídica del Menor* of 15 January 1996 or the Catalan *Llei d'atenció I protecció dels infants I dels adolescents* dating from 1995.[38] These laws developed the rights of the children recognised in the Spanish Constitution and in the UN Convention on the rights of the child which was ratified by Spain in 1990. There are also public law rules dealing with public intervention in the legislation of the seveteen *Comunidades Autónomas* into which Spain is divided.

Legal Texts. The Foundation of a Rule-of-Law State and a Market Economy, The Hague, London: Boston Simmons and Hill Publishing Ltd, , 1998, p. 517- 593.

38 For other Autonomonous Communities see - LEY 14/2002, de 25 de julio, de Promoción, Atención y Protección a la Infancia en Castilla y León. ; LEY 12/2001, de 2 de julio, de la Infancia y la Adolescencia en Aragón.

SWEDEN

In Swedish domestic law, the provisions on parental responsibilities are found in the Swedish Children and Parents Code (1949:381), adopted in 1949 but subject of numerous later amendments. The provisions concerning custody, residence and contact are found in Chapter 6. The rules concerning guardianship are scattered throughout Chapters 9-15, which also includes incapacitated adults. Provisions on the enforcement of judgments and agreements on custody, contact and residence are found in Chapter 21 of the Swedish Children and Parents Code.

SWITZERLAND

The Swiss Code of Civil Law (in the second section: Family Law) Second Division: Kinship; Eighth Subsection: The Effects of the Parent-Child Relationship with a Third Section: Parental Responsibilities and a Fourth Section: The Child's Property, Art. 296 - 327 Swiss CC.

QUESTION 5

A. GENERAL

Give a brief history of the main developments of the law concerning parental responsibilities.

AUSTRIA

The development of parent and child law in Austria began with the introduction of the Austrian Civil Code in 1811. At that time, children born in wedlock were under their father's authority. Parents could use corporal punishment on their children, but in a manner that was not excessive and harmful to their health. Parental responsibilities were divided up: The mother was responsible for the care and education of young children. The father was responsible for their care and education from the age of eight, for supporting the children, and for making all important decisions in matters relating to the children.[1] Illegitimate children, of course, had a right to support from their fathers, but were excluded from the rights of kinship and family (Sec. 165 Austrian CC, original version).

In the course of the family law reforms of the 1970s, illegitimate children were given the same rights as legitimate children.[2] Since then, men and women have also been entitled to equal parental rights (so-called parental authority, Sec. 137(3) Austrian CC). The welfare of the child (*Kindeswohl*) in the sense of the child's best interests was established as the central theme of the Austrian law of parent and child (1977 Child's Act *[Kindgesetz]*).[3]

With the 1989 reform of the law of parent and child,[4] there was a total prohibition against the use of corporal punishment in the parent-child relationship and the introduction of the concept of parental responsibilities instead of parental authority (Sec. 144 Austrian CC), to make it clear that the child should be the recipient of parental care and not the object of parental authority.[5] The UN Convention on the Rights of the Child (20 November 1989) took effect in Austria on 5 September 1992 and is implemented in detail by the

---

1 O. LEHNER, *Kinder-und Jugendrecht*, 2nd Edition, Vienna: Orac, 1998, p. 18.

2 *Bundesgesetz über die Neuordnung der Rechtsstellung unehelicher Kinder* (Federal Act on the New Regulation of the Legal Status of Children Born out of Wedlock), Federal Law Gazette *[Bundesgesetzblatt, BGBl.]* 1970/312.

3 *Bundesgesetz über die Neuordnung des Kindschaftsrechts,* (Federal Act on the New Regulation of the Law of Parent and Child), *BGBl.* 1977/403; W. POSCH, 'Zur Neuregelung der rein persönlichen Rechtsbeziehungen zwischen Eltern und Kindern nach dem BG 10.06.1977 BGBl. 1977/403', in: R. Ostheim, *Schwerpunkte der Familienrechtsreform 1977/78,* Vienna: Manz Verlag, 1979.

4 *BGBl.* 1989/62.

5 *BGBl.* 1996/759. I. HOLZHAMMER/R. HOLZHAMMER, *Ehe und Familie*, 2nd Edition, Freistadt: Plöchl Verlag, 2001, p. 97 *et seq.*

European Council's Convention on the Exercise of Children's Rights of 1 January 1996 (*Übereinkommen zur Ausübung von Kinderrechten*).[6] Since 1996, the Federal Act to Protect Against Domestic Violence (*Bundesgesetz zum Schutz vor Gewalt in der Familie*) has guaranteed swift police and court measures will be taken against violent family members.[7]

The 2001 Act Amending the Law of Parent and Child[8] (*Kindschaftsrechts-Änderungsgesetz*) further expanded the principle of parental responsibilities and enhanced the legal position of minors with respect to having a say and self-determination. The Act included important innovations related to taking the child's wishes into account (Sec. 146(3) Austrian CC), the child's right to have a say in custody proceedings (Sec. 104, 105 Non-Contentious Proceedings Act [*Außerstreitgesetz*]), and a child's independent consent to medical treatments (Sec. 146c-d Austrian CC). In addition, the age of majority was lowered from 19 to 18, the right of contact (*Besuchsrecht*) was also formulated as a right of the child (Sec. 148 Austrian CC) and - after a lengthy discussion on legal policy[9] - the possibility of joint parental responsibilities was created in the case of separation (Sec. 177 *et seq* Austrian CC). Before the Act Amending the Law of Parent and Child took effect on 1 July 2001, the judge had to attribute parental responsibilities to just one parent in divorce, unless the divorced parents continued to live together. Procedurally, the entire law of parent and child is part of non-contentious proceedings (*Außerstreitverfahren*) as of 1 January 2005.[10]

BELGIUM

The regulations on parental responsibilities have been fundamentally reformed over the course of the last decades. Since 1804, both parents have possessed the parental power, but it was only exercised by the father until 1965. The Belgian Law of 8 April 1965 installed the joint exercise of the parental power by both parents during their marriage. In case of disagreement, the will of the father remained predominant but the mother had the ability to appeal to the Juvenile Court to contest the father's decision. The Belgian Law of 1 July 1974 treated both parents as equal holders of parental responsibilities, whereas beforehand the father was dominant. In case of disagreement, either parent had the right to appeal to the Juvenile Court. The Belgian Law of 31 March 1987 changed the terminology from parental power, being a set of rights that could also be in the interests of the holder, to parental authority, being a set of competences that are

---

6 I. MOTTL, *Die Sorge der Eltern für ihre Kinder*, Vienna: Peter-Lang Verlag, 1992, p. 35 *et seq*. For further information see http://www.yap.at; http://www.kinderhabenrechte.at; http://europa.eu.int.

7 *BGBl.* I 759/1996. I. HOLZHAMMER/R. HOLZHAMMER, *Ehe und Familie*, 2nd Edition, Freistadt: Plöchl Verlag, 2001, p. 97 *et seq.*

8 *BGBl.* I 135/2000, http://www.ris.bka.gv.at. S. FERRARI/G. HOPF, *Reform des Kindschaftsrechts*, Vienna: Manz Verlag, 2001.

9 B. GRÜNDLER, 'Die gemeinsame Obsorge nach dem KindRÄG 2001', *Österreichische Juristenzeitung*, 2001, p. 701-717 with further references.

10 *Außerstreitgesetz, BGBl.* I 2003/111, 112. S. Kriwanek, *Das neue Außerstreitverfahren*, Vienna: LexisNexis ARD Orac, 2004.

in the sole interests of the minor. It also made the regulations of parental responsibilities applicable to unmarried couples; the only criterion being a legally determined descent. The Law of 19 January 1990 lowered the age of majority from 21 to 18 years, withdrawing young adults from the scope of parental responsibilities. Notwithstanding the lowering of the age of majority, the maintenance obligation can continue till the young adult has fulfilled his education (Art. 203 Belgian CC). The Belgian Law of 13 April 1995 introduced 'joint-parenthood', being the joint exercise of parental authority over the person and property of their children, whether or not the parents live together. The Belgian Laws of 27 March 2001 and 29 April 2001 made the regulations of parental responsibilities applicable to minors with only one parent, whereas before the property of the minor in these situations was submitted to the guardianship, while the person of the minor was submitted to the parental authority. Finally, the 'reparation' Belgian Law of 13 February 2003 solved a few problems that arose from the Belgian Law of 27 March 2001; among others, those concerning the territorial competence of the Justice of the Peace. In general, the exercise of parental responsibilities is placed more and more under judicial supervision.[11]

BULGARIA

Since 1944 the legal framework of parent-children relationships has been changed three times, but in general the spirit of the major principles and norms adopted is preserved in the current Bulgarian Family Code (1985). The Bulgarian Child Protection Act which regulates issues such as public care for children, intervention in the family and provision of community based services for families and children,[12] was adopted in 2000.

In deciding custody and contact matters the Bulgarian Family Code stipulates the court shall consider 'the interests of the children'.[13] However, the interests of children have never been identified by law as 'a paramount'[14] or 'a primary consideration'[15] in the decisions affecting them. Relevant provisions have even undergone regressive development. One of the few changes in Bulgarian family law since the 1940s came surprisingly, after a period of complete negligence:

---

11 W. PINTENS, 'Die Entwicklung des belgischen Kindschaftsrechts', in D. SCHWAB and D. HENRICH (ed.), *Entwicklungen des europäischen Kindschaftrechts*, Bielefeld: Verlag Ernst und Werner Gieseking, 1996, p. 19-34; W. PINTENS, 'Die Reform des belgischen Kindschaftsrechts aus vergleichender Sicht', *Fam RZ*, 1997, p. 460-464.

12 See more about the Act in: V. TODOROVA, 'The Bulgarian Child Protection Act: The Start of the Child Welfare Reform?', in: A. BAINHAM (ed.), *International Survey of Family Law*, Bristol: Jordans, 2002, p. 91.

13 Art. 106 § 2 Bulgarian Family Code.

14 See Art. 1b Bulgarian Children Act 1989.

15 See Art. 3 § 1 of the UN Convention on the Rights of the Child, ratified by Bulgaria in 1991.

Legislation assigned children the most favoured status in the family law.[16] Since then the tendency is shifting from the rights of children to the expansion and strengthening of parental rights. This is evident both in the development of divorce regulations and in the serial revisions of the legislation regarding parent-children relationships. The interests of children are allocated a more modest position and emphasis is shifted to rights of the parents.

For instance, according to Art. 45, § 1 Bulgarian Marriage Ordinance Act (1945), '... the court shall consider exclusively the interest of children irrespective of the spouses' fault for the divorce'. In the later Bulgarian Persons and the Family Act (1949) the word 'exclusively' is substituted by 'only' (Art. 54). The attribute 'exclusive' is disposed of completely in this rule of the current Family Code, which refers only to the: 'assessment of all circumstances with regard to the interests of the children'.

Another illustration is found in the Bulgarian Persons and the Family Act saying that: 'during the marriage, parental rights and duties shall be exercised by both parents and only in the interest of children (Art. 85)'. Subsequent legislation has abandoned this stipulation.

At the end of the 1950s and the beginning of the 1960s, the focus was shifted to the rights of parents and away from their duties. Gradually the emphasis evolved to cover the autonomy of the parents and the family. A concept was established that parental rights have a standing equivalent to that of parental obligations. Child rearing satisfies parent's personal interests, therefore parental rights need to be protected against the illegal interference by third parties.[17] Thus, the intervention in parent-child relationships remained rather theoretical until very recently. This was also due to the lack of 'child abuse' discourse. The Bulgarian Child Protection Act and the articulation of the 'child abuse' phenomenon created the environment necessary for public debate on the issues of 'parental rights' and state intervention.

CZECH REPUBLIC

After the formation of the Czechoslovak Republic in 1918 the previous civil law effective in the territory of the former Austro-Hungarian Empire *i.e.* the 1811 *Allgemeines Burgerliches Gesetzbuch* was adopted pursuant to the Czech Law No. 11/1918 Coll. The legal regulation of relationships between parents and

---

16 Pieces of legislation such as the Bulgarian Persons Act (1907) where children were regarded as parents' property have been taken into account as have the Acts of 1889 and 1940 regulating illegitimacy.

17 According to T. Tzankova, *Commentary on the Legal Regulation of Parents-Children Relations in the Draft Family Code, Socialist Law*, 1984, p. 11: 'the rearing and upbringing of children is not merely an obligation of the parents. It is their major right... The parents exercise this right in the interest of children, but also in their own interest... The law does not allow the illegitimate interference in parental rights ...'. In the same sense, H. Georgiev, I. Palazov, P. Beshkov and T. Damyanov, *Family Code – Commentary*, 1975, p. 307.

children was based on distinguishing children born in and outside wedlock. The marital father was granted the so-called fatherly power. If the marital father was not alive, or was deprived of parental power, a guardian was appointed for the child.

On 1 January 1950 a new act on family law (Czech Family Law Act) following the ideas of the new Constitution of 9 May took effect. It stipulated equality between man and women in marriage and family, and also defined children born in and out of wedlock as equals. Both parents had the same rights and duties in relation to child regardless of existence of marriage. The total of all rights and duties of parents in relation to a child was labelled 'parental power'. Its contents did not differ considerably from the regulation existing now.[18]

However, Act No. 94/1963 Coll. effective from 1 April 1964 (Czech Family Code) eliminated the concept of parental power saying that the socialist society had disposed of all power elements in the relationship between parents and children, and from then on the concept of parental rights and duties was used. Their exact contents were not determined sufficiently. As an issue of theory as well as judicial practice, individual opinions differed. In particular, the Czech Family Code in its original version did not include regulation of administration of the child's property. That situation was only changed after 1998 when the total of rights and duties of parents were defined and designated in the Czech Family Code as parental responsibility.

DENMARK

The first law reform regarding parental authority was the Act on incapacity and guardianship, *Lov om umyndighed og værgemål*, from 1922.[19] The 1922 Act contained provisions regarding parental authority and contact. The Act was one of the results of the Family Law Commission's work. The Commission was established in 1910 and carried out its work in close co-operation with similarly established commissions in Norway and Sweden.

The main feature of the 1922 Act was that spouses were bestowed with joint parental authority. The father was no longer superior in relation to the children.[20] In the case of divorce parental authority was granted to one of the parents solely. The primary criterion for granting sole parental authority to one parent was the child's well being and only where both parents were equally capable of raising the child was a fault criterion used in order to give parental authority to the parent who was not to blame for the break-up of the marriage.

The parent who was not given parental authority had a principal right to contact. For children born outside of marriage, the situation remained the same as before the law reform; the mother had full parental authority while the father

---

18 J. PETRULAKOVA, *Vychova deti v rodine*, Bratislava: Obzor, 1970, p. 27.

19 Act No. 277 of 30.06.1922.

20 The father remained the sole guardian of the children until 1958.

had no right to contact. As late as in 1964 the Supreme Court confirmed the difficult position of the unmarried father. It was established that, regardless of the circumstances and the father's connection with the child, the father was not granted any contact rights with his child against the mother's wishes.[21]

At the end of the 1960s and in the 1970s three changes to the 1922 Act were designed to give unmarried fathers better rights. In 1969 it was made possible for the unmarried father to obtain a contact order. The conditions were that it was in accordance with the child's well-being and that special circumstances, especially the father's prior contact with the child, indicated that this was beneficial for the child.[22] In 1972 it became possible for the unmarried father to obtain parental authority if the mother had consented to give the child up for adoption. The conditions were similar to those adopted in 1969 regarding contact rights.[23] Finally in 1978 there was a significant improvement for the unmarried father. It was now possible to transfer parental authority to the father, where this was necessary for the well being of the child.[24]

In 1986 the 1922 Act was thoroughly revised on the basis of a Commission report.[25] The main feature of the revision was[26] that joint parental authority became possible after divorce and for unmarried parents. The underlying reasoning was that joint parental authority after divorce was becoming possible in the US and in other Scandinavian countries. Joint parental authority was considered to improve co-operation between parents and to enhance the sense of responsibility as far as parents were concerned. Further, a principal right for all parents to have contact with their children was introduced. Finally, the opinion of a child older than twelve should be obtained before a decision regarding parental authority and contact was made and the authorities now had to offer counselling when there was disagreement on issues of parental authority and contact.

In 1996 the Act was again changed on the basis of a further Commission report.[27] This time the provisions relating to parental authority and contact were placed in a separate Act, namely the Danish Act on Parental Authority and Contact, *Lov om forældremyndighed og samvær*.

The substantive changes introduced by the 1996 Act were the following: the strengthening of the unmarried father's position regarding parental authority, the strengthening of the parents' right to have contact with their child, as well

---

21 *Højesteret*, Supreme Court, 24.03.1964, *Ugeskrift for retsvæsen* 1964.801H.
22 Act No. 257, 04.06.1969.
23 Act No. 280, 07.06.1972.
24 Act No. 244, 08.06.1978.
25 Commission report No. 985/1983.
26 Act No. 230, 06.06.1985.
27 Commission report No. 1247/1994.

as "other" contact rights such as the exchange of letters and improved rights to counselling.

The unmarried father who did not have parental authority over his child, but who had cohabited with the mother for a longer period, was given an equal right to be awarded parental authority when this was applied for and when it had an immediate connection with the break-up of the relationship.

In 2002 an amendment to the Danish Children Act, *Børneloven*,[28] regarding maternity and paternity had implications for the rules on parental authority. A statement made by the parents to the effect that they will care for and be responsible for their child before or at the time of birth establishes paternity. When such a statement is made the unmarried parents automatically have joint parental authority. The procedure is not limited to cohabitating unmarried parents, however.

At the same time a change was made to the effect that it is no longer required, as a formal part of the divorce proceedings, to make a decision regarding parental authority over the children. Joint parental authority continues automatically.[29] The change was suggested by the Justice Department with the following reasoning:[30]

> 'The Justice Department has in that connection stressed that there is no requirement for unmarried cohabitating parents to decide on the issue of parental authority in the case the relationship breaks down. In the light of the general principle of equality between married couples and unmarried cohabitating couples, which forms the basis of the Children Act Proposal, it may seem less appropriate to retain a requirement for married couples to make such a decision. Furthermore, it is a fact that a considerable number of married couples divorcing or legally separating, already agree on joint parental authority'.

ENGLAND & WALES

English child law was fundamentally reformed by the English Children Act 1989 which came into force in October 1991. Prior to that the law was governed by a mixture of common law and statute. Among the key substantive changes made by the 1989 Act and most relevant to this report was to replace the concept of parental rights and duties with the concept of parental responsibility.

Before the English Children Act 1989 statutes referred to 'parental rights and duties' or 'parental power and duties' or to the 'rights and authority' of a parent. Not only were these terms inconsistent with one another but, as the Law

---

28 Act No. 460, 07.06.2001.

29 Act No. 461, 07.06.2001.

30 Notes to the Act, No. 198, p. 11, *Forslag til ændring af retsplejeloven og forskellige andre love.*

Commission commented:[31] "It can be cogently argued that to talk of 'parental rights' is not only inaccurate as a matter of juristic analysis but also a misleading use of ordinary language". In their Report on *Guardianship and Custody*[32] the Commission were concerned that because of the continued use of such terms the law did not adequately promote the view that parenthood is a matter of responsibility rather than of rights. Accordingly, they recommended the introduction of the concept of 'parental responsibility' to replace all the ambiguous and misleading terms employed in statutes. The Government accepted this recommendation and 'parental responsibility' has become a pivotal concept of the 1989 Act.

Since the English Children Act 1989 further reform in relation to the allocation of parental responsibility both to unmarried fathers (see further Q 22b) and step-parents (see further Q 27) has or will be made by the English Adoption and Children Act 2002 which is currently being brought into force in phases and the position is also affected by the recently enacted British Civil Partnership Act 2004 (see Q 27b).

FINLAND

The first important legislative enactments concerning children in Finland were in the 1920s, when the Act concerning children born outside of wedlock was brought into force. In 1936 the first Finnish Child Protection Act was enacted. It followed the Scandinavian model, which was based on the original Norwegian Act concerning Child Protection. In 1930 the Finnish Marriage Act came into force and, at the same time, amendments to the old Finnish Guardianship Act stipulated the best interests of the child together with the guilt of the parent as the criteria for child custody decisions. The first Finnish Enforcement Act concerning child custody decisions was enacted in 1975. The Act included a renewal of mandatory mediation as a part of the enforcement proceedings. This system still prevails in much the same way. The child gained the right to prevent the enforcement at the 15 years of age.

The Finnish Child Custody and the Right of Access Act 1983 was the first Finnish Act defining child custody in the way it is understood today. Before this, only a few rules existed in the former Finnish Guardianship Services Act concerning the granting of custody in divorce and the upbringing of the child. Since the new Finnish Child Custody and the Right of Access Act 1983, children born in wedlock and children born outside of wedlock have been equal in the area of parental responsibility. Before 1984, only parents who were married to each other could have joint custody of their child. Since 1984, the best interests of the child have been the first and paramount consideration in deciding child custody and right of access cases. The importance of the child's right of access to the parent with whom the child is not living and the child's right to be heard

[31] Law Com. Report No. 118 *Illegitimacy* (1982), para 4.18.
[32] Law Com. Report No. 172 (1988).

and have its views taken into consideration in decisions concerning it are also emphasised.[33]

Together with the Finnish Child Custody and the Right of Access Act, a new Finnish Child Protection Act was enacted in 1983. The new Act gives the authorities the ability to consider the child's needs and situation as a whole with the best interests of the child as the leading principle. For example, taking the child into care is no longer bound to certain conditions in a child's behaviour. Furthermore, according to the new Act, the custodian does not lose all custodial rights if the child is taken into care.

The child custody law reform in 1993 was connected to the ratification of the 1980 Hague Child Abduction Convention and the 1980 European Convention concerning the recognition of custody decisions. The Enforcement Act was reformed in 1996. The reform mainly concerned proceedings that were transferred to the court. The enforcement cases had been dealt with by the administrative authorities before. The child retained the right to prevent enforcement, for which right the age limit had already, in 1983, been lowered to the age of 12 years. The guardianship legislation reform followed in 1999. Rules concerning the supervision of the children's property administration were modernised, among other improvements.

FRANCE

Until 1970, parental responsibilities belonged solely to the father (*puisssance paternelle*), who made all decisions concerning the child. A very important reform (Act No. 70-459 of 4 June 1970) put both parents on equal footing; they both had parental responsibilities but had to use them in the child's interest. A reform in 1985 (Law No. 85-1372 of 23 December 1985) abolished the only advantage the father had retained *i.e.* with respect to the administration of the child's property. Act No. 87-570 of 22 July 1987 modified the rules concerning the exercise of parental responsibilities after divorce, as well as for all other non-married parents. Another reform (Law No. 93-22 of 8 January 1993) stated the principle of joint parental responsibilities (*autorité parentale conjointe*) for divorced or separated parents and for non-married parents.

The newest reform is the Act No. 2002-305 of 4 March 2002, which provides a new definition for *autorité parentale* (parental authority): a collection of rights and duties aiming at the child's interest (see Art. 371-1 French CC). This reform also modernises the exercise of parental responsibilities. This reform retained

---

33 K. KURKI-SUONIO, *Äidin hoivasta yhteishuoltoon – lapsen edun muuttuvat oikeudelliset tulkinnat*, Suomalainen Lakimiesyhdistys, Helsinki, 1999 p. 367-557; M. HELIN, T. LINNA and M. RINTALA, Huolto ja tapaamisoikeuden täytäntöönpano, Kauppakaari Oy, Helsinki, 1997, pp. 3-10. See also M. HELIN, 'Enforcement of Custody, Access and Residence Orders, Intercountry Adoptions and Registration of Same Sex Couples', in: A. BAINHAM (ed.), *International Survey of Family Law*, Kluwer Law International: The Hague 1999.

the term 'parental authority' even though many foreign law provisions now use the term 'parental responsibilities'. The French approach insists upon giving the parents an authority to comply with their educational task. The new law follows and improves the principle of equality between the parents (*coparentalité*) in the exercise of their parental responsibilities. The law also very clearly states that all children are equal (the law no longer uses the terms *filiation légitime* and *filiation naturelle* with respect to parental responsibilities. Now all legal provisions concerning parental responsibilities after divorce are put in the section containing the general rules on parental responsibilities under a broad heading concerning the situations of separated parents or parents who do not cohabit).

GERMANY

The German CC of 1896 used the term 'parental authority' (*elterliche Gewalt*). It was, however, the father of a legitimate child who had this authority. As a consequence of altered views on the role of spouses, the German Basic Law (*Grundgesetz*) of 1949 established equality between men and women (Art. 3 para. 2). A transitional provision made it clear that all statutes not in conformity with this principle would cease to be valid as of 31 March 1953 (Art. 117 para. 1 German Basic Law). From then on, the courts struck down an increasing number of family law provisions on the ground that they were unconstitutional (see Q 4). Later, many provisions of substantive family law were recodified by the Act on Equal Rights of Men and Women in the Field of Civil Law (Equal Rights Act; *Gleichberechtigungsgesetz*) of 18 June 1957.[34] These provisions lead to gender equality not only in marriage law, but also in child law as far as legitimate children were concerned. 'Parental authority' was replaced by 'parental care' in a reform law of 1979.[35]

The old provisions on illegitimate children in §§ 1705 *et seq* German CC had also been declared unconstitutional, so a reform became necessary[36] (see Q 4). The Illegitimacy Act of 1969 for the most part called for the equal treatment of legitimate and illegitimate children.[37] Nevertheless there was still a certain amount of discrimination, especially the control of a non-married mother (so-called *Amtsvormundschaf*, a certain kind of administrative curatorship), and there was no custody for the unmarried father.[38] The Civil Code also determined that the biological father of a child born out of wedlock could only exercise a right of access if the mother agreed or the Court of Guardianship so

34 Gleichberechtigungsgesetz of 18.06.1957, *BGBl.* 1957 I p. 609.

35 Gesetz zur Neuregelung der elterlichen Sorge (SorgeRG) of 18.07.1979, *BGBl.* 1979 I, p. 1061.

36 BVerfG, 03.06.1969, *BVerfGE* 26, 44 = *FamRZ* 1969, 401.

37 Gesetz über die rechtliche Stellung der nichtehelichen Kinder of 19.08.1969, *BGBl.* 1969 I, p. 1243.

38 The denial of joint custody was declared unconstitutional in a case of an illegitimate child that was later declared legitimate (§ 1738 old version German CC) by BVerfG, 07.05.1991, *BVerfGE* 84, 168 = *FamRZ* 1991,913.

ordered.[39] For procedural reasons, in two cases a Chamber of the ECtHR found that this denial of the right of contact was discriminatory with respect to the application of the rights protected by Art. 8 of the Human Rights Convention.[40] The Grand Chamber, however, dismissed the claim.[41]

After Germany's reunification, the mother of an illegitimate child in East Germany retained full parental custody according to its former Family Code (*Familiengesetzbuch*; FamGB).[42] The former restrictions of the German CC did not apply in East Germany (Art. 230 para. 1 Introductory Act to the German CC). The reform of legal curatorship - in the past often criticised, as unnecessary State interference - as well as the improvement of the legal position of a father of an illegitimate child were the main objectives of the reform of guardianship law in 1997.[43]

Another fundamental reform also took place through a law of 16 December 1997, which came into force on 1 July 1998 (*Kindschaftsrechtsreformgesetz*; Child Law Reform Act).[44] The Child Law Reform Act mainly changed the rules on parental custody and contact in the event of divorce and for non-married fathers. It broke with the former concept that the father of a child born out of wedlock could not acquire custody and it also introduced the possibility for a non-married father to get parental care. Parental care, however, is still primarily with the mother (§ 1626a German CC), a solution that was recently confirmed by the Federal Constitutional Court.[45] See Q 22. The Child Law Reform Act also established the principle of co-parenting (joint parental responsibility) if married parents separate. Sole custody now represents the exception to the rule of joint custody, see § 1671 German CC. This concept of custody implies that, under the German CC, major decisions concerning the child must be made jointly by the parents. To a certain extent the Child Law Reform Act also recognized the stepfamily. The spouse of the parent (step-parent) got a right to contact (§ 1685 para. 2 German CC).[46]

---

39 See the former §§ 1705, 1711 German CC.

40 ECtHR (Fourth Section), *Sommerfeld* v. *Germany*, 11.10.2001, *Europäische Grundrechte-Zeitschriftt (EuGRZ)* 2001, 588 = *FamRZ* 2002, 381; ECtHR (Fourth Section), *Sahin* v. *Germany*, 11.10.2001, *EuGRZ* 2002, 25.

41 ECtHR (Grand Chamber), *Sommerfeld* v. *Germany*, 08.07.2003, *ECtHR Reports* 2003-VIII No. 71 = *FamRZ* 2004, 337; ECtHR (Grand Chamber), *Sahin* v. *Germany*, 8.07.2003, *ECtHR Reports* 2003-VIII No. 71 = *FamRZ* 2004, 337. See *C. Lenz/J. Baumann*, FPR 2004, 303 *et seq.*

42 Familiengesetzbuch, *Gesetzblatt* (*GBl.*) 1966 I Nr. 1, p. 1, as amended.

43 Gesetz zur Abschaffung der gesetzlichen Amtspflegschaft und Neuordnung des Rechts der Beistandschaft of 04.12.1997, *BGBl.* 1997 I, p. 2846.

44 Gesetz zur Reform des Kindschaftsrechts (Kindschaftsrechtsreformgesetz; KindRG) of 16.12.1997, *BGBl.* 1997 I p. 2942. See R. FRANK, 'Parentage Law Reform,' in: *The International Survey of Family Law*, The Hague: M. Nijhoff Publ., 1999, p. 170 *et seq.*

45 BVerfG, 29.01.2003, BVerfGE 107, 150 = *FamRZ* 2003, 285 = *NJW* 2003, 955.

46 See K. MUSCHELER, 'Das Recht der Stieffamilie', *FamRZ* 2004, 913, 916.

Other amendments became necessary when registered life partnership for same-sex couples was introduced (2001).[47] The legislature gave the registered partner, and also a new spouse of the parent, 'limited parental responsibilities' (see § 9 para. 1(2) Registered Partnership Act; § 1687 b German CC).[48] By an amendment of 2004, adoption of stepchildren by a registered partner was allowed (see §9 para 4 Registered Partnership Act).[49] A minor amendment concerns the legal position of a biological father where parentage is not established legally.[50] Another amendment brought an extension of the persons who have a right to contact. Today there is no longer an enumeration of the persons having the right to contact but instead a general clause, see § 1685 para. 2 German CC (see Q 43c).[51]

GREECE

The first radical reform of the law concerning parental responsibilities was realized in 1983. Before that time the father was solely responsible for the care of the child, the administration of its property, and its legal representation (*patria potestas*).[52] The role of the mother was mostly restricted to cases where paternal authority had come to an end.[53] Law 1329/1983 substituted the term "paternal authority" for "parental care" and significantly reformed the concept along the lines of the constitutional imperatives for equality between men and women (Art. 4 para. 2 Greek CC) and the protection of childhood (Art. 21 para. 1 Greek CC).[54]

Law 2446/1996 put into effect the second major reform of the relevant legal framework. More specifically, it restructured the institutions of adoption and guardianship, so as to grant more effective protection for children. In addition, the same law introduced, for the first time in Greek legal history, the institution of foster care for minors.

---

47 Gesetz über die eingetragene Lebenspartnerschaft (Lebenspartnerschaftsgesetz – LPartG) of 16.02.2001, *BGBl.* 2001 I 266.

48 K. MUSCHELER, 'Das Recht der Stieffamilie', *FamRZ* 2004, 913, 916.

49 See Act to Amend the Law of Registered Partnership (Gesetz zur Überarbeitung des Lebenspartnerschaftsrechts) of 15.12.2004, *BGBl.* 2004, I, p. 3396.

50 Gesetz zur Umsetzung familienrechtlicher Entscheidungen des Bundesverfassungsgerichts of 13.12.2003, *BGBl.* 2003, I, p. 2547. See E. HÖFELMANN, 'Das Gesetz zur Umsetzung familienrechtlicher Entscheidungen des Bundesverfassungsgerichts', *FamRZ* 2004, 65 *et seq.*

51 Gesetz zur Änderung der Vorschriften über die Anfechtung der Vaterschaft und das Umgangsrecht von Bezugspersonen of 23.04.2004, *BGBl.* 2004, I, p. 598.

52 Art. 1500-1501 Greek CC/1940.

53 Art. 1590 Greek CC/1940.

54 P. AGALLOPOULOU, in: A. GEORGIADIS and M. STATHOPOULOS (eds.), *Civil Code commentary, Vol. VIII, Family Law (Arts. 1505-1694)*, 2nd Edition, Athens: Law & Economy, P.N. Sakkoulas 2003, Art. 1510 Greek CC, p. 173-174, No. 4 -5 [in Greek].

HUNGARY

The history of the main developments of the law concerning parental responsibilities can be summarised briefly as follows. The sources of today's parental responsibilities were based on: the Hungarian Guardianship Act, namely the Act No. XX. 1877 and the Hungarian Marriage Act, namely the Act No. XXXI. 1894. These essence of these Acts as they pertained to parental responsibilities remained unchanged until 1945.

These Acts, along with other European rules of the time, regulated paternal authority instead of the jointly exercised parental responsibilities of today. Paternal authority gave the everyday care of the child to the mother, but the father could decide, at least according to the Act, in matters affecting the child. The father also had the powers of the paternal responsibilities. A consequence of divorce, which rarely occurred, the child was placed with the mother. The mother could not have the full parental responsibilities even if the father died. She could be the 'natural and legal guardian of her child' only if the father had not appointed another person as guardian for the child.

The powers of the paternal authority were similar to the powers of today's parental responsibilities. An essential difference between the legal rules of past and today is that the age limit of majority was 24, although there were other ways to obtain majority. The child was generally under paternal responsibilities until reaching the age of 24. If the woman was younger than 24 but married with the proper permission, the marriage resulted in her majority; however, if the man was younger than 24 and married, he remained under paternal authority despite the marriage.

As with other matters of the family law, there was a huge distinction in the duties and powers of parental responsibilities between the child of marriage and the child born out of wedlock. If the child was born out of wedlock, only the mother, the natural and legal guardian of the child, had parental duties and powers. There was no legal relationship between the unmarried father and the child born out of wedlock.

Women were also discriminated against when it came to guardianships. A woman could not be guardian, nor could she exercise parental authority as the guardian of any child other than her own natural and legal child.

Partial legislative changes were enacted in 1945 and 1946, namely before the Family Act in 1952.

In 1945 the paternal authority changed to parental authority but this did not mean that the parents could exercise their authority jointly. The mother's parental authority was subsidiary; the mother could exercise her authority only when a judicial judgment after divorce placed the child with her (a right she did not have earlier), and when the father was prevented from exercising his parental authority.

The age limit of majority was also reduced in 1945 to the age of 20, and marriage, for both women and men, resulted in majority if they were under the age of 20 and married with the proper permission.

The most important change was introduced in 1946. Act No. XXIX. 1946 abolished discrimination against children born out of wedlock, This prevented discrimination in the matter of parental authority, therefore the unmarried father obtained the same parental authority as the married father, provided his legal status was secured. The Act also significantly enlarged the opportunities for the establishment of paternal affiliation.

The Family Act in 1952 gave rules about the parental responsibilities, specifically about the parental 'supervision' rights that both parents had jointly. The Act stressed that these parental responsibilities had to be exercised in the interest of the child. The word 'authority' disappeared from the wording of the Act.

It had not yet been specifically stated in 1952 that the unmarried mother or father's parental responsibilities are the same as those of the married mother and father, or that there is only a difference concerning whether the parents live together or not. There was thus no need to emphasise the 'equality' of unmarried parents and married parents in 1952.

At the same time the Family Act was enacted, the age of majority became 18; the age until which a child was under parental responsibilities also became 18.

The revision of the rules of the Family Act started in the 80's. Some of the changes in the parental responsibilities came from divorced spouses; parents living apart from the child demanded comprehensive rights consisting of more than the exercise of the parental responsibilities in connection with their non-resident child. Nevertheless, although the institution of the joint parental responsibilities after divorce, is known in Hungary,[55] the joint parental responsibilities after divorce was not regulated in the amendment of the Family Act in 1986. The rights of the parental responsibilities of the parents living apart from the child became broader; these parents obtained the right to decide important matters concerning the child together with the holder of the parental responsibilities. These matters were, according to the amendment, the determination of the child's name, residence, education and career.

The United Nation's Convention on the Rights of the Child of 1989 was promulgated in Hungary in 1991. Since that time, but especially since 1995, children's rights have gradually broadened in matters concerning the parental responsibilities; primarily the children's rights to express their views and have due weight given to their views, according to the child's age and maturity. The

---

55 A 1982 decision of the German Constitutional Court was in fact published in Hungary.

joint parental responsibilities after divorce were admitted and regulated during the amendment of the Family Act in 1995.

In the Child Welfare Act of 1997, the child's right to be brought up in its own family is emphasised. The activities provided by the public guardianship authorities and the Child Welfare services were broadened in order to assist the parent holding parental responsibilities to better care for the child, in the hopes that the child would not be taken from its family.

The Child Welfare Act also rejected the rule that allowed public authority to exercise the parental responsibilities over the children taken into state care. Along with this, the Act strengthened the demand for children taken into state care to live with foster parents, and for foster parents, as guardians, to hold parental responsibilities. The supervisors of the children's homes also obtained rights as guardians by limiting the number of children living in a children's home.

IRELAND

The principal statute governing parental responsibilities is the Irish Guardianship of Infants Act 1964. Where the parties are married at the time of the child's birth, both are conferred with joint and equal guardianship rights. Where the parents are not married, rather different considerations apply. While the natural mother of a child is deemed automatically to be a guardian thereof, a natural father who is not the husband of the mother, is not considered to be a guardian. Since the coming into force of Sec. 12 Irish Status of Children Act 1987,[56] the non-marital father may apply for an order conferring on him the status of guardian. Sec. 4 Irish Children Act 1997[57] enables the parties, by agreement, to make a statutory declaration that while not married to each other, the parties are indeed father and mother respectively of the child in question, and that they have agreed that the natural father should be appointed as guardian. Sec. 9 Irish Children Act 1997 makes it clear, should any doubt exist, that it is possible, even where a couple is separated, to award joint custody.

ITALY

The 1965 Code was based on the concept of patriarchy (adultery by a wife was criminal), as was the family. Although both parents had the duty to educate, provide moral guidance and support the child, only the father - explicitly defined as 'head of the family' - exercised the parental responsibilities (so called 'parental authority'); the mother could exercise parental responsibilities only after the father died. External interferences with the family were not tolerated. Fathers had the power to remove a 'rebellious' son from the family, providing him only with the support strictly necessary, or, applying to the court, placing him in a reformatory. It was not possible for children born to an unmarried mother to later be recognised by anyone she married. The

---

[56] No. 26 of 1987.
[57] No. 40 of 1997.

guardianship of orphans was entrusted to a person appointed by the remaining parent, or if there was no remaining parent, by the paternal grandfather.

These provisions influenced the 1942 code, but state interference became stronger within the family's ambit. In particular, parents were obligated to educate and provide moral guidance to their children that 'conformed to the moral principles of fascism and its proper idea of a nation.' During that period, two new judicial institutions were installed: the Family Proceeding Court and the guardianship judge.

The exclusive authority and discipline of the husband-father remained unchanged for many years, even after the robust Italian Constitution in 1948 established the legal and moral equality of the spouses (Art. 3 e 29 § 2), as well as the right and duty of the parents to support, educate and provide the children with moral guidance, even if they were born outside the marriage (Art. 30 § 1). Despite the elimination of reference to fascist nationalism, until the criminal nature of adultery was repealed in 1968, neither Italy's cultural background nor its legal system changed. Changes became progressively more numerous and important following this: in 1970 divorce was introduced, in 1975 the age of consent was lowered to 18 years old (instead of 21) and, above all, the whole of family law was reformed (Law of 19 May 1975, No. 151). Although it is not possible to list all innovations the reform introduced, the modification of Art. 147 stands out. It imposed the parental duty to support, provide moral guidance and educate the child 'taking into account the capacities, natural inclinations and aspirations of the child.' Moreover, the innovation contained in Art. 315 Italian CC dealing with the duty of the children is emblematic because it eliminated the obligation to 'honour' the parents, leaving only the duty to respect them. In addition, the discipline of adoption, introduced in 1983 and modified in 2001 by providing the 'right of the child to grow up within his own family', shows the final and radical change of perspective: from the protected child who was expected to submit to and obey his or her parents, to the minor who is a holder of rights and demands respect.[58] However, an opposing tendency reveals that although the entire discipline supposedly consistently focuses on the interests of the child, the system is still *de facto* based on the traditional vision; consequently the child continues to passively be seen as an 'incidental addressee of a series of decisions taken by others'.[59] It can therefore be observed that an effective change of perspective can't be achieved by legislative reforms alone, but must also be accompanied by conscious jurisprudential practise and a major collaboration of the experts in the field of psychological pedagogy.[60]

---

58 Among the numerous contributions see M. E. QUADRATO, *Il minore tra interesse e diritti: una lettura comparata,* Bari 1995, p. 70.

59 P. CENDON and L. GAUDINO, *I problemi generali,* in: AA.VV., *I bambini e i loro diritti* by P. CENDON, Bologna, 1991, p. 25.

60 AA.VV., *La tutela del minore tra norme, psicologia ed etica* by A. MESTITZ, Milan, 1997.

Still, from this slow evolution, until now *in fieri*, to which the international Conventions for the protection of the minor has contributed (*e.g.* the Convention of New York of 20 November 1980 ratified and implemented in Italy with the Law of 27 May, No. 176), there has emerged a 'flexible' definition of parental responsibilities, whose content and rigour decrease in accordance with the increasing age of the child and his concrete capacity of judgment.

LITHUANIA

During the period of feudalism, family relationships, including parental responsibilities, were regulated by codified sources of law: Lithuanian Statutes of 1529, 1566 and 1588. The Third Lithuanian Statute of 1588 was applied until 1840, when the Russian Imperial Civil Law was introduced. Characteristic of the Statutes was the discrimination against a child born out of wedlock and the dominant position of the father in the family.

During the pre-World War II period of independence (1918-1940), parental responsibilities were regulated by several legal acts applied in different parts of the territory of Lithuania: in the largest part the Russian Imperial Civil Law of 1840 was applied; in Klaipeda region, the German CC; in Uznemune region, the French CC of 1804; in Palanga and Zarasai regions, the Collection of Civil Laws of the Baltic Provinces of 1864.

From 1944 until 1 July 2001, Soviet legislation, including the Code of Family and Marriage of 16 July 1969 was applied. The Code of Family and Marriage of 1969, which was in force until the entry into force of the Lithuanian CC of 2000, did not define parental responsibilities, but the legal aspects of parental authority were given: parental responsibilities and rights in educating their children, maintenance duties of parents *etc.* The Code provided equal rights and duties to both parents and abolished discrimination towards children born out of wedlock.

In 2000 the new Lithuanian CC was adopted. The family law was incorporated into Lithuanian CC as its Third Book. During the preparation of the Lithuanian CC, new tendencies, especially the contemporary developments of international law in the area of parental responsibilities, were taken into account. The United Nation Commission on the Rights of the Child evaluated the new Civil Code as one of the most progressive sources in respect to the protection of the rights of the child. The new Lithuanian CC was enacted on 1 July 2001.

THE NETHERLANDS

As of 1947 the father and the mother have joint parental responsibilities within marriage, before that time only the father had the right. If, however, the parents disagreed after 1947, the will of the father was decisive.[61] The father also retained the administration of the child's assets and the usufruct. If the marriage ended, the joint parental responsibilities were terminated. Since 1995 a

61 This did not change until 1984, Act of 30 August 1984, *Staatsblad* 1984, No. 404.

number of changes have been made in the law relating to parental responsibilities; however, the Government has not reconsidered the general underlying principles of parental responsibilities law. This has resulted in haphazard changes and an extremely complicated and incoherent 'system' of parental responsibilities rules.[62]

The most influential changes in the law with regard to parental responsibilities in the last ten years concern: (1) the continuation of joint parental responsibilities after divorce and separation, (2) the possibility for a parent with sole parental responsibilities to apply for joint parental responsibilities with a new partner, and (3) the attribution by operation of law of parental responsibilities to registered partners and married same-sex couples over children born into their relationship. In 1995 the Custody and Access Act introduced new provisions into the Dutch CC specifying when joint parental responsibilities may be obtained. After divorce parents could request the district court to give them joint parental responsibilities; however, this regulation was deemed to be unsatisfactory because it was easier for unmarried parents to obtain joint parental responsibilities by means of a simple registration procedure, whereas divorced parents had to go to court.[63]

Under the new rule, which came into force on 1 January 1998,[64] joint parental responsibilities continue after divorce unless it is in the best interests of the child to attribute sole parental responsibilities to one of the parents. At the same time it became possible for a parent to obtain joint parental responsibilities with a new partner. According to Art. 1:253t Dutch CC the district court may on the joint application of the parent who is charged with parental responsibilities and a person other than a parent who has a close personal relationship with the child, charge them with joint parental responsibilities. The idea behind this rule is that 'it is in the child's best interest to clarify the position of the social parent'.[65] Paragraph 3 of Art. 253t Dutch CC states that the application must be rejected if, taking into account the interest of the other parent, there is a well-founded fear that the best interests of the child would be neglected. These so called '253t-responsibilities ' can also be granted to a same-sex couple, if one of the partners is the minor's parent. Since the introduction of this Act it is also possible for two people to exercise shared guardianship, whereas before it had only been possible for one person to exercise guardianship. More changes in the

62 See J.E. DOEK, 'Het gezag over minderjarigen. Iets over een doolhof en het zoeken van (rode?) draden', *FJR,* 2000, p. 217-226 and A. NUYTINCK, 'De complexiteit van de gezagsregeling', *FJR,* 2002, p. 190-191 .

63 C. FORDER, 'An Undutchable family law: partnership, parenthood, social parenthood, names and some Art. 8 ECHR case law', in: A. BAINHAM, *The International Survey of Family Law 1997,* p. 259-307; and C. FORDER, 'Re-thinking marriage, parenthood and adoption', in: A. BAINHAM, *International Survey of Family Law 1995*, p. 359-382.

64 Act of 30.10.1997 to amend, *inter alia,* Book 1 Dutch CC in connection with the introduction of shared custody for a parent and his partner and shared guardianship, *Staatsblad* 1997, No. 506.

65 *Kamerstukken Tweede Kamer,* 1995-1996, 23714, No. 6, p. 3.

law relating to parental responsibilities were made in 2002.[66] As of that date partners in a registered partnership or spouses in a same-sex marriage acquire joint parental responsibilities over a child born into their relationship unless the child already has legal family ties with a parent outside the partnership (Art. 1:253aa and 1:253sa Dutch CC).

NORWAY

Parental responsibilities have been attributed to both parents since the 18th century, if the child was born in wedlock. After a divorce, however, until the 1980s only one of the parents was attributed parental responsibilities. Contact rights for the parent not living with the child were acknowledged by the Supreme Court in 1940.[67]

To a child born out of wedlock, until 1915 parental responsibilities were attributed to the person(s) with whom the child lived, irrespective of whether this was the mother or another person. The father at that time normally had no relationship, legal or actual, with the child. Art. 3 of the Norwegian Act on Children born out of Wedlock 1915 (The Castberg Act) vested parental responsibilities in the mother. The father could gain parental responsibilities only if the mother died or was unable to care for the child and agreed that the child should live with the father. (The Norwegian Children Acts 1915, however, eliminated the differences between children born in and out of wedlock with regard to their legal status, for example with regard to inheritance from the father.) According to Art. 35 Norwegian Children Act 1981, the mother still has sole parental responsibilities when the parents are not married. The parents may, however, by mutual agreement also attribute parental responsibilities to the father (or to the father alone). This agreement becomes valid when the National Population Register is notified.

Until the 1980s, the concept of parental responsibilities included the rights of custody after divorce. Today, the question of who the child shall permanently live with is considered separately, according to Art. 36 Norwegian Children Act 1981. After divorce the main rule is joint parental responsibilities. With regard to the question of where the child shall permanently reside, if the parents do not agree the court must decide that the child shall have one permanent place of residence, Art. 36 sec. 2.

The Norwegian Children Act 1981 introduced the term 'parental responsibility' instead of 'parental authority'; a change that reflects a shift in attitude more than a shift in content. The content of parental responsibilities has not undergone any major changes in the last hundred years. The statutory provision that allowed parents to physically punish their children was repealed

---

66 See W. SCHRAMA, 'Reforms in Dutch Family law during the course of 2001: Increased pluriformity and complexity' in: A. BAINHAM, *International Survey of Family Law 2002*, p. 277-304.

67 Rt. 1940 p. 155.

in 1972, and such punishment was explicitly prohibited in 1987. Art. 30 sec. 3 Norwegian Children Act 1981 states that a child must not be subjected to violence or be treated in any way that might harm or endanger his or her mental or physical health.

POLAND

After World War II, the principal regulations in this matter were issued in: the decree of 22 January 1964 - Family Law; the decree of 14 May 1946 - Guardianship Law; and the decree of 21 May 1946 on the proceedings before the guardianship authority (all these acts entered into force on 1 July 1946). Subsequently, the Family Code (statute of 27 June 1950 entered into force on 1 October 1950) and the statute on legal proceedings in family and custody cases issued simultaneously with the Polish Family Code.

Presently, parental responsibility matters are set out in the Family and Guardianship Code (statute of 25 February 1964) and procedural law provisions in the Civil Procedure Code (statute of 17 November 1964). Some of the provisions of the Family and Guardianship Code were amended by the statute of 19 December 1975 (Art. 109, Art. 112^1,112^2, Art. 113 § 2) and the statute of 21 December 2000 (Art. 109 § 2 i § 4, Art. 111 § 1a).

PORTUGAL

The 1867 Portuguese CC regulated the institution of parental responsibility in Title IX (On the Incapacity of Minority and Ways of Compensate it) of Part I (On Civil Capacity) and presented it as a collection of parental rights, designed to regulate the child and administer his or her property (Art. 137). This systematic insertion shows that parental responsibility was understood predominantly as a way to cure the child's incapacity to act while still a minor. This is perfectly attuned to the concept of the absolute power of parents (particularly the father) over their children until majority or emancipation. The legal regulation of this institution thus reflects an authoritarian and hierarchical vision of family relations.

As regards entitlement to parental responsibility, the rule was that both parents were entitled to hold parental responsibility (Art. 137 of the 1867 Seabra Code). However, owing to the relative incapacity of the married woman, the exercise of those powers was shared unequally between the father and mother. As head of the family, the father would direct, represent and defend his children, in and out of court (Art. 138 of the 1867 Seabra Code); the mother would participate and be heard on all matters concerning the child's interests, but had only a 'consultative function', as the mere collaborator of her husband (Art. 138 of the 1867 Seabra Code).

With regards to the personal aspect of parental responsibility, the rights of custody, education and representation were exercised by the father (Art. 137, 138, 143 and 148 No. 2 of the 1867 Seabra Code). The Code did not expressly establish a parental right to correct children. However, most authors agree that this right is included in the collection of rights that make up parental responsibility, considering that the right to correct is an instrumental right included in the rights of custody and education. Indeed, in accordance with Art. 143 of the 1867 Seabra Code, in the event of bad behaviour, serious indiscipline or disobedience from children, parents could apply to the courts to decree the appropriate corrective measures.

As regards the property of minors, the father held exclusive rights of administration (Art. 146 of the 1867 Seabra Code). However, both father and mother enjoyed (legal) use of the child's property (Art. 145 of the 1867 Seabra Code). Parents were not obliged to provide accounts of this administration (Art. 152 of the 1867 Seabra Code); however, they had to support the burden of maintaining and educating their children in a decent manner appropriate to their social status (Art. 148, No.1, *in fine,* and No. 2 of the 1867 Seabra Code). This right to use could be renounced in favour of the children (Art. 149, No. 1 and only § of the 1867 Seabra Code).

Corresponding to these rights that the parents (especially the father) held over the children and their property was the duty of the children to respect and honour their parents (Art. 142 of the 1867 Seabra Code).

The essence of this system of parental responsibility was not altered by the Portuguese CC of 1966. The new Code only changed the location of this information, with parental responsibility now appearing in Chapter 4 (Effects of parenthood) of Title III (On parenthood) of Book 4 (Family Law) of the Portuguese CC. Parental responsibility was presented as one of the main effects of parenthood.

In 1976, the new Constitution of the Portuguese Republic dealt directly with matters concerning the parent-child relationship. The Fundamental Law established various principles that directly affected the regulation of the parent-child relationship. The first of these was the principle of equality of spouses as regards the maintenance and education of the children (Art. 36 No. 3 Portuguese Constitution); this meant that parental responsibility was now held and exercised by both parents (father and mother), with no special powers attributed to either of them (Art. 1901 Portuguese CC). There was also the principle of awarding parents the right and duty to educate and maintain their children (Art. 36, No. 5, Portuguese Constitution), which was manifested as a right and duty to oversee the education of their children (Art. 1878 No. 1 Portuguese CC), not in an authoritarian way, but rather by respecting the child and promoting her or his gradual autonomy (Art. 1874 No. 1 and 1878 No. 2 Portuguese CC); this also translates into a right and duty of parents before the State, namely the right to educate their children in accordance with their own philosophical, ideological, political, aesthetic, moral and religious convictions. This role of the State is thus reduced to helping and collaborating with parents in the exercise of this main right (Art. 67 No. 2c and 68 No. 1 Portuguese Constitution). Finally, there is the principle of inseparability of children from parents (Art. 36 No. 6 Portuguese Constitution). This principle encodes the parent's subjective right not to be deprived of their children or to have their children removed from them, except in those circumstances laid down by law, such as situations when they have not fulfilled their basic duties towards their children, and only then upon judicial decision (Art. 1915 and 1918 Portuguese CC).

Through the direct influence of the Portuguese Constitution of 1976, the Portuguese CC also underwent alterations as regards the regulation of parental responsibility. Effectively, the 1977 Reform of the Portuguese CC established a new concept of the family and consequently of the parent-child relationship. This now included mutual rights and duties for parents and children, namely the duty to respect, help and support (Art. 1874 No. 1 Portuguese CC). The interests of the child was now made into the guiding criterion for the exercise of parental responsibility (Art. 1878 No. 1 Portuguese CC). Another innovation presented by the 1977 Reform led, in the teaching of PEREIRA COELHO and DE OLIVEIRA, to the imposition of a positive duty upon parents to respect their child. Thus, in accordance with the provisions of Art. 1878 No. 2 2nd part Portuguese CC, parents should take their children's opinions into account (in accordance with the child's maturity and understanding) on important family matters, and recognise their autonomy in the organisation of their own lives. The duty of children to obey their parents nevertheless remains (Art. 1878 No. 2 1st part Portuguese CC).

Today, the Portuguese CC does not expressly establish the so-called power to correct. Indeed, the 1977 Reform did not include the wording of the former Art. 1884, Portuguese CC from 1966, which recognised for both parents 'the power to correct their child, within moderation, when she or he was at fault'. Applying the constitutional principle of equality (Art. 13 and 36 No. 4 Portuguese Constitution), the Reform refused the two-part division of parental responsibility according to whether the children were 'legitimate' or 'illegitimate'. The only difference that now existed in the regulation of these two situations was in the way parental responsibility was exercised, because the effective difference in the situations demanded it. The regulation of the property dimension of parental responsibility was not untouched by the Reform. It effectively eliminated the right of parents to use their children' property and established the possibility of parents drawing revenue from their children's property, if that were necessary to cover the expenses of maintenance, safety, health and education of their children, and, within reasonable limits, the needs of the family (Art. 1896 Portuguese CC).

RUSSIA

The main peculiarity of the history of the concept of parental responsibility of Russia is that joint parental responsibility, which didn't make an entrance into Western Europe until the 1990s, was introduced in Russian law in 1918.

Before the Revolution of 1917 the concept of parental responsibility was dominated by a patriarchal vision of the family. Minor and adult children of both sexes were under parental power (Art. 164 (1) *Svod Zakonov Rossiyskoy*

Imperii).[68] Parental power did not cease to exist but only underwent some *de facto* limitations when adult children married or became employed.[69] Although the law spoke of the parental power of both parents, the mother could not execute parental power as long as the father was still alive and legally capable, as she herself was under the power of her husband.[70] The parental power was not total, but was still very broad. In order to enforce the children's obedience, the parents were empowered to apply 'domestic punishments'[71] and could employ the authority of the State to have their children imprisoned for up to four months without investigation by simply issuing 'Orders of Arbitrary Arrest' (*Lettres de cochet*).[72] However, by the end of the nineteenth century this practice was so at odds with modern ideas concerning personal rights of the children that the magistrates were no longer willing to enforce such requests.[73] The parental power can not be discharged even in case of grave abuse thereof.[74]

After the Revolution of 1917 the concept of parental power was entirely revised. The concept of parental power was replaced by the concept of parental rights and duties. The Russian Family Code of 1918[75] first introduced one of the core elements of the Russian concept of parental responsibility: joint parental responsibility. The parental rights of both parents became formally equal irrespective of whether they were or had been married, or whether parentage had been established by way of voluntary recognition or by the court against the father's will.[76] Parental responsibility lasted until boys reached the age of eighteen and girls the age of sixteen.[77] Parental responsibility had to be executed exclusively in the best interests of the child,[78] which was interpreted in such a way that the interests and wishes of the parents did not even need to be

---

68 *Collection of Statutes of the Russian Empire* where family law was placed together with other acts on civil law in the second part of volume X.

69 G. SHERSHENEVICH, *Russkoe grazgdanskoe pravo* (*Russian Civil Law*), Moscow: Spark, 1995, p. 438.

70 G. SHERSHENEVICH, *Russkoe grazgdanskoe pravo* (*Russian Civil Law*), Moscow: Spark, 1995, p. 437.

71 Art. 165 (1) *Svod Zakonov Rossiyskoy Imperii.*

72 Art. 1592 Russian Criminal Code.

73 I. ZAGOROVSKII, *Handbook of Family Law* (*Kurs semeinogo prava),* Moscow: Zerzalo, 2003 , p. 243.

74 I. ZAGOROVSKII, *Handbook of Family Law* (*Kurs semeinogo prava),* Moscow: Zerzalo, 2003 , p. 249. Deprivation of parental rights were, however, provided for in the Bill of the Guardianship Code, which has not become law. *Ibid*, p. 250.

75 *Kodeks Zakonov ob Aktah Grazhdanskogo Sostoianiia, Brachnom, Semeinom i Opekynskom Prave*, of 22.10.1918, *SU RSFSR,* 1918, No. 76, item 818, further referred to as Russian Family Code of 1918.

76 D. GENKIN *et. al.*, *History of Soviet Family Law 1917-1947* (*Istoria sovetskogo grazhdanskogo prava 1917-1947),* Moscow: Juridicheskaia Literatura, 1949, p. 409.

77 A. NETCHAEVA, *Family Law* (*Semeinoe pravo*), Moscow: Jurist, 1998, p. 69.

78 Art. 153 Russian Family Code of 1918.

considered.[79] The content of parental responsibility was similar to what it is now, and included the right and duty of care, education, representation, protection and maintenance of the child.[80] The second Russian Family Code of 1926[81] maintained most of the provisions of its precursor. In the following decennia the family law in general and the concept of parental rights in particular experienced the influence of totalitarian ideology. In line with French positivist LÉON DUGUIT's[82] theory that 'no one has any other right than the right to always fulfil one's duty',[83] parental responsibility was perceived solely as the duty imposed on the parents by the State.[84] Consequently, the notion of parental responsibility was transferred into a concept of parental duties. The parents started to be seen 'solely as educators of a child, appointed by operation of law to fulfil this function' as long as the State found them suitable.[85]

The Russian Family Code of 1969[86] did away with the excesses of the preceding period. Rights and duties of the parents were given a proper balance again.[87] The law no longer required parental responsibility to be executed 'exclusively' in the best interests of the child without any regard of the interests of the parents.

In 1995 the New Russian Family Code was adopted. This Code further shifted the perspective of parental responsibility from the relations between the parents and the State to the relations between parents and children. Before the new Code, minor children were primarily perceived as passive subjects of parental care. The new Code made deliberate efforts to switch from this paternalistic position to the rights-based approach. A new special Chapter 11 dealing with the rights of minor children was incorporated into the court. The new Code bestows on children rights beyond the minimum level provided under the 1989 UN Convention on the Rights of the Child.

The 1995 Code is still based upon the same concept of 'always joint' equal parental responsibility. However, it should be noticed that this concept,

---

79 D. GENKIN *et. al.*, *History of Soviet Family Law 1917-1947 (Istoria sovetskogo grazhdanskogo prava 1917-1947)*, Moscow: Juridicheskaia Literatura, 1949, p. 444.

80 Art. 154-156 Russian Family Code of 1918.

81 *Kodeks zakonov o brake sem'e i opeke*, 19 .11.1926, *SU RSFSR* 1926, No. 82, item 611.

82 The ideas of DUGUIT, although never openly acknowledged by the Soviet legal establishment, had profound influence on legal thinking during the period of totalitarianism.

83 L. DUGUIT, *General Transformations of Civil Law Since the Times of the Code Napoleon* (Obsie preobrazovania *grazhdanskogo prava so vremen kodeksa Napoleona)*, Moscow: 1919, p. 22.

84 D. GENKIN, 'Predmet sovetskogo grazhdanskogo prava', 4 *Sovetskoe gosudarstvo i pravo*, 1939, p. 39.

85 D. GENKIN *et. al.*, *History of Soviet Family Law 1917-1947 (Istoria sovetskogo grazhdanskogo prava 1917-1947)*, Moscow: Juridicheskaia Literatura, 1949, p. 455.

86 *Kodex Zakonov o Brake i Sem'ie RSFSR*, 30.07.1969, *Ved. RSFSR*, 1969, No. 32, item 1086.

87 A. NETCHAEVA, *Family Law (Semeinoe pravo)*, Moscow: Jurist, 1998, p. 84.

revolutionarily when it was first introduced in 1929, no longer seems to be in line with the requirements of our time. According to this concept, parental responsibility is coupled to a link of legal filiation between a parent and child. A legal filiation, with the exception of situations involving donors or a surrogate mother, reflects the biological truth. Coupling parental responsibility to filiation instead of marriage was once very progressive; it facilitated the ultimate equalisation of the rights of the children born in and outside wedlock and the rights of married and unmarried parents. However, the application of this concept in practice has shown that the legislature went too far. The idea that there must be no parental duties without rights has lead to the situation where a biological parent (father) whose paternity has been established by court order against his will and who never had any family relationships with either the child or the mother, acquires full parental responsibility. As the law gives the courts no power to distribute parental responsibility between parents, the only remedy against such 'parent' is the discharge of parental responsibility. Such an 'all or nothing approach' leaves almost nothing[88] in between full parental responsibility and no parental responsibility at all. At the same time, linking parental responsibility to filiation precludes attribution of parental responsibility to social parents (mostly step-parents) who have educated the child all through his or her childhood.

SPAIN

The current regulation of parental responsibilities is mainly a consequence of the Spanish 1978 Constitution. However, legislation was also strongly influenced by developments in other European countries, particularly France, Germany and Italy. The ratification of the UN Convention on the rights of the child in 1990 gave further impulse for reform.

The main points of reform during these years were:

- to establish that *patria potestad* is a function (an *officium*). The concept of *patria potestad* was historically understood to be a power of the father. It gradually evolved in case-law as an institution aiming to protect the child. In the reforms after 1978 it was established as a function by statute.
- to establish that *patria potestad* is to be exercised in accordance with the child's best interests and according to the child's personality.
- to establish a possibility of intervention by public authorities if *patria potestad* is not properly exercised.
- to ensure the observation of the non discrimination principle both in regard to the powers and duties of fathers and mothers and in regard to children born in and out of wedlock.

88 The only exception is the possibility to restrict parental responsibility or take the child away from the parent(s) if living with such parent(s) is dangerous for the child (Art. 73 Russian Family Code).

SWEDEN

The present Swedish legislation concerning parental responsibilities can be traced back to the end of the 1910's and the 1920's when a number of Acts, commonly referred to as 'the Child Acts', were passed.[89] In 1949, these Acts were merged into a comprehensive code, called Swedish Children and Parents Code (*Föräldrabalken*), which entered into force on 1 January 1950.[90] This Code is still in force, but has been the subject of numerous amendments over the course of years. Most of these amendments have concerned issues relating to parental responsibilities, in particular the attribution and exercise of the custody of a child.[91]

In 1966, the parents' right to use corporal punishment was abolished. In 1979, an explicit provision prohibiting it was inserted in Chapter 6 Sec. 1 Swedish Children and Parents Code. In 1973, a major divorce law reform that included abolishing, fault as a ground for divorce was enacted. As a consequence, fault to marriage breakdown also became irrelevant to the outcome of disputes on parental responsibilities. In 1973, the prospects for transferring custody from the child's mother to the child's father, when the parents had not been married to each other, were improved by introducing the same test of suitability to the father as to the mother. Until then, custody could be transferred to the father only if the mother was found unsuitable as a custodian. In 1976, all remaining differences in the legal treatment between children born in and out of wedlock were abolished. Furthermore, joint custody of children became available to both divorced and unmarried parents. Until then divorced or unmarried parents could only have sole custody of a child. In the case of divorce, it had been up to the courts to settle the parents' disputes and award one of them sole custody of the children. In order to strengthen the child's right to contact with the parent with whom the child is not living, since 1983 the law has explicitly stated that it is the child who has the right to contact.[92] Issues of contact re-emerged in 1993, when provisions were enacted obliging the court to regard the risk of child abuse, kidnapping or other harm when contact with a non-custodial parent or other person particularly close to the child takes place.[93]

Since the 1990's, the trend has been to encourage parents to reach agreements concerning their children. With this purpose in mind, in 1990 so-called co-

---

89 These enactments consisted of Act on marital birth (1917), Act on children born out of wedlock (1917), Act on adoption (1917), Act on children born in wedlock (1920) and Act on guardianship (1924).

90 The main *travaux préparatoires* consist of the following committee reports (SOU) or Governmental Bills (Prop.): SOU 1946:49 Ärvdabalkssakkunnigas förslag till föräldrabalk, Prop 1949:93. See also LU 1949:34 Första lagutskottets utlåtande i anledning av dels Kungl. Maj:ts proposition med förslag till föräldrabalk, m.m., dels ock i ämnet väckta motioner.

91 For a comprehensive enumeration of the legislative steps taken, see Å. SALDÉN, *Barn och föräldrar*, Uppsala: Iustus förlag, 2001, 4th Edition, p. 13-26.

92 Prop 1981/82:168, p. 41 *et seq.*

93 Prop 1992/93:139.

operation discussions were introduced to facilitate agreements between the parents.[94] Since a 1998 law reform, a court may also order joint custody against the wish of one of the parents whereas before the reform, joint custody could only be ordered if neither of the parents opposed it.[95] However, the 1998 reform primarily aims at keeping parental responsibilities issues out of court by encouraging parents to reach agreements on custody, contact and the child's residence. Such agreements must be confirmed by the local social welfare committee, if they are compatible with the best interests of the child.

Finally, the enactment of the Registered Partnership Act in 1994,[96] granted a same-sex couple with a registered partnership the same legal rights as a married couple. Originally, the rules concerning parental responsibilities were not applicable to registered partnership, however, since 2003 registered partners may jointly adopt a child, and a registered partner may adopt his or her stepchild. Registered partners may also jointly be appointed as special custodians to a child.

SWITZERLAND

Until the Swiss Code of Civil Law came into effect in 1912 the legitimate parent-child relationship was governed basically by cantonal law. Only in exceptional cases did federal legislation interfere with the cantons' sovereign power to issue laws, as for example in the Federal Act concerning Mixed Marriages with regard to children's religious instruction and in the Federal Act concerning Marital Status and Marriage with respect to naming the child.[97]

After eliminating the diversity among the cantons, the Swiss CC created an order that was progressive for the time: the distinction between a legitimate (defined in the 7th sub-section, 'old' Art. 252-301 Swiss CC) and an illegitimate (defined in the 8th sub-section, 'old' Art. 302-327 Swiss CC) parent-child relationship. This order was also significant to the regulation of parental (not 'paternal') responsibilities. In comparison to the cantonal laws, the Swiss CC introduced a decided improvement for an illegitimate parent-child relationship: parental responsibilities could be conferred on the mother ('old' Art. 324 Swiss CC). Furthermore, it became possible, by means of recognition or adjudication with consequences to the child's status, to create a child-father relationship that

94 Prop 1990/91:8. See: Chapter 6 Sec. 18 Swedish Children and Parents Code, revised in 2001.

95 Prop 1997/98:7.

96 Registered Partnership Act (1994:1117). The Act entered into force on 01.01.1995.

97 A. SILBERNAGEL and P. WÄBER, *Schweizerisches Zivilgesetzbuch, Familienrecht, II. Abteilung: Die Verwandtschaft*. Art. 252 - 359, Bern: Stämpfli & Cie. 1921, p. 3. More also with critical review in H. HAUSHEER, 'Rechte des Kindes und Personensorge als Kontinuum der Rechtsordnung', *ZVW*, 2001, p. 45 *et seq.*

largely corresponded to a legitimate relationship ('old' Art. 303, 323 and 325 Swiss CC).[98]

On 1 January 1978, a formal, material and total revision of children's law came into effect. The principle of a unified parent-child relationship replaced the previous 'legitimate/illegitimate' categories of children's law.[99] The mother's position within marriage was enhanced by the abolition of a father's right to make final decisions in disputes ('old' Art. 274 § 2 Swiss CC) and outside marriage the conferring parental responsibilities through the law (Art. 298 § 1 Swiss CC). Step-parents and foster parents were also granted a share in parental responsibilities (Art. 299 and 300 Swiss CC). The child's welfare and respect for the child's personality were recognised as both goals and restraints with respect to parental responsibilities (Art. 301 - 303 Swiss CC). At the same time, the protection of the child was extended and improved upon (Art. 307 - 315a Swiss CC).[100] In 1981 the provision concerning procedures for providential detainment (Art. 314a Swiss CC) came into force. The comprehensive revision of divorce law, in force since 1 January 2000, brought further formal and material changes to parental responsibilities. For instance, the term 'parental authority' (*Gewalt* in German) was replaced by 'parental responsibilities' (*Sorge* in German),' but above all, joint parental responsibilities may now be conferred on divorced (Art. 133 Swiss CC) and unmarried parents (Art. 298a Swiss CC), taking the child's welfare and other prerequisites into consideration.

---

98 C. HEGNAUER, *Berner Kommentar, Das Familienrecht, Die Verwandtschaft, Die Entstehung des Kindesverhältnisses*, Art. 252 - 269c ZGB, Bern, Stämpfli & Cie., 1984, p. 29.

99 C. HEGNAUER, *Berner Kommentar*, 1984, p. 33; HAUSHEER, 'Rechte des Kindes und Personensorge als Kontinuum der Rechtsordnung', *ZVW*, 2001, 45 *et seq.*

100 C. HEGNAUER, *Berner Kommentar*, 1984, p. 67; HAUSHEER, 'Rechte des Kindes und Personensorge als Kontinuum der Rechtsordnung', *ZVW*, 2001, 45 *et seq.*

QUESTION 6

A. GENERAL

Are there any recent proposals for reform in this area?

AUSTRIA

No.

BELGIUM

Some proposals in support of homosexual couples have recently been made to introduce parental rights and responsibilities for the partner of a biological parent who cares for the latter's child without being a biological parent.[1] The Constitutional Court has appealed to the legislature to meet these wishes.[2] A proposal has also been made to introduce a new article in the Belgian CC that would ban physical and psychological violence towards children, including violence perpetrated by holders of parental responsibilities.[3]

The right to contact between parents and children and between grandparents and grandchildren is being guaranteed by another proposal.[4] Finally, a proposal has been made that would grant every minor who has reached the age of twelve and makes the request, the right to be heard in every dispute that concerns the minor.[5] There is even a proposal which would grant the child the right to intervene in all proceedings that concern it.[6] All the above mentioned proposals are still in the initial stages of the parliamentary procedure.

---

1 Proposition de loi complétant le Code civil par des dispositions relative à la parenté sociale, *Doc. Parl.* Sénat, B.Z. 2003, No. 3-167/1; Proposition de loi complétant le Code civil par des dispositions relative à la parenté sociale, *Doc. Parl.* Chambre, 2003-04, No. 0393/001; Proposition de loi introduisant la parenté sociale dans le Code civil, *Doc. Parl.* Chambre, 2003-04, No. 0815/001.

2 Constitutional Court, 08.10.2003, *Rev. trim. dr. fam.*, 2004, p. 185-201, annotated J.-L. RENCHON; G. VERSCHELDEN, 'Arbitragehof zet de deur open voor zorgouderschap', *Juristenkrant*, 2003, Vol. 78, p. 13; also Juvenile Court of Antwerp, 03.10.2002, *R.W.*, 2002-03, p. 1188-1194, annotated T. ROBERT.

3 Proposition de loi insérant un Article 371 *bis* dans le Code civil, *Doc. Parl.* Sénat, B.Z. 2003, No. 3-149/1.

4 Proposition de loi garantissant le droit aux relations personelles entre parents et enfants et entre grands-parents et petits-enfants, *Doc. Parl.* Chambre, 2003-04, No. 0976/001.

5 Proposition de loi modifiant diverses dispositions relatives au droit des mineurs d'être entendus par le Juge, *Doc. Parl.* Chambre, 25.07.2002, No. 50-1991-01, pour la modification de l'article 931 du Code Judicaire, document 51K0634.

6 Proposition de loi ouvrant l'accès à la justice aux mineurs, *Doc. Parl.* Chambre, 19.07.2002, No. 50-1975/001, pour l'insertion d'un article 1237 *bis* dans le Code Judicaire, document 51K0643.

BULGARIA

No, there are not. There was a new Draft Bulgarian Family Code which was debated by the previous Parliament (1997-2001).

CZECH REPUBLIC

The proposal for a new Czech CC, which is under preparation, returns to the designation of parental rights and duties. However, their contents remain basically the same and only partial issues are more specified.[7]

DENMARK

Major reform is not expected in the near future. Two areas concerning parental authority and contact are currently being scrutinized and commission reports have been published or are expected to be published, which may result in an amendment to the Danish Act on Parental Authority and Contact.

The first report[8] concerns cooperation between the appropriate authorities. In Denmark decisions concerning parental authority are made by the administrative authorities and the courts[9] and contact orders are exclusively determined by the administrative authorities.[10] Child protection measures are decided by another authority: the local authorities. The report describes the degree to which cooperation between the administrative authorities and the local authorities presently takes place and it contains recommendations for the future. Some of the recommendations found in the report may be implemented without changes to the present legislation while others require change.

Secondly, Denmark has acceded to the Hague Convention on jurisdiction, applicable Law, recognition, enforcement and co-operation in respect of parental responsibility and measures for the protection of children.[11] In order to transpose this convention into Danish law, the Ministry of Justice has established a commission that will draft a report covering the necessary

---

7 For more detail see K. ELIAS and M. ZUKLINOVA, *Principy a vychodiska noveho občanského zákoníku*, Prague: Linde, 2002.

8 *Forsøgsprojekt om øget samarbejde mellem kommune og statsamt i sociale og familieretlige sager, Civilretsdirektoratet*, February 2004.

9 The general principle is that cases of conflict are dealt with by the courts and non-conflict cases by the administrative authorities, C.G. JEPPESEN DE BOER, "A comparative analysis of contact arrangements in Denmark and the Netherlands", in: K. BOELE-WOELKI, *Perspectives for the unification and harmonisation of family law in Europe*, Antwerp: Intersentia, 2003, p. 378-401 at 389.

10 The fact that the administrative authorities have exclusive powers means that their decisions are only subject to limited judicial review, i.e. a review limited to ascertaining whether the decision is against the relevant Act or against fundamental administrative principles. In the field of contact only a few cases have been tried and none have been found to be contrary to an Act or administrative principle, S. DANIELSEN, *Lov om forældremyndighed og samvær*, Copenhagen: Jurist- og Økonomforbundets Forlag, 1997, p. 325-329.

11 19.10.1996, Denmark acceded on 01.04.2003.

changes. An aspect that the commission must consider is whether persons other than parents (for example, grandparents) should have a right to contact.[12] The commission must also consider whether Denmark should accede to the Council of Europe Convention on contact concerning children.[13]

ENGLAND & WALES

No.

FINLAND

The bill for the Finnish Child Protection Act reform is expected to be presented to Parliament in the autumn of 2004. The reform will primarily concern the position of children taken into care. A bill concerning assisted reproduction and the paternity of children born as a result of assisted reproduction has been in discussion, but is not expected to be presented to Parliament before 2005 due to some crucial questions on which the Governmental parties have not been able to reach a consensus. Some adjustments are needed to the Finnish Child Custody and the Right of Access Act because of the Brussels IIa Regulation, which Parliament is currently considering (Government Bill 186/2004).

FRANCE

No new recent proposal for reform has been prepared or contemplated since the law of 4 March 2002 has been enacted.

GERMANY

There are no major proposals for reform in the legislative process. However, the consequences and the implementation of the Child Law Reform of 1997, procedural innovations included, are still under debate.[14] Also, after the reform German law primarily reflects biological and genetic parentage. This means that in general the biological parents also have parental responsibilities. However, even under the reformed legal provisions there are still many restrictions for unmarried father which are questionable under constitutional law and European human rights law. Therefore there is a constant debate on the legal position of the unmarried father and the remaining restrictions (see Q 22). Reforms in this respect could happen in the near future. On the other hand, German law has also started to recognise 'social parenthood' more and more, taking into account who the child is living with, and who is taking care of him or her, therefore there are also proposals for an improvement of the legal

12 *Kommisorium for udvalget til gennemførelse af Haagerkonventionen af 19. oktober 1996 om jurisdiktion, lovvalg, anerkendelse, fuldbyrdelse og samarbejde om forældreansvar og beskyttelses foranstaltninger i forhold til børn*, *Tidsskrift for familie- og arveret*, 2004.89.

13 ETS 192, opened for signature 15.05.2003.

14 See Deutscher Bundestag Drucksache (BT-Drucks.) 15/2399 of 28.01.2004, Antwort der Bundesregierung auf die Kleine Anfrage der Abgeordneten M. NOLL, U. GRANOLD, M. EICHHORN, weiterer Abgeordneter und der Fraktion der CDU/CSU - Drucksache 15/2340 - Kindschaftsrechtsreform; http://dip.bundestag.de/btd/15/023/1502399.pdf

position of step-parents.[15] Another issue is the consequence of joint parental responsibility and the limits of contractual agreements of the parents, which is not defined clearly. The new procedural rules, especially in the field of contact, are also under review.

GREECE

There are currently no proposals for reform in this area.

HUNGARY

There is no recent proposal to reform the rules of parental responsibilities. The revision of the Family Act is now in process and the legislature will almost certainly amend the parental responsibilities regulations during this proceeding. Nevertheless, these matters are now open and being debated.

IRELAND

No, there are not.

ITALY

Yes, regarding the separation of spouses and the custody of the child; however, these proposals are not substantial but only limited to formal modifications. Some changes contain explicit definitions of parental responsibilities but these do not add significantly to the practical concepts the legal system has so far developed (*e.g.* the proposal of the law of 9 May 1996, No. 173, on the initiative of the deputies Calzolaio and others).

Projects of reform under discussion mainly concern juvenile justice; a very serious and complex problem concerning the excessive splitting of competences among three different judiciary bodies in our legal system (the Family Proceedings Courts, the ordinary courts, the Guardianship Judge). In particular the proposals of the Law of 8 March 2002, No. 2501 and of the Law of 14 March 2002, No. 2517, after having been approved by the Council of Ministers and forwarded to the Legal Commission of the Chamber, have been unified by proposal No. 2517 with the significant title 'Urgent Measures and delegation to the Government in the field of family law and the law of the minors,' approved with amendments on 8 August 2003.[16]

---

15 See K. MUSCHELER, 'Das Recht der Stieffamilie', *FamRZ* 2004, 913, 919 *et seq.*

16 For a critical analysis of the attempts of reform see e. g. L. ROSSI CARLEO, *La riforma della giustizia minorile: spunti di discussione*, in: *Nuova giur. civ. comm.*, pamphlet No. 3, 2004, p. 149; P. VERCELLONE, 'Profili di riforma della magistratura per i minorenni. La novità sta nel tornare a tanti anni indietro', *Giur. it.*, 2002, p. 1339; M. DOGLIOTTI, 'La giustizia minorile e familiare ad una scelta', *Fam. dir.*, 2003, p. 285 and following; A. PROTO PISANI, 'Ancora sul processo e sul giudice minorile (linee di una possibile legge delega di riforma del processo minorile', *Foro it.*, 2003, V, c.219; P. G. ACQUAVIVA, 'Un passo indietro nella tutela dei minori', *Fam. dir.*, 2002, p. 327 ; G. DOSI, 'Oltre il tribunale per I minorenni verso un nuovo modello di giustizia per la famiglia e per i minori', *Fam. dir.*, 2002, p. 331; A. VACCARO, 'La riforma della giustizia minorile e familiare: due disegni di legge', *Fam. dir.*, 2002, p. 417.

LITHUANIA

There have been no recent proposals for reform in the area of parental responsibilities because the enactment of the new Lithuanian CC means the end of current reforms in this area.

THE NETHERLANDS

In December 2003 a proposal[17] was introduced in Parliament to amend Art. 1:253o Dutch CC in order to give a divorced/separated parent the right to file a unilateral request for the reestablishment of joint parental responsibilities, whereas at the moment such a request is only allowed if it is filed jointly by the two parents. Furthermore in the process of introducing the possibility of an administrative divorce, attention will be paid to the way in which parents exercise their joint parental responsibilities after divorce. A proposal[18] to this end recently introduced in Parliament suggests that the parents must draw up a parenting plan before they can obtain a divorce. The idea behind this parenting plan is that it is in the best interests of the child for both parents to continue to have extensive involvement in the child's life after divorce.

NORWAY

According to Art. 35 sec. 1 Norwegian Children Act 1981 when the mother of a child is not married, she alone is attributed parental responsibilities, if the parents do not agree otherwise. The government has suggested that as a general rule unmarried parents should share parental responsibilities if they live together.[19]

The Ministry of Children and Family Affairs will in the near future probably suggest amendments to the Norwegian Children Act 1981 to prevent a parent who might subject the child to violence from having contact with the child.

POLAND

Apart from the amendments described in the answer to Q 5, in 1995 the Senate (upper chamber of the Polish parliament) presented a bill of amendments, which was rejected in 1996 by the *Sejm* (lower chamber of the Polish parliament). The Codification Commission, operated by the Ministry of Justice, is currently drafting an amendment bill, but it has not yet been published.

---

17 Wijzigingen van enige bepalingen van Boek 1 van het Burgerlijk Wetboek met betrekking tot het het geregistreerd partnerschap, de geslachtsnaam en het verkrijgen van gezamenlijk gezag, *Kamerstukken Tweede Kamer,* 2003-2004, 29353, No. 1-6.

18 *Kamerstukken Tweede Kamer* 2003-2004, 29 676 No. 1-3. There are currently two Bills before Parliament, both proposing the introduction of a parenting plan. The first Bill was introduced by members of parliament. The second Bill has recently been introduced by the Minister of Justice. This Bill does not yet have a parliamentary docket number.

19 St. meld. nr. 29 (2002-2003) p. 7.

PORTUGAL

No.

RUSSIA

Although there is no general awareness that the current concept of parental responsibility and the law it is based upon are deficient, there is a lot of discussion regarding particular problems resulting from it (*e.g.* contact arrangements, abuse of parental rights *etc.*). These discussions, however, have so far not led to any concrete proposals for reforms.

SPAIN

As concerns the Spanish CC regime, the main reforms envisaged are in connection to the regulation of marriage and divorce. The present Government has announced a reform of divorce law which seeks to facilitate divorce. In connection to that there will be reforms to promote joint or shared custody after divorce. As will be seen when dealing with Q 41, although joint custody is not statutorily ruled out, it is very rare in practice. Children normally live with their mothers after divorce, while their fathers have rather reduced contact rights.

The introduction of shared or joint custody after divorce is one of the most contested parts of the envisaged reform. Although it is conceded that shared custody improves the possibility that children will maintain a personal relationship with both parents, it is argued that it is very difficult to implement in practice and even damaging to the child because it deprives him or her of a stable environment.

There are no proposals for reforms in Catalan law, which has a quite recent Family law (1995).

SWEDEN

In June 2002 a parliamentary committee was appointed by the Government to evaluate the effects of the1998 reform,[20] which allows entrusting joint custody to parents even when one parent is against it. The committee is also to evaluate how the local social welfare committees have succeeded in their task to approve parental agreements on custody, contact and the child's residence. The rules on enforcement of decisions and agreements on custody, residence and contact are also to be reconsidered. The committee is expected to present its report and proposals by March 2005.

The Ministry of Justice is currently considering proposals put forth in three memorandums, namely Ds 1999:57,[21] Ds 2002:13,[22] and Ds 2004:19,[23] on specific

---

20 Kommittédirektiv 2002:89 Vårdnad, boende, umgänge.

21 Gemensam vårdnad för ogifta föräldrar samt en språklig och redaktionell översyn av 6 kap. föräldrabalken ('Joint custody for unmarried parents').

issues connected to the attribution and exercise of parental responsibilities. The 1999 memorandum proposes introducing a provision automatically granting unmarried parents joint custody of their child three months after the determination of paternity, provided that neither of the parents expressly opposes joint custody. The 2002 memorandum concerns legislative measures that need to be taken in order to enable Sweden's planned ratification of the European Convention on the Exercise of Children's Rights.[24] The 2004 memorandum proposes that lesbian couples who have registered a partnership or who are cohabiting with each other should be allowed access to artificial insemination at public hospitals in Sweden. If such an insemination results in the birth of a child, both the woman giving birth and her registered partner or cohabitee should be regarded as the child's legal parents, also sharing the parental responsibilities.

SWITZERLAND

The Federal Act on Same-Sex Registered Partnerships, recently passed by the Federal Parliament but still awaiting confirmation by referendum, stipulates the following in Art. 27 § 1: 'If a person has children, their partner will support them in discharging the obligation of maintenance and in fulfilling parental responsibilities in an appropriate manner, and will represent their partner if and when circumstances require.'

Within the revision of the Swiss Code of Civil Law currently underway (preliminary draft regarding adult protection, law concerning persons and children's law) additional selected amendments are planned regarding the parental responsibilities of unmarried parents (VE Art. 298 § 1bis, new Art. 298a § 1bis). In accordance with a (further) preliminary draft of a Federal Act on the Proceedings before the Child Protection and Adult Protection Authority, the competent authority would appoint an official adviser (*Beistand* in German) for the child for the proceedings if necessary (Art. 30).

---

22 Utövandet av barnets rättigheter i familjerättsprocesser ('The exercise of the rights of the child in family law proceedings').

23 Föräldraskap vid assisterad befruktning för homosexuella ('Parenthood in connection with artificial fertilisation of homosexuals')

24 European Treaty Series, No. 160.

QUESTION 7

B. THE CONTENTS OF PARENTAL RESPONSIBILITIES

Describe what the contents of parental responsibilities are according to your national law including case law.

AUSTRIA

In the broader sense, parental responsibilities mean supplying the child's material and non-material needs, including providing support (Sec. 140 Austrian CC). In a narrower sense, parental responsibilities are the supervisory and care relationship between parent and child. This encompasses care and education of the minor child, administration of the child's property, and legal representation in all these areas (Sec. 144 Austrian CC). Care, education, and administration of property constitute the internal relationship between the holder(s) of parental responsibilities and the child; legal representation constitutes the external relationship between the holder(s) of parental responsibilities and third parties.[1]

BELGIUM

Since the legislature uses neither a uniform terminology nor treats the matter as a whole, there is confusion in both the legal literature and the case law about the exact contents of the parental responsibilities. In general, parental responsibilities include the authority over the child (Art. 373-375 Belgian CC), the administration of the child's property (Art. 376-379 Belgian CC), the right to personal contact with the child (Art. 374(4) Belgian CC) and the right of use and enjoyment of the child's property (Art. 384-387 Belgian CC). *Sensu lato* the parental authority encompasses the parental competences concerning the status of the child, including the consent to marriage (Art. 148 Belgian CC) and the agreement to adoption (Art. 348, 368(4) and 349(4), (5) and (6) Belgian CC). The parental responsibilities are not subject to one general regulation, they are treated separately.[2]

BULGARIA

Neither the Bulgarian Family Code nor legal literature provide a list of rights or duties of the parents. Some general provisions in the Bulgarian Constitution and in the Bulgarian Family Code entrust the parents with the care and upbringing of children. Some pieces of legislation, such as the Bulgarian Public Education Act and Bulgarian Law on Health, contain separate duties or rights. For example those connected with the education of children or consent for medical treatment of the child. The family law doctrine has adopted one general

---

1 M. SCHWIMANN, *Familienrecht*, 5th Edition, Vienna: LexisNexis ARD Orac, 2004, p. 70.

2 H. DE PAGE, *Traité élémentaire de droit civil belge*, T. II (Les Personnes), Vol. 2 (by J.-P. MASSON), Brussels: Bruylant, 1990, p. 960.

typology of parental rights and duties – 'rights on personal relationships' and rights/duties on property of the child.[3]

CZECH REPUBLIC

Parental responsibility is defined in the Czech Family Code (Sec. 31 § 1) as the sum total of rights and duties:

- when taking care of a minor, including, in particular, care of its health and physical, emotional, intellectual and moral development,
- when representing a minor,
- when administering its property.

When executing these rights and duties the parents are obligated to protect the child's interests, to control its conduct and supervise the child according to the degree of its development. The parents may use reasonable means of upbringing in such a manner that the child's dignity is not affected and its health and physical, emotional, intellectual and moral development is not jeopardised (Sec. 31 § 2 Czech Family Code). Parents have the decisive role in upbringing their children and they should be models for them through their lives and behaviour (Sec. 32 Czech Family Code).

DENMARK

The holder(s) of parental authority must care for the child and they have the authority to make decisions regarding the child's personal circumstances from the perspective of the child's interests and needs. The holder(s) of parental authority must treat the child respectfully and they have the duty to protect the child against physical and mental harm and other offensive treatment, Art. 2 Danish Act on Parental Authority and Contact.

The content of parental authority is not further elaborated in the Act. It has been considered, however, whether this subject should be further elaborated in the Act. This notion was dismissed, on the one hand, because it was considered difficult to list all duties and powers and to weigh the importance of these various duties and powers against each other. On the other hand, it was also considered that the legal value of such listed duties would be limited as they would be non-enforceable.[4]

The fact that the courts do not have competence to decide on conflicts, for example, concerning residence, the choice of education and medical treatment, between parents who have joint parental authority means that case law offers little guidance as to the content of parental authority.

---

3 See: L. NENOVA, *Family Law of the Republic of Bulgaria*, Sofia, 1994, p. 407.

4 Commission report No. 985/1983, p. 61.

The duty to care for the child does not necessarily entail that the holder(s) of parental authority have the final financial obligation towards the child. This financial obligation is based on legal parenthood and not on parental authority.[5]

ENGLAND & WALES

Sec. 3(1), English Children Act 1989 defines 'parental responsibility' as meaning:

> 'all the rights, duties, powers, responsibilities and authority which by law a parent of a child has in relation to the child and his property'.

This is a generic rather than a specific definition.[6] Indeed, the English Law Commission did not consider it practicable to include a list of what parental responsibility comprises, pointing out,[7] that such a list would have to change from time to time to meet differing needs and circumstances and would have to vary with the age and maturity of the child and circumstances of the case.

However, on the basis of now both pre and post-Children Act, law commentators[8] generally agree that while it may not be possible to state with certainty the precise ambit of responsibility, it comprises at least the following aspects:

- Providing a home for the child;
- Having contact with the child;
- Protecting and maintaining the child;
- Disciplining the child;
- Determining and providing for the child's education;
- Determining the child's religion;
- Consenting to the child's medical treatment;
- Choosing the child's name and agreeing to its subsequent change;
- Consenting to the child's marriage;
- Agreeing or withholding agreement to the child's adoption;
- Applying for or vetoing the issue of a child's passport;

---

5 Art. 13 Danish Act on the Support of Children, *Lov om børns forsørgelse*, Act No. 352 of 15.05.2003.

6 It was described as a 'non definition' by Lord MESTON in the debate on the Children Bill: HL Debs Vol. 502, Col 1172.

7 Law Com Report No. 172, *Guardianship and Custody* (1988), para 2.6. For a critique of this approach see *e.g.* LOWE/DOUGLAS, *Bromley's Family Law*, 1998, 9th Ed., p. 348-349 and LOWE, 'The Meaning and Allocation of Parental Responsibility – A Common Lawyer's Perspective' (1997) 11 *IJLPF* 192.

8 See *e.g.* CRETNEY/MASSON/BAILEY-HARRIS, *Principles of Family Law*, London: Sweet & Maxwell, 2002, 6th Ed., §18-010 *et seq*, HERRING, *Family Law*, Pearson, 2nd Ed., 2004, p. 356 *et seq*, LOWE/DOUGLAS, *Bromley's Family Law*, 1998, p. 350 *et seq* and WHITE/CARR/LOWE, *The Children Act in Practice*, Butterworths, 3rd Ed., 2002, §3.18 *et seq*.

- Taking the child outside the United Kingdom and consenting to the child's emigration;
- Administering the child's property;
- Representing the child in legal proceedings;
- Appointing a guardian for the child; and
- Disposing of the child's corpse.

As most of these aspects are discussed in other answers it is not proposed to say much more about them here. The one exception, however, is choosing the child's name and agreeing to its subsequent change, and particularly since English law is different to that of continental European legal systems it is proposed to discuss the English position on names.

Naming a child and most certainly changing a child's surname is an aspect of parental responsibility. By convention a child born to married parents takes his father's surname though it would seem that the father cannot insist upon this.[9] Conversely, a child whose parents are not married normally takes his mother's name but he may be registered in his father's name[10] although the unmarried father has no right to insist upon this.[11]

It is well established that once the child's name has been registered then neither married parent (a similar position obtains between unmarried parents where each has parental responsibility) may change it without the other's consent or leave of the court, save where the parent is dead.[12] Where only one person has parental responsibility then that person has a unilateral right to change the child's name.[13]

A person in whose favour a residence order (*i.e.* an order determining with whom the child is to live) has been made is *not* entitled to change the child's surname unless he has the written consent of every person who has parental responsibility for the child or the leave of the court.[14]

FINLAND

Reference has been made directly to the relevant sections of the Finnish Child Custody and the Right of Access Act, the Finnish Child Protection Act and in the Finnish Guardianship Services Act which provide the general contents and

---

9 There is nothing in the Registration of Births and Deaths Regulations 1987 SI 1987/2088 requiring the father's name to be given priority and it seems that a mother is entitled to register the child in her name: *D v B (Surname: Birth Registration)* [1979] Fam 38. See also *Re H (Child's Name: First Name)* [2002] EWCA Civ 190, [2002] 1 FLR 973.

10 For an example see, *Re P (Parental Responsibility)* [1997] 2 FLR 722.

11 See *Dawson v Wearmouth* [1999] 2 AC 308, HL.

12 *Re PC (Change of Surname)* [1997[2 FLR 730, *Re T (A Minor)(Change of Surname)* [1998] 2 FLR 620, CA and *Re W, Re A, Re B (Change of Name)* [1999] 2 LFR 930, CA.

13 *Re PC (Change of Surname)*, ibid.

14 Sec. 13(1)(a), Children Act 1989.

goals of child custody, the administration of the child's property and to the child protection.

Finnish Child Custody and the Right of Access Act

Section 1: Child custody
(1) The objects of custody are to ensure the well-being and well-balanced development of a child according to the child's individual needs and wishes, and to ensure close and affectionate human relationships for the child, particularly those between the child and its parents.
(2) A child shall be ensured good care and upbringing as well as the supervision and care appropriate to its age and stage of development. A child should be brought up in a secure and stimulating environment and should receive an education that corresponds to its wishes and talents.
(3) A child shall be brought up in the spirit of understanding, security and love. The child shall not be subdued, corporally punished or otherwise humiliated. The child's growth towards independence, responsibility and adulthood shall be encouraged, supported and assisted.

Section 4: Duties of custodians
(1) Custodians shall safeguard the child's development and well-being as laid down in section 1 of this Act. For this purpose, they are empowered to make decisions on the child's care, upbringing, residence and other matters relating to the person of the child's physical care.
(2) Before a custodian makes a decision on a matter relating to the child's care, the custodian shall, where possible, discuss the matter with the child taking into account the child's age and maturity and the nature of the matter. In making the decision the custodian shall give due consideration to the child's feelings, opinions and wishes.
(3) The custodian has the power to represent the child in matters relating to it, unless otherwise provided by the law.

Child Protection Act

Section 1: The rights of the child
A child is entitled to a secure and stimulating growing environment and to a harmonious and well-balanced development. A child has a special right to protection.

Section 2: Child Protection
The purpose of child protection is to ensure a child the rights mentioned in section 1 by providing a good general growing environment, by assisting the custodians in child upbringing and by providing family-oriented and individual child welfare.

Under all circumstances a child shall be provided such care as stipulated in the Child Custody and Right of Access Act.

Section 9 para. 1: Principles
In family-oriented and individual child protection, the first and paramount consideration shall be the best interests of the child. Parents and others caring for the child shall be assisted in the child's upbringing so as to establish a favourable growing environment for it on a permanent basis.

Section 10 para. 1: Ascertainment of the best interests of the child and hearing of a child
In ascertaining the best interests of a child, the child's wishes and views shall be taken into account, its growing environment shall be studied and due consideration shall be given to the probable effects of alternative child protection measures applicable to the child.

Section 19: Custody of a child in care
When the local social authority takes a child into care, the authority will have the power to decide on care, upbringing, supervision, caretaking in other ways and residence of the child in order to carry out the purpose of the caretaking. The authority shall, however, make every effort to cooperate with the parents or other custodians of the child.

The local social authority or director of a child care institution shall decide on contacts between the child and its parents or other persons close to the child in accordance with sections 24 and 25 of this Act.

Guardianship Services Act

Section 37 para 1: Property management
The guardian shall manage the property of the ward in a manner allowing for the property and the revenue to be used for the benefit of the ward and for the satisfaction of his or her needs. In this task, the guardian shall take conscientious care of the rights of the ward and promote his or her interests.

There is no important case law completing these sections.

FRANCE

In French law, parental responsibilities (*autorité parentale*) encompass the right and the duty of the parents to live with their child (this is part of the *garde*, a term still used by French scholars[15] but no longer appearing in legal provisions). The minor child has the obligation to live together with its parents (Art. 371-3 French CC). *Garde* means living together, cohabitation and more generally the collection of rights and duties of each parent to contact with the child. This encompasses the right of the parents to determine the child's residence. French law (Art. 108 French CC) allows the spouses to have distinct domiciles (one of them is chosen by the spouses as the family home). If the

15 See *e.g.* Ph. SIMLER, 'La notion de garde de l'enfant', *RTDCiv.* 1972, p. 685.

parents have separate domiciles, the child's domicile is the home of the parent with whom he actually lives (Art. 108-2 French CC). The parents can force the minor child to live with them (Art. 371-3 French CC); the child can only be removed from the family home as allowed by law.

Garde is also a parental duty that is based on the idea of protection. Parents who do not comply with the duty can be condemned to civil or criminal sanctions. Civil sanctions are, among others, the discharge of parental responsibilities or measures of educational support (*mesures d'assistance éducative*) that can even consist of the placement of the child with a third person or a social institution (in these cases, the child lives at the third person's home or is put in care at the social institution). Criminal sanctions (see *e.g.* Art. 227-1 French Criminal Code) for the abandonment of a minor under fifteen years of age is punishable by seven years' imprisonment and a fine of €100,000, unless the circumstances of the abandonment assured the health and the safety of the minor.

If a parent does not have parental responsibilities or if the child does not live with the parent, the parent has a right and duty of contact (*droit de visite, d'hébergement et de correspondance*). For joint parental responsibilities, see Art. 373-2 French CC, which states that a father and mother shall maintain the bond with their child regardless of the circumstances of separation. If only one parent is a holder of parental responsibilities, see Art. 373-2-1 French CC (the exercise of contact rights cannot be denied to the parent who is not holder of parental responsibilities except for *motifs graves* (very serious reasons). Both parents shall maintain personal relationships with the child.

(a) Right and duty of care (*soins*, *surveillance*)

The Law No. 2002-305 of 4 March 2002 theoretically suppressed the concept of *surveillance,* but it has maintained the parental duty to lead the family (*direction de la famille,* Art. 213 French CC) and to protect the child's health, safety and morality (Art. 371-1 French CC), which implies some supervision.[16] Since the parents shall control and guide (*diriger*) their minor child they are liable for the damages the child causes (see Art. 1384 para. 4 French CC).[17] The duty of care also requires that parents meet the elementary needs of the child (Art. 203 and 371-2 French CC): food, maintenance and upbringing.

---

16 See Th. FOSSIER, *L'autorité parentale*, 2002, ESF, 2nd Ed., p. 8.

17 Art. 1384 para. 4 French CC: '*Le père et la mère, en tant qu'ils exercent l'autorité parentale, sont solidairement responsables du dommage causé par leurs enfants mineurs vivant avec eux*' (Father and mother, as holders of parental responsibilities, are jointly liable for the damages caused by their minor children living with them). See also French Supreme Court, Civ. II, 19.02.1997, *JCP* 1997.II. 22 848: this liability has become objective because the parents can only be discharged of it if they prove a case of *force majeure* or the fault of the victim. See also French Supreme Court. Crim., 25.03.1998, *JCP* 1998. II. 10 162 annotated HUYETTE; French Supreme Court, Civ. II, 20.01.2000, *Bull. civ.* II, No. 14 (the holder of parental responsibilities remains liable for the damages caused by the child even if the child is put up for a short time at the other parent's or at a third person's home.

The parents have the right to decide upon medical treatment, surgery *etc.* concerning their child. See also the special legal provisions with regard to: interdiction of sterilisation of minor children: Art. L. 2123-1 and L. 2123-2 French Code of Public Health (*Code Santé Publique*); delivery of contraceptive products to minor children: Art. L. 2311-4 and L. 5134-1 French Code of Public Health; voluntary termination of pregnancy by a minor child : Art. L. 2212-4 and L. 2212-7 French Code of Public Health; removal of organs on a minor child see Art. L. 1231-2 and L. 1232-2 French Code of Public Health; biomedical research concerning a minor child, see Art. L. 1121-6 and L. 1122-2 French Code of Public Health. See also Q 8.

(b) Upbringing (*éducation*)

See Art. 371-1 para. 2 French CC. Parental responsibilities belong to the father and mother until the child's majority or emancipation in order to protect the child's safety, health and morality, to ensure his education and to allow his personal development. In France, children must go to school from the age of six to sixteen (Law No. 75-620 of 11 July 1975). The parents can chose which school the child will attend and when the child will stop their studies (after 16 and under some restrictions). The French term *éducation* in the French terminology encompasses the right to control the child's studies, to decide upon his professional future, religious upbringing, *etc.* Parents shall also teach the child respect for the law. Corporal punishment (*châtiments corporels*) can be a part of the parental rights.[18]

If a parent without any legitimate reason does not comply with this duty of *éducation* and the child is seriously endangered, the parent can be condemned to a maximum of two years imprisonment.[19] Art. 227-18 *et seq* French Criminal Code provides for a possible sanction of imprisonment for parents who provoke their child to use drugs unlawfully, to transport, keep, or offer drugs, or regular excessive consumption of alcoholic beverages, or habitually commit felonies or misdemeanours.

(c) Maintenance obligation (*obligation d'entretien*)

Parents shall feed and maintain their child in proportion to each parent's means and to the child's needs (Art. 371-2 French CC). The maintenance obligation of the parents towards the child goes further than the simple vital needs. It encompasses, among others, the affiliation to social security and the duty to get insured for civil liability (*assurance responsabilité civile*). The maintenance

---

18 See French Supreme Court. Crim., 21.02.1967, *Bull. crim.* No. 73 see TGI Paris, 24.05.1972, *Gaz. Pal.* 1972. 2. P. 560. Teachers do not have such a right. The parents are nevertheless not allowed to treat their child in a degrading way, for example by food deprivation, Cass. Crim., 02.12.1998, *Bull. crim.* No°327.

19 Art. 222-17 French Criminal Code: 'Failure by the legitimate, natural or adoptive father or mother, without a legitimate reason, to comply with their legal obligations to the point of seriously endangering the health, safety, morals or education of their minor child is punished by two years imprisonment and a fine of €30,000.'

obligation does not automatically cease when the child reaches majority (Art. 371-2 para. 2 French CC); it still exists when, for example, the child is studying at university and is not yet able to support himself.

The amount of the maintenance is not determined in advance by *barêmes* (tables), such as the German *Tabellen*. When a dispute arises (most frequently when the parents separate) the court decides the amount that shall be paid, so there are some discrepancies in the amounts ordered between the different French courts. All the judges, however, apply some common criteria: income of each parent, property, child's age and needs, exceptional costs of one parent or of both *etc.*

If a parent does not comply with his or her duty to maintain the child, Art. 227-3 French Criminal Code titles the offence *abandon de famille*: 'The non-execution of a judicial decision or a judicially affirmed agreement imposing upon a person an obligation to pay, in the interest of a legitimate, natural or adoptive child, of a descendant, an ascendant or spouse, a pension, a contribution, subsidies or benefits of any nature on the basis of one of the family obligations set out in Titles V, VI, VII and VIII of Book I French CC, by remaining more than two months without fulfilling that duty in its entirety is punished by two years' imprisonment and a fine of € 15,000: 'The offences referred to in the first paragraph of the present article are assimilated to abandoning the family for the purposes of 3° of Art. 373 of the Civil Code'.[20] In some cases the court can release the parents from their duty to maintain (*e.g.* if the child has assets and resources).

(d) Legal administration and right to *jouissance légale*

See Q 10 and 11.

GERMANY

Since there has been no basic legal concept of parental responsibility until now, the contents of a general concept of parental responsibility cannot be defined. While the Civil Code of 1896 originally recognised and regulated 'parental authority' (*elterliche Gewalt*), today parents have 'parental care' (custody; *elterliche Sorge*). This change in terminology reflects the modern principle that the 'best interests' of the child should control and that the increasing ability of the child to act independently has to be taken in account. Although tort law protects the absolute right of parental custody from interference by third parties (§§ 823 par. 1, 1632 par. 1 German CC), the concept appears to be shaped just as much by the parents' duty to the child.[21]

In matters of parental custody, the law distinguishes mainly between the personal and the property interests of the child. 'Personal care' (*Personensorge*)

---

20 Official Translation.

21 U. DIEDERICHSEN, in: PALANDT, *Bürgerliches Gesetzbuch*, 64th Edition, Munich: Beck, 2005, § 1626 German CC No. 1.

includes the right and the duty to care for the child and to determine his or her education and residence. 'Property care' (*Vermögenssorge*) is the care for the child's assets, § 1626 German CC. Another essential concept of German law is that in both of these kinds of care another distinction is made concerning whether the care relates to a more factual acting for the child or to legal representation.

GREECE

Parental responsibilities consist of the physical care of the child, the administration of its property and its legal representation in any matter, transaction, or litigation concerning the child or its property (Art. 1510 para. 1 and 1603 Greek CC). The physical care of the child compromises, in particular, its upbringing, supervision, education and instruction as well as the determination of its residence (Art. 1518 and 1606 Greek CC). This list is not exclusive. So, other responsibilities, such as the determination of the child's name[22], its religious upbringing and its medical treatment unquestionably also fall within the concept of the care of the child.[23]

HUNGARY

The traditional elements of parental responsibilities are: the care and education of the child, the administration of the child's property, the legal representation of the child and the right of the parents to appoint a person as guardian for their child or exclude persons from the guardianship in case of their death. The views of the child capable of judgment, given the child's age and level of maturity, are of the greatest importance, especially when considering the rights of care and education.

Besides the traditional elements of parental responsibilities, the Child Welfare Act defines some further elements, including the rights of the children and parents when children are taken into state care.

The most important right of the children among those stated in the Child Welfare Act is the child's right to be raised in his or her own family environment. This right is provided by several rules of the Child Welfare Act. One of these rules states that a child can be separated from his or her parents or other relatives only if it's in the child's interest and in situations stated in the Act. From cases and methods regulated in an act, another rule says a child cannot be separated from his or her family if the child is only endangered because of financial reasons. One more rule in the Act states that a child taken

---

22 For determining the child's surname there are specific provisions. See Art. 1505-1506 Greek CC.

23 E. KOUNOUGERI-MANOLEDAKI, *Family Law*, Vol. II, 3rd Edition, Athens-Thessaloniki: Sakkoulas, 2003, p. 288-289 [in Greek]; A. POULIADIS, in: A. GEORGIADIS and M. STATHOPOULOS (eds.), *Civil Code commentary, Vol. VIII, Family Law (Arts. 1505-1694)*, 2nd Edition, Athens: Law & Economy, P.N. SAKKOULAS, 2003, Art. 1518 Greek CC, p. 257, No. 4, p. 268-275, No. 50-64, and p. 280-291, No. 86-120.

into state care has the right to initiate the return to his or her family environment and to get support for this from his or her caretaker. The Child Welfare Act also contains regulations concerning parental rights: parents have the right to get the support needed to take care of a child in their family, and if the child has already been taken into state care, the parent has the right to bring the child back into the family, to overcome the cause of the state care, to arrange familiar circumstances and to place back the child in the family.

There is also a duty for parents to do their best to take the child back into the family. A further duty of parents whose child is in state care is to maintain contact with the child and co-operate with the persons and institutions taking care of the child, in the interest of the proper education of the child.

IRELAND

As previously stated, the central concepts governing parental responsibilities are guardianship, custody and access. By virtue of Sec. 11 Irish Guardianship of Infants Act 1964, any person, who is the guardian of a child, may apply to the court for an order on any question relating to the welfare of that child. Once its jurisdiction has been invoked, the court may make such order relating to the welfare of the child in question as it thinks proper. Typically, such an order would concern guardianship and custody of, or right of access to the child, although it is also possible to make an order requiring either the father or mother to make such maintenance payments as the court considers reasonable.

The meaning of the term 'welfare', for the purposes of the Irish Guardianship of Infants Act 1964, is quite widely defined. It includes, according to Sec. 2 thereof, the religious, moral, intellectual, physical and social welfare of the child in question. Sec. 3 of the 1964 Act makes it abundantly clear that in considering an application relating to the guardianship, custody or upbringing of a child, or to the administration of property belonging to, or held in trust for the benefit of that child, or the application of the income of the child, the court must have regard to the welfare of the child. This, the Sec. states, is 'the first and paramount consideration'. Although it is not the only consideration, it is, apparently, the most important one. In his judgment in *G. v. An Bord Uchtála,*[24] WALSH J. stated as follows:

> 'The word 'paramount' by itself is not by any means an indication of exclusivity; no doubt if the Oireachtas had intended the welfare of the child to be the sole consideration it would have said so. The use of the word 'paramount' certainly indicates that the welfare of the child is to be the superior or the most important consideration, in so far as it can be, having regard to the law or the provisions of the Constitution applicable to any given case.'

---

24 [1980] I.R. 32 at 76.

Guardianship means the rights and duties of parents in respect of the upbringing of their children. It encompasses the duty to maintain and properly care for the child and refers to the decisions that must be made during the child's lifetime which relate to the general lifestyle and development of the child. Being a guardian requires a person to partake in the important decisions in a child's life, for example, education, religion and general rearing.

Custody is the right of a parent to exercise physical care and control in respect of the upbringing of their child on a day-to-day basis, per DENHAM J. in *W.O'R. v. E.H.*.[25] The parent who does not obtain custody of a child but remains a guardian is entitled to apply for access to the child. The court will consider an application for access on the basis that the best interests of the child are of paramount importance. The right of access is, ultimately, a right of the child.

Wardship is part of the Irish High Court's inherent jurisdiction over children, whereby the Court assumes the role of a parent in relation to the child (ward).

ITALY

Our legislation has not established the organic or detailed content of parental responsibilities. Taking into account not only the normative facts but also the historical, social, and cultural evolution, the concepts the legal literature elaborates upon confirm that parental responsibility is composed of a number of rights and duties consisting of moral and material support of the minor. More specifically: the support, the moral guidance and education, the protection and care, the protection of the child's health, security and morality; in the promotion of the child's psychological and physical well-being, custody and formation, and the representation and management of his properties. The duties of the parents and the parental authority can be distinguished because it is possible that they will not coincide (*e.g.* in case of termination of the parental authority, the duty to support the child does not expire).

The content of the parental responsibilities is not positively considered in case law (what parents must do is not established) but is rather considered in the negative (it is stated what parents do not have to do). Most judicial proceedings in this field concern (the more serious) cases of omission or violation of the duties related to the parental authority, abuse of the connected rights, or maltreatments, behaviours or decisions that are prejudicial to the children. These behaviours are sanctioned by the limitation or termination of parental authority (see Q 51). Judicial decisions emerge during separation or divorce proceedings; in general, if the parents can't resolve conflicts regarding the education of their children, they mark the start of a more serious crisis affecting the spouses' personal relations and finish with their separation and divorce.

25 [1996] 2 I.R. 248.

LITHUANIA

The content of parental responsibilities (parental authority) according to Lithuanian national law, including case law, includes personal parental responsibilities as well as parental property responsibilities. In general, the content of parental responsibilities is provided for in Part 2 of Art. 3.155 Lithuanian CC. Accordingly, the substance of paternal responsibilities is defined in the following way: parents have a right and a duty to properly educate and bring up their children, care for their health and, having regard to their physical and mental state, to create favourable conditions for their full and harmonious development so that the child will be able to live independently in society. Art. 3.165 Lithuanian CC, supplementing Art. 3.155 Lithuanian CC, defines the substance of personal parental rights and duties as follows:

> Parents shall have a right and duty to bring up their children; they shall be responsible for their children's education and development, their health and spiritual and moral guidance. In performing these duties, parents' rights shall have priority over the rights of other persons;[26]
> Parents must create conditions for their children to learn during their compulsory school age;
> Parents shall decide all questions related to the education of their children by mutual agreement. In the event of the lack of agreement, the disputed matter shall be resolved by the court;
> Parents are under the duty to provide maintenance for their child as well as to provide due management for the property of the child.

THE NETHERLANDS

Dutch statutory law does not contain a concise description of the content of parental responsibilities. Art. 1:247 Dutch CC states that parental responsibility comprises the duty and the right of the parent to care for[27] and raise her or his minor child.[28] This includes the care and responsibility for the mental and physical well being of the child and fostering the development of its personality. Furthermore Art. 1:245 § 4 Dutch CC states that parental responsibilities relate to the minor, the administration of his or her estate and his or her representation in civil acts, both judicially and extra-judicially.[29] The central ideas are that parental responsibilities are attributed to parents in the best interests of their children, and parents have the right and the freedom to raise their children in accordance with their own outlook on life as long as their

---

26 Supreme Court of Lithuania, 19.11.2002, case *Prienu rajono savivaldybe v. G.Sanda, www.lat.lt*

27 *Personen- en familierecht, Tekst en commentaar*, 2004, p. 295.

28 See Supreme Court 15.4.1994, *NJ*, 1994 576.

29 *Personen- en familierecht, Tekst en commentaar* 2004, p. 295.

actions are within the framework of the law.[30] Furthermore, despite the fact that this is not explicitly mentioned in the law, parents must take into account the fact that as the child grows older it increasingly has a say in matters that concern him.[31]

NORWAY

Parental responsibilities shall be exercised on the basis of the child's interests and needs, and consist of a duty to take care of the child, as well as a right to make decisions on behalf of the child. According to Art. 30 Norwegian Children Act 1981, the child is entitled to care and consideration from those who have parental responsibilities. Those who have parental responsibilities are under an obligation to raise and maintain the child properly. They shall ensure that the child receives an education according to its abilities and aptitude, and that it not be subjected to violence or be treated in any other way that could harm or endanger its mental or physical health.

According to Art. 30 Norwegian Children Act 1981, the holders of parental responsibilities have a right and a duty to make decisions for the child in personal matters, within the limits set by Art. 31 (the child's right of co-determination) and Art. 33 (The child's right of self-determination). As the child develops and is able to form his or her own opinions, the parents shall listen to the child's opinions before making decisions for the child on personal matters. They shall pay due regard to the opinions of the child according to its age and maturity. When the child has reached the age of seven, it shall be allowed to state its opinions before decisions are made on personal matters on its behalf, including the question of which of the parents it wishes to live with, according to Art. 31 Norwegian Children Act 1981. When the child has reached the age of twelve, great importance shall be attached to the child's wishes. Parents shall steadily extend the child's right to make its own decisions until its comes of age, according to Art. 33 Norwegian Children Act 1981.

POLAND

Within the regulations of legal relations between parents and children, the provisions governing the legal institution defined as 'parental authority' are of crucial importance. This concept encompasses, in particular, the obligations and rights of the parents to exercise custody over the child and the child's property, and the right to the child's upbringing (Art. 95 § 1 Polish Family and Guardianship Code) and guidance (Art. 96 sentence 1 Polish Family and Guardianship Code). Parental authority obligates the parents to take care of the child's physical and intellectual development and to prepare the child for future work that will benefit society according to the child's abilities (Art. 96 sentence

---

30 ASSER-DE BOER, Mr. C. *Asser's Handleiding tot de beoefening van het Nederlands Burgerlijk Recht. Personen- en Familie Recht*, 2002, No. 818; S.F.M. WORTMANN/J. VAN DUIJVENDIJK-BRAND, *Compendium personen- en familierecht*, 2002, p. 176.

31 S.F.M. WORTMANN/J. VAN DUIJVENDIJK-BRAND, *Compendium personen- en familierecht*, 2002, p. 176. S.F.M. WORTMANN, *Losbladige Personen- en familierecht*, Art. 247 No. 7.

2 Polish Family and Guardianship Code). Parental authority should be exercised in accordance with the child's best interests and the common interest of the society (Art. 95 § 3 Polish Family and Guardianship Code). A child still under parental authority must obey his or her parents (Art. 95 § 2 Polish Family and Guardianship Code).

Irrespective of parental authority, there is a mutual obligation for parents and their children to assist each other (Art. 87 Polish Family and Guardianship Code). The law also lays down the child's obligations to: help meet the needs of the family if the child has income from work and lives with the parents (Art. 91 § 1 Polish Family and Guardianship Code) or help the parents in the household if the child is maintained by the parents and lives with them.

Maintenance obligations *i.e.* the obligation to provide means of subsistence and means of rearing a child, are regulated independently from the parental authority (Art. 128 - 139 Polish Family and Guardianship Code). Parents are obliged to provide subsistence for a child who is not yet able to provide for himself or herself, apart form situations where the income from the child's own property could cover the costs of the child's maintenance and rearing (Art. 133 § 1 Polish Family and Guardianship Code). Parents' right to personal contact with a child is regulated with the regulation of parental authority (Art. 113 Polish Family and Guardianship Code), but exists separately from it.

PORTUGAL

In the terms of Art. 1878 No. 1 Portuguese CC, 'it is the responsibility of the parents, in the interests of their children, to look after their health and safety, provide for them, oversee their education, legally represent them, even while still unborn, and administer their property'. Parental responsibility is made up of a collection of powers and duties, which, according to national legal literature and jurisprudence, includes: the power and duty of custody of children, the power and duty to protect the child's health, the power and duty to provide for them, the power and duty to oversee their education, the power and duty to represent them legally and the power and duty to administer their property. In addition to these functional powers listed in the article, other powers and duties may be considered as included in this one, namely: the power and duty to declare the birth of the child (Art. 97 No. 1a Portuguese Code of Civil Registry) and the power and duty to name the child (Art. 1875 and 1876 Portuguese CC and Art. 103 Portuguese Code of Civil Registry).

RUSSIA

According to Russian law parental responsibility includes the following rights and duties of the parents:

- the right and duty to care for the child (Art. 28 (2) of the Russian Constitution, Art. 63 (1) Russian Family Code);
- the right and duty to maintain personal relationships with the child, including the right and the duty to live with the child (on the part of the residential parent) and the right to maintain contact with the child

(on the part of the non-residential parent). This right includes the right of the parents to reclaim their child from any person who holds the child by any means other than the authorisation of a court order (Art. 68 (1) Russian Family Code);

- the right to determine the child's residence;
- the right to receive information relating to the child from every medical or educational institution, administrative authorities and private persons;
- the right to decide upon questions regarding the child, taking into consideration the opinion of the child, including the right:
  - to determine the religious education of the child;
  - to choose the name and the family name of the child (Art. 58 Russian Family Code), and to change the name and the family name of the child under the age of fourteen (Art. 59 Russian Family Code);
  - to decide upon medical treatment of the child;
  - to take the child abroad including immigration;
  - to change the nationality of the child;
  - to give consent to the adoption of the child;
  - to give consent to the emancipation or marriage of a minor child
- the right and duty to educate the child personally and, taking the opinion of the child into consideration, to choose the form of education and educational institution (Art. 63 Russian Family Code);
- the right and the duty to protect the rights and interests of the child (Art. 64 (1) Russian Family Code);
- the rights and duty to legally represent the child (Art. 64 (1) Russian Family Code);
- the right to administrate the child's property (Art. 60 (3) Russian Family Code, Art. 37 Russian CC);
- the duty to maintain the child (Art. 80-83 Russian Family Code). The duty of maintenance is perceived in Russia as an element of parental responsibility, however, the duty to maintain the child survives the discharge of parental responsibility (Art. 71 (2) Russian Family Code).

SPAIN

As mentioned under Q 1, parental responsibility is not defined in Spanish law. It is described in legal writing and case law as a collection of powers and duties over a child and the child's property, vested equally with the child's father and mother. It's exercise is compulsory; no reason justifies the non-exercise of parental responsibility. It must be exercised in the interests of the child, respecting the child's personality. Children have a right to be informed and listened to, according to their degree of maturity.

As to the contents, Art. 154 Spanish CC and Catalan Family Code enumerate certain specific functions. The statutory functions are personal duties, such as the duty to care for, maintain and educate children. There is also a duty to represent and administer the property of the child. See also Q 8.

SWEDEN

Swedish law distinguishes between the concepts of custody (*vårdnad,* Chapter 6 Swedish Children and Parents Code) and guardianship (*förmynderskap,* Chapters 9-15 in part Swedish Children and Parents Code).

Custody refers to the legal responsibilities that a custodian has for the child's personal circumstances. These include a duty to ensure that the child's needs for care and protection, good upbringing and education are provided. The custodian also has a responsibility to see to that the child is maintained. In personal affairs, the custodian represents the child, and it is the custodian who determines the child's residence. Normally, custody also involves the actual care of the child, meaning that the custodian lives with and looks after the child. However, it is not necessary for the child to live with the custodian. Custody does not necessarily entail an obligation to personally fulfil the responsibilities of a custodian, only to make sure that they are carried out by someone.

A person who has custody of a child is also responsible for ensuring that the child receives necessary supervision, having regard to his or her age, development and other circumstances. In order to prevent the child causing detrimental damage to any other person, the person with custody shall ensure that the child is kept under supervision or that other appropriate steps are taken, Chapter 6 Sec. 2 para. 2 Swedish Children and Parents Code. The child's parents have a joint responsibility to ensure that the child's right of contact with a parent with whom the child is not living is living is met. The custodian shall also ensure that the child's need of contact with any other person particularly close to the child is met, Chapter 6 Sec. 15 Swedish Children and Parents Code.

Guardianship refers to administration of the child's property and legal representation of the child in legal proceedings concerning the property, the Chapters 10, 11 and 13 Swedish Children and Parents Code,. Normally a child's parents are both custodians and guardians to the child. If custody is transferred from a parent or parents to one or two specially appointed custodians, they normally also become guardians to the child. The guardian is obligated to regard the child's needs when determining the appropriate capital needed for education and other expenses.[32]

SWITZERLAND

Art. 301 § 1 and 2 Swiss CC circumscribe the contents of parental responsibilities in general and methodological terms. The content of Art. 301 Swiss CC is supplemented by Art. 272 Swiss CC, which stipulates the obligation between parents and children to give support and show consideration. These general principles are to be taken into account in each case in describing the concrete contents of parental responsibilities. As explained above, Art. 301 § 3

---

[32] G. WALIN and S. VÄNGBY, *Föräldrabalken, En kommentar, Del I, 1-13 kap.,* Stockholm: Norstedts Juridik, 2002, p. 12:3.

Swiss CC deals with the parents' right to determine the child's residence (custody right). Art. 301 § 4 Swiss CC confers on the holder of parental responsibilities the power to give the child a christian name. Parental responsibilities are circumscribed in Art. 302 Swiss CC as the right and obligation to raise the child *i.e.* to provide the child with care and education. The holder or holders of parental responsibilities also basically decide on the child's religious upbringing until the child reaches his or her sixteenth birthday (Art. 303 § 1 and 3 Swiss CC). Under certain circumstances parents without parental responsibilities (*e.g.* mothers who are minors and have a child born outside of wedlock who is under guardianship) may be granted the right to make decisions concerning the child's religious upbringing.

Art. 304 and 305 Swiss CC govern the parents' legal right to represent minor children. Parents are attributed the right of representation to the extent of their parental responsibilities. However, representation without parental responsibilities[33] is also conceivable, as already shown.[34] Moreover, the right to administer the child's property forms part of parental responsibilities (Art. 318 § 1 Swiss CC).

33 See Q 2d.

34 If parental responsibilities are restricted or withdrawn as a result of a measure for the protection of the child, the authority to represent the child ceases. The authority to represent the child does not exist if it concerns matters on which representation is not feasible, including supremely personal rights.

QUESTION 8

B. THE CONTENTS OF PARENTAL RESPONSIBILITIES

What is the position taken in your national law with respect to:
(a) Care;
(b) Education;
(c) Religious upbringing;
(d) Disciplinary measures and corporal punishment;
(e) Medical treatment; and
(f) Legal representation.

AUSTRIA

(a) Care

The care of a minor child includes in particular safeguarding the child's health and physical well-being as well as direct supervision (Sec. 146(1) Austrian CC). The necessary extent of such care is based on the parents' living conditions (Sec. 146(3) Austrian CC). This means both the limits of their financial capacity and other necessities in the parental sphere, such as relocation as the result of a job change.[1]

(b) Education

Education includes the development of the child's physical, mental, psychological, and moral strengths, the fostering of its aptitudes, abilities, inclinations, and developmental capabilities, and its education in school and in an occupation (Sec. 146(2) Austrian CC). The extent of such education is based on the parents' living conditions (Sec. 146(3) Austrian CC). Therefore, it depends on their social position and financial capacity. The parents have the duty to register their children for school at the age of six.[2]
The parents' child-rearing duties also include the task of naming the child,[3] even though this is not mentioned in the statute. If, in so doing, they do not act in the best interests of the child or if they cannot agree, a court can make the necessary disposition in non-contentious proceedings under Sec. 176 Austrian CC.

(c) Religious upbringing

Parents entitled to care for and educate a child jointly determine the child's religion and can jointly change it. If they cannot agree, the court can replace the necessary consent of one of the parents. This also applies if a parent wishes to remove a child from religious instruction (Sec. 154 (2) Austrian CC), Sec. 1 and 2

---

1 J. STABENTHEINER, 'KindRÄG 2001', in: P. Rummel, *ABGB-Kommentar*, suppl. vol. 1, 3rd Edition, Vienna: Manz Verlag, 2003, § 146 Marg. No. 5.

2 *Österreichisches Schulpflichtgesetz*, Federal Law Gazette *[Bundesgesetzblatt, BGBl.]* 1985/76.

3 *Verwaltungsgerichtshof*, 20.04.1983, *EFSlg*. 43.212.

Federal Act on the Religious Education of Children *[Bundesgesetz über die religiöse Kindererziehung]*).

(d) Disciplinary measures and corporal punishment

A minor child must follow his or her parents' orders. In this, parents must pay attention to the child's age, development, and personality. Parents may not use force or inflict bodily or psychological harm (Sec. 146a Austrian CC). In enforcing their orders, parents must initially seek to influence the child's will through positive means. Only if this has failed, may they take reasonable measures to overcome the child's resistance.[4] The prohibition on the use of force forbids any treatment that is unreasonable and detrimental to the welfare of the child. It excludes not only the infliction of physical pain but also any treatment that violates human dignity, even if the child him or herself does not experience this as suffering in the individual case.[5]

(e) Medical treatment

A child who is capable of understanding the situation and making its own judgments can decide on its own whether to consent to medical treatments. If the child is over 14 years of age, it will be assumed that the child understands the situation and can form judgments (Sec. 146c(1) Austrian CC). A medical treatment that is typically accompanied by severe physical or psychological impairment may be provided only if both the child who is capable of understanding the situation and making its own judgments and the person entitled to legal representation in matters of care and upbringing consent (Sec. 146c(2) Austrian CC). Such serious treatments can include taking psychotropic drugs, a cosmetic operation, or tattooing. Having one's ears pierced for earrings is not a serious treatment. Other types of piercing are in dispute.[6]

The consent of a child who is capable of understanding the situation and making its own judgments and of the person entitled to legal representation in matters of care and upbringing are not necessary if the treatment must be provided immediately to avoid the child's death or severe impairment of its health (Sec. 146c(3) Austrian CC).

Neither a minor child nor the child's parents can consent to a procedure that would render the child permanently incapable of reproducing (Sec. 146d Austrian CC). Medically necessary interventions that may have the unavoidable effect of rendering the child permanently incapable of reproduction (*e.g.*

---

4 M. SCHWIMANN in: M. SCHWIMANN, *Praxiskommentar zum ABGB*, Vol. I, 2nd Edition, Vienna: Orac, 1997, § 146a Marg. No. 3.

5 I. HOLZHAMMER/R. HOLZHAMMER, *Ehe und Familie*, 2nd Edition, Freistadt: Plöchl Verlag, 2001, p. 97 *et seq.*; O. MALECKY, 'Zur Strafbarkeit der g´sunden Watschn', *Österreichische Juristenzeitung*, 1993, p. 625.

6 J. STABENTHEINER, 'KindRÄG 2001', in: P. RUMMEL, *ABGB-Kommentar*, suppl. vol. 1, 3rd Edition, Vienna: Manz Verlag, 2003, § 146d Marg. No. 11.; P. Haidenthaller, 'Die Einwilligung Minderjähriger in medizinische Behandlungen', *Recht der Medizin*, 2001, p. 172 *et seq.*

removal of the uterus on account of a tumour)[7] are not subject to this prohibition on sterilization.

(f) Legal representation

Legal representation of minors relates to all matters in which the parents must act vis-à-vis third parties in the interests of the child (Sec. 144 Austrian CC).[8] Generally, each parent is entitled and obliged to represent the child, acting alone. The parent's legal action is valid even if the other parent does not agree (Sec. 154(1) Austrian CC). When legal actions are inconsistent with each other, the one taken first applies. If they are taken simultaneously, both are invalid. Current examples are entering into an apprenticeship contract or including children on the passport of one parent.[9]

Important actions in which a parent represents the child (exhaustively listed in Sec. 154(2) Austrian CC) require the consent of the other parent in order to become legally effective: changing the child's name, joining or leaving a religious denomination, placement in the care of another, acquisition of citizenship or refusal to do so, premature termination of an apprenticeship or employment contract, and recognition of the paternity of a child born out of wedlock.

Acts of representation by a parent in property matters that fall outside the scope of proper business operations require not only the consent of the other parent but also the approval of the court in order to become legally effective. These include, for example, the sale and encumbrance of real estate; the acquisition, transformation, sale, or dissolution of a business; waiver of a right of inheritance, unconditional acceptance or renunciation of an inheritance; acceptance of an encumbered gift or rejection of a proffered gift; certain types of monetary investments (*e.g.* granting a loan or acquiring real estate); filing a complaint and making all procedural dispositions that relate to the matter in dispute (Sec. 154(3) Austrian CC).

BELGIUM

(a) Care

The care of the child is guaranteed by Art. 203 and Art. 372 to 375 Belgian CC, and it is based on descent. According to Art. 203 Belgian CC, both father and mother have the obligation to contribute to accomodation, support, surveillance, upbringing and education of their children according to their possibilities. When the descent from the father is not legally determined, Art.

---

7 I. HOLZHAMMER/R. HOLZHAMMER, *Ehe und Familie*, 2nd Edition, Freistadt: Plöchl Verlag, 2001, p. 70.

8 Notwithstanding existing legal representation and without restricting it, minors under the age of 14 have the legal capacity to undertake certain transactions independently (Sec. 865 Austrian CC); see Q 12(b).

9 I. HOLZHAMMER/R. HOLZHAMMER, *Ehe und Familie*, 2nd Edition, Freistadt: Plöchl Verlag, 2001, p. 72.

336 Belgian CC provides the opportunity for the child to demand an allowance for its support, upbringing and education from the man who had intercourse with the child's mother during the legal period of conception (Art. 336 to 341 Belgian CC). The stepparent can also have obligations towards the children of his or her deceased spouse, but only within the boundaries of what the surviving spouse received out of the latter's estate and out of donations between spouses (Art. 203 (2) Belgian CC). According to Art. 391 *bis* Belgian Penal Code, criminal action can be taken against a parent who has disregarded his or her obligations for at least two months.[10] The specific contents of the right to care include, on one hand, the support and education of the child, encompassing the satisfaction of its material needs *e.g.* the right to nutrition, physical care, housing, heating, clothing, medical care. In addition to the right of the parents to decide on the former, they also have the right to the every day care of the child; to decide on its movements, to determine the extent of the child's contacts with third parties, its correspondance, reading material and use of audiovisual means and entertainment. On the other hand, the right to care also encompasses the satisfaction of the child's moral and intellectual needs, e.g. education, upbringing, assistance, protection and the right of the parents to make fundamental decisions concerning the upbringing of the child. These decisions include the choice of school, as well as the choice of profession, ideology, religion and language. (Art. 374 Belgian CC). Thus, the duty to provide necessary care includes a whole set of financial and personal actions by the parents. This obligation is the largest maintenance obligation of the Belgian legal system. The child need not prove indigence in order for maintenance to be allowed. It has the right to share the same standard of living as its parents. According to Art. 203(2) Belgian CC, this obligation ends only after one's child has finished its education; if required, after its majority.[11]

In the broader sense, the right to care also includes the liability of the parents for damage to third parties caused by a wrongful act of their minor child (Art. 1384(2) Belgian CC). This liability is tied to the parental authority of the parents and their duty to care, educate and supervise the child.[12]

(b) Education

The right to care as mentioned above (See Q 8a) also encompasses the right of the parents to decide on the education of the child (Art. 203 Belgian CC). This right is a part of the authority over the person of the child and includes the right

---

10 J. GERLO, *Onderhoudsgelden*, Antwerp: Kluwer, 1994, p. 160-176; J.-P. MASSON and N. MASSAGER, *Droit des personnes, Chronique de jurisprudence 1994-1998*, Brussels: Larcier, 2000, p. 200-201.

11 H. DE PAGE, *Traité élémentaire de droit civil belge*, T. II (Les Personnes), Vol. 2 (par J.-P. MASSON), Brussels: Bruylant, 1990, p. 960; J. GERLO, *Onderhoudsgelden*, Antwerp: Kluwer, 1994, p. 105-176.

12 Cass., 05.04.1995, *Arr. Cass.*, 1995, p. 377; Cass. 23.02.1989, *Arr. Cass.* 1988-89, p. 721; R. DALCQ, 'Examen de jurisprudence (1987-1993). La responsabilité délictuelle et quasi délictuelle', *R.C.J.B.* 1995, p. 612-617; J. FAGNART, 'La responsabilité civile des parents', *J. dr. jeun.*, 1997, p. 362-371.

to decide on fundamental options such as the philosophical, religious and ideological upbringing of the child, its language, school, type of education and profession, etc. When the parents exercise the parental responsibilities together, they need to agree on the education of their children, including the choice of a school, although the presumption of agreement of Art. 373(2) Belgian CC is applicable (See Q 36). When an agreement is not possible, the disagreement must be presented to the competent authority, who will rule according to the child's interests. Even when the parental authority is exercised by only one parent, the authority may not simply deviate from a previous agreement of the parents. The court will take into account the common intent of the parents at the time they still lived together and/or exercised the parental responsibilities together. According to Art. 203 (2) Belgian CC, it is only after the child has finished its schooling that this obligation ends and, when necessary, the obligation continues after its majority. In the latter case, certain conditions will have to be met by the child in order to receive continuing support, e.g. its schooling needs to take a normal course, and the child's own revenues will be taken into account. Moreover, the respect that the child owes his parents according to Art. 371 Belgian CC will also be considered in order to decide whether it deserves further support.[13]

(c) Religious upbringing

The right to care as mentioned above (See Q 8a) encompasses the right of the parents to decide upon the religious upbringing of the child (Art. 203 Belgian CC). When the parents cannot reach an agreement on the religious education of the child, there is a tendency in the case law to prefer the less radical and stringent profession of faith, although some authors claim that the fundamental right to freedom of religion is endangered when this should lead to an evaluation of the contents of different religions by the courts. In any case, the court will have to rule according to the interests of the child in order to avoid it being torn between its parents' convictions, to avoid confusion if a different religion is imposed by one parent after the parents separate, and in order to ensure that no religion is imposed on the child that will intervene with its development and its right to its own personal convictions when it has reached the age of discernment. Generally, it is assumed that although a parent is allowed to practice his or her faith very strictly, but cannot impose this faith upon his or her minor children. If this happens, the court may limit the parent's right to contact with the child or even take away his parental responsibilities.[14]

---

13 Cass., 24.11.1983, *Rev. Not. B.*, 1984, p. 32, *Pas.* 1994, I, p. 330; Court of Appeal of Brussels, 29.05.1984, *Rev. trim. dr. fam.*, 1986, p. 444; J.-P. MASSON and N. MASSAGER, *Droit des personnes, Chronique de jurisprudence 1994-1998*, Brussels: Larcier, 2000, p. 166-174.

14 Court of Appeal of Gent, 13.02.2003, *R.W.*, 2003-2004, p. 1732; Court of Appeal of Liege, 18.12.2000, *Rev. trim. dr. fam.*, 2002, p. 118-123; P. DE POOTER and F. JUDO, 'De grenzen van de godsdienstvrijheid en het ouderlijk gezag verkend', note to Court of Appeal of Gent, 13.02.2003, *R.W.*, 2003-2004, p. 1732-1736; K. RIMANQUE, *De levensbeschouwelijke opvoeding van de minderjarige – publiekrechtelijke en privaatrechtelijke beginselen*, Brussels: Bruylant, 1980, p. 285 *et seq*. It must be noted that Art. 14 of the

(d) Disciplinary measures and corporal punishment

Since the suppression of the Art. 375-383 Belgian CC by the Belgian Law of 15 May 1912, there have been no explicit references to disciplinary measures and corporal punishment in Belgian legislation. Although these Articles were suppressed, it would be wrong to assume the right of punishment no longer exists. The Belgian Law of 1912 only suppressed the right of the father to be the sole judge of the punishment and its execution, namely imprisonment. Two components of the right to take disciplinary measures and to corporal punishment remain. First, the right to take domestic measures was not suppressed, including the right to use extremely moderate violence when it is absolutely necessary. However, when it is not used with the required moderation, physical violence towards a child may be a reason to award exclusive parental responsibilities to the other parent.[15] Also, a proposal has been made to introduce a new article in the Belgian CC that bans physical and psychological violence towards children, including violence exercised by holders of parental responsibilities.[16] Second, according to Art. 37 Belgian LJP,[17] the parents have the right to ask the Juvenile Court to take measures of custody, guard and education when the child is sued for having committed a punishable offence.[18]

(e) Medical treatment

The right to decide on fundamental options includes those options involving the medical care of the child and is included in a parent's right to authority over the child. The parents may exercise all the rights allowed to the patient according to Art. 12(1) Belgian Law of 22 August 2002 concerning the Rights of the Patients. However, from the moment that the child has the necessary maturity and has reached a reasonable age, it is involved in the decisions. According to Art. 12(2) Belgian Law of 22 August 2002, the child can even independently dispose of all its rights as a patient, once it is able to judge its interests. Some authors talk about a 'medical majority' that is submitted to the judgment of the doctor. However, euthanasia is an exception. According to Art. 3(1) Belgian Law of 28 May 2002 concerning Euthanasia, only a major or an

---

International Treaty on the Rights of the Child of 20.11.1989 provides that the Member States should honour the rights and obligations of the parents or legal guardians to lead the child in exercising its right to freedom of thought, conscience and religion in a way that is reconcilable with the child's developing abilities.

15 Court of Appeal of Mons, 28.06.2000, *Rev. trim. dr. fam.*, 2002, p. 94-97.

16 Proposition de loi insérant un Article 371 *bis* dans le Code civil, *Doc. Parl.* Sénat, B.Z. 2003, No. 3-149/1.

17 Flemish and French-speaking Community: Art. 2 Belgian Law 02.02.1994, *M.B.* 17.09.1994.; Cass., 04.03.1997, *J. dr. jeun.*, 1997, p. 337. For the German Community, this possibility is limited to minors who have committed acts considered to be criminal offences.

18 H. De Page, *Traité élémentaire de droit civil belge*, T. II (Les Personnes), Vol. 2 (by J.-P. Masson), Brussels: Bruylant, 1990, p. 996-998; *Rép. prat. dr. belge*, compl., v° *Puissance paternelle – Autorité parentale*, No. 44.

emancipated minor can request euthanasia. Minor patients are excluded from the field of application of the law. The parents may not make the decision either.[19]

(f) Legal representation

Minors are only incompetent to exercise their rights. Their incompetence does not mean that they do not hold rights. Therefore, to permit minors to participate in legal transactions, the system of legal representation, according to the rules of parental authorities or guardianship, is applicable. This system has been fundamentally reformed by the Belgian Laws of 27 March 2001, 29 April 2001 and 13 February 2003. The right to legal representation must be situated as a part of the right to the administration of the property of the child (See Q 2d), which itself is part of the rights of the parents concerning the goods of their children (Art. 376-379 Belgian CC).[20] The parents may represent their child in all civil actions, including both the material acts of law as well as the child's representative in court as either plaintiff or defendant. A distinction must be made between three types of acts. First, there are acts over which the legal represantative normally has all power. Second, there are acts where the representative needs the specific authorisation of the Justice of the Peace before being able to represent the child. This authorisation will be given if the demand is in the interests of the child. The interests of the child are the only criteria (Art. 378 and 410 Belgian CC. See Q 12a). Third, there are acts which are prohibited. Prohibited acts have such a personal character that representation is excluded (*e.g.* to write a will) or, although not mentioned in the list of Art. 410, represent a risk of impoverishment of the child and are therefore incompatible with the mission of administration of someone's patrimony (*e.g.* to provide bail).[21]

BULGARIA

(a) Care

The main provision in the Chapter 'parent-child relationships' of the Bulgarian Family Code entrusts the parents with the obligation to care for their children: 'Parents are obliged to care for their children and to prepare them for socially useful activity' (Art. 68 § 1). A similar provision exists in the Constitution:

19 J. HERVEG, M.-N. VERHAEGEN and Y. POULLET, 'Les droits du patient face au traitement informatisé de ses données dans une finalité thérapeutique: les conditions d'une alliance entre informatique, vie privée et santé', *T. Gez.*, 2002-2003, p. 82; T. VANSWEEVELT, 'Persoonlijkheidsrechten van de minderjarige en grenzen van het ouderlijk gezag: de toestemming van de minderjarige in een medische behandeling', *R.W.* 1987-88, p. 897-912.

20 The rights of the parents concerning the goods of their children are divided in two categories: the rights concerning the administration of the property of the children (Art. 376-379 Belgian CC) and the right of use and enjoyment of the property (Art. 384-387 Belgian CC). See Q 11.

21 H. CASMAN and J.-P. MASSON, 'La nouvelle législation sur la tutelle', *Rev. trim. dr. fam.* 2002, p. 34, No. 25; S. THIELEN, 'Administration légale et tutelle: Actes soumis à autorisation', in: Y.-H. LELEU (ed.); *Les incapacités*, Liege: CUP, 2003, p. 99.

'Raising and bringing up of children until their age of majority is both a right and an obligation of their parents' (Art. 47 § 1).

The content of the concept of 'care' comprises the care for the physical upbringing of the child and his or her support as well as the care for intellectual and moral development of the child. The following components of 'care' are enlisted in the legislation and in the case law:

- Child's identity - naming the child on the birth certificate (Art. 12 Bulgarian Civil Registration Act). In disputes among parents, the Registrar takes one of the names chosen by the parents. Parents assist the child in obtaining a passport.
- Rights protection.
- Constant supervision of the child. The Bulgarian Child Protection Act stipulates a parent shall not allow a child out of the home without supervision after ten o'clock in the evening. (Art. 8 § 3).
- School attendance.
- Health care.
- Assuring a home (see Supreme Court Decision 5/1976).
- Care for the personal hygiene and clothes (see Supreme Court Decisions 5/1976, 1686/1977).
- Child support.
- Property.

(b) Education

Parents are obliged to educate the child until the child is 16 years old (Art. 53 § 2 Bulgarian Constitution). Parents are liable under administrative law if they do not ensure the child's attendance in school (Art. 47 Bulgarian Public Education Act). As legal representatives, parents choose the school and type of education (Art. 9 Bulgarian Public Education Act). After the age of 14 children may exercise this right on their own.

(c) Religious upbringing

Parents are expected to bring up the child and teach it values. The Bulgarian Law of Religious Beliefs (2002): 'parents and legal guardians have the right to bring up their children according to their own religious beliefs' (Art. 6 § 2). The Bulgarian Child Protection Act however provides for nuances in this rule based on the capacity of children to decide for themselves. According to the Art. 14 'Protection of Religious Beliefs - (1) The attitude of children below 14 years of age towards religion shall be guided by their parents or legal guardians; while those of children between 14 and 18 shall be decided by common consent between them and their parents or their guardians. (2) Where such consent can not be reached, the underage person may refer, through the bodies pursuant to this Act, to the District Court to settle the dispute.'

The protection of children involves a prohibition against 'forcible involvement in political, religious and trade union activities' (Art. 11 § 4). Religious denominations or institutions may only involve minors in their activities with the consent of their parents. Children above this age may only be involved if there is no explicit disagreement from their parents (Art. 7 § 5 Bulgarian Law of Religious Beliefs).

(d) Disciplinary measures and corporal punishment

Legislation does not explicitly ban the corporal punishment of children. The Bulgarian Child Protection Act however provides protection of the child against disciplinary measures that might be harmful and undermining its dignity. Art. 11 § 2 reads that: 'Every child has a right to protection against all methods of upbringing that undermine its dignity; against physical, psychological or other types of violence; against all forms of influence which go against its interests.' In addition, the Act stipulates that: 'A child at risk' is a child: 'b) who has become the victim of abuse, violence, exploitation or any other inhuman or degrading treatment or punishment either in or out of his or her family' (Additional provision No. 5).

(e) Medical treatment

The new Bulgarian Law on Health (in force from January 2005) stipulates for 'informed consent of the patient' for any medical operation (Art. 87). If a child above 14 is concerned, its consent, together with the consent of the parent or guardian, is necessary. If the child is below 14, only the parent provides consent. Prior to giving their consent, both the child and the parent should be duly informed by the medical doctor (Art. 88). In cases where the life of the patient is jeopardised and it is impossible to obtain the informed consent of the parent in time, medical treatment may be performed without consent (Art. 89). The child, as well as its parent, may refuse any treatment at any time with written consent except in cases where the child's life is at stake or where the medical doctor could act on his or her own to save the life (Art. 90). Medical treatment against the will of the patient is possible only if permitted by law (Art. 91).

Theoretically, if the parents are not available or refuse to give consent, the case may be brought to the court in order to terminate the parental rights. A guardian who will consent for the medical treatment should then be assigned to the child. This takes a long time and puts the child at risk. There is no case law on this matter.

(f) Legal representation

Parents are the representatives of their minor children who have not yet reached the age of 14. Children who are between 14 and 18 years old act with the consent of their parents. According to the Art. 73 Bulgarian Family Code, representation and guardian assistance: - (1) 'Each parent is entitled to solely represent his or her minor children, and to give consent only for the legal acts in the interests of his or her adolescent children.' This is applicable not only when dealing with the child's property, but to all legal actions related to the child; legal representation before the court, giving a name, consent for treatment, choice for school *etc.*

CZECH REPUBLIC

(a) Care

The concept of care has several meanings in the Czech Family Code. Firstly, it is understood in the broadest sense to be about deciding essential matters related to the child, secondly, it means upbringing, and, thirdly, it is the physical care of the child. It is considered the most important part of parental responsibility.

(b) Education

Education is not expressly regulated in the Czech Family Code and should be a matter of agreement between the parents.

(c) Religious upbringing

Religious upbringing is not regulated in the Czech Family Code. Czech Act No. 3/2002 Coll. on Freedom of Religious Belief and Legal Status of Churches and Religious Communities establishes only that it is the parents who decide about the religious upbringing of a child under 15 years of age. From the contents of the provision of the Czech Family Code regulating exercise of rights and duties following from parental responsibility, it is possible to deduce that in case of disagreement between the parents about the religious upbringing of the child, the court may decide the issue.

(d) Disciplinary measures and corporal punishment

Parents are obliged to supervise the child according to its degree of development. They have a right to take reasonable disciplinary measures, so long as the dignity of the child is not affected and its physical, emotional, intellectual and moral development is not jeopardised in any way (Sec. 31 § 2 Czech Family Code). Taking 'reasonable disciplinary measures' does not mean that parents are expressly allowed to corporally punish the child. However, the law does not include an express prohibition of corporal punishment, either.

If a parent mistreats his or her child physically or mentally to such an extent that it constitutes a crime, the Czech Family Code imposes the duty on courts to consider whether a procedure to deprive the parent of parental responsibility should be initiated (Sec. 44 § 4 Czech Family Code).

(e) Medical treatment

Medical treatment concerning the child is not regulated by the Czech Family Code, but by the Czech Act No. 20/1966 Coll. on Care of People's Health, as amended. The patient's consent is required for medical examination and treatment. Medical treatment may also be started if such consent can be presumed (Sec. 23). If parents refuse to give their consent to medical treatment of a minor child and an urgent medical examination or treatment is required to save the child's health or live, the doctor is entitled to decide about medical treatment (Sec. 23 § 3). This provision expressly concerns children that cannot judge the urgency of such a treatment due to their intellectual development.

(f) Legal representation

Legal representation is part of parental responsibility. Parents represent their child in legal actions for which the child does not have full capacity (Sec. 56 Czech Family Code). The legal capacity of the child (to act legally) is regulated in Sec. 9 Czech CC. Minors possess the capacity to perform acts in law only if the nature of such acts corresponds to the mental and moral maturity of their age. Thus the current concept of legal capacity of minors follows the principle that either a minor has legal capacity and acts independently, or, regarding the nature of legal act and the minor's age, it lacks legal capacity and one of the parents acts in the child's name.

Parents especially represent their child in legal acts concerning property matters. The legal acts concerning personal matters, representation is usually excluded because of the very nature of such an act. For example, parents cannot represent their minor unmarried mother in her agreement to consent to adoption, or their minor son in a declaration of his paternity.

The Czech Family Code does not regulate in detail the manner in which parents represent a minor child in legal acts. Generally, there is an opinion that either parent may represent the child in ordinary matters. If, in essential matters, or in matters in which representation of both parents is expressly stipulated by legislation, one of the parents does not consent there is an option of a court decision substituting his or her consent (Sec. 49 Czech Family Code).

The legal representative cannot perform all legal acts on behalf of the child, being, by operation of law, restricted in the following two cases. First, if the parent deals with the child's estate in an essential matter, the court's consent is required for such a legal act to be valid (Sec. 28 Czech CC). The court will approve such an act if it is in the interests of the minor (Sec. 179 Czech Code of Civil Procedure). Second, neither parent may represent the child if a conflict of interest between the parents and the child, or a conflict of interests between the children of these parents, may arise. In such a situation the child is represented by a court appointed custodian *ad litem*. This is usually a community authority on social and legal protection of children (a community authority).

A conflict of interest is always probable when the parents and the child are parties to proceedings. This is especially so in proceedings concerning the care of a minor child, but also in probate proceedings, the proceedings on determination or denial of paternity, etc. It is not necessary to determine a custodian for proceedings that qualify a minor to enter into marriage (Sec. 194 Czech Code of Civil Procedure) because in that case the Czech Civil Procedure Code grants the minor full capacity to sue and be sued.

DENMARK

(a) Care

The holder(s) of parental authority must care for the child. This is directly mentioned in the provision on the content of parental authority, Art. 2. According to the *travaux préparatoires* and legal doctrine caring for the child entails feeding and clothing that child, providing him/her with a home, caring for the child in the case of illness and protecting the child against physical and mental harm.[22]

(b) Education

Although education is not directly mentioned in the Danish Act on Parental Authority and Contact, it is generally considered that providing the child with a suitable education is included in the concept of care. According to the Danish Constitution, *Grundloven*, all children have the right to receive free education in a state school. The holder(s) of parental authority is/are obliged to provide education for their children, but are not obliged to send them to school. The obligation can also be fulfilled through teaching the children at home.[23] As such it is not an obligation to attend school but an obligation to learn. The obligation commences in the year that the child becomes 7 years of age and ends when the child has received education for nine years.[24]

(c) Religious upbringing

The holder(s) of parental authority can decide on the child's religion. The holder(s) can decide to baptize the child, to allow him/her to join a particular church/religion or to withdraw the child from a particular church/religion, as the case may be. According to the regulation on the establishment or cession of membership of the Danish State Church a child of 15 must consent to such a move.[25]

(d) Disciplinary measures and corporal punishment

The child has the right to care and safety. It must be treated respectfully and must not be subjected to physical punishment or other demeaning treatment, Art. 2(2) Danish Act on Parental Authority and Contact. This provision was introduced in 1997 and was intended to clearly abolish the unregulated right to smack children, *revselsesretten*. The right to smack meant that parents subject to certain limits could punish their children without risking a conviction for violence. The change to the Act means that violence against children will be punished in the same way as violence against other persons. It also serves to remind parents that physical violence is an unacceptable tool in bringing up children. The same applies to other demeaning treatment such as emotional exclusion or deprivation of liberty for longer periods of time.[26]

---

22 Commission report No. 985/1983, p. 60, I. LUND-ANDERSEN, N. MUNCK and I. NØRGAARD, *Familieret*, Copenhagen: Jurist- og Økonomforbundets Forlag, 2003, p. 9 and L. NIELSEN, J.VORSTRUP RASMUSSEN and F. TAKSØE-JENSEN, *Familieretten*, Copenhagen: Gad Jura, 2001, p. 438.

23 Art. 76 Act No. 169, 05.06.1953 and Art. 35 Danish Act on State Schools, *Lov om Folkeskolen*, Act No. 870, 21.10.2003.

24 Art. 34(1) Danish Act on State Schools.

25 Act No. 57, 24.01.1992, Art. 8.

26 I. LUND-ANDERSEN, N. MUNCK and I. NØRGAARD, *Familieret*, Copenhagen: Jurist- og Økonomforbundets Forlag, 2003, p. 101.

(e) Medical treatment

The holder(s) of parental authority is/are entitled to take decisions concerning the medical treatment of the child. There are no obligatory medical programmes such as, for example, a compulsory vaccination programme. When the child reaches the age of 15 he/she practically has a free choice regarding medical treatment. He/she can decide whether or not to receive treatment.[27] A child of 15 can, for example, go on a hunger strike which must not be interrupted, refuse to have a blood transfusion and refuse treatment when the treatment cannot cure the illness but only prolong his/her life.[28] The holder(s) of parental authority must also receive relevant information concerning the medical treatment and be informed of the child's position on the matter. If a child of 15 is considered not to understand the consequences of his/her decision, consent to the treatment may be given by the holder(s) of parental authority. Children may be given advice on contraception without the consent of the holder(s) of parental authority having been given. A child under the age of 18 needs the consent of the holder(s) of parental authority to obtain an abortion. If such consent cannot be obtained, it is possible to obtain permission from the local authorities instead.

(f) Legal representation

In matters concerning the child which are of a personal nature the holder(s) of parental authority is/are the legal representative(s), Art. 2 Danish Act on Parental Authority and Contact. In matters concerning financial and legal issues, the guardian(s), who are most likely also the holder(s) of parental authority is/are the legal representative(s).[29]

ENGLAND & WALES

(a) Care

As stated in answer to Q 2e those with parental responsibility have a prima facie responsibility to provide a home for the child and to determine where the child should live. In other words such persons will normally have both the right and the responsibility to care for the child. Where responsibility is jointly held, as it will automatically be the case as between married parents (see Q 15) and will commonly be the case between unmarried parents (see Q 20), then in the absence of any court order or agreement this right/responsibility to care for the child will be jointly held. In the event of a dispute over this then application needs to be made to court for what is known as a residence order which is an order determining with whom the child is to live.[30] The granting of a residence order to one person only determines with whom the child is to live and in

---

27 *Lov om patienters retsstilling*, Danish Act on the Legal Position of Patients, Act No. 482, 01.07.1998, Art. 8(1).

28 I. LUND-ANDERSEN, N. MUNCK and I. NØRGAARD, *Familieret*, Copenhagen: Jurist- og Økonomforbundets Forlag, 2003, p. 102.

29 Danish Act on Guardianship, Art. 1(2) and (3).

30 Sec. 8(1), English Children Act 1989.

particular does not deprive the other person of parental responsibility. It does, however, limit the other person's ability to exercise their parental responsibility for not only will the child not live with them but neither are they entitled to interfere with the day to day decisions associated with the child's upbringing, at any rate while the child is living with the residence holder.[31]

(b) Education

As stated in answer to Q 2c providing for a child's education is an incident of parental responsibility. One consequence of this is that there is a duty to ensure that the child receives 'efficient full-time education'.[32] This duty can be discharged by ensuring that children attend independent rather than state schools or even by educating them at home, provided in this latter instance the local education authority is satisfied that the child is receiving efficient and full-time education suitable to his age etc.

Disputes between individuals (usually divorcing parents) about appropriate schooling can be resolved by an appropriate court order, namely, either a specific issue order (under when the court will direct the appropriate school) or a prohibited steps order (under which a party will be prohibited from continuing the child's education at a particular school).[33]

A child's schooling is regarded as belonging to a small group of important decisions that ought not to be carried out by one holder of parental responsibility without the agreement of other holders.[34]

(c) Religious upbringing

A person with parental responsibility has a right to determine the child's religious education, though there is no duty to give a child a religious upbringing. As WALL J said in *Re J (Specific Issue Orders: Muslim Upbringing and Circumcision)*:[35] 'Parental responsibility ... clearly includes the right to bring up children in a particular religious faith, or in none'. Based on the common law,[36] this right to determine the child's religious education is protected to the extent that a local authority cannot cause a child in their care 'to be brought up in any religious persuasion other than that in which he would have been brought up if the order had not been made.[37] Adoption agencies must also, when placing a

---

31 *Cf Re S (Parental Responsibility)* [1995] 2 FLR 648, CA and *Re A (a minor)(parental responsibility)* [1996] 1 FCR 562.

32 See Sec. 7 and 8, English Education Act 1996, discussed at Q 2(c).

33 Specific issue orders and prohibited steps orders are provided for by Sec. 8(1), English Children Act 1989.

34 See *Re G (Parental Responsibility: Education)* [1994] 2 FLR 964.

35 [1999] 2 FLR 678 at 685 – upheld by CA see [2001] 1 FLR 571.

36 *Andrews v Salt* (1873) 8 Ch App 622. The rule, see *e.g. Hawksworth v Hawksworth* (1871) LR Ch App 539, that unless there were exceptional circumstances, children had to be brought up in the religion of their father, was abolished by Sec. 1, English Guardianship of Infants Act 1925.

37 Sec. 33(6)(a), English Children Act 1989.

child for adoption have regard, so far as practicable, to any wishes of the child's parent or guardian as to the child's religious upbringing.[38] Parents with parental responsibility and those caring for the child can require a child's exclusion from religious studies lessons and school assembly.[39]

(d) Disciplinary measures and corporal punishment

Before the Children Act 2004 a person with parental responsibility could lawfully chastise and inflict reasonable corporal punishment upon the child.[40] What was reasonable was a question of fact and depended upon the age and strength of the child and the nature and degree of punishment.[41] The law will, however, be reformed in January 2005 when s 58 of the Children Act 2004 comes into force. Under that section in relation to certain specific offences (namely, wounding and causing grievous bodily harm, assault occasioning actual bodily harm and cruelty to persons under the age of 16) 'battery of a child cannot be justified on the ground that it constituted reasonable punishment'. This has been popularly translated as meaning that if hitting a child leaves a mark on the child then that cannot be reasonable punishment for these purposes.

A person with parental responsibility may lawfully chastise and inflict reasonable corporal punishment upon the child.[42] What is reasonable is a question of fact and will depend upon the age and strength of the child and the nature and degree of punishment.[43]

---

38 Sec. 7, English Adoption Act 1976. But, note under the English Adoption and Children Act 2002, there will be a more general requirement upon adoption agencies to have regard to the child's religious persuasion when placing the child for adoption, rather than specifically having to have regard to parental wishes, see Sec. 1(5).

39 Sec. 71, English School Standards Framework Act 1998.

40 See the review by Elias J in *The Queen on the Application of Williamson v Secretary of State for Education and Employment* [2001] EWHC Admin 900, [2002] 1 FLR 493 at 498, paras [19] et seq decision upheld on appeal at [2002] EWCA Civ 1820, [2003] 1 FLR 726, *R v Hopley* (1860) 2 F & F 202; *R v Woods* (1921) 85 JP 272, CYPA 1933, s 1(7).

41 Where reasonable chastisement is raised as a defence to criminal charges, a judge should direct the jury to consider the following: '(i) the nature and context of the defendant's behaviour; (ii) the duration of that behaviour; (iii) the physical and mental consequences in respect of the child; (iv) the age and personal characteristics of the child; (v) the reasons given by the defendant for administering the punishment.' *R v H (Assault of Child: Reasonable Chastisement)* [2001] EWCA Crim 1024, [2001] 2 FLR 431, CA.

42 See the review by ELIAS J, *The Queen on the Application of Williamson v Secretary of State for Education and Employment* [2001] EWHC Admin 900, [2002] 1 FLR 493 at 498, para. 19 *et seq*, decision upheld on appeal at [2002] EWCA Civ 1820, [2003] 1 FLR 726, *R v Hopley* (1860) 2 F & F 202; *R v Woods* (1921) 85 JP 272, CYPA 1933, s 1(7).

43 Where reasonable chastisement is raised as a defence to criminal charges, a judge should direct the jury to consider the following: '(i) the nature and context of the defendant's behaviour; (ii) the duration of that behaviour; (iii) the physical and mental consequences in respect of the child; (iv) the age and personal characteristics

If it goes beyond what is reasonable it is unlawful and renders the individual criminally liable for assault, or, depending on the gravity, for more serious offences. If it amounts to degrading punishment,[44] or is inflicted without parental consent it is in breach of the European Convention on Human Rights.[45] The power to discipline a child may be delegated[46] but it seems it can only be exercised by those *in loco parentis* to the child.[47] However, corporal punishment is forbidden in all schools,[48] children's homes[49] and foster placements.[50]

(e) Medical treatment

Any person over the age of 16 who has responsibility (in the sense of having de facto control) for a child under the age of 16 has a duty to obtain essential medical assistance for that child.[51]

As a general rule anyone with parental responsibility, including a local authority,[52] can give a valid consent to the child's surgical, medical or dental treatment. Indeed, unless of sufficient age and understanding to consent for him or herself, if the child is under 16 the consent of a person with parental responsibility will normally be required for each treatment.

This general power, however, is subject to a number of qualifications. First, not all those with parental responsibility are in the same position. In particular those having responsibility by virtue of an emergency protection order only have authority to take such action 'as is reasonably required to safeguard or promote the welfare of the child'.[53] Hence, while such persons can give a valid

---

of the child; (v) the reasons given by the defendant for administering the punishment.' *R v H (Assault of Child: Reasonable Chastisement)* [2001] EWCA Crim 1024, [2001] 2 FLR 431, CA.

44 *Cf Costello-Roberts v UK* [1994] ELRI – slippering a seven-year-old held not be 'degrading'.

45 See *e.g.* ECtHR, *A v United Kingdom (Human Rights: Punishment of Child)* [1988] 2 FLR 959, and ECtHR, *Campbell and Cosans v UK* (1982) 4 EHRR 293.

46 Either expressly as in *Sutton London Borough Council v Davis* [1994] 1 FLR 737, or impliedly, as in the case of schools.

47 See *e.g. R v Woods* (1921) 85 JP 272 – unlawful for an elder brother to administer corporal punishment on his sibling where both were living with their father.

48 Sec. 548, Education Act 1996, as substituted by Sec. 131, School Standards and Framework Act 1998 which removes the defence of justification which is necessary if the intentional infliction of physical harm is not to be considered unlawful, rather than prohibits corporal punishment as such.

49 Re. 17(5)(a), English Children's Homes Regulations 2001 (SI 2001/3967), which simply prohibits the use of any form of corporal punishment.

50 Reg. 25(5)(b), Sch 5, point 8, English Fostering Services Regulations 2002 (SI 2002/57) which requires foster parents in England to make a written agreement not to administer corporal punishment.

51 Sec. 1, English Children and Young Persons Act 1933.

52 *T v Kirklees Metropolitan Borough Council, ex p C* [1992] 2 FLR 117.

53 Sec. 44(5)(b), English Children Act 1989.

consent to day-to-day treatment they cannot agree to major elective surgery. In these cases, however, the applicant can seek a court direction.[54]

Secondly, although the power of consent vested in those with parental responsibility extends to most forms of surgical, medical or dental treatment including treatment of drugs or for drug abuse and, by analogy with Sec. 8(2), English Family Law Reform Act 1969, diagnostic procedures such as HIV testing and, by reason of Sec. 21(3) of that Act, (as amended), the taking of bodily samples from the child to be used in tests to determine paternity, and ritual male circumcision,[55] even parents with parental responsibility are not empowered to consent to all forms of treatment. According to Lord TEMPLEMAN in *Re B (A Minor)(Wardship: Sterilisation)*,[56] sterilisation of a girl under 18 should only be carried out with the leave of a High Court judge. In other words, even parents, with parental responsibility cannot give a valid consent. Notwithstanding that Lord TEMPLEMAN was the only Law Lord to suggest this, as Lord DONALDSON MR subsequently put it in *Re W (A Minor)(Medical Treatment)*[57] parties might be well advised to apply to the court for guidance. Whether a similar requirement extends to other forms of treatment has yet to be decided.[58] However, High Court leave is not required to perform an operation for therapeutic reasons even though a side effect (but not the main purpose) will be to sterilise the child.[59] Furthermore, it has been held that notwithstanding that a decision as to sterilisation is a matter for the judge, parents (or others with parental responsibility) nevertheless retain the responsibility for bringing the issue before the High Court.[60]

A third qualification on the power of consent of those with parental responsibility is the age of the child. Although according to *Re W (A Minor)(Medical Treatment: Court's Jurisdiction)*[61] those with parental responsibility retain their power to give a valid consent throughout the child's minority, it seems clear[62] that

---

54 Sec. 44(6)(b), English Children Act 1989.

55 *Re J (Specific Issues Order: Child's Religion Upbringing)* [2000] 1 FLR 571, CA.

56 [1988] AC 199 at 205.

57 [1993] Fam 64, CA.

58 It might conceivably cover all irreversible treatment for non-therapeutic reasons.

59 *Re E (Medical Treatment)* [1991] 2 FLR 585, per Sir BROWN P. Note that in *Re B (A Minor)(Wardship: Sterilisation)* [1988] AC 199, the Law Lords rejected the legal relevance of the notion of a non-therapeutic sterilisation.

60 *Re HG (Specific Issue Order: Sterilisation)* [1993] 1 FLR 587. See also *Practice Note* [1993] 3 All ER 222.

61 [1993] Fam 64, CA.

62 The view was most clearly expressed by Lord DONALDSON MR but seemed also to be accepted by BALCOMBE LJ, both of whom expressly rejected the contention that Lord SCARMAN should have been taken to be saying in *Gillick v West Norfolk and Wisbech Area Health Authority* [1986] AC 112, HL that parents of a 'Gillick competent' child had no right at all to consent to medical treatment of the child.

- a child aged 16 or 17[63] or who is 'Gillick competent'[64] if under the age of 16 can give a valid consent which cannot be countermanded by an adult;[65]
- although in theory a valid consent may be given by an adult with parental responsibility notwithstanding the opposition of the 'Gillick competent' or 16 or 17-year-old child, in practice no treatment should be given without prior court sanction;[66] and
- any decision by a parent can subsequently be overridden by the High Court.[67]

Disputes about a child's medical treatment can be resolved by a court order, namely, a specific issue or prohibited steps order.

(f) Legal representation

As stated in answer to Q 2d it is an aspect of parenthood and presumably, therefore, of parental responsibility to act as the legal representative of the child. It may be that as an exception to the general rule that children cannot conduct their own legal proceedings they can do so in the magistrates' courts.[68] There is also an express right for children of sufficient age and understanding to seek in their own name a Sec. 8 order under the Children Act 1989.[69]

FINLAND

(a) Care

A child's custodian is responsible for the daily care of the child (Sec. 1 Finnish Child Custody and the Right of Access Act). The responsibility for the care of the child does not prevent the custodian from transferring the daily care to another person or body. The local social authority is responsible for the child's care and protection if the child has been taken into care, and the authority is given the power to carry out this task (Sec. 19 para. 1 Finnish Child Custody and the Right of Access Act).

---

63 See Sec. 8, Family Law Reform Act 1969.

64 This was a phrase first coined in *Re R (A Minor)(Wardship: Medical Treatment)* [1992] Fam 11.

65 See Lord DONALDSON in *Re W*, above [1993] Fam at 83-84. The child's consent can, however, be overridden by the court.

66 This, at any rate, was NOLAN LJ's view in *Re W*, above [1993] Fam at 94. Lord DONALDSON MR, at 84, thought that a child's refusal was a very important consideration for parents deciding whether themselves to give consent.

67 See *e.g. Re D (A Minor)(Wardship: Sterilisation)* [1976] Fam 185 overriding parental consent to a child's sterilisation and *Re A (Children: Conjoined Twins: Surgical Separation)* [2001] Fam 147, overriding parental refusal to the surgical separation of conjoined twins.

68 See LOWE/DOUGLAS, *Bromley's Family Law*, 1998, 9th Ed., p. 363.

69 Rule 9.2A, Family Proceedings Rules 1991, added by Rule 6, Family Proceedings (Amendment) Rules 1992.

(b) Education

The custodian has the right to make decisions regarding the education of the child (Sec. 1 para. 2 Finnish Child Custody and the Right of Access Act). The right to make decisions regarding the education of the child when the child has been taken into care has not been regulated by Sec. 19 Finnish Child Protection Act. In legal literature, the local social authority is regarded as having the right to decide upon the education of the child during long-term substitute care, whereas the child's custodians would retain the power to decide upon the child's education if the care is meant to be temporary.[70]

(c) Religious upbringing

A child's religion and his or her membership of a church or other religious group have been regulated in the Finnish Religious Freedom Act, which was reformed in 2003. According to this Act, the custodians are to make decisions regarding the child's religious upbringing together. If they cannot agree, a mother with custody of the child has the sole power to decide regarding the registration of the child in a religious group within the first year after the child is born, unless the court has ordered otherwise (Sec. 3).

The Finnish Religious Freedom Act includes special provisions concerning the child's autonomy. A child aged 15 or older has the right to choose its religious affiliation if the child's custodians give their written consent. The religious affiliation of a child aged 12 or older or more cannot be changed without the child's own consent (Sec. 3). Taking the child into the care of the local social authority does not affect the custodian's right to make decisions regarding the child's religious affiliation (Sec. 19 Finnish Child Protection Act).

(d) Disciplinary measures and corporal punishment

Corporal punishment or other behaviour that causes the humiliation of the child is not allowed (Sec. 1 para. 3 Finnish Child Custody and the Right of Access Act). The same applies to substitute care, since Sec. 2 para 2 Finnish Child Protection Act refers to the Finnish Child Custody and the Right of Access Act. Corporal punishment has been forbidden and criminalized in all circumstances since 1984. In 1993 the Supreme Court of Justice penalised the cohabiting partner of a mother because of corporal punishment. According to the court decision, the partner caused pain to the child by flipping the child and pulling its hair. The child was five years old.[71]

(e) Medical treatment

A child has the right to decide upon his or her own medical treatment if the child has reached an age and a maturity which allow him or her to understand the meaning of the treatment and its consequences (Sec. 7 Finnish Patient Act 785/1992). If this is not the case, the custodian or other legal representative of

---

70 M. MIKKOLA and J. HELMINEN, *Lastensuojelu*, Karelactio Helsinki, 1994, p. 190.

71 Supreme Court of Justice, 26.11.1993, KKO 1993: 151.

the child shall make the decisions concerning the child.[72] However, the custodian or other legal representative has no power to deny necessary treatment when the life or health of a minor is in danger (Sec. 9 Finnish Patient Act). Another legal representative may be the local social authority, for instance, if the child has been taken into care. The Supreme Administrative Court decided on 10 March 2000 that a child whose parents were Jehovah's Witnesses could be taken into care in order to safeguard his or her continuing treatment for lymphoma (KHO 10.3.2000/530). The parents had denied the use of blood products in the treatment of the child.

(f) Legal representation

The custodian has the power to represent the child in matters relating to person of the child, unless otherwise provided by law (Sec. 4 Finnish Child Custody and the Right of Access Act). A custodian preserves his or her right to represent the child if the child has been taken into care (Sec. 19 Finnish Child Protection Act).

According to procedural law, a child aged 15 or older has the right to self-representation in cases relating to its person. The child and its custodian thus both have a parallel right to represent the child in these cases. This arrangement applies both to civil and criminal proceedings as well as to administrative proceedings, such as care proceedings (Chapter 12 Sec. 1 and 2 Finnish Code of Judicial Procedure; Sec. 14 para. 3 Finnish Administrative Procedure Act). In care proceedings, a child whose care is in question has exceptional procedural rights, such as the right to appeal if the child is 12 or more years old (Sec. 35 Finnish Child Protection Act).

The child has the right to independently administer assets which it has purchased with its earnings, as well as to represent itself in civil or criminal proceedings concerning these assets (Chapter 12 Sec. 1 para. 2 Finnish Code of Judicial Procedure). A special guardian can be appointed if there is a considerable conflict of the interest risk between a ward and a guardian (Sec. 11 Finnish Guardianship Act).[73] In social welfare matters, if a conflict of interest can be assumed the local social authority shall *ex officio* take the matter of the appointment of a special guardian to the court or to the guardianship authority (Sec. 10 Finnish Act Concerning the Position and Rights of the Social Welfare Client).

According to a Supreme Court of Justice decision, a guardian for a child should not be appointed in a case that concerns the annulment of the paternity of the child. According to the court, the child should be allowed to consider the consequences of such proceedings by her or himself at an age of maturity. An

---

72 See M. HELIN, *Alaikäisen oikeudet potilaana* J. Kovisto Potilaan oikeudet ja potilasasiamiestoiminta. Suomen Kuntaliitto Helsinki, 1994 p. 90–103; Salla Lötjönen: *Ihmiseen kohdistuva lääketieteellinen tutkimustoiminta*, Lakimies, 1997 p. 856–879.

73 P. VÄLIMÄKI, *Holhoustoimen pääpiirteet*, WSOY Lakitieto, Helsinki, 2003 p. 54.

appointment for this situation was not found to be in the best interests of the child (KKO 2002:13).

FRANCE

(a) Care

In France, care encompasses the *garde* and the *surveillance* (see Q 7) and is part ofparental responsibilities. See definition of *autorité parentale* in Art. 371-1 French CC (the set of rights and duties that ensure the welfare of the child; the aim of parental responsibilities is to protect the child and his security, health and morality, to ensure his education and allow his personal development). The parents are liable (Art. 1384 para. 4 French CC) for the damages caused by their minor child living with them. See also Q 7.

(b) Education

Education is also part of the parental duties. See Q 7. The parents control the minor child's relationships, the letters the child receives *etc.* They also choose the school at which the child will study and decide on the child's professional direction.

(c) Religious upbringing

The parents are free to decide upon the religious upbringing of the child. This is part of the parental responsibilities. Family court case law reflects the many disputes stemming from this right.[74]

(d) Disciplinary measures and corporal punishment

Disciplinary measures and corporal punishment (*châtiments corporels*) can be part of the parental rights,[75] but the punishment must be proportionate and may not consist of maltreatment.

(e) Medical treatment

Parents are entitled to decide on any medical treatment or surgery for their child. In case of serious danger, however, the parents' permission is not required.[76] The parents also generally must give their permission for a minor to terminate a pregnancy,[77] but there are exceptions if the minor child wishes to

---

74 See *e.g.* French Supreme Court, Civ. I, 11.06.1991, *D.* 1991. P. 521 annotated MALAURIE (dispute between the parent about the possible conversion of the child to another religion. The judge decided that the parents must wait until the child's majority); CA Rennes, 18.02.1993, *JCP* 1994. II. 22 210 annotated CHEVALIER.

75 See French Supreme Court, Crim., 21.02.1967, *Bull. crim.*, No. 73; *cf* TGI Paris, 24.05.1972, *Gaz. Pal.* 1972. 2. P. 560. Teachers do not have such a right. The parents are nevertheless not allowed to treat their child in a degrading way, for example by food deprivation, French Supreme Court, Crim., 02.12.1998, *Bull. crim.*, No. 327.

76 See TOUZELIN, 'Le refus de consentement à un traitement par les parents d'un mineur en danger de mort', *JCP*, 1974. I. 2672.

77 But the court may control whether a parent abuses their right to refuse termination of pregnancy in case of incest, CA Bordeaux, 4.12.1991, *D.* 1993. p. 129 annotated DUBAELE.

keep the pregnancy and termination secret (See Art. L-2212-7 French Code of Public Health (*Code de la Santé Publique*)).

See also the special legal provisions with regard to:

- prohibition of sterilisation of minor children : Art. L 2123-1 and L. 2123-2 French Code of Public Health;
- delivery of contraceptive products to minor children : Art. L 2311-4 and L 5134-1 French Code of Public Health; the child does not need the parental authorisation (Art. 4 Law Act of 4 December 1974);
- voluntary termination of pregnancy by a minor child : Art. L 2212-4 and L. 2212-7 French Code of Public Health; the parental authorisation is generally required but Act No. 2001-588 of 4 July 2001 states that if the minor child wants to keep the pregnancy and termination secret from the holders of parental responsibilities or the legal representative, she must be assisted in the choice of the person of majority who will accompany her.[78]
- removal of a minor child's organs, see Art. L. 1231-2 (such removal is not allowed on living minor children) and L. 1232-2 French Code of Public Health (for removal of a dead minor child's organs, both holders of parental responsibilities must give their written authorisation. If one of them cannot be consulted the removal of organs can take place if the other holder of parental responsibilities gives her or his authorisation in writing);
- biomedical research concerning a minor child (see Art. L. 1121-6 and L. 1122-2 French Code of Public Health), is allowed only in very limited cases (see L. 1121-7 French Code of Public Health).

(f) Legal representation

The parents who have parental responsibilities are also the legal representatives of the child (Art. 389 French CC). They are *administrateurs légaux* (statutory administrators) representing the minor child in all civil transactions, except where the law or usage authorises minors to act for themselves (Art. 389-3 para. 1 French CC). When parental responsibilities are jointly exercised by the two parents, they are statutory administrators. In regard to third parties, each parent is deemed to have received from the other the power to act alone in any

---

78 See Art. L 2212-7 Code Santé publique : '*Si la femme est mineure non émancipée, le consentement de l'un des titulaires de l'autorité parentale ou, le cas échéant, du représentant légal est recueilli. Ce consentement est joint à la demande qu'elle présente au médecin en dehors de la présence de toute autre personne.Si la femme mineure non émancipée désire garder le secret, le médecin doit s'efforcer, dans l'intérêt de celle-ci, d'obtenir son consentement pour que le ou les titulaires de l'autorité parentale ou, le cas échéant, le représentant légal soient consultés ou doit vérifier que cette démarche a été faite lors de l'entretien mentionné à l'article L 2214-4. Si la mineure ne veut pas effectuer cette démarche ou si le consentement n'est pas obtenu, l'interruption volontaire de grossesse ainsi que les actes médicaux et les soins qui lui sont liés peuvent être pratiqués à la demande de l'intéressée, présentée dans les conditions prévues au premier alinéa. Dans ce cas, la mineure se fait accompagner dans sa démarche par la personne majeure de son choix.*'

transaction for which a guardian would not normally need authorisation from the court. Statutory administration is outright when the two parents exercise joint parental responsibilities. The administrative powers are placed under supervision of the guardianship court if one of the parents is dead or deprived of the exercise of parental responsibilities (Art. 389-2 French CC). For more details, see Q 10 and 11.

GERMANY

(a) Care

Parental custody includes the care of the child, § 1626 para. 1 German CC. The statute does not go into details; however, it is generally accepted that this includes a general responsibility for the personal welfare of the child; this includes the child's physical, mental and spiritual welfare (health, nourishment, clothing). A distinction has to be made between factual care (*tatsächliche Personensorge*) and representation in personal affairs (*Vertretung in persönlichen Angelegenheiten*).[79]

A certain splitting of care has come from the fact that with joint parental responsibility there are several persons with care who do not necessarily live together. If the child has his or her ordinary residence with one parent, this parent can decide the 'affairs of daily life' (*Angelegenheiten des täglichen Lebens*) alone; § 1687 para. 1 sent. 2 German CC, see Q 36. Also the spouse or the registered partner of the parent with sole custody has a right to decide these daily affairs (see Q 14, 27a), *e.g.* on a one-day school excursion. Personal care includes choosing the child's first name.[80]

(b) Education

Care for the child specifically includes the right and the duty to educate the child, § 1631 para. 1 German CC. The parents shall give special consideration to the aptitude and inclination of the child with regard to matters of schooling and vocation. If there is doubt, the advice of a teacher or of another suitable person should be obtained (§ 1631a German CC). *E.g.*, parents have to decide what school to send their child to;[81] however, routine issues of school attendance are simply 'affairs of daily life' in the sense of § 1687 para. 1 sent. 2 German CC;[82] see Q 8a.

---

79 L. PESCHEL-GUTZEIT, in: STAUDINGER, *Kommentar zum Bürgerlichen Gesetzbuch*, 13th Edition, Berlin: de Gruyter, 2002, § 1626 No. 58 *et seq.*

80 J. GERNHUBER and D. COESTER-WALTJEN, in: *Lehrbuch des Familienrechts*, 4th Edition, Munich: Beck, 1994, § 54 I 6, p. 834.

81 P. HUBER, in: *Münchener Kommentar*, 4th Edition, München: Beck, 2002, § 1631 German CC No. 4.

82 H. OELKERS, 'Die Entwicklung des Sorgerechts bis Ende 2001', *FuR* 2002, 107, 109.

(c) Religious upbringing

Religious upbringing of the child is a part of personal care.[83] The parent with the right of personal care can determine the religious upbringing of the child.[84] There has to be consent between the parents if they have joint parental responsibility. Generally, the religious belief that was common to the parents when they entered into marriage is decisive. If one parent wants a change and the other parent does not agree, the Guardianship Court can decide the dispute.

(d) Disciplinary measures and corporal punishment

Disciplinary measures can be taken, but their content and application is restricted.[85] Whereas the former wording of the German CC was rather vague, stating that degrading disciplinary measures, in particular physical and mental mistreatment, were improper, now § 1631 para. 2 sent. 1 German CC states that children have a right to be educated without violence. Corporal punishment, mental injuries and other degrading measures are inpermissible (§ 1631 para. 2 sent. 2 German CC). Also, 'moderate' corporal punishment is now banned.[86]

(e) Medical treatment

Medical treatment is, as a rule, a question of parental care. The holder of parental care can consent or refuse consent to the child's medical treatment.[87] If the holder, *e.g.*, as a Jehova's Witness refuses a necessary blood transfusion this can amount to a danger for the welfare of the child. Then the family court can take necessary steps according to § 1666 German CC and may substitute the parental consent to medical treatment;[88] see Q 51.

In cases of daily routine (especially day-to-day treatment) and also in cases of emergency, other persons who are not holders of parental care can take the necessary steps; see Q 27a. This is especially the case for the spouse of the parent, i. e. the step-parent (§ 1687b para. 1 and 2 German CC)[89] and the registered partner (§ 9 para. 2 Registered Partnership Act). Neither the parents nor the child can agree to a sterilisation (§ 1631c German CC) because the consequences for a minor child cannot be assessed correctly.

---

83 L. SALGO, in: STAUDINGER, *Kommentar zum Bürgerlichen Gesetzbuch*, 13th Edition, Berlin: de Gruyter, 2002, § 1 RKEG No. 1.

84 L. SALGO, in: STAUDINGER, *Kommentar zum Bürgerlichen Gesetzbuch*, 13th Edition, Berlin: de Gruyter, 2002, § 1 RKEG No. 2.

85 H. OELKERS, ‚Die Entwicklung des Sorgerechts bis Ende 2001', *FuR* 2002, 107, 110 *et seq.*.

86 L. SALGO, in: STAUDINGER, *Kommentar zum Bürgerlichen Gesetzbuch*, 13th Edition, Berlin: de Gruyter, 2002, § 1631 German CC No. 86.

87 L. M. PESCHEL-GUTZEIT, in: STAUDINGER, *Kommentar zum Bürgerlichen Gesetzbuch*, 13th Edition, Berlin: Gruyter, 2002, § 1626 German CC No. 22.

88 See U. DIEDERICHSEN, in: PALANDT, *Bürgerliches Gesetzbuch*, 64th Edition, München: Beck, 2005, § 1666 German CC No. 16.

89 See in more detail B. VEIT, 'Kleines Sorgerecht für Stiefeltern (§ 1687 b BGB)', *FPR* 2004 , 67, 72 *et seq.*

(f) Legal representation

Legal representation means that the parent acts in the name of the child but that the child bears the consequences. In general the parents represent the child jointly. However, in some instances one of the parents may represent the child individually (§ 1629 para. 1 German CC). The parent *e.g.* has the right to sign binding contracts in the name of the child, or the child may sue or be sued in his or her own name. Because the Civil Code distinguishes between care for the person and care for the property, there can be representation in both respects. Representation is generally a consequence of custody. Custody in respect with personal or property matters encompasses representation in these matters, § 1629 para. 1 German CC. However, according to § 1687 b para. 2 German CC, the spouse of a parent with sole parental responsibilities has a 'right of representation in emergency situations' (*Notvertretungsrecht*) in the event of imminent danger. The same applies to registered partners (§ 9 Registered Partnership Act), see Q 27a.

GREECE

(a) Care

The objective of the upbringing of a child is to ensure its material needs, protect it, and to provide for its general physical and mental development.[90] According to Art. 1518 para. 2 Greek CC, parents shall encourage the child to develop its personality responsibly and with a collective conscience, abstaining from any discrimination according to the child's gender. The same is true by analogy in the case of guardianship (Art. 1606 Greek CC).

(b) Education

As regards the education and the professional training of the child, the holders of parental responsibilities should take into consideration the child's particular capabilities and aptitudes (Arts. 1518 para. 3 and 1606 Greek CC). For this purpose they must cooperate with the school authorities, and, if necessary, seek the assistance of the competent public services. They should also take into consideration the child's own opinions with due regard to its maturity (Art. 1511 para. 3 Greek CC applicable, by analogy, in the case of guardianship).

(c) Religious upbringing

In principle, the holders of parental responsibilities determine the religious upbringing of the child, which forms part of the duty of care. The child may form its own religious beliefs if it is sufficiently mature (Art. 1511 para. 3 Greek CC). However, there is no general consent as to when the child becomes sufficiently mature in this respect.[91]

---

90 A. POULIADIS, in: A. GEORGIADIS and M. STATHOPOULOS (eds.), *Civil Code commentary, Vol. VIII, Family Law (Arts. 1505-1694)*, 2nd Edition, Athens: Law & Economy, P.N. Sakkoulas, 2003, Art. 1518 Greek CC, p. 259-260, No.12.

91 It has been claimed that the child is sufficiently mature to reach such a decision at the age of 14, and in any case when the child marries. Other opinions reduce the critical age to 12 years or even to 10 years (A. POULIADIS, in: A. GEORGIADIS and M. STATHOPOULOS (eds.), *Civil Code commentary, Vol. VIII, Family Law (Arts. 1505-1694)*,

(d) Disciplinary measures and corporal punishment

The holders of parental responsibilities can only impose disciplinary measures if these are necessary from a pedagogical perspective and do not impinge on the dignity of the child (Art. 1518 para. 2 and 1606 Greek CC). Corporal punishment conflicts with both of these criteria, and is thus not justifiable.[92]

(e) Medical treatment

Medical treatment forms part of the duty of care. Hence, the holders of parental responsibilities are entitled to make the relevant decisions on behalf of the child. Nevertheless, if the child is sufficiently mature to understand the significance of a certain treatment, it can decide of its own volition.[93] If the parents deny medical intervention although this is urgent and necessary in order to avert a threat to the life of the child, Art. 1534 Greek CC provides that the public prosecutor at the district court may, upon the request of the responsible physician, or the director of the hospital where the child is being treated, or any competent health authority, grant the required permission. The same holds true by analogy when the child is subject to guardianship.

(f) Legal representation

The holders of parental responsibilities represent the child in any matter regarding his person or his property (Art. 1510 para. 1 and 1603 Greek CC). Legal transactions which the minor of a certain age is entitled to enter into (*e.g.* disposing of pocket money, Art. 135 Greek CC), or which are assigned to third persons (*e.g.* the administration of a gift which the child acquired subject to the condition that a third person will administer this gift, Art. 1521 and 1616 para. 2 Greek CC), are exempt from this provision.[94]

2nd Edition, Athens: Law & Economy, P.N. Sakkoulas, 2003, Art. 1518 Greek CC, p. 270, No. 53, fns. 70 and 71). Nonetheless, it is generally accepted that the maturity of the child does not necessarily depend on its age (see, among others, P. AGALLOPOULOU, in: A. GEORGIADIS and M. STATHOPOULOS (eds.), *Civil Code commentary, Vol. VIII, Family Law (Arts. 1505-1694)*, 2nd Edition, Athens: Law & Economy, P.N. Sakkoulas 2003, Art. 1511, Greek CC, p. 208, n. 31, with further references to court decisions; E. KOUNOUGERI-MANOLEDAKI, *Family Law*, Vol. II, 3rd Edition, Athens-Thessaloniki: Sakkoulas, 2003, p. 270-271). Thus we believe that there is no reason to deviate from an *in concreto* examination of the child's maturity.

92 A. POULIADIS, in: A. GEORGIADIS and M. STATHOPOULOS (eds.), *Civil Code commentary, Vol. VIII, Family Law (Arts. 1505-1694)*, 2nd Edition, Athens: Law & Economy, P.N. Sakkoulas, 2003, Art. 1518 Greek CC, p. 263-264, No. 26-27; E. KOUNOUGERI-MANOLEDAKI, *Family Law*, Vol. II, 3rd Edition, Athens-Thessaloniki: Sakkoulas, 2003, p. 290-291.

93 A. POULIADIS, in: A. GEORGIADIS and M. STATHOPOULOS (eds.), *Civil Code commentary, Vol. VIII, Family Law (Arts. 1505-1694)*, 2nd Edition, Athens: Law & Economy, P.N. Sakkoulas, 2003, Art. 1518 Greek CC, p. 291, No. 120, referring to Art. 1511 para. 3 Greek CC.

94 P. AGALLOPOULOU, in: A. GEORGIADIS and M. STATHOPOULOS (eds.), *Civil Code commentary, Vol. VIII, Family Law (Arts. 1505-1694)*, 2nd Edition, Athens: Law & Economy, P.N. Sakkoulas 2003, Art. 1510 Greek CC, p. 189, No. 83; K. PANTELIDOU,

HUNGARY

(a) Care

The position of the Hungarian law concerning the child's care. See Q 2a.

(b) Education

The position of the Hungarian law concerning the child's education. See Q 2c.

(c) Religious upbringing

Hungarian law, following the Hungarian Constitution, does not allow state intervention in the exercise of religious upbringing. In this matter the parents cannot apply for a judgment or decision from either the court or the public guardianship authority.

The Child Welfare Act states that children taken into state care have the right to freedom of religion and conscience, to declare and exercise it and to take part in religious education.

(d) Disciplinary measures and corporal punishment

The Family Act does not regulate disciplinary measures or corporal punishment; however, the Child Welfare Act grants children the right to human dignity, and protection against physical, mental or sexual violence. Extreme cases of corporal punishment may have criminal consequences, too.

(e) Medical treatment

Medical treatment is part of the parental duty to care and protect the child. If medical intervention is needed during the medical treatment that demands the consent of the minor's legal representative, the parent has the right to give consent as the minor's legal representative.

(f) Legal representation

Legal representation of the child includes representation of the child and the child's property. Sometimes there is no possibility of representation; in these situations, the child under parental responsibilities has the right to decide for himself or herself.

The child's age effects the legal representation of a child's property; a child under 14 is legally incapacitated, a child over 14 has restricted legal capacity. The holder of parental responsibilities, as the child's legal representative, concludes contracts for his or her legally incapable child. If the child is over 14, the parent can represent the child in the above mentioned manner or the child may conclude a contract himself or herself, but prior consent or later approval of the child's legal representative is also needed.

---

in: A. GEORGIADIS and M. STATHOPOULOS (eds.), *Civil Code commentary, Vol. VIII, Family Law (Arts. 1505-1694)*, 2nd Edition, Athens: Law & Economy, P.N. Sakkoulas, 2003, Art. 1603 Greek CC, p. 560-562, No. 6, 8, and 9 [in Greek].

Parents do not have the right to legally represent their child in financial matters concerning property of the child that the parents or legal representatives do not have the right to administer. An example of this type of property is the child's salary, if the child is over 14, that the child can dispose of without the consent or approval of his or her legal representative.

The minor's right to deliver a testament is specifically regulated. A minor over 14 who has restricted capability can freely deliver a testament without the approval of his or her legal representative. This possibility is only limited by the rule that the testament must be made by public instrument.

IRELAND

(a) Care

Sec. 11 Irish Guardianship of Infants Act 1964 permits a guardian to apply to the court for its direction on any question affecting the care of a child. Where proceedings are brought before the court which relate to the care of a child, the court is obliged under Sec. 3 Irish Guardianship of Infants Act 1964 to regard the welfare of the child as the first and paramount consideration.

(b) Education

Art. 42 Irish Constitution of 1937 provides as follows:

'1) The State acknowledges that the primary and natural educator of the child is the family and guarantees to respect the inalienable right and duty of parents to provide, according to their means, for the religious and moral, intellectual, physical and social education of their children...

In exceptional cases, where the parents for physical or moral reasons fail in their duty towards their children, the State, as guardian of the common good, by appropriate means shall endeavour to supply the place of the parents, but always with due regard for the natural and imprescriptible rights of the child.'

Clearly, this Art. provides that only in exceptional cases, where parents, for physical or moral reasons, fail in their duty towards their children, can the State as guardian of the common good endeavour to supply the place of the parents. In fact, it is true to say that Art. 42 has more to do with the family than it does with the substantive right to education. It deals with education in a wider sense than simply scholastic education. When it refers to education, it is alluding to the upbringing of the child, which it holds not only to be a right but a duty of parents. This Art. reinforces the decision making autonomy of the family. On examination, it can be seen that the intellectual structure of Art. 42 assigns a strong sense of priority to parental autonomy.

Art. 42.5 Irish Constitution is of particular importance in that it addresses the complete inability of some parents to provide for their children's education. It has been interpreted as not being confined to a failure by the parents of a child to provide education for him/her, but extends in exceptional circumstances, to failure in other duties to satisfy the personal rights of the child.

The Irish Education (Welfare) Act 2000 requires a parent to ensure that his or her child attends a recognised school on each day subject to certain exceptions. A number of limited exceptions to the parents' duty to ensure that their children go to a recognised school exist where:

- the child is registered with the National Educational Welfare Board for education provided outside the recognised system under Sec. 14;
- the child is being educated outside the State or is taking part in a programme of education, training, instruction or work experience prescribed by the Minister for Education under Sec. 14(19);
- the child is receiving a certain minimum education in accordance with Sec. 27(2); or
- another sufficient cause exists for the child's non-attendance.

(c) Religious upbringing

In determining the matter of custody, the court must have regard to the religious upbringing of the child. Generally, the courts have proved anxious not to disturb the religious and moral formation of the child in question. Thus, the courts have often refused to give custody to a parent who was in a relationship with a person of a religious persuasion different to that of the child. In this respect, the courts have an unenviable task to perform. On the one hand, they must be seen to respect the initial decision of the parents regarding the child's religious upbringing. On the other hand, it can hardly be regarded as acceptable that a person will be denied custody of a child on the basis, even in part, of their religious persuasion. Here, as in other areas, one detects a serious tension between the constitutional preference for the promotion of free practice of religion and the constitutional rule against discrimination on the basis of religious profession, status or belief.[95] A different religious inclination is not, however, an absolute bar to custody.

(d) Disciplinary measures and corporal punishment

The Irish law on chastisement by parents and corporal punishment is contained in the Irish Non-Fatal Offences Against the Person Act 1997.[96] Parental chastisement is a defence to both a criminal prosecution and a civil claim. The only defence specifically excluded by the Irish Non-Fatal Offences Against the Person Act 1997 is to be found in Sec. 24 which abolishes any rule of law giving a teacher immunity from criminal prosecution in respect of physical chastisement of a pupil.

---

95 See Art. 44.2.1° and 44.2.3° respectively.

96 No. 26 of 1997.

(e) Medical treatment

Sec. 23 Irish Non-Fatal Offences Against the Person Act 1997 provides that children over the age of 16 can give full consent to medical examination and treatment as if they were of full age. It states:

> '1. The consent of a minor who has attained the age of 16 years to any surgical, medical or dental treatment which, in the absence of consent, would constitute a trespass to his or her person, shall be as effective as it would be if he or she were of full age; and where a minor has by virtue of this section given an effective consent to any treatment it shall not be necessary to obtain any consent for it from his or her parent or guardian.
> 2. In this section, 'surgical, medical or dental treatment' includes any procedure undertaken for the purposes of diagnosis, and this section applies to any procedure (including, in particular, the administration of an anaesthetic) which is ancillary to any treatment as it applies to that treatment.
> 3. Nothing in this section shall be construed as making ineffective any consent which would have been effective if this section had not been enacted.'

The rights of the 'mature child' when in conflict with the rights of parents were examined in the case of *Gillick v. West Norfolk and Wisbech AHA*.[97] In that case a doctor was held to have discretion to prescribe contraceptives to a girl under the age of 16 without the knowledge or permission of her parents, as she had reached an age and had sufficient understanding and intelligence, which rendered her capable of fully understanding what was involved. The House of Lords, by a majority, held that parental rights yield to competent children, even those under the age of 16. Lord SCARMAN stated that it will be a question of fact in each case whether a child has sufficient understanding of what is involved to give a valid consent. Whether such a conclusion would be reached in Ireland is an open question. Arguably, the constitutional rights of parents under Art. 42 Irish Constitution might preclude such a result.

In *A. and B. v. Eastern Health Board*,[98] GEOGHEGAN J. held that the termination of pregnancy was 'medical treatment' within the meaning of the Irish Child Care Act 1991. The case concerned a child, pregnant as a result of rape, who was the subject of an interim care order. The parents objected to the termination of the pregnancy. While GEOGHEGAN J. rejected the contention that the District Judge had failed to take cognisance of the wishes of the parents, he stated:

> '[T]he Court must undoubtedly regard the welfare of the child as the first and paramount consideration but it must do so within a constitutional framework.'[99]

---

97 [1986] A.C. 112.
98 [1998] 1 I.L.R.M. 460.
99 *Ibid.* at page 475.

(f) Legal representation

All the parties involved in disputes concerning parental responsibility will generally be legally represented. Where the parties cannot afford such representation, legal aid may be available under the Irish Civil Legal Aid Act 1995.[100] However, under the 1995 Act, both a means test and a merits test are applied before legal aid can be granted.

ITALY

(a) Care

Art. 30 § 1 of the Italian Constitution and Art. 147 Italian CC impose a parental obligation to support the child. This obligation is for everything necessary to grant the child an adequate standard of living, considering the economic and social conditions of her or his family. The obligation is familial in character, the fulfilment of which both parents are entirely responsible for (Art. 1292 Italian CC), proportional to their respective financial capacities. (Art. 148 § 1 Italian CC) If the parents don't have sufficient means, other legitimate or natural ascendants are obliged to supply the parents with what is necessary to comply with their duties towards the children (Art. 148 § 1 Italian CC). If this duty is not met, the court can order part of the obligated parent's income to be paid directly to the other parent or to the person who supports the child (Art. 148 § 2 Italian CC). These cases derive almost exclusively from the separation or divorce of the spouses, and therefore also involve the parent's division and duration of familial obligations.

(b) Education

Art. 30 § 1 of the Italian Constitution and Art. 147 Italian CC impose the parental obligation to educate the children taking into account the children's capacities, natural inclinations and aspirations. The State has the responsibility to provide structures that allow parents to comply with their obligations, as well as the responsibility to ensure the parent's compliance with their duties (Art. 34 of the Italian Constitution.). Parents and the State are thus co-responsible for the education of minors. In addition, Art. 1 of the Law of 18 June 1986, No. 281 ('Capacity to choose the type of the school and of enrolment in high schools') confers on secondary high school pupils (which in general would be more than 14 years old) the right to choose whether to take part in religious education and optional classes, or in any other cultural and educational activity. The legislature did not fix a precise age, but preferred to refer to the scholastic level of the minor as the criterion for the presumption of the child's judgment capacity. Such a criterion, in a vision shared by a majority of the legal literature,[101] aims to grant greater freedoms of personal choice to the minor and

---

[100] No. 32 of 1995.

[101] See, among others, STANZIONE, *Capacità e minore età nella problematica della persona umana*, Camerino- Naples, 1975, ID, *Diritti fondamentali dei minori e potestà dei genitori*, in *Rass. Dir. Civ.*, 1980, p. 452, F. GIARDINA, headword *Minore*, in *Enc. giur. Treccani XX*, Rome, 1990, p. 1.

therefore recognise the full autonomy of minors capable of judgment, in a number of cases going beyond what is explicitly provided for by the law.

In contrast, choices are reserved to the parents of children in the lower school levels, in view of the children's presumed lack of judgmental capacity; however, considering the parental obligation to respect the children's natural inclinations and aspirations, the parents must still satisfy their children's preferences as long as they are in line with the choices society generally accepts, even when the parents do not share the preferences.

(c) Religious upbringing

Jurisprudence denies parents the coercive power to force a child to conform with their religious practise, recognising a 17 year old boy's capacity, and consequently right, to choose his own religious creed.[102] Following this case, the legislature intervened and conferred the choice of religious education on secondary high school pupils (Art. 1, Law of 18 June 1986, No. 281 'Capacity to choose the type of the school to attend and enrolment in high schools'; see also above, Q 8b Education). The legislature did not fix a precise age, but preferred to refer to the scholastic level of the minor as the criterion for the presumption of the child's judgment capacity. Such criterion, in a vision shared by the majority of legal literature,[103] aims to grant greater freedoms of personal choice to the minor and therefore to recognise the full autonomy of the minor capable of judgment, in a number of cases going beyond what the law explicitly provides. In contrast, choices are reserved to the parents of children in the lower school levels, in view of the children's presumed lack of judgmental capacity; however, considering the parental obligation to respect the children's natural inclinations and aspirations, the parents must still satisfy their children's preferences as long as they are in line with the choices society generally accepts, even when the parents do not share the preferences.

However, the choice of religious education sees more conflicts between parents who profess different religions than with conflicts between parents and child.

(d) Disciplinary Measures

Concerning disciplinary measures and corporal punishment, the Supreme Court established the following principle of law: 'the recourse to violence for the purpose of education cannot be held lawful. The reason has to be found either in the importance that the legal system has attributed to the dignity of man, and so also to the 'minor', now the subject of rights and no longer, as in the past, simply an object for adults to protect; or it has to be found in the fact

---

102 Family Proceedings Court Genoa 09.02.1959, in *Giur. cost.*, 1959, p. 1278.

103 See, among others, P. STANZIONE, *Capacità e minore età nella problematica della persona umana*, Camerino- Naples, 1975, ID, *Diritti fondamentali dei minori e potestà dei genitori*, in *Rass. Dir. Civ.*, 1980, p. 452, F. GIARDINA, headword *Minore*, in *Enc. giur. Treccani XX*, Rome, 1990, p. 1.

that the harmonious development of a personality based on values of peace, tolerance and coexistence cannot be reached by violent means.'[104]

(e) Medical Treatment

The question of medical treatment relates to two aspects of parental responsibility: those treatments that come under parental rights and duties, and those decisions that parents carry out by virtue of the powers of representation of the minor conferred on them by law.[105] It is only during the last decade that decisions have been delivered in this field. They pose two problems: First, if and how, taking the officially recognised treatments into consideration, a 'wrong' decision by the parents can be substituted, (and consequently qualified as an incorrect exercise of the inherent parental authority powers); and second, whose decision prevails if there is a conflict between the parents and the child.

With regard to the first problem between the parents and third persons, our legal system always chooses the right to life. The parent does not have the power to deny necessary treatments for the minor. If this is done, the judge, following indications given by the doctor, can issue a measure he or she considers in the best interests of the minor, pursuant to Art. 333 Italian CC; in this way the judge can make the medical treatment proposed by the doctor lawful.[106] The jurisprudential tendency is to choose the medical treatment sustained by conventional medicine, with the aim to not neglect seriously dangerous situations. Still, decisions have also been made that pay more attention to the minor's will.[107]

With regard to the second issue of familial relationship between the parents and their children, in regard to specific medical treatments Italian legal rules expressly give importance to the minor's will. With a guardianship judge's prior authorisation, a minor can have an abortion (Art. 12 Law of 22 May 1978, No. 194), use contraceptives (Art. 12 Law of 22 May 1978, No. 194) and if addicted to drugs may seek the intervention of appropriate treatments and rehabilitation (Art. 120 of the Consolidated Text on the drugs law). The outcome of an HIV test may be communicated exclusively to the minor if she or he requested the exam (Art. 5 § 4 of the Law 135/1990). Although there are few specific provisions in the Italian legal system, the general principle is to grant

---

104 Supreme Court, 16.05.1996, *Dir.fam.pers.*, 1997, p. 509, with comments by D. BONAMORE.

105 See P. VERCELLONE, *Il corpo del minorenne: i trattamenti sanitari*, in *Trattato di diritto di famiglia* directed by P. Zatti, II, *Filiazione* by G. COLLURA, L. LENTI and M. MANTOVANI, Giuffrè: Milan, 2002, p. 987; G. TURRI, 'Minorenni e 'autodeterminazione in senso debole'. Sintesi di un dibattito', *Questione giustizia*, 2000, p. 1108; A.C. MORO, *Manuale di diritto minorile*, Zanichelli: Bologna, 2000, p. 274.

106 See Family Proceeding Court of Bari 25.10.2000, *Minorigiustizia*, 2001, No. 2, p. 201.

107 Family Proceeding Court of Brescia 18.05.1999, *Nuova giur. civ. comm.*, 2000, I, p. 204; Family Proceeding Court of Appeal of Ancona 26.03.1999, *Fam. dir.*, 1999, p. 467, annotated by B. LENA; Family Proceeding Court of Venezia 07.10.1998, *Dir. fam. pers.*, 1999, p. 693.

full autonomy to a minor capable of understanding any decision of personal character (such as those relating to medical treatments) in areas adjacent to those expressly indicated.

(f) Legal representation

Art. 320 Italian CC confers to parents holding parental authority the powers and duties to represent their children and to manage their properties. The legal representation aims to remedy the minor's inability to represent himself or herself.

In addition, the child, even if incapable to act, can validly perform certain acts (e.g. a child can exercise the rights and duties deriving from an employment contract, pursuant to Art. 2 § 2 Italian CC). Representation also includes the power to act for the protection of the minor's personal rights, such as a civil action for compensation of damages if the minor's rights are violated, or for status actions not implicating conflicts of interest with the minor. Italy's legal system has developed a general principle that grants autonomy to a child for personal acts if the child has the power of judgment, or is mature enough to make decisions with necessary awareness.[108] If the child does not have the requisite maturity, the legislation for the minor's representation contemplates property management (see Q 2f.). The parental rights for these acts include representation of both their born and unborn children (Art. 462 and 784 Italian CC).

LITHUANIA

(a) Care

Part 6 of Art. 38 Lithuanian Constitution, in providing for the main direction of personal parental rights and duties, establishes the following responsibilities within the scope of care: to bring up their children to be honest individuals and loyal citizens, as well as to support them until they come of age. The main parental rights and duties as defined in Art. 3.155 Lithuanian CC include a more detailed list of parental responsibilities in the sphere of care: the duty to properly educate and bring up the children, care for their health and, having regard to their physical and mental state, to create favourable conditions for their full and harmonious development so that the child will be ready for independent life in society.

(b) Education

According to Part 2 of Art. 3.155 Lithuanian CC, parents must create conditions for their children to learn during their compulsory school age (16 years). Law

[108] Concerning the general freedom of the minor having capacity of judgment relating to the exercise of the nonproperty and, more generally, the conduct of his personal affairs, see among others, P. STANZIONE, *Capacità e minore età nella problematica della persona umana,* Camerino- Naples, 1975; ID., 'Diritti fondamentali dei minori e potestà dei genitori', *Rass. Dir. Civ.*, 1980, p. 425; F. GIARDINA, headword *Minore,* in *Enc. Giur. Treccani,* XX, Rome 1990, p. 1.

on Education of 25 June, 1991 (Art. 19-25) is a special legal act which specifies the duties parents owe to their children in creating conditions for education.

(c) Religious upbringing

According to Part 5 of Art. 26 of the Lithuanian Constitution, parents and guardians shall without restrictions ensure the religious and moral education of their children and the children under their guardianship, in conformity with their own convictions. Part 1 of Art. 26 Lithuanian Constitution provides that freedom of religion shall not be restricted: Part 2 of Art. 26 states that everyone shall have the right to freely choose any religion or faith and, either alone or in community with others, in public or private, to manifest his religion or faith in worship, observance, practice or teaching. However, Part 3 of Art. 26 of the Lithuanian Constitution establishes that no one may coerce another person or be subjected to coercion to choose or manifest any religion or faith: Part 4 of Art. 26 Lithuanian Constitution provides that freedom to manifest and spread one's religion or faith may be subject only to limitations as are prescribed by law and only when this is necessary in the interests of public safety, public order, health or morals, or for the protection of fundamental rights and freedoms of others. At the same time, the Lithuanian Constitution (Art. 27) establishes that a person's convictions, manifested religion or faith may not serve as a justification for the commission of a crime or non-compliance with the law. Art. 17 of the Law on Education provides that 'upon the wish of parents (or guardians), children may have religious instruction in school by individuals authorised by church dignitaries of the chosen denomination. Children in ward shall be instructed in the religion which is professed by their families or relatives'.

(d) Disciplinary measures and corporal punishment

When exercising their parental authority, parents may use the necessary disciplinary measures with their child. However, corporal punishment or any other violence against a child, or measures which violate the honour and dignity of a child, are prohibited by Art. 49 of the Law on the Protection of the Rights of the Child of 14 March 1996.

(e) Medical treatment

One of the main personal parental duties is parents' responsibility for the health of their children (Part 1 of Art. 3.165 Lithuanian CC). If a child is 16 years of age or younger, the parents are responsible for all decisions regarding medical treatment of the child. After becoming 16, a child may independently make decisions regarding its medical treatment, except in cases provided for by law when such decisions could be adopted only by persons who have attained 18 years of age (Art. 6.726 Lithuanian CC).

(f) Legal representation

According to Art. 3.157 Lithuanian CC, legally incapable children are represented by their parents, except where the parents have been declared legally incapable by a court judgment. Parents represent their children on the presentation of the child's birth certificate.

According to Art. 2.5 Lithuanian CC, full civil legal capacity is acquired when a person attains 18 years of age. Art. 2.9 Lithuanian CC provides for the possibility of emancipation of persons from 16 years. Minors up to 14 years of age have the right to enter into small transactions (Part 3, Art. 2.7 Lithuanian CC). The special procedure for entering into transactions for minors up to 14 years of age is established by Art. 2.8 Lithuanian CC. Thus, children themselves who have not yet attained the age of majority, if they are not emancipated or married, cannot implement their rights in full.

As has already been mentioned, according to Art. 3.157 Lithuanian CC, legally incapable children are represented by their parents, except where the parents have been declared legally incapable by a court judgment. Parents generally represent their children by entering into transactions (when children are below 14 years of age) or by giving their consent for the child to enter into such transactions (after children reach 14 years). Parents who are recognised by court judgment as legally incapable cannot be representatives under the law. In such cases, children are represented by a guardian (curator) (Part 1, Art. 3.240 Lithuanian CC). Parental representation is not needed where the law provides the minor with the right to enter into certain transactions independently (Part 3, Art. 2.7; Part 2, Art. 2.8 Lithuanian CC). The minor's parents are his representatives under the law not only in civil relationships, but also when deciding upon the child's personal questions or questions of responsibility. For example, when parents give their consent to acknowledge a minor's paternity (Part 3, Art. 3.142 Lithuanian CC), they on the one hand realise their parental authority and, on the other hand, are acting on his or her behalf to represent the interest of the minor. Representation of minor children is one of the aspects of parental authority. Parental authority is based on filiation, therefore no authorszation is needed for a parent to represent their child. Only the presentation of a document which confirms the child's filiation — the child's birth certificate — is required. To confirm their own identity, parents usually present their passport or personal identification card.

THE NETHERLANDS

(a) Care

According to Art. 1:247 Dutch CC, care is the duty and the right of parents with parental responsibilities to care for their children.

(b) Education

Though not specifically mentioned, education is part of the parents' right and duty to foster the personal development of their children, Art. 1:247 § 2 Dutch CC. However, Art. 2 Dutch Compulsory Education Act obliges holders of parental responsibilities to register the child with a school and to ensure that the child attends this school regularly between the ages of 5 and 16.[109]

---

109 Art. 3 Dutch Compulsory Education Act.

(c) Religious upbringing

Parents are free to determine the religious upbringing of their children.

(d) Disciplinary measures and corporal punishment

The Civil Code does not contain a specific regulation concerning violence in the upbringing of children. However, since the autumn of 2001 there have been discussions about whether the Civil Code should ban the corporal punishment of children. The Research and Documentation Centre of the Dutch Ministry of Justice commissioned the Netherlands Institute for Care and Welfare to compile a report of legal standards various European countries have used to eliminate all forms of violence in the upbringing of children.[110] This report contains the following recommendations. Firstly, the Dutch government should be clear in its aims, task and responsibility. Secondly, if the government wants to commit itself to the norm that all forms of violence against children are unacceptable, it should pass legislation that supports this vision. Thirdly, legislation should be supplemented by additional measures in the form of information, support for parents and professionals, and research.

The government has not yet introduced the changes recommended by the committee. Presumably the government adheres to the point of view that 'not every form of violence against children should be qualified as child abuse. This concept includes physical punishment by a parent that is out of proportion or does not serve the upbringing. However, avoiding physical punishment of children is recommended.'

(e) Medical treatment

The law makes a distinction between minors younger than twelve years old, minors between the ages of twelve and sixteen, and minors of sixteen and seventeen.[111] If a parent charged with parental responsibility refuses to consent to necessary medical treatment in order to prevent serious risk to the health of a minor who is under 12 years old, such consent may be replaced by that of the children's court judge on the application of the institution for family guardianship (Art. 1:264 Dutch CC). If a minor between the ages of 12 and 16 requests a necessary medical treatment and the parent or guardian refuses to give his or her consent, no intervention of the children's' court judge is required. If in such a case the doctor is convinced that serious harm for the patient will be avoided, he can act without the parents' consent.[112] The law assumes that children older than twelve are able to decide by themselves, because both their consent and their parents' or guardians' consent is required.[113] The question arises, however, what will happen if a child is not able

---

110 Nederlands Instituut voor Zorg en Welzijn (NIZW), K. KOIJMAN/I. TEN BERGE/A. OOSTVEEN, *Fysieke bestraffing van kinderen, een inventarisatie van wettelijke verboden in vier Europese landen*, 2003.

111 Book 7, Title 7, Section 5: *the agreement on medical treatment* Dutch CC.

112 Art. 7:450, Dutch CC.

113 Art. 7:447, Dutch CC.

to make a well-balanced decision in spite of being twelve. In this case, the institution for family guardianship may nonetheless request a decision of the children's court judge.[114] Art. 1:264 Dutch CC only refers to a parent. If parental responsibilities are exercised jointly, disputes between the parents regarding the medical treatment of a minor child may be submitted to the district court (Art. 1:253a Dutch CC). If the situation is urgent, the court obviously cannot intervene. Since 2001 Dutch law also contains provisions with regard to a minor's request for euthanasia or suicide assistance. If the patient is between 16 and 18 years of age and is capable of a reasonable evaluation of his interest, the doctor may act in accordance with the patient's request for euthanasia or suicide assistance, if the parent(s) or guardian(s) with parental responsibilities over the minor have been involved in the decision making process; their consent is not required. [115]

(f) Legal representation

See Q 2d.

NORWAY

(a) Care

According to Art. 30 Norwegian Children Act 1981, the child is entitled to care and consideration from those who have parental responsibility. Those with parental responsibilities are obliged to properly raise and maintain the child. The child must not be subjected to violence or be treated in any other way that might harm or endanger his or her mental or physical health.

(b) Education

According to Art. 32 Norwegian Children Act 1981, a child of 15 or older may make all decisions on its education. It is the duty of those who are attributed parental responsibilities to ensure that the child receives an education commensurate with its abilities and aptitudes; see Art. 30 sec. 2 Norwegian Children Act 1981.

(c) Religious upbringing

In respect to religious matters, if both parents are members of the Church of Norway, they cannot discontinue the membership of the child. According to Art. 2 Norwegian Constitution, such parents have a duty to educate their children in the Evangelical-Lutheran religion. This means that they must allow the child to attend religious classes in primary schools. This applies until the child reaches the age of 15. After that, the child decides for itself; see Art. 3 No. 5 Norwegian Act on the Church of Norway 1996.

If both parents do not belong to the Church of Norway and the child is under 15, the parents can enter the child in religious societies or discontinue its

---

114 *Personen- en familierecht, Tekst en commentaar*, 2004, p. 358

115 Act concerning assessment of termination of life at request and suicide assistance, *Staatsblad* 2001, No. 194.

membership according to Art. 6 sec. 1 Norwegian Act on Religious Societies 1969. If the child is 12 or older, it should be heard before such a step is taken. This act, in Art. 3, gives a child of 15 or older an independent right to become a member or to discontinue membership of a religious group.

(d) Disciplinary measures and corporal punishment

The general view is that physical punishment of children is prohibited. Art. 30 sec. 3 Norwegian Children Act 1981 states that a child must not be subjected to violence or be treated in any way that might harm or endanger his or her mental or physical health.

(e) Medical treatment

Medical treatment can only be given with the patient's consent, Norwegian Act on Patient Rights 1999, Art, 4 sec. 1. Parents may consent on behalf of a child younger than sixteen years of age. A child older than 16 can consent to treatment independently of its parents' wishes, Art. 4 sec. 3.

(f) Legal representation

It is the guardian who legally represents the child in both personal and economic matters. A child's guardian is normally the one who is attributed parental responsibilities, Art. 3 Norwegian Act on Guardianship 1927.

POLAND

(a) Care

Custody over the child's person and property is the key element of parental authority.

(b) Education

Ensuring the child's education is encompassed within the obligation to prepare the child for future work according to the child's abilities (Art. 96 sentence 2 Polish Family and Guardianship Code).

(c) Religious upbringing

Art. 53 sec. 3 of the Polish Constitution.

(d) Disciplinary measures and corporal punishment

There are no provisions on this matter.

(e) Medical treatment

The duty to provide the child with necessary medical care is encompassed in the obligation of care for the child's physical development (Art. 96 sentence 2 Polish Family and Guardianship Code).

(f) Legal representation

Parents are the legal representatives of children under their parental authority. If a child remains under the joint parental authority of both parents, each of them can act independently as the child's legal representative (Art. 98. § 1 Polish Family and Guardianship Code). The limitation of their representation is prescribed by Art. 98 § 2 Polish Family and Guardianship Code, which states that no parent should represent a child in legal actions involving other children remaining under their parental authority, or in legal actions between a child and the other parent or the parent's spouse (except for the cases when the legal act is gratuitous and for the child's benefit or concerns the means of child's subsistence and upbringing due from the other parent).

PORTUGAL

(a) Care

The concept of care is contained in the legal notion of parental responsibility (Art. 1878 No. 1 Portuguese CC). When the law refers to parents' duty to look after their children's safety, it is specifically referring to one of the powers and duties included in parental responsibility: the power and duty of custody. This functional power should not be understood merely in physical or material terms. The exercise of this power and duty also involves a series of acts carried out by parents with a view to satisfy the material and emotional needs of their children (i.e. feeding them, supplying them with clothing and accommodation, organising their lives, providing attention and affection) that correspond perfectly to the dimension of care. When parents do not act in this way and if their actions are damaging to the children or put their safety, health, moral training or education at risk, then they may be discharged of their parental responsibilities or have them restricted (Art. 1915 and 1918 Portuguese CC).

(b) Education

The power and duty to educate minor children is expressly mentioned in the legal notion of parental responsibility (Art. 1878 No. 1 Portuguese CC). It is therefore the responsibility of parents to promote the physical, intellectual and moral development of their children. Legal literature and jurisprudence have understood that this obligation includes not only the socialisation of their children (that is, promoting the development of their physical and intellectual faculties) but also their moral, religious, civil and political training, and the acquisition of technical and professional skills (Art. 1885 Portuguese CC). However, the level to which children are educated depends not only upon their parents' economic means (Art. 1885 No. 1 Portuguese CC) but also upon the talents and inclinations of the child (Art. 1885 No. 2 Portuguese CC).

(c) Religious upbringing

As regards religious education, the decision whether to give the child a religious education lies with both parents: they choose the religion and decide how it should be taught and practised. This continues until the child reaches sixteen years of age, when the law recognises the child's freedom of self-determination in matters of religion (Art. 1886 Portuguese CC).

(d) Disciplinary measures and corporal punishment

The Portuguese CC does not mention the "power to correct". DE OLIVEIRA claims that the 1977 Reform did not include this expression 'certainly out of deference and respect for minors'.[116] Does this therefore mean that parental orders and advice cannot be enforced against the will of the child? Legal literature seems mostly to accept that parents still have this power, even though it is not explicit. Thus, parents have the right to correct their children, not as an autonomous right, but as one that is subordinate to the powers and duties of overseeing and educating them, and one which should be exercised in a non-punitive way. Physical or psychological abuse of children is today punishable as a criminal offence in Portugal (Art. 152 Portuguese Criminal Code).

(e) Medical treatment

Parental responsibility also involves the power and duty to look after the child's health (Art. 1878 No. 1 Portuguese CC). This involves ensuring that children receive essential medical care, particularly by attending regular check-ups, taking prescribed medicines and receiving care when ill. Consequently, parents may not prevent the performance of compulsory medical procedures ordered for reasons of public health, such as vaccinations and examinations for certain diseases, nor may they omit to follow a doctor's instructions for their child in particular.

The power and duty to look after their child's health also has other implications. It involves the right and duty to make decisions regarding surgery or medical treatment that medical experts recommend for their child. The need for parental permission for surgery or medical-surgical treatment results, therefore, from the general rules of parental responsibility. This principle has its limits, however. One such limit concerns the child's autonomy, proportional to his or her age and capacity for discernment. Art. 38 No. 3 Portuguese Criminal Code establishes that effective consent shall be provided by anyone over 14 years of age who possesses the necessary discernment to assess the significance and implications of their decisions at the moment the decisions are made. An interpretation of this article concludes that the law considers an adolescent of 14 who has the capacity to discern as capable of making decisions regarding medical surgery or treatment to his or her own body. Legal literature has stated that this recognises a 'special majority' rule in matters of healthcare.[117]

(f) Legal representation

It is the parents' responsibility to represent their children's interests even before the children are born (Art. 1878 No. 1 Portuguese CC). The exercise of the power and duty of representation aims to cure the minor's incapacity to exercise rights. According to some legal literature, the power of representation covers not only the child but also the property aspects of parental responsibility. Thus, the power of representation includes the exercise of all the child's rights and the fulfilment of all his or her obligations, except those acts

[116] See G. DE OLIVEIRA, 'Protecção de menores/ Protecção familiar', in: G. DE OLIVEIRA, *Temas de Direito da Família*, Coimbra: Coimbra Editora, 1999, p. 273.

[117] See G. DE OLIVEIRA, 'O acesso dos menores aos cuidados de saúde', in: G. DE OLIVEIRA, *Temas de Direito da Medicina*, Coimbra: Coimbra Editora, 1999, p. 226.

that are purely personal, which the minor has the right to perform personally and freely, and those acts regarding property of which the administration does not belong to his or her parents (Art. 1881 No. 1 Portuguese CC).

RUSSIA

(a) Care

Parents have the right and are under the duty to care for the health, physical, psychological, spiritual and moral development of their children. (Art. 28 (2) of the Russian Constitution, Art. 63 (1) Russian Family Code).

(b) Education

The right and duty to educate their children is regarded as a core element of parental responsibility. It is mentioned by Art. 28 (2) of the Russian Constitution, and developed in Art. 63 Russian Family Code. Art. 63 (1) Russian Family Code, that because of the public-private nature of this right-duty, parents not only have the right but are also responsible for the education of their children. The same Art. also provides that the parental right to educate their children has precedence over the educational rights of any other persons. The educational rights of the parents include the right to educate the child personally and to entrust education temporarily to other persons (family member, babysitters *etc.*) or institutions (kindergarten, *etc.*).[118] While doing this the parents remain fully responsible for the education of the child.[119] Parents are also under the duty to ensure that the child receives basic general education (Art. 63 (2) Russian Family Code). Giving regard to the opinion of the child, parents have the right to choose a school and the form of pre-school education (Art. 63 (2) Russian Family Code and Art. 52 (1) Russian Law on Education[120]). Parents also have the right to give children additional education in music, art, sports, crafts, *etc.* (Art. 40 Russian Law on Education). The right to educate the child also includes the right to make choices regarding religious education of the child.[121]

(c) Religious upbringing

Religious upbringing of the child is regarded in Russia as an element of the parental right to educate the child. The law[122] provides that the 'religious education and upbringing of children is carried out by their parents, taking into consideration the right of the child to freedom of conscience and the freedom of choice of religion.' Therefore parents are obliged to give their child the ability to express his or her opinion on this matter. The general rules (Art. 57 Russian Family Code) regarding the right of the child to express his or her opinion have

118 L. PCHELINTZEVA, *Family Law* (*Semeinoe pravo*), Moscow: Norma-Infra M, 1999, p. 303.

119 L. PCHELINTZEVA, *Family Law* (*Semeinoe pravo*), Moscow: Norma-Infra M, 1999, p. 303.

120 Federal Law in Education of 1992 *Ved. RF,* 1992, No. 30, item 1797 in the reduction of the Law of 13.01.1996 *Sobranie Zakonodatel'stva Rossiiskoi Federatsii,* 1996, No. 3, item 150.

121 M. ANTOKOLSKAIA, *Family Law* (*Semeinoe pravo*), Moscow: Jurist, 1999, p. 207.

122 Art. 5 (5) Federal Law On the Freedom of Conscience and Religious Organisations.

to be followed. If a child is 10 years old or older, the law (Art.57 Russian Family Code) prescribes that his or her opinion must be 'considered'.[123] If the opinion of such a young child is not followed, the parents must sufficiently explain the grounds thereof. The wishes of a child of ten years or older can only be overruled under special circumstances. According to Art. 57, parents are obliged to listen to such a child and, if they do not agree with his or her view, they have to provide the grounds for their disagreement. In such serious personal matters as religious upbringing the weight of a child's opinion grows heavier with age. As the parents are given no ability to impose their decisions concerning religious upbringing on a child against her or his wishes, it can be concluded that in practice the child will always have the last word regarding this matter.

If the parents cannot agree on the religious upbringing of the child, there are no special legal provisions offering resolution. Therefore, such disputes have to be dealt with according to the general rules regarding parental disagreements concerning educational matters (Art. 65 (2) Russian Family Code). The choice as to the religious upbringing have to be made by the parents upon their mutual consent. If parents disagree they can lay their dispute before the Guardianship and Curatorship Department. The Department cannot choose a religion for the child; therefore, it is suggested[124] that the Guardianship and Curatorship Department ask the parents belonging to different religions to provide the child with all possible information about both of them in order to enable the child to make his or her own choice as soon as the child becomes mature enough. The same applies to parental disagreement regarding religious and atheistic upbringing.

(d) Disciplinary measures and corporal punishment

Parents are allowed to apply certain disciplinary measures in order to enforce desirable behaviour from the child. The law does not specify the measures that can be employed.[125] However, these measures must not include treatment denigrating, cruel, offensive, humiliating to human dignity, insult or exploitation of the child (Art. 65 (1) Russian Family Code). Cruel treatment of the child, in general, and physical and mental violence in particular, can lead to the limitation or discharge of parental responsibility (Art. 69 and 73 Russian Family Code). Statutory law, therefore, totally excludes any possibility of the application of corporal punishment. However, in practice, giving a child an incidental smack almost never leads to serious consequences for the parents, and the child normally does not complain.

---

123 See also: *Commentary on the Family Code of the Russian Federation*, I.M. KUZNETZOVA (ed.), Moscow: Jurist, 2000, p. 199-201.

124 M. ANTOKOLSKAIA, *Family Law (Semeinoe pravo),* Moscow: Jurist, 1999, p. 207-208.

125 M. ANTOKOLSKAIA, *Family Law* (*Semeinoe pravo*), Moscow: Jurist, 1999, p. 206-107.

(e) Medical treatment

Parent(s) are entitled to make decisions regarding the medical treatment of a child younger than fifteen. A child older than fifteen is entitled to decide for him or herself.[126]

The parent(s) of a child younger than fifteen have the following rights regarding medical treatment:

- to receive medical information concerning the child's health (Art. 31 Russian Law on Health Protection);
- to give an informed consent to medical treatment of the child (Art. 31 Russian Law on Health Protection);
- to refuse medical treatment of the child. However, if such refusal places the child's life in danger, a medical institution can ask the court to overrule the decision of the parent(s) (Art. 33 Russian Law on Health Protection). It was rightly alleged that giving parents such a broad discretionary power regarding refuse of treatment is contrary to the best interests of a child.[127] It was therefore suggested that the law should provide a possibility to overrule the decision of the parents in every case when refusal of medical treatment can cause serious harm to a child's health;[128]
- to give consent to application of new medicines and techniques not yet recommended for general application, if the child's life is in danger and no other way of treatment is available(Art. 43 Russian Law on Health Protection);
- to protect the interests of the child under psychiatric treatment (Art. 7 Russian Law on Psychiatric Aid); [129]
- to request the placement or to consent to the placement of the child into the psychiatric clinic (Art. 28 (4) Russian Law on Psychiatric Aid).

(f) Legal representation

Parents are the legal representatives of the child by operation of law (Art. 64 (1) Russian Family Code). They are entitled to represent their children in relation to any natural and legal person and in court procedures without a special authorisation (Art. 64 (1) Russian Family Code). The position of legal representatives gives the parents the right to administrate child's property (Art. 60 (3) Russian Family Code), to perform civil transactions on behalf of a child younger than fourteen (Art. 28 (1) Russian CC), and to give consent to

---

126 The Federal Law on Health Protection of 22.06.1993 (*Sobranie Zakonodatel'stva Rossiiskoi Federatsii,* 1993, No. 33, item 318) grants a child older than fifteen the right to receive all medical information directly (art. 31) and to give informed consent to medical treatment to refuse of such treatment (art. 24 (5).

127 M. MALEINA, *Man and Medicine in Contemporary Law* (Chelovek I medicina v sovremennom prave), Moscow: BEC, 1995, p. 71.

128 M. MALEINA, *Man and Medicine in Contemporary Law (Chelovek I medicina v sovremennom prave),* Moscow: BEC, 1995, p. 71.

129 Law of 2 July 1992. *Ved. RF,* 1992, No. 33, item 1913.

performance of transactions that a child from fourteen to eighteen cannot perform without parental consent (Art. 26 (1) Russian CC). In case of conflicts between the interests of the parent and that of the child, the Guardianship and Curatorship Department will appoint a special representative for the child (Art. 64 (1) Russian Family Code). A conflict between the interests of the parent(s) and the child is presumed if the parent(s) represent the child in relation to her- or himself. In the latter case the child also needs to be represented by a special representative.[130]

SPAIN

(a) Care

Both the Spanish CC and Catalan law establish a very widely construed maintenance obligation. This obligation is imposed on parents by reason of parenthood; it does not disappear even if a parent never acquires or is discharged of his or her parental responsibilities. A child's maintenance by his or her parents is not dependent on the child's need, and a parent's inability to pay does not extinguish the obligation. Once a child reaches majority the maintenance obligation is transformed into an ordinary maintenance obligation.

The contents of maintenance depend on the financial abilities of the parents. Maintenance can include not only food, clothes, shelter, medical care and education, but also spare time activities, vacations *etc*. Some authors include moral assistance as well.

Besides the maintenance obligation there is also a duty of care that is generally described as an attitude which informs the implementation of all other more specific obligations that are inherent to parental responsibility. It certainly includes a duty to keep children away from danger and to impede any damage they may cause.

(b) Education

Education is not only a content of parental responsibility but also a fundamental right of the child requiring the possibility of intervention by the Administration. Conflicts between these two aspects of education do not often reach the courts. It is generally understood that it is preferable to be flexible than to risk that children belonging to certain minority groups (gipsies or children of the Islamic religion) cease attending school.

There is case law on two issues that derive from the right of the child to education relating to possible limitations of parental responsibility in the area of education. The first is whether home schooling is admissible as an alternative to attendance at school. The matter was dealt with by the Constitutional Court in STC 260/1994. Although this Judgment is complicated on grounds of procedure and because the parents belonged to a destructive sect, it can still be concluded that in Spanish law the right of parents to educate their children according to

130 See: M. ANTOKOLSKAIA, *Family Law* (*Semeinoe pravo*), Moscow: Jurist, 1999, p. 209-110.

their religious and moral convictions is derivatively limited by the right of the child to attend school. The State must ensure that this right is not infringed by parents. There is even an obligation imposed on school teachers and directors to notify public child protection bodies if a child does not habitually attend school (Art. 13.2 LO 1/1996, *de protección jurídica del menor*). School non-attendance justifies intervention by public child protection bodies (see Q 32).

Another issue courts have dealt with is whether parental responsibility holders can object to their children attending certain classes; for example, classes on sexual education. In a judgment delivered by the Superior Court of Cantabria it was concluded that parents can choose whether they send their child to a State or a private school (which may be religious), but they have no right to object to their child receiving education in a certain subject if they choose a state school (STS Cantabria 23-3-98).

(c) Religious upbringing

A decision by the Spanish Constitutional Court[131] expressly recognised children's right to freedom of conscience and religion; however, the exercise of this right requires for the child to have attained a sufficient degree of maturity.

If the child has attained a sufficient degree of maturity (there is a tendency to assume that children older than twelve are sufficiently mature; see Q 62) and there is a conflict between the parents and the child, the child's opinion will prevail. If the child has not attained a sufficient degree of maturity, Art. 27.3 Spanish Constitution recognises the right of the parents to educate their child according to their religious convictions and moral beliefs.

On the possible conflict with the child's right to receive an education, see Q 8b. See also Q 8e on the refusal of medical treatments on grounds of religion.

(d) Disciplinary measures and corporal punishment

Art. 154 Spanish CC establishes that parental responsibility holders can correct their children moderately and within reason. Catalan law uses more restrictive wording, establishing that sanctions cannot be humiliating or contrary to a child's rights (Art. 143 Catalan Family Code).

Although some authors have tried to argue that corporal punishment is irreconcilable with the child's right to physical integrity, it is generally admitted that corporal punishment is included in the faculties inherent to paternal responsibility. It is even admitted that the faculty to correct a child may serve as a cause of justification in the area of Criminal law. The Spanish Criminal Code distinguishes between delict and fault. The right to correct one's child serves as a cause of justification as regards the faults regulated in Art. 617.2 and 620 Spanish Criminal Code, which refer to the act of beating or mistreating someone without causing a physical or psychological injury.

---

131 STC 141/2000, de 29 de mayo.

(e) Medical treatment

In Catalonia some of the issues were dealt with in the *Ley 21/2000, de 29 de diciembre, sobre los derechos de información concernientes a la salud y la autonomía del paciente, y la documentación clínica.* Art. 7 of that law establishes that parental responsibility holders will give their consent to a medical treatment if their child is intellectually or emotionally unable to understand its consequences. However, the child must be heard in all cases if he or she is older than twelve and, if younger than twelve, if he or she has attained a sufficient degree of maturity. This implies a right of the child to be informed in a manner according to his or her age and maturity.

Children who are emotionally and intellectually able must give their own consent. This is presumed to be the case if the child is emancipated (See Q 3) or older than sixteen. There are, however, certain exceptions regarding abortion, medical research, etc., in which it seems to be necessary to obtain the parental responsibility holder's consent as well. This regulation was adopted throughout Spain in the *Ley 41/2002, de 14 de noviembre, básica reguladora de la autonomía del paciente y de derechos y obligaciones en materia de información y documentación clínica.*

There is a possibility of direct intervention without the patient's informed consent or consent by parental responsibility holders in cases in which there is a risk to the public or an immediate risk for the patient's health.

There have been quite a number of cases dealing with the refusal of medical treatment by parental responsibility holders and children on grounds of belief. In cases of urgency it is possible for doctors to intervene directly; otherwise, a court order is needed. However, these orders are sometimes not complied with. STC 154/2002 dealt with a case in which parental responsibility holders and a child of 13 refused a blood transfusion. The family were Jehovah's witnesses. The court ordered the blood transfusion should be carried out, but the parents did not collaborate in getting the order enforced. The Supreme Court conferred criminal responsibility on the parental responsibility holders. This was denied by the Constitutional Courts because there was no active refusal or obstruction of the court order by the parents.

(f) Legal representation

Art. 162 Spanish CC and 155 Catalan Family Code establish that parental responsibility holders are the legal representatives of non-emancipated children. There are however four exceptions:

- Acts relating to personal rights (see Q 8b, 8c and 8e).
- Acts which by law children can carry out for themselves. Children can marry with judicial authorisation from the age of 14 (Art. 46.1 and 48.2 Spanish CC), they can exercise parental responsibility as regards their own children (Art. 121 Spanish CC and Art. 141 Catalan Family Code), they can dispose of their property *mortis causa* in a will from the age of 14 (Art. 663.1 Spanish CC) and accept donations (Art. 625 Spanish CC).

- Acts in which there is a conflict of interests between parents and children. If the conflict is with one of the parental responsibility holders, the other will represent the child alone (Art. 162 Spanish CC and Art. 157 Catalan Family Code). If there is a conflict of interests with both parental responsibility holders, a third person will be named to defend the child (*defensor*, if it is in a court proceeding it will be a *defensor judicial;* see Art. 163 Spanish CC). There is no statutory definition of conflict of interests; in case law a conflict of interests is nearly always a conflict of economic interests in connection to the administration of the child's property or the succession of a deceased person. The majority position in legal literature also conceives a conflict of interests to be a conflict of economic interests. There is statutory indication of who become legal representatives in this extraordinary situation: it is the same circle of relatives that can become guardians of the child, in the same order (see Q 31), provided that these people have no interest conflicts with the child. If there are conflicts, the judge can depart from this circle and name an unrelated person. The *defensor judicial* is named for a specific issue.
- Acts that relate to goods excluded from the administration of property carried out by parental responsibility holders (see Q 10-12).

SWEDEN

(a) Care

The custodian's responsibility for the care of the child is expressly stated in the Chapter 6 Sec. 1 Swedish Children and Parents Code,. The term 'care' encompasses responsibility to satisfy the child's material, psychological and mental needs, and to decide important issues concerning the child. In this context the custodian's responsibility for the child should not be confused with *de facto* care of the child. In particular in situations where the child's parents have joint custody but do not live together, both parents are jointly responsible for the care of the child, whereas the *de facto* care is normally exercised by the parent with whom the child lives.

It is up to the custodian to ensure that the child's individual needs are met. Thus, the legislature has abstained from introducing an exhaustive list of the custodian's duties. From the introductory provision concerning custody, residence and contact, found in Chapter 6 Sec. 1 Swedish Children and Parents Code: 'Children are entitled to care, security and a good upbringing. They shall be treated with respect for their person and their distinctive character and may not be subjected to corporal punishment or any other humiliating treatment.' The person who has custody of the child is responsible for the child's personal affairs and shall ensure that the child's above-mentioned needs are met.[132] A child's right to security includes the right to live in a stable relationship with an adult whom the child can trust. The right to care and a good upbringing refer to experiencing a feeling of affinity and to develop personal resources in order to

[132] Chapter 6 Sec. 2 para. 2 Swedish Children and Parents Code.

gradually gain independence from the custodian. Furthermore, the custodian is to treat the child with respect, being attentive of the child's individuality and growing needs of personal integrity. All forms of corporal punishment and demeaning treatment are prohibited by law and can constitute a criminal offence.

(b) Education

The custodian is responsible for ensuring that the child receives a satisfactory education, having regard to the child's age, development and other circumstances, Chapter 6 Sec. 2 para. 2 Swedish Children and Parents Code.

(c) Religious upbringing

In Swedish law, a custodian can normally act alone only in matters relating to the daily care of the child. Decisions concerning religious upbringing and membership in a religious community are considered to be of such far-reaching significance for the child's future that they must be made by both parents if the child is under their joint custody.[133] Correspondingly, if the parents' custody rights have been transferred to two specially appointed custodians, they must make the decisions relating to the child's religious upbringing together. If parents sharing custody rights (or the two specially appointed custodians) cannot agree, it is, *e.g.*, not possible to register the child as a member of a religious community or as a pupil in a religious school. This position is confirmed by Art. 2 Additional protocol 1 to the European Convention on Human Rights.[134] It has been suggested in Swedish legal literature that any kind of religious upbringing, such as teaching the child to pray or to follow any religious traditions, requires the consent of both custodians.[135]

Since custodians are to pay regard to the child's wishes depending on the child's age and level of maturity, it follows that the child at a certain point acquires the freedom to make decisions on its own as regards religion. If the child has reached the age of 12 years, the child's consent, in addition to that of the custodian(s) is necessary for entry into or withdrawal from a religious community, the Swedish Act (1998:1593) on Religious Communities (*Lag om trossamfund*) Section 4. However, it is claimed that in practice not all religious communities in Sweden follow the law in this respect.[136]

---

133 J. SCHIRATZKI, *Barnets bästa i ett mångkulturellt Sverige*, Stockholm: Skrifter utgivna av Juridiska fakulteten vid Stockholms universitet, 2000, p. 152-155.

134 Nordisk Børneret II, Forældreansvar, Et sammenlignende studie af dansk, finsk, islandsk, norsk og svensk ret med drøftelser af harmoniseringsmuligheder og reformbehov, Copenhagen: Nordisk Ministerråd, 2003, p. 108.

135 J. SCHIRATZKI, *Barnets bästa i ett mångkulturellt Sverige*, Stockholm, Skrifter utgivna av Juridiska fakulteten vid Stockholms universitet, 2000, p. 154.

136 J. SCHIRATZKI, *Barnets bästa i ett mångkulturellt Sverige*, Stockholm: Skrifter utgivna av Juridiska fakulteten vid Stockholms universitet, 2000, p. 152-153.

(d) Disciplinary measures and corporal punishment

The Children and Parents Code explicitly prohibits subjecting children to corporal punishment or any other humiliating treatment. Neither may this be done in reaction to actions or omissions by the child, Chapter 6 Sec. 1. Such measures can constitute a criminal offence and they may not be used by the custodian as a method of raising the child.[137]

Regarding other forms of disciplinary measures, the law prohibits demeaning treatment of a child, the content of which may differ depending on the age and maturity of the child. Measures such as systematically reading a child's mail[138] or confining the child to his or her room (room arrest) may constitute demeaning treatment, particularly with older children. The prohibition of demeaning treatment aims at measures that can endanger the child's personal development, *e.g.* through ridicule or systematically ignoring the child.[139] A custodian who subjects the child to corporal punishment and other forms of unsuitable treatment shall be deprived of the custody of the child, if the behaviour is considered to constitute a lasting danger to the child's health or development, Chapter 6 Sec. 7 Swedish Children and Parents Code.

(e) Medical treatment

Decisions concerning medical treatment of a child fall within the responsibility of the custodian, to be jointly exercised by parents sharing custody. Nevertheless, it is possible that some decisions could fall under the residential parent's authority to make decisions concerning the child's daily life, *e.g.*, a decision to vaccinate the child. In respect to certain types of medical treatment, the child may decide on its own, on condition that the child is considered to have reached a sufficient level of maturity in relation to the issue. For example, a child considered mature enough has the right to request and be granted contraceptives or an abortion without the knowledge or consent of the custodians.[140] In other areas, such as treatment of mental problems, the consent of the custodians is normally required.[141]

---

137 See: Prop 1978/79:67. Corporal punishment of the child is criminalised if it corresponds to such assault against another person that is criminalised in the Swedish Penal Code. See: G. WALIN and S. VÄNGBY, *Föräldrabalken, En kommentar, Del I, 1-13 kap.*, Stockholm: Norstedts Juridik, 2002, p. 6:6.

138 This prohibition is also included in Art. 16 United Nations Convention on the Rights of the Child.

139 G. WALIN and S. VÄNGBY, *Föräldrabalken, En kommentar, Del I, 1-13 kap.*, Stockholm: Norstedts Juridik, 2002, p. 6:6-6:7.

140 See: E. RYNNING, *Samtycke till medicinsk vård och behandling*, Uppsala: Iustus Förlag, 1994, p. 285-289.

141 J. SCHIRATZKI, 'Custody of Children in Sweden - Recent Developments', *Scandinavian Studies in Law*, Volume 38, Legal Issues of the Late 1990s, p. 262, with reference to *The Yearbook of the Parliamentary Ombudsmen*, 1992/93, p. 439.

(f) Legal representation

The custodian acts as the legal representative of the child in regard to the child's personal affairs, Chapter 6 Sec. 11 and 12 Swedish Children and Parents Code. This includes matters concerning the establishment of parentage and maintenance, as well as the right to medical treatment and education. In matters concerning the administration of the child's property and financial affairs (other than maintenance) the child is represented by his or her guardians, Chapter 12 Sec. 1 Swedish Children and Parents Code. When both parents have rights of custody and guardianship, they have joint authority to represent the child. In some situations, the child may act on his or her own *e.g.* in respect of property which the child has acquired through his or her own labour, Chapter 9 Sec. 3 Swedish Children and Parents Code.

In certain public law proceedings aimed at providing protection for the child, the law provides for appointing a separate representative for the child. This is the case *e.g.* in proceedings initiated by a local social welfare committee concerning the removal of the child from the parents' care without their consent, when the child is under 15 years of age and there is reason to believe that the interests of the custodians and the child are in conflict, Sec. 39 and 36 Swedish Act on the Care of Young Persons (1990:52). On the other hand, a child who has reached the age of 15 years in entitled to speak on his or her own in such proceedings. It is also possible to appoint a separate legal representative to protect the interest of the child, instead of having the (other) custodian representing the child in criminal proceedings against a custodian based on alleged abuse of the child, Swedish Act on Special Legal Representative for Children (1999:997).

SWITZERLAND

(a) Care

Art. 301 § 1 and Art. 302 § 1 Swiss CC oblige parents to care for their child, and raise the child with a view to his or her welfare and to facilitate and protect the child's physical, mental and moral development.

(b) Education

Since parents must raise their child in accordance with their situation and facilitate and protect the child's physical, mental and moral development and have to provide the child, particularly a physically or mentally impaired child, with a general and vocational education that suits the child's abilities and predisposition as far as possible, Art. 302 § 3 Swiss CC obliges parents to cooperate in an appropriate manner with the school and, if circumstances so require, public and community youth welfare services.

(c) Religious upbringing

The parents decide on their child's religious upbringing until the child reaches his or her sixteenth birthday. Subsequently the child may decide his or her own religious beliefs. (Art. 303 § 1 and 3 Swiss CC).

(d) Disciplinary measures and corporal punishment

Parental responsibilities include the use of necessary and appropriate disciplinary measures. Corporal punishment which violates or endangers the child's physical, mental or spiritual integrity is, however, impermissible (see also Art. 9 § 1 and Art. 10 § 2 and 3 Federal Constitution).[142] For example, if a parent repeatedly assaults their child, the parent will be pursued *ex officio* under criminal law (Art. 126 § 2 Swiss Penal Code). Claiming a disciplinary intent will not justify the behaviour.

(e) Medical treatment

Parents are responsible for their child's physical wellbeing. They therefore have the right to give consent for medical treatment if their child is not capable of making an appropriate judgment. Should the parents fail to give their consent, it may be necessary to impose a custodial measure for the protection of the child (Art. 307 *et seq* Swiss CC). Minors who are capable of making an appropriate judgment may exercise those rights to which they are entitled (Art. 19 § 2 Swiss CC). This can lead to delicate issues of demarcation as to what extent a child is capable of making a judgment with regard to medical treatment and whether the child can make decisions on its own in this matter.

(f) Legal representation

Parents represent their child in dealings with third parties by virtue of law to the extent of the parental responsibilities attributed to them (Art. 304 § 1 Swiss CC). Consequently, parents act in the name of their child who is not yet capable of judgment. They grant consent to the legal transactions of their child who is capable of good judgment. 'If both parents hold parental responsibilities, then third persons may in good faith presume that each parent is acting with the consent of the other' (Art. 304 § 2 Swiss CC). Whether a third party's invocation of good faith is to be protected depends on the awareness it was possible to command in the specific circumstances (Art. 3 § 2 Swiss CC). Special care is required if the parents are divorced, unmarried or separated.[143]

---

142 BGE 105 IV 25; 117 IV 18.

143 C. Hegnauer, *Grundriss des Kindesreschts*, p. 202.

QUESTION 9

B. THE CONTENTS OF PARENTAL RESPONSIBILITIES

What is the position taken in respect of the child's right to be heard with regard to the issues mentioned under Q 8a-8f. What relevance is given to the age and maturity of the child?

AUSTRIA

In caring for and rearing the child, the parents must also pay attention to the child's wishes, unless the welfare of the child or the parents' living conditions prevents this. The more the child can understand the reason for and importance of an action and base its wishes on this insight, the more important the wishes of the child (Sec. 146(3) Austrian CC). Expressions of a child's wishes must be taken into account, for example, in planning leisure time as long as this does not involve excessive costs, e.g. for keeping a horse, or jeopardize the child's physical or psychological health, for example, by participating in a black mass.[1]

A child must be heard before the court in proceedings for care and education (*i.e.* in all personal law disputes excluding economic matters). If a child is under the age of 10, suitable persons or institutions (experts, representatives of juvenile court assistance or child welfare agencies) shall be brought in for this purpose, if needed. However, the questioning must stop if the child's interests would be endangered - through the questioning itself or a postponement of the judicial disposition related to it - or if it is obvious that a considered statement about the subject matter of the proceedings cannot be expected due to the child's inability to understand the questions (Sec. 105(2) Non-Contentious Proceedings Act *[Außerstreitgesetz]*). Children over 14 years of age have the capacity to plead in proceedings for care and education (Sec. 104(1) *Außerstreitgesetz*).[2] Therefore, they can independently petition courts for the necessary orders to ensure their interests in matters of care and education if the parent's behaviour endangers the child's interests (Sec. 176(3) Austrian CC).

In addition to these general provisions, special provisions apply to the following matters: A child over the age of 14 who has expressed an opinion to his or her parents about schooling or occupational training without success can have recourse to the courts. The court shall, after carefully weighing the reasons put forth by the parents and the child, make the dispositions that are

---

1 EBRV 296 BlgNR XXI. GP, p. 53 (explanatory notes to Government bill, 296 supplements to the stenographic minutes of the National Assembly, XXI legislative period). J. STABENTHEINER, 'KindRÄG 2001', in: P. RUMMEL, *ABGB-Kommentar*, suppl. vol. 1, 3rd Edition, Vienna: Manz Verlag, 2003, § 146 (3) Marg. No. 5 with further references.

2 See Q 61a.

appropriate for the child's interests (Sec. 147 Austrian CC). For example, in selecting a school, the wishes of the child should not be passed over without a particular reason.[3]

In questions of adherence to a religion, children over the age of 10 must be heard, children over the age of 12 can refuse to change their religious affiliation, and children over the age of 14 are free to choose their religion (Sec. 3(3) and 5 Federal Act on the Religious Education of Children *[Bundesgesetz über die religiöse Kindererziehung]*).

Apart from emergency treatment, medical treatment can be provided only with the consent of a child who is capable of understanding the situation and forming a judgment. For serious treatments the consent of the person entitled to the child's legal representation in matters of care and education is also necessary (Sec. 146c Austrian CC). The capacity of a child to understand the situation and form judgments must always be determined based on the specific individual case. With medical interventions, the physician's assessment is controlling.[4] In doubtful cases, it is presumed that minors over the age of 14 have the capacity to understand situations and form judgments (Sec. 146c(1) Austrian CC).

The question of whose consent to a medical treatment is necessary from the viewpoint of the child's personal rights must be distinguished from the entering into a treatment agreement. Entering into such an agreement depends on the child's capacity to contract, *i.e.* the child's capacity to acquire contractual rights and duties through his or her own actions.[5] In contrast to the capacity to understand situations and form judgments, a minor's legal capacity is subject to certain restrictions, which are graduated based on age group.[6]

If a child lacks the capacity to contract or the necessary capacity to understand the situation and form a judgment with respect to individual matters or a group of matters as a result of noticeably delayed development, a mental illness, or mental handicap, the court will so rule, on its own initiative or at the request of a holder of parental responsibilities. Unless revoked or limited by the court as to duration, the ruling will be effective until the child reaches majority (Sec.

---

3 *Oberster Gerichtshof*, 30.01.1996, *EFSlg.* 80.929.

4 P. HAIDENTHALLER, 'Die Einwilligung Minderjähriger in medizinische Behandlungen', *Recht der Medizin*, 2001, p. 172 *et seq.*

5 J. STABENTHEINER, 'KindRÄG 2001', in: P. RUMMEL, *ABGB-Kommentar,* suppl. vol. 1, 3rd Edition, Vienna: Manz Verlag, 2003, § 146c Marg. No. 10.

6 Children under the age of 7 lack legal capacity. Minors over the age of 7 can execute transactions by which they acquire rights, but not obligations. Minors over the age of 14 can independently enter into employment relationships and make commitments with respect to the income from their employment and dispose of matters that are left to their free disposition (e.g. pocket money) as long as this does not jeopardize their support (Sec. 151, 152, 865 Austrian CC).

154b Austrian CC). A child over the age of 14 can file a petition for revocation on their own accord (Sec. 104(1) *Außerstreitgesetz*).[7]

BELGIUM

See Q 59.

BULGARIA

There is no special legislative text obliging the parents to consult their children in making decisions affecting their lives. However, the law authorises the child to take independent action with legal consequences, and also to be heard in legal and administrative proceedings.

According to Art. 15 Bulgarian Child Protection Act, participation in procedures: '(1) All cases of administrative or judicial proceedings affecting the rights and interests of a child should provide for an obligatory hearing of the child, provided he or she has reached the age of 10, unless it proves harmful to its interests. (2) In cases where the child has not reached the age of 10, it may be given a hearing depending on the level of its development. The decision to hear the child shall be substantiated.'

The regulation creates an imperative general rule for the hearing of children between the ages of 10 and 18. The court or administrative authority should file the hearing through a special order and then express its impressions of the hearing in the reasoning of its decision. The only exception possible is where the hearing would harm the interests of the child. The assessment in this respect shall be made by the court or administrative authority and shall be expressed in a hearing. The law provides only for the personal and direct contact of the child with the hearing authority. This contact may not be substituted by 'conveying the viewpoint of the child' through a third person. If a child has not reached the age of 10, the court or administrative authority shall hear the child with a substantiated decision, depending on the degree of development of the child. The court is vested with the right to make the necessary assessment.

Before the child is given a hearing, the court or the administrative body shall:

1. provide the child with the necessary information which would help it to form its opinion;
2. inform the child about the possible consequences of its opinion, as well as about all the decisions made by the judicial or administrative body (Art. 15 § 3). The hearing and the consultation of a child shall by all means take place in appropriate surroundings and in the presence of a social worker or another appropriate specialist (Art. 15 § 4).

For instance, the child can be provided a hearing in determining the protection measures under the Bulgarian Child Protection Act (placement in public care

---

[7] I. Holzhammer/R. Holzhammer, *Ehe und Familie*, 2nd Edition, Freistadt: Plöchl Verlag, 2001, p. 61.

and termination of this placement), in the administration of parental rights in the case of divorce, in the case of disputes over parental rights and the place of residence of the child, in the case of restricting or terminating parental rights, in the appointment of a custodian or a guardian, in adoption cases, or in the case of a permission of disposing with property, treatment, etc. The legal meaning of the hearing is to consult and inform the respective authority about the opinion of the child when the authority makes a decision on any issue affecting a right of the child or a legally protected interest of the child.

The Bulgarian Child Protection Act stipulates two separate public rights of the child connected with the above right. The child has the right to information and consultation: 'Every child has a right to be informed and consulted by the child protection body even without the knowledge thereof of its parents or of the persons who take care of its rearing and upbringing, should that be deemed necessary in view of protecting its interests in the best possible way and in the situation where informing the said persons might harm the child's interests.' (Art. 13 Bulgarian Child Protection Act). The child also has a right to freedom of expression: 'Every child has a right to freely express his or her opinion on all issues affecting its interests. The child may seek the assistance of the bodies and persons, to whom its protection pursuant to this Act has been assigned' (Art. 12 Bulgarian Child Protection Act).

Attaining the age of 14 considerably broadens the legal capacity of children to take actions with legal consequences, irrespective of the will of their parents or custodians: They can conclude common legal transactions for meeting their current needs, and also dispose of what they have earned with their own labour (Art. 4 § 2 Bulgarian Act on the Persons and the Family).

They can instigate their legal proceedings in person where legal labour relations are involved or where the disputed matter stems from transactions under Art. 4 Bulgarian Act on the Persons and the Family (Art. 16 § 3 Bulgarian CCP). Children over 14 can instigate their legal proceedings in person, but only with the consent of their parents or custodians (Art. 16 § 2 Bulgarian CCP), however they can instigate matrimonial claims on their own (Art. 258 Bulgarian CCP). The consent of the parents or guardians is not required where a 16-year old person wishes to get married (Art. 12 Bulgarian Family Code).

For more serious transactions and medical interventions, the consent of both the child and of the parents or custodians is required. Children determine their religious convictions in accord with their parents (Art. 14 Bulgarian Child Protection Act). According to the Bulgarian Act on Public Education, they can choose the type of school and tuition. They give their consent for adoption (Art. 54 § 1 Bulgarian Family Code).

Legislation does not contain a general provision for solving the conflict between the child and the parents if they hold differing views regarding the above matters. The only express wording in this respect is related to religious conviction (Art. 14 § 2 Bulgarian Child Protection Act): 'Where such consent can not be reached, the underage person may refer through the bodies pursuant to this Act to the district court to settle the dispute.' No obstacles exist that for any matter of dispute, the child would address the 'bodies and persons, to whom its protection pursuant to this Act has been assigned', which are the State Agency for Child Protection and the Child Protection Departments in the municipalities. The latter can be consulted to resolve the dispute or could instigate proceedings at court if the child is at risk or for the purpose of restricting parental rights (Art. 21 § 1 § 14 Bulgarian Child Protection Act). The Child Protection Department, however, may not substitute the missing parental consent. The child must be assigned to a guardian/custodian if parents have had their parental rights waived and they should provide the missing consent.

CZECH REPUBLIC

The 1998 family law reform introduced a provision into the Czech Family Code stating that a child who is able to hold an opinion of his or her own and to consider the consequences of measures related to him or her, given the stage of his or her development, has the right to gain the required information and to free expression on all decisions of his or her parents in essential matters concerning his or her personality and the right to be heard in every proceeding in which such matters are decided (Sec. 31 § 3 Czech Family Code). Czech Act No. 359/1999 Coll. states that the child who is able to articulate his or her own opinions has the right to express these opinions, for purposes of social-legal protection, wherever matters concerning his personality are dealt with, even without the presence of the child's parents or other persons responsible for its upbringing. The opinions expressed by the child shall be duly taken into consideration according to its age and intellectual maturity wherever matters concerning its personality are dealt with (Sec. 8 § 2 Czech Act on Social and Legal Protection).

The extent to which the child's opinion is respected and the child is really heard in a judicial procedure depends considerably on the particular case, as well as on the judge. Court practice differs in this respect, but the child is usually heard before court if he is more than twelve years old. The opinion of a younger child is always investigated by a social worker through a conversation with the child and is also available to the court. The more the child approaches majority the more respect is paid to his opinion by the court as well as the social worker.

DENMARK

There is no general rule giving the child the right to be heard concerning the aforementioned issues. The Danish Act on Parental Authority and Contact provides that decisions must be made from the perspective of the child's interests and needs, but it does not prescribe that the child should be heard, Art. 2(1). In legislation covering issues such as medical treatment, the child practically has a free choice at the age of 15 as he or she must consent to treatment.[8] In matters relating to religion a child of 15 must consent to the

8 Danish Act on the Legal Position of Patients, Act No. 482, 01.07.1998, Art. 8(1).

decision of the holder(s) for that decision to be valid.[9] In matters concerning legal representation, when this concerns the legal and financial matters covered by guardianship, the guardian(s) in principle has/have to consult a child older than 15 before important decisions can be made.[10] In matters of education the child has, in principle, no autonomy and no right to be heard.

ENGLAND & WALES

Outside the context of court proceedings the child has no right to be heard. Consequently insofar as the issues mentioned in Q 8a-8f are the automatic consequence of having parental responsibility and so long as the issues are not contested the child will have no voice. However, where the issue is contested and a Sec. 8 order under the English Children Act 1989 (*viz* a residence order, contact order, specific issue order or a prohibited steps order) is being sought then, pursuant to Sec. 1(3)(a), English Children Act 1989, it is mandatory for the court to have regard to

> 'the ascertainable wishes and feelings of the child concerned (considered in the light of his age and understanding)'.

In any event, according to Sec. 7 of the 1989 Act the court when considering any question with respect to a child under the 1989 Act ask either CAFCASS[11] officer, or a local authority to report to the court "on such matters relating to the welfare of that child as are required to be dealt with in the report". The officers concerned do not represent the child but merely report on the circumstances.

Although it is established that judges have the power to interview children in private[12] the general view seems to be that it is a practice that should not be readily undertaken. In any event it is a matter entirely at the judge's discretion.[13] If a judge does interview a child in private he cannot promise confidentiality and for that very reason should be cautious in agreeing to see the child in such circumstances.[14]

So far as children being directly heard by the court is concerned the normal rule is that a child may begin and prosecute family proceedings only by a next friend and may defend proceedings only by a guardian *ad litem*.[15] However, in any family proceedings where it appears to the court that the child should be

9 Act No. 57, 24.01.1992, Art. 8.
10 Danish Act on Guardianship, Art. 26(1).
11 *I.e.* the Children and Family Court and Advisory Service which, as from April 2001, has been responsible for providing what were formerly known as welfare officers and who are now known as children and family reporters.
12 See *e.g. Re W (Child: Contact)* [1994] 1 FLR 843, and *Re M (A Minor)(Justices' Discretion)* [1993] 2 FLR 706.
13 See *Re R (A Minor)(Residence: Religion)* [1993] 2 FLR 163, CA.
14 *B v B (Minors)(Interviews and Listing Arrangements)* [1994] 2 FLR 489, 496, CA.
15 Rule 9.2, English Family Proceedings Rules 1991.

separately represented,[16] the child can be made a party to the proceedings. In such a case the court will normally refer the matter to CAFCASS Legal.

As mentioned in answer to Q 2d and Q 8f, a child may bring or defend proceedings him or herself where he has obtained leave of the court to do so, or where a solicitor considers that the child is able, having regard to his understanding to give instructions in relation to the proceedings and has accepted instructions from the child to act for him or her.[17] Before granting leave to the child the court has to be satisfied that the child has sufficient understanding to participate as a party to the particular proceedings.[18]

Despite being placed first in the welfare checklist, the child's view is not expressed to be determinative. In other words the court's obligation is to consider the child's wishes and feelings but not necessarily to give effect to them. Clearly, however, the older the child the more weight is likely to be placed on those wishes. As BUTLER-SLOSS LJ put it in *Re P (minors)(wardship: care and control)*[19]

> 'How far the wishes of children should be a determinative factor in their future placement must of course vary on the particular facts of each case. Those views must be considered and may, but not necessarily must, carry more weight as the children grow older'.

FINLAND

Section 4 para. 2 Finnish Child Custody and the Right of Access Act includes a general rule about the task of the custodian to discuss matters relating to the child with the child, giving regard to the child's age and maturity. According to this section the custodian shall give due consideration to the child's feelings, opinions and wishes. There are no specified age limits concerning the custodian's duty to listen to the child, but because the custodian is to support and assist the child's growth towards independence, responsibility and adulthood, the goal of the Act seems to be that the child's right to take part in decisions concerning its own affairs would expand step by step.

The principle expressed in this section covers all custodial decision making, but as it is only a goal or ideal, there are no sanctions if the custodian does not listen to the child. However, the custodian's failure to listen to the child's opinion can be taken into consideration as a relevant factor if the court has to make a decision about the custody of the child according what is deemed to be in accordance with the best interests of the child.

---

16 See the leading case, *Re A (Contact: Separate Representation)* [2001] 1 FLR 715.

17 Rule 9.2A, English Family Proceedings Rules 1991 and *Practice Direction* [1993] 1 FLR 668. See also *Re T (A Minor)(Child Representation)* [1994] Fam 49, CA.

18 See *e.g. Re S (A Minor)(Representation)* [1993] 2 FLR 437, CA.

19 [1992] 2 FCR 681 at 687.

Concerning the relationship between the child and authorities, there are, however, specific rules safeguarding that the child's views will be heard. Such rules concern the child's religious affiliation and the child's medical treatment. The contents of these rules are explained above in Q 8c and 8e.

There are other examples where an authority must take the will of the child into consideration. The child's consent is needed, for instance, if the child's first name or family name is petitioned to be changed and the child is at least 12 years old. A child younger than 12 can prevent the change of its name, if the child demonstrates enough maturity that its will should be taken into consideration (Sec. 33 Finnish Name Act). A child 12 or older can also prevent its own adoption if the child does not consent to the adoption. The will of a younger child can also be taken into consideration (Sec. 8 Finnish Adoption Act). An important right of the child is the right to prevent the enforcement of a decision concerning custody or right of access (Sec. 2 Finnish Act of the Enforcement of a Decision on Child Custody and Right of Access). The child's right to be heard in decisions concerning its custody will be clarified in Q 59 – 62. The rules concerning legal representation can provide a child of 15 or older not only the right to be heard, but also to act as a party with the child's custodian, as explained in Q 8f.

FRANCE

See Art. 388-1 French CC:[20] In any proceeding relating to the minor child, a child capable to understand (*capable de discernement*) can be heard by the judge or by the person appointed by the judge. If the minor child makes a request to be heard, the judge must give special reasons if the request is denied. The minor child can be heard alone or with the assistance of a lawyer or another person of his choice. If the judge thinks the person the child chooses will not represent the child's best interests, the judge can appoint another person. If the child is heard before court, it does not follow that that the child will necessarily become a party to the proceedings.

There are special provisions concerning the right of the child to be heard when the judge decides upon the modalities of the exercise of parental responsibilities (Art. 373-2-11 French CC the judge shall take into account the feelings expressed by the child during proceedings) or when the *juge des enfants* (juvenile court judge) has to decide on possible educational support (Art. 1186 New French Code of Civil Procedure). All legal provisions require the child to be capable of understanding. The judge can deny the child a hearing if the age, health or intellectual skills of the child make the hearing impossible or if the hearing could endanger the child's health, mental health[21] or psychological

20 This legal provision was included in the French CC by the Act No. 93-33 of 03.01.1993.

21 French Supreme Court, Civ. I, 20.02.1985, *Gaz. Pal.*, 1985. 2. 756.

balance.[22] If the child wants to be heard and formulates its request before the court,[23] the court shall state any circumstances of the case, which make the hearing of the child undesirable.[24]

GERMANY

(a) Care

As a general rule, in matters of care and education parents have to take into account the growing abilities and the need for the child to be independent and responsible acting, § 1626 para. 2 sent. 1 German CC. Parents must discuss issues of parental care with the child, as far as it is indicated, and endeavour to come to an understanding. For court proceedings see Q 59, 60.

(b) Education

As far as education is concerned the general rules apply. The parents shall give special consideration to the aptitude and inclination of the child with regard to matters of schooling and vocation, § 1631a German CC. They shall not press the child in a direction which does not conform with the child's aptitude and inclination.[25] Disputes between the parents can be solved by court order, see Q 37.

(c) Religious upbringing

Generally, parents having parental custody decide whether the child should be given a religious upbringing. Under a special statute, a child of fourteen already has complete religious freedom (§ 5 sent. 1 German Act Concerning the Religious Upbringing of Children of 1921).[26] At the age of 12, a child cannot be educated under a different religion than before against his or her will (§ 5 sent. 2 German Law on Religious Upbringing). The child has to be heard when it is ten years old (§ 2 para. 3 sent. 5 German Law on Religious Upbringing).

(d) Disciplinary measures and corporal punishment

Disciplinary measures can be taken. As stated in answer to Q 8 corporal punishment is inadmissible. However, insignificant acts are left out of consideration.

(e) Medical treatment

Medical treatment concerns an issue of parental responsibility and follows the general rules, see (a). One question is how far parents have to take the child's views into account. Another important question is how far the consent of the child is necessary or even sufficient for medical treatment. Generally the consent of the person with parental responsibility is necessary. However, there

---

22 French Supreme Court, Civ. I, 02.11.1994, *Rép. Defrénois* ,1995. 1027 annotated MASSIP.

23 See G. CORNU, *Droit civil, La famille*, No. 90, p. 184.

24 French Supreme Court, Civ. I, 25.06.1991, *Bull. civ.* I, No. 210.

25 U. DIEDERICHSEN, in: PALANDT, *Bürgerliches Gesetzbuch*, 63rd Edition, München: Beck, 2004, § 1631a German CC No. 1.

26 Gesetz über die religiöse Kindererziehung of 15.07.1921, *RGBl.* 1921, p. 939.

can also be cases where the consent of a minor child alone is sufficient. This is especially the case if the medical treatment is of minor importance.[27] The validity of consent to medical treatment will depend on the maturity and understanding of the child. The courts sometimes only require a 'natural understanding' (*natürliche Einsichtsfähigkeit*).[28] However, the conditions under which the consent of a child alone will suffice are a matter of controversy. A stricter view insists that consent of the parents is generally necessary.[29] See also Q 51.

If a pregnant minor chooses to have an abortion, under the conditions of § 218a German Penal Code it is argued that she can decide herself, as long as her maturity and understanding are guaranteed.[30] This is, however, disputed. Other views demand that the consent of the holder of parental responsibility (parents) is always required[31] or that a custodian must be appointed for the affair.[32] If a minor woman wants to have the child and her parents object, the family court can, if necessary, take measures according § 1666 German CC (jeopardy to the welfare of the minor child) and appoint a curator, thus protecting the pregnant woman.[33]

(f) Legal representation

Legal representation is generally a consequence of parental care, therefore the restrictions of parental responsibility also set limits to legal representation. The parent cannot agree to medical treatment against a child's will, as long as the child has the necessary understanding of the treatment's consequences.[34]

GREECE

Art. 1511 para. 3 Greek CC provides that the child should be heard and its opinion should be taken into consideration on every decision pertaining to

---

27 L. PESCHEL-GUTZEIT, in: STAUDINGER, *Kommentar zum Bürgerlichen Gesetzbuch*, 13th Edition, Berlin: de Gruyter, 2002, § 1626 German CC No. 93.

28 BGH 05.12.1958, *BGHZ* 29, 33 = *FamRZ* 1959, 200 annotated by BOSCH.

29 M. COESTER, in: STAUDINGER, *Kommentar zum Bürgerlichen Gesetzbuch*, 13th Edition, Berlin, 2000, § 1666 German CC No. 138.

30 Landgericht (LG) München I 24.07.1978, *FamRZ* 1979, 850 = *NJW* 1980, 646 (16 year old woman); Amtsgericht (AG) Schlüchtern 29.04.1997, *NJW* 1998, 832; L. M. PESCHEL-GUTZEIT, in: STAUDINGER, *Kommentar zum Bürgerlichen Gesetzbuch*, 13th Edition, Berlin: Gruyter, 2002, § 1626 German CC No. 98.

31 Oberlandesgericht (OLG) Hamm 16.07.1998, *NJW* 1998, 3424; U. DIEDERICHSEN, in: PALANDT, *Bürgerliches Gesetzbuch*, 63rd Edition, München: Beck, 2004, § 1626 German CC No. 13.

32 See L. M. PESCHEL-GUTZEIT, in: STAUDINGER, *Kommentar zum Bürgerlichen Gesetzbuch*, 13th Edition, Berlin: Gruyter, 2002, § 1626 German CC No. 1626 No. 101.

33 See AG Dorsten Der Amtsvormund 1978, 131 (16 years old woman); M. COESTER, in: STAUDINGER, *Kommentar zum Bürgerlichen Gesetzbuch*, 13th Edition, Berlin, 2000, § 1666 German CC No. 102; L. M. PESCHEL-GUTZEIT, in: STAUDINGER, *Kommentar zum Bürgerlichen Gesetzbuch*, 13th Edition, Berlin: Gruyter, 2002, § 1626 German CC No.102.

34 L. M. PESCHEL-GUTZEIT, in: STAUDINGER, *Kommentar zum Bürgerlichen Gesetzbuch*, 13th Edition, Berlin: Gruyter, 2002, § 1626 German CC No. 8.

parental care and relating to its interests, provided that the child is sufficiently mature. A child is considered to be sufficiently mature if it can conceptualise its interests.[35] The maturity of the child is related to its age, but is not determined by it. Hence, the degree of maturity must be examined separately in each case.[36] The right of the child to be heard is a basic principle of family law and, as such, it also applies when the child is subject to guardiandhip.[37]

HUNGARY

The Hungarian Family Act states, as a general rule in connection with the exercise of the parental responsibilities, that the parents must guarantee that a child who is capable of forming his or her own views can express these views concerning all decisions that affect him or her, and that the parents should give due weight to these views according to the age and maturity of the child. This rule is to be applied to every matter covered by the parental responsibilities.

Hungarian law has no general rule applicable to every case that states the age at which a child is considered to be capable of forming his or her own views, and so be heard in matters of parental responsibilities. Nevertheless, in some cases it is expressed that according to Hungarian law a child over 14 is capable of forming his or her views in matters under parental responsibilities. There are rules stating that a child under 14 is to be heard if he or she demands it.

Family law rules state that a child older than 12 is capable of forming his or her views if there is conflict between the child and the parents regarding the child's schooling, education or the determination of the child's career. In this situation, the public guardianship authority will rule on the controversy. Moreover, the child over 12 has the right to directly ask the public guardianship authority to rule on this. Similarly, if the child is over 12, she or he is to be heard in the Child Welfare mediation proceeding aimed at determining the arrangement of the contact. The public guardianship authority has the duty to hear any child under guardianship in important matters concerning the child if the child is over 12. If the proceeding is about the placement of the child, the child is to be heard and due weight should be given to his or her views if the child is over 14. According to the Family Act the child is to be heard even if the child is younger than 14 if it is motivated; if the child demands it himself or herself, it is always motivated.

---

35 P. ARVANITAKIS, in: K. KERAMEUS, D. KONDULIS and N. NIKAS (eds.), *Commentary on the Code of Civil Procedure, Vol. II (Arts. 591-1054),* Athens–Komotini: Ant. N. Sakkoulas, Art. 681c Greek Code of Civil Procedure, p. 1311, No. 4 [in Greek]. This opinion is followed by the courts. See Supreme Court Decisions: 15/1997, *Elliniki Dikaiosini* Vol. 38 (1997), p. 1538, 180/1986, *Elliniki Dikaiosini* Vol. 27 (1986), p. 496, 577/1989, *Elliniki Dikaiosini* Vol. 31 (1990), p. 1271.

36 P. AGALLOPOULOU, in: A. GEORGIADIS and M. STATHOPOULOS (eds.), *Civil Code commentary, Vol. VIII, Family Law (Arts. 1505-1694),* 2nd Edition, Athens: Law & Economy, P.N. Sakkoulas 2003, Art. 1511 Greek CC, p. 208, No. 31.

37 See also Art. 3 of the European Convention on the Exercise of Children's Rights (Law 2502/1997).

Although this goes beyond the scope of the Questionnaire, it must be mentioned that Hungarian family law demands not only a hearing for a child over 14, but also the child's consent in two issues: The child's adoption and the paternal affiliation of the child by voluntary recognition.

IRELAND

The Irish judiciary does not favour children being present in court while cases concerning them are taking place. Sec. 11 Irish Children Act 1997, which inserts a new Sec. 25 into the Irish Guardianship of Infants Act 1964, allows the court, as it thinks appropriate and practicable having regard to the age and understanding of the child, to take account of his or her wishes in any proceedings with regard to the issues mentioned under Q 8a-Q 8f. In this regard, the Irish High Court in March 2004 held that children aged 13 and 14 years of age were of an age and maturity to have their wishes taken into account.[38] This case is the first to draw a link between the personal right of a child under Art. 40.3 Irish Constitution to have a decision made in accordance with natural and constitutional justice and the provisions of the Irish Guardianship of Infants Act 1964. As the High Court stated:

> '[S]ection 25 [of the 1964 Act] should be construed as enacted for the purpose of, *inter alia*, giving effect to the procedural right guaranteed by Art. 40.3 to children of a certain age and understanding to have their wishes taken into account by a court in making a decision under the Act of 1964, relating to the guardianship, custody or upbringing of a child.'

The case of *A.S. (orse A.B.) v. R.B.* addressed the issue of a judge seeing a child in chambers. KEANE C.J. urged caution with regard to doing this, noting that the only evidence that should be received by a trial judge is that on oath in the presence of the parties to the case. However, he was of the view that interviews may help the judge in determining the wishes of the child.

Sec. 11 Irish Children Act 1997, which inserts a new Sec. 28 into the Irish Guardianship of Infants Act 1964, should also be noted in that it makes provision in Irish law for the appointment by the court of a guardian *ad litem* to act on behalf of any child in private law proceedings involving guardianship, custody of, or access to, a child. This section is one of two sections of the Irish Children Act 1997 not yet in force. The guardian *ad litem* is, effectively, an independent representative appointed by the court to represent the welfare and wishes of the child. At best, the Irish child's right to be heard in the aforementioned applications is discretionary. The net result of such discretion is a chaotic system of representation for children with significant variations as to the operation of the provision of representation throughout Ireland.

---

38 *F.N. and E.B. v. C.D., H.O. and E.K.*, High Court, 26.03.2004, Finlay-Geoghegan J.

ITALY

The Italian legal system is not homogenous when it comes to the minor's right to be heard (*e.g.* Art. 6 § 9, 1 Italian Divorce law; Art. 4, 10, § 5 1 Italian Adoption Law; Arts. 316 and 348 Italian CC). However, a joint reading of these Articles and a particular consideration of their systematic coordination with the principles established by the international Conventions ratified in Italy (in particular the Convention UNO of 20 November 1989 concerning the child's rights, ratified and implemented in Italy with the Law of 27 May 1981, No. 176 and the 1996 Convention of Strasbourg concerning the exercise of the child's rights, ratified and implemented in Italy with the law of 20 March 2003, No. 176) underlines the Italian legal system's recognition of the minor's right to be heard in procedures effecting the minor's life or development[39] if the minor has the necessary capacity of judgment. Besides cases where this is expressly provided for or deemed 'strictly necessary', the judge may choose to hear the minor under the condition that the minor has the capacity to form her or his own opinion (capacity of judgment). Consequently, the legislature's ability and authorisation to draft specific rules (*e.g.* the limitation of the age) regulating strict and pre-established criteria is negated.

The judge is not forced to consider a minor's opinions because minors are not forced to give them; however, the judge must consider them against other elements when reaching a decision. The necessity to 'hear' the minor and to 'take the minor's opinion into consideration' if the minor has the requisite capacity of judgment is generally accomplished by the minor's participation in decisions regarding himself or herself and by an active involvement in evaluating the minor's awareness and allowing him or her appropriate influence at every chance. In this way consideration of the minor's changed judgment can be confirmed: from being the subject of other's decisions to being an active participant in the decisions.

LITHUANIA

According to Art. 3.164 Lithuanian CC, the child, if capable of formulating his or her views, must be heard directly or, where that is impossible, through a representative. Any decisions related to a child must be taken with regard to the child's wishes unless they are contrary to the child's interests. In making a decision on the appointment of a child's guardian (curator) or on a child's adoption, the child's wishes shall be given paramount consideration.

---

39 The Italian jurisdiction has recognised this principle apart from the existence of an explicit rule. See Supreme Court, 23.07.1997 No. 6899, *Giust. Civ.*, I, p. 2295, which confirmed that in procedures concerning the minor, the necessity to hear the minor is based on the strength of the minor's will and personality. These procedures are based on individual cases and emerge from direct interviews with the interested person, so they cannot be established in advance by general criteria. See also, among others, the Constitutional Court 30.01.2002, No. 1 in *Giust civ.*, 2002, I, p. 1467 with the note of A.G. CIANCI. See also C.M. BIANCA, *Diritto sull'esercizio della potestà*, in: *Trattato di diritto di famiglia* conducted by PAOLO ZATTI, II *Filiazione* by G. COLLURA, L. LENTI and M. MANTOVANI, Giuffrè, Milano, 2002, p. 1039.

If a child considers that his or her parents abuse his or her rights, the child shall have a right to apply to a state institution for the protection of the child's rights or, on attaining the age of 14, to bring the matter before the court.

According to Art. 3.177 Lithuanian CC, when adjudicating on disputes over children, the court must hear the child capable of expressing his or her views in order to ascertain the wishes of the child. According to Part 2 of Art. 3.174 Lithuanian CC, the court must resolve such disputes, having regard to the interest of the child and the child's wishes. The child's wishes may be disregarded only if they are contrary to the best interests of the child *etc.*

The general rule is that the age of the child is not important. Therefore, the abstract criteria is established; the child must be heard only when it is capable of formulating its views, *i.e.* when communicating with the child it is possible to know the child's opinion of the question discussed.

However, the law very often provides norms which establish from what age or in what cases and in what manner a child must be heard. Part 2 of Art. 3.142 Lithuanian CC provides that the acknowledgment of paternity in respect to a child who has become 10 is only possible with the written permission of the child.

THE NETHERLANDS

According to Art. 809 § 1 Dutch Code of Civil Procedure in cases concerning minors a judge will only decide the case after he has given minors twelve or older the opportunity to be heard, unless the case is of minor importance. The judge may hear minors under the age of twelve in a manner to be determined by the judge. In practice, however, children are not heard very often. In particular, where parents agree, children are not heard. Courts recognise that as the child grows older it increasingly deserves a voice in matters that concern him or her. If there is a conflict between the child and the holder(s) of parental responsibilities about issues that are covered by these parental responsibilities, the child according to Art. 1:250 Dutch CC has the right to have a legal guardian appointed.

NORWAY

The basic rule is that the child shall be heard on all matters relating to its situation. According to Art. 31 sec. 1 Norwegian Children Act 1981, as the child develops and matures the parents shall listen to its opinions before making a decision on personal matters for the child. They shall pay due regard to its opinions. For a child of 12 or older, the Article in force up to 2003 stated in Sec. 2 that great importance should be attached to the child's wishes. The same applies to others with whom the child lives or who are associated with the child. This includes public authorities and the courts. When Norway incorporated the UN Child Convention in national law in 2003, Art. 31 Norwegian Children Act 1981 was amended. In addition to what was previously stated, Sec. 2 now says that when a child has reached the age of seven, it shall be given the opportunity to express its opinions before decisions are taken on personal matters, including where it shall live following a separation or divorce.

According to Art. 31 Norwegian Children Act 1981, parents shall steadily extend the child's right to make decisions, as it grows older, until it comes of age. It is expressly stated in Art. 32 Norwegian Children Act 1981 that a child of 15 or older may make all decisions relating to its education. This age is also decisive for self-determination in religious matters.

POLAND

When assessing the child's rights, Art. 72 sec. 3 Polish Constitution provides that all public authorities and persons responsible for the child are obliged to hear the child and, to the extent possible, the child's opinion. This provision is to be applied directly.

PORTUGAL

In establishing the general principles of the regulation of parental responsibility, Portuguese law imposes upon parents a 'positive duty to respect their children', which translates into the duty to take account of their opinion in important family matters, in accordance with their maturity, and the duty to gradually recognise their autonomy in leading their own lives (Art. 1878 No. 2 Portuguese CC).

When there is disagreement between parents on important matters relating to the exercise of parental responsibility, an adolescent of fourteen or over may be heard by the judge (Art. 1901 No. 2 2nd part Portuguese CC). The law also establishes that parents should take their child's wishes into consideration on matters regarding their academic and professional training (Art. 1885 No. 2 Portuguese CC). As regards religious education, parental responsibility comes to an end when the child reaches the age of sixteen. Indeed, the law establishes a special majority in this respect, recognising that a child over sixteen has complete freedom to decide upon their religion (Art. 1886 Portuguese CC). The law also establishes a special majority in regards to medical treatment; an adolescent may validly give their own consent on matters of medical treatment and surgical intervention at fourteen (Art. 38 No. 3 Portuguese Criminal Code).

RUSSIA

Russian legislation follows the UN Convention by granting the child the right to express its opinion, irrespective of the child's age. Therefore, a Russian child has the right to express his or her opinion with regard to any decision made by his or her parents which effects the child's interests as soon as the child is able to formulate such an opinion. The age of the child is only relevant when it comes to evaluating his or her opinion. Art. 12 of the UN Convention urges consideration of a child's opinion in light of the child's ability to formulate it. The Russian Supreme Court, in its Directive No. 10 of 27 May 1998, also obliged judges to investigate whether a child has been unduly influenced by the litigating parties, whether the child is aware of his or her interests, and on what grounds the child has reached his or her opinion.[40]

Opinion of a child under the age of ten. A child that has not reached the age of ten must generally be given the opportunity to be heard; however, the parents are not obliged to follow the child's opinion and provide reasons why they had not followed child's opinion (Art. 57 Russian Family Code). In practice, the wishes of a child under ten years of age are not really taken very seriously.

Opinion of a child of ten years or older. Art. 57 of the Russian Family Code provides that if a child is 10 years old or older, its opinion must be 'considered'.[41] If the child's opinion is not followed, the parents who disregard its opinion must sufficiently explain the grounds therefore. The wishes of a child of ten years or older can only be overruled under special circumstances. According to Art. 57, the parents are obliged to hear such a child and, if they do not agree with his or her view, they have to provide the grounds for their disagreement. Theoretically this means that if a child older than ten year of age has not being given the possibility to express his or her opinion or the parent(s) disregarded this opinion without motivation, the decision of the parent(s) can be subjected to administrative (by the Guardianship and Curatorship Department) or judicial revision. As not hearing a child or not considering its opinion properly can be regarded as an abuse of parental rights the child can initiate such revision her or himself by invoking protection against abuse of parental rights granted to him or her by Art. 56 (2) Russian Family Code. According to this provision a child of any age can complain to and seek protection from the Department of Guardianship and Curatorship upon his or her own initiative. From the age of fourteen, a child is allowed to instigate proceedings against her or his parents directly before the court (Art. 56(2) Russian Family Code). This remains, however, largely only the law in the books as in practice children almost never complain about not being heard or not being taken seriously.

SPAIN

Children have a right to be informed, with regard to their age and degree of maturity, and a right to express their opinion freely on all matters affecting them.[42] There is a corresponding duty for parental responsibility holders to inform the children adequately and to listen to them before making any decision affecting them (Art. 133.2 Catalan Family Code and Art. 154 Spanish

---

40 Item 20 of the Directive of the Supreme Court of the Russian Federation of 27.05.1998 No. 10 'On the Application of the Legislation by Dissolving Cases Relating to the Education and Care for Children', Bulleten' verhovnogo suda RF, 1998, No 7.

41 See also: *Commentary on the Family Code of the Russian Federation*, I.M. KUZNETZOVA (ed.), Moscow: Jurist, 2000, p. 199-201.

42 As for Catalan law 11.1 and 2 Llei d'atenció I protecció dels infants I adolescents; Art. 9 Ley Orgánica de Protección Jurífica del Menor.

CC). A breach of these obligations will not invalidate an act taken; however it will be understood that parental responsibility has not been properly exercised.

Catalan law establishes that children 12 or older must be heard in all cases; younger children will be heard if they have attained a sufficient degree of maturity. The twelve year old age limit also appears in the Spanish CC for specific issues such as the attribution of custody when parents do not live together (Art. 159 Spanish CC) or the regulation of parental responsibility after divorce (Art. 92 Spanish CC), although there is no general rule.

SWEDEN

The child's right to be heard is a fundamental principle in Swedish family law. In assessing questions concerning custody, residence and contact, regard shall be made to the wishes of the child, taking into account the child's age and maturity, Chapter 6 Sec. 2b Swedish Children and Parents Cod. Furthermore, in decisions concerning the child's personal affairs, the person with custody of the child shall, in keeping with the increasing age and maturity of the child, also take the child's views and wishes increasingly into account, Chapter 6 Sec. 11 Swedish Children and Parents Code. As regards the child's economic affairs, the guardian shall hear the child where appropriate if the child is at least 16 and the matter is important, Chapter 12 Sec. 7 Swedish Children and Parents Code. The underlying ideology is that the child is the expert of his or her own situation, all the more so with increasing age and maturity. From this, it follows that very small children are not considered to be able to have clear opinions. Mature children, on the other hand, exercise a considerable autonomy in respect to certain types of medical treatment and participate in the decision-making in other respects.

SWITZERLAND

The Swiss CC states the general principle, in Art. 301 § 1 and Art. 305 § 1 Swiss CC, that parents should include the child in decisions concerning the child in a manner commensurate with the child's maturity. This consultation consists first of all in listening to the child. As the child grows older, parents should guide the child into taking responsibility for shaping her or his own life so that when the child reaches the age of majority she or he will no longer require parental care. In this way the parental authority to make decisions is subject to the child's growing capacity to act, which is not defined by age but by the implication of the legal actions in question. Whereas the child, it is true, owes obedience to its parents, the parents must allow their child the freedom to shape her or his life based on the child's level of maturity, and they must show consideration as far as possible to the child's opinion in important matters (Art. 301 § 2 Swiss CC).

The following applies specifically:

- 'The child may not leave the parental home without the parents' consent' (Art. 301 § 3 sentence 1 Swiss CC).

- Parents must provide the child, particularly a physically or mentally impaired child, with an adequate general and vocational education that is as commensurate as possible with the child's abilities and disposition (Art. 302 § 2 Swiss CC).
- 'Once the child reaches his or her 16th birthday, the child shall decide his or her own religious beliefs' (Art. 303 § 3 Swiss CC).
- The child's age and maturity play an important role in decisions regarding medical treatment because, as already mentioned, minors capable of good judgment may basically exercise those rights to which they are entitled, which includes the field of physical integrity (Art. 19 § 2 Swiss CC).
- A child to whom parental responsibilities apply has the same limited capacity to act as a person under a guardianship (Art. 305 § 1 Swiss CC). This means that a child capable of making a judgment may not, subject to legal exceptions, precipitate any legal effect by his or her actions (Art. 18 Swiss CC). On the other hand, a child capable of making a judgment may enter into a commitment by means of his or her actions, even if this is only the case, with the consent of his or her legal representatives. Without such consent the child may obtain gratuitous advantages and exercise rights to which he or she is entitled (Art. 19 § 1 and 2 Swiss CC).

QUESTION 10

B. THE CONTENTS OF PARENTAL RESPONSIBILITIES

Do(es) the holder(s) of parental responsibilities has(have) the right to administer the child's property?

AUSTRIA

The right and the duty of administering the child's property is an express part of parental responsibilities (Sec. 144, 149, and 150 Austrian CC) and the special provisions governing the exercise of parental responsibilities by other persons (Sec. 229 Austrian CC). The judicial control mechanisms are set forth in greater detail in sections 133-138 of the Non-Contentious Proceedings Act (*Außerstreitgesetz*).[1]

BELGIUM

Yes. The administration of the child's property follows the regulations of the authority over the child. When both parents exercise this authority jointly, they will also administrate the property jointly, except in case of legal exception. When only one parent exercises parental responsibilities, only this parent will administrate the property, except in case of legal exception. Then the other parent has the right to supervise the administration, to be informed and to cease the Juvenile Court (Art. 376 Belgian CC).

BULGARIA

Yes.

CZECH REPUBLIC

The parents are obliged to administer the child's property 'with due care'. The right to administer the child's property is held by both parents on the basis of their mutual agreement. If the child is placed into care of one of the parents, everyday property matters are administered by that parent, but in essential matters the other parent's consent is required. If a parent (parents) deals (deal) with the child's property beyond ordinary matters, court approval is required (Sec. 28 Czech CC).

The parents are obligated to give the child an account of the estate administration if the child requires it within a year after the termination of their administration. The child's rights from damage liability and unjust enrichment remain unaffected (Sec. 37a § 3 Czech Family Code).

---

1 R. FUCIK, 'Die Vermögensverwaltung nach dem KindRÄG 2001: Vom Obervormund zur Missbrauchskontrolle', in: S. FERRARI/G. HOPF, *Reform des Kindschaftsrechts*, Vienna: Manz Verlag, 2001, p. 36 ; S. KRIWANEK, *Das neue Außerstreitverfahren*, Vienna: LexisNexis ARD Orac, 2004, p. 6 and 147-156.

DENMARK

The holder(s) of parental authority is/are almost always also the guardian(s) of the child. The guardian(s) has/have the right to administer the child's property.[2]

ENGLAND & WALES

As stated in answer to Q 2f holders of parental responsibility have, pursuant to Sec. 3(1), English Children Act 1989 "all the rights, duties, powers, responsibilities and authority which by law a parent of a child has in relation to the child *and his property*" (emphasis added) and, pursuant to Sec. 3(2), to such rights as the guardian of the estate, would have had in relation to the child's property.

FINLAND

The custodians of a minor child also act as guardians *i.e.* taking responsibility for the administration of the child's property, unless a special guardian has been appointed by the court or other guardianship authority (Sec. 4 Finnish Guardianship Services Act).

FRANCE

Yes. See Art. 382 French CC, which states that the father and mother have the right to administer and use the child's property (*administration* and *jouissance légale*). It is therefore a kind of usufruct so that the parents have the *usus* and the *fructus* on the child's property. The parents can spend the yields of the child's property without having to justify their expenses. The parents shall use these amounts first to maintain the child and to provide for his education and upbringing (Art. 385(2) French CC).[3] The right to use the property ceases when the child reaches the age of 16 (Art. 384(1) French CC) or when he gets married, while the right of administration ceases when the child reaches the majority (18 years), gets married or is emancipated.

GERMANY

The person holding parental custody (usually the parents) also has to administer the child's property (*Vermögenssorge*, § 1626 para. 1 German CC). Particularly important legal transactions concluded in the child's name, such as the sale of real property, require the approval of the family court (§ 1643 German CC), see Q 12.

GREECE

The management of the child's assets forms an inherent part of parental care (Art. 1510 para. 1 Greek CC) and of guardianship (Art. 1603 Greek CC). Thus the holder of parental responsibilities has the right to administer the child's

---

2 Danish Act on Guardianship, Art. 1(2).

3 *'La nourriture, l'entretien et l'éducation de l'enfant selon sa fortune'* (Art. 385(2) French CC).

property with respect to the best interests of the child (Art. 1511 para. 1 Greek CC).

HUNGARY

The holders of the parental responsibilities have the right to administer the child's property. This is also their duty.

IRELAND

No.

ITALY

Yes, but it is a 'right' connected with a duty to be exercised only in the interest of the minor.

LITHUANIA

Yes, he or she does.

THE NETHERLANDS

Yes. See Q 2f.

NORWAY

Yes. According to Art. 3 Norwegian Act on Guardianship 1927, the guardian(s) are those attributed parental responsibilities.

POLAND

Yes, through the concept of care over the child's property (Art. 95 § 1 Polish Family and Guardianship Code).

PORTUGAL

Parents are the legal administrators of their children's property. Indeed, parents, as holders of parental responsibility, assume the power and duty to administer their children's property.

RUSSIA

Art. 60 (4) of the Russian Family Code states that property of the parents and their children remains separate and that children and parents acquire no right to the property of each other. Parent(s) are entitled to administer the property of the child as the legal representative(s) of the child.

SPAIN

The general rule is that the holder(s) of parental responsibility administer the child's property (Art. 154 Spanish CC and Art. 145 Catalan Family Code). The administration of the child's property is an inexcusable duty of parental responsibility holders.

SWEDEN

The right to administer the child's property belongs to the child's guardian(s), unless the child, by law or otherwise, has acquired a right of disposition. Where property has been given to the child, *e.g.*, as a gift or through a testamentary disposition, the donor or testator may stipulate that the property shall be administered by a person other than the child's guardian, Chapter 12 Sec. 1 Swedish Children and Parents Code.

SWITZERLAND

'Parents have the right and the obligation to administer the child's property if parental responsibilities are attributed to them' (Art. 318 § 1 Swiss CC). However, a child capable of good judgment is also to be introduced to the administration of property for educational reasons, which means that the child is to be included in the decision-making process if there are far-reaching consequences to the decisions (Art. 301 Swiss CC).[4]

[4] P. BREITSCHMID, Art. 318 ZGB, p. 1669 (No. 9), in: H. HONSELL, N.P. VOGT, TH. GEISER (ed.), *Basler Kommentar zum Schweizerischen Privatrecht, Zivilgesetzbuch I*, Art. 1-456 ZGB, Basel: Helbing & Lichtenhahn, 2002.

QUESTION 11

B. THE CONTENTS OF PARENTAL RESPONSIBILITIES

If the answer to Q 10 is yes, explain the content of this right.

AUSTRIA

Parents must administer the property of a minor child with the care of proper parents. Unless the child's interests require otherwise, they must maintain and, if possible, increase the property (Sec. 149(1) Austrian CC). The child's special needs - due to disability or a special talent - can justify the use of property for the child's interests (Sec. 149(2) Austrian CC), *e.g.* using a child's property to equip the home to accommodate the child's disabilities, to finance study abroad, or to purchase a high-quality musical instrument.[1]

In general, a child may be supported only from the earnings of the child's property (Sec. 140(3) Austrian CC). The property itself may be used for support only if the parents are not solvent and the grandparents have no duty to support (Sec. 141 Austrian CC) or the child's needs cannot be covered in some other way (Sec. 149(2) Austrian CC, at the end).[2] Parents must administer their children's property free of charge.[3] However, the costs of administration, including the preservation of the property and the expenditures necessary for proper business operations are to be paid from the property (Sec. 149(2) Austrian CC).

BELGIUM

The rights of the parents concerning the property of their children are divided in two categories: the rights concerning the administration of the property of the children and their legal representation (Art. 376-379 Belgian CC) and the right of use and enjoyment of the property (Art. 384-387 Belgian CC). The administration of the child's property is distinguished by three types of acts: acts in which the legal representative generally has the power to initiate and undertake alone, acts that require the authorisation of the competent authority and acts that are forbidden.

To perform the acts of the first category, the holder(s) of parental responsibilites has complete power, as long as the holder exercises it in the interests of the child. If both parents jointly hold parental responsibilities, when one parent performs certain acts of administration alone there is a presumption of agreement by the other parent towards third parties acting in good faith . This

---

1 EBRV 296 BlgNR XXI. GP, p. 53 (explanatory notes to Government bill, 296 supplements to the stenographic minutes of the National Assembly, XXI legislative period); see *Oberster Gerichtshof*, 26.02.2003, *Juristische Blätter*, 2003, p. 571.

2 *Oberster Gerichtshof*, 13.02.2002, *Österreichischer Amtsvormund, 2002*, p. 83 (U 351).

3 *Landesgericht für Zivilrechtssachen* Vienna, 30.10.1987, *EFSlg*. 53.962.

presumption exists notwithstanding the possibility of one parent addressing the Juvenile Court when there is disagreement with the actions of the other. When the third party knew or reasonably could have known of the disagreement of the other parent, the third party is not protected by the presumption of agreement (Art. 376 Belgian CC).[4] Although Art. 376 Belgian CC concerning the presumption of agreement only mentions the administration of the property and not the legal representation, it is admitted that each parent can act as plaintiff in a case against a third party acting in good faith.[5] When the claim is introduced by a third party, both parents must be involved. When only one parent has parental responsibilities over the child, the other parent has the right to supervise the way the other parent administrates the property of the child (Art. 374(4) and 376(4) Belgian CC).[6] The parent without parental responsibilities may request information from the other parent and third parties, and may address the Juvenile Court when it is in the interests of the child.[7]

The Belgian Law of 29 April 2001, as modified by the law of 13 February 2003, requires authorisation from the Justice of the Peace of the domicile of the child (or its residence) in order to perform a limited list of acts mentioned in Art. 410 Belgian CC (See Q 12a).[8] The only criterion required for the authorisation is that the demand is in the interests of the child. When both parents administrate the property of the child, both parents require the authorisation. There is no presumption of agreement towards third parties of good faith when one parent acts alone. When only one parent requires the authorisation, the other parent is summoned and heard, and becomes a party to the case by this convocation. Although both parents are involved in the procedure, the Justice of the Peace has the ability to authorise one of the parents to act alone when the parents do not agree on the action to be taken, or when one of the parents fails to appear (Art. 378(1)(5) Belgian CC).[9] When only one parent administrates the property of the child, only that parent requires an authorisation, however the other parent will be summoned and heard.[10]

Finally there are the prohibited acts; acts that have such a personal character that representation is excluded (*e.g.* to write a will) or, although not mentioned in the list of Art. 410, represent a risk of impoverishment of the child and,

---

4 A. DUELZ, *Le droit du divorce*, Brussels: Larcier, 2002, p. 170.
5 J. GERLO, *Personen- en Familierecht*, Bruges: Die Keure, 2003, p. 308.
6 P. SENAEVE, *Compendium van het personen- en familierecht*, Leuven: Acco, 2004, p. 130.
7 Juvenile Court of Charleroi, 16.12.1998, *J. dr. jeun.*, 2000, Vol. 198, p. 32.
8 H. CASMAN, 'De nieuwe voogdijwet', *Not. Fisc. M.*, 2001, p. 240-242.
9 T. MOREAU and J. SOSSON, 'La loi du 13 février 2003 modifiant certaines dispositions du Code civil et du Code Judiciaire en ce qui concerne la protection des biens du mineurs', *Rev. trim. dr. fam.* 2003, p. 699.
10 A. WYLLEMAN, 'Enkele specifieke problemen inzake de nieuwe regeling van de uitoefening van het ouderlijk gezag', in: *Gandaius Actueel I*, E. Story-Scientia, 1995, p. 156.

therefore, are incompatible with the mission of administration of someone's patrimony (*e.g.* to provide bail).

Additionally, the parent(s) who administrate(s) the child's property have (has) the legal right of use and enjoyment, which is the right to enjoy the fruits of the property of their children until they reach the age of majority or are removed from guardianship (Art. 384 Belgian CC). In return, the parents are obliged to fulfill the obligations of the usufructary, to raise and educate their children according to their income, to ensure that the capital of the minor remains intact and to pay the costs of the last illness or the funeral of the person from whom the child inherits (Art. 386 Belgian CC). This legal right of use and enjoyment does not include the use and enjoyment of the revenues of property that was given to the child or inherited by the child under the explicit condition that its parents would not have the right of use and enjoyment (Art. 387 Belgian CC), nor the revenues of estates that are attributed personally to the child because its parents are unworthy to acquire them (Art. 730 Belgian CC), nor the salary of the child. Finally, the legal right of use and enjoyment does not include use and enjoyment of the interest of money that is placed in a bank account by or on behalf of the child.[11]

BULGARIA

Being the legal representatives or guardians of their children, the parents, jointly or separately, are entitled to administer the child's property. This option stems from the argument contrary to Art. 73 § 2 Bulgarian Family Code: 'The disposal of real property and chattels, with the exception of fruits and perishables, the encumbering thereof with liabilities and in general the undertaking any transactions related to the property of minors, are allowed with the permission of the district court in the place of residence only in case of necessity or where this is in the child's obvious interests.' Any other actions with the child's property are considered to be actions of administration/management of the property.

The Bulgarian Family Code does not contain any definition of the concept of 'common management'. Any actions on such grounds shall stem either from the interpretation of the above text or from the judicial practice. The Supreme Court deems common management actions to be those actions in which the property is not disposed, but preserved, maintained and used.[12] The assessment regarding the type of action shall be provided for each particular case.

CZECH REPUBLIC

See Q 2f.

---

11 H. CASMAN and J.-P. MASSON, 'La nouvelle législation sur la tutelle', *Rev. trim. dr. fam.* 2002, p. 34, No. 25; F. SWENNEN and K. JANSSENS, 'Het nieuwe voogdijrecht', *R.W.* 2001-2002, 17, No. 86; S. Thielen, 'Administration légale et tutelle: Actes soumis à autorisation', in : Y.-H. LELEU (ed.), *Les incapacités*, Liege: CUP, 2003, p. 99.

12 Decision of the Supreme Court, 91-1974.

DENMARK

The guardian(s) must carry out his/her/their duties in the interest of the child. Income/interest may be used to support the child.[13] In the Guardianship Act there are rules concerning the administration of the child's property and it is also stipulated that transactions regarding property other than the use of income/interest must be approved by the administrative authorities.[14]

ENGLAND & WALES

Although it is generally said that parental responsibility includes the right to administer the child's property the precise extent of this right is obscure. Indeed, at common law there is confusion as to position of a parent *qua* parent and a parent as guardian of the estate.[15] So far as the former is concerned while there may be a right to administer the child's property it is reasonably clear there are no rights as such in the child's property.[16] The Law Commission concluded[17] that 'It may be that the father's powers of control over the child's person would include the power to direct the child in the management of property in the child's possession'.

The position of guardians of the estate was well summarised by the Law Commission. They commented as follows:[18]

> 'A guardian of the estate has, subject to the rights and powers of statutory owners, personal representatives and trustees for sale, the right to recover rents and profits from the minor's land and to manage his personal estate for the duration of the guardianship, *i.e.* he can control the income due to the infant and any of the personal profit to which the infant is legally as well as beneficially entitled, but is not entitled to receive or exercise powers over property to which the infant has only beneficial title, except income as it becomes payable. He must account to the minor for the profits and income of the estate received by him'.

It might be added that property of any value will normally be derived under a settlement or will and legal ownership usually vests in trustees.

FINLAND

The starting point in Finnish guardianship legislation is that guardianship should be as easy as possible for parents or other custodians of children who do

---

13 Danish Act on Guardianship, Art. 25(2).

14 Danish Act on Guardianship, Chapter 5.

15 See the discussion in Law Com Working Paper Report No. 91, *Guardianship*, 1985 at para. 2.32 *et seq*.

16 See BROMLEY, *Bromley's Family Law*, Butterworths, 3rd Ed., 1966, p. 463.

17 Law Com Working Paper Report No. 91 at para. 2.32.

18 Law Com Working Paper Report No 91 at para. 2.23.

not have any special property. Most parents are probably not even aware of the different duties which a guardian may have, but as soon the child receives significant assets or property, or if the child becomes an heir, the actions of the parents or other custodians in the administration of the child's property become an object of supervision by guardianship authorities, the magistrate and the court. In such a situation, the guardianship of the child shall be entered into a register of guardianship affairs (Sec. 65 and 66). The supervision of the guardianship happens in practice mainly by means of accountability (Sec. 50 - 56) and the necessity of asking for permission for certain transactions, and by means of other restrictions.

FRANCE

The *administration légale* (right of administration) belongs equally to both parents if they both hold parental responsibilities. The *administrateur légal* (legal representative) represents the child in all routine daily acts (legal transactions, Art. 389-3 French CC),unless the child is authorised by law or custom to act on his or her own behalf. The child may act alone in some situations: *e.g.* a child who is at least 16 can write his or her last will (*testament*, Art. 904 para. 1 French CC); a child with employment can decide to become a member of a trade union of her or his choice (Art. 411-6 French Employment Code), but one parent can oppose it; the child may also spend his or her own pocket money or, more generally, enter into small contracts.

The legal administrator can act alone for all *'actes d'administration'* (administration acts) *e.g.* remove the child's money from the bank[19] or pay lawyer's fees.[20] Legal administration also means that the parents have the power to represent the child in judicial proceedings. But if the child and the legal administrator seem to have opposite interests in a proceeding, the *juge des tutelles*[21] (guardianship court) or the judge before whom the proceedings are pending shall appoint an *ad hoc* administrator (a special administrator only for the pending proceedings, see Art. 388-2 French CC).

The French legal provisions distinguish between three kinds of judicial acts:

- those that concern the routine day to day management, in which one parent can act alone and is deemed to have received power to act alone from the other parent (Art. 389-4 French CC). This is the *gestion concurrente,* which means that father or mother can act alone.
- those that are important and serious (so called *actes de disposition,* disposition acts), see Art. 389-5 French CC. If the parents cannot reach an agreement, one of them can call the guardianship court judge and petition for the authorisation to act alone;
- those that are so serious that both parents must ask for judicial authorisation even if they agree upon the act to be made (see Art. 389-5

19 French Supreme Court, Civ. I, 20.03.1989, *D.* 1989. 406 with obs. MASSIP.

20 See French Supreme Court, Civ. I, 03.07.2001, *Bull. civ.* I, No. 195.

21 The *juge des tutelles* is a single judge of the *tribunal d'instance.*

para. 3 French CC): to renounce a right in the child's name, to contribute an immovable or a business concern belonging to the child to a partnership, to enter into a loan agreement on the child's behalf *etc.* The guardianship court judge is competent to give the necessary authorisation for such acts.

When only one parent is holder of parental responsibilities (for example in some situations with an extra-marital family, or after divorce or separation), the legal administration is exercised by one parent, but under judicial control (see Art. 389-6 French CC). The holder of parental responsibilities may undertake acts of administration alone but she or he needs judicial authorisation for all acts or disposition (Art. 457 French CC).

GERMANY

The content of the right to administer the child's property is a general obligation to conserve and to augment the child's assets. These assets include everything the child owns and acquires (immovables, movables, income *etc.*).[22] According to the principle of surrogation, the child's assets include anything purchased by the holder of parental care with the child's means, § 1646 German CC. The right to administer the child's property includes the legal representation of the child, § 1629 German CC, see Q 2d.

The Civil Code contains some basic rules on the administration of child's property. Money should be invested in accordance with the principles of 'profitable property management' ('*wirtschaftliche Vermögensverwaltung*') in that it must not to be used to cover expenses, § 1642 German CC. The Civil Code also gives some guidelines as to how the child's assets are to be used. Income is to be used primarily to cover the cost of administrating the property and the cost of maintaining the child. Any remaining income shall not be kept by the parents but be reinvested.[23] If the income is insufficient, the income of the child's gainful employment or independent gainful occupation (*Erwerbstätigkeit*) can be used, § 1649 para. 1 German CC. The original capital may only be touched if the child's maintenance would otherwise be endangered.[24]

If the income is not necessary for the administration of the child's assets and maintenance, it can also be used for two other purposes, i.e. the maintenance of the parents and the maintenance of any unmarried siblings. This possibility is based on the idea of family solidarity. The use of income is restricted, however, by the economic situation of the parties and 'equity'.

---

22 U. DIEDERICHSEN, in: PALANDT, *Bürgerliches Gesetzbuch,* 64th Edition, München: Beck, 2005, § 1626 German CC No. 19.

23 H. ENGLER, in: STAUDINGER, *Kommentar zum Bürgerlichen Gesetzbuch,* 13th Edition, Berlin: Gruyter, 2000, § 1642 German CC No. 7 *et seq.*

24 See U. DIEDERICHSEN, in: PALANDT, *Bürgerliches Gesetzbuch,* 63rd Edition, München: Beck, 2004, § 1642 German CC No. 4.

GREECE

The holder of parental responsibilities has, in principle, the right to administer the property of the child and to enter into any transaction so as to preserve, enhance, develop, or even burden the property.[25] It is worth noting, however, that a guardian is subject to more restrictions than the parents and is controlled by a supervisory council.

HUNGARY

The Hungarian Family Act regulates the administration of the child's property as a right of the parent who is the holder of parental responsibilities, but these rules are also to be applied, with some differences, to the guardians who hold parental responsibilities. Parents administer the child's property without the duty to provide security and account for it, however they must provide the same duty of care in their administration of the child's property as they do to their own matters. They are liable for serious negligence committed during the administration of the property.

There are strong rules regarding the administration of a child's property by guardians who hold parental responsibilities. Guardians have the duty to give an account to the public guardianship authority on a regular basis. When their guardianship comes to an end they must give a final accounting of the child's property. This duty to account is not as severe if the child has no property and the child's regular income does not exceed an amount stated by the Act; it's also easier if the guardian is a close relative of the child.

Both parents and the guardian can allot the income from a child's property to cover the expenses of the property's maintenance and administration, and also to cover the child's necessary expenses *e.g.* schooling, education, medical treatment, etc. There is a special exception if the guardian administers the child's property because the guardian, as opposed to the parent, does not have to maintain the child.

See Q 12 for restrictions to the parent's and the guardian's administration of the child's property.

IRELAND

Not applicable.

ITALY

Parental responsibilities include the right and duty to represent the child and to manage her or his property (Art. 320 Italian CC). If parental responsibilities are exercised jointly, each parent can individually make ordinary acts of disposition of the minor's property; however, extraordinary acts of disposition (alienation,

---

[25] S. KOUKOULI-SPILIOTOPOULOU, in: A. GEORGIADIS and M. STATHOPOULOS (eds.), *Civil Code commentary, Vol. VIII, Family Law (Arts. 1505-1694)*, 2nd Edition, Athens: Law & Economy, P. N. SAKKOULAS, 2003, p. 60, No. 131.

the establishment of pledges or mortgages, acceptation or renouncement of inheritances, legacy and donation; dissolution of common ownerships, contract loans, initiation of court proceedings regarding those acts, reference to an arbitrator, settlements) can only be exercised out of necessity or if they are obviously beneficial for the child and presuppose the authorisation of the guardianship judge (Art. 320 § 3 Italian CC). The collection of principal amounts must also be authorised, and the judge will determine how they shall be invested (Art. 320 § 4 Italian CC). In addition, the continuing operation of a commercial enterprise presupposes the authorisation of the court, given after prior consultation with the guardianship judge (Art. 320 § 5 Italian CC).

If a conflict of interests regarding property arises between the children, or between the children and the parents exercising the parental responsibility, the guardianship judge can appoint a special guardian (Art. 320 § 3 Italian CC). In order to avoid possible conflicts of interest, it is prohibited for the parents to acquire, even through an intermediary, goods or rights of the child that are the object of their parental authority. Acts performed in violation of this rule can be annulled at the request of the parents exercising the authority, or on the request of the child, his heirs or successors in interest (Art. 322 Italian CC); the action is proscribed until five years from the time the child reaches the age of consent.

Parents have the legal usufruct of their child's property for the support of the family and the education and moral guidance of the child (Art. 324 Italian CC).

LITHUANIA

These relationships are regulated by Art. 3.185-3.191 Lithuanian CC establishing parental rights and duties related to the property owned by children. According to Art. 3.185 Lithuanian CC, property owned by underage children shall be managed by the parents under the right of usufruct. The parents' right of usufruct may not be pledged, sold, transferred or encumbered in any way, and no execution may be charged against it; parents shall manage the property that belongs to their underage child by mutual agreement. In the event of a dispute over the management of the child's property, either parent may petition for a judicial order establishing the procedure for the management of the property; where the parents, or one of the parents, cause harm to the child's interests by mismanaging their underage child's property, the state institution for the protection of the child's rights or a public prosecutor may apply to the court for the removal of the parents from the management of the property that belongs to their underage child. Where warranted, the court shall remove the parents from the management of their underage child's property, revoke their right of usufruct to the child's property and appoint another person the administrator of the minor's property. Where the grounds for the removal no longer exist, the court may allow the parents to resume the management of their underage children's property under the right of usufruct.

According to Art 3.186 Lithuanian CC, parents are under the obligation to manage their underage children's property by giving paramount consideration to the interests of the children. The parents may use the fruits and income derived from their underage child's property to meet the needs of the family by taking account of the child's interests. In managing the property of their underage child, the parents have no right to acquire, directly or through intermediaries, this property or any rights to it. This rule shall also be applicable to auctioning a minor's property or interests in it. An action to have such transactions declared void may be brought by the child or the child's successors. The parents of an underage child may not enter into a contract of assignment of claim under which they would acquire the right of claim to their underage child's property or the child's rights to it.

If a transaction causes a conflict of interests between the underage children of the same parents or between an underage child and the child's parents, the court, on the application of either of the parents, shall appoint an *ad hoc* guardian to the transaction.

Where there is a conflict of interests between an underage child and one of the child's parents, the child's interests shall be represented and transactions shall be made by the parent whose interests do not conflict with those of the child. A breach of these rules may cause the court to declare the transaction void in an action brought by the child, one of the child's parents or their successors.

According to Art. 3.189 Lithuanian CC, the parents who manage their underage children's property under the right of usufruct may not transfer, pledge or encumber the right of usufruct in any way. The claims of the creditors of the parents of underage children may not be executed against the property of the underage children or against the right of usufruct of their parents.

According to Art. 3.190 Lithuanian CC, where parental authority is exercised by only one of the parents of a minor, the minor's property shall be managed only by that parent. Where the parents are divorced or separated, the right to manage the minor's property shall belong to the parent with whom the child lives. If a parent of an underage child enters into a new marriage, that parent shall retain the right of usufruct in respect to the underage child's property, but shall be obliged to transfer all the fruits and income derived from the property to the minor's bank account and to maintain separate accounts for the fruits in excess of the expenses for the child's education (training, education, maintenance). If the new spouse of the child's parent adopts the child, he or she shall also acquire the right to manage the underage child's property.

Parents shall lose the right to manage their underage children's property under the right of usufruct, when:

- the minor is emancipated under the law;
- the minor contracts a marriage in the procedure laid down by the law;
- the minor reaches majority;
- the court orders the parents removed from the management of their underage child's property;
- the court separates the children from the parents or limits their parental authority (Art. 3.191 Lithuanian CC).

Where the parents (or one of the parents with whom the child lives) continue to use the child's property after the end of the right of usufruct, they shall be obliged to return the property and all the income and benefits derived from the child's property to the child from the moment when the child or the child's representative demands it.

THE NETHERLANDS

The right to administer the estate of a child includes the right of usufruct (Art. 1:253l Dutch CC). Art. 1:253k Dutch CC determines that a number of articles from Title 14, section 6, paragraph 10 relating to the administration by the guardian (Art. 1:342 § 2, 1:344 up to and including to Art. 1:357 and 1:370 Dutch CC) apply *mutatis mutandis* to the administration of a minor's estate by the holder(s) of parental responsibilities. The right to administer a minor's property includes, according to Art. 1:253l Dutch CC, the right of usufruct over the child's capital, which is not a property right in the strict sense but is considered to be unconditionally personal, and cannot be transferred.[26] This right of usufruct, however, has a few limitations.

NORWAY

The right to administer the child's property is to a large extent limited by Art. 62 and 63 Norwegian Act on Guardianship 1927. All major decisions regarding the child's assets require the consent of the Public Guardian's Office. Financial assets of more than NOK 75,000 shall be managed by the Public Guardian's Office.

POLAND

The scope and contents of the right differ depending on the circumstances *i.e.* whether a child remains under parental authority of both parents, under parental authority of one of the parents (Art. 104 Polish Family and Guardianship Code) or under guardianship (Art. 160-162 Polish Family and Guardianship Code). The parents are obliged to administer the property of a child still under their parental authority with all due care (Art. 101 § 1 Polish Family and Guardianship Code). The net income from the child's property is to be used first to cover the maintenance of the child and his or her siblings'(if they are raised together) and costs of upbringing; the remaining income can be used to cover other reasonable needs of the family (Art. 103 Polish Family and Guardianship Code).

If only one of the parents holds parental authority, the court may order that parent to prepare the inventory of the child's property and notify the court as to all major changes in the property (Art. 104 Polish Family and Guardianship Code).

---

26 *Personen- en familierecht, Tekst en commentaar*, 2004, p. 315.

After the administration of the child's property ceases, the parents are obliged to return the property to the child or to the child's guardian. On the child's (or the guardian's) request, for up to one year following the end of the administration, the parents should present a financial report of the administration. The child, however, cannot demand an accounting with respect to the income realised from property during the exercise of parental authority (Art. 105 Polish Family and Guardianship Code).

A guardian cares for the child and the child's property under the supervision of the family court (Art. 155 § 1 Polish Family and Guardianship Code). In comparison to a person holding parental authority, the guardian's rights are limited. Firstly, the guardian should obtain the court's authorisation in all major issues regarding the minor (Art. 156 Polish Family and Guardianship Code). Additional obligations of the guardian are: to prepare an inventory of the property of the one under guardianship (Art. 160 § 1 Polish Family and Guardianship Code), to deposit specific items with the court (Art. 161 Polish Family and Guardianship Code) and to present an annual financial report of the property administration (Art. 165 Polish Family and Guardianship Code) to be confirmed by the court (Art. 166 Polish Family and Guardianship Code).

With regard to property administration, parents holding parental authority over a fully incapacitated child are subjected to restrictions analogous to those imposed on a guardian (Art. 108 Polish Family and Guardianship Code).

PORTUGAL

Although the law does not expressly stipulate this, legal literature understands parents to hold the power of both ordinary and extraordinary administration. In administering their children's property, parents should use the same diligence they employ when administering their own (Art. 1897 Portuguese CC), although they are not generally obliged to provide accounts of their administration (Art. 1899, Portuguese CC), nor to provide a guarantee (Art. 1898 Portuguese CC).

The power and duty of administration ceases when parental responsibility ends. Thus, when the child reaches majority or is emancipated, parents should hand over all the child's property (Art. 1900 No. 1 1st part Portuguese CC). Parents should hand over moveable property to the child in the state in which they found it. If the property no longer exists, the parents should pay their children for the value of the property unless the child has participated in the consumption of this property, or unless it perished for a reason not imputable to the parents (Art. 1900 No. 2 Portuguese CC).

RUSSIA

While executing the right to administrate the child's property parent(s) have the same rights and responsibilities as the civil law (Art. 37 Russian CC) attributes to a guardian of an legally incapable adult (Art. 60 (3) Russian Family Code).

The content of the parental right to administer the property of the child varies according to the child's age.[27] Children under the age of fourteen are legally incapable, so all acts of administration of property have to be performed by their parents (Art. 28 (1) Russian CC). Children from fourteen to eighteen are partially legally capable and can without parental consent, among others, dispose of their salary, study grants and other incomes, open bank accounts and administrate them (Art. 28 (2) Russian CC). For all other transactions children from fourteen to eighteen need the written consent of their parent(s) (Art. 28 (1) Russian CC).

The parental right of administration of the child's property is generally restricted by the obligation to acquire prior authorisation from the Guardianship and Curatorship Department for concluding or giving consent to conclusion of almost all transactions beyond the disposition of a child's income aimed to provide for the daily needs of the child (Art. 37 (1) Russian CC).

SPAIN

Administration has to be understood in a broad sense. Parents have the ability to take any action which benefits the child. There are, however, some exceptions or limitations concerning certain goods or transactions, which will be developed under Q 12.

Catalan law's degree of diligence is stricter than the Civil Code's. The Spanish CC establishes that parents are to administer their child's property as if it were their own (Art. 164 Spanish CC); the Catalan Family Code requires the administration to be carried out as it would be by a good administrator (Art. 145 Catalan Family Code), although certain duties, like that of keeping a record of the property, are exempted since it is understood that the basis of administration by the parental responsibility holder is trust and good will. If the child is subject to guardianship instead of parental responsibility there is a much stricter control of the administration (see Q 31).

Administration of the child's property by parental responsibility holders is not remunerated although there is a right to compensate necessary expenses. If children own property they are expected to participate in household expenses.

Upon termination of parental responsibility parental responsibility holders will be held accountable, at the request of the child and for a limited time period (three years in the Spanish CC and two years in the Catalan Family Code).

SWEDEN

The guardian is responsible for taking care of the child's property and representing the child in legal proceedings regarding the property, Chapter 12 Sec. 1 Swedish Children and Parents Code. As a main rule, although the guardian is free to decide how the assets shall be handled, the guardian shall

---

27 L. PCHELINTZEVA, *Family Law* (*Semeinoe pravo*), Moscow: Norma-Infra M, 1999, p. 292.

carry out his or her duties prudently, always favouring the best interests of the child.[28] The guardian is liable to compensate the child for any intentional or negligent damage, Swedish Children and Parents Code (Chapter 12, Section 14).

The child's property to a reasonable extent shall be used for his or her living expenses and education, with the remaining part invested in a manner that safeguards the value of the property and provides profits, Chapter 12 Sec. 4 Swedish Children and Parents Code. The guardian's administration of the child's property is supervised by the Chief Guardian (*Överförmyndaren*) who also may order the guardian to account for the administration, Chapter 13 Sec. 18 Swedish Children and Parents Code.

SWITZERLAND

'Parents may use the income from their child's property for the child's maintenance, upbringing and education and, to the extent it is equitable, may also use this income for the needs of the household' (Art. 319 § 1 Swiss CC). Accordingly, parents may obtain relief from their obligation to provide maintenance to the extent of income from the child's property. Income from the child's property not required for the child's maintenance may only be used by the parents for the needs of the household as a whole on condition that their own income does not suffice for this purpose.[29]

'Settlements, compensation for damages and similar benefits may only be partially used, based on the day-to-day requirements for the child's maintenance' (Art. 320 § 1 Swiss CC).

'If it should prove necessary to cover the costs of maintenance, upbringing or education, the guardianship authority may permit parents to draw on the rest of the child's property for certain amounts' (Art. 320 § 2 Swiss CC). For this, the parents must obtain the authority's permission to use the child's property in advance, stating a predetermined amount for a designated purpose.

The child's property and the income from the property may also be used to pay maintenance support to relatives on behalf of the child (Art. 328 § 1 Swiss CC). However, the approval of the guardianship authority is required for drawing on the property in this manner (Art. 320 § 2 Swiss CC). However, a commensurate education for the child may not be endangered as a result thereof.[30]

---

28 Chapter 13 Sec. 1 and Chapter 12 Sec. 3 Swedish Children and Parents Code.

29 Guardianship Division of the High Court of the Canton of Aargau, maintenance support for relatives from minor children for their mothers (Art. 328, 392 Section 2 ZGB), Zeitschrift für Vormundschaftswesen, 1997, p. 137 - 141.

30 C. HEGNAUER, *Grundriss des Kindesrechts*, p. 233.

QUESTION 12

B. THE CONTENTS OF PARENTAL RESPONSIBILITIES

Are there restrictions with respect to:
(a) Certain goods and/or values (inherited property, gift...);
(b) Salary of the child; or
(c) Certain transactions?

AUSTRIA

(a) Certain goods and/or values (inherited property, gift...)

If a minor has a significant amount of property,[1] the court must oversee its administration with the aim of preventing any endangerment of the child's interests (Sec. 133(1) Non-Contentious Proceedings Act *[Außerstreitgesetz]*). If parents, grandparents, or foster parents are entrusted with administration of property as part of their parental responsibilities, the court will generally oversee the administration of the property only if it includes immovables or if the value of the property or the annual income from it significantly exceeds €10,000 (Sec. 133(2) *Außerstreitgesetz*).[2] In any event, the legal representative must gather records of the administration of significant amounts of property, safeguard them, and inform the court if immovables are acquired or if the value of €10,000 is exceeded (Sec. 135(3) *Außerstreitgesetz*).

If a parent or a third party gives property to a minor child and at the same time excludes a parent from administering that property, the other parent shall be responsible for administering it. If both parents or the sole parent entitled to exercise parental responsibilities is excluded, the court shall entrust other persons with administering the property (Sec. 145c Austrian CC).

The authority of a person entrusted with parental responsibilities (other than a parent or child welfare agency) to receive payments on behalf of the child is restricted by statute: Such a person can receive payments to the child that exceed €10,000 and give a receipt for them only if authorized to do so by the court. Without such authorization, the payment made to the representative releases the debtor from its debt only if the payment remains part of the child's property or is used for the child's purposes (Sec. 234 Austrian CC). Banks, in

1 The term "a significant amount of property" was introduced by the 2003 *Außerstreitgesetz*, which took effect on January 1, 2005. It has no statutory definition and has not yet been interpreted by case law. See S. Kriwanek, *Das neue Außerstreitverfahren*, Vienna: LexisNexis ARD Orac, 2004, p. 49.

2 For court control where the best interests of the child are directly threatened, see infra Q 13.

particular, must ensure that the representative has court authorization to withdraw such large amounts from the child's savings or checking account.[3]

(b) Salary of the child

A minor over the age of 14 is entitled to keep the income he (or she) earns: He can administer it and dispose of it and make commitments based on the economic foundation for this income as long as he does not thereby endanger his support (Sec. 151(2) Austrian CC). This also applies to property and rights acquired through the use of this income, e.g. an item purchased, an insurance payment made under private insurance if the premium was paid from the child's income, lotto winnings from a ticket acquired from the child's income. In addition, the legal representative or a third party with the consent of the legal representative can also leave other matters to the child's free disposition (Sec. 151(2) Austrian CC).[4]

(c) Certain transactions

Exceptional representational acts on the part of a parent in property matters require the consent of the other parent and the approval of the court to be legally valid unless the matter is part of proper business operations. This includes, for example, the sale and encumbrance of real estate; the acquisition, transformation, sale, or dissolution of an enterprise; waiver of a right of inheritance, unconditional acceptance or renunciation of an inheritance; acceptance of an encumbered gift or rejection of a proffered gift; certain types of monetary investments (*e.g.* granting a loan or acquiring real estate); filing a complaint and making all procedural dispositions that relate to the matter in dispute (Sec. 154(3) Austrian CC).

Under the special provisions of Sec. 230-230e Austrian CC and Article XVII of the 2001 Act Amending the Law of Parent and Child *(Kindschaftsrechts-Änderungsgesetz)*, monetary assets must be promptly invested in a secure investment that is as profitable as possible – to the extent they are not used for special purposes, such as support. If a person other than a parent is entrusted with parental responsibilities, the remaining movable property that is not needed for or does not appear to be suitable for the satisfaction of the child's present or future needs is to be liquidated at the best possible price. Court approval is required if the market value of an individual item is expected to exceed €1,000 or the total value of the items to be liquidated is expected to exceed €10,000 (Sec. 231 Austrian CC). A person other than a parent who is entrusted with parental responsibilities may sell real estate only in an emergency. It must be sold with court approval for the clear advantage of the child (Sec. 232 Austrian CC).

---

3 I. HOLZHAMMER/R. HOLZHAMMER, *Ehe und Familie*, 2nd Edition, Freistadt: Plöchl Verlag, 2001, p. 89.

4 J. STABENTHEINER in: P. RUMMEL, *ABGB-Kommentar*, suppl. vol. 1, 3rd Edition, Vienna: Manz Verlag, 2000, § 151 Marg. No 5 and 6.

BELGIUM

(a) Certain goods and/or values (inherited property, gift...)

According to Art. 378 Belgian CC, a list of certain acts can only be performed with the prior authorisation of the Justice of the Peace. Art. 378 Belgian CC refers to Art. 410 Belgian CC, which is the article concerning the authorisation required by the guardian of the child when the system of guardianship has replaced the institution of parental authorities. Holders of parental responsibilities and guardians are submitted to (almost) the same rules concerning the administration of the child's property.

An authorisation by the Justice of the Peace, which will only be given in the interests of the child, is required in order (Art. 378 Belgian CC, referring to Art. 410(1), (1) to (6), (8), (9) and (11) to (14)):[5]

- to alienate the goods of the minor (movable and immovable goods); all alienations are concerned (sale, change,[6] contribution in a company ...). There are two legal exceptions: first, the fruits and undeliverable objects; and second, the goods that are administrated by a financial institution. The parents (or the sole parent) who have the right to administrate the property of the child are entitled to the fruits of the goods of their minor children as a result of their legal right of use and enjoyment. They may alienate these goods without authorisation (Art. 384 Belgian CC), given a few exceptions (See Q 11). This regulation gives the parents the opportunity to recuperate some of the costs of the housing, education, maintenance and supervision of the child (Art. 203 Belgian CC), and it avoids complicated bills at the end of the parents' administration of the child's property, since the parents must only account for the administration of the property and of the revenues over which they do not have the legal right of use and enjoyment (Art. 379 Belgian CC) (See Q 13). Art. 410(2) Belgian CC states that souvenirs and other personal goods of the child cannot be alienated unless it is absolutely necessary, and that they are to be kept at the disposal of the

---

5 H. CASMAN and J.-P. MASSON, 'La nouvelle législation sur la tutelle', *Rev. trim. dr. fam.* 2002, p. 48; S. MAERTENS and G. BENOIT (eds.), *Actualia ouderlijk gezag, voogdij en voorlopig bewind*, Bruges: Die Keure, 2004, p. 51-52, 70-88 and p. 93-148; S. MOSSELMANS, 'Art. 378 and 410 Burgerlijk Wetboek', in: X, *Personen en familierecht. Artikelsgewijze commentaar*, Antwerp: Kluwer (looseleaf.), 2003; W. PINTENS, 'De voogdijwet herbekeken - Een eerste toelichting bij de reparatiewet van 13 februari 2003', *T. Vred.*, 2003, p. 129-139; F. SWENNEN and K. JANSSENS, 'Het nieuwe voogdijrecht', *R.W.*, 2001-02, p. 16; S. THIELEN, 'Administration légale et tutelle: actes soumis à authorisation', in: Y.-H. LELEU (ed.), *Les incapacités*, Liege: Edition Formation Permanente CUP, 2003, p. 115 and 118; A. WYLLEMAN, 'De verkoop van roerende en onroerende goederen van minderjarigen', in: P. SENAEVE, J. GERLO and F. LIEVENS (eds.), *De hervorming van het voogdijrecht*, Antwerp: Intersentia, 2002, p. 311-315.

6 C. DE BUSSCHERE, 'Nieuw artikel 411 B.W. - Is ruil van goederen tussen minderjarige en zijn voogd of toeziende voogd wettelijk mogelijk of daarentegen wettelijk absoluut verboden?', *T. Not.* 2002, p. 190.

child until its majority. Second, Art. 410 Belgian CC, referring to Art. 407(1) Belgian CC, states that when the minor's goods (*e.g.* a stock account) are administrated by a financial institution, no authorisation is required for the goods' alienation. Art. 407 Belgian CC provides the conditions under which money and valuables of the minor that are placed under the administration of a financial institution by decision of the Justice of the Peace can be withdrawn by the guardian. It is disputed whether the parents (instead of only the guardian) may also ask the Justice of the Peace for an authorisation to have the goods placed under the administration of a financial institution, now that Art. 378 Belgian CC only refers to Art. 410 Belgian CC, but not to Art. 407 Belgian CC. Certain authors claim that parents may also acquire this authorisation; otherwise a proper administration of the child's property would be unnecessarily difficult. Indeed, placing the child's money and valuables with a financial institution not authorised on demand of the parents would require more authorisations than a guardian must have in order to alienate goods of the minor. Others advocate that no authorisation is necessary for the parents to place the valuables with a financial institution and/or alienate them once they are placed with a financial institution.

- to acquire real estate. Although not mentioned, certain authors consider that personal property also requires authorisation. The majority of the authors, however, conclude that collecting money from the child's account does not qualify as an alienation for which an authorisation is required according to Art. 410(1)(1) Belgian CC;
- to contract a loan and to mortgage or to pledge goods of the minor;
- to enter into a lease of land, a commercial lease or a rental agreement for more than nine years, or to renew a commercial lease;
- to renounce an inheritance or a universal legacy, or accept it, but only under the benefit of inventory; to accept a donation or a specific legacy;
- to conclude a covenant of joint ownership entered into for a period of maximum five years, according to Art. 815 Belgian CC;
- to effect a compromise or to enter into an arbitration agreement;
- to pursue a trading enterprise that is acquired by hereditary succession by operation of law or succession by will;
- to alienate souvenirs and other personal objects, even when they have limited value;
- to dispose of goods which are inalienable according to a decision taken in respect of Art. 379 or 776 Belgian CC; Art. 379 provides that every court decision concerning sums of money that are attributed to the minor must decide that these sums are placed on a personalized bank account of the child; the court has no alternative. Except for the legal right of use and enjoyment of the parents, the account can not be disposed of until the age of majority of the minor; according to Article 776, the same rules apply to assets inherited by the child, although the parents may ask permission from the Justice of the Peace to use the account's assets.

- When only one parent demands the authorisation, the other will be heard or at least convoked. In case of a conflict of interest between the parents or when one parent fails to appear, one parent can be authorised to perform the action alone (Art. 378 Belgian CC).[7]

(b) Salary of the child

The salary earned by the child is its own property. Art. 44 Belgian Law on the Labour Contract confirms that the employer correctly pays the salary directly to the child, except when there is opposition from the mother, the father (or the guardian). Moreover, Art. 387 Belgian CC excludes the professional income of the child, including the revenues from property acquired with its professional income, from the legal right of use and enjoyment of the parents. This exception on the general right of use and enjoyment is justified by the wish to avoid the limitation of the diligence or the sense of initiative of the child. Although the salary is the own property of the child and is excluded from the parent's legal right of use and enjoyment, its administration is submitted to the parental authorities. The child normally can not dispose of its salary.[8]

(c) Certain transactions

Apart from the transactions already mentioned in Q 12a, Art. 378 Belgian CC refers to Art. 935(3) Belgian CC. The latter Article states that the parents and even the grandparents may accept a gift to their minor child without an authorisation from the Justice of the Peace. Thus an exception is made to the required authorisations of Art. 378 in conjucntion with Art. 410 Belgian CC. When the parents both give and accept for the child, a conflict of interest arises, in which case a guardian ad hoc needs to be appointed to act on behalf of the child (Art. 378 Belgian CC).[9]

BULGARIA

(a) Certain goods and/or values (inherited property, gift...)

Yes, there are. The restriction does not apply to the type of rights, but to the type of actions regarding the property of the child. Parents are not entitled to commit actions to the child's property, that change the character of the property right,[10] such as transferring, restricting, transforming, terminating, or relating to

---

7 T. MOREAU and J. SOSSON, 'La loi du 13 février 2003 modifiant certaines dispositions du Code civil et du Code judiciaire en ce qui concerne la protection des biens des mineurs', *Rev. trim. dr. fam.*, 2003, p. 698-699 ; S. MOSSELMANS, 'Art. 378 Burgerlijk Wetboek', in: X, *Personen en familierecht. Artikelsgewijze commentaar*, Antwerp: Kluwer (looseleaf), 2003, p. 42; W. PINTENS, 'De voogdijwet herbekeken - Een eerste toelichting bij de reparatiewet van 13 februari 2003', *T. Vred.*, 2003, p. 128-129.

8 P. DENIS, 'La loi du 3 juillet 1978 relative aux contrats de travail', *Ann. Dr.*, 1978, p. 384; M. TACQUET and C. WANTIEZ, 'La loi sur les contrats de travail (3 juillet 1978)', *J.T.T.* 1978, No. XXXI, p. 295.

9 Justice of the Peace of Houthalen-Helchteren, 28.11.2001, *A.J.T.*, 2001, p. 720, annotated F . DEBUCQUOY; J. VERSTRAETE, 'Schenkingen aan minderjarigen', *Waarvan Akte*, 2002, p. 51.

10 Decision of the Supreme Court, 91-1974.

money withdrawals from the bank accounts of the child. Such action is only possible following permission from the district court for each separate transaction (Art. 73 § 2 Bulgarian Family Code). The court shall issue its permission only where such action is of necessity to the child or where this is in the child's obvious interests. The court makes this assessment in each particular case where such permission is applied for and provisions are made for reviews during judicial holidays too.[11] The Bulgarian Child Protection Act stipulates that the court may request the opinion of the Child Protection Department (Art. 15 § 6), or, if the disposition is carried without the permission of the court, it shall be voidable.[12]

(b) Salary of the child

Yes, according to Art. 4 § 2 Bulgarian Act on the Persons and the Family, children shall have the ability to dispose of what they earn from their own labour.

(c) Certain transactions

Certain actions with the property of children are forbidden by the Bulgarian Family Code. According to Art. 73, § 3: 'The donation, waiver of rights, lending and guaranteeing the debts of third persons by pledge, mortgage or endorsement, effected by children not yet of full age are null and void. This does not apply to the transactions executed by married minors to whom only the limitation of Art. 12 para. 3 is relevant'. Art. 12 § 3 reads: 'With the contraction of marriage a minor becomes competent but can only dispose of real estate with the permission of the district court in the place of the child's residence.'

CZECH REPUBLIC

(a) Certain goods and/or values (inherited property, gift...)

When dealing with the child's estate the parents are only restricted by the general provision of Sec. 28 Czech CC, according to which, in essential matters, the legal representative may deal with the estate of the represented person only with consent of the court. Typically, the court will approve the parents' acting on behalf of the child.

(b) Salary of the child

According to the established practice, the child who has an income from its own work is entitled to deal with it independently within the extent of the child's legal capacity to act (Sec. 9 Czech CC). However, the child cohabiting with its parents and having an income from its own work or estate is obligated to contribute to cover common family expenses (Sec. 31 § 4 Czech Family Code).

---

11 According to Art. 192 § 2 § 4 Bulgarian Law on the Judicial Authority.

12 Art. 27 Bulgarian Act on Obligations and Contracts.

(c) Certain transactions
When dealing with the child's estate the parents are restricted only by the general provision of Sec. 28 Czech CC, according to which, in essential matters, the legal representative may deal with the estate of the represented person only with the consent of the court. Typically, the court will approve the parents' acting on behalf of the child.[13]

DENMARK

(a) Certain goods and/or values (inherited property, gift...)
Transactions whereby the property is dispersed must be approved by the administrative authorities.[14] If certain conditions are laid down in a will or deed of gift then the guardian(s) must respect these.

(b) Salary of the child
A child of 15 is free to spend the salary that he/she has earned as well as any inheritance or gift where this has been stipulated in the will/deed of gift and money which the guardian(s) has/have given him/her to spend.[15]

(c) Certain transactions
Transactions whereby the property is dispersed must be approved by the administrative authorities. There are specific rules stipulating how the property must be administered.[16]

ENGLAND & WALES

(a) Certain goods and/or values (inherited property, gift...)
The law is by no means clear on this but generally it would seem that the responsibility to administer the child's property is a general one. However, one commentary[17] explains that property brought by a child out of his own income remains exclusively that of a child and clothes (and presumably other types of gifts) bought for an older child belongs to that child.

(b) Salary of the child
Again the law is rather under developed but there is some authority for saying that those with parental responsibility have no claim on a child's salary/wages.[18]

(c) Certain transactions
There is no authority to suggest that there are any such restrictions.

---

13 H. NOVA, 'Ochrana majetku nezletilých osob', *Pravni radce*, 6/1997.
14 Danish Act on Guardianship, Art. 39.
15 Danish Act on Guardianship, Art. 42(1).
16 Danish Act on Guardianship, Chapter 5.
17 See BROMLEY, *Bromley's Family Law*, Butterworths, 3rd Ed., 1966, p. 463.
18 See *Williams v Boulton* [1948] 1 All ER 603, cited by BROMLEY, *Bromley's Family Law*, Butterworths, 3rd Ed., 1966, p. 463.

FINLAND

(a) Certain goods and/or values (inherited property, gift...)

The actions of a guardian in the administration of a minor's property are subject to a number of restrictions. Sec. 34 Finnish Guardianship Services Act includes 13 paragraphs describing different actions that the guardian is not entitled to perform without the permission of the guardianship authority. These restrictions encompass proceeds concerning housing property (para. 10 and 11), real property (para. 1, 3 and 12), inheritance and division of marital property (para. 7, 8 and 9).

(b) Salary of the child

An incompetent person, such as a minor, has the right to the proceeds of his or her own work. The guardian has, however, the right to take this property into his or her administration if the incompetent person exercises the right in a manner that is obviously contrary to his or her best interests or in order to prevent the incompetent person from coming to harm if there is an imminent danger (Sec. 25 para. 2 Finnish Guardianship Services Act).

(c) Certain transactions

The actions of a guardian in the administration of a minor's property are subject to a number of restrictions. Sec. 34 Finnish Guardianship Services Act includes 13 paragraphs describing different actions that the guardian is not entitled to perform without the permission of the guardianship authority. These restrictions encompass the incurrence of a loan (other than a student loan guaranteed by the state) or assumption of liability for a bill of exchange or the debt of another person (para. 5 and see also para. 2); business operations in the name of the ward (para. 5) and the purchase of investment targets other than those listed in para. 13a - 13e. The guardian is however entitled to freely invest the ward's property in stocks.[19]

FRANCE

(a) Certain goods and/or values (inherited property, gift...)

Yes for *administration légale* (right of administration) and *jouissance légale* (right to use and enjoyment)(see Q 9). See Art. 389-3 para. 3 French CC for the right of administration: the property given to the child under the condition that it should be administrated by a third person is not subject to legal parental administration.

See also Art. 387 French CC for the right to use and enjoyment: the right to use the child's property does not extend to property acquired by the child through its work, nor to property donated or bequeathed to the child under the express condition that the parents may not have use and enjoyment of the property. If the parents' legal right of use has been expressly excluded by the testator or the donor, the parents still keep the right to administer the property but are not allowed to spend the yields. It is also possible for the testator or the donor to

---

19 P. VÄLIMÄKI, *Holhoustoimen pääpiirteet*, WSOY Lakitieto, Helsinki 2003, p. 93 - 99.

expressly exclude the parents' legal administration of the given or inherited property.[20]

(b) Salary of the child

Yes for the right to use and enjoyment. (see Art. 387 French CC). The salary of the child and the property bought with this salary is not subject to the parental right of use and enjoyment.[21]

(c) Certain transactions

Yes. As seen above (see Q 10) some transactions require the consent of both holders of parental responsibilities (so called *gestion conjointe*, Art. 389-5 para. 1 French CC: this applies to acts of dispositions). If the parents do not agree on the consent, the one who wants to undertake the act must petition the judge of the guardianship court for authorisation.

Some very important and serious transactions require not only the consent of the holders of parental responsibilities, but also the authorisation of the guardianship court (see Art. 389-5 para. 3 French CC); this applies to some sales, credit contracted on the child's behalf, a contribution of an immovable or a business concern belonging to the minor child to a partnership, or a renunciation to a right in the child's name.[22]

GERMANY

(a) Certain goods and/or values (inherited property, gift…)

There is a general restriction for the holder of parental responsibility with respect to the child's property. The parents may only use income from the child's property for their own support and for the support of siblings when it is not needed for the proper management of the property or for the child's maintenance, and if such a use is equitable in view of the assets and income of all the parties involved (§ 1649 para. 2 German CC).

There can also be restrictions to the administration of property concerning certain property, especially those that are inherited. The right and the duty to administer the child's property does not extend to property acquired by the child *mortis causa* or received by him as a gratuitous disposition *inter vivos* under § 1638 para. 1 German CC, if there were dispositions that the parents should not administer the property made by the testator by testamentary disposition or by the donor at the time the gift was given. Anything the child acquires by reason of a right belonging to such property or by way of

---

20 See G. CORNU, *Droit civil, La famille,* 2001, Paris: Montchrestien, 7th Ed., No. 97, p. 191.

21 See G. CORNU, *Droit civil, La famille,* 2001, Paris: Montchrestien, 7th Ed., No. 97, p. 191.

22 See, for example, for the approval of a judgment in the name of the children (the judicial decision concerned the damages suffered by the children. The approval (*acquiescement*) meant renunciation to appeal), French Supreme Court, Civ. I, 03.03.1992, *Gaz. Pal.*, 4-8 sept. 1992. Pan. p. 219. See also French Supreme Court, Civ. I, 06.07.1982, *Bull. civ.* I, No. 252.

compensation for the destruction, damage or deprivation of an item belonging to the property, or through a legal transaction involving the property, similarly may not be administered by the parents, § 1638 para. 2 German CC. If it is determined by testamentary disposition or upon making a gift that one of the parents is not to administer the property, it shall be administered by the other parent; to this extent the latter will represent the child (§ 1638 para. 3 German CC).

Another restriction concerns administration under instructions of third parties. Anything which the child acquires *mortis causa*, or which is given him as a gratuitous disposition *inter vivos*, shall be administered by the parents according to the instructions contained in the testamentary disposition or given at the time of making the gift, § 1639 para. 1 German CC. According to § 1639 para. 2 German CC the parents are permitted to deviate from the instructions to the same extent a guardian is permitted to do so under § 1803 para. 2, 3 German CC.

For all assets acquired by the child *mortis causa* the parents have to draw up an inventory of property, which is then submitted to the family court, § 1640 para. 1 German CC. However, this is not necessary if the value of property does not exceed 15.000 Euros or the testamentary disposition stated that no inventory has to be drawn up, § 1640 para. 2 German CC.

(b) Salary of the child

Where an under age child is employed with the authorisation of his or her parents, the child has the legal capacity to act in respect to the conclusion or dissolution of an employment contract, § 113 German CC. However, the general rules apply to the salary of the child. As far as there is no consent from the holder of the care for the property, the freedom of the child to dispose of his salary is not unlimited.[23] There can be, however, a general consent of the holder of parental responsibility which can also be given implicitly.[24]

(c) Certain transactions

There are several restrictions concerning certain transactions. One category of restrictions are 'subjective limits.'[25] The representation of a child by his or her parents is excluded if the parents' activities give rise to a conflict between their own interests and the interests of their child, §§ 1629 para. 2, 1795 German CC. This is especially the case if the parent represents the child in a transaction with his spouse or a relative in direct line, unless the transaction is only the performance of an existing obligation (§ 1795 No. 1 German CC).

---

23 See U. DIEDERICHSEN, in: PALANDT, *Bürgerliches Gesetzbuch*, 64th Edition, München: Beck, 2005, § 1626 German CC No. 19, 20.

24 L. M. PESCHEL-GUTZEIT, in: STAUDINGER, *Kommentar zum Bürgerlichen Gesetzbuch*, 13th Edition, Berlin: Gruyter, 2002, § 1626 German CC No. 66.

25 H. ENGLER, in: STAUDINGER, *Kommentar zum Bürgerlichen Gesetzbuch*, 13th Edition, Berlin: Gruyter, 2000, vor §§ 1638 - 1665 German CC No. 2.

There can also be no parental representation in the case of § 181 German CC, *i.e.* in a contract between the child and the parent (§ 1795 para. 2 German CC). These restrictions do not apply though, where the transaction can only be beneficial for the child.[26]

§ 1643 German CC lists also finite types of cases where parents may only represent their child if the family court expressly agrees to the legal transactions to be performed in the child's name. The approval of the family court is necessary for important or unusual transactions. The first category are legal transactions involving land or ships (§ 1821 German CC), transactions involving the full property of the child or an inheritance (§ 1822 No. 1 German CC), contracts involving the acceptance or refusal of a purchase or a business contract affecting this purchase (§ 1822 No. 3 German CC), lease contracts and other contracts involving obligations recurring over a year after the child comes of age (§ 1822 No. 5 German CC), credit (§ 1822 No. 8 German CC) and certain credit transactions, including the giving of a guarantee (§ 1822 No. 9 - 11 German CC).

There is also a general prohibition to making gifts. In representing a child the parents may not make gifts; such a contract is void.[27] Excepted are gifts which are deemed to be made under a moral obligation or out of common decency, § 1641 German CC.

GREECE

(a) Certain goods and/or values (inherited property, gift...)

According to Art. 1521 Greek CC parental management does not extend to assets which the child acquires by will or gift subject to the condition that the parents will not administer them. If the testator or the donor has not assigned the management of these assets to a specific person, the court will appoint a special guardian. Art. 1616 para. 2 Greek CC reiterates this provision in the case of guardianship. In addition, Art. 1616 para. 1 Greek CC provides that the guardian should conform to any conditions set by the deceased or the donor.[28]

(b) Salary of the child

Art. 135 Greek CC provides that a minor of 14 years of age or older can freely dispose of his or her earnings gained form employment. Hence, the salary of

---

26 Federal Supreme Court (Bundesgerichtshof; BGH), 27.09.1972, *Entscheidungen des Bundesgerichtshofs in Zivilsachen (BGHZ)* 59, 236; BGH, 16.04.1975, *FamRZ* 1975, 480.

27 H. ENGLER, in: STAUDINGER, *Kommentar zum Bürgerlichen Gesetzbuch*, 13th Edition, Berlin: Gruyter, 2000, § 1641 German CC No. 15.

28 Nevertheless, the donor or the deceased can neither release the guardian from the restrictions laid down under the law, nor relieve him from his responsibilities. See A. POULIADIS, in: A. GEORGIADIS and M. STATHOPOULOS (eds.), *Civil Code commentary, Vol. VIII, Family Law (Arts. 1505-1694)*, 2nd Edition, Athens: Law & Economy, P.N. SAKKOULAS, 2003, Art. 1616 Greek CC, p. 598, No. 3

the child is excluded from management by the holder of parental responsibilities.

(c) Certain transactions

The holders of parental responsibilities may not grant donations out of the child's property, unless these are for a special moral duty or by reason of dignity (Art. 1524 and 1617 Greek CC). Furthermore, both the parents and the guardian need judicial permission before entering into certain transactions which may be detrimental to the property of the child, such as the disposition of property, the sale or purchase of real estate, lending or borrowing, acting as a guarantee for the debts of a third person etc. (Arts. 1526 and 1624 Greek CC). In addition, a guardian needs the permission of the supervisory council before taking any action beyond the ordinary administration of the property (Art. 1619 Greek CC). Moreover, he may not use the property of the child for his own benefit (Art. 1618 Greek CC). This last restriction also applies to the parents. However, they may, in principle, use the income from the child's property to a reasonable extent in order to meet the needs of the family (Art. 1529 Greek CC).

HUNGARY

There are some restrictions with respect to certain goods and valuables of the child's property and also restrictions in respect to certain transactions. These rules are for the most part common to property administrated by either the parent or the guardian.

(a) Certain goods and/or values (inherited property, gift...)

There can be some of the child's property which is not under the parent's administration, and also some property in which the parent's (guardian's) right of administration is restricted.

Property given to a child with a donative clause stating that the property is not to be administered by the parent will not be under the parent's administration, aside from the situation in Q 12b. The donator is not obliged to give the grounds for the clause and can even appoint or propose the person he or she wants to administer the given property. The public guardianship authority will give attention to this proposal, provided it is in the child's interests. If there is no such proposal, the public guardianship authority will appoint a guardian to administer the property.

The parent's (or other holder of parental responsibilities) right to administer the child's property is restricted by the Act. The Act requires following property to be held by the public guardianship authority on behalf of the child:

- money of the child that does not have to be reserved for covering the child's actual expenses or for other grounds;
- valuables of the child, not including jewellery worn by the child;
- museum pieces in the child's ownership which are to be preserved by a museum.

The goods delivered to the public guardianship authority are taken from parental (or of the holder of parental responsibilities) administration only in the sense that they can only be disposed of with the guardianship's approval. The public guardianship authority can approve investing the child's money in assets for the child or investing in state bonds or insurance policies, provided in both cases that this is in the child's interest.

(b) Salary of the child
A child over 14 can freely dispose of his or her salary; it is not under the administration of the holder of parental responsibilities.

(c) Certain transactions
The regulations broadly enumerate transactions for which the holder of parental responsibilities needs the public guardianship authority's approval. These, among others, include:

- the disposal of the child's property which has been delivered to the public guardianship authority;
- transactions affecting movable or immovable property, securities, shares which are in the child's ownership and exceed a statutory amount;
- the alienation or encumbrance of any immovable the child's owns;
- transactions regarding the apartment in which the child has a lease agreement to live;
- certain legal statements regarding assets which are due to the child from inheritance.

IRELAND

(a) Certain goods and/or values (inherited property, gift...)
Yes.

(b) Salary of the child
The Irish Minimum Wage Act 2000 applies to all employees in Ireland including children. That said, sub-minimum rates of pay apply to children and those aged 18 or older if it is their first entry into employment. For children, the minimum wage is 70 % of the standard minimum wage.

(c) Certain transactions
Yes.

ITALY

(a) Certain goods /and or values (inherited property, gift...)
No, the restrictions provided by the Italian legal system do not concern the object but the activity.

(b) Salary of the child
Yes, the minor has the capacity to work pursuant to Art. 2 § 2 Italian CC.

(c) Certain transactions

Yes, extraordinary acts of disposition (alienation, obtaining a lien or mortgage, acceptance or renunciation of inheritances, legacies or donations, dissolution of common ownerships, contract loans, initiation of court procedures relating to these actions, reference of an arbitrator, settlements) can only be performed without the authorisation of the guardianship judge in cases of necessity or if there is an obvious advantage for the child (Art. 320 § 3 Italian CC). If a conflict of interests regarding property arises between the children, or between the children and the parents exercising the parental responsibility, the guardianship judge can appoint a special guardian (Art. 320 § 3 Italian CC). In order to avoid possible conflicts of interest, the parents are prohibited from acquiring, even through an intermediary, goods or rights of the child that are the object of their parental authority (Art. 322 Italian CC).

LITHUANIA

(a) Certain goods and/or values (inherited property, gift...)

Yes. According to Art. 3.187 Lithuanian CC, parents shall have no right to manage the property under the right of usufruct if that property:

- has been acquired for the money earned by the child;
- is intended for the purposes of the child's education, hobbies or leisure;
- has been devolved to the child by donation or succession on condition that it will not be made subject to usufruct.

(b) Salary of the child

Yes. According to Art. 2.7 and 3.187 Lithuanian CC, parents shall have no right to manage under the right of usufruct the salary of the child.

(c) Certain transactions

Yes. According to Parts 3 and 4 of Art. 3.186 Lithuanian CC, in managing the property of their underage child, the parents have no right to acquire, directly or through intermediaries, the property or any rights to it. This rule shall also be applicable to auctioning a minor's property or interests in it. An action to have such transactions declared void may be brought by the child or the child's successors. The parents of an underage child may not assign a claim under which they would acquire the right of claim to their underage child's property or the child's rights to it.

Without the prior leave of the court parents shall have no right to:

- alienate or charge their underage children's property or in any other way encumber the rights to it;
- accept or decline to accept inheritance on behalf of their underage children;
- enter into a lease agreement in respect of their underage children's property for a term exceeding five years;
- enter into an arbitration agreement on behalf of their underage children;

- enter into a loan agreement on behalf of their underage children for an amount exceeding four minimal monthly wages;
- invest the funds of their underage children in excess of ten minimal monthly wages (Art. 3.188 Lithuanian CC).

Art. 3.188 Lithuanian CC provides that if a transaction causes a conflict of interests between the underage children of the same parents or between an underage child and the child's parents, the court, on the application of either of the parents, shall appoint an *ad hoc* guardian to the transaction. Where there is a conflict of interests between an underage child and one of the child's parents, the child's interests shall be represented and transactions shall be made by the parent whose interests do not conflict with those of the child. A breach of the above mentioned rules may cause the court to declare the transaction void in an action brought by the child, one of the child's parents or their successors.

THE NETHERLANDS

(a) Certain goods and/or values (inherited property, gift...)

Art. 1:253m Dutch CC states that the holder of parental responsibilities does not have the right to usufruct of assets that a testator has provided by last will and testament or assets that have been gifted. Nor does it include assets that a minor inherits in his own right because the minor's father or mother is excluded on the basis of unworthiness.[29] In derogation of the general rule of Art. 253i § 1 and 3 Dutch CC according to which the holder(s) of parental responsibilities administer the capital of the minor, Art. 1:253i § 4 (c) Dutch CC, states that a person who donates or bequeaths property to a minor may, by last will and testament provide that another person who is not a holder of parental responsibilities shall conduct the administration of such property.

(b) Salary of the child

According to Art. 1:253l § 1 Dutch CC the general right of usufruct does not include the income from labour of the minor; however, the minor is obliged to contribute in accordance with its means to the costs of the household of the family if it lives with the parents. Neither does this right include incidental income.

(c) Certain transactions

According to Art. 1:345 Dutch CC the holder of parental responsibilities requires authorisation from the sub-district court for the performance of the following transactions for a minor:

(a) entry into contracts for the disposal of property of the minor, unless the transaction relates to money, or when it may be regarded as a normal administrative transaction, or when made pursuant to a judicial order;

(b) a bequest or gift, unless it is usual and not excessive;

---

29 ASSER-DE BOER, Mr. C. *Asser's Handleiding tot de beoefening van het Nederlands Burgerlijk Recht. Personen- en Familie Recht*, 2002, p. 629 No. 838.

(c) the acceptance of a bequest or gift subject to burdens or conditions;
(d) money loans or binding the minor as surety or several co-obligors;
(e) Agreeing that an estate to which the minor is entitled remains undivided for a specific period.

The sub-district court may specify that the guardian requires the court's authorisation to collect the claims of the minor, including disposing of balances at giro- or credit institutions. For the entry into a contract to bring a dispute in which the minor is involved to an end, the guardian does not require authorisation in the case of Art. 87 Dutch Code of Civil Procedure, or if the object of the uncertainty, or the dispute does not exceed a value of €700, or if the contract may be considered as an administrative act. The holder of parental responsibilities may not purchase, rent or lease the minor's property or land without the sub-district court's approval of the contract. Approval for a public sale, letting of property or the lease of land must be applied for within one month thereafter (Art. 1:346 Dutch CC). The minor has the right to invoke nullification of the transactions mentioned in the Art. 1:345 and 1:346 if the holder(s) of parental responsibilities has not asked for authorisation of the sub-district court, except if the legal transaction was gratuitous, the third party acted in good faith and the legal transaction did not cause the minor any harm (Art. 1:347 Dutch CC).

NORWAY

(a) Certain goods and/or values (inherited property, gift...)

All major decisions regarding the child's assets require the consent of the Public Guardian's Office. Financial assets of more than NOK 75,000 shall be managed by the Public Guardian's Office, Art. 62 and 63 Norwegian Act on Guardianship 1927. Inherited property or gifts are subject to these general rules, unless the deceased or the donor has stated that the child shall have the right to dispose of the assets itself, Act on Guardianship, 1927, Article 33.

(b) Salary of the child

A child 15 or older can dispose of money he or she earns from work without the consent of the guardian(s), Art. 33 Norwegian Act on Guardianship 1927.

(c) Certain transactions

The guardians need the consent of the Public Guardian's Office to dispose of real property belonging to the child Art. 49 Norwegian Act on Guardianship.

POLAND

(a) Certain goods and/or values (inherited property, gift...)

Yes. A contract for a gift or a testament of the donor or the testator may stipulate that the objects acquired by the child as a gift or inheritance shall not be administered by the parents. In this situation, the administration is carried out by a curator appointed by the donor or testator. In the absence of such an appointment the curator is to be named by the court (Art. 102 Polish Family and Guardianship Code).

(b) Salary of the child
Yes. The administration of the parents do not cover the child's salary or items given to the child for the child's free use (Art. 101 § 2 Polish Family and Guardianship Code).

(c) Certain transactions
Yes. Parents cannot act without court authorisation in cases exceeding the regular administration, nor can they consent to such acts being performed by the child (Art. 101 § 3 Polish Family and Guardianship Code).

PORTUGAL

(a) Certain goods and/or values (inherited property, gifts etc)
Not all of the child's property is administered by the parents. Parents only administer property that is not excluded by law (Art. 1888 Portuguese CC *a contrario*). The law specifies the categories of property that are not administered by parents. These are: property the child acquires through inheritance, if parental administration has been excluded for reasons of unworthiness or disinheritance (Art. 1888 No. 1(a), 2034 and 2166 Portuguese CC); property the child acquires as a gift or inheritance against the will of his or her parents (Art. 1888 No. 1(b) Portuguese CC); property the child acquires through gift or inheritance if parental administration has been excluded, even if they are otherwise legitimately entitled to do so (Art. 1888 No. 1(c) and No. 2 Portuguese CC).

(b) Salary of the child
Property acquired by a child over sixteen as product of his or her own work (Art. 1888 No. 1(d) and 127 No. 1(a), Portuguese CC).

(c) Certain transactions
Parents may not legally perform certain acts relating to the administration of a child's property without prior permission from the Public Prosecutor's Office (Art. 2 No. 1 Portuguese Law No. 272/2001 of 13 October 2001). Parents may not: sell or mortgage property unless it is subject to loss or deterioration (Art. 1889 No. 1(a) Portuguese CC); vote at a company's general assembly on matters concerning the company's dissolution (Art. 1889 No. 1(b), Portuguese CC); acquire a commercial or industrial establishment or continue to operate one that the child has acquired through inheritance or gift (Art. 1889 No. 1(c) Portuguese CC); form a company in joint name, as a silent partner or through shares (Art. 1889 No. 1(d) Portuguese CC); contract commercial debts resulting from any kind of bill transferable by endorsement (Art. 1889 No. 1(e), Portuguese CC); guarantee or assume debts for others (Art. 1889 No. 1(f) Portuguese CC); contract loans (Art. 1889 No. 1(g) Portuguese CC); contract debts to be discharged after the age of majority (Art. 1889 No.1(h) Portuguese CC); transfer credit rights (Art. 1889 No. 1(i) Portuguese CC); repudiate an inheritance or legacy (Art. 1889 No. 1(j) Portuguese CC); accept an inheritance, gift or legacy with charges, or agree to the extrajudicial sharing of it (Art. 1889 No. 1(l) Portuguese CC); lease property for a period of longer than six years (Art. 1889 No. 1(m) Portuguese CC); enter into agreements or apply for the court for the

division of common property or the liquidation of the share in joint property (Art. 1889 No. 1(n) Portuguese CC); accept compromises, or commit themselves in arbitration about above mentioned acts, or negotiate agreements with creditors (Art. 1889 No. 1(o) Portuguese CC), upon penalty of such acts being declared annullable (Article 1893 Portuguese CC).

If the minor inherits property or a legacy, or is given a gift that must be accepted, the parents should accept it, if they are legally entitled to do so, or apply to the Public Prosecutor's Office within thirty days to accept or refuse it (Art. 1890 Portuguese CC and Art. 4 No. 1 Portuguese Law No. 272/200 of 13 October 2001).

Under the terms of Art. 1892 No. 1 Portuguese CC, parents may not, in principle, rent or acquire, directly or through an intermediary, even in auction, property or rights belonging to a child that is subject to parental responsibility, nor may they become holders of credit or other rights against the child, upon risk of those acts being voidable (Art. 1893 Portuguese CC).

RUSSIA

(a) Certain goods and/or values (inherited property, gift...)

Parent(s) need prior authorisation from the Guardianship and Curatorship Department in order to enter into transactions on behalf of a child under the age of fourteen or to give consent to a transaction of the child from fourteen to eighteen with regard to a dwelling owned or co-owned by the child (Art. 37 (2) Russian CC).

Upon the claim of a parent who is paying maintenance to the child, a court can order the transfer of 50% of such maintenance to the child's bank account (Art. 60 (2) Russian Family Code). This measure is mainly taken if there is a danger of misadministration of the maintenance payments on the part of the child's residential parent. Money accumulated in the child's account is then meant to be administrated by both parents jointly.

(b) Salary of the child

As children from fourteen to eighteen are entitled to dispose of their salary without parental consent (Art. 26 (2) Russian CC), parents normally do not have the right to administrate a child's salary.

However, upon the request of his or her parents, a court can restrict or withdraw the right of the child to administrate his or her salary, if there are sufficient grounds for application of such measure (Art. 28 (4) Russian CC). Sufficient grounds are mainly established when the child profligates his or her salary or uses it to his or her detriment by purchasing alcoholic drinks, drugs or gambling. In such cases the court can order that the child can dispose of his or her salary only with preceding parental consent.

(c) Certain transactions

According to Art. 37 (2) Russian CC parent(s) need prior authorisation of the Guardianship and Curatorship Department in order to conclude on behalf of the child under the age of fourteen; or to give the child from fourteen to eighteen a consent to conclude the following transactions:

- alienation of the child's property, including exchange; donation, renting out, or lending out without consideration, mortgage of child's property or giving it as security;
- other transactions entailing a waiver of patrimonial rights belonging to the child including division of the child's property, or separation of a share thereof;
- other transactions which diminish the child's property, except for transactions made in order to provide for daily needs of the child (like food, closing, education or holydays);
- transactions with themselves except for donating a property to the child or lending the property to the child without consideration.

SPAIN

(a) Certain goods and/or values (inherited property, gift...)

Gifts and inherited goods are excluded from the parental responsibility holder's administration if the deceased person or the donor expressly provided that they were not to be administered by the holder and established who should carry out the administration. It is also permissible to specify rules of administration. Inherited property is excluded from administration by the parental responsibility holder if the child inherited the goods because the parental responsibility holder was excluded from succession for reasons such as indignity.

(b) Salary of the child

The salary of a child older than sixteen is also exempted from ordinary administration by the parental responsibility holder because the child will carry it out himself or herself. However, for acts that go beyond ordinary administration (*e.g.* acts of disposal and long-term engagements) the child will need the parental responsibility holder's consent.

(c) Certain transactions

Certain transactions require judicial authorisation. The general purpose of this rule is to protect the child's property. Catalan law is more precise in its enumeration of the acts requiring authorisation, but the Spanish CC and the Catalan Family Code both basically coincide in requiring authorisation for acts disposing of the child's property, long term engagements like leases of immovable property for more than 15 years, borrowing money or renouncing an inheritance or donation *etc.*, for acts that go beyond the ordinary administration of property and that can substantially affect the child's property.

Authorisation must be requested beforehand. If authorisation is not requested or the transaction is carried out although authorisation was not granted, it is possible to annul the transaction (Art. 154 Catalan Family Code). Catalan law expressly provides that authorisation can refer to a plurality of transactions, whereas the Civil Code regime an authorisation is required for each single transaction.

There is no discretion in the granting of this authorisation. If the parental responsibility holder proves that such a transaction is useful or necessary the judge must grant the authorisation, notwithstanding the fact that there might be a more useful or advantageous course of action. In order to evaluate whether the transaction is useful or necessary the Judge will hear the *Ministerio Fiscal*, a public body similar to the French *Ministère Public*, which usually acts in judicial proceedings representing the child's interests.

The law of Catalonia and Aragon allow for alternative authorisations which can substitute the authorisation of the Judge. The Catalan Family Code, for example, establishes that the child can give the authorisation himself or herself if the child is older than sixteen; or the judge's authorisation can be substituted by the authorisation of two other relatives, one from each branch of the family.

SWEDEN

(a) Certain goods and/or values (inherited property, gift...)

The guardian's right to administer the child's assets may be restricted through stipulations by a third party. This is the case when the child receives property as a gift or through a testamentary disposition on the condition that the property shall be administered by a person other than the guardian.[30] The guardian is also excluded from the right to administer the child's assets if the child has been given the right to dispose of the property.[31] Exceptionally, however, property the child disposes himself or herself may be administered by the guardian. This requires permission from a body supervising administration of the minor's property, the so-called Chief Guardian, if the child has reached the age of 16 years. Such permission should only be granted if it is necessary for the child's upbringing or welfare. The permission may, furthermore, be granted only after the child has been heard.

There are also restrictions on the guardian's administration of the child's property based on the value of the property. The guardian(s) is free to administer the child's property, without involvement of the Chief Guardian, only if the value of the child's property does not exceed the sum of eight so-called 'base amounts', annually fixed by social security law.[32] In 2003, this amounted to approximately €36,000.[33] If the value of the child's property

30 Chapter 12 Sec. 1 Swedish Children and Parents Code.

31 See: Chapter 12 Sec. 1 with reference to Chapter 9 Sec. 3-4 Swedish Children and Parents Code.

32 This is a result of a law reform carried out in 1994. See G. WALIN and S. VÄNGBY, *Föräldrabalken, En kommentar, Del I, 1-13 kap.*, Stockholm: Norstedts Juridik, 2002, p. 12:2.

33 In 2003, one base amount was fixed to 38,600 SEK *i.e.* approximately €4,200.

exceeds this amount, the assets must be placed in a manner stipulated by the law, see Chapter 13 Sec. 2 to 7 Swedish Children and Parents Code. Exceptions may, however, be granted by the Chief Guardian. The guardian must give the Chief Guardian a yearly accounting of the administration of the assets.

A person who gives the child property *e.g.* through a gift or a testamentary disposition, may always stipulate that the administration of that property shall be subject to the same provisions as property exceeding the value of eight base amounts, irrespective of the value of the property.[34]

(b) Salary of the child

A child who has reached the age of 16 years may dispose of property he or she has acquired through his or her own labour if the custodian(s) consent.[35] The guardian may, with the permission of the Chief Guardian, take over the administration of such acquisitions, provided it is necessary for child's upbringing or well-being. Permission should be granted only after the child has been heard.[36]

(c) Certain transactions

Irrespective of the value of the property, certain transactions always require the consent of the Chief Guardian. Dispositions concerning real property of the child, as well as the use of the child's assets for support of family or others close to the child always require the consent of the Chief Guardian. The consent of the Chief Guardian is, furthermore, required for investments in shares. Such a permission is also required if the child is to run a business in his or her name. The relevant provisions are found in the Chapter 13 Sec. 10–13 Swedish Children and Parents Code.

SWITZERLAND

(a) Certain goods and/or values (inherited property, gift...)

Administration of property by the parents is only excluded if this is explicitly stipulated when an allocation is made by a third party (Art. 321 § 2 Swiss CC). To do this, the person making the allocation may designate the party who will be responsible for the administration. If no instructions are issued regarding the administration and if the child is capable of making his or her own judgment, the child shall be entitled to administer the property. If the child is not capable of making a decision, the guardianship authority must appoint an official adviser in accordance with Art. 393 Swiss CC. The child's (legally protected) statutory portion in a testamentary disposition may also exclude the parents from administration (Art. 322 § 1 Swiss CC). The testator may entrust a third

---

34 Chapter 13 Sec. 2 Swedish Children and Parents Code.

35 Chapter 9 Sec. 3 Swedish Children and Parents Code.

36 The child's right to take employment with the consent of the custodian is expressed in Chapter 6 Sec. 12 Swedish Children and Parents Code and the prerequisites of the child's right to handle that property is expressed in Chapter 9 Sec. 3 Swedish Children and Parents Code.

party with the administration until the child reaches majority (Art. 322 § 2 Swiss CC). If the testator does not issue instructions with regard to the administration, the guardianship authority again has to proceed in accordance with Art. 393 Swiss CC.[37]

Furthermore, parents may not use income from the child's property in accordance with the legal provisions described above[38] if an explicit condition to that effect was imposed when the property was allocated to the child or if the property was allocated on the condition that it was to be invested to earn interest or invested as savings (Art. 321 § 1 Swiss CC). This is subject to the consumption of the income from the statutory portion within the limits of Art. 319 § 1 Swiss CC and subsequently subject to drawing on the substance of the statutory portion under the prerequisites contained in Art. 320 § 2 Swiss CC, even if the parents were excluded from the administration in accordance with Art. 321 Swiss CC or Art. 322 § 1 Swiss CC.[39]

(b) Salary of the child

'A child shall be entitled to administer and use whatever the child earns through his or her own work, and any part of the property the child receives from his or her parents, to exercise a profession or a conduct a trade of his or her own' (Art. 323 § 1 Swiss CC). A child capable of good judgment thus becomes capable to act and has the legal capacity to sue to the extent of his or her earnings from gainful employment, after deduction of its own maintenance or rather to the extent of its professional or trade property, if the child's parents have given their consent to an employment contract (Art. 19, 304 and 305 Swiss CC) or child's property has been released to exercise a profession or a trade.[40] The parents' legal right to represent the child in accordance with Art. 304 Swiss CC is excluded to this extent.[41] However, if the child is not capable of good judgment, neither she nor he is capable of acting (Art. 17 and 18 Swiss CC). Consequently, the child is not permitted to administer his earnings from work. The parents are responsible for administration of earnings from work.

(c) Certain transactions

The parents' right of representation is limited by Art. 304 § 3 in combination with Art. 408 Swiss CC: They may not enter into any sureties for the benefit of the child, nor may they make substantial gifts or set up a foundation.

---

37 C. HEGNAUER, *Grundriss des Kindesrechts*, p. 233.

38 Section 11

39 C. HEGNAUER, *Grundriss des Kindesrechts*, p. 233.

40 C. HEGNAUER, *Grundriss des Kindesrechts*, p. 234.

41 BGE 106 II 10.

QUESTION 13

B. THE CONTENTS OF PARENTAL RESPONSIBILITIES

Are there special rules protecting children from indebtedness caused by the holder(s) of parental responsibilities?

AUSTRIA

When necessary to avert a danger directly threatening the interests of a child, the court will supervise the administration of the child's property without regard to whether a significant amount of property is involved (Sec. 133(3) Non-Contentious Proceedings Act *[Außerstreitgesetz]*). To research the property, oversee its administration, and safeguard it, the court can give orders to the legal representative, obtain information from credit institutions or other persons obligated to provide information, order an appraisal, the blocking of bank accounts, or court custody of documents or movable property, and take temporary precautionary measures (Sec. 133(4) *Außerstreitgesetz* and Sec. 229 Austrian CC). The court will also make the necessary dispositions to safeguard the interests of the child if the parents cannot reach agreement on a matter of importance to the child (Sec. 176 Austrian CC)[1]. In particular, the court can substitute its consent for a parent's consent required by law if there is no legitimate ground for withholding consent, and it can take away the right of consent provided by law, the right to administer the child's property, or the parental responsibilities in their entirety (Sec. 176 and 253 Austrian CC). To avert a danger to the interests of the child, the court will give the legal representative a special order to submit a statement of accounts (section 135 (4) *Außerstreitgesetz*).

BELGIUM

There is no general obligation of the parents or sole surviving parent to inventory the property of their minor child. Nevertheless, the parents are held responsible for their administration of the child's property. When their parental responsibilities come to an end, they must justify themselves to the adult child for both the property and revenues of the goods for which they did not have the right of use and enjoyment, but only for the property of the goods for which they did have the right of use and enjoyment, because in the latter case they were entitled to the revenues (Art. 379(1) Belgian CC).

During the parental administration of the property, the law protects the child's property. As already mentioned in Q 12, Art. 379(2) Belgian CC provides that every court decision concerning sums of money attributed to the minor must

---

1 *E.g.*, blocking of a home loan and savings contract in a dispute over whether it was entered into for the benefit of the child or a parent: *Oberster Gerichtshof*, 17.01.1984, *Österreichischer Amtsvormund*, 1985, p. 51 = *EFSlg*. 45.795; judicial deposit: *Oberster Gerichtshof*, 13.02.2002, *Österreichische Juristenzeitung - EvBl*, 2002, No. 128, p. 503.

decide that these sums are placed in a personalized bank account of the child. The court has no choice except to allow the legal right of use and enjoyment of the parents, and the account can not be disposed of until the age of majority of the minor. According to Art. 776 Belgian CC, these same rules apply to assets inherited by the child, although the parents may ask permission from the Justice of the Peace to use the account's assets. All authorisations required by Art. 378 in conjunction with 410 Belgian CC are installed in order to protect the children from indebtedness or irresponsible administration of the child's property (See Q 12).[2]

Whenever a conflict of interest arises between the parents' interests and the administration of the property of the child, the Justice of the Peace will appoint a guardian ad hoc to act on behalf of the child at the request of an interested party, the Public Prosecutor or *ex officio* (Art. 378 Belgian CC).[3]

BULGARIA

No, there are not.

CZECH REPUBLIC

The parents are obliged to administer the child's estate with due care (Sec. 37a § 1 Czech Family Code). If the child's interests in the estate could be put at risk, the court will appoint a special custodian for administration of the child's estate under the supervision of the court. The child's rights resulting from liability or unjust enrichment by the child's parents are governed by the Czech CC. The limitation period for claiming these rights does not begin to run before the child's attains the age of majority (Sec. 114 Czech CC).

DENMARK

There are no special rules. The general principle in Danish law is that the indebtedness of a person does not affect the property of a spouse or children. If the child's property can be properly identified it will not be affected by the indebtedness of the holder(s) of parental authority.

ENGLAND & WALES

As stated in answer to Q 12 holders of parental responsibility are under a duty to account to the child for the profits and income of the child's estate received by him. Beyond this there are no special rules protecting children from

2 Court of Appeal of Brussels, 11.03.1986, *Rev. Not. B.*, 1987, p. 49; M. GRÉGOIRE, 'La loi du 29 avril 2001 modifiant les dispositions légales en matière d'autorité parentale et de tutelle', *Rev. not. b.*, 2002, p. 139; W. PINTENS, 'De voogdijwet herbekeken - Een eerste toelichting bij de reparatiewet van 13 februari 2003', *T. Vred.*, 2003, p. 129-132.

3 C. CAPITAINE, 'Aspects procedureaux et judiciaires du droit de la tutelle et de l'authorité parentale', in: Y.-H. LELEU (ed.), *Les incapacités*, Liege: Edition Formation Permanente CUP, 2003, p.164-165; S. MOSSELMANS, 'Werking van de voogdij inzake het vermogen', in: P. Senaeve, J. GERLO and F. LIEVENS (eds.), *De hervorming van het voogdijrecht*, Antwerp: Intersentia, 2002, p. 147-148.

indebtedness caused by parental responsibility holders, although in the normal course of events children are not liable for their parents' debts.

FINLAND

There are no special rules concerning children as wards, but the Finnish Guardianship Services Act includes general rules concerning how the guardian shall handle the expenses of the ward. The guardian shall take conscientious care of the rights of the ward and promote the ward's interests (Sec. 37-39 Finnish Guardianship Services Act. See Q 7).[4]

The most important way to protect the ward's property is through supervision of the guardianship authorities, which encompass the guardian's duty to provide authorities with an inventory of the assets and liabilities of the ward as well as the guardian's duty to keep records and provide the guardianship authority with a financial record (annual statement and final statement, Sec. 46 - 57). The guardianship authority may, however, decide that a generalised statement of the property is deemed to be sufficient in view of the nature of the property under management (Sec. 55 para. 3).

The guardianship's duty to ask for permission for certain activities and transactions for certain activities is also supervised. The guardian's duty to ask for permission from the authority for the incurrence of any loan, other than a student loan guaranteed by the State or assumption of liability for a bill of exchange or the debt for another person, can be specially be mentioned here (see Q 12).

If the guardian has failed to safeguard the interests of the ward, the court shall appoint another guardian on the petition of the guardianship authority (Sec. 58). The guardian shall bear the responsibility for the damages he or she caused (Sec. 61 - 63).

FRANCE

Art. 389-5 French CC states that both parents who hold parental responsibilities can undertake acts of administration and disposition. Still, some serious acts require judicial authorisation (Art. 389-5 para. 3 French CC). If the act undertaken by the parents causes damage to the child, the parents are jointly liable (para. 4).

GERMANY

There are general rules on the administration of the property of children (see Q 12). As a consequence of a decision by the Federal Constitutional Court,[5] special rules exist to protect children from indebtedness caused by the holders of

4 A child's own assets can be taken into consideration when the extent of the parent's responsibility to maintain the child is estimated (Sec. 2 Finnish Child Custody and the Right of Access Act).

5 BVerfG, 13.05.1986, *BVerfGE* 72, 155 = *FamRZ* 1986, 1859.

parental custody. They were introduced by an Act Limiting the Liability of Minors (*Gesetz zur Beschränkung der Haftung Minderjähriger*), which came into force on 1 January 1999.[6] Today there is a restriction of a child's liability, according to § 1629a German CC, up to the value of the child's property at the moment the child reaches the age of majority. This applies to acts of the parents in the framework of their legal representation.

The restrictions do not apply to obligations of the child arising from the carrying on of an independent gainful occupation permitted under § 112 German CC. The same is true for obligations solely for the satisfaction of his personal needs (§ 1629a para. 2 German CC).

GREECE

In the Greek CC there are several provisions on managing the assets of the child, which restrict the rights of the holders of parental responsibilities and impose certain obligations on them in order to prevent indebtedness. The restrictions pertain to the prohibition of donations (Arts. 1524 and 1617 Greek CC) and the use of the property of the child for their own purposes (Arts. 1529 and 1618 Greek CC).[7] Moreover, both the parents and the guardian are subject to certain formalities when they wish to enter into any transaction which might burden the property of the child (Art. 1526 and 1624 Greek CC: the need to obtain judicial permission, Art. 1619 Greek CC: the requirement that the guardian needs to obtain the consent of the supervisory council).[8]

In addition, the holders of parental responsibilities must draw up an inventory of any asset that falls under their management (Art. 1523 and 1611 Greek CC).[9] They must also use the money of the child productively or invest it without delay (Art. 1525 and 1613 Greek CC). Further, a guardian has an obligation to secure the bonds, the stocks, the valuables, as well as the important legal documents of the child (Art. 1614 Greek CC).[10] Finally, the guardian reports to the supervisory council on a yearly basis (Art. 1626 Greek CC),[11] which is also entitled to audit him (Art. 1643 Greek CC).

---

6 Gesetz zur Beschränkung der Haftung Minderjähriger (Minderjährigenhaftungsbeschränkungsgesetz - MiHbeG) of 25.08.1998, *BGBl.* 1998 I, p. 2487.

7 For further details see the answer to Q 12c.

8 For a complete list of those transactions, see the full text of Art. 1527 and 1624 Greek CC as well as Art. 1619 Greek CC.

9 On the aim of the inventory, see A. POULIADIS, in: A. GEORGIADIS and M. STATHOPOULOS (eds.), *Civil Code commentary, Vol. VIII, Family Law (Arts. 1505-1694)*, 2nd Edition, Athens: Law & Economy, P.N. SAKKOULAS, 2003, Art. 1523 Greek CC, p. 352, No. 1.

10 Nevertheless, the parent who has the right to appoint a guardian upon his death may also exonerate him from these obligations (Art. 1633 Greek CC).

11 The supervisory council may designate a different point in time for the submission of these reports, but this control should take place at least every five years (Art. 1626 Greek CC).

Non-compliance with most of the abovementioned restrictions and obligations lead to the nullity of the relevant actions.[12] The nullity may be relied upon by the father, the mother, the child itself, and its successors, in the case of parental care, and by the guardian, the supervisory council, the child itself, and its successors, in the case of guardianship.

Furthermore, both the parents and the guardian are liable to the child for all their actions (Art. 1531 and 1632 Greek CC).[13] If there is a (serious) conflict of interests between the holder of parental responsibilities and the child, for example in the context of the administration of property, the court will assign a special guardian to represent the child (Art. 1517 and 1627 Greek CC).

HUNGARY

Regarding the protection of the child from indebtedness caused by the holder of parental responsibilities there are only the following rules in the family law:

The public guardianship authority can order supervision of the parents' administration of the child's property on a regular basis if the property is endangered, and can also oblige the parents, as the guardian, to give security or an accounting on a regular basis. The power of the guardian to administer the child's property can be restricted if the child's interest requires it, and the guardian can even be removed if the guardian seriously breaches his or her obligation. These measures do not affect the financial liability of the guardian for the damages caused to the child.

IRELAND

Generally no. However, if a child has been made a ward of court, special rules apply.

ITALY

Yes; acts performed in violation of the rules regarding the administration of the minor's properties can be annulled at the request of the parents holding the parental responsibilities or at the request of the child, the child's heirs or the child's successors in interest (Art. 322 Italian CC); the action is proscribed until 5 years after the child reaches the age of majority. If the minor's property is improperly administrated the court can prescribe conditions to be observed for the administration, can remove both or one of the parents from the administration and can partially or wholly deprive them the legal usufruct of

12 Art. 1528 Greek CC specifies that nullity is the consequence of a violation of the provisions of Art. 1524-1526 Greek CC, whereas the provision under Art. 1630 Greek CC covers any action where the guardian did not follow the required formalities.

13 The parent's level of care is determined by the care which they exercise in organising their own affairs, whereas the liability of the guardian is determined on the basis of objective criteria (Art. 1531 and 1632 Greek CC).

the property. If both parents are deprived, a guardian will be entitled to administrate the child's property (Art. 334 Italian CC).

LITHUANIA

According to Part 1 of Art. 3.189 Lithuanian CC, the parents' right of usufruct may not be pledged, sold, transferred or encumbered in any way, nor may execution be charged against it. The same Article provides that the claims of the creditors of underage children's parents may not be executed against the property of the underage children or against the right of usufruct of their parents.

THE NETHERLANDS

According to Art. 1:350 Dutch CC which concerns the duty of the holder(s) of parental responsibilities to ensure effective investment of the estate of the minor, authorisation by the sub-district court is required to invest the minor's monies. However, the holder(s) of parental responsibilities may, in so far as the sub-district court does not rule otherwise, invest monies in the minor's name with a credit institution that is registered in accordance with the Dutch Credit System Supervision Act 1992. If the required authorisation has not been obtained, the transactions are valid (Art. 1:352 Dutch CC); however, the holder(s) of parental responsibilities may be held liable for bad administration and all attributable loss, unless the enjoyment of the benefits from such capital is conferred by law, pursuant to Art. 1:253j Dutch CC. In order to protect children from the threat of indebtedness the holder(s) of parental responsibilities, or *ex officio*, the sub-district court, may place an estate or part of the estate under administration (Art. 1:370 Dutch CC). This may include the benefits for the duration of the child's minority if this is regarded necessary for the best interest of the minor. Where parental responsibilities are exercised jointly, the placement under administration shall only be decided if both holders make the request jointly.

NORWAY

There are special rules in Art. 55 Norwegian Act on Guardianship 1927 that protect the child from indebtedness caused by the guardian(s). It is not permissible to incur debt on the child's behalf without the consent of the Public Guardian's Office.

POLAND

No. A parent who does not properly administer the child's property may be held liable for damage incurred by the child, based on general regulation of contractual responsibility (Art. 471 and subs. Polish CC).

PORTUGAL

As regards the protection of a child against indebtedness caused by parents, the law only establishes the need to obtain permission from the Public Prosecutor's Office to assume liabilities that will be discharged after the age of majority (Art. 1889 No. 1(h) Portuguese CC).

RUSSIA

No. Transactions concluded by the parent(s) without prior authorisation of Guardianship and Curatorship Department can be declared void by a court order according to the general rules of Civil Law.

SPAIN

If the administration by parental responsibility holders endangers the child's property the judge, at the request of the child, the *Ministerio Fiscal* or any of the child's relatives, can adopt any measure he thinks necessary. This may include naming an administrator (Art. 167 Spanish CC).

SWEDEN

The guardian needs the consent of the Chief Guardian to any transaction that presupposes contracting debts for the child, Chapter 13 Sec. 12 Swedish Children and Parents Code. The same applies if the guardian wants the child to warrant for somebody or the child's property to provide security for the child's or another person's transactions. A consent should only be granted if the measure is necessary to secure the child's other assets, education or living, or for some other special reason. An action taken by the guardian without the consent of the Chief Guardian is not valid, Chapter 12 Sec. 10 Swedish Children and Parents Code.

Although the law aims at protecting children from indebtedness caused by the guardians, parental actions still indebt many children. In many cases in Sweden, the child's debt refers to cars registered by the parents in the child's name *e.g.* unpaid parking tickets. Furthermore, a significant proportion (about 50%) of children's debts originate from the parents' transactions with the child's capital *e.g.* stock investments with the resulting taxes left unpaid. This problem has only recently received the attention of the legislature. Since October 2004, an authority called the Enforcement Service has the duty to report to the Chief Guardian every time a person under the age of 18 years is registered for unpaid fees, etc. The Chief Guardian should then take the measures required by the situation to secure the interests of the child. This entails convincing the parents to take responsibility for debts that are not the child's. The Chief Guardian can also appoint a guardian *ad litem* to initiate court proceedings to have the debts removed or declared invalid. The problem may have accelerated due to parents' lack of knowledge of the law, as well as the limited resources of the Chief Guardian.

SWITZERLAND

Art. 324 and 325 Swiss CC stipulate the following rule for the protection of children's interests in respect of property rights: 'If careful administration is not adequately guaranteed, the guardianship authority will take appropriate measures to protect the child's property' (Art. 324 § 1 Swiss CC). In this capacity the authority must observe the principles of commensurability and subsidiarity. The guardianship authority may issue directives regarding the administration of the property and, if the periodic statement of accounts and reports are not adequate, it may order a deposit and the furnishing of securities (Art. 324 § 2 Swiss CC). Then, if the threat to the child's property cannot be countered in any other way, the guardianship must entrust the administration thereof to an official adviser (Art. 325 § Swiss CC). In this way the parents are divested of the administration of the child's property without it being necessary to deprive them of parental responsibilities.[14]

The inventory and the obligation to render an accounting, submit a report in accordance with Art. 318 § 2 and 3 Swiss CC and submit a statement of account once parental responsibilities come to an end, based on Art. 326 Swiss CC, and the parents' responsibility, within the meaning of Art. 327 Swiss CC, has a preventive effect *i.e.* even if no concrete danger exists. If parents are deprived of their parental responsibilities based on Art. 311 Swiss CC, their general right to administer the child's property lapses. The withdrawal of parental responsibilities consequently acts at the same time as a measure to protect the child's property.

For the rest, protection of the child's assets is provided under criminal law by Art. 138 Swiss Penal Code (embezzlement) and Art. 158 Swiss Penal Code fraudulent conduct of business). Since the child's own property is separate from the parents' property, it does not require any special protection under civil law in the event of the bankruptcy of a parent.[15]

---

14 C. HEGNAUER, *Grundriss des Kindesrechts*, p. 237.

15 P. BREITSCHMID, Art. 318 Swiss CC, p. 1667 (No. 1), in: H. HONSELL, N.P. VOGT and TH. GEISER (ed.), *Basler Kommentar zum Schweizerischen Privatrecht, Zivilgesetzbuch I*, Art. 1-456 ZGB, Basel: Helbing & Lichtenhahn, 2002.

QUESTION 14

B. THE CONTENTS OF PARENTAL RESPONSIBILITIES

Do the contents of parental responsibilities differ according to the holder(s) of parental responsibilities (*e.g.* married, unmarried, parents not living together, stepparents, foster parents or other persons)? If so, describe in some detail how it differs.

AUSTRIA

Married, unmarried, and separated parents, stepparents, and foster parents may all be holders of parental responsibilities under Sec. 144 *et seq* Austrian CC. If - by operation of law, judicial decision, or agreement - they are attributed parental responsibilities, the contents of their parental responsibilities do not differ.

In contrast, a series of special provisions apply to other persons entrusted with parental responsibilities (Sec. 187 *et seq* Austrian CC): They are subject to special court control in administering the child's property, (Sec. 229 *et seq* Austrian CC)[1] and must obtain court approval in the important matters relating to the child listed in Sec. 154(2) Austrian CC,[2] unless there is imminent danger (Sec. 216 Austrian CC). In addition, they are liable to the child for every culpable loss (Sec. 264 Austrian CC). The standard is the care exercised by a proper parent.[3] On the other hand, they are entitled to compensation and reimbursement of their expenses (Sec. 266 and 267 Austrian CC). If, however, the child welfare agency is entrusted with parental responsibilities by operation of law (Sec. 211 Austrian CC), certain allowances are made when it, as a public institution, exercises its parental responsibilities (Sec. 214 Austrian CC): There is no need for court approval in the important matters relating to the child listed in Sec. 154(2) Austrian CC [4] or before investing the child's property, unless the agency chooses a form of investment not included in the statute. The agency can receive payments to the child without the limitation on the amount established in Sec. 234 Austrian CC and is not entitled to compensation or reimbursement of expenses for its activities under Sec. 266 and 267 Austrian CC.

BELGIUM

The contents of parental responsibilities do not differ according to whether the parents are married, whether they live together, or whether there are two

---

1 For details see Q 12a and 12c.

2 For details see Q 8f.

3 See J. STABENTHEINER, 'KindRÄG 2001', in: P. RUMMEL, *ABGB-Kommentar,* suppl. vol. 1, 3rd Edition, Vienna: Manz Verlag, 2003, § 264 Marg. No. 3.

4 For details see Q 8f.

parents or only one. The parental responsibilities of adoptive parents and biological parents are the same (Art. 361(1) and 370(1) Belgian CC).[5]

Although homosexual partners of a parent have tried to acquire parental responsibilities over their partner's child through adoption, a sole adoptive parent can currently only acquire parental responsibilities together with the legal parent by adopting the child of a heterosexual spouse or legal cohabitant (in case of ordinary adoption, Art. 345 until 367 Belgian CC), or a heterosexual spouse or factual cohabitant (in case of full adoption, Art. 368 until 370 Belgian CC).[6] Moreover, the Belgian Law of 13 February 2003 opening the institute of marriage to same-sex partners explicitly mentions that same-sex marriage will have no effect on affiliation or adoption.[7]

If both (adoptive) parents are deceased or unable to exercise their parental responsibilities, a guardianship is created (Art. 375(2) Belgian CC), and a different set of regulations is applicable instead of the regulations on parental responsibilities.[8]

Although only legal and adoptive parents have full parental responsibilities, it is nevertheless possible for persons other than the (adoptive) parents to acquire certain aspects of the parental responsibilities. The grandparents, and every person who can prove having a particular affectionate relationship with a child, have the right to contact with the child. When no agreement between the parties is possible, the Juvenile Court will decide based on the interests of the child, at the request of the parties or the Public Prosecutor (Art. 375 *bis* Belgian CC). However, grandparents have no right to the parental responsibilities involving the material care of their grandchild. Indeed, the judicial right to the material care of the child includes the right to live with the child, to decide on its nutrition, clothing and housing, to administer its contacts with friends, its

5 Court of Appeal of Antwerp, 06.03.2002, *NjW*, 2002, p. 97; M. GRÉGOIRE, 'La loi du 29 avril 2001 modifiant les dispositions légales en matière d'autorité parentale et de tutelle', *Rev. not. b.*, 2002, p. 137-140 ; J.L. RENCHON, 'L'exercice de l'administration légale par le parent survivant - contrôle de la gestion du parent survivant - Responsabilité du parent survivant', in X., *Tutelle et administration légale - Questions d'application de la loi du 29 avril 2001*, Louvain-la-Neuve: U.C.L., 2002, p. 4.

6 Constitutional Court, 28.11.2001, ref. 154/2001, *J.T.*, 2002, p. 82-85, annotated Y.-H. LELEU, *R.W.*, 2001-02, p. 949-951, annotated P. SCHOLLEN; Constitutional Court, 03.05.2000, ref. 49/2000, *J.T.*, 2000, p. 536, annotated Y.-H. LELEU; Constitutional Court, 03.05.2000, ref. 53/2000, *J.L.M.B.*, 2000, p. 1066-1069, annotated D. PIRE; Constitutional Court, 06.11.1997, ref. 67/97, *Rev. trim. dr. fam.*, 1997, p. 410-414; F. SWENNEN, 'Adoptie door de 'feitelijke partner' van een oorspronkelijke ouder', *R.W.*, 2000-01, p. 681-686.

7 Law 13.02.2003, *Belgian Bulletin of Acts and Decrees*. 28.02.2003.

8 N. GALLUS, 'Aspects civiles du nouveau droit de la tutelle', in: Y.-H. LELEU (ed.), *Les incapacités*, Liege: Edition Formation Permanente CUP, 2003, p. 205-219; S. MOSSELMANS, 'Ouderlijk goederenbeheer anno 2003', in: S. MAERTENS and G. BENOIT (eds.), *Actualia ouderlijk gezag, voogdij en voorlopig bewind*, Bruges: Die Keure, 2004, p. 49.

reading material, its entertainment, mail, etc. (See Q 8a), i.e. the daily care over the child. Material care is a parental prerogative. The grandparents have a more limited right to factually keep the child with them during the exercise of their right to personal contact, but they do not exercise any parental authority.[9]

Persons other than the parents may also acquire the material care (factual care) of the child when there is a disfunction in the exercise of the parental responsibilities by the parents, such as when a protective measure is issued by the Juvenile Court (Art. 37(2)(3) Belgian LJP), but this will not include the right to care as a part of the authority over the child (judicial care). The right to educate remains with the parents.[10]

Nevertheless, the Constitutional Court ruled that foster parents who hold the material care over the child are entitled to participate in debates concerning the child before the Juvenile Court. Also, foster parents acquire certain aspects of the parental responsibilities *e.g.* they will have the duty to raise, educate and maintain the child, (Art. 203 Belgian CC), and they also administer its property (Art. 475 *bis* until 475 *septies* Belgian CC), but the right to agree to the child's marriage or adoption (Art. 475 *quater in fine* Belgian CC) still belongs to the parents. Additionally, the Art. 34-35 Belgian LJP appoint a pro-guardian with specific responsibilities towards the child when the parent(s) have been dismissed from parental authority because of bad treatment, abuse of authority, apparent bad behaviour or grave negligence that endangers the health, safety or morality of the child.[11]

In general however, grandparents, stepparents, foster parents or other persons who have no tie of affiliation with the child cannot acquire parental responsibilities, although there are recent proposals for reform (See Q 6). Up until now, the only possibility for persons other than the parents to acquire full parental responsibilities is adoption.[12]

---

9 Cass., 18.02.1993, *R.W.*, 1993-94, p. 157, *J.L.M.B.*, 1993, p. 1453, annotated C. PANIER ; A. DE WOLF, 'Artikel 375 bis Burgerlijk Wetboek', in X., *Personen en familierecht. Artikelsgewijze commentaar*, Antwerp: Kluwer (looseleaf), 1997, p. 12-13 ; K. JACOBS, 'Het omgangsrecht in België en Nederland', *T.P.R.*, 1996, p. 827-902 ; J.L. RENCHON, 'La recevabilité des actions en justice introduites par les grands-parents dans le contexte du règlement de l'excercice de l'autorité parentale à l'égard de l'enfant', *Rev. trim. dr. fam.*, 1989, p. 251 *et seq.*

10 Cass., 19.12.1975, *R.C.J.B.*, 1977, p. 193, annotated F. RIGAUX; S. BECQ, 'Het juridisch statuut van de pleegouders', *R.W.*, 1980-81, p. 2045-2046 and 2051; F. TULKENS and Th. MOREAU, *Droit de la jeunesse*, Brussels: Larcier, 2000, p. 652-657.

11 Constitutional Court, 03.12.1998, ref. 1998/122, *J. dr. jeun.*, 1999, p. 57, annotated T. MOREAU, *J.L.M.B.*, 1999, p. 312; K. DEWEERDT and J. PUT, 'Veertig jaar jeugdbeschermingsrecht. Overzicht van rechtspraak (1965-2004)', *NjW*, 2004, p. 835; J. SMETS, *Jeugdbeschermingsrecht*, Antwerp: Kluwer, 1996, p. 240-245 and 267-294; F. SWENNEN, 'Adoptie door de 'feitelijke partner' van een oorspronkelijke ouder', *R.W.*, 2000-01, p. 686.

12 Constitutional Court, 08.10.2003, ref. 134/2003, *E.J.*, 2003, p. 134-139, annotated P. SENAEVE; Juvenile Court of Antwerp, 03.10.2002, *R.W.*, 2002-03, p. 1188, annotated T.

Finally, certain other persons may hold obligations towards the child. When the descent from the father is not legally determined, Art. 336 Belgian CC provides the child the opportunity to demand an allowance for its support, upbringing and education from the man who had intercourse with the child's mother during its legal period of conception (Art. 336-341 Belgian CC). Also, the step-parent can be held liable to a maintenance obligation towards the children of his or her deceased spouse, but only within the boundaries of what the step-parent received from the deceased's estate and from donations between spouses (Art. 203 (2) Belgian CC).[13]

BULGARIA

Parental rights and obligations pertain to the parents irrespective of their marital status, if the origin of the child is established with regard to such parent(s) in the manner set forth by the Bulgarian Family Code.

As regards the regulation of relations between unmarried parents, no specific provisions exist in the Bulgarian Family Code, especially when such parents do not live together. The Code states that: 'Where the parents do not live together and are unable to reach an agreement as to with whom the children will live, the dispute is resolved by the district court at the place of residence of the children, after the court has heard the children, if they are ten years of age or older. The decision of the court is subject to appeal according to the general rules.' (Art. 71 § 2.) Theoretically, such a claim may be used both by parents who live separately, both married and unmarried.[14] According to judicial practice, however, such claims are filed by parents who have not been married, but live separately.[15] In contrast with divorce, in cases of separation the court can only determine the residence of the child with one of the parents if the parents cannot reach an agreement. This is admitted to be an indirect approach to matters of custody and contact, but the scope is not as broad as in divorce proceedings.[16] The major difference is that the court can make no

---

ROBERT; F. SWENNEN, 'Het ouderlijk gezag en de voogdij. Recente en komende wetgeving', in: CBR (ed.), *Jongeren en Recht*, Antwerp: Intersentia, 2003, p. 55-58.

13 A. HEYVAERT and R. VANCRAENENBROECK, 'Artikel 336-341 Burgerlijk Wetboek', in: X., *Personen en familierecht. Artikelsgewijze commentaar*, Antwerp: Kluwer (looseleaf), 1998, p. 32; M. PUELINCKX-COENE, 'De grote promotie van de langstlevende echtgenote. Beschouwingen bij de integratie van de wet van 14 mei 1981 in het bestaande recht', *T.P.R.*, 1981, p. 699-715; L. RAUCENT, *Les droits successoraux du conjoint survivant*, Brussels: Ed. juridiques Swinnen, 1981, p. 165-172.

14 L. NENOVA, *Family Law of the Republic of Bulgaria*, p. 424-425.

15 Decisions of the Supreme Court (Civil Division) No. 261- 1974, 1781-1978, 1218-1999, etc.

16 Judicial theory and practice admit that by issuing the residence order, the regime of parental rights is solved automatically, despite the absence of explicit regulation. See Cases 261-1974 (Civil Division); 669-1992 (Civil Division); 1218-1999 (Civil Division). Also, an analogy is admissible with divorce arrangements, without the effect of the *ex officio* principle Cases 1781-1978 (Civil Division) and 606-1982 (Civil Division).

pronouncement *ex officio* on parental rights regime if it is not addressed in a dispute over the residence of the child.

Step-parents, foster parents or other persons such as guardians or custodians do not hold parental rights. They only exercise factual care in the raising and the upbringing of the child. According to Art. 68 § 2, 'the stepfather and the stepmother are obliged to assist the parent in the discharge of his or her duties.' The Bulgarian Child Protection Act stipulates that 'The spouses or the person of the foster family do not bear the parental rights and responsibilities' (Art. 31 § 2).

CZECH REPUBLIC

Parental responsibility belongs to both parents, provided they have full legal capacity to act. It does not matter whether the parents are married or divorced or have never been married. If the child's parents do not cohabit and cannot agree, either of them may apply to the court to decide on the regulation of an exercise of their parental responsibility *i.e.* deciding about awarding the upbringing (personal care) of the child to one of them and setting up the amount of maintenance for the other one, or deciding about regulation of contact between one of the parents and the child, or about any other essential matter in which the parents cannot come to an agreement.

The step-parent does not have parental responsibility. Pursuant to Sec. 33 Czech Family Code, he or she only has a duty to participate in the upbringing of the child. He or she does not have a maintenance duty. If the child is placed into foster care, parental responsibility remains with the parents. Foster parents are obliged to take personal care of the child, 'reasonably' exercising the rights and duties of parents. Foster parents have a right to represent the child and administer its matters (assets) in ordinary matters only. If the foster parent believes that a decision of the parent as a legal representative is not in compliance with the child's interest, he or she may seek a judicial decision. Foster parents do not have a maintenance duty in relation to the child; the State provides them with a social allowance for covering the child's needs, an allowance when the child is taken over by them and remuneration for exercise of foster care. The individual allowance amounts are set forth in Czech Act No. 117/1995, Coll., On State Social Benefit. The parents continue to have a maintenance duty; they do not pay the expenses to the foster parents but to the State (Sec. 45c Czech Family Code).

The upbringing of the child may be awarded to a natural person other than the child's parents (Sec. 45 Czech Family Code). Parental responsibility remains with the parents. In such a case the extent of the rights and duties is to be

---

However, it is admitted that regarding the current situation there is a lack of power for the court to make the full arrangements. See L. NENOVA, *Family Law of the Republic of Bulgaria*, Sofia, 1994, and T. TZANKOVA, *Factual Spouse Cohabitation*, Sofia, Feneya 2000, p. 134-6.

determined by a court, which usually awards these persons the right to decide about the child, to represent it and to administer the child's estate but only in ordinary matters. In essential matters, the rights remain with the parents. Most frequently, the upbringing of the child is awarded to the grandparents or other relatives. The parents pay these persons for the expenses as a result of their maintenance duty. The legal theory designates such cases as the factual limitation of parental responsibility.[17]

DENMARK

The content does not differ.

ENGLAND & WALES

There is some difference in the scope of parental responsibility according to who has it and how it is acquired. It is widest when enjoyed by parents or guardians inasmuch as their agreement is required for the child's adoption,[18] they can appoint a guardian[19] and they have a right to bury or cremate the deceased child.[20] It will be noted, however, that there is no difference in the scope of parental responsibility enjoyed by each married parent or, once the unmarried father has acquired it (see Q 22), between each unmarried parent.[21]

Individuals who acquire parental responsibility by means of a residence order (see Q 31) do not have the right to agree or to refuse to agree to the making of an adoption order or to appointing a guardian for the child.[22] A similar position obtains where a local authority acquires parental responsibility by virtue of a care order,[23] but in addition the local authority cannot 'cause the child to be brought up in any religious persuasion other than that in which he would have been brought up if the order had not been made'.[24]

As the law currently stands step-parents are treated like any other individual non parent but this position will change when the English Adoption and Children Act 2002 comes fully into force. Under that Act, step-parents (*i.e.* a

---

17 S. RADVANOVA and M. ZUKLINOVA, *Kurs občanského prava. Instituty rodinneho prava*, Prague: C.H.Beck, 1999; M. HRUSAKOVA and Z. KRALICKOVA, *České rodinne pravo, 2. vyd*, Brno: MU, 2001.

18 Sec. 16, English Adoption Act 1976, prospectively Sec. 47(2), English Adoption and Children Act 2002.

19 The power of guardians themselves to appoint guardians is conferred by Sec. 5(4), English Children Act 1989.

20 See *R v Gwynedd County Council ex p B* [1991] 2 FLR 365, CA.

21 There is, however, one key difference in the case of unmarried fathers in that no matter how he has acquired it, the courts have the power, upon application, to end parental responsibility pursuant to Sec. 4(3), English Children Act 1989 (see Q 51).

22 Sec. 12(3), English Children Act 1989.

23 Sec. 33(6)(b), English Children Act 1989.

24 Sec. 33(6)(a), English Children Act 1989

person who is married to the child's parent with parental responsibility)[25] will be placed in a similar position to unmarried fathers inasmuch as they will be able to acquire parental responsibility by a formal agreement or a court order.[26] The responsibility thus vested will co-extensive with that that enjoyed by the parent.[27]

A similar strategy is to be adopted in the case of a registered partner of a parent with parental responsibility.[28] Parental responsibility is narrowest for those in whose favour an emergency protection order has been made inasmuch as for the duration of the order (*viz* 8 days with the possibility of one extension of up to 7 days) there is authority only to take 'such action in meeting his parental responsibility for the child as is reasonably required to safeguard or promote the welfare of the child (having regard in particular to the duration of the order).[29]

FINLAND

A parent's legal position as custodian does not differ from that of any other custodian (whether the custodian is a stepparent, foster parent, a parent not living with the child *etc.*.). But parents, as parents, have certain privileges as regarding the child's custody. According to the Finnish Child Custody and the Right of Access Act parents have:

- The right to make an agreement about child custody and the right of access, which after the approval of the local social authority has the same effect as a court decision (Sec. 7 and 8);
- A special right to retain custody of their own child, in which case the court can transfer custody from the parents or a parent to one or more other persons where that is deemed to be manifestly in the best interests of the child (Sec. 9 para. 2);
- The right to make an application to the court in order to obtain a decision on child custody or right of access matter as a parent, regardless of the parent's status as custodian (Sec. 14 para. 1).

There are also other special rights for parents:

- The child has a right of access to the parent with whom the child does not live and the right to maintain contact with that parent;

---

25 Sec. 4(A)(1), English Children Act 1989, as prospectively substituted by Sec. 112, Adoption and Children Act 1989.

26 Sec. 4A, English Children Act 1989, as substituted by Sec. 112, English Adoption and Children Act 2002.

27 But as with the case of unmarried fathers the court retains the power upon application to end step-parent's parental responsibility pursuant to Sec. 4(3), English Children Act 1989.

28 See the amendments to be introduced by Sec. 75, British Civil Partnership Act 2004. NB civil partnerships will be restricted to same-sex couples, see Sec. 1, British Civil Partnership Act 2004.

29 Sec. 44(5)(b), English Children Act 1989.

- The parent has a right to be heard in care proceedings regarding the child even if he or she is not the child's custodian. However, the authority is not required to hear a parent if the action not to hear the parent's wishes can be deemed as well-grounded because of the lack of contact between this parent and the child (Sec. 17 Finnish Child Protection Act); and
- The parent's consent is needed for the child's adoption regardless of the parent's status as custodian (Sec. 9 Finnish Child Adoption Act).

If the parents of a child were not married at the time of the child's birth, the father's paternity must be approved according to the Finnish Paternity Act (No. 702/1975).

FRANCE

In principle, the contents of parental responsibilities do not differ according to the holder(s) of parental responsibilities. The definition of parental responsibilities is the same in a family based on marriage as in other families. The exercise of parental responsibilities only differs depending on whether there is one holder of parental responsibilities or two. For example when only one parent holds parental responsibilities, the administration of the child's property takes place under judicial control and all acts of disposition must be expressly authorised by a judge of the guardianship court.

GERMANY

The content of parental custody differs according to the holder(s) of parental responsibilities and to what extent it is acquired. Married parents have full parental custody for their children as long as it is not restricted or taken away, § 1626 para. 1 German CC.

An unmarried mother generally has full sole parental custody, § 1626a para. 2 German CC (see Q 20, 22). An unmarried father has only joint custody if there is a common declaration by the parents on custody (*Sorgeerklärung*), § 1626a para. 1 No. 2 German CC (see Q 22a). In this case he has full joint custody with the mother. Without such joint custody the father only has a contact right, § 1684 para. 1 German CC.

Parents living apart are generally in the same legal position as parents living together. Living together does not give the unmarried father a better legal position.

As stated in the answer to Q 8, a step-parent does not have full parental custody. However, he or she has a right to co-decide 'in agreement' ('*im Einvernehmen*') with the custodian in daily affairs, § 1687b para. 1 German CC (see Q 27a). This attribution of 'limited parental responsibilities' is often called 'small custody' ('*kleines Sorgerecht*').[30] This limited custody, however,

[30] See B. VEIT, ‚Kleines Sorgerecht für Stiefeltern (§ 1687 b BGB)', *FPR* 2004 , 67 *et seq.*

presupposes that there is sole custody of only one of the parents. It is excluded if there is joint custody of the parents. In cases of imminent danger for the child the step-parent can undertake all necessary legal acts in the interests of the child (§ 1687b para. 2 German CC). The custodian has to be informed without delay.

The family court may restrict or exclude the 'limited parental responsibility' (limited custody) of the step-parent if this is necessary for the welfare of the child, § 1687b para. 3 German CC. Limited parental responsibility ends when the spouses no longer live permanently together (§ 1687b para. 4 German CC). The concept of 'limited parental responsibility' also applies to registered partners, § 9 *Lebenspartnerschaftsgesetz* (see Q 27b).

If parents are not willing or able to undertake the child's upbringing, foster care (*Familienpflege*) may be possible. Only sometimes is this possible without a permission of the youth office (§ 44 Social Security Act VIII). The carer (*Pflegeperson*) takes on the factual role of a parent, while parental care remains vested in the parents. However, the caregiver has certain rights. He or she can decide in daily affairs and may represent the child in these affairs (§ 1688 para. 1 sent. 1 German CC), though not against the parents express wishes (§ 1688 para. 3 sent. 1 German CC). The carer also has the right to administer the earnings of the child's gainful employment and to claim for the child's maintenance, insurance and social security payments (§ 1688 para. 1 sent. 2 German CC). On application of the parents or with the parents consent the family court may transfer further rights to the foster caregivers, to the exclusion of the parents (§ 1630 para. 2 German CC).

GREECE

The contents of parental responsibilities correspond to the needs of the child, so they do not depend on who is the holder of these responsibilities. Thus the content of parental care (that the parents are married, natural or adoptive) coincides with that of guardianship. Nevertheless, several legal provisions, especially those which assign powers to the supervisory council, restrain the guardian as regards the exercise of his responsibilities.[31] This circumspection with regard to the guardian is justified because of the fact that the guardian is a third person.

When the holders of parental responsibilities are at least two persons, the parental responsibilities may thereby be distributed between them on the basis of a common decision, according to Art. 1511 para. 1 Greek CC, so that each one is responsible for a distinct part of these responsibilities (*e.g.* one holder is responsible for the care of the child and the other for the management of its property).

---

31 See the answer to Q 13 above as well as the provisions of Art. 1607, 1612, 1619, and 1621 Greek CC.

As regards foster families, these are usually responsible for the actual care of the child and in no case can they have more responsibilities than those relating to the actual care of the child.[32]

HUNGARY

The contents of parental responsibilities do not differ according to the marital status of the parents; however, the contents do differ according to whether the parents who exercise it live together or not. With the exception of joint parental responsibilities, if the parents do not live together only the parent with whom the child resides has full parental responsibilities; the non-residential parent only has the right to decide important matters in conjunction with the holder of the parental responsibilities and the right and duty to contact with the child.

If the child's close relatives exercise parental responsibilities instead of the parents, because of the parents' death or on any other ground, their rights of parental responsibilities are the same as those of the parents with one exception: they have the neither the right to appoint nor to exclude a person as a guardian for the child if they (the relative) should die.

The guardian of the child taken into state care (either the foster parent or the supervisor of the children's home) has the right to administer the child's property only if the public guardianship authority has empowered him or her with this right. Of course, they do not have the right to appoint a person as guardian or exclude persons from the guardianship, either. They do have the obligation to regularly render an account of the child's development to the public guardianship authority. Generally, the professional guardian does not take care of the child personally, but the child's property's administration is one of his or her main tasks.

Although a step-parent, or an unmarried partner of the parent who is not the parent of the partner's child, takes part in taking care of the child every day, he or she does not have any parental responsibility.

IRELAND

Where the parties are married at the time of the child's birth, both are conferred with joint and equal guardianship rights.[33] Where the parents are not married, rather different considerations apply. While the natural mother of a child is deemed automatically to be a guardian thereof, a natural father, who is not the husband of the mother, is not considered to be a guardian unless one of three conditions are met:

---

32 P. SKORINI-PAPARRIGOPOULOU, in: A. GEORGIADIS and M. STATHOPOULOS (eds.), *Civil Code commentary, Vol. VIII, Family Law (Arts. 1505-1694)*, 2nd Edition, Athens: Law & Economy, P.N. SAKKOULAS, 2003, Art. 1659 Greek CC, p. 815-816, No. 15 [in Greek].

33 See Sec. 6 Irish Guardianship of Infants Act 1964.

- a man, not being married to the mother of his child at the time of its birth, may subsequently acquire guardianship by marriage to the aforementioned mother;
- alternatively, the natural father may apply to the court under Sec. 6A of the 1964 Act (inserted by Sec. 12 Irish Status of Children Act 1987) for an order conferring on him the status of guardianship;[34]
- a third, and probably the simplest option, is for the parties, by agreement, to make a statutory declaration stating that while not married to each other, the parties are indeed father and mother respectively of the child in question, and that they have agreed that the natural father should be appointed as guardian. The father must be registered as father on the birth certificate of the child in question to utilise this procedure.[35] Such a declaration must be made in the form prescribed by the Irish Guardianship of Children (Statutory Declaration) Regulations 1998.[36] The parties must, furthermore, have made arrangements regarding the custody of, and/or access to the child in question.

In fact, the term 'father' as used in the 1964 Act, is deemed by Sec. 2 thereof generally to exclude (with certain exceptions) 'the father of a child who has not married that child's mother'. That said, even where the natural father does not have guardianship rights, he may nonetheless apply to the court (by virtue of Sec. 11(4) of the 1964 Act) for an order regarding the custody of, or access to, his child. Thus, notwithstanding Sec. 2, a reference in Sec. 11 to the father or parent of a child, may indeed include the non-marital father of a child, although it seems that such person may only apply for an order of custody or access. The Act seems to preclude such person from applying for an order of maintenance in respect of the child.

Stepparents and foster parents enjoy few rights in Ireland. As far as the natural parent's rights in relation to a child in foster care are concerned, they retain all their rights in relation to their child and can reclaim the foster child at any time. Foster parents must deliver the child to the natural parents in the terms detailed in the Irish Child Care (Placement of Children in Foster Care) Regulations 1995.[37]

ITALY

While the contents of the parental responsibilities differ if the parents are not living together, the parents' marital status has no influence.

Art. 317 Italian CC concerning a child born to an unmarried mother (or born out of the marriage) states that parents who live together exercise the parental

34 See *K. v. W.* [1990] I.L.R.M. 121 and *W. O'R. v. E. H.* [1996] 2 I.R. 248.
35 See Sec. 2 (4) of the 1964 Act.
36 S.I. No. 5 of 1998.
37 S.I. No. 260 of 1995.

responsibilities. Otherwise, the parent with whom the child lives exercises the parental responsibilities while the other parent has the right to supervise the education, moral guidance and conditions of the minor's life.

Art. 316 § 2 regarding a legitimate child (born during the marriage) states that the exercise of the parental responsibilities is based on a common agreement of the parents. The parent to whom the child has been entrusted because of separation, divorce or annulment has full exercise of parental responsibilities, unless the judge provides differently. The parental responsibilities are realised by the power to make decisions with respect to the everyday life of the minor. Both parents must make decisions concerning issues of major importance for the children, otherwise they will be made by the judge. The parent not living with the child has the right and duty to supervise the child's moral guidance and education, and can at any time petition the judge concerning prejudicial decisions the other parent has made concerning the child. The non-residential parent also has the right to visit the child and to keep the child for a certain period, respecting the methods determined by the court. Other members of the family also have the right to visit the child if it is considered necessary for the development of the child (see Q 43-48).

LITHUANIA

According to Part 2 of Art. 3.156 Lithuanian CC, parents have equal rights and duties towards their children irrespective of whether the child was born to a married or unmarried couple, after divorce or judicial nullity of the marriage or separation.

Art. 3.267 Lithuanian CC establishes that a child's guardian (curator) is obliged to:

- ensure the child's physical and mental safety;
- take care of the child's health and schooling;
- educate the child;
- decide issues related to the child's interests in co-operation with the interested central and local government institutions;
- create no obstacles for the child's contact with his or her biological parents provided this is not detrimental to the child's interests;
- maintain contact with the child's parents, inform the child's parents and close relatives, if they so request, about the child's development, health, studies and other important issues;
- organize the child's leisure activities, taking into account the child's age, development level and inclinations;
- prepare the child for independent life and work in the family, civil society and the State.

Art. 3.272 Lithuanian CC establishes that a child's guardian (curator) is the child's statutory representative and defends the child's rights and legitimate interests. A child's guardian (curator) has the right to demand in court the return of the child from any person who unlawfully keeps the child.

The essential content of parental responsibilities does not differ depending on the persons holding the responsibilities. Some differences can be found in the guardian's (curator's) responsibilities, as these persons have the duty to maintain contact with the child's parents, to inform the child's parents and close relatives, if they so request, about the child's development, health, studies and other important issues.

Step-parents and foster parents only have the same responsibilities as the biological parents if they adopt the child. However, according to the literature, the step-parent who has not adopted the child has the obligation to provide maintenance for the child.[38]

THE NETHERLANDS

The content of parental responsibilities is the same for all parents irrespective of their civil status and their living arrangements. A non-parent who exercises parental responsibility with a parent is considered, pursuant to Art. 1:245(5) Dutch CC, to exercise joint parental responsibilities unless there is a contrary statutory provision. Therefore, according to Art. 1:253v Dutch CC almost all of the provisions regarding parental responsibilities[39] and the administration by the parents[40] apply. However, with regard to the joint administration, Art. 1:253v § 2 Dutch CC states that Art. 1:253i Dutch CC is only applicable if the parent charged with parental responsibilities does not conduct the administration pursuant to Art. 1:253i § 4 (a) or (c) Dutch CC. In these cases the administration of the estate has been entrusted to the other parent or a third person. Persons who are not parents and do not exercise joint parental responsibilities with a parent can be attributed with guardianship. Custody includes parental responsibilities and guardianship (Art. 1:245 § 2 Dutch CC). All the rules that specifically require the holder of parental responsibilities to be a parent do not apply to the guardian.[41]

NORWAY

Parental responsibilities do not vary according to the status of the holder(s).

POLAND

The general regulations of parental responsibility are to be applied to the child's parents, with the prerequisite that they have full capacity to perform legal acts (Art. 94 Polish Family and Guardianship Code). If the parents are not married

---

38 V. MIKELENAS, *The Law of Obligations* (in Lithuanian), Vol. I, Vilnius: Justitia 2003, p. 26.

39 Title 14 section 2.

40 Title 14 section 3.

41 For example the general provisions with regard to the administration of the minor's estate can be found in Title 14, section 6, paragraph 10 on the administration by a guardian whereas the complementary regulations for parents with parental responsibilities can be found in the paragraph relating to the administration of parents Title 14, section 2, paragraph 3.

to each other or they are married but live separately, the court may appoint one of them to exercise parental authority, limiting the authority of the other parent to certain obligations and rights with regard to the child (Art. 107 § 1 and 2 Polish Family and Guardianship Code). The person adopting a child obtains parental authority equal to that of a parent (Art. 121 § 1 Polish Family and Guardianship Code).

The scope of parental responsibility held by a guardian is limited by the constant supervision of the family court (Art. 155 § 1 Polish Family and Guardianship Code), according to the rules set forth in Arts. 165 – 168 Polish Family and Guardianship Code. The guardian should obtain the court's authorisation for all major issues regarding the minor before deciding the issues (Art. 156 Polish Family and Guardianship Code). The guardian should hear a child under the guardianship if the state of the minor mental health allows such and, if possible, the guardian should take into consideration the reasonable wishes of the minor (Art. 158 Polish Family and Guardianship Code).

The status of a foster family or a child-care institution is regulated by Art. 112^1 Polish Family and Guardianship Code. This states that unless the family court rules otherwise, the foster family or the child-care institution holds the right and duty to carry out regular custody over a minor placed with them, which includes the right and duty to carry out the minor's upbringing and representation in maintenance cases. Other duties and rights resulting from parental authority are held by the parents.

PORTUGAL

The content of parental responsibility varies only if the child has been entrusted to the care of a third person or to some child-care establishment. In this situation, they hold only those parental powers and rights necessary for the proper performance of their functions (Art. 1907 No. 1 Portuguese CC).

RUSSIA

The contents of parental responsibilities are the same irrespective of whether the parents are or have been married or have never been married; or live or have lived together. In Russia the concept of parental rights is reserved to the rights and duties of natural and adoptive parents only.[42] Step-parents, foster parents and other persons are not regarded under Russian law as bearers of parental responsibility. They acquire legal rights and duties regarding a child only through their appointment as full guardians or guardians with limited capacity. The legal position of such persons is generally modelled upon parental responsibility; they enjoy lesser rights, and are under lesser duties.[43]

---

42 L. MIKHEEVA, *Full and Limited Guardianship* (*Opeka i Popechitel'stvo*), Moscow: Paleotip, 2002, p. 81.

43 L. MIKHEEVA, *Full and Limited Guardianship* (*Opeka i Popechitel'stvo*), Moscow: Paleotip, 2002, p. 81.

SPAIN

As will be seen under Q 31, Spanish law grants parental responsibilities to persons who are not parents in the framework of guardianships (*tutela*). Guardianship comprises the duty to care for the child, provide education, administer the child's property and represent the child legally. This differs from *patria potestad* mostly in that the exercise of guardianship is subject to the control and supervision of the judge, especially regarding the administration of property. There is an obligation to inventory the child's property and a general obligation to present the accounts for judicial approval after the termination of guardianship. The judge can intervene at any time and request the guardian to provide information on the child's situation.

The contents of parental responsibilities do not differ based on the parents' marital status. The content of parental responsibilities does not differ if the parents live apart, although in this situation there certain measures must be established concerning the exercise of parental responsibility. Being a step-parent (a parent, through adoption, of a partner's child) does not affect the rights or duties towards the child. Foster parents do not hold parental responsibilities (See Q 32).

SWEDEN

In Swedish law the contents of parental responsibilities do not differ according to the family status of the holder(s). In part this is due to the fact that a child cannot have more than two custodians at a time. The custodians are always either the child's parents or one or two specially appointed custodians. As long as either one of the parents has custody, no additional person can be appointed as a special custodian. There are no means (other than adoption in certain cases) for example, a step-parent to become a holder of parental responsibilities together with a parent with custody rights.

SWITZERLAND

Parental responsibilities are as circumscribed in a general and abstract manner, and apply equally to married and unmarried parents. However, if one parent exercises parental responsibilities alone, this parent must file an inventory of the child's property with the guardianship authority based on Art. 318 § 2 Swiss CC. The other parent, as already explained,[44] has a status comparable to that of a step-parent or foster parent. Step-parents and foster parents assist or represent the parents in the exercise of their parental responsibilities, in accordance with Art. 299 und 300 Swiss CC.

---

[44] See Q 2d.

QUESTION 15

C. ATTRIBUTION OF PARENTAL RESPONSIBILITIES

I. Married Parents

Who has parental responsibilities when the parents are:
(a) Married at the time of the child's birth; or
(b) Not married at that time but marry later?

AUSTRIA

(a) Married at the time of the child's birth

By operation of law, the married parents are jointly entrusted with parental responsibilities (Sec. 144 Austrian CC).

(b) Not married at that time but marry later

By operation of law, the unmarried mother alone is entrusted with parental responsibilities (Sec. 166 Austrian CC). The child may be legitimized by subsequent marriage to the child's father (Sec. 161 Austrian CC). Therefore, the child is legitimate as of the marriage and from then on both parents are entrusted with parental responsibilities (Sec. 144 Austrian CC).

BELGIUM

(a) Married at the time of the child's birth

Since the Belgian Law of 31 March 1987, the general rule is that both parents exercise their parental responsibilities together, whether they are married (Art. 373 Belgian CC) or whether they live together, as long as the descent from the father has been legally determined.[1] The principle of equality of all children is confirmed by Art. 334 Belgian CC, regardless the parents' relationship of the way the descent was determined. In its judgment of 22 July 2004, the Constitutional Court confirmed this principle of equality between children born of a marriage and children born outside of marriage.[2]

(b) Not married at that time but marry later

See Q 15a.

BULGARIA

(a) Married at the time of the child's birth

Art. 32 § 1 Bulgarian Family Code stipulates: 'the husband of the mother is deemed to be the father of the child who has been born during the marriage or before the elapsing of three hundred days from its dissolution.' The mother is the woman who gives birth to the child (Art. 31 § 1 Bulgarian Family Code).

---

1 M. GRÉGOIRE, 'La loi du 29 avril 2001 modifiant les dispositions légales en matière d'autorité parentale et de tutelle', *Rev. not. b.*, 2002, p. 135.

2 Constitutional Court 22.07.2004, ref. 140/2004, www.arbitrage.be.

(b) Not married at that time but marry later

The later marriage does not establish the fatherhood of the child. The parental responsibilities stem from the legally established affiliation of the child. The origin of the mother is determined by birth. The same applies also in cases where the genetic material (*i.e.* egg) belongs to another woman (Art. 31 § 1 Bulgarian Family Code). The fatherhood of the child born out of the marriage cannot be established by presumption. Instead, there are two other options. The first one is given to the father – he may recognise the child before the civil registry officer.[3] The other option establishes the fatherhood by means of judicial decision. Only the mother and the child may claim fatherhood before the court. According to the Art. 41 Bulgarian Family Code: 'The origin from the father may be established by an action brought by the child up to the elapsing of three years from becoming of full age, and by the mother within three years from the date of birth of the child. Where the action is brought by the child the mother is summoned as a party to the lawsuit.' In cases establishing extra-marital parentage the court makes the custody arrangements. It orders the custody of children (meaning the factual exercise of the parental rights and duties), contact issues and their support *ex officio* (Art. 42 and 106 Bulgarian Family Code).

CZECH REPUBLIC

(a) Married at the time of the child's birth

If the parents are married at the time of the child's birth both of them have parental responsibility provided that their legal capacity to act has not been limited by the court due to their mental illness, or they have not been deprived of legal capacity.

(b) Not married at that time but marry later

Parental responsibility arises for both parents regardless of whether the child is born in or out of wedlock. It also arises, by operation of law, for the father whose paternity has been determined by court. The only precondition for the vesting of parental responsibility is the fact that at the time of the child's birth the parent has full legal capacity to act.

The status of a minor parent, especially of a minor unmarried mother, has been strengthened since the 1998 family law reform. As a result, such a parent does not have parental responsibility by operation of law, but pursuant to Sec. 34 § 3 Czech Family Code, even a minor parent may be judicially awarded parental responsibility in relation to care of the child, if such a parent has attained the age of 16 and is duly qualified for the exercise of rights and duties of parental responsibility. In practice, this provision allows that, in case of the child's parents not cohabiting and not agreeing, the court may award the minor unmarried mother parental responsibility in relation to care of the child and to place the child in her upbringing (personal care) pursuant to Sec. 50 Czech

---

3 Art. 35 *et seq.* Bulgarian Family Code.

Family Code, and to determine maintenance from the father. However, the minor parent is not a legal representative of the child and cannot administer its estate. If the father is of the age of majority, he will have those rights. If both parents are minors, the court must appoint a guardian (Sec. 78 Czech Family Code).

If the parents get married after the child's birth their parental responsibility is not affected. The marriage may only affect the surname of their child because the child will have their common surname or the surname determined for their common children (if each of them keeps their original surnames), compare with Sec. 39 § 1 Czech Family Code.

DENMARK

(a) Married at the time of the child's birth

They have joint parental authority. If the parents were legally separated at the time of birth the mother has sole parental authority by operation of the law, Art. 4 Danish Act on Parental Authority and Contact.

(b) Not married at that time but marry later

When the parents marry they acquire joint parental authority if they did not already have joint parental authority, Art. 4 Danish Act on Parental Authority and Contact.

ENGLAND & WALES

(a) Married at the time of the child's birth

According to Sec. 2(1), English Children Act 1989 where the father and mother of the child were married to each other at the time of the child's birth, they *each* have parental responsibility. The phrase 'married to each other at the time of the child's birth', however, has to be interpreted in accordance with Sec. 1, English Family Law Reform Act 1987.[4] Consequently the phrase refers to a child whose parents were married to each other at any time during the period beginning with insemination or (where there is no insemination) conception and ending with the birth and also a child who is legitimate notwithstanding that the marriage is void,[5] legitimated by the parents' subsequent marriage,[6] adopted, or is otherwise treated in law as legitimate.

(b) Not married at that time but marry later

Provided they married before the child reaches the age of 18, the parents' subsequent marriage will confer full parental responsibility upon the father so that each parent will have parental responsibility.[7]

---

4 Sec. 2(3), English Children Act 1989.

5 *I.e.* provided both or either of the parties reasonably believed that the marriage was valid - see Sec. 1(1), English Legitimacy Act 1976.

6 As provided for by Sec. 10, English Legitimacy Act 1976.

7 Sec. 2(1) and (3), English Children Act 1989 and Sec. 1(3)(b), English Family Law Reform Act 1987.

FINLAND

(a) Married at the time of the child's birth

Parents who are married at the time of the child's birth become *ex lege* joint custodians by the birth of the child (Sec. 6 Finnish Child Custody and the Right of Access Act). If the child's mother is not married at the time of the birth, she will become the sole custodian of her child.

(b) Not married at that time but marry later

If one of the parents has sole custody of a child, when the parents marry they both become joint custodians of the child, presuming that the paternity of the unmarried father has been approved according to the Finnish Paternity Act, either through an approved acknowledgment or a court decision.

FRANCE

(a) Married at the time of the child's birth

In this situation the mother and father have joint parental responsibilities (see the general assertion in Art. 372 para. 1 French CC: Father and mother shall exercise the parental responsibilities in common). This rule of joint parental responsibilities is the general principle for married parents, as well as for separated or divorced parents (except in certain situations).

(b) Not married at that time but marry later

After the marriage both parents hold parental responsibilities. This also applies before the marriage, if they both acknowledge the child (but if the parentage of one parent is established either more than a year after the child's birth or by judicial decision, the other parent who has recognised the child is sole holder of parental responsibilities, see Art. 372 para. 2 French CC).

GERMANY

(a) Married at the time of the child's birth

When the parents are married at the time of the child's birth, they are *ipso iure* the joint holders of parental responsibilities. This situation is presumed to be self-evident in the German CC; although it is not expressly mentioned in the law, it results indirectly from the wording of § 1626 a para. 1 sent. 2 German CC, where it says that parents who are not married at the time of the child's birth are entitled to exercise parental responsibilities if they get married. Parents who are married at the time of the child's birth need not issue a declaration nor can they prevent the fact of joint parental responsibility; joint parental responsibility exists until this legal state is changed by operation of law, for example, by the death of one parent, § 1680 para. 1 German CC, or through a court decision.[8]

(b) Not married at that time but marry later

When the parents are not married to each other at the time of the child's birth but subsequently marry, the mother's sole parental responsibility, which exists

---

[8] D. SCHWAB, *Familienrecht*, 12th Edition, Munich: Beck, 2003, No. 522.

by operation of law, § 1626 a para.1 sent. 2 German CC, is automatically converted into joint parental responsibility in accordance with § 1626 a para. 1 sent. 2 German CC. If prior to the marriage the parents declared, with legally binding effect, in accordance with § 1626 a para. 1 sent. 1 German CC, their willingness to assume joint parental responsibility for the child, the joint responsibility which came into existence as a result of the declarations continues automatically.

GREECE

(a) Married at the time of the child's birth

If the parents are married at the time of the child's birth, the law attributes parental responsibilities to both of them and provides that they have to exercise these responsibilities jointly (Art. 1510 para. 1 Greek CC).

(b) Not married at that time but marry later

If the parents marry after the birth of the child, and the father has recognised the child as his own, the child has in all respects the same status as a child born in wedlock (Art. 1473 Greek CC). Thus, in this case both the parents are holders of parental responsibilities, but the exercise of the relevant duties and responsibilities belongs to the mother, according to Art. 1515 para. 1 Greek CC. Both (still unmarried) parents can exercise parental responsibilities jointly, if this is permitted by the court, respecting the best interests of the child (Art. 1515 para. 2 Greek CC). If the parents subsequently marry, but no recognition of the child takes place, the relationship between the father and the child is not established (*filius nullius*). In this case, therefore, the parental responsibilities belong to the mother alone (Art. 1515 para. 1 Greek CC).[9]

HUNGARY

(a) Married at the time of the child's birth

If parents are married at the time of the child's birth they exercise joint parental responsibilities together. Married parents can arrange the manner of the exercise of parental rights in informal agreement, especially in regard to the everyday care of the child.

There can be an exception to joint parental responsibilities if the parents are factually separated, but it is not always an exception (see Q 16d).

(b) Not married at that time but marry later

If parents are not married at the time of the child's birth but marry later, the subsequent marriage does not in itself result in the father obtaining parental responsibilities; the voluntary recognition of the father during the marriage is also required. Still, this recognition has more conditions. It is not possible to recognise a child during the marriage if the child already has a father, either from the mother's earlier marriage or from an unmarried partnership. The consent of a child over 14 is also needed. Whether there is a factual filiation

[9] See, additionally, the answer to Q 20.

between the child and the man recognising him or her cannot be scrutinised during the proceeding. After the recognition is given during a subsequent marriage, both parents exercise joint parental responsibilities together.

IRELAND

(a) Married at the time of the child's birth

Both parents have parental responsibilities.

(b) Not married at that time but marry later?

The natural mother has parental responsibilities when the parents are not married whereas both parents have parental responsibilities on marriage.

ITALY

(a) Married at the time of the child's birth

Both parents (Art. 316 § 2 Italian CC).

(b) Not married at that time but marry later

Both parents (Art. 280 Italian CC).

LITHUANIA

(a) Married at the time of the child's birth

The married parents themselves. According to Part 3 of Art. 3.137 Lithuanian CC, the filiation of a child is confirmed at birth, and the mutual rights and duties of the child and its parents are based on the child's filiation. Therefore, parental authority is exercised from the child's birth.

(b) Not married at that time but marry later

Firstly, in the situation where the parents are not married, if the unmarried father acknowledges his paternity or his paternity is established by the court judgment, then after the marriage, the married parents. Secondly, the unmarried mother, if the father does not acknowledge his paternity. In the event of the marriage between the child's mother and a man who has not acknowledged his paternity, parental responsibilities belong only to the mother.

A person who was not married to the child's mother and did not acknowledge paternity at the time of the child's birth can acquire the parental responsibilities after the acknowledgement of his paternity or the establishment of his paternity by a court judgment (Art. 3.156, 3.159 Lithuanian CC)

According to Art. 3.156 Lithuanian CC, the father and the mother have equal rights and duties with respect to their children. This equality of rights and duties is irrespective of whether the child was born to a married or unmarried couple, after divorce or judicial nullity of the marriage or separation. This conforms to the principle of equality of all persons provided for by Part 1 of Art. 29 Lithuanian Constitution, the provisions of Art. 14 European Convention on Human Rights and the provisions of Part 1 of Art. 6 Council of Europe Convention on the legal status of children born out of wedlock.

THE NETHERLANDS

(a) Married at the time of the child's birth

The parents have joint parental responsibilities over the child from the moment of birth (Art. 1:251 Dutch CC). The spouses in a female same-sex marriage also have joint parental responsibilities over children born during their marriage, even though they are legally a parent and a non- parent.

(b) Not married at that time but marry later

The wording of Art. 1:251 Dutch CC (During their marriage the parents exercise joint parental responsibilities) is not specific on whether joint parental responsibilities are attributed to the parents, by dint of the marriage, over their children born before the marriage. However, from the legal history it becomes clear that even though Art. 1:251 Dutch CC does not include the words over their children,[10] it is not the intention of the lawmaker to exclude these children from joint parental responsibilities.[11]

The unmarried father is not a parent by operation of law; he must recognise the child with the mother's consent before he becomes a parent.[12] This means that if he did not recognise the child before the marriage he will not automatically be vested with joint parental responsibilities; he is not a legal parent.[13] The person other than a parent in a female same-sex marriage will not automatically be vested with parental responsibilities because, regardless of the fact that the female couple may have raised the child from birth, the mother's partner is also not a legal parent. Since she does not have the right to recognise her partner's child under Dutch law, she will not acquire joint parental responsibilities with the biological mother by dint of their marriage. There are, however, other ways in which these two couples can acquire joint parental responsibilities.[14]

NORWAY

(a) Married at the time of the child's birth

When the parents are married at the time of the child's birth, both parents share parental responsibilities on an equal basis, Art. 34 sec. 1 Norwegian Children Act 1981.

(b) Not married at that time but marry later

If the parents marry after the birth of the child, their parental responsibilities continue to reflect the rules of parental responsibility for unmarried parents.

---

10 The term *their children* also included the children who were legitimized by the marriage itself.

11 *Kamerstukken Tweede Kamer*, 23012 No. 3, p. 36.

12 Art. 1:199 (c) and 1:204 § 1 (c) Dutch CC. The biological father can also recognise his child without the mother's consent; for this purpose he will have to request the court to replace the mother's consent. (Art. 1:204 § 3 Dutch CC. Moreover, he can become a parent by adoption (Art. 1:199 under e Dutch CC) or by judicial establishment of his paternity (Art. 1:199 d Dutch CC).

13 This is a consequence of the fact that children are no longer legitimized by marriage.

14 See Q 21 and 22.

This means that if only the mother had parental responsibilities for the child, she alone continues to have these until the parents agree that they both shall be attributed parental responsibilities. They must then notify the public registrar accordingly.

POLAND

(a) Married at the time of the child's birth

In this situation, both parents hold parental authority, so long as they have the full capacity to perform legal acts. On the existence of parenthood: see Q 1.

(b) Not married at that time but marry later

As a rule, parental authority is held by a child's parents, irrespective of their marital status. An exception is made in the situation where paternity is established by the court, in which case the father generally holds no parental authority (Art. 93 § 2 Polish Family and Guardianship Code). Should the parents later marry, upon the father's request their marriage would be a ground for the court to grant the father parental authority (Art. 93 § 2 sentence 2 Polish Family and Guardianship Code).

PORTUGAL

(a) Married at the time of the child's birth

If the parents are married when their child is born, both exercise parental responsibility (Art. 1901 No.1 Portuguese CC).

(b) Not married at that time but marry later

If the parents are not married when their child is born but marry later, both parents exercise parental responsibility during the marriage (Art. 1901 No. 1 and 1911 No. 1 Portuguese CC), provided the parenthood of both has been legally established.

RUSSIA

(a) Parents are married at the time of the child's birth

According to Russian law parental responsibility is coupled to the legal filial link between the child and the parent, not the marriage between the parents. If parents are married at the time of birth of a child, they both acquire parental responsibility by virtue of a presumption of paternity of the husband of the mother of the child (Art. 48 (1) Russian Family Code).

(b) Parents are not married at that time but marry later

Subsequent marriage of the parents has no influence on their parental responsibility. Russian law bears no trace of legitimisation by subsequent marriage. If the father of the child has recognised the child or his paternity has been established by a court order, he acquires full parental responsibility and shares joint parental responsibility with mother. These acts can take place before or after the marriage of the parents. If those acts did not take place, the marriage of the parents can not substitute them.

SPAIN

(a) Married at the time of the child's birth

Parental responsibility is a consequence of parenthood. Whether the parents are married is therefore irrelevant; what matters is whether parenthood is determined. For married parents, a presumption of parenthood establishes that a child born to a woman after the celebration of marriage or 300 days after legal or factual separation is the common child of both the husband and wife.

(b) Not married at that time but marry later

Patria potestad is vested on both father and mother as a consequence of parenthood regardless of civil status. If parents are not married at the time of the child's birth, the father will have to recognise the child regardless of whether the parents later marry.

SWEDEN

(a) Married at the time of the child's birth

Parents who are married to each other at the time of the child's birth automatically obtain joint custody of the child, Chapter 6 Sec. 3 para. 1 Swedish Children and Parents Code. Married parents who have reached the age of majority (18 years) also automatically become the guardians of the child.

(b) Not married at that time but marry later

When the parents of a child marry after the birth of the child, they both shall have custody of the child from then on, unless a court has previously entrusted custody to one or two specially appointed custodians, Chapter 6 Sec. 3 para. 1 Swedish Children and Parents Code.

SWITZERLAND

(a) Married at the time of the child's birth

'During the marriage the parents jointly exercise parental responsibilities' (Art. 297 § 1 Swiss CC).

(b) Not married at that time but marry later

If the parents marry one another, the parents jointly exercise parental responsibilities in accordance with Art. 259 § 1 Swiss CC, in combination with Art. 297 § 1 Swiss CC, as soon as the husband's paternity has been established by recognition or in a judgment.

QUESTION 16

C. ATTRIBUTION OF PARENTAL RESPONSIBILITIES

I. Married Parents

How, if at all, is the attribution of parental responsibilities affected by:
(a) Divorce;
(b) Legal separation;
(c) Annulment of the marriage;
(d) Factual separation.

AUSTRIA

(a) Divorce

Sec. 177(1) Austrian CC provides that the parental responsibilities of both parents continue after divorce unless the parents agree otherwise, namely that one parent's parental responsibilities are restricted or completely revoked. However, if, in fact, the parents want to continue joint parental responsibilities, they must submit an agreement to the court naming the parent with whom the child will primarily reside (*i.e.* where the centre of the child's life will be). This will ensure that continuity of child-rearing will be maintained to the greatest extent possible.[1] The so-called domicile parent must always be entrusted with all parental responsibilities (Sec. 177(2) Austrian CC). The court will approve the parents' agreement if it is in the best interests of the child (Sec. 177(3) Austrian CC). If the parents fail to reach an (approvable) agreement on the primary residence of the child or the attribution of parental responsibilities within reasonable time, the court will entrust one parent with sole parental responsibilities based on the best interests of the child - after having unsuccessfully tried to reach an amicable solution with the parents (Sec. 177a(1) Austrian CC). The same applies if the exercise of joint parental responsibilities later fails: either parent may petition the court to end joint parental responsibilities without substantiation at any time. Then the court will entrust one parent with sole parental responsibilities based on the best interests of the child unless a reconciliation between the parents may be brought about (Sec. 177a(2) Austrian CC).

When deciding which parent shall be entrusted with sole parental responsibilities the court must *inter alia* consider whether previously the parent has observed the requirement of good behaviour *(Wohlverhaltensgebot)* according to Sec. 145b Austrian CC: In exercising parental responsibilities, each parent must refrain from doing anything that would impair the child's relationship with the other parent and other persons holding rights and duties

---

1 See *Bundesministerium für Justiz*, EBRV 296 BlgNR XXI. GP, p. 95 (explanatory notes to Government bill, 296 supplements to the stenographic minutes of the National Assembly, XXI legislative period).

concerning the child (*e.g.* grandparents) or make it more difficult for these persons to perform their duties with respect to the child. This prohibition encompasses a broad spectrum of behaviour: from insulting statements to physical and/or psychological violence against the other parent or persons.

(b) Legal separation

There is no legal separation under current Austria law.

(c) Annulment of the marriage

If the marriage of the parents of a minor child is annulled or declared invalid[2], the same provisions apply as with divorce (Sec. 177 Austrian CC, see Q 16a).

(d) Factual separation

If married parents separate (without divorce), they are free to structure their parental responsibilities as they wish (Sec. 177b and 177 Austrian CC). Sec. 177b Austrian CC states that the provisions for divorce/annulment/nullification of a marriage apply (see Q 16a and 16c) with the exception that a court will issue a decision entrusting one parent with all parental responsibilities only upon petition.

BELGIUM

(a) Divorce

The parental responsibilities are in principle jointly attributed to both parents, whether they are married, live together, are divorced or are factually separated. According to Art. 373 Belgian CC, both parents hold parental responsibilities when they live together (See Q 15). Art. 374 Belgian CC confirms both parents also hold parental responsibilities when they live apart (See Q 18). The law does not make a distinction based on the parents' relationship. The legislation installs a basic model of joint parental responsibilities, and there are no specific regulations concerning the parental responsibilities of those who have divorced or for the parents of children born out of wedlock. The Constitutional Court confirmed this principle in a recent judgment, stating that since the Belgian Law of 31 March 1987, the parental authorities and responsiblities are no longer regulated on the basis of marriage, but solely on the basis of a legally determined affiliation to, or adoption of, the child.[3]

Although the *attribution* of parental responsibilities is principally not affected by the ending of the parent's relationship through either divorce, separation or annulment of the marriage, or the ending of the unmarried parents' relationship, the *exercise* of those responsibilites may be affected by the ending

---

2 §§ 20-32, 35-42 *Ehegesetz* (Austrian Marriage Act).

3 Constitutional Court 12.05.2004, ref. 81/2004, www.arbitrage.be; J. GERLO, 'De basisregeling van de wet van 13 april 1995 betreffende de gezamenlijke uitoefening van het ouderlijk gezag', in: *Gandaius Actueel I*, Antwerp: Kluwer, 135, No. 220-240; T. MOREAU, 'La loi du 13 avril 1995 relative à l'exercice conjoint de l'autorité parentale', *Div. Act.*, 1995, p. 97; W. PINTENS, 'Die Reform des belgischen Kindschaftsrechts aus vergleichender Sicht', *FamRZ*, 1997, p. 460-464.

of the (un)married parents' relationship (Art. 374 Belgian CC). (See Q 37 and Q 38).

(b) Legal separation
See Q 16a.

(c) Annulment of the marriage
See Q 16a.

(d) Factual separation
See Q 16a.

BULGARIA
(a) Divorce
Divorce does not affect the legal attribution of the parental rights and duties but does affect their factual exercise, which concentrates in the parent with whom the child resides.[4] The other parent is entitled to contact with the child.

In cases of divorce due to marital breakdown based on fault,[5] the court settles all matters regarding the former spouses' relations with their children. In the dissolution of marriages where there are minor children, the court, irrespective of whether the interested party files a claim to this end or not, orders the custody of children (meaning the factual exercise of the parental rights and duties), contact issues and child support as well as the use of the matrimonial home *ex officio* (Art 106 § 1 and 107 Bulgarian Family Code).

With the declaration of the divorce the court orders *ex officio* custody of children, contact measures between the children and the parents, and the support of the children.

The court determines child custody after scrutinising all circumstances in relation to the child's interests. The custody cannot be granted to the spouse who was found guilty in the divorce procedure if this may have negative effect for the rearing and upbringing of the children.

The court hears the parents and the children if they are fourteen years of age or older. Where the court finds it appropriate it can hear the children who are ten years of age or older, and also close relatives and friends of the family. As an exception, where the interests of children require it, the court may decree that the children would live with their grandfather, grandmother or somebody else, with the consent of the latter, or at a social institution.

When a change in the circumstances occurs the court may, at the petition of one of the parents or *ex officio*, change the previously decreed measures and decree

---

4 L. NENOVA, *Family Law of the Republic of Bulgaria*, Sofia, 1994, p. 624-630.

5 Art. 99 § 2 Bulgarian Family Code.

new ones. In cases of divorce by mutual consent or divorce granted on a marital breakdown where the spouses file a request of non-pronouncement for fault, the spouses settle the post-divorce arrangements, including the exercise of the parental rights and duties, through an agreement. The court approves the agreement if it corresponds to the interests of the children.[6]

The court or the agreement should, as a post-divorce arrangement, appoint one of the parents to exercise the parental rights and duties thus also settling the residence of the child with that parent. Measures of personal contact and support are ordered or arranged for the other parent.[7] The arguments on which the regulation is based are the possible practical difficulties generated by the joint custody following the divorce or the separation and the incompatibility of this situation with the interests of children.[8]

Granting the custody means granting the practical day-to-day exercise of parental rights.[9] It is assumed that the duties continue to be fulfilled by both parents.[10] For instance the non-custodial parent still owes duties of support, care and supervision during times of contact with the child.[11] According to theory and judicial practice, the parent in question also preserves the full range of parental rights (the custody). What he or she loses is the opportunity to exercise them in practice.[12] Practically, by granting the custody to one of the parents, the other loses any capacity not only for factual actions (due to their separate residence), but also for legal actions. This follows from the interpretation suggested by the Supreme Court. According to the court the 'exercise of parental rights' means: 'the daily exercise of parental rights regarding the protection, defence and representation of children'.[13] Therefore, the non-custodial parent cannot act as a legal representative of the child and that capacity remains solely with the custodial parent.[14]

---

6 Art. 99 § 3 and Art. 100 § 2 Bulgarian Family Code.

7 Art. 106 § 1 Bulgarian Family Code.

8 L. NENOVA, *Family Law of the People's Republic of Bulgaria*, Sofia, 1977, p. 322. This principle was upheld in 1994: L. NENOVA, *Family Law of the People's Republic of Bulgaria*, Sofia, 1994, p. 637. Judicial practice maintained the same view in Decision of the Supreme Court, 1-1974, § 1. V.N. MLADENOV and P. BRATANOVA, *Family Code: Text, judicial practice, etc*, 1996.

9 The meaning of the phrase 'parental rights' in Bulgarian legislation corresponds to the interpretation of Jonathan HERRING when he discusses the option that the parent might have rights not in his or her capacity of a human being but because he or she is a parent. In J. HERRING, *Family Law* 2001, Longman, p. 325.

10 See HR. GEORGIEV, I. PALAZOV, P. BESHKOV and T. DAMYANOV, *Family Code. Commentary*, Sofia, 1975, p. 203. In the same sense, L. NENOVA, *Family Law of the Republic of Bulgaria*, Sofia, 1994, p. 638.

11 L. NENOVA, *Family Law of the Republic of Bulgaria*, Sofia, 1994, p. 639.

12 A. STANEVA, *Representative and Custodial Functions of Parents*, Sofia, 1992, p. 31.

13 See Decision of the Supreme Court, 1-1974.

14 A. STANEVA, *Representative and Custodial Functions of Parents*, Sofia 1992, p. 32-33. Also the Supreme Court substantiation in Decision of the Supreme Court, 1-1974.

Only the exercise of some rights is preserved for the non-custodial parent, which protect his or her interest rather than the interest of the child: to give consent for adoption, to agree both for a change in the name of the child and for taking the child out of the country.[15] Non-custodial parents also retain another important right: to petition the court for revision of parental custody regime if the circumstances have changed.[16] Another important right of the non-custodial parent is to maintain contact with the child.

In spite of this regulation and practice, the view has been expressed that it is not impossible for the custody to be granted to both parents jointly where the interests of the child so require.[17] This is an isolated statement and no serious discussion has taken place so far in Bulgaria on the issue of joint custody after divorce. Moreover the idea may not be confirmed by the interpretation of the law. It clearly states that: '...the court rules to which spouse the custody shall be granted, orders the measures regarding the ... contact between parents and children'.[18] No case law is known where a joint custody has been granted. To the contrary, the entire practice of the Supreme Court confirms the principle of the sole custody after divorce. In fact the theory tries to claim against the factual dissolution of parentage following the divorce that contrasts the equality of parents' principle articulated explicitly in the law. This discourse distracts attention from the real problems following the divorce. They are connected with the status of non-custodial parent and his or her relations with the child. In reality, the status of that parent depends not on his or her legal position, which is very unclear, but on the factual relations with the custodial parent. If they are bad, as it is in the majority of cases especially in fault divorces, that a parent actually loses the custody of the child. Regardless of the theoretical attempts to provide reasons to the contrary, the current legislation does not provide an opportunity for the non-custodial parent to preserve not only his or her legal but factual position in relation to the child. Lawyers and legal commentators refuse to admit that the law shows a limited capacity even to ensure the contact rights of non-custodial parent and the child.

(b) Legal separation

Bulgarian family law does not provide for a legal separation between spouses.

(c) Annulment of the marriage

Art. 98 Bulgarian Family Code entitled 'consequences arising from the annulment of marriage' stipulates that – 'the rules regarding the consequences of the dissolution of marriage through divorce in connection with the personal property and property relations between the spouses, as well as those about the relations between them and the children are also applicable to the annulment of marriage. The bad faith by annulment of marriage has the same meaning as the

---

15 Art. 54 § 1 Bulgarian Family Code; Art. 45 of the Identification Documents Act.

16 Art. 106 § 5 Bulgarian Family Code.

17 L. NENOVA, *Family Law of the Republic of Bulgaria*, Sofia, 1977, p. 322.

18 Art. 106 Bulgarian Family Code.

guilt by divorce. The children who have been conceived or born during the annulled marriage are deemed as born in wedlock and for them the presumption for fatherhood, under Art. 32, is also applicable.'

(d) Factual separation

The situation is more or less the same in cases of separation between cohabiting (or married) parents where the court grants only the residence of the child. According to Art. 71 § 2: 'Where the parents do not live together and are unable to reach an agreement as to with whom of them the children will live, the dispute is resolved by the district court of the children's residence, after the court has heard the children, if they are ten years of age or older. The decision of the court is subject to appeal according to the general rules.' In cases of separation, the court may only determine the residence of the child with one of the parents if they cannot reach an agreement.

CZECH REPUBLIC

(a) Divorce

Spouses may not divorce until after a judicial decision on the regulation of the relationship between the spouses and their minor children for the period after divorce. This judgment must always include the decision on placing the child into upbringing (personal care, determination of residence) and establishing the amount of maintenance due (Sec. 26 Czech Family Code). In case of the parents' inability to come to an agreement the court may also decide upon the regulation of contact (visits) of the other parent.

The parents' agreement concerning contact with the child need not be approved by the court. As for personal care and maintenance, the court may decide itself or approve the parents' agreement, so long as the agreement does not contravene the child's interests (Sec. 26 § 3 Czech Family Code).

Parental responsibility does not end by divorce for either of the parents; it is only the exercise that is changed. The parent who does not personally care for the child continues to be a legal representative of the child and his or her consent is needed in all essential matters relating to the child.

(b) Legal separation

Czech law does not recognise the concept of legal separation.

(c) Annulment of the marriage

Annulment of the marriage has the same effects in relation to exercise of parental responsibility as divorce of the marriage (Sec. 17 § 2 Czech Family Code).

(d) Factual separation

In case of factual separation the court may award the care of the child to one of the parents and determine that the other parent pay maintenance, if the parents cannot reach an agreement (Sec. 50 Czech Family Code). Parental responsibility remains for both parents and it is only its exercise that is changed. The court may start proceedings (*ex officio*) even without a parent's motion.

DENMARK

(a) Divorce

Joint parental authority continues after divorce.[19] Parents who no longer live together or intend to live separately can demand that the joint parental authority be terminated, Art. 8 Danish Act on Parental Authority and Contact.

(b) Legal separation

Joint parental authority continues after (legal) separation.[20] Parents who no longer live together or intend to live separately can demand that the joint parental authority be terminated, Art. 8 Danish Act on Parental Authority and Contact.

(c) Annulment of the marriage

A marriage may be annulled where the parties are within prohibited degrees of consanguinity, in the case of bigamy, and in some cases where there is a lack of sound mind or deceit.[21] The legal consequences are the same as for divorce, that is, the joint parental authority continues after the annulment.[22] Parents who no longer live together or intend to live separately can demand that the joint parental authority be terminated, Art. 8 Danish Act on Parental Authority and Contact.

---

19 This rule came into force on 1 January 2002, Act No. 461 of 07.06.2001, Art. 2 and 10. Before then a decision regarding parental authority (sole or joint) had to be made in connection with the divorce, Danish Act on Parental Authority and Contact, Art. 7 (old).

20 This rule came into force on 1 January 2002, Act No. 461 of 07.06.2001, Art. 2 and 10. Before then a decision regarding parental authority (sole or joint) had to be made in connection with the separation, Danish Act on Parental Authority and Contact, Art. 7 (old).

21 Danish Act on Formation and Dissolution of Marriage, *Lov om ægteskabs indgåelse og opløsning*, Act No. 147, 09.03.1999, Art. 6, 9, 23 and 24.

22 Danish Act on Formation and Dissolution of Marriage, *Lov om ægteskabs indgåelse og opløsning*, Act No. 147, 09.03.1999, Art. 25(1).

(d) Factual separation

Joint parental authority continues after factual separation. Parents who no longer live together or intend to live separately can demand that the joint parental authority be terminated, Art. 8 Danish Act on Parental Authority and Contact.

ENGLAND & WALES

(a) Divorce

Under English law the attribution of parental responsibility is not affected by divorce.

(b) Legal separation

Under English law the attribution of parental responsibility is not affected by legal separation.

(c) Annulment of the marriage

If a marriage is annulled on the grounds of voidability then it remains valid for all purposes prior to the decree.[23] Consequently, it does not affect the attribution of parental responsibility. Even if a marriage is held void provided either or both spouses reasonably believed the marriage was valid it will not affect the attribution of parental responsibility.[24]

(d) Factual separation

Under English law the attribution of parental responsibility is *not* affected by factual separation.

FINLAND

(a) Divorce

Attribution of custody or any other aspect of parental responsibility is not necessarily affected by the divorce of the parents at all. The court may render a decision about the custody of a child in connection with the divorce proceedings of the parents who have the custody of their child. The court can also deal with the question of the custody of the children *ex officio,* but it cannot render a decision concerning custody without a parental request (Sec. 31 - 32 Finnish Marriage Act No. 411/1987).

(b) Legal separation

Legal separation is not recognised by the Finnish legal system

(c) Annulment of the marriage

Annulment is not recognised by the Finnish legal system, since the reform of the related law in 1987.

---

23 Sec. 16, English Matrimonial Causes Act 1973.

24 See answer to Q 15a.

(d) Factual separation

The factual separation of the parents does not affect their custodial status.

FRANCE

(a) Divorce

In principle the attribution of parental responsibilities is not affected at all by divorce, see Art. 373-2 para. 1 French CC: '[T]he separation of the parents has no consequence to the application of the rules concerning the allocation of parental responsibilities.' The reform Act of 4 March 2002 incorporated a new section into the French CC concerning 'the exercise of parental responsibilities by separated parents.' This section makes no distinction between married and non-married parents who are separated. The criterion chosen by the French legal provisions is the 'separation of the parents'; it does not matter if the separation is a divorce, an annulment, a legal separation or even a factual separation.

In all cases of parental separation both parents generally remain holders of parental responsibilities (Art. 373-2 French CC), and the French CC requires each parent to maintain personal relationships with the child (para. 2). However, if the child's interest so requires, the judge can decide that only one parent shall have the exercise of the parental responsibilities (Art. 373-2-1 French CC).[25] The other parent then has a contact right (*droit de visite et d'hébergement*, see Art. 373-2-1 para. 2 French CC).

The judge is free to discern what is in the child's best interests. The *Cour de cassation* refuses to overrule decisions made under the discretion of the court using this standard,[26] but the *Cour de cassation* requires the family judge to state why the child's interests require that the exercise of parental responsibilities should be attributed to only one parent.[27]

(b) Legal separation

Same rules as above under (a) divorce.

---

25 See *e.g.* the case which was brought before the European Court of Human Rights (ECtHR, 16.12.2003, *Palau-Martinez v. France*, Appl. No. 64927/01: the French court had decided that the children would live with the father because the mother was a member of the religious sect called Jehovah's Witnesses. The European Court of Human Rights criticises the insufficiency of the reasons given by the French court.

26 See French Supreme Court, Civ. II, 28.03.1977, *Gaz. Pal.*, 1977. 2. 602; Civ. I, 20.06.1995, *Bull. civ* I, No. 264.

27 See French Supreme Court, Civ. II, 31.05.1995, *Bull. civ.* II, No. 165 (the decision that attributed the exercise of parental responsibilities to the mother only mentioned that she was more available than the father to take care of the child and that her educational skills were as high as the father's ones). Several decisions insist upon the necessity for the family judge to give reasons concerning the research of the child's interest and its results, see e.g. French Supreme Court, Civ. II, 24.02.1993, *Bull. civ.* II, No. 76.

(c) Annulment of the marriage

Same rules as in case of divorce (see under (a)).

(d) Factual separation

The same rules apply as in case of a divorce (see above under (a)).

GERMANY

(a) Divorce

Until the *Child Law Reform Act* of 1998, a court decision on parental responsibility was compulsory in the event of a divorce,[28] whereas according to the legislation currently in force, a court decision is no longer required. Back in 1982 the Federal Constitutional Court[29] declared the mandatory transfer of parental responsibility to one parent on divorce[30] as null and void, due to the violation of parental rights this involved.[31] Since the Reform Act, therefore, joint parental responsibility is generally maintained despite divorce. No court ruling is required. A parental divorce no longer means that family courts are obliged to deal with the future arrangements regarding parental responsibilities. A court decision on parental responsibility is now only made following an application by one parent. Such an application can always be made if the parents live apart, § 1671 German CC.

At the same time, the state of living apart that results from divorce does change the structure of joint parental responsibility, as the child will usually either live with the mother or the father on account of their spatial separation. The law takes account of this circumstance by means of the special provision in § 1687 German CC. Under the umbrella of the continuance of joint parental responsibility after divorce, which does not describe a reality but is a legal construct[32], issues regarding contact with the child, § 1684 para. 3 German CC, maintenance and upbringing, § 1628 German CC, must be clarified between the parents, pursuant to § 1687 para. 1 German CC. If the child's permanent residence is with one of the parents, as opposed to any other possible arrangement for the sharing of responsibility, § 1687 para. 1 sent. 1 German CC stipulates that the parents' mutual consent is in general no longer required, as otherwise is the case when the parents hold joint responsibility. Mutual consent is only required in matters the regulation of which is of considerable importance for the child. In matters relating to everyday life, the decisions are made solely by the parent with whom the child habitually resides, the habitual residence resulting either from the consent of the other parent or from a court decision. The term 'matters relating to everyday life' refers to frequently occurring situations requiring a decision by the parents, but whose effects on

28 § 1671 German CC (old version), § 623 para. 1 German Code of Civil Procedure (old version).

29 BVerfG 03.11.1982, *BVerfGE* 61, 358.

30 § 1671 para. 4 sent. 1 German CC (old version).

31 Art. 6 para. 2 German Basic Law (*Grundgesetz*).

32 D. SCHWAB, *Familienrecht*, 12th Edition, Munich: Beck, 2003, No. 667.

the child's development can be modified without a great deal of difficulty (*e.g.* § 1687 para. 1 sent. 3 German CC).[33] By contrast, any decisions regarding matters which have an effect on the child's development that can either not be modified or be modified only with difficulty, are of 'considerable importance' for the child.[34]

Above and beyond the provision of § 1687 German CC, both holders of parental responsibilities are authorised in accordance with § 1629 para. 1 sent. 4 German CC to act alone on behalf of the child in the event of imminent danger, § 1687 para. 1 sent. 5 German CC.

(b) Legal separation

German law does not have the legal institution of 'legal separation'.

(c) Annulment of the marriage

Since the annulment of marriage by court decision in accordance with § 1313 German CC has no retroactive effect, the same principles apply as for divorce. This means that joint parental responsibility continues after the annulment of a marriage by court decision.

(d) Factual separation

In the event of a factual separation, too, the previously existent joint parental responsibility continues. This means that there is no difference in comparison with the situation pertaining after a divorce. As shown by § 1671 para. 1 German CC, which refers to 'living apart' and not to 'divorce', it is not the divorce but the separation which forms the jurisdictional basis for the legal provisions.

GREECE

(a) Divorce

Art. 1510 para. 1 Greek CC provides that the parents exercise parental care jointly, without referring to the relations between them *(i.e.* if they cohabit, if they are factually separated, if their marriage has been annulled, or if they are divorced). Thus, the parents continue to exercise joint parental care also after divorcing, unless they submit a petition to the court to regulate parental care.[35]

---

33 BT-Drucks. 13/8511 p. 74 *et seq;* U. DIEDERICHSEN, in: PALANDT, *Bürgerliches Gesetzbuch*, 64th Edition, Munich: Beck, 2005, § 1687 No. 11.

34 U. DIEDERICHSEN, in: PALANDT, *Bürgerliches Gesetzbuch*, 64th Edition, Munich: Beck, 2005, § 1687 No. 7.

35 This is the prevailing opinion which is also followed by the courts. Nevertheless, it has been claimed that the courts should always regulate the attribution of parental care after divorce or the annulment of the marriage. Hence, if the parents continue to exercise parental care jointly, as they did before the divorce or annulment, this is only a *de facto* exercise. On this question see, among others, P. AGALLOPOULOU, in: A. GEORGIADIS and M. STATHOPOULOS (eds.), *Civil Code commentary, Vol. VIII, Family Law (Arts. 1505-1694)*, 2nd Edition, Athens: Law & Economy, P.N. Sakkoulas 2003, Art. 1513-1514 Greek CC, p. 216, No. 2-3.

In this last scenario, the court has a wide range of possibilities: It may grant the exercise of parental care to one of the parents, or to both parents jointly, or it may distribute it between the parents,[36] or attribute it to a third party (Art. 1513 Greek CC). Independent of the court decision on the exercise of parental care, both parents will continue to engage in parental care.

(b) Legal separation
The institution of legal separation does not exist in Greece.

(c) Annulment of the marriage
Greek law does not differentiate between the effects of a divorce and an annulment of the marriage.[37] Hence, the court regulates the exercise of parental responsibilities on the basis of the abovementioned options (Art. 1513 Greek CC).

(d) Factual separation
The provisions on the attribution of parental responsibilities in the case of a divorce and an annulment of the marriage also apply factual separation of the parents (Art. 1514 Greek CC).

HUNGARY
(a) Divorce
Divorce generally affects the attribution of parental responsibilities. Maintaining joint parental responsibilities after divorce is rather exceptional in Hungary.

With a divorce, parental responsibilities, if they are not joint, are attributed by judicial judgment to the parent with whom the child is placed. The non-residential parent has the right to contact and the right to decide important matters affecting the child in conjunction with the holder of the parental responsibilities. If the parental responsibilities of the holder of these rights and duties comes to an end for any reason, e.g. because of the death of this parent, the divorced parent's parental responsibilities will be revived.

(b) Legal separation
Hungarian law does not recognise legal separation.

(c) Annulment of the marriage
The legal consequences of an annulment of marriage are the same as for a divorce. In Hungarian law, a void marriage results in paternal affiliation, so the parental responsibilities of the father are the same as with a valid marriage,

---

36 This distribution may relate to the functions of parental care or to time. P. AGALLOPOULOU, in: A. GEORGIADIS and M. STATHOPOULOS (eds.), *Civil Code commentary, Vol. VIII, Family Law (Arts. 1505-1694)*, 2nd Edition, Athens: Law & Economy, P.N. Sakkoulas 2003, Art. 1513-1514 Greek CC, pp. 230-231, No. 77.

37 See Art. 1382 Greek CC.

with no regard given to the ground of the invalidity. It makes no difference how a marriage is terminated, parental responsibilities are decided regardless of whether the termination is by divorce or annulment. An annulment of marriage is rare in Hungary.

(d) Factual separation

Joint parental responsibilities do not automatically come to an end with a factual separation - their maintenance or termination depends on the agreement of the parents. Nevertheless, each parent has a right to file a claim, without a corresponding petition for divorce, for a judgment on who of them the child is placed with. This judgment will govern issues of parental responsibilities, just as with a judgment made in the course of the divorce proceeding. Therefore, the attribution of parental responsibilities happens as in case Q 16a.

IRELAND

(a) Divorce

The granting of a decree of divorce does not affect the right of the father and mother of a child to continue to be joint guardians of any relevant children.[38] The court, however, may declare either of the parties unfit to have custody of any minor child and, if it does so, that party is not entitled to the right to custody of that minor on the death of the other party.[39]

(b) Legal separation

It is not at all affected by legal separation.

(c) Annulment of the marriage

The fathers of children of annulled marriages remain their guardians under Sec. 2 Irish Guardianship of Infants Act 1964, as amended by the Irish Children Act 1997. The mother has constitutional protection in this regard.

(d) Factual separation

It is not affected at all by factual separation.

ITALY

(a) Divorce

Pursuant to Art. 317 § 2 Italian CC, joint parental responsibilities expire neither as a consequence of separation, divorce or annulment, nor if only one of the parents holds custody of the child. If only one of the parents lives with the child, it is possible to differentiate the other parent's exercise of parental responsibilities[40] (Art. 155 Italian CC and Art. 6 § 4 Italian Divorce law).

---

38 Irish Family Law (Divorce) Act, 1996, Sec. 10 (2), No. 33 of 1996.

39 1996 Act, Sec. 41.

40 M. GIORGIANNI , *Della potestà dei genitori,* in *Commentario al diritto italiano della famiglia* by G. CIAN, G. OPPO and A. TRABUCCHI, IV, Cedam: Padova, 1992, p. 336

The Italian legal system is uniform as far as the actual regulation of the parent-child relationship after separation, divorce or annulment;[41] however, it does not give specific methods because the leading criteria are exclusively the moral and material interests of the minor. Still, the judge has wide discretionary authority in which to examine the minor's interests in each individual case.

The law provides three different types of custody: exclusive custody, joint custody and alternating custody, and thus provides differentiated modalities for exercising parental responsibilities. If there is just cause can the judge order the minor to live with a third party or at an institute for education (Art. 155 Italian CC), or he can order the family custody (Art. 6 § 8 Italian Divorce law).

With exclusive custody, the custodial parent has the right to exercise full parental responsibilities unless the judge provides otherwise. This parent has the right to make all decisions regarding the daily life of the minor. Issues of major importance must be decided by both parents; otherwise the issue is submitted to the judge. The non-custodial parent consequently has limited parental responsibilities; this parent has the right and duty to make major decisions for the child with the other parent and to supervise the child's education and moral guidance. The non-custodial parent can petition the judge when the she or he believes the other parent has made prejudicial decisions; she or he has the right to visit the child and to keep the child for a certain period, according to the court established methods (Art. 155 § 3 and Art. 6 § 4 Italian CC). Other members of the family (*e.g.* grandparents) also have the right to visit the child if it can be considered necessary for the development of the child (see Q 43-48).

Joint custody implies that both parents hold custody and exercise parental responsibilities, even if the child only lives with one of them. Both parents share the same rights and parental responsibilities in respect to decisions regarding the minor. In theory, this form of custody seems to respect the most interests of the minor because the minor has both of his parents; however, this is often not realisable in practise. For a useful application, some conditions are indispensable. The parents should have a good relationship and the capacity to be good parents. They should also live close to each other.

Alternating custody means that one of the parents has custody of the child for predetermined periods. Each parent has the exclusive exercise of parental

---

[41] With regard to children, the legal literature and the courts agree to apply the more recent rule (at the moment the rule concerning divorce). Even if the rules concerning separation (Art. 155 Italian CC) and divorce are formally different and do not correspond, separation and divorce are regarded as the same problem and solutions are based on the same premise: the children must suffer as little as possible from the family crises. Therefore the differences must be exclusively attributed to the different moments in which they were introduced. In addition, if there is an *invalidness of the marriage,* the parent-child relationship is ruled by the separation and divorce rules (Art. 129 § 2 Italian CC).

responsibilities during his or her period of custody. The courts and legal literature dispute whether this type of custody respects the interests of the minor; they consider it potentially harmful because it risks creating insecurity and instability, a particularly serious matter during the evolutionary period of the minor (see Q 41).

These short considerations explain why the practice of custody being granted to only one of the parents is the rule our jurisdiction follows[42] even though the law concedes wide discretionary power to the judge when it comes to the interests of the minor.

(b) Legal separation

See Q 16a.

(c) Annulment of the marriage

See Q 16a.

(d) Factual separation

Parental responsibilities do not expire after a factual separation. The parents can freely decide on the attribution of their relative duties and rights, except for the right of both parents to petition the judge to ascertain the conditions established in the interest of the children.

LITHUANIA

(a) Divorce

According to Art. 3.159 Lithuanian CC, a father's or mother's disclaimer (waiver) of the rights and duties by his or her underage children shall be void. Parents are jointly and severally responsible for the care and education of their children. Parental authority may not be used contrary to the interests of the child. Failure to exercise parental authority shall be subject to legal responsibility under the law. Divorce shall have no legal effect on attribution of parental responsibilities, except with the administration of the property of the child. According to Art. 3.190 Lithuanian CC, if the parents are divorced or separated, the right to manage the minor's property shall belong to the parent with whom the child lives.

However, the divorce of child's parents may cause problems related to the exercise of parental responsibilities *e.g.* regarding the determination of the child's place of residence, contacts with the child, and participation of the parents in the maintenance of the child, *etc.* According to Art. 3.193 Lithuanian CC, on divorce, spouses shall make an agreement providing for the place of

---

42 There are numerous proposals introducing joint custody as the rule when cohabitation of the parents ends as the result of a pronounced separation, divorce or annulment of the marriage. These proposals testify to our jurisdiction's diffuse dissatisfaction towards the choice of granting the custody to only one parent – consistently the mother (see Q 19).

residence of the child and the parents' mutual duties in maintaining their underage children, as well as on the procedure, amount and form of such maintenance. This agreement shall be approved by the court (Art. 3.53 Lithuanian CC). In the absence of this agreement between the divorced parents, all questions shall be decided by the court.

(b) Legal separation

Legal separation, like a divorce, shall not affect the attribution of parental responsibilities, except the administration of property of the child. According to Art. 3.190 Lithuanian CC, where the parents are separated, the right to manage the minor's property shall belong to the parent with whom the child lives.

The separated spouses shall have equal parental responsibilities. However, despite these parental duties, some disputes or conflicts over the attribution of parental responsibilities between the parents living separately may take place: disputes over the child's residence, disputes of separated parents over contacts with the child or involvement in the education of the child, disputes over the child's contact with his or her close relatives, disputes over maintenance duties *etc.* In the event of legal separation, the parents shall make an agreement on the place of residence of the child and their mutual duties in maintaining their underage children, as well as the procedure, amount and form of such maintenance (Art. 3.193 Lithuanian CC). Such agreement shall be approved by the court (Art. 3.53 Lithuanian CC). In the absence of such agreement between separated parents, all questions shall be decided by the court under the application of one of the parents.

(c) Annulment of the marriage

Annulment of the marriage of the parents shall have no legal effect on their children (Part 1, Art. 3.45 Lithuanian CC). However, the annulment of the marriage of a child's parents may cause some problems related to the exercise of parental responsibilities, *e.g.* regarding the determination of the child's place of residence, regarding the contacts with the child, and regarding the participation of the parents in the maintenance of the child *etc.* In such a case, the parents shall make an agreement on the place of residence of the child and their mutual duties in maintaining their underage children, as well as the procedure, amount and form of such maintenance. Such agreement shall be approved by the court (Art. 3.53 Lithuanian CC). In the absence of such agreement between the parents, all questions shall be decided by the court under the application of one of the parents.

(d) Factual separation

Factual separation of spouses shall have no legal effect on their parental responsibilities, except the administration of property of the child. According to Art. 3.190 Lithuanian CC, where the parents are separated, the right to manage the minor's property shall belong to the parent with whom the child is to live. This legal rule shall be applied by the analogy to the factual separation as well.

However, factual separation may cause various disputes between parents regarding the exercise of their parental rights and duties. According to Art. 3.174 Lithuanian CC, petitions for the determination of the child's residence may be filed by the child's father, mother, also by the parents or guardians (curators) of the child's minor-aged parents of limited active capacity. The court must resolve the dispute by giving regard to the interests of the child and the child's wishes. A child's wishes may be disregarded only if they are contrary to the best interests of the child.

According to Art. 3.175 Lithuanian CC, petitions for contact or involvement in the child's education may be filed by the child's father, mother or the parents (guardians/ curators) of the child's legally incapable minor-aged parents. The court shall determine the procedure for the separated parent's contact with the child by taking into consideration the child's interests and by creating a possibility for the separated parent to be involved in the education of the child to the greatest extent possible. Minimal contact with a child may be ordered only in cases where constant maximal contact is prejudicial to the child's interests.

THE NETHERLANDS

(a) Divorce

Since 1998 the parents continue to have joint parental responsibilities after divorce.[43]

(b) Legal separation

With regard to parental responsibilities there is no difference between parents who are divorced and parents who are legally separated. Joint parental responsibilities continue after legal separation.

(c) Annulment of the marriage

Annulment of a marriage has no consequences for the joint parental responsibilities that existed during the marriage. Art. 1:77 § 2 (a) states that the annulment shall have no retrospective effect and have the same effect as a divorce as regards to the children of the spouses. This means that the existing joint parental responsibilities will continue after the annulment.

(d) Factual separation

Factual separation has no influence on joint parental responsibilities. During their marriage parents cannot apply to the court for sole parental responsibilities. If there are disputes between the parents about how to exercise their joint parental responsibilities, they can submit their dispute to the district court. The court will try to obtain an agreement between the parents before it

---

43 This rule came into force on 1 January 1998, Statute of 30.10.1997, *Staatsblad* 1997, No. 506 as a result of the right to family life formulated in Art. 8 of the European Convention of Human Rights.

makes a decision. The court will give an order that is most in keeping with the best interests of the child (Art. 1:253a Dutch CC).

NORWAY

(a) Divorce

As a main rule, a divorce does not have any consequences for the attribution of parental responsibilities, Art. 34 sec. 2 Norwegian Children Act 1981.

(b) Legal separation

As a main rule, a legal separation does not have any consequences for the attribution of parental responsibilities, Art. 34 sec. 2 Norwegian Children Act 1981.

(c) Annulment of the marriage

If the annulment of the marriage should lead to a re-determination of paternity, the parental responsibilities will be affected. As annulment of marriage seldom occurs, the legal situation with regard to re-determination of paternity is not clear.

(d) Factual separation

As a main rule, a factual separation does not have any consequences for the attribution of parental responsibilities, Art. 34 sec. 2 Norwegian Children Act 1981.

POLAND

The listed facts do not affect parental responsibility because parental authority in Polish law is independent from a marriage between the parents. However, if the parents are not married to each other, the court may entrust one of them with the exercise of the parental authority, limiting the other parent's rights and duties to certain activities (Art. 107 § 1 Polish Family and Guardianship Code).

(a) Divorce

In a divorce judgment, the court rules over the parental authority for the common minor children and decides the proportional amount each parent is obliged to contribute to the cost of the child's upbringing and maintenance. The court may, in particular, entrust one of the parents with the exercise of the parental authority, limiting the rights and duties of the other parent to certain activities (Art. 58 § 1 Polish Family and Guardianship Code).

(b) Legal separation

Legal separation results in a situation equivalent to divorce (parental responsibility issues included), unless the law states otherwise (Art. 61^4 § 1 Polish Family and Guardianship Code).

(c) Annulment of the marriage

The legal consequences of divorce (see above, Q 16a are applied when a marriage is declared null and void (Art. 21 Polish Family and Guardianship Code).

(d) Factual separation
A factual separation of the parents should be treated analogous to a situation of parents not married to each other (Art. 107 § 2 Polish Family and Guardianship Code).

PORTUGAL
(a) Divorce
Divorce of the parents has consequences upon the parent-child relationship. These consequences include a new way of exercising parental responsibility (Art. 1905 Portuguese CC).

(b) Legal separation
The same applies in the case of legal separation (Art. 1905 Portuguese CC).

(c) Annulment of the marriage
The same applies when the marriage has been declared void (in the case of a Catholic marriage) or annulled (in the case of a civil marriage) (Art. 1905 Portuguese CC).

(d) Factual separation
The system laid out in Art. 1905 Portuguese CC as to the establishment of a new way of exercising parental responsibility in the event of divorce, legal separation, nullity or annulment of the parents' marriage also applies to cases of factual separation of the parents, through Art. 1909 Portuguese CC.

RUSSIA
(a) Divorce
Divorce has no formal affect on parental responsibility. Parents always retain joint responsibility after divorce. Their parental rights and duties remain formally equal. However, the Russian experience of almost eighty years teaches that when joint parental responsibility is always the case (Art. 61 (1) Russian Family Code), the post-divorce problems shift from the issue of attribution of parental responsibility to the that of determination of the child's residence and the participation of the non-residential parent in the upbringing of the child.

(b) Legal separation
The institution of legal separation does not exist under Russian law.

(c) Annulment of the marriage
The annulment of a marriage has no influence on the rights and duties of the parents regarding their children (Art. 30 (3) Russian Family Code).

(d) Factual separation
Factual separation, like divorce, has no formal affect on parental responsibility. Similar to the situation after divorce, the main problems after the separation of the parents relate to the child's residence and contact arrangements.

SPAIN

(a) Divorce

The attribution of *patria potestad* is unaffected by divorce. However, divorce usually means that the parental responsibility holders do not live together. It is this fact, regardless of whether there was previous cohabitation, that renders certain measures necessary. These measures affect the exercise of parental responsibility. See Q 18.

(b) Legal separation

The attribution of *patria potestad* is unaffected by legal separation. However, legal separation usually means the parental responsibility holders do not live together. It is this fact, regardless of whether there was previous cohabitation, that renders certain measures necessary. These measures affect the exercise of parental responsibility. See Q 18.

(c) Annulment of the marriage

The attribution of *patria potestad* is unaffected by annulment of the marriage of the child's parents. Annulment however usually means that the parental responsibility holders do not live together. It is this fact, regardless of whether there was previous cohabitation, that renders certain measures necessary. These measures affect the exercise of parental responsibility. See Q 18.

(d) Factual separation

The attribution of parental responsibility is a consequence of parenthood and not of civil status nor even of cohabitation. If parents do not live together, regardless of whether they have never lived together or have separated, certain measures must be adopted. These measures will not affect parental responsibility as such, but its exercise. See Q 18.

SWEDEN

(a) Divorce

According to the main rule, the parents' joint custody also continues after divorce, Chapter 6 Sec. 3 para. 2 Swedish Children and Parents Code. The court shall remind the parents in the divorce decree that joint custody still applies. Under certain conditions, however, the joint custody may be dissolved, and sole custody be entrusted to one of the parents.

(b) Legal separation

Legal separation has not existed in Swedish law since 1974.

(c) Annulment of the marriage

Marriage annulment has not existed in Swedish law since 1974. A marriage can only be dissolved by divorce or the death of a spouse.

(d) Factual separation

The factual separation of parents does not in itself affect the previously existing custody. The main rule is that parents who are married to each other have joint custody of their children, irrespective of the living arrangements.

SWITZERLAND

(a) Divorce

In accordance with Art. 297 § 3 2nd sentence Swiss CC, the court must decide on parental responsibilities in accordance with the clauses of the divorce. In so doing there is the possibility to attribute parental responsibilities to one parent or, upon joint petition, to leave parental responsibilities with both parents if this is reconcilable with the child's welfare and the parents have agreed to the division of the maintenance costs and their respective share of taking care of the child in an agreement which is approvable by the court (Art. 133 § 1 and 3 Swiss CC). By way of exception the court will deprive both parents of parental responsibilities, based on Art. 311 Swiss CC in combination with Art. 315a Swiss CC, if the child's welfare is endangered and this danger cannot be avoided in any other manner.

All important facts and circumstances with regard to the child's welfare are to be applied in the allocation of parental responsibilities to one parent (Art. 133 § 2 sentence 1 Swiss CC). The parents' interests are to be considered to be secondary. Consideration is to be shown to a joint petition by the parents (Art. 133 § 2 sentence 2 Swiss CC). If both parents fulfil the same requirements and have an equal ability to raise the child, both parents may be awarded parental responsibilities. 'Preference is given [...] to the parent who, in view of the overall circumstances, offers the best assurance that the child will have the best chance to develop from a mental-psychological, physical and social point of view in a way that does justice to the child's age. If it has been established that both parents fulfil these prerequisites and both also have the ability to take personal care of the child in an approximately equal fashion, the aspect of the stability of family and place of residence and, depending on the children's age, their specific wishes are to be taken into account in any event'.[44]

Attribution of joint parental responsibilities requires, in accordance with Art. 133 § 3 Swiss CC, an examination of the contents of the parents' divorce settlement and a comprehensive appraisal of the circumstances. In this context, the divorce settlement is to be reviewed, especially in regard to whether it can be implemented in practice *i.e.* not just with regard to objective issues (possibilities in terms of living and care, parents' professional activities, economic framework of conditions, needs in terms of schooling and the child's personal requests) but also to subjective aspects (in particular, a certain inner concurrence between the parents). As to its contents, the settlement must state the respective contributions to personal care and financial maintenance (this must moreover be quantifiable in terms of the amount, with a view to enforceability in the event of conflict). It is of crucial import whether the basic concept of joint parental responsibilities (the joint distribution of the burdens involved in raising and caring for the child in such a way that, although each parent may make different contributions in quantitative terms, the burdens are

---

[44] BGE 115 II 206, 209.

shared and balanced as in a partnership) can be jointly realised or whether the primary aim is to obtain control over the other parent and disregard the other's personality. If need be, a partial exercise of parental responsibilities by one parent may be provided (*e.g.* with regard to administration of the child's property). Nonetheless parental joint responsibilities must still consist of shared responsibilities, as in a partnership. It may not amount to simply extended visiting rights.[45]

(b) Legal separation

Since the provisions concerning divorce proceedings are also applicable analogously in the case of legal separation, the court allocates parental responsibilities to one parent or upon joint petition leaves both parents with parental responsibilities (Art. 133 § 1 and 3 Swiss CC). The wording of Art. 297 § 2 Swiss CC makes it possible to leave both parents with parental responsibilities even if the special pre-requisites stipulated in Art. 133 § 3 Swiss CC are not met.[46]

(c) Annulment of the marriage

If the marriage is annulled, the provisions of divorce law apply to the children (Art. 109 § 2 Swiss CC). Consequently, the provisions contained in Art. 133 Abs. 1 and 3 Swiss CC are applicable analogously.

Since the substantive divorce provisions and also those provisions concerning the divorce proceedings are to be applied in both legal separations and annulments of marriage, Art. 133 and Art. 145 Swiss CC are applied in all three cases (at least on a *mutatis mutandis* basis). The maxim of examination by the court and the *ex officio* maxim as stipulated in Art. 145 Swiss CC both apply without reservation in respect to issues pertaining to children, *i.e.* also with regard to parental responsibilities. The necessary dispositions in the interest of the children are therefore withdrawn from the parents' power of disposition in the proceedings. Accordingly the court decides the allocation of parental responsibilities, taking all the important facts relating to the child's welfare into consideration; the court must also clarify *ex officio* the relevant facts in the decision (Art. 145 § 1 Swiss CC). However, the (divorce) court must, in accordance with Art. 133 § 2 Swiss CC, show consideration for any joint petition submitted by the parents. The joint petition is moreover one of the prerequisites for allowing the parents to keep parental responsibilities on a joint basis (Art. 133 § 3 Swiss CC).

---

45 P. BREITSCHMID, Art. 133 ZGB, p. 831 - 832 (No. 18 - 21), in: H. HONSELL, N.P. VOGT, TH. GEISER (ed.), *Basler Kommentar zum Schweizerischen Privatrecht, Zivilgesetzbuch I*, Art. 1-456 ZGB, Basel: Helbing & Lichtenhahn, 2002.

46 I. SCHWENZER, Art. 297 ZGB, p.1574 (No. 10), in: H. HONSELL, N.P. VOGT, TH. GEISER (ed.), *Basler Kommentar zum Schweizerischen Privatrecht, Zivilgesetzbuch I*, Art. 1-456 ZGB, Basel: Helbing & Lichtenhahn, 2002.

(d) Factual separation

In the case of a purely de facto separation, parents still have joint parental responsibilities. If the court is asked to rule with regard to separation (*i.e.* dissolution of the joint household based on Art. 175 *et seq* Swiss CC) in the case of a de facto separation, the so-called marriage protection court must basically ex officio take the necessary measures in accordance with the provisions concerning the effects of the parent-child relationship (Art. 176 § 3 Swiss CC). Accordingly, the marriage protection court may allocate parental responsibilities to one spouse alone (Art. 297 § 2 Swiss CC).

QUESTION 17

C. ATTRIBUTION OF PARENTAL RESPONSIBILITIES

I. Married Parents

To what extent, if at all, are the parents free to agree upon the attribution of parental responsibilities after divorce, legal separation or annulment of the marriage? If they are, are these agreements subject to scrutiny by a competent authority.

AUSTRIA

The following statements apply to both divorce and annulment (there is no legal separation in Austria): Since the 2001 Amendment to the Law of Parent and Child took effect, parents are relatively free to determine their parental responsibilities by agreement. If the parents wish to continue joint parental responsibilities after dissolution of the marriage, they must enter into an agreement deciding with which parent the child will have its primary residence (Sec. 177(2) Austrian CC).

The parents can also agree upon a new allocation of parental responsibilities (section 177(1) Austrian CC). They have the following options for structuring such an allocation: They can agree to give one parent sole parental responsibilities (Sec. 177(1) Austrian CC). It is also possible to entrust one parent with total parental responsibilities and the other parent with only partial parental responsibilities restricted to certain matters (*e.g.* schooling and occupational training, medical treatment, or the administration of particular assets).

Parents are not allowed to divide up the areas of parental responsibilities, *i.e.* to split parental responsibilities in a way that one parent is responsible, *e.g.* for care and education and the other is responsible for administration of property and legal representation. Parents are also not allowed to make a time-based allocation of parental responsibilities, *e.g.* half the year with the mother and half the year with the father. Under settled case law, the continuity of child-rearing practices is important for the welfare of the child.[1]

All the aforementioned agreements require court approval. The court shall approve the agreement if it is in the best interests of the child (Sec. 177(3) Austrian CC). If not, the agreement is invalid and the court will entrust one parent with sole parental responsibilities based on the best interests of the child unless an approvable agreement between the parents may be reached (Sec. 177a(1) Austrian CC).

---

1 *Oberster Gerichtshof,* 31.07.2001, *EFSlg.* 96.672.

BELGIUM

Parental responsibility is an institution created in the interests of the child. It is part of the status of the person; consequently, the applicable rules are those of public policy. Every agreement specifically concerning the attribution (not the exercise; parents can agree on the modalities of the exercise of parental responsibilities) of parental authority is void (Art. 6 Belgian CC). This principle is unanimously accepted.[2]

BULGARIA

In principle the agreement on parental responsibilities is considered by the law as the best solution in cases of separation or divorce. Nevertheless this principle may be applied according to the situation of divorce/annulment of the marriage combined with some intervention by the court.

Divorce by mutual consent is predetermined by an agreement reached and drawn in advance by the spouses as regards all consequences of divorce. As stated in Art. 101 § 1 Bulgarian Family Code: ' In a divorce by mutual consent the spouses have to set forth their settlement as to the child custody, contact with children and the support of the children, and also their property relations, the use of the matrimonial home, the maintenance between them, and the family name. The settlement is ratified by the court after it is satisfied that the interests of the children have been protected.' The court only confirms the agreement after examining 'whether the interests of children are protected'. The court may not on its own motion provide a substitute for a missing agreement similar to that which settles the relations set forth under Art. 101 § 1. The court may only approve the agreement or give the spouses a deadline to improve it in accordance with the requirements of the law.[3]

The court scrutinises the agreement in two ways: completeness (does it cover all issues provided for by the law?) and adequacy as to the interests of children. The court does not examine the interests of the spouses, but the agreement must be compliant with the provisions of law and ethics. Where an agreement does not meet one of the above requirements, the court sends it back to the spouses to correct its deficiencies: 'Where the settlement is not complete or the interests of the children are not well protected the court sets a term during which these defects should be eliminated. Where, within the set term, the defects are not eliminated the divorce petition is dismissed.' (Art. 101 § 2 Bulgarian Family Code).

---

2 Cass., 22.03.1923, *Pas.*, 1923, I, p. 423; Court of Appeal of Gent, 14.03.1894, *Pas.*, 1894, II, p. 363; Court of Appeal of Liege, 18.05.1881, *Pas.* 1881, II, p. 235; H. DE PAGE, *Traité élémentaire de droit civil belge*, T. II (Les Personnes), Vol. 2 (by J.-P. MASSON), Brussels: Bruylant, 1990, p. 951.

3 L. NENOVA, *Family Law of the Republic of Bulgaria*, Sofia, 1994, p. 583 and A. STANEVA, *Representative and Custodial Functions of Parents*, Sofia, 1992, p. 529.

In the case of divorce due to marital breakdown where the spouses file a request of non-pronouncement on fault, they are required to furnish an agreement on all matters regarding relations between themselves and between them and their children after the divorce: 'The court does not pronounce itself as to the fault for the breakdown of the marriage where the spouses request this and submit to the court their agreement regarding the custody of children, the contact and the support of the children, and also about their property relations, the use of the matrimonial home, the maintenance between them and the family name' (Art. 99 § 3 Bulgarian Family Code). The contents of such an agreement overlap in full with its counterpart agreement in the case of divorce by mutual consent.

Though legislation has articulated no express provisions in this respect, both judicial practice and theory admit that the matrimonial court holds the same powers in assessing the agreement as it does in divorce by mutual consent. Bearing in mind that the agreement settles all consequences of divorce, it must guarantee the interests of children, be complete and not contradictory to law. Agreements, which do not meet these requirements, are returned to the parties for the purpose of removing any identified deficiencies.

The Supreme Court has stated that 'the court, as by law provided, has no authority to transform the agreement or substitute it by any terms of its own, it may only instruct the parties as to the removal of deficiencies......'.[4] Thereafter, the court grants a decision by which it dissolves the marriage and reproduces the agreement on the consequences of divorce.

These rules also apply to the annulment of marriage.

CZECH REPUBLIC

An agreement between the parents on placing the child into one's personal care and on the other one's maintenance is always subject to court approval (Sec. 26 § 3 Czech Family Code) and must be made before the divorce. If the marriage is declared void, the court will commence proceedings on regulation of the relationships between the parents and their common children even without a motion.

The court will approve an agreement on care and maintenance if it is in the interests of the child. The agreement between the parents on contact with the child does not require court approval (Sec. 27 § 1 Czech Family Code). Sometimes, such an agreement is submitted to the court for approval, especially if the divorce occurs on the basis of the spouses' agreement pursuant to Sec. 24a Czech Family Code, when that agreement is part of larger agreements on placing the child into someone's care, on maintenance and on settlement of the spouses' property after divorce. In practice, some judges refuse to approve the

4 Decision of the Supreme Court, 60-1987.

agreement, arguing that it does not need a court approval, but only in rare cases.

DENMARK

Parents, whether married or not, are free upon the termination of the relationship to make agreements concerning joint or sole parental authority, and such agreements are not subject to judicial scrutiny, Art. 6, 9(1) and 11(1) Danish Act on Parental Authority and Contact. The agreement is only binding when it has been reported to the administrative authorities, Art. 6, 9(1) and 11(1) Danish Act on Parental Authority and Contact.

ENGLAND & WALES

As the attribution of parental responsibility is fixed by law parents are not free under English law to alter that attribution. However, what they can agree upon is how responsibility should be exercised (see Q 37).

FINLAND

Parents (and only parents) have the right to make agreements upon the attribution of the custody of the child, which can be approved by the local social authority (Sec. 7 Finnish Child Custody and the Right of Access Act). A condition for approval by the authority, however, is that at least one of the parents is also the custodian of the child (Sec. 8 Finnish Child Custody and the Right of Access Act). Parents then may agree,

- that they shall have joint custody of the child;
- that the child shall reside with one parent, if the parents do not live together;
- that one of the parents shall have the sole custody of the child;
- that the child has the right of access to the parent with whom the child does not reside in conformity with the parents' agreement.

The parent's written agreement shall be subject to approval by the local social authority of the child's residence. The authority shall approve the agreement if the agreement is in accordance with the best interests of the child. An approved agreement has the same validity, and is as enforceable, as a court order (Sec. 8 Finnish Child Custody and the Right of Access Act).

FRANCE

In principle, a parent may not waive or transfer his or her parental responsibilities; such a renunciation or cession is void unless confirmed by a judicial decision (Art. 376 French CC). Nevertheless French law does promote parental agreements on the exercise of parental responsibilities in separations and divorce.

See Art. 373-2-7 French CC: Parents can bring a joint petition to the court (more precisely to the *Juge aux affaires familiales (JAF)*, the family court that is competent to hear most issues concerning divorce and parental responsibilities) in order to submit their agreement concerning the modalities of the exercise of parental responsibilities and the financial contribution to the maintenance and the education of the child to the judge. This agreement is subject to scrutiny by the judge who will *homologue* (approve) it unless he thinks the agreement (*convention*) does not protect the child's interests, or that the consent of one parents was not freely given.

The parents' agreement only relates to the modes of exercise of parental responsibilities, not to their allocation, because each parent remains a holder of parental responsibilities even if the parent and child do not live together. The parent who does not have the exercise of parental responsibilities maintains a contact right (see Art. 373-2-1 para. 2 French CC) unless there are very serious reasons preventing it; she or he also keeps the right and the duty to control the child's maintenance and education, and must be informed of important choices relating to the child's life. She or he is also still obliged to contribute to the child's maintenance and education (Art. 373-2-1 § 3 French CC). See also Art. 376-1 French CC (when the family judge makes a decision on the modalities of the exercise of parental responsibilities, on the education of a minor child or decides to entrust the child to a third person, he or she can take agreements made freely between the parents into account, unless one of the parents invokes serious reasons as to why his or her consent should be withdrawn.

GERMANY

After a divorce, annulment of the marriage or factual separation of parents who were previously joint holders of parental responsibilities and who, as has been shown, remain so, each parent can, to the extent that § 1687 German CC applies, grant to the other parent, by means of the relevant authorisations, more scope for action than that which is in accordance with the legal situation governing representation.[5] Such authorisations can, however, always be revoked[6] and do not change the fundamental attribution of parental responsibilities.

In addition to these powers of control, each parent has the option to file an application with the family court, in accordance with § 1671 para. 1 German CC, for the transfer of sole parental responsibility, either in full or in part. The court must grant this application subject to the following preconditions:

Dissolution of joint parental responsibility in accordance with § 1671 German CC requires that the parents have lived apart from each other not just on a temporary basis at the time the decision concerning parental responsibility was taken, the reference point being the date of the last hearing.[7] The parents are considered to 'live apart' within the meaning of § 1671 German CC if the requirements set out in § 1567 para. 1 German CC have been met, i.e. if a

---

5 D. SCHWAB, *Familienrecht*, 12th Edition, Munich: Beck, 2003, No. 672.

6 U. DIEDERICHSEN, in: PALANDT, *Bürgerliches Gesetzbuch*, 64th Edition, Munich: Beck, 2005, § 1629 No. 9.

7 M. Coester, in: STAUDINGER, *Kommentar zum Bürgerlichen Gesetzbuch*, 13th Edition, Berlin: de Gruyter, 2000, § 1671 No. 41.

common household no longer exists and there is no will to re-establish such, or if the parents are divorced.

Joint parental responsibility can only be dissolved on application; the arrangement of parental responsibility upon the court's own motion cannot be based on § 1671 German CC.[8] Only the parents are entitled to file an application.[9]

When deciding on the application, § 1671 para. 2 German CC distinguishes between those applications where parents are in agreement and those that are disputed. In the case of an amicable solution, with which this question is concerned, § 1671 para. 2 No. 1 German CC applies:

If the respondent, i.e. the other parent, agrees, parental rights explicitly take precedence over control by the state. The family court does not have to examine the application to see whether it most nearly corresponds to the best interests of the child;[10] as a rule, the assessment of the child's best interest can be left to the parents who are in agreement regarding the same.[11] This means that the court is bound by the parents' will, as expressed in the application and the consent. The only exception to this is when the child has completed its 14th year and objects to the sought-for attribution of sole parental responsibility, or if attribution of the said responsibility would endanger the welfare of the child (§ 1697 a German CC). Objection by the child does not mean that the court must in all cases be guided by the child's will; if the court arrives at the conviction that granting sole parental responsibility constitutes the best solution, resistance from the child notwithstanding, it will nevertheless grant the application.[12]

In proceedings in accordance with § 1671 German CC, the court can, both when the parents agree and when the application is disputed, either transfer full sole parental responsibility to the proponent of the application or grant the proponent only partial sole responsibility while reaffirming joint responsibility in all other matters. Partial transfer of parental responsibility is an option, particularly if the parents have conflicting views regarding only one area. This is most often the case when it comes to the right to determine the residence of the child.[13]

---

8 Th. RAUSCHER, *Familienrecht*, Heidelberg: C.F. Müller, 2001, No. 998.

9 P. FINGER, in: *Münchener Kommentar zum Bürgerlichen Gesetzbuch*, 4th Edition, Munich: Beck, 2002, § 1671 No. 58.

10 OLG Hamm 31.08.1998, *NJW* 1999, 68.

11 M. COESTER, in: STAUDINGER, *Kommentar zum Bürgerlichen Gesetzbuch*, 13th Edition, Berlin: de Gruyter, 2000, § 1671 No. 65.

12 D. SCHWAB, *Familienrecht*, 12th Edition, Munich: Beck, 2003, No. 676.

13 U. DIEDERICHSEN, in: PALANDT, *Bürgerliches Gesetzbuch*, 64th Edition, Munich: Beck, 2005, § 1671 No. 5.

GREECE

The parents are free to agree upon the attribution of parental responsibilities after divorce or an annulment of the marriage. If the parents wish to deviate from the provision of Art. 1510 para. 1 Greek CC (*i.e.* joint parental care), a court decision should always regulate this issue for the benefit of the child.[14] In deciding, the court shall take into consideration any relevant agreements between the parents (Art. 1513 para. 2 Greek CC), as well as the child's own opinion, depending on its maturity (Art. 1511 para. 2 Greek CC).

The only case where an agreement between the parents is legally required and may temporarily regulate the attribution of parental responsibilities is when they file a petition to the court for a divorce by mutual consent. A prerequisite for this is that they also submit a written agreement on matters of parental care over the children as well as the contact with them. This agreement is subject to the scrutiny of the court and is valid until the court decides on this issue (Art. 1441 para. 3 Greek CC).[15]

HUNGARY

The parents can agree on maintaining joint parental responsibilities either in a divorce or an annulment proceeding. According to law, in this case the parents have to make declarations about how they are going to co-operate with each other, especially on issues regarding the care and education of the child. The parents' agreement about the joint parental responsibilities after divorce needs the judicial approval (the court is the competent authority). Primarily, the court must scrutinise whether the agreement is in the interest of the child.

Nevertheless, although it is rare and the Act is silent about it, the parents can agree, without agreeing on the full joint parental responsibilities, to continue to exercise certain parts of the parental responsibilities together, or that these parts will be exercised by the parent living apart from the child.

See Q 46 about the agreement on contact.

IRELAND

Parties are not free to agree upon the attribution of parental responsibilities after annulment of the marriage. They are, however, free to agree upon the attribution of parental responsibilities after legal separation and divorce. It is possible to have an executed separation agreement on, *inter alia*, the attribution of parental responsibilities, made a rule of court, in either the Circuit Court or the High Court. The ruling of the agreement allows for the remedy of contempt

---

14 P. AGALLOPOULOU, in: A. GEORGIADIS and M. STATHOPOULOS (eds.), *Civil Code commentary, Vol. VIII, Family Law (Arts. 1505-1694)*, 2nd Edition, Athens: Law & Economy, P.N. Sakkoulas 2003, Art. 1513-1514 Greek CC, p. 216, No. 3.

15 A. KOUTSOURADIS, 'Scheidung und nachehelicher Unterhalt in Griechenland', in: HOFER, SCHWAB, HENRICH (eds.), *Scheidung und nachehelicher Unterhalt im europäischen Vergleich*, Bielefeld 2003, p. 123.

of court where breach of the agreement occurs. If the parents agree upon the attribution of parental responsibilities after divorce, the court will endeavour to reflect such agreement in the orders granted after divorce. That said, the ultimate decision is that of the court.

ITALY

Parents are free to make an agreement, but the judge always controls the agreement made. This control, expressly provided by law, aims to verify that the conditions of the agreement are not in conflict with the interests of the child. If they are, the judge can rule against the agreement. If an agreement between the parents cannot be reached, the judge is entitled to make the decision, based exclusively on the moral and material interests of the child.

LITHUANIA

According to Art. 3.51 Lithuanian CC, parents are free to agree upon the exercise of their parental duties and rights after divorce, legal separation or annulment of the marriage. They may agree upon the place of the residence of a child, upon their participation in maintenance of a child, their contact with a child *etc.* Such an agreement must be made in writing and be presented to the court for approval. The court has the duty to investigate the content of the agreement in respect to the interests of the child and the equality of the parents. The court shall refuse to approve the agreement if it contradicts the interests of a child or violates the principle of equality of the rights and duties of parents (Art. 3.53 Lithuanian CC). However, it is prohibited for the parents to waive their rights or duties in respect to the child by means such agreement. Parental responsibilities are statutory obligations and may be not waived. Agreements between parents to disclaim or waive parental duties and rights are void because they violate mandatory rules and are against public policy and good morals (Art. 3.108 Lithuanian CC).

THE NETHERLANDS

Parents are not free to agree upon the attribution of parental responsibilities after divorce, legal separation or annulment of the marriage. If parents wish to end the existing joint parental responsibilities they must apply to the court (Art. 1:251). Either parent or both parents jointly can request the court to attribute sole parental responsibilities to one of them on the ground that this would be in the best interests of the child (Art. 1:251 § 2 Dutch CC). However, the criteria used by the courts for terminating joint parental responsibilities are very strict. If one or both of the parents apply for sole parental responsibilities the court must decide whether terminating joint parental responsibility is in the best interests of the child. If the court decides to terminate the existing joint parental responsibilities it will subsequently need to determine which parent should be vested with parental responsibilities in view of the best interests of the child.

In a judgment of 10 September 1999 the Supreme Court formulated two important criteria.[16] First, a request by one of the parents to be attributed with parental responsibilities to the exclusion of the other is not sufficient ground for terminating joint parental responsibilities. Second, parental responsibilities can only be attributed to a sole parent if the judge finds there is an unacceptable risk the child will be damaged if parental responsibilities continue to be exercised jointly.[17] Communication problems are not sufficient grounds to terminate joint parental responsibilities. The consequence is that is has become very difficult for parents to obtain sole parental responsibilities after divorce since 1998.

In practice a distinction tends to be made between the following situations: (1) one parent files an application for sole parental responsibilities; (2) both parents file applications for sole parental responsibilities; (3) the parents agree that only one of them should hold parental responsibilities. In the first two situations, it is clear that the court has to establish and motivate why attributing sole parental responsibilities to one of the parents is in the best interests of the child(ren). However, with regard to the third situation there is still discussion whether the court has the same comprehensive duty to establish and motivate (*integrale toesting*) or whether it simply needs to establish that the application is not evidently contrary to the best interests of the child (*marginale toetsing*). It has been assumed by lawyers and courts that the latter is the case.[18] However, a recent decision of the Court of Appeal of 's Hertogenbosch and recent legal literature point in a different direction.[19] The Court of Appeal of 's Hertogenbosch denied a request by two parents to attribute parental responsibilities to the mother alone, because the court did not agree with the parent's claim that this would be in the best interests of the children.[20]

---

16 See Supreme Court 10.9.1999, *NJ*, 2000, 20: 'The communication problems between the man and the woman were of such a serious nature that there was an unacceptable risk that the children would become *klem of verloren* (stuck or lost) between the parents and it is not to be expected that the situation would change sufficiently in the foreseeable future.' What the Court in all likelihood meant to convey is that the difficulties between the parents are of such a serious nature that the children run an unacceptable risk of being damaged. There has been discussion about the concepts 'unacceptable risk and the seriousness of the parent's communication problems', but hardly about the meaning of the phrase *klem of verloren*.

17 C. WAMELEN, 'Eenhoofdig gezag na scheiding', *Nemesis*, 2000, p. 58-63.

18 I. JANSEN, *Losbladige Personen- en familierecht*, Art. 2 51 No. 25 and E. BEENEN and P. VLAARDINGERBROEK, 'Doorlopend ouderlijk gezag in de praktijk', *FJR*, 2004, p. 36-38. The authors studied decisions of the District Court of 's Hertogenbosch of 2001 and 2002 on the continuation or termination of joint parental responsibilities after divorce, and found that if both parents agreed that one of them should have parental responsibilities only one request out of the 29 was denied (on technical grounds). In these cases the court did not verify whether termination of joint parental responsibilities was indeed in the best interst of the children.

19 Court of Appeal 's Hertogenbosch 15.4.2004, *LJN*, AO7714 and E. BEENEN and P. VLAARDINGERBROEK, 'Doorlopend ouderlijk gezag in de praktijk', *FJR* 2004, p. 36-38.

20 The parents claimed they did not agree on the proper treatment of their handicapped son and thought it would be best if only the mother would hold parental

However, until the Dutch Supreme Court has judged this issue it remains unclear what the task of the courts in these situations entails.

Once one parent has been attributed sole parental responsibilities after divorce, joint parental responsibilities of both parents can only be re-established on the basis of a joint request to this end by both parents (Art. 1:253o Dutch CC) or remarriage of the parents (Art. 1:253 § 1 Dutch CC). However, on 3 December 2003 a proposal of law was introduced in Parliament that would give the parent without parental responsibilities the possibility to file a request to re-establish joint parental responsibilities without the cooperation of the parent with sole parental responsibilities.[21] The court may re-establish joint parental responsibilities if there has been such a change of circumstances that the child is no longer in danger of being damaged by the possible joint parental responsibilities of its parents.[22]

NORWAY

The parents are free to agree upon the attribution of parental responsibilities after legal separation or divorce, Art. 34 sec. 2 Norwegian Children Act 1981. Their agreement is not subject to public scrutiny. Since 1997, agreements concerning parental responsibilities must be reported to the National Population Register. Agreements concerning parental responsibilities which are not reported to the National Population Register are not valid, Art. 39. If no agreement is reached, the parents continue to have joint parental responsibilities until a court, at the request of one of the parents, decides otherwise. If the parents disagree as to who shall have parental responsibility, either of them may institute legal proceedings, according to Art. 56 and 48.

POLAND

The court is to decide on these issues, but nothing prevents it from taking the parents' opinion into consideration, as long as it is not be contrary to the child's interests.

PORTUGAL

In situations of contentious divorce, contentious legal separation or the declaration of nullity or annulment of marriage, the new system for the exercise of parental responsibility may result from a system established by the parents through an agreement, subject to ratification by the judge (Art. 1905 No. 1

responsibilities. The court held that the child's interests would be best served if decisions about its welfare would be the result of consultation between the parents, even if the parents had different ideas on the subject.

21 *Kamerstukken Tweede Kamer* 2003-2004, 29353 No. 1-3. The Court of Appeal in Leeuwarden 5.2.2003, *NJ*, 2003, 352 already decided that the request of a father without parental responsibilities to re-establish joint parental responsibilities with the child's mother was admissible.

22 No doubt this will make it even more difficult for a parent to obtain joint parental responsibilities with a person other than a parent according to Art. 1:253t Dutch CC.

Portuguese CC and Art. 174, Portuguese Child Protection Law), or from court intervention in those cases where there is little chance of agreement between the parents, or when the agreement presented by them is not in the interests of the children. The new system of parental responsibility is then regulated by judicial decision in keeping with the interests of the child (Art. 1905 No. 2 Portuguese CC and Art. 180 Portuguese Child Protection Law).

In situations of divorce by mutual consent, or legal separation by mutual consent, the parents will agree upon the new system of exercising parental responsibility. Spouses that wish to divorce by mutual consent should present to the Civil Registry Office (Art. 12 No. 1(b) Portuguese Law No. 272/2001 of 13 October 2001), together with the divorce application, three agreements, one of which relates to the future of their children, if those children are minors. The agreement on the exercise of parental responsibility is sent to the Department of Justice, which will, within a period of thirty days, pronounce whether the agreement is in the interests of the children (Art. 14 No. 4 Portuguese Law No. 272/2001 of 13 October 2001). If the Public Prosecutor's Office does not consider the agreement sufficient to protect the interests of the children, the applicants may alter it or present a new agreement for the Public Prosecutor's Office consideration (Art. 14 No. 5 Portuguese Law No. 272/2001 of 13 October 2001). If the Public Prosecutor's Office decides the agreement is in accordance with the interests of the child, or if the parents have altered the agreement to bring it into line with the Public Prosecutor's Office recommendations, the process of divorce by mutual consent will proceed in the Civil Registry Office.

RUSSIA

After the divorce or annulment[23] of their parents, children always formally remain under the joint parental responsibility of both parents. This means that the parental responsibility of divorced spouses, at least on paper, remains equal. However, in reality the parent with whom the children reside after the divorce exercises parental rights almost alone. Therefore the contested issue concerning children in the divorce or annulment procedure is not about parental responsibility but about child's residence.

Parents are free to make agreements about the child's residence after a divorce or annulment of the marriage (Art. 24 (1) Russian Family Code); even if the parents of the child, due to whatever reason, are not living together (Art. 65 (3) Russian Family Code). If the child's residence is being determined other than in the framework of a divorce or annulment procedure, there is no obligatory judicial scrutiny of parental arrangements. Only if parents fail to reach such agreement must the issue be brought before the court (Art. 65 (2) and (3) Russian Family Code).

Agreements made by parents during a divorce or annulment proceeding regarding a child's residence are subject to judicial scrutiny. The judge is

23 The institution of legal separation does not exist under Russian law.

entitled to set aside the parental agreement if it is not in the best interests of the child or one of the spouses (Art. 24 (2) Russian Family Code). The spouses are strongly encouraged to make an agreement which will be accepted by the judge without alteration, because then they can be sure a divorce order will be granted after one month (Art. 23 (2)) without any further problems and costs. According to Art. 65(2), which provides a general guidance for taking decisional in respect of the child, the parents should decide on the child's residence 'according to the child's best interests and taking into consideration the child's wishes'. If the agreement has been not approved by the judge or if the parents fail to reach agreement, then a rather complicated procedure with the participation of the Guardianship and Curatorship Department is commenced in order to enable the court to determine the child's residence. The duty of the court is to find out which of the parents can provide for a more favourable condition for the upbringing of the child.[24] When deciding the child's residence, the judge takes into consideration 'the attachment of the child to each of the parents, brothers and sisters, the age of the child, the moral and other personal qualities of the parents, relations existing between each of the parents and the child, the possibility of creating for the child conditions for nurturing and development (nature of activity, work regime of parents, material and family status of the parents and others)'.[25] The judge's most important source of information concerning such matters is a report by the Department of Guardianship and Curatorship.[26] The inspector of the Department of Guardianship and Curatorship makes inquires as to the above criteria, questioning and conversing with the child and, if necessary, also with the child's relatives and teachers. In difficult cases an expert psychologist may become involved. On the basis of this information the Department of Guardianship and Curatorship draws up its advice for the judge. The judge, of course, is not bound by this advice, but he or she has to provide the due grounds if he or she reaches a different decision. In reality if parents have reached agreement about child's residence, the judge almost never subjects it to deep scrutiny.

SPAIN

Agreements on the attribution of parental responsibility are not permissible because parental responsibility is not disposable. It is only possible to reach agreements on the exercise of parental responsibility. The Spanish CC contemplates agreements in the framework of divorce, annulment and legal separation. Catalan law contains a very similar regulation.

Agreements are presented to the judge, who will approve them unless they are damaging to the child or detrimental to one of the spouses (Art. 90 Spanish CC).

---

24 Item 5 of the Directive of the Supreme Court of the Russian Federation of 27.05.1998 No. 10 'On the Application of the Legislation by Dissolving Cases Relating to the Education and Care for Children', *Bulleten' verhovnogo suda RF*, 1998, No 7.

25 Art.. 65(3) Russian Family Code.

26 Art. 78 Russian Family Code.

The judge will have to justify why agreements are disregarded; there is the possibility to submit new agreements. If the agreements are not approved, the judge will make the decision on the exercise of parental responsibility. It should be kept in mind that the judge will not get any information on the family's situation, nor will he get an explanation about why the agreements were made. He can theoretically ask for evidence in order to carry out the scrutiny according to Art. 777.4 Law of Civil Procedure, but in the ordinary case this will not be done. It has therefore been contended that scrutiny is rather formal and does not take sufficient account of the uniqueness of the case.[27]

Agreements which have not been court approved are not enforceable and do not produce any effect *vis-à-vis* third parties. In practical terms this means that if one of the parties does not comply with the agreement, the other party will have to ask the court to adopt measures for the exercise of parental responsibility. The agreement will be just one of the elements taken into account in order to adopt these measures.

SWEDEN

Parents are free to enter into agreements concerning the attribution of parental responsibilities after divorce. The agreement is valid if it is in writing and approved by the local social welfare committee or by the court, Chapter 6 Sec. 4, 5 and 6 Swedish Children and Parents Code.

The social welfare committee or court should approve the parents' agreement on joint custody, if joint custody is compatible with the best interests of the child. The social welfare committee should also approve an agreement providing for the sole custody of one of the parents, if sole custody is in the best interests of the child. The court formally remains free to decide, based on the best interests of the child, between joint custody or sole custody, even if the agreement stipulates sole custody. Joint custody can not be granted, however, if both parents are opposed to it, Chapter 6 Sec. 5 para. 2 Swedish Children and Parents Code.

SWITZERLAND

If parents were allocated joint parental responsibilities in connection with a divorce, they are free to subsequently change this agreement. However, such an amendment only becomes binding, in accordance with Art. 134 § 3 Swiss CC, once the guardianship authority has granted its approval. The parents may thus at any time jointly apply to the guardianship authority based on this provision of law and request that joint parental responsibilities be revoked and conferred on one parent.

In the absence of an agreement between the parents, the court competent to amend the divorce decree decides, in accordance with Art. 134 § 3 Swiss CC, on new arrangements regarding joint parental responsibilities as well as one

---

27 I. LAZARO GONZALO, *Los menores en el Derecho español*, Madrid, 2002, p. 218-219.

parent's sole parental responsibilities. A significant change in circumstances is a prerequisite in this case.[28]

The same applies to parental responsibilities in connection with *legal separation* in accordance with Art. 117 Swiss CC, and Art. 109 § 2 Swiss CC in connection with the *annulment of the marriage*. With respect to the latter, the provisions concerning divorce apply analogously to the parents as well as their children.

28 On this whole subject as one example to represent many, see: C. HEGNAUER, *Grundriss des Kindesrechts*, p. 188 *et seq.*

QUESTION 18

C. ATTRIBUTION OF PARENTAL RESPONSIBILITIES

I. Married Parents

May the competent authority attribute joint parental responsibilities to the parents of the child even against the wish of both parents/one of the parents? To what extent, if at all, should the competent authority take account of a parent's violent behaviour towards the other parent?

AUSTRIA

Joint parental responsibilities always require an agreement between the parents, at least on the primary residence of the child (Sec. 177 Austrian CC).[1] Therefore, it is not possible to attribute joint parental responsibilities against the will of one or both parents. Once agreed upon, joint parental responsibilities can even not be continued against the will of one of the parents. Either parent can petition the court to end joint parental responsibilities without substantiation at any time (Sec. 177a(2) Austrian CC).

Failing an (approvable) agreement on the primary residence of the child or the attribution of parental responsibilities, the court will entrust one parent with sole parental responsibilities based on the best interests of the child. When deciding which parent to entrust with sole parental responsibilities the court must also take into account a parent's violent behaviour against the other.[2]

BELGIUM

The joint exercise of parental responsibilities is the guiding principle, even when the parents are separated (Art. 374 Belgian CC) and even when it is against their wish.[3] Thus, parents exercise their parental responsibilities jointly by law and without judicial interference. However, the parents can agree on a different exercise (not attribution, see Q 17) of parental responsibilities. Also, when problems arise, such as when the parents can not reach an agreement about an important decision concerning the child (Art. 374(2) Belgian CC), or when the decision made seems to be incompatible with the interests of the child, the competent authority can vest exclusive parental responsibilities in one parent for this decision, while vesting parental responsibilities for certain important decisions concerning the education of the child in both parents.[4]

---

1 See Q 16. *Oberster Gerichtshof*, 22.04.2002, *Österreichischer Amtsvormund*, 2002, p. 274 S 39; J. STABENTHEINER, 'KindRÄG 2001', in: P. RUMMEL, *ABGB-Kommentar*, suppl. vol. 1, 3rd Edition, Vienna: Manz Verlag, 2003, §§ 177-177b Marg. No. 4.

2 See also Q 16 and 17.

3 Court of Appeal of Brussels, 13.06.1997, *Rev. trim. dr. fam.*, 1998, p. 617, annotated J.-L. RENCHON.

4 Court of First Instance of Brussels, 12.09.1997, *Div. Act.*, 1998, p. 4, annotated LIGOT.

Nevertheless, in case of minor disagreements the court can also decide that the joint exercise of parental responsibilities remains in the child's interests, and impose it, even against the wish of the parents[5] (See Q 42a).

Violent behaviour from one parent towards the other is only relevant when it affects the child's interests. If it appears that the behaviour of one parent towards the other has negative consequences on the child, this behaviour will be taken into account. If the violence is not proven, it will be of no relevance.[6] Art. 32(1)(2) Belgian LJP provides that the parent(s) can be dismissed from parental authority in case of bad treatment, abuse of authority, apparent bad behaviour or grave negligence that endanger the health, safety or morality of the child (See Q 51-54).

BULGARIA

No, it may not. The Bulgarian Family Code provides for the attribution of sole custody - one of the parents exercises parental responsibilities and lives with the child. For the other parent, contact should be arranged.

The Bulgarian Family Code requires that in deciding custody issues, the court must review the circumstances with regard to the interests of children. The law does not describe the exact content of children's interests and the manner in which they will be identified in the particular case. These issues have been left to the court discretion to interpret.[7] The leading Supreme Court case in this area dates back to 1974.[8] In this case the court makes the following interpretation of the concept of 'the interests of children': 'the need for the correct rearing and upbringing, the establishment of working habits and discipline, preparation for labour in the interest of the public, including material interests: housing, handling of their property, where the aim is for the child to become a harmoniously developed person and a good citizen'.

The court further states that 'the interests of the child' are not the only criterion for the eligibility of the parent and that the best safeguard to the interests of children has to be exercised in view of 'harmonising their personal interests with those of the family and society'. However, the manner of attaining this harmonisation is not clear, and no regard is given to the potential supremacy of other interests over those of the child.[9]

---

5 W. PINTENS, 'Die Reform des belgischen Kindschaftsrechts aus vergleichender Sicht', *Fam.RZ*, 1997, p. 463.

6 Court of Appeal of Brussels, 12.06.1997, *J.L.M.B.*, 1998, p. 365.

7 See also J. EEKELAAR, *Regulating Divorce*, 1991, p. 123.

8 See Decision of the Supreme Court, 1-1974 and also Cases 3350-1978, 2792-1980.

9 See criticism of this view in V. TODOROVA, 'The Decision on Communication No.27496/95 before the Commission Human Rights in Strasbourg - MM v. Bulgaria and the questions raised for Bulgarian family law', *Human Rights*, issue 1/1999, Appendix - p. 28-29.

The decision cited also offers a list of major circumstances, which need to be examined in determining the interests of children. These are:

(1) the capacity of the parents to bring up their children,
(2) care and attitude of the parents to children,
(3) affection of the children for their parents,
(4) sex and age of the child,
(5) support by third parties,
(6) social environment,
(7) housing and other living conditions, and
(8) the fault in divorce'.

The violent behaviour of the parent towards the other parent is not among these circumstances, but it could be part of the fault in divorce situation if examined.

CZECH REPUBLIC

Joint parental responsibility belongs to both parents regardless of their will. The court may deprive a parent of parental responsibility if he or she abuses his or her parental responsibility or its exercise, or if he or she seriously neglects it (Sec. 44 § 3 Czech Family Code). However, abuse or neglect must be related to the child. Violent behaviour towards the other parent does not affect parental responsibility.

DENMARK

Joint parental authority cannot be attributed to the parents who no longer live together or intend to live separately against the wish of one or both parents, Art. 8 Danish Act on Parental Authority and Contact.

ENGLAND & WALES

As the attribution of parental responsibility is fixed by law and since the courts have no power to divest married parents of parental responsibility this question has no relevance in English law.

FINLAND

A court may order that the parents shall have joint custody if it considers this to be in accordance with the best interests of the child. The disagreement of one or both parents, as such, does not have any effect according to Sec. 10 Finnish Child Custody and the Right of Access Act. According to the *travaux preparatoires* however, the discretion of the court should be based on the fact that the parents agree on the joint custody, although exceptions to this were supposed to be possible.[10] In the beginning of the 1990s nearly 20 percent of the custody cases in Courts of Appeal resulted in joint custody against one parent's

---

10 Governmental Bill (HE 224/82) p. 5; K. KURKI-SUONIO *Äidin hoivasta yhteishuoltoon*, Suomalainen Lakimiesyhdistys Helsinki 1999, p.485; K. KURKI-SUONIO, 'Joint Custody as an Interpretation of the Best Interests of the Child in Critical and Comparative Perspective', *IJLPF*, 2000, Vol. 14, p. 195.

will.[11] In any case, one must bear in mind that in Finland only the court can decide the child shall have its residence at one of the parents' residences, if the parents do not live together (Sec. 9 para. 1 point 2 Finnish Child Custody and the Right of Access Act).

However, since the beginning of the 1990s, courts have become more reluctant to order joint custody against one parent's will.[12] According to the Finnish Child Custody and the Right of Access Act the best interests of the child shall be the first and paramount consideration in settling any matter concerning custody and right of access (Sec. 10 para 1). The court shall pay special attention to the way in which the objectives of custody and the right of access can best be implemented in the future (Sec. 10 Finnish Child Custody and the Right of Access Act). Thus, domestic violence of any kind is not mentioned in the Act. The Supreme Court has also not set any precedents for this question either. Thus the courts must make their decisions *in casu*.[13]

During the last ten years the problem of domestic violence has received attention in academic writings and studies as well as by high authorities and the gravity of the problem has been widely acknowledged. Today the Finnish Government, among others, runs several programs in order to prevent, identify, treat and organise follow-ups for parents and children who are affected by this problem. It is submitted that, unfortunately, public interest does not mean that all social workers or judges possess the necessary skills to deal with the problem of domestic violence in custody and right of access cases, as yet.

FRANCE

The recent reforms in France promote the principle of joint parental responsibilities after parental separation. Art. 373-2 French CC states that the parental separation has no consequence to the allocation of the exercise of parental responsibilities; both parents remain holders of parental responsibilities and continue to act in this respect. If only one parent was holder of parental responsibilities, that parent remains the sole holder.

---

11 K. KURKI-SUONIO 'Joint Custody as an Interpretation of the Best Interests of the Child in Critical and Comparative Perspective', *IJLPF*, 2000, Vol. 14, p. 194, K. KURKI-SUONIO, *Äidin hoivasta yhteishuoltoon*, Helsinki: Suomalainen Lakimiesyhdistys, 1999, p. 501-504.

12 My personal experience is based in my work at the office of the Parliamentary Ombudsman and in functioning as teacher of courses for judges and other court lawyers about child custody decision-making. The courses have been organised by the Ministry of Justice for the last four years.

13 See K. KURKI-SUONIO, 'Joint Custody as an Interpretation of the Best Interests of the Child in Critical and Comparative Perspective', *IJLPF*, 2000, Vol. 14, p. 197-198, where I suggest that the policy of promoting joint custody as a part of a 'concept of the amicable divorce' may underestimate the significance of parental conflicts in child custody decision making, both in court and in mediation.

The legal provisions do not expressly mention whether a judge may attribute joint parental responsibilities to the parents against the wish of one or both parents. The joint exercise of parental responsibilities requires a minimum of good will from both parents, but the judge can attribute the exercise of parental responsibilities to both parents against their wish[14] because this is a legal principle of parental separation and because parents continue to have duties to their child even if they separate.

Art. 373-2-1 French CC states that the family judge can attribute the exercise of parental responsibilities to only one parent if the child's interest requires it. The most important criteria for the judge are the child's interests (see also Art. 373-2-6 French CC); the judge can take all measures to preserve the continuity and strength of the child's bonds with each parent. The family judge tries to promote conciliation between the parents (Art. 373-2-10 French CC); she or he can also propose a mediation procedure in order to find a solution between the parents concerning the exercise of parental responsibilities. The judge can even order the parties to meet with a family mediator (Art. 373-2-10 para. 3 French CC).

A parent's violent behaviour towards the other parent can indirectly be taken into account by the family judge if, in the child's interest, this violent behaviour should exclude the possibility of joint parental responsibilities. The judge can also rely on social inquiry (*enquête sociale*), the spouses agreement and/or hearing, or the child's hearing to decide on the attribution of the exercise of parental responsibilities (see Art. 373-2-11 French CC for all elements the judge can take into account in order to decide upon the attribution of the exercise of parental responsibilities: *e.g.* parental agreement or former practice, feelings expressed by the child, ability of each parent to take on his duties and to respect the rights of the other parent, result of expert testimony, the child's age and all information obtained through social inquiries).

GERMANY

There are several ways in which the courts can become active with regard to the attribution of parental responsibilities against the will of one or both of the parents:

If the parents are living apart not just on temporary basis, the case falls under the scope of the provision contained in § 1671 para. 2 No. 2 German CC. If the parents are not in agreement about the attribution of sole parental responsibility to one parent, the court should grant the application only if it is to be expected that the dissolution of joint responsibility and moreover the transfer of sole responsibility on the proponent correspond most closely to the child's best interests. In this respect, it is still disputed whether the court should

---

14 See Th. FOSSIER, *L'autorité parentale*, 2002, ESF, 2nd Ed., p. 45.

carry out its examination of the child's best interest in two stages[15] - i.e. whether it should initially decide whether joint responsibility or sole responsibility most closely correspond to the child's best interests, followed by an examination as to whether the sole responsibility applied for by the proponent itself most closely corresponds to the child's best interests - or whether such a two-stage procedure is to be rejected.[16] According to the prevailing opinion in this regard, a two-stage examination is called for: The key criterion in the decision to dissolve joint responsibility is the parents' ability and willingness to cooperate.[17] This means that for joint responsibility to be dissolved, considerable impediments to communication must be present; in this context, disputes of a profound nature in matters of upbringing[18] are to be given greater weight than a dispute of a profound nature between the partners which has so far not involved the child. Serious conflict between partners, such as sustained violence[19] between parents or reports of a serious nature to the police, may give rise to dissolution of joint responsibility if these disputes prevent the parents from performing their joint parental responsibilities in accordance with the child's best interests.[20] It would seem that in German judicial practice, violence within a relationship still plays a fairly minor role with regard to court decisions on parental responsibility.[21] However, the Federal Constitutional Court in a more recent decision[22] explicitly ruled that if the child's father has been sentenced with final and binding effect as a result of substantial acts of violence against the child's mother, resulting in substantial psychological problems for the mother, joint parental responsibility cannot be considered a possibility due to the lack of viable social relations between the parents. It is only when joint responsibility is not in the child's best interests that the question as to which parent is to be attributed sole responsibility arises. The valuation criteria used when deciding on the child's best interests are: the principle of the promotion of the child's development and that of continuity, the former having priority. The principle of the promotion of the child's development requires that priority of parental care be given to the parent with whom the child can be expected to receive the most support in the

15 OLG Hamm 25.08.1998, *FamRZ* 1999, 38, 39; OLG Nürnberg 17.11.1998, *FamRZ* 1999, 673, 674;
D. SCHWAB, 'Elterliche Sorge bei Trennung und Scheidung der Eltern, Die Neuregelung des Kindschaftsrechtsreformgesetzes', *FamRZ* 1998, 457, 462.

16 M. COESTER, in: STAUDINGER, *Kommentar zum Bürgerlichen Gesetzbuch,* 13th Edition, Berlin: de Gruyter, 2000, § 1671 No. 104 *et seq.*

17 OLG Zweibrücken 02.03.2000, *FamRZ* 2000, 1042, 1043.

18 KG 21.09.1999, *FamRZ* 2000, 502, 503; OLG Bamberg 10.03.1999, *FamRZ* 1999, 805, 806.

19 OLG Hamm 13.08.1999, *FamRZ* 2000, 501, 502; M. COESTER, in: STAUDINGER, *Kommentar zum Bürgerlichen Gesetzbuch,* 13th Edition, Berlin: de Gruyter, 2000, § 1671 No. 139.

20 BVerfG 18.12.2003, *FamRZ* 2004, 354, 255; KG 18.10.1999, *FamRZ* 2000, 504, 505.

21 H. KINDLER and A. DRECHSEL, 'Partnerschaftsgewalt und Kindeswohl', *JAmt* 2003, 217, 218 *et seq.*

22 BVerfG 18.12.2003, *FamRZ* 2004, 354, 355.

establishment of his or her personality.[23] By contrast, the principle of continuity is guided by the fact that a child's upbringing ought to seek to foster the establishment of behavioural constants[24] and aim to keep the child in that environment where his or her strongest ties lie.

Regardless of whether the parents live apart or not, moreover, § 1628 German CC provides that the family court will, in the case of joint parental responsibility, make a decision if the parents are unable to agree on a specific issue or specific kind of issue relating to parental responsibility, the regulation of which is of considerable importance for the child. Again, the family court will only act upon application (see also the answer to Q 38).

Furthermore, there are cases where the court must intervene upon its own motion and regulate parental responsibility in order to avoid the child being placed in danger. The legal basis for this is found in § 1666 German CC: This provision authorises the family court to take all measures necessary to prevent the jeopardising of the physical, mental or moral welfare of the child as a result of the abusive exercise of parental responsibility, neglect of the child, parents' failure through no fault of their own, or of a third party's behaviour. Accordingly, changes to the arrangements of parental responsibility can be made to the extent that they seem suitable and necessary to avert danger. In this context, the court may withdraw responsibility from one parent, either in part or in full, as a result of which the other parent will then exercise sole responsibility in accordance with § 1680 para. 1 and 3 German CC. Furthermore, the court may withdraw parental responsibility from both parents in part[25] and subsequently appoint a curator for the child.[26] Finally, the court has the option to withdraw all parental responsibilities from both parents[27] and to appoint a guardian for the child.[28] It can be assumed that a child's best interests are in jeopardy if the child is exposed to a present danger to such an extent that it can be predicted with reasonable certainty that he or she will be considerably damaged in his or her further development.[29] In this context, the court must also, under the aspect of jeopardy to the child's best interests by a third party's behaviour, take into account any violence between the partners

---

23 BVerfG 05.11.1980 *FamRZ* 1981, 124, 126; U. DIEDERICHSEN, in: PALANDT, *Bürgerliches Gesetzbuch*, 64th Edition, Munich: Beck, 2005, § 1671 No. 21; P. FINGER, in: *Münchener Kommentar zum Bürgerlichen Gesetzbuch*, 4th Edition, Munich: Beck, 2002, § 1671 No. 28.

24 U. DIEDERICHSEN, in: PALANDT, *Bürgerliches Gesetzbuch*, 64th Edition, Munich: Beck, 2005, § 1671 No. 22.

25 § 1666 a para. 2 German CC.

26 § 1909 para. 1 German CC.

27 § 1666 a para. 2 German CC.

28 § 1773 para. 1 German CC.

29 BGH 14.07.1956, *FamRZ* 1956, 350, 351; BayObLG 03.12.1976, *FamRZ* 1977, 473.

within the family.[30] Given the principle of proportionality, parental responsibility will only be withdrawn from a parent in extreme cases.

GREECE

The court will only attribute joint parental responsibilities to the parents if they both agree to this, and, at the same time, if they determine the location of the child's residence (Art. 1513 para. 1 Greek CC). The guideline for the courts in deciding on the exercise of parental care is the best interest of the child (Art. 1511 para. 2 Greek CC). Within this framework a parent's violent behaviour towards the other parent is certainly a factor to be taken into account.

HUNGARY

The court cannot attribute joint parental responsibilities to the parents against the wish of even one of the parents. An element essential for a decision favouring joint parental responsibilities is that the divorced parents, or the parents living apart, can permanently co-operate with each other in matters concerning the child. The exercise of joint parental responsibilities would be impossible without this co-operation; forcing the parents to exercise their parental rights jointly would not be in the child's interests.

IRELAND

Yes, the competent authority may do so. Sec. 11A Irish Guardianship of Infants Act 1964, as inserted by Sec. 9 Irish Children Act 1997 makes it clear, should any doubt exist, that it is possible, even against the wish of one of the parents, to award custody to both the father and mother jointly. In *E.P. v. C.P.*,[31] MCGUINNESS J. stated that joint custody is ill-advised where there is significant acrimony between the parents. In such circumstances, she felt, that joint custody was not suitable. The reason for this is outlined further by the same learned judge in *D.F.O'S. v. C.A.*,[32] MCGUINNESS J. noting that:

> 'As a general rule where there is deep hostility between the parents I am very reluctant to make an order granting joint custody, due to the probable inability of the parents to co-operate in caring for the child.'

The existence of inter-parental conflict and objections by one or both parents however, is by no means an absolute bar to joint custody. In the latter case, for example, and notwithstanding the existence of conflict and acrimony between the parents, MCGUINNESS J. made an order granting joint custody to both parents. She did so, in the hope that the conferral of joint responsibility would encourage them to 'put their antagonisms behind them'. The learned judge feared, moreover, that the award of sole custody to either parent could exacerbate the sense of bitterness and resentment already existing between the

---

30 U. DIEDERICHSEN, in: PALANDT, *Bürgerliches Gesetzbuch*, 64th Edition, Munich: Beck, 2005, § 1666 No. 33.

31 High Court, 27.11.1998.

32 High Court, 20.04.1999.

parents. Referring to expert evidence submitted at the trial, McGuinness J. observed that despite their tempestuous marital relationship, both parties had maintened an excellent personal relationship with their daughter and thus, under the circumstances, that joint custody was the most appropriate solution.[33] A similar approach was adopted by Herbert J. in *D.McA. v. K.McA.*[34] where he granted joint custody to a father and mother of their children, although he did express the view that the everyday routine of the children should not be circumscribed by the joint custody arrangement.

In the attribution of parental responsibilities, Sec. 20(2)(i) Irish Family Law (Divorce) Act 1996 requires the court to take account of:

> '...the conduct of each of the spouses, if that conduct is such that in the opinion of the court it would in all the circumstances of the case be unjust to disregard it'.

This provision, which mirrors the equivalent provision in the Irish Family Law Act 1995, is a broader version than that contained in the Irish Judicial Separation and Family Law Reform Act 1989, which required the court to disregard the conduct of each spouse, unless it would in all the circumstances of the case, be repugnant to justice to do so. Clearly, the court in the attribution of parental responsibilities, is now afforded greater scope to take account of a parent's violent behaviour towards the other parent and to take account of how that behaviour has affected any children of the marriage. That said, considerations of conduct, including a parent's violent behaviour towards the other parent, are only relevant if the behaviour is 'gross and obvious'. In *T. v. T.*,[35] Denham J. stated that the Irish Family Law (Divorce) Act 1996 did not seek to establish a fault based divorce system. The learned judge considered Sec. 20(2)(i) and stated:

> '[T]he Act of 1996 does not seek to establish a fault system. Thus the concept of 'conduct' established by Sec. 20(2)(i) is of conduct which it would be unjust to disregard'.

ITALY

No; if not expressly provided by law, the judge cannot attribute the joint exercise of parental responsibilities without the consent of both parents. For joint exercise of parental responsibilities, Italian law requires the following conditions: a good relationship between the parents, both need the capacity to

---

33 See also *E.H. v. J.M.*, High Court, 04.04.2000, Kinlen J., and *C.F. v. J.D.F.*, High Court, 16.05.2002, O'Sullivan J.

34 High Court, 17.12.2002, Herbert J.

35 Supreme Court, 14.10.2002.

be good parents and they should live close to each other.[36] It is not possible to order joint parental responsibilities against the wish of the parents or of one of them.[37]

Violent behaviour by one of the parents towards the other (spouse as well as partner) can create prejudice to the violent parent's physical and moral integrity or to his liberty, it may fulfil the elements of Art. 572 Italian Penal Code (maltreatment of family or minors) and it also has relevance in civil terms. At the request of one of the parties the civil judge can order the cessation of this prejudicial behaviour and also for one of the parents to leave the family's house (Art. 342*bis* and 342*ter* Italian CC, recently introduced by the Law No. 154, of 4 April 2001 and modified by Law No. 304, of 6 November 2003). The judge can also order the intervention of a local social service, centre for family mediation or associations who support and receive victims of abuse and maltreatment. The judge can order the periodic payment of an allowance in favour of one of the cohabitants who, because of the ordered removal from the family's house, remains without appropriate means. The judge will establish the methods and terms of the payment and decide if the obligated parent must have his or her employer deduct the relevant amount from his or her salary to be paid directly to the recipient. The judge will establish the duration that one of the cohabitants must stay away from the family's house. This cannot be for longer than 6 months from the removal-order and can only be extended at the request of one party for grave reasons and for a period that is strictly necessary. If there are difficulties or oppositions regarding the execution of the removal order, the judge will order necessary measures, including security forces and the health official.

Whether this form of protection, characterised by urgency and timeliness, presumes a cohabitation[38] of the parents (spouses or non spouses) or if it is also applicable pending or after a factual separation, or during the process of separation, divorce or annulment of the marriage has been discussed. In this case, the order to leave the family's house would also include the prohibition to frequent the victim's habitation or to have contact with her or him.[39] At any rate, it deals with a residual protection which applies when the conditions for the suspension or limitation of the parental responsibilities according to Art. 330 and Art. 333 Italian CC are fulfilled.[40]

---

36 See the Court of Genoa 18.04.1991, *Giust. Civ.*, 1991, I, p. 3095, with note of M. MIGLIETTA; Court of S. Maria Capua Vetere 14.09.1993, *Giur. merito*, 1994, p. 226 with note of G. MANERA; Court of Catania 06.06.1994, *Dir. Fam. pers.*, 1995, p. 222.

37 See the Court of Milan, 14.07.1993, *Gius*, 1994, p. 99.

38 See also the Court of Genoa 07.01.2003, *Fam. dir.*, 2004, p. 387, annotated L. CARRERA; Court of Naples 01.02.2002, *Fam. dir.*, p. 504, annotated A. FIGONE.

39 See the Court of Florence 15.07.2002, *Fam. dir.*, 2003, p. 263, with a critical note of G. DE MARZO.

40 Concerning the possibility of also applying Art. 330 and 333 Italian CC in cases of 'indirect' abuse and maltreatment or in cases where the act is committed towards relatives instead of the minor but (such as the other parent) to whom the minor is so

LITHUANIA

Yes. In deciding such questions, the wishes of one or both parents are irrelevant because parental responsibilities are statutory obligations and their existence or attribution does not depend on the wishes of the parties.

A parent's violent behaviour towards the other parent shall have legal significance only if attribution of joint responsibilities to both parents is against the best interests of the child. In such a case, the violent behaviour of one of the parents may be a ground for the separation of that parent from the child or for the restriction of parental authority of the parent (Art. 3.179 Lithuanian CC). In any case, the attribution of parental responsibilities to only one of the parents is possible in the event of judicial separation of a parent from the child or in the event of judicial restriction of parental authority.

THE NETHERLANDS

The court may reject a request for sole parental responsibilities, which means that the existing joint parental responsibilities will continue, even if this is against the wish of one or both of the parents. The idea is that continued joint parental responsibilities are in the best interest of the child. Even if the parents agree that it would be best for the children if one of them were to have sole parental responsibilities, the court may reject their request if it considers it not to be in the child's best interests to terminate joint parental responsibilities. It has been assumed by the legal literature that in this situation the court simply has to determine that the request is evidently not contrary to the best interests of the child.[41] However, a recent decision by the Court of Appeal of 's Hertogenbosch points in a different direction.[42] The Court of Appeal of 's Hertogenbosch denied a request by two parents to attribute sole parental responsibilities to the mother, because it did not agree with the parent's claim that this would be in the best interests of their children.[43] However, until Dutch

---

close that its 'harmonic and balanced psychophysical upbringing' is compromised, see the Family Proceedings Court L'Aquila 19.07.2002, *Fam. dir.* 2003, p. 482.

41 E. BEENEN and P. VLAARDINGERBROEK, 'Doorlopend ouderlijk gezag in de praktijk', *FJR* , 2004, p. 36-38. The authors studied judgements of the District Court of 's Hertogenbosch of 2001 and 2002 on the continuation or termination of joint parental responsibilities after divorce, and found that in cases where both parents agreed that one of them should have parental responsibilities, only one of the 29 request that come before the court was denied (on technical grounds). In cases like these the court did not verify whether termination of joint parental responsibilities was indeed in the best interest of the children.

42 Court of Appeal 's Hertogenbosch 15.04.2004, *LJN* AO7714 and E. BEENEN and P. VLAARDINGERBROEK, 'Doorlopend ouderlijk gezag in de praktijk', *FJR,* 2004, p. 36-38.

43 The parents claimed that they did not agree about the proper treatment of their handicapped son and thought it would be best if only the mother would hold parental responsibilities. The court held that the child's interests would be best served if decision about his welfare would be the result of consultation between the parents, even if the parents have different ideas on the subject.

Supreme Court has judged this issue, it will remain unclear whether the court has to do more than simply determine the request is evidently not contrary to the best interests of the child.

Violent behaviour of one parent towards the other parent is in itself not a reason to terminate joint parental responsibilities. Only if the violent behaviour of the parent threatens to cause problems of such seriousness that there is an unacceptable risk that the children will be damaged will the court attribute sole parental responsibilities to one of the parents.[44]

NORWAY

According to Art. 48 Norwegian Children Act 1981, the decision of the court shall first and foremost be taken on the basis of what is best for the child. The court may attribute joint parental responsibilities to the parents of the child against the wish of one of the parents, and, in principle, also against the wish of both parents. The main rule is for both parents to share parental responsibilities after a separation or divorce, Art. 34 sec. 2 Norwegian Children Act 1981. If one of the parents wishes sole responsibility, the courts will comply with such a request only if there are special circumstances that support the claim. Such 'special circumstances' will include, for instance, the possibility that the other parent might be considered unsuited to share parental responsibilities. A recent case decided by the Supreme Court illustrates this:[45] A suitable parent was not allowed to continue sharing parental responsibilities. In the judgment concerning an autistic child, the mother was awarded sole parental responsibilities. It was emphasised that the relationship between the parents was poor and, in the view of the court, 'there was a gulf impossible to bridge'. Further, the child's negative reactions to the father, relating to her autism, were of significance, and if he were granted the right of contact, this would exacerbate the disfunctional parental communication and hurt the child. An important issue was that the mother might become unable to care for the child, due to the stress caused by contact with the father.

POLAND

According to the general principle, the competent authority is always obliged to act in accordance with the child's best interests and aim to safeguard the child's wellbeing. While acting to achieve those goals the court may take the facts discussed into consideration (*e.g.* the parents' will, their behaviour towards each other), but they do not have direct legal significance.

PORTUGAL

No. The attribution of joint custody to both parents following a divorce, legal separation, declaration of nullity or annulment of marriage, or factual separation, is restricted to an agreement between the parents to exercise

---

[44] Criterion developed by the Supreme Court in its judgement of 10.9.1999, *NJ*, 2000, 20.

[45] Rt. 2003 p. 35.

parental responsibility jointly as they did while they were living together (Art. 1906 No. 1 Portuguese CC).

The law is silent as to whether the court should take into account the fact that one parent has been the victim of domestic violence. Legal literature, however, seems to consider that this fact should be taken into consideration when determining a new exercise of parental responsibility, by not accepting a (presumed) agreement of the parents as to joint custody and in some cases even refusing the right of contact to the aggressor.[46]

RUSSIA

A judge has no competence to decide upon attribution of parental responsibility, as parents always have joint parental responsibility by operation of law. The only way to end joint parental responsibility is to discharge the parental responsibility of one or both parents who are found guilty of serious misconduct against the child (Art. 69 Russian Family Code). As an intentional crime against the health or life of the other parent constitutes a ground for discharge of parental responsibility (Art. 69), such measure can be applied when one of the parents has been convicted by the criminal court for violence towards the other parent.

SPAIN

Parental responsibility is an effect of parenthood. It is held jointly by the father and mother regardless of their civil status.

If the parents do not live together, as is normally the case upon divorce, legal separation or annulment, it is necessary to adopt measures for the exercise of parental responsibility. Here there are substantial differences between the Spanish CC regime and Catalan law.

The Spanish CC establishes that the parent the child lives with will exercise *patria potestad* (Art. 156 Spanish CC). On the request of the other parent and in the interests of the child, the judge can either establish that *patria potestad* is to be jointly exercised by both parents or distribute its functions among them. Statute does not require that the other parent agrees to this measure. In practice it is not common for parents to share the exercise of parental responsibility after separation. It is even less common for judges to order the joint exercise against the will of one of the parties; it is assumed that then a joint exercise of parental responsibility would, in practical terms, become impossible. It is not possible to decree that parental responsibilities are to be exercised jointly if there is not a request for it by at least one of the parental responsibility holders.

---

46 See C. SOTTOMAYOR, *Exercício do poder paternal relativamente à pessoa do filho após o divórcio ou separação de pessoas e bens*, Oporto: Publicações Universidade Católica, 2003, p. 486 *et seq.*

Catalan law, on the contrary, establishes that after the parent's relationship ends, parental responsibility generally continues to be exercised jointly. Parents can agree that only one of them is to exercise parental responsibility. This agreement may be disregarded by the judge, who can theoretically re-establish the joint exercise of parental responsibility if he or she thinks the agreement is detrimental to the child's best interests. In practice this should be very rare unless one of the parents renounces his or her parental responsibility rights and duties in the agreement. If one of the parents objects to the joint exercise of parental responsibility he or she may go to court. The judge can decide either to maintain the joint exercise or to disregard the legal regime if it is contrary to the child's best interests.

Parliament is currently working on more comprehensive protection for victims of domestic violence. From this will probably come the ability to suspend the exercise of parental responsibility and even contact rights, if the judge decides it to be necessary.[47] See Q 36.

SWEDEN

Since the 1998 law reform, the court may order joint custody of a child against the wish of one of the parents but not if both parents object to it, Chapter 6 Sec. 5 Swedish Children and Parents Code. When deciding the suitable custody position, the court shall regard the best interests of the child. In its judgment NJA 1999 p. 451 the Swedish Supreme Court stated that the present legislation presupposes that joint custody is, as a rule, in the best interests of the child. The *travaux préparatoires*, however, emphasise that there are cases where joint custody is not desirable. This is the case if one of the parents is guilty of violence towards the child or the other parent. Neither is joint custody appropriate in cases where conflict between the parents is so severe and deep that it is impossible for them to cooperate in matters concerning the child.[48] An example of how these exceptions are assessed is provided by the judgment of the Swedish Supreme Court, NJA 2000 p. 345. In the Supreme Court's opinion, the fact that the father had been found guilty of the assault of the mother in 1999 did not make him unfit as a custodian at the time of the proceedings a year later. However, the assault was found to reflect the parents' profound difficulties to cooperate, making it impossible for them to cooperate in issues concerning the children. Custody was therefore granted to the mother alone, with reference to the best interests of the children.

SWITZERLAND

The answer to this is, in principle, negative because a joint petition is a prerequisite for the divorce court to allow the parents to keep joint parental responsibilities, as is explicitly stipulated in Art. 133 § 3 Swiss CC. When

---

47 Art. 63 and 64 *Proyecto de Ley Orgánica de medidas de protección integral contra la violencia de género.*

48 Prop. 1997/98:7 p. 49.

deciding attribution of parental responsibilities, the competent authority must take all the circumstances pertaining to the child's welfare into consideration.

Only in a legal separation in accordance with Art. 117 Swiss CC would it be possible, based on the wording of Art. 297 § 2 Swiss CC, to leave both parents with parental responsibilities even if no joint petition was submitted to this effect and even if further special prerequisites set forth in Art. 133 § 3 Swiss CC are not fulfilled.[49]

---

49 I. SCHWENZER, 'Art. 297 ZGB, p. 1574 (No. 10)', in: H. HONSELL, N.P. VOGT, TH. GEISER (ed.), *Basler Kommentar zum Schweizerischen Privatrecht, Zivilgesetzbuch I*, Art. 1-456 ZGB, Basel: Helbing & Lichtenhahn, 2002.

QUESTION 19

C. ATTRIBUTION OF PARENTAL RESPONSIBILITIES

I. Married Parents

Provide statistical information on the attribution of parental responsibilities after divorce, legal separation or annulment of the marriage.

AUSTRIA

The divorce rate in Austria was 43.2% in 2003. About 16,500 minor children were affected. Since joint parental responsibilities became a possibility on 1 July 2001, about half of those seeking a divorce wished to continue joint parental responsibilities. In almost all other cases, the mother assumed sole parental responsibilities. The probability the mother will receive sole parental responsibilities in custody disputes increases the younger the child is. If the father alone has legal counsel, his chances of being awarded parental responsibilities increase. On average, three weeks' more visitation days are agreed upon with joint parental responsibilities than with sole parental responsibilities. Actually, fathers with joint parental responsibilities spend almost six weeks more time with their children than when mothers have sole parental responsibilities.[1]

BELGIUM

There is no recent, relevant statistical information available.

BULGARIA

The statistical information suggests that the share of children from divorced families is:[2]

1970	1980	1990 - 2000
2% (1 child out of every 50 children)	3.5-4% (1 child out of every 30 children)	6.5% (one child out of every 15 children)

The census of 2001 reveals that there are 144,870 lone parent families in Bulgaria (from the total of 2,392,000), which is 12.4% from the total number of families. The ratio between mother-headed and father-headed families is 4.5:1, respectively, or 84% of lone parent families are headed by the mother and 16%

---

1 Informationsdienst des Österreichischen Instituts für Familienforschung (ed.), 'Akte Scheidung', *Beziehungsweise*, 2004, No. 11 of 1 June 2004, http://www.oif.ac.at/presse/bzw/artikel.asp?Rubrik=3&ID_Art=1&BZWArtikel=743.

2 M. BELCHEVA, *Condition, tendencies and problems of birth rate in the Republic of Bulgaria*, National Statistical Institute, 2003, p. 67.

by the father. Irrespective of the fact that judicial termination of the marriage is only one of the reasons for the existence of single-parent families, this proportion also applies in determining which parent will exercise parental rights and obligations before the court; in most of the cases the mother is the preferred parent.[3]

In fact, the instruction given by the Supreme Court in its leading decision No. 1 of 1974 in making custody arrangements is to examine the qualities of the parents and their environment, but not so much the specific interests of the child. The only indicators for the needs of the particular child mentioned in the instructing decision are 'the sex and the age' of the child and 'his or her attitude to one or the other parent'. Thereupon, that decision delineates specific needs for some children, such as girls, especially during puberty or pre-puberty and small children (babies and very young children) and children with disabilities. The mother is identified as the parent more suitable to satisfy their needs, and so will be regarded as the preferable parent.[4] The recommendation to courts is that: 'the mother is more eligible to rear and bring up children of the female sex and equally, to rear and raise boys'. Following these instructions, in 90% of the cases, courts prefer the mother as the custodial parent, with the father being granted contact with the child. No discontent has been registered with fathers regarding this practice of the court so far.

CZECH REPUBLIC

No answer.

DENMARK

Such statistical information should contain details relating to agreements on parental authority and the judgements by the courts. This information does not exist, however. But statistics do show that 75% of parents who became divorced or legally separated in 1999 agreed on joint parental authority. Since 2002 joint parental authority automatically continues after divorce, so a higher rate is now expected.[5] In 2001 a study showed that the father was awarded parental authority over 42% of the total number of children and the mother over 58% of the total number of children in cases before the lower courts and that the father was awarded parental authority over 36% of the total number of children and the mother over 64% of the total number of children in cases before the appeal courts.[6]

---

3 M. BELCHEVA, *Condition, tendencies and problems of birth rate in the Republic of Bulgaria*, National Statistical Institute, 2003, p. 87-88.

4 Also according to J. EEKELAAR, *Regulating Divorce*, 1991, p. 124.

5 S. DANIELSEN, *Nordisk børneret II*, Copenhagen, Oslo, Uppsala: Nord, 2003, p. 87.

6 M. HØJGAARD PEDERSEN, 'Når den fælles forældremyndighed skal ophøre', *Tidsskrift for familie- og arveret*, 2002, p. 81. The numbers relate to the total number of children involved in the cases and not to the number of cases. A parent may be given parental authority over some but not all of the parents' children.

ENGLAND & WALES

As the answer to Q 16 states, divorce, legal separation, and for the most part, annulment has no affect upon the attribution of parental responsibility. Consequently there are no statistics.

FINLAND

There is no official statistical information about the attribution of child custody by the courts. However, there are statistics about parental agreements that have been approved by local social authorities. When interpreting these statistics one must bear in mind that the most typical situation for drawing up a parental child custody agreement about is the birth of a child to an unmarried cohabiting couple. Most cohabiting couples draw up joint custody agreement during the same visit to the local social office where the father acknowledges his paternity of the newborn baby. Later, the unmarried parents may draw up a new agreement if they separate. So, because the statistics do not differentiate between the different social situations in which parental agreements can be made, they must be carefully interpreted.

In 2003, the local social authorities approved 39,331 agreements. One agreement always concerns one child, thus the number of agreements between parents often parallels the numbers of siblings. There were slightly more agreements in 2003 than in 2002 (38,313) and the trend has been increasing (in 1999 there were 36,254).

Of all these agreements, 91.5% concerned joint custody. Sole custody was given to the mother in 7.5% and to the father in 1%of agreements. In about 81 % of cases (19,458) parents stipulated the child's place of residence as the home of its mother and in 19% as the home of its father.[7]

The latest statistics about court decisions were included in my 1999 doctoral thesis.[8] According to the findings, about 64% of the contested custody cases from three Courts of Appeal (146) concerned sole custody and 36 percent joint custody. The sample concerned cases from the years 1992 and 1993. The child's place of residence was assigned to the mother in 73% of all these cases and to the father in 25% of cases. In 2% of the cases the residences of the siblings were divided between the parents.[9]

---

7 Statistics of the National Research and Development Centre for Welfare and Health, Statistic Information 11/2004, 7.5.2004, (in Finnish and in Swedish).

8 About the sample see, K. KURKI-SUONIO, 'Joint Custody as an Interpretations of the Best Interests of the Child in Critical and Comparative Perspective', *IJLPF*, Vol. 14, 2000, p. 183-205, particularly p. 193.

9 K. KURKI-SUONIO, *Äidin hoivasta yhteishuoltoon*, Helsinki: Suomalainen Lakimiesyhdistys, 1999, p. 501 and 537.

FRANCE

Some statistical information from 1996 can be provided.[10] In 1996, the family courts ordered joint parental responsibilities in 86% of all divorce cases; in 11% of the cases, parental responsibilities were attributed to the mother and in 2% to the father.[11] The child's residence was with the mother in 86% of all cases. An alternating residence between the mother and father's home was ordered in only 1% of all judicial decisions. If the parents disagreed, the family court judge accepted the mother's request in 61% of the cases and the father's request in only 21%.[12] 10% of the children met their father once a week, 25% once a month and 30% never saw their father.

There have been no statistics available since the reform act of 2002 was enacted, but joint parental responsibilities connected with a residence of the child on an alternating basis between the mother and father's home must have increased because the new Law Act states this as the normal rule. The Ministry of Justice provides only a few figures concerning alternating residence (*résidence alternée*):[13] 80.7% of the cases requesting alternating residence are jointly presented by the parents. When the parents disagree, an alternating residence is ordered in 25% of the cases; in 75% of the disputes the residence is fixed at the home of only one parent, usually the mother's. Most of the children for whom an alternating residence is jointly proposed are under 10 years old.

In 2002, the family courts were seized with 99,121 petitions concerning parental responsibilities and contact rights. 18,244 requested modification of either the exercise of parental responsibilities or of the minor child's residence; 9,130 requested a modification of contact rights; 2,640 dealt with the contact right of grandparents or other persons, 908 aimed to solve a dispute about the exercise of parental responsibilities, 3,137 dealt with delegation or regaining of parental responsibilities and 65,062 concerned the exercise of parental responsibilities, the child's residence or the contact rights for children of unmarried parents.[14]

GERMANY

(a) Divorce

A court decision on parental responsibility will only be made following an application by one of the parents, § 1671 para. 1 German CC (see answer to Q 17 for further details). If no application for the attribution of parental responsibilities is filed, joint responsibility continues after the divorce. In the year 2000, this was the case in 69.35 % (87,630 cases in absolute figures) of

10 *Chiffres du ministère de la justice,* direction des affaires générales, 1996.
11 See also http://www.senat.fr/rap/101-071/101-0712.html.
12 See also http://www.senat.fr/rap/101-071/101-0712.html.
13 See http://www.justice.gouv.fr/publicat/etudesst.htm.
14 See *Annuaire Statistique de la Justice 2004*, p. 85.

divorce proceedings involving children.[15] In those cases where parental responsibility was attributed by the court, the breakdown was as follows: in 6.19 % (5,423) of divorce proceedings the courts attributed joint parental responsibility to mother and father; in 21.62 % (18,949) of proceedings, sole parental responsibility was attributed to the mother, while sole parental responsibility was attributed to the father in only 1.52 % (1,334) of proceedings.[16] The latter two figures illustrate that mothers still take precedence when it comes to the attribution of sole parental responsibility. All in all, it can be said that joint parental responsibility predominates and is the usual model. To illustrate, altogether joint parental responsibility accounted for 75.54 % of cases in 2000.

(b) Legal separation

German law does not have the legal institution of 'legal separation'.

(c) Annulment of the marriage

The annulment of a marriage, the consequences of which in accordance with § 1318 para. 1 German CC are largely informed by the provisions governing divorce, is in practice of very little importance. Consequently there is no statistical information on the attribution of parental responsibilities after annulment of the marriage.

GREECE

In Greece no reliable statistics exist on this issue. From an unofficial study of court decisions it appears that the courts usually attribute parental responsibilities after divorce or annulment to the mother.[17]

HUNGARY

Unfortunately we do not have exact statistics on the attribution of parental responsibilities after either divorce or annulment. Legal separation is unknown in Hungary. With regard to an annulment of the marriage it has to be mentioned that lawsuits concerning annulment occur extremely rarely in Hungary.

Nevertheless, there is some statistical information about marriages with common children which ended by divorce. In 2002 the total number of divorces was 25,506. In 10,085 divorces there were no common children alive. In 15,421

---

15 R. PROKSCH, *Begleitforschung zur Umsetzung der Neuregelungen zur Reform des Kindschaftsrechts, 2. Zwischenbericht Teil II*, Bonn, 2001, I.3.3.1 (S. 14), http://www.bmj.bund.de/media/archive/202.pdf.

16 R. PROKSCH, *Begleitforschung zur Umsetzung der Neuregelungen zur Reform des Kindschaftsrechts, 2. Zwischenbericht Teil II*, Bonn, 2001, I.3.3.1 (S. 14), http://www.bmj.bund.de/media/archive/202.pdf.

17 P. AGALLOPOULOU, in: A. GEORGIADIS and M. STATHOPOULOS (eds.), *Civil Code commentary, Vol. VIII, Family Law (Arts. 1505-1694)*, 2nd Edition, Athens: Law & Economy, P.N. Sakkoulas 2003, Art. 1513-1514 Greek CC, p. 224, No. 45, citing numerous court decisions.

divorces there were one (in 8,833 cases), two (in 5,292 cases) or more children affected (in 1,296 cases there were three or more common children). The number of common minor children at the time of the divorce totalled 23,630. Among these children 6,861 were under the age of 6 and 16,769 were between the ages of 7-17.

IRELAND

No such statistical information is available.

ITALY

The mother holds parental responsibilities in 85.5% of separation cases, the father in 8.8%, both parents in 1.6%, in 1.6% the children are separated (one living with the mother and the other one with the father) and in 2.6% of the cases other solutions are made (entrustment to relatives or other institutions).[18] Consequently, the cases in which parental responsibilities are held by the mother dominate[19] (the so called daily exercise). However, arguments concerning the children composed only 18.2% of the cases (in these cases are also those in which the father applied for the parental responsibilities); in 75.7% of these cases the mother holds parental responsibilities and in 15.7% the father. In addition, the mother's parental responsibilities are considered to correspond more closely to the child's interests during early childhood (0-6 years).

LITHUANIA

There is no relevant statistical information available. A survey of court practice carried out by the Supreme Court in 2002 shows that with divorce, the child's place of residence was established with the father in 45% of cases, with the mother in 34%, and with other persons, such as grandparents *etc.* in 21%of the cases.[20]

THE NETHERLANDS

Children in divorce procedures	PARENTAL RESPONSIBILITIES				CONTACT ORDER			
	Continuation	Attribution			Man	Woman	Both	Not known
		Man	Woman	Both				
1993	16	5	76	3	9,1	0,7	0,8	89,5
1995	17	5	71	7	9,3	0,4	0,5	89,8

---

18 The dates are based on research completed by the analysis of Civil Court of Roma decisions regarding judicial separation during 1999. See M. MALAGOLI TOGLIATTI, A. LUBRANO and L. CARAVELLI, 'La CTU per l'affidamento del minore. Una ricerca sulle sentenze di separazione giudiziale emesse dal Tribunale civile diRoma', *Famiglia*, 2004, p. 27.

19 The dates are not very different from those given in previous research made by different Italian Courts, among them also the Court of Rome. See AA.VV., *L'affidamento dei figli nelle sentenze giudiziali* by A. DELL'ANTONIO and D. VINCENTI AMATO GIUFFRÈ, Milano, 1992.

20 Teismu praktika (Court Practice), No. 17, 2002, p. 348.

1997	34	3	59	4	13,9	0,8	0,7	84,6
1999	74	1	16	9	17,2	0,9	1,1	80,7
2001	93	0	5	2	18,6	1,1	1,5	78,9
2003	92	0	3	0	25,7	2,1	2,7	69,4

This data[21] clearly illustrates the history of joint parental responsibilities after divorce. Since the mid-1980s, courts have allowed couples to continue exercising joint parental responsibilities after divorce. This case law was codified in 1995. Since 1998 joint parental responsibilities continue after divorce by operation of law unless one or both of the parents request sole parental responsibilities and the court deems this to be in the best interests of the child. A judgment by the Supreme Court of 10 September 1999 clarified the new law and formulated very strict criteria for attributing sole parental responsibilities after divorce. Hence in over 90% of divorce cases joint parental responsibilities continue after divorce.[22]

NORWAY

There is no official statistical information on the attribution of parental responsibilities after divorce, legal separation or annulment of the marriage. Court decisions on this matter are rare, and there is no public scrutiny of the agreement of the parents. It is the general view that in the great majority of cases the parents agree upon continued joint parental responsibilities.

POLAND

Such information is not available.

PORTUGAL

According to statistics provided by the Ministry of Justice Study and Planning Department in 2002, of the 19,502 cases dealing with the regulation of parental responsibility, 14,471 concerned children born within wedlock, 4,685 concerned children born without wedlock, 346 regarded children of unknown parenthood, 806 decisions awarded custody to the father, 8,856 decisions awarded custody to the mother, 253 decisions awarded custody to the same family, 291 decisions awarded custody to a third party and 64 decisions awarded custody to a welfare or educational institution. Joint custody was decreed in 276 of the decisions.

RUSSIA

Parental responsibility is always attributed to both parents. The child's residence after divorce is, in more than 90% of all cases, attributed to the mother.[23]

---

21 Source: *Centraal Bureau voor de Statistiek*, http://www.statline.cbs.nl. Figures on legal separation and annulment are not available.

22 See also C. VAN ROOIJEN, 'Gescheiden, maar toch gebonden', *FJR*, 2004, p. 270-275.

23 A. PANASIUK, 'Komu peredat'na vospitanie rebenka?', *Rossiyskaia Justitzia*, 1996, No. 9, p. 53-54.

SPAIN

This information is not available.

SWEDEN

The most recent statistics regarding attribution of custody after divorce refer to parents who divorced in 2002.[24] After divorce, the parents had joint custody of 23,512 children; almost 97% of all the concerned children. The mother had sole custody of 759 children; about 3%. The father was entrusted sole custody of 104 children, amounting to approximately 0.4% of the concerned children.

Joint custody, however, does not necessarily say anything about the actual care of the child. Most children lived with their mother after divorce (as well as after separation between unmarried parents).[25] By the end of 2002, 430,070 (83%) of all children with divorced or separated parents lived with their mother (or with the mother and her new partner). 78,636 children lived with their father (or with the father and his new partner), which is about 15% of the concerned children.[26] It was estimated that in 2002 approximately 17% of all children with divorced or separated parents lived alternately with both parents.

SWITZERLAND

The following statistical information is available:

Attribution of parental responsibilities for minor children 1997-2002	1997	1998	1999	2000	2001	2002
Divorces in total	17,073	17,868	20,809	10,511	15,778	16,363
Divorces without any minor children	9,110	9,335	10,870	5,698	8,545	8,830
Divorces with minor children	7,963	8,533	9,939	4,813	7,233	7,533
Attribution of parental responsibilities for minor children to:						
Mother	12,288	13,127	15,067	6,373	8,569	8,463
Father	1,316	1,255	1,534	523	682	826
A third party	38	28	37	22	29	30
Mother with reservation (or a third party)	-	9	14	7	21	14
Father with reservation (or a third party)	-	3	5	3	5	4
Mother and father	-	54	223	1,189	2,861	3,379

24 Statistics Sweden, www.scb.se.

25 Statistics Sweden, www.scb.se.

26 Statistics Sweden, www.scb.se. 9,171 (almost 2%) of all children with divorced or separated parents lived with a person other than a parent.

The attribution of parental responsibilities for minor children has only been in force since 2000. However, some judges already applied this type of attribution as early as in 1998, anticipating the amendment of the law.[27]

[27] Source: BEVNAT (Federal Statistics of Natural Movement of Population).

QUESTION 20

C. ATTRIBUTION OF PARENTAL RESPONSIBILITIES

II. Unmarried Parents

Who has parental responsibilities when the parents are not married?

AUSTRIA

If the parents are unmarried, the mother of the child receives sole parental responsibilities by operation of law (Sec. 166 Austrian CC). However, the parents can agree to exercise joint parental responsibilities (Sec. 167 Austrian CC).

BELGIUM

See Q 15a.

BULGARIA

See Q 15a and 15b.

CZECH REPUBLIC

Both parents have parental responsibility regardless of their mutual relationship. The only requisite condition for parental responsibility is that the parent must have full legal capacity to act. If this condition is met, the mother acquires parental responsibility at the moment of the child's birth and the father acquires it on the basis of a determination of paternity by a consensual declaration of the child's parents or by a court decision.

DENMARK

If the parents are not married, they have joint parental authority if they have made a statement that they will care for and be responsible for the child together, Art. 5(1) Danish Act on Parental Authority and Contact. The statement on care and responsibility is typically made in connection with the establishment of paternity and the registration of birth.[1] The establishment of paternity is not a matter left solely to the parents. The mother is required to provide information about the potential father(s) and the administrative authorities will initiate proceedings concerning paternity if such proceedings are not initiated by the mother, the potential father or the child's guardian.[2] It is also possible for unmarried parents to make an agreement on joint parental authority, Art. 6 Danish Act on Parental Authority and Contact. If no statement relating to care and responsibility or an agreement on joint parental authority

1 Danish Children Act, *Børneloven*, Act No. 460 of 07.06.2001, Art. 2, 14(1), 14(3) and 19.

2 Danish Children Act, *Børneloven*, Act No. 460 of 07.06.2001, Art. 4-7.

have been made then the mother has sole parental authority, Art. 5(2) Danish Act on Parental Authority and Contact.

ENGLAND & WALES

Where the father and mother of the child were not married to each other at the time of the child's birth (effectively meaning where the child is illegitimate) then by Sec. 2(2), English Children Act 1989 the mother but not the father has parental responsibility.

FINLAND

The mother shall be sole custodian of the child if the parents are not married at the time of the child's birth (Sec. 6 Finnish Child Custody and the Right of Access Act).

FRANCE

In principle, and as with married parents, unmarried parents have joint parental responsibilities (Art. 372 French CC); however, this only applies if both parents have acknowledged the child. Nevertheless, Art. 372 para. 2 French CC states that in two cases only one parent has parental responsibilities:

- when the parentage of one parent was established more than a year after the child's birth. If the child was acknowledged earlier by the other parent, this other parent remains sole holder of parental responsibilities.
- The same applies if the second parent's parentage was established by judgment; if the parentage was established by judgment, the parent did not want to spontaneously acknowledge his paternity (or her maternity).

In these two situations parental responsibilities can nevertheless be exercised jointly if both parents make a joint declaration before the Secretary of the Court (*tribunal de grande instance*) or if the family judge issues an order allocating joint parental responsibilities to both parents (Art. 372 para. 3 French CC).

GERMANY

According to § 1626 a para. 2 German CC, when the parents are not married to each other at the time of the child's birth, the mother as a rule has sole parental responsibility. The Federal Constitutional Court established on several occasions that the initial legal attribution of the child to the mother in accordance with § 1626 a para. 2 German CC and the general attribution to her of the right of care and custody of the child do not violate the parental rights of the father of a child born outside marriage resulting from Art. 6 para. 2 German Basic Law.[3] The general attribution of parental responsibilities to the mother is justified on account of the great variety of life circumstances into which children born outside marriage enter; often the mother is the child's only sure 'reference person', i.e. person able to provide a secure reference point for the

---

3 BVerfG 24.03.1981, *BVerfGE* 56, 363, 389; BVerfG 29.01.2003, *NJW* 2003, 955, 956.

child, after its birth. Moreover, the court holds that the mother has a natural connection to her child right from the start, unlike the father, who must begin building it up after birth.[4]

The parents do, however, have the option to both issue a declaration of parental responsibility in accordance with § 1626 a para. 1 No. 1 German CC, which if effective results in the parents being attributed joint responsibility for the child. For such declarations of responsibility to be effective, specific preconditions set out in §§ 1626 b to 1626 e German CC must be met. Declarations of responsibility are unconditional, § 1626 b para. 1 German CC, but can be issued before the birth of the child, § 1626 b para. 2 German CC. Furthermore, a declaration of responsibility is strictly personal, § 1626 c para. 1 German CC, and requires public registration, § 1626 d para. 1 German CC. To obtain joint responsibility, it is not necessary for the parents to live together. Nor are these declarations of responsibility examined with a view to establishing whether joint responsibility corresponds to the child's best interest.[5]

In this regard, it may be worth mentioning a recent decision by the Federal Supreme Court:[6] According to this decision, the fact that the child's mother is still married does not stand in the way of the biological father issuing a declaration of responsibility in accordance with § 1626 a para. 1 No. 1 German CC, if the child is born after the application for divorce was lodged and the biological father has acknowledged paternity in accordance with § 1599 para. 2 German CC. In this case, the declaration of responsibility is invalid for the time being; once the court has granted the petition for divorce and issued a decree absolute the declaration becomes valid.

GREECE

When the parents of the child are not married the exercise of parental responsibilities belongs to the mother. If, however, the father has voluntarily recognised the child as his own, or he has not appeared as a defendant in a case on judicial recognition, he will also take part in the parental care. However, he will only exercise this duty if the mother's parental care has ceased, or if she is unable to do so (Art. 1515 para. 1 Greek CC). The court can, at the father's request, also assign the exercise of parental care to the father in other cases, if the interest of the child merits this. The consent of the mother on this issue constitutes an important, but not decisive factor (Art. 1515 para. 2 Greek CC).[7] It is worth noting that, according to the prevailing opinion, the court may

---

4 BVerfG 29.01.2003, *NJW* 2003, 955, 956.

5 BT-Drucks. 13/4899 p. 59.

6 BGH 11.02.2004, *NJW* 2004, 1595, 1596.

7 M. KARASIS, in: A. GEORGIADIS and M. STATHOPOULOS (eds.), *Civil Code commentray, Vol. VIII, Family Law (Arts. 1505-1694)*, 2nd Edition, Athens: Law & Economy, P.N. SAKKOULAS, 2003, Art. 1515 Greek CC, p. 238, No. 8 [in Greek].

attribute the exercise of parental care to the father alone.[8] Finally, in the case of judicial acknowledgement where the father has appeared as the defendant, he may not take part in the parental care or replace the mother in the exercise thereof (Art. 1515 para. 3 Greek CC).

HUNGARY

The answer for this Question must be seen together with the answer for Q 22.

If the parents are not married, the mother and the father living in a non-formalised partnership exercise parental responsibilities jointly, just as the married partners - provided the legal status of the mother's partner is settled. Hungarian law makes no distinction between the parental responsibilities of married and unmarried parents, provided the legal status of the parents is settled.

IRELAND

The unmarried mother.

ITALY

Both parents, if they have recognised the child together and are still living together. If they do not live together, the parent with whom the child is living is entitled to exercise parental responsibilities. If the child does not live with either parent, the one who first recognised the child has the right of exercising parental responsibilities, unless the judge provides differently in the interests of the child (Art. 317*bis* Italian CC).

LITHUANIA

When the parents are not married, the parental responsibilities are vested with to the unmarried parents if the filiation of the child from those parents is established according to the procedure provided by Art. 3.139-3.148 Lithuanian CC.

THE NETHERLANDS

By operation of law only the unmarried mother has parental responsibilities over her child (Art. 1:253b Dutch CC) unless she lacks the capacity for parental responsibilities at the time she gives birth (Art. 1:253b § 1 and 2 Dutch CC).

NORWAY

If the mother of a child is not married, she alone will have parental responsibilities, Art. 35 sec. 1 Norwegian Children Act 1981.

---

8 M. KARASIS, in: A. GEORGIADIS and M. STATHOPOULOS (eds.), *Civil Code commentray, Vol. VIII, Family Law (Arts. 1505-1694)*, 2nd Edition, Athens: Law & Economy, P.N. SAKKOULAS, 2003, Art. 1515 Greek CC, p. 238, No. 8; E. KOUNOUGERI-MANOLEDAKI, *Family Law*, Vol. II, 3rd Edition, Athens-Thessaloniki: SAKKOULAS, 2003, p. 248, No.10.

POLAND

Both parents, in accordance to the general regulation of Art. 93 § 1 Polish Family and Guardianship Code On the existence of parenthood; see Q 1.

PORTUGAL

When parents are not married to each other and parenthood has only been legally established with one of them, parental responsibility belongs only to that parent (Art. 1910 Portuguese CC). If parenthood has been established with both parents and they were not married when the child was born nor have they married since, then the exercise of parental responsibility falls to the parent who has custody of the child (Art. 1911 No. 1 Portuguese CC). The law presumes that the mother has custody of the child (Art. 1911 No. 2 Portuguese CC), although this presumption may be legally overturned (Art. 1911 No. 2 Portuguese CC).

If the parents were not married but live together, and have declared before the official of the Registry Office that they wish to jointly exercise parental responsibility over their child, then parental responsibility belongs to both (Art. 1911 No. 3 Portuguese CC).

RUSSIA

According to Russian law, parental responsibility is coupled to legal filiation between a child and parent rather than on marriage between the parents. The only difference if the parents are not married is that a father and child cannot acquire legal parentage, and therefore parental responsibility, by virtue of a presumption of paternity by being the husband of the mother of the child (Art. 48 (1) Russian Family Code).

Thus, parental responsibility for a child of unmarried parents belongs to:

- a legal mother of child (a women who has given birth to the child (Art. 48 (1) Russian Family Code) solely, if the legal parentage of the father has not been established;
- to the legal mother and the legal father jointly, if the father has recognised the child (Art. 48 (3) Russian Family Code) or paternity of the reluctant father has been established by a court order (Art. 49); or
- to the legal father of the child solely, if he has recognised the child (Art. 48 (3) Russian Family Code) or his paternity has been established by the court order against his will (Art. 49), if the mother of the child is unknown, has died, or has been declared by a court to have disappeared.

SPAIN

Parental responsibility is not dependent on the nature of the parent-child relationship. It is therefore irrelevant whether the parents are married; what matters is that parenthood has been established. If parenthood is established as regards both parents, parental responsibility is vested equally on both father and mother. The main difference is a presumption which establishes that a child born in wedlock is the child of both husband and wife, whereas in the case of an unmarried couple the father will have to recognise the child.

SWEDEN

The unmarried mother has sole custody, *ex lege*, of the child from the child's birth, Chapter 6 Sec. 3 para. 1 Swedish Children and Parents Code. Unmarried parents with the father's approved acknowledgement of paternity who are in agreement can obtain joint custody by means of registration with the tax authority (the authority in charge of population records in Sweden) after joint notification to the social welfare committee, Chapter 6 Sec. 4 para. 2 Swedish Children and Parents Code.

SWITZERLAND

Primarily the mother is entitled to parental responsibilities by virtue of law (Art. 298 § 1 Swiss CC). However, if the mother is a minor, has been placed under guardianship or has died, or if she has been deprived of parental responsibilities, the guardianship authority, based on Art. 298 § 2 Swiss CC, will confer parental responsibilities on the father or appoint a guardian for the child depending on the requirements of the child's welfare. 'If the parents have agreed, in an agreement which is capable of being approved, on their respective share of taking care of the child and the distribution of the costs of maintenance, the guardianship authority will confer joint parental responsibilities on them upon petition if this is reconcilable with the child's welfare' (Art. 298a § 1 Swiss CC).

QUESTION 21

C. ATTRIBUTION OF PARENTAL RESPONSIBILITIES

II. Unmarried Parents

Does it make a difference if the parents have formalised their mutual relationship in some way (registered partnership, civil union, *pacte civil de solidarité* ...).

AUSTRIA

In Austria, there is no way of formalizing a non-marital partnership (*nichteheliche Lebensgemeinschaft*). Unmarried parents can jointly assume parental responsibilities by entering into an agreement (Sec. 167 Austrian CC).

BELGIUM

No, the nature of the relationship between parents is not relevant. Only the descent of the child is important. See Q 15a.

BULGARIA

Bulgarian legislation does not regulate non-marital relationships.

CZECH REPUBLIC

The parents have parental responsibility regardless of their mutual relationship. The only condition for the arising of parental responsibility is the parent's full legal capacity to act.

DENMARK

The only way of formalizing a relationship under Danish law, besides marriage, is to register a partnership. However, a registered partnership is only open to same-sex partners.[1] A registered partnership is therefore of no relevance to the attribution of parental authority to opposite-sex parents. The only way for two same-sex persons to be parents under Danish law, is if one partner has adopted the other person's child, in other words so-called stepchild adoption, *stedbarnsadoption*. The conditions are the following: the child has not been adopted from a third country and the couple are registered as partners. If this has taken place they have joint parental authority.[2]

ENGLAND & WALES

At the time of writing English law makes no provision for registered partnerships. However, this will change when the British Civil Partnerships Act

---

1 Danish Registered Partnership Act, *Lov om registreret partnerskab*, Act No. 372, 07.06.1989, Art. 1.

2 Danish Registered Partnership Act, *Lov om registreret partnerskab*, Act No. 372, 07.06.1989, Art. 4(1) and Danish Act on Parental Authority and Contact, Art. 4.

2004 is brought into force. However, under Sec. 1 of that Act, partnerships will be restricted to same sex couples. Consequently, short of marriage, there is no mechanism by where the mother and father of a child can formalise their relationship.

FINLAND

In Finland a registered partnership only concerns partners of the same sex (Sec. 1 Finnish Act Concerning Registered Partnership (No. 950/2001)). The rules of the Paternity Act concerning paternity based on marriage shall not be implemented to the registered partnership (Sec. 9 of the same Act). This means that a partner of a mother may not gain the legal position of a parent.

FRANCE

No. French legal provisions do not have regard to this criterion but instead see if both parents acknowledged the child soon enough after the child's birth.

GERMANY

In German law, the only way mixed-sex couples may formalise their relationship is through marriage. The Registered Partnership Act of 16 February 2001, which offers the opportunity to formalise a relationship, applies only to same-sex partners. Since a major reform of the Registered Partnership Act, which took effect on 1 January 2005, a same-sex partner living in a registered partnership can adopt the child of his or her partner, § 9 para. 7 Registered Partnership Act. A bill providing for joint adoption[3] by registered partners was rejected (see answer to Q 28 for further details).

GREECE

In Greece there is no way to formalise or legalise a relationship other than marriage.[4]

HUNGARY

Hungarian law does not recognise any form of the formalised relationship, including registered partnerships, civil unions and *pacte civil de solidarité*.

IRELAND

No, it makes no difference.

ITALY

No, it does not make any difference. Our legal system does not provide any kind of formalised relationship.

---

3 See Art. 2 para. 1 No. 2-9 of the draft legislation prepared by the FDP faction to amend the Registered Partnership Act, dated 11 February 2004, BT-Drucks. 15/2477 pp. 29, 31.

4 An engagement (Art. 1346-1349 Greek CC) is a mere promise to marry and, as such, it cannot be considered as a separate method of formalising a relationship.

LITHUANIA
No, it does not make any difference.

THE NETHERLANDS
When registered partnership was introduced in 1998 it had no legal consequences for the children of the partners. However since 2001, Art. 1:253aa Dutch CC gives parents joint parental responsibilities over children born during their registered partnership. If the biological father has not recognised his child, he will also be attributed joint parental responsibilities with the mother over a child born during their registered partnership, unless legal family ties exist between the child and another parent (Art. 1:253sa Dutch CC).

NORWAY
It does not make any difference if the parents have formalised their mutual relationship.

POLAND
Polish law does not recognise those institutions.

PORTUGAL
No.

RUSSIA
No.

SPAIN
No, as long as parental responsibility is established as reragrds both parents, both will jointly hold parental responsibilities. There is no presumption that a child born to one of the members of a registered partnership is the child of the other partner. The father will have to recognise the child in exactly the same way he would have had to if the parents had not formalised their relationship.

SWEDEN
At present, *ex lege* effect is only given to the parents' marriage. A proposal is under consideration that would automatically grant unmarried parents joint custody of the child three months after the determination of paternity, on the condition that neither of the parents opposes joint custody.[5]

SWITZERLAND
Swiss legislation does not presently contemplate any arrangements of this kind. As to registered partnership of partners of the same sex (which has been passed by both legislative bodies of the Swiss Confederation but still has to be approved in a referendum), a new Art. 27 deals with the position of the partner who is not a parent.[6] Q 27b also refers to this matter.

---

5 See Ds 1999:57, above under Q 6.

6 See Q 6.

QUESTION 22

C. ATTRIBUTION OF PARENTAL RESPONSIBILITIES

II. Unmarried Parents

Under what condition, if at all, can
(a) The unmarried mother obtain parental responsibilities;
(b) The unmarried father obtain parental responsibilities.

AUSTRIA

(a) The unmarried mother obtain parental responsibilities

By operation of law, the unmarried mother is entitled to sole parental responsibilities for the child born out of wedlock (Sec. 166 Austrian CC). If the mother is still a minor, the public youth welfare agency assumes legal representation and administration of the child's property at birth (Sec. 145a and 211 Austrian CC).

(b) The unmarried father obtain parental responsibilities

If the parents live in the same household, they can enter into an agreement that both parents will be entrusted with parental responsibilities in the future. In such a case, the father is always entitled to full parental responsibilities (Sec. 167 (1) Austrian CC).

If the parents do not live in the same household, they can agree that the father will also be entrusted with full or partial parental responsibilities in the future, if at the same time they submit an agreement to the court indicating the parent with whom the child will primarily reside. If the child will primarily reside in the father's household, the father must be entrusted with full parental responsibilities. Despite such an agreement, however, either parent may petition the court to end joint parental responsibilities without substantiation at any time (Sec. 167(2) in conjunction with Sec. 177a(2) Austrian CC).

All the aforementioned agreements must be reviewed by the court based on the best interests of the child and approved if a positive evaluation is made (Sec. 167(1) and (2) Austrian CC).

BELGIUM

(a) The unmarried mother

Being the legal mother is enough to obtain parental responsibilities. See Q 15a.

(b) The unmarried father

Being the legal father is enough to obtain parental responsibilities. See Q 15a.

BULGARIA

(a) The unmarried mother

See Q 15a.

(b) The unmarried father
He can recognise the child. As the Bulgarian Family Code stipulates:

PARENTAGE
Art. 35. Each parent may establish parentage with his or her child. It is also possible to establish parentage with conceived children, as well as deceased children who have left descendants.

FORM OF PARENTAGE
Art. 36. (1) Parentage is established personally with a written declaration submitted to the Civil Registrar or by a declaration with the signature attested by the notary public, filed with the officer for civil status. The declaration may be forwarded through the manager of the establishment where the child has been born.
(2) (New - SG, No. 63 of 2003) The Civil Registrar shall notify the other parent of the establishment of parentage, if he or she is known, the child, if having reached full age, and the Social Assistance Directorate within 7 days from carrying the action.

PROTESTING PARENTAGE ESTABLISHED BY THE OTHER PARENT AND THE CHILD
Art. 37. (1) (Rev. - SG, no. 63 of 2003). The parent or the child may protest the establishment of parentage with a request in writing to the Civil Registrar within three months of the notification. Where parentage is not protested it shall be entered on the birth certificate.
(2) When parentage is protested, the person that has declared it may, within a three-month term of the receipt of notification file a claim for the establishment of origin.
(3) Where, as of the time of the establishment of parentage, the child has not attained the age of majority, he or she may protest such an action within three years of attaining the age of majority or from becoming aware of such an establishment of parentage, if he or she has become aware of it at a later time. If the claim is respected, the establishment of parentage shall be deleted from the birth certificate with the respective note in the certificate.
If the fatherhood has been established in the above way the father acquires parental responsibilities.

CZECH REPUBLIC

(a) The unmarried mother
The unmarried mother acquires parental responsibility at the moment of the child's birth. The only condition for the arising of parental responsibility is the parent's full legal capacity to act.

(b) The unmarried father
The unmarried father acquires parental responsibility at the moment of his paternity determination; this takes place by a consensual declaration of the parents or by a court decision. The proceedings on the determination of paternity are linked with the proceedings on regulation of the relationships

between the parents and the minor child *i.e.* the court decides at the same time on placing the child into someone's upbringing - care (typically, the mother) and on setting up maintenance of the father (Sec. 113 Czech Civil Procedure Code).

DENMARK

(a) The unmarried mother

The unmarried mother either has sole parental authority or joint parental authority, Art. 5 Danish Act on Parental Authority and Contact. If the mother has agreed to transfer parental authority to the father or to another person, or parental authority has been transferred to the father by a court order, the only way to re-obtain parental authority is by means of an agreement with the holder(s) of parental authority (sole or joint) or by a court order (sole), Art. 6, 11 and 13 Danish Act on Parental Authority and Contact. The criteria for transferring sole parental authority by a court order are strict. Special reasons must be present and it must be considered to be the best solution for the child, especially due to changed circumstances, Art. 13 Danish Act on Parental Authority and Contact.

(b) The unmarried father

The unmarried father who does not have joint parental authority can obtain joint parental authority with the agreement with the holder (the mother) of parental authority, Art. 6 Danish Act on Parental Authority and Contact. He can also obtain sole parental authority by way of an agreement with the holder(s) of parental authority, Art. 11 Danish Act on Parental Authority and Contact. Further, he can obtain sole parental authority by way of a court order. There are three separate procedures. The father who has cohabitated with the mother for a longer period, but not shared parental authority, and who applies for sole parental authority immediately after the break-up has an equal right to obtain sole parental authority as the mother, Art. 12(1) Danish Act on Parental Authority and Contact. This procedure gives the unmarried cohabitating father without parental authority the same legal position at the time of the relationship termination as the unmarried cohabitating father who shares joint parental authority with the mother and even as the married father. Secondly, if the father has not cohabitated with the mother for a longer period or seeks sole parental authority long after the relationship has broken up, he may only obtain a court order where the change is better for the child, Art. 12(2). Thirdly, if the father has had sole parental authority and has lost it through an agreement or a court order and seeks to re-obtain sole parental authority, the criteria are strict; special reasons must be present and it must be considered to be the best solution for the child, especially due to changed circumstances, Art. 13 Danish Act on Parental Authority and Contact.

ENGLAND & WALES

(a) The unmarried mother

By Sec. 2(2), English Children Act 1989 all unmarried mothers automatically have parental responsibility.

(b) The unmarried father

Apart from marrying the mother[1] the unmarried father can acquire parental responsibility in a number of different ways. The most likely means of acquiring responsibility is by being named as the father on the child's birth certificate. This is provided for in an amendment to the English Children Act 1989 by the English Adoption and Children Act 2002,[2] which came into force in December 2003.[3] Since under English law, unmarried fathers have no unilateral right formally to register themselves as the father, registration must be done either by the mother or with her written authorisation.[4] Another means by which responsibility can be acquired is by making a formal parental responsibility agreement with the mother.[5] This has to be made on a prescribed form[6] and signed before a court official[7] but is not subject to a formal court scrutiny. Clearly, the need to make agreements has been substantially reduced by conferring responsibility upon those formally registered as the father. An even less common way of acquiring parental responsibility is by being formally appointed as guardian either by the child's mother or by the court in accordance with Sec. 5, English Children Act 1989. Such an appointment can only take effect after the mother's death.

There are two other means for unmarried fathers to acquire parental responsibility, namely, by having a parental responsibility order made in his favour, pursuant to Sec. 4(1)(c) of the 1989 Act, or by having a residence order made in his favour in which case a separate Sec. 4 parental responsibility order must be made.[8] Effectively it is through either of these means that unmarried fathers can hope to acquire responsibility notwithstanding the mother's opposition. The key difference between these proceedings is that in the former the applicant father is only seeking parental responsibility whereas in the latter he is primarily seeking an order by which the child is to live with him with allocation of responsibility only a consequence should the residence order be made. In both proceedings the court is governed by the welfare principle, that is, in determining whether to grant the order, the court must treat the child's welfare as its paramount consideration.[9] However, whereas in parental responsibility order proceedings the court will apply the welfare principle to

---

1 In which case, provided the child is under 18, the father will have brought himself within s 2(1), English Children Act 1989 as interpreted in light of Sec. 1, English Family Law Reform Act 1987 (see Q 15).

2 See Sec. 111, English Adoption and Children Act 2002, amending Sec. 4, Children Act 1989.

3 See English Adoption and Children Act 2002 (Commencement No. 4) Order 2003, SI 2003/3079.

4 See Sec. 10 and 10A, English Births and Deaths Registration Act 1953.

5 See Sec. 4(1)(b), English Children Act 1989.

6 Sec. 4(2), English Children Act 1989.

7 See the English Parental Responsibility Agreements Regulation 1991, SI 1991/1478, as amended.

8 See Sec. 12(1), English Children Act 1989.

9 *I.e.* Sec. 1(1), English Children Act 1989 applies.

determine whether parental responsibility should be granted to the father, in residence order applications the court will apply the welfare principle only to decide with whom the child is to live. As WAITE J commented in *Re CB (A Minor)(Parental Responsibility Order)*:[10]

> 'there is an unusual duality in the character of a parental responsibility order: it is on the one hand sufficiently ancillary by nature to pass automatically to the natural father without enquiry of any kind when a residence order is made in his favour; and, on the other hand, sufficiently independent, when severed from the context of a residence order, to require detailed consideration upon its merits as a free-standing remedy in its own right'.

FINLAND

(a) The unmarried mother

The biological mother of the child is always a custodian at the birth of the child.

(b) The unmarried father

An unmarried father primarily obtains the custody of the child by virtue of an agreement with the mother. A precondition to this is the confirmed paternity of the unmarried father (Sec. 7 and 8 Finnish Child Custody and the Right of Access Act). Normally an unmarried couple makes an agreement concerning joint custody soon after the birth of the child (see Q 19). After the approval of the agreement concerning the joint custody of the parents, their position does not differ in any way from that of married parents. The parents can also agree that the father has sole custody, although this seems to be extremely rare.

An unmarried father can obtain custodial rights through a court decision, if he cannot reach an agreement about custodial rights with the mother. Both parents have the right to submit an application to the court concerning custody or the child's right of access (Sec. 14 and Sec. 9 Finnish Child Custody and the Right of Access Act). The court can vest the custody on both parents jointly or on one of them alone, as it deems, in accordance with the best interests of the child.

FRANCE

(a) The unmarried mother

Most of the time when a child is acknowledged by only one parent, it is by the mother. Therefore if only the mother has acknowledged the child,[11] she is sole holder of parental responsibilities. The same applies if the father acknowledges the child more than one year after the child's birth, or if the paternity is not established by voluntary recognition but instead by judicial decision (Art. 372 §

---

10 [1993] 1 FLR 920 at 929.

11 The recognition by the mother can be implicit when the mother's name is mentioned in the birth certificate and the child has *possession d'état* (because the child has been treated by the woman as her child, it is considered to be hers), see Art. 337 French CC.

2 French CC). In these two situations, only the parent that has acknowledged the child (or the parent that acknowledged first) has parental responsibilities. This is usually the mother. The attribution of parental responsibilities is automatic in such cases and does not require a judicial decision. The parent (mother or father) who is the sole holder of parental responsibilities has almost the same rights and duties as the parents who are both holders of parental responsibilities. Only the legal administration for acts of disposition is subject to some restrictions (see Q 11).

(b) The unmarried father

The same rules apply for the unmarried father. In France it is possible for a woman to deliver a baby anonymously (*accouchement anonyme, sous X*), so it is theoretically possible for a child to be acknowledged by a father alone. In this seldom case the father is automatically sole holder of parental responsibilities.[12] See Art. 372 French CC and also the situations faced in Art. 372 para. 2 French CC. See also the details of the legal provisions under (a).

GERMANY

(a) the unmarried mother obtain parental responsibilities

In line with what was said in the answer to Q 20, German law generally provides that when the parents are not married to each other at the time of the child's birth, the mother of a child born outside marriage has sole parental responsibility, § 1626 a para. 2 German CC.

Where parental responsibilities have been withdrawn from the mother through court proceedings – for example, on the basis of § 1666 German CC (see Q 18) – the mother can reclaim them only in accordance with § 1696 German CC, i.e. through a court decision.

If the parents have made declarations of responsibility in accordance with § 1626 a para. 1 No. 1 German CC, either before or after the child's birth, and are thus jointly responsible for the child, their declarations are binding, which means that joint responsibility cannot subsequently be revoked.[13] Even if the father consents, therefore, the mother can obtain sole responsibility only in those cases where the couple has lived apart, following a court decision in accordance with § 1671 German CC.

(b) The unmarried father obtain parental responsibilities

First of all, the father of a child born out of wedlock can assume joint parental responsibility through the provisions of § 1626 a para. 1 No. 1 German CC, in

[12] For a very complicated case in which the father recognised his paternity before the mother anonymously delivered the child and entrusted it to spouses in order to be adopted by them, see CA Nancy, 23.02.2004, *D.* 2004. P. 2249 annotated POISSON-DROCOURT.

[13] U. DIEDERICHSEN, in: PALANDT, *Bürgerliches Gesetzbuch*, 64th Edition, Munich: Beck, 2005, § 1626 a No. 9.

agreement with the child's mother, by means of the relevant declarations of responsibility. The Child Law Reform Act through § 1626 a para. 1 No. 1 German CC has provided the parents of a child born outside marriage with the opportunity to take joint legal responsibility for the child. The Act is founded on a concept of organising parental responsibilities, the touchstone of which is the parents' consensual desire to assume joint responsibility, being guided by considerations of the child's best interests. The fact that the father is not able to obtain parental responsibility against the will of the mother does not, in the opinion of the Federal Constitutional Court - in contrast to a widely held view in legal literature[14] - violate the parental rights of the father as protected by Art. 6 para. 2 German Basic Law.[15] The joint exercise of parental responsibilities presupposes a functioning social relationship between the parents, requires at least a minimum of consensus between them and must be geared to the child's best interest. In contrast to the case of parents of children born in wedlock, who through marriage undertook to take responsibility for one another and for any common children, the legislature cannot generally assume even today, according to the court, that unmarried parents live in a common household, are able to care for their child, and wish to do so. The child's best interests, however, demand that the child from his or her birth onwards has a person who can take legally binding actions on his or her behalf. This could not be ensured if the question of who is to represent the child were to be, after the child's birth, a matter requiring the clarification of the court. The assignment of parental responsibilities to the mother on principle is, according to the court, also justified because the legislator has afforded unmarried couples who wish to take responsibility for their child together, the opportunity, by way of § 1626 a para. 1 No. 1 German CC, to do so through a joint declaration of responsibility. If such is made, it justifies the assumption that consensual cooperation between them will be possible.[16] The court considers that joint responsibility enforced against the will of one parent has proven to have more disadvantages than advantages for the child.[17] The legislature was justified to assume that in instances where the necessary willingness to cooperate required for joint responsibility existed between parents, parents generally did in fact make use of the opportunity afforded them and legally safeguarded their factual joint responsibility through a legal declaration. Based on this assumption, according to the court, it is not a violation of Art. 6 para. 2 German Basic Law to rule out joint responsibility in the absence of a joint declaration. Still working under the assumption that the lawmakers' prognosis is correct, the Constitutional Court also denies a violation of Art. 6 para. 5 German Basic Law, which mandates that children born out of wedlock be given the same

---

14 M. LIPP, 'Das elterliche Sorgerecht für das nichteheliche Kind nach dem Kindschaftsrechtsreformgesetz', *FamRZ* 1998, 65, 70. ; P. HUBER, in: *Münchener Kommentar zum Bürgerlichen Gesetzbuch*, 4th Edition, Munich: Beck, 2002, § 1626 a No. 39-42.

15 BVerfG 29.01.2003, *NJW* 2003, 955, 956.

16 BVerfG 29.01.2003, *NJW* 2003, 955, 957.

17 BVerfG 29.01.2003, *NJW* 2003, 955, 958.

conditions for their development as children born within. In the court's opinion, neither does the provision of § 1626 a German CC violate the rule of equality under Art. 3 para. 1 German Basic Law.[18] The mother's consent to joint responsibility is required in the case of a father of a child born outside marriage and of a father of a child born within marriage, the difference being that in the latter case, the declaration of consent is given in the consent to marry, while in the former it is given through a declaration of parental responsibility.

The Constitutional Court does, however, see the necessity of reviewing the validity of the lawmaker's prognosis. Should it turn out that in a substantial number of cases, even when the parents live with their children, joint responsibility is not legally secured and that this is not due to reasons connected with the child's welfare, then the denial of the father's right to participate in the child's upbringing does in fact violate his parental rights pursuant to Art. 6 para. 2 German Basic Law.[19]

Furthermore, the family court is obliged to transfer parental responsibility to the father of the child born outside marriage following the death of the mother, who had sole parental responsibility in accordance with § 1626 a para. 2 German CC, provided that this serves the best interests of the child, § 1680 para. 2 sent. 2 German CC.

Finally, the family court can transfer parental responsibility to the father of the child born outside marriage within the scope, and subject to the preconditions, of § 1666 German CC (see Q 18).

Regarding the situation of unmarried couples living apart, see the answer to Q 23.

GREECE

(a) The unmarried mother

The unmarried mother obtains parental responsibilities at the moment of the child's birth (Art. 1515 para. 1 Greek CC).

(b) The unmarried father

Until the father acknowledges the child as his own, his relationship with the child is not established. Thus, the unmarried father can only take part in the parental care if he acknowledges the child as his own. The extent to which he can exercise his parental responsibilities depends on the form of the acknowledgement. For further details see the answer to Q 20.

---

18 BVerfG 29.01.2003, *NJW* 2003, 955, 960.

19 BVerfG 29.01.2003, *NJW* 2003, 955, 956, 959.

HUNGARY

(a) The unmarried mother

An unmarried mother's parental responsibilities arise automatically unless the mother is a minor at the time of the child's birth. The extent of her parental responsibilities are identical to those of a married mother. The unmarried mother either exercises parental responsibilities with the unmarried father or she has sole parental responsibilities, depending on whether the father and mother live together.

If the unmarried mother is a minor when the child is born, a guardian will be appointed to exercise parental responsibilities until the mother reaches majority. This is not a rare occurrence in Hungary. This issue does not emerge for a minor mother who is married, as the minor's marriage results in majority.

(b) The unmarried father

The unmarried father's parental responsibilities do not arise automatically. These come about as the consequence of two conditions: one is that the unmarried father should have legal affiliation towards the child; the other is that the father should live with the mother in a relationship that has not been formalised.

The father's legal affiliation can be established either by voluntary recognition or by judicial decision. The legal status established by recognition has importance with respect to parental responsibilities because a father whose legal affiliation is established by judicial decision generally does not want to take part in the exercise of parental responsibilities. The number of the legal affiliations established by recognition increases parallel to the increasing number of non-formalised partnerships.

The conditions for the recognition of an unmarried father are similar those required for a subsequent marriage. This recognition can be made with respect to the unborn child who is already conceived.

If the recognition is made by a father who is still a minor, which is rarer than mothers under 18 who give birth, the father's parental responsibilities are suspended until he reaches majority.

IRELAND

(a) The unmarried mother

Where a child is born to parents who are not married to each other at the time of birth, only the unmarried mother will be deemed to be a guardian. The Supreme Court has considered the constitutional rights of the unmarried mother in a number of cases. The unmarried mother has a natural right to the custody and care of her child and such other natural personal rights as she may have fall to be protected under Art. 40.3 (personal rights clause) Irish Constitution.

O'HIGGINS C.J. in *G. v. An Bord Uchtála*[20] indicated that the rights of the non-marital mother are neither inalienable nor imprescriptible, unlike the rights of the marital family under Art. 41 Irish Constitution. Her rights can be alienated or transferred in whole or in part and can be lost, if her conduct towards the child amounts to an abandonment or abdication of her rights and duties. In summary, the unmarried mother has a constitutional right (under Art. 40.3 Irish Constitution) and a statutory right (under Sec. 6 Irish Guardianship of Infants Act 1964) to the guardianship and custody of her child.

(b) The unmarried father

The unmarried father has no automatic right to the guardianship or custody of his child. The hardship of this rule is obviated by a series of exceptions:

- a natural father may become guardian of his child upon marriage to the mother thereof, notwithstanding the fact that this occurs after the birth of the child;
- since 1988, the natural father of a child may, notwithstanding the fact that he is not married to its mother, apply to the court to be appointed a guardian under Sec. 6A of the 1964 Act.[21] Such appointment, however, shall not affect the guardianship status of any other person in relation to the child who is the subject of the order.

Despite these new powers, the court is not obliged to grant guardianship status to every natural father. The decision in *J.K. v. V.W.*[22] underlines this point. There the Supreme Court held that while a father is entitled by virtue of Sec. 6A to apply to be made guardian, it did not confer any automatic right to be appointed as such. In a similar vein, the court noted that the insertion of Sec. 6A did not, despite the spirit of equality inspiring the Irish Status of Children Act 1987, confer upon the natural father of a child the automatic rights of guardianship enjoyed by a father of a child born within marriage. In the course of his decision, FINLAY C.J. noted that:

> '...the discretion vested in the Court on the making of such an application must be exercised regarding the welfare of the infant as the first and paramount consideration. The blood link between the infant and the father and the possibility for the infant to have the benefit of the guardianship by and the society of its father is one of the many factors which may be viewed by the court as relevant to its welfare...'.[23]

The matters that will be taken into account in proceedings under Sec. 6A were alluded to in the Supreme Court decision in *W.O'R. v. E.H. and An Bord*

20 [1980] I.R. 32.
21 As inserted by Sec. 12 of the Irish Status of Children Act 1987.
22 [1990] 2 I.R. 437.
23 *Ibid.* at 447.

Uchtála.[24] That case, like *J.K. v. V.W.*[25] involved the adoption of a non-marital child. Amongst the matters that arose was the character and extent of the rights that the natural father had in respect of his child. The Supreme Court, while reiterating the predominant position of the child's welfare in such proceedings, did also consider the weight to be given to the blood link between the father and the child. The blood link alone, it noted, was not a factor sufficient of itself to give rise to a judgment favourable to the father in an application to be appointed guardian under Sec. 6A. Where, however, the child had been born into a stable and established home environment and cared for by both father and mother, the Court suggested that the father's prospects of success were considerably stronger. The blood link, combined with the interest and concern that arose from the father's close connection to the child, might give rise to more substantial rights in respect of the child. In a disputed application to be appointed a guardian under Sec. 6A the court generally looks at a variety of factors which include:

- the circumstances surrounding the birth of the child;
- the relationship between the parents;
- the way in which parental responsibilities have been shared;
- the history of access up to the date of the application.

ITALY

(a) The unmarried mother

The unmarried mother can obtain parental responsibilities if she lives with the child or if she was the first to recognise the child, unless the judge decides that the child's best interests require otherwise.

(b) The unmarried father

The unmarried father can obtain parental responsibilities if he lives with the child or if he was the first to recognise the child, unless the judge decides that the child's best interests require otherwise.

LITHUANIA

(a) The unmarried mother

Parental responsibilities are statutory obligations which arise independently from the existence of marriage. The only source of such statutory obligations is filiation because the mutual rights and duties of the child and its parents shall be based on the filiation of the child *i.e.* on the blood (biological) relationship between a child and the mother. According to Art. 3.139 Lithuanian CC, a woman shall be entered as a child's mother in the records of the Registry of the Civil Status Acts on the basis of the certificate of the child's birth issued by a hospital. Where the child is not born in a hospital, a certificate of the child's birth shall be issued by the medical centre that performs the postnatal examination of the mother and the baby's health. If a child is not born in a hospital and no postnatal examinations of the mother and the baby's health are

---

24 [1996] 2 I.R. 248.

25 [1990] 2 I.R. 437.

made, the certificate of the child's birth shall be issued by a consulting commission of doctors in the procedure laid down by the Government. According to this certificate, the mother of the baby is the woman who the consulting commission of doctors have no doubt gave birth to the baby concerned. If the record of the child's birth contains no data on the child's mother or if the maternity of the child has been successfully contested, the child's mother may be established by a a court action filed by the woman who considers herself to be the child's mother, by the adult child, by the child's father or guardian (curator) or by a state institution for the protection of the rights of the child.

(b) The unmarried father

The unmarried father obtains parental responsibilities in either of the two possible ways:

- by the acknowledgement of his paternity (Art. 3.141-3.145 Lithuanian CC), or
- by the declaration of his paternity by the court judgment (Art. 3.146-3.148 Lithuanian CC). An action for the establishment of paternity may be filed by the man considering himself the father of the child, the child's mother, child's guardian (curator), a state institution for the protection of the child's rights or by the child itself after having attained 18 years, or by the descendants of the child (Art. 3.148 Lithuanian CC).

THE NETHERLANDS

(a) The unmarried mother

The unmarried mother has parental responsibilities by operation of law from the moment of the birth of her child unless she lacks the capacity for parental responsibilities at the moment she gives birth (Art. 1:253b§ 1 Dutch CC). Minors, persons over whom a guardian has been appointed and persons whose mental capacity is disturbed to such an extent that they find themselves in a position where they are unable to exercise parental responsibilities, do not have the capacity to exercise parental responsibilities unless the disturbance is of a temporary nature (Art. 1:246 Dutch CC). A mother who lacks the capacity for parental responsibilities at the time she gives birth will acquire this by operation of law at the time when such capacity is vested in her unless another has already been granted parental responsibilities (Art. 1:253b § 1 Dutch CC).

(b) The unmarried father

If the unmarried mother wishes to exercise parental responsibilities together with the unmarried father, they may file their joint request with the registrar of the Custody Register kept by the District Court. The registrar will make a record of their joint parental responsibilities in the registry unless (Art. 1:252 Dutch CC) either or both parents do not have the capacity to exercise parental responsibilities, one or both parents have been divested consensually or non-consensually of parental responsibilities, custody over the child has been entrusted to a guardian, the provision in the custody of the child has ceased to exist, or the parent who has parental responsibility exercises it jointly with a person other than a parent. The registrar does not have the authority to determine whether joint parental responsibilities are in the best interests of the child, because the assumption is that joint parental responsibilities of the parents are in the best interest of the child.

If the unmarried mother does not want to exercise her parental responsibilities together with the unmarried father he can file a request for sole parental responsibilities with the court to the exclusion of the mother on the basis of Art. 1:253c Dutch CC. He can do so if he has the capacity for parental responsibility and has never exercised joint parental responsibilities with the mother. If at the time of the request the mother has sole parental responsibilities, the court will only grant the father sole parental responsibilities if this is considered to be in the best interest of the child. The Supreme Court ruled in 1998 that when dealing with such a request the court should consider the possibilities that each of the parents offers or can offer to the child without losing sight of the fact that the transfer of parental responsibilities from one parent to the other may in itself have a detrimental effect on the child.[26] It is not enough to establish that the mother is fulfilling her parental responsibilities adequately, without looking into the possibilities the father has to offer.

Recently two courts[27] have granted a father the right to request joint parental responsibilities over the child together with the mother even though the mother objected to this. The judgments were on completely different grounds. The Court of Appeal of 's Hertogenbosch replaced the mother's consent so the registrar could make a record of their joint parental responsibilities in the Custody Register kept by the District Court. The Utrecht District Court judged that if the father can ask for sole parental responsibilities to the exclusion of the mother on the basis of Art. 1:253c Dutch CC he should also be given the opportunity to ask for joint parental responsibilities. However, until the Supreme Court rules on this issue, will remain unclear whether a father does indeed have this right.

NORWAY

(a) The unmarried mother

The unmarried mother obtains parental responsibilities upon the birth of the child, Art. 35 sec. 1 Norwegian Children Act 1981,.

(b) The unmarried father

If the father and mother agree upon joint parental responsibilities and inform the National Population Register of their agreement, the agreement is legally valid, Art. 35 sec. 2 Norwegian Children Act 1981. Since the great majority of unmarried mothers live together with the father of the child, such agreements are very common. If the parents disagree as to who shall have parental

---

26 See Supreme Court 30.10.1998, *NJ*, 1999, 115.

27 Court of Appeal, 's Hertogenbosch 13.1.2004, *NJF*, 2004/273 and District Court Utrecht 28.7.2004, *LJNA*, Q9901.

responsibilities, either of them may initiate legal proceedings on this issue, according to Art. 56. According to Art. 48, the decision of the court shall first and foremost be taken on the basis of what is best for the child.

POLAND

(a) The unmarried mother

The mother always holds parental authority from the birth of the child.

(b) The unmarried father

If the father recognises the child, he always holds parental authority. Should the paternity, on the contrary, be established by the court, the father will hold parental authority only if the court grants the authority in the judgment establishing the paternity, or later (Art. 93 § 2 Polish Family and Guardianship Code).

PORTUGAL

(a) The unmarried mother

As was mentioned in Q 20, if the parents were not married when the child was born but parenthood has been established for both, then the parent that has custody of the child will exercise parental responsibility; the law presumes this to be the mother (Art. 1911 No. 1 and 2 Portuguese CC).

(b) The unmarried father

An unmarried father may exercise parental responsibility if his paternity has been legally established, he has legal custody of the child and he manages to legally overturn the presumption in Art. 1911 No. 2 Portuguese CC.

RUSSIA

(a) The unmarried mother

A mother, irrespective marital status, always acquires parental responsibility by the fact of giving birth to the child.

(b) The unmarried father

An unmarried father acquires parental responsibility if he has recognised the child (Art. 48 (3) Russian Family Code) or his paternity has been established by court order against his will (Art. 49).

SPAIN

(a) The unmarried mother

Parental responsibility is imposed on the mother of a child, regardless of her marital status, as an effect of the birth of the child. Maternity cannot be hidden or kept secret on the mother's request.

(b) The unmarried father

If paternity is established, the unmarried father generally obtains parental responsibility on exactly the same terms as the married father. However, there are two exceptions. Parental responsibility does not arise if the child was conceived as a consequence of a sexual crime, established by a final judgment, or if paternity is established after an investigation of paternity carried out in the framework of a judicial proceeding and the father opposed paternity (Art. 111 Spanish CC). Still, this does not mean that the father has no duties towards the child; the duties to take care of and maintain the child subsist.

SWEDEN

(a) The unmarried mother

The unmarried mother automatically becomes the (sole) custodian of a child from the child's birth, Chapter 6 Sec. 3 para. 1 Swedish Children and Parents Code.

(b) The unmarried father

Unmarried parents can obtain joint custody through a court order or through registration with the tax authority, Chapter 6 Sec. 4 Swedish Children and Parents Code. This registration can be done after a joint notification to the social welfare committee in connection with the father's acknowledgement of paternity, or, in certain cases, through a joint application directly to the tax authority.[28]

If the father alone wishes to change the existing custody position, he must initiate court proceedings, demanding sole or joint custody, Chapter 6 Sec. 6 Swedish Children and Parents Code.

SWITZERLAND

(a) The unmarried mother

The mother is entitled to parental responsibilities by law in accordance with Art. 298 Swiss CC; furthermore, parental responsibilities are attributed exclusively to her unless she is a minor, has been placed under guardianship or has been deprived of parental responsibilities.

(b) The unmarried father

'If the mother is a minor, has been placed under guardianship or has been deprived of parental responsibilities, the guardianship authority will confer parental responsibilities on the father or appoint a guardian for the child, depending on the requirements with regard to the child's welfare' (Art. 298 § 2 Swiss CC). However, the transfer of parental responsibilities to the father does not take place automatically; on the contrary the guardianship authority must examine whether this is also commensurate with the child's welfare. This is because if the mother reached her majority and parental responsibilities had been transferred to the father, parental responsibilities first would have to be withdrawn again from the father, on the strict conditions stipulated in Art. 311 Swiss CC, before parental responsibilities could be transferred to the mother. For this reason, the guardianship authority makes it a rule to wait until the mother reaches her majority so the parents may perhaps agree on joint parental

28 A requirement is that no custody order has previously been issued and that the child and the parents are Swedish citizens.

responsibilities. If no agreement is reached, parental responsibilities are attributed to the mother (who has reached the age of majority) by virtue of law and the guardianship over the child automatically lapses (Art. 298 § 1 Swiss CC).[29]

Based on Art. 298a § 1 Swiss CC the guardianship authority may, upon joint petition, confer joint parental responsibilities on unmarried parents on the condition that they 'have agreed, in an agreement capable of being approved, on their respective shares of the care of the child and the distribution of the costs of maintenance,' and that joint parental responsibilities are reconcilable with the child's welfare.

29 A. RUMO-JUNGO and P. LIATOWITSCH, 'Nichteheliche Lebensgemeinschaft: vermögens- und kindesrechtliche Belange', *Die Praxis des Familienrechts (fampra)*, 2004, p. 907.

QUESTION 23

C. ATTRIBUTION OF PARENTAL RESPONSIBILITIES

II. Unmarried Parents

How, if at all, is the attribution of parental responsibilities affected by the ending of the unmarried parents' relationship?

AUSTRIA

If unmarried parents permanently separate, under Sec. 167(1) Austrian CC, the same provisions apply as for divorce, annulment or nullification of the marriage (Sec. 177 and 177a Austrian CC):[1] previously agreed joint parental responsibilities continue unless the parents agree to restrict or revoke the parental responsibilities of one parent. However, in any case of joint parental responsibilities after the ending of the parents' relationship, the parents must submit an agreement to the court naming the parent with whom the child will primarily reside; this domicile parent must always be entrusted with all parental responsibilities. The court will approve the parents' agreement if it is in the best interests of the child. If the parents fail to reach an (approvable) agreement on the primary residence of the child or the attribution of parental responsibilities within a reasonable time after the ending of their relationship, the court will entrust one parent with sole parental responsibilities based on the best interests of the child - after unsuccessfully having tried to bring about an amicable solution between the parents. In practice, however, the court will usually not learn of the separation and thus not intervene unless one of the parents petitions the court.[2]

If - despite an agreement after the ending of the relationship - the exercise of joint parental responsibilities later fails, either parent may petition the court to end joint parental responsibilities without substantiation at any time. The court will then entrust one parent with sole parental responsibilities based on the best interests of the child unless a reconciliation between the parents may be brought about (Sec. 167 in conjunction with Sec. 177a(2) Austrian CC).

BELGIUM

See Q 16a.

---

1 See Q 16a and 16c.

2 J. STABENTHEINER, 'KindRÄG 2001', in: P. Rummel, *ABGB-Kommentar*, suppl. vol. 1, 3rd Edition, Vienna: Manz Verlag, 2003, § 167 Marg. No. 8.

BULGARIA

The separation of the unmarried couple does not affect the attribution of parental responsibilities.[3] See Q 14.

CZECH REPUBLIC

If the parents of a minor child do not cohabit and do not come to an agreement concerning the upbringing and maintenance of the child, the court may decide, even without a motion, who will be awarded the care of the child and how each of the parents will contribute to the child's maintenance (Sec. 50 Czech Family Code). This regulation also concerns the parents who are married but factually separated.

DENMARK

The attribution is only changed in the sense that the parents may apply for sole parental authority on the basis of the relationship's termination, Art. 8 and 12 Danish Act on Parental Authority and Contact.

ENGLAND & WALES

The ending of the unmarried parents' relationship has in itself no effect upon the attribution of parental responsibility. The unmarried mother automatically has parental responsibility and the court has no power to divest her of it. Once an unmarried father has acquired parental responsibility, it can only be ended by a specific court order to that effect under Sec. 4(3), English Children Act 1989. Such orders can only be made upon application by any person who has parental responsibility for the child (this will include the father himself) or, with leave of the court, the child.[4] In the latter case leave can only be granted if the court is satisfied that the child has sufficient understanding to make the application.[5]

FINLAND

The ending of the unmarried parents' relationship has no legal effect on the custodial rights of the parents.

FRANCE

As with married couples who separate, the attribution of parental responsibilities is not, in principle, affected by the unmarried parents ending

3 Judicial theory and practice admit that by issuing the residence order, the regime of parental rights is solved automatically, despite the absence of explicit regulation. See Cases 261-1974 (Civil Division); 669-1992 (Civil Division); 1218-1999 (Civil Division). Also, an analogy is admissible with divorce arrangements, without the effect of the *ex officio* principle – Cases 1781-1978-I (Civil Division), 606-1982-II (Civil Division). However, it is admitted that, regarding the current situation, there is a lack of power for the court to make the full arrangements. See L. Nenova, *Family Law of the Republic of Bulgaria*, Sofia 1994, p. 424-5 and T. Tzankova, *Factual Spouse Cohabitation*, Sofia, Feneya, 2000, p. 134-6.

4 Sec. 4(3), English Children Act 1989.

5 Sec. 4(4), English Children Act 1989.

their relationship. See Art. 373-2 French CC. Each mother and father maintain personal relationships with the child. But with married couples (see Q 16 and Q 18), the judge can attribute the exercise of parental responsibilities to only one parent 'if the child's interests requires it' (Art. 373-2-1 French CC).

GERMANY

If the mother had sole parental responsibility in accordance with § 1626 a para. 2 German CC before the separation, the situation remains unchanged by the separation. If the parents held joint parental responsibilities before the separation on the basis of § 1626 a para. 1 No. 1 German CC (declarations of responsibility), the joint responsibilities will continue after separation; with respect to the special arrangements regarding joint parental responsibilities in the event of the parents living apart, the provisions of § 1687 German CC must be taken into consideration (see Q 16a).

GREECE

The attribution of parental responsibilities when the parents are not married is not linked to their relationship. Thus the ending of the parents' relationship does not directly affect parental responsibilities. Nevertheless, the ending of the relationship does constitute a change of circumstances and, as such, it entitles each parent to request the court to adjust the decision on parental care according to the new circumstances (Art. 1536 Greek CC). This has a practical significance in the case where the exercise of parental care was initially attributed to both parents.

HUNGARY

If the unmarried parents' relationship comes to an end they are given the legal status of parents who live apart. Their joint parental responsibilities do not automatically come to an end, they can arrange it either by agreement (even by an informal agreement) or by filing an action in the court that decides on the placement of the child.

In this proceeding, similar to a proceeding on the placement of a child after divorce, the court will generally use its discretion to attribute parental responsibilities to the parent with whom the child continues to live. The non-resident parent has the right to decide important matters concerning the child with the parental responsibilities holder and, of course, also has the right and duty to contact with the child.

IRELAND

It is not affected.

ITALY

The ending of a cohabitant's relationship is treated the same as a separation, divorce or annulment of a marriage (see Q 16). The parent holding the custody has full parental responsibility, meaning the right to make all decisions regarding the child's daily life. Both parents must make decisions concerning issues of major importance for the children; otherwise, a solution will be made at the discretion of the judge. The parent not living with the child has the right and duty to supervise the child's moral guidance and education, and can at any time petition the judge concerning decisions the other parent has made which prejudice the child. The non-residential parent also has the right to visit the child and have the child stay with her or him for a certain period, respecting the methods determined by the court. Other members of the family also have the right to visit the child if it is considered necessary for the development of the child (see Q 43-48).

The non-residential parent can obtain limited parental responsibilities. If the judge has not ordered joint parental responsibilities at the request of the parents (see Q 16), the non-residential parent has the right and duty to make decisions with the other parent regarding issues of major importance for the child. The parent not living with the child also has the right and duty to supervise the child's moral guidance and education, and can at any time petition the judge concerning decisions the other parent has made which prejudice the child. The non-residential parent also has the right to visit the child and have the child stay with him or her for a certain period, respecting the methods determined by the court (Art. 155 § 3 and Art. 6 § 4 Italian CC). Other members of the family also have the right to visit the child, if it is considered necessary for the development of the child (see Q 43-48).

LITHUANIA

The ending of the unmarried parent's relationship does not affect the attribution of parental responsibilities. However, it may cause disputes between the parents regarding the exercise of their parental responsibilities. Also, according to Art. 3.190 Lithuanian CC, where the parents are separated, the right to manage the minor's property shall belong to the parent with whom the child lives.

THE NETHERLANDS

The ending of the relationship in itself has no effect on the attribution of parental responsibilities. If the parents have not acquired joint parental responsibilities and the mother has sole parental responsibilities, the father may apply to the court for sole parental responsibility over the child (Art. 1:253c Dutch CC). If the mother exercises parental responsibility over the child the court will only grant the father's application if it is considered to be in the best interests of the child.[6] If the parents have acquired joint parental responsibilities, the ending of the relationship has no effect on the attribution of parental responsibilities. In a recent decision[7] the Supreme Court ruled that even though the joint parental responsibilities had come about by the choice of the parents, a request from one of the parents to terminate the joint parental responsibilities is not a sufficient ground for attributing parental responsibilities

6 Details regarding recent case law are provided under Q 22.

7 See Supreme Court 28.3.2003, *NJ*, 2003, 359.

to one of the parents. Only if the court, after further investigation, determines that it is in the best interests of the child to attribute parental responsibilities to one of the parents, can such a decision be made. The Court based the decision on the fact that Art. 8 of ECHR does not allow for a distinction to be made between joint parental responsibilities that were attributed by operation of law after divorce and joint parental responsibilities that came about by choice without proper justification. This means that the same strict criteria applied after divorce for the attribution of parental responsibilities to one of the parents also apply after the termination of the relationship. If the parents' relationship comes to an end by virtue of the annulment of their registered partnership, this will, contrary to the annulment of a marriage, have consequences for the joint parental responsibilities that have come about by reason of the registered partnership.[8] If a marriage is annulled the consequences with regard to the couple's children are the same as in the case of divorce.[9] On the other hand, should a registered partnership be annulled, the position of the children is as if the registered partnership never existed.[10] When registered partnership was inserted in the Dutch CC in 1998, the legislature failed to accordingly amend important provisions, such as the one that relates to the annulment of a registered partnership.[11]

NORWAY

If an unmarried couple end their relationship and both have parental responsibilities, it does not affect the attribution of their parental responsibilities. But one of the parents, under the same conditions as married couples, may obtain a court decision that grants the said parent sole parental responsibilities, Art. 56 Norwegian Children Act 1981. According to Art. 48, the decision of the court shall first and foremost be taken on the basis of what is best for the child.

If one of the parents had sole parental responsibilities during the relationship, the attribution of parental responsibilities is not affected if the relationship ends. If the parents disagree as to who shall have parental responsibilities in the future, either of them may initiate legal proceedings on this issue, according to Article 56. According to Article 48, the decision of the court shall first and foremost be taken on the basis of what is best for the child.

POLAND

It does not affect the attribution.

---

8 See A. NUYTINCK, 'Nietigverklaard partnerschap en gezag', *FJR*, 2004, p. 81.

9 Art. 77 (2)(a) Dutch CC.

10 Non-application of Art. 77(2)(a) Dutch CC to registered partnerships.

11 A proposal of law (*Kamerstukken Tweede Kamer*, 2003-2004, No. 29353) was introduced in parliament in December 2003 containing a number of changes in Book 1 Dutch CC with regard to registered partnerships. This proposal does not yet however contain changes with regard to the annulment of a registered partnership.

PORTUGAL

The ending of the unmarried parents' relationship also has consequences for the exercise of parental responsibility. If parenthood has been established for both unmarried parents, the rules regulating the exercise of parental responsibility following divorce, legal separation, the declaration of nullity or annulment of marriage and factual separation of parents apply (Art. 1904 to 1907 and 1912 Portuguese CC).

RUSSIA

Ending of the unmarried parents' relationship has no affect on joint parental responsibility of both parents.

SPAIN

As with married couples, paternal responsibility is not affected by the end of a relationship; but since the end of the relationship usually means that parents cease to live together, there will be consequences in regard to the exercise of parental responsibility. See Q 18.

SWEDEN

The ending of the unmarried parents' relationship does not affect the attribution of parental responsibilities. The existing custody position remains after a separation. For it to be changed, a court order or an approved agreement between the parents is necessary.

SWITZERLAND

In principle, the end of the unmarried parents' relationship does not affect the attribution of parental responsibilities. Nonetheless the ending of the relationship may be of significance if the unmarried parents jointly exercised parental responsibilities until this time and if upon dissolution of the joint household a parental partnership of the necessary extent no longer exists. In accordance with Art. 298a § 2 Swiss CC, 'upon the request of one parent, the child or the guardianship authority . . . the attribution of parental responsibilities is to be reorganised by the guardianship authority, if this is necessary for the child's welfare due to significant changes in circumstances' (Art. 298a § 2 Swiss CC).

QUESTION 24

C. ATTRIBUTION OF PARENTAL RESPONSIBILITIES

II. Unmarried Parents

May the competent authority attribute joint parental responsibilities to the parents also against the wish of both parents/one of the parents? To what extent, if at all, may the competent authority take into account a parent's violent behaviour towards the other parent?

AUSTRIA

With unmarried parents as well, there can be no joint parental responsibilities against the will of one or both parents. If despite a previous agreement a parent later petitions the court to end joint parental responsibilities, or if after the ending of their relationship the parents are unable to reach an (approvable) agreement on the primary residence of the child or the attribution of parental responsibilities, the court must attribute sole parental responsibilities to one of them (Sec. 167 and 177a Austrian CC).[1] When deciding which parent to entrust with sole parental responsibilities the court must also take into account a parent's violent behaviour toward the other.[2]

BELGIUM

See Q 18.

BULGARIA

No it may not. It is not possible even when based on the wish of both parents. See Q 18.

CZECH REPUBLIC

Joint parental responsibility arises for both parents by operation of law, regardless of their will, under one condition; that the parent has full legal capacity to act. The competent authority cannot take into account a parent's violent behaviour towards the other parent. The competent authority may take into account only a parent's violent behaviour towards the child, and it does so by depriving the parent of parental responsibility if the parent seriously abuses or neglects his or her parental responsibility or its exercise (Sec. 44 § 3 Czech Family Code). If it is in the interests of the child, the court may restrict or prohibit the contact of such a parent with the child (Sec. 27 § 3 Czech Family Code). This may happen if the child witnesses violent behaviour towards the parent it lives with.

---

1 For details see Q 22, 23 and 25.

2 For the requirement of good behaviour (Sec. 145b Austrian CC) see Q 16 at the end.

DENMARK

Joint parental authority cannot be attributed to parents who no longer live together or intend to live separately against the wish of one or both parents, Art. 8 Danish Act on Parental Authority and Contact.

ENGLAND & WALES

The attribution of parental responsibility to the mother is automatic and the courts have no powers to alter that attribution. As the answer to Q 22b states unmarried fathers can acquire parental responsibility in different ways. Insofar as it is acquired by reason of registration on the birth register as the father it is automatic and the courts' only power to end it is where a specific application is made to that effect under Sec. 4(3), English Children Act 1989. (See Q 23). A similar position obtains in the case of parental responsibility agreements since the court has no power of scrutiny over the making of such agreements. Insofar as applications are made for a parental responsibility order, then the making of the order is governed by the paramountcy of the child's welfare[3] and in that context the parties' wishes and violent behaviour will certainly be factors that are taken into account.[4]

FINLAND

The law does not differentiate between married or unmarried parents in this respect. Refer to Q 18.

FRANCE

Yes. Parental responsibilities are not just a parental right, but also a duty and a responsibility of the parents towards their child. The same rules apply as for married parents. Therefore, see Q 18. When unmarried parents do not separate (or have never lived together), upon request of the mother, the father or the prosecutor (*ministère public*), the family judge can decide that parental responsibilities shall be jointly exercised by both parents in the two situations stated in Art. 372 para. 2 French CC:

- when one parent acknowledged the child more than one year after the child's birth and the other parent did it much earlier; or
- when the parentage of the second parent was been established by judicial decision and not by voluntary acknowledgment. See also Art. 373-2-8 French CC.

---

3 *Viz* Sec. 1(1), English Children Act 1989 applies, see *Re H (Parental Responsibility)* [1998] 1 FLR 855 at 859 per BUTLER-SLOSS LJ.

4 See e.g. *Re T (Parental Responsibility: Contact)* [1993] 2 FLR 450, CA order refused because of the father's violence towards the mother, *Re L (A Child)(Contact: Domestic Violence)* [2001] Fam 200, order refused because of the father's violence and desire to control the child and *Re H (Parental Responsibility)* [1988] 1 FLR 855, CA, order refused because of the father's violence to the child.

GERMANY

In this case there are, once again, various possible courses of action open to the court when it comes to the attribution of parental responsibilities against the wishes of both parents or one of the parents:

- If the parents were jointly responsible for the child before their separation, in accordance with § 1626 a para. 1 No. 1 German CC (declarations of responsibility), each parent can file an application requesting sole parental responsibility in accordance with § 1671 para. 2 No. 2 German CC. Concerning the prerequisites and consequences of a procedure in accordance with § 1671 para. 2 No. 2 German CC, that which has been said in response to Q 18 applies.
- Moreover, the court may make a decision on the basis of § 1628 German CC if the parents are unable to agree on a specific issue or specific kind of issue relating to parental responsibility (see Q 18).
- Finally, the court has the authority, in fulfilment of its official mandate as guardian in accordance with § 1666 German CC, to take any measures required to avert a danger to the child and to reattribute parental responsibilities within this context (see Q 18).

GREECE

Although there is no specific provision in the law on this issue, it is accepted that a prerequisite for the attribution of joint parental responsibilities is the consent of both parents.[5] This opinion is based on the provision of Art. 1513 Greek CC, according to which the attribution of joint parental responsibilities to the parents after divorce or annulment presupposes that they both agree to this. As far as the violent behaviour of one parent towards the other is concerned, the court may take this into account to the extent that affects the interests of the child.

HUNGARY

The court cannot attribute joint parental responsibilities to the parents against the wish of even one of the parents. An element essential for a decision favouring joint parental responsibilities for parents that have never married each other is that they can co-operate with each other in matters concerning the child after their relationship ends. The exercise of joint parental responsibilities would be impossible without this co-operation; forcing the parents to exercise their parental rights jointly would not be in the child's interests.

IRELAND

Yes, it may, although this would be most unusual. In reality, the competent authority has little opportunity to take into account a parent's violent behaviour towards the other parent. In Ireland, a cohabiting couple is not recognised as a 'family' even in circumstances where the parties have lived together for a

---

5 M. KARASIS, in: A. GEORGIADIS and M. STATHOPOULOS (eds.), *Civil Code commentray, Vol. VIII, Family Law (Arts. 1505-1694)*, 2nd Edition, Athens: Law & Economy, P.N. SAKKOULAS, 2003, Art. 1515 Greek CC, p. 238, No. 8.

number of years, or where they have children and effectively live as a family as recognised under the Irish Constitution.

ITALY

No; unless expressly provided by law the judge cannot attribute the joint exercise of parental responsibilities without the consent of both parents. For joint exercise of parental responsibilities, Italian law requires the following conditions: the parents have a good relationship, they should both have the capacity to be good parents and they should live close to each other.[6] It is not possible to order joint parental responsibilities against the wish of the parents or of one of them.[7]

Violent behaviour by one of the parents towards the other (spouse as well as partner) can create prejudice to the violent parent's physical and moral integrity or to his liberty, it may fulfil the elements of Art. 572 Italian Penal Code (maltreatment of family or minors) and it also has relevance in civil terms. At the request of one of the parties the civil judge can order the cessation of this prejudicial behaviour and also for one of the parents to leave the family's house (according to Arts. 342bis and 342*ter* Italian CC, recently introduced by the Law No. 154, of 4 April 2001 and modified by the Law No. 304, of 6 November 2003). The judge can also order the intervention of a local social service, centre for family mediation or associations who support and receive victims of abuse and maltreatment. The judge can order the periodic payment of an allowance in favour of one of the cohabitants who, because of the ordered removal from the family's house, remains without appropriate means. The judge will establish the methods and terms of the payment and decide if the obligated parent must have his or her employer deduct the relevant amount from his or her salary to be paid directly to the recipient.

The judge will establish the duration that one of the cohabitants must stay away from the family's house. This cannot be for longer than 6 months from the removal order and can only be extended at the request of one party for grave reasons and for a period that is strictly necessary. If there are difficulties with or oppositions to the execution of the removal order, the judge will order necessary measures, including security forces and the health official.

Whether this form of protection, characterised by urgency and timeliness, presumes a cohabitation[8] of the parents (spouses or non spouses) or if it is also applicable pending or after a factual separation, or during the process of

---

6 See the Court of Genoa 18.04.1991, *Giust. Civ.*, 1991, I, p. 3095, with note of M. MIGLIETTA; Court of S. Maria Capua Vetere 14.09.1993, *Giur. merito*, 1994, p. 226 with note of G. MANERA; Court of Catania 06.06.1994, *Dir. Fam. pers.*, 1995, p. 222.

7 See the Court of Milan, 14.07.1993, *Gius*, 1994, p. 99.

8 See also the Court of Genoa 07.01.2003, *Fam. dir.*, 2004, p. 387, with a added note of L. CARRERA; Court of Naples 01.02.2002, *Fam. dir.*, p. 504, with a added note of A. FIGONE.

separation, divorce or annulment of the marriage has been discussed. In this case, the order to leave the family's house would also include the prohibition to frequent the victim's habitation or to have contact with her or him.[9] At any rate, it deals with a residual protection which applies when the conditions for the suspension or limitation of the parental responsibilities according to Art. 330 and Art. 333 Italian CC are fulfilled.[101]

LITHUANIA

Yes. In deciding such questions, the wishes of one or both parents are irrelevant because parental responsibilities are statutory obligations and their existence or attribution may not depend on the wishes of the parties.

One parent's violent behaviour towards the other parent shall have legal significance only if the attribution of joint responsibilities to both parents shall be against the best interests of a child. In this situation, violent behaviour of one of the parents may be a ground for the separation of the violent parent from a child or for the restriction of parental authority of that parent (Art. 3.179 Lithuanian CC). This means that in any case, the attribution of parental responsibilities only to one of the parents is possible in the event of judicial separation of such parent from a child or in the event of judicial restriction of parental authority.

THE NETHERLANDS

The court may reject a request for sole parental responsibilities, which means that the existing joint parental responsibilities will continue, even if this is against the wish of both or one of the parents. The idea is that continued joint parental responsibilities are in the best interests of the child. For more detailed information see Q 18 on the attribution of parental responsibilities after divorce; the information given there applies equally to this question.

Violent behaviour of one parent towards the other parent is in itself not a reason to terminate joint parental responsibilities. Only if the violent behaviour of the parent threatens to cause problems of such seriousness that there is an unacceptable risk that the children will be damaged, will the court attribute sole parental responsibilities to one of the parents.[11]

---

9 See the Court of Florence 15.07.2002, *Fam. dir.*, 2003, p. 263, with a critical note of G. DE MARZO.

10 Concerning the possibility to also apply Art. 330 and 333 Italian CC in cases of 'indirect' abuse and maltreatment, or in cases where the act is not committed towards the minor but towards relatives (such as the other parent) to whom the minor is so close that his or her 'harmonic and balanced psychophysical upbringing' is compromised, see the Family Proceedings Court L'Aquila 19.07.2002, *Fam. dir.* 2003, p. 482.

11 Criterion developed by the Supreme Court 10.9.1999, *NJ*, 2000, 20.

NORWAY
According to Art. 48 Norwegian Children Act 1981, the decision of the court shall first and foremost be taken on the basis of what is best for the child. The court may attribute joint parental responsibilities to the parents of the child against the wish of one the parents, and, in principle, even against the wishes of both parents. If one of the parents wishes sole responsibility, the court will comply with the request only if there are special circumstances to support the claim. Such 'special circumstances' will include, for instance, the possibility that the other parent might be considered unsuited to share parental responsibilities, and in this judgment the court may take into account a parent's violent behaviour towards the other parent.

POLAND
The authority is obliged to safeguard the child's best interests and wellbeing. To achieve those goals it may take the described facts into consideration, but they do not have legal significance.

PORTUGAL
The judge may not award joint custody to unmarried parents unless they both agree (Art. 1906 No. 1 and 1912 Portuguese CC). As to whether the existence of domestic violence influences the custody decision, see Q 18 above.

RUSSIA
A judge has no competence to decide upon attribution of parental responsibility, as parents always have joint parental responsibility by operation of law.

The only way to end joint parental responsibility is to discharge the parental responsibility of one or both parents who are found guilty of serious misconduct against the child (Art. 69 Russian Family Code). As an intentional crime against the health or life of the other parent constitutes a ground for discharge of parental responsibility (Art. 69), such measure can be applied when one of the parents has been convicted by the criminal court for violence towards the other parent.

SPAIN
See Q 18.

SWEDEN
Unmarried parents are subject to the general rules regarding any change in the custody position. The court may, upon application, also order joint custody against the wish of one of the parents, but not if both parents are opposed to joint custody, Chapter 6 Sec. 5 Swedish Children and Parents Code. A parent's violent behaviour towards the other parent may be a reason not to grant joint custody, at least in conjunction with a conflict between the parents so severe

and deep that it makes it impossible for them to cooperate in matters concerning the child, see NJA 2000 p. 345.[12]

SWITZERLAND

The answer to this is negative because a joint petition by the parents is a prerequisite for the guardianship authority to confer joint parental responsibilities on them (Art. 298a § 1 Swiss CC). The competent authority must take all the circumstances relating to the child's welfare into account. Violent behaviour towards the other parent in the parental relationship would, therefore, *a priori* routinely preclude the attribution of joint parental responsibilities.

---

12 This Supreme Court judgment was described above under Q 18. Although the judgment concerned children of parents that had been married to each other, there is no reason to assume the outcome would have been different had the parents never been married to each other.

QUESTION 25

C. ATTRIBUTION OF PARENTAL RESPONSIBILITIES

II. Unmarried Parents

To what extent, if at all, are unmarried parents free to agree upon the attribution of parental responsibilities after the ending of their relationship?

AUSTRIA

In the event the parents separate, Sec. 167 Austrian CC, which governs the attribution of parental responsibilities between unmarried parents, refers to the provisions on divorce, annulment or nullification of the marriage (Sec. 177 and 177a Austrian CC).[1] That means that joint parental responsibilities can be maintained despite the dissolution of the common household if the parents submit an agreement as to the child's primary residence to the court and the court approves it. The parents can also agree to partial continuation of joint parental responsibilities whereby the parental responsibilities of one of them are restricted to certain matters. This is permissible only if it is agreed that the child's primary residence will be with the other parent who has full parental responsibilities. Finally, the parents can agree that one of them will have sole parental responsibilities. In the last two cases as well, the agreement on parental responsibilities must be approved by the court.[2]

BELGIUM

See Q 17.

BULGARIA

They are free to agree on the attribution of parental responsibilities after the ending of their relationship. The agreement is a purely private matter since neither scrutiny nor any registration or approval of the agreement are envisaged by law.

CZECH REPUBLIC

Whether the parents are married is not essential. If the parents of a minor child do not cohabit and do not come to an agreement, the court may decide, even without a motion, on the regulation of the relationship between the parents and the child, *i.e.* about placing the child into the personal care of one of the parents and setting up maintenance obligations of the other (Sec. 50 Czech Family Code). The court may approve the parents' agreement on the measures. The parents' agreement on contact with the child does not require a court approval (Sec. 27 § 1 Czech Family Code).

---

1 See Q 16a and 16c.

2 J. STABENTHEINER, 'KindRÄG 2001', in: P. Rummel, *ABGB-Kommentar*, suppl. vol. 1, 3rd Edition, Vienna: Manz Verlag, 2003, § 167 Marg. No. 8.

DENMARK

Parents whether married or not, are free upon the ending of their relationship to make agreements about joint or sole parental authority, and such agreements are not subject to judicial scrutiny, Art. 6 and 9 Danish Act on Parental Authority and Contact.

ENGLAND & WALES

The mother's parental responsibility is fixed by law and its attribution cannot be changed either by agreement or a court order. Once the unmarried father has acquired parental responsibility it cannot subsequently be altered by agreement. It can, however, upon application of anyone with parental responsibility or, with leave of the court, of the child, be brought to an end by a court order.[3]

FINLAND

The ending of the unmarried parents' relationship does not affect their right to draw up agreements about their child's custody (Sec. 7 Finnish Child Custody and the Right of Access Act, see Q 17).

FRANCE

To the same extent as married couples who separate or divorce, because the same rules apply. See Art. 373-2 French CC. The reform Act of 4 March 2002 introduced the same rules for all kinds of couples (married, unmarried, *Pacs etc.*), therefore the same legal provision set in Art. 373-2-7 French CC apply with regard to the parental agreements on the exercise of parental responsibilities. Parents (married or not) may enter into agreements about parental responsibilities and the contribution to the child's maintenance and education. They may present a request to the family judge aiming at the *homologation* (judicial approval) of this agreement. The family judge (*juge aux affaires familiales, JAF*) will approve the parental agreement unless it does not protect the child's interests or the consent of one parents was not freely given (see Art. 373-2-7 para. 2 French CC).

See also Art. 376-1 French CC (when the family judge makes a decision on the modalities of the exercise of parental responsibilities, on the education of a minor child or on the entrustment of the child to a third person, the judge can take agreements the parents freely made between themselves into account, unless one of the parents invokes serious reasons for withdrawing her or his consent.)

GERMANY

If the parents were jointly responsible for the child before their separation through declarations of responsibility in accordance with § 1626 a para. 1 No. 1 German CC, this joint responsibility on principle continues after separation (see Q 23).

By contrast, if the mother had sole parental responsibility in accordance with § 1626 a para. 2 German CC before the separation, the parents are still able to file declarations of responsibility in accordance with § 1626 a para. 1 No. 1 German CC after separation, as living together is not a prerequisite for the obtaining of joint

---

3 Under Sec. 4(3), English Children Act 1989, on which see *Re P (Terminating Parental Responsibility)* [1995] 1 FLR 1048.

responsibility (see Q 20). The father can obtain sole responsibility only if he files an application for transfer of responsibility in accordance with § 1672 German CC. Through this provision, the legislature of the German Child Law Reform Act replaced the method of attribution of parental responsibility to the father, which in earlier legislation could be achieved only through a declaration of legitimacy[4] or through adoption[5], by a parental responsibility arrangement that is not concerned with personal status or descent.[6] This change in the attribution of parental responsibilities presupposes the filing of an application by the father and the mother's consent; failure by the mother to give her consent results in the application being rejected as inadmissible out of hand.[7] Unlike § 1671 para. 2 No. 1 German CC, § 1672 German CC does not follow the parents' joint assessment, making rather changes in the attribution of parental responsibilities dependent on an additional positive examination of the child's best interests, through a decision of the family court; the application will be granted if the transfer of responsibility serves the child's best interests, § 1672 para. 1 sent. 2 German CC. Once a reattribution of parental responsibilities has taken place, joint parental responsibility can no longer be established by means of a declaration of responsibility, but only through the decision of the family court, § 1696 German CC.

The compulsory requirement of the mother's consent for the transfer of sole responsibility to the father is regarded by many as open to objection from a constitutional law point of view,[8] given that a child who has lived with both parents is likely to have developed emotional ties with his or her father. Failing to raise any objections on principle against the norm of § 1626 a German CC from a constitutional law point of view, the Constitutional Court also declared § 1672 German CC to be constitutional.[9] According to the Constitutional Court, an incompatibility of § 1626 a German CC - and hence as a logical consequence, of § 1672 German CC - with German Basic Law exists only to the extent that there is a lack of transitional arrangements for those parents who have lived with their child born outside marriage and have jointly cared for their child, but who separated before the Child Law Reform Act came into force on 1 July 1998:[10] Such parents, particularly the fathers, must be given the opportunity to have their case examined by the court to decide whether joint parental responsibility can be established in consideration of the child's best interests, the other parent's will to the contrary notwithstanding. The legislator has since created such a transitional provision regarding the German Child Law Reform Act for parents who are not married to each other.[11] Under this arrangement, the family court can, on application, substitute the declaration of responsibility of the parent holding parental responsibilities, subject to certain conditions.

4 § 1723 German CC (old version).
5 § 1741 German CC.
6 Th. RAUSCHER, *Familienrecht,* Heidelberg: C.F. Müller, 2001, No. 1011.
7 Th. RAUSCHER, *Familienrecht,* Heidelberg: C.F. Müller, 2001, No. 1012.
8 U. DIEDERICHSEN, in: PALANDT, *Bürgerliches Gesetzbuch,* 64th Edition, Munich: Beck, 2005, § 1672 No. 3.
9 BVerfG 23.4.2003, *FamRZ* 2003, 1447.
10 BVerfG 29.01.2003, *NJW* 2003, 955, 956.
11 BGBl 2003/I p. 2547 *et seq.*

GREECE

The parents are free to agree upon the attribution of parental responsibilities after the ending of their relationship. The court must decide on any deviation from the initial regulation on parental responsibilities. Both parents can request an adjustment to the initial court decision if there are any new circumstances (Art. 1536 Greek CC). See also the answer to Q 17.

HUNGARY

Unmarried parents are free to agree upon the attribution of parental responsibilities after their relationship ends. They can agree to continue with their joint parental responsibilities or they can agree that one of them will now have the sole exercise of parental responsibilities. There is an important difference between this agreement and the agreement during a divorce proceeding: while the arrangement of parental responsibilities in a divorce proceeding requires judicial approval and is therefore the subject of inquiry, unmarried couples are not obliged to obtain approval from either the court or any other authority.

IRELAND

Sec. 2(4) Irish Guardianship of Infants Act 1964, as amended by Sec. 4 of the Children Act 1997, allows the unmarried mother and father by agreement to make a statutory declaration conferring upon the father the status of guardian.[12] Both parties must have agreed to the appointment and are required to have made arrangements concerning the custody of and/or access to the child in question. The natural father must be named as father on the birth certificate of the child. There are practical difficulties with the operation of this Sec.. For example, where does one 'file' the declaration? Furthermore, if the father is not registered on the birth certificate and presents the statutory declaration to the Registrar, it is likely that the Registrar will not accept the declaration and will require a court order.[13] The main difficulty, of course, arises when the father's wish and application to be appointed a joint guardian is contested by the natural mother. The position in relation to these applications has not been altered by Sec. 4 of the 1997 Act.

ITALY

Parents are free to make an agreement, but the judge always controls the agreement made. This control, expressly provided by law, aims to verify that the conditions of the agreement are not in conflict with the interests of the child. In they are, the judge can rule against the agreement. If the parents cannot reach an agreement, the judge is entitled to make the decision; he must exclusively take the moral and material interests of the child into consideration.

The only difference between married and unmarried parents concerns the competent judicial authority deciding custody and the methods of the exercise of the parental responsibilities. With married parents, the Ordinary Court is competent (the court competent for the procedures of separation, divorce and

---

12 See S.I. No. 5 of 1998.

13 See Ord. 59 of the Circuit Court Rules 2001 (S.I. No. 510 of 2001) which requires the father to be registered as the father in a register maintained under the Births and Deaths Registration Acts 1863-2004.

annulment of the marriage); for unmarried parents the Family Proceedings Court is the competent authority (see Q 55).

LITHUANIA

According to Art. 3.51 Lithuanian CC, parents are free to agree upon the exercise of their parental duties and rights after divorce, legal separation or the annulment of the marriage. This rule is applied by analogy to unmarried parents as well. The unmarried parents may agree upon the place of the residence of a child, upon their participation in maintenance of a child, their contact with a child *etc.* after the ending of their relationship. Such an agreement must be made in writing and must be presented to the court for approval. The duty of the court is to investigate the content of the agreement in respect to the interest of the child and the equality of the parents. The court shall refuse to approve the agreement if it contradicts the interests of the child or violates the principle of equality of the rights and duties of parents (Art. 3.53 Lithuanian CC). However, in no case may the parents, by such agreement, disclaim (waive) their rights or duties in respect to the child. Parental responsibilities are statutory obligations and may not be waived. Agreements between parents to disclaim (waive) parental duties and rights are void because they violate mandatory rules and are against public policy and good morals (Art. 1.80, 1.81 and 3.159 Lithuanian CC).

THE NETHERLANDS

If unmarried partners want to terminate the existing joint parental responsibilities after the ending of their relationship, it is not enough for them to agree on the attribution of their duties. They need to apply to the court.

NORWAY

After ending their relationship, unmarried parents are free to agree upon the attribution of parental responsibilities. There is no public scrutiny of such an agreement. Agreements concerning parental responsibilities which are not reported to the National Population Register are not valid; Art. 39 Norwegian Children Act 1981.

POLAND

They are not, to any extent.

PORTUGAL

When the parents' relationship ends, the need to regulate a new system of parental responsibility arises. This new system may result from an agreement between the parents subject to ratification by the judge (Art. 1905 No. 1 and 1912 Portuguese CC and Art. 174 *ex vi* Art. 183 Portuguese Child Protection Law), or it may result from court intervention if the parents are unable to arrive at an agreement or if the agreement they have presented is not in the interests of the children. Parental responsibility will then be regulated by a legal decision made in accordance with the interests of the child (Art. 1905 No. 2 and 1912 Portuguese CC and Art. 180 Portuguese Child Protection Law).

RUSSIA

Unmarried parents, as with married ones, cannot decide to attribute parental responsibility to only one of them, as joint parental responsibility always survives the breakdown of their relationships.

SPAIN

Parental responsibility is non-disposable, which means that the possibility to agree on the attribution of parental responsibility does not exist. It is however possible to agree on the exercise of parental responsibility.

Spanish courts apply the regulation on agreements established in connection to divorce, annulment and legal separation as well to unmarried couples. See Q 17. However, it should be noted that since ending an informal relationship does not require a judicial procedure, these agreements often do not reach the courts and are neither scrutinised nor judicially approved. If these agreements are not complied with voluntarily they cannot be enforced through the court system.

SWEDEN

Upon and after the termination of their relationship, unmarried and married parents have the same right to enter into agreements concerning custody, residence and contact.[14] Such an agreement must be in writing and approved by the social welfare committee. The parents' agreement may also be confirmed by court order.

SWITZERLAND

Parents are not free to agree upon the attribution of parental responsibilities. Even after the ending of their relationship the previous arrangement concerning parental responsibilities still remains in operation. If joint parental responsibilities were attributed to the parents (Art. 298a § 1 Swiss CC), a request for a new arrangement with regard to the attribution of parental responsibilities may be called for, in accordance with Art. 298a § 2 Swiss CC as a result of significant changes in circumstances for the sake of the child's welfare. The guardianship authority decides these requests.

14 See answer to Q 17.

QUESTION 26

C. ATTRIBUTION OF PARENTAL RESPONSIBILITIES

II. Unmarried Parents

Provide statistical information available regarding the attribution of parental responsibilities for unmarried parents.

AUSTRIA

In 2003, 1.4 million families, with 2.4 million children, lived in Austria: 50 % of them were married, 37% were in (heterosexual) life partnerships, and 13% were single parents. About 85% of the approximately 286,300 single parents raising children were mothers. The proportion of single fathers raising their children was related to the age of the child.[1]

BELGIUM

No statistical information is available.

BULGARIA

There is no information available on this matter.

CZECH REPUBLIC

No answer.

DENMARK

Such statistical information should contain details relating to of care and responsibility statements resulting in joint parental authority, agreements on parental authority and judgements by the courts. This does not exist, however. What is known is that 44.9% of all children born in 2003 were born to unmarried mothers.[2] Statistics from the administrative authorities from 1999 showed that 81% of unmarried parents who lived together chose joint parental authority at the time of birth.[3] This was before the care and responsibility procedure was introduced and it is expected that more unmarried parents now have joint parental authority.

ENGLAND & WALES

There are no overall statistics on how many fathers have parental responsibility. All that can be said is that according to the Judicial Statistics (Department of Constitutional Affairs, 2004, Table 5.3) 9524 parental responsibility orders were made in 2003. It is estimated that in 2002 82% of births outside marriage were

---

1 http://www.statistik.at; http://www.oif.ac.at; R. SCHIPFER, *Familien in Zahlen*, Vienna: Österreichisches Institut für Familienforschung, 2003, p. 16.

2 Statistics Denmark.

3 S. DANIELSEN, *Nordisk børneret II*, Copenhagen, Oslo and Upsala: Nord, 2003, p. 92.

registered jointly by both parents (ONS 2004, Birth Statistics, Series Fm No. 31) which would now be sufficient to give the unmarried father parental responsibility (see Q 22b).

FINLAND

As explained above, it is impossible to differentiate between married parents or unmarried parents in the statistical information (see Q 19).

FRANCE

There is no statistical information available regarding the attribution of parental responsibilities for unmarried parents. It seems to frequently be disputed; the *Annuaire statistique de la Justice* for 2004[4] mentions that in 2002, 65,062 petitions were filed concerning the exercise of parental responsibilities, the determination of the minor child's residence or the contact rights for children of unmarried parents. Theses statistics do not give more details on how the issues were solved by the family courts.

GERMANY

If the parents are not married to each other at the time of their child's birth, the mother has sole responsibility (§ 1626 a para. 2 German CC) unless both parents have filed a declaration of responsibility in accordance with § 1626 a para. 1 No. 1 German CC (see Q 15b for further details). As far as the frequency of these declarations is concerned, no statistical data are available. In 2004 the statistical recording of the number of declarations became a legal requirement, § 58 a para. 2 SGB XIII, which means that this number will be included in the Youth Welfare Statistics (*Jugendhilfestatistik*) from 2005 onwards. Then it will be easier to assess whether the legislator's prognosis was accurate, i.e. that parents living together legally secure their factual joint responsibility through the filing of declarations of responsibility (see Q 22b).

GREECE

No official statistics exist on this issue in Greece.

HUNGARY

Unfortunately, we do not have exact statistical data on the attribution of parental responsibilities for unmarried parents. We do have statistics on the number of the paternal recognitions. In 2003 the number of the minors whose family status was settled by the public guardianship authority was 7,736. Among these, 5,302 were paternal recognitions.

IRELAND

No such statistics are available.

---

[4] P. 85.

ITALY

There is no information available; however, it can be assumed the statistics would be comparable to those collected with reference to married couples (see Q 19).

LITHUANIA

There is no relevant statistical information available.

THE NETHERLANDS

There is no statistical information available with regard to this question.

NORWAY

There is no statistical information on this matter. Since the great majority of unmarried mothers live with the father of the child, agreements on joint parental responsibilities are very common.

POLAND

Such information is not available.

PORTUGAL

The statistics available reveal only the number of cases relating to the regulation of parental responsibility concerning children born out of wedlock. See Q 19.

RUSSIA

Parental responsibility is always attributed to both parents. No information's is available regarding attribution of child's residence.

SPAIN

Statistics are not available.

SWEDEN

The most recent statistics regarding the attribution of custody after separation of unmarried parents refers to parents who separated in 2002.[5] The unmarried parents who separated that year had joint custody of 16,157 children; almost 89% of the concerned children. The mother had sole custody of 1,987 children; about 11%. The father had sole custody of 46 children; 0.3%. Swedish statistics show that joint custody is the most common form of custody for both divorced and separated parents, the figures being slightly higher among divorced parents than among separated parents who have not been married to each other.[6]

SWITZERLAND

No statistical information is available.

---

5 Statistics Sweden, www.scb.se.

6 See the statistics provided above under Q 19.

QUESTION 27

C. ATTRIBUTION OF PARENTAL RESPONSIBILITIES

III. Other Persons

Under what conditions, if at all, can the partner of a parent holding parental responsibilities obtain parental responsibilities, when, he or she is:

> **(a) Married to that parent;**
> **(b) Living with that parent in a formalised relationship (registered partnership, civil union, *pacte civil de solidarité…*); or**
> **(c) Living with that parent in a non-formalised relationship?**

AUSTRIA

(a) Married to that parent

Apart from stepparent adoption (Sec. 179 *et seq* Austrian CC), case law and legal writing does not regard joint parental responsibilities with equal rights and duties between a biological parent and a stepparent to be permissible.[1] Due to the stepparent's close actual relationship to the child, a stepparent is considered to be a foster parent under Sec. 186 Austrian CC;[2] this is a person who actually carries out the care and education of the child and with whom the child has a relationship similar to that with a biological parent. A foster parent may apply to the court for a transfer of parental responsibilities (Sec. 186a Austrian CC). However, according to predominant view such a transfer of parental responsibilities has the effect that the previous holder(s) of parental responsibilities lose them to the extent they pass to the new holder of parental responsibilities.[3]

(b) Living with that parent in a formalised relationship (registered partnership, civil union, *pacte civil de solidarité…*);

In Austria, there is no formalised relationship between unmarried partners.

(c) Living with that parent in a non formalised relationship

As to the question whether a partner of a parent holding parental responsibilities may obtain parental responsibilities, the same reasoning applies for marital as well as for non-marital partnerships:[4] The new partner is

---

1 *Oberster Gerichtshof,* 25.09.2002, *Österreichische Juristenzeitung - EvBl,* 2003, No. 16, p. 102 = *ÖJZ-LSK* 2003/2; M. SCHWIMANN, *Familienrecht,* 5th Edition, Vienna: LexisNexis ARD Orac, 2004, p. 80.

2 See Q 31.

3 *Oberster Gerichtshof,* 25.09.2002, *Österreichische Juristenzeitung - EvBl,* 2003, No. 16, p. 102 = *ÖJZ-LSK* 2003/2; M. SCHWIMANN, *Familienrecht,* 5th Edition, Vienna: LexisNexis ARD Orac, 2004, p. 80.

4 See also Q 27a.

considered to be a foster parent under Sec. 186 Austrian CC due to his or her close actual relationship to the child. However, joint parental responsibilities between a parent and a foster parent are regarded not permissible. A judicial transfer of parental responsibilities to the foster parent (Sec. 186a Austrian CC) would have the effect that the previous holder(s) of parental responsibilities would lose their rights and duties, to the extent they passed to the foster parent as new holder of parental responsibilities[5]. Thus, the only possibility for the parent's partner to obtain joint parental responsibilities is by means of an adoption (Sec. 179 *et seq* Austrian CC).[6]

BELGIUM

(a) Married to that parent

Only the parents can hold parental responsibilities, unless the child has been adopted or the parents have been discharged of their responsibilities by the Juvenile Court. Except in case of custodianship (See Q 31), the partner of a parent can never hold these responsibilities, regardless of the relationship he or she has with the parent (marriage, formalised relationship or non formalised relationship). Persons not the parent of a child can only obtain custody of the child by agreement of the parents or after intervention of the Juvenile Court, which acts on the request of the parent(s) or the Public Prosecutor.[7] See Q 6 regarding the introduction of parental rights and responsibilities for a partner who cares for a biological parent 's child without being the biological parent.

(b) Living with that parent in a formalised relationship (registered partnership, civil union, *pacte civil de solidarité*...)

See Q 27a.

(c) Living with that parent in a non formalised relationship

See Q 27a.

BULGARIA

(a) Married to that parent

There are two possibilities. If the child has established parentage to only one parent, the partner of the parent may either recognise the child or adopt it. Where a child has an established origin with regard to a second parent, the only alternative for the partner is adoption. For this purpose, the consent of the second parent is required. As the Bulgarian Family Code states: Aoption by the spouse of the parent: 'By an adoption under the provisions of Art. 61 and Art. 62 of a child by the spouse of the parent the rights and obligations between this

---

5 *Oberster Gerichtshof*, 25.09.2002, *Österreichische Juristenzeitung - EvBl*, 2003, No. 16, p. 102 = *ÖJZ-LSK* 2003/2; M. SCHWIMANN, *Familienrecht*, 5th Edition, Vienna: LexisNexis ARD Orac, 2004, p. 80. For details see Q 31.

6 J. STABENTHEINER in: P. RUMMEL, *ABGB-Kommentar*, Vol. I, 3rd Edition, Vienna: Manz Verlag, 2000, § 182 Marg. No 4.

7 Cass. 26.04.1979, *R.W.*, 1979-80, F. RIGAUX, 'La délégation de l'autorité parentale, création jurisprudentielle?', *R.C.J.B.*, 1977, 206.

parent and his or her relatives on one hand, and the adopted and his or her descendants on the other hand, are preserved' (Art. 63).

(b) Living with that parent in a formalised relationship (registered partnership, civil union, *pacte civil de solidarité*...)

No such regulation exists in Bulgaria.

(c) Living with that parent in a non formalised relationship

The only possibility is if the child does not have an established parentage to other parent. In this case the partner may recognise the child.

CZECH REPUBLIC

(a) Married to that parent

The spouse of the child's parent cannot have parental responsibility as it belongs only to the child's parents, who are recorded in the register of births as being the parents. The Czech Family Code only imposes a duty on the step-parent to participate in the upbringing of the child if he or she lives with the child (Sec. 33 Czech Family Code).

(b) Living with that parent in a formalised relationship (registered partnership, civil union, *pacte civil de solidarité*...)

Czech legislation does not recognise the concept of a formalised relationship. Even the proposed act on registered partnership of persons of the same sex does not take into account any rights or duties of the partner in relation to the child.

(c) Living with that parent in a non formalised relationship

The partner of the child's parent living with that parent in a non-formalised relationship has no rights or duties in relation to the child.

DENMARK

(a) Married to that parent

The married partner of a parent who has sole parental authority can obtain parental authority by agreement with the parent. The agreement must be approved and approval is granted if it is not considered to be inconsistent with what is best for the child, Art. 11 Danish Act on Parental Authority and Contact. Permission cannot be expected if the other parent does not consent to the transfer of parental authority.[8]

(b) Living with that parent in a formalised relationship (registered partnership, civil union, *pacte civil de solidarité*...)

It is not possible.

(c) Living with that parent in a non formalised relationship

It is not possible.

---

8 I. LUND-ANDERSEN, N. MUNCK and I. NØRGAARD, *Familieret*, Copenhagen: Jurist- og Økonomforbundets Forlag, 2003, p. 76.

ENGLAND & WALES

(a) Married to that parent

In its current form the English Children Act 1989 makes no special provision for step-parents (whether married or not to the parent) to acquire parental responsibility. Accordingly, they do not have parental responsibility automatically but they can acquire it principally[9] upon being granted a residence order (which is an order determining the person with whom the child is to live). In that context it is possible for the parent and sep-parent jointly to apply for a residence order. However, it is to be stressed that the principal concern of the court will be to determine whether it is in the child's interests to live with the applicant. In other words the application for a residence order should not be regarded simply as a means of allocating parental responsibility to the step-parent.[10]

According to Sec. 12(2), English Children Act 1989 any person (who is not a parent or guardian) in whose favour a residence order has been made has parental responsibility for the duration of the order, though, by Sec. 12(3), this will not entitle him or her to agree to the child's adoption nor to appoint a guardian.

This position will change when the English Adoption and Children Act 2002 comes fully into force since that Act prospectively amends the English Children Act 1989[11] to permit a step-parent who is married (*i.e.* cohabitation is insufficient) to the child's parent who has parental responsibility to obtain responsibility either by agreement or by a court order.

So far as agreements are concerned if both parents have parental responsibility then the agreement will have to be made with both. Presumably the formalities for making these agreements will be the same as for those made between the parents.

It may be noted that unlike for married fathers no provision is made for the automatic making of a parental responsibility order following the making of a residence order in a step-parent's favour. Consequently unless the step-parent already has a separate parental responsibility order in his favour parental responsibility will cease upon the ending of a residence order.

---

9 It can also be acquired upon a formal appointment as a guardian in accordance with Sec. 5, Children Act 1989 following the death of the parent or parents with parental responsibility (see Q 34) or upon being granted an emergency protection order under Sec. 44(4), (5) of the 1989 Act. In the latter case not only is responsibility short lived (it only lasts as long as the order, *i.e.* a maximum of 15 days) but it is also limited in effect, see Sec. 44(4)(c) and 44(5)(b); and the answer to Q 14.

10 See *Re WB (Residence Orders)* [1995] 2 FLR 1023 but cf *Re H (Shared Residence: Parental Responsibility)* [1995] 2 FLR 883.

11 Sec. 112 prospectively inserting Sec. 4A, English Children Act 1989.

(b) Living with that parent in a formalised relationship (registered partnership, civil union, *pacte civil de solidarité* ...)

English law currently makes no provision for registered partnerships. However, this will change when the Civil Partnerships Act 2004 comes into force. Under that Act it will be possible for same-sex couples only to formally register their partnership.[12] Where an individual is the registered partner of a parent with parental responsibility he will be in the same position as a heterosexual step-parent who is married to a parent with parental responsibility and therefore such persons will be able to acquire parental responsibility by making a formal parental responsibility agreement with all those having parental responsibility or by applying for a court order.[13]

(c) Living with that parent in a non formalised relationship

The only way an individual living with a parent in a non formalised relationship can acquire parental responsibility is by obtaining a residence order (see Q 27a).[14]

FINLAND

(a) Married to that parent

A married partner of a parent may obtain custody of the child. This can only happen by means of a court order. A court may order that one or more persons who have consented thereto shall have the custody of a child instead of, or together with, the parent or parents (Sec. 9 para. 1 point 4 Finnish Child Custody and the Right of Access Act). The application to the court can be made by the parent(s), by the child's custodian(s) or by the local social authority (Sec. 14 para. 1).

If the court should at the same time transfer the custody from a parent, the court must consider the condition expressed in Sec. 9 para. 2 Finnish Child Custody and the Right of Access Act. According to this condition, the transfer is only possible if it is manifestly in the best interests of the child. This condition does then not apply if the custody is not to be transferred from a parent. As referred to above, the child may also have more than two custodians.

(b) Living with that parent in a formalised relationship (registered partnership, civil union, *pacte civil de solidarité*...)

The registered partner of a parent may obtain custody of the child under the same conditions explained above in point (a). Registered same-sex partnership is the only form of a formalised relationship known in Finnish legislation.

---

12 Sec. 1, British Civil Partnership Act 2004.

13 Sec. 75, British Civil Partnership Act 2004, prospectively amending Sec. 4, English Children Act 1989.

14 But note the points made in Q 25 above.

(c) Living with that parent in a non formalised relationship

The partner of the parent in a non - formalised relationship may obtain custody of the child under the same conditions explained above in point (a).

FRANCE

(a) Married to that parent

Only one legal provision deals indirectly with this issue: Art. 371-4 French CC. This provision states that the child has the right to personal relationships with his *ascendants* (grandparents and great grandparents) and that only very serious reasons can hinder this right. Para. 2 of the same provision adds that if it is in the child's interest, the family judge can determine the mode of the relationship between the child and a third person who may or may not be a relative. The judge will therefore only allow a partner who is married to a parent holding parental responsibilities some personal relationship rights to the child, such as contact rights (visiting, lodging right *etc.*).[15] The partner can never obtain parental responsibilities.

In some cases (and especially when one parent is deprived from the exercise of parental responsibilities) the family judge can order that the child shall be entrusted to a third person (see Art. 373-2 French CC). Usually this third person is a grandparent; it will very seldom be the partner of a parent. When the child is entrusted to a third person's care, the parental responsibilities are still exercised by their holder; the third person undertakes all ordinary acts related to the child's supervision and upbringing (Art. 373-4 *French CC*).

(b) Living with that parent in a formalised relationship (registered partnership, civil union, *pacte civil de solidarité*...)

The same rules apply as under (a). But a very recent court order (*Tribunal de Grande Instance Paris*, 7 July 2004)[16] determined that two female same-sex partners can have joint parental responsibilities. First, only the mother of the three daughters had parental responsibilities, but her female partner adopted the three children (so called *adoption simple* which does not destroy the official bonds between the adopted child and the child's biological parents). The adoption normally transfers parental responsibilities to the adoptive parent. The women brought a petition to obtain joint parental responsibilities, which was accepted by the civil court. Sometimes (although a very recent evolution of French judicial practice),[17] the homosexual partner of a parent can obtain part of parental responsibilities through a delegation of parental responsibilities by the parent who is his or her partner.

---

15 The judge is free to decide whether the third person should be allowed to personal relationships with the child. Even if the situation is exceptional a visiting right can be denied if this corresponds to the child's interest; the court must give reasons for its decision, see French Supreme Court, Civ. I, 10.05.1977, *Bull. civ.* I, No. 213; 16.07.1997, *Dr. famille* 1997 n° 173 with obs. Murat. For a *droit d'hébergement* (housing, lodging right), v. French Supreme Court, Civ. I, 05.05.1986, *Bull. civ.* I, No. 112.

16 http://www.legalnews.fr.

17 See *Le Monde* 23.09.2004, p. 12.

(c) Living with that parent in a non formalised relationship

The same rules apply as under (a) and (b).

GERMANY

(a) Married to that parent

The spouse of the parent holding parental responsibilities can participate in or obtain parental responsibilities in the following ways:

First of all, the spouse of the parent holding parental responsibilities has the option of obtaining parental responsibilities for the child of his or her spouse through adoption. In accordance with § 1741 para. 2 sent. 3 German CC, a spouse can, on their own, adopt the child of his or her spouse. Subsequently the child will acquire the legal position of a joint child of the spouses, § 1754 para. 1 German CC. This situation also leads to the spouses obtaining joint responsibility for the child, § 1754 para. 3 German CC. For an adoption to be effective, a number of declarations of consent must be obtained, namely that of the child who is to be adopted, that of his or her parents and, if applicable, that of the spouse; these declarations of consent must be recorded by a notary, they are absolute and valid indefinitely and must, with a few exceptions, be made in person and are irrevocable (§ 1750 para. 1 - 3 German CC); furthermore, they become ineffective if the application for adoption is withdrawn or refused (§ 1750 para. 4 sent. 1 German CC).[18] According to § 1741 para. 1 sent. 1 German CC, adoption must always serve the child's best interests. In most cases, however, so-called 'stepchild adoption' does not serve the child's best interests as long as the other parent is alive. Stepchild adoption must not destroy the child's relationship with the other parent, who as former partner of the parent caring for the child might seem to that parent worth displacing.[19] Only in cases where a personal relationship with the other parent has never existed, or no longer does so, or where it has at least become considerably less close, can stepchild adoption serve the child's best interests.[20] In accordance with § 1752 para. 1 German CC, the declaration of adoption of the child is made by the guardianship court on application by the adopting parent.

In all other cases, that is, without recourse to adoption, there is no change to the original attribution of parental responsibilities; this means that the spouse of the parent holding parental responsibilities does not, for example, obtain (joint) parental responsibility for the latter's child as a result of marriage. However, by virtue of the *Gesetz zur Beendigung der Diskriminierung gleichgeschlechtlicher Gemeinschaften: Lebenspartnerschaften* (Law to end discrimination against same-sex partnerships: registered partnerships), which came into force on 8 August 2001, the legislature has created a provision for the specific arrangements of

---

18 D. SCHWAB, *Familienrecht*, 12th Edition, Munich: Beck, 2003, No. 702.

19 Th. RAUSCHER, *Familienrecht*, Heidelberg: C.F. Müller, 2001, No. 1153.

20 H.-U. Maurer, in: *Münchener Kommentar zum Bürgerlichen Gesetzbuch*, 4th Edition, Munich: Beck, 2002, § 1741 No. 32.

parental responsibility both in the cases under discussion here, i.e. marriage by one parent (§ 1687 b German CC) and, in § 9 Registered Partnership Act, the cases where a parent enters into a registered partnership with a same-sex partner.

According to § 1687 b para. 1 German CC, the spouse of a parent with sole parental responsibilities is entitled to participate in decision-making on matters relating to the child's everyday life, - the so-called 'limited parental responsibilities' (*kleines Sorgerecht*), - and, in accordance with § 1687 b para. 2 German CC, a 'right of representation in emergency situations' (*Notvertretungsrecht*) in the event of imminent danger. According to § 9 German Registered Partnership Act, the same applies to registered partners.

§ 1687 b para. 1 sent. 1 German CC and/or § 9 para. 1 German Registered Partnership Act refers to 'the spouse of the parent holding sole parental responsibility, who is not a parent of the child' being entitled to 'participate in decision-making' on 'matters relating to the child's everyday life' in 'agreement' with the parent holding parental responsibility. According to § 1687 b para. 3 German CC and/or § 9 para. 3 Registered Partnership Act, the family court can limit or rule out the rights provided for in § 1687 b para. 1 German CC (§ 9 para. 1 German Registered Partnership Act), if this is necessary in the interests of the child's best interests.

The provisions of § 1687 b para. 1 German CC and/or § 9 para. 1 German Registered Partnership Act are not uncontroversial as far as their interpretation and importance in terms of legal policy is concerned. For instance, the legal literature has often criticised the lack of clarity concerning the exact nature of the acts constituting 'limited parental responsibilities'.[21]

One of the difficulties is the interpretation of the term 'consent' from the point of view of the binding effect of the 'consent' once it has been granted. Some have cited the way legislative procedure[22] was used to create the legal provision in question as proof that the intention of the legislature was that, once granted, the consent becomes binding. By virtue of the provision added in § 1687 b para. 3 German CC (§ 9 para. 3 German Registered Partnership Act), (only) the family court can restrict the rights provided for in § 1687 b para. 1 (§ 9 para. 1 German Registered Partnership Act) if this is necessary in the best interests of the child; continuous disputes between partners can harm the child's best interests.[23] According to predominant opinion, however, the requirement of 'consent' is not meant to be qualified by any restriction on the parental responsibilities of

21 D. SCHWAB, *Familienrecht*, 12th Edition, Munich: Beck, 2003, No. 604; Th. RAUSCHER, *Familienrecht*, Heidelberg: C.F. Müller, 2001, No. 1134.

22 See BT-Drucks. 14/3751, p. 39.

23 D. SCHWAB, 'Eingetragene Lebenspartnerschaft - ein Überblick', *FamRZ* 2001, 385, 394.

the parent who holds responsibility; for this reason, the opinion of the parent with sole responsibility is decisive in the event of a dispute.[24]

The legal scope of the term 'participation in decision-making' also raises problems. A right to participate in decision-making must mean more than merely the right to a hearing. This right to a hearing, in fact, already results from § 1353 para. 1 German CC (§ 2 German Registered Partnership Act) - duty to conjugal community, bearing of mutual responsibility - to the extent that the arrangements of the step-parent's marriage to the parent holding responsibility or the arrangements of the registered partnership are affected.[25] From this results the question whether the parent holding responsibility must come to an agreement with the step-parent, especially, regarding whether the former will cease to be the sole external representative of the child.[26]

Furthermore, the phrase 'matters relating to everyday life' requires interpretation. This terminology refers back to the legal definition of § 1687 para. 1 sent. 3 German CC (see Q 16 a). However, the situation outlined in § 1687 b German CC (§ 9 Registered Partnership Act) is different from that of § 1687 German CC, in that in § 1687 German CC the parents' right to decide becomes concentrated in one person due to their separation, in spite of their continuing to hold joint responsibility, whereas the provision of § 1687 b German CC (§ 9 German Registered Partnership Act) is based on the partners cohabiting, with only one partner holding sole responsibility.[27]

Finally, it is disputed under which conditions a parent can be deemed to hold sole parental responsibilities, which is necessary for the so-called limited parental responsibilities to come into play. Some, in an extensive interpretation, understand a parent to hold *sole* parental responsibility even in cases of joint responsibility where one parent had sole right to decide in matters relating to everyday life until they married or entered a registered partnership, either as a result of parental consent or of a court decision.[28] Although the requirement of sole parental responsibility does not appear meaningful due to the limited scope of the authorisation,[29] given the unambiguous wording and legislator's

---

24 G. Brudermüller, in: PALANDT, *Bürgerliches Gesetzbuch*, 64th Edition, Munich: Beck, 2005, § 9 LPartG No. 1.

25 Th. RAUSCHER, *Familienrecht*, Heidelberg: C.F. Müller, 2001, No. 1134.

26 D. SCHWAB, 'Eingetragene Lebenspartnerschaft - Ein Überblick', *FamRZ* 2001, 385, 395; Th. RAUSCHER, *Familienrecht*, Heidelberg: C.F. Müller, 2001, No. 1134.

27 G. BRUDERMÜLLER, in: PALANDT, *Bürgerliches Gesetzbuch*, 64th Edition, Munich: Beck, 2005, § 9 LPartG No. 1.

28 See St. MOTZER, 'Die neueste Entwicklung von Gesetzgebung und Rechtsprechung auf dem Gebiet von Sorgerecht und Umgangsrecht', *FamRZ* 2001, 1034, 1040; G. Brudermüller, in: PALANDT, *Bürgerliches Gesetzbuch*, 64th Edition, Munich: Beck, 2005, § 9 LPartG No. 1.

29 N. DETHLOFF, 'Die Eingetragene Lebenspartnerschaft - Ein neues familienrechtliches Institut', *NJW* 2001, 2598, 2602.

intention it indeed appears to be a requirement that the parents do not hold joint responsibilities.

Despite the objections against the 'limited parental responsibilities'[30] raised in legal literature from a constitutional law point of view, the Constitutional Court has ruled the provision of § 9 para. 1 German Registered Partnership Act, which corresponds to § 1687 b para. 1 German CC, to be compatible with the constitution.[31] It ruled that in entrusting 'limited parental responsibilities' to the spouse or registered partner, the legislature does not interfere with the parental rights resulting from Art. 6 para. 2 German Basic Law, which belong to the parent who does not hold parental responsibilities. It was not the 'limited parental responsibilities' derived from the sole parental responsibility of a parent that deprive the parent who does not hold parental responsibility of his or her responsibilities, but the decisions by the family court which transferred sole responsibility to one parent rather than another. The rights of a parent who does not have parental responsibility cannot be affected if a third person living with the child were to exercise joint parental responsibilities in part, in agreement with the parent holding sole parental responsibility.

The right of representation in emergency situations stipulated in § 1687 b para. 2 German CC (§ 9 para. 2 German Registered Partnership Act) corresponds to an actual need, that is, to the enabling of the step-parent to act in the best interests of the child in the event of imminent danger; because the parent holding parental responsibility must be notified immediately, this does not produce conflict with the parental rights.[32] This competence in emergency situations has an effect on the outside world and includes legal representation, for example in the case of medical treatment after an accident.[33]

(b) Living with that parent in a formalised relationship (registered partnership, civil union, *pacte civil de solidarité*...)

Since mixed-sex couples under German law do not have the opportunity to legally formalise their relationship other than by marriage, this question is not applicable. Regarding the situation of same-sex partners, see the answer to Q 28.

(c) Living with that parent in a non formalised relationship

'Non-marital step-parenthood' does not offer the partners of parents holding sole parental responsibility the option to obtain joint parental responsibility. Declarations of responsibility in accordance with § 1626 a para. 1 No. 1 German CC (see Q 20), stating the assumption of joint responsibility for a child, can only be made by the biological parents. Furthermore, partners in non-formalised relationships cannot adopt the biological child of a partner with sole parental

---

30 Th. Rauscher, *Familienrecht*, Heidelberg: C.F. Müller, 2001, No. 1134.
31 BVerfG 29.01.2003, *NJW* 2002, 2245, 2250.
32 Th. Rauscher, *Familienrecht*, Heidelberg: C.F. Müller, 2001, No. 1134.
33 BT-Drucks. 14/3751 p. 39.

responsibility; § 1741 para. 2 sent. 3 German CC applies only to spouses. Finally, the parent holding sole parental responsibility is not allowed to transfer part of his or her parental responsibility to the other partner or to grant him or her the authority to care jointly for the child in the context of an agreement; parental responsibility is a highly personal duty.[34] The parent with sole responsibility does, however, have the option to involve his or her partner in the fulfilment of his or her duties on a revocable basis; the essence from a legal point of view in this respect is the consent of the parent with parental responsibilities. The matter of the consent is the permission to fulfil parental care functions; it constitutes a legally recognised justification for the involvement of third parties, that is otherwise not permitted.[35]

GREECE

(a) Married to that parent

The partner of the parent can only obtain parental responsibilities if she or he adopts the child. For this purpose a court decision is required. The court ascertains whether the adoption serves the interests of the child and whether further conditions laid down by the law have been met (Art. 1558 Greek CC). These conditions refer to the consent of the holders of parental responsibilities (Art. 1550 Greek CC), to the consent of the child itself, if the child is above 12 years old (Art. 1555 Greek CC), as well as to the age difference between the adoptive parent and the child, which should never be less than 15 years (Art. 1544 para. 3 Greek CC). When the judgement becomes final, the two spouses (*i.e.* the adoptive parent and the natural parent) have parental responsibilities (Art. 1562 in connection with Art. 1510 para. 1 Greek CC), whereas the relations between the child and its other natural parent are invariably interrupted (Art. 1561 Greek CC).

(b) Living with that parent in a formalised relationship (registered partnership, civil union, *pacte civil de solidarité*...)

In Greece there is no formalised relationship other than marriage.[36]

(c) Living with that parent in a non-formalised relationship

The partner of a parent in a non-formalised relationship can only obtain parental responsibilities if he adopts the child. Nevertheless, in practice this is not an option since it results in an interruption to the relations of the child with both its natural parents. Art. 1562 Greek CC, which provides that the relations of the child with the natural parent, who is the partner of the adoptive parent, still prevail, is not applicable in this case, since it presupposes that the partners are married. In spite of the prevailing opinion in the legal literature,[37] according to which the provisions of the Civil Code on marriage can be applied, by

---

[34] D. SCHWAB, *Familienrecht*, 12th Edition, Munich: Beck, 2003, No. 593.

[35] D. SCHWAB, *Familienrecht*, 12th Edition, Munich: Beck, 2003, No. 593.

[36] See An engagement (Art. 1346-1349 Greek CC) is a mere promise to marry and, as such, it cannot be considered as a separate method of formalising a relationship.

[37] P. AGALLOPOULOU, 'Cohabitation and one-parent Families According to Greek Law', *International Family Law*, 2003, p. 24-28 at 25, with further references.

analogy, during cohabitation, the courts are rather reluctant to do so.[38] Thus, in practice, adoption is not really an option.

HUNGARY

(a) Married to that parent

A partner who is married to a parent with parental responsibilities (this married parent is the step-parent according to the Hungarian law) generally doesn't have any right to the parental responsibilities. Of course he or she can take part in the everyday care of the child, without legal regulation. He or she does not have the right to legally represent child or administer the child's property, especially if a third person is involved.

Whether the step-parent can take part in decisions having to do with the education and schooling of the child obviously depends on how old the child is when the step-parent marries the holder of the parental responsibilities.

Nevertheless, a partner who is married to a holder of the parental responsibilities can have rights of parental responsibilities in certain cases or with regard to certain aspects:

- A step-parent can obtain full parental responsibilities through step-parent adoption, which has conditions that are simpler than those of an adoption by persons who are not relatives or not step-parents. Nevertheless the consent of the child's other parent and the consent of a child over 14 to the adoption are requirements even to an adoption by a step-parent. These consents are required because the other parent's parental responsibilities, including the right to contact, come to an end with an adoption, even in an adoption by a step-parent.
- If the spouse of a parent is related to the child, the spouse's right to contact with the child remains even if the child is placed with the other parent or with third persons.
- If both parents die or the parental responsibilities of both persons end by any other reason, the spouse of the parent with parental responsibilities (a person who has a familial relationship with the child) is among the persons the public guardianship authority will consider when a guardian for the child is appointed.

(b) Living with that parent in a formalised relationship (registered partnership, civil union, *pacte civil de solidarité*...)

Hungarian law does not recognise any form of formalised relationship.

(c) Living with that parent in a non formalised relationship

A partner who lives with the parent in a relationship that is not formalised does not have the right to the parental responsibilities, similar the situation in Q 27a. He or she can take part in the care of the child without legal regulation, the

---

[38] This reluctance on the part of the Supreme Court can be seen in decision 14/2004, accessible at www.dsanet.gr.

partner does not have any other right or duty simply because he or she is the parent's partner.

Among the rights enumerated in Q 27a, this parent can only have the one mentioned under point 3. If both parents die or the parental responsibilities of both persons end by any other reason, the partner of the parent with parental responsibilities (a person who has a familial relationship with the child) is among the persons the public guardianship authority will consider when a guardian for the child is appointed. He or she does not have the right to step-parent adoption or to contact with the child.

IRELAND

(a) Married to that parent

Adoption is the only way of investing the partner of a parent holding parental responsibilities with parental responsibilities in respect of that child. To achieve this, however, the natural parent must also adopt his or her own child even though he or she has parental responsibilities in respect of the child. There is no mechanism within the existing adoption code whereby the natural parents can continue a legal parenting regime, and, at the same time, allow the custodial parent to adopt the child with his or her partner. The Irish Adoption Board has called for a change in the legislation to facilitate a new spouse of a natural parent obtaining joint guardianship rights with the mother, while at the same time facilitating the continuation of any factual relationship of the non-custodial natural parent with the child. The introduction of a divorce jurisdiction in Ireland in 1996 has not distorted the pattern of adoptions, and will not do so as stepparent adoptions will not arise. Under the current divorce legislation neither parent loses guardianship on divorce.[39]

(b) Living with that parent in a formalised relationship (registered partnership, civil union, *pacte civil de solidarité*...)

Not at all.

(c) Living with that parent in a non formalised relationship

Not at all.

ITALY

(a) Married to that parent

In such a situation, the partner can apply to the Family Proceedings Court for a particular form of adoption of the minor (Art. 44 (b)). This adoption does not break the ties between the adopted minor and his family of origin, but confers the *status* of an adopted child on the minor and attributes full parental responsibility, identical in content to that of the biological parent-spouse, to the person who adopts the child.

---

39 Sec. 10 (2), Irish Family Law (Divorce) Act 1996.

(b) Living with that parent in a formalised relationship (registered partnership, civil union, *pacte civil de solidarité* ...)

The Italian Legal system does not provide for such formalised relationships. Consequently such situations are allow neither the possibility of adoption (Art. 44 (b)), Italian Adoption Law), nor the possibility to obtain the parental responsibility.

(c) Living with that parent in a non formalised relationship

The partner that lives with the parent cannot apply for the adoption if it is not one of the particular situations described by Art. 44 (b)) Italian Adoption Law; adoption is only allowed for the biological parent. Therefore, neither is it possible to obtain parental responsibility.

LITHUANIA

(a) Married to that parent

According to the Lithuanian law, marriage is possible only between persons of different sex. In the event of marriage, a spouse of the parent can obtain parental responsibilities in either of two possible ways:

- if he or she is the biological parent of a child, by acknowledgement of paternity (maternity) or by the establishment of paternity by court judgment;
- if he or she is not the biological parent of a child, by the adoption of the child.

(b) Living with that parent in a formalized relationship (registered partnership, civil union, *pacte civil de solidarité ...*)

According to the Lithuanian law, the registered partnership is possible only between a man and a women *i.e.* only between persons of different sex (Art. 3.229 Lithuanian CC). In the event of registered partnership, the partner of the parent can obtain parental responsibilities in either of the two possible ways:

- if he or she is the biological parent of a child, by acknowledgement of paternity (maternity) or by the establishment of paternity by court judgment;
- if he or she is not the biological parent of a child, by the adoption of the child.

However, adoption in such a case will be complicated because according to Art. 3.210 Lithuanian CC, the right to adopt a child may be exercised only by married couples. An unmarried person may be allowed to adopt a child only in exceptional cases.

(c) Living with that parent in a non formalized relationship

In the event of a man and a woman living in a non formalised relationship, the partner of the parent can obtain parental responsibilities in either of two possible ways:

- if he or she is the biological parent of a child, by acknowledgement of paternity (maternity) or by the establishment of paternity by court judgment;

- if he or she is not the biological parent of a child, by the adoption of the child.

However, the adoption in such a case will be complicated because according to Art. 3.210 Lithuanian CC, the right to adopt a child may be exercised only by married couples. An unmarried person may be allowed to adopt a child only in exceptional cases.

THE NETHERLANDS

(a) Married to that parent

Since 2001 a parent and his or her spouse who is not a parent exercise joint parental responsibilities over a child born during a marriage by operation of law unless legal family ties exist between the child and another parent (Art. 1:253 sa Dutch CC).

(b) Living with that parent in a formalised relationship (registered partnership, civil union, *pacte civil de solidarité* ...)

When registered partnership was introduced in 1998 it had no legal consequences for the children of the registered partners. However, since 2001 Art. 1:253sa Dutch CC grants registered partners joint parental responsibilities over children born during their partnership unless legal family ties exist between the child and another parent.[40] If a biological father has not recognised his child, he will also be attributed joint parental responsibilities with the mother over a child born during their registered partnership on the basis of this Article, unless legal family ties exist between the child and another parent. Should he recognise his child at a later date, the parents' joint parental responsibilities will then be based on Art. 253aa Dutch CC. When registered partnership was inserted into the Dutch CC in 1998, the legislature failed to accordingly amend important provisions, such as the one that relates to the annulment of a registered partnership.[41]

(c) Living with that parent in a non-formalised relationship

The parent and his or her partner may file an application for joint parental responsibilities with the court pursuant to section Art. 1:253t Dutch CC. The court will only grant the application if the parent's partner has a close personal relationship with the child. Furthermore, if legal family ties exist between the child and another parent, the application will only be granted if prior to the application the parent and the other person have jointly cared continuously for the child for at least one year, and the parent who makes the application has been vested with sole parental responsibilities for at least three continuous

---

40 See M.J. VONK, 'One, two or three parents? Lesbian co-mothers and a known-donor with 'family life' under Dutch Law', *International Journal of Law, Policy and the Family*, 2004, Dutch Vol. 18, p. 103-117.

41 A proposal of law (*Kamerstukken Tweede Kamer*, 2003-2004, No. 29353) was introduced in parliament in December 2003 containing a number of changes in Book 1 of the Dutch Civil Code with regard to registered partnerships. This proposal does not yet however contain changes with regard to the annulment of a registered partnership.

years. The application will be rejected if, in the light of the interests of the other parent, there is a well-founded fear that the best interests of the child would be neglected if it were granted. Art. 1:253t Dutch CC makes no distinction between same-sex partners and opposite sex-partners.

As a consequence of the introduction of continued joint parental responsibilities after divorce, termination of a registered partnership or separation, and the strict criteria maintained by the courts for attributing parental responsibilities to only one of the parents, it is in practice very difficult for the partner of a parent to obtain joint parental responsibilities as only two people can have parental responsibilities over a child under Dutch law.

NORWAY

(a) Married to that parent

No person other than the legal father or mother can obtain parental responsibilities, except after the death of a parent.

(b) Living with that parent in a formalised relationship (registered partnership, civil union, *pacte civil de solidarité* ...)

No person other than the legal father or mother can obtain parental responsibilities, except after the death of a parent.

(c) Living with that parent in a non formalised relationship

No person other than the legal father or mother can obtain parental responsibilities, except after the death of a parent.

POLAND

(a) Married to that parent

Should the parent's spouse adopt the child, the prior parental authority does not cease (Art. 123 § 2 Polish Family and Guardianship Code), since the adoption of the child is held jointly by the parent and the parent's spouse who adopted the child.

(b) Living with that parent in a formalised relationship (registered partnership, civil union, *pacte civil de solidarité* ...)

These institutions are not present in Polish law.

(c) Living with that parent in a non formalised relationship

An informal relationship with the parent of a child does not form a prerequisite to the granting of parental authority.

PORTUGAL

(a) Married to that parent

Through full adoption of the spouse's child (Art. 1979 *et seq* especially 1986 Portuguese CC).

(b) Living with that parent in a formalised relationship (registered partnership, civil union, *pacte civil de solidarité* ...)

Within the Portuguese legal system, there is no legal situation that may be subsumed into the concept of 'formalised relationship' such as 'registered partnership', 'civil union' and '*pacte civil de solidarité*'.

(c) Living with that parent in a non formalised relationship

In accordance with Art. 7 Portuguese Law No. 7/2001 of 11 May 2001, the right of adoption is recognised for partners of different sexes that live together under the terms laid down in Art. 1979 Portuguese CC. Thus, one of the cohabiting partners may adopt the child of the other (full adoption) if she or he is over 25 years of age and less than 60, and if the age difference between the adopter and adoptee is not more than 50 years (Art. 1979 No. 1 and 4 Portuguese CC).

Legal literature does not consider it necessary to verify that the couple have cohabited for the minimum period;[42] two years under the terms of Art. 1 Portuguese Law No. 7/2001 of 11 May 2001.

RUSSIA

Russian law couples parental responsibility to a legal filial link, not social parentage. Therefore the rights of the spouse or the partner of the child's parent who participates in the education of child are not legally protected. It has been noticed[43] that by leaving a person who has had close family links with the child without legal protection, Russian law disregards the right to protection of family life safeguarded by Art. 8 European Convention on Human Right and Fundamental Freedoms.

(a) Married to a parent of a child

A person married to the parent of the child can only obtain parental responsibility by through adoption.

(b) Living with a parent of a child in a formalised relationship (registered partnership, civil union, *pacte civil de solidarité* ...)

Russian law does not provide for formalised relationships for persons living together without marriage.

(c) Living with the parent of a child in a non formalised relationship

A person living with the parent of the child in a non formalised relationship can only obtain parental responsibility by through adoption.

SPAIN

(a) Married to that parent

If parental responsibility vests with both the father and mother, the husband or wife of either can not acquire parental responsibility unless one parental responsibility holder consents to adoption by the other parental responsibility holder's spouse.

---

42 F. PITÃO, *União de facto no Direito Português*, Coimbra: Almedina.

43 By M. ANTOKOLSKAIA, *Family Law* (*Semeinoe pravo*), Jurist, Moscow: 1999, p. 192.

If parental responsibility is held individually by the father or mother, parental responsibility can be acquired by either the husband or wife through adoption. There is a simplified procedure for step-parent adoption. The husband or wife might also acquire parental responsibility upon the death of the parent, if he or she is appointed guardian of the child (see Q 34), although the judge is free to disregard this appointment if it is not in the child's best interests.

(b) Living with that parent in a formalised relationship (registered partnership, civil union, *pacte civil de solidarité* ...)

The situation is basically the same as under Q 27a. The registered partner of a parent cannot acquire parental responsibility if it is jointly held by both parents unless the parent who is not his or her partner consents and relinquishes parental responsibility.

If there is only one holder of parental responsibility, his or her partner can adopt the child. Step-parent adoption is not confined to the spouse of a parent but also possible for a different-sex cohabitant, regardless of whether they are registered partners (Art. 115 Catalan Family Code). For same-sex partners see Q 28.

The parent's partner may also acquire parental responsibility upon the death of the parent if he is appointed by that parent as a guardian of the child (see Q 34), although the judge is free to disregard this agreement in consideration of the child's best interests.

(c) Living with that parent in a non formalised relationship

See above under Q 27b.

SWEDEN

(a) Married to that parent

According to Swedish law parental responsibilities are almost exclusively a right and an obligation of the parents. A child can have no more than two legal custodians or guardians at a time. As long as one or both parents are fit custodians, no other custodian can be appointed. It follows that it is not possible for a step-parent to obtain parental responsibilities as long as these belong to a parent. Adoption of the child is the only exception to the rule, Chapter 4 Sec. 3 Swedish Children and Parents Code. This requires, in addition to the general conditions for adoption, that the other spouse is the sole custodian of the child and consents to the adoption.

(b) Living with that parent in a formalised relationship (registered partnership, civil union, *pacte civil de solidarité* ...)

Since 2003, a registered partner may adopt his or her partner's child and thereby obtain full parental responsibilities.[44] The same conditions apply as when a spouse wishes to adopt the other spouse's child.

---

[44] SFS 2002:603.

(c) Living with that parent in a non-formalised relationship

A person living in a non-formalised relationship with the child's parent is excluded from obtaining parental responsibilities in respect of the child.[45] In Swedish law, cohabitees cannot adopt each other's children.

SWITZERLAND

(a) Married to that parent

Step-parents do not have parental responsibilities unless they have adopted a stepchild. However, each spouse must 'provide the other with assistance in an appropriate manner in the exercise of parental responsibilities in relation to the other spouse's children and stand in for the other if circumstances require' (Art. 299 Swiss CC).

Since the biological parent requires the consent of the step-parent to include the child in the household, the corresponding authority is also, as a rule, granted when duties are divided between the spouses.[46] The step-parent may moreover represent the biological parent in respect to parental responsibilities, if the latter is, for instance, ill or absent and an urgent matter so requires. On the other hand, if the law requires the consent of the parents, the step-parent is not authorised to act (Art. 90 § 2, 260 § 2, 265a § 1 Swiss CC). If a biological parent cannot exercise his or her parental responsibilities on a continuing basis, the step-parent does not simply take the other spouse's place. On the contrary, parental responsibilities must be taken away from the biological parent and a guardianship must be established. However, the step-parent may also be taken into consideration as a guardian.

By adopting a stepchild, the spouse of the holder of parental responsibilities may likewise obtain (joint) parental responsibilities. A person may adopt his or her spouse's child if the spouses have been married for at least five years (Art. 264a § 3 Swiss CC). In order for the adoption to be approved by the competent authority the other prerequisites for an adoption must also be fulfilled (Art. 264 *et seq* Swiss CC). The adoption of a stepchild gives rise to a joint parent-child relationship with respect to the biological parent and his or her spouse (Art. 267 Swiss CC).[47] Consequently, the spouses have joint parental responsibilities.[48]

---

45 The only exception relates to a duty to maintain the child, under certain conditions. Issues of maintenance, however, fall outside the scope of this Report.

46 C. HEGNAUER, *Grundriss des Kindesrechts*, p. 181 *et seq.*

47 P. BREITSCHMID, Art. 267 ZGB, p. 1418 (No. 7), in: H. HONSELL, N.P. VOGT, TH. GEISER (ed.), *Basler Kommentar zum Schweizerischen Privatrecht, Zivilgesetzbuch I*, Art. 1-456 ZGB, Basel: Helbing & Lichtenhahn, 2002.

48 P. BREITSCHMID, Art. 267 ZGB, p. 1420 (No. 17), in: H. HONSELL, N.P. VOGT, TH. GEISER (ed.), *Basler Kommentar zum Schweizerischen Privatrecht, Zivilgesetzbuch I*, Art. 1-456 ZGB, Basel: Helbing & Lichtenhahn, 2002.

(b) Living with that parent in a formalised relationship (registered partnership, civil union, *pacte civil de solidarité* ...)

Currently no such arrangements exist under Swiss legislation. With regard to the registered partnership of couples of the same sex, which is not yet valid in law, please refer to Q 6 and Q 21.

(c) Living with that parent in a non formalised relationship

The partner in a non-formalised relationship may not be the holder of parental responsibilities. Art. 299 Swiss CC may be applied analogously, if need be.[49]

[49] I. SCHWENZER, Art. 299 ZGB, p. 1583 (No. 1), in: H. HONSELL, N.P. VOGT, TH. GEISER (ed.), *Basler Kommentar zum Schweizerischen Privatrecht, Zivilgesetzbuch I*, Art. 1-456 ZGB, Basel: Helbing & Lichtenhahn, 2002.

QUESTION 28

C. ATTRIBUTION OF PARENTAL RESPONSIBILITIES

III. Other Persons

Does it make any difference if the partner of the parent holding parental responsibilities is of the same sex?

AUSTRIA

A homosexual partner cannot obtain parental responsibilities for the biological child of his or her partner, neither upon application nor via an adoption. In 2002 the Supreme Court rejected the application for joint parental responsibilities in the case of a lesbian couple.[1] Whether a homosexual partner may be regarded as a foster parent under Sec. 186 Austrian CC and thus have the right to petition the court in matters of care and education as well as in contact proceedings has been left open by the above mentioned Supreme Court decision.[2]

BELGIUM

Not relevant. See Q 27

BULGARIA

There is neither legislation nor practice on same sex couples in Bulgaria.

CZECH REPUBLIC

Czech legislation has not yet recognised registered partnership of persons of the same sex. The act is under discussion in the Parliament. Even if adopted, the act on registered partnership of persons of the same sex does not take into account any rights and duties of one partner in relation to the other partner's child.

DENMARK

Yes, only married partners may obtain parental authority and marriage is only open to opposite sexes.

ENGLAND & WALES

Under the current law same-sex partners of a parent with parental responsibility are treated no differently to any other individual. They can acquire parental responsibility principally by obtaining a residence order under (see Q 27a).[3]

---

1 *Oberster Gerichtshof,* 25.09.2002, *Österreichische Juristenzeitung - EvBl,* 2003, No. 16, p. 102 = *ÖJZ-LSK* 2003/2.

2 See also M. SCHWIMANN, *Familienrecht,* 5th Edition, Vienna: LexisNexis ARD Orac, 2004, p. 80; Q 27a, 27c and Q 31.

3 But note the points made in Q 25 above.

Under the British Civil Partnerships Act 2004 (which is not yet in force) it will be possible for the same-sex partners (but no-one else) to formally register their partnership and those that do will be able to acquire parental responsibility either by making a formal parental responsibility agreement with other holders of parental responsibility or by applying to court for a parental responsibility order (see Q 27b).[4]

FINLAND

The sex of the partner has no significance according to the Finnish Child Custody and the Right of Access Act. Same-sex partners have also in practice been able to obtain joint custody of the other partner's biological (or adoptive) child. On 19 October 2001 the Supreme Court of Justice assigned custody of two siblings to the female partner of their mother after her death instead of to the father of the children. The mother had had the sole custody of the children, aged 12 and 14 at the time of the decision, who had been living with the mother and her female partner in Finland for several years. The father was living abroad and the children resisted moving to live with him. The father would not have been able to obtain an enforcement order against the will of the children and the court therefore found such a custody order not to be in the best interest of the children (KKO 2001:110).

FRANCE

No. The partner of the parent holding parental responsibilities can only try to obtain a contact right from the family judge (*juge aux affaires familiales*) (see Art. 371-4 para. 2 French CC). The judge will discern the child's interests. This visiting right (or more generally the '*relations*,' or relationships, between the child and the third person) can be decided by the judge without regard to the gender of the parent's partner.[5]

GERMANY

Since a major reform of the Registered Partnership Act, which took effect on 1 January 2005, a same-sex partner living in a registered partnership can adopt the child of his or her partner, § 9 para. 7 Registered Partnership Act. The child thus obtains the legal position of a joint child of the same-sex partners in accordance with § 1754 para. 1 German CC.

Moreover, the registered partner of a parent with sole parental responsibilities is entitled to participate in decision-making on matters relating to the child's everyday life, § 9 para. 1 Registered Partnership Act. Please refer to the comments on limited parental responsibilities in answer to Q 27a.

---

4 *Viz* pursuant to the changes to be introduced by the British Civil Partnerships Act 2004, see Q 27.

5 See, for example, CA Aix-en-Provence, 12.03.2002, *D.* 2003. 1528 with annotation by CADOU: attribution of visiting rights to the female former-partner of the mother.

If the same-sex partner does not cohabit with the parent holding sole parental responsibilities on a formalised basis, i.e. without having established a registered partnership, he or she may only be granted the exercise of individual duties of parental responsibility within the context of the revocable consent granted by the parent holding sole parental responsibilities. In such cases, no limited parental responsibilities exist. In addition, that which has been said in answer to Q 27c applies.

GREECE

The issue is the same as in Q 27c. In other words, the partner of a parent can only obtain parental responsibilities if he adopts the child. In such a case, however, the relations of the child with both its natural parents are interrupted. The exception under Art. 1562 Greek CC only applies to married couples. However, same-sex marriage is still not possible in Greece,[6] and the courts deny the application of Art. 1562 Greek CC by analogy in the case of cohabitation. In any event, it is questionable whether adoption would serve the interests of the child in such a case.

HUNGARY

This question has no meaning in the Hungarian law with regard to the above mentioned; both the married partner of a holder of parental responsibilities and a partner living in a non-formalised relationship with the parent have very restricted rights.

IRELAND

No.

ITALY

Yes. The Italian legal system only permits adoption to the spouse of the biological parent and does not foresee formal union to people of the same sex (registered partnership, civil union, *pacte civil de solidarité*).

LITHUANIA

Yes. Lithuanian law does not recognise partnerships between persons of the same sex. If the partners are of the same sex, the court will refuse the adoption of a child to the partner on the basis of the best interests of the child.[7] A partner who is the same sex as the parent of a child may not obtain parental responsibilities.

---

6 Although the relevant articles of the Civil Code do not explicitly provide that different sexes is a prerequisite for marriage, same-sex marriage is excluded, according to prevailing opinion. On this issue see E. KOUNOUGERI-MANOLEDAKI, *Family Law, Vol. I*, 3rd Edition, Athens-Thessaloniki: Sakkoulas, 2003, p. 64, with further references [in Greek].

7 See also Judgment of the European Court of Human Rights in the case *Fretté v. France*, 26.02.2002.

THE NETHERLANDS

No, neither Art. 1:253sa nor Art. 1:253t Dutch CC distinguish between whether the spouse or (registered) partner is of the same sex or the opposite sex. The only existing difference is that in a female-female marriage, only the woman who gives birth to the child is a parent by operation of law. By operation of law, joint parental responsibilities will be attributed to both women, just as with a heterosexual married couple, unless the child already has legal family ties to another parent. (Art. 1:253sa § 1 Dutch CC).

NORWAY

It does not make any difference if the partners with parental responsibilities are of the same sex.

POLAND

No. There are no formalised same-sex relationships under Polish law. Neither does a non-formalised same-sex relationship (nor any non-formalised relationship) form a prerequisite to the granting of parental authority (see Q 27).

PORTUGAL

Yes. According to Art. 7 Portuguese Law No. 7/2001 of 11 May 2001, mentioned above, the right to adopt under conditions analogous to those of spouses (Art. 1979 Portuguese CC) is only possible for people of differing sex who live together.

RUSSIA

A partner of the child's parent can never obtain parental responsibility other than through adoption. Russian law contains no formal obstacles for a same-sex partner of a child's parent to adopt the child.[8] However, such adoption is unlikely to be allowed. The law grants a court broad discretional power to decide whether or not adoption is in the best interests of the child and, particularly, whether or not such adoption would be favourable for the physical, psychological, spiritual and moral development of a child (Art. 124 (1) and 125 Russian Family Code). There is little doubt that, considering the current low level of acceptance of same-sex relationships in Russia, the court would most likely deem upbringing in a same-sex union as being not in the best interests of the child.[9]

---

8 N. ALEKSEEV, *Gay-Marriage: A XXIst Century Puzzle. Family status of same-sex couples in International, National and Local Law, (Gey-brak. Semeinii status odnopolikh par v mezgdynarodnom, natsional'nom I mestnom prave),* Moscow: BECK, 2002, 388.

9 A similar pessimistic prediction was made by N. ALEKSEEV regarding the prospect of same-sex partners to be appointed as guardians or foster parents. N. ALEKSEEV, *Legal Regulation of the Status of Sequel Minorities. Russia in the light of the perceives of the International organisation and national legislation of the foreign countries (Pravovoe regulirovanie polozgenia sexual'nikh men'shinstv. Rossia v svete praktiki mezgdynarodnikx opganizaii I natsional'nogo zakonodatel'stva stran mipa),* Moscow: BECK, 2002, p. 219.

SPAIN

For the moment, adoption by same-sex partners is only possible in the Basque Country, Navarra and Aragon. Catalonia will introduce this possibility before the end of 2004. Same-sex adoption will also be possible under the Spanish Civil Code regime if an announced reform is carried out. It will then make no difference, at least in written law.

SWEDEN

Since 2003, there are no differences in treatment between heterosexual and homosexual step-parents as regards parental responsibilities.

SWITZERLAND

The law concerning registered partnerships which, as mentioned, is still subject to a referendum, contains the following provision: 'If a person has children, his or her partner will assist his or her partner in fulfilling their obligation in respect of maintenance and in discharging parental responsibilities in an appropriate manner and shall stand in for his or her partner if circumstances require' (Art. 27 § 1). In terms of contents this corresponds to the provision with respect to step-parents (Art. 299 Swiss CC).

QUESTION 29

C. ATTRIBUTION OF PARENTAL RESPONSIBILITIES

III. Other Persons

How, if at all, is the attribution of parental responsibilities in the partner affected by the ending of his/her relationship with the parent? Distinguish according to the different relationships referred to in Q 27 and Q 28.

AUSTRIA

Since it is not possible for a spouse or life partner of a parent to participate in parental responsibilities, the end of the relationship has no effect on parental responsibilities. However, after the relationship ends, the child may be granted the right to maintain contact with the former spouse or life partner of the child's parent, if the break-up would endanger the interests of the child (Sec. 148(4) Austrian CC).[1]

BELGIUM

The partner of a parent can never get parental responsibilities. The kind of relationship between the parent and the parent's partner (marriage, formalised relationship, non formalised relationship) is of no relevance. The most the partner of a parent can hope for, once the relationship with the parent has ended, is contact with the child, if he or she can prove the existence of a significant affectionate relationship with the child and if it appears that this contact is in the interests of the child (Art. 375 *bis* Belgian CC). However, the law recognises 'custodianship'; the voluntary transfer of (most of the) parental responsibilities, during the life of the parent(s), on a contractual basis. (Art. 475*bis* - 475 *septies* Belgian CC). (See Q 30- 31).

BULGARIA

Within the relationships described in Q27, the parentage established by recognition or by adoption remains after the separation of the couple. The adoption could be challenged if there are additional grounds, '... a serious offence committed by one of the parties or in the presence of other circumstances which deeply upset the relations between the adoptive parent and the adopted person' (Art. 64 § 1 § 2 and 3 Bulgarian Family Code).

CZECH REPUBLIC

The partner of the child's parent does not have any rights or duties in relation to the child after their relationship is ended.

---

1 For details see Q 44c.

DENMARK

Joint parental authority between a parent and his or her partner is only possible when they are married and marriage is only open to opposite-sex partners. If they have obtained joint parental authority and they end their relationship, the situation is the same as for married parents. Joint parental authority continues after legal separation, divorce and the termination of the relationship. When they no longer live together or intend to live separately, they can demand that the joint parental authority be terminated, see the principle in Art. 8 Danish Act on Parental Authority and Contact.

ENGLAND & WALES

The ending of the relationship with the parent does not in itself affect the attribution of parental responsibility. In the case of married parents both parents retain their responsibility notwithstanding their divorce or separation and the court has no power to divest them of that responsibility. A similar position obtains in relation to unmarried mothers.

Insofar as parental responsibility is acquired by an unmarried father living with the mother then again separation does not per se affect that allocation. However, it is open both to the mother (and indeed the father) to seek a court order under Sec. 4(3), English Children Act 1989 to end the father's parental responsibility. A similar position will obtain in relation to step-parents[2] and registered partners[3] who (prospectively) obtain parental responsibility by a formal agreement or court order.

For those partners who acquire parental responsibility following the making of a residence order (which under the current law is effectively the only way partners whether married or not to the parent with parental responsibility can acquire such responsibility) while the ending of the relationship with the parent will not itself end responsibility, it will be open to the parent to seek to end their partner's residence order which in turn will terminate parental responsibility.

FINLAND

The ending of any of the relationships mentioned above in Q 27 and Q 28 does not, as such, have an impact on the custody of the child.

FRANCE

The partner of the parent holding parental responsibilities cannot obtain parental responsibilities. The end of the partner's relationship with the parent therefore has no special consequence on parental responsibilities. The partner can go to court (the family judge (*juge aux affaires familiales*) is competent for such issues) to obtain a visiting right or a housing right (*droit d'hébergement*); the

---

2 *Viz* pursuant to the changes to be introduced by the British Civil Partnerships Act 2004, see Q 27.

3 *Viz* pursuant to the changes to be introduced by the British Civil Partnerships Act 2004, see Q 27.

judge will decide the issue with regard to the child's interests (Art. 371-4 French CC), especially taking into consideration the feelings the child has developed towards the previous partner of his parent.

GERMANY

Relationship of the type in Q 27a (spouse of the parent):

Here a distinction must be made according to the various permutations possible:

- If an adoption has already been completed, on divorce or annulment of the marriage the adopting spouse and the biological parent they were married to continue, on principle, to exercise joint parental responsibilities. Consequently, § 1687 German CC applies. In this context, please refer to the comments made in the answer to Q 16a.
- If there has been no adoption and if the spouse of the parent holding sole parental responsibility enjoyed only 'limited parental responsibilities', the following applies: The 'limited parental responsibilities' of the step-parent must always 'protect and secure' the care for and raising of the child;[4] therefore in accordance with § 1687 b para. 4 German CC they end once the spouses live apart on a permanent basis.

Relationship of the type in Q 27b:

This question is not applicable (see Q 27b above).

Relationship of the type in 27c (unmarried partner of the parent):

In the case of 'non-marital step-parenthood' the partner cohabiting with the parent holding parental responsibility without being married to him or her can only - as shown in answer to Q 27c - be assigned the exercise of individual areas of parental responsibility, as shown in answer to Q 27c, and that by way of consent, i.e. a revocable authorisation. The termination of the relationship, i.e. the separation of the unmarried cohabiting partners, is generally accompanied by an - implied, at least - revocation of any authorisations previously granted with regard to the exercise of specific aspects of parental responsibility.

Relationship of the type in Q 28:

Here the following distinction must be made:

If a same-sex partner cohabits with a parent holding sole parental responsibility in a registered partnership in accordance with the Registered Partnership Act, then § 9 para. 1 Registered Partnership Act applies, as shown in the answer to Q 28, and provides the registered partner with 'limited parental responsibilities'. If the registered partners live apart on a permanent basis, the 'limited parental responsibilities' end in accordance with § 9 para. 4 Registered Partnership Act, as the purpose associated with them, i.e. to secure and protect the care for and upbringing of the child by this step-parent, has ceased to exist.

---

4 BT-Drucks. 14/3751 p. 39.

With cohabitation that has not been formalised through a registered partnership, the termination of the relationship does not affect the attribution of parental responsibilities. Just as in the case of termination of a relationship between unmarried cohabiting mixed-sex partners, however, the termination of the relationship generally includes an implied revocation of any authorisations previously granted with regard to the exercise of specific aspects of parental responsibility.

GREECE

The partner of the parent can only obtain parental responsibilities if he adopts the child. This is not linked to the relationship between the parents, so it does not directly affect the attribution of parental responsibilities. Nevertheless, in view of the new circumstances, the holders of parental responsibilities may request the court to regulate this issue. For the case where the partner and the parent have been married, see the answer to Q 16a and for the case where they remained unmarried see answer to Q 23. The court will decide on this issue in the interest of the child by taking into consideration all the relevant factors. Under these circumstances, the attribution of parental responsibilities to the natural parent may be more probable, in view of the normally stronger ties of the child with its natural parent.[5]

HUNGARY

The rights of a partner when the partnership ends is an issue that has a very restricted meaning in Hungarian law because the partner of a holder of parental responsibilities has very restricted rights even during a marriage or partnership.

If a partner was the spouse of a holder of parental responsibilities:

- If the step-parent adopted the child, the adoption remains even if the marriage to the parent comes to an end.
- The Act does not regulate whether the parent's spouse retains the right of contact with the child when a relationship ends. This will be judged based on whether the marriage ended by the death of the holder of the parental responsibilities or by divorce. If the marriage ended as a consequence of the parent's death, it is logical to assume that the contact of the step-parent should remain, but if it ended by divorce the step-parent's contact with the child seems to be reasonable only if there was a strong emotional relationship between the child and the parent's ex-spouse.
- The appointment of a parent's partner as the child's guardian can result from the death of the holder of the parental responsibilities, provided that the other parent is also deceased or is not able to exercise parental responsibilities for some other reason. Nevertheless,

---

5 P. AGALLOPOULOU, in: A. GEORGIADIS and M. STATHOPOULOS (eds.), *Civil Code commentary, Vol. VIII, Family Law (Arts. 1505-1694)*, 2nd Edition, Athens: Law & Economy, P.N. Sakkoulas 2003, Art. 1513-1514 Greek CC, p. 226-227, No. 55.

> the awakening of the other parent's parental responsibilities will always take priority. If the relationship of the step-parent and the parent ended by divorce, the appointment of the ex step-parent as guardian can never occur.

If the partner lived together in a non-formalised relationship with the parent holding parental responsibilities, only one possibility can emerge among the above mentioned. The ex-partner can be appointed as guardian, provided of course, that there is no other parent able to exercise the parental responsibilities.

IRELAND

Not at all.

ITALY

If Art. 44 (b) Italian Adoption Law grants the spouse of a parent's the right to adopt, ending the marriage will have the same consequences to the attribution of parental responsibility as those that follow from a separation, divorce or annulment of the marriage (see Q 16). As the attribution of the parental responsibility to the unmarried partner of the parent is not possible, the termination of their relationship does not have any consequences.

LITHUANIA

In the event of Q 27, the answer is as follows: if the partner acknowledged his (or her) paternity (maternity) or has adopted a child *i.e.* he or she has acquired parental authority, the ending of relationship has no effect on his or her parental responsibilities. However, the ending of such a relationship may cause some problems related to the exercise of parental responsibilities *e.g.* regarding the determination of the child's place of residence, the contacts with the child, and the participation of the parents in the maintenance of the child *etc.* In such cases Art. 3.193 Lithuanian CC should be applied by analogy: parents shall make an agreement on the place of residence of the child and their mutual duties in maintaining their underage children, as well as on the procedure, amount and form of such maintenance. Such agreement shall be approved by the court (Art. 3.53 Lithuanian CC). In the absence of such agreement between the parents, all questions shall be decided by the court on the application of one of the parents. In respect of Q 28, the question does not have any relevance because partnerships between persons of the same sex are not allowed, and the partner may not obtain parental authority.

THE NETHERLANDS

Not at all in all cases mentioned under Q 27 and Q 28. Either one of the holders of parental responsibilities may apply for sole parental responsibilities. Again, the court will only attribute parental responsibilities to one of the ex-partners if this is in the best interests of the child. There are no presumptions that the legal parent is automatically the one to be granted sole parental responsibilities. If the parents' relationship comes to an end by virtue of the annulment of their registered partnership, this will, contrary to the annulment of a marriage, have consequences for the joint parental responsibilities that have come about by reason of the registered partnership.[6] If a marriage is annulled the consequences with regard to the couple's children are the same as in the case of divorce.[7]

NORWAY

Not relevant.

POLAND

Q 27a: A person married to the child's parent who adopted the child acquires parental authority over the child. If then divorced, the person is still treated as a parent, which leads to a situation analogous to that created by the divorce of the child's biological parents (see Q 16a).
Q 27b: Those institutions are not present in Polish law.
Q 27c: An informal relationship with a child's parent does not create a prerequisite for the grant of parental authority. Termination of such a relationship therefore has no legal significance.

PORTUGAL

The ending of a heterosexual relationship in which a natural parent and adopter live together with both holding and exercising parental responsibility over the child requires the regulation of parental responsibility similar to that described in Q 23 onwards.

RUSSIA

It has no influence at all.

SPAIN

Since the acquisition of parental responsibilities by the parental responsibility holder's partner requires the adoption of the child by that partner, the situation basically equates to that of the end of the parent's relationship, which has been discussed under Q 18. The attribution of parental responsibility is unaffected although it will be necessary to adopt measures that reflect that the parental responsibility holders do not live together anymore.

No differences derive from the fact that the relationship which ended was a marriage, a formal or registered partnership or a factual cohabitation if there has been an adoption of the child by the parental responsibility holder's partner.

In most cases, the father's or mother's spouse or partner will not have acquired parental responsibility through adoption. Notwithstanding this fact he or she has a right to maintain a personal relationship with the child after the relationship ends, which will be further discussed under Q 44.

---

6 See A. Nuytinck, 'Nietigverklaard partnerschap en gezag', *FJR*, 2004, p. 81.

7 Art. 77 (2)(a) Dutch CC.

SWEDEN

In Swedish law, it is only through adoption that a step-parent can obtain full parental responsibilities over a child. Where an adoption has taken place, the end of the relationship between the parent and his or her partner has no legal effect on the adoptive parent's parental responsibilities.

A child, on the other hand, has the right to contact with persons particularly close to him or her. The person with custody of the child is responsible for ensuring that the child's need of contact is met, Chapter 6 Sec. 15 Swedish Children and Parents Code. The child's right to contact primarily aims at ensuring contact between the child and his or her relatives *e.g.* grandparents, but can also include other persons emotionally close to the child, such as a former step-parent.[8] It should be noted that a step-parent[9] who wishes to have contact with the child does not have an independent right to initiate proceedings to obtain a contact order. Proceedings can be initiated only by the local social welfare committee, Chapter 6 Sec. 15a Swedish Children and Parents Code. There are no published cases on this.

The legal nature of the former step-parent's (former) relationship to the holder of parental responsibilities is irrelevant in these respects.

SWITZERLAND

The persons referred to in Q 27 and Q 28 are not entitled to parental responsibilities in principle. They therefore also lose their authority to exercise parental responsibilities as a stand-in when their relationship with the parent ends. If a person obtained parental responsibilities as a result of the adoption of a stepchild (see Q 27a), the explanations given in response to Q 16 -18 apply when the relationship ends.

---

8 G. WALIN and S. VÄNGBY, *Föräldrabalken, En kommentar, Del I, 1-13 kap.*, Stockholm: Norstedts Juridik, 2002, p. 6:33.

9 The term 'stepparent' is used here to describe the partner of a parent holding parental responsibilities, regardless of the status of the relationship. Thus step-parenthood denotes the 'social parenthood' between the adult and the child due to marriage, cohabitation or partnership registration between the child's parent and the stepparent. For a discussion concerning the role of social parenthood de lege lata and de lege ferenda, see: A. SINGER, *Föräldraskap i rättslig belysning,* Uppsala: Iustus Förlag, 2000, p. 536-542.

QUESTION 30

C. ATTRIBUTION OF PARENTAL RESPONSIBILITIES

III. Other Persons

To what extent, if at all, is the parent holding parental responsibilities and his or her partner free to agree upon the attribution of parental responsibilities after the ending of his or her relationship with the parent? Distinguish according to the different relationships referred to in Q 27 and Q 28.

AUSTRIA
Since there is no possibility for a spouse or life partner to obtain parental responsibilities during his or her relationship with the parent holding parental responsibilities, there is also no autonomy to agree upon the attribution of parental responsibilities after the ending of the relationship.

BELGIUM
In principle, no agreement is possible upon the attribution of parental responsibilities (See Q 17). A parent cannot transfer all parental responsibilities to his or her partner, except through custodianship (Art. 475 *bis* - 475 *septies* Belgian CC). This institution supposes the existence of an agreement between the partner (candidate-custodian) and the child, if it has reached the age of 15 years or, if not, its parent(s) or guardian (See Q 29 and 31)

BULGARIA
The common rules apply if the child has established parentage towards both partners. The separation calls for arrangements on custody/residence and contact. If the partner of the parent does not have established parentage towards the child, the separation does not create any additional rights for the partner. The holder of parental responsibilities remains the parent of the child. The parent can not transfer any parental responsibility to his or her former partner.

CZECH REPUBLIC
The partner of the child's parent does not have any rights or duties in relation to the child after his or her relationship with that parent is ended.

DENMARK
Joint parental authority between a parent and his/her partner is only possible when they are married and marriage is only open to opposite-sex partners. If they had made an agreement on joint parental authority which had been approved, they would be free to continue this agreement. They could also agree on attributing sole parental authority to one parent, see the principle in Art. 9(1) Danish Act on Parental Authority and Contact.

ENGLAND & WALES

Since the allocation of parental responsibility is a matter of law it is not open to the parent with parental responsibility and his or her partner (of whatever status) to agree to change that formal allocation. However, what can be agreed upon is how parental responsibility should be exercised. In the case of formal relationships, namely marriage, and prospectively, civil partnerships there is power of the court upon divorce or the formal ending of the partnership to interfere with such agreements in the interests of the child but this is a minimal power.[1] Outside this context there is no formal power of court scrutiny. However, in cases of dispute it is always open to either partner to apply to court for an appropriate order (see Q 38).

FINLAND

Only the child's legal parents have the right to make effective agreements concerning the custody of the child. The partner of the parent can only obtain custodial rights if the court so orders, as explained in Q 27a. Thus, the ending of the relationship between the parent and his or her partner does not affect the legal situation in any way.

FRANCE

This question has no relevance under French law since the partner of the parent holding parental responsibilities cannot obtain parental responsibilities. Therefore there is no reason for an agreement between the partner and the parent of the child. It is only a possible contact right that could be agreed on.

But a very recent court order (*Tribunal de Grande Instance Paris*, 7 July 2004)[2] determined that two female same-sex partners can have joint parental responsibilities. First, only the mother of the three daughters had parental responsibilities, but her female partner adopted the three children (so called *adoption simple* which does not destroy the official bonds between the adopted child and the child's biological parents). The adoption normally transfers parental responsibilities to the adoptive parent. The women brought a petition to obtain joint parental responsibilities, which was accepted by the civil court. If the partners separate, they might enter into an agreement on parental responsibilities, but this agreement would be, as in any other case, scrutinised by the family judge.

---

1 In the case of divorce, pursuant to Sec. 41, English Matrimonial Causes Act 1973, the court must consider the proposed arrangements for the children's future after the divorce and whether it should exercise any of its powers under the Children Act 1989. A similar position will apply to the dissolution of a civil partnership, see prospectively, Sec. 63, British Civil Partnerships Act 2004.

2 http://www.legalnews.fr.

GERMANY

Relationship of the type in Q 27a:

After a divorce, annulment of the marriage or factual separation both the adopting spouse and the biological parent generally remain jointly responsible. Moreover they may, within the scope of § 1687 German CC as outlined in the answer to Q 16a, grant to the other parent by means of the relevant authorisations more scope for action than that which is in accordance with the legal provisions governing representation, but subject to the premise of revocability. In addition to these powers of control, each parent has the option to file an application with the family court, in accordance with § 1671 para. 1 German CC, requesting the transfer of sole parental responsibility, either in full or in part. With regard to the prerequisites and consequences of a procedure on the basis of § 1671 para. 1 German CC, please refer to the appropriate comments found in the answer to Q 17.

If the stepchild was not adopted, § 1671 para. 1 German CC does not apply; there is no way for the (former) spouse of the biological parent to obtain the transfer of the parental responsibilities or joint parental responsibilities. This applies even if he or she has in fact cared or jointly cared for the child over a prolonged period of time, even as far back as the child's birth, and has close emotional ties with the child. The parent holding sole parental responsibility only has the option to transfer to the other parent, as to any other third party, the exercise of aspects of parental responsibility by way of consent, while the attribution of parental responsibilities remains otherwise unchanged.

Relationship of the type in Q 27b:

In the absence of possibilities other than marriage which might be used to legally formalise a relationship between mixed-sex partners, this question is not applicable (see Q 27b).

Relationship of the type in Q 27c:

In the event of the termination of extramarital cohabitation between a parent and his or her partner, the general attribution of parental responsibilities remains unaffected, just as it was while the relationship was intact. If the parent holding sole parental responsibility has transferred to the partner the exercise of certain areas of parental responsibility by granting the relevant authorisations, the separation will generally be viewed as including at least an implied revocation of such authorisations. The parent holding sole parental responsibility is, however, free on termination of the relationship with his or her partner to include the ex-partner, as they could any other third party, in the exercise of aspects of parental responsibility by means of consent.

Relationship of the type in Q 28:

With regard to the powers of control on termination of a registered partnership or the *de facto* separation of registered partners, the only option available to the parent holding sole parental responsibility is, once again, to grant the authorisation mentioned above.

GREECE

The parent of the child and his partner holding parental responsibilities can decide on the attribution of parental responsibilities after the ending of their relationship. The court may decide on this issue, in order to ensure that the interests of the child are ensured. For further details, see the answers to Q 17 (for married couples) and Q 25 (for unmarried couples).

HUNGARY

The partner of the holder of the parental responsibilities, either living together in marriage or in an non-formalised partnership, has very limited rights even during a marriage or partnership, so there is not much of a possibility to agree upon the attribution of the parental responsibilities if the relationship ends. There is one exception: A parent has a right, as part of his or her parental responsibilities, to appoint a person as guardian for the child in case of the death of the parent. A parent can therefore appoint his or her partner, either the new spouse or the person living with him or her in a non-formalised partnership, as guardian. Nevertheless, if the other parent's parental responsibilities can be revived, the designated person cannot be appointed as guardian.

IRELAND

Not at all.

ITALY

If Art. 44 (b) Italian Adoption Law grants the parent's spouse the right to adopt, the biological parent and the adoptive parent are free to agree upon the attribution; but in every case the attribution is be controlled by the judge with regard to the agreement's compatibility with the minor's interests. In all other cases nothing inhibits the consensual subdivision of duties that flow from the parental responsibility, respecting the fact that the Italian legal system confers parental responsibility to neither the partner nor the ex-partner of the biological parent.

LITHUANIA

In the event of Q 27, the answer is as follows: if the partner has acknowledged his (or her) paternity (maternity) or has adopted a child *i.e.* he or she has acquired parental authority, the parents may agree on the exercise of their parental rights and duties in respect of their child. The rules which regulate the legal consequences of divorce shall be applicable by analogy. Parents shall have the right to make an agreement on the place of residence of a child and their mutual duties in maintaining their underage children as well as on the procedure, amount and form of such maintenance. The court shall refuse to approve such an agreement if this agreement contradicts the interests of the child or violates the principle of equality of the rights and duties of parents (Art. 3.53 Lithuanian CC). However, in no case may the parents waive their rights or duties in respect of the child by means of such agreement. Parental responsibilities are statutory obligations and may be not waived. Agreements between parents to disclaim or waive of parental duties and rights are void because they violate mandatory rules and are against public policy and good morals (Art. 1.80, 1.81, 3.159 Lithuanian CC).

In respect to Q 28, the question does not have any relevance because partnerships between persons of the same sex are not allowed, and the partner may not obtain parental responsibilities.

THE NETHERLANDS

The parent and the partner are not free to agree upon the attribution of parental responsibilities regardless of their civil status or living conditions. Joint parental responsibilities can only be terminated by a court order or by the death of one of the holders. The mere desire of a holder to terminate joint parental responsibilities is not grounds enough to terminate the existing joint parental responsibilities; the best interests of the child is the only ground on which such a decision can be taken by the court.

NORWAY

Not relevant.

POLAND

Q 27a: A person married to the child's parent who adopted and acquired parental authority over the child is to be treated as a parent. As with the parents' divorce, the issue of parental responsibility is decided by the court, which may take the parents' opinion into consideration (see answer to Question 16a).
Q 27b: Those institutions are not present in Polish law.
Q 27c: No.

PORTUGAL

See the answer to Q 25, concerning heterosexual cohabitation.

RUSSIA

A parent holding parental responsibilities and his or her partner cannot decide upon the attribution of parental responsibility to one of them. If the partner has adopted the child, joint parental responsibility always survives the breakdown of their relationships. If the partner has not adopted the child, he or she has no rights at all.

SPAIN

If the parent's partner has acquired parental responsibilities through the adoption of his or her partner's child, the freedom to make agreements is exactly the same as that described under Q 17 and Q 25. There are no differences depending on whether this relationship is a marriage, a registered partnership or cohabitation.

SWEDEN

Unless the child was adopted by the parent's spouse or registered partner, no such agreements can be entered into. A custodial parent cannot validly attribute custody rights to a former step-parent.[3]

SWITZERLAND

It is not possible for the holders of parental responsibilities and their partners in the different relationships referred to in Q 27 or Q 28 to enter into any agreements regarding parental responsibilities.

---

3 G. WALIN and S. VÄNGBY, *Föräldrabalken, En kommentar, Del I, 1-13 kap.*, Stockholm: Norstedts Juridik, 2002, p. 6:34 and 6:61.

QUESTION 31

C. ATTRIBUTION OF PARENTAL RESPONSIBILITIES

III. Other Persons

Under what conditions, if at all, can other persons not being a parent or a partner of a parent holding parental responsibilities, obtain parental responsibilities (*e.g.* members of the child's family, close friends, foster parent...)? Specify, where such other persons may obtain parental responsibilities, if it is in addition to or in substitution of existing holder(s) of parental responsibilities.

AUSTRIA

Parental responsibilities can be obtained by persons other than the natural parents if parents are prevented from exercising the same, whether in whole (*e.g.* upon discharge of parental rights, Sec. 176 Austrian CC or in the event of death, Sec. 145 Austrian CC)[1] or in part (*e.g.* because they are under age, Sec. 145a Austrian CC).[2] The court must then entrust one or both grandparents or foster parents with the parental responsibilities (Sec. 145 Austrian CC). Not only stepparents but also relatives, friends, and other persons who have close ties to the child and plan to care for and make the child a part of their household on a permanent basis in a close relationship similar to a parent-child one are considered for the role of foster parent(s). If no parents, grandparents, or foster parents are to be found, Sec. 187 *et seq* Austrian CC provide that another holder of parental responsibilities must be appointed. Eligible parties include private individuals who are deemed suitable for this purpose (relatives, godparents, or other trusted third parties) or, as a last resort, the youth welfare agency.[3] The final selection is made in accordance with the best interests of the child. Since all these persons may obtain parental responsibilities only if the natural parents become unable to exercise the same, they act in substitution of the parents and not in addition to them.

If the natural parents are not prevented from exercising parental responsibilities for the above-mentioned reasons, they may place the child in the care of a foster parent or foster parents on a contractual basis. In this case, however, the foster parents' rights are generally restricted to the entitlement to file petitions in custody proceedings concerning the child (Sec. 186 Austrian CC). A judicial transfer of parental responsibilities to foster parents[4] would have the effect that the parents would lose the parental responsibilities to the extent they passed to

---

1 See Q 33.

2 *Oberster Gerichtshof,* 25.09.2002, *Österreichische Juristenzeitung - EvBl,* 2003, No. 16, p. 102.

3 See Q 32.

4 For details see Q 49, 50.

the foster parents as new holders of parental responsibilities.[5] In such a case, the natural parents would only retain communication rights (Sec. 148 and 178 Austrian CC).[6]

BELGIUM

The law recognises voluntary transfer of (most of the) parental responsibilities, during the life of the parent(s), on a contractual base: 'custodianship' (Art. 475 *bis* - 475 *septies* Belgian CC). The transferee obtains parental responsibilities in substitution of the existing holder(s) of parental responsibilities. The transfer of parental responsibilities is submitted to two conditions, namely an agreement between the candidate-custodian and the child, if it has reached the age of 15 years or, if not, its parent(s) or guardian and the candidate-custodian must be at least 25 years old. All the parental responsibilities are transferred except the right of use and enjoyment of the property, the parental competences concerning the status of the person and the right to decide about the fundamental options concerning the child.

BULGARIA

There are no such conditions. Adoption and the establishment of parentage are the only options for persons who are not biological parents to obtain parental responsibility. Other persons such as members of the child's family, close friends or foster parent cannot obtain parental responsibility. They can only exercise parental rights and duties if the child has been placed with them by a court, but they do not become holders of parental responsibilities. Bulgarian family law regards the relatives of the child has already having a legal relation to him or her and there is no need to substitute it by parental responsibilities. There are two possibilities for a child to be placed under the care of relatives (members of his or her family) - in private and public law.

The Bulgarian Family Code states that in cases of divorce: 'Where the interests of children require it, as an exception, the court may place them with their grandparents, other relatives or close friends, with the consent of the latter, or at a specialized social institution' (Art. 106 § 4). Neither of these persons becomes a holder of parental responsibilities.

Providing public care for the child, he or she may be placed outside the family of origin. The Bulgarian Child Protection Act lays down: Placement out of the family 'The placement of a child with a family of relatives or friends, as well as placement of a child to be reared by a foster family or a specialised institution shall be done by the court. Until the court comes out with a ruling, the social assistance directorate at the current address of the child shall provide for a temporary placement by administrative order' (Art. 26 § 1). Art. 31 § 2 of the

---

5 *Oberster Gerichtshof*, 25.09.2002, *Österreichische Juristenzeitung - EvBl*, 2003, No. 16 = *ÖJZ-LSK* 2003/2; M. Schwimann, *Familienrecht*, 5th Edition, Vienna: LexisNexis ARD Orac, 2004, p. 80.

6 See Q 44.

same Act explicitly states that foster parents do not obtain parental responsibilities.

CZECH REPUBLIC

Parental responsibility as a right to decide about the child belongs only to the parents and cannot be awarded to another person. Even in case of foster care or placing the child into the upbringing of another person, parental responsibility remains for the parents. It is only restricted in the sense that personal care, representation and administration of the child's estate in ordinary matters belongs to the foster parent or third person whose upbringing the child was placed into by court.

DENMARK

If such other persons were to obtain parental authority it would be in substitution of existing holder(s) of parental authority. The only way for such persons to obtain parental authority would be by agreement with the holder(s) of parental authority, and such agreement would need to be approved, Art. 11 Danish Act on Parental Authority and Contact, or upon the death of one or both holder(s) of parental authority, Art. 14 Danish Act on Parental Authority and Contact.

ENGLAND & WALES

Any individual who is not a parent or guardian can acquire parental responsibility upon being granted a residence order (an order determining with whom the child is to live). As stated in answer to Q 27 the application for a residence order should not be regarded as a means of allocating parental responsibility rather the principal concern of the court will be to determine whether it is in the child's interests to live with the applicant. Another means of obtaining parental responsibility is being formally appointed (by a holder of parental responsibility) as a guardian but this appointment will only take effect upon death of the parent or parent with parental responsibility.[7] It should be noted that without a residence order or a formal appointment as a guardian an individual, even one looking after a child, such as a foster parent does, not have parental responsibility.

The acquisition of parental responsibility by an individual through a residence order does not affect the legal position of parents who will continue to have parental responsibility. In other words, the acquisition of parental responsibility is in addition to or not in substitution of existing holders of responsibility.

FINLAND

As the rules concerning another person's right to custody of the child applies to anyone, regardless of the relationship to the parent of the child, the legal rules are the same as already explained in Q 27a. The substitution of a parent or

---

7 See Sec. 5, English Children Act 1989. See further Q 34.

parents as custodians is only possible under the condition that the arrangement would be manifestly in the best interests of the child concerned, as pointed out.

FRANCE

Generally, when the parents (or at least one parent) are alive and holders of parental responsibilities, no other person can obtain parental responsibilities. Only in a few special cases can a third person obtain these responsibilities. When both parents are dead or are not able to exercise personal responsibilities or when neither the father nor mother has voluntarily acknowledged the child (see Art. 373-5 and 390 French CC), the *juge des tutelles* (guardianship court) shall order a *tutelle* (guardianship). The *tuteur* (guardian) will have the same rights and duties as a holder of parental responsibilities but under the supervision and the direction of the board of guardians (see Art. 449 and 450 French CC).

Also if only one parent is holder of parental responsibilities and has legal administration under judicial supervision, the judge of the guardianship court can, either on his own motion or upon request of relatives or of the prosecutor, order that a guardianship shall be established (Art. 391 para. 1 French CC). If both parents are holders of parental responsibilities, the guardianship court may only order the opening of a guardianship for serious reasons (Art. 391 para. 2 French CC). In such cases, the parent(s) generally keeps his or her parental responsibilities, except for the legal administration[8].

The parents (or one of them) can make a joint petition with a third person in order to delegate some of their rights and duties of parental responsibilities to this third person (see Art. 377 French CC and Q 49 and 50). A third person, an institution or the *service départemental de l'aide sociale à l'enfance* (social institution, public body) can also bring a petition before the family judge to obtain total or partial delegation of the exercise of parental responsibilities. In this case only the exercise of parental responsibilities (or of some rights and duties belonging to parental responsibilities) is delegated; the parent(s) remain holders of parental responsibilities.

When a parent is discharged of her or his parental responsibilities (*retrait de l'autorité parentale*) because of serious fault and when the other parent is dead or has lost the exercise of parental responsibilities, the court shall appoint a third person who will temporarily take care of the child and request a guardianship. The court can also decide to entrust the child to a social institution, see Art. 380 French CC and more details in Q 51.

---

[8] See French Supreme Court, Civ. I, 13.12.1994, *Rép. Defrénois* 1995, p. 325 annotated MASSIP (the judicial decision to open a guardianship has no influence on the parental responsibilities); comp. French Supreme Court, Civ. I, 8.11.1982, *Gaz. Pal.* 1983.2 p. 517 annotated MASSIP (the guardianship is limited to the legal administration of the child's property but only under the condition that the father is able to exercise his parental responsibilities despite his imprisonment).

GERMANY

Once again, the parents holding parental responsibilities may involve third parties, on a revocable basis, in the exercise of the tasks associated with parental responsibility. The essence of the permitted involvement of third parties from a legal point of view lies in the consent granted by the parents holding parental responsibility. The parental responsibility as such does, however, remain with the parent(s) holding parental responsibility.

Where parents are not able, or perhaps not even willing, to bring up their child themselves, they have the option to give their child up for adoption. Moreover, they may entrust the child to a foster family for a shorter or longer period, or possibly even on a long-term basis.

The adopting third party will, in accordance with § 1754 para. 3 German CC, be granted parental responsibility for the minor he or she has adopted. In return, the biological parents who have given their child up for adoption will lose their parental responsibilities.

By contrast, when the child is received into a foster family the foster parent is not attributed any direct parental responsibilities for this child. The parental responsibilities of the biological parents remain undiminished by any contractual foster care arrangements and any mediated by the youth welfare office.[9] If the child is in foster care over a prolonged period, the foster parent is, however, authorised, in accordance with § 1688 para. 1 sent. 1 German CC, to decide on matters relating to everyday life and to act for the holder of parental responsibility to this extent. Moreover, the foster parent is entitled, in accordance with § 1688 para. 1 sent. 2 German CC, to administer any remuneration for work the child may receive and to claim and administer any maintenance, insurance, public support and other social benefits on behalf of the child. The holder of parental responsibility may, however, in accordance with § 1688 para. 3 sent. 1 German CC, preclude such authorisations by 'declaring otherwise'; furthermore, the family court, in accordance with § 1688 para. 3 sent. 2 German CC, may limit or preclude the foster parent's said authorisations. Subject to the consent of the parents holding parental responsibility, the foster parent may be granted a legal position which exceeds § 1688 German CC: for instance, the family court has the option, in accordance with § 1630 para. 3 sent. 1 German CC and upon application by the parents, to transfer matters of parental responsibility to the foster parent if the child is in foster care over a prolonged period. The transfer may concern matters having to do with responsibility for the child's person and for the child's property; the phrase 'matters of parental responsibility' does not limit the scope, which

9 Th. RAUSCHER, *Familienrecht*, Heidelberg: C.F. Müller, 2001, No. 1129.

means that a full transfer of parental responsibility, especially of responsibility for the child, can take place in individual cases.[10]

In addition to the options outlined so far, there are two further ways in which third parties can obtain parental responsibility: guardianship and curatorship.

Guardianship *(Vormundschaft)* usually refers to the legally regulated, comprehensive care for a person unable to safeguard his or her interests. Today guardianship only exists for minors. A prerequisite of guardianship is that the parents do not act as legal representatives. According to § 1773 German CC, the minor is entrusted to a guardian if he or she is not subject to parental responsibility or if the parents are not entitled to represent the minor legally, either in the area of responsibility for the child's person or for the child's property. This is the case, for example, if both parents die, if parental responsibility has been suspended or if it has been withdrawn from the parents in accordance with § 1666 German CC. The guardianship court must furthermore place the child under the care of a guardian if the personal status of the minor cannot be established, i.e. if the child is a foundling.

Guardianship replaces parental responsibility; as a result, in accordance with § 1793 para. 1 sent. 1 German CC it generally includes full responsibility for the child's person and the child's property and the authorisation to represent the child legally. In exceptional cases the guardian may not be granted full parental responsibility, for example, if in accordance with § 1673 para. 2 sent. 2 German CC the under-age mother is entitled *de facto* to care for the child alongside the guardian. In general, guardianship is ordered and the guardian chosen by the guardianship court; if the family court has withdrawn parental responsibility from the parents, then this task falls to the family court. The guardian is chosen primarily on the basis of the person named by the parent in accordance with §§ 1776, 1777 German CC (see answer to Q 34), and secondly, i.e. in the absence of such, by the court, using criteria of suitability. An examination of suitability takes into account the personal life situation as well as the assets and other circumstances of the person in question; for instance, the court will deem unsuitable any person who forced the court to intervene in matters to do with the care for and upbringing of his or her own children, or any person who might have been sentenced for child abuse.[11] Although the law assumes guardianship by a single guardian to be the norm, the youth welfare office or even an association can be, and often is, appointed as guardian.

Curatorship (*Pflegschaft*) means the holding of parental responsibility for a limited number of matters; structurally it is modelled on guardianship, and the

---

10 U. DIEDERICHSEN, in: PALANDT, *Bürgerliches Gesetzbuch*, 64th Edition, Munich: Beck, 2005, § 1630 No. 19.

11 Th. WAGENITZ, in: *Münchener Kommentar zum Bürgerlichen Gesetzbuch,* 4th Edition, Munich: Beck, 2002, § 1779 No. 5.

rules of guardianship law are largely applicable to it, in accordance with § 1915 para. 1 German CC.

In this context, it is particularly the 'supplementary curatorship' (*Ergänzungspflegschaft*), in accordance with § 1909 para. 1 German CC, that is of importance: It supplements parental responsibility or guardianship if and to the extent that the parents or guardian are either factually (*e.g.*, due to geographical distance) or legally (*e.g.*, due to self-dealing in accordance with § 181 German CC) prevented from looking after specific matters on behalf of the child. In the case of § 1909 German CC, the curator is not chosen according to the provisions governing the appointment of a guardian. As a result, the court can make its choice without being bound by parental wishes, once again guided by criteria of suitability. In comparison with parental responsibility and the responsibility of a guardian, the remit of a curator's scope for action is limited.[12] Insofar as the inability of parents and guardian to assume their responsibilities results directly from the law, no further measures by the court are required for the appointment of a curator in accordance with § 1909 para. 1 sent. 1 and 2 German CC. If, however, the law provides for parental responsibility to be restricted by a court decision, *e.g.* in the case of § 1666 German CC (see Q 18), a partial withdrawal of parental responsibility or of the guardian's power of representation is necessary if a curator is to be appointed. Since parents and curators or guardians and curators must per force work alongside each other with regard to parental responsibility in questions which affect both their respective areas, differences of opinion which cannot be decided by a clear allocation of competence may arise. In these situations, § 1630 para. 2 German CC stipulates that in such cases the family court will be appointed to settle the dispute. The court cannot make this decision upon its own motion, but only following an application by a parent, the guardian or the curator.

GREECE

Other persons, not being parents of the child, may obtain parental responsibilities as a substitute to the parents if these parents do not have or are unable to exercise parental care (Art. 1589 Greek CC). A lack of parental care will arise when the child is of unknown parents, or the parental care of both parents has ceased because they have died, they have been declared to be missing persons, or they have forfeited this right (Art. 1538 Greek CC). Further, the court may only deprive the parents of parental responsibilities if it is of the opinion that they have abused their rights, violated their duties, are not in a position to be able to carry out this task (Art. 1532 para. 1 Greek CC), or, after divorce, annulment or factual separation, they are unsuitable for this purpose (Art. 1513-1514 Greek CC)[1]. Finally, the court can, at the request of the parents, discharge them from the exercise of parental care on important grounds (Art. 1535 Greek CC).

---

12 D. SCHWAB, in: *Münchener Kommentar zum Bürgerlichen Gesetzbuch*, 4th Edition, Munich: Beck, 2002, § 1909, No. 41.

A guardian is always appointed by the court and he or she may be, in order of precedence: the spouse of the minor; a person appointed by the parent who was holding parental care until his death;[13] or any other person whom the court considers suitable, preferably from among the relatives of the child (Art. 1592 Greek CC). When the parents request that parental care be attributed to a third person on the basis of Art. 1535 Greek CC they will also nominate the guardian. The court appoints a supervisory council at the same time, whose tasks may be to consult, control or take decisions, depending on the circumstances.[14] This council is composed of three to five members, who are acquaintances or relatives of the parents (Art. 1634 Greek CC).

If the holders of parental responsibilities, be they parents or guardians, require assistance in the exercise of parental responsibilities, they may assign the actual care of the child to third persons *i.e.* foster parents.[15] The court may, in addition, attribute the entire physical care of the child to a foster family, especially when the parents cannot effectively exercise parental care.[16] Foster care is an institution which is supplementary to parental care and guardianship (or even to adoption). Thus, it does not affect, in principle, the attribution of parental responsibilities (Art. 1655 Greek CC).[17] Nevertheless, if the child has been integrated into the foster family for a long period and at the same time its ties with its parents or its guardian have weakened, the foster parents may request the court that they be assigned, wholly or partly, with parental responsibilities. If the court accepts their request, it will appoint them as guardians (Art. 1660 and 1661 Greek CC).

HUNGARY

This matter is discussed fully in Q 51 'Discharge of parental responsibilities'.

If a parent is temporarily prevented from exercising parental responsibilities, the parent can initiate the relocation of their child to the home of another family for this period, and the person who takes the child into his or her household will exercise the parental responsibilities as the child's guardian. This person can be a member of the child's family or any other person.

---

13 See also Art. 1535 Greeek CC.

14 For a more detailed description of the powers of the supervisory council see K. PANTELIDOU, in: A. GEORGIADIS and M. STATHOPOULOS (eds.), *Civil Code commentary, Vol. VIII, Family Law (Arts. 1505-1694)*, 2nd Edition, Athens: Law & Economy, P.N. SAKKOULAS, 2003, Art. 1642 Greek CC, p. 713, No. 1.

15 The guardian also needs the permission of the supervisory council (Art. 1607 Greek CC).

16 See also Art. 1533 Greek CC.

17 As mentioned above, only the court may entrust the physical care of the child to a foster family. This is only the case if it is considered necessary in order to prevent harm to the physical, psychological or mental health of the child and provided that there are no less drastic means to ensure this. See also Art. 1533 para. 1 and 4 Greek CC.

A judicial decree can also rule that the child shall live with a third person and that this person will exercise parental responsibilities as the child's guardian. The court usually chooses this person from among the members of the child's family, nevertheless a condition of this solution only is that the child live with third person. the condition of chosing a third person (with whom the child should live) is that this third person demands it.

The public guardianship authority can state that a child endangered by living with his or her parental family should live with a third person, chosen among the child's relatives. If there is no such person, the child will be taken into state care by the guardianship authority and live with foster parents or in a children's home. In these situations, the foster parent or the head of the children's home will usually exercise parental responsibilities as the child's guardian.

Parental responsibilities are suspended if an unmarried mother is a minor. In this case the parental responsibilities are exercised usually by the mother's family members; the child is taken into state care only if there is no suitable person in the mother's family to act as the child's guardian.

In the enumerated cases, a guardian has full parental responsibilities but nevertheless the parents retain some rights: they can have contact with the child, and they have the right and duty to follow the child's upbringing and to support the persons and institutes taking care of the child.

If the reason the child is taken into state care is that his or her parent consented to an adoption by an unknown person, or if the court terminated both parents' parental responsibilities because of their serious parental negligence, the child's guardian will substitute the parents in their parental responsibilities and all parental rights end. Nevertheless, in case of the judicial abolition of parental responsibilities, the parents' right to contact with the child can be maintained to the limited extent that it is in the child's interest.

IRELAND

Art. 41 and 42 Irish Constitution, which recognise the natural rights and duties of marital parents in respect of their children, describe such rights and duties as 'inalienable' and 'imprescriptible', essentially preventing marital parents from surrendering their parental rights to others. While Art. 41 and 42 represent a legal impediment to state intrusion into the marital family, no such impediment arises in the context of the non-marital family where the best interests of a non-marital child will take precedence over all other matters. That said, it is only possible for either a parent (including an unmarried father) or guardian to seek a custody order under the Guardianship of Infants Act 1964. Currently, adoption and invoking the wardship jurisdiction of the Courts are the only options available to substitute parents who seek to establish a stable legal relationship with a child and acquire parental responsibilities.

ITALY

Art. 343 Italian CC states that if both biological parents die or are prevented from the exercise of their parental responsibilities for another reason, guardianship can be exercised at the minor's residence by the legal authority. This means that the parents' rights and duties are conferred on a third person, the guardian, who exercises the parental responsibilities in the absence, impossibility or incapacity of the parents. As has been clarified (see note 2), although the guardianship is modelled after parental authority, there are significant differences between the two due to the absence of rapport between the guardian and the minor.

With regard to the choice of the guardian, Art. 348 Italian CC provides for the judge to appoint the person designated by the last parent to exercise parental responsibilities (by testament, public act or authenticated private deed). If there is no indication or if it is not possible to appoint the indicated person due to serious reasons, the guardian is preferably chosen from the minor's relatives or next of kin. The appointed person must be of irreproachable conduct and fit for the task. Moreover, he or she must be able to provide moral guidance and education to the minor taking the minor's abilities, natural inclinations and ambitions into account.

LITHUANIA

Two different situations must be distinguished. Firstly: the parents of a child are not separated from the child and their parental authority is not restricted by the court judgment. In this case, some other persons may obtain some elements of parental authority in addition to the holder(s) of parental authority, but only in exceptional cases. Secondly: the parents are separated from the child or their parental authority is restricted by a court judgment. In this case, guardians or curators substitute the parents of the child.

In the first case, when a child has parents whose parental authority is not restricted by the court, nor there are separated from the child, no other persons may obtain parental responsibilities, save in very few exceptional cases:

- if the parents of a child are minors, a guardian shall be appointed to the child. In such cases, the guardian shall obtain the parental responsibilities in addition to the parental responsibilities of the parents (Art. 3.158 Lithuanian CC);
- close relatives of a child, *e.g.* the grandparents, adult brothers or sisters of the child shall have the right to contact the child if such contacts are consistent with the child's interests (Art. 3.172, 3.176 Lithuanian CC);
- circumstances permitting, an adult sibling and grandparents of a child shall maintain their minor sibling and grandchildren deprived of parents maintenance (Art. 3.236 Lithuanian CC). In this case, the duty of maintenance is additional to the parents' duty.

In the second case, if the parents are separated from a child or their parental authority is restricted by a court judgment, the person appointed as a guardian or curator of the child shall obtain parental responsibilities in substitution of the parental authority of the child's parents (Part 2, Art. 3.160 Lithuanian CC).

THE NETHERLANDS

Pursuant to Art. 1:253t Dutch CC, a parent may apply for joint parental responsibilities together with a person who is not a parent. As the law does not specify that this non-parent must be the partner of the parent, the parent can apply for joint parental responsibilities with any person who has a close personal relationship with the child, for instance a family member of the parent.[18] For the other situations it is important to point out that Dutch law makes a distinction between parental responsibilities, which can be exercised by one parent alone, by two parents jointly or by a parent and his or her partner jointly, and guardianship, which can be exercised by a person or persons other than the child's parents. The umbrella term is custody (Art. 1:245 § 2 and 3 Dutch CC). All the regulations relating to custody (*gezag*) apply to parental responsibilities (*ouderlijk gezag*) as well as guardianship (*voogdij*). Pursuant to Art. 1:245 § 1 Dutch CC all minors are subject to custody.

Guardianship can be attributed to two persons who are not parents,[19] to one person who is not a parent and to a legal person.[20] Guardianship can be obtained by operation of law (Art. 1:253x Dutch CC), by the last will of a parent with parental responsibilities, or by court order. The last two possibilities will be discussed, as the first option is mainly[21] a matter of terminology: a person other than a parent who has joint parental responsibilities with a parent will be become the child's guardian after the death of the parent (Art. 1:253x Dutch CC).

The parent may provide by last will and testament which person or which two persons will exercise custody over his or her children as guardian or joint guardians (*tutela testamentaria*) after the parent's death (Art. 1:92 Dutch CC). Guardianship will be vested in the person(s) appointed at the moment the person accepts the guardianship. Furthermore the sub-district court will appoint a guardian over minors who are not subject to parental responsibilities and for whose guardianship no provision has been lawfully made (*tutela dativa*). This may be the case after the death of the parent(s) with parental responsibilities or when the parent(s) with parental responsibilities is discharged of his responsibilities towards the child. During such a procedure,

18 See District Court Dordrecht 13.1.1999, *FJR*, 1999, No. 50, p. 107, in which case a father and his brother were vested with joint parental responsibilities since the child had lived with the brother and his wife since the death of its mother.

19 Possible since 1998, a court cannot appoint two guardians at the same time. If two people want to obtain joint guardianship they will have to apply to the court in a procedure akin to Art. 1:253t Dutch CC.

20 See for more information Q 32.

21 There are however some small, though not entirely unimportant, differences. For instance, a guardian cannot name a guardian for the children by last will and testament.

each person capable of exercising guardianship can request the court to grant them guardianship. Art. 1:275 § 2 Dutch CC. Moreover, this section states that in the case of consensual discharge, the court will preferably appoint a person or persons who have cared for the child for one year or more as a guardian Art. 1:275 § 3 Dutch CC. This subsection implies that the foster parents will preferably be given guardianship unless they do not have the capacity to act. A person who has cared for and raised a minor as a member of the family for one year or more with the consent of the guardian, other than under a supervision order or under an interim guardianship, may apply to the court to appoint him or her as a guardian (Art. 1:299a Dutch CC).

NORWAY

No person other than the legal father or mother can obtain parental responsibilities, except after the death of a parent, compare Art. 38 and 63 Norwegian Children Act 1981. See Q 33.

POLAND

A guardian is appointed for a child when the child does not remain under parental authority (*e.g.* when the parents are unknown, have died or have been deprived of parental authority). The guardian must possess the full capacity to perform legal acts, and cannot have been deprived of public rights, parental rights or guardianship rights. A person who presumably will not be able to fulfil the guardian's duties cannot be appointed to be a guardian (Art. 148 Polish Family and Guardianship Code).

A person the parents recommend may be appointed as a guardian, if the parents were not deprived of parental authority and such an appointment it is not contradictory to the child's interests. (Art. 149 § 1 Polish Family and Guardianship Code). Otherwise, another person from among the child's relatives or persons close to the child or the child's parents (Art. 149 § 2 Polish Family and Guardianship Code) may be appointed. If there is a need to appoint a guardian for a child placed with a foster family, the court should, if possible, appoint the foster parents as guardians (Art. 149 § 4 Polish Family and Guardianship Code).

A guardian may only be appointed for children who are not subject to parental responsibility, thus excluding the possibility of the two institutions existing together with regard to one child.

PORTUGAL

Only in exceptional circumstances. The child is only entrusted to a third person (Art. 1905 No. 2 Portuguese CC) if the parents have been found guilty of infringing their duties towards their children, causing serious harm to them; or if, through inexperience, infirmity, absence or other reasons, they are unable to perform those duties (Art. 1915 Portuguese CC and 194 Portuguese Child Protection Law), that is, when they have been discharged of parental responsibility by the court; or if the parents' behaviour puts the safety, health, moral training and education of the child at risk, and the court has formally ordered the restriction of parental responsibility (Art. 1918 Portuguese CC).

When the child has been entrusted to a third person or to a child-care establishment, then that person or establishment will hold the parental powers and duties required for the performance of their functions (Art. 1907 No. 1 Portuguese CC). As regards those powers and duties that are not considered necessary for the adequate performance of those functions, the court shall decide which parent shall exercise them (Art. 1907 No. 2 Portuguese CC and Art. 180 No. 4 Portuguese Child Protection Law).

RUSSIA

A person other than the parent or the partner of the parent of the child can only obtain parental responsibility through adoption. In case of an adoption by one person, one parent of the child can retain parental responsibility (Art. 137 (3) Russian Family Code). In case of an adoption by a married couple, legal relationships between the child and his or her parents cease to exist (Art. 137 (2) Russian Family Code).

Adoption is possible when the child is left without parental care. Adoption is allowed only upon consent of the parents (Art. 129 Russian Family Code), except for the following cases:

- when the parent(s) are unknown;
- when the parent(s) has been declared by court to have disappeared;
- when the parent(s) has been declared by court legally incapable;
- when the parent(s) has been discharged of parental rights;
- when the parent(s), for reasons considered insufficient by the court, have not lived with their child for six or more months and neglect their duty to educate and maintain the child (Art. 130 Russian Family Code).

SPAIN

Non-parents can obtain parental responsibilities in the framework of '*tutela*' or guardianship. A guardian will be named if the child is not subject to *patria potestad* (for example because both parents died). The guardian therefore substitutes any other parental responsibility holder.

There is an obligation to request the naming of a guardian by those relatives that are called upon in order to become guardians as well as by any person in whose company a child has been left. If this obligation is not complied with these people will be jointly held responsible to pay damages (Art. 229 Spanish CC). Other persons are obliged to communicate the situation to the *Ministerio Fiscal* or the judge with jurisdiction in the territory were the child is (Art. 230 Spanish CC).

The *Ministerio Fiscal*, a special body acting in the interests of children, must promote guardianship and Judges must establish guardianship on their own motion if they discover children residing in their jurisdiction who are not subject to *patria potestad* (Art. 228 Spanish CC).

Guardianship is established by the judge after hearing the child (if he or she is older than twelve or, if younger, if the child has attained a sufficient degree of maturity), the relatives of the child and any other person the judge determines to be helpful.

The judge supervises and controls the exercise of guardianship in a way he or she does not with parents holding parental responsibility. A judge can, for example, request the guardian to provide information on the child's situation at any time. Upon the termination of guardianship, the guardian must give an accounting of his or her administration of the child's property to the judge for approval, whereas in the case of administration by parents who hold parental responsibility, judicial control will only proceed on the request of the child who has reached majority. The judge can name one or more guardians, although the latter is the exception. Guardians can be actual or legal persons (*e.g.* charities); However, there is a preference for choosing an actual person as a guardian, if such persons are available.

In the case of actual persons, the judge is obliged to choose among certain predetermined people. The Spanish CC names the child's spouse, the child's parents, persons named by the child's parents in their will (see Q 34) and relatives in the ascending line. The judge is allowed to alter the order, or even choose someone other than the listed persons if it is in the child's interests. The judge will, however, have to justify the choice if this is done. It is statutorily preferable to name as guardian a person with whom the child can actually live.

The named guardian is obliged to accept the judge's designation; there are only a limited number of permissible reasons for rejecting the post. As seen under Q 3, emancipated children still need their parents' consent for certain acts if their capacity is not complete. If the parents are missing, a curator will be named. The rules for constituting a curatorship and the persons who can become curator are basically the same as those who can become guardians.

SWEDEN

According to Swedish law a child cannot have more than two legal custodians at a time. Entrusting custody to persons other than the parents denotes a transfer of custody, the existing holder(s) of parental responsibilities being substituted by other custodians.

Custody can be entrusted to a non-parent in three situations: (1) when the parents are unfit to exercise custody, (2) when the child has been cared for in a home other than the parental home and it is in the best interests of the child that custody be transferred to the persons who have been caring for the child, and (3) when the parents die. (This last situation is dealt with under Q 33).

The first situation arises when the parent exercising custody of a child is guilty of abuse or neglect or is otherwise behaving in a manner that entails an enduring risk to the child's health or development, Chapter 6 Sec. 7 Swedish Children and Parents Code. If both parents have custody and this behaviour only applies to one of them, the court shall entrust sole custody to the other parent. If both parents are wanting in their behaviour, the court shall transfer custody to one or two specially appointed custodians. In practice it is very seldom that custody is transferred from the parent(s) on this ground; the child is considered to be sufficiently protected through child protection measures such as placing the child in another home for care.[22] The person receiving the child for care will be in charge of the daily care of the child. The local social welfare committee has the duty to contribute to the child's good care and upbringing, a favourable living environment and suitable education. To this end, the social welfare committee shall provide the custodians and the persons caring for the child with advice, support and other necessary assistance, Chapter 6 Sec. 7 Swedish Social Services Act. It should however be emphasised that neither the person receiving the child for care in another home nor the social welfare committee obtain parental responsibilities according to the Children and Parents Code.[23]

The second situation arises when social welfare authorities place the child for care in another private home according to the Swedish Social Services Act (2001:453) or the Swedish Care of Young Persons Act (1990:52). Normally, such a placement is also the result of the parents' abuse or neglect of the child and the placement often becomes of long duration. On the condition that it is manifestly in the best interests of the child to secure continuity in the caring of the child, the court may transfer the custody of the child to the person(s) in charge of the child's care ('family home parents'), Chapter 6 Sec. 8 Swedish Children and Parents Code. The 'family home parents' (foster parents) will in this case be specially appointed custodians for the child.[24] This possibility of transferring custody is only rarely used in practice.[25] This has to do with an unwillingness to deprive parents of custody (thus regarding them unsuitable), as well as a fear that transferring custody from the parents would negatively affect the child's contact with them. In addition there is an overall uncertainty as to how the child's best interests should be assessed in a situation like this. Thus, the 2003 reform of the Swedish Care of Young Persons Act obliging the

---

22 G. WALIN and S. VÄNGBY, *Föräldrabalken, En kommentar, Del I, 1-13 kap.*, Stockholm: Norstedts Juridik, 2002, pp. 6:38-6:39; A. SINGER, *Föräldraskap i rättslig belysning*, Uppsala: Iustus Förlag, 2000, p. 474.

23 Swedish law could be criticised for leaving the child in a 'legal vacuum'. Legal custody, which carries with it the responsibility for the custodian to care for the child's personal affairs, is not in line with the real situation where somebody else cares for the child.

24 Chapter 6 Sec. 8 Swedish Children and Parents Code. Special regard is to be paid to the wishes of the child.

25 See: SOU 2000:77, p. 252 *et seq.* According to statistics from the late 1990's, custody was tranferred from the parent(s) only in approximately 50 cases per year.

social welfare committee to consider, as soon as the placement of the child in a particular private home has lasted for three years, if there are reasons to transfer custody to the foster parents, has had a limited effect.[26] Questions concerning transfer of custody to foster parents will be considered by the court on application of the social welfare committee. The foster parents cannot by themselves initiate a transfer of custody, but they have to consent to a transfer.

Normally, a specially appointed custodian also becomes the child's guardian, but exceptionally another person can be appointed as guardian, Chapter 10 Sec. 3 Swedish Children and Parents Code. It is also possible to appoint several guardians *e.g.* if the child's economic affairs are complex, or if the parents with custody are not suitable to act as guardians, Chapter 10 Sec. 8 Swedish Children and Parents Code.

SWITZERLAND

Parental responsibilities are non-transferable. Only the exercise of parental responsibilities may be entrusted to third parties within the limits of Art. 299 and 300 Swiss CC.

---

26 Sec. 13 Swedish Care of Young Persons Act. See also: Prop. 2002/03:53. Oral information by the National Board of Health and Welfare, SUZANNE JUHLIN.

QUESTION 32

C. ATTRIBUTION OF PARENTAL RESPONSIBILITIES

III. Other Persons

Under what conditions, if at all, can a public body obtain parental responsibilities? Specify, where it is so obtained, if it is in addition to or in substitution of existing holder(s) of parental responsibilities.

AUSTRIA

The *Jugendwohlfahrtsträger* (this is the respective federal state in its capacity as a youth welfare agency; the implementing bodies are the district youth welfare offices *[Bezirksjugendämter]* as regional authorities) is the last body to be entrusted with parental responsibilities if neither the natural parents, nor any suitable grandparent or foster parent, nor any other suitable person is able to exercise parental responsibilities (statutory third-party custody *[gesetzliche Fremdobsorge]* = public custody *[Amtsobsorge]*, Sec. 213 Austrian CC). In practice, the youth welfare office frequently transfers the actual exercise of parental responsibilities by empowering third parties (*e.g.* a children's home director), and only assumes advisory and supervisory duties[1]. Furthermore, by operation of law the youth welfare agency is responsible for the legal representation and administration of property of a child whose parents are still minors (Sec. 145a, 211 sentence 2 Austrian CC), and finally it is entitled to full parental responsibilities for parentless children found within Austria (Sec. 211 sentence 1 Austrian CC).[2] In all these cases, the youth welfare agency will act in lieu of – and not in addition to – other persons holding parental responsibilities.

In the following cases, the youth welfare agency has to support the legal representative, usually the mother, of a child born in Austria: Based on the legal representative's assent in writing the youth welfare agency will act as the child's representative for the determination and/or enforcement of the child's maintenance claims, when applicable also for the determination of paternity; for other matters only, if it is willing to do so (Sec. 212(1) - (3) Austrian CC). As the child's representative the youth welfare agency may also apply for provisional measures of protection against domestic violence (Sec. 382b, 382d Enforcement Code *[Exekutionsordnung]*) if the ordinary legal representative has not filed the required petition immediately (Sec. 215(2) Austrian CC). Moreover, the youth welfare agency is generally authorized to petition the court for orders to preserve the child's interests (Sec. 176(2), 215(1) sentence 1 Austrian CC); however, in case of increased danger in any delay (*e.g.* when school registration

---

1 E. STREINESBERGER/Th. HACKER, '*Jugendwohlfahrtsrecht*,' in: O. LEHNER, *Kinder- und Jugendrecht*, 2nd Edition, Vienna: Orac, 1998, p. 172.

2 Parental responsibilities may only be transferred to resurfacing parents by a judicial decision to that effect (Sec. 250 Austrian CC).

is pressing or in case of violence against the child), the agency itself may take action on a temporary basis to provide for the child's care and/or education until the court has rendered a decision (Sec. 215(1) Austrian CC).

BELGIUM

The Public Social Welfare Centre has guardianship over two categories of children:

- children over whom nobody exercises parental responsibilities or guardianship, and over whom nobody exercices custody (Art. 396 Belgian CC and Art. 63 Belgian Law on the Public Social Welfare Centre); and
- children who are already under custody of the Public Social Welfare Centre and whose parents are partly or totally discharged of parental responsibilities.

This institution, governed by public law, acts in substitution of existing holder(s) of parental responsibilities and has a residuary competence. The guardianship over unaccompanied foreign minors is determined by the Belgian Program Law of 24 December 2002. According to this law, the guardianship over these unaccompanied foreign minors is organised by the Guardianship Service, an institution governed by public law (Art. 3(1)(1)). The Service designates, retributes and controls the guardian. The guardian exercises following tasks: physical care over the child (Art. 10(1)), contact with the minor for the purpose of creating a relationship based on mutual trust, general representation (Art. 9(1)(11)), administration of the child's property in respect of Art. 410 Belgian CC and to present a report and the financial statement of the guardianship.[3]

BULGARIA

There is not such an option under the Bulgarian legislation.

CZECH REPUBLIC

Public bodies cannot obtain parental responsibility.

DENMARK

A public body cannot obtain parental authority.

ENGLAND & WALES

Local authorities can only acquire parental responsibility in one of two ways, namely, by having a care order or an emergency protection order made in their

---

[3] C. CASTELEIN, 'De wet voogdij over niet-begeleide minderjarige vreemdelingen', in P. SENAEVE and F. SWENNEN, *De hervormingen in het personen- en familierecht 2002-2003*, Antwerp: Intersentia, 2003, p. 41.

favour. Both orders require the local authority to satisfy fairly stringent conditions before they can be made.[4]

Upon the making of a care order, local authorities share parental responsibility with any parent or guardian (*i.e.* the responsibility conferred is in addition to, and not in substitution of, existing holders of responsibility).[5] However, if they are satisfied that it is necessary to do so to safeguard or promote the child's welfare, however, they may determine the extent to which a parent or guardian of the child may meet his parental responsibility for him.[6] In no event, however, will a local authority be empowered to change the child's religion, to consent to an order freeing him for adoption, or to appoint a guardian.[7] Local authorities also acquire parental responsibility to the same limited extent as individuals upon being granted an emergency protection order (see Q 14).

FINLAND

If the child has been taken into the care of the local social authority (under the conditions of Sec. 16 or Sec. 18 Finnish Child Protection Act), the local social authority obtains *ex lege* the right to decide on the care, upbringing, supervision, other welfare and place of residence of the child (Sec. 19 para. 1 Finnish Child Protection Act). Thus, once the child has been taken into care, the custodian no longer has the right to decide regarding these matters, unless the care is terminated through a decision of the local social authority or of the administrative court. The local social authority shall in any case, make efforts to cooperate with the parents or other custodians of the child (Sec. 19 para. 2 Finnish Child Protection Act). The custodian of the child remains a holder of some custodial rights despite the care order, such as the right to make decisions regarding the child's religious affiliation and name.[8] Taking the child into care does not affect the custodian's or other guardian's right to administrate the child's property.

In any case, the local social authority always has the right to submit an application to the court to review the child's custody (Sec. 14 para. 1 Finnish

---

4 *I.e.* for a care order, the court must be satisfied as a minimum that the so-called threshold provisions under Sec. 31(2), English Children Act 1989 have been proved, or in the case of emergency protection orders that there is reasonable cause to believe that they will be satisfied, pursuant to Sec. 44(1).

5 Sec. 33(3)(a), English Children Act 1989.

6 Sec. 33(3)(b) and (4), English Children Act 1989.

7 Sec. 33(6), English Children Act 1989.

8 It has been argued that the purpose for which the child has been taken into care has an influence on the division of the custodial rights between the custodian and the local social authority. The authority would not have the right to exercise custodial rights to a larger extent than what is necessary to avoid the risks to the child's well-being that were the reasons for the caretaking procedure. The interpretation is based on the wording of the section. The translation into English is unfortunately not quite precise in this respect. M. MIKKOLA and J. HELMINEN: *Lastensuojelun pääpiirteet*, Karelactio, Helsinki, 1994 p. 189-192.

Child Custody Act). The local social authority also has the right to bring to the court the matter concerning the appointment of a guardian for a minor, if a suspicion arises about the misuse of the right to administrate the child's property, for instance (Sec. 72 para. 2 Finnish Guardianship Services Act).

FRANCE

The French legal provisions distinguish between:

- delegation of parental responsibilities: see Art. 377 French CC; the mother and father can jointly or separately request for the court to order the partial or total delegation of parental responsibilities to a third person. This third person can be a member of the family, a reliable close person (*proche digne de confiance*), an institution approved to take children in or the *service départemental de l'aide sociale à l'enfance* (departmental Children's Aid Service). The last of the three mentioned above is a public body. The institutions approved to take children in can be either private or state operated.
- If a parent's parental responsibilities have been discharged (*retrait de l'autorité parentale*) and the other parent is dead or has also lost parental responsibilities, the court can appoint a third person to temporarily take care of the child. The court can also entrust the child to the departmental Children's Aid Service (see Art. 380 French CC).

GERMANY

It is possible to appoint the youth welfare office, being a public body, as guardian or curator of the child, subject to the general conditions governing the appointment of guardians or curators mentioned in the answer to Q 31.

According to § 1791 b para. 1 German CC, in cases where there is no suitable candidate to be individual guardian, the youth welfare office can be appointed guardian. However, the youth welfare office is the last resort, utilised if no suitable individual guardian can be found despite intensive efforts.[9] The guardianship court alone has the power to appoint the youth welfare office as guardian; the parents cannot appoint it guardian with legal effect, § 1791 b para. 1 sent. 2 German CC. The appointment procedure is an abridged one, which is why a written order by the guardianship court suffices.[10] Guardianship is to be transferred to the youth welfare office with local jurisdiction. According to § 87 c para. 3 sent. 1 German Social Security Code (*Sozialgesetzbuch*) VIII, it is the youth welfare office in whose area the child or teenager has his or her habitual residence that has local jurisdiction. The youth welfare office will in turn transfer the exercise of the duties of guardian to one or more of its civil servants or employees, § 55 para. 2 sent. 3 German Social Security Code (*Sozialgesetzbuch*) VIII.

---

[9] LG Flensburg 18.02.2000, *FamRZ* 2001, 445.

[10] Th. WAGENITZ, in: *Münchener Kommentar zum Bürgerlichen Gesetzbuch*, 4th Edition, Munich: Beck, 2002, § 1791 b No. 6.

Furthermore, in accordance with § 1791 c para. 1 German CC, the youth welfare office becomes guardian at the birth of a child whose parents are not married to each other and who requires a guardian, if the child's habitual residence is within the territory of application of the German CC. This legal provision regulates the guardianship of the youth welfare office; the guardianship comes into effect immediately by operation of law, the so-called 'legal *ex officio* guardianship'. This type of guardianship is used exclusively for children born outside marriage who are not subject to parental responsibilities at their birth. No letter of appointment is issued; all the guardianship court must do is confirm in writing, by way of a declaration, that the guardianship has come into force, § 1791 c para. 3 German CC.

If no suitable candidate for individual curatorship is available, the youth welfare office can be appointed curator.[11]

GREECE

If the court determines that there is no natural person who is suitable to obtain parental responsibilities, it may assign the guardianship of the child to a special foundation or society, or else to the competent social services (Art. 1600 Greek CC). These bodies cannot reject this assignment (Art. 1599 Greek CC).

HUNGARY

Hungary uses strong efforts to prevent the exercise of parental responsibilities by public bodies, even with respect to children who are in state care.

Hungarian law recognises the 'professional guardian', which is not seen as public body in the closest sense of the word, who exercises his or her tasks as guardian mostly as a civil servant or working in some other paid position. The task of a professional guardian can be narrowed so as to only include the administration of those children's property whose guardians, especially foster parents and the heads of the children's homes, are not empowered with this power. However, even a professional guardian cannot be the guardian of more than forty children.

IRELAND

Where a health board (i.e. local authority) is of the opinion that a child who resides in or was found in its area is in need of care or protection which he or she is unlikely to receive unless an appropriate order is made by the court, it shall be the duty of the health board to make an application to the court for a care order. The effect of a care order is to commit the child in need of care or protection to the care of the health board for so long as he or she remains a child or for a shorter period. Sec. 18 Irish Child Care Act 1991 authorises the court on the application of the health board to make a care order where it is satisfied that:

---

11 D. SCHWAB, *Familienrecht*, 12th Edition, Munich: Beck, 2003, No. 811.

the child has been or is being sexually assaulted, ill-treated, neglected, or sexually abused; or
the child's health, development or welfare has been or is being avoidably impaired or neglected; or
the child's health, development or welfare is likely to be avoidably impaired or neglected, and that the child requires care and protection which he is unlikely to receive unless the order is made.

The court is further entitled to extend that 'shorter' period upon its own motion or the application of another person, if it is satisfied that the grounds for the making of the order continue to exist.

Sec. 18 (3) Irish Child Care Act 1991 provides that where a care order is in force, the health board has control over the child as if it were his or her parent. The health board is further obliged to do what is reasonable in all the circumstances to safeguard and promote the child's health, development or welfare. In particular, the health board has authority to decide the type of care to be provided for the child. Where a child has been placed in the care of a health board, the health board has a number of placement options. Sec. 36 Irish Child Care Act 1991 specifies three options, which are, foster care, residential care and placement with relatives. By virtue of Sec. 36(1)(c) of the 1991 Act a health board can place a child who may be eligible for adoption 'with a suitable person with a view to his adoption.'

ITALY

A public or private body can obtain parental responsibilities only if the parents die, or if neither of them can hold such responsibilities. Art. 354 Italian CC provides that if there are no next of kin or persons able to hold the guardianship in the place the minor resides, the judge can assign the child to a private or public body located in the city where the minor resides. The private or public body delegates to one of its members the exercise of the guardianship.

LITHUANIA

Yes. Such a situation is possible through the establishment of an institutional guardianship (curatorship) of a child in the case of the separation of the parents from a child or in the event of the restriction of the parents' parental authority by a court judgment (Art. 3.261 Lithuanian CC). However, such form of guardianship (curatorship) is used only in those cases when there is no possibility of placing the child under guardianship (curatorship) in a family (Art. 3.261 Lithuanian CC).

When the child is separated from the parents, the parents lose their right to live together with the child or demand the return of the child from other persons. The parents may exercise their other rights in so far as that is possible without living together with the child (Art. 3.180 Lithuanian CC). This means that parental responsibilities of a public institution exist in addition to, as well as in substitution of, the parental authority of parents.

In the event of temporary or unlimited restriction of parental authority of parents, the parents lose their rights. However, they shall retain the right of visitation, except where that is contrary to the child's interests. This means that in such cases the parental responsibilities of the public body exist in substitution to the parental authority of the parents.

THE NETHERLANDS

The court may appoint a public body as guardian if the institution for guardianship is subsidised thereto by virtue of Art. 60 § 1(a) Dutch Juvenile Assistance Act. When appointing a legal person as guardian the court has to take the religion of the child concerned into account.

NORWAY

A public body can never obtain parental responsibilities.

POLAND

Parental responsibilities may be obtained by a foster family; the institution is a form of limiting parental authority.

PORTUGAL

A child may be entrusted to a child-care establishment under the exceptional circumstances mentioned in the previous question. As for the powers held by those institutions and their implications, see the answer to the previous Q 2.

RUSSIA

A public body can never obtain parental responsibility under Russian law. It can only fulfil the functions of child's guardian (Art. 147 (1) Russian Family Code).

SPAIN

If a child is declared to be bereaved or abandoned, the public child-protection organisation will automatically assume parental responsibilities over the child (an administrative guardianship). This will suspend the *patria potestad* or ordinary guardianship held by the child's parents or other persons according to the rules of Civil Law. The declaration of bereavement will specify the protection measures decreed by the public authority (*e.g.* whether the child is taken in by a foster family or should live in an institution, and any other educational or therapeutic measures considered necessary).

The concept of bereavement or *desamparo* differs according to the legislation in force in each of the seventeen Autonomous Communities into which Spain is divided. A child will be declared to be bereaved if parental responsibilities are not properly exercised because of the following:[12]

---

12 I. LAZARO GONZALO, *Los menores en el Derecho español*, Madrid, 2002, p. 355

- if the child has been voluntarily abandoned by his or her family,
- if the child does not habitually attend school,
- in cases of ill-treatment (physical or psychological) by the parental responsibility holder, or by a third person with the parental responsibility holder's consent or acquiescence,
- economic exploitation of the child, or
- mental disorders, alcoholism or drug addiction of the parental responsibility holder which do not allow a proper exercise of parental responsibilities.

The declaration of abandonment or bereavement is the result of an administrative procedure which is regulated differently throughout the Autonomous Communities. However, it is generally initiated by the public authority on its own motion after receiving notice of the situation. The parental responsibility holders and the child should be allowed to participate in this administrative procedure. Reports drawn up by social workers, psychologists *etc.* are given a decisive role, although it is sometimes not expressly provided in the regulation itself.[13] The declaration of bereavement can be challenged before court in a judicial proceeding.

SWEDEN

When a child, through measures taken by social welfare committee, is removed from the parents' care in order to protect the child from abuse or neglect, the daily care of the child is entrusted to the person in charge of the home receiving the child.[14] In most cases, however, the parents retain their legal custody of the child. The social welfare committee has the duty to contribute to the child's good care and upbringing, a favourable living environment and suitable education. To this end, the social welfare committee shall provide the custodians and the persons caring for the child with advice, support and other necessary assistance, Social Services Act, Chapter 6, Section 7.

In these situations it might be possible to claim that the social welfare committee obtains certain parental responsibilities, but not according to provisions of the Children and Parents Code.[15] Generally speaking, however, the idea of entrusting parental responsibilities to a public body does not fit at all into the Swedish system and terminology, based on a division of rights to custody and guardianship.

SWITZERLAND

If the child is not under any parental responsibilities, then guardianship authorities (Art. 360 Swiss CC) take over the corresponding function; in accordance with Art. 368 § 1 Swiss CC, all minors for whom nobody holds

---

13 I. LAZARO GONZALO, *Los menores en el Derecho español*, Madrid, 2002, 357.

14 Such placements take place in accordance with the Swedish Social Services Act (2001:453) or the Swedish Care of Young Persons Act (1990:52).

15 See answer to Q 31.

parental responsibilities need to be placed under guardianship. Parental responsibilities and guardianship mutually exclude one another. A minor child, therefore, only needs to be placed under guardianship if parental responsibilities do not exist (any more). Nevertheless, parental responsibilities take precedence because these cannot be waived as a matter of principle.[16]

The following circumstances result in the establishment of a guardianship for minor children due to the absence of parental responsibilities:[17]

- both parents who held parental responsibilities have died or have been placed under guardianship (Art. 296 § 2 Swiss CC);
- the sole holder of parental responsibilities has died or been placed under guardianship and it is not possible or advisable to confer parental responsibilities on the other parent (Art. 296 § 2, 297 § 3 Swiss CC);
- the unmarried mother is a minor or has been placed under guardianship and it is not possible or advisable to confer parental responsibilities on the father (Art. 298 § 2 Swiss CC);
- the father's position as the sole holder of parental rights no longer applies as a result of a successful challenge to the presumption of the husband's paternity (Art. 256 Swiss CC), recognition in accordance with Art. 259 § 2 Swiss CC or as a result of the annulment of a marriage;
- the adoptive parents' position as parents is set aside by means of a successful challenge to the adoption and the biological parents cannot exercise parental responsibilities;
- parental responsibilities are taken away from both parents (Art. 311 § 2, § 312 Swiss CC);
- parental responsibilities are taken away from the sole holder of parental responsibilities and it is not possible or advisable to confer them on the other parent (Art. 298 § 2 Swiss CC);
- in the case of a foundling there are no parental responsibilities in the first place

Administrative authorities and courts must report to the guardianship authority in accordance with Art. 368 § 2 Swiss CC as soon as they become aware of a guardianship case in the course of their official activities. The establishment of the guardianship and the appointment of a guardian usually take place at the same time.

---

16 E. LANGENEGGER, Art. 368 ZGB, p. 1809 (No. 4), in: H. HONSELL, N.P. VOGT, TH. GEISER (ed.), *Basler Kommentar zum Schweizerischen Privatrecht, Zivilgesetzbuch I*, Art. 1-456 ZGB, Basel: Helbing & Lichtenhahn, 2002.

17 E. LANGENEGGER, Art. 368 ZGB, p. 1809 (No. 6), in: H. HONSELL, N.P. VOGT, TH. GEISER (ed.), *Basler Kommentar zum Schweizerischen Privatrecht, Zivilgesetzbuch I*, Art. 1-456 ZGB, Basel: Helbing & Lichtenhahn, 2002.

QUESTION 33

C. ATTRIBUTION OF PARENTAL RESPONSIBILITIES

III. Other Persons

To whom are the parental responsibilities attributed in the case of:
(a) The death of a parent holding parental responsibilities;
(b) The death of both parents of whom at least one was holding parental responsibilities at the time of the death?

AUSTRIA

(a) The death of a parent holding parental responsibilities

Upon the death of a parent who held parental responsibilities jointly with the other parent, the parental responsibilities automatically pass solely to the other, surviving parent by virtue of law.[1] This parent can demand a judicial declaration to this effect (Sec. 145(1) sentence 1 and 145(2) Austrian CC).

Upon the death of a parent who held sole parental responsibilities, the court has to decide whether the other parent or grandparent(s) or foster parents and, if applicable, which grandparent(s) or foster parent(s) are to be entrusted with parental responsibilities (Sec. 145(1) sentence 2 Austrian CC). Pursuant to the legislator's intention none of the mentioned potential holders of parental responsibilities has priority by reason of his, her or their status; they are all on an equal footing.[2] Which person the court will in fact select as holder of parental responsibilities in an individual case depends solely on the child's emotional and social relationship with these persons. The decisive factor is what will serve best the child's interests. If, for instance, both the unmarried father and the stepfather as foster parent wish to obtain parental responsibilities, the court should attribute parental responsibilities primarily to the stepfather who has already had close ties to the child and not to the biological father who has previously had no or only very loose contact with the child.[3]

---

1 The same applies in the event that the parent's whereabouts have been unknown for at least six months or that the court has revoked his/her parental responsibilities.

2 Contra some older precedents recognising a priority based on the degree of consanguinity, *e.g. Oberster Gerichtshof,* 19.06.1997, 6 Ob 170/97m, *EFSlg* 84.247; still in this tradition *Oberster Gerichtshof,* 27.02.2002, 7 Ob 31/02p, http://www.ris.bka.gv.at/jus/, *EFSlg* 100.189-100.191.

3 EBRV 296 BlgNR XXI. GP, p. 54 (explanatory notes to Government bill, 296 supplements to the stenographic minutes of the National Assembly, XXI legislative period); *Oberster Gerichtshof,* 28.05.2002, EFSlg 100.188; SCHWARZL, 'Obsorge, Kindeswohl und Sachwalterschaft nach dem KindRÄG 2001', in: S. FERRARI/G. HOPF, *Reform des Kindschaftsrechts,* Vienna: Manz Verlag, 2001, p. 23. See also *Oberster Gerichtshof,* 27.07.1995, *Juristische Blätter,* 1996, p. 381 = *EFSlg.* 77.968; *Oberster Gerichtshof,* 27.05.1993, *Juristische Blätter,* 1994, p. 328 = *Österreichischer Amtsvormund,* 1994, p. 27.

If none of the aforementioned persons (parent, grandparent(s), foster parent(s), Sec. 145(1) sentence 2 Austrian CC) is able to assume parental responsibilities, the court is required to entrust another suitable person[4] with the parental responsibilities, taking into account the best interests of the child in selecting that person (Sec. 187 Austrian CC). The child's relatives will be considered first and only then other persons in a position of trust. Persons who are especially suited for legal representation or the administration of property include attorneys, caretakers, and notaries. As a last resort, the youth welfare agency *(Jugendwohlfahrtsträger)* will be the holder of parental responsibilities (Sec. 213 Austrian CC).

(b) The death of both parents of whom at least one was holding parental responsibilities at the time of the death?

Also upon the death of both parents (or in the event that their whereabouts have been unknown for at least six months or that the court has revoked their parental responsibilities), the court must transfer the parental responsibilities to the grandparent(s) or one or both foster parents; the decisive factor is what will serve best the child's interests (Sec. 145 (1) sentence 2 Austrian CC). If none of these persons may assume parental responsibilities, the court has to entrust another suitable private person or, as a last resort, the youth welfare agency with parental responsibilities, taking into account the best interests of the child in selecting that person (Sec. 187 Austrian CC).[5]

BELGIUM

(a) The death of a parent holding parental responsibilities

On the death of a parent, the child stays under parental responsibilities of the remaining parent.[6]

(b) The death of both parents of whom at least one was holding parental responsibilities at the time of the death

When both parents are dead, legally unknown or are unable to exercise their parental responsibilities due to permanent incapacitation, parental responsibilities are not transferred to a third person.[7] The system of parental responsibility is replaced by the system of guardianship (Art. 389 Belgian CC). The guardian exercises authority over the person of the minor, administrates its property and represents it (Art. 405 Belgian CC), but has no legal right of use

4 Individuals who are under a legal disability or are personally unfit are inappropriate (Sec. 188 Austrian CC).

5 For details see Q 33a, paragraph 2.

6 This applies, when one of the parents is dead, absent, incapable to exercise his parental responsibilities or (juridically) unknown.

7 Except in case of adoption. In that situation, the parental responsibilities are attributed to the adoptive parent(s), as a consequence of the adoption, but not as a consequence of the death of the parent(s).

and enjoyment. The guardian's competences are exercised under the supervision of the Justice of the Peace.[8]

BULGARIA

(a) The death of a parent holding parental responsibilities

Where there is another parent, the parental rights and responsibilities are passed over solely to him or her. In case both parents are deceased, no other person may be attributed with parental rights, except through the adoption of the child.

(b) The death of both parents of whom at least one was holding parental responsibilities at the time of the death

If both parents have died or the child is being raised by a single parent, no opportunity exists for the parental rights to pass over to another person, except through the adoption of the child.

CZECH REPUBLIC

(a) The death of a parent holding parental responsibilities

In case of the death of one of the parents, parental responsibility is attributed to the other parent.

(b) The death of both parents of whom at least one was holding parental responsibilities at the time of the death

If the child's parents have died there is no one to hold parental responsibility. The court is obligated to appoint a guardian of the child who will bring up and represent the child and administer his or her estate on behalf of the parents. The same applies if the parents have been deprived of parental responsibility, the exercise of parental responsibility has been suspended or the parents lack full legal capacity to act (Sec. 78 Czech Family Code). The guardian is subject to the court's supervision. All the guardian's decisions in essential matters concerning the child must be approved by court (Sec. 80 § 4 Czech Family Code). The guardian does not have parental responsibility; the Family Code establishes that the relationships between the guardian and the child are adequately governed by provisions on rights and duties of parents and children. The guardian does have maintenance duty in relation the child, though (Sec. 81 Czech Family Code).

DENMARK

(a) The death of a parent holding parental responsibilities

If both had parental authority and the child resided with the surviving parent, parental authority remains with this parent, Art. 14(1) first sentence Danish Act on Parental Authority and Contact. If, however, the child did not reside with the surviving parent then another person may apply for parental authority. The application from a third party will only be accepted if it is considered to be not

---

8 W. PINTENS, 'De voogdijwet herbekeken. Een eerste toelichting bij de Reparatiewet van 13 februari 2003', *T. Vred.* 2003, 127.

consistent with what is best for the child to allow parental authority to remain with the surviving parent, Art. 14(1) second and third sentence Danish Act on Parental Authority and Contact.

If the deceased parent had sole parental authority, then parental authority must be placed with the remaining parent or others. If the remaining parent applies for parental authority he or she is given priority, Art. 14(2) Danish Act on Parental Authority and Contact.

(b) The death of both parents of whom at least one was holding parental responsibilities at the time of the death

When both parents are deceased, sole parental authority may, upon application, be granted to a family member or friend, or joint parental authority may be granted to a married couple, who has/have close personal relationships with the child. If there is more than one application, a decision will be made considering what is best for the child, Art. 14(2), first sentence. If there are no applications for parental authority, the local authorities must assist in finding a suitable person/married couple to fulfil this role.[9]

ENGLAND & WALES

(a) The death of a parent holding parental responsibilities

Upon the death of one parent holding parental responsibility, that responsibility simply continues to be held by the other holder(s). If there are no other holders then in the absence of any appointment of a guardian (see Q 34) no one has parental responsibility for the child. There is in short no mechanism by which upon death responsibility is automatically transferred to someone else, though as already intimated, it is open to a parent with parental responsibility to appoint a guardian to take effect after their and the surviving parent with parental responsibility's death (see Q 34) and any individual can seek to be appointed as a guardian by the court.[10]

(b) The death of both parents of whom at least one was holding parental responsibility at the time of the death

The allocation of parental responsibility following the death of both parents is the same in principle as following the death of one of them. Accordingly, following the death responsibility will continue to be held by any other holder and in the absence of any other holder and in the absence of any appointment of a guardian (see Q 34) no one will have parental responsibility for the child.

FINLAND

(a) The death of a parent holding parental responsibilities

The Finnish Child Custody and the Right of Access Act actually has no rules for the case of a custodian's death except Sec. 14 para. 2, according to which a

---

9 S. DANIELSEN, *Lov om forældremyndighed og samvær*, Copenhagen: Jurist- og Økonomforbundets Forlag, 1997, p. 279.

10 Pursuant to Sec. 5, English Children Act 1989.

relative or another person close to the child has the right to submit an application to the court concerning the custody of the child, if the child has been left without any custodian because of the death of his custodian. Consequently, if one custodian dies, the other custodian will remain as sole custodian and exercise the custodial rights alone.

(b) The death of both parents of whom at least one was holding parental responsibilities at the time of the death

The Finnish Child Custody and the Right of Access Act actually has no rules for the case of a custodian's death except Sec. 14 para. 2, according to which a relative or another person close to the child has the right to submit an application to the court concerning the custody of the child, if the child has been left without any custodian because of the death of his custodian. Consequently, if both parents die and the child is left without a custodian, the procedural rules explained above enable the relatives of the child, for instance, or other close persons, to submit an application to the court to have a custodian appointed for the child. In such a situation the local social authority shall contact persons close to the child in order to examine whether it should make the application to the court and, in case an application is needed, do so (Sec. 10 Finnish Child Custody Decree).

FRANCE

(a) The death of a parent holding parental responsibilities

If a parent is alive and has not been discharged of parental responsibilities she or he remains the holder of parental responsibilities (Art. 373-1 French CC). The same rule applies if one parent is discharged of her or his parental responsibilities. The same rule also applies when the parents are separated (Art. 373-3 French CC). But in this situation if there are exceptional circumstances and if the child's interest requires it, the judge may order the child to be entrusted to a third person's care, preferably a relative (Art. 373-3 para. 2 French CC). In exceptional circumstances, the family judge who decides how to implement the exercise of parental responsibilities after the parents' separation can order that if a parent holding parental responsibilities dies, the child shall not be entrusted to the other parent (Art. 373-3 para. 3 French CC).[11]

(b) The death of both parents of whom at least one was holding parental responsibilities at the time of the death

In this case the judge of the guardianship court shall order a guardianship (Art. 373-5 and 390 French CC). The guardian will exercise parental responsibilities under the direction and the supervision of the board of guardians.

---

[11] See *e.g.* CA Pau, 12.12.1995, *Rép. Defrénois* 1997.996 annotated MASSIP (exceptional circumstances: the mother is very seriously ill and divorced from a man of Zairean nationality who was expelled from France after a criminal condemnation).

GERMANY

(a) The death of a parent holding parental responsibilities

Here the following distinction ought to be made:

- If the parents held joint parental responsibility and one parent dies, parental responsibilities will in future be attributable to the surviving spouse, § 1680 para. 1 German CC. Application is irrespective of whether joint parental responsibility existed by virtue of the parents' marriage or as a result of declarations of parental responsibility (§ 1626 a para. 1 No. 1 German CC).
- If a parent who was entitled to sole parental responsibility in accordance with § 1671 or § 1672 para. 1 German CC (see also answers to Q 17, 18 and 25) dies, the family court must attribute parental responsibility to the surviving parent, unless this is contrary to the child's best interests, § 1680 para. 2 sent. 1 German CC.
- If the mother was entitled to sole parental responsibility in accordance with § 1626 a para. 2 German CC (see Q 20), the family court must attribute parental responsibility to the father if this serves the child's best interests, § 1680 para. 2 sent. 2 German CC. The procedures in accordance with § 1680 German CC are initiated upon the court's own motion, which means that even in the case of para. 2 sent. 1 and 2 they do not require an application to be made by the surviving parent who claims his or her sole parental responsibility or demands the assignment of parental responsibilities.[12]

(b) The death of both parents of whom at least one was holding parental responsibilities at the time of the death

If both parents die, at least one of whom held parental responsibility for the child, parental responsibility for the child ends at the parents' death.[13] At this, there is an absence of parental responsibility, which means that a guardian must be appointed for the child in accordance with § 1773 para. 1 German CC. Concerning the conditions for and consequences of the guardian's appointment, see Q 31.

GREECE

(a) The death of a parent holding parental responsibilities

In the case of the death of a parent holding parental responsibilities, parental care devolves exclusively to the other parent, provided that he or she has also taken part in the parental care (Art. 1510 para. 2 Greek CC). The law provides an exception to this rule if the child was born out of wedlock and the father had appeared as a defendant judicial acknowledgement proceedings (Art. 1515 para. 3 Greek CC); then the father is not entitled to exercise parental care even after the death of the mother, unless the court, at his request, enables him to

---

12 P. FINGER, in: *Münchener Kommentar zum Bürgerlichen Gesetzbuch*, 4th Edition, Munich: Beck, 2002, § 1680 No. 23.

13 Th. WAGENITZ, in: *Münchener Kommentar zum Bürgerlichen Gesetzbuch*, 4th Edition, Munich: Beck, 2002, § 1773 No. 7.

exercise such care, taking into consideration the interests of the child. If the other parent does not have or is not able to exercise parental care, the court will appoint a guardian. For further details see the answer to Q 31.

(b) The death of both parents of whom at least one was holding parental responsibilities at the time of the death

If both parents die, the court will assign parental responsibilities to a guardian. For further details see the answer to Q 31.

HUNGARY

(a) The death of a parent holding parental responsibilities

If a parent holding parental responsibilities dies, the responsibilities are primarily attributed to the other parent. If the parents exercised their parental responsibilities jointly, the surviving parent's parental responsibilities remain unchanged. If they did not exercise them jointly, the surviving parent's responsibilities are revived. This happens more frequently because joint parental responsibilities are not common after divorce in Hungary.

After the death of a custodial parent, the public guardianship authority is obliged to call the non-custodial parent to exercise his or her parental responsibilities. If another person (*e.g.* the new spouse or partner of the custodial parent or the grandparent) takes care of the child when the parent dies, the public guardianship authority orders them to give the child to the surviving parent, who then exercises his or her rights.

In this situation a third person can be empowered with the right to exercise parental responsibilities; a guardian for the child can be appointed, but only if the non-custodial parent cannot exercise parental rights due to a reason stated in the Act.

(b) The death of both parents of whom at least one was holding parental responsibilities at the time of the death

If both parents die and at least one was holding parental responsibilities at the time of death, a guardian appointed for the child by the public guardianship authority will exercise parental responsibilities. In this situation, if the parent did not previously name the person as guardian in the case of his or her death, the public guardianship authority will generally appoint a guardian from among the child's relatives or persons who are in a family relationship with the child. A 'family relationship' includes persons who took care of the child. Also, a child who is capable of forming his or her own views has the right to express them in this issue and the public guardianship authority should give a due weight to the child's views with respect to the person according to the child's age and maturity.

Only if there is no suitable person among the child's relatives can anyone else be appointed guardian.

IRELAND

(a) The death of the parent holding parental responsibilities

In the case of all children born to parents who, at the relevant time, are married to each other, Sec. 6(1) of the 1964 Act confers joint and equal rights of guardianship on both the father and the mother. If either parent should die during the lifetime of the other, the latter will be deemed guardian of their children either alone or together with such person as is appointed by will by the deceased spouse or by the court.[14] An unmarried father may also be appointed guardian by deed or will on the death of the unmarried mother or other guardian.[15]

(b) The death of both parents of whom at least one was holding parental responsibilities at the time of the death

Where a child has no guardian any person or persons may, by virtue of Sec. 8(1) of the 1964 Act, apply to the court to be appointed as guardian(s) of the child.

ITALY

(a) The death of a parent holding the parental responsibilities

To the other parent (Art. 317 § 1 Italian CC).

(b) The death of both parents were of them was the holder of the parental responsibilities at the time of his death

To the guardian nominated by the guardianship judge (Art. 343 *et seq* Italian CC).

LITHUANIA

(a) The death of a parent holding parental responsibilities

To the surviving parent, if his or her parental authority is not restricted or he or she is not separated from the child *i.e.* to another parent holding parental responsibilities. If the surviving parent is separated from the child, or his or her parental authority is restricted, the parental responsibilities shall be attributed to the guardian (curator) of the child.

(b) The death of both parents of whom at least one was holding parental responsibilities at the time of the death

To the guardian (curator) of the child.

THE NETHERLANDS

(a) The death of a parent holding parental responsibilities

If another person holds parental responsibilities at the time of the parent's death, be it a parent (Art. 1:253f Dutch CC) or a person other than a parent (Art. 1:253x Dutch CC), this person will from then on exercise sole parental responsibilities (the other parent) or guardianship (the person other than a parent) by operation of law. However, if a person other than a parent becomes a

14 See Sec. 6(2) and (3) Irish Guardianship of Infants Act 1964.
15 See Sec. 7 of the 1964 Act.

guardian pursuant to Art. 1:253x § 1 Dutch CC, the court may at any time, on the application of the surviving parent, provide for the surviving parent to be charged with parental responsibilities if he or she has the capacity to exercise it.

If the deceased parent was vested with sole parental responsibilities, the court will attribute parental responsibilities to the surviving parent or to a third person (Art. 1:253g Dutch CC). The court will do so on application of the Child Care and Protection Board, the surviving parent or *ex officio*. The surviving parent's request will only be denied if there is a well-founded fear that the best interests of the child(ren) would be neglected were it to be granted (also Art. 1:293 under a Dutch CC). If the parent with parental responsibilities had by last will and testament appointed a person other than the surviving parent as guardian, the court will give preference to the surviving parent if so requested.

(b) The death of both parents of whom at least one was holding parental responsibilities at the time of the death

If at the death of both parents one of the parents was holding parental responsibilities with a non-parent, the non-parent will become the guardian (Art. 1:253x Dutch CC). If one of the parents was holding sole parental responsibility and appointed a guardian in his or her last will and testament, the appointee will become the guardian if he or she accepts his appointment. A parent without parental responsibilities cannot appoint a guardian. If both parents had parental responsibilities at the time of their death and appointed the same person as guardian in their last will and testament, this person will become the children's' guardian at the moment the appointment is accepted. Problems will arise if the parents have appointed different guardians and it is unclear which parent died first. In such a situation the court will decide *ex officio* which appointment will take effect (Art. 1:292 § 3 Dutch CC). If neither parent appointed a guardian in their last will and testament, the court will appoint a guardian (Art. 1:295 § 1 Dutch CC).

NORWAY

(a) The death of a parent holding parental responsibilities

Upon the death of one of the parents having parental responsibilities, the other parent, if he or she had already shared these, will hold sole parental responsibilities, Art. 38 sec. 1. If the child lived with both parents at the time of the death, the surviving parent will be attributed parental responsibilities even if the deceased alone had these, Art. 38 sec. 2 Norwegian Children Act 1981. If the parent who acquires parental responsibilities pursuant to the Art. 38, sec. 1 did not live with the child, or the parent who acquires parental responsibilities pursuant to Art. 38, sec. 2 did not have parental responsibilities when the other parent died, other persons may within six months of the death initiate legal proceedings to claim parental responsibilities and the right to live permanently with the child, according to Art. 63 sec. 1. In these cases, the court may allow one person to have sole parental responsibilities or allow a man and woman who are cohabitants to share it. If any person other than the surviving father or mother is given parental responsibilities, the court shall also decide whether the father or mother shall continue to share in the parental responsibilities according Art. 63 sec. 5 Norwegian Children Act 1981.

(b) The death of both parents of whom at least one was holding parental responsibilities at the time of the death

If the death of both parents results in no one having parental responsibilities, the local police or district court shall be notified on the death certificate, Art. 38 sec. 3 Norwegian Children Act 1981. The decision shall first and foremost be taken on the basis of what is best for the child, Art. 48. If only one claim for parental responsibilities is received, the court shall grant the claim except when there is a risk that the child will not be given proper care and upbringing, or that the child will suffer harm in some other way. Rejection of a claim for parental responsibilities shall be done by court order and may be appealed, according to Art. 63 sec. 3.

POLAND

(a) The death of a parent holding parental responsibilities

If both parents hold parental authority and one parent dies, the surviving parent will be vested with sole parental authority (Art. 94 Polish Family and Guardianship Code). If parental authority was held only by the parent who died, a guardian is to be appointed.

(b) The death of both parents of whom at least one was holding parental responsibilities at the time of the death

A guardian is to be appointed.

PORTUGAL

(a) The death of a parent holding parental responsibilities

If the parents were married and one of them dies, parental responsibility passes to the surviving parent (Art. 1904 Portuguese CC). If an unmarried parent dies who has cohabited and has declared their desire to jointly exercise parental responsibility before the official of the registry office, the situation is the same (Art. 1904 and 1911 No. 3 Portuguese CC).

(b) The death of both parents of whom at least one was holding parental responsibilities at the time of the death

If both parents die, the child is subject to compulsory guardianship (Art. 1921 No. 1(a) Portuguese CC). Guardianship is one of the ways to compensate for the lack of parental responsibility.

RUSSIA

(a) In case of the death of a parent holding parental responsibilities

In case of the death of the parent holding parental responsibilities, parental responsibility rests upon the other parent alone, if her or she has not been discharged of parental responsibility by a court order.

(b) The death of both parents of whom at least one was holding parental responsibilities at the time of the death

If both parents of the child have died:

- the child can be placed for adoption; the adoptive parent(s) will obtain parental responsibility over the child (Art. 124 (1) and 137 (1) Russian Family Code);
- the Department of Guardianship and Curatorship can appoint a guardian for the child (Art. 145 Russian Family Code and Art. 35 Russian CC). Rights and duties of the guardians, although modelled upon parental responsibility, are of more limited nature and fall outside the concept of parental responsibility.[16]
- The child can be placed with foster parents (Art. 151 Russian Family Code). Rights and duties of the foster parents also fall outside the concept of parental responsibility.

SPAIN

(a) The death of a parent holding parental responsibilities

If parental responsibility was held jointly with another person, this person will become the sole holder of parental responsibility. If parental responsibility was held solely by the deceased parent, parental responsibility is extinguished and it will become necessary to name a guardian as described under Q 31.

(b) The death of both parents of whom at least one was holding parental responsibilities at the time of the death

Parental responsibility is extinguished in this case. It will therefore become necessary to name a guardian as described under Q 31.

SWEDEN

(a) The death of a parent holding parental responsibilities

If both parents have custody of a child and one of them dies, the other parent becomes sole custodian of the child, Chapter 6 Sec. 9 Swedish Children and Parents Code. If the sole custodian of a child dies, the court shall, upon the application of the other parent or upon notification by the social welfare committee, entrust custody to the other parent. In the latter case, if it is considered more appropriate, the court may instead entrust custody to one or two specially appointed custodians. In an appellate court decision *RH 1983:53*, the sole custodial parent of an eleven-year-old boy died. The dead father's cohabitee was appointed as custodian of the child in accordance with the child's wishes.

The person having custody of the child is also guardian to the child, Chapter 10 Sec. 2 to 3 Swedish Children and Parents Code.

---

16 L. MIKHEEVA, *Full and Limited Guardianship (Opeka i Popechitel'stvo)*, Moscow: Paleotip, 2002, p. 81.

(b) The death of both parents of whom at least one was holding parental responsibilities at the time of the death

If both parents die, the court shall, upon notification by the social welfare committee or when the situation otherwise becomes known, entrust custody to one or two specially appointed custodians, Chapter 6 Sec. 9 para. 1 Swedish Children and Parents Code.

SWITZERLAND

(a) The death of a parent holding parental responsibilities

After the death of a spouse the parental responsibilities are attributed to the surviving spouse (Art. 297 § 3 sentence 1 Swiss CC).

If an unmarried mother (or an unmarried father) dies, the guardianship authority conveys parental responsibilities to the father (or respectively to the mother) or appoints a guardian for the child, depending on what is required for the child's welfare (Art. 298 § 2 Swiss CC).

(b) The death of both parents of whom at least one was holding parental responsibilities at the time of the death

A guardian must be appointed in accordance with Art. 368 § 1 Swiss CC for any minor person for whom nobody holds parental responsibilities. 'The guardianship authority must appoint a person as guardian who seems suited to this office' (Art. 379 § 1 Swiss CC). 'If there are no substantial reasons for acting to the contrary, the authority when making its choice has to give preference to a suitable close relative [...] of the child to be placed under guardianship, taking their personal circumstances and the vicinity of their place of residence into consideration' (Art. 380 Swiss CC). Suitable close relatives must, therefore, be shown due consideration in the selection procedure and will be shown preference if there are several applicants of approximately equal degrees of suitability.[17]

---

[17] CH. HÄFELI, Art. 380/381 ZGB, p.1882 (No. 3), in: H. HONSELL, N.P. VOGT, TH. GEISER (ed.), *Basler Kommentar zum Schweizerischen Privatrecht, Zivilgesetzbuch I*, Art. 1-456 ZGB, Basel: Helbing & Lichtenhahn, 2002.

QUESTION 34

C. ATTRIBUTION OF PARENTAL RESPONSIBILITIES

III. Other Persons

To what extent, if at all, may the holder(s) of parental responsibilities appoint a new holder(s) upon his, her or their death? If such an appointment is permitted, must it take place in a special form *e.g.* will?

AUSTRIA

The transfer of parental responsibilities to other persons via a private legal transaction is not possible; instead, the court will make a decision in this regard in accordance with the best interests of the child (Sec. 145, 176, 186a, 187, 213 Austrian CC). Consequently, parents cannot prospectively make any binding disposition regarding the awarding of parental responsibilities even in the case of death.[1] Rather the court has to entrust a suitable person with parental responsibilities according to the rules laid down in Sec. 145 and 187 Austrian CC, taking into account the best interests of the child.[2]

BELGIUM

Both parents can appoint a guardian by a declaration before the Justice of the Peace or before a notary, as long as they act jointly. Their declaration, which takes effect on the death of both parents, may be modified at any time by making a new one (Art. 392(2)). Each parent has the right to revoke the declaration before the authority who received it,[3] without the intervention of the other parent (Art. 392(4)). After the death of one of the parents, the declaration remains valid so long as the surviving parent has not revoked it or so long as another guardian has not been designated by will or declaration as foreseen in Art. 392(1) Belgian CC (Art. 392 (3)). According to Art. 392(1) Belgian CC, the parent who last exercised parental authority may appoint a guardian by will, by declaration before the Justice of the Peace or by declaration before a notary. If the person designated by the parent(s) accepts the guardianship,[4] the Justice of the Peace will approve the designation, unless serious reasons concerning the child's interests prevent the Justice of the Peace from respecting the choice of the parent(s).

---

1 *Oberster Gerichtshof*, 27.02.2002, 7 Ob 31/02p, http://www.ris.bka.gv.at/jus/, *EFSlg* 100.189-100.191; see also *Oberster Gerichtshof*, 19.06.1997, 6 Ob 170/97m, *EFSlg* 84.247.

2 See Q 33(a) and (b).

3 When the declaration is initially made before a notary, another notary can be chosen for the revocation. The notary so chosen will inform the notary who received the declaration. The Law does not provide the same possibility when a declaration is made before the Justice of the Peace.

4 According to Art. 396(1) Belgian CC, he has no obligation to do so.

If there is no parental choice, the Justice of the Peace will appoint a guardian, preferably, a member of the immediate family (Art. 393 Belgian CC). According to Art. 394 Belgian CC, the Justice of the Peace will hear a minor who is at least twelve years old, its grandparents, its brothers and sisters who have reached majority, its uncles and aunts and all other persons who could give useful advice, before the approval or the appointment of the guardian.

BULGARIA

There is no such legal option. Parental rights may not be transferred from the parents to any other persons even in the case of death. In the case of death, a parent may only express his or her wish, without legal effect, as to which person is to be appointed guardian or custodian of the child and with whom the child should be placed for upbringing and education. No special form is required for this action (which is of no legal significance) although it may be part of the will. The wish of the parent may be taken into consideration by the Guardianship authority or by the Child Protection Department.

CZECH REPUBLIC

Parental responsibility belongs only to the parents or to the adoptive parents. In case of the death of the child's parents a guardian of the child must be appointed by court. Preference is given to the person recommended by the parents. The form of recommendation is not prescribed; it is not excluded that the will may include such a recommendation. The court is not bound by such a recommendation; it must first examine whether the recommended guardian has full legal capacity to act, if he or she agrees with his or her appointment, and he or she must guarantee that their exercise of guardianship will be in the interests of the child. The guardian does not have parental responsibility and is subject to supervision of the court.

DENMARK

The holder(s) of parental authority cannot appoint a new holder(s) upon death but can make a statement stating his/her/their intention/preference upon death. This statement will be respected unless it is against what is best for the child, Art. 15 Danish Act on Parental Authority and Contact. A statement does not alter the priority given to the surviving parent. The statement is not required to have a special form such as in a will. However, the statement is often contained in a will to ensure its existence at the time of death.

ENGLAND & WALES

Parents with parental responsibility and guardians can appoint a guardian in accordance with Sec. 5, English Children Act 1989. No one else has this power under the current law[5] though it is open to any individual following the death of the parents or other holders of parental responsibility to apply to court to be appointed a guardian (see below).

---

5 Though prospectively under the Sec. 114, English Adoption and Children Act 2002, special guardians will also be able to appoint a guardian.

Any parent with parental responsibility (*i.e.* not an unmarried father without such responsibility nor other individuals having parental responsibility by reason of a residence order being made in their favour) and any guardian may appoint an individual to be the child's guardian.[6] Although reference is made to an 'individual', it is clear that more than one person may be appointed as a guardian.[7] Furthermore an additional guardian or guardians can be appointed at a later date.[8] There is nothing to prevent an appointment being made by two or more persons jointly.[9]

There is no restriction or control on who may be appointed (even another child, it seems, could be appointed)[10] nor are there any means of scrutinising an appointment unless a dispute or issue is subsequently brought before the court.[11] Appointments can be made only in respect of children under the age of 18.[12]

Under Sec. 5(5), English Children Act 1989, it is sufficient that the appointment 'is made in writing, is dated and is signed by the person making it'. This simple method of appointment is intended to encourage parents (particularly young parents who are notoriously reluctant to make wills) to appoint guardians.[13] Sec. 5(5) does not preclude appointments being made in a will or deed, since clearly such means will satisfy the minimum prescribed requirements.[14] An appointment made by will but not signed by the testator, will be valid if it is signed at the direction of the testator in accordance with Sec. 9, English Wills Act 1837.[15] An appointment will also be valid in any other case provided it is signed at the direction of the person making the appointment, in his presence and in the presence of two witnesses who each attest the signature.[16] These latter provisions cater for the blind or physically disabled persons who cannot write, but not for those who are absent or mentally incapacitated.[17]

Under Sec. 5(7), the appointment only takes effect immediately upon the death of the appointing person where:

---

6 Sec. 5(3) and (4), English Children Act 1989.
7 This is implicit in Sec. 6(1) which refers to "an additional guardian".
8 Sec. 6(1).
9 Sec. 5(10).
10 Although it may seem questionable for one child to have parental responsibility over another, there are occasions when such a power could be useful, see *Re A, J and J (Minors)(Residence and Guardianship Orders)* [1993] Fam Law 568.
11 *Viz* under Sec. 6, English Children Act 1989.
12 Sec. 105(1).
13 See the Law Commission's comments at Law Com Report No. 172, para 2.29.
14 See Lord MACKAY LC's comments at 502 HL Official Report (5th Series), col 1199.
15 Sec. 5(5)(a).
16 Sec. 5(5)(b).
17 *Cf* Guidance and Regulations, Vol 1, Court Orders, para 2.18.

- following that death the child has no parent with parental responsibility[18] (but it will take effect where a non-parent has responsibility, for example, by having a residence order in their favour); or
- there was a residence order (or existing custody order)[19] in favour of the person making the appointment immediately before his death (unless a residence or 'existing custody order' was also made in favour of the surviving parent).[20]

In this latter instance, the surviving parent has no right to object but he can apply to the court for an order ending the appointment.[21] Where the child does have a parent with parental responsibility, the appointment will take effect only upon the death of that person.[22]

For the sake on completion it should be added that the court also has power to appoint an individual to be the child's guardian. According to Sec. 5(1), English Children Act 1989 this power arises if, (a) the child has no parent with parental responsibility for him; or (b) a residence order has been made with respect to the child in favour of a parent or guardian of his who has died while the order was in force.

Under Sec. 5(2) this power of appointment may be exercised in any family proceedings[23] either upon application or "if the court considers that the order should be made even though no application has been made for it".

FINLAND

Before the present Finnish Child Custody and the Right of Access Act came into force in 1984, it was possible for the custodian to determine in a will who was to take custody of his or her child in case of death. However, according to the present Finnish Child Custody and the Right of Access Act such a determination has no legal effect, because child custody and the right of contact shall be decided solely on the basis of what is considered to be in the best interests of the child (Sec. 10).

FRANCE

In general, if a parent holding parental responsibilities dies, the other parent automatically becomes the sole holder of parental responsibilities (Art. 373-1

---

18 It will, therefore, take effect if the child's unmarried father is still alive, unless he has obtained parental responsibility.

19 Sch 14, para 8(2).

20 Sec. 5(9) and Ch. 14, para 8(2).

21 Sec. 6(7).

22 Sec. 5(8).

23 This is widely defined by Sec. 8(3), English Children Act 1989 and includes most proceedings under the 1989 Act but also adoption and domestic violence proceedings.

French CC). A parent could express a wish to appoint, upon his or her death, someone other than the other parent as holder of parental responsibilities, but such a wish expressed in a will or any other document will usually be of no direct consequence.

If the parents were separated before the death of the parent who exercised parental responsibilities, the family judge who determines the implementation of the exercise of parental responsibilities can order, in very exceptional circumstances, the child not to be entrusted to the other parent. The family judge can also determine to whom the child will be temporarily entrusted in this situation (Art. 373-3 para. 3 French CC). Therefore it is only when the parents are separated that the holder of parental responsibilities (or more precisely if there are two holders, the parent who has the exercise of parental responsibilities) can bring a petition before the family judge to appoint a third person to whom the child should be entrusted if the claiming parent dies. There is no other legal possibility.

If only one parent is still alive, that parent can mention in a document to whom he would like the child to be entrusted in case of this parent's death. On his death a guardianship will be ordered by the guardianship court judge. The judge may take the wish expressed by the parent who held parental responsibilities before his or her death into account, but the judge is not obliged to do so.

GERMANY

The relevant provisions are contained in §§ 1776, 1777 German CC:
§ 1776 para. 1 German CC attributes to the parents holding parental responsibilities the right to designate the person who is to be appointed guardian of their under-age child, this includes the case of the parents' death. This right to designate a guardian is an expression of parental responsibilities both in terms of responsibility for the child's person and for the child's property.[24] In accordance with § 1777 para. 1 German CC, parents can designate a guardian for their child only if they hold parental responsibility for the child's person and the child's property at the time of their death. The contents of the designation must ensure that the identity of the person being designated is safely concluded; alternatively, the parents could merely limit the group of people from among whom the guardian is to be chosen.[25]

In accordance with § 1777 para. 3 German CC, designation is by means of a will, § 1937 German CC, or by means of a contract of inheritance (*Erbvertrag*), § 1941 German CC; such a designation is unilaterally obligating only - i.e. it is not interdependently or contractually binding even if it is made in a joint will or in a contract of inheritance. A will can, in accordance with § 2221 German CC, be

24 BayObLG 04.05.1992, *FamRZ* 1992, 1346, 1348.

25 Th. WAGENITZ, in: *Münchener Kommentar zum Bürgerlichen Gesetzbuch*, 4th Edition, Munich: Beck, 2002, § 1776 No. 9.

drafted as a holographical will (§ 2247 German CC) or in the form of a public will (*öffentliches Testament*) (§ 2232 German CC). According to § 2276 para. 1 sent. 1 German CC, a contract of inheritance must be recorded in writing by a notary in the presence of both parties.

The designation may be revoked at any time with legally binding effect; for this reason, a parent, may after a joint designation, unilaterally designate another person by making a new disposition.[26] In the event of diverging designations by the parents holding parental responsibility the special provision of § 1776 para. 2 German CC applies, whereby each parent's designation is valid even if the father and the mother designate different persons, subject to the proviso that the designation by the parent who died last applies; this means that any dispute between parents during their lifetime is irrelevant.

As a consequence of the valid designation as guardian in accordance with § 1776 German CC, the guardianship court must appoint the designated person guardian, provided that he or she is willing and that there is no impediment or reason to pass over this person. In accordance with § 1778 para. 1 German CC, the person appointed guardian pursuant to § 1776 German CC can be passed over without his or her consent only if that person in their very person presents a hindrance, if he or she is factually prevented from assuming guardianship not only on a temporary basis, if the assumption of guardianship is delayed, if his or her appointment would threaten the best interests of the ward or if the ward has completed his or her 14th year and objects to the appointment, unless the ward has no legal capacity to contract.

GREECE

Only a parent may appoint a new holder of parental responsibilities upon his or her death. The appointment may be included in a will or declared to a notary or to a justice of the peace. A condition for the validity of this appointment is that the parent held parental responsibilities both at the time of the declaration and at the time of his or her death (Art. 1592 para. 2 Greek CC). It is worth mentioning that if one parent is still alive at the time of the other's death, parental care will devolve to him or her exclusively (see the answer to Q 33a), so any appointment by the deceased will have no effect.[27]

---

26 W. ZIMMERMANN, in: SOERGEL, *Großkommentar zum Bürgerlichen Gesetzbuch*, 13th Edition, Stuttgart: Kohlhammer, 2000, § 1776 No. 4.

27 K. PANTELIDOU, in: A. GEORGIADIS and M. STATHOPOULOS (eds.), *Civil Code commentary, Vol. VIII, Family Law (Arts. 1505-1694)*, 2nd Edition, Athens: Law & Economy, P.N. SAKKOULAS, 2003, Art. 1592-1594 Greek CC, p. 538, No. 4. See also No. 5, where it is mentioned that if the parent who died first appointed a guardian and the other parent did not, the appointment of a guardian by the first parent is not binding on the court after the death of the latter.

HUNGARY

The parents, as holders of parental responsibilities, have the right to appoint a guardian to exercise parental responsibilities upon their death. A guardian who was appointed by only one of the parents can take over the parental responsibilities if both parents die.

The appointment for a guardian has to be made in a testament or a public instrument. The latter is usually performed in a recorded declaration before the public guardianship authority.

A guardian appointed by the parent holding parental responsibilities will not automatically become the guardian of the child. The public guardianship authority appoints the guardian of the child. The public guardianship authority can disregard a person appointed by the parent only if he or she cannot be a guardian by a reason stated in the Act, or if his or her appointment would endanger the child's interests.

The guardian, as opposed to the parent, is under the control of the public guardianship authority while exercising parental responsibilities. Nevertheless, if the child's guardian is one of the child's close relatives, the guardian's activity is closer to the parent's parental responsibilities than that of the foster parent or the head of the children's home.

IRELAND

Any parent who is also the guardian of a child may, by deed or will, appoint any person or persons, to take the former's place as guardian or guardians, in the case of the death of that parent.[28] Such appointee (the 'testamentary guardian') shall, on the death of the parent in question, act together with any other surviving guardians. A surviving parent may, however, object to such appointment. In such a case, the testamentary guardian cannot act as guardian unless, on application to the court, the court grants an order that the testamentary guardian shall act as guardian, either jointly with the surviving parent or indeed to the latter's exclusion.[29] In making such an order, the court may also, at its discretion, make such orders relating to the custody of or access to children as to it appear proper.[30]

ITALY

Art. 348 Italian CC provides that the judge must appoint as guardian the person the last parent who held parental responsibilities indicated by will, public deed or authenticated private deed, unless it is not possible to appoint the designated person due to serious reasons.

---

28 Sec. 7 of the 1964 Act.
29 Sec. 8(5) of the 1964 Act.
30 Sec. 8(6) of the 1964 Act.

LITHUANIA

Despite the fact that the appointment of a guardian (curator) of a child is the exclusive competence of a court (only in exceptional cases *i.e.* in the event of temporary guardianship (curatorship), the guardian (curator) may be appointed by the local government (municipality) (Art. 3.264 Lithuanian CC), the parents are allowed to express their wishes regarding the guardian (curator) of the child in the event of their death. These wishes must be established in a will. According to Part 4 of Art. 3.265 Lithuanian CC, the guardian (curator) of the child shall be appointed taking into consideration the wish of the child's deceased parent(s) as expressed in his (their) will. However, such wishes are not obligatory for the court or municipality. The court or municipality may appoint another person as a guardian (curator) of a child if the person designated by the dead parents of a child does not correspond to the requirements established by Art. 3.269 Lithuanian CC (*e.g.* the person is older than 65 years or is suffering from chronic alcoholism *etc.*), or if the appointment of such person as a guardian (curator) will be against the interests of the child.

THE NETHERLANDS

A parent with parental responsibilities can appoint a new holder upon his or her death by means of his last will and testament. A parent without parental responsibilities has no such rights. The person(s) appointed will become the guardian(s) at the moment the appointment is accepted.

NORWAY

A parent cannot appoint a new holder of parental responsibilities in the case of his or her death. If the parents have stated in writing who they wish to have parental responsibilities after their deaths, importance should be attached to their wish, according to Art. 63 sec. 5 Norwegian Children Act 1981.

POLAND

A person the parents recommend may be appointed as an guardian, if the parents were not deprived of parental authority and such an appointment it is not contradictory to the child's interests (Art. 149 § 1 Polish Family and Guardianship Code). No specific form is required for the recommendation, but it is not binding for the court.

PORTUGAL

Yes. The parents may, in a will or other authentic or authenticated document, appoint a guardian (or guardians) for their child in the event of their death or disability (Art. 1928 Portuguese CC). The guardian indicated by the parents must be confirmed by the juvenile court (Art. 1925 No. 2 Portuguese CC), which will oversee the exercise of the guardianship (Art. 1925 No. 1 Portuguese CC).

RUSSIA

A holder of parental responsibility cannot appoint a new holder of parental responsibility in case of her or his death. However, the wish of the parent is always respected in appointing a guardian.

SPAIN

The child's parents, provided they hold parental responsibility, can appoint the person they wish to become a guardian if they die, or specify the persons they wish to exclude as guardians of their children. It is possible to appoint supervisory bodies, to specify who is to become a member of such a supervisory body and to give instructions as concerning the children and the children's property. This has to be done in either a will or a public document (Art. 223 Spanish CC and Art. 173-176 Catalan Family Code).

The judge will follow the parents' appointments and or instructions, unless he or she considers them contrary to the child's best interest. In this case there is an obligation to depart from the parents' wishes.

There are rules that deal with contradictory appointments and/or instructions. The Spanish CC establishes that the Judge must try to reconcile them; if this is impossible he may select those that are more appropriate to the best interests of the child. Catalan law provides a different criterion in that it establishes that the more recent appointment or instruction is to be given higher consideration.

SWEDEN

If the court is to appoint a custodian after the death of the child's parents and the parents (or one of them) have made known who they wished to be appointed custodian, the court shall appoint that person, unless it is inappropriate to do so, Chapter 6 Sec. 10a para. 4 Swedish Children and Parents Code. Although the parents' wishes are normally respected, the best interests of the child must be the primary consideration of the court. If the child has reached a sufficient degree of maturity and is opposed to the appointment of the person chosen by the parents, it is not appropriate to appoint that person.[31] It is also possible that the circumstances changed to such an extent, after the stipulation was made, that it is no longer appropriate to follow it.

The provision regarding guardianship in case of the death of both parents is identical to the one on custody and found in Chapter 10 Sec. 7 Swedish Children and Parents Code. The persons suggested by the parents shall be appointed guardian, unless it is inappropriate to do so.
The manifestation of the parents' will concerning custody and guardianship does not have to take place in a special form, but it does need to be expressed with reasonable certainty.[32]

---

31 G. WALIN and S. VÄNGBY, *Föräldrabalken, En kommentar, Del I, 1-13 kap.*, Stockholm: Norstedts Juridik, 2002, p. 6:47.

32 G. WALIN and S. VÄNGBY, *Föräldrabalken, En kommentar, Del I, 1-13 kap.*, Stockholm: Norstedts Juridik, 2002, p. 10:12.

SWITZERLAND

Art. 381 Swiss CC has the following to say in this respect: 'If the person to be placed under guardianship, or said person's father or mother, names somebody as the guardian in whom they can trust, then this suggestion should be complied with unless there are significant reasons to the contrary.' The guardianship authority is under an obligation to comply with the suggestion of a guardian whom the family trusts if no important reasons go against doing so, in particular if the person named is not *a priori* unsuited to the office. No particular formal requirements apply to the suggestion and it may also be submitted orally.[33]

[33] CH. HÄFELI, Art. 380/381 ZGB, p. 1883 (No. 9), in: H. HONSELL, N.P. VOGT, TH. GEISER (ed.), *Basler Kommentar zum Schweizerischen Privatrecht, Zivilgesetzbuch I*, Art. 1-456 ZGB, Basel: Helbing & Lichtenhahn, 2002.

QUESTION 35

D. THE EXERCISE OF PARENTAL RESPONSIBILITIES

I. Interests of the Child

In exercising parental responsibilities, how are the interests of the child defined in your national legal system?

AUSTRIA

Parents must see to the upbringing of their children and promote their welfare in general (Sec. 137(1) Austrian CC). In assessing the child's welfare *(Kindeswohl)*, i.e. their interests, it is necessary to give due consideration to the child's personality and needs, especially his or her aptitudes and abilities, predispositions and developmental potential, as well as to the parents' living conditions (Sec. 178a Austrian CC). This notion also includes the physical, mental, and emotional welfare of the child. Therefore, parental love, care and the imparting of security are the basis for realizing the child's welfare.[1]

BELGIUM

The parental authorities are a purposive competence that must be exercised in the interests of the child. The notion of 'interests of the child' dominates family law and stems from public policy; it justifies the intervention of the authorities. Some authors consider the interests of the child as a general principle of law, that the judge should take into account even when the Law does not explicitly mention it, but there is no unanimity on this point of view. Although the interests of the child guide the exercise of parental responsibilities, they are not really determined; it is a subjective standard. A general definition of the interests of the child refers to an effective advantage for the child (positive component), combined with a negative component, namely the absence of any disadvantage for the child. Interests of the child are a changing notion because of the changing personal situation of the child and as an evolutive notion, according to the sociological context. Indeed, the precise implications of the principle will vary over time according to an individual child's situation. The definition may be filled in positively (in the sense that it represents a real advantage for the child) or negatively (in the sense that it causes no disadvantage to the minor), but defining the interests of the child in general rules is not only impossible, it is dangerous for the child.

The notion of 'interests of the child' has changed substantially during the last years. Where, it had been considered that the child was absolutely incapable of exercising its own rights, there is now a tendency to give the child a certain right of participation. 'Protection, provision and participation' dominate the

---

1 *Oberster Gerichtshof* 22.10.1986, *Sammlung der Entscheidungen des Obersten Gerichtshofs in Zivilrechtssachen (SZ)*, Vol. 59, No. 184; LG Eisenstadt 29.11.2001, EFSlg. 96.695.

approach of the child in the legal system without, however, giving the child the sovereignty to determine its destiny. The competent authority will take certain criteria into account, such as the existing situation, the stability of the child, the maintenance of a sustained relationship between the child and its parents, the desires of the child, the age of the child, the educational capacity of the parents, the availability of the parents and the material conditions of the parents. The judgment of the competent authority will vary according to the context, the time and the place. In certain cases, it may depend on the vision of the judge. In case of conflict between the interests of the child and the interests of its parents, the interests of the child will prevail.[2]

BULGARIA

The Bulgarian Family Code does not explicitly define the link between the exercise of parental responsibilities and the interests of children. See Q 7f.

CZECH REPUBLIC

Despite a frequent use of the concept of interests of the child, the Czech Family Code does not expressly define what is meant by 'interests of the child'. The interpretation of 'interests of the child' is then left to judicial practice and theory.[3] Generally, it may be deduced from the contents of individual provisions that the parents have a decisive role in upbringing the children and are supposed to be models for the children by their personal life and behaviour (Sec. 32 Czech Family Code), and that the exercise of parental responsibility should lead to an all-round development of the child.

DENMARK

There is no general definition of the best interests of the child with respect to the exercise of parental authority. The Danish Act on Parental Authority and Contact does, however, specify that decisions must be made from the perspective of the child's interests and needs, Art. 2.

ENGLAND & WALES

The overarching principle of English child law is that provided by Sec. 1(1), English Children Act 1989, namely

> 'When any court determines any question with respect to:
> the upbringing of the child; or
> the administration of the child's property or the application of any income arising from it,
> the child's welfare shall be the court's paramount consideration'.

---

2 E. De Kezel, 'Het begrip 'het belang van het kind'', *R.W.*, 1998-99, p. 1165; M. Steennot, 'Het belang van het kind', *R.W.*, 1974-75, p. 1733; A.-C. Van Gysel, 'L'intérêt de l'enfant, principe général de droit', *T.B.B.R.*, 1988, p. 186-206.

3 M. Hrusakova, *Dite, rodina, stat.* Brno: MU, 1993.

However, this paramountcy principle only applies, if at all, in the course of litigation. It does not, therefore, directly apply[4] to parents or other individuals in the exercise of their parental responsibility insofar as it is not the subject of litigation. As one commentator has put it[5]

> 'It can hardly be argued that parents, in taking family decisions affecting a child, are bound to ignore completely their own interests, the interests of other members of the family and, possibly, outsiders. This would be a wholly undesirable, as well as an unrealistic objective'.

Accordingly, parents are not bound to consider their children's welfare in deciding, for example, whether to make a career move, to move house or whether to separate or divorce.[6]

FINLAND

The Child Custody Act includes general principles that define certain goals or ideals for the factual contents of the custody, *i.e.* for exercising the rights and the duties of a custodian. The Act does not call these principles a definition of the best interest of the child, but they can be interpreted as such.[7] Sec. 1 Finnish Child Custody and the Right of Access Act concerns principles relating to the custody of the child and Sec. 2 to the right of access. (Sec. 4 concerns principles relating to the custodian's duty to listen to the child's opinions, which has already been illuminated in Q 9). See also Q 7.

According to Sec. 2 the child shall be ensured the right to meet the parent with whom the child is not living. It also stipulates that the parents of the child shall aim to ensure the implementation of this right in mutual understanding and while taking the best interests of the child into consideration. The Finnish Child Protection Act values the 'best interests' principle.

FRANCE

French law provisions mention *l'intérêt de l'enfant,* in singular, as a general and vague concept that must be recognised in every case involving holders of parental responsibilities and, if there is dispute, by the court. If the court has to make a decision on the exercise of parental responsibilities, it must always search for the child's best interests.[8] The *Cour de cassation* does not control the

---

4 Of course, if the issue does come before the court then the conduct of the parental responsibility holder(s) will be judged in the light of the paramountcy principle.

5 A. BAINHAM, *Children: The Modern Law*, 2004, Jordans, p. 38, 2nd Ed.

6 See B. DICKENS, 'The Modern Function and Limits of Parental Rights' (1981) 97 *LQR* 462 at 471, who asserts that parental responsibility is not to do positive good but to avoid harm.

7 As M. HELIN, 'Lapsen huolto', in: H. MATTILA, *Lapsioikeuden pääpiirteet 1984*, Juridica, Helsinki, 1984.

8 See also Art. 373-2-6 French CC, which states that the family judge decides on issues of parental responsibilities in particular over the safeguarding of the minor children's interests.

recognition of the child's interests but requires inferior courts to justify their recognition (*appréciation souveraine*) of the child's interests.[9]

See Art. 371-1 French CC for the definition of parental authority and its aims as being a collection of rights and duties aimed at the child's interests. It belongs to the father and mother until the child reaches majority or becomes emancipated, in order to protect the child's safety, health and morality, to provide for his education and to allow for his or her personal development. The parents shall help the child to make decisions that concern the child's life; taking into account the child's age and maturity.
This legal provision shows how parental responsibilities are to be used and what kinds of interests of the child are to be protected: safety, health, morality, education *etc.*

Other provisions give more detailed provisions on other aspects of the child's interests:

- Art. 371-2 French CC obliges the parents to contribute to support and to provide for education to the child (in proportion to their means, to those of the other parent and to the child's needs). This obligation does not automatically cease when the child reaches majority. It is in the child's interest to study and have professional education even if the child has reached majority.
- Art. 371-3 French CC: the child cannot be taken away from the family home, except for those necessary situations mentioned in the legal provisions. In principle, it is in the child's interests to live with her or his parents.
- Art. 371-4 French CC: It is normally in the child's interests to have personal relationships with his or her grandparents, and even with the great grandparents.
- Art. 371-5 French CC: the child should not be separated from his brothers and sisters unless it is impossible to keep them together or the child's interests requires another solution. If they are separated, the judge shall determine the modalities of the personal relationships between brothers and sisters.
- Art. 373-2-6 French CC: concerning the decisions made by the family judge on issues of parental responsibilities: para. 2 of this provision insists upon the measures that the judge can order 'to protect the continuity and strength of the bonds between the child and each parent'. This shows the supposition of French law that it will usually be in the child's interests to keep personal relationships with both parents.

---

9 See *e.g.* French Supreme Court, Civ. II, 15.04.1981, *Gaz. Pal.*, 1982. 2. 583 annotated VIATTE; Civ. I, 20.06.1995, *Bull. civ.* I, No. 264; Civ. II, 31.05.1995, *Bull. civ.* II, No. 165. The court must examine concretely what the child's interests are with regard to all circumstances of the case, French Supreme Court, Civ. I, 13.10.1993, *Bull. Civ.* I, No. 275.

GERMANY

The best interests of the child constitute the guiding principle of parental responsibility, § 1697 a German CC. It is the highest guiding principle for the exercise of parental responsibility by the parents; at the same time, it also constitutes the yardstick and legal basis for any court decisions.

This undefined concept of law is assumed in many norms of the German CC: For instance, § 1671 para. 2 sent. 2 German CC names the best interests of the child as a criterion to be taken into account by the family court in deciding whether sole parental responsibility can be attributed to one parent when the parents live apart. Furthermore, in accordance with § 1680 para. 2 German CC the best interests of the child are to be taken into account in deciding whether parental responsibility is to be attributed to the surviving parent should the parent holding sole parental responsibility die. Furthermore, a threat to the best interests of the child can constitute the reason for the child's being ordered to reside in the joint household of the parent not holding parental responsibilities and another reference person, § 1682 German CC.

What constitutes the best interests of the child is, however, only specified by law in individual instances. § 1666 para. 1 sent. 1 German CC makes a distinction between the physical, mental and moral welfare of the child to achieve a protection of the child that is as comprehensive as possible, but specifies only certain types of behaviour, such as neglect of the child, as being a threat to the child's best interests. Any closer definition of the term is generally guided by the question as to whether certain objective developmental standards which have absolute application, for example, as set out in the German Social Security Code (*Sozialgesetzbuch*), have been assured for the child. It is further guided by objective educational principles, which include: the promotion of the child's development, the raising of the child to become a person who is able to take responsibility for himself or herself and live in community,[10] the continuity and stability of the circumstances in which the child is cared for, and the respect for the child's internal ties.[11] Furthermore, the circumstances of the individual in question must be taken into account, such as his or her social milieu and age.[12]

In view of parental autonomy with regard to education, as enshrined in Art. 6 German Basic Law, the best interests of each child are to be determined primarily by the parents themselves, using the criteria set out above, taking into particular account the child's personal rights pursuant to Art. 2 para. 1 German

---

10 § 1 German Social Security Code VIII.

11 Th. RAUSCHER, *Familienrecht*, Heidelberg: C.F. Müller, 2001, No. 958.

12 U. DIEDERICHSEN, in: PALANDT, *Bürgerliches Gesetzbuch*, 64th Edition, Munich: Beck, 2005, § 1666 No. 15.

Basic Law.[13] An objective external assessment is required only where a court decision is necessary.

Moreover, § 1626 para. 3 German CC includes a positive approach to filling in the definition, which stipulates that a constituent part of the child's welfare is contact with both parents and, provided that it promotes the child's development, with other persons to whom the child is close. Finally, the definition is and will be shaped by the findings of child and family psychology, which are continually in development.[14]

GREECE

In Greek family law there is no determined legal definition of the interests of the child. This concept is somewhat vague and thus flexible, so it can be adapted to the particular circumstances of each case (*in concreto*).[15] As for the content of this concept in general, doctrine distinguishes between the moral and the material interests of the child.[16] The first include safeguarding its psychological, mental, and physical health, the development of its personality, as well as the protection of its fundamental rights and liberties. The material interests refer to the property of the child. Important criteria for the specification of the interests of the child can de derived from international law (for instance, the European Convention on Human Rights or the Convention for Children's Rights), the provisions of national law, as well as from the findings of modern psychology and child psychiatry.[17]

HUNGARY

The Hungarian Family Act states among its fundamental principles that the child's interests must always be taken into account when the Act is applied, and that the child's rights are always to be ensured. This general statement is repeated specifically in the VIII Chapter of the Act concerning parental responsibilities and state care. The VIII Chapter repeats one of the fundamental principles of the Act. The parental responsibilities are always to be exercised in

---

13 L. M. PESCHEL-GUTZEIT, in: STAUDINGER, *Kommentar zum Bürgerlichen Gesetzbuch*, 13th Edition, Berlin: Gruyter, 2002, § 1627 No. 20; Th. RAUSCHER, *Familienrecht*, Heidelberg: C.F. Müller, 2001, No. 958.

14 Th. RAUSCHER, *Familienrecht*, Heidelberg: C.F. Müller, 2001, No. 958.

15 S. KOUKOULI-SPIMIOTOPOULOU, in: A. GEORGIADIS and M. STATHOPOULOS (eds.), *Civil Code commentary, Vol. VIII, Family Law (Arts. 1505-1694)*, 2nd Edition, Athens: Law & Economy, P. N. SAKKOULAS, 2003, p. 94, No. 206-207; P. AGALLOPOULOU, in: A. GEORGIADIS and M. STATHOPOULOS (eds.), *Civil Code commentary, Vol. VIII, Family Law (Arts. 1505-1694)*, 2nd Edition, Athens: Law & Economy, P.N. Sakkoulas 2003, Art. 1511 Greek CC, p. 205-206, No. 17, citing numerous court decisions.

16 S. KOUKOULI-SPILIOTOPOULOU, in: A. GEORGIADIS and M. STATHOPOULOS (eds.), *Civil Code commentary, Vol. VIII, Family Law (Arts. 1505-1694)*, 2nd Edition, Athens: Law & Economy, P. N. SAKKOULAS, 2003, p. 93, No. 204.

17 S. KOUKOULI-SPILIOTOPOULOU, in: A. GEORGIADIS and M. STATHOPOULOS (eds.), *Civil Code commentary, Vol. VIII, Family Law (Arts. 1505-1694)*, 2nd Edition, Athens: Law & Economy, P. N. SAKKOULAS, 2003, p. 95-109, No. 211-238.

the interest of the child, This is also guaranteed by the rule that gives the child who is capable the right to be heard and have due weight be given to his or her view in every important matter affecting him or her.

The rules regulating the rights and duties of the parents are properly applicable to the rights and the duties of the guardian according to the Act; therefore, a guardian must also exercise the parental responsibilities in the best interests of the child.

It has to be mentioned that the Family Act contains the term 'the interest of the child' instead of 'best interest' but the legal literature and practice unambiguously holds the wording of the Act to be understood as the 'best interests of the child'.

IRELAND

The interests of the child are defined by reference to the principle that the best interests of the child must take precedence in all matters concerning the child's welfare. 'Welfare' is defined by Sec. 2 Irish Guardianship of Infants Act 1964 as comprising the religious, moral, intellectual, physical and social welfare of a child. Sec. 3 of the 1964 Act makes it abundantly clear that in considering an application relating to the guardianship, custody or upbringing of a child, or to the administration of property belonging to or held in trust for the benefit of that child, or the application of the income of the child, the court must have regard to the welfare of the child. This, the Sec. states, is 'the first and paramount consideration.' Although this has been qualified by the constitutional preference for the marital family, the ostensible rule is that where there is a conflict between the welfare of the child and other considerations (such as the rights of parents), the welfare of the child takes precedence over all other matters. This is sometimes known as the 'best interests test', although Sec. 3 refers specifically to the welfare of the child.[18] This principle is in line with Ireland's international obligations, in particular under the UN Convention on the Rights of the Child 1989.[19] O'FLAHERTY J. in applying this principle in *Southern Health Board v. C.H.*[20] stated that:

> 'It is easy to comprehend that the child's welfare must always be of far graver concern to the court. We must, as judges, always harken to the constitutional command which mandates, as a prime consideration, the interests of the child in any legal circumstances.'

---

18 See WALSH J. in *G. v. An Bord Uchtála* at page 76, who appears to suggest that the two terms may differ in meaning in certain contexts. With utmost respect, it is submitted that the distinction suggested is perhaps rather fine.

19 The UN Convention on the Rights of the Child 1989 was ratified by Ireland on 21.09.1992.

20 [1996] 2 I.L.R.M. 142.

Later, in his judgment, O'FLAHERTY J. observed that 'the first point to note about this case is that the judge is in essence required to inquire as to what is in the best interests of the child.' No individual factor can, in itself, be considered conclusive. WALSH J. highlighted this in his judgment in *S. v. S.*, [21] which was cited favourably by MCGUINNESS J. in *C.C. v. P.C.*,[22] wherein the learned judge stressed the merits of assuming an overall view:

> 'All the ingredients which the Act stipulates are to be considered globally. This is not to be decided by the simple method of totting up the marks which may be awarded under each of the five headings. It is the totality of the picture presented which must be considered ... the word 'welfare' must be taken in its widest sense.'[23]

The welfare of a child must be judged by reference to all relevant matters. While the welfare of the child as defined by the Irish Guardianship of Infants Act 1964 is deemed to be a paramount consideration, it is nonetheless possible (and sometimes necessary) to look outside the strict confines of the definition in Sec. 2 of the 1964 Act. Other factors have been found relevant to the consideration of the court.

A factor not mentioned by the 1964 Act, but nonetheless of importance, is the question of emotional welfare. This was highlighted most recently by the decision of MCGUINNESS J. in *D.F.O'S. v. C.A.*.[24] There the learned judge, referring to supporting precedent, noted the recognition of this added factor.[25] This 'most important aspect of welfare', though not explicitly mentioned in the 1964 Act, should be taken into account in determining applications under the Act. In the case cited, MCGUINNESS J. suggested that the emotional welfare of the child would be better served by the parents attending counselling sessions.

In Ireland, it has generally been accepted, that, where a child is of 'tender years' (which generally means under the age of seven), all else being equal, that the child in question should reside in the custody of its mother. In *B. v. B.*,[26] for instance, O'DÁLAIGH C.J. ruled that '... in view of his tender age, there can be no doubt that the younger son [of the parties] should continue in the custody of his mother.'

The more generally applicable comments of BUDD J. in *B. v. B.*[27] reveal the reasoning behind the court's decision noting that 'young children are

---

21 (1974) 110 I.L.T.R. 57.

22 [1994] 3 Fam. L.J. 85.

23 See also *D.F.O'S. v. C.A.*, unreported, High Court, McGuinness J., 20.04.1999.

24 Unreported, High Court, 20.04.1999.

25 See also *M.B. O'S. v. P.D. O'S.* (1974) 110 I.L.T.R. 57; *MacD. v. MacD.* (1979) 114 I.L.T.R. 66, *per* GRIFFIN J.; *S. v. S.* [1992] I.L.R.M. 732.

26 [1975] I.R. 54 at 59.

27 *Ibid.* at 67.

notoriously nearer to their mother than their father'.[28] His later comments seem to suggest that he believed that only the mother in that case could attend to her son's physical needs and give him the attention he required. Indeed, at one point, the principle seemed to have evolved into something approaching a presumption of law.[29] In *H. v. H.*[30] PARKE J. noted the 'ample judicial support' for the proposition that a 'child of tender years should be entrusted to the custody of his mother unless she had so gravely failed in her duty as a mother as to forfeit such right'. In *MacD. v. MacD.*,[31] HENCHY J. expressed the preference for the mother as follows:

> 'In the case of very young children ... the person *prima facie* entitled to their custody, where the parents are estranged, is the mother, for by reason of her motherhood she will usually be the person primarily and uniquely capable of ministering to their welfare.'

In more recent times, however, this approach has been somewhat more restrained. It is arguable that this principle, besides compounding gender stereotypes, ignores the growing prevalence and acceptance of men who play an enhanced parenting role in their respective families. In fact, the principle is not invariable and in light of changing parenting patterns the courts have proved increasingly willing, as in *J.J.W. v. B.M.W.*,[32] to make an order of custody relating even to young children in favour of their father. In this regard, a recent dictum of MCGUINNESS J. is most instructive. In *D.F.O'S. v. C.A.*,[33] the learned judge, in deciding to grant joint custody of a four-year old child, noted that she:

> '...[did] not entirely accept the old *tender years* principle: modern views and practices of parenting show the virtues of shared parenting and the older principles too often meant the automatic granting of custody to the mother virtually to the exclusion of the father.'

The question of parental capacity is closely allied to the last factor, although it relies on the surer footing of individual characteristics rather than resorting to crude gender stereotypes. The court is required to ensure that the parent being granted guardianship, custody or access has sufficient mental and physical resources to perform the duties envisaged. This is not to say that the more capable spouse will always be granted custody. Nor should it suggest that parents with needs of their own, owing for instance to disabilities, should be denied custody. In *E. v. E.*[34] and *A.H.S. v. M.S.*,[35] for instance, custody was

---

28 See also his comments, *ibid*, at 70.
29 See also the *dicta* of Walsh J. in *E.K. v. M.K.*, unreported, Supreme Court, 31.07.1974.
30 Unreported, High Court, PARKE J., 04.02.1976.
31 (1979) 114 I.L.T.R. 66.
32 (1971) 110 I.L.T.R. 49.
33 Unreported, High Court, MCGUINNESS J., 20.04.1999.
34 Unreported, High Court, 03.02.1977.

granted to women who, despite a history of mental illness, were shown to have overcome their difficulties to an extent sufficient to allow their having custody.[36]

Where a parent, however, is manifestly incapable of carrying out this role, the court will lean heavily against such an order. In *C.(C.) v. C.(P.)*,[37] MCGUINNESS J. declined to make an order of custody in favour of a father. The evidence showed that the roles of child and parent had largely reversed in this case. In response to his father's difficulties, the child, it seemed, had taken on the role of parent, generally looking out for and protecting his father. In such a case there was a danger, in the words of the judge, of the child becoming 'parentified', of taking on the mantle of responsibility for a family well before his time.

ITALY

Our legal system requires that judges must exclusively take a minor's moral and material interests into account in decisions affecting minors, but it neither defines nor clarifies the content of these interests. The elasticity of this legal formula is intentional, as the formula must be adjusted to the facts of each case. The interests can only be the interests relating to each individual case.

LITHUANIA

According to Part 3 of Art. 3.159 of Lithuanian CC, parental authority may not be used contrary to the interests of a child. Art. 3.164 Lithuanian CC provides a general rule that all questions related to a child must be decided exclusively in the interests of the child. The positive law does not provide a legal definition of the notion 'interests of the child'. The content of this notion is explained by the legal literature and court practice. In general, the interests of the child are defined as a complex of material, living, educational, emotional and other circumstances which are most favourable for the development of the personality of the child.[38]

THE NETHERLANDS

With respect to the exercise of parental responsibilities, the Dutch CC provides no explicit or general definition. Taking into account the legislation[39] and the childcare protection system the exercise of parental responsibilities must meet a certain minimum standard, but this is not necessarily the equivalent of the best interests of the child.

---

35 Unreported, High Court, 12.11.982.

36 Although in the former case the order was made subject to subsequent review.

37 [1994] 3 Fam. L.J. 1985.

38 V. MIKELENAS *et. al.*, *Commentary of Book Three of the Civil Code of Lithuania*, Vilnius: Justitia 2002, p. 313-314

39 See Art. 1:247 and Art. 1:253j Dutch CC.

NORWAY

The interests of the child are not directly defined in Norwegian legislation. But when the UN's Child Convention was implemented as national law with priority over other legislation, the reference to 'the best interests of the child principle' in Art. 3 was also the foundation of national law. It is reflected in respect to parental responsibilities in the various articles in Norwegian Children Act 1981, which give the child the right to be heard in personal matters from the age of seven, and which attach great importance to the child's wishes. It should also be noted that any form of violence or other action that could harm or endanger his or her mental or physical health is forbidden.

POLAND

According to Polish law, the principle of the child's interests has the same contents and scope as are found in the Convention on the rights of a child of 29 October 1989 and in the normative acts of domestic law, in particular the Polish Family and Guardianship Code and the Polish Civil Procedure Code.[40] It is emphasised that the minor child's best interests remain the basic aim of family law. However, this does not mean that the parents' best interests are completely disregarded.[41]

PORTUGAL

The exercise of parental responsibility is always subordinate to the interests of the child (Art. 1878 No. 1 Portuguese CC). The law does not define the interests of the child, nor does it offer criteria for defining it. The child's interests are, therefore, a vague legal concept. Despite the extreme difficulty that legal literature has had in defining it, this concept is particularly expressive and acquires more defined contours when referring to the circumstances of a particular child, since there exist as many different interests as there are children. The child's interests is a cultural concept, profoundly dependent upon the system of values in force at any given moment and in each society, concerning the person of the child, his or her material and emotional needs, and the conditions necessary for his or her healthy development. Thus, the notion can only be specified in reference to those values and by means of a systematic interdisciplinary study of the child's real-life situation.

RUSSIA

Art. 65 (1) Russian Family Code states that 'execution of parental responsibility should not contravene the interests of the child' and that 'safeguarding of the child's interests should be the parent's paramount consideration'.

Unlike the family codes of 1918 and 1926, current legislation no longer speaks of execution of parental responsibility 'exclusively' in the best interests of the child. This transformation has been interpreted in the sense that the current law presupposes finding a balance between the interest of the child and the interests

---

40 Supreme Court judgment of 12.12.2000, V CKN 1805/00.

41 Supreme Court judgment of 05.05.2000, II CKN 765/00.

of his or her parents. Only in cases when the conflicts between the interests of the child and his or her parent(s) are so serious that no compromise can be found, should priority be given to the interest of a child.[42]

The law does not specify the best interests of the child. Art. 65 (1), however, identifies a number of patterns of parental behaviour that are always presumed to contravene the best interests of the child. Thus, execution of parental responsibility may not harm physical or psychological health of the child or be detrimental to the child's moral development. Methods of education should exclude treatment that is denigrating, cruel, offensive or humiliating to human dignity, nor insulting or exploitative to the child (Art. 65 (1) Russian Family Code).

Determination of what is in the best interests of the child is normally reserved to the parent(s). If the parents can not agree or there is an indication that their decisions are against the best interests of the child, the best interests of the child can be delineated by the Department of Guardianship and Curatorship or by a court. A child of any age is given the possibility to express his or her opinion concerning what he or she considers as his or her best interests (Art. 57 Russian Family Code). However, the child's subjective vision of his or her best interests does not always coincide with what is objectively in the best interests of that child. Therefore the parents and the authorities are allowed not to follow the child's opinion if they come to a conclusion that the child is not able to reasonably assess his or her best interest. If a child is under the age of ten, the parents or authorities do not need to note why they depart from the child's opinion. If a child is older than ten, the law prescribes that his or her opinion should be considered and followed, unless it is not in the child's best interests (Art. 57 Russian Family Code). This requirement imposes on the parents and the authorities the duty to prove due motivation, whether they have considered child's best interests in their decision.[43]

Execution of parental responsibility against the best interests of the child can lead to restriction or discharge of parental responsibility (Art. 65 (1), Art. 69 and 73 Russian Family Code), and/or administrative and criminal[44] responsibility of the parents.

SPAIN

Spanish law does not provide a list of legal criteria in order to determine the best interests of the child but instead operates with a general clause. There is an exception in the framework of the divorce, annulment and separation

---

42 M. ANTOKOLSKAIA, *Family Law* (*Semeinoe pravo*), Jurist, Moscow: 1999, p. 195-196.

43 L. PCHELINTZEVA, *Commentary on the Family Code of Russian Federation,* Moscow: Norma, 1998, p. 215-217.

44 Art. 156, introduced in the Criminal Code of The Russian Federation in 1997, provides for criminal punishment for parents who neglect or abuse their parental rights if parental misconduct was involved cruelty towards the child.

procedure. Here, the one criterion mentioned is that siblings should not be separated (Art. 92 Spanish CC).

In legal writing the best interests of the child are often equated to his or her fundamental rights, but this is not a sufficient criterion to make choices if, as often happens, all the alternatives are in compliance with the child's rights. In practice, the determination of the best interests of children poses difficulties, especially if there is disagreement between the father and mother. Judges usually tend to ratify technical reports provided by psychologists, social workers *etc* or apply criteria which are shared by the majority of the population.[45]

SWEDEN

The best interests of the child are the primary consideration when determining issues concerning custody, residence and contact. No specific definition is given on how the notion of the best interests of the child is to be understood because its content may vary depending on the prevailing values and morals of the society as well as the circumstances of the individual case. The point of departure is found in Children and Parents Code, Chapter 6, Section 1, stating that children are entitled to care, security and good upbringing. Children are furthermore to be treated with respect and may not be subjected to corporal punishment or other humiliating treatment.

Certain basic considerations characterise the Swedish position, *i.e.*, (1) respect of the child's human dignity and need of special protection due to his or her vulnerable position,[46] (2) assessing the child's best interests on the basis of the circumstances of each individual case,[47] and (3) having regard to the wishes of the child while taking into account the child's age and maturity.

The present legislation is based on the assumption that joint custody, generally speaking, is in compliance with the best interests of the child and that the child needs close and good contact with both parents. Parental agreements are encouraged, the aim being to keep parental disputes out of court as far as possible.

SWITZERLAND

In respect to children, the child's welfare is the ultimate maxim in the entire law. Consequently, it is also to be taken into account as the decisive guideline in exercising parental responsibilities. As an indeterminate legal term, it is not

45 J. FERRER RIBA, 'Comentari a l'article 133', in: EGEA FERNANDEZ-FERRER RIBA, *Comentaris al Codi de Familia, a la Llei d'unions estables de parella i a la Llei de situacions convivencials d'ajuda mutua*, Madrid, 2000, 615.

46 Huvudbetänkande från Barnkommittén, SOU 1997:116 Barnets bästa i främsta rummet, p. 127-129.

47 Prop 1997/98:7 p 34 and 105. See also: *Vårdnad, Boende och Umgänge*, Stockholm: Socialstyrelsen (National Board of Health and Welfare), 2003, p. 74.

possible to give a more precise definition in respect to its contents. Art. 302 § 1 Swiss CC only defines one core area of the child's welfare, the effort to facilitate the child's physical, mental and moral development. Federal legislation specifically demands that the child be given the possibility to develop, from a mental-psychological, physical and social point of view, in a way which consistently does justice to the child's age at the time, where the best possible solution for the child is to be aimed at, taking all circumstances into account.[48]

48 BGE 129 III 250, 255.

QUESTION 36

D. THE EXERCISE OF PARENTAL RESPONSIBILITIES

II. Joint Parental Responsibilities

If parental responsibilities are held jointly by two or more persons, are they held equally?

AUSTRIA

The rights and duties of joint parental responsibility holders are generally equal (Sec. 137(3) Austrian CC). The only exception is if one parent is partially prevented from exercising parental responsibilities, *e.g.* if he or she has been partially discharged of his or her parental responsibilities or if he or she is a minor. In that case, the other parent independently assumes the parental responsibilities in the respective matters, *e.g.* in case of a parent's minority, the other parent takes over the administration of the child's property and legal representation (Sec. 145 and 145a Austrian CC).

BELGIUM

Yes. Both parents equally hold the parental responsibilities. This equality is realised by the system of joint exercise of parental responsibilities, according to Art. 373(1) Belgian CC. However, it is unthinkable that both parents must always act together. Therefore, Art. 373(2) Belgian CC provides a legal presumption that each parent acts with the agreement of the other, even if the other parent is not present. This presumption pertains to all acts concerning the authority over the child, including routine as well as important decisions, excepting those legally excluded (Art. 373(2) Belgian CC).[1] The presumption is rebuttable, but only in relation to *bona fide* third parties. Third parties are presumed to be bona fide as long as they have no knowledge and, according to the standard of due care, could not reasonably be expected to have any knowledge of the disagreement of the other parent.[2]

BULGARIA

Yes. Holders of parental responsibilities are both parents if known and alive. As Art. 72 Bulgarian Family Code states: 'Both parents exercise parental rights and obligations jointly and separately'.

---

1 In fact, only one exception exists, namely the authorisation of both parents in case of removal of an organ. In this situation, the agreement of the other parent is never presumed (Art. 7 Belgian Law of 13 June 1986 concerning the Organ Transplantation).

2 W. PINTENS, 'Die Reform des belgischen Kindschaftsrechts aus vergleichender Sicht', *Fam.RZ*, 1997, p. 457-464.

CZECH REPUBLIC

Parental responsibility is always held jointly by the parents, provided they have full legal capacity to act and the court has not deprived one (or both) parents of parental responsibility or has not suspended its exercise (Sec. 44 Czech Family Code). Both parents have the same rights and duties in relation to the child and the Czech Family Code presumes that they will agree on exercise of rights and duties. If they do not come to an agreement on an essential matter, either of them may apply to the court for a decision.

DENMARK

Yes, although there may be differences in their rights based on parenthood, for example, the right to obtain a contact order based on parenthood and not parental authority.

ENGLAND & WALES

The general answer to this question is yes where responsibility is held by two or more individuals, it is held equally. This is subject to two qualifications. First, as explained in Q 14, certain individuals, namely those non parents who acquire parental responsibility by means of having a residence order in their favour do not acquire the right to agree to the child's adoption or to appoint a guardian and clearly those rights are not shared with those of any existing parents with parental responsibility. Secondly, where a local authority acquires parental responsibility upon the making of a care order (see Q 32) then, on the one hand, while the authority does not thereby acquire the right to agree to the child's adoption or to appoint a guardian or to change the child's religion, on the other, [3] if they are satisfied that it is necessary to do so to safeguard or promote the child's welfare they may determine the extent to which a parent or guardian may meet his parental responsibility for the child.[4]

FINLAND

Legally joint custodians, no matter how many, are equal when not otherwise ordered by the court.

> The custodians shall be jointly responsible for the exercise of custody and shall jointly make all decisions relating to the child unless otherwise provided by the law (Sec. 5 para 1)

The court has the power to modify the custodial rights of two or more custodians. The court may attribute to one of the joint custodians the sole power to decide about a custodial issue. This can be the right to decide alone about the child's residence or religious affiliation, for instance.

> Where necessary, a court may issue directions on the attribution of duties rights and responsibilities of a person or persons assigned

---

3 Sec. 33(6), English Children Act 1989.

4 Sec. 33(3)(b) and (4), English Children Act 1989.

custody of a child and if there are more persons, may decide on the distribution of responsibilities between them. (Sec. 9 para. 3 Finnish Child Custody and the Right of Access Act).[5]

The court shall make the decision according to what it finds to be in accordance with the best interests of the child (Sec 10 para. 1 Finnish Child Custody and the Right of Access Act). Judges sometimes try to seek settlements in custody disputes by modifying the joint custody. The court may thus, for example, grant both of the parents the position as a legal custodian, although one parent may be given somewhat reduced powers, if both of the parties find this solution acceptable. The court may also give such an order against the will of the parties.[6]

If the child has been taken into care, the custodial powers are divided between the local social authority and the custodian or custodians. The division of powers has been explained above in Q 32.

FRANCE

Yes. Art. 372 French CC states that the father and mother are to exercise communal parental authority. This joint exercise is based on the full equality of both parents.[7] For all usual and ordinary acts concerning the child, each parent is deemed to act with the agreement of the other parent towards third persons in good faith (Art. 372-2 French CC).[8] If the parents cannot agree on more important decisions, they (or one of them) can bring a petition before a family judge who will try to bring the parents to agreement; if this is not possible the judge will decide on the issue.

GERMANY

If the parents hold joint parental responsibilities, the mother and father are entitled and obliged to exercise their parental responsibilities equally; on principle, each parent is entitled to care for the child's person and for the child's

---

5 The Supreme Court has granted a non-custodial parent the right to obtain information concerning the child from the authorities. The court did not find it necessary to attribute the custody of the child to both parents jointly, when the only reason for that would have been to make it possible to the other parent to get the right to obtain information from authorities (KKO 2003:7).

6 On the role of judges in promoting settlements in family matters in Finland, see, A-K. AALTONEN, 'Tuomari sovinnontekijänä perheoikeusasioissa', in: S. POHJONEN, *Sovittelu*, WSLT: Helsinki, 2001, p. 353-369.

7 See G. CORNU, *Droit civil, La famille*, 2001, Paris : Montchrestien, 7th Ed., No. 80, p. 169: '*situation d'égalité et de coopération sur la supposition idéale sinon idyllique, au moins optimiste – d'une entente entre époux*'.

8 See *e.g.* TGI Paris, 06.11.1973, *Gaz. Pal.*, 1974.1.299 annotated BARBIER (light surgery); CA Dijon, 19.06.1996, *JCP*, 1998. IV. 3145 (blood expertise). School insurance, vaccination, authorisation given to go camping *etc.* are usual decisions. For serious surgery, change of school, or some trips abroad it will depend on the circumstances, see G. CORNU, *Droit civil, La famille*, 2001, Paris: Montchrestien, 7th Ed., No. 83, p. 174.

property in all their constituent elements.[9] This also includes representation of the child, which in accordance with § 1629 para. 1 sent. 2 clause 1 German CC is also effected jointly.

In exceptional cases, a parent may, subject to the conditions laid out in § 1678 para. 1 clause 1 German CC, exercise sole parental responsibility despite the parents holding joint parental responsibility if the other parent is factually prevented or if that parent's parental responsibility has been suspended. Such a suspension can, for example, be caused by legal or actual incapacity and results in the parent concerned being prevented from exercising their parental responsibilities on a temporary basis, §§ 1673-1675 German CC.

If the parents live apart, the parent with whom the child has its legitimate habitual residence is moreover authorised, in accordance with § 1687 para. 1 sent. 2 German CC, to decide alone on matters relating to everyday life. According to § 1687 para. 1 sent. 4 German CC, such decisions are those that recur frequently and whose effect on the development of the child can easily be modified (see also the answer to Q 16). The other parent then only has the authority to make decisions alone during the period in which the child is temporarily and legally with him or her. This authority is limited to matters of actual care, § 1687 para. 1 sent. 4 German CC. Matters of actual care concern, for example, questions of diet, of rest and of TV consumption and thus also constitute matters relating to everyday life.[10] In the area of actual care there is no comprehensive right to sole representation. Instead, in accordance with § 1687 para. 1 sent. 5 German CC the right of representation in emergency situations stipulated in § 1629 para. 1 sent. 4 German CC applies accordingly.

GREECE

When two (or more) persons hold parental responsibilities,[11] they hold them equally. Although there is no explicit provision on this issue in the Civil Code, this result is derived from the spirit of equality, which runs through Greek family law, and is manifested by the absence of any provision to the contrary.

HUNGARY

Two cases have to be distinguished with regard to the joint parental responsibilities, the parental responsibilities exercised by parents living together and by parents living apart from each other. In the legal sense, parents hold parental responsibilities equally in both cases. Practically, if the parents

9 U. DIEDERICHSEN, in: PALANDT, *Bürgerliches Gesetzbuch*, 64th Edition, Munich: Beck, 2005, § 1626 No. 7; W. SCHLÜTER, *Familienrecht*, 10th Edition, Heidelberg: C.F. Müller, 2003, No. 353.

10 U. DIEDERICHSEN, in: PALANDT, *Bürgerliches Gesetzbuch*, 64th Edition, Munich: Beck, 2005, § 1687 No. 13.

11 If the court does not specifically regulate the distribution of parental responsibilities among the holders of this responsibility, it is assumed that joint parental responsibilities are attributed (Art. 1510(1) and 1604 Greek CC).

live apart it is not easy to agree on the placement of the child. The Act does not say anything about it but the judicial practice unambiguously holds that even in the case of joint parental responsibilities after divorce the child has to have one residence with one of the parents, of course with their agreement.

IRELAND

No. Sec. 9 of the Children Act 1997 amends Sec. 11 of the Guardianship of Infants Act 1964 by inserting a Sec. 11A which makes it clear that in appropriate cases, custody of a child may be granted by the court to a father and mother jointly. Joint custody in Ireland generally involves a child residing with each parent for a stipulated period of time, *e.g.* spending weekdays with the mother and weekends with the father. In *B. v. B.*,[12] for instance, Ó'DÁLAIGH C.J. appeared to suggest that joint custody was a desirable option in certain cases, in that case suggesting that the unity of the children would be best served 'by allowing them to reside for half the year with one parent, and the other half with the other.' Such an arrangement should not, however, be such as to cause significant disruption to a child's life, as, for instance, where one parent lives a significant distance from the school at which the children normally attend. In *D.McA. v. K.McA.*[13] Herbert J. granted joint custody although he did express the view that the everyday routine of children should not be circumscribed by joint custody. Each decision depends, of course, on the individual facts of each case. Joint custody in Ireland tends, however, to be the exception rather than the rule. The practicalities of family life in Ireland are such that most often children will reside with one parent while exercising access rights with the other parent.

ITALY

Yes (Art. 316 § 2 Italian CC).

LITHUANIA

Yes. The constitutional principle of equality (Art. 29 of the Lithuanian Constitution) in family law means that parental responsibilities, when held by two or more persons, are held equally (Art. 38 of the Lithuanian Constitution, Art. 3.156 Lithuanian CC).

THE NETHERLANDS

Yes, they are. However, there might be differences in the exercise of these rights and duties due to factual circumstances. For example, when parents with joint parental responsibilities do not live together, the parent who usually lives with the child will have a bigger share of the actual care and daily decision-making process than the non-resident parent, even though he or she has parental responsibilities as well.[14]

---

12 [1975] I.R. 54.

13 High Court, 17.12.2002, HERBERT J.

14 The same applies *mutatis mutandis* to other holders of parental responsibilities, see for example Art. 1:253sa § 2 Dutch CC and Art. 1:253v § 1 Dutch CC.

NORWAY

When parental responsibilities are jointly held by two persons, they are held equally.

POLAND

The parents have joint parental authority over their child; each of them is obligated and authorised to exercise it. In so doing, the parents may act individually (Art. 97 § 1 Polish Family and Guardianship Code). Decisions of major importance are an exception to the rule, since they should be take unanimously by both parents (Art. 97 § 2 Polish Family and Guardianship Code). Only spouses may exercised joint guardianship (Art. 146 Polish Family and Guardianship Code).

PORTUGAL

With regards to a child born to married parents, parental responsibility belongs equally to the father and mother and is exercised by both (Art. 1901 No. 1 and 2 Portuguese CC). The principle of equality between spouses imposes this solution (Art. 1671 Portuguese CC). Art. 36 No. 3 Portuguese Constitution establishes that spouses have equal rights and duties regarding to the maintenance and education of their children.

In those exceptional circumstances in which parental responsibility is awarded to a third person or to a child-care establishment, the situation arises in which there is simultaneous exercise of parental responsibility by the parents, on the one hand, and by the third person or institution to which the child has been entrusted, on the other. Art. 1907 Portuguese CC specifically stipulates that the third party or establishment concerned acquires the parental powers and duties necessary to properly perform his, her or its functions; and No. 2 of the same article establishes that the court will decide which parent will exercise those powers and duties not exercised by the third party or institution.

RUSSIA

Two persons (under Russian law, this can only be two natural or adoptive parents) holding joint parental responsibility hold it equally (Art. 38 (2) Russian Constitution and Art. 61(1) Russian Family Code).

There are, however, the following exceptions to this rule; if one of the parents of the child is under age and the parents are not married, the minor parent does not acquire full legal capacity. Family law, however, grants a minor unmarried parent who has reached the age of sixteen full parental responsibility (Art. 62 (2)). This leads to an inconsistency: this person is regarded by civil law as just partially legally capable and is him- or herself under guardianship and not allowed to perform certain legal acts without consent of his or her parents or guardians.[15] Therefore it is difficult to imagine that a minor parent can enter

---

15 Children from fourteen to eighteen years of age are partially legally capable and can, without parental consent, dispose of their salary, study grants and other incomes,

into transactions on behalf of the child that he or she is not allowed to enter on behalf of him- or herself.[16] If the minor unmarried parent is under the age of sixteen, the child must be appointed a guardian until the minor parent reaches the age of sixteen (Art. 62 (2) Russian Family Code). The child's guardian raises the child with the minor parent and represents the child as his or her legal representative. A minor parent under the age of sixteen has the right to live with the child and to participate in the child's upbringing. Disagreements between the child's guardian and the minor parent are resolved by the Department of Guardianship and Curatorship (Art. 62 (2) Russian Family Code). The law allows but does not require appointing a guardian to a child whose parent is under the age of sixteen.[17] If the child has a second legal parent of full age that has good contact with the minor parent, the appointment of a guardian can be superfluous. In this situation, the child would be educated by the two parents formally holding joint parental responsibility, while the right and duties of one of them would be restricted due to his or her age.

The court can declare one of the parents legally incapable because he or she cannot understand and direct the significance of his or her acts due to a mental disorder (Art. 29 Russian CC). Such a parent will be appointed a guardian. The court can also restrict the legal capacity of a parent if he or she gravely detriments his or her family's financial wellbeing due to alcohol or drug abuse. In both cases the parent does not automatically lose parental responsibility. However, restriction of legal capacity precludes the execution of some parental rights (*e.g.* representation of the child or administration of child's property), because those acts require full legal capacity. If living with a parent addicted to drugs or alcohol is dangerous for the child, a court can restrict the parent's parental responsibility and take his or her child away (Art. 73 Russian Family Code).

If one of the holders of parental responsibility lives apart from the child, his or her rights remain formally equal, save for a few exceptions.[18]

However, this is mainly just the law on the books. In reality, the parent with whom the children resides exercises parental rights almost alone. Russian law prescribes that the judge must treat both parents equally in respect to the

open bank accounts and administer them (Art. 28 (2) Russian CC). For all other transactions, children from fourteen to eighteen years of age need the written consent of their parents or guardians (Art. 28 (1) Russian CC).

16 M. ANTOKOLSKAIA, *Family Law* (*Semeinoe pravo*), Moscow: Jurist, 1999, p. 205-206.

17 M. ANTOKOLSKAIA, *Family Law* (*Semeinoe pravo*), Moscow: Jurist, 1999, p. 204.

18 One of these exceptions is that the name or family name of the child who lives with both parents can only be changed upon their mutual consent (Art. 59 (1) Russian Family Code), while a name or family name of the child who is living with only one of the parents can be changed without the consent of the parent living apart from the child. The Department of Guardianship and Curatorship is only obliged to consider the opinion of the non-residential parent when contemplating a decision concerning the change of the child's name (Art. 59 (2) Russian Family Code).

options for the child's residence after divorce; however, in more than 90% of all cases the child is placed with his or her mother after divorce.[19] In practice, a parent (mostly a father) who is not living with a child can hardly exercise most of his educational rights because he does not have daily contact with the child.

SPAIN

If parenthood is established for both the father and mother, parental responsibility vests equally on both of them.

Parental responsibilities are not exercised equally if the parents do not live together. The Spanish CC and the Catalan Family Code differ in their regulation of the exercise of joint parental responsibilities in the case of separation. Art. 156 Spanish CC establishes that if parents live separately, parental responsibility is exercised by the parent with whom the child lives unless the non-resident parent requests a joint exercise or a distribution of functions between parental responsibility holders. The judge will decide the issue in view of the best interests of the child. In practice this is not granted frequently unless there is agreement between the parties.

Catalan law, on the contrary, establishes a preference for a joint exercise of parental responsibility if the parents are separated or have never lived together. Each of the parents will care and protect the child when the child is with him or her, either because the child lives with that parental responsibility holder or because the child is visiting the non-resident parent. Certain important decisions regarding the choice of education, a change of domicile or acts concerning the disposal of the child's property must be taken jointly. Catalan law guides situations in which communication between parental responsibility holders is difficult by providing that once a parent is informed that the other parent intends to make a decision, he or she has the right to veto the decision. If he or she does not exercise the veto right within thirty days of having been informed, the other parent will be allowed to proceed (Art. 139 Catalan Family Code). Parents objecting to this regulation can agree on a different type of exercise of parental responsibilities. The agreement will only become enforceable through the court system if it is approved by the judge, which requires that the agreement is not contrary to the child's best interests. If one parent objects to the joint exercise of parental responsibilities after separation, he or she may request another type of exercise of parental responsibilities in a judicial proceeding.

SWEDEN

When parents have joint custody of their child, parental responsibilities are equally held, and the parents are, in principle, obligated to decide all issues concerning the child jointly, Chapter 6 Sec. 13 Swedish Children and Parents

---

19 A. PANASIUK, 'Komu peredat'na vospitanie rebenka?', *Rossiyskaia Justitzia*, 1996, No. 9, p. 53-54.

Code. The same applies as regards guardianship, Chapter 12 Sec. 12 Swedish Children and Parents Code.

SWITZERLAND

In a marriage, each parent is entitled to parental responsibilities as an independent and entirely equal right. In accordance with Art. 297 § 1 Swiss CC, these parental responsibilities are, however, exercised jointly. This does not mean that the parents must always act jointly. It is sufficient for the other parent to give their prior or subsequent, explicit or implicit consent (see also Art. 304 § 2 Swiss CC). An agreement on the division of duties between parents frequently results in the authority of one parent to act on his or her own.[20]

[20] I. SCHWENZER, Art. 297 ZGB, p. 1572 (No. 2), in: H. HONSELL, N.P. VOGT, TH. GEISER (ed.), *Basler Kommentar zum Schweizerischen Privatrecht, Zivilgesetzbuch I*, Art. 1-456 ZGB, Basel: Helbing & Lichtenhahn, 2002.

QUESTION 37

D. THE EXERCISE OF PARENTAL RESPONSIBILITIES

II. Joint Parental Responsibilities

If parental responsibilities holders cannot agree on an issue, how is the dispute resolved? For example does the holder of parental responsibilities have the authority to act alone? In this respect is a distinction made between important decisions and decisions of a daily nature? Does it make any difference if the child is only living with one of the holders of the parental responsibilities?

AUSTRIA

The holders of joint parental responsibilities, *i.e.* parents, grandparents or foster parents (hereinafter parents), should act by mutual assent in fulfilling their rights and duties (Sec. 144 Austrian CC).[1] However, the legislature does not require unreasonable efforts[2]. If an agreement cannot be reached, each parent is normally authorized to make decisions and represent the child independently, *e.g.* to enter into an apprenticeship contract or to include the child on his or her passport (Sec. 154(1) Austrian CC).[3] When the parents' legal actions are inconsistent with each other, the one taken first will be valid; if they are taken simultaneously, neither will be valid.

The case is different regarding certain important matters that are enumerated exhaustively in Sec. 154(2) Austrian CC and require the consent of the other parent in order to be legally effective. These matters comprise changing the child's name, joining or leaving a religious denomination, placement in the care of another, acquisition of citizenship or refusal to do so, premature termination of an apprenticeship or employment contract, and recognition of the paternity of a child born out of wedlock.

Representative acts in property-related matters that fall outside the scope of proper business operations require not only the consent of the other parent but also the approval of the court in order to become legally effective. This includes, for example, the sale and encumbrance of real estate; the acquisition, transformation, sale, or dissolution of a business; waiver of a right of inheritance, unconditional acceptance or renunciation of an inheritance; acceptance of an encumbered gift or rejection of a proffered gift; certain types of monetary investments (*e.g.* granting a loan or acquiring real estate); filing a

1 *Oberster Gerichtshof,* 04.04.1978, *EFSlg.* 31.222.

2 *Oberster Gerichtshof,* 28.8.1997, *Sammlung der Entscheidungen des Obersten Gerichtshofs in Zivilrechtssachen (SZ),* Vol. 70, No. 163 = *Juristische Blätter,* 1998, p. 243.

3 I. HOLZHAMMER/R. HOLZHAMMER, *Ehe und Familie,* 2nd Edition, Freistadt: Plöchl Verlag, 2001, p. 72.

complaint and making all procedural dispositions that relate to the matter in dispute (Sec. 154(3) Austrian CC).

If the parents cannot agree on a matter involving the child and thereby endanger the child's interests, the court will issue such orders as are necessary to safeguard the interests of the child (Sec. 176 Austrian CC).[4]

The above stated rules regarding the child's legal representation (Sec. 154 Austrian CC) apply regardless of which parent the child is living with most of the time. If the parents have permanently separated (after divorce, annulment of the marriage, ending of a non-marital partnership, or permanent separation of married parents) or have never lived in a common household, however, each parent may petition the court to revoke joint parental responsibilities without substantiation at any time (Sec. 167, 177a (2), 177b Austrian CC). In such a case, the court will entrust one parent with sole parental responsibilities based on the best interests of the child, unless a reconciliation between the parents may be brought about (Sec. 177a (2) Austrian CC).[5]

BELGIUM

When the parents live together, joint exercise of parental responsibilities is the principle. Consequently, when they do not agree on an issue, they do not have the right to act alone. They must try to reach a consensus. If they do not succeed, one of them can bring the conflict before the Juvenile Court (See Q 38). Although a parent normally has no right to act alone, in practice most of the issues brought before the Juvenile Court concern demands of a parent to undo decisions that have been taken without consent (*a posteriori*).[6] Art. 373 Belgian CCdoes not make a distinction between different types of parental decisions.

The joint exercise of parental responsibilities is also the principle for separated parents (Art. 374 Belgian CC). Separated parents are submitted to exactly the same standard as parents who live together. Consequently, when they do not agree on an issue, they do not have the right to act alone. They must bring the conflict before the Juvenile Court. However, the joint exercise of parental authorities is not easy for parents who live separately. It only has a chance to succeed if the parents can reach a consensus on the most important questions concerning the education, namely the organisation of the housing and problems concerning the health, the education, the school, the recreation and the religious or ideological choices of the child. (See Q 23).

BULGARIA

Any parent has the authority to act alone even when the decision could be an important one *e.g.* consent for medical treatment and issuing of a passport of the child. This is explicitly set out concerning the representation of the child. As

---

4 For details see Q 38.

5 See Q 16, 18, 22b, 23.

6 Court of Appeal of Liège, 17.10.2000, *J.T.*, 2001, p. 473.

Art. 73 § 1 Bulgarian Family Code stipulates 'Each one of the parents is entitled to solely represent his or her minor children, and to give consent for the legal acts of his or her minor children only in their interest.' There are two exceptions to this rule. The adoption of the child requires the consent of both parents (Art. 54 § 1 § 2 Bulgarian Family Code). In this case neither parent can act alone. The second exception is the removal of the child from the jurisdiction – both parents must agree on the issuing of a passport for the child and agree to the child leaving the country (Art. 76 § 9 Bulgarian Act on Identity Documents).

If the other parent disagrees or parental responsibilities holders cannot agree on an issue they may bring the dispute (including the one on issuing a passport) to the court: '... the dispute is resolved by the District court after hearing the parents, and where necessary also the child. The decision may be appealed according to the general rules' (Art. 72 Bulgarian Family Code).

Administrative solutions for dispute resolution are envisaged for specific disagreements *e.g.* if parents cannot agree on the name of the child, the civil registrar could select one of the names suggested by the parents (Art. 12 § 2 Bulgarian Civil Registration Act). Disputing parents could also seek assistance to resolve the conflict from the Child Protection Department (Art. 23 § 4 Bulgarian Child Protection Act).

CZECH REPUBLIC

If the child's parents cannot agree on an essential matter concerning the child, either of them may apply to the court for a decision (Sec. 49 Czech Family Code). In ordinary matters either of the parents may act on his or her own. Cohabiting parents usually act in harmony. If the child's parents do not cohabit and the court has placed the child into care of one of them, the other parent is usually excluded from deciding ordinary matters. However, an agreement of both parents is always required in essential matters, or the parent may apply to the court for a decision (Sec. 49 Czech Family Code).

DENMARK

The basic principle is that the holder(s) of parental authority must agree on all issues of importance. If they cannot agree they must seek sole parental authority. The only exception concerns contact, here the parent who does not live with the child can apply to an authority for an order also when they have joint parental authority, Art. 16 Danish Act on Parental Authority and Contact.

ENGLAND & WALES

In cases of disagreement over any issue concerning a child's upbringing it is always an option to seek a resolution of the dispute before a court (see Q 38). According to Sec. 2(7), English Children Act 1989, however, notwithstanding that parental responsibility is shared each person who has it 'may act alone and without the other (or others) in meeting that responsibility' except where a statute expressly requires the consent of more than one person in a matter affecting the child. This latter qualification preserves, for example, the embargo imposed by Sec. 1, English Child Abduction Act 1984, against one parent taking the child (under the age of 16) outside the United Kingdom without the other's consent and maintains the need to obtain each parent's agreement to an adoption order as laid down by Sec. 16, English Adoption Act 1976.[7] Another qualification on the power to act independently is, pursuant to Sec. 2(8), a person with parental responsibility is not entitled to act in any way that would be incompatible with a court order. A final qualification is that there are a group of important decisions that ought not to be carried out or arranged by even the one-parent carer in the absence of agreement of those with parental responsibility. According to case-law this group of decisions includes, the child's schooling, changing the child's surname, male circumcision and issues of immunisation.[8]

This general ability to act independently was intended to mean not simply that neither parent has a right of veto but also that there is no legal duty upon parents to consult each other since, in the Law Commission's view[9] such a duty was both unworkable and undesirable. It was expressly contemplated that even where a residence order had been granted in one parent's favour, subject to not acting incompatibly with a court order, each parent could still exercise that responsibility without having to consult the other and with neither having a right of veto over the other's action. Referring to the example of child living with one parent and going to a school nearby the Law Commission considered that while it would be incompatible for the other parent to arrange for the child to have his hair done in a way which would exclude him from the school, it would be permissible for that parent to take the child to a sporting occasion over the weekend, no matter how much the parent with whom the child lived might disapprove.[10] According to the Commission the intended independence of each parent was to be seen as part of the general aim of encouraging both parents to feel concerned and responsible for the welfare of the children.[11]

On the other hand case-law concerning the granting of a parental responsibility order to unmarried fathers also establish the point that the granting of such an order does not entitle the father to interfere with the day-to-day running of affairs affecting the child at any rate whilst the child is living with another carer.[12]

---

7 Prospectively Sec. 47(2), English Adoption and Children Act 2002.

8 See respectively, *Re G (A Minor)(Parental Responsibility: Education)* [1994] 2 FLR 964, CA; *Re PC (Change of Surname)* [1997] 2 FLR 230, *Re J (Specific Issue Orders)(Muslim Upbringing and Circumcision)* [2000] 1 FLR 571, and *Re C (Welfare of Child: Immunisation)* [2003] EWCA Civ 1148, [2003] 2 FLR 1095.

9 Report on Guardianship and Custody, Law Com Report No. 172 (1988) para 2.11.

10 Report on Guardianship and Custody, Law Com Report No. 172 (1988) para 2.11.

11 Report on Guardianship and Custody, Law Com Report No. 172 (1988) para 2.10.

12 See *Re S (a minor)(parental responsibility)* [1995] 3 FCR 564, *Re A (a minor)(parental responsibility)* [1996] 1 FCR 562 and *Re P (A minor)(Parental Responsibility Order* [1994] 1 FLR 578.

In summary, the position under English law is that where there is more than one holder of parental responsibility then, subject to some restrictions, each can act independently of the other but where the child is living with one of them that does not entitle the non carer to interfere in the day-to-day decision making.

FINLAND

As it is not possible in practice for legally equal custodians who do not live together to act jointly in every single matter, it has been argued that the custodian with whom the child resides should have the sole power to make decisions of minor importance in the everyday life of the child. In any case, decisions which have a major importance to the child's future should be made jointly whenever possible.[13]

> If one of the custodians is unable to take part in the making of a decision owing to absence, illness or some other reason and if a delay in deciding the matter would be detrimental, his or her consent on the matter shall not be necessary. A matter of great importance for the future of the child, however, may only be decided jointly by the custodians unless it is manifest that the best interests of the child otherwise require (Sec. 5 para. 2).

Thus, the Finnish Child Custody and the Right of Access Act allows the custodians to mutually arrange the way they wish to jointly exercise their custodial rights. If they fail to find this understanding, however, the Act gives few guidelines.[14] In the legal literature, and in *travaux préparatoires* decisions concerning the child's residence, education, health care or religious affiliation are considered to require a joint decision by both parents. Special legislation, such as the Finnish Name Act, for instance, may include prescriptions concerning requirements of participation for both custodians in decision-making.[15]

---

13 M. SAVOLAINEN, *Lapsen huolto ja tapaamisoikeus,* Suomen Lakimiesliiton Kustannus Oy, Helsinki, 1984 p. 30-31; M. HELIN, 'Lapsen huolto', in: H. MATTILA, *Lapsioikeuden pääpiirteet 1984,* Juridica: Helsinki 1984, p. 133; E. GOTTBERG, 'Lapsen huolto, huoltoriidat ja pakkotäytäntöönpano', Turun yliopiston oikeustieteellisen tiedekunnan julkaisuja, Yksityisoikeuden julkaisusarja A:93, Turku 1997, p. 30-31; K. KURKI-SUONIO, 'Kotimaiset ja kansainväliset riidat lapsen huollosta', *Defensor Legis,* 2000, Vol. 5, p. 753.

14 See, for instance, Norwegian Child Law. DANIELSEN, *Nordisk borneret II, Foraeldreansvar* Nord 2003:14, Nordisk Ministerråd : Copenhagen 2003, p. 108-110.

15 Government Bill HE 224/1982; M. HELIN, 'Lapsen huolto', in: H. MATTILA, *Lapsioikeuden pääpiirteet 1984,* Juridica: Helsinki, 1984, p. 134; E. GOTTBERG, 'Lapsen huolto, huoltoriidat ja pakkotäytäntöönpano', Turun yliopiston oikeustieteellisen tiedekunnan julkaisuja, Yksityisoikeuden julkaisusarja A:93, Turku 1997, p. 31-32; K. KURKI-SUONIO, 'Kotimaiset ja kansainväliset riidat lapsen huollosta', *Defensor Legis,* 2000, Vol. 5, p. 753-754; Finnish Name Act 694/1985 Sec. 4, 4a and 5.

Neither a disagreement between joint custodians nor any other reason permits one custodian to exercise custodial powers alone, with the exception of urgent matters where delay would be detrimental, as stipulated in Sec. 5 para. 2.[16] The only possibility for joint custodians to obtain an authoritative resolution for their mutual dispute is to ask the court to render a decision concerning the division of powers according to Sec. 9 para. 3, as illuminated above in Q 36. Consequently, the court may issue an order regarding the division of powers, according to which one of the custodians obtains the sole power to act for that particular issue. The court may also in this connection vest the entire custodial powers in one of the custodians alone. The court may not, however, decide on the substance of the issue in question (except in cases where the dispute concerns the child's right of access to the other parent).

FRANCE

If both parents are holders of the parental responsibilities, one of them is allowed to act alone for 'usual decisions relating to the person of the child'. With regard to third persons in good faith, the parent who has acted is deemed to have acted with the agreement of the other holder of parental responsibilities: Art. 372-2 French CC. This rule does not apply for important decisions.[17] Both holders of the parental responsibilities must reach agreement for such decisions. If this is impossible, either one or both of them can make a petition before the family judge (*juge aux affaires familiales*). Before the reform of 4 March 2002, Art. 372-1-1 French CC stated that if the parents could not agree on what the child's interests required, they had to follow whatever practice they followed before in similar situations. When no former practice existed or when it was contested, one parent (or both jointly) could bring a petition before the family judge who would first try to conciliate the parents; if the conciliation failed the judge had to decide upon the contested issue. This provision was suppressed by the Act of 4 March 2002 and was replaced by Art. 373-2-11 French CC, which states more generally that the judge who determines the implementation of the exercise of parental responsibilities shall take into account:

- the usual practice previously followed by the parents, or the agreements they had entered into before;
- the feelings expressed by the minor child;
- the ability of each parent to take on his duties and to respect the rights of the other parent;
- the result of the expert testimony possibly ordered and presented (with regard to the child's age);

---

16 There is however a special regulation in the Passport Act for cases concerning custodial dispute, Sec. 5 Finnish Passport Act 642/1986, with the amendments of 14/1998. Sec. 3 Finnish Religious Freedom Act provides that the mother may decide upon the child's religious affiliation if parents cannot agree. See above Q 8c).

17 *E.g.* for a circumcision, which is a serious decision, see French Supreme Court, Civ. I, 26.01.1994, *D.* 1995.226: unilateral decision by the father. Sanction given by the court: the father is deprived from any contact right.

- the information obtained through potential social inquiries.

The fact that the child is only living with one of the holders of parental responsibilities does not always play a role because the other parent, in principle, remains a holder of the parental responsibilities and therefore also continues to hold part of the exercise of the parental responsibilities.[18] It depends on the situation; if the child lives primarily with one parent and only occasionally with the other,[19] this other parent must be consulted for important decisions concerning the child.[20]

Another situation occurs if the parent with whom the child does not live is deprived of the exercise of the parental responsibilities and has instead only contact rights. In this situation, the parent who has the exercise of the parental responsibilities will make the decisions alone but the other parent keeps the right and duty to supervise the maintenance and the education of the child. He or she must be informed of the important choices concerning the child's life (Art. 373-2-1 para. 3 French CC). Neither parent has the power to make these decisions without the other.

GERMANY

In principle, the parents ought to come to an agreement in questions concerning the care for and upbringing of the child, § 1627 German CC. In accordance with § 1687 para. 1 sent. 1 German CC, this applies to matters of considerable importance, even if the parents live apart. Such an agreement might also take the form of a mutual authorisation to permit one of the holders of parental responsibility to make decisions alone - both those of a daily nature and those concerning important matters.[21]

Without such an agreement a parent has the right to make decisions on his or her own authority only in the event of imminent danger, as provided for with regard to representation in § 1629 para. 1 sent. 4 German CC. With regard to this right to make decisions in the event of imminent danger, it is immaterial whether the parents are or were married to each other and whether they

---

18 For example he must normally be consulted about the choice of a school for the child, see CA Paris, 20.04.1988, *D.* 1988. IR. p. 317; 25.10.1991, *JCP* 1992. IV. P. 203.

19 The model proposed by the reform of 04.03.2002 is that after the parents' separation, the family judge should, if possible and consistent with the child's interests, determine the residence of the child alternately at the father's and the mother's home in a more or less equal way depending on the child's interest. If this is not possible, the child's residence can be set mainly (*à titre principal*) at one parent's home and secondarily at the other parent's residence, see Th. FOSSIER, *L'autorité parentale,* 2002, ESF, 2nd Ed., p. 43.

20 See Th. FOSSIER, *L'autorité parentale,* 2002, ESF, 2nd Ed., p. 50.

21 U. DIEDERICHSEN, in: PALANDT, *Bürgerliches Gesetzbuch*, 64th Edition, Munich: Beck, 2005, § 1687 No. 8.

cohabit or live apart.[22] Imminent danger can be said to exist if the participation, particularly the consent, of the other parent cannot be obtained without frustrating the purpose of the intervention.[23] For this to be the case the mere possibility of the child's best interests being threatened is insufficient; rather, the child must be threatened with health or economic disadvantages of a considerable extent requiring immediate intervention.[24]

If the parents live apart, § 1629 para. 2 sent. 2 German CC, furthermore, enables the parent with whom the child lives to be the sole representative of the child when asserting maintenance claims against the other parent. Further rights of a parent to make his or her own decisions in matters of a daily nature or of actual care for the child can result from § 1687 para. 1 German CC if the parents live apart (see Q 16 and 36).

GREECE

If the parents who hold joint parental responsibilities cannot agree on an issue related to the exercise of parental care, although it is necessary to reach a decision thereon, in order to protect the interests of the child the court shall decide (Art. 1512 Greek CC). A lone parent can only regulate pressing or day to day matters relating either to the usual care of the child, or to the ongoing administration of its property (Art. 1516 para. 1 Greek CC). As a matter of fact, if the child lives with only one parent, the latter will often have to act alone. Nevertheless, this does not alter the above provision, which stems from the nature of joint responsibilities.

If the child is subject to co-guardianship, the supervisory council will decide on any dispute between the guardians. If a guardian disagrees with the decision of the supervisory council he or she may bring the case before the courts (Art. 1605 Greek CC). Nevertheless, the guardians may determine that they can decide by majority decision on certain issues, provided that they are at least three in number.[25] In any case, the abovementioned provisions concerning joint parental care may also apply to co-guardianship by analogy.[26] It is worth noting, however, that normally the court will appoint a sole guardian (Art. 1594 Greek CC).

---

22 U. DIEDERICHSEN, in: PALANDT, *Bürgerliches Gesetzbuch*, 64th Edition, Munich: Beck, 2005, § 1629 No. 17.

23 BGH 12.02.1962, *JZ* 1962, 609, 610; L. M. PESCHEL-GUTZEIT, in: STAUDINGER, *Kommentar zum Bürgerlichen Gesetzbuch*, 13th Edition, Berlin: de Gruyter, 2002, § 1629 No. 53.

24 P. Huber, in: *Münchener Kommentar zum Bürgerlichen Gesetzbuch*, 4th Edition, Munich: Beck, 2002, § 1629 No. 27.

25 See K. PANTELIDOU, in: A. GEORGIADIS and M. STATHOPOULOS (eds.), *Civil Code commentary, Vol. VIII, Family Law (Arts. 1505-1694)*, 2nd Edition, Athens: Law & Economy, P.N. SAKKOULAS, 2003, Art. 1604-1605 Greek CC, p. 567, No. 1.

26 K. PANTELIDOU, in: A. GEORGIADIS and M. STATHOPOULOS (eds.), *Civil Code commentary, Vol. VIII, Family Law (Arts. 1505-1694)*, 2nd Edition, Athens: Law & Economy, P.N. SAKKOULAS, 2003, Art. 1604-1605 Greek CC, p. 567, No. 1.

HUNGARY

With regard to joint parental responsibilities, two situations have to be differentiated: when the parents live together and when they live apart. If the parents live together and they cannot agree on an issue they can petition the public guardianship authority to decide it, excluding issues having to do with the freedom of religion and conscience.

If parents exercising joint parental responsibilities after a divorce can not agree on an issue of parental responsibilities, the competent authority to decide the issue is the court, with the exception of one matter: the public guardianship authority has the authority to determine the residence of a minor over 16.

With regard to the administration of the child's property and the legal representation of the child in financial matters, these can be exercised jointly by the parents, not only for parents with full joint parental responsibilities (either by the parents living together or after divorce) but also if the non-custodial parent is empowered with the right and duty to administrate the child's property and can represent him or her legally.

The parents can give each other the sole and full authorisation to exercise the legal representation of the child in his or her financial matters through a public instrument or a private document. A parent who represents the child's day-to-day financial transactions of low importance can be regarded to have the authorization of the other parent by third persons acting in good faith. The authorisation of the other parent is not possible for the child's personal matters.

IRELAND

If parental responsibilities holders cannot agree on an issue, the dispute is resolved by the court. Sec. 11 of the Guardianship of Infants Act 1964 permits any person to apply to the court for its direction on any question affecting the welfare of the child.
Although the holder of parental authorities does not have the authority to act alone with respect to important decisions, he or she is entitled to make such decisions if they are of a daily nature. In this respect, it is important whether the child is living with one of the holders of parental responsibilities.

ITALY

Art. 316 Italian CC describes the exercise of the parental responsibilities regardless of the parents marital status (in describing the exercise of parental responsibilities by natural parents, Art. 317 *bis* Italian CC makes express reference to the applicability of the rules contained in Art. 316 Italian CC). This provision of law states that if issues of minor importance are concerned (those issues relating to daily life), the parents holding the parental responsibilities are free to decide individually. However, if the issues are of major importance (for example the selection of the religious creed, the type of school to attend, the medical treatment, the decision to allow the child to travel abroad, to the decision of permitting him to participate to TV shows *etc*) both parents can petition the judge (of the Family Proceeding Court). In case of imminent danger, the father can make urgent decisions or those which cannot be delayed.[27] The judge suggests the most suitable decisions in the interests of the minor and of the family unity. If there is still disagreement, the judge will confer the power to make a decision to the parent who, in each particular case, she or he considers more suitable to pursue the best interests of the minor. If the child lives with only one parent, the ways in which the parental responsibilities are exercised are differentiated. The decisions relating to daily life are made only by the parent living with the minor, while the other can supervise the child's education and moral guidance, and can petition the judge if he or she feels that decisions prejudicial to the interests of the minor have been taken. In case of disagreement on important decisions (which the parents must make jointly) both parents can petition the judge.

In this situation, the determination of the competent Court is a real problem. It is disputed whether Art. 316 Italian CC is applicable only to the 'united' family or also to the 'divided' family, with special reference to the parents that obtained a separation, a divorce or an annulment of marriage decision. It is not only a theoretical dispute, it has important practical consequences since the courts that issue the decision are different: The Family Proceeding Court pursuant to Arts. 316, or the Ordinary Court pursuant to 155 Italian CC and Art. 6 Italian Divorce law, which issues orders concerning the custody of the children in separations, divorces or annulments of marriage.[28]

LITHUANIA

The father and the mother shall have equal rights and duties with respect to their children (Art. 3.156 Lithuanian CC). Because of this, all questions related to parental responsibilities shall be decided by the parents by mutual agreement. In the event of lack of agreement, the disputed matter shall be

---

27 Such provision of law is the last remaining option which constitutes the expression of a different historical context and must be regarded as inconsistent with the principle of moral and legal parity of the parents. It therefore should also be applicable for the mother.

28 On one side it is felt that Art. 316 Italian CC can be applied in difficult situations between the parents (separated or divorced) when there is a partial joint exercise of the parental responsibilities. (M. GIORGIANNI, *Della potestà dei genitori*, in: CIAN, OPPO and TRABUCCHI, *Commentario al diritto italiano della famiglia*, IV, 1992, p. 757; M. MANTOVANI, headword *Separazione personale dei coniugi, I) Disciplina sostanziale*, in: *Enc. giur. Treccani*, XXVIII, Roma, 1992, p. 24; see Case Law Supreme Court 07.02.94, No. 1401, in *Dir. fam. pers.*, 1994, p. 1383). On the other, it is felt that Art. 316 Italian CC can only be applied to parents who live together. (GRASSETTI, in: CIAN, OPPO and TRABUCCHI *Commentario al diritto italiano della famiglia*, II, Padova, 1992, p. 699; BONILINI, TOMMASEO, 1997, Case Law, see Supreme Court, united sections, 02.03.1983, No. 1151, *Dir. fam. pers.*, 1983, p. 38, and 02.03. 1983, No. 1152, *Foro it.*, 1983, I, 826). Therefore, considering the loss of the family unit due to separation or divorce, possible conflicts between separated or divorced parents have to be solved by the Ordinary Court. In practice, the second solution has prevailed. (see also Q 55).

resolved by the court or by another competent authority, such as a state institution on the protection of the rights of the child.

In the event of a dispute, the daily decisions may be taken by one of the parents. However, important decisions, *e.g.* surgery of a child, can only be made by both parents. If the parents disagree regarding an important decision, one of them may apply for a court order enabling them to make such a decision without the consent of the other of the parent.

The fact that the parents live separately has no legal importance in respect to the adoption of important decisions. However, decisions of daily nature are, in such cases, made by the parent with whom the child lives.

THE NETHERLANDS

They may both request a decision of the district court (Art. 1:253a Dutch CC). The court will first try to reconcile the parents and will then, if still necessary, make a decision it deems to be in the best interests of the child.[29] In principle, there is no authority to act alone when there is no agreement, but a distinction is made between when the child is living with both parents and when this is not the situation. In the first situation both parents have to agree on all issues. If they cannot reach an agreement, the dispute must be submitted to the court. This rarely happens in practice. In the second situation there is a difference between important decisions and decisions of a daily nature. The non-resident parent with parental responsibilities must agree only on important decisions (school choice, important medical treatment, religious upbringing, choice of profession, place of residence). Matters of a daily nature may be decided alone by the parent the child lives with.[30]

NORWAY

When two holders of parental responsibilities do not agree on issues concerning the child, as long as they live together there are no rules on how such disputes should be resolved. It is considered that such disputes should remain inside the home; one of the parents has to give in. The Norwegian Children Act 1981 has no provisions on the matter. There is no legal distinction between important decisions and decisions of an everyday nature.

However, as regards financial matters, Art. 3 Norwegian Act on Guardianship 1927 allows for the possibility of one parent giving the other the power of attorney to act on behalf of both parents. According to Art. 3 sec. 2, all warnings and communication during the case should be directed to both parents. If only

---

29 The same applies *mutatis mutandis* to other holders of parental responsibilities, see for example Art. 1:253sa § 2 Dutch CC and Art. 1:253v § 1 Dutch CC.

30 *Kamerstukken Tweede Kamer*, 1996-1997, 23 714, No. 11, p. 12. E.J. NICOLAI, 'De juridische positie van de niet-verzorgende ouder na echtscheiding', *NJ*, 1998, p. 698 is critical on this point, since in his view the result is that the parental responsibilities of the non-caring parent are curtailed.

one signs the necessary documents and meets in court on behalf of the child, he or she is considered as having the consent of the other parent unless the court is otherwise informed.

If the child lives permanently with one of the two parents holding parental responsibilities, the situation changes. According to Art. 37 Norwegian Children Act 1981, the parent who does not live with the child may not object to the one with whom the child lives making decisions concerning important aspects of the child's care, such as questions as to whether the child shall attend a day-care centre, where in Norway the child shall live, and other major decisions concerning everyday life. However, both parents must agree to a change of residence to another country, Art. 40 sec. 2.

POLAND

The unanimous decision of both parents is required for major issues (*i.e.* those of major importance for the child), regardless of whether the child lives with both parents, so long as both parent's parental authority has not been limited. If the parents cannot reach an agreement on them, the court is to decide (Art. 97 § 2 Polish Family and Guardianship Code).

PORTUGAL

Parental responsibility is exercised jointly by married parents while they are married (Art. 1901 No. 1 Portuguese CC). The joint exercise of parental responsibility involves daily agreement regarding the child and the child's property. If the parents are unable to agree on matters of particular importance, either spouse may petition the court to settle the problem (Art. 1901 No. 2 Portuguese CC).

In demanding the parents' agreement on the exercise of parental responsibility, the law does not necessarily require that both parents intervene in every act. Either parent may act alone; the law will presume they have the other's consent. However, this presumption does not apply to acts for which the law requires the express consent of both parents (*i.e.* to file lawsuits representing the minor (Art. 10 No. 2 Portuguese Code of Civil Procedure)) or for acts of particular importance (Art. 1902 No. 1 Portuguese CC). With an act of normal importance, a non-consenting parent cannot oppose a third party acting in good faith that there is parental agreement (Art. 1902 No. 1 *in fine* Portuguese CC). The third party's good faith is removed by knowledge of the lack of agreement between the parents or if the act in question is considered an act of particular importance (Art. 1902 No. 2 Portuguese CC).

If the child lives only with one parent, this might function as a way of removing the good faith of the parent that committed the act, to the extent that it is not reasonable to suppose they were both in agreement, given that they do not live together.

RUSSIA

If the holders of parental responsibility cannot agree on a certain issue they can bring their dispute before the Department of Guardianship and Curatorship or before the court (Art. 65 (2) Russian Family Code). The law makes no difference between important decisions and the decisions of a daily nature. In practice, each parent is generally allowed to make decisions of a daily nature alone; the silent consent of other parent is presumed.[31] However, the other parent always has the right to contest or block a decision that was made without his or her consent. The law makes no distinction whether the parents live together with the child or apart. However, in practice a parent who lives with the child normally makes all decisions of a daily nature alone.

SPAIN

The basic idea is that if parental responsibilities are jointly vested on both the father and mother, they are to be exercised jointly, or by one with the express or tacit consent of the other. *Vis a vis* third parties there is actually a *iuris et de iure* presumption that each of the parental responsibility holders acts with the consent of the other.

There is authority to act alone in decisions of a daily nature, such as authorising a son or daughter to go to the cinema or to visit a friend or relative, and also in regard to urgent decisions, such as if the child urgently needs medical treatment.

If there is disagreement between parental responsibility holders they will have to apply to the court. This is further developed under Q 38. If parental responsibility holders do not live together they are not granted an equal exercise of parental responsibilities (see Q 36).

SWEDEN

The starting point is that parents with joint custody (or specially appointed custodians) shall jointly decide on issues concerning the child, Chapter 6 Sec. 13 Swedish Children and Parents Code. If they cannot agree on relevant issues, the ultimate solution is to apply for a court order on sole custody of the child.[32]

When the child lives with only one of the parents having joint custody, the residential custodian may make decisions of a daily nature without the consent of the other custodian. This right includes decisions regarding the child's meals, clothing, bed-time routines and leisure-time activities. A suggestion to clarify the decision-making power of the residential parent was turned down in

---

31 A. NETCHAEVA, 'Commentary to art. 65 Russian Family Code', in: I. KUZNETZOVA (ed.), *Commentary on the Family Code of Russian Federation*, Moscow: Jurist, 2000, p. 224.

32 See also answer to Q 39.

connection with the law reform of 1998, and uncertainty remains as to its scope.[33]

The child's guardians are also to act jointly. The law does not give one of the guardians the right to make decisions alone. However, in case of disagreement it is possible to turn to an authority called 'Chief Guardian' (*överförmyndaren*) for a decision.

SWITZERLAND

In contrast to the earlier law, the currently valid version of the law (which has been in force 1978) dispenses with a 'final decision or casting vote' in favour of one parent if the parents cannot agree on an issue with respect to a child. If the parents cannot agree on (vitally) important issues, they may call upon the marriage protection court, jointly or individually, to mediate in this matter (Art. 172 § 1 and 2 Swiss CC). If the child's welfare is endangered by (lasting) disagreement between the parents, measures for the protection of the child are to be taken in accordance with Art. 307 *et seq* Swiss CC.

One party may only act unilaterally and without the consent or knowledge of the other if this is necessary to protect his person and the interests of the child and the other parent are not violated by doing so. One parent may only act against the declared will of the other parent if this is unquestionably in the child's interest and a delay would result in danger.[34] If the child lives only with one parent with parental responsibilities, the authority of this parent to act alone may be derived from the agreed upon division of duties. If one parent is awarded custody by the court as a result of the dissolution of the joint household (Art. 176 § 3 Swiss CC), the parent who has custody has the right to determine the child's place of residence and consequently also to decide a large number of day-to-day matters.

---

[33] See: Prop 1997/98:9, p. 55.

[34] C. HEGNAUER, *Grundriss des Kindesrechts*, p. 184 *et seq*.

QUESTION 38

D. THE EXERCISE OF PARENTAL RESPONSIBILITIES

II. Joint Parental Responsibilities

If holders of parental responsibilities cannot agree on an issue, can they apply to a competent authority to resolve their dispute? If applicable, specify whether this authority's competence is limited to certain issues e.g. residence or contact.

AUSTRIA

If no agreement is reached concerning an important matter involving the child (Sec. 154(2) and (3) Austrian CC) or if the child's interests are jeopardized by the inconsistent or independent action of one parent[1], the matter may be brought before the court for a decision (Sec. 176 Austrian CC). Either parent, the grandparents, and where applicable even the foster parents, the youth welfare agency, and a minor child over 14 years of age himself or herself will have standing to file the petition (Sec. 176(2) Austrian CC); other persons may only make proposals to the court. If one parent's consent is withheld unjustifiably, i.e. in the absence of convincing reasons to do so, the court may substitute that consent on a case-by-case basis. The court is also authorized to permanently revoke parental rights of assent and consent if the child's interests are at risk (Sec. 176(1) Austrian CC), *e.g.* in the event of a categorical refusal to a blood transfusion by Jehovah's Witnesses[2]. The court's competence is not limited to certain issues.

If the parents have permanently separated (after divorce, annulment of the marriage, ending of a non-marital partnership, or permanent separation of married parents) or have never lived in a common household, each parent may petition the court to end joint parental responsibilities without substantiation at any time (Sec. 167, 177a(2), 177b Austrian CC). Then the court will entrust one parent with sole parental responsibilities based on the best interests of the child, unless a reconciliation between the parents may be brought about (Sec. 177a(2) Austrian CC).

---

1 See Q 37.

2 *Oberster Gerichtshof,* 04.06.1996, *Juristische Blätter,* 1996, p. 714 = *EFSlg.* 81.134; European Court of Human Rights, *ECHR, series A No. 255-C,* 23.06.1993, pp. 45 et seq. (Hoffmann v. Austria); see I. Fahrenhorst, 'Sorgerecht und Religion', *Europäische Grunderechtezeitschrift,* 1996, pp. 633 et seq.; H. Pichler, 'Zeugen Jehovas', *Österreichischer Amtsvormund,* 1994, p. 171; see O. Maleczky, 'Unvernünftige Verweigerung der Einwilligung in die Heilbehandlung', *Österreichische Juristenzeitung,* 1994, p. 681.

BELGIUM

As mentioned in Q 37, the competent authority for this matter is the Juvenile Court. Its competence is not limited to certain issues. Every dispute may be brought before the Juvenile Court, whether the parents live together and whether the dispute concerns important decisions or decisions of daily nature. According to Art. 373(3) Belgian CC, only the Juvenile Court is competent for disputes concerning the authority over the child when the parents live together. Although Art. 376 Belgian CC does not explicitly mention it, it is generally admitted that the Juvenile Court is also competent for acts concerning the administration of the property.[3]

When parents live together a discussion may be brought before the Court when they can not reach a consensus on a certain point. Normally, the dispute must be brought to the Juvenile Court before the decision is made, because decisions made without the consensus of the parents are in conflict with the law. However, in practice most disputes concern decisions already made by one of the parents without the consent of the other. The Juvenile Court has different solving-mechanisms: it can solve the problem itself in the interests of the child and leave all remaining joint exercise of parental authority to both parents, it can give authorisation to one of the parents to act alone for one or more specific decisions, it can determine which decisions concerning the education of the child can only be made with the consent of the other parent or it can charge one of the parents with the exclusive exercise of all parental authority.[4]

When the parents live separately, the same rules are principally applicable and the Juvenile Court remains the competent authority (Art. 374(3) Belgian CC). However, when the question of parental responsibilities arises in a context of interim measures between spouses, the Justice of the Peace is the competent court (Art. 221-223 Belgian CC). It will take all the interim measures into account, including the problem of the children and the parental responsibilities. When an action for divorce has been introduced in court (Art. 1280 Belgian Judicial Code) or when a plaintiff can prove that the dispute is urgent (Art. 584(1) Belgian Judicial Code), the President of the Court of First Instance (judge sitting in chambers to deal provisionally with matters of special urgency) is competent. When one of the parents wants to end the system of joint exercise of parental authorities or when he or she can not reach a consensus with the other parent on a decision that must be taken, he or she can bring the dispute before the competent court. When it seems that parents disagree on one or more important aspects of the education of the child (and only then), the competent court can attribute exclusive parental responsibilities to one parent, but this is

---

3 G. Verschelden, 'Ouderlijk gezag en omgangsrecht', *T.P.R.*, 2001, 1978.

4 D. Deli, 'De uitdrukkelijke wettelijke erkenning van de gezamenlijke uitoefening van het ouderlijk gezag en van het recht op persoonlijk contact', *R.W.*, 1996-1997, p. 2-3; T. Moreau, 'La loi du 13 avril 1995 relative à l'exercice conjoint de l'autorité parentale', *Div. Act.*, 1995, p. 97; J.-L. Renchon, 'La nouvelle réforme législative de l'autorité parentale', *Rev. trim. dr. fam.*, 1995, p. 361.

not obligatory. According to Art. 374(2) Belgian CC, important decisions consist of the organisation of the housing and problems concerning the health, the education, the school, the recreation and the religious or ideological choices of the child. (See Q 23). The competent court also has the ability to impose an arranged exercise of parental responsibilities. This may be used in a situation where parental responsibilities are primarily exercised jointly, but certain decisions may be made exclusively by one of the parents. Another possibility is a situation where exclusive exercise is excepted for certain decisions that must be made jointly (Art. 374(3) Belgian CC). Only the interests of the child are relevant. In any case, the court shall make any decision concerning the housing of the child and its inscription will be published in the Registers of Population (Art. 374 *in fine* Belgian CC).

BULGARIA

If the holders of parental responsibilities cannot agree on an issue, they can apply to the district court to resolve their dispute. The competence of the court under this Art. 72 is not limited to certain issues. The court is competent to resolve any dispute over parental rights and obligations brought before it.

CZECH REPUBLIC

Either of the parents (holders of parental responsibility) may apply to the court for a decision if the parents are not able to agree on any essential matter concerning the child (Sec. 49 Czech Family Code). A change of residence agreement by the parents must be approved by court. The court may decide a change of upbringing environment if a material change of circumstance has occurred. Either of the parents may apply to the court for a decision when there is disagreement between the parents about contact with the child. The parents' agreement on regulation of contact does not require a court approval (Sec. 27 § 1 Czech Family Code).

DENMARK

Neither the courts nor the administrative authorities have competence to settle disputes between parents. The only exception is that disputes regarding contact can be decided by the administrative authorities, Art. 16 Danish Act on Parental Authority and Contact.

ENGLAND & WALES

In cases of dispute over a child's upbringing, holders of parental responsibility can always seek a remedy from the courts.[5] Parents, guardians and those with a residence order in their favour are entitled to apply for any Sec. 8 order (see below) which means that they do not have to seek the leave of the court to bring an action.[6]

---

5 Courts for these purposes means court of any level, *viz* magistrates' courts, county court or High Court: Sec. 92(7), English Children Act 1989.

6 Sec. 10(4), English Children Act 1989.

The Sec. 8 orders referred to above are wide ranging and application may be made to (a) determine with whom the child lives (a residence order), (b) determine what visiting or other contact arrangements there should be (a contact order) and (c) to resolve any other dispute, the example, over the child's education or medical treatment or name (a prohibited steps order or a specific issue order).

FINLAND

The possibility of obtaining a court order about the division of custodial powers has been explained above in Q 36 and 37.

Concerning the child's right of access to his or her parent, the court can give detailed orders (Sec. 9 Finnish Child Custody and the Right of Access Act). Whether the parent to whom the child has the right of access is a custodian or not does not have a legal effect on the detailed orders concerning this issue.

FRANCE

See Q 37. The family judge is competent for issues concerning the parental responsibilities (see Art. 373-2-11 French CC). The competence of this authority is not limited to some issues. The family judge can be called when the holders of the parental responsibilities cannot agree on decisions for which their joint agreement is necessary. For more details, see Q 36 and 37.

GERMANY

If the parents are unable to agree on a specific issue or specific kind of issue relating to parental responsibility, the family court may, in accordance with § 1628 sent. 1 German CC, assign the decision to one parent, following an application by the father or the mother. To avoid the parents offloading their responsibility onto the family court,[7] however, this only applies to matters that are of considerable importance for the child. Whether a matter is of considerable or merely minor importance depends on its effect on the child. Furthermore, its field of application with regard to the subject matter is limited to matters of parental responsibility with a specific reference to the given situation.[8] Parent/child conflicts are not covered by § 1628 German CC, nor are disputes between the parents concerning the carrying of the child to term, i.e. decisions for or against birth.[9]

---

7 BT-Drucks. 8/2788 p. 46; BVerfG 29.07.1959, *FamRZ* 1959, 416, 421; L. M. PESCHEL-GUTZEIT, in: STAUDINGER, *Kommentar zum Bürgerlichen Gesetzbuch*, 13th Edition, Berlin: de Gruyter, 2002, § 1628 No. 26.

8 P. HUBER, in: *Münchener Kommentar zum Bürgerlichen Gesetzbuch*, 4th Edition, Munich: Beck, 2002, § 1628 No. 8, 10.

9 P. HUBER, in: *Münchener Kommentar zum Bürgerlichen Gesetzbuch*, 4th Edition, Munich: Beck, 2002, § 1628 No. 8-9; L. M. PESCHEL-GUTZEIT, in: STAUDINGER, *Kommentar zum Bürgerlichen Gesetzbuch*, 13th Edition, Berlin: Gruyter, 2002, § 1628 No. 20; Th. RAUSCHER, *Familienrecht*, Heidelberg: C.F. Müller, 2001, No. 964.

It is doubtful whether the rule applies to questions relating to the child's residence. The application of the rule has been rejected by some[10] to avoid the circumvention of more specific provisions. The prevailing opinion[11] does, however, assume that § 1628 German CC also applies in matters relating to residence. It is true that this results in a certain amount of overlap with the field of application of § 1671 German CC, according to which the family court can, following an application by the father or the mother, decide which parent should be attributed parental responsibilities following a separation. But just because the same or a similar result can be achieved through § 1628 German CC and § 1671 German CC, this does not mean that an application in accordance with § 1628 German CC in the same matter - relating to the child's residence - is inadmissible; it must, however, be remembered that they differ with regard to their prerequisites and provisions.[12]

If a parent has been assigned the decision in accordance with § 1628 German CC, this parent will alone represent the child, in accordance with § 1629 para. 1 sent. 3 alt. 2 German CC.

GREECE

If the holders of joint parental care cannot agree on an issue they may apply to the court to settle their dispute, provided that, in view of the interests of the child, a decision on a particular issue is necessary (Art. 1512 Greek CC). In the case of co-guardianship, the supervisory council will settle the dispute. If a guardian does not agree he may bring the case before the court (Art. 1605 Greek CC). Both the court and the supervisory council may decide on all the relevant matters in the interest of the child, without having to conform to the opinion of one of the holders of parental responsibilities.[13]

HUNGARY

If parents who live together cannot agree on an issue of parental responsibilities they can apply to the public guardianship authority. If they exercise parental responsibilities after a divorce, they can apply to the court. Either of the parents can apply to the judge that decides in an out-of-court proceeding. The court has the power to determine the residence of the child if one of the parents wants to

---

10 U. DIEDERICHSEN, in: PALANDT, *Bürgerliches Gesetzbuch*, 64th Edition, Munich: Beck, 2005, § 1628 No. 2.

11 P. HUBER ber, in: *Münchener Kommentar zum Bürgerlichen Gesetzbuch*, 4th Edition, Munich: Beck, 2002, § 1628 No. 11-12; D. SCHWAB, *Familienrecht*, 12th Edition, Munich: Beck, 2003, No. 679; idem, 'Elterliche Sorge bei Trennung und Scheidung der Eltern', *FamRZ* 1998, 457, 467 *et seq*, 471 *et seq*.

12 D. SCHWAB, *Familienrecht*, 12th Edition, Munich: Beck, 2003, No. 679.

13 P. AGALLOPOULOU, in: A. GEORGIADIS and M. STATHOPOULOS (eds.), *Civil Code commentary, Vol. VIII, Family Law (Arts. 1505-1694)*, 2nd Edition, Athens: Law & Economy, P.N. Sakkoulas 2003, Art. 1512 Greek CC, p. 213 No. 9; K. PANTELIDOU, in: A. GEORGIADIS and M. STATHOPOULOS (eds.), *Civil Code commentary, Vol. VIII, Family Law (Arts. 1505-1694)*, 2nd Edition, Athens: Law & Economy, P.N. SAKKOULAS, 2003, Art. 1604-1605 Greek CC, p. 569, No. 7.

place the child either with a person or institute away from the child's permanent residence, or abroad, either permanently or longer than a year.

The resolution of a dispute regarding contact can be determined by either the court or the public guardianship authority if the partners can not agree. The court has the power to decide, if the contact emerges in a divorce case, a case on the placement of the child or from a change of contact arranged in a judgment, provided that the suit is brought within two years from the earlier judgment or judicial consent to the partners' settlement.

If a claim for the arrangement of contact doesn't emerge in a divorce case, in a case on the placement of the child or at least two years from an earlier judgment, the public guardianship authority has the power to settle or re-settle the matter.

IRELAND

If holders of parental responsibility cannot agree on an issue, Sec. 11 Irish Guardianship of Infants Act 1964 permits an application to the court for its direction on any issue affecting the welfare of the child.

ITALY

Yes, in case of disagreement on an important decision, both parents, living together or not, can petition the judge. The judge will suggest the most suitable decision in the interests of the minor and the family unity. If the disagreement persists, the judge is supposed to confer the power to make the decision to the parent who, in each case, he or she considers most suitable to pursue the interests of the minor. The judge can decide on any important issue that generates a dispute between the parents, such as the determination of the domicile or the conditions of the visitation rights.

LITHUANIA

Yes. In the event of a dispute, either of the parents may apply to a court for the resolution of their dispute (Art. 30 of the Lithuanian Constitution and Art. 3.165 Lithuanian CC). The court is a competent authority to make decision regarding all disputes between the parents *i.e.* the court's authority in this respect is unlimited.

THE NETHERLANDS

Yes, holders of parental authorities may both apply to the court in order to resolve a dispute. The court will have to attempt to reach an agreement between the parties and may make any decision it deems to be in the child's best interests (Art. 1:253a Dutch CC), even if this is not a solution proposed by one of the parental responsibilities' holders.[14] The court's competence is not limited to certain issues.

[14] See Supreme Court 15.12.2001, *NJ*, 2001, 123 annotated S. WORTMANN.

NORWAY

If the parents holding equal parental responsibilities do not agree on an issue, there is no public authority to whom they can apply to resolve the dispute so long as they live together. If they do not live together, parents may initiate court proceedings concerning the extent of the right of contact, according to Art. 56 Norwegian Children Act 1981. The same applies to the question of who the child shall permanently reside with, compare Art. 36.

POLAND

See Q 37. There is no specification of issues other than that one described.

PORTUGAL

As described in Q 37, if parents are unable to agree on issues of particular importance, the court will settle the matter (Art. 1901 No. 2 Portuguese CC). The court will first and foremost try to persuade the parents to resolve their differences by fostering agreement between them. If this proves impossible, the court will decide. Before doing so, however, the judge shall hear any child over fourteen years of age, unless there are circumstances that militate against this (Art. 1901 No. 2 *in fine* Portuguese CC).

RUSSIA

If the holders of parental responsibility cannot agree on a certain issue they can bring their dispute before either the Department of Guardianship and Curatorship or before the court (Art. 65 (2) Russian Family Code).

The competence of the Department of Guardianship and Curatorship is not limited to certain kinds of disagreements between the parents. However, unimportant disputes regarding the issues of daily routine fall outside the scope of legal regulation and are deemed to be resolved by the parents themselves.[15] The law explicitly mentions that the Department is competent to resolve parental disputes regarding choosing a child's name and family name (Art. 58 (4) Russian Family Code). The parents are also free to put before the Department of Guardianship and Curatorship a disagreement of purely pedagogical or ethical nature,[16] like religious upbringing or choice of a school. The main objective of the Department is to discover and explain to the parents which decision is in the best interests of the child. If necessary the Department can invite an expert in pedagogy or child psychology for consultation.[17] In case

---

15 L. PCHELINTZEVA, *Commentary on the Family Code of Russian Federation*, Moscow: Norma, 1998, p. 248.

16 L. PCHELINTZEVA, *Commentary on the Family Code of Russian Federation*, Moscow: Norma, 1998, p. 248.

17 A. NETCHAEVA, 'Commentary to art. 79 Russian Family Code', in: I. KUZNETZOVA (ed.), *Commentary on the Family Code of Russian Federation*, Moscow: Jurist, 2000, p. 225.

of purely pedagogical and ethical disagreements the Department gives the parents instructions and recommendations which are not legally enforceable.[18]

The competence of the court is limited to adjudication of a dispute regarding child's residence (Art. 65 (3) Russian Family Code) and the execution of parental rights by the parent living apart from the child (Art. 66(2) Russian Family Code).

SPAIN

If there is a disagreement between the holders of parental responsibility either of them can apply to a judge to resolve the dispute. The court will hear both parents and the child; in all cases if he or she is older than sixteen and also for those younger, if they have attained a sufficient degree of maturity. There is also the possibility to hear other persons and to ask for expert reports.

As a result of this procedure, the judge will confer the power of decision on one of the parents. The law does not provide any specific criteria to make the choice. The judge cannot substitute the parents and decide the dispute by imposing his or her own views (Art. 156 Spanish CC) unless he or she thinks the decisions proposed by both partners constitute a danger for the child. The fact that the judge confers the power of decision onto one of the parents does not hinder them from later agreeing to decide otherwise.

Catalan law basically has the same regulation. The main difference is that the judge has the discretion to order mediation (Art. 79 Catalan Family Code) and the result of the procedure can be appealed whereas it is final in the Spanish CC regime. Catalan law also offers an alternative to judicial intervention by providing that the parents can agree to substitute judicial intervention with the intervention of two relatives, one from each branch of the family.

If disagreements become common or the joint exercise of parental responsibility is seriously disturbed the judge can temporarily confer the exercise of parental responsibility to one of the parents or distribute its functions between them (Art. 156 Spanish CC and Art. 138 Catalan Family Code).

Statute does not limit judicial intervention to conflicts over certain issues.

SWEDEN

Parents with joint custody can receive assistance in the form of cooperation discussions, supervised by the local social welfare committee, to enable them to agree on issues concerning custody, residence and contact, Chapter 6 Sec. 18 Swedish Children and Parents Code. If the parents fail to reach an agreement on such an issue, the remaining option is to take the matter to court.

---

18 L. PCHELINTZEVA, *Commentary on the Family Code of Russian Federation,* Moscow: Norma, 1998, p. 248.

There is no authority competent to resolve disputes other than attribution of custody or concerning residence and contact, *e.g.*, the child's education or religious upbringing. The only solution is to apply for sole custody.[19] It is, however, not certain that the court will grant such an application, unless both parents are opposed to joint custody.

If the guardians are in disagreement about what actions are to be taken in respect to the child's property, the matter can be referred to the Chief Guardian, Chapter 12 Sec. 12 Swedish Children and Parents Code. The opinion supported by the Chief Guardian will then prevail.

SWITZERLAND

If parents cannot agree on (vitally) important issues, they may, as already explained in Q 37, jointly or individually call upon the marriage protection court to mediate in this matter (Art. 172 § 1 and 2 Swiss CC). If the child's welfare is endangered by the parents' disagreement, then the protection of the child is to be ensured by measures for the protection of the child in accordance with Art. 307 *et seq* Swiss CC, possibly also by means of restrictions with regard to personal contact (Art. 273 § 2 and 274 § 2 Swiss CC).[20]

19 Å. SALDÉN, *Barn och föräldrar*, Fourth Edition, Uppsala: Iustus förlag, 2001, p. 77.
20 C. HEGNAUER, *Grundriss des Kindesrechts*, p. 184 *et seq.*

QUESTION 39

D. THE EXERCISE OF PARENTAL RESPONSIBILITIES

II. Joint Parental Responsibilities

To what extent, if at all, may a holder of parental responsibilities act alone if there is more than one holder of parental responsibilities?

AUSTRIA

Pursuant to Sec. 154(1) Austrian CC, either holder of joint parental responsibilities is generally authorized to represent the child independently, *i.e.* he or she may even act alone. In the event of contradictory declarations by the parental responsibilities holders, the following principle applies: the action taken by the first parental responsibilities holder to act will be legally valid; simultaneous declarations that contradict each other will cancel each other out, whereby nothing is deemed to have been declared.[1] However, the consent of both holders of parental responsibilities is required for important matters concerning the child (Sec. 154(2) Austrian CC, *e.g.* change of religion or name or placement of the child in the care of a third party) as well as for representative acts in property-related matters that fall outside the scope of the ordinary enterprise (Sec. 154(3) Austrian CC).[2]

BELGIUM

Concerning the relationship between the parents, normally they may only act alone if they have reached a consensus. When, there is no consensus even after discussion, the discussion must be submitted to the Juvenile Court that will make the decision (See Q 37 and Q 38). In relation to other persons, a distinction is made between acts concerning the authority over the person and the administration of the property of the child.

For acts concerning the authority over the person of the minor, Art. 373(2) Belgian CC provides a legal presumption that one parent is acting with the consent of the other parent, even if the other parent is not present. The presumption is rebuttable to all bona fide persons other than the parents. These persons are presumed to be bona fide so long as they have no knowledge, and could not reasonably be expected to have any knowledge, of the disagreement of the other parent. This presumption applies to all acts concerning the authority over the child, apart from the legally provided exceptions.[3] When the contracting party is bona fide, the recourse of one parent to the Juvenile Court will not lead to the nullification of the contested act; the Juvenile Court will

---

1 J. STABENTHEINER, 'KindRÄG 2001', in: P. Rummel, *ABGB-Kommentar*, suppl. vol. 1, 3rd Edition, Vienna: Manz Verlag, 2003, § 154, 154a Marg. No. 3; see Q 8f.

2 For details see Q 8f and 37.

3 See Q 42.

only judge the ramifications of the act and consequently order the other parent to pay any resulting damages to the child. If the third party is not bona fide, the presumption will not be applicable and the act will be voidable.[4]

Art. 376(2) Belgian CC provides the same presumption for acts involving administration of the child's property. Although Art. 376(2) Belgian CC concerning the presumption of agreement only mentions the administration of the property and not the legal representation, it is agreed that each parent can act as plaintiff in a case against a third party acting in good faith. When the claim is submitted by a third party, both parents must be involved.[5]

BULGARIA

As Art. 72 Bulgarian Family Code states: 'Both parents exercise parental rights and obligations jointly and separately'. In the exceptional cases of adoption and removal from the jurisdiction, the parent that has not consented could claim termination of adoption or ban the child from leaving the country.

CZECH REPUBLIC

The law presumes that if both parents hold parental responsibility they will agree on the exercise of individual rights and duties. Both parent's consent is always required in essential matters; if there is no agreement either of the parents may apply to the court for a decision (Sec. 49 Czech Family Code).

DENMARK

The competence of one holder of parental authority is not regulated, unlike the situation with regard to guardianship.[6] It is generally accepted that decisions of a daily nature such as clothing and feeding the child and attending to his/her health can be made by one parent while decisions such as a change of school, medical treatment which is not eminent, for example an eye correction operation or the use of strong medication, must be decided jointly.[7]

ENGLAND & WALES

According to Sec. 2(7), English Children Act 1989, notwithstanding that parental responsibility is shared each person who has it 'may act alone and without he other (or others) in meeting that responsibility' except where a statute expressly requires the consent of more than one person in a matter affecting the child. This latter qualification preserves, for example, the embargo imposed by Sec. 1, English Child Abduction Act 1984, against one parent taking the child (under the age of 16) outside the United Kingdom without the other's consent and maintains the need to obtain each parent's agreement to an

---

4 G. VERSCHELDEN, 'Ouderlijk gezag en omgangsrecht', *T.P.R.*, 2001, 1978.

5 W. PINTENS, 'Die Reform des belgischen Kindschaftsrechts aus vergleichender Sicht', *Fam.RZ*, 1997, p. 457-464.

6 Danish Act on Guardianship, Art. 3.

7 S. DANIELSEN, *Nordisk Børneret II*, Copenhagen, Oslo and Uppsala: Nord, 2003, p. 107.

adoption order as laid down by Sec. 16, Adoption Act 1976.[8] Another qualification on the power to act independently is, pursuant to Sec. 2(8), a person with parental responsibility is not entitled to act in any way that would be incompatible with a court order. A final qualification is that there are a group of important decisions that ought not to be carried out or arranged by even the one-parent carer in the absence of agreement of those with parental responsibility. According to case-law this group of decisions includes, the child's schooling, changing the child's surname, male circumcision and issues of immunisation.[9]

FINLAND

The custodian has the right to make a decision alone concerning the child in case of emergency (see Sec. 5 para. 2, described in Q 37). If the matter is of great importance for the future of the child, the power to act alone because of the other parent's absence or illness is sanctioned only in those situations where the child's best interests manifestly so require. About the residential custodian's right to act in daily matters, see above Q 37.

FRANCE

See Q 36. A holder of parental responsibilities may act alone if the decision concerns a 'usual decision on issues of parental responsibilities relating to the child'. In this situation the parent acting alone is presumed to act with the agreement of the other holder of parental responsibilities (Art. 372-2 French CC). Usual decisions are, for example, decisions concerning school insurance, holidays, choice of the school (but not always a change of school if it would change the child's life), registration at a sporting club, request for a passport *etc.*

GERMANY

Regarding the question as to when a holder of parental responsibilities may act alone, please see the answer to Q 37.

In the event of imminent danger, the parent entitled to represent the child in emergency situations may, in accordance with § 1629 para. 1 sent. 4 German CC, perform all acts necessary in the interests of the child. Subsequently, however, the other parent must be informed immediately, *i.e.*, without culpable delay, § 1629 para. 1 sent. 4 clause 2 German CC. In the absence of specific provisions in § 1629 German CC, the reimbursement of expenses incurred and any other compensation claims are governed by the general provisions.[10]

---

8 Prospectively Sec. 47(2), English Adoption and Children Act 2002.

9 See respectively, *Re G (A Minor)(Parental Responsibility: Education)* [1994] 2 FLR 964, CA; *Re PC (Change of Surname)* [1997] 2 FLR 230, *Re J (Specific Issue Orders)(Muslim Upbringing and Circumcision)* [2000] 1 FLR 571, and *Re C (Welfare of Child: Immunisation)* [2003] EWCA Civ 1148, [2003] 2 FLR 1095.

10 P. HUBER, in: *Münchener Kommentar zum Bürgerlichen Gesetzbuch*, 4th Edition, Munich: Beck, 2002, § 1629 No. 31; U. DIEDERICHSEN, in: PALANDT, *Bürgerliches Gesetzbuch*, 64th Edition, Munich: Beck, 2005, § 1629 No. 18.

Where the assertion of maintenance claims in accordance with § 1629 para. 2 sent. 2 German CC is concerned, the scope of the authorisation to act alone is wide: The parent in whose care the child is can assert the child's maintenance claims in and out of court.[11] Assertion in court includes both active and passive representation in all disputes concerning the child's maintenance claims against the other parent, i.e. including an application for the variation of an order for periodical payments, action for temporary judicial relief or action for a negative declaration by the other parent.[12]

§ 1687 German CC generally grants authorisation not only for legal actions but also for all actual arrangements concerning the matters of parental responsibility in question.[13] The power of the parent who merely exercises his or her right to contact to act alone resulting from § 1629 para. 1 sent. 4 German CC, is extended in scope with regard to prolonged visits by the child corresponding to the requirements of the length of the visit.[14] § 1687 para. 1 sent. 5 German CC refers for both parents to § 1629 para. 1 sent. 4 German CC, which means that in these cases, too, subsequent mutual notification is required. Furthermore, reference is made to § 1684 para. 2 German CC, which says that the parents must refrain from anything that might adversely affect the child's relationship with the other parent and/or with the person in whose care the child is, or which might render the raising of the child more difficult. This means that the father and mother are obliged to mutual loyalty and must not refuse to participate in the decisions required of them.[15]

GREECE

A parent can only act alone in matters of a usual nature (referring either to the care of the child or to the ongoing administration of its property), or in pressing matters (Art. 1516 para. 1 Greek CC). In addition, a lone parent may receive a

---

11 OLG Hamburg 13.02.1981, *FamRZ* 1981, 490; L. M. PESCHEL-GUTZEIT, in: STAUDINGER, *Kommentar zum Bürgerlichen Gesetzbuch*, 13th Edition, Berlin: Gruyter, 2002, § 1629 No. 341; P. Huber, in: *Münchener Kommentar zum Bürgerlichen Gesetzbuch*, 4th Edition, Munich: Beck, 2002, § 1629 No. 91.

12 H.-W. STRÄTZ, in: SOERGEL, *Großkommentar zum Bürgerlichen Gesetzbuch*, 12th Edition, Stuttgart: Kohlhammer, 1987, § 1629 No. 42; L. M. PESCHEL-GUTZEIT, in: STAUDINGER, *Kommentar zum Bürgerlichen Gesetzbuch*, 13th Edition, Berlin: de Gruyter, 2002, § 1629 No. 340.

13 BT-Drucks. 13/4899 p. 107; Jaeger, in: *Kommentar zum Eherecht*, 4th Edition, Munich: Beck, 2003, § 1687 No. 2.

14 Jaeger, in: *Kommentar zum Eherecht*, 4th Edition, Munich: Beck, 2003, § 1687 No. 8.

15 Jaeger, in: *Kommentar zum Eherecht*, 4th Edition, Munich: Beck, 2003, § 1687 No. 10; U. DIEDERICHSEN, in: PALANDT, *Bürgerliches Gesetzbuch*, 64th Edition, Munich: Beck, 2005, § 1687 No. 15.

disposition addressed to the child. The same holds true, by analogy, in the case of co-guardianship.[16]

HUNGARY

In one specified situation the holder of the parental responsibilities can act alone when there are joint parental responsibilities: in the child's financial matters - but with the presumption that the parent acts not only in his or her name but also in the name of the other parent. The Act distinguishes between the important financial matters (a formulated authorisation is needed) and the matters of low importance and of daily nature (the authorisation is presumed if the third party acts in good faith).

IRELAND

In a case where there is more than one holder of parental responsibilities, a holder of parental responsibilities can only act alone in respect of the physical care and control of the child on a day-to-day basis.

ITALY

The holder of the parental responsibilities can only act alone with respect to decisions of minor importance (of daily nature), or to urgent measures and to those which can't be delayed without prejudice. The other parent has the power to petition the judge when he thinks that such decisions are prejudicial to the interests of the minor (Art. 316 and 155 Italian CC).

LITHUANIA

Part 3 of Art. 3.165 Lithuanian CC provides that parents decide all questions by their mutual agreement. This means that one of the parents may act alone only in respect to matters of daily nature and only until the other parent makes an objections.

THE NETHERLANDS

There is no general provision on this subject in the Dutch CC. In principle the holders of parental responsibilities have to agree on decisions and actions concerning the child. It may be presumed that when a holder of parental responsibilities acts alone, the other holder will implicitly agree on it. With respect to the administration of the capital of the child and its representation in civil law acts, Art. 1:253i § 1 Dutch CC explicitly provides that the parents with parental responsibilities should act together, but that they may act alone as well, if the other one raises no objections. If one of the holders objects to a specific decision or action, he or she will have to request the court to settle the dispute or to give a decision (Art. 1:253a Dutch CC).

---

[16] K. PANTELIDOU, in: A. GEORGIADIS and M. STATHOPOULOS (eds.), *Civil Code commentary, Vol. VIII, Family Law (Arts. 1505-1694)*, 2nd Edition, Athens: Law & Economy, P.N. SAKKOULAS, 2003, Art. 1604-1605 Greek CC, p. 567, No. 1.

NORWAY

With regards to financial matters, Art. 3 Norwegian Act on Guardianship 1927 allows for the possibility of one parent giving the other the power of attorney to act on behalf of both parents. According to Art. 3 sec. 2, all warnings and communication during the case should be directed to both parents. If only one signs the necessary documents and meets in court on behalf of the child, he or she is considered as having the consent of the other parent unless the court is otherwise informed.

If the child lives permanently with one of the two parents holding parental responsibilities, the parent who does not live with the child may not object to the one with whom the child lives making decisions concerning important aspects of the child's care, such as questions as to whether or not the child shall attend a day-care centre, where in Norway the child shall live, and other major decisions concerning everyday life, according to Art. 37 Norwegian Children Act 1981. However, both parents must agree to a change of residence to another country, Art. 40 sec. 1.

POLAND

When parental authority is held by both parents, they are both authorised and obligated to exercise it (Art. 97 § 1 Polish Family and Guardianship Code). All major decisions with regard to the child should, however, be agreed upon by both parents (Art. 97 § 2 Polish Family and Guardianship Code)

PORTUGAL

It appears that, in practice, when a child has been entrusted to a child-care establishment, the director of that establishment may apply to the court for permission to perform those acts of particular importance for the life of the child.

RUSSIA

A holder of parental responsibility is generally allowed to act alone in all cases if the law does not require an explicit consent of the other parent. When a holder of parental responsibility acts alone there is a reversible presumption of consent of the other holder.[17] The explicit consent of the other parent is required to:

- take the child abroad,[18] including immigrating with the child,
- change the child's name or family name,[19]

---

17 A A. NETCHAEVA, 'Commentary to art. 79 Russian Family Code', in: I. KUZNETZOVA (ed.), *Commentary on the Family Code of Russian Federation*, Moscow: Jurist, 2000, p. 224.

18 Art. 21 Federal Law On Departure from and Entrance of the Russian Federation of 22.08.1996, *Sobranie Zakonodatel'stva Rossiiskoi Federatsii*, 1996, No. 34, item 4029.

19 Art. 59 (1) Russian Family Code. The consent of the parent who lives apart from the child is not required. The Department of Guardianship and Curatorship is only

- change the child's nationality,[20]
- allow the adoption of the child[21]

Considering that joint parental responsibility is always the case under Russian law, granting a parent (almost always a father) whose paternity has been established against his will such a wide scope of rights sometimes proves to lead to considerable problems. Such a parent usually does not have an effective bond with the child and is rather reluctant to fulfil his parental responsibilities. In the best case, this parent does nothing. In the worst case the parent uses every opportunity to abuse the right to refuse consent as a revenge for instigating a paternity suit against him.[22]

SPAIN

It is useful to distinguish whether the parents live together.
If they live together the power to act alone is granted only for decisions of a daily nature and for urgent decisions (see Q 37), or if the judge has solved the dispute among the parental responsibility holders by attributing the power to act alone to one of them (see Q 38). There is also a power to act alone if there is a conflict of interest between one of the parental responsibility holders and the child. In this situation, the other parental responsibility holder acts alone (see Q 8e).

If the parental responsibility holders do not live together, the Civil Code regime and Catalan law differ. The Spanish CC confers the exercise of parental responsibility to the parent the child lives with, unless the judge provides otherwise. This parent is therefore granted a general power to act alone. Catalan law, on the contrary, establishes that both parental responsibility holders must continue to jointly exercise parental responsibility, but that each of them is to take care of and protect the child when the child is with him or her (see Q 36). In this respect one can say that parental responsibility holders have an alternating power to act alone that is confined to a small number of areas (attention to the physical and psychological needs of the child, duty of surveillance), because decisions on important issues like the type of education or the domicile require the consent of both parents. This regime can be disregarded by the judge (see Q 36).

---

obliged to consider his or her opinion when changing the child's name (Art. 59 (2) Russian Family Code).

20 Art. 25 Federal Law on Nationality of Russian Federation of 19.04.2002.

21 Adoption is only allowed with the consent of both parents (Art. 129 Russian Family Code) unless the parents are unknown or have been declared by a court to have disappeared, to be incapable, to have been discharged of parental rights, or, due to reasons considered by a court not serious, have not being living with the child for six or more months and neglect their duty to educate and maintain a child (Art. 130 Russian Family Code).

22 M. ANTOKOLSKAIA, *Family Law* (*Semeinoe pravo*), Moscow: Jurist, 1999, p. 198.

There is also a power to act alone if it is impossible to act jointly because the parental responsibility holder is not available, incapable or absent (Art. 156 Spanish CC and Art. 137.3 Catalan Family Code). These concepts are to be restrictively interpreted.

SWEDEN

If owing to absence, illness or some other reason, one of the persons with custody is prevented from participating in custody decisions relating to the child and the decision cannot be postponed without inconvenience, the other person may make such a decision alone, Chapter 6 Sec. 13 para. 2 Swedish Children and Parents Code. However, that person may not make a decision alone that has far-reaching significance for the child's future unless it is manifestly required by the best interests of the child.

When the child is living with only one of the parents it is acknowledged that the residential custodian has the right to make certain decisions regarding the daily life of the child, without the consent of the co-custodian.[23] Decisions regarding the child's economic interests are to be made jointly by the guardians. The law does not give one of the guardians the right to decide alone.

SWITZERLAND

One parent may, as already explained in Q 37, only act unilaterally and without the consent and knowledge of the other parent if this is necessary for the protection of the child's person and the interests of the child and the other parent are not violated thereby. Unilateral action on the part of one parent contrary to the declared will of the other is only permissible if the child's interest unquestionably requires such action and a delay would endanger the child.[24]

---

23 See above, Q 37.

24 C. HEGNAUER, *Grundriss des Kindesrechts*, p. 184 *et seq.*

QUESTION 40

D. THE EXERCISE OF PARENTAL RESPONSIBILITIES

II. Joint Parental Responsibilities

Under what circumstances, if at all, may the competent authority permit the residence of the child to be changed within the same country and/or abroad (so-called relocation) without the consent of one of the holders of parental responsibilities?

AUSTRIA

Holders of joint parental responsibilities, *i.e.* parents, grandparents or foster parents (hereinafter parents), who are entitled to care for and educate the child also have the right to determine the child's residence. In exercising their right they should act by mutual assent (Sec. 144 and 146b Austrian CC).[1] If an agreement cannot be reached, the determination of the parent who acts first will be valid. The court may generally only interfere with this right to determine the child's residence - as with other parental rights - if the child's interests are at risk.[2] In such a case the court will render the decisions necessary to safeguard the interests of the child (Sec. 176(1) Austrian CC), and therefore may also permit the residence of the child to be changed without the consent of one holder of parental responsibilities. It may even issue an order on the child's residence against the determination of both parental responsibilities holders.

However, if the parents have permanently separated (after divorce, annulment of the marriage, ending of a non-marital partnership, or permanent separation of married parents) or have never lived in a common household, each parent may petition the court to end joint parental responsibilities, without substantiation, at any time. Unless a reconciliation between the parents may be brought about, the court will entrust one parent with sole parental responsibilities based on the best interests of the child (Sec. 167, 177a(2), 177b Austrian CC). Then, of course, this holder of sole parental responsibilities also has the sole right to determine the child's residence.

BELGIUM

The guideline for the determination of the residence of a child is the interests of the child. If it appears that it is in the child's interests to change its residence, the competent authority will make this decision, regardless of whether both parents consent.

---

1 M. SCHWIMANN in: M. SCHWIMANN, *Praxiskommentar zum ABGB*, Vol. I, 2nd Edition, Vienna: Orac, 1997, § 146b Marg. No. 1.

2 J. STABENTHEINER in: P. RUMMEL, *ABGB-Kommentar*, Vol. I, 3rd Edition Vienna: Manz 2000, § 137a Marg. No. 10.

BULGARIA

If parents do not live together (unmarried and not living together, living together but separated, married but separated) the court, based on the application of either parent, will decide on the residence of the child (Art. 71 § 2 Bulgarian Family Code). As stated above, the decision on the residence affects the exercise of parental rights, the resident parent will be exercising parental responsibilities. There is no special regulation on giving a permit from the non-resident parent in order for the residence of the child to be changed.

If a parent wants to relocate the child, he or she must have the consent of the other parent. Both parents must apply for issuing a passport for the child (Art. 45 Bulgarian Act on Identity Documents). If the parent has not given written consent for the child to leave the country, the border police may stop the child from passing the border (Art. 76 § 9 of the Act on Bulgarian Identity Documents). If the relocation of the child is disputed any parent may make a claim before the court (Art. 72 Bulgarian Family Code). The court order may replace the missing consent of the parent.

CZECH REPUBLIC

If the child is placed into personal care of one of the parents due to a court decision or due to an agreement approved by the court, no consent of the other parent or the court is needed for the parent to move the child to another town within the same country. If the parent wants to move the child to another country no approval of the court is needed, either provided the other parent agrees (even tacitly) with the move. If the other parent who does not live with the child disagrees with the move, he or she can apply to the court for a change of upbringing environment so that the child may be placed into his or her care. The reason for a change of the court decision on the child's upbringing is a material change of circumstance in which the child lives (Sec. 28 Czech Family Code). It is arguable, though, whether he or she would be successful because the court will consider the interests of the child first, including continuity of the child's upbringing environment. However, the court may not expressly forbid the parent to move the child.

DENMARK

It is not possible for a holder of parental authority to obtain permission from a competent authority to relocate. The notion is that the holder(s) must agree on all matters, when they have joint parental authority, including the child's residence or, if this is not possible they will have to seek sole parental authority. If a parent relocates without the consent of the other, the other parent can seek sole parental authority, Art. 8 Danish Act on Parental Authority and Contact. If one or both of the parents want(s) to have sole parental authority and they disagree on this issue, they must both consent to the child leaving the country, Art. 3 Danish Act on Parental Authority and Contact. Any relocation abroad is in this situation illegal.

ENGLAND & WALES

Disputes as to with whom the child should live can be resolved by means of a residence order obtained from the court. In resolving such disputes the court must, pursuant to Sec. 1(1), English Children Act 1989, treat the child's welfare as its paramount consideration and applying that principle can grant a residence in favour of one party against the wishes of the other. Before granting any order the court must, pursuant to Sec. 1(5) of the 1989 Act, be satisfied of the benefit to the particular child of any order sought, but in cases of dispute this requirement is normally satisfied. In determining the outcome of a contested residence order application (and indeed of any contested application for a Sec. 8 order) it is incumbent upon the court to apply the so-called statutory checklist.[3] This requires the court to take into account the following:

> '(a) the ascertainable wishes and feelings of the child concerned (considered in the light of his age and understanding);
> (b) his physical, emotional and educational needs;
> (c) the likely effect on him of any change in his circumstances;
> (d) his age, sex, background and any characteristics of his which the court considers relevant;
> (e) any harm which he has suffered or is at risk of suffering;
> (f) how capable each of his parents, and any other person in relation to whom the court considers the question to be relevant, is of meeting his needs; and
> (g) the range of powers available to the court under this Act in the proceedings in question'.

Space forbids detailed discussion of the application of the checklist etc. Instead readers are referred to the numerous commentaries on this subject.[4] A residence order only determines with whom the child is to live not *where* the child should live. If it is sought to limit where the child and carer should live it is necessary to seek an order to that effect (either a specific issue or prohibited steps order or, the adding of a condition to a residence order pursuant to Sec. 11(7), English Children Act 1989). It is now established that a distinction should be drawn between so-called internal relocation and external relocation. So far as the former is concerned, it is established[5] that it is only in exceptional circumstances that the courts should restrict where a carer and child should live within the United Kingdom. In other words, it is for the person seeking the restriction to convince the court why it is in the child's interests to restrict where the carer

---

3 The checklist is contained in Sec. 1(3), English Children Act 1989. The requirement to apply it in contested cases is contained in Sec. 1(4)(a).

4 See *e.g.* CRETNEY/MASON/BAILEY-HARRIS, *Principles of Family Law*, 2003, §20-011 *et seq*, HERRING, *Family Law*, 2004, 2nd Ed., p. 440 *et seq* and LOWE/DOUGLAS, *Bromley's Family Law*, 1998, 9th Ed., Ch 12.

5 See *Re S (a child)(residence order: condition)* [2001] EWCA Civ 847, [2001] 3 FCR 154 and *Re H (Children)(Residence Order: Condition)* [2001] EWCA Civ 1338, [2001] 2 FLR 1277.

and child should live.[6] In contrast, in so-called external relocation cases it is established that the burden is on those seeking to relocate abroad to justify doing so.[7] The governing principle is the paramountcy of the child's welfare but the test generally applied[8] is that provided the request is reasonable (*i.e.* reasonably well thought out and planned)[9] and bona fide (*i.e.* not motivated by a desire to prevent contact with the other parent)[10] then leave to remove the child will generally be granted unless it can be shown to be against the particular child's interests.

FINLAND

If the child has two (or more) joint custodians the child's residence should always be a matter for all custodians to decide, unless the court has given (according to Sec. 9 para. 3) one custodian the sole power to make the decision concerning the child's residence (See above Q 36).

However, if the residential custodian changes the child's place of residence within the country of Finland without the consent of the other custodian, the non-consenting custodian cannot require the enforcement of a move back to the child's past residence. She or he can only apply for the sole custody of the child or a residential order in a normal custody court dispute in order to get the child's place of residence changed to that of his or her place of residence.

If the residential custodian takes the child abroad without the consent of the other custodian, (and there is no order about the residential custodian's sole power to decide the child's country of residence,) the non-consenting custodian can ask for the return of the child according to the Hague Child Abduction Convention of 1980 (see Sec. 32 Finnish Child Custody and Right of Access Act, amendment 186/1994).

FRANCE

In principle, after the parents separate both parents remain holders of the parental responsibilities and shall also maintain personal relationships with the child. Nevertheless, the family judge can attribute the exercise of parental responsibilities to only one parent even if both are holders of parental

---

6 For examples see *Re S (a child)(residence order: condition)(No.2)* [2002] EWCA Civ 1795, [2003] 1 FCR 138 – mother of a child suffering from Down's Syndrome with a serious heart condition and respiratory problems and who had frequent contact and a close relationship with her father (from whom the mother was divorced) forbidden to move from Croydon to Cornwall; and *B v B (Residence: Condition Limiting Geographic Area)* [2004] 2 FLR 979 – mother seeking to move to the north of England, which was geographically distant from the father, primarily to frustrate her child's contact with him, was forbidden to do so.

7 See *Re H (Children)(Residence Order: Condition)* [2001] EWCA Civ 1338, [2001] 2 FLR 1277.

8 See *Payne v Payne* [2001] EWCA Civ 166, [2001] 1 FLR 1051.

9 See *e.g. Re T (Removal From Jurisdiction)* [1996] 2 FLR 352, CA.

10 See *e.g. Tyler v Tyler* [1989] 2 FLR 158, CA.

responsibilities (Art. 373-2-1 French CC). Each parent, even the one with whom the child lives, can change his residence even if this modifies the way the parental responsibilities will be exercised. But Art. 373-2 § 2 French CC requires the parent who changes residence to inform the other parent in advance and in due time. If the informed parent does not agree with the methods of exercise of her or his parental responsibilities the change of residence causes, she or he can call the family judge who will make a decision based on the child's interests. The decision can modify these methods; it could even change the attribution of the exercise of parental responsibilities. If the residence of one of the holders of parental responsibilities changes, the family judge can also order the parents to share the travelling expenses and consequently adjust the contribution of the parent with whom the child does not live to the child's maintenance and education.

If a danger exists that one parent could take the child abroad and never return him or her to France, the family judge can, on petition, order an entry on the passport of both parents prohibiting the child's departure from the territory without both parents' authorisation (Art. 373-2-6 para. 3 French CC). However, the family judge cannot impose such entry on a foreign passport.[11]

GERMANY

According to § 1631 para. 1 German CC, the obligation and right to determine the child's place of residence form part of the responsibility for the child and thus of parental responsibility, in accordance with § 1626 para. 1 sent. 2 German CC. If the father and mother hold joint parental responsibility, it is generally not possible for a court to make a decision regarding a change in the child's place of residence against the will of one of the persons holding parental responsibility. A unilateral decision by one parent regarding the child's place of residence is generally only possible if this parent has been attributed, by the court, sole responsibility for the child or the sole right to determine the child's place of residence.[12]

If a parent changes the child's place of residence against the will of the other parent, who is entitled to determine the same, the latter is, in the case of wrongful retention of the child, entitled to claim the child's return as a result of § 1632 para. 1 German CC. The decision as to whether or not such an illegal act has been committed is guided, in relations where parents hold joint parental responsibility, exclusively by the best interests of the child.[13] If the best interests of the child demands it, the family court may, in exceptional cases, even where the parents hold joint parental responsibility, refuse the parent filing the application his or her claim for return of the child. Although the right to return of the child serves the enforcement of responsibility for the child, it cannot

11 See CA Paris, 03.04.2003, *AJ Famille* 2003. 277.
12 BGH 27.05.1992, *NJW-RR* 1992, 1154.
13 OLG Düsseldorf 06.09.1973, *FamRZ* 1974, 99; U. DIEDERICHSEN, in: PALANDT, *Bürgerliches Gesetzbuch*, 64th Edition, Munich: Beck, 2005, § 1632 No. 6.

automatically be derived, of its own and without the need for a factual examination, from the attribution of parental responsibility.[14]

GREECE

If the parents do not agree on the residence of the child, they may apply to the court or the supervisory council resolve their dispute (Art. 1512 Greek CC). The guideline for the court in deciding on this matter is the interests of the child. After evaluating all the relevant factors the court may permit a change to the child's residence within the same country or abroad. It is worth mentioning that this disagreement between the parents, as well as the change of residence of the child constitute new circumstances. This may indicate that the exercise of joint parental responsibilities is no longer advantageous and thus a new regulation is needed. The same holds true, by analogy, in the case of co-guardianship with the difference being that the dispute is, at least initially, resolved by the supervisory council (Art. 1605 Greek CC).

HUNGARY

If joint parental responsibilities are exercised by parents living together, the public guardianship authority has competence to decide their disputes. If they live apart, the court has competence. If one of the parents wants to change the child's residence within the country and the other parent does not agree to it, the competent authority scrutinises the new residence and the child's maintenance. The competent authority must hear all interested persons, get the opinions of experts, if needed, and can make a study of surroundings as well. The same rules are applied if the child moves abroad.

A child's permanent relocation abroad is specifically regulated. The permission of the public guardianship authority is needed irrespective of whether the child moves alone or with his or her parents, and regardless of whether there is agreement between the parents. The public guardianship authority must scrutinise whether the child will be taken care of and whether his or her education, maintenance and schooling is provided abroad. The possibility of exercising the right to contact is also taken into account. If the parents do not live together, the court's decision is needed.

IRELAND

The Irish courts have stated that the parent with sole custody has the right to determine the residence of the child as part of his or her 'rights' as the custodial parent.[15] Where a parent is not actually exercising 'rights of custody' but merely holds the rights 'on paper' the onus is on the parent asserting such rights to

---

[14] BayObLG 01.07.1976, *FamRZ* 1977, 137, 139; U. DIEDERICHSEN, in: PALANDT, *Bürgerliches Gesetzbuch*, 64th Edition, Munich: Beck, 2005, § 1632 No. 6.

[15] See *W. v. W.* [1993] 2 I.R. 476, *H.I. v. M.G.* [1999] 2 I.L.R.M. 22 and *W.P.P. v. S.R.W.* [2001] 1 I.L.R.M. 371.

show that they are actually exercised.[16] Removal of the child by one party during the course of an application (under the Irish Guardianship of Infants Act 1964) to determine issues of child custody and guardianship in the District Court is not permissible.[17]

Where a parent applies to court for permission to relocate, the court determines the question under the general heading of 'best interests of the child' as a paramount consideration. However, the court must also consider other matters such as the question of freedom of movement. Where the rights of individuals are in conflict, the court must balance the interests of the parties carefully and conscientiously.

Where the consent of one of the holders of parental responsibilities is not forthcoming in Ireland, the test appears to be for the court to focus on what is best for the child. It determines what benefits the child will have and what detriments the child will suffer in a move, and, additionally, what consequences will follow from an order restricting movement.

ITALY

The competent authority, taking the interests of the minor into consideration, may permit the child to change residence within the same country and/or abroad (so called relocation) without the consent of the other holder of the parental responsibilities if the parents don't live together or if they are separated, divorced or if their marriage has been annulled.

LITHUANIA

In a dispute concerning a child's place of residence, the residence may be changed by the court judgment without the consent of the other parent if such a change is necessary for the protection of the interests of the child (Art. 3.169 Lithuanian CC). The basis for such judgment may be exceptional circumstances such as illness of one of the parents, violence against the child *etc.*

THE NETHERLANDS

The court may permit the residence of the child to be changed, both within the same country and abroad. The best interests of the child are decisive. As a change of residence abroad may have more implications for the child and for the other holder of parental responsibilities/parent, the court will probably take this into consideration. The court may also determine the place of residence of the child without terminating joint parental responsibilities.[18]

---

16 See McGuinness J. in *C.M. and O.M. v. Delegacion de Malaga and Others* [1999] 2 I.R. 363.

17 See *H. (Abduction: Rights of Custody)* [2000] 1 F.L.R. 201.

18 See Supreme Court 15.12.2000, *NJ*, 2001, 123 annotated S. Wortmann.

NORWAY

The courts cannot direct that a child shall change its place of residence within the country or permanently move abroad. The parent with whom the child lives may without consent of the other parent move within the country, but may move to another country only if that parent alone is the holder of parental responsibilities, according to Art. 37 and 40 sec. 1 Norwegian Children Act 1981.

POLAND

No.

PORTUGAL

No answer.

RUSSIA

The law does not contain any definition of the child's residence; legal literature interprets the term 'residence' as living together with one of the parents whenever she or he decides to set up home.[19] If the child's residence is determined by a court order, the term residence is understood in this sense. This interpretation gives a parent the possibility to move with the child not only within one city or area but all over the country without consent of the other parent and without asking for alteration of a court order. Considering the size of the Russian Federates the decision of a parent with whom the child resides to move far away from the place where the other parent lives can effectively deprive the child and the other parent from the possibility to maintain regular contacts. At the moment the law provides no remedy for this situation. The other parent can always ask the court to transfer the child's residence to him or her, but in order to make this claim successful he or she needs to provide evidence that the transfer of residence would be more beneficial to the child than remaining with the other parent.[20] This proves rather difficult, considering the fact that a court has already once evaluated which parent better fits the residential interests of the child. The non-residential parent cannot prohibit the residential parent from moving the child's residence within the country.

---

19 This conclusion can be derived from: A. NETCHAEVA, 'Commentary to art. 65 Russian Family Code', in: I. KUZNETZOVA (ed.), *Commentary on the Family Code of Russian Federation*, Jurist, Moscow: 2000, p. 225; L. PCHELINTZEVA, Commentary on the Family Code of Russian Federation, Moscow: Norma, 1998, p. 251.

20 According to Art. 65 (3) Russian Family Code, the judge's decision must consider the opinion of the child and 'tak[e] into account the attachment of the child to each of the parents, brothers and sisters, the age of the child, the moral and other personal qualities of the parents, relations existing between each of the parents and the child, the possibility of creating for the child conditions for nurturing and development (nature of activity, work regime of parents, material and family status of the parents and others)'.

If the residence of the child has been determined by an agreement between the parents (Art. 24 (1) and 65 (3) Russian Family Code), the parents are free to stipulate in their agreement that the child should reside with one of them in a certain place and that the residence cannot be changed without the consent of the non-residential parent. However, the enforceability of this will always depend on judicial scrutiny. In such scrutiny the court should take into consideration not only the best interests of the child but also the interests of the parents (Art. 24 (2) Russian Family Code). However, the outcome of such scrutiny would most likely be the same as it was when the residence was determined by a court order.

If the parent, with whom the child resides wishes to establish himself or herself abroad, the explicit consent of the non-residential parent is required.[21] If the consent is refused, the residential parent can ask the court to decide the issue.[22] This court should decide giving paramount consideration to the best interests of the child and at the same time taking into account the interests of both parents.

SPAIN

There is a different regulation between the Spanish CC regime and Catalan law.

The Spanish CC basically confers the exercise of parental responsibility to the parent with whom the child lives. This parental responsibility holder can change residence without the other parent's consent unless the parental responsibility holders had previously agreed that a change of residence should be consented by both. If a change of residence is subject to the consent of both parental responsibility holders and they do not agree, it will be necessary to bring the matter before the court (see Q 38). A judge can also subject changes of residence to previous judicial authorisation according to Art. 103.1 and 158.3 c) Spanish CC. These provisions were introduced in a law dealing with Child Abduction.[23] These measures are therefore conceived as preventive measures, meaning that there must be a risk of child abduction.

In Catalan law, both parental responsibility holders must always consent to a substantial change of residence, even if they are separated; provided the judge has not ruled otherwise. There is a duty to inform the non-resident parent, who can object to the change of residence. If within 30 days after having been informed he or she does not object to the change of residence, the residential parent is allowed to proceed. If he or she wishes to object he or she has to bring the matter to the court (see Q 38).

---

21 Art. 21 Federal Law On Departure from and Entrance of the Russian Federation of 22.08.1996.

22 Art. 21 Federal Law On Departure from and Entrance of the Russian Federation of 22.08.1996.

23 Ley Orgánica 9/2002, de 10 de diciembre, de modificación de la Ley Orgánica 10/1995, de 23 de noviembre, del Código Penal, y del Código Civil, sobre sustracción de menores.

Statute does not provide criteria to decide whether a change of residence should be authorised. Case law gives the impression that in most cases attention is focused on readjusting the regulation of contact after the change of residence and on determining how travel expenses are to be distributed.

SWEDEN

If the custodians cannot reach an agreement on the child's residence the question of who the child will live with can be referred to the court, Chapter 6 Sec. 14a Swedish Children and Parents Code. The court's power is limited to decide with whom the child will reside, and does not include deciding where the child will live. In deciding who the child will live with, the court shall consider the best interests of the child, including possibilities of contact with both parents. A change of the child's residence within the same country or abroad requires the consent of the co-custodian.[24] If such consent cannot be received, application of sole custody remains the ultimate solution. In Swedish law, a sole custodian is in principle free to change the child's residence, even if it means moving to another country, but should respect the child's right to a close and good contact with the other parent. Relocation orders permitting *e.g.* a child to move abroad with a custodial parent, are not possible under Swedish law.

SWITZERLAND

If a child is under parental responsibilities, its residence is determined in accordance with Art. 25 Swiss CC. Parental responsibilities include custody and, consequently, the right to determine the child's place of residence. Parents may in this way also leave the exercise of the actual custody to third parties. On the other hand, legal custody as such is non-transferable and cannot be renounced. In accordance with Art. 301 § 3 Swiss CC, the child may not leave the parental household without the parents' consent. Nevertheless, parents must allow the child the freedom to shape its life in line with the child's maturity and parents must take the child's opinion into account (see also Q 8).[25]

Only for the protection of the child (Art. 307 *et seq* Swiss CC) may the competent authority (depending on the nature of the proceedings this is the guardianship authority or a court) revoke parental custody (in fact and in law) against the parents' will and place the child in an appropriate manner with third parties, if a danger to the child cannot be prevented in any other way (Art. 310 § 1 Swiss CC). The same provision of law also renders it possible to change placement from one place to another. Finally the competent authority may also revoke parental custody at the request of the parents or of the child and place the child in an appropriate manner with third parties if the relationship between the child and its parents has broken down so severely that the child

24 G. WALIN and S. VÄNGBY, *Föräldrabalken, En kommentar, Del I, 1-13 kap.*, Stockholm: Norstedts Juridik, 2002, p. 6:55.

25 C. HEGNAUER, *Grundriss des Kindesrechts*, p. 195 *et seq.*

cannot reasonably be expected to remain in the joint household and there is no other way of helping the child in view of the circumstances (Art. 310 § 2 Swiss CC).

QUESTION 41

D. THE EXERCISE OF PARENTAL RESPONSIBILITIES

II. Joint Parental Responsibilities

Under what conditions, if at all, may the competent authority decree that the child should, on an alternating basis, reside with both holders of parental responsibilities (*e.g.* every other month with mother or father)?

AUSTRIA

In the best interests of the child, the legislature deems it necessary that permanently separated parents who want to hold joint parental responsibilities must agree on which parent the child is to reside with most of the time, i.e. the location of the child's "home base" (Sec. 177(2) and 167 Austrian CC)[1]. If the parents are unable to reach such an agreement on the primary residence of the child, the court must attribute sole parental responsibilities including the right to determine the child's residence to one of them (Sec. 167, 177a and 177b Austrian CC). A division of parental responsibilities whereby the child changes his or her residence, *e.g.* alternating every month from the child's father's home to the mother's home, is neither permissible by way of agreement nor by judicial decree.[2]

BELGIUM

Until the beginning of the nineties, alternating the residence of the child was exceptional, and generally only allowed if both parents agreed.[3] Even then some judges refused it. Since the Belgian Law of 13 April 1995, alternating the child's residence is no longer the exception; certain Juvenile Courts consider it the common rule.[4] The guideline used for judging the alternating system is always the interests of the child. Therefore, unless it is obviously against the interests of the child, it will be enacted if both parents agree. When the parents cannot agree, the decision will be made after examination of the interests of the child. The disagreement of the parents is no longer a determining element. The competent authority may designate an expert to investigate and give an opinion concerning the residence of the child. Generally, it is assumed that the advise of the expert will be followed by the compentent authority, but the expert's advise is not binding. The competent authority cannot delegate its competence to an expert. Included in the relevant factors are the distance between the parents' houses, the age of the child, their relationship with the child, the aptitude of the

---

1 See Q 16, 17, 22b, 23 and 25.

2 See J. STABENTHEINER, 'KindRÄG 2001', in: P. RUMMEL, *ABGB-Kommentar*, suppl. vol. 1, 3rd Edition, Vienna: Manz Verlag, 2003, §§ 177-177b, Marg. No. 6 *et seq.*

3 Court of Appeal of Liege, 21.01.1985, *Rev. trim.dr. fam.*, 1986, p. 238.

4 Juvenile Court of Brussels, 08.06.1998, *R.W.*, 1998-99, p. 822, *J.D.J.*, 1999, No. 1985, p. 42; A. DUELZ, , *Le droit du divorce*, Brussels: Larcier, 2002, p. 171.

parents to communicate with each other, the personal situation of both parents (*e.g.* their availability according to their professional situation) and the distance to the school. If the alternating system of residence is admitted, it will usually be on a weekly rather than monthly basis, but this is not a legal certainty. It is considered that a prolonged separation is not ideal, especially with younger children.[5]

BULGARIA

It is not possible under the legislation in force.

CZECH REPUBLIC

Czech legislation has recognised the possibility of alternating upbringing since the 1998 reform. Sec. 26 § 2, establishes that if both parents are qualified for the child's upbringing and they wish to do so the court may place the child into common (joint) or alternating upbringing (care) of both parents if it is in the interests of the child and if his or her needs are better satisfied in that manner. Placing the child into common upbringing (joint custody) means, in Czech law, that the situation of the child is not regulated in any manner after the divorce or factual separation of its parents. Even though the wording of the law allows for the possibility for the court to hold against the will of one the parents, judicial practice tends to view such a decision as not being in the interests of the child. Therefore, courts approve agreements on common upbringing. In practice, common upbringing appears quite rarely, usually when children approach the age of majority.

Alternating upbringing is, also not awarded against the will of one of the parents; courts only approve the parental agreement. The length of alternating upbringing is not regulated by the law. In practice, the parents alternate at monthly intervals; with children of tender years the interval is often weekly. Opinions on alternating upbringing are varied ('a child with a suitcase in hand, constantly travelling'). In practice, courts hold the view that the child should not change its school, circle of friends and leisure interests.[6]

DENMARK

This is not possible.

ENGLAND & WALES

It is within the courts' powers to grant what is known as a shared residence order, that is, an order made in favour of two persons who do not live together. Shared care arrangements can take different forms, for example, the child living during term-time with one parent and school holidays with the other or spending weekdays with one and weekends with the other or spending

---

5 N. DOPCHIE, 'Considérations sur l'adéquation psychologique de l'octroi d'un droit de garde alternée en cas de séparation ou de divorce', *Rev. trim. dr. fam.*, 1981, p. 367.

6 M. HRUSAKOVA, *Zákon o rodine. Komentar. 2. vyd.* Prague: C.H.Beck, 2001, p. 179.

alternative weeks or months with each of the parties. It is now accepted[7] that whether or not to make a shared residence order is determined solely according to the child's welfare. It is quite likely to be made in cases where the child has been happily living with each parent so that in effect all the court is doing is confirming the status quo.[8]

FINLAND

An order concerning the child's residence can only concern one of the parents, if the parents do not live together (Sec. 7 and 9 Finnish Child Custody and Right of Access Act).[9] However, it is possible that although a child resides with one parent, his or her right of contact is so great that the child practically resides with both custodians (such as a division of two weeks and two weeks). This arrangement can be settled by means of a parental agreement or a court order. Such arrangements are not to my knowledge very common in Finland. No statistical information exists about their frequency.

FRANCE

The most recent French reform of 4 March 2002 has opted for this kind of exercise of parental responsibilities as the best possible solution. In principle, the parents' separation does not affect the rules related to the exercise of parental responsibilities. Each parent shall maintain personal relationships with the child (Art. 373-2 French CC). The principle is therefore joint parental responsibilities after any type of parental separation. The new Art. 373-2-9 French CC states that the child's residence can be 'fixed on an alternating basis at both parent's domicile or at the domicile of one of the parents'. Priority is given to parental agreements, if they are not contrary to the child's interests (Art. 373-2-7 French CC), that agree to an alternating residence of the child, at both parent's domiciles.

Art. 373-2-9 French CC also states that on the claim of one parent or if the parents disagree on the child's residence, the family judge can issue an interim order for the child's residence to alternate between the domiciles of each parent for a certain duration. At the end of this period the judge will make a definitive decision on the child's residence, either on an alternating basis at each parents' domicile or at the domicile of one parent. This shows the aim of the French

7 See *D v D (Shared Residence Order)* [2001] 1 FLR 495, CA. At once time such orders were thought exceptional, see *Re H (A Minor)(Shared Residence)* [1994] 1 FLR 717 or at least unusual, see *Re H (Shared Residence: Parental Responsibility)* [1995] 2 FLR 883, but this is no longer the case.

8 As in *D D v D (Shared Residence Order)* [2001] 1 FLR 495. See also *A v A (children: shared residence order)* [2004] EWHC 142 (Fam), [2004] 3 FCR 201. But note *Re F (Shared Residence Order)* [2003] EWCA Civ 592, [2003] 2 FLR 397 where neither findings adverse to one parent nor the fact that the parents were living in separate jurisdictions (*i.e.* Scotland and England) precluded the making of a shared residence order.

9 This is not so in Sweden, for instance, according to DANIELSEN, *Nordisk Borneret II, Foreldreansvar*, Nord 2003:14, Nordisk ministerråd, Kobenhavn 2003, p. 189.

reform to promote the alternating residence of the child as a way to encourage the continuing personal relationships with both parents even after their separation[10] (as stated in Art. 373-2 French CC). However, if this model does not correspond to the child's interests the family judge shall decide another solution.

GERMANY

Parents who live apart and hold joint parental responsibilities have a choice of various different models for caring for the child. The law assumes the so-called residence model, but it may, subject to the parents' consent, allow a dual-residence, alternating or nest model.[11]

However, the court cannot order the alternating residence model for the child against the will of the parents; it may, at most, beyond the scope of § 1666 German CC, order partial sole parental responsibilities on an alternating basis with regard to the right to determine the child's residence.[12]

In case of conflict it is, moreover, conceivable that the family court may decide on the scope of the right to contact, § 1684 para. 3 sent. 1 German CC. In this context, according to § 1697 a German CC the best interest of the child is the sole yardstick for its decision. Provided that it corresponds to the child's best interest, the court may, instead of periodical contact of short duration with the parent living apart, order contact over prolonged blocks of time.[13] However, due to the fact that § 1684 German CC has been drafted without reference to parental responsibility, no particular provisions apply in the case of joint parental responsibility, for example, in the direction of a more generous provision of contact, for the period of the contact provision.[14] As a result, it is not possible for the court to order an alternating residence model using this avenue of approach.

GREECE

Such a case usually arises after the divorce, annulment of the marriage, or the factual separation of the parents. The court may decide that the child should reside on an alternative basis with both holders of parental responsibilities either when it attributes joint parental responsibilities to the parents, who have

---

10 Under the Act No. 87-570 of 22.07.1987 the judge had to determine the parent at whose domicile the child would have his 'principal residence'; the child had in this case only a secondary residence at the other parent's domicile.

11 See AG Hannover 13.10.2000, *FamRZ* 2001, 846; B. VEIT, in: Bamberger and Roth, *Kommentar zum Bürgerlichen Gesetzbuch*, 1st Edition, Munich: Beck, 2003, § 1687 No. 3; H. Oelkers, 'Das gemeinsame Sorgerecht nach Scheidung in der Praxis des Amtgerichts Hamburg – Familiengericht', *FamRZ* 1994, 1080, 1082.

12 See AG Hannover 13.10.2000, *FamRZ* 2001, 846.

13 U. DIEDERICHSEN, in: PALANDT, *Bürgerliches Gesetzbuch*, 64th Edition, Munich: Beck, 2005, § 1684 No. 15.

14 Th. RAUSCHER, in: STAUDINGER, *Kommentar zum Bürgerlichen Gesetzbuch*, 13th Edition, Berlin: de Gruyter, 2000, § 1684 No. 200.

already agreed on this issue,[15] or when it determines that parental responsibilities should rotate between the parents.[16] In any case, the court has to take the interests of the child into consideration.

HUNGARY

Hungarian legal practice and literature unambiguously hold that for a child to reside with the child's parents on an alternating basis would harm the child's requirement for stability, which has great importance in the life of the minor. Although it may happen factually through an informal agreement of the parents, the competent authority will not decree the placement of the child on an alternating basis.

IRELAND

The court has absolute discretion in this matter.

ITALY

The competent authority can decree that the child should reside on an alternating basis with each holder of parental responsibilities whenever the authority deems it to be in the interests of the child. In practise, this never happens. Neither case law nor legal literature consider alternating custody of the child to be in the interests of the minor. On the contrary it is considered potentially prejudicial and to provoke serious uncertainty and instability during the minor's growth (see Q 16).

LITHUANIA

Such court judgments are possible if this corresponds to the interests of the child. Everything depends on the wishes of the child and the possibilities of each holder of parental responsibilities to provide adequate livening, educational and other conditions for the child.

THE NETHERLANDS

There is no specific provision in the Civil Code on this subject and there is little case law. The best interests of the child will be decisive and it is hard to imagine that such a decree would be made if the parents do not agree to such an arrangement. In 2001 the District Court in Zutphen decreed that the children should alternatively reside two years with the mother and two years with the father. The Court of Appeal, Arnhem, decided that the children should reside

---

15 The court may only attribute joint parental responsibilities to the parents if they both agree to and, at the same time, they determine the residence of the child. (See the answer to Q 18.) In any event, the court is not bound by any agreement between the parents. See P. AGALLOPOULOU, in: A. GEORGIADIS and M. STATHOPOULOS (eds.), *Civil Code commentary, Vol. VIII, Family Law (Arts. 1505-1694)*, 2nd Edition, Athens: Law & Economy, P.N. Sakkoulas 2003, Art. 1513-1514 Greek CC, p. 229-230, No. 71.

16 P. AGALLOPOULOU, in: A. GEORGIADIS and M. STATHOPOULOS (eds.), *Civil Code commentary, Vol. VIII, Family Law (Arts. 1505-1694)*, 2nd Edition, Athens: Law & Economy, P.N. Sakkoulas 2003, Arts 1513-1514 Greek CC, p. 232, No. 83-87.

with the mother in order to meet their needs of safety, stability and continuity. Although the father appealed to the Supreme Court, it did not give a judgment on this question, due to procedural errors.[17]

NORWAY

The competent authority, *i.e.* the court, may not order that the child should reside with both holders of parental responsibilities on an alternating basis (*e.g.* every other week, month *etc*) A child must have permanent residence with one of the parents unless they, by mutual agreement, decide otherwise, Art. 36 sec. 2 Norwegian Children Act 1981.

POLAND

There is no specific regulation on this issue; the law permits that the child may only stay with one of the parents (Art. 26 § 2 Polish CC). It should be stated that this is a decision of major importance. Therefore, in the absence of parental unanimity the family court is to decide.

PORTUGAL

Alternating custody is rarely applied by courts. The court may only ratify an agreement between parents relating to the future exercise of parental responsibility after divorce, legal separation, the declaration of nullity or annulment of a marriage, which establishes a system of alternating custody as a way of exercising joint parental responsibility if that is in the interests of the child (Art. 1905 No. 1 and 1906 No. 1 Portuguese CC). The Public Prosecutor's Office shall operate in the same way (Art. 14, No. 4 Portuguese Decree-Law No. 272/2001 of 13 October 2001).

RUSSIA

It is not customary in Russia for a child's residence to alternate after divorce. Post-divorce arrangements mostly provide for the child to reside with the mother, with the father granted a limited possibility to visit the child and/or to have the child with him for short periods of time during weekends and summer holidays. This practice is based on the dominant opinion that 'a child of any age needs a single stable educational patron, and should live according to familiar rules and in a trusted environment.'[18]

SPAIN

Both in Catalan law and the Civil Code regime it is possible for parents to agree on such a scheme. Judge's are not prevented from decreeing that children reside on alternating basis with each parent, if this is in the child's best interests. However, from case law decisions it is much more common that these arrangements are not permitted because they are considered detrimental to the

17 See Supreme Court 29.10.2004, *LJN* AR1213, R 03/081HR.

18 A. NETCHAEVA, 'Commentary to Art. 66 Russian Family Code', in: I. KUZNETZOVA (ed.), *Commentary on the Family Code of Russian Federation*, Moscow: Jurist, 2000, p. 228.

child's best interests due to the lack of stability for the child. Still, this matter is currently being discussed in an announced reform of divorce law. The Government wishes to promote shared custody because it allows children to exercise their right of contact with both parents more fully.

SWEDEN

If both parents have joint custody of a child, the court may, upon the application of one or both of them, decide with which of them the child shall live, Chapter 6 Sec. 14a, para. 1 Swedish Children and Parents Code. The court may also decree that the child shall live with both parents alternately. The best interests of the child shall be decisive. Alternate living normally presupposes that the parents live close to one another, considering that frequent travelling is tiresome and challenging for a child and that a child needs continuity in school attendance and in relations with friends.[19] Where the parents live close to each other it is not uncommon in Sweden that children live on a weekly basis alternating between both parents.

Swedish research shows that a prerequisite for a functioning alternate living with both parents is that the parents can cooperate in questions concerning custody.[20] This is seldom the case when the parents are not able to agree on alternate living arrangements for the child. In Sweden, the suitability for children under the age of three to live with both parents alternately has been questioned.[21]

Parents are free to agree on alternate living arrangements concerning their children, but to be valid such an agreement must be in writing and approved by a local social welfare committee, Chapter 6 Sec. 14a para. 2 Swedish Children and Parents Code.

SWITZERLAND

As long as the parents are married they jointly determine the child's residence. They are also free to agree, if it is reconcilable with the child's welfare, that the child should reside with both holders of parental responsibilities on an alternating basis, if they do not have a joint place of residence.

In a divorce, the court in principle confers parental responsibilities on one parent. If the relevant prerequisites such as, among other conditions, an agreement that can be approved are fulfilled, it may also confer the parental responsibilities jointly on both parents (Art. 133 § 3 Swiss CC; see also Q 16). In the agreement the parents may also agree on the child residing on an

---

19 G. WALIN and S. VÄNGBY, *Föräldrabalken, En kommentar, Del I, 1-13 kap.*, Stockholm: Norstedts Juridik, 2002, p. 6:59.

20 G. EWERLÖF, T. SVERNE and A. SINGER, *Barnets bästa. Om föräldrars och samhällets ansvar*. 5:e uppl. Stockholm: Norstedts Juridik 2004 p. 57.

21 G. WALIN and S. VÄNGBY, *Föräldrabalken, En kommentar, Del I, 1-13 kap.*, Stockholm: Norstedts Juridik, 2002, p. 6:60.

alternating basis with the mother and father, if this is reconcilable with the child's welfare. Legal literature and court practice both show certain reservations in connection with this in view of the stability of the child's situation.[22] In any case joint parental responsibilities are not based on the premise of alternating custody in the sense that parents each take turns in doing their half of the duty of caring for their children.[23]

22 See inter alia U. TSCHÜMPERLIN, *Die elterliche Gewalt in Bezug auf die Person des Kindes*, Freiburg: Universitätsverlag, 1989, p. 166 *et seq.*

23 More details in this respect *inter alia* in R. REUSSER, *Die Stellung der Kinder im neuen Scheidungsrecht, in: Vom alten zum neuen Scheidungsrecht*, Bern: Stämpfli-Verlag, 1999, marginal notes 4.35 *et seq.*

QUESTION 42

D. THE EXERCISE OF PARENTAL RESPONSIBILITIES

III. Sole Parental Responsibilities

Does a parent with sole parental responsibilities have full authority to act alone, or does he or she have a duty to consult:
(a) The other parent;
(b) Other persons, bodies or competent authorities?

AUSTRIA

(a) The other parent

The parent with sole parental responsibilities has the sole right to make decisions, while the other parent is limited to the right to be informed and to express his or her opinion (Sec. 178 Austrian CC).[1] In the event of sole representation by operation of law, the requirement of the other parent's consent will not apply even to important matters concerning the child (Sec. 154(2)(b) Austrian CC).[2]

(b) Other persons, bodies or competent authorities

Transactions in property-related matters that fall outside the scope of the ordinary enterprise always require the court's approval (Sec. 154(3)(b) Austrian CC). These matters include, *inter alia,* the sale and encumbrance of real estate; the acquisition, transformation, sale, or dissolution of a business; waiver of a right of inheritance, unconditional acceptance or renunciation of an inheritance; acceptance of an encumbered gift or rejection of a proffered gift; certain types of monetary investments (e.g. granting a loan or acquiring real estate); filing a complaint and making all procedural dispositions that relate to the matter in dispute.[3]

BELGIUM

(a) The other parent

In principle, he or she has full authority to act alone and has no duty to consult the other parent. It should be noted that, excepting very grave reasons to the contrary, the other parent still retains the right to contact with the child and retains the right to supervise the way the other parent exercises parental authority and administrates the property of the child (Art. 374(4) and 376(4) Belgian CC). He or she may request information from the other parent and third parties, and may address the Juvenile Court when it is in the interests of the

---

1 See Q 44b.

2 M. SCHWIMANN in: M. SCHWIMANN, *Praxiskommentar zum ABGB*, Vol. I, 2nd Edition, Vienna: Orac, 1997, § 154 Marg. No. 10.

3 See also Q 8f.

child.[4] In any case, either parent or the Public Prosecutor may utilize the Juvenile Court any time a problem should arise. In the interests of the child, the court may impose or change any regulations concerning the parental responsibilities (Art. 387 *bis* Belgian CC).

However, in some cases concerning the parental authority *sensu lato*, the agreement of both parents is required, namely for parental consent in case of adoption (Art. 348(1), 349(4), (5) and (6) and 368(4) Belgian CC), custodianship (Art. 475 *bis* Belgian CC) and marriage (Art. 148(1) Belgian CC), for the request of judicial removal from guardianship (emancipation) (Art. 477 Belgian CC) and for the state of prolonged minority (Art. 487 *ter* (1) Belgian CC), to assist with a (change of) marriage contract (Art. 1397 Belgian CC)[5] and to appoint a testamentary guardian in case an only parent should die (Art. 392 Belgian CC).[6] The authorisation of both parents is also required in case of removal of an organ (Art. 7 Belgian Law of 13 June 1986 concerning the Organ Transplantation).

A discussion exists regarding the demand for a change of name (Art. 2(2) Belgian Law of 15 May 1987 on Surname and First names). Since the judgment of the Council of State of 30 July 1985,[7] it is admitted that the demand for change of name is not a part of the parental administration of the child's property, but instead a part of the competence of legal representation of the child which is not limited to proprietary acts. Some authors consider the demand for a change of name as a part of the parental authority *sensu lato*, which requires the intervention of both parents.[8] However, according to certain authors, the demand for a change of name is, by lack of a different legal regulation, part of the parental authority *sensu stricto* and, therefore, follows the general rules of Art. 373-374 Belgian CC concerning joint or sole parental responsibilities, including the presumption of agreement of the other parent towards third parties acting in good faith.[9]

(b) Other persons, bodies or competent authorities

Yes, he or she has full authority to act alone and has no duty to consult other persons, bodies or competent authorities.

---

4 Juvenile Court of Charleroi, 16.12.1998, *J. dr. jeun.*, 2000, Vol. 198, p. 32.

5 Y.-H. LELEU, 'Le contrat de mariage', in *Rép. Not.*, V-II, p. 504-504, No. 508.

6 See Q 34.

7 Council of State, 30.07.1985, *J.T.*, 1986, p. 47, annotated J. DE GAVRE.

8 H. CASMAN, *Notarieel Familierecht*, Ghent: Mys & Breesch, 1991, n° 600.

9 W. PINTENS, *Naam*, in *A.P.R.*, Gent: Story-Scientia, 1981, No. 129; J. SOSSON, 'Une procédure peu connue: le changement de nom par la voie administrative. Conditions, modalités et effets', *Ann. Dr. Louvain*, 1994, p. 107, confirmed by Council of State 27.05.1994, *R.A.C.E.*, 1994, 12-15; D. VAN GRUNDERBEECK, *Artikelsgewijze commentaar met overzicht van rechtspraak en rechtsleer personen- en familierecht* (Naamwet), Antwerp, Maklu, 1997, Art. 2-8 – 2-14.

BULGARIA

(a) The other parent

This is possible only if one of the parents has been deprived of parental rights. In this situation the other parent as a single holder of parental responsibilities may act without consulting or notifying the other parent. The only exception is in the case of adoption of the child - the parent deprived of parental rights shall provide an opinion for the adoption of the child.

(b) Other persons, bodies or competent authorities

No. That parent should not consult anybody.

CZECH REPUBLIC

(a) The other parent

The parent who is the sole holder of parental responsibility has no duty to consult with the parent who has been deprived of parental responsibility or whose exercise of parental responsibility has been suspended.

(b) Other persons, bodies or competent authorities

If one parent has been deprived of parental responsibility or his or her exercise of parental responsibility has been suspended, the parent who is the sole holder of parental responsibility has full authority to act alone with two exceptions. Dealing with the child's estate in essential matters always requires court approval (Sec. 28 Czech CC) and a parent cannot represent the child if there is a danger of a conflict of interests between the child and the parent or between children of the same parent (Sec. 37 Czech Family Code).

DENMARK

(a) The other parent

There is no duty to consult.

(b) Other persons, bodies or competent authorities

There is no duty to consult.

ENGLAND & WALES

(a) The other parent

The short answer to this question is that a parent with sole parental responsibility has full authority to act alone in respect of all aspects of parental responsibility (including changing the child's name)[10] and is not obliged to consult anyone.

(b) Other persons, bodies or competent authorities

A parent with sole parental responsibility is not obliged to consult any person, body or competent authority when exercising parental responsibility.

---

10 See *Re P C (Change of Surname)* [1997] 2 FLR 730.

FINLAND

(a) The other parent

The sole custodian has the power to use his or her custodial rights without consulting the other parent. However, the sole custodian's consent for the adoption of the child is not sufficient, because the Act concerning adoption requires the consent of both parents (Sec. 9).

Additionally, courts often give practical guidelines to the parents concerning the exercise of the child's right of access. The parents may be obliged to consult each other about certain conditions, such as work shifts, summer holidays or other practical arrangements, regardless of the attribution of the custodial rights to one or both parents (Sec. 9 para. 3 Finnish Child Custody and the Right of Access Act).

(b) Other persons, bodies or competent authorities

Before the 1974 reform concerning the position of children born out-of-wedlock, there were restrictions on an unmarried mother's right to exercise her custodial rights. All restrictions on an unmarried mother's position were removed when the present Finnish Paternity Act came into force in 1976.

The restrictions concerning the power of the guardian in the administration of the child's property also concern the sole custodian if he or she is functioning as the guardian of the child, if no special guardian has been appointed. About these restrictions, see above (Q 12). The custodian shall consult the child in the way explained in Q 9.

FRANCE

(a) The other parent

French law distinguishes between two situations:

- the parent who is sole holder of parental responsibilities; and
- the parent who holds parental responsibilities with the other parent, but has sole exercise of these responsibilities (*e.g.* after separation or divorce).

In the first situation the parent has full authority to act alone. She or he does not have to consult the other parent who is deprived of parental responsibilities. Some restrictions exist but they concern only the legal administration which takes place under judicial control. The parent can act alone on all *actes d'administration* (acts of administration) but must ask judicial permission for all *actes de disposition* (acts of disposition).

In the second situation, where both parents hold parental responsibilities but only one has the exercise of them, the parent who does not have this exercise nevertheless keeps the right and duty to supervise the child's maintenance and education and must be informed of all important choices relating to the child's life (Art. 373-2-1 para. 3 French CC). He therefore does not have to be consulted but only informed of important matters.

(b) Other persons, bodies or competent authorities

For the legal administration only, the parent with sole parental responsibility must ask for judicial permission for all acts of disposition (Art. 457 French CC). The *juge des tutelles* (guardianship court) is competent to deliver such permissions. See (a) and Q 11.

GERMANY

(a) The other parent

§ 1627 German CC provides that the parents must exercise their parental responsibilities in mutual agreement and that they must attempt to reach an agreement the event of a dispute. This norm, however, applies only when the parents hold joint parental responsibility.[11] By contrast, in the case of sole parental responsibility, just as in the case of factual or legal inability by one of the two joint holders of parental responsibilities,[12] there is no such duty to consult.

The concentration of parental responsibility in one parent by necessity results in the disenfranchisement of the other parent, who does not hold parental responsibility, although the latter retains his or her position as parent, which is protected by the constitution, Art. 6 para. 2 German Basic Law.[13] Family law does, however, take account of these parental rights through the institution of the right to contact and through the option to have one's parental responsibilities reinstated at a later date if, for example, sound reasons of the child's best interests argue in favour of such a change in parental responsibility, § 1696 German CC. Furthermore, each parent is entitled to be informed by the other parent of the child's personal circumstances, § 1686 sent. 1 German CC.

Moreover, in the case of sole parental responsibility the parent who does not hold parental responsibility can of course pa rticipate in the care for the child, provided that the parents wish it; the parent holding sole parental responsibility does, however, remain solely responsible from a legal aspect.[14]

(b) Other persons, bodies or competent authorities

Parental responsibility is generally, irrespective of whether it is exercised by one parent alone or jointly by both parents, subject to certain limits (see Q 12). One particular feature for the married parent holding sole parental responsibility results from § 1687 b German CC, which stipulates that the spouse of this parent has the right to participate in decision-making on matters

---

11 H.-W. STRÄTZ, in: SOERGEL, *Großkommentar zum Bürgerlichen Gesetzbuch*, 12th Edition, Stuttgart: Kohlhammer, 1987, § 1627 No. 3; P. Huber, in: *Münchener Kommentar zum Bürgerlichen Gesetzbuch*, 4th Edition, Munich: Beck, 2002, § 1627 No. 3.

12 J. GERNHUBER and D. COESTER-WALTJEN, in: *Lehrbuch des Familienrechts*, 4th Edition, Munich: Beck, 1994, § 64 II, III, pp. 1024-1026.

13 J. GERNHUBER and D. COESTER-WALTJEN, in: *Lehrbuch des Familienrechts*, 4th Edition, Munich: Beck, 1994, § 65 III 3, p. 1039.

14 J. GERNHUBER and D. COESTER-WALTJEN, in: *Lehrbuch des Familienrechts*, 4th Edition, Munich: Beck, 1994, § 65 III 3, p. 1040.

relating to everyday life, the so-called 'limited parental responsibilities' (see Q 27a).

GREECE

(a) The other parent

If a parent has sole parental responsibilities, he or she never has a (legal) duty to consult the other parent. It is worth noting, however, that the parent to whom parental care is not entrusted, has the right to demand information concerning the child and its property (Art. 1513 para. 3 Greek CC).

(b) Other persons, bodies or competent authorities

Parents need the permission of the court before entering into certain transactions concerning the management of the child's assets (Art. 1526 Greek CC which refers to Art. 1624 and 1625 Greek CC). This restriction is applicable to all cases and is not confined to those instances where sole parental responsibilities are attributed.

HUNGARY

(a) The other parent

If there are no joint parental responsibilities, one of the parents exercises sole parental responsibilities; still, the other parent can have, more or less, rights and duties. If the other parent's parental responsibilities are not restricted or terminated by the court, although the parent's parental responsibilities are suspended he or she has the right to contact and to decide important matters affecting the child together with the holder of parental responsibilities. Consequently, the holder of parental responsibilities is obliged to consult the other parent when deciding the above-mentioned matters.

The non-custodial parent can be empowered by the court to administrate the child's property and to represent him or her legally. In this case the holder of parental responsibilities has the duty to consult with the other parent.

(b) Other persons, bodies or competent authorities

There are instances the holder of parental responsibilities has to consult with the competent authority, namely the public guardianship authority, irrespective of whether the parent exercises the parental responsibilities alone or jointly with another parent. The authority's consent is needed for certain issues in connection with the administration of the child's property and for the child's legal representation.

The money and goods of the child, if these do not have to be held in reserve to cover the actual expenses or for other grounds, are to be delivered to the public guardianship authority for the child, according to the Act. A parent can dispose of them only with the public guardianship authority's approval.

The Hungarian Civil Code and the Order of Guardianship enumerates which of the parent's legal declarations need the consent of the public guardianship authority. Generally these are transactions affecting the child's assets, money or maintenance.

IRELAND

(a) The other parent

A parent with sole parental responsibilities does not have to consult the other parent.

(b) Other persons, bodies or competent authorities

A person with sole parental responsibilities does not have to consult other persons, bodies or competent authorities.

ITALY

(a) The other parent

A parent can hold sole parental responsibilities only if the other parent is dead or has been deprived of authority pursuant to Art. 330 Italian CC. (see Q 51) Therefore, the parent holding sole parental responsibilities has full authority to act alone, without the need to consult the other parent.

(b) Other persons, bodies or competent authorities

A parent can hold sole parental responsibilities only if the other parent is dead or has been deprived of parental authority pursuant to Art. 330 Italian CC (see Q 51). Therefore, the parent holding sole parental responsibilities has full authority to act alone, unless there are extraordinary acts of disposition of the minor's property. Then the authorisation of the guardianship judge is needed and in its absence such acts can be voided (Art. 320 Italian CC).

LITHUANIA

(a) The other parent

Yes, he or she has full authority to act alone. He or she has no duty to consult the other parent, because the other parent does not have parental authority.

(b) Other persons, bodies or competent authorities

No, except in those cases where court leave (permission) is obligatory even if both parents have parental authority.

THE NETHERLANDS

(a) The other parent

A parent with sole parental responsibilities has full authority to act alone. However, he/she is under a duty to inform the other parent of important matters as regards the child and the child's estate, and must consult with the other parent on decisions to be taken in this respect (Art. 1:377b § 1 Dutch CC). Consultation does not imply a right of decision.[15] Important matters are, for

[15] S.F.M. WORTMANN, *Losbladige Personen- en familierecht*, Art. 377b, 1. See also District Court Breda 9.7.1996, *NJ*, 1999, 38 where the father unsuccessfully tried to prevent the circumcision of his sons.

instance, school choice, choice of profession, school results, important medical treatment, important matters relating to religious upbringing and the financial situation of the child.[16] If the parents cannot agree on the duty of information and consultation, they may apply to the court for an arrangement (Art. 1:377b § 1 Dutch CC). Only if it would be against the best interests of the child may the court determine – *ex officio*[17] or on the application of the parent with parental responsibilities – that such a duty is not applicable (Art. 1:377b § 2 Dutch CC).[18] The legislation does not provide for a right to information for the child itself in respect to the non-resident parent, which has been criticised in the legal doctrine.[19]

(b) Other persons, bodies or competent authorities

There is no legal provision in this respect. Even a biological or social parent who is not living with the child has no legal right to be informed or consulted by the parent with parental responsibilities, since Art. 1:377b Dutch CC only applies to a legal parent. However, the Supreme Court[20] held that the begetter had a right to information on the basis of Art. 8 ECHR, if he has family life with the child. This also applies to other persons with family life with the child.[21] It is unclear whether a right of consultation could also be based on Art. 8 ECHR.

NORWAY

(a) The other parent

A parent with sole parental responsibilities has full authority to act without consulting the other parent. This includes changing residence to another country.

(b) Other persons, bodies or competent authorities

A parent with sole parental responsibilities has full authority to act without consulting other persons, bodies, or competent authorities.

---

16 ASSER-DE BOER, *Mr. C. Asser's Handleiding tot de beoefening van het Nederlands Burgerlijk Recht. Personen- en Familie Recht*, 2002, No. 1022.

17 The position of the child aged twelve or older, or younger but able to appraise his or her interests, is regulated by Art. 1:377g Dutch CC. The court may *ex officio* terminate the duty to inform and consult the other parent if it appears to the court that the child appreciates this.

18 See for such a decision: Court of Appeal Arnhem 25.11.2003, *LJN*, AO4893, where the father's right on information and consultation was terminated, because the children objected to it.

19 C.M.A. LEENEN, 'Het recht van het kind op informatie over ouders, broers en zussen,' *FJR*, 1999, p. 58-60.

20 See Supreme Court 17.12.1993, *NJ*, 1994, 360.

21 See ASSER-DE BOER, Mr. *C. Asser's Handleiding tot de beoefening van het Nederlands Burgerlijk Recht. Personen- en Familie Recht*, 2002, No. 1022a; M.J.C. KOENS & C.G.M. VAN WAMELEN, *Kind en Scheiding*, 2001, p. 123; S.F.M. WORTMANN, *Losbladige Personen- en familierecht*, Art. 377b, No. 2c.

POLAND

(a) The other parent

No.

(b) Other persons, bodies or competent authorities

No. The principle of general protection is formulated in Art. 109 Polish Family and Guardianship Code by establishing specific court competencies in situations where the wellbeing of the child is endangered.

PORTUGAL

(a) The other parent

The parent that does not exercise parental responsibility has the right to oversee the education and living conditions of the child (Art. 1906 No. 4 Portuguese CC). The custodial parent does not have full freedom of action. His or her actions within the sphere of parental responsibility are subject to the control of the non-custodial parent. However, this does not mean that the custodial parent may only act with the prior agreement of the non-custodial parent. Rather, it means that the right of the non-custodial parent only operates indirectly, through court appeal. The control exercised by the non-custodial parent is thus the power to appeal to the court in order to impugn the actions of the custodial parent, when those actions endanger the child's interests.

(b) Other persons, bodies or competent authorities

For the performance of the acts stipulated in Art. 1889 and 1890 Portuguese CC, the custodial parent requires the permission of the Department of Justice. See Q 12c.

RUSSIA

(a) The other parent

Provided that Russian law always attributes joint parental responsibility to both parents, a parent can have sole parental responsibility only if:

- the other parent has died;
- the parentage of the other parent has never been established;
- the other parent is declared by court to have disappeared;
- the other parental is discharged of the parental responsibility

In all those cases there is no other *de facto* or *de jure* parent to consult.

While executing his or her right to administrate a child's property a parent with sole parental responsibility needs the consent of the Department of Guardianship and Curatorship for entering certain transactions; on the same basis as when parents with joint parental responsibility administrate their child's property (Art. 37 (2) Russian CC).[22]

22 See answer to the Q 12c.

(b) Other persons, bodies or competent authorities

If one of the parents of the child is under age and the parents are not married, the minor parent does not acquire full legal capacity. Family law, however, grants a minor unmarried parent who has reached the age of sixteen full parental responsibility (Art. 62 (2)). This leads to an inconsistency: this person is regarded by civil law as just partially legally capable and is him- or herself under guardianship and not allowed to perform certain legal acts without consent of his or her parents or guardians.[23] Therefore it is difficult to imagine that a minor parent can enter into transactions on behalf of the child that he or she is not allowed to enter on behalf of him- or herself. If the minor unmarried parent is under the age of sixteen, the child must be appointed a guardian until the minor parent reaches the age of sixteen (Art. 62 (2) Russian Family Code). The child's guardian raises the child with the minor parent and represents the child as his or her legal representative. A minor parent under the age of sixteen has the right to live with the child and to participate in the child's upbringing. A minor parent cannot make decisions concerning the child without consulting the child's guardian. Disagreements between the child's guardian and the minor parent are resolved by the Department of Guardianship and Curatorship (Art. 62 (2) Russian Family Code). The law allows but does not require appointing a guardian to a child whose parent is under the age of sixteen. If the child has a second legal parent of full age that has good contact with the minor parent, the appointment of a guardian can be superfluous. In this situation, the child would be educated by the two parents formally holding joint parental responsibility, while the right and duties of one of them would be restricted due to his or her age.

The court can declare one of the parents legally incapable because he or she cannot understand and direct the significance of his or her acts due to a mental disorder (Art. 29 Russian CC). Such a parent will be appointed a guardian. The court can also restrict the legal capacity of a parent if he or she gravely detriments his or her family's financial wellbeing due to alcohol or drug abuse. Such a parent is also appointed a guardian, with a more limited capacity. In both cases the parent does not automatically lose parental responsibility. However, restriction of legal capacity precludes the execution of some parental rights (*e.g.* representation of the child or administration of child's property), because those acts require full legal capacity. Thus the child will have his or her own guardian appointed (Art. 71 (5) and 74 (4) Russian Family Code). A parent who is declared legally incapable or whose legal capacity is restricted cannot make decisions concerning the child without consulting the child's guardian. The guardian would involve the parent in the child's education and raising as far as such involvement is in the best interests of the child. The law does not provide for the resolution of disagreements between the child's guardian and such a parent; however, the rule on resolution of the disputes between the child's guardian and the minor parent of the child (Art. 62 (2) Russian Family Code) can be applied by analogy.

---

23 M. ANTOKOLSKAIA, *Family Law* (*Semeinoe pravo*), Moscow: Jurist, 1999, p. 205-206.

SPAIN

A parent can have sole parental responsibility in four cases:

- because parenthood was established only for that parent or there was a single-person adoption, which is permissible in Spanish Law,
- because parental responsibility was granted only for that parent because the parenthood was resulted from a sexual crime or was established in a judicial procedure which that parent opposed,
- because the other parent was discharged of parental responsibility, or
- because the other parent died or was declared absent or dead.

A parent with sole parental responsibility has full authority to act alone unless a public protection measure has been decreed. However, this might also happen if parental responsibility is held jointly.

SWEDEN

(a) The other parent

A sole custodian, as a rule, has full authority to act alone in all matters concerning the child. If the child has the same surname as the non-custodial parent, the child's surname can only be changed by consent of the non-custodial parent or by decision of a court, Sec. 6 Swedish Act on Names (1982:670). An application by the custodial parent's spouse or registered partner to adopt the child can only be granted after hearing the non-custodial parent (and on condition that all the other conditions for adoption are met), Chapter 4 Sec. 10 para. 3 Swedish Children and Parents Code.

(b) Other persons, bodies or competent authorities

The sole custodian's authority can be limited by the child's own right to decide in certain issues, a right which increases with the child's increasing age and maturity.

SWITZERLAND

(a) The other parent

The parent who is the holder of parental responsibilities has the sole authority to take decisions. Nonetheless, the other parent has the right based on Art. 275a § 1 Swiss CC to be informed about special events in the life of the child and to have their opinion heard prior to decisions which are of special importance for the overall development of the child. However, this does not mean that the parent who has no parental responsibilities has the right to interfere in general in the child's upbringing.

(b) Other persons, bodies or competent authorities

In principle the person who is the sole holder of parental responsibilities may act alone. With regard to the child's property; however, Art. 318 § 2 Swiss CC imposes an obligation to submit an inventory of the child's property to the guardianship authority.

QUESTION 43

E. CONTACT

Having regard to the definition by the Council of Europe (see above), explain the concepts of contact used in your national legal system.

AUSTRIA

Sec. 148 Austrian CC ensures the maintenance of the child's personal contact with his or her parent and other persons who do not live in a common household with the child, but are nevertheless very close to him or her. This so-called visitation right *(Besuchsrecht)* is regarded as a fundamental right in the parent-child relationship.[1]

Regarding the child-parent and child-grandparent(s) relationship, the concerned persons should arrange the exercise of contact by mutual assent. If an agreement cannot be reached, at the request of the child, a parent or grandparent the court will regulate the exercise of contact according to the child's bests interest taking into account the needs and wishes of the child (Sec. 148(1) and (3) Austrian CC). Regarding the child-third person (other person than parent or grandparent) relationship the court will only take action to regulate the exercise of contact, if the interests of the child would be at risk without such contact (Sec. 148(4) Austrian CC).

The extent of the right of contact is not regulated in the law but rather depends on the individual case. The following standards have developed in the case law: the right of contact generally exists twice a month; the intensity and duration of the visit increases with the child's age. Beginning at three years of age, a child can already stay with the other parent for an entire day, while children over six years of age can spend an entire weekend, including an overnight stay, with the other parent.[2] The right to personal contact includes not only visits but also all other forms of communication, such as telephone calls, letters, faxes, e-mail, *etc.*[3]

In addition to the right of contact, the parent who does not hold parental responsibilities also has the right to be informed of important matters

---

1 *E.g., Oberster Gerichtshof,* 11.05.1994, *EFSlg.* 77.972; M. Roth, 'Europäische Menschenrechtskonvention und Privatrecht: Landesbericht Österreich', *Rabels Zeitschrift für ausländisches und internationales Privatrecht (RabelsZ),* 1999, p. 735 with further references.

2 *Landesgericht für Zivilrechtssachen Vienna,* 01.01.1998, *EFSlg.* 86.883 et al.; I. Mottl, 'Umfasst das Besuchsrecht auch Telefonanrufe?', *Österreichischer Amtsvormund,* 1994, pp. 173-174.

3 *Landesgericht für Zivilrechtssachen Vienna,* 27.01.1995, *EFSlg.* 78.007; *Landesgericht für Zivilrechtssachen Vienna,* 30.3.2000, *EFSlg.* 92.939.

concerning the child and to express his or her opinion on the same (Sec. 178 Austrian CC).

BELGIUM

The concept of contact refers to the right for certain adults to have contact with a child on a regular basis. This contact can consist of hosting the child, letting it reside during limited periods, paying it a visit, writing it, calling it or sending it by mail or e-mail.

BULGARIA

The Bulgarian Family Code uses the term 'personal relations' rather then 'contact'. 'Personal relations' means 'the relations between the child and the parent who does not live with the child'.[4] The law does not establish forms of personal relations thus leaving this to the discretion of the court. As for case law - '... the ways and the forms of personal relations could be various. Seeing the child and taking the child are inseparable parts of maintaining personal relations.'[5] Courts are instructed to provide a sufficiently detailed description of terms/conditions so as to avoid conflicts and disputes between the parents. Court practice has adopted various forms of contact: personal, through letters and postcards, by phone. Since the adoption of the Bulgarian Child Protection Act, contact under the supervision of a social worker has been possible.

CZECH REPUBLIC

If the child's parents do not cohabit, regardless of being divorced, married or the child being born out of wedlock, the form of contact of the parent who does not live with the child in a common household is not regulated by the Czech Family Code and it is up to the parents to reach a contact agreement. Only if the parents are not able to agree will the court determine the extent of the child's contact with the other parent. The extent of the contact depends on the child's age, the distance of the other parent's residence and a number of other individual circumstances. A typical judicial regulation of contact between a child and parent is to allow contact every other week-end (either from Friday until Sunday, or one day only), a week or two weeks during summer holidays, one day during Christmas holidays and one day during Easter holidays.

DENMARK

The Danish concept is *samvær* which is best translated as contact. It typically encompasses the child staying with the parent with whom he/she does not live for a certain amount of time. It may also encompass other forms of contact such as correspondence by letter or telephone conversations. A parent who has no parental authority has the right to obtain information about the child from schools, childcare institutions, health and social authorities, private hospitals, doctors and dentists, Art. 19(1) Danish Act on Parental Authority and Contact.

---

4 See L. NENOVA, *Family Law of the Republic of Bulgaria*, Sofia 1994, p. 640.

5 Decision of the Supreme Court, (Civil Division) 1-1974, § 4 § 2.

ENGLAND & WALES

The English concept of contact very much accords with that embraced by the Council of Europe both in its White Paper and, more especially, in its 2003 Convention on Contact Concerning Children (ETS 192). According to Sec. 8(1), English Children Act 1989 a contact order

> 'means an order requiring the person with whom the child lives, or is to live, to allow the child to visit or stay with the person named in the order, or for that person and the child otherwise to have contact with each other'.

In general terms contact orders provide for the child to visit or stay with the person named in the order the emphasis thus being on the child rather than parent. Contact orders embrace both physical and non-physical contact and may therefore range from long or short visits to contact by letter or telephone.[6] Indirect contact can also be by email or even video recording.[7]

Orders may provide for the child to have contact with any person (including, where appropriate, a sibling) and more than one contact order may be made in respect of a child. A contact order can be the sole order even between parents and may be appropriate where there is no dispute as to the person with whom the child is to live. Orders can provide for contact to take place at Contact Centres. The role of these Centres has been said[8] to be 'one of the most important developments of the last ten years'. They are useful as a means of providing a temporary venue for supported contact in cases where the parents are unable to provide an alternative. Orders can also provide for contact to take place abroad.[9] Contact orders requiring one parent to allow the child to visit the other parent[10] will automatically lapse if the parents subsequently live together

---

6 For examples of contact by post see *Re P (minors)(contact: discretion)* [1999] 1 FCR 566, *A v L (Contact)* [1998] 1 FLR 361 and *Re M (Contact: Conditions)* [1994] 1 FLR 272, each involving letter contact with a father in prison; *Re P (Contact: Indirect Contact)* [1999] 2 FLR 893 indirect contact with a father who had just been released from prison: *Re L (Contact: Transsexual Applicant)* [1995] 2 FLR 438 – indirect contact with a transsexual father; *Re D (Parental Responsibility: IVF Baby)* [2001] EWCA Civ 230, [2001] 1 FLR 972, CA, indirect contact with a man deemed to be the father under the Human Fertilisation and Embryology Act 1990, ss 28(3) and 29(1B). For examples of indirect contact being ordered with violent or abusive parents, see *Re S (Violent Parent: Indirect Contact)* [2000] 1 FLR 481, *Re H (Contact: Domestic Violence)* [1998] 2 FLR 42, CA and *Re M (Sexual Abuse Allegations: Interviewing Techniques)* [1999] 2 FLR 92.

7 See 'Indirect Contact via Video-tape' [1997] Fam Law 310, which might be a particularly useful way of re-establishing contact'.

8 See *Making Contact Work* (A Report to the Lord Chancellor by the Advisory Board on Family Law, Children Act Sub-Committee, 2002), Ch 8.

9 *Re F (A Minor)(Access Out Of Jurisdiction)* [1973] Fam 198.

10 Note: if the order is directed against someone other than a parent or if the child is permitted contact with a third party it will not lapse because of the parents' cohabitation.

for a continuous period of more than six months.[11] While the child is with a parent on a contact visit that parent may exercise parental responsibility, at any rate with respect to short-term matters, without consulting the other provided he does nothing that is incompatible with any existing court order (see Q 37).

FINLAND

There are two concepts that can be taken into account. The first, and arguably more important concept is the child's right of access to its parents according to the Finnish Child Custody and the Right of Access Act (private law). The second concept, provided by the Finnish Child Protection Act (public law), is the child's right to maintain contact with persons close to the child. This concept concerns a child who has been taken into the care of the local social authority.

The child has a right of access, which encompasses the right to meet and keep contact with the parent with whom the child does not live with (Sec. 2 Finnish Child Custody and the Right of Access Act). The Enforcement Act gives the non-residential parent the ability to ask for the child's right of access to be enforced if the child's custodian does not allow the non-residential parent to meet with the child. The enforcement is given because the right of access determined in a parental agreement has been approved by the social local authority or in a court decision.

A child who has been voluntarily placed in substitute care or has been taken into care of the authority has the right to meet and keep in touch with its parents and other persons close to it (Sec. 24 Finnish Child Protection Act). The local social authority can for, safety or security reasons, decide upon restrictions concerning this right of a child who has been taken into care of the authority (Sec. 25 Finnish Child Protection Act).[12] The decision of the local social authority is subject to appeal in the administrative court.

FRANCE

If both parents are holders of parental responsibilities but do not have the joint exercise of parental responsibilities, the parent who is not in charge of this exercise has contact rights called *droit de visite et d'hébergement*. The parent cannot be deprived of this right except for serious reasons, see Art. 373-2-1 French CC. He or she keeps the right and the duty to supervise the child's maintenance and education and shall be informed of all important choices in the child's life.

Contact rights encompass visiting and lodging rights. The court takes the child's behaviour into account when determining the exercise of these rights,[13]

---

11 Sec. 11(6), English Children Act 1989.

12 A director of a childcare institution can make a decision with effects for a maximum length of one month (Sec. 9 para. 2 Finnish Child Protection Decree).

13 See French Supreme Court, Civ. II, 23.05.1984, *Gaz. Pal.* 1985. 1. Pan. 69 annotated GRIMALDI.

but the judge will not delegate his power to decide what is in the child's best interests when it comes to the exercise of contact rights.[14] In order to guarantee the effectiveness of contact rights the court is allowed to pronounce an *astreinte* (civil fine) against the parent with whom the child lives.[15]

Only very serious reasons can justify the deprivation of a parent's contact rights if a parent does not have the exercise of parental responsibilities. That the children do not wish to see their father again is not a sufficient reason for a deprivation of contact rights.[16] The family judge of the tribunal of Paris[17] has decided that for a husband who claimed a contact right with the children, his violent behaviour was a reason enough to deny him such a right. Another judicial decision suspended the lodging right of the father because he placed moral and psychological religious pressure on the child (the father wanted the daughter to wear the Islamic veil).[18]

GERMANY

Contact (*Umgang*) means access to the child. This kind of contact is factual. It can be realised through different means, especially personal contacts, visits and stays (weekend-visits, holidays, day-visits *etc.*).[19] It can also be effected via telephone, letters, e-mail *etc.*[20] Contact is often limited in time (see Q 47). The right to contact is a separate legal position based on the natural right of parents and protected by Art. 6 para. 2 German Basic Law.[21] Today it is accepted that there exists not only a right of the parent, but also a duty of the parent to contact, § 1684 para. 1 German CC. Contact is also a right of the child. The statute, however, does not mention that the child has a duty to contact, see § 1684 para. 1 German CC. As a rule the rights and duties to contact exist irrespective of who actually holds parental care. A parent who is not entitled to personal custody nevertheless retains the right to personal contact (*persönlicher Umgang*) with his or her child (§ 1684 para. 1 German CC). He or she may also demand information about the personal condition of the child, in so far as this is compatible with the child's welfare (§ 1686 German CC). This right to

---

14 French Supreme Court, Civ. II, 07.10.1987, *Bull. civ.* II, no. 190; 22.10.1997, *Bull. civ.* II, No. 255.

15 CA Rennes, 18.03.1982, *D* 1983. IR. 449. If the parent with whom the child lives does not allow the other parent to make use of his contact rights he will have to pay this civil fine to the parent having contact rights.

16 French Supreme Court, Civ. II, 29.04.1998, *Bull. civ.* II, No. 133.

17 TGI Paris, 16.07.1976, *JCP* 1976. II. 18502.

18 French Supreme Court, Civ. I, 24.10.2000, *Bul. Civ.* I, No. 262.

19 P. FINGER, in: *Münchener Kommentar,* 4th Edition, München: Beck, 2002, § 1684 German CC No. 21.

20 U. DIEDERICHSEN, in: PALANDT, *Bürgerliches Gesetzbuch,* 64th Edition, München: Beck, 2005, § 1684 German CC No. 2.

21 T. RAUSCHER, in: STAUDINGER, *Kommentar zum Bürgerlichen Gesetzbuch,* 13th Edition, Berlin: Gruyter, 2000, § 1684 German CC No. 62.

information also exists independently of the right of parental care and the right of contact.[22]

GREECE

The right to contact is regulated in Art. 1520 Greek CC. This right is not included in the concept of parental care, but is a distinct right stemming from the ties of kindred between the child and its family.[23] Nevertheless, contact relates to the physical care of the child.[24] Thus, the provision in Art. 1520 Greek CC gains practical significance for the parent to whom the court has not attributed such parental responsibilities. The concept of contact encompasses personal or telephone communication, correspondence, the offer of a gift, or any other kind of modern communication[25] and it can also be realised through a third person.[26]

HUNGARY

The concept of the contact is the following: there are two main types of contact in Hungarian law and legal practice: in one, the non-custodial parent and this parent's relatives maintain contact with a child who lives with the other parent, and in the other case the parents and other relatives maintain contact with the child who is taken out of the family and put into state care. This has great importance both for the child living apart from one or both of her or his parents and for the parent living apart from the child. The issues of contact are regulated partially in the Family Act and partly in the Order of Guardianship. The non-custodial parent's right to contact is regulated primarily in the Family Act, but the particulars are contained in the Order of Guardianship. The Order of Guardianship also emphasises the contact between the child and his or her grandparents, his or her brother or sister who has reached majority and also the

---

22 U. DIEDERICHSEN, in: PALANDT, *Bürgerliches Gesetzbuch*, 64th Edition, München: Beck, 2005, § 1686 German CC No. 1.

23 S. KOUKOULI-SPILIOTOPOULOU, in: A. GEORGIADIS and M. STATHOPOULOS (eds.), *Civil Code commentary, Vol. VIII, Family Law (Arts. 1505-1694)*, 2nd Edition, Athens: Law & Economy, P. N. SAKKOULAS, 2003, p. 70, No. 154, with further references.

24 S. KOUKOULI-SPILIOTOPOULOU, in: A. GEORGIADIS and M. STATHOPOULOS (eds.), *Civil Code commentary, Vol. VIII, Family Law (Arts. 1505-1694)*, 2nd Edition, Athens: Law & Economy, P. N. SAKKOULAS, 2003, Introductory Remarks on Art. 1505-1541 Greek CC, p. 74, No. 159 [in Greek]; A. POULIADIS, in: A. GEORGIADIS and M. STATHOPOULOS (eds.), *Civil Code commentary, Vol. VIII, Family Law (Arts. 1505-1694)*, 2nd Edition, Athens: Law & Economy, P.N. SAKKOULAS, 2003, Art. 1520 Greek CC, p. 308-309, No. 16.

25 A. POULIADIS, in: A. GEORGIADIS and M. STATHOPOULOS (eds.), *Civil Code commentary, Vol. VIII, Family Law (Arts. 1505-1694)*, 2nd Edition, Athens: Law & Economy, P.N. SAKKOULAS, 2003, Art. 1520 Greek CC, p. 310-311, No. 19-26.

26 A relevant example is where the parent sends a good friend to visit the child on his or her behalf. This may be crucial when the parent lives far away and the child is very young, so that other means of contact are not satisfactory. See E. KOUNOUGERI-MANOLEDAKI, *Family Law*, Vol. II, 3rd Edition, Athens-Thessaloniki: SAKKOULAS, 2003, p. 297.

contact between the child and the parent's spouse and the child's aunts and uncles.

The aim of the contact is to maintain the personal and familiar relationship between the child and the parent and the child's other close relatives that have a right to contact and to allow the other parent that ability to continuously watch the development of the child and be supportive of the child. The forms of the contact are: the continuous and periodical contact with the right to remove the child from the child's residence and the duty to return the child back to the child's residence, meeting the child at the child's residence and other forms of communication, such as correspondence, telephone-connection, presentation and sending a package. Continuous contact means regular contact (*e.g.* in every second week-end), periodical contact means irregular contact (*e.g.* two weeks in the summer holiday).

IRELAND

The concept of contact (access) as used in Ireland may be described as a right and duty of visitation, allowing the person having access to visit with and communicate with a child on a temporary basis. The court will consider an application for access on the basis that the best interests of the child are of paramount consideration. Recent Irish legislation reinforces the duty upon the Irish courts to consider all matters of access primarily by reference to what is in the child's best interests. Sec. 9 Irish Children Act 1997 added a new Sec. 11D to the Irish Guardianship of Infants Act 1964 which requires that the court, in considering making any contact order, have regard to whether the child's best interests would be promoted by maintaining personal relations and direct contact with both his or her father and mother on a regular basis. The Irish legislature regards access to both parents as invariably being in the best interests of a child. It is, indeed, exceptionally uncommon for an application for access to be refused. The case of *A.MacB. v. A.G.MacB.*[27] exemplifies the strong judicial tendency in favour of granting access. There, a father was granted access to his children despite strong evidence that the children were afraid of him. This was despite the additional fact that the father was alleged to have caused malicious damage to property. BARRON J., nonetheless, considered that it was 'essential that the children know that they have a father and … that their father is able to take the place of a father in their lives.'[28]

ITALY

The Italian system recognises the minor's right to have enduring, steady and serene contacts with both parents even if there are marital problems or their cohabitation ends. The Italian legal system considers contact with the parent who does not reside with the child to be a minor's fundamental right. This concept is broader than the one defined in the EC Regulation No. 2201/2003, as

---

27 High Court, 06.06.1984.

28 *Ibid* at page 13.

it includes the right to meet the child and take him or her to a place other than the child's habitual abode for a limited period of time.

Such contact is also a right and duty of a parent who does not have custody or live with the child (Art. 155 § 2 Italian CC and Art. 6 § 3 Italian Divorce law). Since this parent maintains parental responsibilities (even if they are exercised differently from the parent that resides with the child), she or he also keeps the fundamental right and duty to have a relationship with the child. The non-residential parent can only maintain the relationship through frequent and constant contacts, which also discharges the parent's obligation to supervise and to cooperate with the growth of the child and with the child's education and moral guidance. The contact is a primary obligation of the parent, to be observed in the moral and material interests of the child even before it constitutes a parental right.[29]

Maintaining continuous, permanent and untroubled contacts with both parents is in the interests of the minor. Because the peaceful growth of the child requires both parents, the right and duty of contact is recognised even in the absence of a specific judicial order. Judges tend to describe the conditions of visitation in a precise and clear way in order to help the non-residential parent exercise this right and in order to avoid additional sources of friction with the other parent.[30] The parent the child lives with must permit the non-residential parent to exercise visiting rights within the limits of the interests of the minor, which prevail if there is a conflict over the parental rights (see Q 47). The visiting right generally implies frequent and regular meetings with the minor (usually once a week as well as every other weekend); moreover the non-residential parent has the right and duty to keep the child for specific periods during the year (for example during the holiday seasons and the summer holidays).

Even in the absence of a precise provision of law the judge can also prohibit or grant visiting rights to other relatives (such as the grandparents, the brothers or the sisters) if this is in the child's interests (see Q 44c).

LITHUANIA

The right of contact is a personal right of the parent who lives separately from the child to see the child, to communicate with the child, and to be involved in the child's education. On the other hand, this is also a personal right of a child whose parents are separated to have constant and direct contact with both parents irrespective of their place of residence (Art. 3.170 Lithuanian CC). The father or the mother with whom the child resides may not interfere with the other parent's contact with the child. The right to contact also includes the right of the father or mother who lives separately from the child to receive

29 G. F. BASINI, *Lo scioglimento del matrimonio,* sub *art. 6 L. 898/70,* in *Il Codice Civile. Commentario* founded by P. SCHLESINGER and directed by F.D. BUSNELLI, Giuffrè, Milan, 2004, p. 742.

30 Supreme Court, 03.05.1986, No. 3013, *Mass. Giust.,* 1986, p. 850.

information about the child from all the institutions and authorities concerned with the child's education, training, health care, protection of the child's rights *etc.*[31]

Parents may also maintain contact and be involved in the education of a child who is placed in a special situation (detention, arrest, imprisonment, in-patient clinic *etc.*) in the procedure laid down by special laws (Art. 3.171 Lithuanian CC).

THE NETHERLANDS

Contact (*omgang*) is a general and legal term (Art. 1:377a Dutch CC) used for any form of contact, either physical or by means of telephone, e-mail *etc.* The term contact refers both to contact between a parent and a minor and contact between other adults/minors with a minor child, if the child normally lives with another person (parent/other person). Art. 8 ECHR and the interpretation thereof in the case law of the European Committee and the European Court of Human Rights have had a great influence in this field of law.[32] Contact has to be distinguished from the right to information and consultation, for which other provisions apply (Art. 1:377b and c Dutch CC).

NORWAY

The concept of contact in Art. 42 sec. 1 Norwegian Children Act 1981 is expressed as follows: 'The child has the right of access to both parents, even if they live apart. The parents have mutual responsibility for implementing the right of access.' The child is entitled to care and consideration from the parent the child is with, Art. 42 sec. 2.

POLAND

There is no specific regulation on this. Personal contact with a child is covered by the more general regulation of Art. 95 § 1 Polish Family and Guardianship Code *i.e.* the parents' duty and right to exercise custody over the child and the child's property. According to Art. 96 Polish Family and Guardianship Code, the parents raise and guide the child under their parental authority. Personal contact with the child is necessary to exercise those rights and fulfil those duties.

Polish law emphasises that the parents' personal contact with the child may only be prohibited in exceptional cases *e.g.* when it poses a danger to the child's life, health, or safety, or may demoralise the child[33]

31 Supreme Court of Lithuania, 27.11.2002, case *F.Baskiene v. V. Miniotas*, www.lat.lt

32 ASSER-DE BOER, Mr. C. *Asser's Handleiding tot de beoefening van het Nederlands Burgerlijk Recht. Personen- en Familie Recht*, 2002 No. 1004; M.J.C. KOENS & C.G.M. VAN WAMELEN, *Kind en scheiding*, 2001, p. 82-83.

33 Supreme Court judgment of 07.07.2000, I CKN 1115/00.

PORTUGAL

Today, the right of contact in the context of a divorce or legal separation is understood very broadly. It consists of the right of the non-custodial parent to relate to and spend time with the child, not only through occasional contacts but also by providing accommodation for the child for short periods of time (such as weekends, holidays) and by corresponding with the child (by letter, e-mail, telephone, or through an intermediary).

RUSSIA

The concept of contact encompasses the mutual rights of the child, and the parent who is living apart from the child and the other relatives of the child to maintain personal relationships with each other.

SPAIN

Spanish law uses the concept of access (*derecho de visita*) rather than contact, whereas Catalan law establishes a right to maintain personal relationships (*dret de relacionar-se personalment*). However, the difference is more a difference in terminology because both concepts include a right to visit, that is: to temporarily see the child without the other parental responsibility holder's presence, a right to communicate with the child by post, phone, electronically or by other means and a right to stay with the child at the place (his or her domicile, a hotel) chosen by the person having contact rights *vis a vis* the child.

Contact is described in case law and legal writing as both a right and a duty that is subordinate to the child's best interests. An agreement whereby one parent renounces his or her right and duty to maintain a personal relationship with the child is not permissible. The exercise of access cannot be delegated to a third party, such as the grandparents.

SWEDEN

Rules on contact were first introduced into Swedish law in 1915, the purpose being to ensure, by court order, the non-custodial parent's right to see the child. The concept of contact in modern Swedish law focuses on the child's need to close and good contact with both parents, Chapter 6 Sec. 2a Swedish Children and Parents Code. The child's need of contact with relatives and other important persons in the child's life is also to be met. The interests of a parent are not explicitly considered when deciding in contact issues.[34] It is the best interests of the child that shall prevail over all other concerns in matters regarding contact. The child's own wishes shall be taken into account, increasingly with the increasing age and maturity of the child.

Basically the same approach also prevails in legislation protecting children. When a child is placed in care in another home, the social welfare committee

---

[34] *Vårdnad, Boende och Umgänge*, Stockholm: Socialstyrelsen (National Board of Health and Welfare), 2003, p. 74.

has the duty to ensure, as far as possible, that the child's need of contact with parents and custodians is met, Sec. 14 Swedish Care of Young Persons Act.[35]

SWITZERLAND

Parents who do not have parental responsibilities or custody mutually share a right with the child to adequate personal contact (Art. 273 § 1 Swiss CC). This right does not require the parent in question to have any parental responsibilities; it is a right to which every parent who has no custody rights is entitled.

35 See also: Chapter 6 Sec. 1 and 5 Swedish Social Services Act (2001:453).

QUESTION 44

E. CONTACT

To what extent, if at all, does the child have a right of contact with:
(a) A parent holding parental responsibilities but not living with the child;
(b) A parent not holding parental responsibilities;
(c) Persons other than parents (*e.g.* grandparents, step-parents, siblings *etc*)?

AUSTRIA

(a) A parent holding parental responsibilities but not living with the child

Pursuant to Sec. 148 Austrian CC, a child has a right of contact with a parent who does not live in the same household with the child, irrespective of whether this parent holds parental responsibilities or not.[1]

(b) A parent not holding parental responsibilities

The child has the same right to personal contact with a parent not holding parental responsibilities as with a parent holding parental responsibilities, but not living in the same household with the child (Sec. 148(1) Austrian CC).[2]

In addition to this right to contact, the parent who does not hold parental responsibilities also has the right to be informed and the right to express his or her opinion (Sec. 178 (1) sentence 1 Austrian CC). These rights concern the important matters of Sec. 154 (2) and (3) Austrian CC (*e.g.* language-course vacations abroad, a change of school, graduation from school or vocational training, marriage, serious illnesses or accidents, alcohol or drug addiction, or the like)[3] and are closely related to the actual exercise of contact: The less regularly the parent not holding parental responsibilities has personal contact with the child (despite that parent's willingness to have such contact), the more extensive the parent's right to be informed and to express his or her opinion will be, and these rights may be extended to less important matters concerning the child (Sec. 178 (1) sentence 2 Austrian CC). Thus, for example, the father may also personally obtain information from the doctor or teachers regarding the welfare of his child if he does not learn about these matters promptly or within a reasonable time from the mother holding parental responsibilities (*e.g.* with respect to the child's specific end-of-the-year report cards, recreational activities, athletic achievements, circle of friends, *etc*).[4]

---

1 For details see Q 43; G. WALLISCH, 'Der andere Elternteil und das Besuchsrecht', *Österreichische Juristenzeitung*, 2002, p. 487.

2 For details see Q 43.

3 See Q 37.

4 P. HAIDENTHALLER, 'Schwerpunkte der Kindschaftsrechts-Reform 2001', *Juristische Blätter*, 2001, pp. 628-630; U. Aichhorn, *Das Recht der Lebenpartnerschaften*, Vienna/New York: Springer Verlag, 2003, p. 83.

(c) Persons other than parents (e.g. grandparents, stepparents, siblings *etc*)

The child also has a right of contact with his or her grandparents.[5] However, if the exercise of this right disturbs the family life of the parent(s) or their relationship with child, it must be restricted or prohibited (Sec. 148 (3) Austrian CC).

The child may also be granted personal contact with third parties to whom he or she has close emotional ties if interrupting the contact would be disadvantageous to the child (Sec. 148(4) Austrian CC). In this manner the child's contact with a stepparent(s), foster parent(s), and also with a former partner of the parent holding parental responsibilities, as well as with siblings, aunts, uncles, godparents, etc. can be established or maintained, even against the will of the parental responsibilities holder. The right of contact with third parties does not depend on a kinship relationship. Entitled to petition the court are the child's parents, the youth welfare agency, and the child him or herself, but not the third party; also the third party is not entitled to standing as a party in the contact proceedings. However, the court may take action *ex officio*.

BELGIUM

(a) A parent holding parental responsibilities but not living with the child

Basically, the child has the right of contact with both of its parents, regardless of whether both parents exercise the parental responsibilities. Both parents may work out every thinkable system of contact between a child and themselves. If no agreement can be reached by the parents, the competent authority will design a contact-scheme at the request of one of the parents or at the request of the Public Prosecutor.[6] It can also work out every thinkable scheme. The decisive factor will be the interests of the child.

(b) A parent not holding parental responsibilities

Unless there are exceptional reasons to the contrary, a child has the right of contact with a parent, even when the parent does not hold any parental responsibilities. These exceptional reasons are interpreted very strictly. A parent that has been discharged, will only have a right of contact when it can be proven that it is in the interests of the child to see the parent and the child has a significant, affectionate relationship with the parent. This right of contact is based on Art. 375 *bis* Belgian CC. (See Q 53).

(c) Persons other than parents (*e.g.* grandparents, step-parents, siblings *etc*)

According to Art. 375 *bis* Belgian CC, a child has the right of contact with its grandparents when it is proved that it is in the child's interests. For all other persons (including brothers and sisters of the child), it must also be proved that

---

5 See also Q 43.

6 See Q 61a for the competence of the Public Prosecutor.

the child has a significant, affectionate relationship with the persons seeking the right.[7]

BULGARIA

(a) A parent holding parental responsibilities but not living with the child

It is difficult to discuss the personal right of the child to contact a parent given the lack of any explicit rights of children in relation to parents, except for the right to support as provided by the Bulgarian Family Code. On the other hand, it is admitted that the child has an indisputable interest in the contact with the non-custodial parent. In spite of the lack of regulation, theory and judicial practice have always placed an emphasis on the interests of the child in contact with the parent. The interests of the child matter not only in the arrangement of contact, but also in the substantiation of its rejection: '...the interests of the child have priority to those of its parents', and where these interests so require, contact will not be adjudicated other than in the order of exception.[8] During the 1950s and the 1960s, the court ruled both in favour of the contact with both parents as they were deemed 'necessary for the strengthening of the relations between themselves, and the nourishment of the love and respect needed',[9] and for the denial of contact between the child and its parent, where there was risk that the parent would harm the child.[10] At the end of the 1970s, the court even started to state: 'contact is the right of the child to communicate with the other parent... and it satisfies the child's need to communicate with both parents'.[11]

(b) A parent not holding parental responsibilities

At this stage, two hypotheses must be discussed: when a person has no parental rights and obligations because no origin has been established in relation to him or her and when a parent has been deprived of parental rights and obligations.

De facto family relations are not recognised as a basis for contact arrangements. A person claiming to be a parent but without established parentage can not claim for contact with the child. When a parent has been deprived of parental rights, the court, at its own discretion, may rule on measures for personal relations between that parent and the child. As the Art. 76 Bulgarian Family Code sets forth: 'In all cases of restriction or depriving of parental rights the court also decrees the measures for the personal relations between the parents

---

7 A. De Wolf, *Artikelsgewijze commentaar met ovezricht van rechtspraak en rechtsleer personen- en familierecht* (Art. 375 *bis* Belgian CC), Antwerp:Maklu, 1997, p. 1-21.

8 L. Nenova, *Family Law of the Republic of Bulgaria*, Sofia, 1994, p. 641.

9 See Decision of the Supreme Court, 2021-1960.

10 See Decision of the Supreme Court, 189-1959: – the father is in prison and suffers from a nervous disorder; and Case 3314-1959: the father has abandoned the pregnant mother and has not seen the child for 10 years. Contact is rejected where the behaviour of the parent jeopardises the personal integrity, the upbringing or the health of the child, Case 758-1973 (Civil Division).

11 Case 3717-1979 (Civil Division).

and the children.' In this case, according to legal theory the court is entitled to rule against contact if it is not in the interests of the child.[12]

(c) Persons other than parents (*e.g.* grandparents, step-parents, siblings *etc*)

The right of grandparents to contact with the child is comparatively new for Bulgarian family law, irrespective that the Supreme Court announced its recognition of this right as early as 1957 (Decision 47/1957). The Bulgarian Family Code of 1985 created the provision of Art. 70 § 2, according to which: 'The grandfather and grandmother are entitled to personal relations with their grandchildren who are minor. Where there are obstacles in the way of maintaining personal relations, the district court at the place of residence of the grandchildren, will, at the request of the grandfather or the grandmother, decree measures for personal relations with their grandchildren, except where this is not in the interests of the children.'

This right may only be brought through a judicial claim procedure if the contacts are being hampered. The competent court is the District Court at the permanent residence of the grandchildren. The contact is ruled by the court in a manner similar to the contact with the non-resident parent in a divorce. The court may refuse to arrange the contact if this is in the interest of the child.

No legal regulation exists for stepparents, nor may the court review the matter. The right to contact between siblings is realised by their placement together after the divorce. The Supreme Court generally requires all children to be placed with the same parent. Separate placement of the children is admissible only by exception, where required by overriding circumstances which affect the children's interests. These may be: a big difference in their age, lack of mutual interests and affiliation, long-lasting separate life, or hatred of one of the parents. If separation of the children is needed, the court has to settle the contacts in such a manner that the children meet when parents contact each other.[13]

CZECH REPUBLIC

(a) A parent holding parental responsibilities but not living with the child

If the child's parents do not cohabit, regardless of them being divorced, married or the child being born out of wedlock, the form of contact of the parent who does not live with the child in a common household is not regulated by the Family Code and it is up to the parents to agree on the contact. Only if the parents are not able to agree will the court determine the extent of the child's contact with the other parent. A typical judicial regulation of the contact between the child and the non-custodial parent is to allow contact every other week-end, one to four weeks during summer holidays, one day during Christmas holidays and one day during Easter holidays.

---

12 L. NENOVA, *Family Law of the Republic of Bulgaria*, Sofia, 1994, p. 641.

13 Cases 1-1974, 1601-1972, 535-1977, 3980-1981.

(b) A parent not holding parental responsibilities

The parent not holding parental responsibility does not have the right of contact with the child.

(c) Persons other than parents (*e.g.* grandparents, step-parents, siblings *etc*)

On the basis of the 1998 family law reform the court may regulate the child's contact with grandparents and siblings, if regulation is needed for the interests of the child or due to the family situation (Sec. 27 § 4 Czech Family Code). The extent of the contact will depend on the child's age and particular circumstances but it is usually narrower than the contact allowed between the parent and the child.

DENMARK

(a) A parent holding parental responsibilities but not living with the child

The child's right to contact with both parents is sought to be maintained by allowing the parent to have a right of contact. The child has no right of contact. A parent who does not live with the child has a right of contact, Art. 16 Danish Act on Parental Authority and Contact. It is not relevant if that parent has parental authority or not.

(b) A parent not holding parental responsibilities

The child's right to contact with both parents is sought to be maintained by allowing the parent to have a right of contact. The child has no right of contact. A parent who does not live with the child has a right of contact, Art. 16 Danish Act on Parental Authority and Contact. It is not relevant if that parent has parental authority or not.

(c) Persons other than parents (*e.g.* grandparents, step-parents, siblings *etc*)

In Denmark only parents have a right of contact with their children. No provisions provide for the possibility of contact with other family members irrespective of the role they may have played in the child's life. Grandparents, aunts, uncles, step-parents or siblings who may have played an active role in the child's life or even have raised the child for a considerable time, have no right of contact. A step-parent recently made a request for contact. The administrative authorities as well as the administrative appeal authority *Civilretsdirektorat* denied the request because Art. 8 of the ECHR, which has been incorporated into Danish law by an Act, "did not empower the administration to make a decision on contact".[14] The issue of contact rights to persons other than parents has been considered by various Danish Commissions preparing legislation in the field of parental authority and contact legislation and this has been rejected, not because it was not seen as important

---

14 *Civilretsdirektoratet*, 14.05.2001, No. 2000-540-2707, *Tidsskrift for famile- og arveret*, 2001, p. 500.

for a child to have contact with close relatives, but because contact was only seen to be in the best interests of the child when it is arranged in accordance with the parent who has parental authority. Further, it was stressed that more controlled contact arrangements may result in hesitation as it may be difficult for the child to have normal leisure time when he/she has to use up many weekends in order to meet the requirements of several contact arrangements.[15]

ENGLAND & WALES

(a) A parent holding parental responsibilities but not living with the child

Although the British Human Rights Act 1998 directly incorporates into English domestic law the European Convention on Human Rights, and consequently promotes the idea of rights, traditionally English law has tended to eschew developing Family Law in terms of rights and still has a tendency to think and develop in terms of remedies. Hence, although there are cases which talk about a child's "right" of contact with each of his parents[16] the general approach is to consider the issue of denying contact between a child and a parent on an individual case by case basis and according to the particular child's welfare. That said, denying contact between a child and a parent is regarded as a very serious issue. As BUTLER-SLOSS LJ pointed out in *Re R (A Minor)(Contact)*,[17] the principle of continued contact is underlined by Art. 9(1), United Nations Convention on the Rights of the Child 1989 and endorsed in the English Children Act 1989. Furthermore as the European Court of Human Rights held in *Glaser v UK*,[18] Art. 8, Human Rights Convention 'includes a right for a parent to have measures taken with a view to his or her being reunited with the child and an obligation of national authorities to take measures' both in public and private law proceedings. However, the court also acknowledged that the obligation of national authorities to take measures to facilitate contact by a non-custodial parent after divorce was not absolute and that where it might appear to threaten the child's interests or interfere with his or her Art. 8 rights, it was for those authorities 'to strike a fair balance between them'.

The general approach, established by *Re H (Minors)(Access)*,[19] is for the judge to ask himself whether there are cogent reasons why the child should be denied contact with a parent. It has since been said to be helpful to cast the relevant principles into the framework of the welfare checklist, namely, to consider whether the fundamental need of every child to have an enduring relationship with both parents is outweighed by the depth of harm that, might thereby be caused.[20]

---

15 Commission report 1279/94, p. 125-127

16 See *M v M (Child: Access)* [1973] 2 All ER 81. See also Sec. 34, English Children Act 1989 which provides: "Where a child is in the care of a local authority, the authority shall (subject to the provisions of this section) allow the child reasonable contact with [*inter alia*] his parents'.

17 [1993] 2 FLR 762 at 767.

18 [2001] 1 FLR 148 at 168.

19 [1992] 1 FLR 148 at 152C, per BALCOMBE LJ, CA.

20 *Re M (Contact)* [1995] 1 FLR 274, CA.

(b) A parent not holding parental responsibilities

In principle the same approach applies with regard to contact regardless of whether the parents are married to each other and regardless of whether the father has parental responsibility.[21] In other words, as the answer to Q 44a shows, it is necessary to establish why in the child's interests some form of contact should not be granted. Nevertheless in practice it might be easier to persuade a court to deny contact to an unmarried father particularly where he does not have parental responsibility.[22]

(c) Persons other than parents (*e.g.* grandparents, step-parents, siblings *etc*)

There is no presumption of contact either with step-parents[23] or with grandparents[24] and consequently in these cases it will have to be shown to be in the child's interests to preserve contact.

There is no direct authority on the position of contact between siblings though provided there is a meaningful relationship between them the court would be reluctant to cut off contact between them, though ultimately the issue will be determined according to the children's welfare.[25]

FINLAND

(a) A parent holding parental responsibilities but not living with the child

In legal terms the custodial position of the non-residential parent makes no difference regarding the child's right of access. In practice, non-residential parents who have joint custody seem to meet with their children more than parents without custodial rights.

(b) A parent not holding parental responsibilities

The child has an equal right to meet its non-residential parent who does not have custody as with a parent who is its custodian, as explained above.

---

21 See also Sec. 34, English Children Act 1989, under which notwithstanding a care order, there is a presumption of reasonable contact with the parents (See 'Indirect Contact via Video-tape' [1997] Fam Law 310, which might be a particularly useful way of re-establishing contact'), no distinction is made between those with or without parental responsibility.

22 See *e.g.* the comment at [1994] Fam Law 484.

23 *Re H (A Minor)(Contact)* [1994] 2 FLR 776. Cf *Re C (A Minor)(Access)* [1992] 1 FLR 309, CA.

24 *Re A (Section 8 Order: Grandparent Application)* [1995] 2 FLR 153, CA. See also *Re W (Contact: Application By Grandparent)* [1997] 1 FLR 793 and *Re S (Contact: Appeal)* [2001] Fam Law 505.

25 But note *Re F (Contact: Child in Care)* [1995] 1 FLR 510 which shows that in the public law context at least the applicant's child's interests might not always be paramount.

(c) Persons other than parents (*e.g.* grandparents, step-parents, siblings *etc*)

The objectives of custody are, among others, to ensure close and affectionate human relationships for a child, in particular those between a child and its parents (Sec. 1 para. 1 Finnish Child Custody and the Right of Access Act). Thus, the Act principally encourages the custodian to allow the child to meet and have contact with other persons close to the child, such as siblings, grandparents and other relatives. However, only the right of access between the child and its parent can be subject to an approved agreement, court decision or enforcement.

If the child has been taken into care, the right of the child to maintain contact with any person close to the child can be subject to scrutiny and a decision by the administrative court (see above Q 43).

FRANCE

(a) A parent holding parental responsibilities but not living with the child

In general the child has a right of contact with a parent holding parental responsibilities but not living with the child. If this parent holds parental responsibilities but does not have the exercise of them, the court may deprive him from contact rights only for very serious reasons (see Art. 373-2-1 para. 2 French CC and the case law cited in Q 42).

(b) A parent not holding parental responsibilities

For the situation of the parent who holds parental responsibilities but does not have exercise of them, see (a). If a judgment discharges all parental responsibilities, the parent will retain no contact rights (Art. 379 French CC). If the discharge is only partial, the court will specify which parental responsibilities are discharged (Art. 379-1 French CC). If the parent has delegated (*délégation d'autorité parentale*) his parental responsibilities (in part or totally) he still keeps some rights and duties. He keeps the contact right (*i.e.* visiting and lodging rights).

(c) Persons other than parents (e.g. grandparents, step-parents, siblings *etc*)

For grandparents[26] see Art. 371-4 French CC: The child has the right to have personal relationships with his grandparents. This right can be suppressed only for very serious reasons. The provision concerns all *ascendants* (ancestors) of the child, so great grandparents also have a contact right with the child. Only the relatives that are concerned have standing to bring a claim before court.[27]

---

26 See G. SUTTON, 'Du droit des grands-parents aux relations avec leurs petits-enfants', *JCP* ,1972. I. 2504; Th. GARE, *Les grands-parents dans le droit de la famille*, CNRS, 1989; H. BOSSE-PLATIERE, 'La présence des grands-parents dans le contentieux familial', *JCP*, 1997. I. 4030.

27 French Supreme Court, Civ. II, 20.07.1983, *Bull. civ.* II, No. 154. The divorced mother is not entitled to bring a claim with respect to contact rights before court in the name of her parents (the child's grand-parents)

Generally the courts presume that personal relationships between the child and the child's grandparents are in the child's interests.[28] Lower courts are free to discern (without possibility of appeal on this issue) whether to grant contact rights to the grandparents;[29] the *Cour de cassation* does not control this discretion.[30]

Other possible reasons to deny contact rights could be: condemnation of the grandparent because of affront to public decency (*outrage aux bonnes mœurs*) related to minor children; morbid atmosphere at the grandparents' home because of illness; systematic criticism of the parents by the grandparents, *etc.*. However, a simple disagreement between parents and grandparents does not justify the denial of contact rights to the grandparents.

Other third persons: For all other third persons Art. 371-4 para. 2 French CC states that in the child's interests the family judge can determine the *modalités des relations* (modes of relationship) between the child and a third person who may or may not be a relative.[31]

GERMANY

(a) A parent holding parental responsibilities but not living with the child

According to the general provision that it is in the interests of the child to have contact with both parents (§ 1626 para. 3 sent. 1 German CC), the child has a right of contact with a parent holding parental responsibilities but not living with the child. A non-resident parent retains the right and duty to contact in addition to his or her continuing duties of parental responsibility. The parent with parental custody also has the right to contact, *e.g.*, when the child stays for a longer period of time with the other parent.[32]

(b) A parent not holding parental responsibilities

The child has a right of contact with a parent not holding parental responsibilities; § 1684 para. 1 German CC. The right of contact exists especially in cases where there is no parental care. This is also true for the unmarried father.

---

28 French Supreme Court, Civ. I, 01.12.1982, *Bull. civ.* I, No. 346.

29 French Supreme Court, Civ. I, 13.12.1989, *Bull. civ.* I, No. 389.

30 For a case of denial of contact rights to a grandparent because of a very difficult family past, see CA Lyon, 14.03.2000, *Dr. famille,* 2000, No. 126 annotated BERTHET.

31 See *e.g.* CA Aix-en-Provence, 12.03.2002, *D.* 2003. 1528 annotated CADOU (contact rights granted to a transsexual ex-partner of the mother). See also French Supreme Court, Civ. I, 05.05.1986, *Bull. civ.* I, No. 112 (a lodging right (*droit d'hébergement)* can in exceptional circumstances be granted to third persons who are not the child's grandparents); Civ. I, 11.05.1976, *D.* 1976. P. 521 annotated HOVASSE (a third person who provided for the child's upbringing for a while); Civ. I, 17.05.1993, *Bull. civ.* I, No. 475 (a husband who is not the child's father but who took care of the child).

32 P. FINGER, in: *Münchener Kommentar,* 4th Edition, München: Beck, 2002, § 1684 German CC No. 5.

(c) Persons other than parents (*e.g.* grandparents, step-parents, siblings *etc*)

Since the 1998 child law reform, additional persons have been vested with a legal right of contact with the child. Grandparents and siblings have this right to contact. There is a pre-condition for the exercise of a contact right, however, that it is in the interests of the child (§ 1685 para. 1 German CC). According to § 1685 para. 2 sent. 1 German CC, a person with a close relationship with the child (*enge Bezugsperson*) also has a right to contact with the child if this person bears or bore factual responsibility for the child. Under these circumstances a socio-familial relationship (*sozial-familiäre Beziehung*) exists. A bearing of factual responsibility generally exists if the person lived with the child in the same household over some length of time (§ 1685 para. 2 sent. 2 German CC). This provision is the result of Federal Constitutional Court case law, which gave biological but non-legal fathers a right to contact.[33] However, a precondition is that the biological father must have, for a certain amount of time, actually bore responsibility for the child and that a social relationship between him and the child developed.[34]

Under the new version of § 1685 para. 2 German CC there is no longer an exclusive enumeration of the different persons with a right to contact.[35] It is agreed however that also the spouse of the parent (step-parent) has a right of personal contact. The same is true for the former spouse and the former partner of a non-marital relationship. The registered partner or former registered partner has also such a right of contact. Other persons can have such a right when they acted as foster carers over some length of time.[36]

GREECE

(a) A parent holding parental responsibilities but not living with the child

Art. 1520 Greek CC formulates the right of contact as a right belonging to the parent. Nevertheless, Art. 8 of the European Convention on Human Rights establishes the protection of the child's family life. An integral part of this is the right of the child to contact its family and, above all, its parents. Likewise, Art. 9 para. 3 of the Convention on the Rights of the Child explicitly provides the child with the right to contact its parents. Greece has signed and ratified both conventions. This calls for a wide interpretation of Art. 1520 Greek CC, so that the child itself has the right to contact its parents.[37] Nevertheless, the courts

33 BVerfG, 09.04.2003, *BVerfGE* 108, 82 = *FamRZ* 2004, 1705 annotated C. Huber = *NJW* 2003, 2151.

34 BVerfG, 31.08.2004, *FamRZ* 2004, 1705.

35 For the former version of § 1685 para. 2 German CC see I. RAKETE-DOMBEK, 'Das Umgangsrecht des Stiefelternteils zu seinem Stiefkind gem. § 1685 II BGB', *FPR* 2004, 73 *et seq.*

36 H. HOLZHAUER, 'Familienrecht', in: R. HAUSMANN/G. HOHLOCH (ed.), *Das Recht der nichtehelichen Lebensgemeinschaft*, 2nd Edition, Berlin: E. Schmidt, 2004, No. 6-95, 98.

37 S. KOUKOULI-SPILIOTOPOULOU, in: A. GEORGIADIS and M. STATHOPOULOS (eds.), *Civil Code commentary, Vol. VIII, Family Law (Arts. 1505-1694)*, 2nd Edition, Athens: Law & Economy, P. N. SAKKOULAS, 2003, p. 87-88, No. 184.

seem to deny this interpretation of Art. 1520 Greek CC. In the majority of court decisions, no such right is recognised as belonging to the child.[38]

(b) A parent not holding parental responsibilities

According to the prevailing opinion, the aim of the abovementioned right of the child is to protect its ties with its family. Hence, it is not dependent on whether or not its parent has parental responsibilities.[39]

(c) Persons other than parents (*e.g.* grandparents, step-parents, siblings *etc*)

The European Convention on Human Rights interprets the notion of the family somewhat widely. Thus, the family not only includes the parents and the child, but all persons with whom the child has real ties, for example its grandparents, siblings, as well as other close relatives.[40] Hence, the right of the child must be interpreted accordingly. Nevertheless, the courts do not recognise any right of contact with the child.[41]

HUNGARY

(a) A parent holding parental responsibilities but not living with the child

A parent holding parental responsibilities but not living with the child is found when parents exercise their parental responsibilities jointly after divorce. An agreement of the parents is the basis of the joint parental responsibilities; they also have to agree on the time and manner of contact. As the parents have to agree on the residence of the child (namely on the placement of the child according to the Family Act) and the permanent residence has to be one of the parent's residence, they must consequently agree on the contact.

(b) A parent not holding parental responsibilities

The child's right to contact with the non-custodial parent is stated in the Act and in the Order. A parent who does not exercise parental responsibilities still has broad rights. It is important for the child to be in contact with the non-custodial parent, both when the child lives with the custodial parent and when the child lives with a third person or in state care.

---

38 Decisions of the Court of Appeals of Athens: 10/1988, *Elliniki Dikaiosini* Vol. 35 (1994), p. 129, 11697/1989 *Elliniki Dikaiosini* Vol. 33 (1992), p. 157, 1908/1992, accessed at www.lawdb.intrasoftnet.com. Similar is the decision of the Court of Appeals of Piraeus 203/1994 *Elliniki Dikaiosuni* Vol. 35 (1994), p. 1690.

39 S. KOUKOULI-SPILIOTOPOULOU, in: A. GEORGIADIS and M. STATHOPOULOS (eds.), *Civil Code commentary, Vol. VIII, Family Law (Arts. 1505-1694)*, 2nd Edition, Athens: Law & Economy, P. N. SAKKOULAS, 2003, p. 70, No. 154, with further references.

40 S. KOUKOULI- SPILIOTOPOULOU, in: A. GEORGIADIS and M. STATHOPOULOS (eds.), *Civil Code commentary, Vol. VIII, Family Law (Arts. 1505-1694)*, 2nd Edition, Athens: Law & Economy, P. N. SAKKOULAS, 2003, p. 25-26 No. 48.

41 Decisions of the Court of Appeals of Athens: 10/1988, *Elliniki Dikaiosini* Vol. 35 (1994), p. 129, 11697/1989 *Elliniki Dikaiosini* Vol. 33 (1992), p. 157, 1908/1992, accessed at www.lawdb.intrasoftnet.com. Similar is the decision of the Court of Appeals of Piraeus 203/1994 *Elliniki Dikaiosuni* Vol. 35 (1994), p. 1690.

According to the Child-Welfare Act the child has the right to maintain contact with both of his or her parents even if they live in different states and the child is in state care, either temporarily or permanently. It is also in the child's interest that if the exercise of this right is a harmful influence to the child, the parents' or other close relatives' right to contact can be restricted or terminated.

The child has the right to maintain a personal and direct contact with his or her non-custodial parent. The non-custodial parent also has the right and the duty to maintain personal and direct contact with his or her child.

The child has the right of contact with the non-custodial parent if this parent's parental responsibilities are suspended and the child is placed with a third person (if the residence by either of the parents endangers the child's development) or if the child is taken into a third person's household with the permission of the public guardianship authority. The child has also the right to contact if he or she is taken out of the family and lives in state care. Even the parent whose parental responsibilities are terminated by the court because of serious harm to the child or because the parent consented to an 'incognito adoption' can have the right to contact with the child if it's in the child's interests.

(c) Persons other than parents (e.g. grandparents, stepparents, siblings *etc*)

The child's right to contact with persons other than the parents is also regulated. The Child-Welfare Act says the child generally has the right to grow up in his or her family and mentions the child's right to maintain the personal relationships.

According to the Order of Guardianship, the right to contact with the child is attributed to the parent, the grandparent and the brother or sister who has reached the age of majority. The brother or sister of the parent and the parent's spouse has the right to maintain the contact with the child only if the parent and grandparent died, they are prevented in maintaining contact on a permanent basis or they do not exercise the right of contact through fault of their own. The guardian of the child taken into state care can allow that the child could maintain his or her personal relationships with other relatives as well. If there is a dispute on it between the child and the guardian, the public guardianship authority decides.

IRELAND

(a) A parent holding parental responsibilities but not living with the child

The child has a right of contact with a parent holding parental responsibilities but not living with the child if such contact is in the child's best interests.

(b) A parent not holding parental responsibilities

The parent who does not obtain custody of a child but remains a guardian is entitled to apply for access to the child. The right of access in this context is ultimately a right of the child. If there is a conflict between what is in the best interests of the applicant parent and the child, the rights of the child will take precedence. It should be remembered that an access order is never a final order. It is always open to either parent to apply to the court to vary the access order if this is in the best interests of the child.[42]

(c) Persons other than parents (*e.g.* grandparents, stepparents, siblings, *etc*)

Until 9 January 1998, only a parent or guardian of a child could apply for access to a child. Since the commencement of Sec. 9 Irish Children Act 1997, however, certain additional persons may now apply to the court to be afforded access to a child. These persons include the relative of a child or a person who has acted *in loco parentis* in respect of the relevant child. This was made possible by Sec. 11B of the 1964 Act. While initial drafts of the legislation confined the meaning of the word 'relative' to persons related by blood only, this definition was subsequently abandoned. For these purposes, then, the term 'relative' includes such persons as are related to the child by marriage or adoption as well as by blood, for instance, a relative of the child's adoptive parents. A person *in loco parentis* may include, for instance, a former foster parent, or the cohabiting partner of a parent. The degree of care required of a person *in loco parentis* is not clear, although it is submitted that this subsection does not include persons *in loco parentis* by virtue of their occupation, for instance, day-care minders and teachers.

Any such order may be accompanied by such terms and conditions as the court sees fit. Such an application is, however, conditional upon the court initially granting leave to apply to make such an application. In deciding whether to grant such leave, the court will have regard to all relevant circumstances including but not restricted to the nature of the relationship and connection between the applicant and the child, and the risk, if any, that the application would disturb the child to the extent that the latter would be harmed. The court must also have regard to the wishes of the child's guardians. The reasons for this two-tier process are not obvious and it is arguable that the insertion of the 'application for leave' stage creates an added burden and expense upon the relatives of a child. It is submitted, however, that this additional requirement is useful in filtering out claims of an unmeritorious nature.

ITALY

(a) A parent holding the parental responsibilities but not living with the child

The minor has the right to enduring, steady and serene contacts with both parents because both of them contribute to the healthy growth of the child. The visitation right is therefore a fundamental right of the minor's which must be observed whenever the minor shows interest, providing it does not interfere with the child's educational obligations, sporting activities and recreational

---

[42] Sec. 12, Irish Guardianship of Infants Act 1964.

activities. The right of visitation generally implies frequent and regular meetings with the minor (usually once a week as well as during every other weekend); moreover the non-residential parent has the right and duty to keep the child for specific periods during the year (for example during the holiday seasons and the summer holidays).

(b) A parent not holding the parental responsibilities

In our legal system, a parent without parental responsibilities either is deceased or has been decreed in forfeiture of his or her parental responsibilities pursuant to Art. 330 Italian CC. This is applied because of disrespect or neglect of the duties pertaining to the responsibilities, or in case of abuse of the powers pertaining to it along with serious damage to the child (see Q 51). The parent whose forfeiture has been decreed as 'incapable to act as parent' is deprived of all parental rights and duties, with the exception of the obligation to support the child. In this case, the judge may also order the child to be taken away from the family home due to the seriousness of the situation or order the parent mistreating or abusing the minor to leave the family home. However, forfeiture of parental responsibilities does not automatically imply the loss of any contact with the minor (see Q 53). Contact is not necessarily linked to parental responsibilities and can therefore be granted to persons that do not hold it. The judge has broad discretion through which he will determine the means, limits and exclusions of contact in the exclusive interests of the minor.

In general, if the forfeiture decree is based on mistreatment or abuse, the parent is denied visitation rights; if instead the decree is based on neglect the visiting right can be recognised with limits and cautionary measures which take the interests of the minor into account.[43]

(c) Persons other than parents (*e.g.* grandparents, step-parents, siblings *etc*)

Even in the absence of a precise provision of law, the judge can grant or prohibit the visiting 'rights' of other relatives (such as the grandparents, the brothers or the sisters) by taking the interests of the minor into account. Since these relatives have neither parental responsibilities nor their exercise, they are not recognised as holders of rights but rather as 'having an interest deemed by the law as important.'[44] Periodical contacts between grandparents and the minor grandchildren is normally recognised due to the fundamental right of the minor to maintain a relationship with her or his grandparents. This relationship

---

43 Cout of Appeal of Rome 27.02.95, *Dir. fam. pers.*, 1995, p. 1450. In this case of first instance, the judge disposing the divorce granted the father the right to contact, notwithstanding that he had been discharged of the parental responsibilities before the divorce. The appellate judges decided to grant the father the right to contact only if both the minor and the mother consented.

44 Supreme Court, 09.06.90, No. 5636, *Giust. civ.*, 1991, I, p. 1545. In this case, the Court voided the arrangements the parents made during their separation that prohibited all contact between their children and the children's grandparents.

can only be limited or denied if there is evidence to the effect that the continuation of this relationship can be prejudicial to the minor.[45]

LITHUANIA

(a) A parent holding parental responsibilities but not living with the child

The child has such a right, except in cases when, under the judgment of the court, the contact with the parent not living with the child is against the interests of the child.

(b) A parent not holding parental responsibilities

The child has such a right if the contact with the parent not holding parental responsibilities (*e.g.* parent whose parental authority is restricted) is not against the interests of the child (Art. 3.179-3.180 Lithuanian CC).

(c) Persons other than parents (*e.g.* grandparents, step-parents, siblings *etc*)

Parents shall be obliged to create conditions for the children to associate with their close relatives (grandparents, adult siblings *etc.*) and other relatives provided that it is consistent with the children's interests (Art. 3.172 Lithuanian CC).

THE NETHERLANDS

(a) A parent holding parental responsibilities but not living with the child

The situation in which a parent has joint parental responsibilities but does not usually live with the child may occur during a marriage of the parents (Art. 1:251 § 2 Dutch CC), a registered partnership of the parents (Art. 1:253aa Dutch CC), after a divorce (Art. 1:251 § 2 Dutch CC) or when parents who never have been married to each other share parental responsibilities (Art. 1:252 and 253aa Dutch CC). There is no explicit provision in the Dutch CC that attributes a right to contact in these situations, either to the child or to the parent.[46] The legislature deemed it unnecessary, since parental responsibilities presuppose direct contact with the child.[47] Although the Dutch CC does not contain an explicit right, Art. 1:377h Dutch CC determines that the court may make an arrangement for the right of contact between the child and the non-resident parent.[48]

---

45 Court of Rome, 07.02.87, *Dir. fam. pers.*, 1987, p. 739.

46 C.G. JEPPESEN DE BOER, 'A comparative Analysis of Contact Arrangements in The Netherlands and Denmark', in: K. BOELE-WOELKI (ed.), *Perspectives for the Unification and Harmonisation of Family Law in Europe*, EFL series No. 4, 2003, p. 385.

47 *Kamerstukken Tweede Kamer*, 1992-1993, 23 012, No. 3, p. 16.

48 The position of the child aged twelve or older, or younger but able to appraise his or her interests, is regulated by Art. 1:377g Dutch CC in conjunction with Art. 1:377h Dutch CC. This implies that the court may *ex officio* decree a contact arrangement if it appears to the court that the child appreciates this.

(b) A parent not holding parental responsibilities

Art. 1:377a § 1 Dutch CC provides for the right of contact between the child and the parent without parental responsibilities. This article relates to all situations in which one parent has no parental responsibilities, regardless whether it concerns a situation after a divorce, a never married couple, a parent who has no capacity to exercise parental responsibilities *etc.* A prerequisite is that the parent is a legal parent. This means that the unmarried father must have recognised the child in order to have a right to contact on the basis of this provision.[49] It is not necessary that a legal parent has family life with the child. The right to contact is attributed to both the child and the parent.

The parents can agree on the exercise of the right of contact, but if they do not agree, they may both apply to the court for an arrangement, which might be of a temporary nature (Art. 1:377a § 2 Dutch CC).

(c) Persons other than parents (*e.g.* grandparents, step-parents, siblings *etc*)

Persons other than the parents may apply for a contact order if they have a close personal relationship with the child (Art. 1:377f Dutch CC). This provision does not mention the child's right to contact with these persons.[50] However, the court may *ex officio* decree a contact arrangement if it appears to the court that a child aged twelve or older (or younger but sufficiently mature) appreciates such an arrangement (Art. 1:377g in conjunction with Art. 1:377f Dutch CC). The term 'close personal relationship' is an equivalent of 'family life' in Art. 8 ECHR. Several categories of persons may qualify: the biological father who did not recognise his child,[51] grandparents,[52] other siblings,[53] other persons[54] as well the 'social parent' who was a partner of the parent.[55] With respect to the close personal relation between a social grandmother and a child, stringent rules apply.[56] It has been argued in the legal literature that the distinction between parents in Art. 1:377a Dutch CC and other persons with family life with the minor in Art. 1:377f Dutch CC might in some cases be contrary to the Art. 14 and 8 ECHR. A biological father or a social parent with family life with the child might on this basis claim that Art. 1:377a Dutch CC is applicable.[57]

---

49 See Supreme Court 15.11.1996, *NJ*, 1997, 423 annotated J. DE BOER: a biological father is not a parent as meant in Art. 1:377a Dutch CC.

50 J.E. DOEK, 'De 'definitieve' regeling van het omgangsrecht: een weerbarstige kwestie', *FJR*, 1992, p. 32-33 who favoured an explicit and independent right to contact for the child in the Dutch CC.

51 See e.g. Supreme Court 19.5.2000, *NJ*, 2000, 545 annotated S. WORTMANN and Supreme Court 29.9.2000, *NJ* 2000, 654.

52 See Supreme Court 25.6.1993, *NJ*, 1993, 628.

53 Like a brother or sister, see *e.g.* District Court Breda 30.5.1991, *NJ* 1992, 451.

54 See Supreme Court 20.12.1987, *NJ*, 1988, 281 with respect to members of a commune.

55 See Supreme Court 5.12.1986, *NJ*, 1987, 957 annotated E. ALKMENA.

56 See Supreme Court 29.3.2002, *NJ*, 2002, 269.

57 S.F.M. WORTMANN, *Losbladige Personen- en familierecht*, Art. 377a, 3 and 377f, 2. See Supreme Court 15.11.1996, *NJ*, 1997, 423 annotated J. DE BOER.

NORWAY

(a) A parent holding parental responsibilities but not living with the child

A parent holding parental responsibilities but not living with the child has a right of contact with the child (visiting rights). Parents usually decide the extent of the right of contact. If they do not agree, then this is determined by the courts and done on an individual basis, taking family circumstances into consideration. The extent of the right of contact, if agreed as an 'ordinary right of contact', entitles the parent to spend one afternoon a week, every other weekend, two weeks of the summer holiday, and Christmas or Easter with the child, Art. 43 sec. 2 Norwegian Children Act 1981.

(b) A parent not holding parental responsibilities

A parent not holding parental responsibilities has a right of contact to the same extent as a parent sharing parental responsibilities, see (a) above.

(c) Persons other than parents (*e.g.* grandparents, step-parents, siblings *etc*)

Persons other than the parents may be given a right of contact under certain limited conditions, Art. 45 Norwegian Children Act 1981. When one or both of the parents are deceased, relatives of the child or persons who are close to the child may request the court to establish whether they have a right of contact with the child, and the extent of such contact. In cases where a court has denied a parent's right of contact, that parent may request that the court determines whether his or her parents shall have a right of contact with the child and the extent of such contact. Contact by grandparents may be granted only on the condition that the person who has been denied contact is not allowed to be with the child.

POLAND

(a) A parent holding parental responsibilities but not living with the child

There are no limitations in this respect. In exceptional cases, if a child is placed with a foster family, the court may limit the parent's personal contact with the child. (Art. 113 § 2 Polish Family and Guardianship Code).

(b) A parent not holding parental responsibilities

A parent holds the right to contact irrespective whether he or she is vested with parental authority. The court may prohibit a parent deprived of parental authority from maintaining personal contact with the child, should the child's wellbeing so require (Art. 113 § 1 Polish Family and Guardianship Code).

(c) Persons other than parents (*e.g.* grandparents, step-parents, siblings *etc*)

Apart from the duty of maintenance, Polish law does not regulate relations between a child and her or his more distant relatives.

PORTUGAL

Portuguese law does not expressly consecrate any right for the child to relate with one of its parents or with other relatives. The right of contact is established as a right belonging to adults. However, more recent legal literature has understood that the institution of visiting rights is not only a right, but also contains an element of duty that corresponds to the rights of the child.

(a) A parent holding parental responsibilities but not living with the child

Thus, in a situation in which parental responsibility is exercised jointly but the child resides with only one parent, it appears that the other parent and correspondingly, the child, enjoy free right of contact with each other.

(b) A parent not holding parental responsibilities

In a situation of sole custody, the law only refers to the child's interest in maintaining a close relationship with the non-custodial parent (Art. 1905 No. 1 Portuguese CC). In these cases, the non-custodial parent's right of contact is restricted to the terms of a system established by agreement, ratified by the judge, appreciated by the Public Prosecutor's Office and deemed to be in the interests of the child, or else it is decreed by the court. This right includes a duty to the child, and therefore constitutes a right of the child. The law appears to recognise this right of the child, although only indirectly. Indeed, in the event of failure to comply with the system of contacts established through the creation of obstacles by the custodial parent, the other may apply to the court, invoking non-compliance with the system of exercise of parental responsibility, for coercive measures to be taken and for the punishment of the parent that is at fault, by means of a fine and compensation to the child (Art. 181 No. 1 Portuguese Child Protection Law). If it is the non-custodial parent who has failed to comply, then the custodial parent may raise the matter of non-compliance.

(c) Persons other than parents (*e.g.* grandparents, step-parents, siblings *etc*)

Portuguese Law No. 84/95 of 31 August 1995 expressly established a limit to parental responsibility in respect to control of the child's personal relationships. Art. 1887-A Portuguese CC establishes that parents may not unreasonably deprive their children of contact with their siblings or ascendants. This rule appears to give rise to a right of contact with siblings, grandparents and other ascendants and consequently, a right of the child to relate to those relatives.

RUSSIA

(a) A parent holding parental responsibilities but not living with the child

A child has the right to maintain contact with his or her parents, irrespective whether they live with the child (Art. 55 (1) Russian Family Code).

A child has the right but no duty to maintain contact with his or her parents. This means that the child can refuse to have contact with one his or her parents.[58] The contact rights of the parent can not be enforced against the will of

[58] The Russian Supreme Court in its Directive No. 10 of 27.05.1998 has, however, urged the judges to investigate whether the decision of the child has been unduly

the child. On the other hand, the child can independently enforce his or her right to contact even against the will of one of his or her conflicting parents. Therefore, a child of any age can use his or her right to complain to the Guardianship and Curatorship Department (Art. 56 (2) Russian Family Code) or insist on being heard during the process of making contact arrangements (Art. 57 Russian Family Code). A child of fourteen years or older can also independently apply to court (Art. 56 (2) Russian Family Code).

(b) A parent not holding parental responsibilities

A parent always holds parental responsibility unless his or her responsibility has been discharged. Parent(s) discharged of parental responsibility lose their right to maintain contact with the child (Art. 71 (1) Russian Family Code). On the contrary the child retains the right to maintain contact with such parent; however, he or she can no longer demand time and attention from the parent(s), as they are no longer under a legal duty to maintain personal relationships with the child.[59]

(c) Persons other than parents (*e.g.* grandparents, step-parents, siblings *etc*)

A child has the right to maintain contact with his or her grandparents, brothers, sisters and other relatives (Art. 55 (1) Russian Family Code). A child can enforce this right independently and even against the will of his parent(s). Therefore a child of any age can use his or her right to complain to the Guardianship and Curatorship Department (Art. 56 (2) Russian Family Code), or insist on being heard regarding the process of making contact arrangements (Art. 57 Russian Family Code). A child of fourteen or older can also independently apply to court (Art. 56 (2) Russian Family Code). The child has no duty to maintain contact with his or her relatives, therefore their contact rights cannot be enforced against child's will.

The law speaks only of the right to maintain contact with relatives and not with other persons with whose child may have had family life (*e.g.* step-parents, foster parents). It has been suggested that such a limitation contravenes the rights of the child and those persons to the protection of family life, safeguarded by Art. 8 European Convention on Human Right and Fundamental Freedoms.[60]

---

influenced by one of the parents. Item 20 of the Directive of the Supreme Court of the Russian Federation of 27.05.1998 No. 10 'On the Application of the Legislation by Dissolving Cases Relating to the Education and Care for Children', *Bulleten' verhovnogo suda RF*, 1998, No 7.

59 M. ANTOKOLSKAIA, *Family Law* (*Semeinoe pravo*), Moscow: Jurist, 1999, p. 219.

60 M. ANTOKOLSKAIA, *Family Law* (*Semeinoe pravo*), Moscow: Jurist, 1999, p. 192.

SPAIN

(a) A parent holding parental responsibilities but not living with the child

A child has the right to maintain personal relationships with his or her parents (Art. 160 Spanish CC and Art. 135.1 Catalan Family Code), regardless of whether they hold parental responsibilities. In a divorce, annulment or separation procedure there is an obligation to regulate the contact of the child's non-resident parent, even if the parties do not it (Art. 90a, 94 and 103.1 Spanish CC.) This regulation is applicable to unmarried couples as well, although in this case courts often do not intervene since the end of the relationship does not require a judicial procedure.

(b) A parent not holding parental responsibilities

Children have a right to maintain personal relationships with their parents regardless of whether the parents hold parental responsibilities, unless a judicial decision provides otherwise or the child has been adopted by another person or persons. The suspension or discharge of parental responsibility does not necessarily imply a suspension or discharge of contact; that will depend on whether it is in the child's best interest to have contact with the parent (see Q 53)

(c) Persons other than parents (*e.g.* grandparents, step-parents, siblings *etc*)

Catalan law establishes that parents must facilitate contact between the child and other relatives, as well as between the child and other close persons (such as the former partner of the parent), and that the parents cannot without justification impede contact. There is authority to support that the right of the child to maintain contact with other relatives and close persons is an actionable right; if this contact is unjustifiably impeded, a Judge will remedy the situation. The Spanish CC was recently modified to clarify this. Art. 160 Spanish CC, which contained a regulation similar to that of Catalan Law, was modified in order to specifically provide for such an action.[61]

SWEDEN

(a) A parent holding parental responsibilities but not living with the child

A child has the right to contact with a parent with whom the child is not living, irrespective of whether that parent has custody rights or not, Chapter 6 Sec. 15 para. 1 Swedish Children and Parents Code. The child's parents have a joint responsibility to ensure that the child's need of contact with a parent with whom the child is not living is met.

(b) A parent not holding parental responsibilities

The child's right to contact with a parent with whom the child is not living also applies when that parent does not have custody rights, Chapter 6 Sec. 15 para. 1 Swedish Children and Parents Code. The child's parents have a joint

61 Ley 42/2003, de 21 de noviembre, de modificación del Código Civil y de la Ley de Enjuiciamiento Civil en materia de relaciones familiares de los nietos con los abuelos.

responsibility to ensure that the child's need of contact with a parent with whom the child is not living is met. When a child is placed for care in another home, the social welfare committee has the duty to ensure, as far as possible, that the child's need of contact with parents and custodians is met, Sec. 14 Swedish Care of Young Persons Act.[62]

(c) Persons other than parents (*e.g.* grandparents, step-parents, siblings *etc*)

A person with custody of a child has a responsibility to ensure that, as far as possible, a child's need of contact with any other person particularly close to the child is met, Chapter 6 Sec. 15 para. 3 Swedish Children and Parents Code. This provision aims at encouraging the child's contact not only with persons the child knows well and misses, but also with *e.g.*, relatives who enrich the child's development. If contact is requested by a person other than the parents and the custodian does not agree, proceedings may only be initiated by the social welfare committee, Chapter 6 Sec. 15a para. 1 Swedish Children and Parents Code. Such proceedings are very rarely if ever, initiated, mainly because a contact order against the will of the parents is feared to increase the level of conflict, which would be detrimental to the interests of the child.

SWITZERLAND

(a) A parent holding parental responsibilities but not living with the child

As long as the parents are married, the child has the right to have unlimited contact with the parent who does not live in the household. If the parents dissolve their joint household and call upon the marriage protection court to rule with regard to separation, this court may confer this custody or parental responsibilities for the child to one parent (176 § 3 in combination with Art. 297 § 2 Swiss CC). At the same time, the marriage protection court must rule on the mutual claim to adequate personal contact between the child and the parent who no longer has custody (Art. 273 § 1 Swiss CC). The same applies in the case of awarding of custody as a provisional measure in divorce proceedings (Art. 137 § 2 Swiss CC).

What is deemed to be adequate personal contact is assessed according to the circumstances of the specific case. The guideline to be followed in organising this contact is the child's welfare. Factors of relevance may be the child's age and personality, the child's own wishes, the relationship of the child to the person entitled to visiting rights, the distance between the places where the parties involved live, the amount of time the parties concerned have at their disposal, etc.

(b) A parent not holding parental responsibilities

The child and the parent who holds neither parental responsibilities nor custody have a mutual right to adequate personal contact (Art. 273 § 1 Swiss

62 See also: Chapter 6 Sec. 1 and 5 Swedish Social Services Act (2001:453).

CC). With regard to adequate personal contact please refer to the previous Q 44a).

(c) Persons other than parents (*e.g.* grandparents, step-parents, siblings *etc*)

Other persons may be granted a right to personal contact in accordance with Art. 274a Swiss CC, if there are exceptional circumstances and this is for the benefit of the child's welfare. Such circumstances are deemed to be given if, for example, as a result of change in the family's situation it becomes impossible for a child to have personal contact with persons with whom they had an especially close relationship. Most third parties do not claim the right to personal contact in competition with parents who are able and entitled to have personal contact with the child, but only if the latter are absent or not in a position to maintain personal contact with their own child. Third parties can, for instance, be grandparents who on the death of their child are refused contact with their grandchild by the child's other parent, or siblings who live in different places as a result of their parents' divorce or separation. It may also be a question of a step-parent whose marriage to the parent with custody rights has been dissolved or foster parents after the dissolution of the placement with these foster parents or the biological parents who placed the child with foster parents with an aim to adopt, or agreed to adoption, or godparents.

QUESTION 45

E. CONTACT

Is the right to have contact referred to in Q 43 also a right and/or a duty of the parent or the other persons concerned?

AUSTRIA

The right to personal contact is also worded as a right of the respective parent and the grandparent(s) (Sec. 148(1) and (2) Austrian CC), and it is also understood as a duty of these persons to take their responsibility towards the child seriously.[1] Persons other than the respective parent and the grandparent(s) to whom the child has close emotional ties are not entitled to petition the court for regulating the exercise of contact or to standing as a party in the respective proceedings; thus they do not have an independent "right of contact".[2]

Neither a child over the age of 14 years nor the respective parent can be forced to exercise contact (Sec. 108 Non-Contentious Proceedings Act [*Außerstreitgesetz*]), since maintaining the contact is only beneficial to the child's welfare if it is done so on a voluntary basis. However, upon rejecting the right of contact, one also loses the right to be informed and the right to express one's opinion (Sec. 178(3) last sentence Austrian CC). Moreover, there are consequences under the law of succession, as well: Sec. 773a Austrian CC generally enables the testator to reduce a child's entitlement to a compulsory portion to one-half if a close family relationship never existed between them. However, this option does not apply if the testator unjustifiably refused to have contact with the child.

BELGIUM

The right of contact referred to in Q 43 is a right of the parents. However, according to Art. 375 *bis* Belgian CC, two other categories of persons have the right to have contact with a child, namely its grandparents and every other person, with the additional condition that the person seeking the contact can prove the existence of a significant, affectionate relationship with the child. The use of a uniform terminology, namely 'right of contact', allows the judge to define precisely the modalities of the right of contact whether it concerns a parent, a grandparent or every other person. This contact can consist of hosting the child, letting it reside during limited periods, paying it a visit, writing to it,

---

1 *E.g., Oberster Gerichtshof,* 10.04.1997, *Österreichischer Amtsvormund,* 1997, p. 168 (Udo Jürgens Case); M. ROTH, 'Europäische Menschenrechtskonvention und Privatrecht: Landesbericht Österreich', *Rabels Zeitschrift für ausländisches und internationales Privatrecht (RabelsZ),* 1999, p. 735 *et seq.* with further references.

2 For details see Q 44c paragraph 2.

calling it or sending it by mail or e-mail.[3] Although the possible modalities of the right of contact are the same, the grandparents or other persons never exercise parental authority. They have a right with its own aim, namely to maintain an affectionate relationship with the child.[4]

BULGARIA

Irrespective of the lack of an explicitly articulated right, the right to contact is agreed to be a subjective right of the parent that is part of parental rights and duties. It is accepted that the parent is entitled to a claim for contact and that it cannot, in general, be rejected. The theory also argues that, although contact is also an obligation of the parent, it cannot be enforced. The non-performance of this obligation, however, may result in the deprivation of parental rights.[5]

The first legal regulation of Bulgarian family law on the right to personal contact was connected to the first regulation of divorce by the Bulgarian Marriage Ordinance Act (1945). It said that the non-custodial parent 'is entitled to maintain appropriate personal relations with them (the children)'.[6] In 1949 a more neutral wording still in use today, replaced the 'right's' language: the court orders 'measures regarding the personal relations between children and parents'.[7]

Family law theory emphasises the importance of the interests of both parties (the parent and the child) in the adjudication of personal contact: 'the contact, on one hand, provides the parent with an opportunity to satisfy his or her parental feeling, ... but it is mostly necessary for children, who experience the need to communicate with their parents'.[8] In this context, irrespective of the premise that the right to contact pertains to the parent, because of the prioritisation of the child's interests the court may decide not to arrange measures for personal relations, if the interests of the child require it.

CZECH REPUBLIC

The parent who is a holder of parental responsibility and does not live with the child in a common household has a right to contact with the child but contact is not a duty. The parental agreement on contact with the child does not require a court approval (Sec. 27 § 1 Czech Family Code).

---

3 J. SOSSON, 'Note – Quand l'enfant vit au loin ... L'avènement du droit aux relations cyber-personnelles ?', *Rev. trim. dr. fam.*, 1998, p. 86.

4 A. DE WOLF, *Artikelsgewijze commentaar met ovezricht van rechtspraak en rechtsleer personen- en familierecht* (Art. 375 *bis* Belgian CC), Antwerp:Maklu, 1997, No. 27-31.

5 In this sense, a parent deprived of their parental rights does not hold an autonomous subjective right to contact. See L. NENOVA, *Family Law of the Republic of Bulgaria*, Sofia, 1994, p. 641.

6 Art. 45 § 2.

7 See Art. 54 of the Act on the Persons and the Family (1949), Art. 29 Bulgarian Family Code (1968) and Art. 106 Bulgarian Family Code (1985).

8 See L. NENOVA, *Family Law of the Republic of Bulgaria*, Sofia, 1977 and 1994, p. 324 and p. 640.

DENMARK

No.

ENGLAND & WALES

Although it would be wrong to place too much emphasis on 'rights' in this context (see Q 44a), the general approach of English law is to judge the issue of contact very much from the child's perspective. Nevertheless the de facto position is that the predisposition to preserve contact between a child and each of his parents even where it is disputed can equally be seen as preserving the parents' position. Furthermore, outside the context of disputes, as has been discussed (Q 26b), parental responsibility certainly embraces the notion of the "right" to have continued contact with the child.

As stated in Q 2b whether a parent has an obligation to maintain contact with the child can be debated. In theory there is clearly a case for saying there is such an obligation but as a matter of practicality it would be difficult to enforce a contact order against an unwilling parent and no authority exists for saying that such orders should be made.

FINLAND

A child's right of access also means that the residential custodian has a duty to allow the child to use its right of access as agreed or ordered by the court, or the Enforcement Act authorises use of enforcement measures against the custodian.

The parent with whom the child has a right to meet has, however, no enforceable duty to meet with the child. This was confirmed by the Supreme Court of Justice in 1991 (KKO 1991: 36). It is questionable whether an enforced contact between the child and its parent would serve the best interests of the child.

If the local social authority and the persons close to a child who has been taken into care cannot agree on how the child should maintain contact, the authority has, according to the Deputy Parliamentary Ombudsman, an obligation to decide how contact should be maintained. This decision can be an object of scrutiny of the administrative court.[9]

FRANCE

The contact right is also a duty for the parent who does not have the exercise of parental responsibilities. Art. 373-2 §2 *C.C.* states that after the parental separation each parent must maintain personal relationships with the child and respect the bonds that the child has with the other parent. Contact is therefore a right and a duty. It is also a duty when a measure of educational support has been ordered by the court in the child's interest: in this case, the parents shall exercise the rights and duties they have kept (see Art. 375-7 French CC) If they

9 See the attitude of the Deputy Parliamentary Ombudsman (since 2002 Parliamentary Ombudsman) RIITTA-LEENA PAUNIO in the Annual Report from 1998, p. 180.

have not exercised them for two years they can be discharged of their parental responsibilities (Art. 378-1 para. 2 French CC).

More generally, a decision of first instance stated that the contact right is also a duty of the parent to whom it is granted; if this parent does not make use of this contact right she or he can be liable on the basis of Art. 1382 French CC (torts).[10] The right to contact can be denied to the parent only for serious reasons, see Art. 373-2-1 para. 2 French CC.

GERMANY

According to § 1684 para. 1 German CC, the child has a right of contact with each parent and each parent has a right of contact and is obliged to contact with the child. Therefore for parents contact is not only a right but also a duty (*Pflichtrecht*)[11]. For the other persons mentioned in § 1685 para. 1, 2 German CC (grandparents, siblings and persons with a close relationship) who have a right of contact, no corresponding duty exists.

GREECE

Contact with the child relates to its care.[12] Thus, the holder of this responsibility would not be exercising this duty properly if he or she does not contact the child. The provision in Art. 1520 para. 1 Greek CC, which establishes the right of a parent to contact the child, gains practical significance when the court has not entrusted the care of the child to the parent. This right in Art. 1520 para. 1 Greek CC does not constitute a part of parental care, but is a distinct right.[13] Therefore, it does not matter whether or not the parent holds parental responsibilities. It is also of no relevance if the parent is adoptive or natural.

Moreover, Art. 1520 para. 2 Greek CC provides that the parents have no right to prevent the child from having contact with its further ascendants (*i.e.* grandmothers, grandfathers), unless this is justified by serious reasons. This article does not seem to assign the right of contact to the ascendants of the child,

---

10 See TGI Poitiers, 15.11.1999, *BICC*, 15.11.2000, No. 1294.

11 S. MOTZER, 'Elterliche Sorge', in: D. SCHWAB, *Handbuch des Scheidungsrechts*, 5th Edition, München: Vahlen, 2004, Part. III No. 232.

12 S. KOUKOULI-SPILIOTOPOULOU, in: A. GEORGIADIS and M. STATHOPOULOS (eds.), *Civil Code commentary, Vol. VIII, Family Law (Arts. 1505-1694)*, 2nd Edition, Athens: Law & Economy, P. N. SAKKOULAS, 2003, Introductory Remarks on Art. 1505-1541 Greek CC, p. 74, No. 159 [in Greek]; A. POULIADIS, in: A. GEORGIADIS and M. STATHOPOULOS (eds.), *Civil Code commentary, Vol. VIII, Family Law (Arts. 1505-1694)*, 2nd Edition, Athens: Law & Economy, P.N. SAKKOULAS, 2003, Art. 1520 Greek CC, p. 308-309, No. 16.

13 S. KOUKOULI-SPILIOTOPOULOU, in: A. GEORGIADIS and M. STATHOPOULOS (eds.), *Civil Code commentary, Vol. VIII, Family Law (Arts. 1505-1694)*, 2nd Edition, Athens: Law & Economy, P. N. SAKKOULAS, 2003, p. 70, No. 154, with further references.

but it does impose a duty not to impede such contact on the parents.[14] Nevertheless, according to the prevailing opinion of the courts and the doctrine, the ascendants of the child are entitled to contact the child.[15]

The Greek CC does not establish a right for other persons to contact the child. On the other hand, the normal psychological and sentimental development of the child may call for contact with other relatives, like the child's aunts, uncles etc. Depriving the child of this contact may indicate that parental responsibilities are not being properly exercised. Likewise, if an adopted child had lived for many years with its natural family before being adopted, its interests may also require that some contact be maintained.[16]

Finally, the right to contact the child does not entail a corresponding duty.[17] In any event, it is doubtful whether forced contact with the child would serve its best interests.

HUNGARY

With regard to the parent: the non-custodial parent has both the right and the duty to maintain contact with the child and to keep in touch with him or her on a regular basis. If the child is taken into state care temporarily, the parent has such a right to contact with the child the failure of which can be even sanctioned. The other close relatives - the grandparent, the brother or sister of full age, the parent's brother or sister and the parent's spouse - have right to contact with the child.

With regard to the custodial parent or other person: the person, usually the parent is obliged to ensure that the contact is untroubled.

IRELAND

While the order for access is often coined in terms of parental rights, the Irish legislature now regards access as a right of the child. In *M.D. v. G.D.*[18] CARROLL

---

14 A. POULIADIS, in: A. GEORGIADIS and M. STATHOPOULOS (eds.), *Civil Code commentary, Vol. VIII, Family Law (Arts. 1505-1694)*, 2nd Edition, Athens: Law & Economy, P.N. SAKKOULAS, 2003, Art. 1520 Greek CC, p. 327 No. 98.

15 See, among others, E. KOUNOUGERI-MANOLEDAKI, *Family Law*, Vol. II, 3rd Edition, Athens-Thessaloniki: SAKKOULAS, 2003, p. 301; S. KOUKOULI- SPILIOTOPOULOU, in: A. GEORGIADIS and M. STATHOPOULOS (eds.), *Civil Code commentary, Vol. VIII, Family Law (Arts. 1505-1694)*, 2nd Edition, Athens: Law & Economy, P. N. SAKKOULAS, 2003, p. 89, No. 187.

16 S. KOUKOULI- SPILIOTOPOULOU, in: A. GEORGIADIS and M. STATHOPOULOS (eds.), *Civil Code commentary, Vol. VIII, Family Law (Arts. 1505-1694)*, 2nd Edition, Athens: Law & Economy, P. N. SAKKOULAS, 2003, p. 77 No. 164.

17 This is the prevailing opinion in the doctrine and the court decisions. See A. POULIADIS, in: A. GEORGIADIS and M. STATHOPOULOS (eds.), *Civil Code commentary, Vol. VIII, Family Law (Arts. 1505-1694)*, 2nd Edition, Athens: Law & Economy, P.N. SAKKOULAS, 2003, Art. 1520 Greek CC, p. 309, No. 17, also with references to the opposite opinion (fn. 20).

J. held, *inter alia*, that the welfare of the child being the paramount consideration in this area, it is the right of the child to access with which the court is concerned and not the right of the adult. In *W.(S). v. W.(F).*,[19] a Circuit Court decision, McGuinness J. made an order restraining the respondent from bringing further applications for custody/access without leave of the court and pointed out that access is primarily the right of the children to enable them to maintain a relationship with the non-custodial parent and an order is made strictly on the basis of the welfare of the children. In the earlier case of *N.A.D. v. T.D.*,[20] Barron J., in a similar vein, remarked that his function 'is to see whether or not it would be for the benefit of these children to see their mother.'[21]

ITALY

The visitation right is also a duty for the parent, but not for the other relatives. The right of contact is a duty even before it is a right; a duty parents have in order to observe the fundamental moral and material interests of the child. It is only through frequent and continual visits that a caring, personal relationship can be maintained with the non-residential parent. Through these visits, the non-residential parent can observe his obligations to look after the child's education and moral guidance and cooperate in the child's psychological and physical growth (see Q 43). It is a duty which cannot be legally enforced if it is not observed, but its non-observance (such as, for example, the total or the enduring lack of interest with respect to the minor) may result in the reduction of the parental authority pursuant to Art. 333 Italian CC, its forfeiture pursuant to Art. 330 Italian CC, or constitute the behaviour contemplated by the crime 'Breach of duty of family assistance' pursuant to Art. 570 Italian Criminal Code.

LITHUANIA

Yes, it is both a right and a duty of the parents having parental responsibilities, because effective performance of parental responsibilities is possible only if there is effective contact between a child and his parents. Other persons have the right of, but not the duty to, contact.

THE NETHERLANDS

Both a parent holding parental responsibilities but not living with the child and a parent not holding parental responsibilities have a right to contact. The Dutch CC does not yet contain a duty to contact. There is hardly any case law[22] and the legal literature does not deal with this question.[23] The Minister of Justice

---

18 High Court, 30 .07.1992, Carroll J.

19 [1995] 1 F.L.J. 32.

20 [1985] I.L.R.M. 153 at 156.

21 Emphasis and italics added.

22 The District Court Maastricht (12.12.1988, *RN* 1990, 85) refused to condemn a father without parental responsibilities to pay a fine for not complying with the contact order, since there would be no duty to contact for the parent without parental responsibilities.

23 See, however, P. Vlaardingerbroek *et al*, *Het Hedendaagse Personen- en Familierecht*, 2004, p. 357, where it is stated that a legal parent cannot be forced to have contact.

recently introduced a Civil Code Bill including an explicit duty for both parents to contact regardless whether they have parental responsibilities.[24] A third person with a close personal relationship also has a right to contact, even though Art. 1:377e Dutch CC does not explicitly provide for such a right, but only mentions the possibility to apply for a contact order.[25] The Minister of Justice's proposal does not include third persons with family life with the child. If the child wants contact with its biological father, family life in the sense of Art. 8 ECHR is required, but the conditions might be easier met than when the father wants contact with the child. The biological father without family life with the child cannot be forced to have contact with the child.[26]

NORWAY

The right of contact is mutual. The child has a right of contact with both parents, Art. 42 Norwegian Children Act 1981, and the parent with whom the child does not live, has a right of contact with the child, Art. 43 Norwegian Children Act 1981. It should be added, however, that the child's right of contact cannot be legally enforced upon a parent that does not wish to have contact with the child.

POLAND

No answer.

PORTUGAL

As regards the parents, yes. The non-custodial parent's right of contact also has the nature of a duty. As was mentioned in Q 44b, if the non-custodial parent does not comply with the system of visits, then that parent may be ordered to pay a fine and compensate the child (Art. 181 No. 1 Portuguese Child Protection Law).

RUSSIA

Parents who live apart from their child have the right and duty to maintain contact with the child. (Art. 66 Russian Family Code). The right of the parent to maintain contact with the child includes the opportunity to spend time with the child, to execute his or her right to the education of the child and to participate in decisions on the child's education.

The right of a parent who lives apart from the child to maintain contact with the child is reinforced by the right to receive information concerning the child from every educational, medical, social or related institution (Art. 66 (4) Russian Family Code).

---

24 *Kamerstukken Tweede Kamer*, 2003-2004, 29 520, No. 1, p. 5.

25 Critical: J.E. DOEK, 'De 'definitieve' regeling van het omgangsrecht: een weerbarstige kwestie', *FJR*, 1992, p. 30.

26 See Supreme Court 22.12.1995, *NJ*, 1996, 419.

Grandparents, brothers, sisters and other relatives also have the right to maintain contact with the child (Art. 67 Russian Family Code). The right of the relatives is mainly restricted to the possibility to see the child. Relatives other than the parents have no duty to maintain contact with the child.

SPAIN

In the case of parents, case law has clearly established that contact is both a right and a duty of the parent. Parents can neither delegate nor renounce the exercise of contact because it is established in the interests of children. It will therefore not take place if it is not in the best interests of the child.

Protection is weaker for those who are not parents. If parents unjustifiably impede other's contact with the child there is a court action to enforce contact (see Q 44). One cannot speak of a duty that these people have to the child.

SWEDEN

The starting point in Swedish law is that contact is the right of the child; the parents are responsible to ensure that this right is met, Chapter 6 Sec. 15 para. 2-3 Swedish Children and Parents Code.

Nevertheless, in regard to enforcing the right to contact it remains more accurate, in a parent-child relationship, to describe contact as a right of the parent not living with the child. Only a parent not living with the child can initiate proceedings concerning contact, Chapter 6 Sec. 15a Swedish Children and Parents Code. That parent also has an exclusive right to request enforcement of agreements or court decisions concerning contact.[27] The child has no corresponding, legally recognised right! The parent with whom the child lives may, according to a judgment by the Supreme Court, NJA 1994 p 128, initiate court proceedings if the purpose is to restrict a previously determined contact with the other parent, in the best interests of the child.

If contact with the child is requested by any other person and the custodian does not agree to it, a court order remains the only solution. Court proceedings can, however, only be commenced by the social welfare committee, Chapter 6 Sec. 15a Swedish Children and Parents Code, which rarely happens. It follows that the rights and duties concerned remain weak.

SWITZERLAND

Parents are entitled to have personal contact by virtue of their rights of person. This right is utterly personal and may therefore not be transferred or renounced. Since this right is in the final analysis constituted and also limited

---

27 J. SCHIRATZKI, 'Custody of Children in Sweden – Recent Developments', *Scandinavian Studies in Law*, Volume 38, 1999, p. 258.

by the child's welfare, it appears as a right and a duty for both the child and the parent concerned.[28]

[28] C. HEGNAUER, *Grundriss des Kindesrechts*, p. 128. More details in H. HAUSHEER, 'Die drittüberwachte Besuchsrechtsausübung', *Zeitschrift für Vormundschaftswesen*, 1998, p. 17 *et seq.*

QUESTION 46

E. CONTACT

To what extent, if at all, are the parents free to make contact arrangements? If they can, are these arrangements subject to scrutiny by a competent authority?

AUSTRIA

The parents and the child may and even should arrange the exercise of contact by mutual assent (Sec. 148(1) Austrian CC). For a contact arrangement to be implemented by force, it must be approved by the court (Sec. 109 and 110 Non-Contentious Proceedings Act *[Außerstreitgesetz]*). Thus, according to predominant opinion a contact arrangement is not legally binding until it has been approved in this manner.[1] The overriding criterion for the court's scrutiny are the child's best interests (Sec. 148(1) Austrian CC).[2]

BELGIUM

There is a distinction between contact arrangements between the parents, and contact arrangements between the parents and every other person. Concerning contact arrangements between the parents, since the joint exercise of parental responsibilities is considered to be the principle, regardless of whether the parents live together, parents who do not (or no longer) live together are not obliged to make an explicit contact arrangement,[3] but they may.[4] The Law does not provide for parental contact agreements, but does not exclude them either. Therefore, refering to the general principles, such agreements are possible and binding; they can be oral or written. However, the contractual freedom and binding effect of the agreement will be limited by the interests of the child. An agreement will only apply so long as the interests of the child do not require its modification. Unless otherwise legally required (see *infra*), parents are not obliged to go to court; the interference of the judge must be the exception. When arrangements are submitted to the Juvenile Court, it is not bound by them; however, it can include these arrangements in a judgement, after advice of the Public Prosecutor[5] and so long as these arrangements respect the interests of the child and the rules of parental authority (See Q 17). After ratification of

---

1 J. STABENTHEINER, 'KindRÄG 2001', in: P. RUMMEL, *ABGB-Kommentar*, suppl. vol. 1, 3rd Edition, Vienna: Manz Verlag, 2003, § 148 Marg. No. 1c with further references.

2 See *Oberster Gerichtshof*, 13.07.2000, *EFSlg.* 92.901; M. Friedrich, 'Was ist das Optimum des Kindeswohls', in: Schriftenreihe des Bundesministeriums für Justiz (Hg), *Gemeinsame Obsorge - Chance oder Scheinlösung?*, Vienna: 1996, p. 63.

3 Excepted in case of divorce by mutual consent.

4 Court of Appeal of Brussels, 07.05.1999, *Rev. trim. dr. fam.*, 2000, p. 637-643, annotated J.L. RENCHON; Court of Appeal of Ghent, 03.05.1999, *E.J.*, 2000, p. 56, annotated K. BROECKX.

5 Art. 765 Belgian Judicial Code and see Q 61a.

the agreement, Art. 1043 Belgian CC concerning the judgments of agreement will be applicable.

Can an agreement modify an agreement? As long as an agreement has not been submitted to the scrutiny of the Juvenile Court, it can be modified by another agreement. Once a judgment has been pronounced, the judgment will apply so long as it has not been replaced by another judgment[6] or by an agreement in case of divorce by mutual consent. A notarial deed or a judgment can also be modified by a judgment when it can be proven the agreement or judgement denies the interests of the child.[7]

Certain legal dispositions explicitly regulate contact arrangements between parents. The parents may conclude a partial or complete agreement concerning the person, the maintenance and the property of their children during a divorce based on fault (Art. 229-231 Belgian CC) or separation (Art. 232 Belgian CC). The Court of First Instance will ratify the agreement when it deems ratification proper (Art. 1258(2) Belgian Judicial Code).[8] Art. 1043 Belgian CC concerning the judgments of agreement is applicable for decisions that ratify an arrangement (Art. 1258(2)(3) Belgian Judicial Code). If there is no ratification of an agreement, the Court of First Instance sends the case to the President of the Court of First Instance (Art. 1258(2)(4) Belgian Judicial Code). In case of a divorce by mutual consent, the parents are obliged to work out an agreement concerning the authority over the person and the administration of the property of their child (Art. 1288(2) Belgian Judicial Code), as well as the contribution of each parent in the maintenance of the child (Art. 1288 (3) Belgian Judicial Code). The agreement must include an arrangement for during the divorce and for after the divorce is finalised. The Court of First Instance will review the agreement after the Public Prosecutor offers a written advice (Art. 1289 *ter* Belgian Judicial Code). The Court may suggest a change to the agreement when certain aspects of it seem contrary to the interests of the minor children, and it may decide to hear the children (See Q 59). The Court may alter or ban parts of

6 Cass. 05.09.1979, *R.W.* 1979-80, 1863, annotated L. DUPONT.

7 Court of Appeal of Brussels, 07.05.1999, *Rev. trim. dr. fam.*, 2000, p. 637-643, annotated J.L. RENCHON; Court of Appeal of Ghent, 03.05.1999, *E.J.*, 2000, p. 56, annotated K. BROECKX; J. GERLO, 'Overeenkomsten over kinderen', annotated cass. 16.01.1997, *R.W.* 1997-98, p. 118-120; B. MAINGAIN, 'Le pacte de séparation de fait : un mode de règlement licite du conflit familial', *Rev. Trim. Dr. Fam.* 1983, 248-249; J-L. RENCHON, 'Les conventions entre parents relatives à leurs droits et obligations à l'égard de leurs enfants', *Rev trim. dr. fam.*, 1988, p. 297.

8 It must be noted that according to Art. 232 Belgian CC, the pronouncement of the divorce based on a two year factual separation is submitted on the condition that the divorce will not tenderly affect the material condition of the minor children. By a judgment of 12.05.2004, the Constitutional Court has judged that this condition was against the principle of equality foreseen in the Art. 10 and 11 Belgian Constitution, because this condition was not provided in a case of divorce based on fault according to Art. 229 and 231 Belgian CC (Constitutional Court 12.05.2004, *Rev. not.* 2004, p. 354).

the agreement that are manifestly contrary to the interests of the children (Article 1290 Belgian Judicial Code). Finally, the Court will ratify the agreement (Art. 1298 Belgian Judicial Code).[9]

According to Art. 387 *bis* Belgian CC, these arrangements can always be modified. When a dispute arises, the competent authority is not bound by the existing arrangement, but will judge according to the interests of the child. The judge will then determine where the child will reside and where it will be registered in the Registers of Population (Art. 374 Belgian CC).[10]

Concerning contact arrangements between parents and other persons, Art. 375 *bis* Belgian CC provides that the Juvenile Court decides on the right of contact 'in the absence of agreement between the parties'. This implies that contact arrangements can be made, moreover, that the Juvenile Court will only be competent when no agreement can be reached between the parents and the other person. Therefore, in case of Art. 375 *bis* Belgian CC, it is impossible to present an agreement to the Juvenile Court (*e.g.* to preserve the future) when no discussion exists between the parents and the other person at the moment of the introduction of the dispute before the judge.[11] When an agreement is reached pending the dispute before the Juvenile Court, the judge can confirm it in its judgment.[12]

BULGARIA

The parents are free to make contact arrangements to the extent that they are free to make parental responsibilities agreements. If parents are not married and do not live together they are free to arrange both the residence of the child and contact. The same applies to a married couple that decides to live apart. The freedom to decide on contact is limited only in cases of divorce. See Q 17.

---

9 Some authors consider that discrimination exists between spouses who want to divorce by mutual consent and the others because only in case of divorce by mutual consent, must the parents have a written convention which is submitted to judicial scrutiny while other parents are free to make an agreement which will not directly be submitted to the scrutiny of the court (J. GERLO, E. DE GROOTE and A. WYLLEMAN, 'De uitoefening van het ouderlijk gezag en omgangsrecht', in *Gandaius Actueel I*, Antwerp: Story-Scientia, 1995, No. 240; *differently* F. BUYSSENS, 'Echtscheiding door onderlinge toestemming', in P. SENAEVE and W. PINTENS, *De hervorming van de echtscheidingsprocedure en het hoorrecht van de minderjarige*, Antwerp: Maklu, 1997, p. 287, footnote 209).

10 In case of divorce by mutual consent, Art. 1288 *in fine* and 1293 Belgian Judicial Code explicitly provide for this possibility, when the situation of the parents or the children changes due to new circumstances irrespective of the will of the parties, the competent authority may review the agreement, both during the divorce procedure as afterwards.

11 This confirmes the principles of Art. 17 and 18 Belgian Judicial Code.

12 A. DE WOLF, *Artikelsgewijze commentaar met overzicht van rechtspraak en rechtsleer personen- en familierecht* (Art. 375 *bis* Belgian CC), Antwerp: Maklu, 1997, p. 14-16.

CZECH REPUBLIC

The parental agreement on contact with the child does not require the approval of the court (Sec. 27 § 1 Czech Family Code) or any other state authority. However, the court will regulate contact between the parents and child if the parents cannot agree. The extent of the regulation depends on the child's age, his or her interests, the distance of the residence of both parents *etc.*

DENMARK

Parents are free to make contact arrangements and these are not subject to public scrutiny. In practice many cases at the administrative authorities are solved through an agreement between the parents resulting in a decision with the consent of the parents. An agreement allocating each parent half of the time will not be accepted as a contact arrangement, because the child is considered to be living with both parents.[13]

ENGLAND & WALES

The general policy of English law is to encourage parents to reach agreement themselves on their child(ren)'s upbringing and this is no less true of making contact arrangements. This policy is underscored by Sec. 1(5), which enjoins the court not to make any order unless it thinks in doing so it will benefit the child.

The extent to which the court has a power of scrutiny over any agreed contact arrangements varies according to the context in which they are made. Outside the context of litigation, for example on the parent's separation, there is, in the absence of any challenge, no power of scrutiny. Even where issues over a child's upbringing are litigated then outside the context of divorce, unless the issue of contact is specifically raised, the court will not necessarily be concerned to look at the contact arrangements. In the context of divorce, however, there is a general power of scrutiny, at any rate, to consider the arrangements as to the child's upbringing, pursuant to Sec. 41, English Matrimonial Causes Act 1973 (see Q 30).

FINLAND

A child's parents shall, by mutual understanding and having the best interests of the child as the first and paramount consideration, make every effort to ensure the implementation of the purpose of access in conformity with the principles stated in Sec. 1 Finnish Child Custody and the Right of Access Act. (Sec. 2 para. 2 Finnish Child Custody and the Right of Access Act)

Thus, the wording of the Child Custody Act seems to place parental cooperation and unofficial mutual agreements as ideals, especially concerning the exercise of access. If enforcement is needed, however, a parental agreement must be approved by the social local authority (Sec. 7 Finnish Child Custody and the Right of Access Act). The local social authority shall give due weight to the best interests of the child when considering the approval of the agreement.

---

[13] *Civilretsdirektoratet*, 13.12.1996, *Tidsskrift for familie- og arveret*, 1998.132.

The condition of the approval is that at least one of the parents has custody of the child.

FRANCE

It depends on the kind of separation: in the case of judicial separation (divorce, legal separation, annulment of marriage), the parents can make contact arrangements but they must submit them to the family judge who will approve the agreement unless it does not protect the child's interests or the consent of one parent was not freely given (Art. 373-2-7 French CC).

Parents are not obliged to go to court if there is a factual separation. They may make their own contact arrangements. Only if one parent does not agree with the arrangements proposed by the other[14] or if both parents want their contact arrangement to become official through judicial approval[15] does one or both parent(s) bring a petition before the family judge, who will then make a decision based on the child's interest.

GERMANY

Generally co-operation of the parents is needed and they are encouraged to reach contact arrangements.[16] However, a total renunciation of contact is against good morals (§ 138 German CC)[17] and prohibited (§ 134 German CC). It is argued that an agreement is invalid unless the non-exercise of contact is in the best interests of the child.[18] In general these arrangements are not necessarily subject to scrutiny by the family court,[19] however, the parents can submit their agreement to the court, which will then make a ruling on the agreement under § 1684 para. 3 German CC.[20] Under these circumstances there is also the possibility of the scrutiny of the court. There can also be arrangements in the framework of court proceedings. Where there is a dispute between parents a special mediation procedure in the family court can take place; see Q 57. In the framework of this procedure arrangements by the parents

---

14 See Art. 373-2-8 French CC: a parent can request the family judge to determine the modalities of exercise of parental responsibilities and the contribution to the child's maintenance.

15 See Art. 373-2-7 French CC. The same rules apply in every kind of separation (factual, judicial separation, divorce, *etc.*).

16 See S. HAMMER, *Elternvereinbarungen im Sorge- und Umgangsrecht*, Bielefeld: Gieseking, 2004

17 S. HAMMER, *Elternvereinbarungen im Sorge- und Umgangsrecht*, Bielefeld: Gieseking, 2004, p. 63.

18 See OLG Frankfurt a.M., 12.03.1986, *FamRZ* 1986, 596 (no contact of father against child support arrangement in favour of father); U. DIEDERICHSEN, in: PALANDT, *Bürgerliches Gesetzbuch*, 64th Edition, München: Beck, 2005,§ 1684 German CC No. 3.

19 S. MOTZER, 'Elterliche Sorge', in: D. SCHWAB, *Handbuch des Scheidungsrechts*, 5th Edition, München: Vahlen, 2004, Part. III No. 236.

20 OLG Düsseldorf, 27.09.1982, *FamRZ* 1983, 90, 91; S. MOTZER, 'Elterliche Sorge', in: D. SCHWAB, *Handbuch des Scheidungsrechts*, 5th Edition, München: Vahlen, 2004, Part. III No. 236.

can be made which have to be included in the proceedings, § 52a para. 4 German Act on Voluntary Jurisdiction.

With a divorce based on the consent of the parties there has to be a declaration of the parents that there will be no application on custody and contact (§ 630 para. 1 No. 2 alt. 1 German Code of Civil Procedure) or, if there will be an application on custody and contact, that the other spouse agrees (§ 630 para. 1 No. 2 alt. 2 German Code of Civil Procedure). One parent can get parental custody if the other spouse agrees and the child is not over 14 years, if the child objects (§ 1671 para. 2 No. 1 German CC). An application to end joint parental custody will be successful if it is in the best interest of the child (§ 1671 para. 2 No. 2 German CC). As a consequence of such an order an order on contact will also be issued (§ 1684 para. 3, 4 German CC).

GREECE

Art. 1520 para. 3 Greek CC provides that the court can regulate the exercise of the right to contact with the child. Nevertheless, it is accepted that the parents may enter into an agreement on this issue. Their contract is binding, but cannot be enforced, unless the court affirms it.[21]

HUNGARY

Parents are free to make arrangements about how to maintain contact with their child. If they exercise the parental responsibilities jointly they have to agree on the particulars, including issues of contact. If only one parent is holds parental responsibilities, the law prefers their agreement to the contact. The agreement has special importance in a divorce by consent as the arrangement of contact is one of the issues which the parties have to agree on. The court scrutinises whether this arrangement is in the interests of the child.

If there is no arrangement between parents on the contact, either the court or the public guardianship authority will resolve the case, primarily by establishing a settlement between the parents. The settlement will be approved if the contact is in the interests of the child and convenient to the aim of contact.

IRELAND

Sec. 20 Irish Guardianship of Infants Act 1964 places a positive duty upon a solicitor acting on behalf of the applicant seeking access to discuss with the applicant the existence of alternative means of dispute resolution, including the possibility of entering into an agreement with the respondent, by deed or otherwise in writing, dealing with the matter of access. If it appears to the court, during the course of proceedings, that agreement between the parties may be possible, Sec. 22 Irish Guardianship of Infants Act 1964 allows the court to

---

21 A. POULIADIS, in: A. GEORGIADIS and M. STATHOPOULOS (eds.), *Civil Code commentary, Vol. VIII, Family Law (Arts. 1505-1694)*, 2nd Edition, Athens: Law & Economy, P.N. SAKKOULAS, 2003, Art. 1520 Greek CC p. 314, No. 34-39. For the case of contact after a divorce by mutual consent see the answer to Q 17.

adjourn proceedings with a view to facilitating such agreement. Where an adjournment is obtained under Sec. 22, the parties may make attempts, either unaided or with the assistance of a third party, to seek an agreed solution to the access issue.

Any agreement in respect of access resulting from the negotiations outlined above can be made a rule of court by virtue of Sec. 24 Irish Guardianship of Infants Act 1964, although this is not necessary. This gives such agreement the like force and application of a court order and may be especially effective where there are strong fears of non-compliance. The court may accede to a request under Sec. 24 of the 1964 Act, however, only if it is satisfied that the agreement is fair and reasonable and, in all the circumstances, adequately protects the interests of the parties and the child.

ITALY

Parents are free to make contact arrangements; however, the arrangements made are subject to judicial scrutiny. The law provides this scrutiny (Arts. 158 Italian CC and Art. 4 § 13 Italian Divorce law) to ensure that arrangements made are not prejudicial to the interests of the child. The law attributes broad discretional powers to the judge, who can void the agreement made by the parents.[22]

LITHUANIA

Yes, parents are free to make contact arrangements. These agreements are subject to court control. The court takes control if these agreements violate the rights of the child or the rights of one of the parents.

THE NETHERLANDS

Parents are free to make contact arrangements; there are no special provisions applicable. The Minister of Justice proposes to introduce a duty for parents who want a divorce to substantiate their application for a divorce decree.[23] The proposals are aimed at an increase of the number of parents who come to terms on the consequences of their divorce and contact themselves.[24] Contact arrangements are subject to scrutiny by the court in so far that any party to the contract may request the court to change the existing arrangement on the ground that circumstances have changed. The court may request the Child Care and Protection Board to give advice on contact arrangements (Art. 810 Dutch Code of Civil Procedure). Recently, it has been suggested by experts and political organisations that parents who want a divorce should first agree on a

---

22 Supreme Court, 09.06.90, No. 5636, *Giust. civ.*, 1991, I, p. 1545. In this case the Court voided the arrangements the parents made during their separation which prohibited all contact between their children and the children's grandparents.

23 See Q 48.

24 *Kamerstukken Tweede Kamer*, 2003-2004, 29 520, No. 1, p. 3-4.

'parenting plan' (*ouderschapsplan*) and contact should be one of the issues on which parents should reach agreement.[25]

NORWAY

The parents are free to make contact arrangements, Art. 43 sec. 2 Norwegian Children Act 1981. They may also agree that the child shall live with the parents on an alternating basis, even if such an arrangement cannot be imposed by the court against the will of one of the parents. Parental agreements are not subject to scrutiny by any authority.

POLAND

In this situation, the general rule allowing the parents' free decision (within the child's best interest) is applied. The parent's freedom of decisions is controlled by the court in accordance to general rules.

PORTUGAL

The contact system is one of the aspects affected by the regulation of the new way of exercising parental responsibility. Thus, parents may decide what specific system will apply in the agreement established between them about the regulation of parental responsibility, to be ratified by the judge or appreciated by the Department of Justice.

RUSSIA

Parents are free to make a contact agreement (Art. 66 (2) Russian Family Code). The agreement must be in writing. The arrangements are not subject to scrutiny by a competent authority. The law does not explicitly state what happens if one of the parents violates a contact agreement. According to an influential opinion, such agreements are not legally enforceable, their violation 'cause no legal consequences,'[26] and the agreement is no more than 'a piece of evidence'.[27] This point of view, however, seems to be controversial. Treating contact agreements as not legally binding would mean that if one parent applies to court regarding the agreement's violation, the court would automatically set the agreement aside and decide upon contract arrangements as if no agreement has been made. Comparison of contact agreements with other agreements relating to children allows for the conclusion that this is definitely not the case. Even in cases where parental agreements are made in the framework of divorce procedure and are subject to obligatory judicial scrutiny, such as those

---

25 PVDA (Labour party), ''Ouder blijf je', Notitie april 2004, over ouderschap en scheiding', Den Haag. *Kamerstukken Tweede Kamer*, 2003-2004, 29 676, No. 1-3; C. DE HOOG/W.Q.J.M. ORBONS, *Integriteit van het ouderschap, Manifest of experts*, April 2004.

26 A A. NETCHAEVA, 'Commentary to Art. 66 Russian Family Code', in: I. KUZNETZOVA (ed.), *Commentary on the Family Code of Russian Federation*, Moscow: Jurist, 2000, p. 230.

27 A. NETCHAEVA, 'Commentary to Art. 66 Russian Family Code', in: I. KUZNETZOVA (ed.), *Commentary on the Family Code of Russian Federation*, Moscow: Jurist, 2000, p. 230.

regarding child maintenance or residence (Art. 24 (2) Russian Family Code), the court's starting point is to approve the parental agreement. Only if the agreement is against the interests of the child or one of the parents can it be set aside by the court. It is rather illogical to suggest that when the law does not prescribe obligatory judicial scrutiny to contact arrangements, the court is supposed to disregard the agreement without even investigating the possibility of its approval. Thus, if a contact agreement is violated by one of the parents, he or she can ask the court to approve and enforce the agreement. By doing this the court can scrutinise the agreement and refuse its enforcement only in case of violation of the interests of the child or one of the parents.

SPAIN

See Q 17 and 25. Agreements are permissible unless the child was declared to be bereaved or abandoned. See Q 32. Agreements must be approved by the judge, who can reject them if they are not in the child's best interests or detrimental to one of the parents. Scrutiny in practice, however, is rather formal because the judge will not have sufficient knowledge of the family's situation or why the agreements were made. Private agreements are not enforceable through the court system if they are not voluntarily complied with. If the agreements are breached, there is an action to ask for a court decision on contact. The agreement will be just one of the elements taken into account when the judge makes the decision.

SWEDEN

If the parents have joint custody of a child, or if one of them has sole custody, they may enter into an agreement concerning the child's right to contact with the non-residential parent. The agreement is valid if it is in writing, signed by both parties and approved by the social welfare committee. The social welfare committee shall approve of the agreement if it complies with the best interests of the child, Chapter 6 Sec. 15a Swedish Children and Parents Code.

SWITZERLAND

If (for example in connection with a parent-child relationship which still has to be established) no dispositions have been issued yet by the authority in regard to the father and mother's right, then in accordance with Art. 275 § 3 Swiss CC, personal contact may not be exercised against the will of the person who has parental responsibilities and/or custody. The person who has custody rights may therefore under these circumstances, until the authority has issued its dispositions, take decisions *de facto* on his or her own with regard to exercise of personal contact. This legal position also allows parents to make mutual arrangements to exercise personal contact. However, such arrangements are not enforceable. For this reason the father or mother may request that their right to personal contact (based on Art. 275 § 1 and 2 Swiss CC) be regulated by the competent authority in a binding manner (Art. 273 § 3 Swiss CC).

In a divorce ruling concerning personal contact, all important circumstances regarding the child's welfare are decisive. Consideration is to be shown to a joint petition by the parents, and also as far as possible to the child's opinion (Art. 133 § 2 Swiss CC).

QUESTION 47

E. CONTACT

Can a competent authority exclude, limit or subject to conditions, the exercise of contact? If so, which criteria are decisive?

AUSTRIA

The court may restrict or even revoke the exercise of contact if the child's interests are at risk, *i.e.* if a specific physical or emotional threat to the child's welfare exists (Sec. 148(2) and 176 Austrian CC). This applies, *e.g.* in the case of alcohol dependency,[1] relevant criminal conviction,[2] abuse of the relationship of authority,[3] but also in the case of sporadic exercise of the contact if the child is regularly disappointed by it.[4] The same is true if the parent entitled to contact interferes with the child's relationship with the other parent or other important contact persons; this concerns especially gross violations of the requirement of good behaviour set forth in Sec. 145b Austrian CC,[5] such as incitement of the child, insulting statements and physical or psychological violence against the other parent or contact persons.

Furthermore, the grandparents' exercise of contact may be restricted if this becomes necessary in order to prevent interference with the parents' family life or their relationship with the child (Sec. 148(3) Austrian CC). This is the case, for instance, if conflicts arise between the parents and the grandparents concerning the child's upbringing.[6]

If problems arise, any party to the proceedings, i.e. a parent or a child over 14 years of age, can petition the court for a visit escort *(Besuchsbegleitung,* section 111 Non-Contentious Proceedings Act *[Außerstreitgesetz]*): a suitable person, e.g., a relative, teacher, social worker, or employee of the youth welfare office, attends the meeting between the parent holding contact rights and the child, usually on neutral ground (a so-called "visit cafe" *[Besuchscafé]*).

---

1 *Landesgericht für Zivilrechtssachen* Vienna, 01.10.1996, *EFSlg.* 81.018.

2 *Landesgericht für Zivilrechtssachen* Vienna, 29.08.1985, *EFSlg.* 48.347, and 07.05.1987, *EFSlg.* 53.912.

3 *Landesgericht für Zivilrechtssachen* Vienna, 26.05.1994, *EFSlg.* 75.045.

4 *Oberster Gerichtshof,* 15.09.1981, *EFSlg.* 38.286.

5 See also Q 16 at the end.

6 *Landesgericht für Zivilrechtssachen Vienna,* 16.01.1996, *EFSlg.* 81.051; *Landesgericht Linz,* 22.12.2000, *EFSlg.* 93.001 et al.

BELGIUM

Yes, it can. It can even work out a solution that has not been asked for/proposed by the parents. The only decisive criteria are the interests of the child.[7]

BULGARIA

Yes, the court may exclude, limit or subject to conditions the exercise of contact on the basis of two criteria: interests of the child or conduct of the parent that is not living with the child.

There are two main arguments for revision of the measures related to the behaviour of the child: (a) where the child does not have an opportunity for the forcible enforcement of the contact order, and (b) change in circumstances connected with the contact arrangements. Thus, for instance, the definite refusal of a 'grown-up child not having reached full age' to fulfil the contact order, constitutes grounds for its revision'.[8] However, where there is proof that such attitude is instilled by the other parent's manipulation of the child, it will not constitute grounds for the revision of measures. Where there is a failure to enforce the contact order for reasons such as delay, incapacity to perform due to change in circumstances or in the interests of the child, the order may be revised. In all cases, however, the claim can only be enforced successfully if the change of circumstances definitely affects the interests of children, i.e. a change in circumstance does not automatically substantiate a change of measures, but there must also be an assessment from the perspective of the situation of the child.[9] Deterioration in the child's health may also constitute grounds for the revision of contact measures.[10]

The conduct of the parent fulfilling the measure of contact is also important. The court may limit the contact where 'the parent's behaviour jeopardizes the personality, upbringing or health of the child'.[11] Unfortunately, the court very rarely assesses the interests of a child in contact where the parents are in conflict or in situations where a parent is a perpetrator of violence.

The conduct of the parent who lives with the child may also constitute a ground for revisions of the contact order. This applies when the custodial parent obviously impedes the contact between the child and the other parent or instils the child with an attitude adverse to the other parent. With the first hypothesis, the possible change is aimed at limiting contact, in terms both of regularity and

---

7 Q. FISCHER, 'Les pouvoirs du juge qui fixe les modalités d'hébergement d'un enfant chez chacun de ses parents. Quelques réflexions sur les principes directeurs de l'instance', *Div. Act.*, 2002, p. 71.

8 Cases 473-1980; 2774-1980.

9 Cases 1571-71, 721-1974, 80-1978, 2929-1982, 1287-1983, 809-1983, etc. V.N. MLADENOV and P. BRATANOVA, *Family Code: Text, judicial practice etc*, 1996, p. 342-3.

10 Case 75-1970.

11 Case 758-1973, 1915-1970.

duration, or even termination. In the second hypothesis, a change of measures can be undertaken *i.e.* a change of the custodial/resident parent. The court has established that one parent's manipulation of the child against the other constitutes grounds for the revision of the measures in favour of the aggrieved parent.[12] The conduct of that parent however is also important: if he or she provokes fear in or manipulation of the child, no grounds will exist for the revision of measures.[13]

CZECH REPUBLIC

The court may limit or prohibit the parent's contact with the child if the interests of the child require it (Sec. 27 § 3 Czech Family Code). Limitation of contact means the original court decision regulating the parent's contact with the child is changed so that the extent of the originally regulated contact is made narrower. The court may also forbid the parent to keep contact with the child. These are situations where contact between the child and the other parent is traumatising for the child, or even dangerous, if the other parent is not able to guarantee due care of the child when the child is with him or her, or the relationship between the child and the other parent is seriously disrupted and the child refuses contact with the parent (*e.g.* if the parent committed a serious crime).

It is possible for the court to decide that the contact will take place in the presence of the parent who lives with the child (especially if the child is of tender years). Even though Czech legislation does not regulate the contact between the parent and the child in the presence of a third person (psychologist, social worker etc.), some courts have recently decided that the contact between the parent and the child in difficult cases is to take place in a special non-governmental institution which provides the parents and the child with help in making contact. For the time being, such a practice is unique, though.

DENMARK

The administrative authorities can exclude the exercise of contact if this is necessary for the child, Art. 17(3) Danish Act on Parental Authority and Contact. In 2001 statistics from the administrative authorities showed that a decision on contact was made in 96% of first time applications for contact and that contact was rejected in 6% of cases.[14] Statistics from 2003 show that exclusions contained a reference to the following main groups: the child's own opinion 57%, the child's age 29%, special circumstances relating to the contact parent 22%, lack of previous contact 8%, special circumstances relating to the child 19%, expert evidence 19%, sibling-related issues 6%, violence/incest 2%, risk of abduction 1%, the contact parent's inactivity 15%, other reasons 9%.[15]

---

12 Case 2130-71, SCCD- 1-1974, Case 2464-71, Case 1248-1982, Case 261-1984.

13 Cases 1212-1980 and 2774-1980-II (Civil Division).

14 Statistical report from *Civilretsdirektoratet*, June 2002, p. 10.

15 Statistical report from *Civilretsdirektoratet*, February 2004, p.16.

The administrative authorities decide on the amount of contact and how this should be exercised, Art. 17(1) Danish Act on Parental Authority and Contact. Consequently, contact may be limited or subjected to conditions such as supervised contact. Supervised contact may only be ordered where unsupervised contact is not possible, and should only be used where it is necessary for the child.[16] The administrative authorities may also impose other conditions for the exercise of contact such as conditions concerning the costs and manner of transportation.[17] More unusual conditions are sometimes stipulated, such as the stipulation that the contact parent should not take the child to a religious event during contact.[18]

ENGLAND & WALES

Yes, the court can exclude, limit or subject to conditions the contact between a child and a particular parent or other individual. The general governing principle is the child's welfare, which by Sec. 1(1), English Children Act 1989 is the court's paramount consideration.

As discussed in Q 43, contact can be limited to indirect contact, for example by post,[19] or it can be supervised. So far as prohibiting contact altogether is concerned, this will be based on what is determined to be best for the child. Examples of where contact has been denied altogether include

- *Re C (Contact: No Order for Contact)*[20] in which indirect contact was refused with a father who had been absent over a three year period and against whom the child had an extreme adverse reaction;
- *Re F (minors)(denial of contact,)*[21] in which contact with a transsexual father was refused primarily because of the children's (boys aged 12 and 9) own wishes;

---

16 Departmental order No. 874 of 24.10.2002, Art. 27(1).

17 I. LUND-ANDERSEN, N. MUNCK and I. NØRGAARD, *Familieret*, Copenhagen: Jurist- og Økonomforbundets Forlag, 2003, p. 83.

18 *Civilretsdirektoratet*, 10.04.2001, No. 1998-540-84, *Tidsskrift for familie- og arveret*, 2001.419.

19 See for examples of contact by post see *Re P (minors)(contact: discretion)* [1999] 1 FCR 566, *A v L (Contact)* [1998] 1 FLR 361 and *Re M (Contact: Conditions)* [1994] 1 FLR 272, each involving letter contact with a father in prison; *Re P (Contact: Indirect Contact)* [1999] 2 FLR 893 indirect contact with a father who had just been released from prison: *Re L (Contact: Transsexual Applicant)* [1995] 2 FLR 438 – indirect contact with a transsexual father; *Re D (Parental Responsibility: IVF Baby)* [2001] EWCA Civ 230, [2001] 1 FLR 972, CA, indirect contact with a man deemed to be the father under Sec. 28(3) and 29(1B), Human Fertilisation and Embryology Act 1990. For examples of indirect contact being ordered with violent or abusive parents, see *Re S (Violent Parent: Indirect Contact)* [2000] 1 FLR 481, *Re H (Contact: Domestic Violence)* [1998] 2 FLR 42, CA and *Re M (Sexual Abuse Allegations: Interviewing Techniques)* [1999] 2 FLR 92.

20 [2002] 2 FLR 723.

21 [1993] 2 FLR 677, CA.

- *Re H (children)(contact order (No 2)*,[22] where, contrary to the children's wishes, no contact order was made with a father who was suffering from Huntingdon's disease and who had in the past threatened to kill himself (and unknown to them) the children, it being found that the mother was at risk of suffering a nervous breakdown if a contact order was made;
- *Re T (a minor)(parental responsibility: contact)*,[23] in which an unmarried father was denied contact because of his violence towards the mother and his blatant disregard for the child's welfare;
- *Re C and V (Parental Responsibility and Contact)*,[24] in which the child had severe medical problems requiring constant and informed medical attention which the mother, but not the father, was able to give, and
- *Re D (a minor)(contact: mother's hostility)*[25] and *Re H (a minor)(parental responsibility)*[26] in which respectively the mother's and the stepfather's implacable hostility towards contact with an unmarried father was held to justify prohibiting contact.

FINLAND

According to the Finnish Child Custody and the Right of Access Act the court may order that a child shall have the right of access to the non-residential parent (Sec. 9 para. 1 point 5). The court shall issue directions on the conditions for access when deciding on the right of access (Sec. 9 para. 3).

These provisions of the Act have also been interpreted by the court to mean that the child does not have a right of access with the parent in question, if the contact is considered not to be in the best interest of the child. The exclusion of the right of access has, however, been regarded as very exceptional. A close and affectionate relationship between the child and its parent is an ideal that is generally considered to be in the best interests of the child (See Q 35).[27]

In cases where there is a risk that contact could harm the child, the courts often order that the child shall meet the parent under a third person's supervision, if this can be realised in practice. Although such an arrangement is not regulated in legislation, most communities and some private organisations provide

---

22 [2000] 3 FCR 385. This was the rehearing of the case remitted by the Court of Appeal reported as *Re H (children)(contact order)* 2[001] 1 FCR 49. *Cf Re M (Contact: Parental Responsibility: McKenzie Friend)* [1999] 1 FLR 75, CA, in which previously successful contact was overshadowed by the mother's fear of the father, though in this case, indirect contact was still granted.

23 [1993] 2 FLR 450, CA.

24 [1998] 1 FLR 392, CA.

25 [1993] 1 FLR 484.

26 [1993] 1 FLR 434. See also *Re B (a minor)(contact: stepfather's opposition)* [1997] 2 FLR 579, CA, in which the dismissal of the father's contact application was justified because of the child's stepfather's threat to reject the child and the mother.

27 M. SAVOLAINEN, *Lapsen huolto ja tapaamisoikeus*, Suomen Lakimiesliiton Kustannus Oy: Helsinki, 1984, p. 127-130.

opportunities for children to meet with their parents in controlled circumstances under supervision.

If the child has been taken into care, the child's right to maintain contact with any person close to it may be restricted on the following conditions:

1) If such contact clearly endangers the development or safety of the child; or
2) if such restriction is necessary for the safety or security of the parents, or of the family where the child is cared for or for the children or personnel at the institution, where the child is cared for. (Sec. 25 Finnish Child Protection Act).

FRANCE

The exercise of contact can only be denied for serious reasons, see Art. 373-2-1 para. 2 French CC. But the court can subject the exercise of this right to conditions, especially when the contact right will be exercised abroad.[28] The court may also allow a contact right to visit without any lodging right. The central criteria used by the judges are the child's interests. More generally the family judge may make an interim decision on the exercise of parental responsibilities and after a test period make a final decision (see, for example, Art. 373-2-9 para. 2 French CC).

GERMANY

The family court can decide on the existence and the extent of a right of contact. This includes the exercise of this right; also vis-à-vis third parties, § 1684 para. 3 German CC. The court can give injunctions to urge persons to fulfil their obligations under § 1684 para. 2 (§ 1684 para. 3 German CC); see Q 45. The family court can also restrict the right of contact or the execution of a former contact decision, insofar as this is in accordance with the welfare of the child, § 1684 para. 2 sent. 1 German CC. The circumstances of the individual case are decisive.

The court can determine how often and in what intervals contact shall take place.[29] Orders often give a contact right one or two weekends in a month. Visits during school holidays and holidays are also common. The appropriate place is generally the home of the parent (or person) with the contact right.[30]

---

28 See *e.g.* TGI Paris, 25.06.1982, *Gaz. Pal.*, 1982. 2. 396 (the parent having contact right can take the child abroad but will have to pay a 5,000 French Francs *astreinte* (fine) per day if the parent does not bring the child back at the end of the period fixed for the holidays). See also French Supreme Court, Civ. I, 03.02.1982, *Gaz. Pal.*, 1982. 1.342 (contact right limited to French metropolitan territory). The decisive criterion is the existing risk that the child could be abducted abroad and never returned to the parent having the exercise of parental responsibilities.

29 U. DIEDERICHSEN, in: PALANDT, *Bürgerliches Gesetzbuch*, 64th Edition, München: Beck, 2005, § 1684 German CC No. 15.

30 BGH 13.12.1968, *BGHZ* 51, 219, 224 = *NJW* 1969, 422; OLG Brandenburg, 08.08.2001, *FamRZ* 2002, 414 (two year old girl).

Often even the details of taking and returning the child have to be regulated.[31] The court can also try to prevent a jeopardy to the welfare of the child (§ 16666 German CC) by appointing a special curator (*Ergänzungspfleger*) for the regulation of the details of contact.

Among other things, the family court may determine that contact shall only occur when a third person prepared to collaborate is present, § 1684 para. 4 sent. 3 German CC (*betreuter* or *begleiteter Umgang*). This third party can be a natural person, but may also be a youth welfare institution or an association. The association then determines which single person fulfils the task, § 1684 para. 4 sent. 4 German CC. Supervised contact generally means that the non-custodial parent may visit the child at a particular time and in a particular place. This is one method of preventing the other parent from taking the children away without consent of the custodian.[32] It is also uses in cases where there was previous domestic violence.

The governing principle for contact orders is the welfare of the child. The custodian's interest in a family life with a new spouse (partner) without the disturbance of having contact with the other parent is left out of account.[33] The child's wishes have some influence. Although the overriding question will always be what is in child's welfare, the court has to take into account that contact with a parent is the general rule. The court has to strike a balance between the right of the child's self-determination and the right of the parent seeking contact.[34] Therefore, the factual reasons for a refusal are decisive. The child does not have the final say and it will be the court's decision just how much consideration is to be given to the child's wishes. This depends on the child's age, maturity, and the quality of the reasons.[35] The will of the child can be disregarded if it is obviously only the result of a parent's power of suggestion.[36]

The family court can also totally exclude the right of contact. *E.g.* a parent's violent behaviour towards the other parent can lead to a restriction or exclusion of the right to contact.[37] However, a decision which restricts the right of contact or its execution for a longer period, or permanently, may only be rendered if the

---

31 OLG Zweibrücken, 28.07.1998, *FamRZ* 1998, 1465.

32 OLG Brandenburg, 23.06.1999, *FamRZ* 2000, 1106; U. DIEDERICHSEN, in: PALANDT, *Bürgerliches Gesetzbuch*, 64th Edition, München: Beck, 2005, § 1684 German CC No. 28.

33 U. DIEDERICHSEN, in: PALANDT, *Bürgerliches Gesetzbuch*, 64th Edition, München: Beck, 2005, § 1684 German CC No. 21.

34 U. DIEDERICHSEN, in: PALANDT, *Bürgerliches Gesetzbuch*, 64th Edition, München: Beck, 2005, § 1684 German CC No. 23.

35 OLG Bamberg, 24.03.1999, *FamRZ* 2000, 46 (contact order despite resistance of the child).

36 BVerfG, 02.04.2001, *FamRZ* 2001, 1057 (six year old girl).

37 R. PROKSCH, *Rechtstatsächliche Untersuchung zur Reform des Kindesrechts*, Köln: Bundesanzeiger Verlag, 2002, p. 233 *et seq*; A. Will, ‚Gewaltschutz in Paarbeziehungen mit gemeinsamen Kindern', *FPR* 2004, 233, 235 *et seq*.

welfare of the child would otherwise be endangered, § 1684 para. 4 sent. 2 German CC. Therefore the family court will ask why it is in the child's interests for some form of contact not to be maintained or granted.

In practice, the person caring for an illegitimate child, *e.g.*, the mother, decides under what circumstances the father will have contact. If the parents cannot agree on the terms of contact, the father may apply to the family court to determine whether personal contact would endanger the child's welfare (§ 1684 German CC).

GREECE

The court specifically regulates the exercise of contact (Art. 1520 para. 3 Greek CC). Thus it may limit such contact, subject it to certain conditions,[38] or in extreme cases even exclude it.[39] In its decision, the court must weigh the interests of both the parents and the child *in concreto*, giving priority to those of the latter.[40] Within this framework, the effect of contact on the physical, mental and psychological health of the child is a decisive factor.[41]

HUNGARY

Both the public guardianship authority and the court have the power to limit or withdraw the right of contact of a parent who shows imputed behaviour or to order the right's interruption in the interests of the child.

The competent authority will reject a petition to rule on contact if the claimant seriously endangered the child's physical, mental, psychical and moral development or did not consistently perform his or her parental obligations through his or her own fault, or neglected them and did not change this behaviour.

---

38 A. POULIADIS, in: A. GEORGIADIS and M. STATHOPOULOS (eds.), *Civil Code commentary, Vol. VIII, Family Law (Arts. 1505-1694)*, 2nd Edition, Athens: Law & Economy, P.N. SAKKOULAS, 2003, Art. 1520 Greek CC p. 314, No. 45.

39 S. KOUKOULI- SPILIOTOPOULOU, in: A. GEORGIADIS and M. STATHOPOULOS (eds.), *Civil Code commentary, Vol. VIII, Family Law (Arts. 1505-1694)*, 2nd Edition, Athens: Law & Economy, P. N. SAKKOULAS, 2003, p. 81-82, No. 175.

40 A. POULIADIS, in: A. GEORGIADIS and M. STATHOPOULOS (eds.), *Civil Code commentary, Vol. VIII, Family Law (Arts. 1505-1694)*, 2nd Edition, Athens: Law & Economy, P.N. SAKKOULAS, 2003, Art. 1520 Greek CC, p. 313-314, No. 42, as well as the following decisions: Supreme Court, 534/1991, *Elliniki Dikaiosini* Vol. 32 (1991), p. 1505, District Court of Thessaloniki, 3253/1988, *Armenopoulos* Vol. 42 (1988), p. 989. See, however, S. KOUKOULI-SPILIOTOPOULOU, in: A. GEORGIADIS and M. STATHOPOULOS (eds.), *Civil Code commentary, Vol. VIII, Family Law (Arts. 1505-1694)*, 2nd Edition, Athens: Law & Economy, P. N. SAKKOULAS, 2003, p. 80, No. 172 who claims that the interest of the child is the only relevant criterion and cites relevant decisions of the European Court of Human Rights in support of this.

41 A. POULIADIS, in: A. GEORGIADIS and M. STATHOPOULOS (eds.), *Civil Code commentary, Vol. VIII, Family Law (Arts. 1505-1694)*, 2nd Edition, Athens: Law & Economy, P.N. SAKKOULAS, 2003, Art. 1520 Greek CC, p. 313-314, No. 42.

The competent authority will limit the right of contact if the entitled person abuses the right, causing damage to either the child or the person taking care of the child. This power of the authority cannot be exercised *ex officio* but only upon application. According to the law an abuse is realised if the entitled person exercises a right of contact that is not in compliance with a ruling, or does not maintain contact for a period of six months through his or her own fault. The limitation also means a change to the form of contact, its frequency or its length.

An interruption of contact can also be ordered, upon application, for the reason that the entitled person abused the right of contact by causing serious damage to either the child or the person taking care of the child. The maximum length of the interruption is six months, according to the law.

The most severe sanction, the termination of the right of contact, is also a consequence of the entitled person's behaviour: the competent authority withdraws this right if the entitled person not only seriously abuses this right, but also seriously endangers the child's upbringing and development. The entitled person can apply for the court or the public guardianship authority to re-establish the terminated, or restore the limited, right of contact and the authority can allow this claim if the circumstances the sanction was based on have changed.

IRELAND

The general rule in Ireland seems to be that contact between a child and his or her parent is to be maintained wherever practical. Where immediate direct contact cannot be ordered, the court is more likely to order supervised or indirect contact.

Where conditions are attached to an access order by an Irish court, they are normally properly related to the issue of access rather than injunctive type orders designed mainly to appease the custodial parent's need for protection.

In *O'D. v. O'D.*,[42] for example, the Irish High Court made it a condition of access by a father accused of sexual abuse of his child that one of the father's four sisters be present at all times. GEOGHEGAN J. pointed out that the primary matter to be considered by the court in determining access rights to a child was the welfare of the child. A substantial risk of abuse would have to be taken into account, but a parent's 'right to access' cannot be made dependent upon a finding of whether there was or was not, sexual abuse. A genuine risk, falling well short of probability, has to be considered relevant in the exercise of discretion in the determination of access rights, unless it is possible to exclude the possibility of sexual abuse on the balance of probabilities. This poses obvious difficulties for the parent accused of misbehaviour towards their child. It may take considerable time to investigate the allegation, and in the

[42] [1994] 3 Fam.L.J. 81.

intervening period the parent making the allegation may have exclusive care and control of the child. This can be surmounted in the intervening period by the granting of supervised access. In exercising its discretion in making orders for access, the court must separate the determination of any issue of sexual abuse from the exercise of such discretion. However, in practice, in Ireland, once an allegation of child sexual abuse is made against a parent by the other parent, the access of the accused parent to the child in question is either suspended or made subject to strict supervision pending the investigation of the allegation. Supervised access facilities are, unfortunately, practically non-existent and unless an agreed supervisor can be found, it is likely that there will be no access pending the completion of the investigation.

ITALY

The parental right to contact is protected so long as it is not prejudicial to the prevailing moral and material interests of the minor. Therefore the judge, within the broad discretionary powers attributed to him by the law, may limit or even exclude the exercise of this right by taking the pre-eminent interests of the child into consideration; for example, if the visit could cause harm to the child's physical or psychological growth. The court decisions underline that this neither constitutes a sanction against the parent nor terminates the parental rights[43] unless the behaviour is serious enough to create a judicial order of termination of the parental responsibility pursuant to Art. 330 Italian CC (see also Q 44b). Again, the decisive and exclusive criteria is always the moral and material interests of the minor.

LITHUANIA

Yes, the court shall have the right to exclude or limit the parents right of contact if the child's interests so require. The main criteria in such cases are the interests of the child. Such measures may be used as provisional measures of protection (Art. 3.65 Lithuanian CC), also in the event of separation of the parent from the child due to objective reasons (*e.g.* serious illness of the parent), as well as in the cases of restriction of parental authority (Art. 3.179-3.180 Lithuanian CC). Minimal contact with the child may be ordered only in cases where constant maximal contact is prejudicial to the child's interests.

THE NETHERLANDS

It depends on the situation. With two parents, both with parental responsibilities, it is not clear whether the court may disallow the right to contact of parent and child. The text of Art. 1:377h Dutch CC does not give that possibility,[44] but legal literature has argued that the court may disallow the

---

43 Supreme Court, 17.01.1996, No. 364, *Fam. dir.*, 1996, p. 227; Supreme Court 25.09.1998, No. 9606, *Fam. dir.*, 1999, p. 17. In this case, the Court granted the right of contact to a parent addicted to drugs, as this was not considered prejudicial to the minor.

44 ASSER-DE BOER, *Personen- en familierecht*, 2002, No. 1000.

right of contact when it is in the best interests of the child.[45] It seems also possible for the court to refuse to make a contact arrangement.[46] Further, changes might be achieved by a change in the exercise of parental responsibilities (Art. 1:253n Dutch CC).

If only one parent has parental responsibilities, the court may only disallow a right of contact on the limited grounds of Art. 1:377a § 3 Dutch CC. All these grounds are directly connected with the interests of the child. The right of contact may be denied if its granting would cause a serious detriment to the mental or physical development of the child, or if the parent is manifestly unfit or considered unable to have contact (for example caused by alcohol or drugs addiction of the parent), or when a child aged twelve or older has serious objections against contact or contact would otherwise be contrary to paramount interests of the child (for example because of the large travelling distance). The last ground is in practice the most important. The fact that the parent with parental responsibilities raises objections to contact is not decisive.[47] The court may not *ex officio* disallow the right of contact.[48] A temporary exclusion of the right of contact is possible[49] as is deferring the decision in order to obtain the advice of the Child Care and Protection Board.[50] The court may also limit the exercise of the right of contact by ordering experimental contacts (*proefcontacten*) that may be supervised by the Child Care and Protection Board. The court applies a different test to contact with a third person in a close personal relationship with the child. The court may disallow a contact order if it is against the best interests of the child or when the child aged twelve or older objects. This test is less stringent than the one applied in case of a parent, where it is more difficult to deny contact.

NORWAY

Either of the parents may at any time ask the court to deny the right of contact. The court may also upon request of one of the parents change the visiting rights the parents have agreed to. The decisive criteria are the interests of the child, Art. 48 Norwegian Children Act 1981, and the wishes of the child.

Visiting rights are paramount. They will only be denied under special circumstances. The Norwegian Children Act 1981 has no provisions on the issue, but the criteria formulated by the Supreme Court are that the right of contact should only be denied if there is a reasonably strong possibility that it

---

45 S.F.M. WORTMANN, *Losbladige Personen- en familierecht*, Art. 377h No. 3.

46 P. VLAARDINGERBROEK *et al*, *Het Hedendaagse Personen- en Familierecht*, 2004, p. 369. District Court Zutphen, 19.11.2002, *LJN* AF 7216.

47 ASSER-DE BOER, Mr. C. *Asser's Handleiding tot de beoefening van het Nederlands Burgerlijk Recht. Personen- en Familie Recht*, 2002 No. 1009-1010; S.F.M. WORTMANN, *Losbladige Personen- en familierecht*, Art. 377a, No. 4.

48 See Supreme Court 8.12.2000, *NJ*, 2001, 648 annotated J. DE BOER.

49 See Supreme Court 28.11.1997, *NJ*, 1998, 166.

50 See Supreme Court 17.11.2000, *NJ*, 2001, 121 annotated S. WORTMANN.

could be seen as undesirable for the child.[51] In one case, two children 11 and 13 did not wish to see their father, and the court held that this was a case where contact between father and children was impossible to enforce; hence contact had to be placed on a voluntary basis.[52] If there were a risk that the parent would abduct the child, right of contact would also be denied.[53]

POLAND

The parental limitation of personal contact with the child may be ordered if their parental authority was limited by placing the child with a foster family or a child-care institution (Art. 113 § 2 Polish Family and Guardianship Code). The contact prohibition may also be effected with regard to a parent deprived of parental authority, should the child's wellbeing so require (Art. 113 § 1 Polish Family and Guardianship Code).

PORTUGAL

The court may modify, suspend or suppress the right of contact in the event of a change of circumstances (Art. 183 Portuguese Child Protection Law). The law does not determine in which cases the right of contact may be modified, suspended or suppressed; however, case law has provided some indications. In situations of serious illness, mental disorder of the non-custodial parent, lack of information about the residence of that parent, change of residence of the non-custodial or of the custodial parent, or lack of interest on the part of the child as a result of long periods without contact *etc.*, the court may decree an alteration or suspension of contact rights. Cases of suspension occur, specifically in cases where the non-custodial parent is an alcoholic or drug-addict, given that such addictions are very destabilising for the child, since the parent may take the child to places where the child's safety, health or moral education is at risk; this is not, however, true for contacts with a child that has greater maturity and discernment.

RUSSIA

There is no specific legal provision empowering a competent authority to exclude or limit the exercise of contact, or to subject it to certain conditions. However, the law gives the parent who lives with the child the ability to refuse another parent contact with the child if 'such contact causes physical or psychological harm to the child or is detrimental to child's moral development' (Art. 66 (1) Russian Family Code). The parent living apart from the child who does not agree with the refusal of contact upon this ground can bring the case to the court. The court is then entitled to scrutinise whether the invocation of the aforementioned provision has been justified. If the court finds that the contact can indeed constitute a danger for physical or psychological health of the child, or to its moral development, it can exclude or limit the contact, or subject the contact to certain conditions. The Supreme Court has urged the courts to

51 Rt. 1976 p. 1497.
52 Rt. 1987 p. 456.
53 Rt. 1983 p. 897.

understand that every case of refusal or limitation of contact needs serious motivation.[54]

Art. 66 (1) has been designated as a measure to protect a child against serious danger, such as incest, influence of criminal parents, parents addicted to drugs or alcohol, *etc.* However, in practice it often is misused by a parent, mostly a mother, in order to put an end to the father's personal relationship with the child. If such a mother is well-advised and persuasive enough she can always collect sufficient evidence that the child 'gets a cold every time it goes out with the father', 'sleeps badly' or 'is distressed' after meeting with the father. She then has a good chance to win the case. This situation has given rise to grievance on the part of the fathers, who justly feel themselves to be *de facto* excluded from exercising their parental rights.[55] The statistical evidence shows that only 33% of divorced fathers often see their children, while 17% of children of divorced parents actually lose all contact with their father.[56]

The right of the parent(s) to maintain contact with the child can be effected by the decision of a court to restrict their parental rights and to take the child away from them according to Art. 75 Russian Family Code. The contacts between the child and the parent whose parental responsibility has been restricted are conditioned upon the permission of the Guardianship and Curatorship Department, another parent, guardian, foster parents of the child or the administration of the institution for children without parental care (Art. 75 Russian Family Code). The contacts can be allowed only if they do not negatively influence the child (Art. 75 Russian Family Code).

SPAIN

The competent authority can limit, suspend or subject contact to conditions if there are serious circumstances justifying this measure or if the duties imposed in the judicial decision are gravely and repeatedly not complied with (Art. 94 Spanish CC and Art. 135.2 Catalan Family Code). A total and irrevocable exclusion of contact is not permissible because circumstances may change, and it may then be possible to recover contact if it is in the best interests of the child.

The Spanish CC and the Catalan Family Code allow for the suspension, modification or limitation of contact if parents do not fulfil their duties. These duties are clearly the duties implicit in the exercise of contact, such as the duty to return the child or to act loyally towards the other parental responsibility

---

54 Item 8 of the Directive of the Supreme Court of the Russian Federation of 27.05.1998 No. 10 'On the Application of the Legislation by Dissolving Cases Relating to the Education and Care for Children', *Bulleten' verhovnogo suda RF*, 1998, No 7.

55 Such fathers have established an association called 'Fathers and Children' which is actively campaigning for 'fathers' rights'. See the site of the association: http://www.orc.ru/otcydeti/jurists.

56 *Demoscope weekly*, N 09-10, 26.02.2001- 11.03.2001.

holder. Contact cannot be restricted because the maintenance obligation was not fulfilled.

Contact can also be modified on grounds of other serious circumstances such as sexual harassment, serious mental illness or drug addiction. The child's wishes are also used a criterion to limit contact, especially in the case of older children.

In practice, courts tend to be very restrictive in limiting contact, whereas it is quite common to supervise contact, or subject contact to conditions such as surveillance by psychologists or social workers. Bigger cities have *Puntos de encuentro*, which are places in which contact can take place.

SWEDEN

When deciding issues concerning contact, the best interests of the child shall always be the primary consideration. In this respect, the law mentions certain factors to be taken into account, Chapter 6 Sec. 2a and b Swedish Children and Parents Code. These include the child's need for close and good contact with both parents, and the risk of the child abuse, kidnapping or other harm. Regard shall be given to the child's wishes, taking into account the child's age and maturity. Therefore, ensuring of the best interests of the child presupposes a right for the court to submit the exercise of contact to certain conditions and, in some cases, to even exclude contact with a parent.

Decisive criteria for excluding contact include the risk of the child being abused, unlawfully removed or detained, or otherwise suffering harm. It has been suggested in the legal literature that the risk of unlawful removal or detention of the child might lead to full exclusion of contact.[57] Also a conflict deep and ongoing enough to prevent them from cooperating regarding the child may result in the exclusion of contact, at least for a limited time.[58] Furthermore, the child's opinion shall be regarded, bearing in mind that a decree on contact generally cannot be enforced against the wish of a child who has reached the age of twelve.[59]

Swedish courts are generally very reluctant to exclude contact with a parent altogether, since such a decision is perceived as an infringement on the child's right to a close and good contact with both parents. The balance between the child's need of contact with both parents and the risk the contact might entail arose in a case examined by the Supreme Court, NJA 2003 p. 372. The father of a three-year-old girl requested contact; the mother had sole custody. In the Court's opinion the father's personality (at the time of the decision) entailed a concrete risk that the child could be psychically harmed by contact with the

---

57 G. WALIN and S. VÄNGBY, *Föräldrabalken, En kommentar, Del I, 1-13 kap.*, Stockholm: Norstedts Juridik, 2002, p. 6:69.

58 G. WALIN and S. VÄNGBY, *Föräldrabalken, En kommentar, Del I, 1-13 kap.*, Stockholm: Norstedts Juridik, 2002, p. 6:67.

59 Chapter 21 Sec. 5 Swedish Children and Parents Code.

father. This risk could, however, be neutralized if contact were limited to three hours every other week, which the Court also ordered. In addition the Court ordered that the contact should take place in the presence of a representative from the social welfare committee. Such restrictions are not unusual measures, ordered to prevent abusive contact. The court can also stipulate conditions regarding where the contact shall take place, Chapter 6 Sec. 15 para. 3 Swedish Children and Parents Code. In case the non-residential parent lives abroad, it might be necessary for the court to order that contact may only take place within the country of the forum.

When parents contact the social welfare committee for approval of their agreement on contact, all of the stipulations must be approved by the committee, save stipulations for travel costs resulting from the exercise of contact.[60] The social welfare committee can, with reference to the best interests of the child, require that certain issues are regulated in detail in the agreement.[61]

SWITZERLAND

If the exercise or non-exercise of personal contact proves to have a detrimental effect on the child, the competent authority may issue warnings or instructions to the parents or the child (Art. 273 § 2 Swiss CC). The authorities may for example regulate visiting arrangements if this was not previously done, or modify unsuitable visiting arrangements or forbid the person in question to get in touch with the child outside the visiting rights granted.

'If the child's welfare is endangered as a result of personal contact, if the parents do not fulfil their duties in exercising parental contact, if they do not take proper care of the child or if there are other just causes, they may be refused or deprived of the right to personal contact' (Art. 274 § 2 Swiss CC). It is deemed to be a failure to fulfil duties if for example there is a breach of the duty of loyalty as defined in Art. 274 § 1 Swiss CC when visiting rights are exercised, or if instructions concerning visiting rights are not complied with or if visiting rights are only exercised irregularly and haphazardly.[62]

When interpreting the criterion 'not taking proper care of the child', Art. 265c Section 2 Swiss CC is to be consulted in view of the use of the same term.[63] For example, a parent who does not contribute to his or her child's welfare, who continuously leaves the care of his child up to other persons and who does not make any effort to build up or maintain an active relationship with the child is deemed not to be taking proper care of the child.[64]

---

60 G. WALIN and S. VÄNGBY, *Föräldrabalken, En kommentar, Del I, 1-13 kap.*, Stockholm: Norstedts Juridik, 2002, p. 6:71-6:72.

61 G. WALIN and S. VÄNGBY, *Föräldrabalken, En kommentar, Del I, 1-13 kap.*, Stockholm: Norstedts Juridik, 2002, p. 6:61.

62 BBl 1997 II 55.

63 BGE 118 II 21, 25.

64 BGE 118 II 21, 25; Pra 1993, 365, 367.

Examples of 'other just causes' are: if the child who is capable of good judgment consistently rejects the contact without any influence being exerted,[65] if there is reasonable suspicion of sexual abuse and no other way to avert danger,[66] if the child is neglected, physically or mentally abused[67] or if the tension between the parents is such that it triggers irresolvable conflicts of loyalty; above all in the case of younger children.[68]

Since the right to personal contact is now a basic constitutional right, great restraint is to be exercised in ordering a total deprivation of this right. In many cases it is possible to alleviate an existing conflict by having a third party supervise the exercise of this right.[69]

---

65 BGE 126 III 219, 222; 111 II 405, 407; 107 II 301, 303.

66 BGE 120 II 229, 232 *et seq*; 119 II 201, 205 *et seq.*

67 BGE 122 III 404, 407.

68 BGE 120 II 177, 181; 115 II 317, 320; 115 II 206, 210.

69 See, among others, H. HAUSHEER, 'Die drittüberwachte Besuchsrechtsausübung – Rechtliche Grundlagen', *Zeitschrift für Vormundschaftswesen* 1998, p. 17 *et seq.*

QUESTION 48

E. CONTACT

What if any, are the consequences on parental responsibilities, if a holder of parental responsibilities with whom the child is living, disregards the child's right to contact with:
(a) A parent;
(b) Other persons?

AUSTRIA

(a) A parent

The parent with whom the child is living is obliged to enable and support the other parent's exercise of his or her right of contact. A violation of this duty to afford the other parent regular contact with the child will by operation of law expand the other parent's right to be informed and to express his or her opinion about important matters involving the child (Sec. 178(1) sentence 2 Austrian CC)[1]. To enforce the right of contact, the court must primarily order compulsory measures, which may range from reprimands and fines all the way to detention (Sec. 110 (2) in conjunction with Sec. 79(2) Non-Contentious Proceedings Act *[Außerstreitgesetz]*)[2]. If these measures fail, the parental responsibilities may even be totally or partially revoked as a last resort (Sec. 176(1) Austrian CC)[3].

(b) Other persons

In this case as well, to enforce the right of contact in relation to other persons the court will adopt compulsory measures (Sec. 110(2) in conjunction with Sec. 79(2) Non-Contentious Proceedings Act *[Außerstreitgesetz]*) and, as a final resort, may even - at least partially - revoke the parental responsibilities (Sec. 176(1) Austrian CC).[4]

---

1 See Q 44b.

2 See Q 58.

3 M. SCHWIMANN in: M. SCHWIMANN, *Praxiskommentar zum ABGB*, Vol. I, 2nd Edition, Vienna: Orac, 1997, § 148 Marg. No. 20. The recalcitrant parent may also lose his/her spousal maintenance (Sec. 74 Austrian CC); *Oberster Gerichtshof*, 21.21.1995, *EFSlg.* 78.714 = *Juristische Blätter*, 1996, p. 402 = *Österreichischer Amtsvormund*, 1996, p. 170; M. ROTH, 'Europäische Menschenrechtskonvention und Privatrecht: Landesbericht Österreich', *Rabels Zeitschrift für ausländisches und internationales Privatrecht (RabelsZ)*, 1999, p. 735.

4 STABENTHEINER, 'KindRÄG 2001', in: P. RUMMEL, *ABGB-Kommentar*, suppl. vol. 1, 3rd Edition, Vienna: Manz Verlag, 2003, § 148 Marg. No. 10.

BELGIUM

(a) A parent

If a parent disregards the child's right of contact with its parent, it will not have any direct consequence on parental responsibilities. However, this attitude can be considered as being against the interests of the child so that, if claimed by the Public Prosecutor or the other parent, the competent court has the possibility to decide that the child should live with the other parent. Besides, the right to contact can be enforced in different ways. However, only judgments are enforceable; whithout a court decision,[5] the disregard of the child's right to contact cannot be enforced. First, the court decision can be submitted to forced execution, by a bailiff, if necessary '*manu militari*'. Although it is possible, it is not considered to be opportune, certainly not for older children. In practice, it does not happen anymore. Second, the court can submit the right of contact to the payment of a fine. If the right of contact is not respected, a certain financial compensation will be due every time the right of contact is disregarded according to Art. 1385 *bis* Belgian Judicial Code.[6] A third enforcement-system is the system of damage. Indeed, compensation can afterwards be claimed if it has appeared that the right conferred by court decision has been disregarded.[7] A fourth option is a criminal action that can be taken against the parent who disregards someone's right of contact, according to Art. 432 Belgian Penal Code.[8] This parent may be sentenced to imprisonment for a term of eight days to one year and be fined to €26 to €1000. Finally, Art. 1322 *bis* - 1322 *octies* Belgian Judicial Code organise the procedural issues concerning the enforcement and protection of international rights of contact in the context of the Hague Convention of 25 October 1980 on the Civil Aspects of International Child Abduction and the European Convention of 25 May 1980 on Recognition and Enforcement of Decisions concerning Custody of Children and on Restoration of Custody of Children, namely by providing simplified proceedings commenced by an application before the President of the Court of First Instance of the place of residence of the child at that moment. The

---

5 This is for example when the parents or their lawyers have made a provisional agreement pending the decision of the judge.

6 P. SENAEVE, in *Comm. Pers.*, 'de dwangsom' (Art. 1385 *bis*-1385 *nonies* Belgian Judicial Code) (1998); J. VAN COMPERNOLLE, 'L'astreinte', *Rép. not.*, Brussels: Larcier, 1992, T.XIII, L. IV-6; K. WAGNER, 'Dwangsom en omgangsregeling', *A.J.T.*, 2001-2002, p. 337.

7 H. DE PAGE, *Traité élémentaire de droit civil belge*, T. II (Les Personnes), Vol. 2 (by J.-P. MASSON), Brussels: Bruylant, 1990, p. 991.

8 Art. 432 Belgian Penal Code, formerly Art. 369 *bis* Belgian Penal Code; Cass. 02.12.1997, *Div. Act.*, 1998, p. 102; Cass. 28.10.1987, *J.T.*, 1988, p. 144; M.-A. BEERNAERT, 'Droit pénal de la famille - Chronique de jurisprudence 1992-1997', *Div. Act.*, 1998, p. 98; J. DE GAVRE, 'A propos de l'arrêt de la Cour de Cassation du 22 octobre 1980 et de l'article 369 *bis*, al. 4 du Code Pénal', in *Mélanges offerts à Robert Legros*, Brussels: Ed. ULB, 1985, p. 151-164; J. MESSINE and M. HIRSCH, 'Propos sur le délit de non-présentation d'enfant', in: *Mélanges offerts à R. Vander Elst*, Brussels: Nemesis, 1986, p. 643; L. STEVENS, 'Over strafrecht, uit de echt gescheiden ouders en hun kinderen. Een decennium rechtspraak m.b.t. art. 369 *bis* Sw. (1989-1999)', *E.J.*, 1999, p. 130-142'.

President will settle the case as in interim injunction proceedings (Art. 1322 *sexies* Belgian Judicial Code); the defendant will have no right to submit a counterclaim (Art. 1322 *octies* Belgian Judicial Code).

(b) Other persons

There are no consequences for parental responsibilities if the parent with whom the child is living disregards the right of contact of that child with other persons. The possibilities to enforce performance of the right of contact are the same as described under Q 48a.

BULGARIA

(a) A parent

The fulfilment of the contact regime is one of the points of conflict between parents. For the aim of preventing conflict, the court has always emphasised that additional obligations arise for the parent with whom the child is living: to observe correct contact with the other parent, not to manipulate the attitude of children against him/her and not to infringe upon his or her reputation.[9] The parent obstructing the establishment of contact bears criminal liability[10] and also risks the enforcement of measures for the limitation or termination of parental rights,[11] or the revision of the court orders regarding parental rights. The latter practice is of highest incidence.

(b) Other persons

If the parent, with whom the child lives, impedes contact with the grandparents, the latter are entitled to request the court to arrange contact with the child (Art. 70 § 2 Bulgarian Family Code). Such a regime can only be ruled inasmuch as it corresponds to the interests of the child. If the parent deters the fulfilment of the court decision, the only unfavourable legal consequence is the penal liability for the non-performance of a court decision.

CZECH REPUBLIC

(a) A parent

Preventing the other parent from contact with the child has been a debated problem for some time the Czech court practice. Provisions on execution of a judgment regulated by the Civil Procedure Code are little effective in such situations. For that reason the 1998 reform supplemented Sec. 27 § 2 Czech Family Code, with a provision establishing that disregarding the entitled parent's right to contact with the child, if repeatedly unjustified, is considered as a change of the child's situation requiring a new decision on upbringing environment. On the basis of this provision the court may decide on placing the

---

9 Supreme Court (Civil Division) Decision 1/1974. Current judicial practice also emphasises the obligation of the custodial parent to ensure contact with the other parent (Case 2416-1981 (Civil Division), including through a motivating influence over the child (Cases 313-1982 (Civil Division), 1713-1982 (Civil Division)).

10 According to Art. 270 Bulgarian Criminal Code.

11 According to Art. 74 and 75 Bulgarian Family Code.

child into the other parent's care. However, in practice, the provision does not stop problems concerning the contact between the parent and the child[12] either, as the court would have to take into consideration whether such a change of upbringing environment is in the interests of the child. In one particular case, a court came to the conclusion that a parent had been repeatedly and without justification prevented from maintaining contact with the child, but the child refused the parent (syndrome of rejected parent), in fact he did not know the other parent any more and had a deep emotional bond with the parent living with him in a common household. In that situation the court decided that it was not in the interests of the child to be placed into the care of a parent with whom the child refuses contact.

(b) Other persons

The court may regulate contact of the child with grandparents or siblings if the interests of the child and the family situation require it (Sec. 27 § 4 Czech Family Code). When someone prevents this contact with the child, the court may proceed to impose fines for non-compliance with a judgment, pursuant to Sec. 272 and 273, Czech Code of Civil Procedure.

DENMARK

(a) A parent

If a parent disregards the child's or rather the other parent's right to contact, the other parent may turn to the enforcement court. Enforcement measures consist of fines, detention of the guilty parent or the physical fetching of the child.[13] These measures do not directly affect parental authority. The other parent may, however, seek sole parental authority or seek to have parental authority transferred from the guilty parent. In 1996 the obstruction of contact was inserted in the provision concerning the transfer of parental authority as the only mentioned consideration.[14] The general criterion of the provisions on the transfer of parental authority is what is best for the child, Art. 12 and 13 Danish Act on Parental Authority and Contact. A number of high-profile cases concerning the transfer of parental authority have since 1996 dealt with the obstruction of contact, but in none of the cases has parental authority been transferred on the basis of obstruction alone.[15]

---

12 M. Kralik, 'De verborum significatione aneb zamysleni nad novelizovanym ustanovenim § 27 odst. 2 zákona o rodine', *Pravni praxe*, 7/1999.

13 Danish Civil Procedural Act, *Lov om rettens pleje*, No. 815 of 30.09.2003 with later amendments, Art. 497(2).

14 This consideration was not contained in the first draft of the Act but was added in the course of the parliamentary debate on the Act, although it was mentioned amongst other considerations in the comments, Commission report 1279/94, p. 145. The consideration is popularly known to be the hallmark of fathers' rights movements.

15 For example, *Højesteret*, Supreme Court, 30.10.2000, U2001.153H.

(b) Other persons

Other persons do not have a right of contact. Disregarding a child's contact with such persons will not have any direct impact on parental authority, although disregarding contact may have a bearing on the parent's parenting abilities.

ENGLAND & WALES

(a) A parent

There are no consequences, as such, on the parental responsibility of a holder of parental responsibility with whom the child is living, if he or she disregards a child's "right" of contact with a parent but the issue can be taken to court and if it is then denied contrary to a court order then action can be taken to punish that person for contempt of court (that can be imprisonment and/or a fine) (See Q 58). An alternative sanction is to transfer residence.[16]

The disobedience or frustration of a contact order is a particularly key issue of contemporary importance in English law and has been the subject of much litigation[17] and comment and the Government have promised to strengthen the sanctions.[18]

(b) Other persons

One key difference between parents and other persons is that unlike the former, the latter have no prima claim of contact. The position is different if they have a contact order in their favour. If a holder of parental responsibility disobeys or seeks to frustrate a contact order they are liable to the sanctions for contempt of court (principally imprisonment or a fine - see Q 58) but notwithstanding that contempt, there is no direct consequence, as such, on the position with regard to parental responsibility.

FINLAND

(a) A parent

The court may order the enforcement of a court decision or approved parental agreement concerning a child's right of access with the other parent. The order may concern a threat of a fine under which the custodian shall allow the child to meet with its parent. Since 1996 it has also been possible for the court to issue a *fetc.*hing order. The child may then be brought to meet with its parent by the executor (in the presence of a social worker) for a special occasion.[19] If the child has been taken into care, the parents and other persons close to the child who

---

16 See *e.g.* *V v V (Contact: Implacable Hostility)* [2004] EWHC 1215 (Fam), [2004] 2 FLR 851.

17 See the excellent analysis by BRACEWELL J in *V v V (Contact: Implacable Hostility)* 2004] EWHC 1215 (Fam) and by MUNBY J in *Re D (Intractable Contact Dispute: Publicity)* [2004] EWHC 727 (Fam), [2004] 1 FLR 1226.

18 See the Government Green Paper: *Parental Separation: Children's Needs and Parental Responsibilities* Cm 6273 (July 2004), discussed at Q58.

19 See M. HELIN, 'Enforcement of Custody, Access and Residence Orders, Intercountry Adoptions and Registration of Same Sex Couples', in: A. BAINHAM (ed.), *International Survey of Family Law 1997,* The Hague: Kluwer, 1999, p. 156.

have been subject to a restriction of contact with the child can appeal to the administrative court. The child may appeal if it is 15 years old (Sec. 10 para. 2 Finnish Child Protection Act).

(b) Other persons

There are no coercive measures to be taken in the case the custodian is not providing the child with the possibility of keeping contact with persons the child is close to other than the parents. If the child has been taken into care, the parents and other persons close to the child who have been subject to a restriction of contact with the child can appeal to the administrative court. The child may appeal if it is 15 years old (Sec. 10 para. 2 Finnish Child Protection Act).

FRANCE

(a) A parent

Each parent must respect the relationship the child has with the other parent (Art. 373-2 para. 2 French CC). If a holder of parental responsibilities with whom the child is living disregards the child's right to contact with a parent, the holder could be condemned by a criminal court on the ground of Art. L 227-5 French Criminal Code (*non-représentation d'enfant.* Possible sanctions: 'The unlawful refusal to produce a minor child to the person who has the right to require the production of the child is punished by one year imprisonment and a fine of €100,000'), or Art. L 227-6 French Criminal Code (if the parent with whom the child lives has not informed the other parent of his change of domicile).[20] The criminal court (*tribunal correctionnel*) is competent. If the impossibility for the parent to exercise his contact right is caused by the child's behaviour (*i.e.* the child refuses to see the parent), the other parent must try to convince the child to have contact with his father or mother. Only if the child's refusal is insurmountable will the holder of parental responsibilities not be subject to criminal condemnation.[21]

The family judge (as a civil court) could also, upon the request of the parent having contact rights, modify the exercise of parental responsibilities by amending a prior decision. The judge can also order an *astreinte* (civil fine) that the holder of parental responsibilities will have to pay to the other parent if she or he does not let the other parent exercise his contact right.[22]

---

20 Art. 227-6 French Criminal Code: 'The failure of a person whose children habitually reside with him to notify those persons who pursuant to a judgment or a judicially affirmed agreement are entitled to exercise visiting or residence rights over such children, of his change of address within one month from the date of such change is punishable by six months imprisonment and a fine of €7,500'.

21 French Supreme Court, Crim., 25.02.1964, *D.* 1964. P. 414; 13.04.1988, *D.* 1989. P. 461 annotated RENUCCI.

22 See CA Rennes, 18.03.1982, *D.* 1983. IR. p. 449.

(b) Other persons

The offence of refusal to produce a child, Art. L 227-5 French Criminal Code, applies to all cases in which the holder of parental responsibilities disregards a contact right that belongs to the child who lives with him or her.

GERMANY

(a) A parent

According to § 1684 para. 2 German CC, each parent shall refrain from impairing the child's relationship with the other parent (*Wohlverhaltensgebot*). If the holder of parental responsibilities with whom the child is living disregards the child's right of contact with a parent, the consequences on parental responsibilities depend on the situation. The other parent can make an application to the family court; then the court has to look for an understanding or to the use of counselling (§ 52 German Act on Voluntary Jurisdiction), see Q 57. Where a court order already exists, a special court conciliation procedure can take place (§ 52a German Act on Voluntary Jurisdiction), see Q 57. If this procedure remains unsuccessful the court can make various orders (§ 52a para. 5 German Act on Voluntary Jurisdiction). It can use coercion, and there can be modifications of the contact regulation or the regulation of parental care, see Q 58.

(b) Other persons

The child has a right of contact with his or her grandparents and siblings, if it is in the interests of the child, § 1685 para. 1 German CC. However, if the parents disregard this right or prevent the grandparents from seeing their grandchild German courts do not enforce the grandparents' right. Quite to the contrary, they generally argue that a serious conflict between parents and grandparents is not in the interests of the child.[23] Therefore, care of the parents is given priority and the grandparents cannot make use of their right of contact, which can be completely excluded (see § 1685 para. 1, 3, § 1684 para. 4 German CC).

The child has also a right of contact with the spouse or the former spouse, and the registered partner or former partner of a parent, § 1685 para. 2 German CC. There can also be conflicts in these situations, and the best interests of the child prevail.

GREECE

(a) A parent

If the parent with whom the child is living disregards the child's right to contact the other parent, he or she will not be properly exercising his or her rights and responsibilities. Thus this behaviour may lead to the adjustment of the court decision on parental responsibilities in view of the new circumstances (as

---

23 See OLG Koblenz, 29.09.1999, *FamRZ* 2000, 1111; OLG Hamm, 23.06.2000, *FamRZ* 2000, 1601 annotated by Liermann *FamRZ* 2001, 704.

provided by Art. 1536 Greek CC).[24] The consequences for a guardian are similar. If the child is under foster care, Art. 1656 Greek CC explicitly provides that the foster parents must facilitate the parents' or the guardian's contact with the child, provided that this does not substantially damage the child's interests.

(b) Other persons

The answer is in principle the same in this case too. Nevertheless, when the court decides on this problem, it may be of importance that the holder of parental responsibilities disregards the right of the child to contact a person other than its parent, so that the consequences of this infringement are less weighty.

HUNGARY

(a) A parent

There can be consequences affecting parental responsibilities if a holder of parental responsibilities disregards the child's right to contact with the other parent, but only if the measures of enforcement enumerated in the Order of Guardianship remain unsuccessful. Therefore, if the parent living with the child continually turns the child against the other parent and does not allow performance of the contact order in spite of enforcement measures, it is possible to petition for a change of the child's residence. However evidence must be introduced that the parent turns the child against the other parent. Judicial practice gives great emphasis to the fact that one of the parents continually prevents the maintenance of contact as a result of his or her own fault.

(b) Other persons

A parental responsibilities holder's disregard of child's right to contact with other persons, usually with the child's close relatives, will not in itself affect the parental responsibilities. There are cases in which grandparents apply for contact with the child and consequently for a change of the child's residence (placement), but these claims are rejected if the parent properly exercises their parental responsibilities.

IRELAND

(a) A parent

The options of the Irish court for dealing with a case where the holder of parental responsibilities with whom the child is living, disregards the child's right to contact with a parent, are quite limited. It may fine or imprison the parent in breach of an order for access.[25] A summons may have the desired

---

[24] E. KOUNOUGERI-MANOLEDAKI, *Family Law*, Vol. II, 3rd Edition, Athens-Thessaloniki: SAKKOULAS, 2003, p. 296-297; Decision of the Court of Appeals of Thessaloniki 2773/1992, *Armenopoulos* Vol. 46 (1992), p. 1229.

[25] Sec. 5 of the Courts Act (No. 2) 1986 created the offence of failure of, or refusal to comply with, the requirements of a direction given in an order under Sec. 7 or Sec. 11 of the Guardianship of Infants Act 1964. On conviction, the court may impose a fine of €254 and/or imprisonment of six months: see District Court Rules 1997, Ord.58, r.8.

effect of bringing to the attention of the custodial parents that they are obliged to comply with a court order and facilitate access as ordered, to the non-custodial parent. The court may also award custody to the other parent.

The duty of the Irish court in custody disputes is to review the factors comprising 'welfare' set out in Sec. 2 Irish Guardianship of Infants Act 1964 in order to evaluate the respective qualifications of the parents as custodians. When the debits and credits on each side have been taken into account, the court makes the order that can be predicted to be in the best interests of the child. The ability of a parent to put the child's needs over and above their own needs is a very important issue. It is of significant concern to the Irish court, if the custodial parent is unable to promote the welfare of the child by encouraging access to the non-custodial parent because of personal antipathy towards that parent. However, in practical terms, as the focus is on the 'welfare of the child' this will tilt the balance in favour of the existing custodial parent in most cases.

(b) Other persons

The options available to the Irish court for dealing with a case where the holder of parental responsibilities with whom the child is living, disregards the child's right to contact with other persons, are more limited than in respect of a parent. It may fine or imprison the parent in breach of an access order.[26]

ITALY

(a) A parent

A parent may petition the judge for a determination of visitation conditions in order to induce the other parent to respect the non-residential parent's rights.[27] Unjustified opposition to the visiting right by the parent who lives with the child can be regarded as prejudicial behaviour that gives the non-resident parent the right to request the judge to limit the parental responsibilities pursuant to Art. 333 Italian CC.[28] Although infrequently granted in practice,

---

26 Sec. 5 of the Courts Act (No. 2) 1986.

27 In this case, the competent authority is the tutelary judge who controls the application of court judgments relating to the exercise of the parental responsibilities and the administration of the minor's property pursuant to Art. 337 Italian CC. Moreover, the tutelary judge has the power to call parents at any time to obtain necessary information. This is normally requested by one of the parents and aims to restore relations between the parent not holding the custody (that is the parent who doesn't live with the child) and the minor and also to ensure that the measures given by the Court have been followed. In these cases the tutelary judge has the difficult task of listening to the complaints of the parents, ensuring that both parents observe the measures imposed by law and the Court and finally ensuring that the parents reach an agreement in order to properly exercise their parental duties. The tutelary judge normally writes notes on the agreement but this record doesn't represent an execution judgment, so the obligations expressed in the agreement can only be applied by petitioning the Court.

28 In this case the competent authority is the Family Proceeding Court.

such limitation can terminate the custody of the minor and consequently entrust the child to the aggrieved parent.[29] If the parent the child lives with consistently disregards the non-residential parent's visitation rights, the court may award compensation for the damages suffered by the non-residential parent.[30]

(b) Other persons

Even in the absence of a specific provision of law, relatives (for example the grandparents) who wish to have a caring relationship with the minor can apply to the judge pursuant to Art. 333 Italian CC. The judge, after ascertaining the interests of the child and the unjustified refusal of the parent, will grant an order limiting parental responsibilities by granting permission for the grandparents to have periodic contacts with the minor.[31]

LITHUANIA

(a) A parent

In this situation, a parent living separately from the child has the right to apply to a court for judgment and enforcement of his or her and the child's right to contact by means of compulsory execution of the court judgment (Art. 3.170 Lithuanian CC).

(b) Other persons

Other persons, such as grandparents, have the right to apply to the state institution for the protection of the right of contact with the child. If the parents fail to comply with the decision of the state institution for the protection of the rights of the child, these persons have the right to apply to the court for a court judgment.

THE NETHERLANDS

(a) A parent

In practice the compliance with a contact arrangement after a divorce is regularly problematic (about 25% of the children does not have contact with the non-resident parent).[32] There are several possibilities in the current legislation, of which changing parental responsibilities is just one. However, this option is not used regularly as it does not generally serve the best interests of the child.

---

29 In this case the competent authority to change the custody is the judge who previously decided it. If the parents are not married the competent authority is the Family Proceeding Court, but if the parents are married or have been married the competent authority is the Ordinary Court, which is competent *ratione materiae* upon proceedings concerning separation, divorce or annulment of marriage.

30 Court of Rome, 13.06.2000, *Dir. fam. pers.*, 2001, p. 209, annotated M. DOGLIOTTI, *ivi*, 2002, p. 61.

31 Supreme Court, 24.02.1981, No. 1115, *Dir. fam. pers.*, 1981, p. 697; Court of Taranto 19.04.1999, *Fam. dir.*, 1999, p. 373.

32 E. SPRUIJT *et al*, *Het verdeelde kind, Literatuuronderzoek Omgang na scheiding*, Utrecht 2002, p. 28.

Obstruction of a contact order does not in itself justify a change of the parental responsibilities.[33]

Different ideas have been presented in Parliament and the legal literature. (Mandatory) mediation in cases where the parents cannot agree on contact,[34] a minimum standard norm for contact in the Dutch CC,[35] making disregard of a contact arrangement punishable,[36] the introduction of a parenting plan, mandatory supervision of a divorce in an early stage by experts and financing more child contact centres (*omgangshuizen*) where the parent with a right of contact may meet the child in a neutral place.[37] The Minister of Justice proposes a duty for spouses to substantiate, in the request for a divorce decree, the way in which they want to deal with parental responsibilities after the divorce and on which matters there is (no) agreement. Non-compliance could justify the court to send back a unilateral application. The court could also refer them to a mediator on a voluntary basis or condemn the non-cooperating parent to pay the legal costs.[38] Further, a duty to contact will be introduced, mediation will be stimulated[39] and the function childcare facilities may play with respect to child contact centres[40] will be investigated.

(b) Other persons

Although in theory the same consequences apply as under (a), in practice there are few consequences, since this situation does not often give rise to problems. Generally speaking, disregarding the right of contact with a third person will be of less importance than disregarding the right of contact with a parent.

The Minister of Justice's future proposals only relate to contact with children after a divorce, which makes the plans rather weak since there is increasingly not a divorce, but instead a factual break-up of the partners. It is unclear what will happen to the children of these break-ups.

---

33 See Supreme Court 10.9.1999, *NJ*, 2000, 20; Supreme Court 13.7.2001, *NJ* 2001, 514. ASSER-DE BOER, *Mr. C. Asser's Handleiding tot de beoefening van het Nederlands Burgerlijk Recht. Personen- en Familie Recht*, 2002, No 1012.

34 See the results of mediation between spouses after a divorce: B. CHIN-A-FAT, *Scheiden: (ter)echter zonder rechter?, Een onderzoek naar de meerwaarde van scheidingsbemiddeling*, 2004.

35 *Kamerstukken Tweede Kamer*, 2003-2004, 29 520, No. 1-3: a minimum right of 48 hours. Critical: S.F.M. WORTMANN, 'Kroniek van het personen- en familierecht', *Nederlamds Juristenblad* 2004, p. 1654.

36 *Kamerstukken Tweede Kamer*, 2002-2003, 28 600, VI, No. 5.

37 M.L.C.C. DE BRUIJN-LÜCKERS/M.J. VOS, 'Weinig wetgevingsinitiatieven op terrein echtscheidings- en omgangsrecht op stapel', *Echtscheidingsbulletin* 2003, No. 2, p. 28-29.

38 *Kamerstukken Tweede Kamer*, 2003-2004, 29 520, No. 1-5. Critical: S.F.M. WORTMANN, 'Kroniek van het personen- en familierecht', *NJB*, 2004, p. 1654.

39 *Kamerstukken Tweede Kamer*, 2003-2004, 29 528, No. 1.

40 *Kamerstukken Tweede Kamer*, 2003-2004, 29 5280, No. 3, p. 1 and No. 6, p. 4.

NORWAY

(a) A parent

If the parent with whom the child permanently lives denies these rights of contact, according to Art. 65 Norwegian Children Act 1981, they may be enforced by a coercive fine, according to the general rules of enforcement in Chapter 13 Norwegian Enforcement Act 1992. This means that the parent with whom the child lives will have to pay a fine of a given amount for each day the visiting right is denied. The parent whose visiting rights are obstructed may also request the court to permanently move the child to live with him or her. There are several examples of this.[41] Thus, it is considered important that a child maintains contact with both parents.

(b) Other persons

According to Art. 45 sec. 3 Norwegian Children Act 1981, the rules described under (a) also apply when the child's right to contact with other persons is disregarded.

POLAND

(a) A parent

This situation is not specifically regulated. Art. 109 Polish Family and Guardianship Code allows the court to issue appropriate orders if the child's wellbeing is endangered. It may, in particular oblige the parents and the minor to specific behaviour and appoint control over the orders to a third person (Art. 109 § 2 point 1 Polish Family and Guardianship Code).

(b) Other persons

As in Q 48a.

PORTUGAL

(a) A parent

As has already been stated, Art. 181 Portuguese Child Protection Law regulates situations of failure to comply with the system of exercise of parental responsibility agreed by the parents or established by the court in point No. 1, which establishes that, if one of the parents does not comply with the agreement or decision, the other may apply to court for measures to be taken to enforce compliance and for the parent at fault to be sentenced to a fine and compensation to the child, to the applicant or both. The judge will summon both parents to a meeting where the parents may agree to alter the system of parental responsibility in accordance with the interests of the child. (Art. 181 No. 2 and 3 Portuguese Child Protection Law). If the parents do not come to an agreement, the judge will decide (Art. 181 No. 4 Portuguese Child Protection Law. The judge may summon only the parent that is at fault and then make allegations that the judge sees fit. This will be followed by a summary inquiry and any other measures that are deemed necessary, and then the judge will decide (Art. 181 No. 2, 3 and 4 Portuguese Child Protection Law).

---

[41] Rt, 1982 p. 116; Rt. 1991 p. 1148.

(b) Other persons

It appears that, if the custodial parent impedes the exercise of the right of contact with siblings, grandparents and other ascendants (Art. 1887-A Portuguese CC), then the system established for situations of non-compliance established in Art. 181 Portuguese Child Protection Law described in part (a) will apply.

RUSSIA

(a) A parent

If a residential parent disregards the contact arrangements, the non-residential parent can ask the court to approve and enforce the agreement by the court order. The court has discretion to refuse its enforcement in case of violation of the interests of the child.

If the parents were not able to agree on contact arrangements, the arrangements can be made by the court upon the advice of the Guardianship and Curatorship Department (Art. 66 (2) Russian Family Code).

If a residential parent does not obey the contact arrangements laid down in the court order, the enforcement measures of civil procedural are applicable. A court bailiff in charge of the order's execution can impose a fine on a disobedient parent of up to two-hundred times the minimum wage.[42] After a fine is paid the bailiff sets up a new term for complying with the court order.[43] If the parent disobeys again, the fine can be doubled. As the law does not limit the number of times the fine can be increased,[44] in principle the disobeying parent can be financially ruined.

No physical force can be used against the child in order to facilitate contact between the parent and the child.

If the parent persistently deliberately disobeys the court order, the judge, taking into consideration the opinion of the child, can order a transfer of the child's residence to the other parent if such transformation is not against the best interests of the child (Art. 66 (3) Russian Family Code). This measure is not usually applied, but the mere threat of its application can compel most uncompromising parents to respect the right of the child to maintain contact with another parent.[45]

---

42 Art. 83 (1) Federal Law On Execution Proceedings of 21.07.1997, *Sobranie Zakonodatel'stva Rossiiskoi Federatsii*, 1997, No. 30, item 3591.

43 A. NETCHAEVA, 'Commentary to art. 79 Russian Family Code', in: I. KUZNETZOVA (ed.), *Commentary on the Family Code of Russian Federation*, Moscow: Jurist, 2000, p. 278.

44 A. NETCHAEVA, 'Commentary to art. 79 Russian Family Code', in: I. KUZNETZOVA (ed.), *Commentary on the Family Code of Russian Federation*, Moscow: Jurist, 2000, p. 278.

45 M. ANTOKOLSKAIA, *Family Law* (*Semeinoe pravo*), Moscow: Jurist, 1999, p. 202.

(b) Other persons

If a parent, with whom the child resides, disregards the contact arrangements with the child grandparents, brothers sisters of other relatives (art. 67 (1) FC), those persons can ask the court to approve and enforce the agreement by the court order. The court has discretion to refuse its enforcement in case of violation of the interests of the child.

If the parents and the afore mentioned persons not able to agree on contact arrangements the arrangements can be made by the court upon the advise of the Guardianship and Curatorship Department.

If the parent living together with the child does not obey the contact arrangements laid down in the court order, the enforcement measures of civil procedural law are applicable. A court bailiff in charge for the execution of the order could impose on disobedient parent a fine up to 200 minimum wages.[46] After a fine is paid the bailiff sets up a new term for complying with the court order.[47] If the parent keeps disobeying the fine could be doubled. As the law does not limit the instances of application of a (each time increasing) fine,[48] the disobeying parent could be in principle financially ruined.

No physical force could be used against the child in order to facilitate the contact between the parent and the child.

On contrast to disobeying the contact arrangements with the other parent, frustrating the implementation of contract arrangements with the relatives of the child could never lead to the transfer of the child's residence.[49]

SPAIN

(a) A parent

It basically depends whether contact rights had previously been determined in a judicial decision or in an agreement ratified by the court.

Once there is a court decision on the matter there is a possibility to ask for the enforcement of contact. See Q 58. In cases in which non compliance with the judicial decision is especially grave a criminal offence may have been

46 Art. 83 (1) Russian Federal Law On Execution Proceedings of 21.07.1997, *Sobranie Zakonodatel'stva Rossiiskoi Federatsii*, 1997, No. 30, item 3591.

47 A. NETCHAEVA, 'Commentary to Art. 79 Russian Family Code', in: *Commentary on the Family Code of* Russian *Federation*, I. KUZNETZOVA, (ed.), Moscow : Jurist, 2000, p. 278.

48 A. NETCHAEVA, 'Commentary to Art. 79 Russian Family Code', in: *Commentary on the Family Code of* Russian *Federation*, I. KUZNETZOVA, (ed.), Moscow : Jurist, 2000, p. 278.

49 A. NETCHAEVA, 'Commentary to Art. 79 Russian Family Code', in: *Commentary on the Family Code of* Russian *Federation*, I. KUZNETZOVA, (ed.), Moscow : Jurist, 2000, p. 278.

committed (*delito o falta de desobediencia a la autoridad* Arts. 556 and 634 Spanish Criminal Code). This however requires that the exercise of contact rights as fixed in a judgment have been repeatedly opposed and that all possibilities provided by the Law of Civil Procedure have been exhausted.

If there is no judgment on contact there will be no possibility to enforce contact rights. The course of action then would be to go to the court and ask for a judgment on contact, which will then become enforceable.

(b) Other persons

Spanish law recognises that the child has the right to contact with relatives and close persons (see Q 44). If contact with these persons is impeded there is the possibility to have the exercise of contact rights established in a judicial decision. This decision is then enforceable.

SWEDEN

(a) A parent

The child's right to contact with the non-residential parent is considered very important. In several relatively recent judgments, the Supreme Court has addressed what effect is to be given to the residential parent's disregard of the child's contact with the other parent. In NJA 1989 p. 335 concerning a custody dispute between the parents of a seven-year-old girl, (sole) custody was entrusted to the father since the mother had obstructed contact between the child and her father and it was assumed she would continue to do so, if custody continued to be entrusted to her. Of relevance to the outcome was that the child was considered to be able to deal with the changes resulting from moving to the father.

However, with the best interests of the child as the primary consideration, factors other than obstruction of contact may be considered more important. The decision of the Supreme Court in NJA 1998 p. 675, concerning custody of a three-year-old boy, illustrates this. The boy had lived all of his life with his mother, who systematically denied contact between the boy and his father. The father requested a court order granting him sole custody. The Court found that the boy had a great need for contact with his father but that a transfer of custody to the father would entail a total change of the boy's life, which would not be in accordance with his best interests. As a result, the mother maintained sole custody of the child.

(b) Other persons

A person with custody of a child has a responsibility to ensure that, as far as possible, the child's need for contact with persons particularly close to the child is met.[50] If a custodian neglects this duty, it is up to the social welfare committee to initiate court proceedings. A condition is that the committee finds contact to

50 Chapter 6 Sec. 15 para. 3 Swedish Children and Parents Code.

be in the best interests of the child.[51] There are no published cases where contact has been granted as a result of a social welfare committee's decision to take the issue to court.

SWITZERLAND

(a) A parent

When it comes to conferring parental responsibilities in the case of a divorce, if both have equal abilities and potential in regard to the child's upbringing, the parent that shows the greater willingness to enable the other to exercise his or her right to personal contact can be of decisive importance.[52]

If the parent who holds parental responsibilities and lives in the same household as the child disregards the child's right to personal contact with the other parent, the competent authority may issue a warning or instructions to the parent in question in accordance with Art. 273 § 2 Swiss CC. A measure for the protection of the child within the meaning of Art. 307 *et seq* Swiss CC needs to be ordered if the child's welfare is endangered and this danger cannot be averted by any other means. Some measures for the protection of the child hardly impose any restrictions on parental responsibilities (such as *e.g.* warnings or instructions, Art. 307 § 3 Swiss CC); other measures impose a total withdrawal (Art. 311 and Art. 312 Swiss CC). Coercive measures carried out by the police are conceivable in principle but are virtually unenforceable. However, if the exercise of extended holiday rights is rendered impossible (on a purely *de facto* basis), this means a larger burden in terms of child support since the respective contribution of support in kind by the parent entitled to exercise visiting rights does not come to bear. Nevertheless, there is no general mutual interdependency between the right to personal contact and child support sspayments.

(b) Other persons

If the parent who holds parental responsibilities and lives in the same household with the child disregards the child's claim to personal contact with third parties in accordance with Art. 274a Swiss CC, the parent may (as with the right of the other parent to personal contact with the child) receive a warning in accordance with Art. 273 § 2 Swiss CC or instructions may be issued to the parent. If the child's welfare is endangered thereby and if this danger cannot be averted by any other means, the competent authority may order a measure for the protection of the child in accordance with Art. 307 *et seq* Swiss CC. Some measures for the protection of the child hardly impose any restrictions on parental responsibilities (such as *e.g.* warnings and instructions, Art. 307 § 3 Swiss CC) while others impose a total withdrawal (Art. 311 and Art. 312 Swiss CC).

---

[51] G. WALIN and S. VÄNGBY, *Föräldrabalken, En kommentar, Del I, 1-13 kap.*, Stockholm: Norstedts Juridik, 2002, p. 6:63.

[52] BGE 117 II 353, 359; 115 II 317, 320; 115 II 206, 210.

QUESTION 49

F. DELEGATION OF PARENTAL RESPONSIBILITIES

To what extent, if at all, may the holder(s) of parental responsibilities delegate its exercise?

AUSTRIA

Parental responsibilities as such may only be transferred to another person by operation of law or by court order in accordance with the child's best interests (Sec. 145, 176, 186a, 187, and 213 Austrian CC).[1] However, one possibility to freely relinquish the actual exercise of parental responsibilities for the child with respect to his or her care and education is the contractual placement of the child in the care of foster parents (Sec. 186 *et seq* Austrian CC).[2]

Transferring the child into the care of a third party requires the consent of both parents (Sec. 154(2) Austrian CC); in the event of unjustified refusal by one parent, such consent may be substituted by the court's decision (Sec. 176(1) Austrian CC). Moreover, for children over 16 years of age an administrative approval by the public youth welfare agency that verifies the suitability of the foster parents must be obtained (Sec. 14 and 16(1) Youth Welfare Act *[Jugendwohlfahrtsgesetz]*).[3] While the child may be transferred into foster care without the required approval, this will result in an administrative penalty (Sec. 35(3) No. 2 *Jugendwohlfahrtsgesetz*). In spite of the child's placement in the care of foster parents the parental responsibilities holders retain full parental responsibilities by operation of law; they fulfil their duties by engaging the foster parents who carry out the actual care and education of the child. Foster parents are entitled to petition the court in matters of care and education as well as in contact proceedings. However, only under certain circumstances do foster parents have the right to obtain parental responsibilities (Sec. 186a Austrian CC).[4]

BELGIUM

Parental responsibility is an institution created in the interests of the child. It is part of the status of the person; consequently, the applicable rules are of public policy. Every agreement which transfers or modifies the exercise of parental

---

1 See Q 33 and 51. 'Erklären die Eltern oder ein Elternteil einen ausdrücklichen Verzicht auf ihre Elternrechte, so wird dies von der Rechtssprechung als kindeswohlgefährdend beurteilt', *Landesgericht für Zivilrechtssachen* Vienna, 22.08.1985, *EFSlg*. 48.405.

2 See R. HOLZHAMMER/M. ROTH, *Bürgerliches Recht*, 6 th Edition, Vienna: LexisNexis ARD Orac, 2004, p. 372 *et seq*.

3 O. LEHNER, *Kinder- und Jugendrecht*, 2nd Edition, Vienna: Orac, 1998, p. 177 *et seq*.

4 For details see Q 50.

authority is void (Art. 6 Belgian CC). This principle is unanimously accepted.[5] The parental competences concerning the status of the person, including the permission to marriage (Art. 148 Belgian CC), the permission for adoption (Art. 348, 368(4) and 349(4-6) Belgian CC), and the demand of judicial removal of the minor from custodianship (emancipation) (Art. 477 Belgian CC), cannot be transferred.

However, custodianship (Art. 475 *bis* – 475 *septies* Belgian CC) is a strictly regulated institution that offers the possibility to transfer a part of the parental responsibilities, under judicial control, to a person who takes over the parental duties and certain parental prerogatives. It is similar, but not equal, to adoption. The custodian has the right to administer the property (Articles 376-379 Belgian CC), but has no right of its use and enjoyment (Art. 384-387 Belgian CC). It includes the right of housing as long as the child has its usual domicile with the custodian (if not, that right still belongs to the parent(s)).

BULGARIA

The Bulgarian Family Code does not provide for such an option.

CZECH REPUBLIC

Parents may temporarily place a child into the care of a third person, very often the grandparents, but that does not deprive the parents of responsibility for the child's upbringing. Parents cannot directly confer the right of the child representation on third persons. Only a general representation by means of a power of attorney is possible. As for administration of the child's estate, the parents need not administer the estate personally, they may authorise a third person by means of a power of attorney. The parents are not allowed to delegate the duty of maintenance on another person.

DENMARK

Parental authority cannot be delegated. If a child younger than 14 is to stay for longer than 3 months with persons other than the parents, the local authorities must approve the foster parents.[6]

ENGLAND & WALES

Whilst preserving the previous position that a person with parental responsibility may not surrender or transfer that responsibility to another person save by a court order, Sec. 2(9), English Children Act 1989 permits those with parental responsibility to delegate some or all of their responsibility to one

---

5 Court of Appeal of Ghent, 14.03.1894, *Pas.*, 1894, II, p. 363; Court of Appeal of Liege, 18.05.1881, *Pas.* 1881, II, p. 235; H. DE PAGE, *Traité élémentaire de droit civil belge*, T. II (Les Personnes), Vol. 2 (by J.-P. MASSON), Brussels: Bruylant, 1990, p. 951.

6 I. LUND-ANDERSEN, N. MUNCK and I. NØRGAARD, *Familieret*, Copenhagen: Jurist- og Økonomforbundets Forlag, 200, p. 105.

or more persons acting on their behalf. As the Department of Health's Guidance and Regulations states:[7]

> 'Informal arrangements for the delegation of parental responsibility are covered by Sec. 2(9), which provides that a person with parental responsibility cannot surrender or transfer any part of their responsibility to another, but may arrange for some or all of it to be met by one or more persons acting on his behalf'.

Such delegation can be made to another person who already has parental responsibility[8] or to those who have not, such as schools[9] or holiday camps. This provision is primarily intended to encourage parents (regardless of whether or not they are separated) to agree among themselves on what they believe to be the best arrangements for their children. Sec. 2(9) does not, however, make such arrangements legally binding. Consequently, they can be revoked or changed at will. Furthermore, as Sec. 2(11) provides, delegation will not absolve a person with parental responsibility from any liability for failure on his part to discharge his responsibilities to the child.[10] While the child is with a parent on a contact visit that parent may exercise parental responsibility, at any rate with respect to short term matters, without consulting with the other provided he does nothing that is incompatible with any existing court order (see Q 37).

FINLAND

The custodian of the child may transfer the daily care of the child to a third person or body. Those situations other than normal day care are considered below.[11] Holidays taken, or time spent as a guest with grandparents, or with other relatives or close persons are excluded.

Empowering the non-residential parent, particularly in an intact family, to make certain decisions alone, for instance, can be regarded as a normal way to exercise custodial rights. The reason for the delegation can also be the placement of the child into foster care. The length of time a custodian may delegate his or her rights and responsibilities as well as the question in which form this should be done (written or oral *etc*) has to be decided *in casu*.[12]

---

7 'Introduction to the Children Act 1989', HMSO 1989, para 2.10.

8 Sec. 2(10).

9 But note the embargo on inflicting corporal punishment in schools, see Q8(d).

10 For example, not to neglect, abandon or cause or procure a child under the age of 16 to be assaulted or ill-treated *etc.*, under Sec. 1 and 17, English Children and Young Persons Act 1933.

11 Parents have a subjective right to communal day care for their child (Sec. 11a, Finnish Day Care Act).

12 M. HELIN, 'Lapsen huolto', in: H. MATTILA, *Lapsioikeuden pääpiirteet*, Juridica: Helsinki 1984, p. 133 - 134, M. SAVOLAINEN, *Lapsen huolto ja tapaamisoikeus*, Vammala: Suomalainen Lakimiesyhdistys: Helsinki, 1984, p. 31 - 37.

Following is an explanation of the regulation of private foster care or a substitute care as a voluntary child protection measure.

The care of a child by someone other than its custodian over a certain period of time can be arranged as a voluntary child protection measure, if the child is 12 years old. The child can be taken into an institution or into a family for a maximal period of 6 months (Sec. 14 Finnish Child Protection Act, amendment 139/1990).[13]

There can also be a private arrangement for a child to be cared for by a third person. The local social authority shall oversee the functioning of private foster families. Both the custodian and the foster parent shall notify this authority about the child's placement in the foster family. The local social authority shall clarify whether the circumstances of the child are properly qualified and in accordance with the best interests of that child. The authority has the power to prohibit a particular foster family from the care of the child (Sec. 41 Finnish Child Protection Act).

A permanent arrangement for the care of the child by a person other than the custodian is supposed to be exceptional, although it may in some cases prove to be in the best interests of the child. If the arrangement is permanent and if another arrangement for the custody of the child is considered to be reasonable regarding the best interests of that child, local social authorities shall take measures to arrange for the custody of a child through a parental agreement or court decision (Sec. 11 Finnish Child Custody and Right of Access Decree, No. 556/1990).

FRANCE

See Art. 376 to 377-3 French CC, Delegation of Parental Authority. In principle parental responsibilities cannot be subject to renunciation or cession unless confirmed by a court decision (Art. 376 French CC). When the family judge must determine the methods of the exercise of parental responsibilities, the child's education or when the judge entrusts the child to a third person, she or he can take parental agreements into account, unless one of the parents invokes serious reasons to withdraw his or her consent (Art. 376-1 French CC). The holders of parental responsibilities can therefore agree upon a delegation of the exercise of parental responsibilities to a third person, but this agreement is subject to the court's discretion and needs a court judgment to have legal effect.

If circumstances require, the father and mother can also (jointly or separately) bring a petition before the family judge to delegate all or part of their parental responsibilities to a third person (Art. 377 French CC). This third person can be a family member, a *proche digne de confiance* (reliable close person), an institution

13 A child who is younger than 12 years old can be taken into substitute care only with his or her parents, in the case the child has not been taken into care (Sec. 14 Finnish Child Protection Act, amendment 139/1990).

approved to take children in or a public body (*service départemental de l'aide sociale à l'enfance,* departmental Children's Aid Service). The family judge can order a full or partial delegation. The judgment can also decide that for the necessity of the child's education, the father and mother, or one of them, will share all the parental responsibilities or part of them with the delegated third person (Art. 377-1 French CC). Such a share requires the agreement of the parent(s) as holder(s) of parental responsibilities (Art. 377-1 para. 2 French CC). If difficulties arise because of this shared exercise of parental responsibilities, the court (the family judge is competent) can be asked to solve them (para 3).

Sometimes (this seems to be a very recent evolution of French judicial practice),[14] same-sex partners bring a joint petition before the court to obtain some of the parental responsibilities through *délégation*; the partner who is the father or the mother of the child proposes to delegate some of his parental duties and rights to his or her partner. Some courts of first instance seem to have accepted such a petition.

GERMANY

As a rule parental care is strictly personal. It cannot be transferred, as a whole, to a third party.[15] However, parents can vest others with certain rights in relation to the child, as *e.g.* in the case of relatives, kindergarten, schools, boarding schools, holiday camps or neighbours caring for the children.[16] In this sense, the holders of parental responsibilities may only partially delegate its exercise.[17] This also applies to the administration of assets.[18]

GREECE

Parental responsibilities are strictly personal (*ius personalissimum*). Thus the holders of such responsibilities cannot delegate them to others.[19] This does not, however, exclude the possibility to delegate concrete aspects of the exercise of parental responsibilities to others. This is necessarily the case when, for

---

14 See *Le Monde* 23.09.2004, p. 12.

15 L. M. PESCHEL-GUTZEIT, in: STAUDINGER, *Kommentar zum Bürgerlichen Gesetzbuch*, 13th Edition, Berlin: Gruyter, 2002, § 1626 German CC No. 24 *et seq*.

16 U. DIEDERICHSEN, in: PALANDT, *Bürgerliches Gesetzbuch*, 64th Edition, München: Beck, 2005, § 1626 German CC No. 3.

17 L. M. PESCHEL-GUTZEIT, in: STAUDINGER, *Kommentar zum Bürgerlichen Gesetzbuch*, 13th Edition, Berlin: Gruyter, 2002, § 1631 German CC No. 15.

18 H. ENGLER, in: STAUDINGER, *Kommentar zum Bürgerlichen Gesetzbuch*, 13th Edition, Berlin: Gruyter, 2000, vor §§ 1631 *et seq* German CC No. 7.

19 S. KOUKOULI- SPILIOTOPOULOU, in: A. GEORGIADIS and M. STATHOPOULOS (eds.), *Civil Code commentary, Vol. VIII, Family Law (Arts. 1505-1694)*, 2nd Edition, Athens: Law & Economy, P. N. SAKKOULAS, 2003, p. 50, No. 108; P. AGALLOPOULOU, in: A. GEORGIADIS and M. STATHOPOULOS (eds.), *Civil Code commentary, Vol. VIII, Family Law (Arts. 1505-1694)*, 2nd Edition, Athens: Law & Economy, P.N. Sakkoulas 2003, Art. 1510 Greek CC, p. 187, No. 75.

instance, the child attends school, or a summer camp.[20] Likewise, the holders of parental responsibilities may appoint a foster family and assign the actual care of the child to them.[21]

HUNGARY

The possibility for a holder of parental responsibilities to delegate the exercise of these rights is exceptional in Hungarian law. Two situations allow for this possibility.

The delegation of parental responsibilities is partial and temporary when parents, because of their health, reasoned absence or any other family reason, initiate the transfer of their child to another family. This other family then takes over the care of the child, and the parents' parental responsibilities are suspended. They are then exercised by the persons who have taken the child into their household as the child's guardians. The parents have right to contact with the child and to make decisions with these persons about all important matters affecting the child. The consent of the public guardianship authority is needed to transfer a child into another person's household; the public guardianship authority governs whether the persons designated by the parents are suitable to exercise the parental responsibilities and whether it is in the child's interests to take him or her into another person's household. When the circumstances for taking the child into another household cease, the parents take the child back into the parental family and their parental responsibilities are revived. (If the help of other persons (usually a grandparent, or the sister or brother of the parent) is temporarily required temporarily to take care of the child, this is not seen by family law as a delegation of parental responsibilities and does not affect the parents' parental responsibilities.)

The other possibility for the delegation of the parental responsibilities arises when a parent gives his or her consent to the adoption of his or her child, whether the consent is for an adoption by an unknown person (so-called incognito adoption) or by a person known to the parent. If the parent does not know the person adopting the child, the parent's parental responsibilities end with the consent itself. The public guardianship authority will then take the child into care, with the parental responsibilities exercised either by a foster parent or children's home until the adoption. If the parent knows the person adopting his or her child, the parent's parental responsibilities remain until the

---

20 P. AGALLOPOULOU, in: A. GEORGIADIS and M. STATHOPOULOS (eds.), *Civil Code commentary, Vol. VIII, Family Law (Arts. 1505-1694)*, 2nd Edition, Athens: Law & Economy, P.N. Sakkoulas 2003, Art. 1510 Greek CC, p. 187, No. 75.

21 P. SKORINI-PAPARRIGOPOULOU, in: A. GEORGIADIS and M. STATHOPOULOS (eds.), *Civil Code commentary, Vol. VIII, Family Law (Arts. 1505-1694)*, 2nd Edition, Athens: Law & Economy, P.N. SAKKOULAS, 2003, Art. 1655 Greek CC, p. 797, No. 5. Art. 1659 Greek CC provides that the foster parents may only regulate pressing matters or matters of a day to day nature, unless the law or a court decision assigns more responsibilities to them.

adoption. After the adoption, the adoptive parents will exercise parental responsibilities.

IRELAND

The holders of parental responsibilities may not delegate the exercise of parental responsibilities.

ITALY

In the Italian legal system the exercise of parental responsibilities cannot be delegated or transferred to others except in exceptional circumstances. Due to 'the parent's duty to support, educate and provide moral guidance to the children' (Art. 30 § 1 of the Constitution of the Republic of Italy), and to 'the right of the minor to be brought up and to receive moral guidance in the ambit of his own family' (Art. 1 § 1 the Italian Adoption Law), the Italian system contemplates the possibility to delegate the exercise of parental responsibilities to other persons only in case of a 'disability' or 'impossibility' of the parents.

A kind of delegation is foreseen by Art. 8 § 1 Italian Adoption Law, which excludes the possibility of abandoning of the child when there are relatives within the fourth degree of consanguinity who can attend to the child's moral and material care. In this situation, therefore, the fundamental right of the minor to be brought up in his own family is realised.

Art. 30, § 2 of the Constitution of the Republic of Italy provides that 'in case of the inability of the parents, the law provides for the exercise of such duties.' Therefore, in order to prevent abandonment and in order to facilitate the moral guidance of the minor within his own family, the law states that the Government, the regions and the local agencies must give support in favour of families at risk by appropriate actions that do not prejudice the family's autonomy and are within their financial resources (Art. 1 § 3 Italian Adoption Law).

When the family (the parents and the relatives within the fourth degree of consanguinity) is not in a position to raise and provide moral guidance to the minor, the Italian Adoption Law provisions apply. Among these provisions is the institution of the 'custody of children' that can be regarded as a type of delegation of the parental responsibilities. It consists in the temporary attribution of the task to assist the minor 'who is lacking an appropriate family atmosphere' to another family, a single person or a public or private assistance institution (Art. 2 § 1 and 2 Italian Adoption Law).[22] The custody is a remedy

---

[22] With regard to the institution of custody, see AA.VV., sub *artt. 2-5, Law 28.03.2001, No. 149 which modifies the Law 4 .05.1983, No. 184*, in: C.M. BIANCA and L. ROSSI CARLEO, *Commentario*, in *Nuove leggi civili comm.*, 2002; A. and M. FINOCCHIARO, *Adozione e affidamento dei minori, Commento alla nuova disciplina*, in Quaderni di diritto e giustizia, Milan, 2001; L. ROSSI CARLEO, *L'affidamento e le adozioni*, in *Trattato di diritto privato* directed by Rescigno, 4, III, Utet, Turin, 1997, p. 462.

designed to protect the minor. It should be used for a limited period to remedy a temporary, difficult situation in the minor's family of origin. Therefore, it neither implies an adoption relationship nor modifies the familial status of the minor.[23] During the period of custody, the parents continue to hold parental authority unless there is a judicial order terminating it (Art. 330 Italian CC) or requiring the parent to leave the family home (Arts. 342 *bis* and 342 *ter* Italian CC). The custodians must take the guidance of the parents into consideration (or of those of the judicial authority which provided for the custody) and must facilitate their relationship with the minor with the view to help the child's reintegration back into her or his family of origin (Art. 5 § 1 Italian Adoption Law).[24]

The judicial order providing temporary custody must indicate the reasons for the decision, the duration of the custody, the way in which it must be exercised, the powers conferred upon the custodian and the way in which the parents and the other family members may maintain their relationship with the minor. The judicial order must also mention the public welfare service institution that will be responsible for the assistance program exercising control, informing the judicial authority of any relevant events and drawing up a semi-annual report on the progress of the program (Art. 4 § 3 Italian Adoption Law).

This custody may be terminated if the momentary difficulties of the family of origin cease, if the continuation of the custody proves prejudicial for the minor or if the duration foreseen for the custody has expired. These circumstances do not automatically determine the termination of custody. A specific judicial order based on the interests of the minor, issued by the Family Proceeding Court that originally provided for the custody, is always necessary. The Family Proceeding Court is supposed to provide for additional measures in the interest of the minor, if advisable (Art. 4 para. 5 and 6 Italian Adoption Law).

---

23 The discipline concerning custody provided by Art. 2-5 of the Law 184/83 has been partially modified owing to the reform enacted with Law No. 149, dated 28.03.2001. This Law first imposed a maximum period of custody for 24 months. A Family Proceeding Court decision can extend this when the interruption is considered to be prejudicial to the minor (Art. 4 § 4 Italian Adoption Law); second, it imposed custody to an assistance institution as near as possible to the family residence when it is not possible to grant custody of the child to other families or similar communities (Art. 2 § 2 Italian Adoption Law); third, it disposed of the prohibition to admit children above the age of six into institutions and also eliminated every institutional admission by the end of 2006 (Art. 2 § 4 Italian Adoption Law); fourth, it indicated more precisely the powers and faculties of the holders of custody (Art. 5 § 1 Italian Adoption Law); and finally, it ended the extension of all parental rights relating to absence from work, and also leaves for the holders of the custody.

24 Parental custody is different from pre-adoption custody, which is the first step towards adoption. It is also different from temporary custody, which can be dispensed by the judge owing to serious reasons in case of separation, divorce or annulment of marriage (Art. 155 § 6 Italian CC and Art. 12 Italian Divorce law) or when the parents' conduct is considered prejudicial for the child (Art. 333 Italian CC).

LITHUANIA

Delegation of the exercise of parental responsibilities is not allowed because these responsibilities are personal and statutory obligations which may only be exercised by the holder of parental responsibilities. If the holder of parental responsibilities is not able to exercise these responsibilities because of objective reasons *e.g.* serious illness, he or she must be separated from the child, and a guardian (curator) of the child must be appointed.

THE NETHERLANDS

If a minor grows up in a manner that constitutes a serious threat to his or her moral or mental interests or his or her health, and other means for aversion of such threats have failed, or if it is foreseeable that these will fail, the children's court judge may vest his or her care and supervision with an institution for family guardianship[25] (Art. 1:254 § 1 Dutch CC). The judge may do so on the application of a parent (Art. 1:254 § 2 Dutch CC). The children's court judge shall specify the duration of the care and supervision, although this may not exceed one year (Art. 1:256 § 1 Dutch CC). Extension is possible each time for at most one year. (Art. 1:256 § 2 Dutch CC). The institution for family guardianship shall supervise the minor and ensure that assistance and support is offered to the minor and the parent charged with parental responsibilities, in order to avert the threat to moral or mental interests or to the health of the minor (Art. 1:257 § 1 Dutch CC). The institution for family guardianship may, when fulfilling its tasks, give written directions with regard to the care and upbringing of the minor (Art. 1:258 § 1 Dutch CC). The parent who is charged with parental responsibilities and the minor must act in accordance with such directions (Art. 1:258 § 2 Dutch CC).

NORWAY

Neither of the parents may delegate parental responsibilities to others.

POLAND

No. The exercise of parental authority is the personal right and duty of the parents.

PORTUGAL

In accordance with Art. 1882 Portuguese CC, parents may not renounce parental responsibility nor any of the rights that it specifically confers upon them, without prejudice to the provision on adoption. If we are to understand that the delegation of parental responsibility includes the renunciation of that responsibility, then it is prohibited under Portuguese law.

---

[25] Art. 60 Dutch Juvenile Assistance Act, *Wet op de Jeugdzorg*, *Staatsblad* 2004, No. 306

RUSSIA

There are no specific legal provisions on delegation of parental responsibility. However, the right to delegate parental responsibility has been derived from the right of the parents to educate their children. According to this interpretation, the educational rights of the parents include the right to educate the child personally and to entrust the education temporarily to the other persons (family member, babysitters) or institutions (kindergarten, *etc.*).[26] While delegating their educational responsibilities, the parents remain primarily responsible for the education of the child.[27]

SPAIN

If the holders of parental responsibility are private persons and cannot fulfil the obligations implicit to parental responsibility, there is the possibility to delegate the exercise of parental responsibility to a public body (so called *guardia administrativa* or administrative custody). The aim of this delegation is to re-establish the conditions necessary for parental responsibility to be properly exercised. Such a delegation is only possible if there is a serious reason for the inability to exercise parental responsibility and the reason is transitory.

Spanish law does not directly contemplate the possibility for parental responsibility holders to delegate the exercise of parental responsibility into the hands of other private persons. Since these situations occur in practice there are some rules on so called *guardia de hecho*, but in these cases there is *strictu sensu* no delegation of parental responsibility.

When parental responsibility is held by a public child protection body (see Q 32), parental responsibility is delegated either on a foster family with whom the child resides or, if a foster family cannot be found, on the director of the child protection institution in which the child lives. In the case of a foster family only the duties as regarding the child will be delegated; that is, the foster family will acquire a duty to care for, protect, maintain and educate the child. The delegation of parental responsibilities to a foster family must be in writing, and requires the consent of the child, if he or she is older than sixteen, and of the child's parents or guardians, the foster family and the public child protection body. If there is opposition by the child's parents or guardians the delegation of the exercise of parental responsibilities to the foster family will require a judicial judgment; otherwise it will be the result of an administrative procedure.

There are different types of foster situations depending on whether the situation is more or less transitory and on whether an adoption by the foster family is in view. If the foster situation is a long term situation, the judge can grant a broader delegation of parental responsibilities that includes legal representation.

---

26 L. PCHELINTZEVA, *Family Law* (*Semeinoe pravo*), Moscow: Norma-Infra M, 1999, p. 303.

27 L. PCHELINTZEVA, *Family Law* (*Semeinoe pravo*), Moscow: Norma-Infra M, 1999, p. 303.

SWEDEN

A custodial parent may, in co-operation and with approval of the local social welfare committee, entrust the care of the child to persons in a private home other than the parental home according to the Swedish Social Service Act (2001:453). Although the child in this case does not live with the custodial parent, the parent retains his or her legal right of custody. The daily care of the child, on the other hand, is entrusted to the person(s) in the home that has received the child for care and is supervised by the social welfare committee.

SWITZERLAND

Because parental responsibilities are an utterly personal right they are non-transferable and cannot be renounced. However, step-parents, similar to foster parents, have the authority (basically only on mutually exclusive basis) to stand in for the parents in exercising parental responsibilities: 'Each spouse must assist the other in an appropriate manner in the exercise of the other's parental responsibilities towards his or her children and must stand in for the other, if circumstances require' (as stipulated in Art. 299 Swiss CC). 'If a child is entrusted to third party foster parents, they represent the parents, subject to instructions to the contrary, in the exercise of parental responsibilities, to the extent which is appropriate to perform their duties properly' (Art. 300 § 1 Swiss CC).

QUESTION 50

F. DELEGATION OF PARENTAL RESPONSIBILITIES

To what extent, if at all, may a person not holding parental responsibilities apply to a competent authority for a delegation of parental responsibilities?

AUSTRIA

Foster parents have a right to the transfer of parental responsibilities and thus may petition the court to this effect, if they are to assume the child's care for the long term, the transfer is consistent with the child's best interests, and the parent(s) or grandparent(s) holding parental responsibilities consent to the transfer (Sec. 186a(1) Austrian CC). The transfer may only be ordered against the will of the parent(s) or grandparent(s) if the interests of the child are at risk (Sec. 186a(2) Austrian CC).[1] However, according to predominant views such a transfer of parental responsibilities has the effect that the previous holder(s) of parental responsibilities lose them to the extent they pass to the new holder of parental responsibilities.[2]

Besides, a transfer or delegation of parental responsibilities may only be ordered if the child's interests are at risk. In this case the court must intervene *ex officio* and discharge the holder(s) of his, her or their parental responsibilities, in part or in whole, and transfer them to another suitable person or persons (Sec. 176(1) Austrian CC), regardless of who brought the matter before it.[3]

BELGIUM

It is generally agreed that parental authority belongs only to the parents, and not to other persons.[4] Therefore, other persons can not initiate an action for the transfer of (a part of) parental authorities. It is inadmissible, except in the specific context of custodianship, where the candidate-custodian must ask the Juvenile Court to uphold the agreement between him orher and the child, if it has reached the age of 15 years or, if not, its parent(s) or guardian (Art. 475 *bis* Belgian CC).[5] Also, see Q 32 concerning the intervention of the Public Social

---

1 On the other hand, the transfer of parental responsibilities has to be revoked, if this is consistent with the best interests of the child (Sec. 186a (3) Austrian CC).

2 *Oberster Gerichtshof*, 25.09.2002, *Österreichische Juristenzeitung - EvBl*, 2003, No. 16 = *ÖJZ-LSK* 2003/2; M. SCHWIMANN, *Familienrecht*, 5th Edition, Vienna: LexisNexis ARD Orac, 2004, p. 80. See also Q 27.

3 For details see Q 51 and 52.

4 H. DE PAGE, *Traité élémentaire de droit civil belge*, I, Brussels: Bruylant, 1962, p. 717.

5 K. HERBOTS, *Artikelsgewijze commentaar met ovezricht van rechtspraak en rechtsleer personen- en familierecht* (Art. 387 *bis* Belgian CC), Antwerp: Maklu, 1997, n°18; J.-L. RENCHON, 'La recevabilité des actions en justice introduites par les grand-parents dans le contexte du règlement de l'exercice de l'autorité parentale à l'égard de l'enfant', *Rev. Trim. Dr. Fam.* 1989, p. 255, No. 8. See Q 31 concerning custodianship.

Welfare Centre and Q 51-54 concerning the discharge of parental responsibilities.

BULGARIA

The delegation of parental responsibilities is not allowed under the Bulgarian Family Code.

CZECH REPUBLIC

Czech law does not recognise the delegation of parental responsibility.

DENMARK

That is not possible. Foster parents have no independent rights in respect of parental authority over the child.

ENGLAND & WALES

Under English law it is not possible to apply to a court or any other body for a delegation of parental responsibility. However, if it is possible both to challenge a parent's exercise of responsibility and to seek authority to exercise at least some specific aspect of parental responsibility by seeking a Sec. 8 order under the Children Act. Individuals who are neither parents or guardians and who do not have a residence order in their favour, nor have provided a home for the child for three years, and who do not have the consent of every person with parental responsibility, will need the leave of the court to seek a Sec. 8 order.[6]

FINLAND

The child's parents, regardless of their custodial status, are always entitled to submit an application to the court concerning child custody or the right of access. The local social authority also has the right to submit an application to the court in child custody matters (Sec. 14 para. 1 Finnish Child Custody and the Right of Access Act). Consequently, the court may use all the alternatives given in Sec. 9 Finnish Child Custody and the Right of Access Act, including the possibility of transferring the custodial rights to the applicant. The court can also decide to distribute the rights and responsibilities between custodians. Certain custodial rights such as the right to obtain information may even be given to the non-custodial parent (see above Q 36).

If the child has remained without a custodian because of the death of custodian(s), the relatives or other persons near to the child are empowered to make an application to the court concerning the custody (see above Q 33).

FRANCE

See Art. 377 para. 2 French CC. In two circumstances a third person, an institution or the public body (*service départemental de l'aide sociale à l'enfance*) that has taken the child in can bring a claim before the court (the family judge,

6 Sec. 10(2) and (4), English Children Act 1989.

juge aux affaires familiales, is competent) in order to obtain full or partial delegation of the exercise of parental responsibilities:

- in case of the parent's manifest uninterest towards the child; or
- if the parents are unable to exercise all parental responsibilities or part of them.

In these two situations the parents must receive notice of the claim and be called to the proceedings (Art. 377 para. 3 French CC). When a measure of educational support has been made concerning the child, the judicial delegation of parental responsibilities cannot take place before the *juge des enfants* (special judge who is competent in matters of educational support) has been heard. This judge expresses his opinion about the delegation.

GERMANY

An application for a delegation of personal responsibility as such is not possible. However, a person not holding parental responsibilities may apply to the family court for a decision on parental responsibilities. Nevertheless, an application to get personal care can only be successful if the person holding parental care will loose (or has to share) it. Third parties can obtain total parental care when they become guardian to a child (*Vormund*, §§ 1773 *et seq* German CC). A third party can also become a custodian (*Pfleger*, § 1630 para. 1, 2 German CC) who is responsible for certain affairs. It is also possible that a third party can be a foster parent (see § 1632 para. 4 German CC) or act as a special curator (*Beistand*; §§ 1712 *et seq* German CC).[7]

GREECE

Any interested person may apply for the delegation of parental responsibilities to the relevant body falling under the Ministry of Health and Welfare. The competent authority will scrutinise the application in order to conclude whether the family is suitable to care for the child. If this is the case, the family is formally recognized by a decision of the Minister. In exceptional cases an application by single persons may also be considered.[8]

HUNGARY

A non-custodial parent who applies to the competent authority for the delegation of the parental responsibilities can, at the same time, apply to change the judicial decision about the child's placement. If the court changes the earlier decision, the non-custodial parent will become the custodial parent and the other parent will exercise the rights and duties of the non-custodial parent. No third person can file a claim concerning the child's placement.

If both parents die, the guardian the parents appointed through use of their parental responsibilities can petition the public guardianship authority for the

---

7 U. DIEDERICHSEN, in: PALANDT, *Bürgerliches Gesetzbuch*, 64th Edition, München: Beck, 2005, § 1626 German CC No. 6.

8 Art. 9 para. 1 and 4, Law 2082/1992 (as reformed by Art. 65 of Law 2447/1996).

delegation of the parental responsibilities and to be appointed as guardian. If there is no such person, the child's close relatives can petition the public guardianship authority for the delegation of the parental responsibilities and to be appointed as guardian. In this latter case, the issue of who amongst the close relatives should be appointed as guardian and be delegated with the parental responsibilities is within the discretion of the public guardianship authority.

IRELAND

Such a person may apply to the court for its direction by virtue of Sec. 11 Irish Guardianship of Infants Act 1964.

ITALY

Custody can be requested by parents holding parental responsibilities or by the guardian. In this situation, the local welfare service will make the decision, which must ask for the minor's opinion if the minor is more than twelve years old, or even younger taking the minor's judgement capacity into consideration. The guardianship judge must ratify the decision issued by the public welfare service (Art. 4 § 1 Italian Adoption Law).

In the absence of the consent of the parents holding parental responsibilities or of the guardian, the Family Proceeding Court makes the custody decision upon request of the public prosecutor (Art. 9 Italian Adoption Law). Any person is entitled to inform the competent authorities (police, judicial authority, welfare services) of any serious abandonment situation involving minors, as well as situations involving the lack of an appropriate family atmosphere (Art. 9 Italian Adoption Law). The law requires public officers, those in charge of a public service and those who carry out an activity of public interest that during the course of their activities, who become aware of similar situations to inform the competent officer of the Family Proceeding Court (Art. 9 Italian Adoption Law). The public prosecutor is the main officer in the system of judicial protection of the rights of the minor.[9] He or she is the person in charge of receiving any notice or complaint issued by public institutions or private citizens, for controlling the public and private assistance institutions and for applying to the Family Proceeding Court (see Q 52).

If the Family Proceeding Court provides for the child's custody without the consent of the parents, they are deprived of their parental authority pursuant to Art. 330 Italian CC (Art. 4 § 2 Italian Adoption Law).

LITHUANIA

No person may apply for such delegation because these responsibilities are not subject to delegation. However, every interested person shall have the right to inform the state institution for the protection of the rights of the child about the

---

9 P. VERCELLONE, *Il controllo giudiziario sull'esercizio della potestà*, in *Trattato di diritto di famiglia* directed by P. ZATTI, II, *Filiazione* by G. COLLURA, L. LENTI and M. MANTOVANI, Giuffrè: Milan, 2002, p. 1033.

necessity of the establishment of guardianship (curatorship) for a child whose rights and interests need protection.

THE NETHERLANDS

Pursuant to Art. 1:254 § 2 Dutch CC, another person who cares and raises the minor as a member of the family, the Child Care and Protection Board or the Public Prosecution Service may apply for a delegation of the parental responsibilities (Care and Supervision Order) if a minor grows up in a manner which constitutes a serious threat to his or her moral or mental interests or his or her health, and other means for aversion of such threats have failed, or if it is foreseeable that these will fail. Where it is necessary, in the interest of the care and upbringing of the minor, or for an examination of his or her mental or physical condition, the children's court judge may authorise the institution for family guardianship, on its application, to instruct the minor to stay elsewhere during the day and overnight (Art. 1:261 § 1 Dutch CC). The authorisation may also be granted on the application of the Child Care and Protection Board or the Public Prosecution Service (Art. 1:261 § 2 Dutch CC). The children's court judge shall specify the duration of the care and protection order for the minor, although this may not exceed one year. On the application of the institution for family guardianship or of the Child Care and Protection Board, the judge may always extend such duration for no more than one year (Art. 1:262 Dutch CC)

NORWAY

A person not holding parental responsibilities cannot apply to any authority for a delegation of parental responsibilities.

POLAND

No.

PORTUGAL

No answer.

RUSSIA

A parent not holding parental responsibility has no possibility to apply for its delegation.

SPAIN

There is no direct possibility of going before a competent authority and asking for a delegation of parental responsibility in one's favour. But in the framework of the institution of guardianship there is an obligation to initiate a guardianship procedure if a child is not subject to *patria potestad*. The law imposes this obligation on the persons listed in order to become guardians.

SWEDEN

If only one of the parents has custody of the child and the other parent wishes the custody to be changed, he or she can make an application to court asking for joint or sole custody, Chapter 6 Sec. 5 Swedish Children and Parents Code. This right applies only to the child's parents. The only situation in Swedish law where another person may request the right to take part of parental responsibilities is when a person close to the child contacts the social welfare committee, asking it to initiate court proceedings for the establishment of contact.[10]

SWITZERLAND

Within the framework of measures for the protection of a child, the child as well as the parents may apply, based on Art. 310 § 2 Swiss CC, for the revocation of parental responsibilities if the relationship between the parents and the child is so seriously disturbed that the child may not reasonably be expected to remain in the joint household and there is no other way to help under the circumstances. At the same time, the guardianship authority must also consider appointing an official adviser within the meaning of Art. 308 Swiss CC.

The parents may also, in accordance with Art. 312 § 1 *et seq* Swiss CC, submit a request to the guardianship authority for the termination of parental responsibilities for 'just cause' (see Q 51).

---

10 See answer to Q 48b.

QUESTION 51

G. DISCHARGE OF PARENTAL RESPONSIBILITIES

Under what circumstances, if at all, should the competent authorities in your legal system discharge the holder(s) of his, her or their parental responsibilities for reasons such as maltreatment, negligence or abuse of the child, mental illness of the holder of parental responsibilities *etc.*? To what extent, if at all, should the competent authority take into account a parent's violent behaviour towards the other parent?

AUSTRIA

If the holder(s) of parental responsibilities threaten the child's interests, the court must intervene and issue the orders necessary to safeguard these interests; in particular the court may totally or partially discharge the holder(s) of his, her or their parental responsibilities, if necessary (Sec. 176 Austrian CC). According to precedent, the child's interests are threatened if the parents neglect their duty to bring up the child or if they abuse their child-rearing authority,[1] violate the prohibition against corporal punishment (Sec. 146b Austrian CC),[2] or in the event of sexual abuse,[3] psychological torture, the failure to obtain necessary medical treatment for the child[4] or the violation of the duty to support the child;[5] also the mother's alcohol addiction or mental illness can lead to the revocation of her parental responsibilities.[6]

The revocation of parental responsibilities can only be ordered as the most extreme emergency measure if no other alternative exists to protect against a specific and genuine threat to the child's interests.[7] Thus, for example, the existence of a risk to the child's interests solely because the parent holding parental responsibilities was a member of the Jehovah's Witnesses or the Church of Scientology was rejected:[8] therefore, the withholding of consent to a

---

1 *Landesgericht für Zivilrechtssachen Vienna,* 11.05.1982, *EFSlg.* 40.878 (child left alone at night); *Oberster Gerichtshof,* 04.06.1996, Juristische Blätter, 1996, p. 714; *Oberster Gerichtshof,* 27.11.2001, *Österreichische Juristenzeitung - EvBl,* 2002, No. 82, p. 335 = *Juristische Blätter*, 2002, p. 374.

2 *Landesgericht für Zivilrechtssachen* Vienna, 29.08.2001, *EFSlg.* 96.644.

3 *Oberster Gerichtshof,* 13.01.1994, *Österreichische Juristenzeitung - EvBl,* 1994, No. 123, p. 594 = *EFSlg.* 15.149.

4 *Oberster Gerichtshof,* 16.12.1992, *EFSlg.* 68.799.

5 E. GITSCHTHALER, *Unterhaltsrecht,* Vienna: Manz Verlag, 2001, Marg. No. 31-35. M. SCHWIMANN & W. KOLMASCH, *Unterhaltsrecht,* 3rd Edition, Vienna: LexisNexis ARD Orac, 2004, p. 95.

6 *Landesgericht für Zivilrechtssachen* Vienna, 13.05.1987; *EFSlg.* 54.019; contra *Landesgericht für Zivilrechtssachen Vienna,* 20.03.1985, EFSlg. 48.411.

7 *Oberster Gerichtshof,* 04.06.1996, *EFSlg.* 96.626.

8 J. STABENTHEINER, 'KindRÄG 2001', in: P. RUMMEL, *ABGB-Kommentar*, suppl. vol. 1, 3rd Edition, Vienna: Manz Verlag, 2003, § 176 Marg. No. 2 with further references.

blood transfusion (that was not actually medically necessary) for the child for reasons of faith does not warrant a precautionary revocation of parental responsibilities because a revocation of this sort would violate Art. 8 European Convention on Human Rights.[9] The revocation of parental responsibilities because of a one-time suicide threat by the parent holding parental responsibilities or because of relationship problems was also denied.[10]

Prior to the revocation of parental responsibilities, a less severe option is the furnishing of assistance with child rearing, e.g. advice on child rearing, therapeutic measures, placement with a child-minder, nursery, children's clinic, or with foster parents (*Erziehungshilfe,* Sec. 27 and 28 Youth Welfare Act *[Jugendwohlfahrtsgesetz]*).

Pursuant to Sec. 145b Austrian CC, a parent must refrain from any act that impedes the child's relationship to other persons holding rights and duties concerning the child or their performance of their duties with respect to the child (requirement of good behaviour *[Wohlverhaltensgebot]*). This prohibition encompasses a broad spectrum of behaviour: from insulting statements to physical and/or psychological violence against the other parties. Any violation against this prohibition may be penalized, if necessary, by restricting or revoking parental rights, i.e. parental responsibilities (Sec. 176, 253 Austrian CC) and/or the right of contact (Sec. 148 Austrian CC).

If a parent behaves in an uncooperative manner in exercising his or her parental responsibilities, this violates the principle of mutual assent specified in Sec. 144 Austrian CC; in this case too, the parental responsibilities can be revoked as a last resort in terms of the specific areas in which no agreement can be reached, e.g., administration of property, education, or medical treatment.[11] In practice, however, such cases are rare.

BELGIUM

Art. 32 Belgian LJP provides that the holder(s) of parental responsibilities can be discharged of all or a part of the responsibilities if:

---

9 *Oberster Gerichtshof,* 04.06.1996, *Juristische Blätter,* 1996, p. 714 = *EFSlg.* 81.134; Case Hoffmann v. Österreich, ECHR, series A No. 255-C, 23.06.1993, pp. 45 et seq.; see I. FAHRENHORST, 'Sorgerecht und Religion', *Europäische Grundrechtezeitschrift,* 1996, p. 633 *et seq;* MALECKY, 'Unvernünftige Verweigerung der Einwilligung in eine Heilbehandlung', *Österreichische Juristenzeitung,* 1994, p. 681; H. PICHLER, 'Die Kinder der Zeugen Jehovas - Probleme der Obsorgezuteilung und der Bluttransfusion', *Österreichischer Amtsvormund,* 1994, p. 171.

10 M. SCHWIMANN in: M. SCHWIMANN, *Praxiskommentar zum ABGB,* Vol. I, 2nd Edition, Vienna: Orac, 1997, § 176 Marg. No. 7; J. STABENTHEINER, 'KindRÄG 2001', in: P. RUMMEL, *ABGB-Kommentar,* suppl. vol. 1, 3rd Edition, Vienna: Manz Verlag, 2003, § 186a Marg. No. 3; E. STREINESBERGER/Th. HACKER, 'Jugendwohlfahrtsrecht', in: O. Lehner, *Kinder- und Jugendrecht,* 2nd Edition, Vienna: Orac, 1998, p. 169.

11 J. STABENTHEINER, 'KindRÄG 2001', in: P. RUMMEL, *ABGB-Kommentar,* suppl. vol. 1, 3rd Edition, Vienna: Manz, 2003, § 176 Marg. No. 4, 10. See also Q 38.

- the father or the mother has been condemned to a criminal penalty for an act perpetrated against the child, or with the help of a child or its descendents;
- the father or the mother who, by maltreatment, abuse of authority, obvious bad behaviour or serious negligence, has endangered the health, security or morality of the child;
- the father or the mother marries a person who has been discharged of their parental responsibilities.

So long as the violent behaviour of a parent is only towards the other parent, this behaviour is not an assessment criterion.[12]

BULGARIA

The Bulgarian Family Code provides for two types of discharge of parental responsibilities: restriction and deprivation. The grounds for this are two types of parental behaviour, which affect the interests of children. The first is the faulty behaviour of the parent: '...where the behaviour of the parent jeopardises the personality, upbringing, health or property of the child' (Art. 74 § 1). The second is non-faulty behaviour, which, however, creates risk for the child: '... where the parent, due to long physical or mental illness, or to prolonged absence or other objective reasons is unable to exercise his or her parental rights' (Art. 74 § 2). Under such assumptions the court 'decrees appropriate measures in the interests of the child and where necessary places the child in a suitable place'. The restriction of parental rights constitutes a temporary seizure of some parental authorities in the interests of the child.

Art. 75 Bulgarian Family Code states: 'The parent may be deprived of parental rights: (1) In exceptionally severe cases under the Art. 74; (2) Where, without a valid reason, he or she consistently does not care for the child and does not support it; (3) Where he or she has placed the child for rearing at a specialised institution and has not taken the child back within six months.'

It is evident from these texts that the restriction or deprivation of parental rights and obligations is based on the parent's behaviour towards the child and not on the behaviour of one parent towards the other. Although there is no explicit legislation, in general, the violence of one parent against the other may jeopardise the personality and the development of the child, and therefore provides grounds for the restriction or deprivation of parental rights. Court practice assumes that a measure of restricting parental rights is the removal of a parent from the family home. Usually in cases of domestic violence, the restriction of parental rights justifies a placement of the child outside the family.

A Bill on Protection against Domestic Violence has been, since 2003, pending a second reading in Parliament. It provides for the removal of the violent parent

---

12 H. DE PAGE, *Traité élémentaire de droit civil belge*, T. II (Les Personnes), Vol. 2 (by J.-P. MASSON), Brussels: Bruylant, 1990, p. 1030-1044; F. TULKENS and T. MOREAU, *Droit de la jeunesse*, Brussels: Larcier, 2000, p. 607-615.

(partner) from the household, thus ensuring the rights and safety of the child. Removal under that law would not constitute a separate ground for restriction of parental rights but could definitely be brought under the circumstances of the Art. 74 § 1 Bulgarian Family Code.

CZECH REPUBLIC

The exercise of parental responsibility may only be changed by a court (Sec. 42 Czech Family Code). The court may suspend the exercise of parental responsibility for the parent or both parents, limit his or her parental responsibility or completely deprive the parents of parental responsibility (Sec. 44 Czech Family Code).

If the parent is hindered in the exercise of parental responsibility by a serious obstacle and the interests of the child so require, the court may suspend the exercise of parental responsibility (Sec. 44 § 1 Czech Family Code). These are situations where the parent serves a long prison term, stays abroad, or is in a curative institution for a long time *etc.* If the exercise of parental responsibility has been suspended for one of the parents, the other parent becomes its sole holder. If the exercise of parental responsibility is suspended for both parents or for the only living parent, the court will appoint a guardian of the child (Sec. 78 Czech Family Code).

If a parent does not duly execute duties following from parental responsibility and if the interests of the child require it, the court will limit his or her parental responsibility, always establishing the extent of rights and duties affected by the limitation (Sec. 44 § 2 Czech Family Code). If both parents, or the only living parent, are limited in the exercise of parental responsibility, the court will appoint a custodian for the extent of limitation.

If a parent abuses his or her parental responsibility, or its exercise, or seriously neglects it, the court will deprive him or her of parental responsibility (Sec. 44 § 3 Czech Family Code). If the parent committed a crime against the child or used the child younger than fifteen to commit a crime or committed a crime as an accessory or counselled the child to be a party to an offence, the court will always consider whether there are reasons for starting proceedings on the deprivation of parental responsibility (Sec. 44 § 4 Czech Family Code).

All the abovementioned types of judicial intervention with parental responsibility are always in relation to an individual parent and an individual child. The fact that the parent has been deprived of parental responsibility in relation to one child does not mean that he or she does not have parental responsibility to his or her other children. If the parent, due to a mental illness, has been limited by court in legal capacity, or has been deprived of it, his or her parental responsibility also ceases to exist.

DENMARK

The local authorities are obliged to supervise the conditions of children living in the area.[13] If a child is being maltreated, neglected or abused it may be necessary to intervene with child protection measures and possibly to place the child in care. Such a measure can be voluntary as far as the parent is concerned or it can be enforced.[14] Such a measure diminishes the powers and duties of the holder(s) of parental authority, but does not as such discharge the holder(s) of their parental authority. If the maltreatment, neglect etc. is being carried out by one of the parents and the parents do not live with each other, the other parent may seek sole parental authority or seek to have the (sole) parental authority transferred, Art. 8, 12 and 13 Danish Act on Parental Authority and Contact. It is possible to discharge the holder(s) of guardianship of their rights as guardians, for example in the case of the incapacity of one or both guardians.[15]

ENGLAND & WALES

Insofar as parental responsibility is automatically conferred at the time of the child's birth, that is in the case of each married parent (see Q 15) and the unmarried mother (see Q 20), it is not possible for the court to divest that responsibility, though in any family proceedings it is possible to limit the exercise of that responsibility by means of making a Sec. 8 order in favour of someone else.

In contrast, no matter how an unmarried father acquires parental responsibility (for which see Q 22b) nor prospectively that acquired by step-parents (see Q 27a) or civil partners (see Q 27b) by reason of a parental responsibility agreement or order the court does have power, upon application, to end that responsibility.[16] In such applications the court is bound to treat the child's welfare as its paramount consideration[17] and in so doing will certainly take account of any violence of the defendant either towards the parent or child.[18]

---

13 Danish Act on Social Services, *Lov om social service,* Act No. 708 of 29.06.2004, Art. 6.

14 I. LUND-ANDERSEN, N. MUNCK and I. NØRGAARD, *Familieret*, Copenhagen: Jurist- og Økonomforbundets Forlag, 2003, p. 111-120.

15 Danish Act on Guardianship, Art. 2.

16 Sec. 4(3), English Children Act 1989.

17 *Viz* Sec. 1(1), English Children Act 1989 applies, see *Re P (Terminating Parental Responsibility)* [1995] 1 FLR 1048.

18 See *Re P (Terminating Parental Responsibility)* [1995] 1 FLR 1048, in which responsibility conferred by a parental responsibility agreement with the mother was terminated because the father had inflicted appalling injuries upon the child. Parental responsibility orders have been refused in the first place because, for example, the father's violence towards the mother, see e.g. *Re T (Parental Responsibility: Contact)* [1993] 2 FLR 450 as well as because of violence towards the child, see *Re L (A Child)(Contact: Domestic Violence)* [2001] Fam 260 and *Re H (Parental Responsibility)* [1998] 1 FLR 855, CA and there is no reason to suppose that such considerations are equally relevant to ending parental responsibility.

FINLAND

Maltreatment, negligence or abuse of the child may constitute legal reasons for child protection measures. If the child's health or development is seriously endangered by a lack of care or other conditions at home, the local social authority shall take the child into care and provide it with substitute care. According to the Child Protection:

> The local social authority shall take a child into care and provide substitute care for it, if the child's health or development is seriously endangered by lack of care or other conditions at home, or if the child seriously endangers its health or development by abuse of intoxicants, by committing an illegal act other than a minor offence, or by other comparable behaviour, if the measures stated in Chapter 4 (*i.e.* assistance in open care) are not appropriate or have proved to be inadequate, and if substitute care is considered to be in the best interest of the child. (Sec. 16)

If a child has been taken into care, the local social authority has the power to decide on the child's care, upbringing, supervision, residence and other welfare of the child (Sec. 19 para. 1 Finnish Child Protection Act). Thus, the custodian will be discharged of exercising the rights mentioned above as a consequence of the care procedure.

There is no special civil court procedure for discharging a custodian because of his or her behaviour or lack of parental competence. A custody decision or approved agreement can be reviewed if the circumstances have changed after the decision or agreement has been made or if the change in custody is deemed appropriate (Sec. 12 Finnish Child Custody and the Right of Access Act).

The violent behaviour of one parent towards the other parent is not mentioned, as such, in the Finnish Child Protection Act or in the Finnish Child Custody and the Right of Access Act, as a reason to be taken into consideration in decision-making. However, if it is proved that the parent's violent behaviour is referred to in Sec. 16 Finnish Child Protection Act as a serious danger for the child's health or development, the violent behaviour should be taken into consideration. Not being in accordance with the best interest of the child, such behaviour can impact the decision-making concerning the custody in the same way, according to Sec. 10 Finnish Child Custody and the Right of Access Act.

FRANCE

In French law, discharge of parental responsibilities can be partial or complete. See Art. 378 to 381 French CC. Two legal provisions state the cases in which parents can be discharged of parental responsibilities:

- Art. 378 French CC: A criminal judgment can discharge the parents of their parental responsibilities (completely or only parts of them) when the parents are sentenced as offenders, co-offenders or accomplices of a crime or offence with respect to their child, or of a crime or offence committed by their child. In this situation the discharge is decided by a criminal court in the same judgment which condemns the parents.

- Art. 378-1 para. 1 French CC: A complete or partial discharge of parental responsibilities can also be ordered by a civil court[19] in the following circumstances: maltreatment, usual and excessive consumption of alcoholic beverages, drug addiction, notorious misconduct, misdemeanour, lack of care or lack of guidance. The legal provision requires that such parental behaviour endangers the child's security, health or morality.
- Art. 378-1 para. 2 French CC: A total or partial discharge can also be decided by the civil court[20] when a measure of educational support has been made in favour of the child and when the parents have voluntarily refrained from exercising the rights and fulfilling the duties of parental responsibilities they still have[21] for more than two years.[22]

The discharge can be claimed by the prosecutor (*ministère public*), a family member or the guardian (*tuteur*) of the child. For some examples of reasons to discharge or not discharge parents from their parental responsibilities, see:

- serious and long psychiatric illness;[23]
- mentally ill and dangerous mother who treated her child so badly that the child became disabled (*infirme*), discharge of parental responsibilities even if the mother was not sentenced by the criminal court because of her insanity;[24]
- father condemned because of murder was a serious danger for the child;[25]
- no proved danger for the child in the case of a father sentenced because of drug traffic;[26]
- no proved danger for the child although the father was condemned because of the sexual abuse of his 15-year old niece;[27]
- generally the *Cour de cassation* requires inferior courts not to rely on possible (and unproved) danger for the child.[28]

19 See Art. 378-1 para. 3 French CC.

20 See Art. 378-1 para. 3 French CC.

21 Parents keep all rights and duties of parental responsibilities which are not consistent with the measure decided by the judge.

22 This legal provision must be interpreted strictly because a discharge can only be justified by an essential requirement corresponding to the child's interests', see ECtHR, 07.09.1996, *D.* 1997. Somm. P. 210 annotated FRICÉRO; French Supreme Court, Civ. I, 15.07.1999, *Bull. civ.* I, No. 237.

23 French Supreme Court, Civ. I, 13.01.1998, *Dr. famille* 1998, No. 97 annotated MURAT: the mother did not voluntarily refrain from exercising her rights and duties (see Art. 378-1 para. 2 French CC) because she was seriously mental ill.

24 French Supreme Court, Civ. I, 14.04.1982, *D.*, 1983. 294.

25 French Supreme Court, Civ. I, 15.05.1990, *Bull. civ.* I, No. 107.

26 French Supreme Court, Civ. I, 06.03.2001, *RJPF*, 2001, 6/35 annotated BLANC.

27 CA Lyon, 22.05.2001, *JCP*, 2002. II. 10 177 annotated GARÉ.

The assertion of the mental fragility of the mother is not sufficient if the court has not researched whether the mother's illness or behaviour endangers the child's safety, health or morality.[29]

Each year between 450 and 600 discharges are decided by judgment. From ten to thirty cases concerning restitution of parental responsibilities are also decided each year.[30]

GERMANY

If the physical, mental or spiritual welfare or the property interests of a child are in jeopardy, the family court is obliged to take the necessary protective steps (§§ 1666 *et seq* German CC), see also Q 18. The family court also has jurisdiction if the issues relating to children are raised in the context of divorce proceedings. As a basis for a court order the danger can result from various causes. The main cases are abuse of parental care (mistreatment,[31] serious educational deficits,[32] sexual abuse *etc.*),[33] negligence of the child (malnutrition, no medical treatment)[34] and inadvertent behaviour of the holder of parental care, § 1666 para. 1 German CC.

Mental illness of the holder of parental responsibilities as such is not enough. However, if the state of health endangers the welfare of the child, mental disorder, paranoia, alcoholism, *etc.* are sufficient reasons for intervention.[35] There was, however, a case where German courts deprived parents of parental custody for their daughters because the parents had learning disabilities. German authorities not only argued that the parents' intellectual capacities were insufficiently developed to permit them to raise their children but also took the children away. However, the parents were successful in a proceeding at the ECtHR. The European Court ruled that the total revocation of the parents' legal custody, and the circumstances of the execution of this measure, constituted a deprivation of parental care that did not satisfy the condition of

---

28 French Supreme Court, Civ. I, 06.07.1999, *Dr. famille,* 2000, No. 4 annotated MURAT.

29 French Supreme Court, Civ. I, 14.06.1988, *Bull. civ.* I, No. 186.

30 See Th. FOSSIER, *L'autorité parentale,* 2002, ESF, 2nd Ed., p. 81.

31 *E.g.* BayObLG, 21.11.1996, *FamRZ* 1997, 572; M. COESTER, in: STAUDINGER, *Kommentar zum Bürgerlichen Gesetzbuch,* 13th Edition, Berlin, 2000, § 1666 German CC No. 92 *et seq.*

32 *E.g.* OLG Köln, 18.02.2002, *JAmt* 2003, 548.

33 For more details see U. DIEDERICHSEN, in: PALANDT, *Bürgerliches Gesetzbuch,* 64th Edition, München: Beck, 2005, § 1666 German CC No. 21 *et seq.*

34 U. DIEDERICHSEN, in: PALANDT, *Bürgerliches Gesetzbuch,* 64th Edition, München: Beck, 2005, § 1666 German CC No. 30; M. COESTER, in: STAUDINGER, *Kommentar zum Bürgerlichen Gesetzbuch,* 13th Edition, Berlin, 2000, § 1666 German CC No.98 *et seq.*- But see OLG Hamm, 22.06.2001, *FamRZ* 2002, 691 (a child's repeated head lice infestation was not sufficient for court measures).

35 OLG Karlsruhe, 14.03.2000, *JAmt* 2001, 192; U. DIEDERICHSEN, in: PALANDT, *Bürgerliches Gesetzbuch,* 64th Edition, München: Beck, 2005, § 1666 German CC No. 32.

proportionality. As a result, the Court held that Art. 8 of the Human Rights Convention had been violated.[36]

Though fault is not necessary for a court order, the parents must be either unwilling or unable to avert the danger themselves.[37] The family court can take into account a parent's violent behaviour towards the other parent; this can lead – at least when it occurs repeatedly and in a aggravated form - to restrictions or a total discharge.[38] Also, the conduct of third parties can be relevant (§ 1666 para. 1 German CC). Court orders have to follow the principle of reasonableness and must be proportionate to the impending danger (see § 1666a para. 1, 2 German CC).

The family court may substitute declarations of the holder of parental care (§ 1666 para. 3 German CC, see Q 8). As far as a consent of the holder of parental responsibility is deemed necessary, it is accepted that the court may substitute the consent if the parent unreasonably refuses to give it.[39] The Civil Code does not specify which other 'measures' the court may take according to § 1666 para. 1 German CC. It is generally accepted that the family court enjoys a broad discretion to make the appropriate orders. These may range from orders on specific issues, modification of custody, placing the child under institutional or foster care, to other orders.

The court also possesses powers in financial affairs. The family court may make an order if the child's assets are put into jeopardy by abuse of parental care, neglect, inadvertent behaviour of the parents or the conduct of third parties. Care for the child and care for the child's property are different issues which must be examined separately.[40] The child's economic interests are endangered if the parents act blatantly contrary to economic principles or from motives of self-interest. Where there is a risk of diminishing or losing the child's fortune or a danger of indebtedness the court may take appropriate actions. § 1666 para. 2 German CC expressly mentions three cases: (1) the parent has violated the right

---

36 ECtHR, 26.02.2002, *Kutzner* v. *Germany*, Request No. 46544/99, *FamRZ* 2002, 1393. - See C. BRÜCKNER, 'Die Überprüfung von Sorgerechtsentziehungen durch den Europäischen Gerichtshof für Menschenrechte', *Familie und Recht (FuR)* 2002, 385 *et seq*; C. HOSS, 'Family Matters: European Court of Human Rights Finds German Parenting Rights Decisions to be in Violation of Art. 8 of the Convention', *German Law Journal* Vol. 3 No. 4 – 01.04.2002. http://www.germanlawjournal.com/

37 U. DIEDERICHSEN, in: PALANDT, *Bürgerliches Gesetzbuch*, 64th Edition, München: Beck, 2005, § 1666 German CC No. 31 *et seq*.

38 KINDLER/DRECHSEL, 'Partnerschaftsgewalt und Kindeswohl', *JAmt* 2003, 217 *et seq*. A. WILL,' Gewaltschutz in Paarbeziehungen mit gemeinsamen Kindern', *FPR* 2004, 233 *et seq*.

39 OLG Hamm 16.07.1998, *NJW* 1998, 3424; U. DIEDERICHSEN, in: PALANDT, *Bürgerliches Gesetzbuch*, 63rd Edition, München: Beck, 2004, §1666 German CC No. 13. See also M. COESTER, in: STAUDINGER, *Kommentar zum Bürgerlichen Gesetzbuch*, 13th Edition, Berlin, 2000, § 1666 German CC No. 103.

40 BayObLG, 09.05.1996, *FamRZ* 1996, 1352.

of the child to receive support, (2) the parent has violated his or her duties in the administration of the child's property or (3) the parent did not follow a court order in respect with the administration of the child's property. In this area the court also enjoys broad discretion.[41] An appropriate measure is often at least a partial deprival of parental custody in financial affairs.

As a matter of last resort, the parents may be deprived, either totally or in part, of their parental custody. As far as possible other measures, including those under public law, must be used (§ 1666a para. 2 German CC). Those measures which involve the separation of a child from his or her paternal family are permissible only if the jeopardy for the child may not be countered in another manner (§ 1666a para. 1 German CC). A detailed catalogue of additional powers of the youth welfare authorities is contained in the Children and Young Persons Assistance Act of 1998. However, intervention must always be limited to what is really necessary (§ 1666a German CC). In a recent case, parents successfully complained to the ECtHR that their parental rights were withdrawn when their children were taken into foster care without giving the parents a fair hearing.[42]

In cases of emergency or where the child or young person asks for it, the youth office can take children or young persons into provisional custody. The holder of parental responsibility has to be informed. If he or she objects, the child or young person must be returned or the youth office has to apply to the family court (§ 42 German Children and Young Persons Assistance Act).

GREECE

According to Art. 1537 Greek CC a parent forfeits parental care when he or she has been finally sentenced to a term of imprisonment for at least one month for a fraudulent offence against the child, or because of any offence against the child's life or health. This is a result of the conviction, without any need for a special provision in the relevant court decision. Under these circumstances, the court may also discharge the parent from the parental care of all his or her children.

In addition, Art. 1532 para. 1 Greek CC provides that if a parent abuses his rights (*e.g.* by maltreating the child),[43] violates his duties (*e.g.* by neglecting the child),[44] or is not in a position to be able to carry out this task (*e.g.* because of a mental illness),[45] the court may only deprive him of the exercise of parental

---

[41] See U. DIEDERICHSEN, in: PALANDT, *Bürgerliches Gesetzbuch*, 64th Edition, München: Beck, 2005, § 1667 German CC No. 3.

[42] ECtHR, *Haase* v. *Germany*, 08.04.2004, *NJW* 2004, 3401 (Taking seven children into care on an emergency basis, including a seven day old baby, without providing parents an opportunity to contest the court order).

[43] Decisions of the Single Judge District Court of Thessaliniki: 954/1990, *Armenopoulos* Vol. 45 (1991), p. 449 and 229/1991, *Armenopoulos* Vol. 46 (1992), p. 20.

[44] Single Judge District Court of Athens 17182/1997, *Elliniki Dikaiosini* Vol. 41 (2000), p. 204, Court of Appeals of Athens, 871/1970, *Armenopoulos* Vol. 24 (1970), p. 884.

[45] Court of Appeals of Thessaloniki 276/2000, *Armenopoulos* Vol. 54 (2000), p. 1385.

care. As regards a parent's violent behaviour towards the other parent, although this behaviour is not directly aimed at the child, it may imply an insufficient exercise of parental care if it has a detrimental effect on the child itself.[46] In any case, Art. 1533 para. 1 Greek CC provides that the court may only discharge a parent from the care of the child if all other available measures are insufficient, or do not suffice in order to prevent any danger to the physical, mental or psychological health of the child (*ultimum remedium*).

If the child is subject to guardianship, the parental responsibilities of the guardian will immediately cease when he or she loses, wholly or partly, his or her capacity to enter into judicial acts (Art. 1650 Greek CC). Moreover, the court may discharge him/her from these tasks, on important grounds, particularly when it determines that the continuation of the guardianship may imperil the interests of the child (Art. 1651 Greek CC).

HUNGARY

Hungarian family law discharges parental responsibilities by ordering the suspension or termination of parental responsibilities.

The court can terminate parental responsibilities if a parent's behaviour seriously damages or endangers his or her child's interests, especially their physical, mental or moral development. This happens specifically if a parent commits an intentional criminal offence against his or her child, but any other mistreatment or abuse of a child may also lead to termination. A parent's violent behaviour towards the other parent is not regulated separately by the Act.

Suspension by judicial decision or by the order of the public guardianship authority is a lesser form of discharge of parental responsibilities, usually also ordered as the consequence of parental failure. Two situations belong here: one is when the court places the child with a third person because it sees that one of the parents would endanger the child, the other is when the public guardianship authority takes the child into institutional care because his or her family endangers his or her growth and the situation can not be solved in any other way, *e.g.* by designating a family caretaker.

In these cases the discharge of parental responsibilities does not leave the family without rights. The parents retain some rights and duties of parental responsibilities, both with respect to children living with third person and children living in institutional care.

IRELAND

Marital parents in Ireland who are involved in a parental responsibilities dispute will only be discharged of their parental responsibilities in exceptional

46 Single Judge District Court of Thessaloniki 165/1992, *Armenopoulos* Vol. 46 (1992), p. 632.

circumstances or for other 'compelling reasons'. Indeed, this parental preference is reflected in Sec. 3(2)(b) Irish Child Care Act 1991 where a health board charged with promoting the welfare of children in its jurisdictional area must have regard 'to the rights and duties of parents, whether under the Constitution or otherwise.'[47]

The majority Supreme Court decision in *North Western Health Board v. H.W. and C.W.*[48] set the threshold for discharging the holders of parental responsibilities (who are married) at a very high level.

In that case DENHAM J. established the requisite test for state intervention in the following terms:

> 'The question is whether the defendants, while exercising their responsibility and duty to P. [the child who was the subject matter of the proceedings in the case] under the Constitution (Art. 41), failed in their duty to him, so that his constitutional rights (including the right to life and bodily integrity) were or are likely to be infringed. In analysing this, P's rights to and in his family are a factor. Consideration has to be given as to whether the State (whether it be a health board or other institution of the State) as guardian of the common good should by appropriate means endeavour to supply the place of the parents to ensure that the welfare of the child is the paramount consideration, but always with due regard to the natural and imprescriptible rights of the child including his rights in and to his family. ... It is only in exceptional circumstances that courts have intervened to protect the child to vindicate the child's constitutional rights. The court will only intervene, and make an order contrary to the parents' decisions, and consent to procedures for the child, in exceptional circumstances. An example of such circumstances in relation to medical matters may be a surgical or medical procedure in relation to an imminent threat to life or serious injury.'[49]

The comments of DENHAM J. in the last sentence should be noted in the context of the recent decision of ABBOTT J. in the Irish High Court.[50] In that case, the Court directed that a five-month-old baby undergo heart surgery, overruling opposition on religious grounds from her mother, who was a member of the Jehovah's Witness community.

The comments of HARDIMAN J. in *North Western Health Board v. H.W. and C.W.* should also be noted:

---

47 See DUNCAN, 'The Child's Right to a Family-Parental Rights in Disguise', (1986) 8 D.U.L.J. 76.

48 [2001] 3 I.R. 622.

49 *Ibid.* at p. 727.

50 Unreported, High Court, 05.08.2004.

> 'Art. 42.5 is in the nature of a default provision. Under its terms, the State may, in exceptional circumstances, upon a failure of parental duty for physical or moral reasons, become a default parent. The sub-article does not constitute the State as an entity with general parental powers.'[51]

MURPHY J. adopted the following approach:

> 'In my view the subsidiary and supplemented powers of the State in relation to the welfare of children arise only where either the general conduct or circumstances of the parent is such as to constitute a virtual abdication of their responsibilities or alternatively the disastrous consequences of a particular parental decision are so immediate and inevitable as to demand intervention and perhaps call into question either the basic competence or devotion of the parents.'[52]

While Art. 41 and 42 Irish Constitution have led to a high threshold for State intervention into the marital family, no such impediment arises in the context of the non-marital family where the best interests of the child will take precedence over all other matters.

Where there are issues of domestic violence, parental responsibilities will be viewed by the Irish court from the perspective of the child. Parental contact with children in cases where there has been domestic violence attracts a significantly different approach to that which would obtain where domestic violence was not a feature of the case. In each case involving a parent's violent behaviour towards the other parent, the risk to the child will be assessed before custody or access is agreed, ordered or discharged. The normal rule of thumb, that access is in the best interest of the child, does not automatically follow where there are issues of domestic violence. The primary question to be considered in such cases by the Irish courts is whether the child needs to be protected.

ITALY

The judge can decree termination of the parental responsibilities when the parent either does not observe or neglects the duties connected with her or his parental authority, or abuses her or his powers by causing serious prejudice to the child (Art. 330 Italian CC). In general, the termination of parental responsibilities is a remedy against the failure to comply with the duties connected to child. The failure to observe the duties relating to the management of the child's property implies (Art. 334 Italian CC) the termination of the management powers (see Q 13). Therefore, not only are actions relevant for the termination of parental responsibilities, but also omissions (such as the

---

51 *Ibid.* at p. 757.

52 *Ibid.* at p. 733.

continuous and total lack of interest towards the child). A single event can be relevant, such as the non-observance of parental duties, if the harm to the child caused by the event is very serious. Prejudicial behaviour of the parents that is not so serious but is constantly repeated can also be relevant. Voluntary prejudicial behaviour is not a requirement since the termination can also be decreed if the holder's mental incompetence causes serious damages to the child.

The Italian legal system, therefore, does not determine *a priori*, in detail, the events that justify the termination of the parental authority, leaving broad discretion to the judge. The facts of each given case are numerous and very different in nature.[53] Instances of 'indirect' abuse or mistreatment, such as the mistreatment of the minor's close relatives (for example, against the other parent) that may prejudice the harmonious psychological and physical growth of the child can be included by analogy in Art. 330 and 333 Italian CC.[54]

The parent whose forfeiture has been decreed because the parent is 'incapable to act as parent', is deprived of all parental rights and duties, with the exception of the obligation to support. If one or of both parent's behaviour is serious enough to justify a decree of termination of parental authority pursuant to Art. 330 Italian CC, but to do so would nonetheless be deemed prejudicial for the child, the judge may grant a decision that is deemed appropriate under the circumstances (Art. 333 Italian CC). In both cases, the judge, for serious reasons, may also decide to remove the child from the family or order to the abusing parent to leave the family home.

LITHUANIA

There are two forms of discharge of parental responsibilities in Lithuanian family law: separation of the parents from their child and the restriction of parental authority.

Separation of the parents from the child is possible without the fault of the parents if the parents do not live with the child and are unable to exercise their parental responsibilities for objective reasons, *e.g.* mental or other serious illness of the parents (Art. 3.179 Lithuanian CC).

---

53 For example, cases of discharge of parental responsibilities due to drugs addiction are numerous. In these cases the discharge is not due simply to drug addiction but is dispensed when the parent addicted to drugs is negligent to his children and doesn't seem to be able to rehabilitate (Court of Appeal of Bologna 11.05.1980, *Dir. fam. pers.*, 1989, p. 602). Moreover the discharge is also dispensed when the parent has been convicted of incest, to life sentence (Art. 564 of the Criminal Code), or in case of forgery and concealment of personal status by way of altering public birth registers, etc. (Art. 566-568 Italian Criminal Code), sexual crimes (Art. 609 *bis*, 609 *ter*, 609 *quater*, 609 *quinquies*, 609 *octies* of the Criminal Code) or in case of children involved in begging activities (Art. 671 Italian Criminal Code).

54 Family Proceeding Court of L'aquila 19.07.2002, *Fam. dir.*, 2003, p. 482.

The restriction of parental authority (temporary or unlimited) is possible only on the basis of the fault of the parent(s). The restriction of parental authority is possible where the parent(s) fail in their duties to raise their children, abuse their parental authority, treat their children cruelly, cause harm to their children by reason of immoral behaviour, or do not care for their children (Art. 3.180 Lithuanian CC). A parent's violent behaviour towards the other parent is treated as immoral behaviour which causes harm to the child and, as a rule, is taken into account by the court when deciding these cases.[55]

Unlimited restriction of parental authority is possible only where the court makes a conclusion that the parent(s) inflicts very great harm on the development of the child or does not care for the child, and no change in the situation is forthcoming.

THE NETHERLANDS

Title 14, section 5 Dutch CC contains two different measures to discharge the parental responsibilities: consensual and non-consensual. Provided this is not contrary to the best interests of the children, the district court may discharge a parent of parental responsibilities over one or more of his or her children on the ground that such a parent is unfit or unable[56] to fulfil the duty of caring or raising the child (Art. 1:266 Dutch CC). In principle consensual discharge may not be pronounced when it is opposed by the parent, however, Art. 1:268 contains the following exceptions:

(a) if it appears after the implementation of a care and supervision order of six months or more, or from the execution of a care and protection order pursuant to Art. 1:261 Dutch CC of more than eighteen months, that there is a well-founded fear that such a measure, due to the parent being unfit or powerless to fulfil his or her duty of care and upbringing of the child, will be insufficient to remove the threat referred to in Art. 1:254 Dutch CC;[57]

(b) if, without the consensual discharge of one parent, the discharge of the other parent would not prevent the children from being subjected to the latter's influence;

(c) if the mental faculties of the parent are so disturbed that he or she is unable to determine his or her will or the significance of his or her statement;

---

55 Supreme Court of Lithuania, 23.10.2002, case *R. Ceplinskiene v. S. Kavaliauskas*, www.lat.lt.

56 Unfit or unable can also be interpreted as unfit or unable to care and raise a specific child, which can be the result of special characteristics of the child or special circumstances of the child, Supreme Court 29.6.1984, *NJ* 1984, 767. This line of reasoning has been used by the courts to discharge a surrogate mother of her parental responsibilities, Court of Appeal 19.2.1998, *NJ kort* 1998, 32 and Court of Appeal Den Haag 21.8.1998, *NJ* 1998, 865.

57 See Rechtbank Groningen 17 June 2004, *LJN* AP 4368 for a recent decision on this ground.

(d) if, after the care and upbringing of the child with the consent of the parent, otherwise than pursuant to a care and supervision order or a placement under an interim guardianship of one or more years by a family other than the parental family, a continuation thereof is necessary since if the child were to return to the parent serious prejudice to the child's interests is feared.

If the well-founded fear, mentioned in Art. 1:268a that gave reason to the vestment of family guardianship and the instruction to stay elsewhere during the day and overnight, would revive, non-consensual discharge is possible.[58] However, non-consensual discharge is not possible if the parents are willing to have the child raised in the home or family appointed by the children's court judge.[59] The parents' approval must be unambiguous and must not be withdrawn in the near future.[60]

Art. 1:269 Dutch CC states that if the District Court considers it necessary in the best interest of the children, it may non-consensually discharge a parent of parental responsibility over one or more of their children on grounds of:

(a) Abuse of parental responsibilities, or gross neglect of the care or raising of one or more children;
(b) Irresponsible behaviour;
(c) Irrevocable conviction:
    (1) on account of wilful participation in a criminal offence with a minor under his or her authority;
    (2) on account of the commission of a criminal offence vis-à-vis the minor described in Titles 13–14 and 18-20 of Book 2 of the Penal Code;
    (3) to a custodial sentence of two years or more;
(d) The serious disregard of the directions of the institution for family guardianship or obstruction of a care and protection order pursuant to the provision of Art. 261;
(e) A well-founded fear of neglect of the best interests of the child because of the parent reclaiming or taking the child back from others who had assumed the care and upbringing of the child.

NORWAY

The question as to whether one of the parents may be freed of his or her parental responsibilities is, in Norway, of practical importance only after a separation or divorce. The main rule is that both parents continue to have parental responsibilities. A discharge may be based on an agreement between the parties, or on a court decision. Such a decision shall be made in the best interests of the child, Art. 48 Norwegian Children Act 1981. It is generally

58 Court of Appeal 's Hertogenbosch 22.4.1999, *FJR* 2002, 48.
59 See Supreme Court 25.4.1997, *NJ* 1997, 596.
60 See Supreme Court 7.4.2000, *NJ* 2000, 563.

agreed that it will be best for the child if both parents continue to hold parental responsibilities.

According to the practice of the courts parental responsibilities may be taken away from the parent not living with the child if it is considered undesirable for that parent to continue participating in such responsibilities. Examples are where the parent's general behaviour is considered to be harmful to the child: maltreatment, violence, suspicion of sexual abuse *etc.* We have no case on the issue of mental illness.

In some cases the relationship between the parents may be a reason for relieving one of the parents of his or her responsibilities. If the parents cannot co-operate in any way, it could be damaging to the child. A recent case decided by the Supreme Court illustrates this:[61] A suitable parent was not allowed to continue sharing parental responsibilities. In the judgment concerning an autistic child, the mother was awarded sole parental responsibility. It was emphasised that the relationship between the parents was poor and, in the view of the court, 'there was a gulf impossible to bridge'. Further, the child's negative reactions to the father, relating to her autism, were of significance, and if he were to be granted the right of contact, this would exacerbate the disfunctional parental communication and hurt the child. An important issue was that the mother could become unable to care for the child, due to the stress caused by contact with the father.

POLAND

There are differences in the way Polish law deals with the suspension of the parental authority (Art. 110 Polish Family and Guardianship Code), its limitation (Art. 107 and 109 Polish Family and Guardianship Code) and deprivation (Art. 111 Polish Family and Guardianship Code).

The court may rule on the suspension of parental authority if there is a temporary obstacle to its exercise (Art. 110 § 1 Polish Family and Guardianship Code). Should the obstacle cease, the court is to revoke the suspension (Art. 110 § 2 Polish Family and Guardianship Code).

If parental authority is held by unmarried parents parental authority may be limited in such a way that the court entrusts one of the parents with the exercise of parental responsibility, limiting the rights and duties of the other parent in certain activities (Art. 58 § 1 Polish Family and Guardianship Code). The provisions are also applicable if the parents are married to each other, but live separately (Art. 107 § 2 Polish Family and Guardianship Code).

The second case of the limitation of the parental authority is, as described in Art. 109 Polish Family and Guardianship Code, a danger posed to the child's wellbeing which requires the court to issue specific orders; in particular, to:

---

61 Rt. 2003 p. 35.

- oblige the parents to specific behaviour and establish a control mechanism in that respect;
- specify which activities cannot be performed by the parents without court authorisation, subject the parents to other form of limitation equivalent to those applicable to a guardian, or subject the parents to constant curator's supervision;
- place the minor with an organisation or institution responsible for children's custody or prepare them for future work; or
- place the minor with a foster family or a child-care institution. The family court may also appoint a curator for the administration of the minor's property.

Polish law emphasises that a prerequisite for the limitation of parental authority is a danger posed to the child's wellbeing. In this situation, the court does not require a parent's guilt and the act is not of a repressive nature.[62]

The prerequisite for depriving one or both parents of parental authority is:

- an permanent obstacle in its exercise (the law defines such an obstacle as one wherein the exercise of parental authority is excluded[63]),
- the abuse of parental authority, or
- the negligence of the parental obligation with regard to the child, in particular, one placed in a foster family or child-care institution.

Since the Polish Criminal Code of 1997 was enacted, a criminal court cannot rule on the deprivation of parental authority, the power is vested in a family court. Polish law emphasises that substantial danger to the child's wellbeing induced by a parent may justify depriving the parent of parental authority without first limiting it.[64]

PORTUGAL

When parents do not comply with their fundamental duties towards their children, they may be discharged of parental responsibility. In certain situations, the law stipulates that parents are automatically discharged of parental responsibility as a consequence of certain facts, presuming that in those circumstances, the parents are in no condition to fulfil their basic duties towards their children. The discharge of parental responsibility may take one of two forms: *ex lege* discharge of parental responsibility and judicial discharge of parental responsibility.

In cases of *ex lege* discharge, certain circumstances are involved that affect the parents and lead the law to presume that it is impossible for them to fulfil their duties towards their children, irrespective of their actual behaviour towards them (*i.e.* definitive condemnation for a crime to which the law attributes this

62 Supreme Court judgment of 13.09.2000, II CKN 1141/00.
63 Supreme Court judgment of 02.07.2000, II CKN 960/00.
64 Supreme Court judgment of 11.01.2000, I CKN 1072/99.

effect, Art. 1913 No. 1(a) Portuguese CC; legal incapacity or disability due to mental disorder, Art. 1913 No. 1(b) Portuguese CC; if the parent is a non-emancipated minor or is legally disabled or incapacitated for a reason other than mental disorder, Art. 1913 No. 2 Portuguese CC).

In situations of judicial discharge, however, the law takes into account the relationship between parents and children and the behaviour of the parents towards their children, particularly the severity of the harm caused by the parents ' actions to their children. Art. 1915 Portuguese CC uses a general clause which covers not only behaviour with *mens rea* by parents that leads to serious harm to the child (Art. 1915 No. 1 1st part Portuguese CC and Art. 192 Portuguese Child Protection Law) but also involuntary harmful behaviour, such as that resulting from inexperience, illness or absence (Art. 1915 No. 1 2nd part Portuguese CC and Art. 192 Portuguese Child Protection Law).

As to the question of whether the mistreatment of a parent influences the decision to discharge the aggressor of parental responsibility, the law is silent. However, it appears that this fact should be taken into consideration when it is severe enough to harm the child.

RUSSIA

Art. 69-72 Russian Family Code entitle the court to discharge the parent(s) of parental responsibility. This Article is only applicable to legal, not adoptive, parents. Adoption can be terminated in a similar fashion, but according to different provisions (Art. 140-143 Russian Family Code). Discharge of parental responsibility is a sanction which is only applicable if the parent(s) have been proven guilty of certain kinds of misconduct. If the parent(s) have perpetrated misconduct without being guilty due, for instance, to a metal illness; discharge of parental responsibility cannot be applied.[65] In such cases, if the behaviour of a parent(s) is dangerous for the children, parental responsibility can be restricted by court order and the children can be taken away according to Art. 73 Russian Family Code. Other than discharge of parental responsibility, termination of adoption is also possible if the adoptive parent(s) have misbehaved against the children without being guilty.[66] Discharge of parental responsibility under Russian law is thus not only a measure of child protection but also a sanction for culpable behaviour of the parents, and is strongly modelled upon criminal sanctions. Therefore, it has been suggested that this measure be transferred into the criminal code in order to enable parents to enjoy all the rights and safeguards granted by criminal law to persons under suspicion of wrongdoing (presumption of innocence, *etc.*).[67]

---

65 M. ANTOKOLSKAIA, *Family Law* (*Semeinoe pravo*), Moscow: Jurist, 1999, p. 211-212.

66 I. KUZNETZOVA, 'Commentary to Art. 141 Russian Family Code', in: I. KUZNETZOVA (ed.), *Commentary on the Family Code of Russian Federation*, Moscow: Jurist, 2000, p. 400.

67 M. ANTOKOLSKAIA, *Family Law* (*Semeinoe pravo*), Moscow: Jurist, 1999, p. 218-219.

Discharge of parental responsibility is applicable in the following cases, exhaustively listed in Art. 69 Russian Family Code:

- Parent(s) in neglect of their parental duties, in particular, those who gravely neglect their duty to provide maintenance for a child. Such neglect can be established if parents leave a young child without supervision and care, creating a dangerous situation for the child. Not providing a child with food, clothing, housing and other necessities of life is another example of such neglect. Systematic non-payment of maintenance, agreed between the parents or determined by the court order, is also deemed sufficient for the discharge of parental rights upon this ground.
- Parent(s) who refuse, without serious reasons, to take their children from a maternity hospital or other medical, educational, social protection or other institution. As parents are under the duty to live with their children, a refusal to take the child from one of these institutions is interpreted as a special case of neglect of parental duties. Such a refusal most often implies *de facto* rejection of parental responsibility on the part of the parent(s).

  It is important to bear in mind that parents under Russian law are not allowed to ask authorities to discharge them of parental responsibility.[68] Thus, the only way for parents to get rid of parental responsibility is to perform a misconduct which leads to the discharge of parental rights. This is why the law regards a simple refusal to take a child from the aforementioned institutions as a special ground for discharge of parental responsibility, without indirectly encouraging them to commit more serious offences against their children in order to be released from them. However, courts have been urged to carefully investigate whether or not a temporary reluctance to take a child from an institution resulted from financial, health-related or other serious problems. Special caution is recommended regarding unemployed or homeless parents, asylum seekers, refugees and unmarried minor mothers.[69]
- Parent(s) who abuse their parental right. Abuse of parental rights can take the form of keeping a child away from school; involving a child in criminal activity, prostitution, drug and alcohol abuse; forcing a child into a sect dangerous for the child's physical and mental health; exploitation of a child, exposing the child to sexual abuse, *etc.* An extreme case of improper use of a child's maintenance, pension or property can also be qualified as an abuse of parental rights.
- Parent(s) who treat their child cruelly, including physical and mental violence, and sexual abuse of the child.

---

68 For a critical account thereof see: M. ANTOKOLSKAIA, *Family Law* (*Semeinoe pravo*), Moscow: Jurist, 1999, p. 197.

69 M. ANTOKOLSKAIA, *Family Law* (*Semeinoe pravo*), Moscow: Jurist, 1999, p. 213.

- Parent(s) who are chronically addicted to drugs or alcohol. This ground is applied only when the intensity of addiction is such that parent(s) are no longer capable to take care for and educate the child.
- Parent(s) who committed an intentional crime against the health or life of their children or another spouse. For application of this ground the parent must have been convicted by a criminal court. A victim of the crime can be the child in question, his or her (step)brothers and (step) sisters, or a (step)parent.

If the parent(s) have performed one or more of the acts listed in Art. 66 Russian Family Code (most often abuse or neglect or parental responsibility, acts of cruelty, crimes against the child of the (step)parent) without fault due to a mental illness, discharge of parental rights cannot be applied. In this case the court can restrict the parental rights of the parent(s) and take the child away from them (Art. 73 (2) Russian Family Code). Parental right can also be restricted if the presence of the child with the parent(s) is dangerous because of the parent(s)' mental or physical illness, or material conditions (Art. 73 (2) Russian Family Code), for instance, if the parent is homeless and has no income. Restriction of parental rights can also be applied as the first stage of discharge of parental responsibility. This can be the case if the behaviours of the parent(s) meet the requirements for discharge of parental responsibility but there is a hope that the parent(s) would improve their behaviour (for instance an addicted parent has consented to treatment). If the situation does not improve within six months, the Guardianship and Curatorship Department must apply to the court for discharge of parental responsibility (Art. 73 (2) Russian Family Code). If the interests of the child so require, the Department can move up the application for the discharge of parental responsibility.

Grounds for the termination of adoption listed in Art. 141 (1) Russian Family Code are mostly the same as for the discharge of parental responsibility, namely if the adoptive parent(s):

- neglect their parental duties,
- abuse their parental right,
- treat their child cruelly, or
- are chronically addicted to drugs or alcohol.

On the top of that, Art. 141 (2) allows the court 'to terminate adoption upon other grounds considered to be in the best interests of the child and the child's opinion.' Under this open norm fall the grounds for discharge of parental responsibility not listed in Art. 141 (1), for instance, an adoptive parent committing by an intentional crime against the health or life of their children or the other spouse. However, there is a clear difference between the expositive list of the fault grounds that can lead to discharge of parental responsibility of the parents and the open list of the grounds for termination of adoption. Unlike parental responsibility, adoption can be terminated in case of the incapacity of the adoptive parent(s) to fulfil their parental duties without fault, for instance due to a serious illness.[70] Adoption can also be terminated when personal relationships between the child and the adoptive parent(s) grows so bad that the continuation of the adoptive relationship is not in the best interests of the child.[71]

SPAIN

The discharge of parental responsibilities can take two forms. The first is the so called *privacion de la patria potestad,* that is privation of *patria potestad*. Both Art. 170 Spanish CC and Art. 136 Catalan Family Code establish that parental responsibility holders can be deprived of parental responsibility if they seriously or repeatedly fail to comply with their obligations as parental responsibility holders. This refers to conducts such as mistreatment, sexual abuse, exploitation, induction to crime, or non compliance with the obligations of care (malnutrition *etc*).

The measure must be decreed by a judge as a consequence of a special judicial procedure. It can be decreed in the framework of criminal or matrimonial proceedings as well. In criminal law, deprivation of *patria potestad* is conceived as a preventive measure to protect the child; in civil law it is a measure of protection as regards he child, although there are some authors who still conceive it as a sanction.

It is necessary to establish that the decree of this measure is convenient to the child's best interests. Mental illness, drug addiction, etc. do not *per se* suffice for the discharge of parental responsibility; it must moreover be established that this is the best way to protect the child. Judges are extremely cautious in this respect because deprivation of *patria potestad* means that parental responsibility holders loose all rights and faculties, and that the adoption of the child will be possible.

Another less harsh possibility is the so called *declaración de desamparo,* which does not imply the loss of *patria potestad* but the suspension of the exercise of some or all of the faculties or rights inherent to *patria poestad*. As a consequence, the public child protection body assumes the functions implicit to guardianship. A declaration of bereavement or abandonment usually means the child will not be allowed to continue living with the parents, meaning that the child will either live with a foster family or in a child protection institution. For further explanations, see Q 32 and 49.

SWEDEN

The court shall entrust custody to the other parent alone or to one or two specially appointed custodians if the parent who is exercising custody of a child

70 I. KUZNETZOVA, 'Commentary to Art. 141 Russian Family Code', in: I. KUZNETZOVA (ed.), *Commentary on the Family Code of Russian Federation*, Moscow: Jurist, 2000, p. 401

71 I. KUZNETZOVA, 'Commentary to Art. 141 Russian Family Code', in: I. KUZNETZOVA (ed.), *Commentary on the Family Code of Russian Federation*, Moscow: Jurist, 2000, p. 401

is guilty of abuse or neglect or is otherwise behaving in a manner that incurs an enduring risk to the child's health or development, Chapter 6 Sec. 7 Swedish Children and Parents Code.[72]

The transfer of custody stipulated by this provision to one or two specially appointed custodians is very rarely used.[73] Restriction of its application is, instead, recommended. It is normally considered sufficient for social welfare authorities to take measures to protect the child *e.g.* removing the child from the abusing or negligent parents' care. The child is then placed in care in a private home authorised to receive children for care. The child is considered to be sufficiently protected through these measures, stipulated in the Swedish Social Services Act (2001:453) and Swedish Care of Young Persons Act (1990:52), and the parents retain their legal custody.

Furthermore, a transfer of custody according to Chapter 6 Sec. 7 Swedish Children and Parents Code, presupposes that there is a person willing to take over the responsibility. That person must also have a close relationship with the child, so that the child accepts him or her as a custodian. A decision to immediately discharge a parent of custody is usually only made if the other parent is suitable to take sole custody of the child. If this is not the case, custody is usually not transferred unless the child has resided in another home for at least three years,[74] the placement has worked out satisfactorily and the person in charge of the child's care is willing to be entrusted custody.[75]

Often the issue of what effect a parent's behaviour will have on custody of the child (and contact) arises in connection with a custody dispute between the parents. The Supreme Court judgment, NJA 2000 p. 345, concerns the effect to be given to a parent's violent behaviour towards the other parent. The Court stated that a parent's violent behaviour towards the child or the other parent constitutes a factor making that parent unfit as a custodian. However, one prior case of assault on the child's mother was not considered enough to make the father unfit as a custodian.[76]

---

72 If custody has been entrusted to one or two specially appointed custodians, questions concerning transfer of custody are governed by Chapter 6 Sec. 10b and 10c Swedish Children and Parents Code.

73 G. WALIN and S. VÄNGBY, *Föräldrabalken, En kommentar, Del I, 1-13 kap.*, Stockholm: Norstedts Juridik, 2002, p. 6:38-6:39; A. SINGER, *Föräldraskap i rättslig belysning*, Uppsala: Iustus Förlag, 2000, p. 474.

74 Sec. 13 para. 4 Swedish Care of Young Persons Act (1990:52), as revised by Act 2003:406.

75 G. WALIN and S. VÄNGBY, *Föräldrabalken, En kommentar, Del I, 1-13 kap.*, Stockholm: Norstedts Juridik, 2002, p. 6:39.

76 See: Chapter 3 Sec. 6 Swedish Social Services Act (2001:453). This condition was applied in *NJA 1995 p. 727*, in order to prevent the father from unlawfully removing the children abroad.

SWITZERLAND

A *de facto* (*i.e.* objective) permanent inability on the part of the parents is a prerequisite condition for the termination of parental responsibilities. There need not be an element of negligence. Withdrawal is only permissible if other measures for the protection of the child, in accordance with Art. 307 to 310 Swiss CC (*i.e.* including withdrawal of custody within the meaning of Art. 310 Swiss CC), cannot ensure the child's welfare or if they appear *a priori* inadequate.[77] Withdrawing parental responsibilities is, therefore *ultima ratio* and this measure must satisfy the principle of commensurability.

Art. 311 § 1 Section 1 states the objective grounds for termination due to the parents' inadequacy, Art. 311 § 1 Section 2 deals with the parents' failure to perform their duties.

The termination of parental responsibilities in accordance with Art. 312 Swiss CC (if the parents apply for termination for 'just cause' or they have consented to a future adoption of the child by unnamed third parties) is often referred to in legal literature as a 'simplified withdrawal'. This should not belie the fact that the same prerequisites must be fulfilled in connection with this as with an Art. 311 Swiss CC termination. Only the proceedings for termination are different in that they tend towards non-contested proceedings, perhaps involving a change in the competent authority.

The extent to which the violent behaviour of one parent towards the other is to be taken into account as a reason for terminating parental responsibilities depends on whether the child's welfare (in the broadest sense) is endangered and whether this danger can be averted by any other means than terminating parental responsibilities.

---

77 C. HEGNAUER, *Grundriss des Kindesrechts*, p. 217.

QUESTION 52

G. DISCHARGE OF PARENTAL RESPONSIBILITIES

Who, in the circumstances referred to in Q 51, has the right or the duty to request the discharge of parental responsibilities?

AUSTRIA

If holders of parental responsibilities threaten the child's interests, then the court must intervene *ex officio* and issue the necessary orders (including the revocation of parental responsibilities), regardless of who brought the matter before it, *e.g.* a neighbour or relative, *etc* (Sec. 176 (1) Austrian CC). Agents of the school authority (i.e. teachers and educators), security forces, and hospitals are required to report to the youth welfare agency if they suspect that the child's interests are at risk (Sec. 37(1) and (2) Youth Welfare Act *[Jugendwohlfahrtsgesetz]*).[1] The parents, grandparents and foster parents, a minor child over 14 years of age, and the youth welfare agency each have an individual right to petition the court (Sec. 176(2) Austrian CC). Persons who bring matters before the court but do not pertain to the group of persons authorized to file petitions do not thereby gain standing as parties or to file appeals.

BELGIUM

According to Art. 32(3) Belgian LJP, the discharge of parental responsibilities must be demanded by the Public Prosecutor.[2]

BULGARIA

As Art. 74 Bulgarian Family Code stipulates, these are: the district court *ex officio*, the other parent or the public prosecutor. The Child Protection Act also authorizes the Child Protection Department of the Municipal Social Assistance Directorate to bring claims to the court for restriction or deprivation of parental rights in the interests of the child. The same body may also enter as a party into court proceedings that have been already commenced (Art. 21 § 14 Bulgarian Child Protection Act).

CZECH REPUBLIC

Proceedings on judicial intervention with parental responsibility may be started by a court even without a specific motion (*ex officio*) as soon as the need for intervention is known to the court. In practice, a motion is usually filed by an authority in charge of social and legal protection of children, which is entitled to do so by Czech Act No. 329/1998 Coll. On Social and Legal Protection of

---

1 O. LEHNER, *Kinder- und Jugendrecht*, 2nd Edition, Vienna: Orac, 1998. p. 164.

2 Court of Appeal of Brussels, 29.06.1927, *Pas.*, 1928, II, p. 156; Court of First Instance of Brussels, 27.11.1948, *J.T.*, 1949, p. 327.

Children, or the motion may be filed by a Prosecuting Attorney (Sec. 35 Czech Code of Civil Procedure).

DENMARK

Parental authority cannot be discharged, but the other parent may seek sole parental authority or to have the (sole) parental authority transferred, Art. 8, 12 and 13 Danish Act on Parental Authority and Contact. A decision to place the child in care is made by a standing committee under the local authorities and is subject to administrative as well as court review. Such a care order does not, however, discharge the holder(s) of his/her/their parental authority.

ENGLAND & WALES

Insofar as it is possible to seek to end or discharge parental responsibility (on which see Q 51), then the following persons can apply, namely:

> any person who has parental responsibility for the child (this will include the father himself) or,
> with leave of the court, the child himself.[3]

In the latter case, the court may grant leave only if it is satisfied that the child has sufficient understanding to make the proposed application.[4] The court may not end a Sec. 4 order while a residence order in favour of the unmarried father remains in force.[5] While the above mentioned persons are empowered to seek an order terminating parental responsibility, they are not under a duty to do so.

FINLAND

The care order can be initiated by the competent local social authority, which is, in practice, the communal social worker or social workers. The child's parents and custodians may submit an application to the court concerning child custody. The local social authority has the same power (Sec. 14 para. 1 Finnish Child Custody and the Right of Access Act, see above Q 50).

FRANCE

See Art. 378-1 para. 3 French CC: the public prosecutor, a member of the family or the guardian of the child.

GERMANY

The proceedings under § 1666 German CC may be initiated *ex officio*.[6] Therefore no formal application is necessary and any person with relevant facts can

---

3 Sec. 4(3), English Children Act 1989.
4 Sec. 4(4).
5 Sec. 12(4).
6 U. DIEDERICHSEN, in: PALANDT, *Bürgerliches Gesetzbuch*, 64th Edition, München: Beck, 2005, § 1684 German CC No. 56.

apply.[7] However, a parent or other relatives can make a request. The youth office is a very important institution, having the right and duty to investigate and to give notice (§ 50 para. 3 German Children and Youth Protection Act). The youth office may also request the discharge of parental responsibilities.

GREECE

If the parent forfeits his or her rights because of a criminal conviction, or the guardian loses his or her full capacity, the discharge of parental responsibilities is immediate, without the need for any further court decision. In the remainder of cases, the court may discharge a parent from parental care at the request of the other parent, the close relatives of the child, or the public prosecutor (Art. 1532 Greek CC). It may also discharge a guardian of his responsibilities at the request of the supervisory council (Art. 1651 Greek CC). The court may also decide on these issues of its own motion (Art. 1532 and 1651 Greek CC). It is worth noting that the law does not entitle the child itself to bring such a case before the court.[8]

HUNGARY

The court holds exclusive power to terminate parental responsibilities. Those persons having the right to file an action to terminate the parental responsibilities are: the other parent, the child, the public guardianship authority and the public prosecutor. The court is the competent authority to decide on the placement of the child. The public guardianship authority is the competent authority to order the child into institutional care; in this case the child will live in foster parent or a children's home.

IRELAND

Sec. 11 Irish Guardianship of Infants Act 1964 enables any person, being the guardian of a child, to apply to the court for an order on any question relating to the welfare of that child. All custody and access decisions are 'interlocutory' by nature. Thus, a decision is never final and conclusive but is instead open to variation should the welfare of the child so demand. The original decision may be changed should altered circumstances or new information require it. Indeed, Sec. 12 of the 1964 Act enables a court to vary or discharge any previously made custody or access order in respect of a child. DENHAM J. further underlined the variable nature of parental responsibilities orders when she noted in *C. v. B.*[9] that:

---

7 M. COESTER, in: STAUDINGER, *Kommentar zum Bürgerlichen Gesetzbuch,* 13th Edition, Berlin, 2000, § 1666 German CC No. 206.

8 The child may, however, intervene in the proceedings (Art. 80 Greek Code of Civil Procedure). Relevant is the decision of the Court of Appeals of Athens 10659/1998, *Elliniki Dikaiosini* Vol. 35 (1994), p. 129, which recognised this possibility in a case concerning the right of contact. In addition, according to Art. 4 of the (1996) European Convention on the Exercise of Children's Rights (Law 2502/1997), the child itself has the right to apply for the appointment of a special guardian to represent it.

9 [1996] 1 I.L.R.M. 63.

'[t]he decision relating to custody of a child, especially a baby ... is never final but evolves with the child, retaining in changing times the fundamental concept of the welfare of the child.'

ITALY

The termination or the limitation decrees pursuant to Arts. 330 and 333 Italian CC may be requested by the other parent, by relatives or by the public prosecutor (Art. 336 § 1 Italian CC). Nobody else is entitled to act; neither the child, nor social services nor the Family Proceeding Court (except on its own initiative or for temporary measures in case of urgent needs) (Art. 336 § 3 Italian CC). Anyone aware of prejudicial facts can inform the competent authorities (police, judicial authority, welfare services), not only in the most serious situations of abandonment of the minors, but also in situations deemed prejudicial to the minors (Art. 9 Italian Adoption Law).

The law obligates public officers, persons entrusted with a public service and those who carry out a public service to reveal any serious situations concerning abandonment of minors to the public prosecutor before the Family Proceeding Court (Art. 9 Italian Adoption Law). The public prosecutor is therefore at the centre of the system of judicial protection of the minor's rights.[10] He or she is the person in charge of receiving any notice or complaint issued by public institutions or by private citizens, for controlling the public and private assistance institutions and for applying to the Family Proceeding Court

LITHUANIA

Such a right and a duty are granted to the state institution for the protection of the rights of the child, a public prosecutor, one of the child's parents or close relatives of the child (Part 1, Art. 3.182 Lithuanian CC).

THE NETHERLANDS

Consensual discharge (*ontheffing*) may only be pronounced on the application of the Child Care and Protection Board or of the Public Prosecution Service (Art. 1:267 § 1 Dutch CC). In some cases,[11] the person who has cared for and raised the child for one or more years at the time of the application may also apply for consensual discharge (Art. 1:267 § 2 Dutch CC). Non-consensual discharge (*ontzetting*) of parental responsibilities shall be pronounced only at the request of the other parent, one of the relatives by blood or by marriage of the children up to and including the fourth degree, the Child Care and Protection Board or the Public Prosecution Service (Art. 1:270 § 1 Dutch CC. In some cases,[12] the

---

10 P. VERCELLONE, *Il controllo giudiziario sull'esercizio della potestà*, in *Trattato di diritto di famiglia* directed by P. ZATTI, II, *Filiazione* by G. COLLURA, L. LENTI and M. MANTOVANI, Giuffrè: Milan, 2002, p. 1033.

11 Art. 1:268 § 2 (d) Dutch CC.

12 Art. 1:269 § 1 (e) Dutch CC.

person who has assumed the care and upbringing of the child may also apply for a non-consensual discharge (Art. 1:270 § 2 Dutch CC).

NORWAY

The only person that has the right to request the court that a parent be discharged of his or her responsibilities is the other parent.

POLAND

According to the provisions of the Polish Constitution, anyone may require the public authorities to protect a child from violence, cruelty, abuse and demoralisation (Art. 72 sec. 1 sentence 2 Polish Constitution). The Family court may initiate proceedings *ex officio* (Art. 570 Polish Civil Procedure Code). Anyone who has information on circumstances which justify initialising *ex officio* proceedings is obliged to report it to the family court (Art. 572 § 1 Polish Civil Procedure Code).

PORTUGAL

The Public Prosecutor's Office, any relative of the minor or any person who has custody of the child in fact and in law may petition the court for parental responsibility to be discharged (Art. 1915 No. 1 Portuguese CC and Art. 194 Portuguese Child Protection Law).

RUSSIA

The right to initiate the procedure of discharge of parental responsibility belongs, according to Art. 70 (1) Russian Family Code, to the following persons and institutions:

- a child of fourteen years and older (Art. 56 (2) Russian Family Code),[13]
- another parent, adoptive parent or guardian of the child,
- a public prosecutor,
- the Guardianship and Curatorship Department,
- other authorities and institutions charged with child protection: *e.g.* a local Commission of Minors Affairs of the Home Office, institutions for children without parental care *etc.*

SPAIN

Parental responsibility holders are deprived of *patria potestad* through a judicial procedure. It can either be an *ad hoc* procedure or decided in a matrimonial or criminal procedure. In a criminal procedure, the measure will be adopted by the judge on his own motion or on request of the *Ministerio Fiscal*. The civil procedure in order to deprive a parental responsibility holder of *patria potestad* can be initiated by the child himself or herself, the father or mother, certain

---

13 A child of fourteen or older is not mentioned in Art. 70 (1) Russian Family Code as being among the persons entitled to initiate the process of discharge of parental responsibility. However, such right is given to a child by Art. 56 (2) Russian Family Code, which grants a child fourteen or older a general right to independently apply to court for protection of his or her rights.

relatives of the child, the *Ministerio Fiscal* or the public child protection body (Art. 134,2 Catalan Family Code and Art. 158; 167 Spanish CC). In a matrimonial procedure, the measure can be decreed by the judge on his own motion, on request of the *Ministerio Fiscal* or of one of the spouses (Art. 92 Spanish CC), if it is discovered that there is reason for privation of *patria potestad*.

The administrative procedure in order to decree a declaration of bereavement is initiated by the competent public child protection body. The public child protection body will intervene on its own or at the request of any other public administration. Any person who comes to know that the child is in a situation of risk has the obligation to inform the competent child protection body. The child him or herself can also request public intervention.

SWEDEN

Questions concerning a change of custody in these circumstances shall be considered by the court, on the application of the social welfare committee, Chapter 6 Sec. 7 para. 4 Swedish Children and Parents Code. In divorce cases between the parents or when the custody otherwise is being considered by the court, the court shall on its own motion consider any necessary change in custody. A parent wishing to discharge the other parent of parental responsibilities may furthermore apply for sole custody in court, Chapter 6 Sec. 5 Swedish Children and Parents Code.

SWITZERLAND

Regardless of actual requests by the child involved and its parents within the meaning of Art. 310 § 2 and 312 § 1 Section 1 Swiss CC, anybody is entitled to initiate the proceedings by filing a report with the authority in question. As soon as the authorities become aware of a danger to a child, they must intervene *ex officio*.

Even 'persons to whom a duty of official or professional secrecy applies, may report any criminal offences committed on minors to the guardianship authorities, if such notification is in the interest of the victim' (Art. 358ter Swiss Penal Code).

Guardianship authorities, officials in the registry office, administrative authorities and courts are obligated to report (Art. 368 § 2 Swiss CC), as well as criminal justice officers (Art. 53 § 2, 358bis Swiss Penal Code). Depending on which cantonal law is applicable, authorities and officials such as teachers, members of the police force, doctors, social welfare works are also obligated to file a report.

QUESTION 53

G. DISCHARGE OF PARENTAL RESPONSIBILITIES

To what extent, if at all, are rights of contact permitted between the child and the previous holder of parental responsibilities after the latter has been discharged of his/her parental responsibilities?

AUSTRIA

Following the revocation of parental responsibilities, a parent or grandparent retains the right to personal contact with the child by operation of law (Sec. 148(1) Austrian CC); in addition the parent holds the right to be informed and to express his or her opinion concerning important matters involving the child (Sec. 178 Austrian CC). However, these rights must be restricted or prohibited if the threat to the child's interests that resulted in the revocation of parental responsibilities continues to exist by maintaining contact with the child (Sec. 148(2), 178(3) Austrian CC).[1] The reactions of the child (who by this point often demonstrates abnormal behaviour and developmental disturbances) and the child's utterances are of special importance in this case.[2] The maintenance of personal contact with other previous holders of parental responsibilities (than parents or grandparents), however, is only permitted if the child's interests are at risk otherwise, *i.e.* without the contact (Sec. 148(4) Austrian CC).

BELGIUM

The right of contact is tied to parental responsibility.[3] Consequently, when a parent is discharged of parental responsibilities, the parent cannot claim a right of contact as part of parental responsibility. However, according to Art. 375 *bis* Belgian CC, any person that can prove a significant, affectionate relationship with a child, can ask a right of contact. This right of contact will be attributed to the person if it is proven that it is in the interests of the child. Using this judicial fiction, a parent that has been completely discharged of his or her parental responsibilities can obtain a right of contact with the child if it is in the child's interests.[4] Even before the introduction of Art. 375*bis* Belgian CC, the Belgian Supreme Court had already judged that it was not contradictory to pronounce the discharge of parental responsibility and still maintain a right of contact with the discharged parent.[5]

---

1 J. STABENTHEINER, 'KindRÄG 2001', in: P. Rummel, *ABGB-Kommentar*, suppl. vol. 1, 3rd Edition, Vienna: Manz, 2003, § 178 Marg. No. 4.

2 O. LEHNER, *Kinder- und Jugendrecht*, 2nd Edition, Vienna: Orac, 1998, p. 173.

3 A. DE WOLF, 'De nieuwe regeling van het omgangsrecht', in: P. SENAEVE (ed.), *Co-ouderschap en omgangsrecht*, Antwerp: Maklu, 1995, No. 354-355.

4 Court of First Instance of Liege, 08.12.1999, *Rev. trim. dr. fam.*, 2000, p. 701.

5 Cass. 19.04.1989, *Arr. Cass.* 1988-89, 957; K. DEWEERDT and J. PUT, 'Veertig jaar jeugdbeschermingsrecht - Overzicht van rechtspraak: 1965-2004', *NjW*, 2003-2004, p. 835.

BULGARIA

Art. 76 Bulgarian Family Code stipulates that in all cases of restriction or deprivation of parental rights the court shall also arrange the personal relations between the parents and the children. The legal theory suggests that it is for the court to decide whether to arrange a contact between the child and a parent with discharged parental rights, depending on the interests of the child. However, the deciding factor here is not to the right of contact of the parent, but of an assessment of the court, which is governed by the interests of the child/children.[6] According to Art. 77, the contact arrangements may be changed or modified.

CZECH REPUBLIC

Being deprived of parental responsibility automatically results in a prohibition of contact between the parent and the child.

DENMARK

Parental authority cannot be discharged, but the other parent may seek sole parental authority or to have the (sole) parental authority transferred, Art. 8, 12 and 13 Danish Act on Parental Authority and Contact, or the child may be placed in care by the local authorities. If the child lives with the other parent, the parent may seek a contact order, which will only be excluded if it is necessary for the child, Art. 17(3) Danish Act on Parental Authority and Contact. If the child has been placed in care by the local authorities, the parents/holder(s) of parental authority retain the right to contact and the local authorities are obliged to facilitate this contact.[7]

ENGLAND & WALES

Unless the father (or prospectively the step-parent or registered partner) has a separate contact order in his favour, once his parental responsibility has been brought to an end in accordance with Sec. 4(3), Children Act 1989 (see Q 52) then all his rights/responsibilities including any "right" to have contact comes to an end. Where he does have a separate contact order then in theory the ending of parental responsibility does not ipso facto end the contact order but it seems inconceivable that the court would not also terminate the contact order.[8]

FINLAND

Whether a parent is a previous custodian or not does not have an impact on the child's right of access. The interests of the child shall be the first and paramount consideration in making a decision about the child's right of access (Sec. 2 and 9

---

6 L. NENOVA, *Family Law of the Republic of Bulgaria*, Sofia, 1994, p. 443.

7 I. LUND-ANDERSEN, N. MUNCK and I. NØRGAARD, *Familieret*, Copenhagen: Jurist- og Økonomforbundets forlag, 2003, p. 121.

8 In Sec. 4(3) proceedings, the court would have power under its own motion to terminate the contact order pursuant to Sec. 10(1)(b), Children Act 1989.

Finnish Child Custody and the Right of Access Act). See Q 47, above, about the conditions for restricting a child's right of access or maintaining contact.

FRANCE

The answer depends on the kind of discharge that has been ordered by the court. If the discharge is total the parent who is discharged automatically loses all rights connected with parental responsibilities (Art. 379 French CC). These consequences apply for all children already born when the judgment is given unless the judgment expressly limits the discharge to one or more of the children. Therefore, in case of total discharge, the discharged parent does not have any contact right.

If the discharge is partial the judgment specifies the parts of parental responsibilities the parent is discharged of. It can also specify that the judgment will only apply for some of the already born children (Art. 379-1 French CC). In both situations if the other parent is dead or has also lost the exercise of parental responsibilities, the court shall appoint a third person to whom the child will be temporarily entrusted and who will request a guardianship from the judge of the guardianship court. The court can also prefer to entrust the child to a public body, see Art. 380 French CC. The court has the same powers if the parental responsibilities only belong to one parent because of a discharge pronounced against the other parent.

GERMANY

Since contact and parental care concern different rights, rights of contact may, as a rule, be exercised between a child and the previous holder of parental responsibilities after the previous holder has been discharged of his or her parental care.[9] However, the holder of the right of contact can also be discharged of this right in the interests of the child (§ 1684 para. 4 sent. 1 German CC). A decision restricting or excluding the right to contact for a longer period, or which excludes it totally, can only be ordered if the welfare of the child would otherwise be endangered (§ 1684 para. 4 sent. 2 German CC). Therefore it is important whether the ground for the discharge of parental custody still persists and would also influence contact with the child and the child's welfare. Existence of a contagious disease or violent behaviour, *e.g.*, may well lead also to an exclusion of contact.[10] In other cases different kinds of restrictions and measures of control are possible.[11] *E.g.*, the family court can order that a third person is present when there is contact (*begleiteter Umgang;* § 1684 para. 4 sent. 3 German CC). Such a third person can be a youth welfare

---

9 See U. DIEDERICHSEN, in: PALANDT, *Bürgerliches Gesetzbuch,* 64th Edition, München: Beck, 2005, § 1684 German CC No. 4.

10 See in more detail L.M. PESCHEL-GUTZEIT, 'Die Regelung des Umgangs nach der Herausnahme des Kindes aus dem Elternhaus, §§ 1666 , 1666a BGB', *FPR* 2003, 290 *et seq.*

11 See U. DIEDERICHSEN, in: PALANDT, *Bürgerliches Gesetzbuch,* 64th Edition, München: Beck, 2005, § 1684 German CC No. 26 *et seq.*

institution or an association. The association then determines which single person fulfils the task of being present (§ 1684 para. 4 sent. 4 German CC).

GREECE

The right of contact is distinct from parental responsibilities.[12] Thus the discharge of parental responsibilities does not necessarily lead to the exclusion of the right to contact the child. Nevertheless, the court will regulate the exercise of the right of contact (Art. 1520 para. 3 Greek CC). In doing so, the reasons as to why the parent does not have parental responsibilities will be of importance.[13] Particularly in the case where the parent has forfeited his responsibilities because of an offence against the child, contact with the child should rather be exceptional.[14] The main guideline to decide this issue is the best interests of the child.

HUNGARY

This matter is regulated differently depending on whether the parental responsibilities end or are only are suspended. If parental responsibilities are terminated, the right of contact between the child and the previous holder of parental responsibilities is permitted only in exceptional cases. If parental responsibilities are suspended, the Act grants the previous holder of parental responsibilities not only right, but also demands the duty of contact with his or her child. Failure to exercise this right can be sanctioned. In this situation, the right of contact also means the right to watch the shaping of the child.

IRELAND

Contact, under Irish law, is the right of the child rather than that of the parents. Where a custody order in favour of a parent, who is a guardian of the child, has been discharged, such a parent is entitled to apply to the court for access to the child. The court will consider an application for access on the basis that the best interests of the child are of paramount importance. Sec. 11D Irish Guardianship of Infants Act 1964 requires the court, in considering an application for access, to have regard to whether the child's best interests would be promoted by maintaining personal relations and direct contact with the applicant on a regular basis. It is extremely unusual for an Irish court to refuse a parent access to his or her own child.

---

12 See S. KOUKOULI-SPILIOTOPOULOU, in: A. GEORGIADIS and M. STATHOPOULOS (eds.), *Civil Code commentary, Vol. VIII, Family Law (Arts. 1505-1694)*, 2nd Edition, Athens: Law & Economy, P. N. SAKKOULAS, 2003, p. 70, No. 154, with further references.

13 S. KOUKOULI- SPILIOTOPOULOU, in: A. GEORGIADIS and M. STATHOPOULOS (eds.), *Civil Code commentary, Vol. VIII, Family Law (Arts. 1505-1694)*, 2nd Edition, Athens: Law & Economy, P. N. SAKKOULAS, 2003, p. 77, No. 165.

14 S. KOUKOULI- SPILIOTOPOULOU, in: A. GEORGIADIS and M. STATHOPOULOS (eds.), *Civil Code commentary, Vol. VIII, Family Law (Arts. 1505-1694)*, 2nd Edition, Athens: Law & Economy, P. N. SAKKOULAS, 2003, p. 77, No. 177.

Until 9 January 1998, only a parent or guardian could apply for access to a child. With the commencement of Sec. 9 Irish Children Act 1997 on that date, certain additional persons may now apply to the court to be afforded access to a child. These persons include the relative of a child or a person who has acted *in loco parentis* in respect of the particular child.

ITALY

Termination of parental responsibilities does not automatically imply the loss of every visiting right. Indeed, the right of visitation is not necessarily connected to parental responsibilities, so persons who do not hold parental authority can also exercise it. The judge has wide discretionary powers, used exclusively in the best interests of the minor, to determine the conditions, limitations and exclusion of the visiting right,. In case of termination of the parental responsibilities the judge may, for serious reasons, decide to remove the child from the family or may order to the abusive parent to leave the family home (Art. 330 § 2 Italian CC). In general, if the termination decree is due to abuse or maltreatment, the parent is deprived of visiting rights; if the termination decree is due to negligence the parent can exercise his visiting right even though the right can be subject to limitations and cautionary measures exclusively aimed at the protection of the minor's interest.[15]

LITHUANIA

The parent, who was separated from the child, or whose parental authority was restricted, retains the right of contact with the child, except where that is contrary to the child's interests. The court makes the relevant decisions.

THE NETHERLANDS

The child and the parent in whom no parental responsibilities are vested have the right to contact with each other (Art. 1:377a § 1 Dutch CC). According to Art. 1:377a § 3 Dutch CC the court shall only disallow a right of contact if:

(a) contact would cause a serious detriment to the mental or physical development of the child, or
(b) the parent is manifestly unfit or clearly not in a position to have contact, or
(c) a child aged twelve or older has demonstrated, on its being heard, to seriously object to contact with the parent, or
(d) contact is otherwise contrary to the paramount interests of the child.

NORWAY

The fact that one parent is discharged from parental responsibilities does not in itself affect the other aspects of his or her relationship with the child. The right

---

15 Court of Appeal of Rome 27.02.95, *Dir. fam. pers.*, 1995, p. 1450. In this case of first instance, the divorce judge granted the father the right to contact notwithstanding that he had been discharged of parental responsibilities before the divorce. The appellate judges decided to grant the father the right to contact only with the consent both of the minor and the mother.

to have contact with the child is not influenced by such a decision. However, the reasons for discharging the parent from parental responsibilities may be relevant to the issue of contact; however, the two issues are legally independent.

POLAND

As a rule, parents should have the right to personal contact with their child in this situation. If the child's best interests so require, the family court may prohibit the parents deprived of parental authority to contact the child in person (Art. 113 § 1 Polish Family and Guardianship Code).

PORTUGAL

Rights of contact are not prohibited by law; in these cases the decision to allow contact is subjected to the criteria of the best interests of the child.

RUSSIA

Parent(s) discharged of parental responsibility lose all their rights[16] regarding the child, including the right of contact (Art. 71 (1) Russian Family Code). The child, on the contrary, retains the right to maintain contact with such parent(s); however, he or she can no longer demand time and attention from the parent(s) as they are no longer under duty to maintain personal relationships with a child.[17]

If parental rights have been restricted and the child has been taken away from the parents, such parent(s) can be allowed to maintain contact with the child only if it does not influence child negatively (Art. 75 Russian Family Code). Such contacts can be allowed by the Guardianship and Curatorship Department, another parent, the guardian, the foster parents of the child or the administration of the institution for children without parental care (Art. 75 Russian Family Code).

SPAIN

Spanish law does not relate rights of contact to parental responsibility. For parents, rights of contact are a consequence of parenthood (Art. 137 Catalan Family Code and Art. 160 Spanish CC); for other relatives or close persons, contact is established because and if it is in the child's best interests (see Q 44).

The fact that a parental responsibility holder has been discharged of his or her parental responsibility does therefore not *per se* impede contact. With a declaration of bereavement or abandonment, it is quite common to establish contact because the situation is considered to be transitory. One of the necessary

---

16 Only the duty to pay a child's maintenance and the right of the child to inherit from his or her parents survive the discharge of parental rights (Art. 71 (2) and (4) Russian Family Code).

17 M. ANTOKOLSKAIA, *Family Law* (*Semeinoe pravo*), Moscow: Jurist, 1999, p. 219.

conditions a foster family must agree with is contact with parents. With the privation of *patria potestad* contact it is, in practice, less commonly granted although still possible in theory. As shown above under Q 51 privation of *patria potestad* is an extreme measure that applies to situations in which contact is not commendable.

SWEDEN

When the child is placed in care due to measures taken by the social welfare committee, the committee has an obligation to ensure, as far as possible, that the child's need for contact with the parents and custodians is met, Sec. 14 Swedish Care of Young Persons Act. If necessary, the social welfare committee may decide upon how the child's contact with the parents (and custodians) shall be exercised. The social welfare committee may also decide that the child's residence shall not be disclosed to the parents or custodians.

When a parent has lost custody of the child, sole custody having been entrusted to the parent with whom the child is living, the reasons the parent was discharged of custody is given weight. A factor such as a parent's violent behaviour towards the child or the other parent can be decisive to the outcome in contact proceedings, justifying contact to be limited or subjected to certain conditions.[18] The point of departure is always to ensure the child's right to contact with a parent with whom the child is not living, Chapter 6 Sec. 15 Swedish Children and Parents Code. This duty rests on the custodial parent or, where special custodians have been appointed, on the latter.

SWITZERLAND

In principle the withdrawal of parental responsibilities does not affect the right to personal contact. Nevertheless the facts which resulted in parental responsibilities being withdrawn may be so momentous that they may result in restrictions in or withdrawal of the right to personal contact (see Art. 274 § 2 Swiss CC).

---

18 See answer to Q 18.

QUESTION 54

G. DISCHARGE OF PARENTAL RESPONSIBILITIES

To what extent, if at all, can the previous holder(s) of parental responsibilities, who has been discharged of his/her parental responsibilities, regain them?

AUSTRIA

Parental responsibilities may be restored to a previous holder of the same if the reasons that led to their revocation no longer exist, *i.e.* if the child's interests are no longer threatened.[1] Before coming to a decision whether parental responsibilities should be restored to their previous holder or not, the advantages and disadvantages of both options have to be weighed.[2]

BELGIUM

Parental responsibilities can be regained at any time, if *ex-officio* pronounced by the Juvenile Court or if proposed by the Public Prosecutor at the Juvenile Court (Art. 60(1) Belgian LJP). A previous holder can also ask to regain parental responsibilities after one year has passed since the judicial decision of discharge has become definitive (Art. 60(2) Belgian LJP). Parental responsibilities can only be regained if it is proved that this is in the interests of the child. The fact that the discharged parent has improved himself or herself is not enough. The discharged parent must also prove that he or she has re-established a harmonious relationship with the child.[3]

BULGARIA

As Art. 77 Bulgarian Family Code stipulates, with a change of circumstances the court may alter the measures decreed under Art. 74, 75 and 76 (restriction and termination of parental rights or contact arrangements). The parent may request the court to restore his or her parental rights where the grounds of deprivation no longer exist.

The main ground for regaining the parental responsibilities is the expiry of the substantiation for their discharge. Such restoration is always made through a

---

1 O. LEHNER, *Kinder- und Jugendrecht*, 2nd Edition, Vienna: Orac, 1998, p. 176; *Oberster Gerichtshof*, 4.6.1996, *Juristische Blätter*, 1996, 714; *Oberster Gerichtshof*, 27.11.2001, *Österreichische Juristenzeitung - EvBl*, 2002, No. 82, p. 335.

2 M. SCHWIMANN in: M. SCHWIMANN, *Praxiskommentar zum ABGB*, Vol. I, 2nd Edition, Vienna: Orac, 1997, § 176 Marg. No. 5; 06.09.1984, *EFSlg*. 45.858; *Oberster Gerichtshof*, 28.08.1985, *EFSlg*. 48.419; *Oberster Gerichtshof*, 09.04.1991, *Österreichischer Amtsvormund*, 1991, p. 140; B. VERSCHRAEGEN, 'Das Kind "Helene", in: Franz Matscher/Ignaz Seidl-Hohenveldern (eds.), Europa im Aufbruch - Festschrift für Fritz Schwind zum 80. Geburtstag, Vienna: Manz, 1993, p. 227-238.

3 Court or Appeal of Brussels, 16.02.1998, *J.D.J.* 1998, No. 174, annotated R. LOOP.

court decision. Only the discharged parent is entitled to request the restoration of his or her rights.

CZECH REPUBLIC

The law does not exclude the possibility of regaining full parental responsibility for the parent who has been deprived of parental responsibility or whose exercise of parental responsibility has been suspended, if an essential change of the situation occurs (Sec. 163 § 2 Czech Code of Civil Procedure). In practice, this happens very rarely.

DENMARK

Parental authority cannot be discharged, but the other parent may seek sole parental authority or to have the (sole) parental authority transferred, Art. 8, 12 and 13 Danish Act on Parental Authority and Contact, or the child may be placed in care by the local authorities. If the child lives with the other parent who has sole parental authority, the parent may seek to have the parental authority transferred, Art. 13 Danish Act on Parental Authority and Contact. The criteria for transfer are strict. If the child has been placed in care, the holder(s) of parental authority can have the child returned when the reasons for the care order are no longer present.[4]

ENGLAND & WALES

There is no specific embargo against an unmarried father (or prospectively a step-parent or registered partner) from seeking to regain parental responsibility after it has been terminated. However, given that a termination of responsibility is a drastic order likely to be made only in extreme circumstances, it seems unlikely that a court would be prepared subsequently to grant a parental responsibility order, but it is possible for the parental responsibility agreement with the mother to be made.

FINLAND

The local social authority shall discharge a child from care when the need for care and substitute placement no longer applies, unless the discharge is clearly contrary to the best interests of the child (Sec. 20 Finnish Child Protection Act). If a decision is made that the child shall be released from care of the authorities, the custodian automatically regains his or her previous custodial rights.[5]

---

4 I. LUND-ANDERSEN, N. MUNCK and I. NØRGAARD, *Familieret*, Copenhagen: Jurist- og Økonomforbundets forlag, 2003, p. 122.

32 The European Court of Human Rights has, in its decisions *K & T v. Finland* and *K. A. v. Finland*, pointed out that the social authorities should periodically examine whether the reasons for the caretaking decision still prevail. The present Finnish Child Protection Act does not impose a direct obligation on the authorities to carry out such periodic examination as, Art. 25 of the Convention of the Rights of the Child requires.

A former custodian may, of course, regain his or her rights if the court reviews the child custody decision or the parents draw up a new agreement according to which a prior sole custody decision is now decided to be joint custody, or the sole custody is vested on the former custodian. (Sec. 12 Finnish Child Custody and the Right of Access Act).

FRANCE

See Art. 381 French CC: A father and mother who have been totally or partly discharged of their parental responsibilities can make a request before court in order to regain all or part of them. The claim must be brought before the civil court and the parents must invoke and prove new circumstances. For example, a parent can use a medical certificate to prove that she or he no longer drinks alcohol or takes drugs. In most cases the public prosecutor will order an inquiry; the court may also do so in order to obtain more information about the 'change of circumstances'. The claim may not be brought for one year after the judgment ordering the discharge has become irrevocable. If the court dismisses the claim, a new claim cannot be brought for one year. If the child has been entrusted to a third person's home in order to be adopted by him or her, the claim is not admissible. If the court decides that the parent(s) may regain parental responsibilities the prosecutor can request that measures of educational support shall be ordered (Art. 381 para. 3 French CC).

GERMANY

In these cases the general rules of non-contentious proceedings apply.[6] The family court has to modify its orders any time it holds that doing so serves the interests of the child. However, serious reasons must exist which affect the interests of the child (§ 1696 para. 1 German CC). Measures under § 1666 German CC and § 1667 German CC must be revoked if a danger to the interests of the child no longer exists (§ 1696 para. 2 German CC). Long-lasting measures under § 1666 German CC and § 1667 German CC must be examined at reasonable intervals *ex officio* (§ 1696 para. 3 German CC). Where the measure discharging the parent of parental care is revoked, the parent regains parental care according to the legal provisions of §§ 1626 *et seq* German CC. Paramount consideration is always the interests of the child. The specific facts and circumstances of each individual case are decisive. Serious reasons for a modification can be an alteration of the underlying facts for the previous court order. There can also be a change in legal provisions or case law.[7]

GREECE

In the case of parental care, if a parent has forfeited the office, he or she cannot regain it. If, however, the court had only deprived him/her of the exercise of parental responsibilities, it may revoke or amend the relevant decision, in view

---

6 U. DIEDERICHSEN, in: PALANDT, *Bürgerliches Gesetzbuch*, 64th Edition, München: Beck, 2005, § 1666 German CC No. 60.

7 U. DIEDERICHSEN, in: PALANDT, *Bürgerliches Gesetzbuch*, 64th Edition, München: Beck, 2005, § 1696 German CC No. 18 *et seq.*

of a change of circumstances, provided that any of the parents, the close relatives, or the public prosecutor request this (Art. 1536 Greek CC). This article introduces an exception to Art. 321 Greek Code of Civil Procedure, which refers to the *res judicata* effect.

If the court discharges the guardian from office, there is no provision which might enable him/her to regain his or her responsibilities. In this case the problem will arise whether or not Art. 1536 Greek CC may apply by analogy. Taking into account the fact that Art. 1536 Greek CC establishes an exception, its application, by analogy, to other cases is methodologically flawed. Moreover, the interests of the child, and particularly the need for the child to live in a stable environment, as well as the fact that the guardian is a third person point in the same direction.

HUNGARY

If parental responsibilities are terminated by judicial decision, they can also be revived in this way. The court can re-establish the parental responsibilities if the reason for the termination no longer exists and there is no other reason for the termination. Persons who have a right to file an action to re-establish parental responsibilities are: either parent, the child, the public guardianship authority and the public prosecutor.

If parental responsibilities were suspended and the reason upon which the court decided on the child's placement with a third person ceases and the circumstances upon which the judgment was based change, the parent or parents can petition to change the judgment.

The legislature intended for the taking of a child into institutional care by the public guardianship authority because of his or her endangerment in the family to be a temporary solution. The competent authorities are obliged to support the parents in changing their circumstances by helping them to become able to take care of their child themselves, and the parents are demanded by the law to do their best to change their circumstances so that they can take their child back. The public guardianship authority is legally obliged to review the justification of the child's institutional care from time to time. The parental responsibilities of the parent awaken as a consequence of the authority's order in these cases.

IRELAND

As previously stated, all custody and access decisions are 'interlocutory' by nature. Thus, a parental responsibilities decision is never final and conclusive. It is open to variation should the welfare of the child so demand. Sec. 12 Irish Guardianship of Infants Act 1964 enables a court to vary or discharge any parental responsibilities order previously made should altered circumstances or new information require it.

ITALY

The judge may reinstate parental responsibilities to a parent who had been deprived of them (Art. 330 Italian CC) when the reasons for the termination of the parental responsibilities cease and there is no risk of further prejudice to the child (Art. 332 Italian CC). The reinstatement request can also be filed by an interested parent. Reinstatement involves the reacquisition of all rights and duties connected with parental responsibilities.

LITHUANIA

This is possible in the event of the separation of a parent from the child if there is a substantial change of circumstances in the reason for the separation, *e.g.* in the event of recovery from illness. In the event of temporary restriction of parental authority, regaining of parental responsibilities is possible if the parent substantially changes his or her behaviour in respect of the child. In the event of unlimited restriction of parental authority, regaining of parental responsibilities is not possible (Art. 3.180 Lithuanian CC).

THE NETHERLANDS

Where the district court is convinced a minor may again be entrusted to its consensually or non-consensually discharged parent, the court may reinstate the parent with parental responsibilities on the parent's request. If parents who are not married to each other wish to exercise joint parental responsibilities, they must apply to do so (Art. 1:277 § 1 Dutch CC). If, on the occasion of the non-consensual or consensual discharge of parental responsibilities the other parent was vested with parental responsibilities, the district court shall not again vest parental responsibilities in the divested parent who applies alone, unless the circumstances have changed since the order vesting the other parent with the responsibility or, unless at the time of the order, it was based on incorrect or incomplete information (Art. 1:277 § 2 Dutch CC).

NORWAY

A parent who has been discharged from parental responsibilities may regain them through an agreement between the parents, or by a court decision. The court will evaluate the request according to the actual situation at the time the decision is made.

POLAND

Should the ground which led to deprivation of parental authority cease to exist, the family court may return parental authority (Art. 111 § 2 Polish Family and Guardianship Code).

PORTUGAL

Full discharge ends when the inability or incapacity is lifted and by the ending of the period of guardianship (Art. 1914 Portuguese CC). In cases of judicial discharge of parental responsibility, this will be lifted when the causes that gave rise to it cease (Art. 1916 No. 1 Portuguese CC). Application for it to be lifted may be made by the Public Prosecutor's Office at any time, or by either parent a year after the transit of the discharge sentence or the sentence that has refused another application for discharge to be lifted (Art. 1916 No. 2 Portuguese CC).

RUSSIA

The restoration of parental responsibility is possible by a court order, upon an application of the parent(s) whose parental responsibility has been discharged. The ground for the restoration is a definitive change of behaviour, way of life and (or) attitude towards the education of the child on the part of the parents (Art. 72 (1) Russian Family Code). The parent(s) can simultaneously request that the child should be returned to them (Art. 72 (3) Russian Family Code). The public prosecutor and the Guardianship and Curatorship Department participate in the proceeding in order to safeguard the interests of the child (Art. 72 (2) Russian Family Code).

Even if the court finds that the behaviour of the parents has definitely changed, it can refuse to restore parental responsibility if such restoration is not in the best interests of the child (Art. 72 (4) Russian Family Code). This can be the case if the child is still traumatised by the previous behaviour of the parent(s), is happy in the new family, *etc.* A child older than ten has an absolute veto regarding the restoration of parental responsibility (Art. 72 (4) Russian Family Code). In order to safeguard the stability of the child's upbringing, the law prohibits restoration of parental responsibility if a child is adopted and the adoption has not been terminated (Art. 72 (4) Russian Family Code).

Restoration of parental responsibility leads to a restoration of all rights and duties attributed to the parents. It should be noticed that restoration of parental responsibility is a rather exceptional event.

SPAIN

A parent who has been deprived of parental responsibility can regain parental responsibility if it is established in a court proceeding that the situation which caused deprivation has disappeared (Art. 170.3 Spanish CC and Art. 136 Catalan Family Code) and that recovery of *patria potestad* is in accordance with the child's best interests. In practice this is very uncommon.

The fact that a parent regains parental responsibility does not necessarily mean that the parental responsibility holder will be allowed to exercise parental responsibility. This requires an independent decision in which the child's best interests are paramount.

The declaration of bereavement has less harsh effects because it affects the exercise of parental responsibilities. The exercise of parental responsibilities will be regained if it is established that the parental responsibility holder has regained his capacity to exercise them properly. There may be a need to establish a transitory phase for the child's adjustment to the new situation.

SWEDEN

If custody has been transferred to one or two specially appointed custodians according to Chapter 6 Sec. 7 Swedish Children and Parent Code, and one of the parents wishes custody to be transferred to him or her, or both so wish, the court shall decide in accordance with the best interests of the child, Chapter 6 Sec. 10 Swedish Children and Parents Code. Questions concerning transfer of custody in this situation shall be considered on the application of one or both parents or on the application of the social welfare committee.

A parent who has lost custody, residence or contact in a dispute with the other parent, for whatever reason, is free to commence new proceedings concerning the matter and request a change in the current position at any time, Chapter 6 Sec. 5 and 15a Swedish Children and Parents Code.

SWITZERLAND

If circumstances change, the measures for the protection of the child are to be adjusted to suit the new situation. Parental responsibilities may in no case be reinstated before a year has gone by since they were withdrawn' (Art. 313 Swiss CC).

QUESTION 55

H. PROCEDURAL ISSUES

Who is the competent authority to decide disputes concerning parental responsibilities, questions of residence of the child or contact? Who is the competent authority to carry out an investigation relating to the circumstances of the child in a dispute on parental responsibility, residence or contact?

AUSTRIA

Custodial matters comprise disputes concerning parental responsibilities (Sec. 144 *et seq* Austrian CC), questions regarding the child's primary residence (Sec. 167 and 177 Austrian CC) and the right of contact (Sec. 148 Austrian CC), including additional rights of communication of the parent not holding parental responsibilities pursuant to Sec. 178 Austrian CC. These matters must be resolved through non-contentious court proceedings (Sec. 104 *et seq* Non-Contentious Proceedings Act *[Außerstreitgesetz]*). The authority that is competent to make these decisions is the district court having jurisdiction over the domicile in which the minor normally resides (Sec. 104a and 109 Jurisdictional Norm *[Jurisdiktionsnorm]* 1895). In custodial matters, specially trained court employees, so-called judicial officers *[Rechtspfleger]*, have broad authority including the power to approve the agreements concerning the exercise of a parent's or grandparent's right to have contact with the child as well as the parents' agreements concerning the primary residence of the child and the exercise of parental responsibilities (Sec. 19(1), 19(2) No. 2 Judicial Officers Act *[Rechtspflegergesetz]* 1985). However, all other procedures for regulating the personal rights and duties emanating from family relations, and in particular the procedures for the (partial) revocation of parental responsibilities as well as for the substitution of assents and consents by the court (Sec. 176 Austrian CC) are reserved for the judge (Sec. 19(2) No. 2 *Rechtspflegergesetz*).

The youth welfare agency (to be precise the district youth welfare office of the minor's domicile) should be heard before the court issues orders in proceedings concerning care and education of the child and the arrangement of his or her personal contacts, or before it approves an arrangement on these matters unless the child's interests would be threatened by a delay associated with this (Sec. 106 *Außerstreitgesetz*). Also, the offices of the juvenile court assistance can be utilized as a source of information (Sec. 48 Juvenile Court Act *[Jugendgerichtsgesetz]* 1988).[1]

---

1 http://www.soziales.at.

BELGIUM

The competent authority is the Juvenile Court. According to Art. 387 *bis* Belgian CC, this Court has a general competence for all disputes concerning minors, including disputes concerning parental responsibilities, questions of residence of the child or contact.[2] However, when a dispute arises in certain situations, other authorities are competent. There is a distinction between married parents, parents who cohabitate legally and unmarried parents.

When a question of parental responsibilities arises between married parents (*e.g.* in case of factual separation, but not necessarily), the Justice of the Peace is the competent court for determining interim measures between spouses (Art. 221-223 Belgian CC). It will take all elements of the factual separation into account, including problems of the children. When a divorce procedure has been introduced in court (Art. 1280 Belgian Judicial Code) the President of the Court of First Instance is competent to pronounce interim measures. Measures between legally cohabitating parents, including measures concerning the children, are pronounced by the Justice of the Peace (Art. 1479 Belgian CC).

Unmarried parents who did not formalise their relationship cannot invoke the competence of the Justice of the Peace; only the Juvenile Court is competent, unless urgency can be proven. When the plaintiff can prove the dispute is extremely urgent, the President of the Court of First Instance is competent according to Art. 584(1) Belgian Judicial Code concerning interim injunction proceedings to take measures concerning the children. This competence applies nothwithstanding the relationship between the parents.[3]

BULGARIA

The competent authority to decide these matters is the District Court, which is the court of first instance. The competent District Court is the one where the current residence of the child is, in cases of residence; or where the parent resides in cases of restriction or termination of parental rights and contact with the child (Art. 71 § 2, 74, 75 Bulgarian Family Code).

The Bulgarian Child Protection Act imposes an obligation of the Child Protection Department of the Social Assistance Directorate to investigate the circumstances of the child. The law requires that in each case 'the court … shall notify the Social Assistance Directorate at the current address of the child. The Social Assistance Directorate shall send a representative of its own to the case, who shall express a viewpoint, and if it becomes impossible, he/she shall present a report. (Art. 15 § 6). The parents or the person who takes care of the child shall have access to the report prior to its submission to the requiring body (Art. 21 § 15).

---

2 Other articles of the Belgian Civil Code confirm it for specific matters, *cfr.* Art. 373(3), 374(2), 375*bis* (2) and 376 (4) Belgian CC.

3 K. HERBOTS, *Artikelsgewijze commentaar met ovezricht van rechtspraak en rechtsleer personen- en familierecht* (Art. 387 bis Belgian CC) Antwerp: Maklu, 1997, No. 11-14.

In cases of restriction and deprivation of parental responsibilities it is still possible for the court and the prosecutor to undertake their own investigation (Art. 74-75 Bulgarian Family Code). This possibility however is rather theoretical due to the new professional bodies that have appeared under the Child Protection Act from 2001 onwards; namely the Child Protection Departments mandated with drafting social reports on the child and his or her family situation.

CZECH REPUBLIC

The court is the only authority competent to decide disputes concerning parental responsibilities, questions of residence of the child or contact. The competent court is the one in whose jurisdiction the child has residence on the basis of a parental agreement, a judicial decision or other decisive facts (Sec. 88 § (c) Czech Code of Civil Procedure). In all proceedings concerning the child, the child must be represented by the custodian *ad litem*, whose role is usually played by an authority in charge of social and legal protection of children (a community with extended powers). Pursuant to Czech Act No. 359/1999 Coll. On Social and Legal Protection of Children, such an authority is charged to provide the court with information on all important facts so the court will be able to make an informed decision. The proceedings on matters concerning care of minors are considered non-contentious proceedings, which means that the court is obliged to furnish itself with all necessary evidence for its decision and is not bound by the parties' motions to call in evidence.

DENMARK

An administrative authority, the *Statsamt,* has sole competence in matters of contact, Art. 17 Danish Act on Parental Authority and Contact. The *Statsamt* may make use of expert evaluations and opinions concerning the parent-child relationship.[4] Decisions of the *Statsamt* may be appealed to another administrative authority.[5] Competence in the field of parental authority is split between the ordinary courts and the *Statsamt*. The general principle is that non-conflict cases are dealt with by the *Statsamt* and conflict cases by the courts. When joint parental authority must end and the parents do not agree as to which of them should have parental authority, the decision is always made by the court, Art. 19(2) Danish Act on Parental Authority and Contact. An enforcement court decides whether measures enforcing contact should be taken. The Enforcement Court may deny enforcement where the child's mental

4 The experts may have a background as psychologists, psychiatrists, social workers or similar and may be employees of the *Statsamt* or external.

5 On 2 August 2004 the field of family law was transferred from the Ministry of Justice to the new Ministry for Family and Consumer Affairs. The administrative appeal authority used to be Department of Private Law, *Civilretsdirektoratet*. All administrative appeal matters relating to family law have now been transferred to a new administrative body called Department of Family Affairs, *Familiestyrelsen,* under the new Ministry for Family and Consumer Affairs.

or physical health is subject to serious danger and it may require an expert opinion and postpone enforcement where there are doubts.[6] The courts use external (private practice) experts.

ENGLAND & WALES

In English law there are three levels of court with original jurisdiction to hear family matters, namely, (in descending hierarchal order) the High Court (Family Division), the county court (principally divorce county courts and family hearing centres) and the magistrates' courts (family proceedings court). No other competent authority can authoritatively adjudicate disputes concerning parental responsibility *etc.*

Each of the above mentioned courts can make Sec. 8 orders under the Children Act 1989[7] which, as discussed in Q 38, cover all aspects of parental responsibility including residence and contact. In so-called freestanding applications, that is, proceedings solely concerning the child's upbringing, there is in general freedom of choice as to the level of court in which to bring proceedings. There are, however, some instances where in the private law context it is established that free-standing proceedings should be begun in the High Court. These include, most relevantly for the purposes of this report, applications by children for leave to apply for Sec. 8 orders,[8] applications to sterilise the child,[9] cases in which a blood test is being disputed[10] and cases in which HIV tests for children are being sought.[11] In addition there are provisions for transferring applications from one level of court to another.[12]

Where the issues relating to children are raised in the context of divorce proceedings between the parents (which will commonly be the case) then the matter must be brought in the first instance in the divorce county court,[13] though again there is provision to transfer the case to a higher level.[14]

Once legal proceedings are in train the responsibility for deciding what, if any, investigation needs to be made into the child's circumstances rests with the court. By Sec. 7, Children Act 1989 a court considering any question with

---

6 Danish Civil Procedural Act, Art. 536(1).

7 'Court' for the purposes of the 1989 means the High Court, a county court or a magistrates' court - Sec. 92(7).

8 *Practice Direction (applications by children: leave)* [1993] 1 All ER 820 (but only the application for leave and not necessarily the substantive application).

9 *Re HG (Specific Issue Order: Procedure)* [1993] 587, *Practice Note (Official Solicitor: Sterilisation)* [1996] 2 FLR 111.

10 *Re F (A Minor)(Blood Tests: Parental Rights)* [1993] Fam 314, CA.

11 *Re HIV Tests* [1994] 2 FLR 116.

12 See Art. 8-12, Children (Allocation of Proceedings) Order 1991 (SI 1991 11677).

13 Sec. 33, Matrimonial and Family Proceedings Act 1984.

14 Sec. 38, Matrimonial and Family Proceedings Act 1984.

respect to a child may ask either a CAFCASS officer[15] or a local authority "to report to the court on such matters relating to the welfare of that child as are required to be dealt with in the report". Before a welfare report is ordered consideration should be given to the court's power to refer the parties to mediation.[16] The court is not bound to order welfare reports in every case and in any event should not do so where there is no live issue under the Children Act. Even where there is a live issue if delay would prejudice the child's welfare, the court will have to balance the advantages to be gained from a report against the disadvantage of the time it takes to obtain it.[17] There are national standards of practice to be followed by a children and family reporter.[18]

It is normal practice for welfare reports to contain recommendations but these are not binding on the courts although if a court departs from a recommendation it is incumbent upon the judge to state the reasons for so doing.[19]

FINLAND

Child custody disputes and the right of access are dealt with by the district court of the child's residence (Sec. 13 Finnish Child Custody and the Right of Access Act). The issues can also be handled together in the divorce case of the child's parents (Sec. 32 § Finnish Marriage Act; Sec. 10 Chapter 10 Finnish Procedural Code). The decisions are open to appeal. The court shall request the local social authority to make a report to the court unless it is evident that a report is not necessary (Sec. 16 Finnish Child Custody and the Right of Access Act). In practice, a report most often will be requested in disputed cases.

Parental agreements concerning child custody and/or the right of access shall be presented for approval at the local social authority in the commune or municipality where the child has residence (Sec. 8 Finnish Child Custody Act).[20]

---

15 *I.e.* the Children and Family Court and Advisory Service which, as from April 2001, has been responsible for providing what were formerly known as welfare officers. These officers are now known as children and family reporters.

16 *District Judge's Direction, Children: Conciliation)* [2004] 1 FLR 974 by which all s 8 order applications are to be listed in the so-called conciliation list operative nationwide since 22 March 2004 (see Q 57).

17 *Re H (Minors)(Welfare Reports)* [1990] 2 FLR 172, CA.

18 First published in Children Act Advisory Committee's annual report for 1993/4 and republished in the Committee's *Handbook of Best Practice in Children Act Cases* (1997).

19 See *e.g. Re V (Residence: Review)* [1995] 2 FLR 1010, CA and *Re L (Residence: Justices Reasons)* [1995] 2 FLR 445.

20 From 1st March 2005 the implementation of the Brussels IIa decree will impact the regulation of the competent authority. According to the proposal the competent authority is the local social authority in the municipality of Helsinki, if neither the parents nor the child is habitually resident in Finland (HE 186/2004).

The care proceedings in cases where the caretaking is opposed by the custodian, or by the child who is at least twelve years old, are subject to submission to the administrative court. Thus, the administrative court deals with the issue of this question (Sec. 17 para. 2 Finnish Child Protection Act). Besides the custodians, the parents and the person(s) providing caregiving immediately before the caretaking procedure are entitled to appeal the caretaking decision of the local social authority to the administrative court, and then to the Supreme Administrative Court (Sec. 35 para. 2 and Sec. 37 Finnish Child Protection Act). The local social authority is responsible for the investigation in the care proceedings.

The proceedings concerning the administration of the property of the child are handled by the district court of the child's residence (Sec. 70 Finnish Guardianship Services Act). The guardianship authority shall be given the opportunity to be heard in the proceedings.

FRANCE

Three kinds of judges can be competent depending on the issues which have to be solved:

- The *juge aux affaires familiales* (*JAF*, family judge) is a member of the civil court called *tribunal de grande instance*. She or he is competent to decide on the exercise of parental responsibilities in all cases of separation (divorce, legal, factual separation, *etc.*.). This judge also determines the parental contribution for the child's maintenance if the child is living with the other parent. She or he also solves all kinds of disputes concerning the attribution or the exercise of parental responsibilities between parents, or concerning the delegation of parental responsibilities. More generally the family judge must protect the child's interests. Most of the time (but not in case of a legal separation or of divorce) she or he can be seized directly by written declaration at the courts' office; a lawyer is not necessary. The court cannot be seized by the minor child himself. For questions concerning the child's residence and contact, the family judge is usually the competent court. In a dispute over parental responsibilities the judge can carry out an investigation relating to the circumstances of the child (he can order an expert testimony or a social inquiry (*enquête sociale*)).
- The *juge des enfants* (juvenile-court judge) is also a member of the *tribunal de grance instance* and has exclusive jurisdiction in matters of educational support and protection of the child.[21] If the education of the child presents a danger, the judge can order educational support

[21] For statistical information about the activity of the juvenile court judge in civil matters of educational support and protection of children, see *Infostat Justice* September 2004, *L'activité des tribunaux pour enfants en 2003*: in 2003 the juvenile court judges were seized for 105,400 minor children in danger (2% less than in 2001). 58,000 inquiry measures and 250,000 protection measures have been ordered.

measures.[22] In this situation he or she can order that the child shall be entrusted to a third person and the parents will no longer exercise all parental responsibilities. The judge can also order protective measures for a young child. The judge can be called either by a lawyer or directly by a written declaration. The minor child can also call him directly. The parents, the person with whom the child lives or the prosecutor (*procureur de la République*) can also call him or her; the judge can also act on his or her own motion. The *juge des enfants* is also competent for some offences committed by minor children. He or she can carry out an investigation relating to the existing danger for the child's safety, health or morality (he can order an expert testimony, a social inquiry (*enquête sociale*), a personality study of the child *etc.*).

- The *juge des tutelles* (guardianship-court judge) is a member of the civil court called *tribunal d'instance*. She or he is competent to order the opening of a guardianship and to supervise the administration of the child's property and the functioning of the guardianship.

GERMANY

The competent authority in matters of parental responsibility is the family court. This is a department of the local court (*Amtsgericht*), see § 23b Court Organisation Act (*Gerichtsverfassungsgesetz*). The family court has to decide disputes concerning parental responsibilities (§ 1628 sent. 1 German CC). This court also decides questions of the child's residence, which generally are framed as an issue of parental care (§ 1671 German CC). The family court is also competent for questions of contact (§§ 1684, 1685 German CC).

There can be an injunction of the family court in the context of a divorce proceeding. The court can make an injunction on the application of one of the parties for the parental custody of a common child (§ 620 No. 1 German Code of Civil Procedure), contact of a parent with the child (§ 620 No. 2 German Code of Civil Procedure) or the surrender of a child to the other parent (§ 620 No. 3 German Code of Civil Procedure). Such an injunction on parental custody, contact or the surrender of a child is also possible in an isolated proceeding on these questions (§ 621g German Code of Civil Procedure in conjunction with § 621 para. 1 No. 1 - 3 German Code of Civil Procedure). In a contact proceeding, an order to surrender the child to the other parent for the purpose of enforceable contact is also possible.[23]

As far as necessary the family court has to carry out an investigation relating to the circumstances of the child in a dispute on parental responsibility, residence

---

22 These measures can modify the contents of a judicial order made by the family judge with regard to the exercise of parental responsibilities, see French Supreme Court, Civ. I, 12.01.1994 and 23.02.1994, *JCP*, 1994. II. 22 341 annotated BERNIGAUD.

23 OLG Karlsruhe, 16.10.2001, *FamRZ* 2002, 1125; OLG Frankfurt 03.09.2002, *FamRZ* 2002, 1585.

or contact. The legal basis is § 12 German Act on Voluntary Jurisdiction. According to this provision the court can undertake an *ex officio* investigation.

The court can use a variety of possibilities to investigate the facts. Often reports of the youth office are used. In most matters concerning children the youth office has to be heard, especially in relation to tasks of foster parents (§ 49a para. 1 No. 3 German Act on Voluntary Jurisdiction), support of parents for personal care (§ 49a para. 1 No. 4 German Act on Voluntary Jurisdiction), contact with the child (§ 49a para. 1 No. 7 German Act on Voluntary Jurisdiction), jeopardizing the welfare of the child (§ 49a para. 1 No. 8 German Act on Voluntary Jurisdiction), parental care after separation of the parents (§ 49a para. 1 No. 9 German Act on Voluntary Jurisdiction) and parental custody after deprival of custody (§ 49a para. 1 No. 12 German Act on Voluntary Jurisdiction). The court can also use expert evidence (psychologists, medical practitioners).[24] Especially in the case of contact disputes with children under ten years of age a psychological opinion may be necessary.[25] However, a parent cannot be forced to have contact with his or her child under the supervision of an expert who has to prepare a report for the court.[26]

GREECE

The competent authority to settle disputes concerning parental responsibilities, questions of the child's residence or contact is always the district court. Depending on the proceedings the case may be heard by a single judge (this is usually the case when the dispute refers to the care of the child)[27] or by a bench of three judges (if the dispute is joined with matrimonial disputes or disputes concerning the relationship between the parents and children).[28] The territorial competence of the court is determined by the domicile of the defendant (Art. 22 Greek Code of Civil Procedure).[29] Finally, Greek courts have international

---

24 U. DIEDERICHSEN, in: PALANDT, *Bürgerliches Gesetzbuch,* 64th Edition, München: Beck, 2005, Einf. § 1626 German CC No. 7.

25 See LENZ/J. BAUMANN, *FPR* 2004, 303 *et seq*; F. FINKE, 'Die rechtlichen Grundlagen der Sachverständigentätigkeit in der Familiengerichtsbarkeit nach der Kindschaftsrechtsreform vom 1. 7. 1998', *FPR* 2003, 503,505 *et seq.*

26 BVerfG, 20.05.2003, *FamRZ* 2004, 523.

27 Art. 17 para. 1 Greek Code of Civil Procedure.

28 Art. 681b para. 2 Greek Code of Civil Procedure. Matrimonial disputes are those relating to divorce, annulment of the marriage, declarations on the existence or non-existence of marriage, and the personal relationship of the spouses during the marriage (Art. 592 para. 1 Greek Code of Civil Procedure). Disputes concerning the relationship between parents and children are those relating to a challenge to paternity, the recognition of the existence or the non-existence of a parent and child relationship, or of parental care, the acknowledgement of paternity of children born out of wedlock or a challenge to such a voluntary acknowledgement, the recognition or the non-recognition of the nullity of adoption or its termination, and the recognition or non-recognition of the existence or non-existence of guardianship, (Art. 614 para. 1 Greek Code of Civil Procedure).

29 If the dispute on parental responsibilities is joined with matrimonial disputes, the *forum matrimonii* will apply. (Art. 39 Greek Code of Civil Procedure).

jurisdiction when they have territorial competence[30] as well as when any of parties, *i.e.* the parents or the child, are Greek citizens.[31] This depends, of course, on any relevant provisions of European or International law, which prevail as *leges superiores*.[32]

The competent authority to carry out an investigation relating to the circumstances of the child is the social service. The establishment of this social service is provided by Law 2447/1996 (Art. 49-54), but it has not yet been established.[33]

HUNGARY

Disputes concerning parental responsibilities, questions of residence (and placement) of the child and the contact are partly in the court's power and partly in the power of the public guardianship bodies, which work not as courts but as administrative authorities in Hungary.

If the parents live together, matters of parental responsibilities are to be decided by the public guardianship authorities according to the law. It is questionable whether parents living together really go to the authorities for the disputes' resolution. Disputes concerning parental responsibility matters between parents not living together are to be resolved by judges in out-of-court proceedings. This can be especially important concerning parental rights attributed to non-custodial parents. There is one issue of parental responsibilities that parents, living together or apart, can not petition either the court or to the public guardianship authority about: it is the child's religious education. Both the Constitution of the Hungarian Republic and the Family Act state that no State intervention is allowed in this matter, even if the parents dispute it.

Usually, courts have the power, in a lawsuit, to decide disputes concerning the placement of the child.

---

30 Art. 3 para. 1 Greek Code of Civil Procedure.

31 Art. 622, Greek Code of Civil Procedure. See S. KOUKOULI- SPILIOTOPOULOU, in: A. GEORGIADIS and M. STATHOPOULOS (eds.), *Civil Code commentary, Vol. VIII, Family Law (Arts. 1505-1694)*, 2nd Edition, Athens: Law & Economy, P. N. SAKKOULAS, 2003, p. 111, No. 243.

32 See, for instance, Art. 8 of Council Regulation (EC) No. 2201/ 2003 Concerning Jurisdiction and the Recognition and Enforcement of Judgments in Matrimonial Matters and the Matters of Parental Responsibility (2003) OJL 338/1, or Art. 5 para. 1 of the (1996) Hague Convention on Jurisdiction, Applicable Law, Recognition, Enforcement and Co-operation in Respect of Parental Responsibility and Measures for the Protection of Children which provide that jurisdiction is, at least in principle, determined by the child's habitual residence.

33 S. KOUKOULI- SPILIOTOPOULOU, in: A. GEORGIADIS and M. STATHOPOULOS (eds.), *Civil Code commentary, Vol. VIII, Family Law (Arts. 1505-1694)*, 2nd Edition, Athens: Law & Economy, P. N. SAKKOULAS, 2003, p. 129, No. 272.

Both the court and the public guardianship authority have the power to decide the resolution of a dispute concerning contact. The court has power to decide, if the claim for the arrangement of the contact emerges in a divorce case or a case on the placement of the child, or if the subject of the lawsuit is a change of contact arranged in a judgment, provided that the lawsuit is within two years from the earlier judgment or the judicial consent to the parents' settlement. If the claim for an arrangement of contact emerges in another context, the public guardianship authority has power to settle or re-settle the matter. The enforcement of the decision, regardless of whether it was court's or the authority's decision, is always in the power of the public guardianship authority.

Both courts and the public guardianship authorities should make their decisions in these cases on the basis of the parents' arrangements, and the parents should be induced to agree on the arrangements themselves. In case of divorce by consent both the agreement on the placement of the child and on the contact are legal prerequisites of filing the action.

IRELAND

The court is the competent authority to decide disputes concerning parental responsibilities, questions of residence of the child or contact.

The court has the power to direct an investigation to be carried out relating to the circumstances of the child in a dispute on parental responsibility, residence or contact. Despite the strictures of the adversarial approach, it is the frequent practice of the Irish courts to request social reports in respect of children who are the subject of proceedings concerning parental responsibility, residence or contact. These allow evidence relating to the child's welfare to be collected, without necessarily requiring the child to appear in court. Such reports are generally prepared and carried out by social workers. The jurisdiction to do so was put on a formal statutory footing by Sec. 47 Irish Family Law Act 1995. This Sec. empowers the Irish Circuit Court or High Court, as the case may be, to order a social report relating to any party to proceedings or any other person to whom they relate, including the children of the parties. Such a report may also be requested on an application by a party to the proceedings, although it is worth noting that the court may request the procurement of such a report of its own motion, without necessarily being requested to do so by a party. Sec. 47 may be invoked in respect of proceedings in a wide range of contexts as listed below:

- Irish Guardianship of Infants Act 1964;
- Irish Family Law (Maintenance of Spouses and Children) Act 1976;
- Irish Family Home Protection Act 1976;
- Irish Domestic Violence Act 1996;
- Irish Status of Children Act 1987;
- Irish Judicial Separation and Family Law Reform Act 1989;
- Irish Child Abduction and Enforcement of Custody Orders Act 1991;
- an application for a decree of nullity; and
- under the Irish Family Law Act 1995 itself.

By virtue of Sec. 42 Irish Family Law (Divorce) Act 1996, the social report facility also applies to proceedings taken under the Divorce Act. Sec. 26 Irish Guardianship of Infants Act 1964,[34] furthermore, once in force, will allow such a report to be procured in proceedings before the District Court taken under the 1964 Act.[35]

Such reports may, and sometimes do, tend to approach the circumstances of the family from the perspective of the adults as they relate to their children rather than focusing on the children's interests in and of themselves. Great care is needed by the Irish judiciary to ensure that the ultimate purpose of the proceedings - to secure the welfare of the child - is not obscured or diluted.

ITALY

Judicial protection of minors in the Italian legal system contemplates an irrational partition of tasks between three different judicial authorities: the Family Proceeding Court, the Ordinary Court and the Guardianship Judge. As a consequence, determining the competent judge may prove very complex and controversial due to the absence of certain and reliable criteria. For this reason, reform projects are currently under discussion (see Q 6) to reduce, if not to eliminate, this excessive fragmentation.

In general, the supervision and power to issue decisions that affect the exercise of parental responsibilities for both married and unmarried parents is exclusively entrusted to the Family Proceeding Court. This Court is competent, pursuant to Art. 316 Italian CC, to settle disagreements between parents on important issues or when orders limiting or terminating parental responsibilities have been requested pursuant to Art. 330 and 333 Italian CC.

The situation is complicated for married parents when a separation, divorce or an annulment decision has been entered. In such cases, the Family Proceeding Court may be asked to issue decisions in connection with the separation, divorce or annulment of the marriage that will modify a situation established by the Ordinary Court. The Ordinary Court is empowered, pursuant to Art. 155 Italian CC, to issue 'any order relating to the children' (therefore also relating to a change custody decision) and to issue new decisions upon the application of the non-residential parent who believes that the previous decisions were prejudicial to the interest of the child. It is clearly difficult to establish between the prejudicial conduct mentioned in Art. 333 Italian CC, which implies the jurisdiction of the Family Proceeding Court, and the prejudicial decision mentioned in Art. 155 Italian CC , which implies the jurisdiction of the Ordinary Court.[36]

---

34 Inserted by Sec. 11 Irish Children Act 1997.

35 This section is one of the two sections Irish Children Act 1997 not yet in force.

36 In practice, the parent not holding parental responsibilities often decides to petition the Family Proceeding Court to request the child's separation from the parent

It is also disputed whether jurisdiction in disagreements on issues of major interest pertains to the Family Proceeding Court pursuant to Art. 316 Italian CC, or if instead it pertains to the Ordinary Court that decided custody following the separation, divorce or annulment of the marriage pursuant to Art. 155 Italian CC.[37] In practice the Ordinary Court has prevailed: the Supreme Court has established, after a number of conflicting decisions, that the Ordinary Court is entitled to modify any order issued concerning the children in connection with the separation, divorce or annulment of marriage decisions while the Family Proceeding Court has jurisdiction only in connection with the termination or the limitation of the parental responsibilities pursuant to Art. 330 and 333 Italian CC.[38]

Recently an additional solution has been adopted: the Family Proceeding Court has jurisdiction with regard to both unmarried and married parents but with married parents, Art. 333 Italian CC may be applied only if a decision on the separation, divorce or annulment has not been issued. If a proceeding on the separation, on the divorce or on the annulment is pending or has been decided, Art. 317 § 2 Italian CC and Art. 155 Italian CC should apply and the jurisdiction of the Ordinary Court should be recognised.[39]

---

holding the parental responsibilities because of behaviours prejudicial to the minor, pursuant to Art. 333 of the Civil Code, instead of modifying the decision concerning the custody and consequently petitioning the competent ordinary Court which first disposed custody pursuant to Art. 155 of the Civil Code.

37 It is stated that Art. 316 of the Civil Code can be applied even in difficult situations between parents (separated or divorced) if there is a joint exercise of the custody (M. GIORGIANNI, *Della potestà dei genitori*, in *Commentario al diritto italiano della famiglia* by G. CIAN, G. OPPO and A. TRABUCCHI, IV, Cedam, Padova, 1992, p. 336-337; M. MANTOVANI, headword *Separazione personale dei coniugi, I) Disciplina sostanziale*, in *Enc. giur. Treccani*, XXVIII, Foro Italiano, Roma, 1992, p. 24; in case law see Supreme Court 07.02.94, No. 1401, *Dir. fam. pers.*, 1994, p. 1383). A different point of view states that Article 316 of the Civil Code can be applied only in case of cohabitation. In this case, the authority competent to decide disagreements between separated or divorced parents is the Ordinary Court, as separation or divorce provokes a loss of the family unity (C. GRASSETTI, in: G. CIAN, G. OPPO and A. TRABUCCHI, *Commentario al diritto italiano della famiglia*, II, Cedam, Padova, 1992, p. 699; N. SCANNICCHIO, sub *art. 6*, in *Commentario alla l. 6 marzo 1987, No. 74* by N. LIPARI, in *Nuove leggi civ. comm.*, 1987, p. 949; in case law see Supreme Court 03.11.2000, No. 14360, in *Fam. dir.*, 2001, p. 38 and following, annotated by F. TOMMASEO).

38 Supreme Court, full bench, 02.03.1983, No. 1151, *Dir. fam. pers.*, 1983, p. 38 and Supreme Court 02.03.1983, No. 1152, in *Foro it.*, 1983, I, p. 826).

39 Supreme Court, 11.04.1997, No. 3159, in *Fam. dir.*, 1997, p. 431. Such a drastic solution, which understandably has not been followed by subsequent decisions, is not convincing since it excludes the possibility for the separated or divorced parents, or for the spouse in case of annulment of the marriage, to request the Judge (of the Family Proceeding Court) to reduce the powers conferred upon the parent which holds the custody pursuant to Art. 333 Italian CC whenever it is deemed in the interest of the child.

The following pattern prevailed with regard to conflicts between separated or divorced parents concerning decisions of minor importance relating to the children (for example the exercise of the visiting right), parents not cohabiting (whether they hold the custody or not) must apply to the guardianship judge who, pursuant to Art. 337 Italian CC, has the task of supervising the conditions established by the Court in connection with the exercise of parental responsibilities and management of the minor's properties. In the most serious cases, when conduct caused a serious prejudice to the minor pursuant to Art. 330 Italian CC or in case of a conduct that is in prejudicial pursuant to Art. 333 Italian CC, the Family Proceeding Court has jurisdiction provided that the separation proceeding has already been already completed; otherwise the jurisdiction of the Ordinary Court should be recognised. Finally, with regard to the decisions ordering a parent to leave the family home, pursuant to Art. 342 *bis* and 342 *ter* Italian CC, the Ordinary Court has jurisdiction unless the above-mentioned order was issued during a proceeding terminating or limiting the parental authority pursuant to Art. 330 and 333 Italian CC.

Usually, the competent judicial authority requires psychological and pedagogical experts to perform comprehensive inquires on the family situation and propose possible solutions, taking into consideration the fundamental moral and material interests of the minor.

LITHUANIA

The competent authority to decide the above-mentioned disputes is the court of first instance (Art. 26 Lithuanian Code of Civil Procedure). The competent authority for the investigation of the above-mentioned matters is the state institution for the protection of the rights of the child, which functions in each region (local government) (Art. 3.178 Lithuanian CC). This institution also takes mandatory participation in all court cases involving the rights of the child.

THE NETHERLANDS

The District Court is competent to decide disputes between the parents concerning parental responsibilities (1:253a Dutch CC), consensual and non-consensual discharge (Art. 1:266 and 1:269 Dutch CC), and contact (if, however, proceedings for the granting of custody are pending at the sub-district court, an application to provide for an arrangement of contact in connection therewith may be made to the sub-district court (Art. 1:377a § 4 Dutch CC). The children's court judge is competent to vest an institution for family guardianship with the minor's care and supervision (Art. 1:254 § 1 Dutch CC) and to authorise the institution to instruct the minor to stay elsewhere during the day and night (Art. 1:261 § 1 Dutch CC).

NORWAY

Disputes concerning parental responsibilities, questions of residence of the child and contact rights, are handled by the lower courts, Art. 48 Norwegian Children Act 1981. The parent who is unhappy with the existing situation initiates the proceedings, Art. 56 Norwegian Children Act 1981.

According to Art. 61 No. 6 Norwegian Children Act 1981, the court may obtain statements from the Child Welfare Office and the Social Welfare Office whenever necessary.

The court shall as a main rule summon the parties to one or more preliminary meetings in order to clarify their differences, to discuss the issues, and to try to obtain agreement between the parties. In doing so, the Court can appoint an expert to give his opinion of the case, Art. 61 No. 1 and 3 Norwegian Children Act 1981.

POLAND

Such legal disputes are to be decided by a family court *i.e.* (according to Art. 569 Polish Civil Procedure Code) the district court of the place of residence of the person concerned (in this situation, the child); in the absence of a permanent place of residence, the family court where the person stays. The court may order the court curator to investigate into the social environment of a case (Art. 570^1 Polish Civil Procedure Code).

PORTUGAL

The competent authority to decide matters concerning the regulation of parental responsibility, the alteration of the respective system, rights of contact and custody is the court in the child's residence; this might be a special court, if the child resides within the area of jurisdiction of one of the family and juvenile courts, or the district court, if the child's residence is outside the jurisdiction of the family and juvenile courts (Art. 149, 154 and 155, Portuguese Child Protection Law).

The concept of the child's residence is not identical to the concept of legal domicile (Art. 85 Portuguese CC). The child's residence is understood to be the place where the child has his life organised in a stable and permanent way. The investigation into the circumstances and needs of the child and the preparation of the respective report are the responsibility of the social services of the Institute for Social Rehabilitation.

RUSSIA

The authority competent to resolve disputes concerning discharge, restriction and restoration, of parental responsibility (attribution thereof is not possible under Russian law as parents always have joint parental responsibility); residence and contact is the court.

Russia does not have specialist courts for juvenile or family matters. All aforementioned cases are dealt with by a court of first instance with general jurisdiction in normal civil proceedings. Specialisation amongst the judges of those courts is also not common. Furthermore, no special training in juvenile and family psychology is required for a judge.

Investigation of the circumstances relating to the child is carried out by the Guardianship and Curatorship Department (Art. 78 Russian Family Code). This body is supposed to have experts specialised in child psychology and family sociology at its disposal.[40] In practice, however, the Department is constantly understaffed due to the low wages offered, and is largely staffed by persons without the necessary education. The Guardianship and Curatorship Department advises judges as to the welfare of particular children in disputes concerning their residence and contact arrangements, drafts reports on the suitability of each of the parents as the educators of the children, investigates the circumstances constituting grounds for discharge of parental rights, estimates whether the wishes of a child are against its best interests, and so on.

SPAIN

The competent authority to decide disputes is a judicial authority. Judges are also responsible for carrying out the investigation. Matters dealing with parental responsibilities are normally heard by a first instance judge specialising in civil matters unless a public child protection body intervenes, causing a shift of jurisdiction to courts specialising in administrative matters. There is some confusion as to which matters belong to each kind of court.

If the matter is in the competence of a civil court it might be heard by a special family court. These exist in larger populations where there is more than one court dealing with civil matters. Special family courts are supported by a multidisciplinary team of psychologists, social workers and Doctors.

SWEDEN

Disputes concerning custody, residence or contact shall be considered by the district court in the place where the child habitually resides or, if raised in conjunction with an application for divorce, by the competent divorce court, Chapter 6 Sec. 17 para. 1 Swedish Children and Parents Code. The court shall ensure that questions concerning custody, residence and contact are properly investigated, Chapter 6 Sec. 19 Swedish Children and Parents Code. Before deciding such an issue, the court shall give the social welfare committee the opportunity to submit information. The committee has the duty to supply the court with any information which could be of significance for the assessment of

---

40 In Moscow the legal norm is one employee of the Department of Guardianship and Curatorship per 5,000 minor children. See: Art. 7 of the Act of the City of Moscow 'On Execution of Custody and Guardianship in the city of Moscow ('Ob obespechenii paboti po opeke i popechitel'stvu v gorode Moskve'), Vedomosti Moskovskoi Dumi, 1997, No. 6.

the question. If further inquiries are necessary, the court may instruct the social welfare committee or some other body to appoint a person to investigate the child's situation. The court may lay down guidelines for this investigation and set a date by which it is to be completed.

Questions concerning change of guardian are decided by the district court, Chapter 10 Sec. 13 Swedish Children and Parents Code. Questions concerning the guardians' administration of the child's assets are handled by the Chief Guardian in the community where the child has his or her habitual residence, Chapter 16 Sec. 2 Swedish Children and Parents Code.

SWITZERLAND

With unmarried parents, guardianship authorities are competent to issue rulings regarding parental responsibilities and personal contact.

For married parents who are separated or divorced parents, depending on whether only parental responsibilities, the child's residence or personal contact with the child are a matter of dispute in themselves or whether these issues are decided in connection with a marital dispute, either the court or a guardianship authority is competent to decide.[41]:

Married but separated parents or divorced parents		
	Court	Guardianship authority
Parental responsibilities	▪ Allocation of custody or parental responsibilities upon dissolution of the joint household or upon separation, Art. 297 § 2 Swiss CC. ▪ Allocation of parental responsibilities to one parent in the case of divorce, Art. 133 § 1 Swiss CC. ▪ Approval of the agreement between the parents regarding joint parental responsibilities upon dissolution of the household, separation or divorce, Art. 133 § 3, 176 § 3 Swiss CC. ▪ Amendment of a marriage-law judgment in the event of dissention between the parents, Art. 134 § 3 Swiss CC.	▪ Approval of new arrangements with respect to parental responsibilities by way of amendment of a marriage-law judgment if the parents are both in agreement, Art. 134 § 3 Swiss CC. ▪ Approval of new arrangements with respect to parental responsibilities by way of amendment of a marriage-law judgment after the death of one parent, Art. 134 § 3 Swiss CC.
Personal contact	▪ Approval of the agreement entered into by the parents in	▪ New arrangements concerning personal contact, regardless of

41 Source: CH. HÄFELI, 'Zur Abgrenzung der Zuständigkeiten von Gerichten und vormundschaftlichen Behörden zur Regelung von Kinderbelangen', *Zeitschrift für Vormundschaftswesen*, 1999, p. 224 - 226.

	divorce proceedings, Art. 135 Swiss CC. ▪ Arrangements for personal contact between the child and the parent who does not have parental responsibilities in a divorce, Art. 133 § 1 Swiss CC and within the framework of provisional measures, Art. 137 § 2 Swiss CC. ▪ Arrangements for personal contact between the child and the parent who does not hold parental responsibilities or custody in proceedings for the protection of a marriage, Art. 176 § 3 Swiss CC. ▪ New arrangements for personal contact in contested amendment proceedings regarding a change in parental responsibilities, Art. 134 § 4 Swiss CC.	whether the parents are in agreement with one another or not (approval of agreement or decision), unless parental responsibilities and/or support contributions have at the same time to be decided anew in contested proceedings, Art. 134 § 4 Swiss CC.
Unmarried parents		
	Guardianship authority	Guardianship supervisory authority
Parental responsibilities	▪ Transfer of parental responsibilities to the father if the mother is a minor, has been placed under guardianship or has died or if parental responsibilities have been withdrawn from her, Art. 298 § 2 Swiss CC. ▪ Allocation of joint parental responsibilities based on the prerequisite conditions of Art. 298a § 1 Swiss CC. ▪ Approval of new arrangements if the parents are in agreement by analogy to Art. 134 § 3 Swiss CC.	▪ New arrangements in regard to parental responsibilities, if necessary, with a view to the child's welfare due to a significant change in circumstances, Art. 298a § 2 Swiss CC
Personal contact	▪ Arrangements upon application by the father, the mother, the child who is capable of judgment or the official adviser/guardian, Art. 275 Abs. 1 Swiss CC ▪ Restriction, refusal or withdrawal based on the prerequisite conditions of Art. 274 § 2 Swiss CC	

The facts are clarified in each case by the competent authority *ex officio*. However, the authority is free to consult experts or make inquiries if necessary *e.g.* addressed to the guardianship authority or the child welfare services (see *e.g.* 145 § 2 Swiss CC).

QUESTION 56

H. PROCEDURAL ISSUES

Under what conditions, if any, may a legally effective decision or agreement on parental responsibilities, the child's residence or contact, be reviewed by a competent authority? Is it, *e.g.*, required that the circumstances have changed after the decision or agreement was made and/or that a certain period of time has passed since the decision or agreement?

AUSTRIA

In matters of parental responsibilities, the child's residence and contact there is no revision of a legally effective decision in the sense of a reopening of the proceedings (Sec. 107(1) No. 3 *Außerstreitgesetz*); however, a subsequent change of circumstances may be asserted by means of a new petition.[1] Thus, for instance, an arrangement on the exercise of contact may be reviewed via a new petition, if the child's age-related needs have changed.[2] Generally, the court may only interfere with parental rights and thus modify a legally effective decision or agreement on the above stated matters if there is a specific threat to the child's interests (Sec. 176 and 148(2) Austrian CC).[3] The revocation or restriction of parental rights must be a necessary measure to secure the child's best interests; the court has to apply a high standard.[4] The argument that other methods of childrearing are "better" or "more progessive" will not suffice for that purpose nor the fact that the child's upbringing by a third party would be better than a proper upbringing by the child's parents,[5] since the continuity of the child's upbringing is considered to be extremely important.[6] On the other hand, an expected substantial amelioration of the child's developmental potential[7] or the genuine desire of a minor over 14 years of age to be assigned to

---

1. S. KRIWANEK, *Das neue Außerstreitverfahren*, Vienna: LexisNexis ARD Orac, 2004, p. 128.
2. U. AICHHORN, *Das Recht der Lebenpartnerschaften*, Vienna/New York: Springer Verlag, 2003, p. 73 et seq.
3. See also Q 40, 47 and 51.
4. J. STABENTHEINER, 'KindRÄG 2001', in: P. RUMMEL, *ABGB-Kommentar*, suppl. vol. I, 3rd Edition, Vienna: Manz, 2003, § 176 Marg. No. 3, § 177 Marg. No. 16.
5. *Landesgericht für Zivilrechtssachen* Vienna, 21.12.1995, *EFSlg.* 78.215; J. STABENTHEINER in: P. RUMMEL, *ABGB-Kommentar*, Vol. I, 3rd Edition, Vienna: Manz Verlag, 2000, §§ 137, 137a Marg. No 10.
6. *Oberster Gerichtshof*, 05.12.1989, *EFSlg.* 59.774; *Oberster Gerichtshof*, 30.01.2001, *Österreichischer Amtsvormund*, 2002, p. 268 S 37; *Oberster Gerichtshof*, 31.07.2001, *EFSlg.* 96.672.
7. *Oberster Gerichtshof*, 27.11.2001, *Österreichische Juristenzeitung - EvBl*, 2002, No. 82, p. 335, and 26.06.1991, *Österreichische Juristenzeitung - EvBl*, 1991, No. 168, p. 737.

the other parent may be considered as sufficient reason for a review of the attribution of parental responsibilities.[8]

However, the legal situation is different in the event of (full or restricted) joint parental responsibilities if the parents have permanently separated (after divorce, annulment of the marriage, ending of a non-marital partnership or permanent separation of married parents) or have never lived in a common household:[9] In these cases, each parent may petition the court to end joint parental responsibilities without substantiation at any time. Then, the court must entrust one parent with sole parental responsibilities based on the best interests of the child unless a reconciliation between the parents may be brought about (Sec. 167, 177a(2) and 177b Austrian CC).

BELGIUM

As provided by Art. 387 *bis* Belgian CC, every legally effective decision or agreement concerning the child may be reviewed from the moment there is a change in the circumstances from which the previous decision was taken. The invoked circumstances must have changed after the legally effective decision or agreement. Circumstances known or even existing (and unknown) at the moment of the previous decision or agreement are not enough to obtain a modification.[10]

BULGARIA

The court decision or the agreement on parental responsibilities, child's residence or contact may only be reviewed on the ground of change in the circumstances: 'Actions on the exercise of parental rights and on the support of children after the divorce by mutual consent are admissible where a change in the circumstances has occurred.' (Art. 101 § 3 Bulgarian Family Code). 'When a change in the circumstances occurs (after the divorce due to a marital breakdown) the court may, at the petition of one of the parents or ex officio, change the previously decreed measures and order new ones.' (Art. 106 § 5 Bulgarian Family Code).

CZECH REPUBLIC

If the circumstances have changed, the court, even without a motion, may change its decision regarding the parental agreement on exercise of parental

8 *Oberster Gerichtshof,* 08.05.1996, *Juristische Blätter,* 1996, p. 714; *Oberster Gerichtshof,* 27.11.2001, *Österreichische Juristenzeitung - EvBl.,* 2002, No. 82, p. 335.

9 Such joint parental responsibilities are based either directly on a legal provision (§ 177 (1) sentence 1 Austrian CC) or on the parents' agreement (§§ 167, 177 (1) Satz 2 and 3, 177b Asutrian CC); they cannot be attributed by judicial decree, see Q 18 and 24.

10 Cass., 14.12.1989, *Pas.,* 1990, I, p. 477; Court of Appeal of Mons, 03.04.1990, *Pas.,* 1990, II, p. 198; P. HOFSTRÖSSLER, 'De wet van 13 april 1995 betreffende de gezamenlijke uitoefening van het ouderlijk gezag', *A.J.T.,* 1995-96, p. 34; J.-L. RENCHON, 'La nouvelle réforme législative de l'autorité parentale', *Rev. Trim. Dr. Fam.,* 1995, 405.

rights and duties (Sec. 28 Czech Family Code). This also applies to the maintenance duty the parents owe the children. It must be a material change of circumstances, either on the part of the child or on the part of the parents.

DENMARK

If the parents have joint parental authority and they no longer live together or intend to live separately each parent can demand that the joint parental authority be terminated, Art. 8 Danish Act on Parental Authority and Contact.

If one parent has sole parental authority on the basis of an agreement or a judgement by the court, the court can transfer parental authority to the other parent, only where there are special reasons, if it is best for the child and especially when conditions have substantially changed. Obstructing the other parent's contact is a consideration, which is taken into account, Art. 13(1) Danish Act on Parental Authority and Contact.

Contact orders and agreements can be amended if the change is best for the child especially when conditions have substantially changed, Art. 17(2) Danish Act on Parental Authority and Contact.

No authority has the power to make decisions on residence and agreements on residence cannot be reviewed.

ENGLAND & WALES

Formal parental responsibility agreements (see Q 22b) can be brought to an end upon a specific application[11] to that effect made to a court pursuant to Sec. 4(3), Children Act 1989 (see Q 51). Informal agreements made in respect of the exercise of parental responsibility with respect to a child's upbringing can subsequently always be challenged in court proceedings.

All court orders made under the Children Act 1989 (including Sec. 8 orders, and parental responsibility orders made under Sec. 4) can, regardless of the level of court that made them, be appealed.[12] Sec. 8 orders can also, save where a specific embargo is imposed under Sec. 91(14) of the Children Act,[13] always be subsequently varied or brought to an end.[14] There are no formal requirements

[11] Applications can be made by *any* person who has parental responsibility (including, therefore, the father) or, with leave of the court, the child: Sec. 4(3).

[12] Sec. 94, Children Act 1989.

[13] Under this provision, a court can direct that "no application for an order under this Act of any specified kind may be made with respect to the child concerned by any person named in the order without leave of the court". Such orders should not be readily granted since they represent a substantial interference with a citizen's right of unrestricted access to the court's, which must be weighed in the balance against the child's welfare, see the leading case of *Re P (A Minor)(Residence Order: Child's Welfare)* [2000] Fam 15 at 37-38.

[14] See Sec. 8(2), Children Act 1989.

as to when a variation can be sought but clearly to justify a variation there has to have been a change of circumstances.

FINLAND

A court decision or an approved parental agreement can be reviewed by the court if there has been a change of circumstances or where it is otherwise deemed appropriate (Sec. 12 Finnish Child Custody and the Right of Access Act). The Act gives no special conditions for making a new parental agreement. Thus, it is a question of parental agreement. The conditions for reviewing a care order are explained above in Q 54.

FRANCE

In general, a legally effective decision on parental responsibilities can be modified or supplemented at any time by the family judge on request of one or both parents, or of the prosecutor, see Art. 373-2-13 French CC. If a prior agreement on parental responsibilities was accepted by the court, the same rule applies: the rules contained in the agreement and all judicial decisions relating to parental responsibilities can be modified or supplemented by the family judge on request of one or both parents, or of the prosecutor who can be called by a third person (child's relative or not), see Art. 373-2-13 French CC.[15] If in a divorce on joint petition of the spouses, the spousal agreement did not foresee any financial contribution from the father to the child's maintenance, the mother can later claim such a financial contribution because the duty to maintain a child is a legal obligation for the parents.[16] See also for a modification of the amount of the child's maintenance (stated in the spousal agreement) in case of a change of circumstances, French Supreme Court, Civ. II, 21.04.1982, *Bull. civ.* II, No. 57.

Also if the domicile of one parent changes, the other parent can call the family judge to can modify the methods of the exercise of parental responsibilities due to the change of residence (see Art. 373-2 para. 3 French CC). More generally the family judge will review the decision or the parental agreement that had been accepted by the court only if there is a change of circumstances.[17] The legal provisions do not require a certain period to time pass after the decision or the agreement. In the special case of discharge of parental responsibilities, the parent can regain them if he or she can prove a 'change of circumstances' (see Art. 381 French CC). A claim can be brought before the *tribunal de grande instance*. The court will examine the claim and decide whether the parent shall

---

15 See *e.g.* French Supreme Court, Civ. II, 04.03.1987, *Bull. civ.* II, No. 60.

16 See also French Supreme Court, Civ. II, 02.05.2001, *Bull. civ.* II, No. 80.

17 See *e.g.* CA Aix-en-Provence, 30.05.1995, *JCP*, 1996. II. 22 566 annotated GARÉ: the court modifies its decision on the exercise of parental responsibilities because of the children's insurmountable refusal to reside with the parent as stated in the court order. See also a modification of the judicial decision because of the expatriation project of one parent, CA Montpellier, 08.01.1998, *JCP*, 1999. IV. 2621.

regain parental responsibilities. At least one year must pass after the discharge decision has become legally effective and irrevocable.

GERMANY

A legally effective decision or agreement on parental responsibilities, the child's residence or contact many always be reviewed by a family court.

The family court has to modify its orders at anytime if this it is necessary because of reasons seriously affecting the welfare of the child (§ 1696 para. 1 German CC). The court is also under an obligation to do so whenever the danger to the child's welfare ceases to be imminent (see § 1696 para. 2, 3 German CC). Also, according to the general rules of non-contentious proceedings, a court decision can be modified if there is a change of circumstances (§ 18 German Act on Voluntary Jurisdiction). That a certain period has elapsed since the decision or agreement is irrelevant.

GREECE

Art. 1536 Greek CC provides that one or both parents of the child, or the child's close relatives, or the public prosecutor may request the court to review the decision, provided that circumstances have changed after the initial decision. This provision refers only to parental care. For the possibility of applying it, by analogy, in the case of guardianship, see the answer to Q 54.

HUNGARY

An essential change of circumstances can result in a change to either the placement of the child or parental contact with the child, by either agreement or decision. Another condition of the change is that it should be in the child's interests. If the interests of the child demand the change, it is not necessary for any period of time to elapse. Nevertheless, especially with regard to the residence (placement) of the child, it is emphasised that a repeated claim for the change will be reviewed to determine whether the claim is unnecessary harassment.

IRELAND

All parental responsibilities decisions are subject to variation should the welfare of the child so demand. Sec. 12 Irish Guardianship of Infants Act 1964 enables a court to review, vary or discharge any decision or agreement on parental responsibilities, the child's residence or contact, should altered circumstances or new information require it. There is no requirement that a certain period of time has passed since the decision or agreement.

Where an agreement on parental responsibilities, the child's residence or contact has been made a rule of court by virtue of Sec. 24 Irish Guardianship of Infants Act 1964, such agreement has the like force and application of a court order. It may thus be varied, as detailed above, should altered circumstances or new information require it.

ITALY

A court decision or an agreement between the parents confirmed during the course of a judicial proceeding can be reviewed only if the circumstances which were the basis of the decision have subsequently changed, unless the law expressly provides for a specific duration (such as, for example, in case of the judicial order to the parent to leave the family home pursuant to Arts. 342 *bis* and 342 *ter* Italian CC; in this case the duration can be extended in case of serious reasons). Also, the interests of the minor must be taken into consideration.

LITHUANIA

Part 3 of Art. 3.53 Lithuanian CC provides for the single ground for the review of the agreement or court judgment in such cases *i.e.* a substantial change of circumstances. For instance, the agreement or court judgment regarding the place of residence of the child may be changed if instances of violent behaviour against the child by the parent with whom the child lives are proved (Art. 3.169 Lithuanian CC). Agreement or court judgment regarding the maintenance of the child may be changed in the event of the illness or injury of the child, a substantial change of the financial situation of one of the parents *etc.* (Art. 3.201 Lithuanian CC).

THE NETHERLANDS

The children's court judge shall specify the duration of the care and protection order for the minor, although this may not exceed one year. On the application of the institution for family guardianship or of the Child Care and Protection Board, the judge may always extend such duration for no more than one year (Art. 1:262 Dutch CC). If, on the occasion of the non-consensual or consensual discharge of parental responsibilities the other parent was vested with parental responsibilities, the district court shall not again vest parental responsibilities in the divested parent who applies alone, unless the circumstances have changed since the order vesting the other parent with the responsibility or, unless at the time of the order, it was based on incorrect or incomplete information (Art. 1:277 § 2 Dutch CC).

NORWAY

A legally effective decision or an agreement between the parties may at any time be reviewed by the court. The parents may also change the residence of the child, the allocation of parental responsibilities and contact rights by mutual agreement, Art. 64 sec. 1 Norwegian Children Act 1981. If the issues have already been decided by the court, a new case may only change the former decision if there are special circumstances that favour such a change. If the court finds that there are no such circumstances, it may decide the case without a full hearing, Art. 64 sec. 2 and 3 Norwegian Children Act 1981. It is not required that a certain period of time must pass after the first decision. However, the existence of special circumstances will seldom occur shortly after the first decision.

POLAND

The family court may change its decisions at any time, even decisions which are final, at any time, should the wellbeing of the person concerned so require (Art. 577 Polish Civil Procedure Code).

PORTUGAL

In the event of non-compliance with the parental agreement or with the court's decision on the system of parental responsibility, or when there are supervening circumstances justifying alterations to the established system, the court may review the matter upon the request of one of the parents or the Public Prosecutor's Office. (Art. 182 No. 1 Portuguese Child Protection Law).

RUSSIA

The law does not contain any provisions on this matter. However, in practice the parents are free to ask the court to review a decision regarding a child's residence or contact arrangement if the circumstances have changed. In these cases, the circumstances are never the same: a child grows older, the family situation of the parents or their residence changes *etc.* such application is almost always possible. A special case of revision of a child's residence is mentioned in the Art. 66 (3) Russian Family Code: a parent, living apart from the child, can ask the court to transfer the child's residence if the other parent persistently and deliberately disobeys the court order concerning contact of the claimant with the child.

SPAIN

Art. 775 Spanish Law of Civil Procedure establishes that legally effective decisions which have been decreed in matters of parental responsibility can be reviewed if there has been a substantial change of circumstances. This applies both to measures decreed by the Judge and to agreements approved by the Judge. If the agreement is private it will be possible to ask for a change of the agreement at any time because such an agreement is not enforceable through the court system. Once it is not voluntarily complied with, it is always possible to go to the court and ask for a decision on the matter.

SWEDEN

In principle, a party unhappy with a court decree on custody, residence or contact, is free to initiate new court proceedings on the same issue at any time. The fact that the court's decision is legally effective and, as a result, enforceable does not in any way limit the right to initiate new proceedings. An agreement between the parents on custody, residence and contact, approved by the social welfare committee and, thus, enforceable may also be replaced at any time by a new agreement between the parents. To be legally effective, the new agreement must also be approved by the social welfare committee.[18] A valid agreement

---

18 In addition, an agreement on parental responsibilities must always be in writing and signed by the parents.

between the parents on custody, residence and contact does not prevent a parent from taking the issues to court. It is also possible to alter a previous court decree through an agreement, on the condition that the agreement is approved by the social welfare committee.[19]

Swedish law does not require for circumstances to have changed after the decision or agreement was made, or that a certain period of time has passed after the initial decision or agreement.[20] According to the Swedish outlook any other approach could be detrimental to the interests of the child. However, it can be assumed that a parent needs to claim that the circumstances have changed in some respect, although the burden of proof in this respect must be kept low. According to the Chapter 42 Sec. 5 Swedish Code of Civil Procedure (*Rättegångsbalken*), the court may give a judgment without conducting a full hearing when it is clear that the claim is unfounded. This provision can be used to prevent a parent from abusing the right to initiate court proceedings without reason.

As regards the parents' right to replace an earlier agreement with a new agreement, there are no explicit provisions stating that a certain period of time must have passed. However, agreements concerning parental responsibilities should aim at providing long-term solutions for the child and should therefore be carefully prepared before they are approved by the social welfare committee. Agreements concerning contact are often limited in time and more frequently renegotiated, which is justified due to the fact that a child's need of contact with the non-residential parent may vary depending on the child's age.[21]

SWITZERLAND

With divorced, married but separated or unmarried parents, the allocation of parental responsibilities may be reviewed at the request of one parent, the child or the guardianship authority, if this is necessary for the sake of the child's welfare in view of significant changes in the circumstances (Art. 134 § 1 Swiss CC, Art. 298a § 2 Swiss CC).

If the court has to issue judgments for divorced, married but separated or unmarried parents regarding a change in parental responsibilities or the support contribution for a minor child, it will also, if necessary, review personal contact (Art. 134 § 4 sentence 1 Swiss CC).

In the other cases the guardianship authority must review personal contact *ex officio* if the arrangements subsequently turn out to be inappropriate and not in harmony with the child's welfare.

---

19 Prop 1997/98:7 p. 83.

20 Prop 1997/98:7 p 85. See also the ruling of the Supreme Court in *NJA 1993 p. 226*.

21 *Vårdnad, Boende och Umgänge*, Stockholm: Socialstyrelsen (National Board of Health and Welfare), 2003, p. 133.

QUESTION 57

H. PROCEDURAL ISSUES

What alternative dispute-solving mechanisms, if any, e.g. mediation or counselling, are offered in your legal system? Are such mechanisms also available at the stage of enforcement of a decision/agreement concerning parental responsibilities, the child's residence or contact?

AUSTRIA

Throughout the proceedings on parental responsibilities, the child's residence or the exercise of contact, the court must take steps to ensure the parties reach an amicable agreement (Sec. 13(3) Non-Contentious Proceedings Act *[Außerstreitgesetz]*, Sec. 177a(1) and (2) Austrian CC for proceedings on the attribution of parental responsibilities, Sec. 108 AußStrG for contact proceedings). If an amicable agreement might be expected via the support of an out-of-court institution, in particular via counselling or mediation,[1] the proceedings should be suspended for a relevant length of time not exceeding six months, unless a delay in the decision would impair public or private interests protected by the proceedings (Sec. 29 *Außerstreitgesetz*). Therefore a stay is excluded, *e.g.* in a proceeding concerning the discharge of parental responsibilities because the child's interests are threatened or if one parent obviously intends to delay the proceedings.[2]

Besides counselling and mediation, parents may be granted varied assistance with child rearing *(Erziehungshilfe)*, *e.g.* therapeutic measures, placement with a child-minder, nursery, children's clinic, or with foster parents (Sec. 27 and 28 Youth Welfare Act *[Jugendwohlfahrtsgesetz]*). To support the exercise of contact in problem cases, any party to the proceedings (parent, grandparent, minor over 14 years of age) can petition the court for a *Besuchsbegleitung* (Sec. 111 *Außerstreitgesetz*): A suitable person (*e.g.* a relative, teacher, social worker, or employee of the youth welfare office) then attends the meeting between the parent entitled to contact and the child, usually on neutral ground such as a child-protection facility (so-called "visit cafe" *[Besuchscafé]*).

The mentioned mechanisms and measures are generally also available at the stage of enforcement of a decision or agreement concerning parental responsibilities, the child's residence or contact (Sec. 13(3) *Außerstreitgesetz:* "at any stage of the proceedings"). However, the court may only refrain from

---

1 See Act on Mediation in Civil Matters *[Zivilrechtsmediationsgesetz]* 2004, Federal Law Gazette *[Bundesgesetzblatt, BGBl.]* I 2003/29, http://www.ris.bka.gv.at; M. ROTH/K. MARKOWETZ, 'Bundesgesetz über Mediation in Zivilrechtssachen - Ein Überblick über die neuen Bestimmungen', *Juristische Blätter,* 2004, p. 296-302.

2 A. DEIXLER-HÜBNER, 'Die neuen familienrechtlichen Verfahrensbestimmungen', in: S. FERRARI/G. HOPF, *Reform des Kindschaftsrechts,* Vienna: Manz Verlag, 2001, p. 124.

continuing enforcement if and as long as the child's interests are at risk (Sec. 110(3) *Außerstreitgesetz*).

BELGIUM

According to the Belgian Law of 19 February 2001 concerning family mediation (Art. 734 *bis* - 734 *sexies* Belgian Judicial Code), the Judge has the ability to designate a mediator in the following cases (Art. 734 *bis* Belgian Judicial Code): disputes concerning the consequences of marriage,[3] divorce,[4] parental authority,[5] legal cohabitation[6] (Art. 734 *bis* (1) and (2) Belgian Judicial Code) and factual cohabitation (Art. 734 *bis* (3) Belgian Judicial Code). This takes place at the request of the concerned parties. The judge can also designate a mediator on his or her own initiative; in this case, the agreement of the concerned parties (on the principle as well as on the name of the mediator) is required. The judicial procedure is suspended during the mediation.[7]

At the stage of enforcement of a decision/agreement, no alternative disputes solving mechanisms are legally organised, however, in practice the competent authority can choose this solution in case of international parental kidnapping.

BULGARIA

The Child Protection Act provides for the opportunity of counselling of parents in disputes over parental responsibilities; as Art. 23 § 6 stipulates, the Child Protection Department should '...conduct social work to facilitate child-parent relations and to support resolving of conflicts and crises. Assistance, support and services in a family environment shall be rendered by the Social Assistance Directorate [actually by its Child Protection Department] upon the request of parents, or persons entrusted with parental functions, of the child, as well as by discretion of the Social Assistance Directorate.' (Art. 24 § 1). These are the only alternative mechanisms for resolving of disputes among parents. A Bill on Mediation has been pending in the Parliament from the beginning of this year.

CZECH REPUBLIC

Alternative mechanisms of solving disputes between the parents are not yet regulated by Czech law. The role of mediator is played to a certain extent by a

---

3 Art. 203-223 Belgian CC.

4 Art. 295-307*bis* Belgian CCand Art. 1254-1310 Belgian Judicial Code.

5 Art. 371-387*bis* Belgian CC.

6 Art. 1475-1479 Belgian CC.

7 B. COMPAGNION, 'La médiation légale dans le cadre d'une procédure judiciaire', *Div. Act.*, 2001, p. 98; I. HACHEZ, 'La médiation familiale à l'heure de sa consécration légale', *Rev. trim. dr. fam.*, 2001, p. 207; A. THILLY, 'De la pratique à la loi du 19 février 2001 à la médiation en matière familiale dans le cadre d'une procédure judiciaire', *J.T.*, 2001, p. 665. Also see the proposal of law according to which the mechanism of mediation is extended to all disputes that can be solved by settlement (Proposition de loi complétant le Code Judiciaire par une septième partie relative à la procédure de médiation extrajudiciaire, *Doc. Parl.* Chambre 08.01.2004; see www.lachambre.be, document 51S0442).

good certified expert who is authorized by the court to provide an expert's opinion on regulation of contact between the parent and the child, or an expert witness who answers the court's question which of the parents is better qualified for upbringing and whose care the child should be placed into because of that. Such experts attempt to make the parents to come to an agreement but it is not a general rule.

DENMARK

Experiments in counselling[8] in relation to contact and parental authority started at the beginning of the 1980s. Since 1986 the administrative authorities must offer counselling in cases concerning contact and parental authority, Art. 28(1) Danish Act on Parental Authority and Contact. The offer is directed towards parents and children, is free of charge and is available at all stages. It is not a condition that both parents and/or the child participate. Counselling may take place with one parent and/or the child alone. Counselling takes place at the administrative authorities.[9] The offer can be made during divorce proceedings if the divorce is administrative or in the course of a contact case. Counselling is independent of the decision making of the administrative authorities and the result of the counselling is not reported to the case officer unless the parents agree otherwise or the case officer has participated in the counselling upon the request of the parents. Counselling has been a success in Denmark. In approximately 60% of cases a positive outcome has been reported.[10] From 2001 mediation has been offered as an alternative to counselling. Both parents must participate and it is a condition that a case concerning contact has terminated before mediation may take place.[11] In 64% of mediations a complete solution has been found and in 18% of cases the conflict has been partly solved.[12] Alongside the offers of counselling and mediation offered by the administrative authorities, mediation experiments have started in some courts.[13]

ENGLAND & WALES

English law has long recognised the importance of alternative dispute resolution mechanisms in helping to solve family problems. Such mechanisms are initially referred to as conciliation schemes but have now become known as mediation. A clear lead for having an alternative mechanism to the court for helping couples deal with the consequences of divorce was given by the Finer Report on One Parent Families,[14] which reported in 1974. Following this report and an even earlier *Practice Direction*[15] which encouraged the courts to refer a

---

8 *Børnesagkyndig rådgivning* (Children expert counselling).

9 The counsellors will have special expertise regarding children. Counsellors are most often psychologists or social workers.

10 Statistical report from *Civilretsdirektoratet*, February 2004, p. 42.

11 *Konfliktmægling* (Mediation) on the website of the *Statsamt* www.statsamt.dk.

12 Statistical report from *Civilretsdirektoratet*, May 2003, p. 39.

13 For example, the lower court in Copenhagen, *Årsberetning for Københavns byret*, 2001.

14 Cmnd 5629.

15 [1971] 1 All ER 894.

case to the court welfare officer (now known as the children and family reporter) when it was considered that conciliation might be helpful, a scheme to incorporate this approach was launched in the Bristol County Court in 1977. Bristol also pioneered the very first out of court conciliation service in 1978. Both types of schemes were subsequently adopted in other parts of the country.

More recently in 1997 the Children Act Advisory Committee published a *Handbook of Best Practice in Children Act Cases* on which they advised[16] that consideration should first be given to 'whether the dispute between the parties could be resolved in any way other than litigation. Most areas have a mediation service which would be able to attempt to deal with disputes by way of negotiation and agreement. *There is rarely anything to be lost, and normally much to be gained, by mediation*'. (Emphasis added).

Building on a scheme first introduced in the Principal Registry in London, there is now (that is from March 2004) a nation wide scheme[17] under which *all* applications for a Sec. 8 order (including variations) under the Children Act have to be listed in a conciliation list unless specifically removed by the district judge concerned. As stated in para. 4.2 of the *Direction*:

> 'It is essential that both parties and any legal advisers having conduct of the case attend the appointment. The nature of the application and matters in dispute will be outlined to the district judge and the CAFCASS officer. The conciliation appointment will be conducted with a view to the parties reaching an agreement, and if appropriate, discussion away from the court room will be facilitated. Conciliation is a legally privileged occasion. All the discussions will be privileged and will not be disclosed on any subsequent hearing (other than at a further conciliation appointment) or upon any later application'.

Children aged 9 or over are also generally expected to attend the conciliation hearing. Where agreement is reached, the district judge will make such orders, if any, as are appropriate. If no agreement is reached then directions are given for an early hearing and disposal of the application. Neither the district judge nor the CAFCASS officer involved in the conciliation process can be involved in any subsequent substantive hearing of the dispute. It has been stressed[18] that mediation/conciliation is vital at all stages of the court process including an appeal.

---

16 Children Act Advisory Committee, June 1997, para 38.

17 *District Judge's Direction - Children: Conciliation)* [2004] 1 FLR 974. For further details see Brasse G 'Conciliation is Working' [2004] Fam Law 722.

18 *Al-Katib v. Masry and others* [2004] EWCA Civ 1353, [2004] 3 FCR 573.

A recent Government Green Paper, *Parental Separation: Children's Needs and Parental Responsibilities*[19] proposes even more emphasis to be placed on mediation in children cases, including referral to information meetings *etc*.[20]

FINLAND

The primary manner for solving family disputes should be a negotiation between the family members that leads to a mutually favourable agreement. This is an important principle in Finnish family law, explicitly articulated in Chapter 5, Sec. 20 Finnish Marriage Act (amendment 411/1987). Communal family counselling and mediation services are available for all families regardless of the marital status of the parents. Private organisations, communities and foundations may also serve as family mediators under the supervision of County Governments (Sec. 22 Finnish Marriage Act).

In 1996 an amendment was made to the Finnish Marriage Act in order to assure that family mediators' and counsellors' services may also be available to solve problems arising from the implementation of an approved agreement or court decision on child custody or right of access (Sec. 20 para. 3 Finnish Marriage Act).

A custody dispute can result in the local social authority approving a parental agreement if it becomes apparent during the preparation of the report that the parents are able to reach a settlement (Sec. 16 para. 2 Finnish Child Custody and the Right of Access Act). It has been argued that social workers may actually function as mediators in preparing the report or instead of preparing a report, because the court may ask the local social authority to clarify whether the case could be solved with a settlement.[21]

The local social authority has an obligation to provide parents with assistance and counselling in drafting agreements regarding child custody and the right of access. In fact, social workers in many communes also offer counselling or even mediation in cases in which parents settling on an agreement difficult. (Sec. 17 Finnish Social Welfare Decree).

The most powerful impact of mediation has been seen at the stage of the enforcement of custody or right of access agreements or decisions. The relevant court shall first appoint a mediator for the case. There are only a few exceptions to this: cases with a recent decision or approved agreement (of less than 3

19 Cm 6273 (July 2004).

20 For an outline of the proposals see "Contact Paper" [2004] Fam Law 630 at 632. See also Q 58.

21 M. SAVOLAINEN, *Lapsen huolto ja tapaamisoikeus*, Suomen Lakimiesliiton Kustannus Oy: Helsinki, 1984, p. 219-220. Critically, with justice, to the social workers' mediation function in connection of making the report: M. AALTONEN, 'Sosiaalitoimen roolit selvitystyössä', in: M. LITMALA, *Lapsen asema erossa,* WSOY Lakitieto: Helsinki, 2002, p. 122-123.

months), urgent cases, and cases where enforcement mediation has already failed (Chapter 2, Finnish Act of the Enforcement of a Decision on Child Custody and Right of Access). According to the empirical results of a research carried out by RISTO JAAKKOLA, in more than half (52%) of the cases where a mediator was appointed, a case was settled, recalled or otherwise laid down. A solution was found in only 39% of cases with no mediator.[22] The results suggest that parties benefit from the help of a mediator.

FRANCE

If the parents cannot agree on the exercise of parental responsibilities, the family judge is called on request of both parents or of one of them. Art. 373-2-10 French CC states that in such a situation of parental disagreement the family judge shall first try to conciliate the parents. Therefore the first task of the judge is to try to find a settlement between the parties. The French Code of Civil Procedure more generally states that the judge can at any stage of the proceedings try to help the parties to find a settlement (Art. 21).[23]

Art. 373-2-10 para. 2 French CC adds that in order to facilitate an agreement between the parents on the exercise of parental responsibilities the judge can propose mediation. If the parents agree, the judge can appoint a mediator. The judge can also order the parents to meet a family mediator who will inform them about the matter and the unfolding of the mediation.[24]

Such mechanisms do not seem to be available at the stage of enforcement of a decision or agreement concerning parental responsibilities, child's residence or contact. The bailiff who will have to enforce the court order will try to get the parents to find a compromise and settle, but this is not an official mediation or conciliation.

GERMANY

It is widely accepted that arbitration proceedings are not admissible for matters of parental responsibility.[25] Alternative dispute solving mechanisms are as such not generally recognised in German law; however, there have been some pilot projects where, with the consent of the parties, family judges act as mediators

---

22 The sample concerned the years 1997-2001. R. JAAKKOLA, 'Lapsen huolto- ja tapaamisoikeuspäätösten täytäntöönpano vuosina 1998-2001', *Lakimies,* 2002, p. 879-901.

23 It shall be part of the duties of the judge to conciliate the parties.

24 See *e.g.* CA Paris, 11.09.2002, *D.* 2002. IR. 3241. See also TGI La Rochelle, 17.02.1988, *D.* 1991.411 with annotated LIENHARD (the family judge appointed a mediator to help with methods of reviving personal relationships between a child and his grandparents).

25 See K. SCHUMACHER, 'Schiedsgerichtsbarkeit und Familienrecht', *FamRZ* 2004, 1677, 1780.

and the court procedure as such is suspended.[26] Most efforts to use mediation in disputes on custody and on contact are supported not only by associations of mediators, but also by attorneys. These more or less private efforts are also beginning to influence traditional dispute mechanisms.[27] They are also available at the enforcement stage of a decision or agreement concerning parental responsibilities, the child's residence or contact. Their effect differs according to the stage of proceedings and the co-operation of the parties. Counselling on issues of partnership, separation and divorce, and also other issues is given not only by the youth office[28] but also by other institutions and associations.

According to § 52 para. 1 sent. 1 German Act on Voluntary Jurisdiction, the family court has to make efforts to come to an understanding in matters concerning the child. This *Vermittlung* has to occur at the earliest possible moment and at every stage of the proceedings. The court has to hear the parties at the earliest possible moment and has to draw attention to the possibility of counselling by the youth welfare institutions, with the goal to develop an agreed concept for custody and parental responsibility (§ 52 para. 1 sent. 2 German Act on Voluntary Jurisdiction). As far as there is no delay detrimental to the welfare of the child, the court can also order a stay of the proceedings if the parties are prepared for counselling or if there are prospects for an understanding between the parties.

Where there is a dispute between the parents a special mediation procedure (*Vermittlungsverfahren*) in the family court can take place. Where one parent claims that the other parent prevents the implementation of a court order on contact, the family court conciliates on the application of one of the parents, § 52a para. 1 German Act on Voluntary Jurisdiction. Despite the fact that these proceedings are often time consuming and not always successful they are used in practice.[29] In such proceedings the personal appearance of the parents can be ordered and in appropriate cases the youth office can also take part (§ 52a para. 3 German Act on Voluntary Jurisdiction). The court will discuss the consequences of an omission of contact for the child and also the legal consequences for the parents (§ 52 a para. 4 German Act on Voluntary Jurisdiction). In the framework of this procedure, arrangements of the parents can be made which have to be included in the procedure, § 52a para. 4 German Act on Voluntary Jurisdiction. Where there is no understanding on contact or on the use of counselling, or where at least one parent does not appear in the proceedings, the court will make an order stating that the conciliation

---

26 See for courts in Lower Saxony F. ENTRINGER, 'Projekt Gerichtsnahe Mediation in Niedersachsen - Praktische Erfahrungen mit Familienmediation', *FPR* 2004, 196 *et seq.*

27 W. GOTTWALD, 'Alternative Streitbeilegung (Alternative Dispute Resolution, ADR) in Deutschland', *FPR* 2004, 163 *et seq.*

28 See § 17 Children and Young Persons Assistance Act (Social Security Code VIII).

29 R. PROKSCH, *Rechtstatsächliche Untersuchung zur Reform des Kindesrechts*, Köln: Bundesanzeiger Verlag, 2002, p. 242 *et seq.*- See also D. MORAWE, 'Die Vermittlung nach § 52a FGG und die Güteverhandlung nach § 278 ZPO', *FPR* 2004, 193 *et seq.*

procedure was unsuccessful (§ 52a para. 5 German Act on Voluntary Jurisdiction).

A conciliation is still possible at the stage of enforcement. However, according to § 52a para. 5 German Act on Voluntary Jurisdiction, the conciliation procedure of the court takes place before coercion is used. On the other hand, the use of coercion granted by § 33 German Act on Voluntary Jurisdiction is not dependent on a previous attempt of conciliation according to § 52a German Act on Voluntary Jurisdiction.[30]

GREECE

In Greece there is no way to settle issues of parental responsibilities or contact with the child other than court proceedings. Nevertheless, Art. 681c para. 2 Greek Code of Civil Procedure, provides that in a mandatory pre-trial stage the competent social service will investigate the living conditions of the child and will submit the relevant report to the court. Furthermore, the judge may not proceed to hear the case before an attempt at conciliation has been made between the parties. This is for the benefit of the child.

HUNGARY

Mediation is available as an alternative dispute solving mechanism in issues of parental responsibilities, residence of the child and contact. Nevertheless, during a divorce proceeding a mediation agreement entered in to by the parties is to be approved by the court.

There is a special 'child-welfare mediation' that can help parents arrange the matter of contact if they cannot agree on the manner or the time of the contact. This child-welfare mediation is also available in the enforcement stage of the decision or agreement. This proceeding can be applied for by the parties or can be initiated by the public guardianship authority with the consent of the parties.

IRELAND

Sec. 11 Irish Children Act 1997 introduced a variety of measures designed to promote alternative dispute solving mechanisms in the attribution of parental responsibilities. These are contained in Sec. 20-24 Irish Guardianship of Infants Act 1964. In certain respects, they mirror similar provisions contained in Sec. 5-7 Irish Judicial Separation and Family Law Reform Act 1989 and Sec. 6-8 Irish Family Law (Divorce) Act 1996.

Sec. 20 of the 1964 Act relates to advice that should be given to an applicant in proceedings under Sec. 6A (provision for the natural father to be appointed guardian in respect of the child), Sec. 11 and Sec. 11B (access to relatives) of the 1964 Act. It places a positive duty upon a solicitor acting on behalf of the

---

30 OLG Bamberg, 29.06.2000, *NJWE-FER* 2001, 24; OLG Rostock, 29.10.2001, *FamRZ* 2002, 967.

applicant to discuss the existence of alternative means of dispute resolution including:

- the possibility of counselling to assist in coming to an agreement regarding guardianship, custody or access or any other question affecting the welfare of a child. For this purpose the solicitor should furnish the names and addresses of persons suitably qualified to give such counselling;
- the possibility of mediation to assist in coming to such an agreement. For this purpose the solicitor should furnish the names and addresses of persons suitably qualified to provide a mediation service;
- the possibility of entering into an agreement with the respondent, by deed or otherwise in writing, dealing with matters of custody, access or any question affecting the welfare of the child.

A similar requirement is outlined in Sec. 21 of the 1964 Act in respect of a solicitor who has received instructions from a respondent involved in proceedings under Sec. 6A, 11 or 11B of the Act.

Sec. 20(3) and 21(3) of the 1964 Act require the respective solicitors involved to furnish evidence of compliance with the requirements of Sec. 20(2) and 21(2) of the Act. When the solicitor for the applicant is lodging the original documents to initiate proceedings, a certificate, signed by the solicitor, indicating that he or she has observed the requirements of the relevant section, must accompany these documents. A copy of this certificate should accompany any copy of the original documents served on any person in respect of the proceedings. In a like manner, the solicitor for the respondent, when formally responding to the institution of proceedings, must indicate in writing that the obligation placed on him or her by Sec. 21(2) of the 1964 Act has been fulfilled. A copy of the certificate indicating compliance should be delivered to the applicant in the proceedings. In both cases, however, compliance will not be necessary where the parties have already satisfied Sec. 5(2) of the Judicial Separation and Family Law Reform Act 1989 or Sec. 6(4) Irish Family Law (Divorce) Act 1996.[31] These Sec. place a like duty upon solicitors in proceedings for judicial separation and divorce, respectively. Thus, this saver prevents unnecessary duplication of advice regarding alternative means of dispute resolution.

Further provision is made where proceedings under Sec. 6A, 11 or 11B of the 1964 Act have already commenced. If it appears to the court, during the course of proceedings, that agreement between the parties may be possible, Sec. 22 of the 1964 Act allows the court to adjourn proceedings with a view to facilitating such agreement. This is in addition to, and not as a substitute for, any other power that the court may have to adjourn proceedings. Where an adjournment is obtained under Sec. 22, the parties may make attempts, either unaided or with the assistance of a third party, to seek an agreed solution to the matter being considered by the court. Such adjournment will end, however, where

[31] See Sec. 20(4) and 21(4) of the 1964 Act.

either party requests that the court resume hearing the proceedings, which is as obvious an indication as any that the negotiations have failed.[32]

In order to encourage attempts at agreement, Sec. 23 of the 1964 Act stipulates that certain oral or written communications between a party to the proceedings and any third party will not be admissible as evidence in the proceedings to which they relate. Any record of such communication is equally inadmissible. The communications contemplated are those made for the purposes of seeking help to reach agreement regarding matters of custody, access or any question relating to the welfare of a child. This will be so, regardless of whether any such communication was known to, or made in the presence of, the other party to the proceedings.

Any agreement resulting from the negotiations contemplated by Part IV of the 1964 Act (outlined above) can be made a rule of court by virtue of Sec. 24 of the Act. The agreement must relate either to the custody rights of the parties or to access arrangements agreed by them, or both. In such a case, either party may apply to the court for an order rendering the agreement a rule of court. The court may accede to such a request, however, only if it is satisfied that the agreement is fair and reasonable and, in all the circumstances, adequately protects the interest of the parties and the child. Any such order shall be deemed to be an order under either Sec. 11(2)(a) or 11B of the 1964 Act, as appropriate.

Alternative disputes solving mechanisms are not available at the stage of enforcement of a decision/agreement concerning parental responsibilities, the child's residence or contact.

ITALY

The Italian legal system doesn't foresee the possibility of family mediation for alternative dispute resolution, except in situations provided for by Art.. 342 *bis* and 342 *ter* Italian CC (which state that the judge, to end prejudicial conduct by ordering a parent to leave the family home, may also order the intervention of the welfare services operating in the territory or the intervention of a family mediation centre). In practice, judges normally suggest that the parties contact the family mediation centres in order to ensure the observation of the provisions concerning the parental responsibilities.

LITHUANIA

There are no special alternative dispute resolution mechanisms provided in the law. However, Art. 3.54 Lithuanian CC and Art. 231 and 376 Lithuanian Code of Civil Procedure impose a general duty on the court to take all necessary measures to reconcile the parties in family disputes. Such settlement is possible at any stage, including the enforcement procedure. However, the judge does not act as a mediator is such cases.

---

32 This, of course, is subject to any other power of the court to adjourn the proceedings.

THE NETHERLANDS

Following the report of the Commission for the Amendment of Divorce Proceeding in 1995, the State Secretary established the supervisory commission on Divorce Conciliation. This commission was charged with supervising experiments carried out in 1999-2001 at the District Court in Amsterdam, Leeuwarden, Den Bosch and The Hague, involving conciliation in divorce and parental access matters.[33] The evaluation of the experiments demonstrated that utilization of mediation instead of traditional judicial proceedings turned out to be a success. One of the members of the evaluating committee defended her dissertation in 2001 on the added value of divorce mediation.[34] Whether the government will introduce a national divorce mediation system partly or completely funded by the state is still under discussion. However, on 13 April 2004 the Minister of Justice informed Parliament about his prospective policies in the field of divorce. Agreement about the exercise of parental responsibilities will be obligatory to the introductory petition to divorce. The court may refer the spouses to a mediator if they have not reached agreement on all the obligatory subjects.[35] CHIN-A-FAT states, however, that the current mediation procedure and its position in the legal process also need to be reconsidered. In particular, she concludes that the current mediation procedure in the Netherlands pays insufficient attention to the position of minor children. Even though children are often used as a reason to choose divorce mediation, in practice and in research they are almost invisible. The fact that children are kept out of the entire divorce procedure is not only not in line with reality but also a violation of their rights. Children should have the right to give their opinion on issues that relate to their lives; this is not only based on Dutch Law but also on international treaties.[36]

NORWAY

The general view is that an agreement reached between the parents regarding parental responsibilities, the child's residence and contact rights is in the child interests. Therefore, parents having children younger than 16, cannot obtain a separation decree from the competent authorities unless they have been through mediation, Art. 26 Norwegian Marriage Act 1991. If an agreement is not reached, the courts will settle the dispute. According to Art. 59 sec. 2 Norwegian Children Act 1981, the judge shall continually assess the possibility of obtaining an agreement between the parents and prepare the way for this.

---

[33] For a more extensive description of the developments see K. BOELE-WOELKI/O. CHEREDNYCHENKO/L. COENRAAD, 'Dutch Report on the Grounds for Divorce and Maintenance Between Former Spouses', in: K. BOELE-WOELKI/B. BRAAT/I. SUMNER, *European Family Law in Action – Volume I, Grounds for Divorce*, EFL series No. 2, 2003, p. 63-65.

[34] B.E.S. CHIN-A-FAT, *Scheiden (ter)echter zonder rechter, een onderzoek naar de meerwaarde van scheidingsbemiddeling*, 2004.

[35] *Kamerstukken Tweede Kamer* 2003-2004, 29520, No. 1.

[36] B.E.S. CHIN-A-FAT, *Scheiden (ter)echter zonder rechter, een onderzoek naar de meerwaarde van scheidingsbemiddeling*, 2004, p. 432-433.

Art. 61 No. 1 Norwegian Children Act 1981 states that the court shall summon the parties to one or more preliminary meetings and attempt mediation. The court may, according to Art. 61 No. 2, recommend that the parties meet with a certified mediator or another person with knowledge of the case. The intent of mediation, according to Art. 52 Norwegian Children Act 1981, is to have the parents reach a written agreement. Although the parents are supposed to appear at the mediation at the same time, the mediator may decide for them to appear separately. He may also decide that one or both of the parents may bring an advisor.

POLAND

Such alternative measures are not provided for. A family having difficulties fulfilling its duties, or the child of such a family, may be assisted in the form of family counselling (Art. 70 of the Polish statute of 2003 on social assistance).

PORTUGAL

In 1997, the project 'Family Mediation in Situations of Parental Conflict' was created by Order No. 12368/97. This aimed to set up family counselling on matters of parental responsibility on an experimental basis. The service is limited to the Lisbon district and operates alongside the courts. The work of family counselling is carried out by multidisciplinary teams.

RUSSIA

Mediation of counselling is one of the tasks of the Guardianship and Curatorship Department. Such mediation can be applied at the stage of the decision-making by the parents as well as during the execution of the agreements and judicial decisions concerning execution of parental responsibilities, the child's residence or contact.

SPAIN

Some Autonomous Communities such as Catalonia, Valencia, Galicia and Canary Islands have legislated Family Mediation, whereas in others these alternative dispute settlement mechanisms exist on an informal basis or do not exist at all. It is therefore difficult to give an answer which is valid throughout Spain.

The Catalan Law on Family Mediation provides that family mediation can be chosen by the parties as a dispute solving mechanism before a judicial procedure has begun. Once a judicial procedure has begun it is still possible to resort to mediation but only if the proceedings have been suspended (Art. 8.2). Mediation is not available once there is a firm judicial decision on an issue, even if difficulties arise in the enforcement phase of the decision. It is, however, expressly provided that mediation is possible if the matter is reopened because there has been a substantial change of circumstances (Art. 5.1.1(e) and 5.1.2(d)). See Q 56.

SWEDEN

Parents can receive assistance in form of cooperative discussions with a view to reaching an agreement on questions of (attribution of) custody, residence and contact, Chapter 6 Sec. 17a and 18 Swedish Children and Parents Code.[37] The court where an issue on custody, residence or contact is pending may instruct the social welfare committee to arrange for cooperative discussions and adjourn the case for a certain period of time.[38] The parents can also receive counselling, focusing on their relationship and trying to solve their conflicts.[39] The cooperative discussions are voluntary and the parents cannot be forced to participate. If the parents cannot reach an agreement, the court must decide.

At present, applications for enforcement of a court decree or an agreement on custody, residence or contact are handled by administrative courts.[40] Although the court is expected to act speedily, it is also recognised that it is always in the best interests of the child to seek voluntary solutions. The court may therefore instruct a member of the social welfare committee, or certain other persons, to ensure that the person with the child in his or her care voluntarily carries out the decision or agreement, Chapter 21 Sec. 2 Swedish Children and Parents Code. A person given such instructions should report back to the court within two weeks on steps that have been taken and on any other circumstances that may have emerged.

SWITZERLAND

In accordance with Art. 171 Swiss CC, the cantons ensure that spouses can individually or jointly turn to marriage or family counselling agencies if they are experiencing difficulties in their marriage. In addition to protection of the child under civil law, parents are also free to turn to voluntary child protection services (family counselling agencies, youth welfare services). It is possible to resort to these options at any time, but no compulsion of any kind is involved. Depending on the canton in question, specially trained personnel and aid services are available to provide support in connection with actual enforcement measures.

---

37 This provision, as revised in 2001, refers to Chapter 5, Section 3 Swedish Social Services Act (2001:453).

38 Chapter 6 Sec. 18 para. 2-3 Swedish Children and Parents Code.

39 *Vårdnad, Boende och Umgänge*, Stockholm: Socialstyrelsen (National Board on Health and Welfare), 2003, p. 109.

40 It is however expected that issues of enforcement will in the future be tranferred to the general courts, in charge of disputes on parental responsibilities.

QUESTION 58

H. PROCEDURAL ISSUES

To what extent, if at all, is an order or an agreement on parental responsibilities, the child's residence or contact enforceable and in practice enforced? Describe the system of enforcement followed in your national legal system. Under what conditions, if at all, may enforcement be refused?

AUSTRIA

To enforce arrangements on parental responsibilities, the child's residence or contact, the court will employ coercive measures, including reprimands, fines, coercive detention, compulsory appearance before the court or taking possession of important documents, e.g. a passport (Sec. 110(2) in conjunction with Sec. 79(2) Non-Contentious Proceedings Act *[Außerstreitgesetz]*). The court may refrain from continuing a coercive measure *ex officio* if and as long as the child's interests are threatened (Sec. 110(3) *Außerstreitgesetz*).

Direct coercive measures may only be employed to enforce an arrangement on parental responsibilities and the child's residence, but not a contact arrangement (Sec. 110(2) Non-Contentious Proceedings Act *[Außerstreitgesetz]*). Hence, taking delivery of the child in order to enforce the right of contact is not permissible; this is regarded as a disproportionate measure that would be detrimental to the child's interests.[1] Also, the court has to refrain from other coercive measures to enforce the right of contact if a minor over 14 years of age or the parent entitled to have contact refuses to exercise the contact and an instruction on their rights and duties and the importance of the contact for the child's welfare as well as an attempt at reconciliation remains unsuccessful (Sec. 108 *Außerstreitgesetz*).[2]

When enforcing an order or an agreement on parental responsibilities or the child's residence, for the sake of preserving the child's interests a public welfare institution (youth welfare agency or juvenile court assistance office) may be called in to render support, in particular to care for the child on a temporary basis. Direct coercive measures to enforce the order, *e.g.* the delivery of the child in the event the parent not holding parental responsibilities refuses to surrender the child, may only be carried out by court officials (bailiffs) and public-safety officers (policemen) who have been called in (Sec. 110(4) *Außerstreitgesetz*, 146b Austrian CC). However, any physical impact on the child should be a last resort.

---

1 S. KRIWANEK, *Das neue Außerstreitverfahren*, Vienna: LexisNexis ARD Orac, 2004, p. 130.

2 *Oberster Gerichtshof*, 29.06.1994, *EFSlg*. 75.001.

BELGIUM

If disregarded, a child's right to contact may only be enforced if this right is contained in a judgment. Agreements made by the parents or their lawyers *e.g.* pending the decision of the judge, are not enforceable unless they are confirmed by judgment.[3]

The judgment can be enforced in different ways. Namely, the decision can be submitted to forced execution by a bailiff, the court can submit the violation of the right of contact to the payment of a penalty, damages can be claimed afterwards and criminal action can be taken against the parent who disregards another's right of contact (See Q 48a).

BULGARIA

The law provides neither for an enforcement mechanism nor for an enforcement authority of the contact order/agreement.[4] Where there is no voluntary observation of the contact order the enforcement of the order or the agreement is possible through a Judge Executive, who organises the 'factual transfer of the child'.[5] The participation of that judge, however, cannot always be effective, due to the sensitive nature of the actions. The Supreme Court underlines that the child is not simply a commodity to be transferred. If the parent does not observe the order, the Judge Executive can ask for assistance by the Guardianship authority, by the police inspector or by the Child Protection Department,[6] but only where other means have proved of no effect or 'the interests of the child require immediate enforcement'. The instructions of the Supreme Court are that consideration must be made of 'the specific circumstances, the age, the affiliation and the condition of the child, not allowing for psychological stress.' The Bulgarian Civil Procedure Code provides that a parent who impedes the enforcement may be fined (Art. 421 and 422). Such a parent is also criminally liable[7] and risks either restriction, deprivation of parental rights or change in the custody and contact arrangements in favour of the other parent. The obstruction of enforcement of a court order is considered to be a change in the circumstances that justifies a change in the custody and contact arrangements.

The enforcement may be refused in exceptional circumstances, 'for reasons such as delay to enforce the contact order, incapacity to perform due to change in circumstances or in the interests of the child'.[8] In such cases the order may be

---

3 D. DELI, 'De uitdrukkelijke wettelijke erkenning van de gezamenlijke uitoefening van het ouderlijk gezag en van het recht op persoonlijk contact', *R.W.* 1996-1997, p. 3.

4 L. NENOVA, *Family Law of the Republic of Bulgaria*, Sofia, 1994, p. 652.

5 See Supreme Court Procedural Rules – 4 1962, V.N. MLADENOV and P. BRATANOVA, *Family Code: Text, judicial practice etc*, 1996, p. 328-9.

6 After the coming into effect Bulgarian Child Protection Act, Art. 21.

7 Art. 270 Bulgarian Penal Code.

8 See Supreme Court Procedural Rules – 4/6 1962, V.N. MLADENOV and P. BRATANOVA, *Family Code: Text, judicial practice etc*, 1996, p. 328-9.

revised. Revision of the measures is recommendable especially where the child does not give an opportunity for the forcible enforcement of the decision. Thus, for instance, the definite refusal of a 'grown-up child not having reached full age' to fulfil the contact order, constitutes grounds for its revision'.[9]

CZECH REPUBLIC

The Czech Civil Procedure Code includes a special provision on enforcement of the decision on upbringing of minor children (Sec. 272 and 273a). If a judicial decision, or a court approved agreement relating to upbringing of the child (residence) and contact with the child, or a decision on placing the child back into care of one of the parents, is not respected voluntarily the court first calls on the obligated parent to voluntarily obey the judicial decision or fulfil the court approved agreement (Sec. 272 Czech Code of Civil Procedure). The court also has a duty to inform the obligated parent about consequences of not fulfilling his or her duties. If the call remains unsuccessful the court may repeatedly impose fines not exceeding 50,000 CZK. The fines are received by the state. The judge may also order the child to be removed from the person with whom the child should not be, according to the judicial decision or the court approved agreement, and may order the child to pass to the entitled parent (Sec. 273 § 1 Czech Code of Civil Procedure). The factual removal of the child takes place in the presence of the judge, a social worker and the judicial guard.

In case of taking the child away the above mentioned call need not be made if it is clear that the call would not force the obligated person to voluntarily fulfil his or her duty, or if the enforcement of the decision could be obstructed (Sec. 273 § 2 Czech Code of Civil Procedure) *e.g.* if there is a danger of the obligated parent hiding with the child, etc.

DENMARK

An Enforcement Court, the *fogedretten*, decides whether measures enforcing parental authority or contact should be taken. The Enforcement Court may deny enforcement where the child's mental or physical health is subject to serious danger and it may require an expert opinion and postpone enforcement where there are doubts.[10] A recent report from the Ministry of Justice's research unit investigated 1224 cases concerning parental authority and contact from the Enforcement Court.[11] Some 13.6% concerned parental authority and some 72.5% contact. The outcome of the cases were that 46.8% were settled, 19.1 resulted in a judgement, 8.3% of cases were rejected, 24.1% of cases were called back, and 1.65 had another outcome. Of the judgements 4.1% contained the decision that contact must be continued, 6.9% imposed a fine, in 1.6% of cases the child was

---

9 Case 473-1980 (Civil Division).

10 Danish Civil Procedural Act, Art. 536(1).

11 *Justisministeriets forskningsenhed, Undersøgelse af fogedretternes praksis i samværs- og forældremyndighedssager*, May 2004.

physically fetched by the Enforcement Court, in 4.2% of cases enforcement was rejected and 2.3% of cases had a different outcome.[12]

ENGLAND & WALES

The only binding agreement that can be made in this context is a formal parental responsibility agreement made under Sec. 4, Children Act 1989 (see Q 22b) which confers parental responsibility on the unmarried father (and prospectively step-parents and registered partners). That can only be undone by a formal court order under Sec. 4(3). As agreements cannot otherwise be bindingly made, their formal enforcement is not an issue under English law.

Court orders are enforceable either under Sec. 34, Family Law Act 1986 or more generally by the imposition of penal sanctions. Under Sec. 34 where a person is required by a Sec. 8 order to give up a child to another person (this will most commonly apply to the enforcement of a residence order) and the court that made the order is satisfied that the child has not been given up, it may make a 'search and recovery' order authorising an officer of the court or a constable to take charge of the child and deliver him to that other person.

So far as penal sanctions are concerned, these are provided by the law of contempt in the case of the High Court and county court and by Sec. 63(3), Magistrates' Courts Act 1980 in the case of the magistrates' courts.

So far as the High Court and county court are concerned the breaking of an order constitutes a contempt of court for which the contemnor may be fined (there are no prescribed maximum limits) imprisoned (up to a maximum of two years)[13] or have their assets frozen (this remedy is known as sequestration). Magistrates have more circumscribed powers under Sec. 63(3) of the 1980 Act limited to a fine not exceeding £50 for every day in default up to a maximum of £5,000 and imprisonment for a maximum of two months.

It is recognised that in the family context that none of these penal sanctions are entirely appropriate and in any event should only be resorted to as a last resort.[14] Nevertheless in an important ruling in *A v N (Committal: Refusal of Contact)*[15] it was held that in considering whether to commit a mother for her persistent and flagrant breach of a contact order with the father, the child's

---

12 *Justitsministeriets forskningsenhed, Undersøgelse af fogedretternes praksis i samværs- og forældremyndighedssager*, May 2004, p. 12.

13 Sec. 14(1), Contempt of Court Act 1981.

14 See *Ansah v Ansah* [1977] Fam 138 at 143, CA and *Hale v Turner* [2000] 1 WLR 2377 at para. 25, CA. An alternative to imposing a penal penalty for breaching a contact order would be to transfer the residence order to another person but this must be in the child's interests. See *e.g. V v V (Contact: Implacability Hostility)* [2004] EWHC 1215 (Fam), [2004] 72 FLR 851 where a transfer was ordered. Note also *Re S (Uncooperative Mother)* [2004] EWCA Civ 597, [2004] 2 FLR 710 – adverse inferences can be drawn from a mother's refusal to re-engage in a process of family therapy.

15 [1997] 1 FLR 533, CA.

welfare was a material but *not* the paramount consideration. In that case the mother was committed to prison for 42 days.[16]

Instances of committal to prison for disobeying a contact order are relatively unusual and there is a general recognition that the enforcement powers particularly of contact orders are often inadequate.[17] The Government Green Paper on *Parental Separation: Children's Needs and Parental Responsibilities*[18] proposes to extend the court's enforcement power inter alia to allow a referral of a defaulting parent to information meetings, meetings with a counsellor or to parenting programmes; to impose community based orders and the award of financial compensation from one parent to another (for example where the cost of a holiday has been lost).

FINLAND

The enforcement of an approved agreement and a court decision concerning child custody, residence or right of access is possible. The enforcement application shall be addressed to the court of first instance, primarily in the area where the child is staying (Sec. 4 Finnish Act of the Enforcement of a Decision on Child Custody and Right of Access). In most cases the mediation explained above (Q 57) constitutes the first stage of the enforcement proceedings. If the efforts of the mediator do not result in a settlement, the mediator delivers his or her report to the court.

The court may decide to accept or reject the application concerning the enforcement, and it may hear witnesses. The court may then order that the defendant shall let the child meet with the applicant, or leave the child to his or her care under a threat of a fine. The court may also issue a fetc.hing order, although these kinds of orders seem to be exceptional in practice, especially if the enforcement concerns the child's right of access, where a fetc.hing order is possible only under special conditions.

A custody or residence order made no longer than three months ago can be executed directly by the executor as a fetc.hing order. The executor may however transfer the case to the court, if he or she finds it reasonable on the grounds of a change of circumstances or for another reason (Sec. 22 Finnish Act of the Enforcement of a Decision on Child Custody and Right of Access).

---

16 See also *F v F (Contact: Committal)* [1998] 2 FLR 237, CA – committal order for 7 days suspended for six months.

17 See the trenchant criticism by MUNBY J in *Re D (Intractable Contact Dispute: Hostility)* [2004] EWHC 727 (Fam), [2004] 1 FLR 1226, in which the judge said that the father had been let down by the system. See also the valuable analysis by Bracewell J in *V v V (Contact: Implacable Hostility)* [2004] EWHC 1215 (Fam), [2004] 2 FLR 851, in which the judge called for legislation to strengthen the sanctions that can be imposed for breaching court orders.

18 Cm 6273 (July 2004).

The court shall reject the application in cases where a child of 12 years of age resists the enforcement. The same effect may be given to the resistance of a younger child if the child has reached such maturity that the child's will can be taken into consideration. The application can also be rejected if the enforcement would be contrary to the best interests of the child because of a change in circumstances or for another reason (Sec. 2 and 14 Finnish Act of the Enforcement of a Decision on Child Custody and Right of Access).

Enforcement measures concerning the child shall be conducted carefully and without upsetting the child. The removal of the child can be postponed, for instance, if the situation upsets the child too much. (Sec. 3 Finnish Act of the Enforcement of a Decision on Child Custody and Right of Access). The mediator or a social worker shall be present when the f*etc.*hing order is realised, and a doctor or other expert may be present as well, if needed (Sec. 24 Finnish Act of the Enforcement of a Decision on Child Custody and Right of Access).[19]

FRANCE

Theoretically a court order (or an agreement on parental responsibility which has been officially approved by the court) can be enforced with the assistance of the police[20]. The bailiff (*huissier de justice*) could call the police (*force publique)* and ask for their assistance in enforcing the order. In practice, the bailiffs are much more cautious. The parent who has a contact right must bring the court order, which states this right to the bailiff. The bailiff will then first go alone to the other parent's residence and explain the possible legal consequences of refusing to let the other parent have contact with the child. The bailiff tries to get the contact order enforced *à l'amiable* (out of court). Sometimes the child spontaneously gives his or her opinion, but the bailiff should not ask the child for it. If the parent still refuses to let the other parent exercise his contact right, the bailiff never physically takes the child under constraint to bring him to the other parent. He makes a record of the difficulties met with and gives this record to the parent who wanted to exercise the contact right. With the record, the parent can go before court in order to show that the other parent will not comply with the court order. The family court may then modify the exercise of parental responsibilities. It may also order an *astreinte* (a civil fine which the parent who does not comply with the order will have to pay per day, week or month of delay). If the parent finally accepts the exercise of the contact right by the other parent, the bailiff brings the child to the other parent.

---

19 See M. HELIN, 'Enforcement of Custody, Access and Residence Orders, Intercountry Adoptions and Registration of Same Sex Couples', in: A. BAINHAM, *International Survey of Family Law 1997*, The Hague: Kluwer Law International, 1999, p. 153.

20 At the end of September 2004 the French mass media mentioned the case of an American judgment allocating parental responsibilities to the American father. The French mother did not comply with this judgment and the French police tried to take the four-year-old child from the school in France in order to give the child back to the father. The teachers and other parents opposed to this.

GERMANY

An order on parental responsibilities is enforceable under § 33 German Act on Voluntary Jurisdiction. The system of enforcement of such a court order is one of non-contentious proceedings. § 33 German Act on Voluntary Jurisdiction deals with cases where the act or the omission of an act depends solely on the will of a person. According to this provision the court can determine a payment by way of a penalty (*Zwangsgeld*; § 33 para. 1 German Act on Voluntary Jurisdiction). There can also be an arrest order (*Zwangshaft*; § 33 para. 1 sent. 2 German Act on Voluntary Jurisdiction), and as an *ultima ratio* the use of force is admissible (*Gewalt*; § 33 para. 2 German Act on Voluntary Jurisdiction).

Before the penalty is determined there has to be a warning by the court. The statutory maximum penalty amount is 25,000 Euros (§ 33 para. 3 German Act on Voluntary Jurisdiction). However, in practice there is often only a threat of a penalty of 5,000 Euros. For the determination of the amount, the circumstances of the individual case, the financial abilities of the party, the degree of disregard of former court orders and the amount of fault have to be taken into account.[21] In the case of a contravention the court fixes the final sum; sometimes a penalty with an amount of 5.000 Euros, but often only 250 - 500 Euros is determined.[22] According to empirical data courts often hesitate to fix a penalty; arrest orders seem not to be used.[23] The use of force is a measure of last resort. It can only be ordered in the surrender of a child where other means of coercion have been unsuccessful.[24] For the execution by force the court can use the help of the bailiff (*Gerichtsvollzieher*). He can, without an additional order, use the police to help (§ 33 para. 2 sent. 3 German Act on Voluntary Jurisdiction).[25]

The use of force against a child who opposes the exercise of contact has been excluded since the reform of parent and child law in 1998 (§ 33 para. 2 German Act on Voluntary Jurisdiction). In a proceeding for the surrender of a child, the use of force is, in principle, admitted. The family court, however, has to take the will of the child into account.

If the parent having parental custody consistently and without reason denies the other parent contact with the child, a partial[26] or even a total termination of

---

21 W. ZIMMERMANN, in: K. KEIDEL, T. KUNTZE and J. WINKLER, *Freiwillige Gerichtsbarkeit*, 15th Edition, München: Beck, § 33 FGG No. 20a.

22 BayObLG, 12.01.1996, *FamRZ* 1996, 878 (10.000 German Marks); BayObLG, 10.02.1998, *NJWE-FER* 1998, 184 (1.000 German Marks); OLG Karlsruhe, 16.10.2001, *FamRZ* 2002, 1125 (400 German Marks).

23 R. PROKSCH, *Rechtstatsächliche Untersuchung zur Reform des Kindesrechts*, Köln: Bundesanzeiger Verlag, 2002, p.237 *et seq.*

24 OLG Brandenburg, 11.10.2000, *NJW-RR* 2001, 1089.

25 For more details see W. ZIMMERMANN, in: K. KEIDEL, T. KUNTZE and J. WINKLER, *Freiwillige Gerichtsbarkeit*, 15th Edition, München: Beck, § 33 FGG No. 40.

26 OLG Brandenburg, 25.10.2001, *FamRZ* 2002, 1273 (deprival of the right to determine the residence of the child); OLG Dresden, 25.04.2002, *JAmt* 2002, 310 (Sorgerechtspfleger); OLG Frankfurt a.M., 03.09.2002, *FamRZ* 2002, 317.

parental custody can be ordered.[27] In such a situation, it is argued, the behaviour of the parent is against the best interests of the child. However, if the holder of parental custody has used all reasonable efforts to persuade the child to grant contact, it is no longer reasonable for the parent to follow the contact order.[28] It cannot be expected for the parent to use force against the child.[29]

For the court order to be enforceable, it must contain an exact order for the type of behaviour the parent or the third party is asked. A simple agreement of the parents alone, even when it is made in the framework of court proceedings, is not sufficient. Only when the content of the agreement is confirmed and transformed into a court order is there an enforceable order.[30] The court order must be detailed enough that it can actually be enforced. Especially in contact cases the exact kind of contact, the location, the period and the frequency of contact must be fixed.

There is no express statutory provision dealing with cases where a contact order against the parent with the obligation to contact his or her child is not followed. However, in court practice some situations are recognised.[31] Where the person having the right and the obligation to contact, usually the father, does not perform this duty it is contested whether a penalty can be determined. Some courts use the possibility of a penalty.[32] Their main argument for this position is that the child is entitled to contact and the parent having the contact duty can be influenced by the penalty. Other courts and the majority in legal literature are against the use of penalty orders.[33] An amelioration of the relationship between the child and an unwilling parent cannot be expected by such an enforcement.

GREECE

The Greek Code of Civil Procedure provides different enforcement proceedings depending on the content of the relevant claim. Art. 950 Greek Code of Civil

---

27 AG Besigheim, 16.01.2002, *JAmt* 2002, 137; AG Frankfurt a.M., 18.02.2003, *FamRZ* 2004, 1595.- For a more restrictive view however M. COESTER, in: STAUDINGER, *Kommentar zum Bürgerlichen Gesetzbuch,* 13th Edition, Berlin, 2000, § 1666 German CC No. 131.

28 OLG Karlsruhe, 05.02.2001, *FamRZ* 2002, 624.

29 OLG Zweibrücken, 23.10.1986, *FamRZ* 1987, 90; OLG Köln, 17.02.1998, *NJWE-FER* 1998, 163.

30 OLG Köln, 17.02.1998, *FamRZ* 1998, 961; OLG München, 02.09.1998, *FamRZ* 1999, 522; OLG Brandenburg, 11.10.2000, *FamRZ* 2001, 1315 (surrender of a child); W. ZIMMERMANN, in: K. KEIDEL, T. KUNTZE and J. WINKLER, *Freiwillige Gerichtsbarkeit,* 15th Edition, München: Beck, § 33 FGG No. 10.

31 OLG Nürnberg, 11.06.2001, *FamRZ* 2002, 413 already refuses a contact order because this would not be in the interest of the child.

32 See OLG Celle, 21.11.2000, *Monatsschrift für Deutsches Recht* (*MDR)* 2001, 395; OLG Köln, 15.01.2001, *FamRZ* 2001, 1023.

33 C. KRAEFT, ‚Vollstreckungsprobleme nach § 33 FGG', *FPR* 2002, 611, 612; D. SCHWAB, *Familienrecht,* 12th Edition, Munich, 2003, No.691.

Procedure introduces special proceedings for the enforcement of the obligation to deliver a child and to allow contact with that child.

More specifically, in such cases the court orders the parent to deliver the child. The parent's compliance with the court's decision is induced by adding a clause ordering the payment of a fine and/or imprisonment for a period of up to one year upon default. If the child is not found, the parent may be compelled to take the "oath of manifestation", certifying that he or she does not know where the child may be found.[34] Similar is the enforcement of agreements or decisions referring to contact with the child.[35]

At this point it is worth mentioning that the abovementioned provisions were introduced by Law 2721/1999. Until then, the enforcement of the decision to deliver the child was direct, meaning that the bailiff removed the child from the one parent in order to deliver it to the other. This (abated) proceeding was detrimental to the child and was thus incompatible with the protection of its interests.

HUNGARY

In practice, the enforcement of a decision or agreement on parental responsibilities, the child's residence (placement) or contact is a problematic matter.

With respect to parental responsibilities and the child's residence (placement), the parent can file an action and claim the obligation of the person (usually the other parent) who illegally withholds the child to give the child back. The regulations of the Execution Act are to be applied to the enforcement of the judicial decisions. According to these rules, the first step is to request the public guardianship authority to promote voluntary performance. If this is unsuccessful, enforcement is provided through a penalty or the assistance of the police.

With respect to the enforcement of contact, the first step is to encourage the parties to take part in the child-welfare mediation. There are also 'contact-services' all around the state which, with its experts, aim to help contact function properly when it breaks down. It may help to have proper rooms available for contact. If these solutions are unsuccessful, administrative sanctions are available against a custodial parent who prevents contact. The last

---

34 By analogy from Art. 941 para. 2 Greek Code of Civil Procedure, concerning the obligation of the debtor to deliver a movable property. See G. NIKOLOPOULOS, in: K. KERAMEUS, D. KONDULIS and N. NIKAS (eds.), *Commentary on the Code of Civil Procedure, Vol. II (Arts. 591-1054)*, Athens - Komotini: Ant.N. Sakkoulas, Art. 950 Greek Code of Civil Procedure p. 1833 No. 1 [in Greek].

35 See Art. 950 para. 2, Greek Code of Civil Procedure, which also refers to the provision of Art. 947 Greek Code of Civil Procedure concerning the enforcement of an obligation not to perform or not to oppose a specific act.

sanction can be the claim for a change of the child's residence, but, of course, only if it is in the child's interests.

A published final judgment of first instance regarded a parent's right to contact with his child to also be the non-custodial parent's personal right and stated that this parent was entitled to damages because of the violation of his personal right.

Instead of refusing enforcement, a revision of the residence or contact decision is possible.

IRELAND

The options of the Irish court in terms of enforcement of an order or an agreement on parental responsibilities, the child's residence or contact are limited. In reality, the Gardaí[36] and social services facilitate the enforcement of such orders. Ultimately, the court may fine or imprison the holder of parental responsibilities or parent in breach of an order or an agreement on parental responsibilities, the child's residence or contact. Sec. 5 of the Courts Act (No. 2) 1986 makes it an offence to fail or refuse to comply with the requirements of a direction given in an order under Sec. 11 of the Guardianship of Infants Act 1964. On conviction, the court may impose a fine of €254 and/or imprisonment of six months.[37] The court may also award custody to the other parent.

The problems with enforcement are compounded where, for example, a child absolutely refuses to have access to a non-custodial parent. This alienation can be due to overt or covert actions by the custodial parent designed to turn the child against the absent parent. The custodial parent may maintain that he or she is in favour of access but will not force the child to go if he or she does not wish to do so. He or she may be unwilling to obey a court order for access, citing the distress of the child, even though he or she may acknowledge that in the long term it is better for the child to have access to and contact with the other parent. If the child steadfastly refuses to comply with an access order, the Irish court may consider an application to take into account the wishes of the child.[38] If the access is determined not to be conducive to the child's best interests, enforcement may be refused.

ITALY

The Court decisions or the agreements confirmed in a judicial proceeding can be enforced through the intervention of the guardianship judge (see footnote to Q 48a) of welfare services (both of them perform very valuable services and mediation activities) or by the police. The Court orders must be observed and cannot be refused so long as they are not modified or revoked.

36 The Irish police force.

37 See District Court Rules 1997, Ord. 58, r.8.

38 Sec. 25 Irish Guardianship of Infants Act 1964.

LITHUANIA

Court judgments, agreements approved by the court, and settlement agreements approved by the court in the above-mentioned cases are enforceable documents which are enforced under the general procedure laid down by Part VI of the Lithuanian Code of Civil Procedure of 2002.

In practice, those documents are enforced. The enforcement procedure is executed by private bailiffs. When enforcing enforceable documents, the bailiffs may request support from the police *e.g.* in the event one of the parents does not execute the court judgment to place the child for the supervision of the other parent. If the child is involved in the enforcement procedure, the bailiff must inform the state institution for the protection of the rights of the child. In such cases, the employees of this institution take part in the enforcement proceedings (Art. 764 Lithuanian Code of Civil Procedure).

THE NETHERLANDS

The legislature has not deemed it necessary to include specific sanctions regarding the enforcement of an agreement or judicial decision on matters concerning parental responsibilities. In particular with regard to contact arrangements, the Minister of Justice has declared that criminal provisions should be regarded as an *ultimum remedium,* and are not appropriate instruments for enforcing contact.[39] The general enforcement sanctions of the Dutch Code of Civil Procedure may be used, whereby the interests of the child are of paramount importance. Therefore, the court may refuse to enforce a contact order, which is not contrary to Art. 8 ECHR.[40] The sanctions for non-compliance with contact arrangements are:[41] imprisonment, the court will order the handing over of the child if necessary with the help of the police, a fine in the event of non-cooperation, reduction or termination of partner maintenance, temporary suspension of child maintenance, care and supervision order, change of parental responsibilities (Art. 1:253c), acceptance of the status quo.[42]

NORWAY

Decisions by the court on parental responsibilities, where the child shall live and on contact rights are enforceable, Art. 65 Norwegian Children Act 1981. In practice, enforcement is necessary in certain cases. The general rules of enforcement in Chapter 13 Norwegian Enforcement Act 1992 apply. In those cases where the child must change residence, three means of enforcement are available. First, force may be used by the enforcement officer. This is a drastic solution, but it is used in practice. Second, the parent with whom the child shall live may collect the child, but in that case no force can be exercised. Third, the court may determine that a coercive fine be levied for each day the parent

39 *Kamerstukken Tweede Kamer* 2002-2003, 28600VI, No. 105.

40 See Supreme Court 24.3.2000, *NJ,* 2000, 356.

41 U. HEEFFER, 'De effectuering van een omgangsregeling', *FJR,* 2001, p. 74-80.

42 J.A.E. VAN RAAK-KUIPER, 'Omgang, informatie en consultatie', in: P. VLAARDINGERBROEK *et al, Het hedendaagse personen- en familierecht,* 2004, p. 360-363.

refuses to give the child to the other parent. It also determines the amount of this fine.

Enforcement by means of a daily fine may not be chosen if it is considered 'impossible' to enforce such a decision, see the general rule in Art. 13-8 sec. 4 Norwegian Enforcement Act 1992. This follows from decisions of the Supreme Court in cases on the child's residence and contact rights. Such impossibility is present if enforcement might result in serious psychological problems for the child.[43] It is further considered an impossibility if a somewhat older child strongly opposes contact with the other parent.[44] That the parent with whom the child lives is strongly against contact with the other parent does not qualify.

POLAND

The only specific provisions are to enforce the removal of a person remaining under parental authority or under guardianship (Art. 598^1 – 598^{13} Polish Civil Procedure Code, added by the statute of 19 July 2001). The exercise of such a judgment may be suspended if it might endanger the person's wellbeing, but only until the danger ceases.

PORTUGAL

See answer to Q 48a. Consideration of the child's interests may lead the court to abstain from decreeing coercive compliance with the established system.

RUSSIA

The enforceability of decisions regarding child's residence.

If the parents of the child, due to whatever reason, do not live together, they are free to determine their child's residence by agreement (Art. 65 (3) Russian Family Code). If the child's residence is being determined other than in the framework of a divorce or annulment procedure, there is no obligatory judicial scrutiny of the parental arrangements. If one of the parents violates the agreement, the issue must be brought before the court (Art. 65 (2, 3) Russian Family Code). After scrutinising the agreement the court has two options: to approve the agreement by a court order or to disapprove the agreement and determine the child's residence by a court order. If the parents fail to reach an agreement they can ask the court to determine child's residence by a court order.

The parents can also agree upon the child's residence if it is being determined during a divorce or annulment procedure (Art. 24 (1) Russian Family Code Russian Family Code); however, in this case judicial scrutiny of their agreement is obligatory. As in the previously described case, the court is entitled to set parental arrangement aside if the agreement in not in the best interests of the child or one of the spouses (Art. 24 (2) Russian Family Code), and the court will

43 Rt. 1970 p. 703.
44 Rt. 1963 p. 1369.

then determine the child's residence by a court order. If the court approves the parental agreement, it will be incorporated into the divorce or annulment order.

Therefore, enforcement of the decisions regarding child's residence always takes the form of an execution of court orders. The procedure of such execution is set down in the Federal Law on the Execution Proceedings, and the Federal Law on the Court Bailiffs.[45] The peculiarity of the execution of the decisions relating to children is the obligatory participation of the Guardianship and Curatorship Department in the executions proceedings (Art. 79 (2) Russian Family Code). The need to enforce the decisions relating to the child's residence arises if the non-resident parent refuses to transfer the child to the resident parent, or abducts the child. In both cases, the child must be taken from one parent to be transferred to the other. This action is considered to be extremely problematic, and requires great caution.

If the parents keep the child against court order and refuse to voluntarily transfer him or her to the other parent, the court order is sent to a court bailiff for enforcement. The bailiff is obliged to accomplish the execution within two months.[46] According to law (Art. 9 (2) Russian Law on the Execution Proceedings) the court bailiff first gives the parent a term (up to five days) to voluntarily comply with court order. If the parent refuses the bailiff can first try to facilitate a peaceful settlement by letting the Guardianship and Curatorship Department to mediate between the parents one more time.[47] If the mediation provides no result, the bailiff can ask the court that issued the residence order to impose a fine on the disobedient parent of up to two-hundred times the minimum wage .[48] After the fine is paid the bailiff sets up a new term for complying with court order.[49] If the parent disobeys again, the fine can be doubled. As the law does not limit the number of times a fine can be increased and reapplied,[50] in principle the disobeying parent can be financially ruined. If fines do not help, the bailiff can try to take the child against the will of the parent. The bailiff may ask experts in child psychology, psychiatry or a

---

45 Law of 21.07.1997, *Sobranie Zakonodatel'stva Rossiiskoi Federatsii*, 1997, No. 30, item 3590.

46 Art. 13 (1) Russian Law on the Execution Proceedings. In case of an illness of the child or other serious reasons, execution can be delayed.

47 A. NETCHAEVA, 'Commentary to Art. 79 Russian Family Code, in: I. KUZNETZOVA (ed.), *Commentary on the Family Code of Russian Federation*, Moscow: Jurist, 2000, p. 277.

48 Art. 83 (1) Federal Law on Execution Proceedings.

49 A. NETCHAEVA, 'Commentary to Art. 79 Russian Family Code', in: I. KUZNETZOVA (ed.), *Commentary on the Family Code of Russian Federation*, Moscow: Jurist, 2000, p. 278.

50 A. NETCHAEVA, 'Commentary to Art. 79 Russian Family Code', in: I. KUZNETZOVA (ed.), *Commentary on the Family Code of Russian Federation*, Moscow: Jurist, 2000, p. 278.

education to advise on the best way to execute and perform this action.[51] Taking a child away is processed in the presence of a representative of the Guardianship and Curatorship Department and the parent with whom the child resides. It is recommended not to take the child away from the residence of the persisting parent but on the neutral territory: school, kindergarten, medical institution.[52] If a direct transfer of the child from one parent to another parent is psychologically difficult for the child, the court may order that the child can be temporarily placed in a child protection institution (Art. 79 (2) Russian Family Code). If necessary, the bailiff can also use police assistance to neutralise the resistance of the parent (Art. 79 (2) Russian Family Code). Application of force to the child is not allowed. The task of the representative of the Guardianship and Curatorship Department is to supervise that this does not happen. If the child resists the execution of the decision, the bailiff has to postpone the execution or report to the court that the execution turned out to be impossible.[53]

The enforceability of decisions regarding contact

The enforceability of parental agreements regarding contact is a matter of controversy. The law does not explicitly state what happens if one of the parents violates a contact agreement. According to an influential opinion, such agreements are not legally enforceable, their violation 'cause no legal consequences',[54] and the agreement is no more than 'a piece of evidence'.[55] This point of view, however, seems to be controversial. Treating contact agreements as not legally binding would mean that if one parent applies to court regarding the agreement's violation, the court would automatically set the agreement aside and decide upon contract arrangements as if no agreement has been made. Comparison of contact agreements with other agreements relating to children allows for the conclusion that this is definitely not the case. Even in cases where parental agreements are made in the framework of divorce procedure and are subject to obligatory judicial scrutiny, such as those regarding child maintenance or residence (Art. 24 (2) Russian Family Code), the court's starting point is to approve the parental agreement. Only if the

---

51 A. NETCHAEVA, 'Commentary to Art. 79 Russian Family Code', in: I. KUZNETZOVA (ed.), *Commentary on the Family Code of Russian Federation*, Moscow: Jurist, 2000, p. 277.

52 A. NETCHAEVA, 'Commentary to Art. 79 Russian Family Code', in: I. KUZNETZOVA (ed.), *Commentary on the Family Code of Russian Federation*, Moscow: Jurist, 2000, p. 277.

53 A. NETCHAEVA, 'Commentary to Art. 79 Russian Family Code', in: I. KUZNETZOVA (ed.), *Commentary on the Family Code of Russian Federation*, Moscow: Jurist, 2000, p. 278.

54 A. NETCHAEVA, 'Commentary to Art. 79 Russian Family Code', in: I. KUZNETZOVA (ed.), *Commentary on the Family Code of Russian Federation*, Moscow: Jurist, 2000, p. 230.

55 A. NETCHAEVA, 'Commentary to Art. 79 Russian Family Code', in: I. KUZNETZOVA (ed.), *Commentary on the Family Code of Russian Federation*, Moscow: Jurist, 2000, p. 230.

agreement is against the interests of the child or one of the parents can it be set aside by the court. It is rather illogical to suggest that when the law does not prescribe obligatory judicial scrutiny to contact arrangements, the court is supposed to disregard the agreement without even investigating the possibility of its approval. Thus, if a contact agreement is violated by one of the parents, he or she can ask the court to approve and enforce the agreement. By doing this the court can scrutinise the agreement and refuse its enforcement only in case of violation of the interests of the child or one of the parents.

If the residential parent does not obey the contact arrangements laid down in the court order, the enforcement measures of civil procedural are applicable. The court bailiff in charge of the execution of the order can impose a fine on the disobeying in the fashion similar to the above described cased relating to the child's residence. No physical force can be used to facilitate the contact between the parent and child. If there is persistent and deliberate disobedience of the court order, the judge, taking into consideration the opinion of the child, can order a change of the child's residence to the other parent, if it is not against the best interests of the child (Art. 66 (3) Russian Family Code). This measure is not usually applied, but the mere threat of its application can compel most uncompromising parent to respect the right of the child to contact the other parent.[56]

Execution of decisions regarding taking the child away after the restriction or discharge of parental rights.
Execution of these decisions is very similar to the execution of the decisions regarding the child's residence. There are, however, two peculiarities. If living with the parent(s) constitutes an acute danger for the child, a court order can enjoin immediate execution (Art. 13 (2) Russian Law on the Execution Proceedings). In case of acute danger, taking the child away can be facilitated by the application of force to the child.

SPAIN

Twenty days after a decision on parental responsibilities, each of the parties to a dispute can ask the judge to order the execution of that decision. The judge will request the other party to comply with the decision within a certain time, which the judge can determine freely. It is possible to establish that if the decision is not complied within the time limit there will not only be an enforcement of the decision but other consequences will arise *e.g.* a fine will be imposed.

Within the required time, it is possible for the party against which execution has been ordered to present his or her objections to execution. It is thereby possible to obtain a refusal of enforcement because time limits have not been respected, documents are missing, etc. Art 158 Spanish CC and Art. 134 Catalan Family Code also allows the judge to adopt any measure necessary in order to protect the best interests of the child. This includes not enforcing a court order.

---

56 M. ANTOKOLSKAIA, *Family Law* (*Semeinoe pravo*), Moscow: Jurist, 1999, p. 202.

If the requirement, which has to be seen as a second chance to comply with the court order voluntarily, does not succeed, the court can, on request of the party asking for the execution, order any appropriate measure to obtain the execution of the court decision. This can include imposing a fine that is payable each month or even modifying the previous custody or access regime in order to obtain execution (Art. 776 LEC). It is also possible for the police intervene; not complying with a court order can amount to a criminal offence (see Q 48a).

Although decisions on parental responsibilities are enforceable, it is generally admitted that enforcement is very difficult in this area; in practice it is possible that an enforceable decision will not be enforced. This is due to a variety of reasons. The Spanish court system is too slow and bureaucratic; it is sometimes said that it offers too many chances to block judicial action. Specifically there is also a reluctance of courts in this area to resort to criminal law or force because that is considered contrary to the child's best interests.

SWEDEN

Court orders, as well as agreements between the parents on custody, residence and contact are enforceable.[57] An agreement must, however, be in writing, signed by both parents and approved by the social welfare committee to be enforceable. At present, applications of enforcement are sent to administrative county courts. It is possible that a future law reform will transfer issues of enforcement to the district courts.

Enforcement shall be effected speedily and, as far as possible, voluntarily with the assistance of the social welfare committee. If voluntary efforts are found to be fruitless, the county administrative court may attach a penalty of a fine for non-compliance with the enforcement order, or decide that the child is to be collected by the police authority, Chapter 21 Sec. 3 para. 1 Swedish Children and Parents Code. As to custody, residence or surrender of a child, a decision regarding collection of the child may be given if enforcement cannot be achieved in any other way or if collection is necessary to prevent the child from suffering serious harm, Chapter 21 Sec. 3 para. 2 Swedish Children and Parents Code. As regards a judgment or decision concerning contact between the child and a parent with whom the child is not living, collection of the child may be ordered on the condition that it is the only way to achieve enforcement and the child has a particularly strong need for contact with that parent, Chapter 21 Sec. 3 para. 3 Swedish Children and Parents Code.[58]

The administrative county court may refuse enforcement if the circumstances have manifestly changed after the judgment or decision on custody, residence or contact was made or after the parents' agreement was approved by the social

57 The relevant provisions are found in Chapter 21 Swedish Children and Parents Code.

58 Chapter 21 Sec. 3 Swedish Children and Parents Code.

welfare committee and it is in the best interests of the child that the issue is reviewed (in this case by the district court). A review by the district court presupposes an application by a person who was a party to the case concerning enforcement at the county administrative court or an application by the social welfare committee, Chapter 21 Sec. 6 para. 1 Swedish Children and Parents Code. The county administrative court also may refuse enforcement if there is a significant risk of harm to the child's physical or mental health, Chapter 21 Sec. 6 para. 2 Swedish Children and Parents Code. The extent of the court's authority to refuse enforcement is limited, the main principle being that a decision or an agreement shall be enforced unless circumstances have manifestly changed or the child's best interests demand a review.[59]

In cases concerning enforcement of agreements or court orders regarding custody, residence or contact, special attention shall be paid to the child's own wishes. Consequently, Chapter 21 Sec. 5 Swedish Children and Parents Code provides that enforcement against the wishes of a child who has reached the age of twelve, or a corresponding level of maturity, cannot be ordered unless it is necessary with regard to the best interests of the child. The provision is applicable when the administrative county court decides questions concerning enforcement of orders or agreements on custody, residence or contact, as well as when the police execute decisions on collection in these cases.[60]

SWITZERLAND

Personal contact: Among other possibilities, instructions (Art. 273 § 2 Swiss CC) or the appointment of an official advisory in accordance with Art. 308 § 2 Swiss CC serve the purpose of enforcing personal contact. In particular, the party who has parental responsibilities for the child to whom the visiting right applies must make the necessary preparations so that the right to personal contact may be exercised. This party may be bound over to do so by means of cantonal enforcement law or by the threat of a penalty for failure to obey the order (imprisonment or fine) in accordance with Art. 292 Swiss Penal Code. The party entitled to exercise visiting rights may not be forced into the visits,[61] but must, if the non-exercise of visiting rights means a failure to contribute in-kind support, as already explained,[62] expect to receive possible subsequent claims for additional maintenance support contributions. If the party entitled to exercise visiting rights acts on his or her own authority to enforce personal contact or does not hand the child over after the visiting time has ended, he or she is deemed to have committed the offence of having absconded with the child (Art.

---

59 G. WALIN and S. VÄNGBY, Föräldrabalken, En kommentar, Del II, 14-21 kap. och internationell föräldrarätt, Stockholm: Norstedts Juridik, 2002, p. 21:26.

60 G. WALIN and S. VÄNGBY, *Föräldrabalken, En kommentar, Del II, 14-21 kap. och internationell föräldrarätt*, Stockholm: Norstedts Juridik, 2002, p. 21:23.

61 BBl 1996 I 159.

62 See Section 48 above.

220 Swiss Penal Code) or in some cases even of having kidnapped the child (Art. 183 *et seq* Swiss Penal Code.[63]

The exercise of the right to personal contact may be simplified by semi-private organisations who supervise the exercise of visiting rights in more or less closed 'neutral' rooms (so-called days of supervised visiting rights).

Parental responsibilities, custody: In principle the judgments *in rem* concerning custody are enforceable under cantonal procedural law.[64] However, extreme restraint is to be exercised in the use of coercive measures due to the child's welfare. The judge competent to rule on enforcement may first obtain an expert opinion regarding any enforcement measures.[65] Constraint is primarily to be used in an indirect manner by the authorities *e.g.* if an enforcement order to hand over a child is combined with the threat of a penalty. However, this only makes sense if it is not the child himself or herself who is offering resistance. Execution by substitution *i.e.* the handing over the child with the assistance of a third party, should only be ordered if all other measures have been tried and have proved fruitless. If the child is of an age to form his or her own judgment about whether he or she wishes to return to the custodial parent or the parent with parental responsibilities, execution by substitution may not be used as a coercive measure of enforcement.[66]

---

63 BGE 118 IV 61; 110 IV 35; 108 IV 22; 119 IV 216 *et seq.*

64 G. Leuch, O. Marbach, F. Kellerhals and M. Sterchi, *Die Zivilprozessordnung für den Kanton Bern*, Bern: Stämpfli Verlag AG, 2000, p. 899-901.

65 BGE 111 II 313.

66 BGE 111 II 313, 315.

QUESTION 59

H. PROCEDURAL ISSUES

To what extent, if at all, are children heard when a competent authority decides upon parental responsibilities, the child's residence or contact, e.g., upon a dispute, when scrutinising an agreement, when appointing or discharging holder(s) of parental responsibilities, upon enforcement of a decision or agreement?

AUSTRIA

Children are heard in person in proceedings concerning their care and education including the arrangement of the child's residence, as well as in proceedings on the right to personal contact unless the child lacks the necessary capacity to understand, as in the case of a small child. The only exception is if questioning the child or any delay associated with doing so would threaten the child's interests (Sec. 105 Non-Contentious Proceedings Act *[Außerstreitgesetz]*).

BELGIUM

Different systems for hearing children must be distinguished.

The Belgian Law of 30 June 1994 has provided a common right, or more precisely, a possibility, of hearing the child, by introducing Article 931 (3-7) in the Belgian Judicial Code.[1] According to Art. 931(3), every minor[2] who has enough discernment can be heard in every dispute in which it is concerned.[3] Art. 931(3)-(7) Belgian Judicial Code is applicable to all courts[4] and to all the proceedings in which children are concerned, whether it concerns their person, their property, their status or their maintenance. The hearing of the child does not require the child to be a party to the dispute.[5] It can take place *ex officio* or on the demand of the child, by the competent authority or by the person it

---

1 J. DE GAVRE, 'La loi du 30 juin 1994 modifiant l'article 931 du Code Judiciaire et les dispositions relatives aux procédures du divorce', *J.T.*, 1994, p. 593; P. DONNY, 'L'audition de l'enfant, pratiques et dérives', *Rev. dr. ULB*, 1996, p. 169; B. POELMANS, 'Het hoorrecht van minderjarigen', in: P. SENAEVE and W. PINTENS, *De hervorming van de echtscheidingsprocedure en het hoorrecht van de minderjarige*, Antwerp: Maklu, 1997, p. 64-122.

2 Children who have reached the age of 18 years have no right to be heard, even if they may be concerned as to disputes between their parents *e.g.* the interim measure concerning the separated residences.

3 Also see Q 61 about the proposal made in Parliament in this matter.

4 Justice of the Peace, Court of First Instance, President of the Court of First Instance and exceptionally Juvenile Court, when Art. 56 *bis* Belgian LJP is not applicable.

5 Art. 931(7) Belgian Judicial Code; Court of Appeal of Liege, 09.01.1996, *J.L.M.B.*, 1996, p. 663, annotated V. D'HUART.

designates. Confusion exists on the interpretation of 'discernment';[6] the judicial authority decides in a sovereign manner and has the right to refuse to hear the child, but if the hearing has been asked by the child the judge must justify his refusal by refering to the criterion of discernment of the child. No appeal is possible from this decision.[7]

Aside from this common right of Art. 931 (3-7) Belgian Judicial Code, Art. 56 *bis* LJP,[8] provides a specific right of hearing before the Juvenile Court. The Juvenile Court has the obligation to call up the child, if it has reached the age of twelve when this court decides upon parental responsibilities, the child's residence or contact, or the administration of its property.[9] If the child has not reached the age of twelve, the Juvenile Court can decide to hear the child, or refuse it by a decision justified according to the general right of hearing in proceedings mentioned in Art. 56 *bis* Belgian LJP[10] (Art. 51(1) Belgian LJP that refers to Art. 931 Belgian Judicial Code).

The Belgian Law on Guardianship of 29 April 2001 has installed a specific right to be heard in procedures before the Justice of the Peace concerning guardianship and parental responsibilities (Art. 1233(1) Belgian Judicial Code). The Justice of the Peace must call upon the minor in order to hear it, if the child is at least twelve years old, in procedures that concern its person, and when it is at least fifteen years old in procedures that concern its property (Art. 1233(1)(2) Belgian Judicial Code). The child is also heard in procedures involving the designation of its guardian, after it has reached the age of twelve, and about all decisions personally concerning the child. The specific procedure of Art. 1233

6 For the hearing of a child of 9-10 years: Court of Appeal of Brussels, 09.02.1999, *J.D.J.*, 2000, No. 194, p. 43; Court of Appeal of Ghent, 19.06.1995, *R.W.*, 1995-96, p. 1356; Court of Appeal of Antwerp, 15.06.1995, *R.W.*, 1995-96, p. 1356; Court of First Instance of Brussels, 29.12.1995, *Rev. trim. dr. fam.*, 1996, p. 442. Against the hearing of a child of 6-7 years : Court of First Instance of Brussels, 12.06.1996, *Rev. trim. dr. fam.*, 1996, p. 464; Court of First Instance of Brussels, 14.05.1996, *Rev. trim. dr. fam.*, 1996, p. 464; Court of First Instance of Mons, 22.03.1995, *Rev. trim. dr. fam.*, 1995, p. 690.

7 Court of Appeal of Liege, 17.12.2002, *J.L.M.B.*, 2003, afl. 36, p. 1577; G. Baeteman, J. Gerlo, E. Guldix, A. Wylleman, G. Verschelden and S. Brouwers, 'Overzicht van rechtspraak (1995-2000): Personen- en familierecht', *T.P.R.*, 2001, p. 1996-2000 and 2005.

8 Cass., 04.09.2002, *Rev. trim. dr. fam.*, 2003, p. 555-558 ; Court of Appeal of Antwerp, 15.06.1995, *J.dr.jeun.* , 1996, p. 383, annotated J. Jacqmain; Court of Appeal of Gent, 19.06.1995, *R.W.*, 1995-96, p. 1356; M. Grognard, 'L'audition de l'enfant depuis l'application des articles 931 nouveau du Code Judiciaire et art. 56bis de la loi du 8 avril 1965 relative à la protection de la jeunesse', *Div. Act.*, 2002, p. 149-159.

9 Contrary to Art. 931 Belgian Judicial Code that provides that the Judge has the possibility to refuse to hear the child, if the Judge refers to 'discernement' as a criterion and also provides that the child can be heard in all the proceedings by which it is concerned.

10 Article 931 Belgian Judicial Code can not be applied to other proceedings before the Juvenile Court, e.g. adoption, because other specific rules concerning the hearing of the child are applicable.

Belgian Judicial Code is not applicable when parents ask for an authorisation according to Art. 410 Belgian Civil Code, however Art. 378 Belgian CC refers to Art. 410 Belgian CC. There is no obligation to hear the child. Only Art. 931 Belgian Judicial Code is applicable.[11]

A child of the age of fourteen can also attend proceedings when the court decides upon parental responsibilities, unless the court decides that according to the circumstances it is better to forbid the presence of the child.[12] (Also see Q 61 concerning the voluntary intervention of the child).

BULGARIA

The Bulgarian Child Protection Act introduced a general rule for participation of the child in judicial and administrative procedures. Art. 15 says: (1) All cases of administrative or judicial proceedings affecting the rights and interests of a child shall provide for an obligatory hearing of the child, provided it has reached the age of 10, unless that proves harmful to the child's interests. (2) In cases where the child has not reached the age of 10, it may be given a hearing depending on the level of the child's maturity. The decision to hear the child shall be substantiated.'

More specifically, the Bulgarian Family Code provides for hearing the child in cases of divorce where the issue of parental responsibilities is decided (Art. 106 § 3): 'The court hears the parents and the children, if they are at least fourteen years of age. Where the court finds it appropriate it can hear from the children who are ten years of age, and also from close relatives and friends of the family.'

The court should also hear the child when deciding on the residence of the child where parents live apart (Art. 71 § 2). 'Where the parents do not live together and are unable to reach an agreement as to with whom of them the children will live, the dispute is resolved by the District Court at the place of residence of the children, after the court has heard them where they have completed ten years of age.'

The Bulgarian Family Code does not provide for an opportunity the child to be heard in two cases: an agreement on parental responsibilities and a contact regime in divorce based on mutual consent and in procedures for discharge of parental responsibilities. However, the general rule of the Child Protection Act (Art. 15) could be applied also in these cases.

---

11 F. APS, 'De procedures inzake voogdij en het hoorrecht van minderjarigen', in: P. SENAEVE, J. GERLO and F. LIEVENS (eds.), *De hervorming van het voogdijrecht*, Antwerpen: Intersentia, 2002, p. 269-291; H. CASMAN, 'De nieuwe voogdijwet', *Not. Fisc. M.* 2001, p. 245.

12 Art. 75 Belgian LJP as modified by Belgian Law of 10.03.1999; K. HERBOTS, 'De minderjarige als toeschouwer in de rechtszaal. Beschouwingen aangaande de Wet van 10 maart 1999', *E.J.*, 1999, p. 82.

CZECH REPUBLIC

Generally, the child has a right to be heard in any proceedings that relate to essential matters relating to the child (Sec. 31 § 3 Czech Family Code). In practice, the child is heard before the court if the parents dispute about placing the child into personal care (determination of residence) or when the parents dispute regulation of contact with the child. When the court approves a parental agreement the hearing of the child is not usually required, but the child's opinion is investigated by a social worker. When the court determines parental responsibility, the child's opinion is not found out in practice; the same applies to enforcement of the decision.

DENMARK

A child aged 12 or older must be heard before a decision is taken in a case concerning parental authority or contact unless this is considered detrimental to the child or without importance to the case, Art. 29 Danish Act on Parental Authority and Contact. If the child is younger than 12 he or she must be heard if the child is sufficiently mature and it is relevant for the case, Art. 29(2) Danish Act on Parental Authority and Contact. The provision also applies to decisions concerning enforcement. If the holder(s) of parental authority reaches/reach an agreement, the child is not heard as this does not constitute "a decision". Appointing (a) new holder(s) of parental authority will constitute "a decision". Parental authority cannot be discharged, but if child protection measures are taken, such as the placement of the child in care, the child must be heard regardless of his or her age the sufficient maturity of the child being the only criterion.[13] If the child is 15 or older he or she also has a right to legal representation in cases concerning child protection measures.[14]

ENGLAND & WALES

Outside the context of court proceedings the child has no right to be heard. However, where the issue is contested and a Sec. 8 order under the Children Act 1989 (*viz* a residence order, contact order, specific issue order or a prohibited steps order) is being sought then, pursuant to Sec. 1(3)(a) of the Children Act 1989, it is mandatory for the court to have regard to

> 'the ascertainable wishes and feelings of the child concerned (considered in the light of his age and understanding)'.

In any event, according to Sec. 7 of the 1989 Act the court when considering any question with respect to a child under the 1989 Act ask either CAFCASS[15] officer, or a local authority to report to the court "on such matters relating to the

---

13 Art. 58 Danish Act on Social Services.

14 Art. 60(3) Danish Act on Social Services.

15 *I.e.* the Children and Family Court and Advisory Service which, as from April 2001, has been responsible for providing what were formerly known as welfare officers and who are now known as children and family reporters.

welfare of that child as are required to be dealt with in the report". The officers concerned do not represent the child but merely report on the circumstances.

Although it is established that judges have the power to interview children in private[16] the general view seems to be that it is a practice that should not be readily undertaken. In any event it is a matter entirely at the judge's discretion.[17] If a judge does interview a child in private he cannot promise confidentiality and for that very reason should be cautious in agreeing to see the child in such circumstances.[18]

So far as children being directly heard by the court is concerned the normal rule is that a child may begin and prosecute family proceedings only by a next friend and may defend proceedings only by a guardian ad litem.[19] However, in any family proceedings where it appears to the court that the child should be separately represented,[20] the child can be made a party to the proceedings. In such a case the court will normally refer the matter to CAFCASS Legal.

As mentioned in answer to Q 2d and Q 8f, a child may bring or defend proceedings him or herself where he has obtained leave of the court to do so, or where a solicitor considers that the child is able, having regard to his understanding to give instructions in relation to the proceedings and has accepted instructions from the child to act for him or her.[21] Before granting leave to the child the court has to be satisfied that the child has sufficient understanding to participate as a party to the particular proceedings.[22]

FINLAND

The way and extent children are heard depends on the case. One can differentiate four situations:

1. Parents are in agreement about custody and/or right of access.
2. Parents are not in agreement about custody, residence or right of access, or the child does not live with its parents.
3. Enforcement proceedings.
4. Care proceedings.

In cases concerning child custody or right of access (situation 1), the wishes and opinions of the child shall only be sought if the parents are not in agreement, if the child has actually been cared for by someone who is not a parent, or if the child's clarification is deemed to be well-founded in considering the best

16 See *e.g. Re W (Child: Contact)* [1994] 1 FLR 843, and *Re M (A Minor)(Justices' Discretion)* [1993] 2 FLR 706.

17 See *Re R (A Minor)(Residence: Religion)* [1993] 2 FLR 163, CA.

18 *B v B (Minors)(Interviews and Listing Arrangements)* [1994] 2 FLR 489, 496, CA.

19 Rule 9.2, Family Proceedings Rules 1991.

20 See the leading case, *Re A (Contact: Separate Representation)* [2001] 1 FLR 715.

21 Rule, 9.2A, Family Proceedings Rules 1991, and *Practice Direction* [1993] 1 FLR 668. See also *Re T (A Minor)(Child Representation)* [1994] Fam 49, CA.

22 See *e.g. Re S (A Minor)(Representation)* [1993] 2 FLR 437, CA.

interests of the child (Sec. 11 Finnish Child Custody and Right of Access Act). Thus, if the parents bring a mutual agreement to the court, the child's views or wishes are normally not sought. The same applies to the local social authority when it approves the parental agreement (Sec. 8 Finnish Child Custody and Right of Access Act). However, parents are supposed to take the views and wishes of their child into consideration when they make decisions on his or her custody (Sec. 4 para. 2 Finnish Child Custody and Right of Access Act, see Q 9 above).

The views and wishes of the child shall be sought if the court is dealing with a child custody or right of access dispute (situation 2). The child's opinion shall be carefully clarified in a way that does not harm the child's and parents' mutual relationship (Sec. 11 para. 2 Finnish Child Custody and the Right of Access Act). Normally the child's views are clarified by social workers or a psychologist in connection with the preparation of the social report.

The child's views have a special importance in enforcement proceedings (situation 3), as the enforcement may not happen against the child's will if the child is 12 years of age or has reached such a maturity that its will can be taken into consideration (Sec. 2 Finnish Act of the Enforcement of a Decision on Child Custody and Right of Access).[23]

In care proceedings a child of 12 years of age has a sort of party position (situation 4). If a child of that age has not been heard or opposes being taking into care, the decision of the local social authority shall be submitted to the administrative court (Sec. 17). A child of 12 also has the right to appeal against certain decisions, such as against a care order (Sec. 35 para. 2 Finnish Child Protection Act). According to the general principles of the Finnish Child Protection Act the child's views and wishes shall be taken in consideration in connection with all child protection measures (Sec. 9 and 10 Finnish Child Protection Act).

FRANCE

The new principle stated in Art. 388-1 French CC (since the Act of No. 93-22 of 8 January 1993) is that the minor child can be heard before the court or before the person appointed by the court, in any proceedings related to the child. The only condition is that the child is *capable de discernement* (capable to understand). If the child requests to be heard, the judge can only deny this hearing with a specifically reasoned decision. The child can be heard alone, with a lawyer or

---

23 The Supreme Court of Justice decided in 2001 to vest the custody of two siblings to the female partner of their deceased mother instead of their biological father who lived abroad. The children, who were 12 years old and above, had repeatedly expressed their will not to leave Finland, where they had been staying with their mother for several years (KKO 2001:110). The court found that it was according to the best interests of these children not to give the custody to the father because this kind of decision could not have been enforced against the children's will anyway.

another person of his choice. If this choice does not appear to be consistent with the child's interests, the judge can appoint another person. The child does not become party to the proceedings even if she or he is heard (Art. 388-1 para. 3 French CC).[24]

In some proceedings the child's interests can be contrary to the ones of his legal representatives. In such cases the guardianship court judge or the court that has the power to decide on the claim shall appoint a special administrator for the child. The special administrator will then represent the child in the pending proceedings (Art. 388-2 French CC). This special administrator does not have more powers than the child. This is why neither the minor child nor the administrator are allowed to file a third party opposition (*tierce opposition)* to the judicial decision on parental responsibilities (since the legal provisions do not mention the child under the persons entitled to claim for a modification of the exercise of parental responsibilities).[25] The court appointed special administrator can himself or herself appoint a lawyer to represent the child and defend his interests in the pending proceedings.[26] The child automatically obtains legal aid (Art. 9.1 , Act of 10 July 1991).

In the more special cases in which the family judge has to decide on the methods of the exercise of parental responsibilities (and also contact rights) she or he can take into account (under several possible and additional criteria) the 'feelings expressed by the child under the conditions of Art. 388-1 French CC'. Therefore the child can be heard before court (either by the family judge or by a person appointed by this judge)[27] and be asked about his or her own feelings concerning the exercise of parental responsibilities. (Art. 373-2-11 French CC) The child's hearing does not oblige the court to take into account or to follow the child's wishes concerning the exercise of parental responsibilities[28]. If the child has already been heard before the court of first instance, the appellate court is not obliged to hear him again and will decide whether a new hearing would be useful or not.[29] If the court hears the child, it must specify in its decision whether the feelings expressed by the child during the hearing have been taken into account.[30]

---

24 The child is therefore not entitled to recourse against the judicial decision, see French Supreme Court, Civ. II, 25.10.1995, *Bull. civ.* II, No. 253; the child cannot require a modification of the decision, French Supreme Court, Ch. mixed, 09.02.2001, *JCP,* 2001. II. 10 514 annotated FOSSIER.

25 See French Supreme Court, Ch. mixed, 09.02.2001, *Bull. civ.* No. 1.

26 TGI La Roche-sur-Yon, 29.07.1993, *BICC,* 01.03.1994, No. 302.

27 See French Supreme Court, Civ. II, 05.06.1991, *Bull. civ.* II, No. 173: the judge must not personally hear the child himself. It is sufficient for him or her to mention in the decision that the child has been heard during the social inquiry.

28 French Supreme Court, Civ. II, 25.05.1993, *Bull. civ.* II, No. 185; CA Paris, 07.04.1999, *D.* 1999. IR. 142.

29 French Supreme Court, Civ. I, 02.04.1996, *Bull. civ.* No. 163.

30 French Supreme Court,. Civ. II, 20.11.1996, *D.* 1997. 192 annotated BENHAMOU; 25.02.1993, *Bull. civ.* II, No. 185 : the judge is not obliged to follow the child's feelings.

GERMANY

As regards the hearing of children in custody proceedings, § 50b Act on Voluntary Jurisdiction stipulates that the court shall hear a child personally in proceedings concerning the child's care or the administration of the child's assets if the inclination, ties or will of the child are of importance for the decision, or if it is indicated that the court have a direct impression of the child in order to determine the facts, § 50b para. 1 German Act on Voluntary Jurisdiction.

If the child is over fourteen the court must always hear the child personally in a proceeding on the child's care (§ 50b para. 2 sent. 1 German Act on Voluntary Jurisdiction). However, in court practice younger children are also heard regularly,[31] see Q 62. The residence of the child is an issue of the child's care. According to empirical data, in 88% of the cases the children were not heard where there was no application for sole custody. Where there was an agreed application for sole custody in nearly 70% of the cases the children were heard and in contested cases the children were regularly heard.[32] In proceedings concerning the child's assets the child must be personally heard, as far as this is indicated according to the nature of the affair (§ 50b para. 2 sent. 2 German Act on Voluntary Jurisdiction).

As far as no detriments for his or her development or education have to be feared, the child has to be informed on the subject of the proceedings and the possible outcome of the proceedings; the child has to be given an opportunity for expression, § 50b para. 2 sent. 3 German Act on Voluntary Jurisdiction. The court may refrain from a hearing only for serious reasons. This is indicated where the hearing itself could already harm the psychological balance of the child.[33] Where there is no hearing due to an imminent danger, there has to be a hearing at a later time, § 50b para. 3 German Act on Voluntary Jurisdiction. Since there is no precise enumeration of cases where children are heard this should occur in almost all cases relevant for their personal welfare.

GREECE

According to Art. 681c para. 3 Greek Code of Civil Procedure, the court, before deciding on issues concerning parental responsibilities or contact, will consider the opinion of the child, due attention being paid to the child's maturity. This is

---

31 See R. PROKSCH, *Rechtstatsächliche Untersuchung zur Reform des Kindesrechts*, Köln: Bundesanzeiger Verlag, 2002, p.269.

32 See R. PROKSCH, *Rechtstatsächliche Untersuchung zur Reform des Kindesrechts*, Köln: Bundesanzeiger Verlag, 2002, p 270 *et seq*. See also K. KOSTKA, 'Die Begleitforschung zur Kindschaftsrechtsreform - eine kritische Betrachtung', *FamRZ* 2004, 1924, 1932 *et seq*. - Former research showed that less than half of the children in child protection proceedings were heard personally. A quarter of those aged 14 to 17 were not heard. J. MÜNDER, B. MUTKE and R. SCHONE, *Kindeswohl zwischen Jugendhilfe und Justiz – Professionelles Handeln in Kindeswohlverfahren*, Münster: Votum 2000, p. 130 *et seq*.

33 H.-U. MAURER, 'Das Verfahren der Familiengerichte', in: D. SCHWAB, *Handbuch des Scheidungsrechts*, 5th Edition, München: Vahlen, 2004, Part. I No. 458 *et seq*.

in accordance with Art. 1511 para. 3 Greek CC, which provides that the opinion of the child must be sought and taken into consideration before any decision is taken concerning parental care (Art. 1511 para. 3 Greek CC), at the same time expanding its field of application, so that it not only covers issues of parental care but also any matter which has an impact on the child. The hearing of the child is obligatory as far as the court is concerned, even in cases concerning conservatory measures, provided that the child has sufficient maturity.[34] Nevertheless, the Supreme Court considers that the maturity of the child is a factual matter, so that final decisions are not subject to an appeal in cassation. It further accepts that the courts do not need to justify explicitly why the child has not been heard: when the child is not heard, it is assumed that the court has determined that the child was not sufficiently mature in order to form an opinion on the issue in question.[35] In this way the importance of hearing the child is moderated. This has therefore been criticised by legal literature.[36]

HUNGARY

A dispute can emerge not only between the parents, but also between the parents and a child in the matter of parental responsibilities, the child's residence or the contact. If the competent authority is to decide these cases, or if the parents' agreement concerning these matters requires the consent of the authority, a minor capable of forming his or her own views must be heard. This rule has to be applied in cases before both the court and the public guardianship authority, both in the original decision and in a revision of the decision or the approved agreement.

The court is obliged to hear a child over 14; a child younger than 14 is also to be heard if the child is capable of judgment and the child demands it. It seems to be an exception from the rule for the child over 14 to be heard concerning his or her residence (placement) if the parents' have an agreement on the issue. This exceptional rule has application in a divorce by consent, as one of the legal conditions of the divorce by consent is that the parents agree on the residence of the child and contact with the child.

---

34 P. ARVANITAKIS, in: K. KERAMEUS, D. KONDULIS and N. NIKAS (eds.), *Commentary on the Code of Civil Procedure, Vol. II (Arts. 591-1054)*, Athens–Komotini: Ant. N. Sakkoulas, Art. 681c Greek Code of Civil Procedure, p. 1311, No. 4 [in Greek]. This opinion is followed by the courts. See Supreme Court Decisions: 15/1997, *Elliniki Dikaiosini* Vol. 38 (1997), p. 1538, 180/1986, *Elliniki Dikaiosini* Vol. 27 (1986), p. 496, 577/1989, *Elliniki Dikaiosini* Vol. 31 (1990), p. 1271.

35 Relevant decision of the Supreme Court: 15/ 1997, *Elliniki Dikaiosini* Vol. 38 (1997), p. 1538, 283/1986, *Elliniki Dikaiosini* 27 (1986), p. 1288, 577/1989, *Elliniki Dikaiosini* Vol. 31 (1990), p. 1271, 180/1986, *Elliniki Dikaiosini* Vol. 27 (1986), p. 496.

36 See among others, S. KOUKOULI-SPILIOTOPOULOU, in: A. GEORGIADIS and M. STATHOPOULOS (Eds.), *Civil Code commentary, Vol. VIII, Family Law (Arts. 1505-1694)*, 2nd Edition, Athens: Law & Economy, P. N. SAKKOULAS, 2003, p. 126-127 No. 268-271; E. KOUNOUGERI-MANOLEDAKI, *Family Law*, Vol. II, 3rd Edition, Athens-Thessaloniki: SAKKOULAS, 2003, p. 272.

If the contact is arranged through the child-welfare mediation, a child over 12 is to be heard and children below 12 who are capable to form their own views are to be heard only if it is proposed by the parties or the public guardianship authority. Generally, if contact is not arranged in a mediation proceeding, a child over 14 is to be heard and children younger than 14 who are capable of forming their own views will only be heard at the discretion of the judge. A claim for arranging contact can even be filed by a child himself or herself if the child is over 14.

IRELAND

Sec. 25 Irish Guardianship of Infants Act 1964 allows the Irish court to hear children (when it decides upon parental responsibilities, the child's residence or contact), as it feels appropriate and practicable having regard to the age and understanding of the child. That said, in the light of the negative impact of court hearings upon children, the overriding preference of Irish judges has been to exclude children from legal proceedings. Indeed, both the Irish Child Care Act 1991[37] and the amended Irish Guardianship of Infants Act 1964[38] allow the court to hear cases concerning the welfare of children in those children's absence. While a child may apply to be present at a hearing, the court may exclude such child if, having regard to his or her age and the nature of the proceedings, it feels that it would not be in the child's interest to allow him or her to be present. The preference in Ireland is to hear children indirectly through either a specially appointed expert or evidence gathered by means of a social report.

ITALY

A minor with the ability to maturely judge has the right to be heard in all proceedings that can affect his or her life and growth, according to the principles established by the Convention of New York of 1989 dealing with the rights of the child.

LITHUANIA

According to Art. 3.164 Lithuanian CC, in considering any question related to a child, the child, if capable of formulating his or her views, must be heard directly or, where that is impossible, through a representative. Thus it is the duty of a court (as well, as of any other institution, including bailiffs), imposed by mandatory legal rule, to hear the child in all the above-mentioned cases, including the enforcement procedure.

THE NETHERLANDS

In cases concerning minors, the judge will not decide before having offered the possibility to the minor of twelve years or older to express its opinion, unless in the judge's view it is a case of minor importance. The judge may offer the minor

---

37 Sec. 30 Irish Child Care Act 1991.

38 Sec. 27 Irish Guardianship of Infants Act 1964, as inserted by Sec. 11 Irish Children Act 1997.

a possibility to express its opinion in a way that the judge will decide (Art. 809 § 1 Dutch Code of Civil Procedure). In practice children are not always heard.[39] In particular, where parents agree on these issues, judges tend not to hear the children concerned. However, in divorce proceedings the court may give an order *ex officio* when it appears to the court that a minor aged twelve or older may appreciate this. Practice in the various courts differs with regard to the minimum age a child can be heard. The District Court in Arnhem always hears children older than 12.[40]

NORWAY

When the court decides on parental responsibilities, residence or contact, the child has a right to be heard. The general rule in Art. 31 Norwegian Children Act 1981 is that from the age of seven, the child shall be heard before decisions are taken in personal matters. It is expressly stated that this shall be done in cases concerning the permanent residence of the child. It is further added that when the child has reached the age of twelve 'great importance shall be attached to the child's wishes'. In a recent case[41] where the issue was whether a decision on contact rights should be reviewed, the question arose as to whether the child's right to be heard should be an absolute right, or if this right could be set aside where it was contrary to the best interests of the child. It was decided that the best interests of the child should be given priority.

POLAND

Art. 72 sec. 3 Polish Constitution formulates a general rule, according to which provides that when assessing a child's rights, the public authorities and persons responsible for the child should hear and, to the extent possible, take the child's opinion into consideration. The family court may order the presence of a person under parental authority or under guardianship, as well as forcibly bring the person to a court session (Art. 574 Polish Civil Procedure Code). The court may also exclude the minor from being present during the proceedings, should it find the minor's presence inappropriate (Art. 573 § 2 Polish Civil Procedure Code).

Legal literature indicates that to safeguard the minor's interest, the court should inquire about the child's opinion, taking into consideration the child's maturity and the character of the case.[42]

PORTUGAL

Under the terms of Art. 175 No. 1 Portuguese Child Protection Law, the judge may authorise the child to attend the meeting in which parental responsibility will be regulated, taking into account his or her age and maturity. The law does

---

39 B.E.S. CHIN-A-FAT, *Scheiden (ter)echter zonder rechter, een onderzoek naar de meerwaarde van scheidingsbemiddeling*, 2004, p. 432-433.

40 M.J.C. KOENS/C.G.M. VAN WAMELEN, *Kind en scheiding*, 2001, p. 79.

41 Rt. 2004 p. 811.

42 Supreme Court judgment of 15.12.1998, I CKN 1122/98.

not establish an age at which a minor may or should be heard. As regards the other situations, although the law is silent it appears that the judge should hear the minor unless there are ponderous circumstances that militate against it.

RUSSIA

The level of the child's participation in reaching an agreement between his or her parents and in resolving problems in court is largely the same. Russian legislation follows the UN Convention of granting children the right to express their opinion, irrespective of the child's age. Therefore, a child has the right to express his or her opinion with regard to any decision made by the parents which effects the child's interests, as soon as the child is able to formulate such an opinion (Art. 57 Russian Family Code). The child has the same right in any administrative or court procedure. The age of the child is only relevant when it comes to evaluating his or her opinion.

SPAIN

The general right of the child to be heard is established in the UN Convention on the rights of the child, which was ratified by Spain in 1990, and in further legislation on the rights of children like Art. 9 *Ley Orgánica de protección jurídica del menor* or its Catalan Counterpart, Art. 11 *Llei d'atenció a la infancia i l'adolescència*.

The right of the child to be heard is, however, implemented inconsistently by the courts because there are no clear general guidelines on how and when children must be heard. In matrimonial procedures, for example, it is established that children are always to be heard if they are older than twelve or have attained a sufficient degree of maturity in the case of younger children. When it comes to the discharge of parental responsibilities there is no such provision and the Supreme Court has held that children need not necessarily be heard even if they are older than twelve.[43]

SWEDEN

Regard shall be paid to the wishes of the child, taking the child's age and maturity into account, Children and Parents Code, Chapter 6, Section 2 b. The obligation to investigate the wishes of the child, as far as possible, applies to court proceedings concerning custody, residence and contact, as well as to the work of the Social Welfare Committee.[44]

Paying regard to the wishes of the child does not, however, necessarily entail that the child is personally heard. The court shall ensure that questions regarding custody, residence and contact are properly investigated by instructing the social welfare committee to appoint a person to make inquiries into the matter, Chapter 6 Sec. 19 Swedish Children and Parents Code. The person conducting inquiries shall, if it is not inappropriate, seek to ascertain the

---

43 STS of 25 June 1994.

44 G. WALIN and S. VÄNGBY, *Föräldrabalken, En kommentar, Del I, 1-13 kap.*, Stockholm: Norstedts Juridik, 2002, p. 6:22.

views of the child and report them to the court (para. 4). In less complicated matters *e.g.* in connection with cooperative discussions where there is no deep conflict between the parents, an indirect picture of the child's situation through the parents' descriptions can be sufficient. However, direct contact with the child is often required in order to secure the child's right to be heard in matters concerning the child.[45] Furthermore, the child may be heard before the court if there are special reasons for doing so and it is clear that it will not harm the child to be heard (para. 5). Research indicates, however, that children are not heard to the extent desirable.[46] In 2002, a parliamentary committee was appointed to consider rules guaranteeing children the opportunity to be heard and have their wishes taken into account.

As to enforcement, the present law contains no explicit provision on the child's right to be heard, save the provision in Chapter 21 Sec. 5 Swedish Children and Parents Code. According to this provision, enforcement may not be ordered contrary to the wishes of a child who has reached the age of twelve years, unless the administrative county court considers the enforcement necessary for the best interests of the child. The same also applies in respect to a younger child who has attained such a degree of maturity that his or her wishes should be taken into account.

SWITZERLAND

Based on the direct applicability of Art. 12 UN Convention of the Rights of the Child (CRC), the child must be heard in all proceedings in which issues concerning the child are dealt with, unless the child's age or other just causes go against hearing the child. This principle is also explicitly established in Art. 144 § 2 Swiss CC and Art. 314 Section 1 Swiss CC.

---

45 *Vårdnad, Boende och Umgänge*, Stockholm: Socialstyrelsen (National Board of Health and Welfare) 2003, p. 83.

46 See: L. DAHLSTRAND, *Barns deltagande i familjerättsliga processer*, Uppsala 2004.

QUESTION 60

H. PROCEDURAL ISSUES

How will the child be heard (e.g. directly by the competent authority, a specially appointed expert or social worker)?

AUSTRIA

Generally, the child will be heard directly by the judge. However, the child may also be heard by the youth welfare agency, by representatives of the juvenile court assistance office or by other appropriate means, such as by experts (*e.g.* persons trained in education and psychology or social workers), if the child has not yet reached the age of 10 years, if his or her development or health condition so requires, or if it is not expected that the child will otherwise express his or her sincere and uninfluenced opinion (Sec. 105 (1) Non-Contentious Proceedings Act *[Außerstreitgesetz]*).

BELGIUM

Variances exist between the child's different rights to be heard. Art. 931 Belgian Judicial Code represents the 'general law' of the hearing of the child and is generally applicable. The hearing of the child according to Art. 51(1) Belgian LJP takes place according to this principle. Art. 1233 Belgian Judicial Code explicitly refers to Art. 931(6)-(7) Belgian Judicial Code. The other modalities according to Art. 931(3)-(5) Belgian Judicial Code are not automatically applicable, except when the child is heard between the ages of 12 or 15 years.[1] When Art. 56 *bis* Belgian LJP does not provide specific rules concerning the modalities of hearing, the Juvenile Court can apply the common modalities of Art. 931 Belgian Judicial Code, as long as these are compatible with the specific rules of the Belgian LJP.[2]

Art. 931(3) Belgian Judicial Code explicitly states that the child can be heard directly by the competent authority or by the person this authority designates. The competent authority is free to designate the person he judges qualified (doctor, psychologist, social worker, ...), excepting the Public Prosecutor. Neither Art. 56*bis* Belgian LJP nor Art. 1233 Belgian Judicial Code provides this possibility. Therefore it is agreed that the child must be heard by the competent

---

1 F. APS, 'De procedures inzake voogdij en het hoorrecht van minderjarigen', in: P. SENAEVE, J. GERLO and F. LIEVENS (eds.), *De hervorming van het voogdijrecht*, Antwerp: Intersentia, 2002, p. 270, No. 613 and p. 284, No. 642.

2 B. POELMANS, Het hoorrecht van minderjarigen in P. SENAEVE and W. PINTENS, *De hervorming van de echtscheidingsprocedure en het hoorrecht van de minderjarige*, Antwerp: Maklu, 1997, p. 78.

authority; no other person can be designated.[3] The hearing will happen in a suitable place.[4]

Neither the parties, nor their lawyers, nor the Public Prosecutor can be present during the hearing, whether the child is heard by the competent authority or by another designated person (Art. 931(3) Belgian Judicial Code). This refusal to admit the parties or their lawyers during the hearing of the child is criticised because it would be against the principles of of a fair trial (Art. 6(1) ECHR).[5] Although the child is principally heard alone, Art. 931(6) Belgian Judicial Code provides that the child can be assisted by a doctor, a social worker, a psychologist, a lawyer if it appears to be opportune. When the competent authority hears the child itself, a registrar must be present to make a record.

The competent authority must make a written record of the hearing of the child (Art. 931(7) and 1233 Belgian Judicial Code). This is necessary to respect the rights of defense of the parties, who must have the ability to respond to the hearing, and for the Judge on appeal, who must take notice of this hearing. The parties, as well as their lawyers, may take notice of the record of hearing, but no copy may be delivered. Art. 931 Belgian Judicial Code does not explicitly provide that the hearing must be recorded in its entirety. Therefore, some authors consider that, not only is there no obligation to do so, the child has the ability to ask that certain declarations not be recorded.[6] This tendency is criticised by the majority of the authors, who consider that this is against the rights of defense and the principles of a fair trial.[7] In practice, it appears that the judges are reluctant to record the whole hearing and mostly limit the record to a

3 Court of First Instance of Liege, 27.01.1995, *J.D.J.*, 1997, No. 164, p. 170; Juvenile Court Ghent, 14.12.1994, *E.J.* 1995, 92, annotated A. WYLLEMAN; F. APS, 'De procedures inzake voogdij en het hoorrecht van minderjarigen', in: P. SENAEVE, J. GERLO and F. LIEVENS (eds.), *De hervorming van het voogdijrecht*, Antwerp: Intersentia, 2002, p. 285, No. 646; B. POELMANS, 'Het hoorrecht van minderjarigen', in: P. SENAEVE and W. PINTENS, *De hervorming van de echtscheidingsprocedure en het hoorrecht van de minderjarige*, Antwerp: Maklu, 1997, p. 97 No. 143.

4 Art. 931(7) and 1233 Belgian Judicial Code, but also Art. 56*bis* Belgian LJP by lack of other legal regulation.

5 S. DEMARS, 'Questions controversées relatives à l'application de la loi du 30 juin 1994 modifiant les procédures de divorce', *J.T.* 1995, p. 825; J. VAN COMPERNOLLE, 'La justice familiale et les principes fondamentaux du droit judiciaire', in: *Familles et Justice, Justice civile et évolution du contentieux familial en droit comparé*, Brussels: Bruylant, 1997, p. 396.

6 C. MAES, C. STAPPERS, L. BOUTELIGIER, D. DEGRANDE and J. VAN GILS, *Mogen wij nu iets zeggen ? Over kinderen, echtscheiding en hun recht om gehoord te worden*, Bruges: Die Keure, 1996, 28.

7 B. POELMANS, 'Het hoorrecht van minderjarigen', in: P. SENAEVE and W. PINTENS, *De hervorming van de echtscheidingsprocedure en het hoorrecht van de minderjarige*, Antwerp: Maklu, 1997, p. 108-109, No. 169-171; J. VAN COMPERNOLLE, 'La justice familiale et les principes fondamentaux du droit judiciaire', in: *Familles et Justice, Justice civile et évolution du contentieux familial en droit comparé*, Brussels: Bruylant, 1997, p. 396.

summarizing of the hearing.[8] If the child is heard by another person, this person also has the obligation to make a written report of the hearing. The problem of the rights of defense when the hearing is not completely recorded does not rise in this case, because the competent authority does not possess more information than the parties.

BULGARIA

The child should be heard directly by the court but in the presence of social worker. As the Child Protection Act stipulates in Art. 15:

> '(3) Before the child is given a hearing, the court or the administrative body shall:
>
> 1) provide the child with the necessary information, which would help him or her form his or her opinion;
>
> 2) inform the child about the possible consequences of his or her desire, of the opinion supported by him or her, as well as about all the decisions made by the judicial or administrative body.
>
> (4) The hearing and the consultation of a child shall by all means take place in appropriate surroundings and in the presence of a social worker or another appropriate specialist.'

CZECH REPUBLIC

The manner in which the child is heard in proceedings depends on the age of the child, the individual matter and the judge's view. Individual courts differ in approach, but the child over twelve is usually heard directly before the court in matters relating its placement of care if the parents disagree, or in matters relating to regulation of contact between the parent and the child. The child's opinion (even of the younger one) is always ascertained orally by a social worker when an authority of social and legal protection prepares a report for the court. When there is a dispute over placing the child into personal care the court often orders an expert's opinion to be made, then a certified expert talks to the child. However, the court is not bound by conclusions of the expert's report.

DENMARK

The idea is that it takes the form of a conversation, Art. 29 Danish Act on Parental Authority and Contact. The child will be heard by the judge or in cases before the administrative authorities by a caseworker. It is possible in more complicated cases to have assistance from a social worker or an appointed expert. In some cases the expert may hear the child alone. For older children experts are used less often.[9]

---

8 *E.g.* Juvenile Court of Brussels; see B. POELMANS, 'Het hoorrecht van minderjarigen', in P. SENAEVE and W. PINTENS, *De hervorming van de echtscheidingsprocedure en het hoorrecht van de minderjarige*, Antwerp: Maklu, 1997, p. 109-110, No. 171.

9 I. LUND-ANDERSEN, N. MUNCK and I. NØRGAARD, *Familieret*, Copenhagen: Jurist- og Økonomforbundets Forlag, 2003, p. 88-89.

ENGLAND & WALES

Unless the child is made a party to proceedings or unless the child is interviewed in privately by the judge (which, as the answer to Q 59 points out, is generally discouraged) the child is not directly heard by the court at all. Instead his views will be reported to the court in a welfare report ordered under Sec. 7, Children Act 1989. In other words those views are conveyed to the court by a CAFCASS officer (the Children and Family Reporter) or by a social worker on behalf of the local authority. It is also possible that a child's views could be reported upon to the court by any expert appointed to act in the case.

If the child is made a party to the proceedings[10] then, unless he is of sufficient understanding to give instructions when he or she can appear in person, he will be represented by a guardian ad litem.

FINLAND

If a child custody or right of access dispute is dealt with by the court, the child can only be heard by the court in special circumstances. The hearing of the child must be necessary for the resolution of the case, and the child must agree to be heard by the court. Moreover it must be evident that the hearing cannot harm the child in question (Sec. 15 para. 2 Finnish Child Custody and the Right of Access Act).

Normally the child is heard by the social worker connected with the preparation with the report for the court. Many communities and municipalities also use psychologists, and in difficult cases child psychiatrists, to clarify the child's wishes and views as well as to discover the child's inner bonds with parents and siblings.[11]

In an enforcement procedure the child is heard by the mediator who has been appointed for the enforcement dispute (Sec. 7 Finnish Act of the Enforcement of a Decision on Child Custody and Right of Access). If a mediator is to be appointed for the case, the hearing of the child must be resolved *in casu*. In the care procedure, a child of 12 years of age or more is heard by a social worker. The hearing shall be officially documented (Sec. 17 para. 1 Finnish Child Protection Act).

FRANCE

The child can be heard either directly by the judge who decides on parental responsibilities or by a person appointed by this judge. This person can be, among others, a social worker in charge of the social inquiry[12] or another judge at the court. See Art. 388-1 French CC.

---

10 The power to do this is conferred by Rule 9.2, Family Proceedings Rules 1991 and see *Re A (Contact: Separate Representation)* [2001] 1 FLR 715.

11 S. TASKINEN, *Lapsen etu erotilanteessa,* Oppaita 24, STAKES Sosiaali- ja terveysalan tutkimus- ja kehittämiskeskus: Helsinki, 2001, p. 71-75.

12 See French Supreme Court, Civ. II, 05.06.1991, *Bull. civ.* II, No. 173.

GERMANY

Where the child in the situations of § 50b para. 1, 2 sent. 1 and 2 German Act on Voluntary Jurisdiction must be personally heard, this means that the court itself shall, as a rule, hear the child personally. Generally, the family judge will talk with the child.[13] The child has a constitutional right to be heard personally, generally orally.[14] As far as it is possible the child has to be informed in an appropriate manner about the subject and the possible results of the proceedings (§ 50b para. 2 sent. 2 German Act on Voluntary Jurisdiction).

GREECE

According to Art. 681c para. 2 Greek Code of Civil Procedure, the competent social service will investigate the living conditions of the child. This may include seeking the opinion of the child. Nevertheless, from the formulation of Art. 681c Greek Code of Civil Procedure it is concluded that the judge should also hear the child him or herself during the (main) proceedings.

HUNGARY

Of course the child has to be heard directly and personally during the Child-Welfare mediation. In other cases it is up to the discretion of the court or the public guardianship authority whether the child is heard personally or indirectly through experts. In proceedings before the public guardianship authority the expert can be also the education advising service, but in judicial proceedings the expert may only be the specially appointed psychologist. Both the court and the public guardianship authority can order that the child has to be heard in the absence of the parents.

In proceedings concerning the child's residence, expert opinions are not only demanded with regard to children being capable of forming their own views; lacking a parental agreement, the court's judgment is usually based on these experts' opinions.

IRELAND

Sec. 11 Irish Children Act 1997, which inserts a new Sec. 25 into the Guardianship of Infants Act 1964, allows the Irish Court, as it thinks appropriate and practicable having regard to the age and understanding of the child, to take account of his or her wishes in any parental responsibilities proceedings. The overall strategy in Ireland is to minimise the child's exposure to the court process, which, on occasion, occurs at the expense of ensuring that the child is adequately represented in court. Consequently, children are rarely heard directly in court unless they are of sufficient age and understanding. Instead, other methods are used to enable a child's voice to be heard in the judicial process, without requiring the child to be physically present in court. Such methods include a specially appointed child expert. Alternatively, and

---

13 See H.-U. MAURER, 'Das Verfahren der Familiengerichte', in: D. SCHWAB, *Handbuch des Scheidungsrechts*, 5th Edition, München: Vahlen, 2004, Part. I No. 452 *et seq.*

14 BVerfG, 14.08.2001, *FamRZ* 2002, 229.

more frequently in Ireland, the court may request a social report in respect of children who are the subject of parental responsibilities proceedings. Such a report allows evidence relating to the children's welfare to be collected, without necessarily requiring the children to appear in court. These reports are normally carried out by social workers and may be requested on an application by a party to the proceedings, although, as previously stated, the court may request such a report of its own motion.

Provision is also made in Irish law for the appointment by the court of a guardian *ad litem* to act on behalf of any child in private law proceedings involving:

- the custody of, or access to, a child; or
- an application for guardianship by a natural father.

That said, Sec. 28 Irish Guardianship of Infants Act 1964, as inserted by Sec. 11 of the Children Act 1997, which allows for such an appointment to be made, is not yet in force. The circumstances in which a guardian *ad litem* may be appointed in such proceedings are, however, very limited. The court must be satisfied that 'special circumstances' exist necessitating the appointment of the guardian *ad litem*, a formula that obviously precludes such an appointment being made in all but the most pressing of cases. In parental responsibilities proceedings and in disputes concerning the child's residence or contact there is no explicit provision allowing for the addition of a child as a party to the proceedings. The Irish courts, however, possess a residual jurisdiction to do so, and moreover, can appoint a solicitor to act on the child's behalf. However, the prospect of such an occurrence taking place is quite slim.

ITALY

The minor can be heard either directly by the judge or by an expert appointed by the judge.

LITHUANIA

As a general rule, the child must be heard directly by the judge in oral proceedings. In the interests of the protection of the child's private life, such hearings are normally closed. If the court so decides, the teachers of the child or psychologist may take part in such a hearing. However, in exceptional circumstances *e.g.* in the event of the hospitalisation of the child, the child may be heard by the employees of the state institution for the protection of the rights of the child. In such a case, the state institution for the protection of the rights of the child shall present to the court all the necessary information (minutes *etc*).

THE NETHERLANDS

The child will be heard directly by the competent authority. Due to the fact that the court is under no duty to hear the child and there is no right of the child to be heard, there are no specific rules as to how the judge should hear the child.

If, however, the court has decided to hear the child, it does so in chambers and the judge will not wear a gown.[15]

NORWAY

Usually the child's opinion is given to the judge in a closed session, where none of the parties or their lawyers is present, Art. 61 No. 4 Norwegian Children Act 1981. The court may also appoint an expert or other suitable person to hear what the child has to say.

POLAND

A minor may be heard outside the courtroom, if deemed appropriate (Art. 576 § 2 Polish Civil Procedure Code).

PORTUGAL

The law says nothing about this (Art. 175 No. 1 Portuguese Child Protection Law). Jurisprudence has understood that the child may be heard either directly by the judge or indirectly through someone from the social services, and, in certain circumstances, by an expert.

RUSSIA

The problem is that the law grants the child the right 'to be heard in any judicial or administrative procedure' that affects its interests (Art. 57 Russian Family Code), but does not oblige the judge to involve the child. In practice this means that if the child is aware of his or her rights and asks the judge to be heard, the judge is obliged to hear that child; but the judge is not obliged to take the initiative himself or herself. The judge is also not obliged to inform the child of his or her right to be heard. Unfortunately, judges often consider it a waste of time to hear the child if the parents have already reached an agreement or if the child is younger than ten years old. The judges do not usually call young children to give evidence. A child is mostly heard by an inspector of the Department of Guardianship and Curatorship. A judge will only hear a child younger than ten himself or herself if there are special reasons to do so or if the child insists on being heard (which of course almost never occurs). Even in cases where no agreement as to the child's residence or contact has been reached by the parents, the judge often prefers to leave the hearing of the child to the Department of Guardianship and Curatorship in order to save court time and to spare the child from the emotional experience of being questioned in court. In cases regarding discharge or restriction of parental authority the children are heard by a judge more often. However, even there the judge is frequently satisfied with a report of the child's hearing made by the Department of Guardianship and Curatorship while investigating the circumstances of the child. Thus, if the child does not insist on being heard by the judge personally (even when he or she is not aware of this right), then being heard by the Department of Guardianship and Curatorship is considered to be acceptable. This Department is supposed to have experts specialised in child

---

15 M.J.C. KOENS/C.G.M. VAN WAMELEN, *Kind en scheiding*, 2001, p. 80.

psychology capable of hearing of children of different ages. In practice, however, this is not always the case, especially in the countryside.

SPAIN

Legislation on this matter is very scarce. The law just establishes that the child's right to privacy has to be protected (Art. 9 *Ley Orgánica de protección jurídica del menor*). The child is usually heard by the competent authority, the judge, in court but often not in an open court session. If the judge orders it, the child might be heard by an expert (psychologist or social worker) if such an expert is available, but there are no clear guidelines on the matter.[16]

SWEDEN

The child can be heard in various ways. Most frequently one or both parents report the opinion of the child to the deciding authority. The social welfare committee may decide to talk with the child on its own initiative, *e.g.*, in connection with cooperative discussions taking place between the parents.[17] When deciding upon custody issues , residence and contact the court may instruct the social welfare committee to appoint somebody to make inquiries, including the child's opinions unless it is inappropriate, and report it to the court.[18] The child may also be heard by the court, if there are special reasons for doing so and it is clear that it will not harm the child. This possibility is to be applied restrictively, the idea being that it is normally sufficient to present the child's viewpoint through an inquiry conducted by *e.g.* a social worker.[19]

SWITZERLAND

The child will be heard in person in a suitable manner by the competent (court) authority or by a third party appointed by the authority (Art. 144 § 2 and Art. 314 Section 1 Swiss CC). Consequently, it is up to the competent authority's discretion, which it is duty bound to exercise, whether the hearing should be carried out by the authority itself or by a third party. This depends on the age of the child in question and on the need for special knowledge in hearing the child. The Federal Supreme Court decided that as a rule the child is to be heard in person by the (court) authority and that this hearing should only be delegated in exceptional circumstances.[20] Nonetheless, a hearing by a(n) (external) specialist may be sufficient if the child was already heard in an assessment for an expert opinion (frequently carried out by medical specialist).

---

16 GUZMAN FLUJA- CASTILLEJO MANZANARES, *Los derechos del menor de edad en el ámbito del proceso civil*, Madrid, 2000, 105-118.

17 Cooperation discussions are described under Q 57.

18 Chapter 6 Sec. 19 para. 3 and 4 Swedish Children and Parents Code.

19 *Vårdnad, Boende och Umgänge*, Stockholm: Socialstyrelsen (National Board of Health and Welfare), 2003, p. 87.

20 BGE 127 II 295, 296 *et seq*; confirmed in the unpublished decision of the Federal Supreme Court of 18.12.2003, 5P.322/2003.

If possible, the child should be spared having to be heard several times by various specialists and authorities.[21]

[21] A. RUMO-JUNGO, 'Das Kind und die Scheidung seiner Eltern: ausgewählte Fragen', in: C. KAUFMANN and F. ZIEGLER (ed.), *Kindeswohl. Eine interdisziplinäre Sicht*, Zürich/Chur: Verlag Rüegger, 2003, p. 153.

QUESTION 61

H. PROCEDURAL ISSUES

How, if at all, is the child legally represented in disputes concerning:
(a) Parental responsibilities;
(b) The child's residence; or
(c) Contact?

AUSTRIA

(a) Parental responsibilities

In proceedings concerning parental responsibilities, each parent holding parental responsibilities is independently entitled to represent the child. If the parents fail to reach an agreement or the court fails to appoint one parent or a third party as representative pursuant to Sec. 176 Austrian CC, the parent who takes the first procedural step will be the child's representative (Sec. 154a Austrian CC). The right of sole representation based on taking the first action lasts until the decision that concludes the proceedings takes legal effect[1]. For minors represented in court by a legal representative, a special guardian (*Kollisionskurator,* Sec. 271 Austrian CC) must be appointed if a conflict of interests arises. However, this cannot be the youth welfare agency.[2]

In addition to the authority of the minor's legal representative to conduct legal proceedings in the name of the minor, minors over 14 years of age may also take legal actions on their own in proceedings concerning their care and education, including the arrangement of their residence as well as in proceedings on the right of contact, but not in proceedings on matters concerning the administration of property (Sec. 104(1) Non-Contentious Proceedings Act *[Außerstreitgesetz]*). The court must instruct and advise the minor appropriately as required by his or her capacity to understand; also, the child must be informed of any opportunities for advice that exist (Sec. 104(1) *Außerstreitgesetz*). In the event of contradictions between the substantive motions of the minor and those of the child's legal representative, the court is required to make the decision that best serves the interests of the child (Sec. 104(2) *Außerstreitgesetz*). A minor over 14 years of age who is capable of representing him- or herself in court proceedings independently may also independently select a representative, e.g. an attorney, for such proceedings. In practice, however, the youth welfare agency is most often used as a representative since no legal professional duty exists for custody proceedings and complicated legal problems seldom arise (Sec. 212(3) - (5) Austrian CC).[3]

---

1 I. HOLZHAMMER/R. HOLZHAMMER, *Ehe und Familie*, 2nd Edition, Freistadt: Plöchl Verlag, 2001, p. 73.

2 *Oberster Gerichtshof,* 25.02.2004, *Österreichische Juristenzeitung - EvBl,* 2004, No. 115, p. 557.

3 A. DEIXLER-HÜBNER, 'Die neuen familienrechtlichen Verfahrensbestimmungen', in: S. FERRARI/G. HOPF, *Reform des Kindschaftsrechts*, Vienna: Manz Verlag, 2001, p. 120.

(b) The child's residence

Since the arrangement of the child's residence constitutes part of the parental responsibilities, the comments made to Q 61a likewise apply to legal representation in disputes of this nature.

(c) Contact

The comments made to Q 61a likewise apply to legal representation in disputes regarding contact.

BELGIUM

(a) Parental responsibilities

Normally, a child is not personally and legally represented in disputes concerning parental responsibilities. It has the right to be heard in the circumstances described in Q 60, but is not a party to the case. Neither does it become a party to the case because of its hearing (Art. 931(7) Belgian Judicial Code).[4]

The interests of the child are represented by the Public Prosecutor, who is always present in hearings at the Juvenile Court and in hearings including children in front of the President of the Court of First Instance.[5] The Public Prosecutor has three determined tasks. First, he is the principal party every time public policy (the interests of the child) is threatened.[6] According to Art. 387*bis* Belgian CC, he has a general right of action before the Juvenile Court, notwithstanding the relationship of the parents. Beside that, Art. 138(2) Belgian Judicial Code provides that the Public Prosecutor intervenes in civil proceedings by legal action every time the law provides it and every time public policy requires it. Second, he is a joined party when he gives advice in the interests of the child.[7] That task is confirmed by Art. 138(2) Belgian Judicial Code, which provides that the Public Prosecutor can intervene not only by legal action, but also by advice. Third, he is the instructor of the civil procedure when, according to Article 872 Belgian Judicial Code, he collects the information demanded by the competent court.[8]

The possibility for a child to intervene voluntary in a dispute directly concerning it arose before the introduction of the right of hearing of the child by the Belgian Law of 30 June 1994. It had been suggested to tolerate the voluntary intervention of the child in order to give it the opportunity to be heard,

---

4 Court of Appeal of Brussels 09.02.1999, *J.T.* 2000, 150.

5 No Public Prosecutor is present at the court of the Justice of the Peace when interim measures between spouses are discussed.

6 According to Art. 1388 Belgian CC, the parental authority is from public policy.

7 When no advice is given by the Public Prosecutor, the judgment is null, according to Art. 765 Belgian CC.

8 Cass., 13.12.1990, *Pas.*, 1991, I, p. 367; Cass., 13.06.1997, *Pas.* 1997, I, p. 671, annotated A.-Ch. VAN GYSEL; A.-Ch. VAN GYSEL and J.-C. BROUWERS, 'Le rôle du ministère public dans les procédures civiles concernant l'enfant', *Rev. dr. ULB*, 1996, p. 35.

according to Art. 12 of the International Convention on the Rights of the Child.[9] This point of view had been accepted by certain courts.[10] However, since the introduction of the Belgian Law of 30 June 1994, this possibility must be excluded. Indeed, according to Art. 931(3)-(7) Belgian Judicial Code, the child has the possibility to ask to be heard when it is concerned by a dispute; that is the way it must express its point of view.[11] Moreover, once it has been heard the child has no right to intervene in the dispute opposing its parents.

The question of whether the child has the right to take the initiative of a legal action has been discussed. According to the classic theory, the incapacity of the minor does not exclude its action, but it must be protected. The action of a minor, therefore, does not cause the inadmissibility of its action, but must be regularized by its legal representative. The child acts correctly when it is represented by its legal representatives, but not when it acts itself.[12] When there is a conflict of interest between the child and its parents, Art. 378 Belgian CC provides that an *ad hoc* guardian must be designated by the competent authority. Certain courts even accept the voluntary intervention of the child,[13] referring to Art. 12 of the International Convention on the Rights of the Child, whose immediate applicability is recognised, but this is very exceptional, because a child is not qualified to act in justice. Finally, a proposal has been made according to which the child should have the right to intervene in proceedings that concern it (See Q 6).[14]

(b) The child's residence

See Q 61a.

(c) Contact

See Q 61a.

---

9 C. PANIER, 'Faire entendre sa parole en justice : un droit pour l'enfant?', *J.L.M.B.* 1992, 149-150; B. POELMANS, 'Het hoorrecht van minderjarigen', in: P. SENAEVE and W. PINTENS, *De hervorming van de echtscheidingsprocedure en het hoorrecht van de minderjarige*, Antwerp: Maklu, 1997, p. 116.

10 Court of Appeal of Liege 24.06.1992, *J.L.M.B.*, 1992, 1087; Court of Appeal of Mons 10.10.1993, *R.R.D.* 1993, 401; Court of Appeal of Antwerp 14.04.1994, *J.D.J.* 1995, No. 147, 322; also see C. PANIER, 'Faire entendre sa parole en justice: un droit pour l'enfant?', *J.L.M.B.*, 1994, p. 522-523.

11 For an application, see Court of Appeal of Liege, 09.01.1996, *J.L.M.B.*, 1996, 664.

12 Th. MOREAU, 'L'autonomie du mineur en justice', in: *L'autonomie du mineur*, Brussels: Publications des Facultés Universitaires Saint-Louis, 1998, p. 170.

13 Liege 23.04.2000, *J.L.M.B.*, 2000, p. 1085.

14 Projet de loi ouvrant l'accès à la justice aux mineurs, *Doc. Parl.* Chambre 19.07.2002, No. 50-1975/001, pour l'insertion d'un article 1237 *bis* dans le Code Judicaire; see www.lachambre.be, document 51K0643.

BULGARIA

(a) Parental responsibilities

No participation of a representative of the child is provided for in the proceedings with regard to parental rights (after the divorce, in the case of parent's separation, *etc.*). The child is not a party of the proceedings in such cases. It can only be given a hearing so that the court would be familiarised with the child's opinion if the requirements of Art. 15 of the Child Protection Act are involved. In Art. 15, § 7 of the Bulgarian Child Protection Act there is a provision that the Social Assistance Directorate may represent the child in cases provided for by law, however, no legislative act has yet provided for this type of opportunity.

(b) The child's residence

The child is not a party to the process. It can only be given a hearing so that the court will be familiarised with their opinion if the requirements of Art. 15 of the Child Protection Act are involved.

(c) Contact

The child is not a party to the process. It can only be given a hearing so that the court will be familiarised with their opinion if the requirements of Art. 15 of the Child Protection Act are involved.

CZECH REPUBLIC

(a) Parental responsibilities

It is a proceeding in matters relating to judicial care of minors (Sec. 176 and subs., Czech Code of Civil Procedure). The Czech Civil Procedure Code requires that the child shall always be a party to these proceedings. Due to the child's lack of capacity to sue and be sued, it must be represented in the proceedings. However, as a conflict of interest between the parents and the child might occur, the child must be represented by a custodian *ad litem* who defends the child's interests in the proceedings (Sec. 37 Czech Family Code).

(b) The child's residence

It is the proceeding in matters relating to judicial care of minors (Sec. 176 and subs., Czech Code of Civil Procedure). The Czech Civil Procedure Code requires that the child shall always be a party to these proceedings. Due to the child's lack of capacity to sue and be sued, he or she must be represented in the proceedings. However, as a conflict of interest between the parents and the child might occur, the child must be represented by a custodian *ad litem* who defends the child's interests in the proceedings (Sec. 37 Czech Family Code).

(c) Contact

It is the proceeding in matters relating to judicial care of minors (Sec. 176 and subs., Czech Code of Civil Procedure). The Czech Civil Procedure Code requires that the child shall always be a party to these proceedings. Due to the child's lack of capacity to sue and be sued, it must be represented in the proceedings. However, as a conflict of interest between the parents and the child might occur, the child must be represented by a custodian *ad litem* who defends the child's interests in the proceedings (Sec. 37 Czech Family Code).

DENMARK

(a) Parental responsibilities

The child has no other legal representation than the general representation of the holder (s) of parental authority.

(b) The child's residence

It is not possible to bring a dispute concerning residence before a court or administrative authority.

(c) Contact

The child has no other legal representation than the general representation of the holder (s) of parental authority.

ENGLAND & WALES

(a) Parental responsibilities

Unless the child is made party to proceedings, he or she will not be legally represented in proceedings concerning disputes over the exercise of parental responsibility. If the child is made a party to proceedings then he or she will be represented by a guardian *ad litem*, unless of sufficient understanding to instruct a solicitor him or herself, when proceedings can be brought in his or her own right.[15]

(b) The child's residence

Unless the child is made party to proceedings, he or she will not be legally represented in proceedings concerning disputes over residence. If the child is made a party to proceedings then he or she will be represented by a guardian ad litem, unless of sufficient understanding to instruct a solicitor him or herself, when proceedings can be brought in his or her own right.[16]

(c) Contact

Unless the child is made party to proceedings, he or she will not be legally represented in proceedings concerning disputes over contact. If the child is made a party to proceedings then he or she will be represented by a guardian

---

15 Rule 9.2A, Family Proceedings Rules 1991, and *Re T (A Minor)(Child Representation)* [1994] Fam 49, CA. But note even if a child is found competent leave might not always be granted see e.g. *Re H (Residence Order: Child's Application For Leave)* [2000] 1 FLR 789 in which leave was refused because it was felt that the child's views could be adequately represented in court by the father.

16 Rule 9.2A, Family Proceedings Rules 1991, and *Re T (A Minor)(Child Representation)* [1994] Fam 49, CA. But note even if a child is found competent leave might not always be granted see e.g. *Re H (Residence Order: Child's Application For Leave)* [2000] 1 FLR 789 in which leave was refused because it was felt that the child's views could be adequately represented in court by the father.

ad litem, unless of sufficient understanding to instruct a solicitor him or herself, when proceedings can be brought in his or her own right.[17]

FINLAND

(a) Parental responsibilities

In custody and right of access disputes the child is not positioned as a party and is therefore not represented in the dispute. In care proceedings the child is a party and may act as a party from the age of 15. The child may have its own attorney, if necessary. The social worker who is responsible in the case shall help the child, to obtain an attorney (Sec. 10 para. 3 Finnish Child Protection Act). The custodian is also the legal representative of the child, and in cases in which the child has gained the parallel right to represent itself at the age of 15, the custodian and the child may act independently. A child aged 12 or more has a right to be heard and a right to appeal against a care order. The care order shall be submitted to the administrative court if the child (12 or older), or the custodian of the child resists taking the child into care (Sec. 17 Finnish Child Protection Act).

In connection to care proceedings it is worth noting that the local social authority may make an application for a special appointed guardian for the child. The authority has a duty to take such measures if the custodian of the child does not seem to be able to represent the child because of an assumed conflict of interest between the custodian and the child (Sec. 10 Finnish Act concerning the Position and Rights of the Social Welfare Client). In enforcement proceedings the child is not considered a party and is thus not represented. In proceedings concerning the appointment of a guardian for a child, a child aged 15 or older must be given a possibility to be heard (Sec. 73 Finnish Guardianship Services Act).

(b) The child's residence

The rules concerning a custody dispute also apply to a dispute over a child's place of residence, as it is understood to be part of the concept of the custody of the child (see above). The same applies to the enforcement of the child's residence.

(c) Contact

The rules concerning the custody dispute of the child (see above point (a)) are also applicable to the private law dispute concerning contact or right of access. If the child has been taken into care and restrictions concerning its right to maintain contact are made, the general rules concerning the taking of the child's views into consideration according to the Finnish Child Protection Act (Sec. 10)

---

17 Rule 9.2A, Family Proceedings Rules 1991, and *Re T (A Minor)(Child Representation)* [1994] Fam 49, CA. But note even if a child is found competent leave might not always be granted see e.g. *Re H (Residence Order: Child's Application For Leave)* [2000] 1 FLR 789 in which leave was refused because it was felt that the child's views could be adequately represented in court by the father.

and to the Finnish Administrative Procedure Act (Sec. 14 para. 3) shall be applied.

FRANCE

(a) Parental responsibilities

In all issues of this kind, the child can be represented by his parents (holders of parental responsibilities). But if in any proceeding the minor child's interests appear to be contrary to those of his legal representatives (normally the father and mother) the guardianship-court judge or the judge who will decide on the issue raised in the proceedings shall appoint a special administrator (*administrateur ad hoc*) who will represent the child in the pending proceedings. The ad hoc administrator will be entitled to appoint a lawyer who will defend the child's interests.[18]

(b) The child's residence

Same answer as under Q 61a.

(c) Contact

Same answer as under Q 61a.

GERMANY

(a) Parental responsibilities

The child himself or herself is not a party in custody proceedings.[19] The child can, however, lodge an appeal without the help of a legal representative (§ 59 para. 1, 3 German Act on Voluntary Jurisdiction; see Q 62). In order to prevent a child from being simply the object of other persons' proceedings, the Child Law Reform Act of 1997 introduced the institution of a curator (*Verfahrenspfleger*) who shall act as an 'attorney of the child' (*Anwalt des Kindes*). The child can be legally represented in proceedings concerning parental responsibilities by appointment of such a curator, § 50 para. 1 German Act on Voluntary Jurisdiction. The court has to appoint a curator in proceedings concerning the 'person' of the child if it is necessary to safeguard the interests of the child. Proceedings concerning the 'person' are interpreted very broadly so that basically only proceedings concerning the assets of the child are not covered.[20]

The statute lists three different situations in a nonexclusive manner. The first situation, formulated as a general clause, is if there is a conflict of interests between the legal representative and the child (No. 1). The second is if there are measures necessary which can lead to a child's separation from his or her family, or to a total deprivation of parental care (No. 2). This can be a

---

18 TGI La Roche-sur-Yon, 29.07.1993, *BICC*, 01.03.1994, No. 302; CA Rouen, 25.05.1993, *BICC* ,01.11.1993, No. 1222.

19 BVerfG, 20.08.2004, *FamRZ* 2004, 86 = *NJW* 2003, 3544.

20 See A. HANNEMANN and P.-C. KUNKEL, 'Der Verfahrenspfleger - das ‚unbekannte Wesen', *FamRZ* 2004, 1833, 1834 note 15; R. PROKSCH, *Rechtstatsächliche Untersuchung zur Reform des Kindesrechts*, Köln: Bundesanzeiger Verlag, 2002, p. 248.

proceeding under § 1666 German CC (jeopardy to the welfare of the child).[21] The third situation concerns the removal of the child from a foster caregiver (§ 1632 para. 4 German CC) or the spouse, the registered partner or a person with a contact right (see § 1682 German CC). If the court does not appoint a curator it has to justify this in its decision concerning the child (§ 50 para. 1 sent. 2 German Act on Voluntary Jurisdiction). An appointment of a curator is not necessary or no longer necessary where the interests of the child can be reasonably represented by an attorney or another person in the proceedings (§ 50 para. 3 German Act on Voluntary Jurisdiction).

The institution of this special curator is not well defined in the law. Because the goal is not clear, it is not clear who is best to perform the task. It is also not clear what kind of qualifications or professional skills a curator should have.[22] There is also no clear guidance as to whether the curator must act for the actual interests of the child as they exist or should rather act with respect to the objective best interests of the child that are already represented by the youth office.[23] Therefore it is also not clear what direction the activities of the curator should take. The family courts appoint different groups of persons as curators, *e.g.* social workers, but also attorneys and in some cases even officials of the youth offices.[24] The courts sometimes seem to be reluctant to appoint such a curator.

(b) The child's residence

In the situations set out by § 50 para. 2 No. 2 German Act on Voluntary Jurisdiction, the welfare of the child is in jeopardy (§§ 1666, 1666a), see (a). By court order a separation from the family can be ordered. Therefore such a proceeding also concerns the child's residence. In the case of removal of the child from a foster person, the spouse, the registered partner or a person with a contact right (§ 50 para. 2 No. 3 German Act on Voluntary Jurisdiction), the residence of the child must also be decided. The appointment of a curator is also

---

21 M. COESTER, in: STAUDINGER, *Kommentar zum Bürgerlichen Gesetzbuch,* 13th Edition, Berlin, 2000, § 1666 German CC No. 210.

22 A. HANNEMANN and P.-C. KUNKEL, 'Der Verfahrenspfleger - das ‚unbekannte Wesen', *FamRZ* 2004, 1833, 1835.

23 For a child centered and against a 'neutral' position A. HANNEMANN and P.-C. KUNKEL, 'Der Verfahrenspfleger - das ‚unbekannte Wesen', *FamRZ* 2004, 1833, 1835. – See also L. M. PESCHEL-GUTZEIT, in: STAUDINGER, *Kommentar zum Bürgerlichen Gesetzbuch,* 13th Edition, Berlin: Gruyter, 2002, vor §§ 1626 *et seq* German CC No. 78. A. HANNEMANN and P.-C. KUNKEL, 'Der Verfahrenspfleger - das ‚unbekannte Wesen', *FamRZ* 2004, 1833 *et seq.* See also R. PROKSCH, *Rechtstatsächliche Untersuchung zur Reform des Kindesrechts,* Köln: Bundesanzeiger Verlag, 2002, p. 247 *et seq.*

24 A. HANNEMANN and P.-C. KUNKEL, 'Der Verfahrenspfleger - das ‚unbekannte Wesen', *FamRZ* 2004, 1833 *et seq.* See also R. PROKSCH, *Rechtstatsächliche Untersuchung zur Reform des Kindesrechts,* Köln: Bundesanzeiger Verlag, 2002, p. 247 *et seq.*

possible if there is a parental dispute that concerns only the residence of a child.[25]

(c) Contact

A proceeding on contact also concerns the 'person' of the child. Therefore the statutory provision on the appointment of a curator also applies here.[26]

GREECE

(a) Parental responsibilities

The child, in principle,[27] has no capacity to litigate in its own name and therefore needs to be represented in any proceedings in which it takes part. Normally, the holders of parental responsibilities are the legal representatives of the child (Art. 1510 para. 1 and 1603 Greek CC). Nevertheless, when litigation concerns issues of parental responsibilities, there is a conflict of interests between the parents and the child. In such cases the court will appoint a special guardian, whose task it is to represent the child in the particular dispute (Art. 1517 and 1627-1628 Greek CC). If the holders of parental responsibilities are more than one person and the conflict refers only to one of them, the other(s) may be appointed special guardian(s) in this case.[28] Relevant is also the provision of Art. 4 of the (1996) European Convention on the exercise of children's rights, which Greece has signed and ratified,[29] according to which the child itself has the right to apply for the appointment of this special representative.

(b) The child's residence

The determination of the child's residence forms an integral part of the care of the child. See above the answer to Q 61(a).

(c) Contact

The courts do not recognize a right of the child to contact. Nevertheless, the child may intervene in the relevant proceedings.[30]

---

25 See R. PROKSCH, *Rechtstatsächliche Untersuchung zur Reform des Kindesrechts*, Köln: Bundesanzeiger Verlag, 2002, p. 247.

26 See A. HANNEMANN and P.-C. KUNKEL, 'Der Verfahrenspfleger - das ,unbekannte Wesen', *FamRZ* 2004, 1833, 1836;

27 Nevertheless, the child who has limited capacity to enter into a transaction may litigate in its own name in the relevant disputes (Art. 63 para. 1 Greek Code of Civil Procedure).

28 P. AGALLOPOULOU, in: A. GEORGIADIS and M. STATHOPOULOS (eds.), *Civil Code commentary, Vol. VIII, Family Law (Arts. 1505-1694)*, 2nd Edition, Athens: Law & Economy, P.N. Sakkoulas 2003, Art. 1517 Greek CC, p. 250, No. 5, 8, and 9.

29 Law 2502/1997.

30 The child may, however, intervene in the proceedings (Art. 80 Greek Code of Civil Procedure). Relevant is the decision of the Court of Appeals of Athens 10659/1998, *Elliniki Dikaiosini* Vol. 35 (1994), p. 129, which recognised this possibility in a case concerning the right of contact. In addition, according to Art. 4 of the (1996) European Convention on the Exercise of Children's Rights (Law 2502/1997), the

HUNGARY

(a) Parental responsibilities

There is no general rule concerning how a child is legally represented in disputes concerning parental responsibilities. Nevertheless, when the court decides about hearing the minor as an interested person in a proceeding concerning parental responsibilities, it appoints a guardian *ad litem* for the child at the same time if it is reasonable.

(b) The child's residence

There is also no general rule concerning how a child is legally represented in disputes concerning the child's placement and the change of the decision on the placement. Nevertheless, when the court decides about hearing the minor as an interested person in a proceeding concerning the child's residence or the change of such a decision, it appoints a guardian *ad litem* for the child at the same time if it is reasonable.

(c) Contact

There is no special rule in this case, either.

IRELAND

(a) Parental responsibilities

A child is rarely legally represented in disputes concerning parental responsibilities. Where a child is legally represented, he or she is usually represented by a solicitor or a barrister.

(b) The child's residence

A child is rarely represented in disputes concerning the child's residence. Where a child is legally represented, he or she is normally represented by a solicitor or a barrister.

(c) Contact

A child is rarely represented in contact disputes. Where a child is legally represented, he or she is normally represented by a solicitor or a barrister.

ITALY

Despite ratification of the 1996 Strasbourg Convention on the rights of the child by means of the Law No. 77 of 20 March 2003, in the Italian legal system the complete implementation of the minor's rights to participate in legal proceedings that affect her or him (namely the right to request to be assisted, the right to appoint her or his own representative, if appropriate a lawyer, to exercise the rights of a party as well the power of the judge to appoint a representative for the minor) requires our legislature to adopt a number of internal instruments which at the moment have not yet been organised (see also

---

child itself has the right to apply for the appointment of a special guardian to represent it.

third footnote to Q 1). Therefore, Italian law totally ignores rights that, even if formally recognised, lack the instruments necessary for their implementation.

LITHUANIA

(a) Parental responsibilities

The child shall be represented by the parent with whom he lives or by the guardian (curator).

(b) The child's residence

The child shall be represented by the parent with whom he lives or by the guardian (curator).

(c) Contact

The child shall be represented by the parent with whom he or she lives or by the guardian (curator). In all the three above-mentioned situations, the court shall have the right to appoint an *ad hoc* guardian (curator) of the child if there is a conflict between the interests of the child and the parent with whom the child lives. In all the above-mentioned situations, the participation of the state institution for the protection of the rights of the child is mandatory.

THE NETHERLANDS

(a) Parental responsibilities

Normally the parent(s) vested with parental responsibilities legally represent the minor (Art. 1:245 Dutch CC). In case of conflicting interests between parent and minor, a special guardian will be appointed to look after the minor's interests. (Art. 1:250 Dutch CC).

(b) Child's residence

Normally the parent(s) vested with parental responsibilities legally represent the minor (Art. 1:245 Dutch CC). If the child is placed in a closed institution pursuant to Art. 1:261 § 3 Dutch CC, it has a right to lodge an appeal by itself.[31]

(c) Contact

In cases concerning contact, the child has informal access to the court (by means of a letter or a phone call to the judge). When the child is twelve years or older or considered able to reasonably appraise his or her interests in the matter, the judge may act *ex officio* (Art. 1:377g and 1:377h Dutch CC). However, the child is not a party in the proceedings. These regulations also apply to the right to information and consultation.

NORWAY

(a) Parental responsibilities

A dispute concerning parental responsibilities is a dispute between parents. The child is not a party in these cases. However, according to Art. 61 No. 5 Norwegian Children Act 1981, the court may appoint a lawyer or another

---

31 Court of Appeal Den Haag 14.6.2000, *LJN* AB0088.

representative to protect the interests of the child. The person who is appointed shall hear the child's opinion on the dispute between the parents and convey the child's opinion to the court. He or she has the right to see all documents relating to the case and may bring suggestions regarding the procedures either in writing or to a court hearing and provide advice as to how the case might best be handled. The court can decide whether the person may be present at the court hearing and, if so, the length of time. When the lawyer or representative is present, he or she may put questions to the parties and the witnesses.

(b) The child's residence
See Q 61a.

(c) Contact
See Q 61a.

POLAND

(a) Parental responsibilities
In legal proceedings before a court a child may be represented by each of his or her parents (Art. 98 § 1 Polish Family and Guardianship Code). In legal actions between a child and a parent or the parent's spouse (except in cases regarding maintenance or upbringing) a child is represented by a curator appointed by the court.

(b) The child's residence
Same as Q 61a.

(c) Contact
Same as Q 61a.

PORTUGAL

(a) Parental responsibilities
The child does not take part in processes of regulation of parental responsibility and is therefore not represented by either his or her parents or by some special representative. The child's interests are considered to be protected by the Public Prosecutor's Office, which intervenes in these processes.

(b) The child's residence
See answer to Q 61a.

(c) Contact
See answer to Q 61a.

RUSSIA

(a) Parental responsibilities
In the disputes regarding discharge, restriction or limitation of parental responsibility the child is represented by:

- another parent if the aforementioned measures concern only one parent (Art. 70 (1) Russian Family Code; Art. 64 Russian Family Code);

- a guardian, if one has been appointed (Art. 70 (1) Russian Family Code);
- institutions for children without parental care (Art. 70 (1) Russian Family Code, Art. 73 (3) Russian Family Code; Art. 147 (1) Russian Family Code)
- the Department of Guardianship and Curatorship, which safeguards the interests of the child (Art. 70 (2) Russian Family Code, Art. 73 (4) Russian Family Code; Art. 72 (2) Russian Family Code).

(b) The child's residence

In the disputes regarding the child's residence the child is represented by:

- the parents (Art. 64 Russian Family Code);
- the Department of Guardianship and Curatorship, which safeguards the interests of the child (Art. 79 Russian Family Code).

(c) Contact

In the disputes regarding contact the child is represented by:

- the parents (Art. 64 Russian Family Code);
- the Department of Guardianship and Curatorship, which safeguards the interests of the child (Art. 79 Russian Family Code).

SPAIN

The child is represented by his or her legal representative. It is possible to name an *ad hoc* legal representative if both parents have a conflict of interests with the child, but the notion of conflict of interests only refers to a conflict as regards property (see Q 8e).

The child's interests are moreover defended by the *Ministerio Fiscal,* a body equivalent to the French *Ministère Public* that is always party to the procedure if it relates to a child. It is generally admitted that the *Ministerio Fiscal* lacks resources in order to adequately carry out this function.

SWEDEN

(a) Parental responsibilities

According to Swedish law, the child is not a party to disputes concerning custody, residence or contact, but has the right to be heard. The interests of the child are protected by the court, which has the duty to ensure that questions concerning custody, residence and contact are properly investigated through assistance of the social welfare committee. Disputes on parental responsibilities are outside the parties' rights of disposal and the court must ex officio regard the child's best interests, independently of the requests of the parties.

The child's legal representation is somewhat different in proceedings governed by the Social Services Act (2001:453) and the Care of Young Persons Act (1990:52). Parties to such proceedings are the child's custodians and the social welfare committee. Children who have reached the age of 15 years are entitled to speak on their own in the proceedings.[32] Younger children have the right to a legal representative of their own, replacing the custodian as the child's legal representative. These children also have the right to be heard if it can benefit the investigation and it can be presumed that the child will not suffer harm from being heard.[33]

Normally, the custodian is also the guardian of a child. The guardian represents the child in proceedings concerning the child's property, Chapter 12 Sec. 1 Swedish Children and Parents Code. A child who has reached the age of sixteen has the right to apply to court for the discharge or appointment of a guardian. The child may be heard in the case, but he or she is not a party to the proceedings, Chapter 10 Sec. 18 Swedish Children and Parents Code.

(b) The child's residence

The child is not a party to the dispute but has the right to be heard. The court protects the child's interests ex officio, see above under Q 61a.

(c) Contact

The child is not a party to the proceedings but has the right to be heard. The court protects the child's interests ex officio, see above under Q 61a.

SWITZERLAND

If there are just causes, legal representation may be ordered for the child in divorce proceedings. The law lists examples of just causes in Art. 146 Swiss CC; for instance, ordering the appointment of an official adviser is to be examined if the parents submit different petitions with regard to parental responsibilities or important issues with regard to personal contact. It is mandatory to order legal representation for a child who is capable of making a judgment if the child makes a request to this effect.

Independent representation for a minor child is not explicitly stipulated in other proceedings. However, legal literature recommends that a legal adviser should be appointed for the child in all legal marriage proceedings which have such permanent consequences on the child's interests that it is necessary for just cause for the child to have an independent safeguard in the proceedings with regard to issues pertaining to the child's rights of person.[34]

Art. 146 Swiss CC is not directly applicable outside of marriage-law proceedings. On the other hand, the child's salary may be the subject of a measure for the protection of a child within the meaning of Art. 307 *et seq.* In particular, independent representation for the minor child is both possible and

---

32 Sec. 36 para. 1 Swedish Care of Young Persons Act (1990:52).

33 Sec. 36 para. 3 Swedish Care of Young Persons Act (1990:52).

34 P. BREITSCHMID, Art. 146/147 ZGB, p. 887 (No. 6), in: H. HONSELL, N.P. VOGT, TH. GEISER (ed.), *Basler Kommentar zum Schweizerischen Privatrecht, Zivilgesetzbuch I*, Art. 1-456 ZGB, Basel: Helbing & Lichtenhahn, 2002.

advisable based on Art. 308 § 2 and Art. 392 § 2 and 3 Swiss CC, if decisions are pending which are important with regard to the child's future and the safeguarding of the child's interests is not assured by the holder of parental responsibilities. As a rule this includes revocation of parental custody (Art. 310 Swiss CC) and the termination of parental responsibilities (Art. 311 Swiss CC).[35]

[35] C. HEGNAUER, *Grundriss des Kindesrechts*, p. 225.

QUESTION 62

H. PROCEDURAL ISSUES

What relevance is given in your national legal system to the age and maturity of the child in respect of Q 59-61?

AUSTRIA

Minors must be heard in person in proceedings concerning their care and education including the arrangement of their residence, as well as in proceedings on the right to contact unless a well-considered statement on the subject matter of the proceedings obviously cannot be expected given the minor's limited capacity to understand. If the minor has not attained 10 years of age, or if his or her development or health condition otherwise so requires, then in addition to being questioned by the court, the child can also be heard by the youth welfare agency, by representatives of the juvenile court assistance office or through other suitable means, such as by experts (Sec. 105 Non-Contentious Proceedings Act *[Außerstreitgesetz])*.

Minors who have attained 14 years of age are capable of representing themselves in proceedings regarding their care and education including the arrangement of their residence, as well as in proceedings on the right to contact (Sec. 104(1) *Außerstreitgesetz*). Nevertheless, in a given case, the court may declare that a child lacks the necessary maturity to do so (Sec. 154b Austrian CC).[1] In this instance, the parents are normally responsible for representing the minor (Sec. 154a Austrian CC).[2] Majority (Sec. 21 Austrian CC) and full legal capacity to conduct legal proceedings in one's own name (Sec. 2 Austrian Code of Civil Procedure *[Zivilprozessordnung]*) begins at age 18.

BELGIUM

The age and maturity are relevant for hearing the child in disputes concerning it. Indeed, the Belgian Law of 30 June 1994 has provided a general right, or more precisely, a possibility, of hearing the child. According to Art. 931(3)-(7) Belgian Judicial Code, every minor who has adequate discernment can be heard in every dispute by which it is concerned. Art. 56 *bis* Belgian LJP provides a specific obligation of hearing before the Juvenile Court, if the child has reached the age of twelve, when the court decides upon parental responsibilities, the child's residence, or contact, or the administration of its property. When the child has not reached the age of twelve, the Juvenile Court can decide to hear the child or refuse it by motivated decision, according to the common right of

---

1 See Q 9.

2 C. FISCHER-CZERMAK, 'Zur Handlungsfähigkeit Minderjähriger nach dem Kindschaftsrechtsänderungsgesetz 2001', *Österreichische Juristenzeitung*, 2002, p. 297; J. WEITZENBÖCK, 'Die Handlungsfähigkeit Minderfähiger nach dem KindRÄG 2001', in: S. FERRARI/G. HOPF, *Reform des Kindschaftsrechts*,Vienna: Manz Verlag, 2001, p. 7.

hearing in proceedings mentioned in Art. 56*bis* Belgian LJP (Art. 51(1) Belgian LJP). The Law on guardianship of 29 April 2001 has installed a specific right to be heard in actions before the Justice of the Peace concerning guardianship and parental responsibilities (Art. 1233(1) Belgian Judicial Code). The Justice of the Peace must call upon the minor, when the child is twelve years old in actions that concern its person, and when it is fifteen years old in procedures that concern its property (Art. 1233(1)(2) Belgian Judicial Code).[3]

A child of the age of fourteen also has the right to attend hearings when the court decides upon parental responsibilities, unless the court decides that according to the circumstances it is better to forbid the presence of the child.[4] Finally, a proposal has been made in Parliament according to which every minor who has reached the age of twelve, and asks, must be heard in every dispute that concerns it.[5] This proposal would have the advantage of uniformising the hearing of the child making it imperative (and no longer a right in certain cases, as now) and by introducing one criterion of age (now, the age of discernment, fourteen years and fifteen years are other criteria).

BULGARIA

The participation of the child in judicial proceedings depends on the age of the child. A child aged 10 is regarded as having attained sufficient maturity child to appear in court and to express its opinion. The only exception is if the interests of the child would be harmed. The court has the discretion to decide if the child's participation would harm it. Art. 15 § 1 stipulates that 'all cases of administrative or judicial proceedings affecting the rights and interests of a child should provide for an obligatory hearing of the child, provided it has reached the age of 10, unless that proves harmful to the child's interests'.

A child younger than 10 could also participate in the court hearings but only after an assessment of its level of maturity. The court decides on the hearing of a child under 10: '(2) In cases where the child has not reached the age of 10, the child may be given a hearing depending on the level of its development. The decision to hear the child shall be substantiated ' (Art. 16 § 5 § 2).

---

3 F. APS, 'De procedures inzake voogdij en het hoorrecht van minderjarigen', in: P. SENAEVE, J. GERLO and F. LIEVENS (eds.), *De hervorming van het voogdijrecht*, Antwerpen: Intersentia, 2002, p. 269-291; P. SENAEVE and W. PINTENS, *De hervorming van de echtscheidingsprocedure en het hoorrecht van de minderjarige*, Antwerp: Maklu, 1997, p. 78-79.

4 Art. 75 Belgian LJP as modified by Belgian Law of 10.03.1999; K. HERBOTS, 'De minderjarige als toeschouwer in de rechtszaal. Beschouwingen aangaande de Wet van 10 maart 1999', *E.J.*, 1999, p. 82.

5 Projet de loi modifiant diverses dispositions relatives au droit des mineurs d'être entendus par le Juge, *Doc. Parl.* Chambre 25.07.2002, No. 50-1991-01, pour la modification de l'article 931 du Code Judicaire, www.lachambre.be, document 51K0634.

CZECH REPUBLIC

This problem is solved in Czech legislation by very general wording that the child's opinions and information should be 'taken into consideration' (*e.g.* Sec. 47 § 2 Czech Family Code, Sec. 8 § 2 Czech Act No. 359/1999 Coll. On Social and Legal Protection of Children). Neither the court nor the social worker is bound by the child's opinion. However, in practice, the court will usually respect the child's opinion if the child's age approaches majority. It will always depend on the particular situation, the child's age and, among other factors, on the personality and life experience of the judge.

DENMARK

Age and/or maturity are the relevant criteria, which determine a child's right to self-determination, the right to be heard and the right to legal representation. The criteria are found in various different acts and these are not always congruent. Nor are the results always logical, for example, a child of 15 almost has complete autonomy in respect of medical treatment, but in theory no rights in respect of education choices.[6]

ENGLAND & WALES

Clearly, the older the child the more relevant and persuasive are his or her views and wishes. Nevertheless, in all cases it is the court's responsibility to evaluate those views and wishes in the light of all the circumstances. As BUTLER-SLOSS LJ put it in *Re P (minors)(wardship: care and control)*[7]

> "How far the wishes of children should be a determinative factor in their future placement must of course vary on the particular facts of each case. Those views must be considered and may, but not necessarily must, carry more weight as the children grow older".

Other key differences according to the age and maturity of the child are that it can determine (a) whether or not a child should be given leave to bring proceedings for a Sec. 8 order[8] and (b) whether or not a child can bring proceedings in his own right or via a guardian *ad litem* (see Q 61).

FINLAND

The age limits of 12 and 15 in care proceedings have been explained above, as well as the age limit of twelve concerning enforcement proceedings (Q 59). In disputes concerning custody (including residence) and right of access there are no age limits. The wishes and views of the child shall be taken into consideration with regard to the maturity that the child has reached. In practice,

---

6 I. LUND-ANDERSEN, N. MUNCK and I. NØRGAARD, *Familieret*, Copenhagen: Jurist- og Økonomforbundets Forlag, 2003, p. 103.

7 [1992] 2 FCR 681 at 687.

8 See Sec. 10(8), Children Act 1989 and *Re S (A Minor)(Representation)* [1993] 2 FLR 437, CA.

social workers tend to talk with the children of school age alone. The younger children are met accompanied by each parent separately.[9]

The child has the power to prevent the enforcement of custody or a right of access decision/agreement from the age of 12. The opinion of a younger child can have the same effect if the child has reached such a maturity that its will can be taken into consideration (Sec. 2 Finnish Act of the Enforcement of a Decision on Child Custody and Right of Access).

FRANCE

For the child's hearing, Art. 388-1 French CC requires that the child shall be able to understand the situation, the questions he will be asked by the judge or by a person appointed by the court. No precise age is mentioned in this legal provision. Under the former law act of 22 July 1987, the court had to hear the child if he or she was at least 13 years old. This rule does not apply anymore, but in practice, most family courts will want to hear a child of this age because he will be in most cases 'capable to understand'. Since the Law Act of 8 January 1993, a child who is capable of understanding can request to be heard alone, with a lawyer or with another person of his or her choice. If the child requests to be heard the court cannot deprive him from this right without mentioning in its decision the reasons for this refusal. The court makes its decision not with regard to the child's age but only with regard to his health and his intellectual skills.[10]

GERMANY

The age and maturity of the child influence the child's procedural position. A child over fourteen must always be personally heard in proceedings concerning the child's care (§ 50b para. 2 sent. 1 German Act on Voluntary Jurisdiction),[11] see Q 59. Such a child can also lodge an appeal without the help of a legal representative § 59 para. 1, 3 German Act on Voluntary Jurisdiction. Where the child is younger, a legal representative is necessary. Any decision against which the child can lodge an appeal must be made known to the child personally. The reasons shall not be communicated to the child, however, where detriments for his development or education have to be feared, § 59 para. 2 German Act on Voluntary Jurisdiction.

The age and maturity of a child also influence whether a hearing of the child could be dangerous to him or her (see § 50b para. 3 German Act on Voluntary Jurisdiction) and to what extent appropriate information shall be given (§ 50b para. 2 Act on Voluntary Jurisdiction). A statutory rule on a certain age does not

---

9 S. TASKINEN, *Lapsen etu erotilanteessa* Oppaita 46, STAKES Sosiaali- ja terveysalan tutkimus- ja kehittämiskeskus: Helsinki 2001, p. 71-75.

10 French Supreme Court,. Civ. I, 20.02.1985, *JCP,* 1985. IV. 159; 26.06.2001, *JCP,* 2002. I. 101, No. 18 annotated FOSSIER (six-year-old child).

11 H.-U. MAURER, 'Das Verfahren der Familiengerichte', in: D. SCHWAB, *Handbuch des Scheidungsrechts*, 5th Edition, München: Vahlen, 2004, Part. I No. 445 *et seq.*

exist. There is contradictory case law about which age it is best to hear children. Some courts argue that the child is to be heard at the age of three.[12] Other courts and authors propose the age of four[13] or of five years.[14] Above this age limit there seems to be consensus that a hearing generally must take place.[15]

GREECE

The hearing of the child is obligatory for the court, even in proceedings concerning conservatory measures, provided that the child has sufficient maturity. The child should be old enough to understand its interest in the specific case.[16] The maturity of the child is not necessarily determined by its age, but has to be examined in each particular case.[17] For further details see the answer to Q 59.

HUNGARY

In certain cases the child has to be heard if the child is 12 or older, in other cases from the age of 14. The maturity of the child can be stated as the important factor for a child that is even younger, according to the circumstances of the case. It has special import for a child under 12 to himself or herself demand his or her hearing.
See Q 59.

IRELAND

An Irish court will only have regard to the wishes of the child where such child is of sufficient age and maturity. Indeed, Sec. 25 of the Guardianship of Infants Act 1964 provides that the court shall take into account the child's wishes

---

12 OLG Frankfurt a.M., 22.05.1996, *FamRZ* 1997, 571; OLG Brandenburg, 14.10.2002, *FamRZ* 2002, 624.

13 BayObLG, 15.12.1987, *FamRZ* 1988, 871, 873; 30.04.1996, *FamRZ* 1997, 223, 224.

14 OLG Zweibrücken, 12.08.1996, *FamRZ* 1997, 687; U. MAURER, in: SCHWAB, *Handbuch des Scheidungsrechts*, 5th Edition: Vahlen, 2004, Part. I No. 450. - Contra KG, 10.02.1999, *FamRZ* 1999, 808, 809 annotated by LIERMANN.

15 OLG Karlsruhe, 21.01.1993, *FamRZ* 1994, 393 (6 years); OLG Hamm, 22.09.1995, *FamRZ* 1996, 421, 422 (6 years).

16 P. ARVANITAKIS, in: K. KERAMEUS, D. KONDULIS and N. NIKAS (eds.), *Commentary on the Code of Civil Procedure, Vol. II, (Arts. 591-1054)*, Athens-Komotini: Ant. N. Sakkoulas, Art. 681c Greek Code of Civil Procedure, p. 1311, No. 4 [in Greek]. This opinion is followed by the courts. See Supreme Court Decisions: 15/1997, *Elliniki Dikaiosini* Vol. 38 (1997), p. 1538, 180/1986, *Elliniki Dikaiosini* Vol. 27 (1986), p. 496, 577/1989, *Elliniki Dikaiosini* Vol. 31 (1990), p. 1271. It is claimed, however, that it is not necessary that the child is able to understand the full consequences of the court decision, but it is sufficient if it can provide any relevant information on the matter in dispute. See S. KOUKOULI- SPILIOTOPOULOU, in: A. GEORGIADIS and M. STATHOPOULOS (eds.), *Civil Code commentary, Vol. VIII, Family Law (Arts. 1505-1694)*, 2nd Edition, Athens: Law & Economy, P. N. SAKKOULAS, 2003, p. 126, No. 267.

17 P. AGALLOPOULOU, in: A. GEORGIADIS and M. STATHOPOULOS (eds.), *Civil Code commentary, Vol. VIII, Family Law (Arts. 1505-1694)*, 2nd Edition, Athens: Law & Economy, P.N. Sakkoulas 2003, Art. 1511 Greek CC, p. 208, No. 31.

'having regard to the age and understanding of the child'. In *Cullen v. Cullen*[18] for instance, the wishes of a 17-year-old girl seemed to have played a significant part in the decision of the court to award custody to her mother. Similarly, in *P.C. v. C.G. (No.2)*[19] the court refused an application for custody by the mother of a 13-year-old boy, ELLIS J. noting the strong preference of the latter to remain in the care of his father.

The Irish courts are anxious to ensure that impressionable children are not unduly influenced by a parent. The case of *J.C. v. O.C.*,[20] concerned the custody of three young children, aged 11, 9 and 5 respectively. The father argued that if the children were interviewed, they would, most likely, be subject to the persuasion of their mother. The court accepted that the children should only be interviewed by the judge after the decision regarding custody had been made by the court.

In the recent case of *F.N. and E.B. v. C.D., H.O. and E.K.*,[21] FINLAY-GEOGHEGAN J. held that children aged 13 and 14 were of an age and maturity to have their wishes taken into account. This is a significant Irish High Court judgment which draws a useful link between the personal right of a child under Art. 40.3 Irish Constitution to have a decision made in accordance with natural and constitutional justice and the provisions in the Irish Guardianship of Infants Act 1964 which deal with parental responsibilities, the child's residence and contact.

ITALY

They are criteria which are regarded as relevant to ascertain the minor's ability to judge and therefore are relevant as to whether the child is entitled to be heard in all the proceedings that affect him or her.

LITHUANIA

The age of the child has no relevance in those cases. The decisive role is the capability of the child to express his or her opinion, views and wishes. *E.g.*, if a child of 4 years is able to express its opinion, such a child must be heard. The decision about the child's capability to formulate its views is adopted by the judge on the basis of the facts of the case. The judge, when deciding this question, may order psychological expertise or ask the opinion of the child's teachers or other persons related to the child.

THE NETHERLANDS

Every child twelve years or older must be heard in disputes concerning it. Minors under twelve may be heard in those disputes if the judge considers them able to reasonably appraise their interests in the matter (Art. 809 Dutch Code of Civil Procedure).

---

18 High Court, 12.11.1982.
19 High Court, 12.07.1983.
20 High Court, 10.07.1980.
21 High Court, s26.03.2004.

NORWAY

The age and maturity of the child are relevant to all decisions on personal matters. As stated in Art. 31 Norwegian Children Act 1981, as the child matures, not only the parents, but all decision-makers shall hear the child's opinions. Due regard is to be given to the child's wishes according to its age and maturity.

POLAND

Polish legislation does not differ in regard to the child's age or maturity.

PORTUGAL

The law does not indicate at what age a child may be heard. However, Art. 1901 Portuguese CC establishes that the judge should hear children over fourteen in cases of parental disagreement over the exercise of parental responsibility; and Art. 1981 No. 1(a) Portuguese CC requires the consent of a child older than 12 and the non-opposition of a child of 12 to adoption. As a presupposition of intervention of authorities with competence in matters concerning children and juveniles and of the protection committees demanded by Art. 10 Portuguese Law No. 147/99 of 14 September (Portuguese Law Protecting Children and Young People at Risk), the age above which there are few doubts as regards whether a child should be heard is situated between 12 and 14. Below these ages, the hearing of a child should be seriously considered.

RUSSIA

The Russian law follows the recommendation of UN Convention to consider the child's opinion in the light of the child's ability to formulate it.[22] A child that has not reached the age of ten must generally be given the opportunity to be heard; however, neither the parents nor the judge are obliged to follow the child's opinion. The wishes of a child under ten are, in practice, not really taken very seriously. However, if a judge has doubts as to the suitability of one of the parents to provide a residence for the young child and the child is also strongly against this, the child's wish can be the decisive argument.

Art. 57 Russian Family Code provides that if the child is ten years old or older, his or her opinion must be 'considered'.[23] If the child's opinion is not followed, those who disregard his or her opinion must sufficiently explain the grounds therefore. The wishes of a child ten or older can only be overruled when they are against the child's best interests. According to Art. 57, the parents and a judge are obliged to hear such a child and, if they do not agree with his or her view, they must provide the grounds for their disagreement.

---

22 UN Convention, art. 12.

23 Family Code 1995, Art. 57. See also: I. KUZNETZOVA (ed.), *Commentary on the Family Code of Russian Federation*, Moscow: Jurist, 2000, p. 199-201.

The law grants a child older than ten an absolute veto regarding restoration of parental responsibility (Art. 72 (4) Russian Family Code). If such a child is against the restoration, his or her decision cannot be overruled.

SPAIN

There is a general tendency to consider that a child who is twelve or older has attained a sufficient degree of maturity. As to younger children, there are big differences in practice, depending on the issue at stake.

SWEDEN

According to Chapter 6 Sec. 2b Swedish Children and Parents Code, the child's wishes, with the child's age and maturity taken into account, shall be regarded when determining questions concerning custody, residence and contact. There is no explicit age-limit specifying when the wishes of the child should be given special regard. In a case decided by the Supreme Court, NJA 1995 p. 398, the clearly expressed wishes of a thirteen-year-old girl were decisive for entrusting her father with sole custody, in spite of the fact that there were doubts, according to the Court, as to the father's suitability as a custodian.

The weight given to the child's wishes in this case is in line with the rules concerning enforcement of court orders or parental agreements on custody, residence and contact. According to Chapter 21 Sec. 5, enforcement may not be ordered against the wishes of a child who has reached the age of twelve or a corresponding level of maturity, unless enforcement is necessary with regard to the best interests of the child. The same applies when the police authority is to execute a decision on collection of the child. The relevance given to the wishes of a child under the age of twelve is assessed individually. There are no official guidelines in this respect.

SWITZERLAND

The child's age and maturity play a role in the representation of the child. If the child is of a very young age, this may on the one hand mean no representation is appointed. On the other hand, it may be precisely the child's lack of ability to make judgments which constitutes just cause within the meaning of Art. 146 § 1 Swiss CC and which may necessitate representation. If the child is capable of making a judgment and requests representation, the court must appoint a legal adviser (Art. 146 § 2 Swiss CC).

The child must be heard if its age or other reasons do not go against this. The law does not stipulate any particular age limit. It is basically up to the discretion of the divorce court, which is duty bound to decide whether the child's age goes against the child being heard. Opinions vary largely in legal literature as to the age at which a child should be heard.[24] The Federal Supreme Court has in any case established the standing guideline that the child in question must, from the

[24] See also the summary in the unpublished decision of the Federal Supreme Court of 18.12.2003, 5P.322/2003.

point of view of the child's age and development, be in a position to give a binding statement of intent. The judge should forego a hearing if it could result in impairing the child's health or mental balance.[25] However, the hearing of a six-year old child does not seem to be excluded as a matter of principle,[26] nonetheless it is to be used more for the purpose of clarifying facts which are relevant to the decision than in participating in a decision regarding an issue which will have a crucial affect on the child's future, such as for instance in connection with conferring parental responsibilities on just one parent.

---

25 Unpublished decision of the Federal Supreme Court of 18.12.2003, 5P.322/2003.

26 BGE 124 III 90, 94.

www.ingramcontent.com/pod-product-compliance
Ingram Content Group UK Ltd.
Pitfield, Milton Keynes, MK11 3LW, UK
UKHW051924100926
8556IPUK00022B/1360

9 789050 954433